HANDBOOK OF
PEDIATRIC
PRIMARY CARE

Marilyn P. Chow, R.N., D.N.S.
Associate Executive Director
California Nurses Association

Barbara A. Durand, R.N., C., M.S., F.A.A.N.
Clinical Professor
Director, Pediatric Nurse Practitioner Program
Department of Family Health Care Nursing
University of California
San Francisco, California

Marie N. Feldman, R.N., C., B.S.
Formerly Director, Pediatric Nurse Practitioners
Kaiser Permanente Medical Clinics, San Francisco

Marion A. Mills, R.N., C., M.S.
Pediatric Instructor
Samuel Merritt Hospital College of Nursing
Oakland, California

HANDBOOK OF PEDIATRIC PRIMARY CARE

SECOND EDITION

Marilyn P. Chow

Barbara A. Durand

Marie N. Feldman

Marion A. Mills

A WILEY MEDICAL PUBLICATION
JOHN WILEY & SONS
New York • Chichester • Brisbane • Toronto • Singapore

Cover design: Wanda Lubelska
Production Supervisor: Audrey Pavey

Library of Congress Cataloging in Publication Data
Main entry under title:

Handbook of pediatric primary care.

  (A Wiley medical publication)
  Includes index.
   1. Pediatric nursing—Handbooks, manuals, etc.
2. Pediatrics—Handbooks, manuals, etc. 3. Ambulatory
medical care for children—Handbooks, manuals, etc.
I. Chow, Marilyn P. II. Series. [DNLM: 1. Nurse
practitioners—Handbooks. 2. Pediatric nursing—Handbooks. 3. Primary nursing care—Handbooks. WY 159 H236]
RJ245.H33 1984   610.73′62   83-26038
ISBN 0-471-86944-9

Printed in the United States of America

10 9 8 7 6 5 4 3 2 1

To my parents, Alice and Bill, and to John

Marilyn Chow

To Ron, Dennis, Mike, Mary, and Jim

Barbara Durand

To Jane, Laurie, Jennifer, and Amy

Marie Feldman

To Marian C. Fraticelli and Kathryn
M. Rudnicki

Marion Mills

Preface

The health care system of the 1980s is facing major social, political, economic, and technological changes that are affecting the health needs of the population. At a time when society is demanding more and better health services, economic depression and political imperatives to reduce government spending have resulted in ever-shrinking resources. One effect of cost containment efforts is a change in hospital utilization. Increasingly, hospitals are treating primarily those patients with acute conditions requiring highly technical care. Hospital stays are shorter, and more chronic illness care is being delivered in ambulatory settings, as evidenced by the number of specialty clinics associated with any major medical center. At the same time, societal concern over health and fitness is increasing, and the need for primary health care services is great.

The nursing profession has kept pace with these changes, and the nurse specialist or nurse practitioner in primary care is now well established as a highly competent, legitimate, and cost-effective primary care provider. In addition to the continued demand for "traditional" nurse practitioners, a significant demand has emerged over the last few years for master's-prepared clinical specialists with nurse practitioner skills to work with subspecialty populations such as children with developmental disabilities, children with hematologic problems, and children discharged from high-risk neonatal intensive care nurseries. These nurses are valued because of their background in family-centered, health-oriented pediatric primary care, which complements illness-focused care and helps maintain an emphasis on the healthy, normal aspects of the child.

The second edition of *Handbook of Pediatric Primary Care* attempts to provide pediatric nurse practitioners and other primary care providers—including pediatricians, family nurse practitioners, family physicians, school nurses, camp nurses, office nurses, maternity and perinatal nurse specialists, physician's assistants, and child health associates—with essential and current information on comprehensive pediatric primary care.

With increasing emphasis on primary care in undergraduate and graduate nursing curricula, we believe that this book will be a useful tool for nursing students preparing to practice pediatrics. We also anticipate that students in other health professional schools will find this book to be a comprehensive introduction to pediatric primary care. Finally, since we believe that parents are the true primary managers of their children's care and should therefore be as informed as possible, this book can serve as a useful resource for parents.

The philosophy that guided us in creating the first edition remains unchanged. We believe that all children and parents deserve access to quality primary care services delivered by competent and accountable professionals; that nursing services focused on health promotion through teaching, counseling, guidance, and support are essential to primary care; that parent participation in joint problem solving and decision making is mandatory for the most effective health care outcomes; and that the primary care provider serves as client advocate in dealings with the health care system.

We have made several significant changes in the book since the first edition. Part One, Assessment and Management of the Healthy Child, has undergone major reorganization. Separate chapters (Chapters 5–7) now contain essential information for providing comprehensive health maintenance care for specific age groups: infant, toddler and preschooler, and school-age child. These chapters use a similar format to present information in five sections: comprehensive schedule for well-child care, growth and development, feeding, accident prevention and safety, and common clinical problems. Chapter 8, Health Care of the Adolescent, has been expanded to include family planning and a section on sexually transmitted diseases. This departure from the basic format of the book, which covers specific illnesses in Part Two, was dictated by the requirements for health teaching for today's adolescents. Other chapters in Part One have been completely updated. Guidelines for family assessment, including cultural variables, have been added to Chapter 1, Child Health Assessment. Information on informed consent regarding immunizations has been expanded in Chapter 2. Material on health education has been extensively revised in Chapter 10 to emphasize incorporation of individual and group health teaching in primary care. To reflect current societal realities, a new chapter, Parenting in Special Circumstances, addresses the needs of certain groups under stress: parents of chronically ill children, single parents, working mothers, and adolescent parents (Chapter 9).

Part Two, Assessment and Management of Common Clinical Problems, continues to define the illness component of our practice. The content is presented with the strong belief that collaboration with physicians and other health professionals is an essential element of our practice and strengthens the quality of health care available to children and families. We have presented guidelines for referral and specified the assessment and management role of the pediatric nurse practitioner. The suggested interventions are meant to be used as guides, not as complete answers. All chapters have been updated and new material has been added. In response to the increasing chronic illness component of contemporary practice, we have added a new chapter, Approach to Chronic Illness (Chapter 12). In this chapter, comprehensive assessment and management of children and families coping with the impact of long-term illness are illustrated using the example of a child with asthma. New sections in other chapters include cardiovascular risk factors in children, hypertension, Reye's syndrome, infant botulism, vaginitis, changes in standards for cardiopulmonary resuscitation techniques in infancy, and greatly expanded communication assessment information related to speech and language development.

Overall, this handbook is organized to be most efficiently used through the index. Extensive cross-referencing within the text allows for quick, easy access to needed information.

In conclusion, we wish to express our gratitude to all who provided suggestions and constructive critique for this edition, especially Sharon S. Hayes, R.N., M.S., P.N.P., School of Nursing, University of Wisconsin. Her meticulous and detailed review assisted us greatly.

Marilyn P. Chow
Barbara A. Durand
Marie N. Feldman
Marion A. Mills

Contents

ASSESSMENT AND MANAGEMENT OF THE HEALTHY CHILD

The nurse practitioner exercises professional judgments and accepts responsibility for the delivery of primary health care. Mutual trust and collaboration among health care providers and families form the bases for effective delivery of quality care. Incorporated in this framework of care are the concepts of prevention, health promotion, and health maintenance. Teaching and counseling are strongly emphasized.

Delivery of primary care requires a continuous relationship between the health professional and the family. The child and family are the primary focus and they are encouraged to become responsible partners in their care.

Part One provides information necessary to maintain and promote the *health* of the child from birth through adolescence and to assess and to manage specific common concerns and conditions of the healthy child. It also presents pertinent information for parent–child teaching and counseling.

1

Child Health Assessment

The provision of pediatric primary care requires mastery of the knowledge and skills of data gathering, namely, the history and the physical examination, as well as the ability to communicate this information through the chart to other health professionals. This chapter provides general guidelines for the interview, history, physical examination, and problem-oriented record.

INTERVIEW GUIDE

The interview is the basic tool for assessment. It is often the key to solving many presenting concerns and in helping formulate a diagnosis. Mastery in the art of interviewing requires the ability to weave observation and communication skills into an accurate picture of a situation. The interview sets the stage for future contacts with the family and allows for the reciprocal transfer of pertinent information between the family and primary care provider. In addition, it provides an excellent opportunity to learn about the family's attitudes toward health and their strengths and vulnerabilities and to provide appropriate health teaching and counseling.

Interview

Clients and the nurse practitioner come to interviews with their own agendas of concerns and with their own ideas of possible solutions. In addition, the client comes with the expectation of being helped. During the interview, the expectations of the client and the nurse practitioner are clarified so that each person understands what is expected and what can be provided. A useful question to ask the client is: What do you think I can do for you today?

The interview should be conducted in a courteous, unhurried, friendly, and sincere manner. The questions should be asked using discretion and tact, particularly when probing into areas the client considers sensitive. The nurse practitioner must listen carefully to the parent and to the child and, in particular, must observe the nonverbal messages. It is essential to use open-ended, nonjudgmental questions, to avoid the use of technical language, and to be aware of personal biases. While the initial focus is on the client's presenting concerns, the nurse practitioner must be cognizant of the possibility that the stated reason for the visit might not be the primary reason for the visit. The nurse practitioner must be keenly sensitive to the client's real problem(s). For example, the nurse practitioner might discover that a client presenting with a complaint of "noisy breathing" is really worried about sudden infant death syndrome (SIDS) because the neighbor's infant recently died suddenly.

CLIENT–NURSE PRACTITIONER RELATIONSHIPS

The inclusion and active participation of clients in their care are important aspects of delivering primary care. Client–nurse practitioner relationships should emphasize the mutual participation of clients in identifying and managing their needs and problems. Continuity of care by the nurse practitioner establishes a therapeutic relationship with the family. While each nurse practitioner develops an individual style of establishing and maintaining supportive relationships, the following guidelines are useful (Hymovich and Chamberlain, 1980, pp. 73–74):

1. Personalize the interactions by introducing yourself to the child and parent by name and addressing them by their names.

2. Use language that is clearly understood.
3. Consider the situation from the client's perspective.
4. Inform the parents of your availability and be accessible by telephone in times of stress.
5. Allow the expression of feelings and concerns of parents about their child and themselves.
6. Listen to parental and child concerns, and guide them without prejudice or annoyance.
7. Focus on parental needs as well as those of the child.
8. Establish consensus with the family regarding problems and priorities for action.
9. Provide positive reinforcement through support, praise, and reassurance of those areas the parents are handling well.
10. Reinforce the ideas of the parents as appropriate and encourage them to develop their own plans of action (Korsch and Aley, 1973).
11. Provide information as appropriate.

TELEPHONE

The telephone is a frequently used device for seeking and obtaining health care. It increases accessibility and expedites communication between the caretaker and the nurse practitioner. The telephone is useful for determining whether the child needs to be seen, for monitoring the progress of an illness, and for providing information such as results of laboratory tests. It has the potential of decreasing the costs of health care. (See Chapter 11, Approach to Illness.)

Caplan (1983, p. 32) identifies five essential tasks when communicating with caretakers by phone:

1. Determine the primary concern and the reason for the call.
2. Arrive at a working diagnosis or problem.
3. Determine the severity of the problem.
4. Determine the sociomedical setting for the call, such as significant health history, parental expectations, and parental competence.
5. Make a disposition.

Telephone protocol manuals are available (Levy, 1979; Strasser, 1979; Schmitt, 1980; Katz, 1982) and serve to standardize this aspect of health care delivery.

Questions to Ask Yourself As the Interviewer

IMMEDIATE ENVIRONMENT

Does everyone look relaxed? Is there privacy? Does the parent look rushed? How is the child responding to me? Is the child comfortable? How does the child react in this situation? How does the child use the play equipment?

PRESENT CONCERNS

Is this the problem? Is the information accurate and reliable? What do the parent and child expect from me? What are the parent and the child trying to tell me? What does this tell me about the family's style of interaction?

OBSERVATIONS

What are the facial expressions, body gestures, tone of voice, and tone of the replies? Are there signs of stress, anxiety, and anger reactions? What are the family's responses to them?

HEALTH HISTORY GUIDE

The history is a longitudinal and cumulative process. The amount and type of history information obtained depend on the purpose of the visit and on the concerns of the parents. This section discusses the components of the history data base. For a discussion of an acute problem history, the reader is referred to Chapter 11, Assessment of the Presenting Symptom.

Obtaining a complete health history (see Table 1-1) on the first visit is time consuming because an initial base of information is collected in addition to eliciting the present concerns. The initial data base varies according to the age of the child, but it includes

Table 1-1
Summary of Health History

1. Identifying information	4. Child profile (*Cont.*)
Name	Review of systems
Address	Head
Phone number	Skin
Clinic number	Eyes, ears, nose, throat
2. Present concerns	Dentition
3. Family profile	Heart and lung
Family characteristics	Blood
Family history	Gastrointestinal
Family development	Genitourinary
Family interaction	Skeletal
Support systems	Neuromuscular
Culture	Personality
4. Child profile	The child as a person
Past medical history	Interaction
Gestation	Development
Birth history	Language
Neonatal period	Fine motor
Immunizations and	Gross motor
laboratory tests	Nutrition
Infectious diseases	Sleep
Operations/hospitalizations	Elimination
Accidents	School
Allergies	Past utilization of health
Current medications	care
	Special concerns of the
	adolescent
	24-hour history

information in areas that are stable and unlikely to change, such as family health history, past medical history, and developmental milestones. Some health care facilities have successfully developed parent questionnaires as a way of solving this problem. In facilities where questionnaires are unavailable the nurse practitioner may find it necessary to gather the health history over a period of time. The purpose of the visit, the interval since the last visit, and the presenting concerns will determine the type and amount of information collected.

Present Concerns

Elicit the chief concerns of the visit and obtain a detailed history of each one. Indicate how each concern affects the child's ability to function (eat, sleep, play) as appropriate. *Remember:* A parent or child's first stated concerns may not be the primary reason for the visit. In eliciting the concerns of the parent, the parent and the child are allowed to tell their story from their own perspectives. An opening question might be: What has been concerning you about your child? Other questions to ask are: What brings you here this particular day? What worries you most and why? What do you think would be helpful? What ideas do you have about the cause of the problem? What did you hope I could do for you today? What questions do you have?

Family Profile

Obtain information that provides an overall picture of the family's strengths and vulnerabilities, dynamics, and patterns of coping.

FAMILY CHARACTERISTICS

Inquire about demographic information (family's name and address, size of family, generations present in the family, ethnicity), socioeconomic status (education, occupation, sources of income, religious affiliation), and physical environment (neighborhood, living space, transportation). Sample questions include: Who else shares your household? Do you live in an apartment or a house? What kind of work do you do? Your spouse? What year of school did you complete?

FAMILY HISTORY

Ask about family relationships (blood, marriage, or adoption), the age, sex, and health status of each family member (natural parents, grandparents, relatives, and siblings), the chronological order of each pregnancy, the dates of important family events (death, marriages, divorces), familial and communicable diseases (e.g., diabetes, epilepsy, hypertension, sickle cell anemia, tuberculosis), family tragedies, and behavioral and social problems of family members.

Draw a kinship diagram using symbols for drawing pedigrees, (Fig. 1-1), and indicate the age and health status of each family member. Useful questions include: How would you describe your own health? Are there any serious illnesses in the family such as convulsions, diabetes, heart disease, hypertension, mental problems, or tuberculosis? Is this your first pregnancy? Does anyone in the family have a lot of problems?

FAMILY DEVELOPMENT

Identify the stage of family development (Table 1-2) using the structure of the family and the age of the oldest child as guideposts. Inquire about the previous stage of family development and about the family's ability to master previous stage-specific developmental tasks (Lamberton, 1980, p. 486). Inquire about the mother's satisfaction with her current balance of mother, wife, and personhood. Helpful questions are: How many children do you have? What is the age of the oldest child? Can you describe what happened when your child first went to school? Have you ever experienced financial difficulties? If so, how did you handle the situation?

FAMILY INTERACTION

Inquire about the interactions among family members (verbal and nonverbal communication, functional and dysfunctional patterns, crisis situations) and their major contacts with outside systems (school, health care, social networks). Questions include: How do you and your spouse settle arguments? What do you argue about? Do you feel you have enough support? If not, how do you manage? Do you have a favorite child? Does your spouse? How do the children get along with each other?

SUPPORT SYSTEMS

Elicit information of the parent's style of coping and whether supportive resource people are available. Suggested questions are: How do you manage? Who and what are sources of pressure or support for you? For your child? How do you react to all these pressures? How does your child react? What do you do when things get rough? Do you ever have time for yourself? Are there extended family or close adult relationships in your life? In the

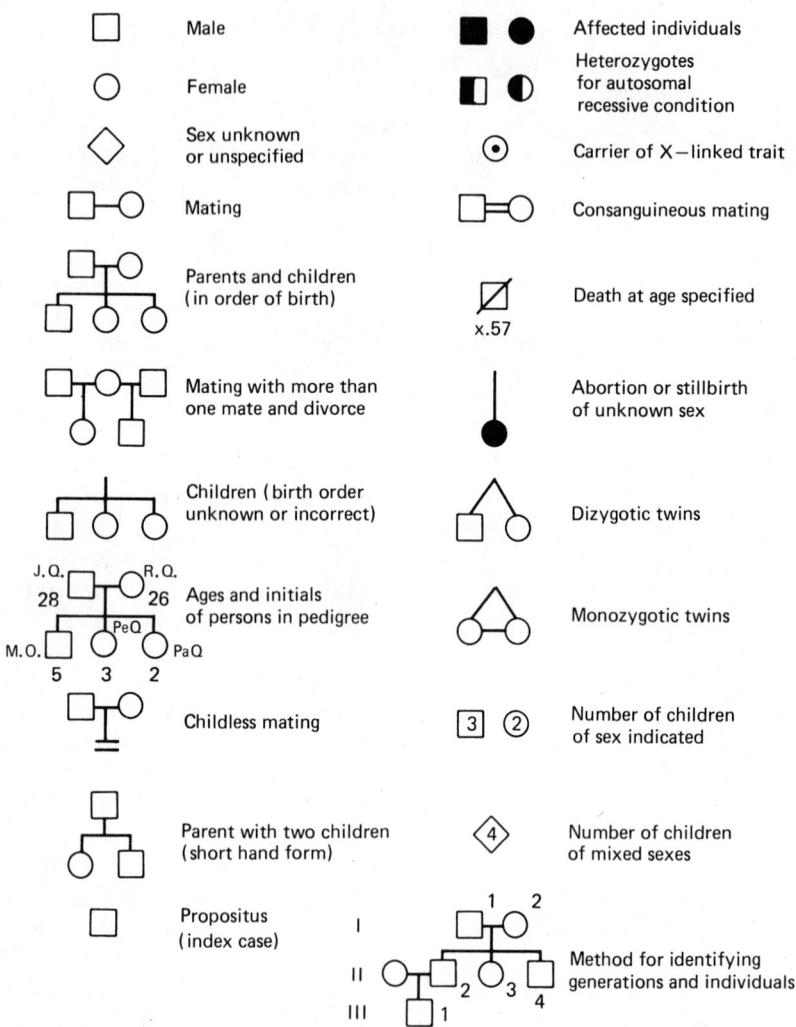

Figure 1-1 Symbols used in drawing pedigrees. (From A. Rudolph, ed., *Pediatrics*, 17th ed. East Norwalk, CT: Appleton-Century-Crofts, 1982. P. 234.)

Table 1-2
Developmental Stages and Developmental Tasks of Families

Stage of Development	Developmental Tasks
1. Newly married couple	Redirecting primary gratification from parents and friends into the marriage
	Fitting into a new kin network
	Planning for establishment of a family
	Establishing and maintaining first home
	Establishing mutually satisfactory ways of economic and emotional support
	Attempting role negotiation
	Beginning to establish identity as a family in the community
2. Childbearing	Solidifying marriage
	Having, adjusting to, and encouraging the development of infants
	Negotiating and establishing parental roles
	Establishing family as a stable unit
	Reconciling conflicting developmental tasks of individual family members
	Providing mutual support and growth
	Establishing constructive patterns of family interaction
3. Parents of preschool-age child(ren)	Continuing modification and adjudication of family roles
	Encouraging individualization of each member over time
	Adapting to the critical needs and interests of preschool children in stimulating, growth-promoting ways
	Maintaining constructive patterns of family interaction

Table 1-2 *(Continued)*

Stage of Development	*Developmental Tasks*
	Supplying adequate space, facilities, and equipment for the maturing family
	Establishing economic stability
	Interacting with the community
	Beginning to establish family values and to make plans for the future
4. Parents of school-age child(ren)	Fitting into the community in constructive ways
	Encouraging children's educational achievement
	Providing for privacy of family members
	Keeping financially solvent
	Planning for the future
	Furthering socialization and growth of family members
5. Parents of teenage child(ren)	Maintaining family integrity as some members seek to identify with others outside the family
	Beginning to establish postparental interests and careers as growing parents
	Providing facilities for widely divergent needs within the family
	Keeping the marriage relationship in focus
	Continuing kinship relationship
	Supporting and tolerating family members
6. Launching center	Reworking of parental roles to becoming parents of adult children
	Releasing young adults into work, military service, college, marriage, and so forth with appropriate rituals and assistance
	Maintaining a supportive home base
	Rearranging physical facilities and resources
	Meeting economic obligations

Table 1-2 (Continued)

Stage of Development	Developmental Tasks
	Continuing to build and modify the marriage relationship
	Accepting new members into the family
7. Middle-aged parents	Integrating and maintaining ties with both older and younger generations
	Assuming role of children of aging parents
	Planning for retirement
	Resolving the empty-nest syndrome
	Accepting illness, disability, and death of first-generation family members (parents' parents)
	Assuming role of grandparents
8. Aging family members	Accepting social, economic, and physical changes that occur with old age
	Adjusting to retirement
	Deciding on living arrangements of older family members
	Accepting a new family generation
	Adapting to loss and death

Source: M. Lamberton, "Alterations in Family Dynamics." In L. M. Shortridge and E. J. Lee, editors, *Introduction to Nursing Practice.* New York: McGraw-Hill, 1980. Pp. 487–488. Adapted from E. M. Duvall, *Marriage and Family Development,* 5th ed, Philadelphia: J. B. Lippincott, 1977.

child's? Do you get any help caring for your child? With whom do you talk when you have a problem? Who is your chief critic?

CULTURE

Obtain information that will increase sensitivity and understanding about the family's cultural background, beliefs, practices, food preferences, eating habits, concepts of health and illness (style of handling health and illness, such as pain, and crying), use of lay healer and folk medicine, sensitivity to personal problems, and experience with preventive health care (Hymovich and Chamberlain, 1980; Mercer, 1981). Consider the following important factors in assessing the culture of an emigrant family: country of origin (ecology, social structure), receiving country (similarities and differences of receiving country and country of origin, such as ecology and social structure, language, skin color, style of dress, and importance of association with people from the country of origin), and individuality (reasons for emigration, adaptability to change, and acculturation) (Mercer, 1981). Useful questions are: What were the reasons for deciding to leave the country of origin? Why did the family choose to immigrate to this country? How long has the family been in this country? Is the family willing to learn a new language or skill? What stresses are the family facing as a result of their emigration? How is the present culture different? What cultural differences does the family find most distressing? What do they miss the most?

Child Profile

Obtain information that provides a picture of the child's strengths and vulnerabilities, roadblocks and frustrations, and style of coping with problems.

PAST MEDICAL HISTORY

Obtain information that establishes the relationship of gestational and perinatal events and past health problems to the child's present state of health.

Gestation   Questions to ask include: In what month did you start prenatal care? How was your health during the pregnancy? Were there any unusual stresses during the pregnancy? Was this a planned pregnancy? Illnesses? Accidents? X-rays? Special diets? Hospitalizations? Medications? How many months did the pregnancy last? How much alcohol was ingested each day? Did you smoke during your pregnancy?

Birth History   See Chapter 5, Health Care of the Infant. Questions to ask include: How many hours was the labor? Was any anesthesia used? What type of delivery was it (breech, cesarean section, vaginal)? Were forceps used? Was the birth of the baby unusual? What was the baby's condition at birth? Did the baby have any trouble breathing? Was the baby's color yellow? What was the birth weight? Was anyone else present at the delivery? How soon after the birth did the parent(s) touch the baby? Was the baby delivered at home? Alternative birth center?

Neonatal Period See Chapter 5, Assessment of the Newborn. Questions to ask are: Did the baby have any problems in the nursery? Was the baby's color ever yellowish or blue? Did the baby have any problems with feedings? When did the baby go home? Did the mother and baby go home together? What was the baby's weight at discharge? Did the baby have any illnesses or problems in the first month of life?

Immunizations and Laboratory Tests See Chapter 2, Immunizations, and Chapter 19, The Hematopoietic System. Questions to ask are: Has the baby received any baby shots? At what age? Did the child have any reactions to the immunizations? If yes, can you describe them? Has the child ever had a tuberculin test? What was the reaction? Has the child had any other skin tests? Has the child ever had a blood test? What was the result? Has the child been screened for sickle cell anemia? For G6PD?

Infectious Diseases See Chapter 27, Infectious Diseases. Questions to ask include: Has the child had chickenpox? Measles? Mumps? Has the child had any streptococcal infections?

Operation/Hospitalizations Describe each one by diagnosis, indications for surgery or for hospitalization, results, and known residual problems. Questions to ask include: Has the child ever had any operations? If yes, for what reasons? What happened? How is the child now? Has the child ever spent any time in the hospital? For what reasons? What was the child's response during the hospitalization? Is the problem resolved?

Accidents/Safety See Chapter 28, Emergencies. Questions to ask include: Has the child ever had an accident? What happened? Can you describe what occurred? What was done for the child? How did the child respond? Is your home child-proofed? What safety measures do you use at home? Do you use car seats?

Allergies See Chapter 26, Allergies. Questions to ask include: Is the child allergic to any foods? If yes, what types of food? What is the reaction? Has the child had any reactions to insect bites, medications, immunizations? What happened?

Current Medications See Chapter 13, Approach to Medications in Childhood. What medications do you give your child regularly? Is your child receiving any medications for any illnesses?

Review of Systems Record problems not previously identified according to the body part or system. List the symptoms, treatments, and known sequelae.

HEAD Does your child complain of headaches? Has your child ever fallen and remained unconscious? (See Chapter 28, Head Injury.)

SKIN See Chapter 14, The Skin. Has your child ever had a severe skin reaction? Has your child ever been treated for a skin infection? What was the diagnosis and treatment?

EYES, EARS, NOSE, AND THROAT See Chapter 15, The Eye, and Chapter 17, The Respiratory System. Do your child's eyes ever cross? Does your child have trouble seeing? Can your child see the chalkboard at school? Do the eyes tear excessively? Does your child have trouble reading? In what position and at what distance does your child watch television? Does your child have frequent earaches? Ear infections? Do you think your child has trouble hearing? Has your child been screened for vision or hearing? If yes, what were the results? Does your child have persistent nosebleeds? Does your child have nasal congestion or stuffiness? Does your child have frequent streptococcal sore throats?

DENTITION See Chapter 16, The Mouth and Teeth. How many teeth does your child have? Has your child ever had any extra teeth removed? When was your child's last dental check-up? Is your child a thumbsucker? Do you have trouble understanding your child's speech? (See Chapter 25, Language and Learning Disabilities.)

HEART AND LUNG See Chapter 18, The Heart, and Chapter 17, The Respiratory System. Can your baby finish a 3- to 4-ounce feeding without tiring? Does your child have any trouble breathing? Describe what occurs. Does your child turn blue? Does your child have trouble with active participation in playground activities? Does your child tend to self-limit play activities?

BLOOD See Chapter 19, The Hematopoietic System. Has your child ever been anemic? Has your child ever had a blood transfusion? Describe the circumstances.

GASTROINTESTINAL See Chapter 20, The Gastrointestinal System. Does your child have problems with diarrhea? Constipation? Does your child have black, tarry stools? Has your child ever complained of anal itching? Does your child complain of stomach aches?

GENITOURINARY See Chapter 21, The Urinary System, and Chapter 22, The Genitalia. Does your child have a strong urinary stream? Does your child have urinary frequency? Has your child complained of pain on urination? When was your child toilet trained? Does your child sleep through the night without wetting the bed? *For girls over 10* (see Chapter 8, Health Care of the Adolescent): At what age did menstruation start? Note date, frequency, duration, and intensity. Do you have any vaginal discharge? Itching?

SKELETAL See Chapter 23, The Skeletal System. Has your child ever broken any bones? Has your child ever sprained any joint? Has your child complained of pain, redness, or swelling around the joints?

NEUROMUSCULAR See Chapter 24, The Neuromuscular System. Has your child ever had convulsions? Has your child ever had a fainting spell? Does your child have tremors? Twitches? Blackouts? Dizzy spells? Frequent headaches? Does your child have night terrors? Sleepwalk? Has your child complained of weakness in the extremities? Does your child appear awkward and clumsy?

PERSONALITY

The Child As a Person Elicit descriptions of the child's personality (activity, attention span, intensity of reactions, adaptability, strengths, sensitivities, fears, crying patterns, impulse control, and frustration levels) and independence (eating, separation, self-care, responsibilities, special and outside interests, and talents). Questions to ask include: How would you describe your child? How does your child spend the day? What do you see as your child's strengths and vulnerabilities? How would you describe your child's ability to

handle new situations? Does your child withdraw or actively participate? Is your child easily frustrated? What happens when this occurs? What upsets him/her? Can you describe his/her behavior?
What calms him/her down? How would you compare him/her to
the siblings? What does he/she do when you leave? What activities
does he/she engage in outside of the home?

Interaction   See Chapter 4, Assessment of Parent–Child Interaction. Elicit descriptions of the quality of the interaction with family
members and peers, limit setting, and discipline. Questions to ask
include: Can you leave the children alone in a room together? How
would you describe the older child's behavior toward the baby?
When was the first time you had to discipline your child? Do you
remember what happened? How often do you find that you need
to discipline your child? (If a situation presents itself in which the
parent attempts to discipline the child ask: Does that usually work?)
Does your child have playmates?

DEVELOPMENT

Perform the Denver Developmental Screening Test regularly to
obtain a longitudinal developmental picture. See Chapter 24, The
Neuromuscular System.

Language   See Chapter 25, Language and Learning Disabilities.
Elicit information about communication patterns, comprehension,
speech, and reading. Questions to ask include: Can you understand your child? Does your child follow directions? Does your
child get confused? Does your child repeat words? Does your child
stutter? How does your child let you know that he or she wants
something?

Fine Motor   Elicit information about manual dexterity, drawing,
dressing, tying, and writing. Questions to ask include: Does your
child scribble? Can your child use a pencil? Can your child tie shoe
laces? Button clothes? Does your child have difficulty writing
school assignments?

Gross Motor   Inquire about developmental landmarks such as sitting alone, standing, walking, riding a tricycle or bicycle. Questions

to ask include: What does your child do for fun? Does your child enjoy playing on the playground in the schoolyard? Does your child have trouble manipulating the parallel bars? Does your child have any difficulty walking? Running? How old was your child when she used a tricycle?

Personal/Social See previous discussion in this chapter, Personality.

NUTRITION

See Chapter 3, Nutrition in Infancy and Childhood. Elicit information according to age, presence of illness, and symptoms. Minimum information includes an evaluation of feeding during the first year and present nutritional status. Determine the gross quantification of protein, iron, and vitamin intake for crucial ages such as infancy and adolescence. If the parent is a poor historian, obtain a detailed 24-hour nutrition history of the day before this visit. Questions to ask include: How would you describe your child's appetite (good, poor)? How would you describe the eating environment at home? What is the feeding schedule? What kind of milk does your child drink? How much milk is consumed in 24 hours? How is the milk prepared? What solids does the child eat (fruit, vegetables, sweets) and in what quantities? Does the child self-feed? Can the child use utensils? Does the child drink from a cup? How do you handle the messiness? Is the child taking any vitamins?

SLEEP

Obtain information about the length of sleep and naps and about the character of sleep. Questions to ask are: Do you think your child is getting enough sleep? How many hours of sleep in a 24-hour period? When does your child awaken and go to bed? Does your child take naps during the day? How long are they? Does the child awaken at night? If yes, how often? What do you do? Does the child have any nightmares or night terrors?

ELIMINATION

See Chapter 6, Health Care of the Toddler and Preschooler. Inquire about patterns and toilet training. Questions to ask are: What are the child's bowel patterns? Frequency? Does the child complain of any discomfort? Is the child toilet trained? At what age was this accomplished? Does the child have any accidents? If so, is it during the day or night? How often does it happen?

SCHOOL

See Chapter 7, Health Care of the School Age Child and Chapter 25, Language and Learning Disabilities. Inquire about the ability to function in school. Questions include: What grade is your child in? Does your child like school? What is the favorite school subject? The least favorite? Has your child missed much school? What are your expectations as a parent for your child's school performance? Is your child enrolled in a special class?

PAST UTILIZATION OF HEALTH CARE

Where has the child usually gone for health care? How often do you take your child to a health care facility? For what reasons?

SPECIAL CONCERNS OF THE ADOLESCENT

See Chapter 8, Health Care of the Adolescent.

24-HOUR HISTORY

Obtain a detailed hourly history if the information is vague and contradictory. Questions might be: What is a typical day like for your child? What time did your child awaken yesterday? What happened then? When did you serve breakfast? And then what happened?

PHYSICAL EXAMINATION

A skillful physical examination is done with a minimum of trauma to the child. It is done with sensitivity to the child's behavior, activity level, and responses, and it takes advantage of opportunities such as crying by quickly looking into the mouth.

Usually a child under 2 years of age is best examined on the

Table 1-3
Summary of Physical Examination

Measurements and vital signs
General condition
Skin
Lymph nodes
Head
  Face
  Eyes
  Ears
  Nose
  Mouth
  Throat
Neck
Chest and lungs
Heart
Abdomen
Genitalia
Rectum and anus
Skeletal
Neuromuscular

parent's lap. Whenever possible, time is allowed for the child to manipulate the intrusive instruments. At some point during the examination the child should be completely undressed to permit a thorough look. Attention is given to ensuring a warm environment and using warm instruments and hands.

There are four basic techniques: auscultation, palpation, percussion, and observation. Of these four techniques, systematic, thorough observation is the most important one.

This section provides information on the general physical examination. Table 1-3 summarizes the physical examination. For more detailed information on physical examination techniques and physical findings according to body system, the reader is referred to the appropriate chapter.

Measurements and Vital Signs

Obtain the following measurements: height, weight, head circumference, temperature, respiration rate (see Chapter 17), pulse rate

Table 1-4
Mnemonics (Weech) for Approximate Height and Weight of Infants
and Children

(a) At birth:	Weight (W) in lb	= 7 lb 6 oz (7.35 lb)
(b) From 3 to 12 months:	W (lb)	= age (mo) plus 11
(c) From 1 to 6 years:	W (lb)	= (age [yr] × 5) plus 17
(d) From 6 to 12 years:	W (lb)	= (age [yr] × 7) plus 5

Note: (c) and (d) give the same value (47 lb) at 6 years. 48 lb is a closer approximation of average. The following mnemonic is suggested: "Up to 5: 5A^a plus 17. From 7 on: 7A plus 5. At 6: use either one, but add 1."

(e) At birth:	Length = 20 in
(f) At one year:	Length = 30 in
(g) From 2 to 14 years:	Height (in) = (age [yr] × 2½) plus 30

Source: From V. C. Vaughan and R. J. McKay, *Nelson Textbook of Pediatrics,* 10th ed., p. 25, © 1975 by the W. B. Saunders Company, Philadelphia.
^{a}A = age [yr]

(see Chapter 18), and blood pressure (see Chapter 18). Table 1-4 approximates the height and weight of infants and children, and Table 1-5 lists the expected increments of head circumference in average full-term infants.

General Condition

Note *appearance* (alert, happy, sick, distressed, pained), *activity level* (lethargic, playful, active, tired), *development,* and *behavior in relation to age and state of nutrition.*

Skin

Inspect *color* (jaundice, pallor, cyanosis), *hair* (texture, location, amount, distribution), *scalp* (oily, dry), *nails* (clubbing, unusual markings), and *lesions* (color, type, location, distribution, shape, size). Observe for *purpura, petechiae, hemangiomas, scarring, mongolian spots, pigmentation,* and *evidence of trauma.* Palpate for *temperature*

Table 1-5
Head Circumference in Term Infant[a]

Period	HC Increments	
First 3 months	2 cm/month =	6 cm
4–6 months	1 cm/month =	3 cm
6–12 months	0.5 cm/month =	3 cm
First year		12 cm

Source: Reprinted with permission from J. A. McMillan, et al, *The Whole Pediatrician Catalog*, (Philadelphia: The W. B. Saunders Company, © 1977), p. 6.
[a] Expected head circumference (HC) during infancy can be estimated by remembering that the average full-term infant will show the following increments in head growth.

(hot, cold), *texture* (edematous, rough, moist, clammy), *turgor*, and *lesions*. See Chapter 14, The Skin.

Note

1. Fingernails are replaced every 5½ months.
2. Toenails are replaced every 18 months.

Lymph Nodes

Inspect and palpate for *tenderness, consistency* (soft, hard), *size, shape, location, mobility, temperature,* and *inflammation.* Palpate the suboccipital, preauricular, anterior cervical, posterior cervical, submaxillary, sublingual, axillary, epitrochlear, and inguinal lymph nodes.

Note Normal ranges of lymph node sizes and characteristics:

1. Nodes up to 3 mm
2. Nodes up to 1 cm in the cervical and inguinal area
3. Nodes that are nontender, cool, and mobile

Head

Inspect and palpate for *shape, size, symmetry* (paralysis, weaknesses), *fontanels* (measurements, tension, intracranial pressure, delayed or premature closure), *sutures* (overriding), *molding, prominences* (cephalohematoma, caput succedaneum, frontal "bossing"), *lesions, craniotabes, position, movement,* and *dilation of veins.* See Chapter 5, Health Care of the Infant.

Note

1. Measurement of the head circumference is best done with a flexible, narrow steel tape measure placed around the largest occipitofrontal circumference. Check for accuracy by repeating this procedure a second time. Take the largest of the two measurements if there is a difference.
2. Transillumination of the head is done in a completely darkened room using a standard flashlight with a soft rubber collar attached to the lighted end placed flush against the skull at various points.
3. The mean anterior fontanel for the newborn is 2.1 cm with 2 SD above and below, 0.6 and 3.6 cm, respectively. The anterior fontanel closes between 4 to 26 months. Figure 1-2 shows the mean anterior fontanel size during the first postnatal year.

FACE

Inspect for *size, shape, symmetry, positioning of eyes, nose, mouth* in relation to each other, *clefts, dimples, paralysis, mandibular size, swelling, hypertelorism,* and palpate for *sinus tenderness.*

EYES

Observe external eye for *shape, symmetry, placement, lids* (position, eyelashes, tear ducts, ptosis, styes, squinting, swelling, redness, tenderness, epicanthic fold, paralysis, crusting, edema, nodules, scaling, discharge, symmetry), *conjunctiva, sclera* (icterus, hemorrhages), *cornea* (cloudiness, ulceration), *iris* (pigmentation, rings of white specks around the periphery, defects), and *pupil* (color, size, symmetry, roundness, reaction to light, and accommodation). Inspect for *conjugate gaze, extraocular movements* (nystagmus) and test for *visual acuity.* Inspect internal eye for *red reflex* and *fundus.* See Chapter 15, The Eye.

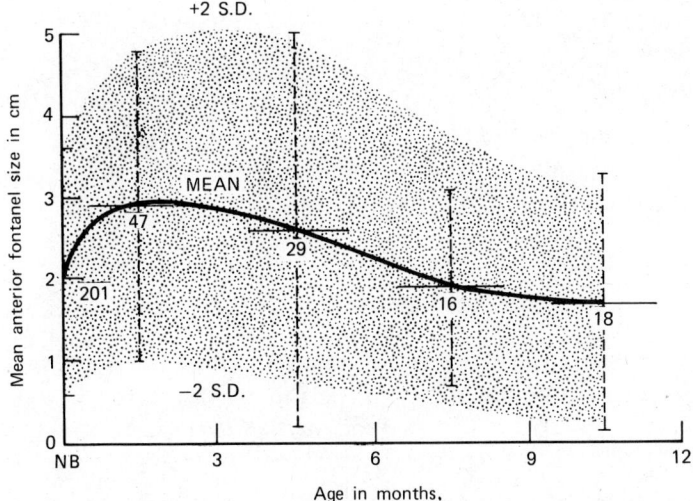

Figure 1-2 Mean anterior fontanel size during the first postnatal year. Beyond the newborn period (NB) the data are averaged at 3-month intervals with the number of persons in each group indicated. (From G. A. Popich and D. W. Smith, "Fontanels: Range of Normal Size," *J Pediatr 80*:749–752, 1972.)

Note

1. To see the red reflex in a sleepy infant, place the infant over the parent's shoulder.
2. Tearing starts several weeks after birth.

EARS

Inspect the *pinna* (shape, size, malformations, nodules, lesions, placement, skin tags, swelling, tenderness), *canal* (patency, discharge, narrowing, redness, pain, foreign bodies, cerumen), and *tympanic membrane* (short process, umbo, long process, light reflex, color, bullae, bulging, foreign bodies, perforation, retraction, mobility). See Chapter 17, The Respiratory System. Test hearing (see Chapter 25).

Note

1. To visualize the tympanic membrane, be sure the child's head is tilted *away* from the examiner toward the other shoulder, and insert the speculum toward the child's eyes.

NOSE

Inspect external nose for *shape* (straight) and *nares* (symmetry, flare, obstruction, discharge). Inspect internal nose for *color of mucosa* (pale, boggy, edematous, reddened), *turbinates, discharge* (purulent, bloody, crusty, amount), *foreign body, polyps, tumors,* and *perforation.* See Chapter 17, The Respiratory System.

MOUTH

Inspect *lips* (symmetry, paralysis, fullness, thinness, cleft, fissures, pallor, color), *mucosa* (bleeding, Stensen's duct, Koplik's spots, petechiae), *gums* (bleeding, discoloration, swelling), *dentition* (number, malocclusion, caries, discoloration, mottling, notching), *uvula, palates* (high arching, Epstein's pearls, petechiae, cleft), *tongue* (geographic, color, movements, size, coated, deviation, fissures, protuberant), *mandibular size,* and *salivary glands* (parotid, submandibular, sublingual). Note *breath odor* and *mouth breathing.* See Chapter 16, The Mouth and Teeth.

Note

1. Salivary production increases to full capacity during the third month of life.

THROAT

Inspect *color of mucosa* and *tonsils* (exudate, inflammation, size, color). Note *voice* (pitch, hoarseness, stridor, grunting) and *cry* (shrill, high-pitched, whiny, weak, hoarse, aphonia). See Chapter

16, The Mouth and Teeth, and Chapter 17, The Respiratory System.

Neck

Note *positions* (torticollis, opisthotonos), *control, range of motion, excessive pulsations, symmetry, stiffness, webbing.* Palpate for *cysts, sternocleidomastoid muscle masses* (shape, size, location, mobility), and *thyroid* (size, tenderness, texture, nodules).

Chest and Lungs

Inspect for *color* (cyanosis), *respirations* (quality, depth, effort, rate, rhythm), *type of breathing* (abdominal, costal), *chest, size, symmetry, shape* (pectus excavatum, barrel chest, slope), *breast appearance* (areola, nipple placement, spacing, presence or absence in relation to age), *respiratory distress* (expiratory grunting, nasal flaring, retractions), *dyspnea* (restlessness, apprehension, rib retractions), and *cough.* Palpate the *general chest configuration, breasts* (see Chapter 8 for Tanner Staging), *scapulas,* and *clavicles.* Auscultate for *breath sounds* (presence or absence, intensity, quality, duration, vesicular, bronchovesicular, bronchial) and note *abnormal chest sounds* (rales, rhonchi, wheezes, pleural friction rub). Percuss for *dullness* and *lung size.* See Chapter 17, The Respiratory System.

Note

1. Respirations:
   - Ratio of respiration to pulse should be 1:4.
   - Short periods of apnea can be normal in newborns.
   - Respiratory movement is abdominal until around 6 years of age, when it becomes predominantly thoracic.

2. Auscultation:
   - Sound is best conducted through solid matter, passes less well through water, and passes least well through air (Delaney, 1975).
   - To check for transmitted breath sounds, block the nasal passages.

3. Breasts:

- Breasts usually develop asymmetrically.
- They are examined after the menstrual period so premenstrual engorgement and tenderness will not be misleading.

Heart

Observe *activity level* (fatigability). Inspect *color* (pallor, cyanosis), *clubbing, prominent veins,* and *precordial bulging.* Palpate for the point of *maximal impulse* (PMI), *pulses* (femoral, radial), and presence of *thrills* or *heaves.* Auscultate *heart sounds* (S_1, S_2, rate, rhythm) and *murmurs* (location, rhythm, radiation, intensity, timing, quality, pitch, effect of positional change). See Chapter 18, The Heart.

Note

1. Thrill is best detected with the edge of the palm.
2. In the young child the apex beat is outside the nipple line in the fourth interspace. In the older child it is more nearly in the adult position.
3. The key to auscultation is to listen to one heart sound at a time:

   - Aortic valve is best heard in the second right intercostal space.
   - Pulmonic valve is best heard in the second left intercostal space.
   - Tricuspid valve is best heard in fifth right intercostal space near the sternum.
   - Mitral valve is best heard in fifth left intercostal space near the midclavicular line.
   - S_1 is louder at the apex.
   - S_2 is louder at the base.
   - Bell of stethoscope detects low-frequency sounds.
   - Diaphragm of stethoscope detects high-frequency sounds.

Abdomen

Check *size, shape,* and *symmetry.* Inspect *protuberance, lesions, umbilicus* (color, hernia, nodules, fistulas, discharge), *distention, distended veins, guarding, facial expression,* and *body movements of child.* Check movements (breathing, peristaltic waves). Auscultate *bowel sounds* (peristalsis, tympanitic, dull, absent). Palpate for *softness, rigidity, pain, tenderness, masses* (location, size, consistency, configuration, tenderness, mobility, fluctuation), *hernias, diastasus rectus, muscle tone, tissue turgor,* and *rebound tenderness.* Palpate *liver, spleen, bladder,* and *kidneys.* Percuss for *liver edges, tympany,* and *shifting dullness.* See Chapter 20, The Gastrointestinal System.

Note

1. In examining a child with a complaint of a tender abdomen, do not begin the examination with the tender area. While doing the examination, observe the child's reactions: Is the child guarding? Is the reaction voluntary or involuntary?
2. A cough may bring out bulge in hernias of the abdominal wall.

Female Genitalia

Inspect external genitalia for *color, labia* (majora, minor), *clitoris, urethral meatus,* and *pubic hair* (presence or absence). Note *odor,* presence of *adhesions, bleeding, discharge, ulcerations, edema,* and *imperforate hymen.* Inspect *vagina* and *cervix.* Palpate the *uterus.* Note *position of uterus, presence of foreign body,* and *discharge.* See Chapter 22, The Genitalia, and Chapter 8, Health Care of the Adolescent.

Note

1. A pelvic examination is usually not done until puberty.
2. A small amount of vaginal discharge, occasionally blood tinged, is normal in newborns, a result of withdrawal from the high levels of maternally derived estrogen (Gundy, 1981, p. 106).

Male Genitalia

Inspect the external genitalia for *penis* (size, glans, shape), *foreskin* (circumcision, retraction, phimosis, paraphimosis), *urethra* (ulceration, position of meatus), *scrotum* (hydrocele, hernia), and *pubic hair.* Palpate *testes, epididymis,* and *spermatic cord.* See Chapter 22, The Genitalia, and Chapter 8, Health Care of the Adolescent.

Rectum and Anus

Inspect *muscle tone, sensation,* and *patency.* Note *presence of foreign body, bleeding, fissures, skin tags, pilonidal dimple, stool,* and *masses.* See Chapter 20, The Gastrointestinal System.

Note

1. Examine the anus with the fifth finger, noting sphincter tone.

Skeletal

Observe *gait* (opposing arm and leg swing, normal heel-to-toe gait), *gross deformities, posture,* and *symmetry.* Examine *spine and back* (body alignment, curvature, rigidity, costal vertebral angle (CVA) tenderness, tufts of hair, lesions, pilonidal dimple, kyphosis, scoliosis), *joints* (range of motion, tightness, contractures, edema, tenderness, redness, nodules, abnormal prominences), *hips* (abduction, internal rotation), *knees* (length, symmetry, contour), *forefoot* (abduction), *fingers and toes* (number, spacing, length, curvatures, palmar creases, webbing, clubbing). See Chapter 23, The Skeletal System.

Neuromuscular

Observe *mental status* (orientation, alertness), *motor development* (Romberg's sign, ability to do knee bend, to hop, to walk on toes and heels, to maintain the arms held forward, to grip the examiner's fingers), *muscle tone* (strength, symmetry, spasticity, hypotonia, hyperreflexia), *cerebellar function* (gait, posture), *sensory* (light touch on the limbs, stereognosis in the hands, pain and vibration in hands and feet), *reflexes* (see Tables 24-1 and 24-2), and *cranial nerves.* See Chapter 24, The Neuromuscular System, and Chapter 25, Language and Learning Disabilities.

LABORATORY AND SCREENING RESULTS

Results of laboratory tests, such as complete blood count (CBC) and urinalysis (UA), and screenings, such as sickle cell, glucose 6-

phosphate dehydrogenase (G-6-PD), vision, and hearing, are usually recorded after the physical examination.

PROBLEM-ORIENTED HEALTH RECORD

Problem-oriented recording is the current form of written communication among health professionals. While there are variations in the implementation of the problem-oriented form of recording, this chapter offers a foundation from which to build expertise with it. Figure 1-3 diagrams the problem-oriented system, and Figure 1-4 outlines the schema of the problem-oriented record. A summary of the format for recording visits is listed in Table 1-6.

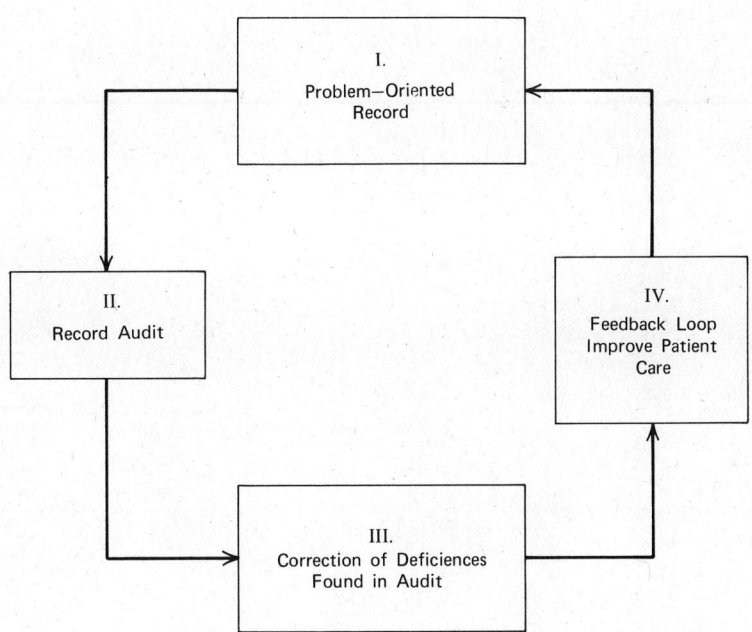

Figure 1-3 Problem-oriented system.

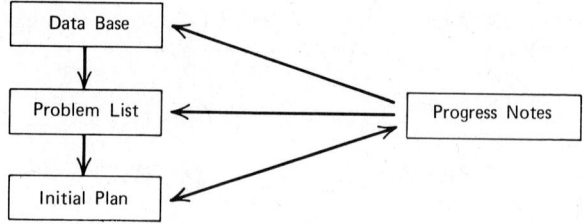

Figure 1-4 Schema of problem-oriented record.

Table 1-6
Format for Recording Visits

Initial Visit
1. Identifying information—date of visit
2. History (see Table 1-1)
3. Physical examination (see Table 1-3)
4. Laboratory and screening results
5. Problem #1—health supervision (*Note:* The entire problem list is
   written on the master problem list located at the front of the record.)
       Initial plan
           Yearly screening tests
           Immunization
           Nutrition
           Growth and development
           Accident prevention
           Safety
6. Problem #2
       Initial plan
           Diagnostic
           Therapeutic
           Patient education
           Follow-up
Subsequent visits
1. Date, problem title, and problem number
2. Subjective
3. Objective
4. Assessment
5. Plan
       Diagnostic
       Therapeutic
       Patient education
       Follow-up

Data Base

The data base is the first component of the problem-oriented system. It consists of *standardized* and *defined* elements of the history, physical examination, and laboratory tests. The nurse practitioner gathers the information as soon as possible, so that the problem list can be completed. The comprehensive initial data base is located at the front of the record. Interval data are located within the body of the chart.

COMMON QUESTIONS

How are changes recorded in the areas of health supervision, such as nutrition and growth and development which obviously change as the child grows?
There are two alternatives:

- Write a progress note under Problem #1 including specific changes in areas of health supervision such as nutrition and growth and development.
  OR
- Use a periodic update data base sheet designed specifically for well-child care.

How is the initial data base updated?
It is either updated in the progress notes or updated on the initial data base form.
What is an incomplete data base?
This term is used when it is not possible for the defined data base to be completed, as in an emergency. In such a situation the term should be listed as problem #1 to serve as a reminder that the problem(s) may be dealt with out of context.

Problem List

The problem list is the *index* to the record. It is located at the front of the record to provide an overall perspective of the client's problems. The provider who obtains the initial data base usually formulates the problem list as well. Other health professionals may add to the list as other problems develop. Each problem is numbered and titled on the master problem list (see example in sample record).

Health supervision is always listed as Problem #1 as a constant reminder to health providers that wellness does require surveillance and management.

COMMON QUESTIONS

What is a problem?
A situation identified by either client or health provider that requires management.
How are problems formulated for the problem list?
A problem statement:

• Does not contain "rule-outs," "probably," or question marks ("Rule-out" is an approach to the solution of a problem and so belongs under Initial Plan.)
• Does not state any guesses
• Is a symptom, a finding, or a diagnosis
• Is specific
• Is stated at the highest level of understanding
• Is stated succinctly
• Reflects only what is known from reviewing the data base

How are problems categorized?
Problems are categorized by type and status.

Type:

1. Medical (physiologic finding, symptom, or abnormal laboratory value) ("Probable," questionable diagnoses, and "rule-outs" are not included here.)
2. Social (finances, housing, employment)
3. Psychiatric
4. Behavioral
5. Environmental

Status:

1. Active problem (currently requiring management)
2. Inactive or resolved problem (one that either no longer requires management or is stable but may recur)
3. Temporary problem (minor problem identified in progress

notes). May be listed on the "short-term problem list" using letters rather than numbers for identification.

Are temporary or short-term problems listed on the problem list?
There are two options:

1. Use a separate sheet titled "short-term problem list." See example in sample record.
   OR
2. Note problems in progress notes using letters to identify them as temporary. If a problem has more than two entries in the progress notes, a decision is made about listing the problem on the problem list.

How are changes recorded on the problem list?
The following are examples of common changes:

1. Reformulation of problems
   Corrected statement

Date	No.	Problem Title		
3/7/83	3	Hb 9.0 gm/dl	3/8/83 ——→	Iron-deficiency anemia

Combination of problems

Date	No.	Problem Title		
4/6/83	4	Acute abdominal pain		
4/6/83	5	Nausea	4/7/83	#4 Appendicitis
4/6/83	6	Elevated WBC	——→	

Once a problem number has been used, it cannot be used again; so in the above example, numbers 5 and 6 cannot be reused.

2. Change of status

Date	No.	Problem Title		Date Resolved
3/7/83	3	Hb 9.0 gm/dl	3/8/83 ——→	6/8/83 Iron-deficiency anemia

Initial Plan

The initial plan organizes the plan of management for the problem. It is written when the problem is first identified by the health care provider. The initial plan has several components:

1. *Diagnostic:* A list of probable causes and specific plans to rule out each cause
2. *Therapeutic:* Palliative or curative measures for alleviation of the problem
3. *Patient education:* Explanation of the problem and therapeutics
4. *Follow-up:* Plans for the client to return to health care facility

Each plan is numbered and titled according to corresponding problem number and title on the problem list. Subsequent plans are written in the progress notes for each problem. See progress notes written in the sample record.

Progress Notes

Progress notes are the mechanism for monitoring the progress of each problem. Progress notes are divided into three types: narrative notes, flow sheets, and discharge summaries.

NARRATIVE NOTES

Commonly referred to as SOAP notes, the format of the narrative notes is as follows:

Date, Problem Title, and Problem Number
*S*ubjective: Interval history from client regarding problem
*O*bjective: Information gathered from physical examination, laboratory results, screening tests, and observation of child's behavior and interaction.
*A*ssessment: Conclusion or comparison stated to level of knowledge, the sum of subjective and objective information.
*P*lan: A description of plans (given above)

The narrative notes are written with attention to previous progress notes. See sample record for examples.

FLOW SHEETS

Several variables can be monitored at a glance with the use of flow sheets, providing a concise picture of the client's progress. Flow sheets are usually kept for routine care or for monitoring stable diseases, such as diabetes. Examples include vital signs and medication sheets.

DISCHARGE SUMMARY

If the client decides to change care providers, each problem is summarized by problem number, title, and plans.

SAMPLE RECORD

NAME ____Juliette D._____
BIRTH DATE ___12/10/1981___
CHART NO. ___00-00-00_____

MASTER PROBLEM LIST

DATE ONSET	NO.	ACTIVE PROBLEMS	INACTIVE/ RESOLVED PROBLEMS	DATE RE- SOLVED
6/12/83	1	Health supervision		
6/12/83	2	Hb 9.0 gm/dl Iron-deficiency anemia		12/83
6/12/83	3		H/O PDA	3/82
6/12/83	4	Inadequate housing		12/83

NAME __Juliette D.__
BIRTH DATE __12/10/81__
CHART NO. __00-00-00__

SHORT-TERM PROBLEM LIST

LETTER	PROBLEM	DATES OF OCCURRENCE
A	Upper respiratory infection	6/82 9/82 1/83
B	Acute otitis media	2/83
C	Tinea corporis	3/83

NAME __Juliette D.__
BIRTH DATE __12/10/81__
CHART NO. __00-00-00__

Date: 6/12/83
PRESENT CONCERNS: well-child visit, no particular problems or questions
FAMILY PROFILE:

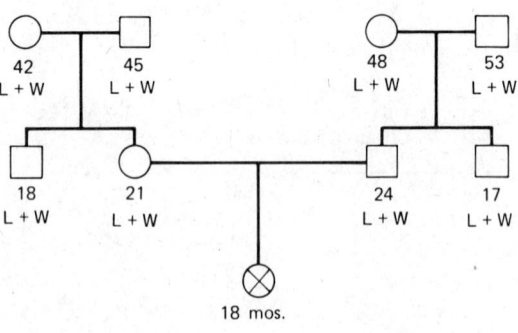

(Continued)

Parents in good health, no significant family medical history, family lives in studio apartment across from maternal grandmother, father employed as baker, no stated financial difficulties, health insurance through employer.

Mother completed tenth grade and father completed high school.

Extended family reported to be positive support system; mother expresses desires to get out more frequently by herself.

CHILD PROFILE:

Past Medical History

Gestation: 1st pregnancy for P_1G_1 woman who initiated care in third month of pregnancy, attended Lamaze classes; no illnesses or unusual strains during pregnancy.

Birth history: 12-hr labor, vaginal delivery with paracervical block given; infant delivered spontaneously. Mother breast-fed in delivery room.

Neonatal period: BW 6 lb 10 oz, spontaneous cry, no respiratory difficulties, jaundice on 2nd day. Follow up with blood tests revealed no further problems. Mother and child discharged on third day.

Immunizations: DPT × 3 and TOPV × 2; M-M-R at 15 months; tine test.

Infectious disease: None.

Operation/hospitalization: None.

Accidents: None.

Current medications: None.

Review of systems: Negative except for the following:

Skin: History of "ringworm" in March 1983, treated with Tinactin cream.

Ear, Nose, Throat: Three episodes of colds, treated with ↑ fluids, and acetaminophen prn. Dates were 6/82, 9/82, 1/83. One episode of acute otitis media bilaterally at 14 months of age, treated with Ampicillin and a decongestant.

Heart: Mother states a heart murmur noted at the first well-child visit. Family told that murmur was due to transition from fetal circulation to independent circulation. Normal ECG. Mother told murmur "was gone" at 3 months of age.

Personality: Very active, "happy" child, cries little. Seems to adapt well to changes in environment. Extremely inquisitive. Parents attempt to set limits but at times become very frustrated.

Development: Sat alone at 6 months, stood alone at 10 months, took first steps at 11 months, walks up steps, drinks from cup without spilling much, eats with hands, content to play by herself at

(Continued)

times, very verbal, can say 2 words such as "bye-bye," seems to hear well, plays with small objects.

Nutrition: 8 oz whole milk × 5/day; three meals a day but eats little fruits, meats, vegetables; no vitamins or minerals taken.

Sleep: Sleeps well, usually from 8:00 PM to 7:00 AM; nap 1/day for 1½ hours. Sleeps in own bedroom.

Elimination: BM × 1/day, usually after breakfast, normal consistency.

Past utilization of health care: Formerly seen by private pediatrician, Dr. L. Brolyn, on Mission St.

PHYSICAL EXAMINATION: Height 82 cm. Weight 12.5 kg. HC 46.5 cm. HR: 116. RR: 30.

General appearance: Well-developed child in no acute distress who clung to mother during the examination.

Skin: Fair; nail beds pink, good turgor, hair evenly distributed, without lesions.

Head: Normocephalic, symmetrical. AF and PF closed.

Lymph nodes: None palpable.

Eyes: Grossly normal, PERRLA; cover test normal, red reflex noted bilaterally, sclera and conjunctiva clear.

Ears: Nl position, light reflex and bony landmarks seen bilaterally.

Nose: No abnormalities noted, mucosa pink, no bleeding noted, clear watery discharge seen.

Mouth and throat: 8 teeth present, dentition normal, moist mucous membranes, tongue shows no deviation, uvula rises symmetrically.

Neck: Supple, without adenopathy or masses.

Chest: No evidence of respiratory distress, lungs clear throughout.

Heart: NSR. PMI at 4th ICS, MCL. No thrills, heart sounds S_1 and S_2 nl. No murmurs noted, femoral pulses palpated bilaterally.

Abdomen: Soft without tenderness, without masses. Liver, spleen not palpable.

Genitalia: Nl female, external structures intact, no discharge or foul odor.

Rectum and anus: No lesions noted, good sphincter tone.

Skeletal: No obvious deformities, straight spine, full ROM of extremities.

Neuromuscular: Alert, responsive child. See DDST for development, cranial nerves II–XII normal.

Parent–child interaction: Mother responsive to child's needs, able to set limits but needs much support with this. Child responds warmly to mother.

(Continued)

LABORATORY AND SCREENING RESULTS:
Hemoglobin: 9.0 gm/dl
Urinalysis: pH 5
   neg. for glucose, ketone, protein, blood
   0–1 WBC/HPF
   0 RBC/HPF
Vision and hearing screenings: completed, normal

PROBLEMS
Problem: #1—health supervision. Normally developing 18 mo. old, with low hemoglobin. See Problem #2.

a. Yearly screening tests
   Initial Plan
       Diagnostic: UA, CBC—done.
       Therapeutic: None.
       Patient education: Discussed with parent the rationale for these tests.
       Follow-up: See Problem #2.

b. Immunizations not up to date
   Initial Plan
       Diagnostic: None.
       Therapeutic: Given DPT in ® anterior lateral thigh and TOPV.
       Patient education: Reviewed with parent the immunization schedule, side effects of DPT, and support measures.
       Follow-up: (1) Discussed return for DPT and TOPV boosters prior to entering school. (2) Send for records from private physician.

c. Nutrition
   Initial Plan
       See under Problem #2

d. Accident prevention/safety
   Initial Plan
       Diagnostic: None.
       Therapeutic: Dispense Ipecac.
       Patient education: Discuss common accidents of toddlers and safety measures to prevent them. Telephone no. of clinic and ER given to mother. Advised her to call in case of ingestion.
       Follow-up: Discuss at next well-child visit in 6 months.

e. Growth and development
   Initial Plan
       Diagnostic: None.
       Therapeutic: None.

Patient education: Anticipatory guidance re: independence and autonomy of child, toilet training. Discussed language stimulation.

Follow-up: Discuss at next well-child visit in 6 months.

Problem: #2—hemoglobin of 9.0 gm/dl
Initial Plan
Diagnostic: R/O anemia, probably iron deficiency anemia—obtain CBC, blood smear, and retic. count.
R/O blood loss—obtain stool guaiac.
Therapeutic: No medication at this time.
Patient education: (1) Discuss lab finding and need for further blood tests to identify cause of low Hb. (2) ↓ milk to 24 oz/day. Suggest offering food before milk to encourage the child to eat more. (3) Review sources of iron-containing foods. List given to mother.
Follow-up: 1. Obtain further lab studies today. 2. Call mother re results and future plans.

Problem: #4—inadequate housing
Initial Plan
Diagnostic: None.
Therapeutic: Support move to a larger apartment.
Patient education: None.
Follow-up: Check on progress next well-child visit.

PROBLEM PROGRESS FORM

Patient name __Juliette D.__ Date __8/15/83__
Chart No.: 00-00-00
Problem: #2—hemoglobin of 9.0 gm/dl ⟶ iron deficiency anemia
Subjective: Mrs. D. is regularly giving iron-containing foods such as meats, eggs, beans, raisins. She has noted that Juliette's BMs are black; Juliette does not "like the medicine, but I mix it with her juice."
Objective: Repeat Hb today is 11.0 gm/dl; Retic. count was 3%.
Assessment: Problem resolving.

(Continued)

Plan: Therapeutic: Continue to include iron-containing foods in diet. Continue Fer-In-Sol 1.2 cc tid × 1 mo.

Patient education: Reassure mother that problem is resolving and continue with diet supports. Review side effects of Fer-In-Sol.

Follow-up: Encourage Mrs. D. to call if any questions or changes. Repeat Hb in December at next well-child visit.

Problem: #4—inadequate housing

Subjective: The apartment situation is the same. Space is totally inadequate for three persons. Mrs. D. has not found time to look for a larger place but plans to look this weekend. She's pessimistic about finding something she can afford.

Objective: Made home visit last week. Apt. is well kept despite lack of space. No medicines or household toxins are kept where children can get them.

Assessment: Problem unstable.

Plan: Have arranged for Mrs. D. to speak with Center social worker about possible housing resources.

Follow-up: Will contact Mrs. D. by phone in 2 weeks.

PROBLEM PROGRESS FORM

Patient Name __Juliette D.__ Date __12/16/83__

Chart No.: 00-00-00

Problem: #1—health supervision

Subjective:

a. *Family:* Warm, stimulating environment in home. Mrs. D. has been spending more time with Juliette on weekends and is getting out herself more than before.

b. *Child rearing:* Mrs. D. no longer having significant concerns. Has been using discipline more judiciously and consistently.

c. *Nutrition:* Well-balanced diet with adequate sources of protein. Mrs. D. has tried cutting down on sweets and has ↑ iron-containing foods for whole family.

d. *Development:* See Denver Developmental Screening Test in chart. Normal language development for age. Toilet training completed.

e. *Child safety:* Mrs. D. has not been able to get harness auto restraint for Juliette.

f. *Immunizations:* Complete for age. Will need boosters before starting kindergarten.

g. *Dental:* Brushing teeth with help from mother.

Objective: Height 87 cm. Weight 13.75 kg. HC 49.5 cm. See growth chart. Physical examination normal.[a]

Assessment: Problem is stable. I feel that things are going relatively well in family at present. Healthy 2 yr. old.

Plan:

1. Encourage to get auto harness restraint and to keep Juliette in back seat until then.
2. Suggestions for fostering language development given.
3. RTC in 6 months.

Problem: #4—inadequate housing

Subjective: Parents found 1-bedroom apartment. Rent is a little more than they expected to pay, but they feel they can manage.

Objective: None.

Assessment: Problem resolved.

Plan: None.

[a]The physical findings are recorded as illustrated in the initial data base. In clinical practice, the complete physical examination is recorded at each visit.

Resource Information

Many audiovisual resources are available for learning the skills of the physical examination. Only selected resources are presented here.

Eye

1. Colenbrander Ophthalmoscopy Mannequin: Model with slides for simulating normal and abnormal conditions of the eye.
2. Ophthalmoscopy Unit: Self-instructional units for ophthalmology
   Part I: Tape/slide and handouts
   Both items 1 and 2 are available from:
   Hansen Ophthalmic Development Laboratory, P.O. Box 613, Iowa City, IA 52240.

Heart

1. Cardiac Auscultation Records, Heart Sounds
   Merck, Sharp and Dohme, West Point, PA 19486.
2. Index of Heart Sounds and Murmurs
   National Medical Audiovisual Center, Video Duplication Service, 1600 Clifton Road, N.E., Atlanta, GA 30333.
3. Heart Sounds Access Tape
   American College of Cardiology, 9650 Rockville Pike, Bethesda, MD 20014.

4. Recording of Stethoscopic Heart Sounds
   Service of Roerig, Division of Pfizer, Inc., 235 E. 42nd Street, New York, NY
   10017.

5. Sounds of Pediatric Cardiology, Pediatrics, Vol. 18, No. 5
   Audio Digest Foundation, 1250 So. Glendale Avenue, Glendale, CA 91205.

6. Stethoscopic Heart Record, Heart Recordings
   Columbia 91B02058 (Collector Series)
   Columbia Special Products, 51 West 52nd Street, New York, NY 10019.

7. The Evaluation of a Child with a Heart Murmur
   National Audiovisual Center, General Services Administration, Washington,
   DC 20409.

Physical Examination

1. Series on Physical Assessment of the Well Adult (cassette slides)
   Wiley Biomedical, Wiley, 605 Third Avenue, New York, NY 10016.

2. Series on Programmed Learning Approach to the Physical Examination
   Blue Hill Educational Systems, Inc., 52 South Main Street, Spring Valley, NY
   10977.

3. Physical Assessment of a Four-Year-Old Female
   University of Minnesota, School of Public Health, Pediatric Nurse Associate
   Program, Patricia Woodbury, Instructor.

4. Physical Examination of the School Age Child (Series)
   Trainex Corporation, P.O. Box 116, Garden Grove, CA 92642.

5. Introduction to Pediatric Screening S-2885
   National Audiovisual Center, General Services Administration, Washington,
   DC 20409.

References

Alexander, M. and M. Brown. *Pediatric History Taking and Physical Diagnosis for Nurses.* New York: McGraw-Hill, 1979.

Athreya, B. H. *Clinical Methods in Pediatric Diagnosis.* New York: Van Nostrand Reinhold, 1980.

Bates, B. *A Guide to Physical Examination,* 3rd ed. Philadelphia: J. B. Lippincott, 1983.

Berni, R. and H. Readay. *Problem-Oriented Medical Record Implementation.* St. Louis: C. V. Mosby, 1974.

Bonkowsky, M. "Adapting the Problem Oriented Medical Record to Community Child Health Care." *Nurs Outlook 20*:515–518, August 1972.

Caplan, S. "The Telephone in Pediatric Practice." In A. J. Moss, editor, *Pediatrics Update: 1983 Edition.* New York: Elsevier Biomedical, 1983. Pp. 27–37.

Delaney, M. "Examining the Chest, Part 1: The Lungs." *Nursing 75 5*:12–14, August 1975.

Delaney, M. "Examining the Chest, Part 2: The Heart." *Nursing 75* 5:41–46, September 1975.

Froelich, R. E. and F. M. Bishop. *Clinical Interviewing Skills.* St. Louis: C. V. Mosby, 1977.

Green, M. *Green & Richmond Pediatric Diagnosis,* 3rd ed. Philadelphia: W. B. Saunders, 1980.

Gundy, J. *Assessment of the Child in Primary Health Care.* New York: McGraw-Hill, 1981.

Hansen, M. F. and C. R. Aradine. "The Changing Face of Primary Pediatrics." *Pediatr Clin North Am 21*:245–256, 1974.

Hurst, J. W. and H. K. Walker, editors. *The Problem Oriented System.* New York: Medcom Press, 1972.

Hymovich, D. and R. Chamberlain. *Child and Family Development.* New York: McGraw-Hill, 1980.

Katz, H. P. *Telephone Manual of Pediatric Care.* New York: Wiley, 1982.

Korsch, B. and E. F. Aley. "Pediatric Interviewing Techniques." *Curr Prob Pediatr 111*:3–42, 1973.

Lamberton, M. M. "Alterations in Family Dynamics." In L. Shortridge and E. J. Lee, editors, *Introduction to Nursing Practice.* New York: McGraw-Hill, 1980. Pp. 475–503.

Levy, J. C. et al. "Development and Field Testing of Protocols for the Management of Pediatric Telephone Calls: Protocols for Pediatric Telephone Calls." *Peds 64*:558–563, November 1979.

Malasanos, L. et al. *Health Assessment,* 2nd ed. St. Louis: C. V. Mosby, 1981.

McMillan, J. A., P. I. Nieburg, and F. A. Oski. *The Whole Pediatrician Catalog.* Philadelphia: W. B. Saunders, 1979.

Mercer, E. et al. "A 'Professional' Approach to Helping Immigrants and Refugees." *Can Nurse 77*:20–23, March 1981.

Popich, G. A. and D. W. Smith. "Fontanels: Range of Normal Size." *J Pediatr 80*:749–752, May 1972.

Schmitt, B. D. *Pediatric Telephone Advice.* Boston: Little, Brown, 1980.

Stewart, R. and C. McGill. "Maximizing the Nursing Role in Public Health." Excerpt on teaching aids from Report of Work Conference Series sponsored by the University of Texas School of Nursing at San Antonio, 1974.

Strasser, P. H. et al. "Controlled Clinical Trial of Pediatric Telephone Protocols." *Peds 64*:553–557, November 1979.

Vaughan, V. C. et al. *Nelson Textbook of Pediatrics,* 11th ed. Philadelphia: W. B. Saunders, 1979.

Waring, W. W. and L. O. Jeansonne III. *Practical Manual of Pediatrics.* St. Louis: C. V. Mosby, 1975.

Weed, L. *Medical Records, Medical Education, and Patient Care.* Cleveland: Case Western Reserve University Press, 1971.

Woody, M. and M. Mallison. "The Problem Oriented System for Patient Centered Care." *Am J Nurs 73*:1168–1175, July 1973.

2

Immunizations

The use of immunizations to control and prevent specific infectious diseases is an established component of comprehensive health care. In fact, the antibody formation induced by immunizing agents is the most specific tool the practitioner has to prevent illness. Nurse practitioners involved in primary care of infants and children will be participating in the planning and implementation of immunization programs and in the education of families and communities regarding the rationale for immunizations. It must be kept in mind that, although familiar to health professionals, immunization procedures and their rationale are not necessarily understood by parents and families. To provide the preventive and protective benefits of immunizations to the largest possible number of children and persons at risk, it is essential that primary care providers conduct the teaching necessary to ensure the fullest informed participation of their clients.

This chapter presents information on immunization procedures and content necessary to understand and to explain the need for such procedures. See Chapter 27, Infectious Diseases, for discussion of common infections in childhood. Concepts of immunology are discussed also in Chapter 26, Allergies.

IMMUNITY

The Immune System

The major function of the immune system is to protect the body from the effects of harmful agents. The regulation of the immune system is extremely complex, involving several immune mechanisms (Wara and Ammann, 1976).

Antibody-Mediated Immunity An antibody is a specific protein (immunoglobulin) produced by a fixed plasma cell in response to exposure to a specific antigen and having the ability to react to that antigen. Of the several classes of immunoglobulins, IgA, IgG, and IgM are of major importance (see Chapter 27, Primary Immunodeficiency Disease, for further discussion). IgE is responsible for most allergic reactions (see Chapter 26, Allergies).

Cell-Mediated Immunity T-cells, or thymus-derived lymphocytes, circulate in the peripheral blood and protect against the spread of viral, fungal, and microbial organisms. They attract macrophages into the affected area and then modify the antigen for further immune response.

Phagocytosis and Complement Phagocytic white blood cells (WBCs) ingest and destroy foreign antigens. Before phagocytosis can occur, bacteria and other antigens must be prepared by interacting with specific antibodies and complement (a substance in normal serum).

Antigen An antigen is a substance not normally present in the body that, when introduced, stimulates production of an antibody that reacts specifically with it.

Types of Protective Immunity

ACTIVE IMMUNITY

Active immunity is long-lasting immunity produced by natural or artificial stimulation that enables the body to produce its own antibodies.

Natural Active Immunity This immunity is produced by an attack of the specific disease (e.g., measles).

Artificial Active Immunity This immunity is produced by the introduction of vaccines and toxoids (e.g., measles vaccine).

PASSIVE IMMUNITY

Passive immunity is a state of temporary nonsusceptibility to certain microorganisms produced by provision of ready-made antibodies.

Natural Passive Immunity This immunity is produced by the maternal transfer of specific antibodies of the IgG type through the placenta to the fetus.

Artificial Passive Immunity This immunity is produced by injecting antibodies of the following types:

1. *Human immune serum globulin (ISG, gamma globulin):* This antibody is prepared from pooled plasma for general use and is given to reduce the severity of disease or to prevent the disease (e.g., measles, viral hepatitis A, viral hepatitis B if specific hepatitis B immune globulin not available). It is also used as replacement therapy in children with hypogammaglobulinemia.
2. *Specific human immune serum globulin:* This antibody is prepared from plasma of convalescing patients with known antibody content for a specific illness (e.g., tetanus, pertussis, hepatitis B, mumps, varicella zoster).
3. *Animal antiserum or antitoxin:* This antibody is prepared from animal serum (horses, cows) and carries with it the danger of foreign serum reactions. It is not given without testing to determine hypersensitivity. Examples are tetanus antitoxin and diphtheria antitoxin.

Types of Agents Conferring Active Artificial Immunity

TOXOID

A toxoid is a bacterial toxin that has been treated by heat or by chemicals to decrease its virulence without destroying its ability to stimulate antibody production (e.g., tetanus, diphtheria). The antibodies developed act against the foreign toxin.

VACCINE

A vaccine is a suspension of attenuated or killed microorganisms. There are several forms:

1. Live attenuated bacteria (e.g., BCG)
2. Killed bacteria (e.g., typhoid, pertussis)
3. Killed virus (e.g., Salk polio, influenza)
4. Live attenuated virus (e.g., measles, mumps, rubella, Sabin polio, smallpox, varicella)

ADJUVANTS

Adjuvants are substances added to the immunizing agent to enhance the antigenic effect (e.g., alum, aluminum phosphate, aluminum hydroxide). These "depot" antigens retain the antigens at the depot site and release them slowly, thus enhancing the response by prolonging contact. They are given intramuscularly and are more likely to produce local reactions at the site of injection. Diphtheria toxoid–tetanus toxoid–pertussis vaccine (DTP) is a depot antigen. See subsequent discussion in this chapter, DTP.

FLUID TOXOIDS AND VACCINES

These agents have no adjuvant and are more rapidly absorbed, so they produce a more rapid secondary response. That is why fluid tetanus toxoid is given after injury in persons who have completed the initial series.

Intervals Between Immunizations

INTERVALS BETWEEN DOSES

Primary Response   After the first injection (DTP is an example), antibody is produced relatively slowly and in small concentration, but the antibody-producing mechanisms are so altered that with subsequent injection of the same antigen they recognize and remember the antigen and react with the secondary response (see Fig. 2-1).

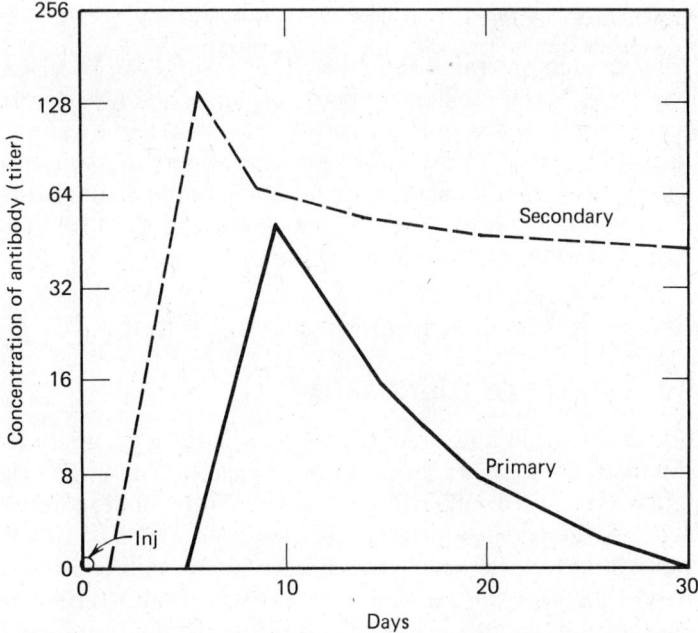

Figure 2-1 Comparison of secondary and primary antibody responses.

Secondary Response   Once the body recognizes the antigen, antibodies are produced much faster and in higher concentration than after the first injection. In other words, the system is capable of responding with increased intensity to future challenges by the same antigen.

Interruption in a Series   Because of the secondary response phenomenon, if the intitial series is interrupted, *regardless of length of time elapsed,* the series does *not* have to be restarted.

BOOSTERS

Once the initial series is completed and sound immunity is achieved, all that is necessary is to keep the concentration of antibody at a reasonable level by subsequent "boosters" at appropriate times of increased risk. The response is usually excellent.

LIVE VIRUS VACCINES

It has been demonstrated that live virus vaccines can be given simultaneously with excellent antibody responses and no increase in reactions, as in measles–mumps–rubella (M–M–R) and trivalent oral poliovirus vaccine (TOPV). However, when giving single live virus vaccines at different times, at least 1 month should elapse between administration in order to avoid interference of the first vaccine with the immune response to the second.

Initiation of Artificial Immunization in Infancy

IMMUNE STATUS OF THE NEWBORN

Although the immune system is developing by the twentieth week of gestation, the neonate is at risk for infection because the system is poorly developed at birth and too immature to respond with sufficient antibody production. The passive transfer of maternal IgG antibodies to the fetus provides the infant with resistance to infectious diseases for the first few weeks or months after birth. This protection is only against diseases for which the mother has developed sufficient antibodies and is only temporary. An adequately immunized mother passively transfers antibodies to the infant for measles, diphtheria, tetanus, and poliomyelitis. Little to no pertussis immunity is transmitted though the placenta. Since IgM does not cross the placenta, newborns are susceptible to bacterial infections. If a newborn has high levels of IgM, an intrauterine bacterial infection is the cause.

AGE TO BEGIN IMMUNIZATIONS

In the normal infant most maternal antibodies have disappeared by 3–6 months of age. Since the immune system is capable of responding with adequate antibody production by 2 months of age, this is the recommended age to begin artificial immunizations.

UNIMMUNIZED CHILDREN

Occasionally children will be encountered who have had no immunizations and whose exposure to ongoing primary care services is doubtful. In such situations, when the likelihood of follow-up poses serious questions, it is valid to administer *simultaneously* the following agents:

- DTP (or Td if the child is over 6 years of age)
- TOPV
- M–M–R
- Tine test (American Academy of Pediatrics, 1980)

Contraindications to Routine Immunization

GENERAL RULES

1. Any acute febrile illness is reason to defer immunization. Minor infections not associated with fever are not contraindications according to the American Academy of Pediatrics. However, if such a child receives an immunization and subsequently develops fever in the next 24–48 hours, it is difficult to assess etiology, especially by telephone, and will require an additional visit to the health care facility for evaluation. Children with upper respiratory symptoms on an allergic basis (e.g., chronic rhinitis, rhinorrhea, postnasal mucous discharge with associated cough) are safe candidates for immunization.

2. Persons with the following conditions are not immunized routinely, especially with live virus vaccines, and medical consultation is required before instituting any immunization procedures:

   - Pregnant women
   - Persons with leukemia, lymphoma, or other generalized malignancy
   - Persons on immunosuppressive therapy (e.g., steroids, irradiation, antimetabolites, alkylating agents)
   - Persons with immunodeficiency diseases, for example, children with cellular immunodeficiencies must not receive bacillus Calmette-Guérin (BCG) or live virus vaccines due to risk of overwhelming infection
   - Persons with marked sensitivity to eggs, chickens, or neomycin, as they are theoretically at risk to live virus vaccines prepared in media containing these substances (Medical consultation should be obtained if marked sensitivity exists.)
   - Persons who have had recent administration of immune serum globulin, plasma, or blood (It is advised to wait 3 months before administering immunizations.)

SPECIFIC CONTRAINDICATIONS

These are discussed under each specific immunizing agent in the Guide for Use of Common Immunizing Agents, presented after the next section of this chapter.

IMMUNIZATION SCHEDULES

Considerations in Planning Immunizations

Recommendations for immunizations are meant to be general guidelines and may need to be modified to meet individual or community needs. Factors to be considered include the following:

1. Risk of a particular disease for an individual or special population (e.g., pertussis in infants, rubella in pregnant women)
2. Risk of the disease for the "herd" or community at large (e.g., polio)
3. Time when optimum immune effect can be obtained (e.g., measles at 15 months of age)
4. Time when risk from the vaccine is minimal (e.g., diphtheria toxoid in childhood)
5. Legal requirements (e.g., in California all children are required to have DTP, polio, measles, mumps, and rubella immunizations before entry into nursery schools, day care centers, and public schools)
6. Efficacy, effectiveness, and safety of specific immunizing agents

Recommended Schedules

The Committee on Infectious Diseases of the American Academy of Pediatrics recommends immunization schedules for children and periodically revises them as new knowledge emerges. Table 2-1 gives the current recommendations for normal infants and children, and Table 2-2 gives data for children not immunized in infancy.

Table 2-1

Recommended Schedule for Active Immunization of
Normal Infants and Children

Recom- mended Age	Vaccine(s)	Comments
2 mo	DTP,[a] OPV[b]	Can be initiated earlier in areas of high endemicity
4 mo	DTP, OPV	2-month interval desired for OPV to avoid interference
6 mo	DTP (OPV)	OPV optional for areas in which polio might be imported (e.g., some areas of Southwest United States)
12 mo	Tuberculin test[c]	May be given simultaneously with MMR at 15 months
15 mo	Measles, mumps, rubella (MMR)[d]	MMR preferred
18 mo	DTP, OPV	Consider as part of primary series —DTP essential
4–6 yr[e]	DTP, OPV	
14–16 yr	Td[f]	Repeat every 10 years for lifetime

Source: Reprinted with permission from American Academy of Pediatrics, *Report of the Committee on Infectious Diseases,* 19th ed., Evanston, IL, 1982. P. 7.

[a]DTP: Diphtheria and tetanus toxoids with pertussis vaccine.

[b]OPV: Oral, attenuated poliovirus vaccine contains poliovirus types 1, 2, and 3.

[c]Tuberculin test: Mantoux (intradermal PPD) preferred. Frequency of tests depends on local epidemiology. The Committee recommends annual or biennial testing unless local circumstances dictate less frequent or no testing.

[d]MMR: Live measles, mumps, and rubella viruses in a combined vaccine.

[e]Up to the seventh birthday.

[f]Td: Adult tetanus toxoid (full dose) and diphtheria toxoid (reduced dose) in combination.

For all products used, consult manufacturer's brochure for instructions for storage, handling, and administration. Biologics prepared by different manufacturers may vary, and those of the same manufacturer may change from time to time. The package insert should be followed for a specific product.

Table 2-2

Recommended Immunization Schedules for Infants and Children Not Initially Immunized at Usual Recommended Times in Early Infancy[a]

Timing	Preferred Schedule	Recommended Schedules	Alternatives[b]		Comments
		#1	#2	#3	
First visit	DTP #1, OPV #1 Tuberculin test (PPD)	MMR, PPD	DTP #1, OPV #1, PPD	DTP #1, OPV #1, MMR, PPD	MMR should be given no younger than 15 mo old.
1 mo after first visit	MMR	DTP #1, OPV #1	MMR, DTP #2	DTP # 2	
2 mo after first visit	DTP #2, OPV #2	—	DTP #3, OPV #2	DTP #3, OPV #2	—
3 mo after first visit	(DTP #3)	DTP #2,	—	—	In preferred schedule DTP #3 can be given if OPV #3 is not to be given until 10–16 mo.

4 mo after first visit	DTP #3 (OPV #3)	—	(OPV #3)	(OPV #3)	OPV #3 optional for areas for likely importation of polio (e.g., some southwestern states).
5 mo after first visit	—	DTP #3, (OPV #3)	—	—	—
10–16 mo after last dose	DTP #4, OPV #3, or OPV #4	DTP #4, OPV #3, or OPV #4	DTP #4, OPV #3, or OPV #4	DTP #4, OPV #3, or OPV #4	—
Preschool	DTP #5, OPV #4, or OPV #5	DTP #5, OPV #4, or OPV #5	DTP #5, OPV #4, or OPV #5	DTP #5, OPV #4, or OPV #5	Preschool dose not necessary if DTP #4 or #5 given after fourth birthday.
14–16 years old	Td	Td	Td	Td	Repeat every 10 yr.

Source: Reprinted with permission from American Academy of Pediatrics, *Report of the Committee on Infectious Diseases*, 19th ed., Evanston, IL, 1982. Pp. 18–19.

[a] For all products used, consult manufacturer's brochure for instructions for storage, handling, and administration. Biologics prepared by different manufacturers may vary, and those of the same manufacturer may change from time to time. The package insert should be followed for a specific product.

[b] Alternative #1 can be used in those more than 15 months old if measles is occurring in the community. Alternative #2 allows for more rapid DTP immunization. Alternative #3 should be reserved for those whose access to medical care is compromised by poor compliance.

Abbreviations: DTP = Diphtheria and tetanus toxoids with pertussis vaccine. OPV = Oral, attenuated poliovirus vaccine contains types 1, 2, and 3. Tuberculin test = Mantoux (intradermal PPD) preferred. Frequency of tests depends on local epidemiology. The Committee recommends annual or biennial testing unless local circumstances dictate less frequent or no testing. MMR = Live measles, mumps, and rubella viruses in a combined vaccine. Td = Adult tetanus toxoid (full dose) and diphtheria toxoid (reduced dose) in combination.

COMMON IMMUNIZING AGENTS

Immunizations are such a routine part of health maintenance care that they are, perhaps, given too routinely. Ongoing research and study continually result in new data that affect immunization procedures in terms of administration, efficacy, and safety. The Guide for the Use of Common Immunizing Agents, which follows, provides current information on the administration of routine immunizing agents. Current recommendations for immunization against other diseases (e.g., cholera, plague, rabies, typhoid, typhus, yellow fever) and for international travelers can be obtained by consulting local health departments. Active immunization against tuberculosis, meningitis, and influenza and passive immunization against hepatitis, measles, and varicella–zoster infections are discussed in Chapter 27, Infectious Diseases. Pneumococcal vaccine is discussed in Chapter 17, The Respiratory System.

DTP

AGENTS

Diphtheria toxoid, tetanus toxoid, and pertussis vaccine combined with aluminum phosphate adsorbed.

AGE TO ADMINISTER

Begin at 2 months of age. Do not give over 6 years of age.

TECHNIQUE OF ADMINISTRATION

Primary course: Three doses of 0.5 cc each at 8-week intervals followed by a fourth dose of 0.5 cc approximately 1 year after the third dose

Booster dose: One dose of 0.5 cc at 4–6 years of age (before school entrance) and thereafter Td 0.5 cc every 10 years (see Table 2-3).

In infants and young children doses are given intramuscularly in the mid-lateral or mid-anterior thigh muscles. In older children dorsogluteal, ventrogluteal, and deltoid sites may be used.

Table 2-3
Guide to Tetanus Prophylaxis in Wound Management

History of Tetanus Immunization (Doses)	Clean, Minor Wounds		All Other Wounds	
	Td^a	TIG^b	Td	TIG
Uncertain	Yes	No	Yes	Yes
0–1	Yes	No	Yes	Yes
2	Yes	No	Yes	No^c
3 or more	No^d	No	No^e	No

Source: Reprinted with permission from S. Krugman, R. Ward, and S. L. Katz, editors, *Infectious Diseases of Children*, 6th ed., St. Louis: C. V. Mosby, 1977. P. 488.

^{a}Td: adult type tetanus-diphtheria toxoid.
^{b}TIG: tetanus immune globulin.
^{c}Unless wound more than 24 hours old.
^{d}Unless more than 10 years since last dose.
^{e}Unless more than 5 years since last dose.

COMMENTS

• The fourth dose is an integral part of the basic immunizing course. Basic immunization cannot be considered complete until the fourth dose has been given.

• Reactions to DTP. Recent studies (Barkin and Pichichero, 1979; Cody et al., 1981) reveal that reactions to DTP vaccine occur very frequently. Local reactions (redness, swelling, pain) develop in 50–72 percent of children, behavioral changes (primarily irritability) in up to 80 percent, and fever in approximately 50 percent. Severe reactions were few, and no encephalitis, seizures, or hospitalizations occurred. These reaction rates are higher than previously expected and underscore the need for adequate instruction of parents.

1. *Local reaction:* Redness, induration, and/or a nodule may develop at the injection site. Discomfort may be relieved by placing the child in a soothing warm bath. Nodules occasionally persist for several weeks. Rotate injection sites during the primary course.

2. *Systemic reaction:* Mild to moderate temperature elevations and irritability may occur soon after injection and usually do not

persist past 24–48 hours. If severe febrile or local reactions occur modification of the schedule and dosage must be considered. Fractional doses of one half to one fourth of the recommended dose may be given. Parents should be fully informed of possible reactions and questioned carefully at subsequent visits about occurrence and nature of reactions. Treatment of reactions is usually not indicated but acetaminophen may be prescribed for fever over 38.5°C (101.3°F). Age-appropriate doses are given in Chapter 11, Approach to Minor Illness.

- *Pertussis:* The pertussis component is thought to be the major contributor to reactions to DTP injections. Controversy exists over its continued use, especially in Great Britain (Robinson, 1981). In the United States the Centers for Disease Control have reported that the protective benefits of pertussis vaccination outweigh the risks (serious reaction estimated at 1:100,000 children), but that there is need to develop a less toxic vaccine. Before giving persussis vaccine, a history of central nervous system (CNS) problems should be ruled out. Pertussis vaccine should not be repeated if any CNS disorder (convulsions, prolonged screaming for more than 3 hours, prolonged drowsiness, fever 40.5°C or over) develops after a DTP injection. Consultation with a physician is indicated. The series is continued using DT.

- *Exposure to disease:* Upon exposure to diphtheria or pertussis an emergency booster dose of the appropriate single antigen is indicated unless the fourth dose or a booster dose has been given within the past year. Since the too-frequent use of tetanus toxoid has resulted in an increased incidence of hyperimmunity and severe reactions, the current recommendations for tetanus prophylaxis are presented in Table 2-3.

DT: Pediatric

AGENTS

Diphtheria toxoid and tetanus toxoid combined with aluminum phosphate adsorbed.

AGE TO ADMINISTER

For children under 6 years of age.

TECHNIQUE OF ADMINISTRATION

Same as for DTP.

COMMENTS

- DT–pediatric is for use in infants and young children under 6 years of age when contraindications to the use of pertussis vaccine exist.
- It contains a larger amount of diphtheria antigen than does Td.

Td: Adult Type

AGENTS

Diphtheria toxoid and tetanus toxoid combined with aluminum phosphate adsorbed.

AGE TO ADMINISTER

For children over 6 years of age and adults.

TECHNIQUE OF ADMINISTRATION

Primary course: Two doses of 0.5 cc each at 8-week intervals followed by a third dose of 0.5 cc 6 to 12 months after the second dose

Booster dose: One dose of 0.5 cc at 14 to 16 years and thereafter every 10 years

COMMENTS

- It contains no pertussis vaccine, since the risk of the disease decreases with age.
- It contains less diphtheria antigen, since reactions to diphtheria antigen increase with age.

OPV

AGENTS

Poliovirus vaccine, live, oral, trivalent (TOPV)
Poliovirus vaccine, live, oral, type 1

Poliovirus vaccine, live, oral, type 2

Poliovirus vaccine, live, oral, type 3

AGE TO ADMINISTER

Begin at 2 months. Do not give to persons over 18 years of age.

TECHNIQUE OF ADMINISTRATION

Primary course: Two doses at 8-week intervals within the first 6 months of life followed by a third dose at 18 months of age (In areas endemic for polio, a third dose within the first 6 months is indicated.)

Booster dose: One dose at 4–6 years of age (before school entrance)

Primary course for children and adolescents under 18 years of age: Two doses at 8-week intervals followed by a third dose 10–16 months after the last dose (see Table 2-2)

COMMENTS

- TOPV (Sabin) is suitable for breast-fed infants. It is not necessary to withhold breast-feeding before or after giving TOPV.
- Vaccine must be kept frozen. If unopened vaccine thaws, it may be refrozen provided the temperature does not exceed 8°C (46°F) during the thaw period. See manufacturer's insert for details.
- There are reportedly no reactions to the vaccine.
- The population at risk has to be defined. Before the introduction of polio vaccines, most of the population were exposed and developed immunity to polio through contact with wild natural polio virus strains. Most of these infections were mild or subclinical (see Chapter 27, Infectious Diseases, under Poliomyelitis). The widespread use of polio vaccines since the early 1960s and especially the use of OPV (which simulates natural infection and also induces local immunity in the intestinal tract) have provided mass immunity. In particular, the quantity of wild virus circulating in the general population has been reduced and has resulted in "herd immunity" (i.e., a barrier is present in the community to protect susceptible persons). At least 80 percent of the community (herd) must be immune to provide an effective barrier to the

wild virus. Thus, the use of vaccines, while reducing and even eradicating polio, makes it essential that all infants and children be immunized. The wild virus population has declined and no longer will contribute significantly to maintaining immunity. If a significant number of children are not vaccinated, especially in the 0- to 4-year age group, they will be susceptible to the wild virus; the wild virus could circulate among them and result in epidemics when a virulent strain is introduced.

• Epidemics can be controlled by giving the monovalent vaccine of the same serotype as that causing the outbreak.

• As for risks of the vaccine, live virus persists in the GI tract of the vaccinee for 4–6 weeks after vaccination, and cases of paralytic disease in vaccinees and their household contacts have appeared. A large percentage of affected persons have been found to have unusual immunodeficiency disorders. The incidence of vaccine-associated paralytic disease, while tragic, is very low, with a risk calculated at 1:3.6 million doses of vaccine (Krugman and Katz, 1981). Some authorities (Salk and Salk, 1977) are advocating the return to inactivated polio vaccine, citing safety and effectiveness in several European countries. Current recommendations in the United States are for use of inactivated poliovirus vaccine (Salk) in children with immune deficiency diseases and their siblings and for adults over 18 years of age who have had no previous polio immunization. In considering the issue of unimmunized adult household contacts of infants scheduled to receive OPV, the American Academy of Pediatrics recommends either proceeding with routine OPV administration or using inactivated polio vaccine for adults monthly for 3 months, and, at the third monthly dose, initiating OPV administration to the child.

• See Contraindications to Routine Immunization, this chapter.

Measles

AGENTS

Measles virus vaccine, live, attenuated

Also in combination:

Measles–rubella virus vaccine, live, attenuated

Measles–mumps–rubella virus vaccine, live, attenuated

AGE TO ADMINISTER

Begin at 15 months of age. See below, Comments.

TECHNIQUE OF ADMINISTRATION

One subcutaneous injection. Vaccine supplied as a single-dose vial of lyophilized vaccine with a disposable syringe containing diluent. Inject total volume of reconstituted vaccine.

COMMENTS

• Inactivated measles vaccine, first licensed in 1963, is no longer recommended and is no longer available in the United States, for the following reasons:

1. The immunogenic and protective effects of the vaccine were transient.
2. Atypical measles including symptoms of high fever, edema of the extremities, and pneumonitis occurred on exposure to measles virus later on.

• Live vaccines were also licensed in 1963 and until 1969 were given with gamma globulin. Live vaccines used commonly today are further attenuated forms of the original Enders-Edmonston B strain.

• Vaccine is prepared by growing virus in chick embryo cultures. Hypersensitivity reactions occur rarely and are usually minor, consisting of wheal and flare or urticaria at the injection site. However, there have been three reported cases of immediate allergic reactions in children with histories of anaphylactoid reactions to egg ingestion. Children with such histories should not be vaccinated without medical consultation (CDC, 1982).

• One injection confers long-lasting immunity. Antibody titers are lower than those following natural measles, but the protection is durable according to follow-up evidence, which now extends over 20 years.

• Reactions. The vaccine produces a mild or inapparent noncommunicable infection. Fifteen percent of vaccinated children have symptoms which include fever, faint rash, and minor toxicity. Symptoms usually occur 5–12 days after vaccination. Significant central nervous system reactions, thought to be associated with measles vaccine, occur approximately once for every million doses.

- Recent outbreaks. Cases of measles have been reported in groups of children and adolescents who:

  1. Have never had measles and have never received live attenuated measles vaccine
  2. Received live attenuated vaccine before 12 months of age
  3. Received live measles vaccine that had been inactivated by exposure to light, inadequate refrigeration, or use of wrong diluent (Do not store vaccine in refrigerator door.)
  4. Received too large a dose of gamma globulin with the measles vaccine when immunized before 1969
  5. Received killed measles vaccine

- Indications for measles immunization and re-immunization are as follows:

  1. Routine measles immunization should be deferred until 15 months of age. This is a recommendation based on studies that show that seroconversion rates of 80 to 85 percent occur in children immunized at 12 months, as compared with seroconversion rates of more than 95 percent in children immunized after 13 to 14 months of age (Krugman, 1977, p. 6).
  2. Measles vaccine should be given any time after 6 months of age during measles outbreaks if the infant is at risk of exposure. A second vaccination should then be given after 15 months of age.
  3. If doubt exists about the details of immunization status, another inoculation of measles vaccine should be given.
  4. Children vaccinated with simultaneous administration of gamma globulin at any age should be revaccinated.
  5. Children vaccinated with inactivated vaccine should be reimmunized.
  6. Children vaccinated before 12 months of age should be reimmunized (Halsey et al., 1979).
  7. For children vaccinated at 12 to 14 months, there is no universal agreement on the need for reimmunization. Since most of

these children will have seroconverted, the decision needs to be individualized on the basis of the amount of measles in the community, the probability of vaccine failure, the risks and consequences of the disease, and the risks and costs of revaccination (Shelton et al., 1978; Marks et al., 1978). Krugman (1980), however, recommends reimmunization of children who were immunized at 12 to 13 months unless the parent can document a reaction to the vaccine. His rationale is that the 10 to 15 percent who did not seroconvert will probably not get measles as youngsters, since their peers are immunized, and will remain susceptible in their older years.

8. Because of recent outbreaks of measles among young children of migrant workers in Texas (CDC, May 1981), the CDC and the Office of Migrant Health recommend that all migrant dependents born since 1957, regardless of where they live, should have documentation of immunity to measles (either documented history of live measles vaccination after 1 year of age or physician-diagnosed measles). It is also recommended that for this population infants aged 6 months through 14 months be vaccinated and those vaccinated before their first birthday be revaccinated when they are 15 months of age.

• Tuberculin testing

1. It is recommended that tuberculin testing be done before administration of measles vaccine because of the hazard of the possible exacerbation of undiagnosed, untreated tuberculosis (see Chapter 27, Tuberculosis). Since this possibility is remote, and since the value of protection against natural measles exceeds the theoretical hazard of exacerbation of tuberculosis, the recommended procedure should not interfere with community-wide immunization programs where the risk of natural measles is high.

2. Measles vaccine may alter immune mechanisms and temporarily depress tuberculin sensitivity. This could result in a false-negative tuberculin test. If measles vaccine precedes TB testing, 4–6 weeks should elapse before administering a tuberculin test.

3. It has been demonstrated that it is valid to administer M–M–R vaccine and tuberculin skin testing simultaneously.

• In unvaccinated normal infants and children live measles vaccine can usually prevent the disease if administered within 2 days after exposure to natural measles. Otherwise give a preventive dose of immune serum globulin as soon as possible (within 5 days) and 3 months later vaccinate unless the infant is under 15 months of age.

• Children with underlying illness that contraindicates the use of live vaccine should be protected on exposure by the use of immune serum globulin. See Table 27-3. In such high-risk children, it is advisable to immunize their regular contacts.

Rubella

AGENTS

Rubella virus vaccine, live, attenuated
  Also in combination:
  Measles–rubella virus vaccine, live, attenuated
  Mumps–rubella virus vaccine, live, attenuated
  Measles–mumps–rubella virus vaccine, live, attenuated

AGE TO ADMINISTER

Begin at 15 months. Do not give to pregnant women. See below, Comments

TECHNIQUE OF ADMINISTRATION

Same as for measles.

COMMENTS

• The vaccine was licensed in 1969. In 1979 a vaccine prepared in human diploid cell culture replaced the former duck embryo vaccine and is thought to be more stable and more immunogenic. Primary rationale for use is to prevent congenital rubella syndrome (see Chapter 27). Two population groups are targets for immunization:

  1. Children between the ages of 15 months and onset of puberty to reduce the spread of natural rubella infection

2. Susceptible nonpregnant women on a selective basis. Although largely successful, recent reports (Lawless et al., 1980) indicate that approximately 15 percent of adolescents and adults remain susceptible to rubella. This includes unimmunized persons as well as those who are vaccine failures. Several authorities are now recommending that increased emphasis be placed on vaccinating susceptible adolescent and adult females of child-bearing age (CDC, February 1981). Others (Krugman, 1980) are suggesting that all children receive two doses of rubella, the second (booster) dose during preadolescence designed to cover those who were vaccine failures after the first dose.

- Vaccination of women of child-bearing age (including adolescents):
  1. Perform serologic testing—hemagglutination inhibition test (HI titer). Passive hemagglutination, hemolysis in gel, and enzyme-linked immunosorbent assay (ELISA) tests are more sensitive measures than the HI test to determine immunity (CDC, February 1981).
  2. If rubella antibodies are present and immunity is confirmed, do not vaccinate. A titer of 1:8 or higher indicates adequate protection.
  3. If susceptible and nonpregnant, vaccination is advised only if the woman understands that she *must not* become pregnant for 3 months after vaccination. An acceptable method of contraception must be followed.
  4. An ideal time to vaccinate susceptible women is in the immediate postpartum period.
- Reactions and side effects:
  1. Rash and lymphadenopathy occur rarely
  2. Transient arthritis and arthralgia occur frequently in women who are vaccinated but rarely in children. It occurs 1 to 3 weeks post vaccination, persists for 1 to 3 days, and rarely recurs.
- Communicability. After vaccination, rubella virus is shed and excreted from the pharynx for 2 or more weeks but a number of studies (CDC, February 1981) have confirmed that immunized children are not contagious. There is no contraindication to the

use of rubella vaccine in children of pregnant mothers. In fact, susceptible children of pregnant mothers *should* be immunized.

- Risk of vaccine to the fetus. Although there may be theoretical risks, all available data on women inadvertently vaccinated within 3 months before, or 3 months after, conception indicate that the risk of teratogenicity, if any, is very small (CDC, February 1981). The Immunization Practices Advisory Committee believes that inadvertent rubella immunization during pregnancy should not be a reason to recommend abortion on a routine basis.

- Reinfection. Reinfection can and does occur more commonly after vaccination than after natural rubella. Viremia has *not* been detected during reinfection. Consequently it is unlikely that fetal infection will occur in association with reinfection.

- Pregnant woman exposed to rubella. When a pregnant woman whose immune status is unknown is exposed to rubella two facts must be established:

1. Whether or not the woman is immune to rubella
2. If not immune, whether or not she has contracted the current infection

The procedure recommended is as follows:

1. Obtain an HI titer as soon as possible (within 1 week of exposure).
2. If antibodies are present in adequate amounts (HI titer ≥ 1:8) the woman can be reassured.
3. If antibody is not detectable, gamma globulin may be given and a second HI titer is obtained 3 to 4 weeks later. If antibodies are then detectable it indicates current rubella infection. Gamma globulin has not proven effective in preventing rubella, but it is worth the try if abortion is not an acceptable alternative. If the HI titer remains < 1:8, no infection is present and this woman should be vaccinated immediately postpartum.
4. If more than 1 week has elapsed before the first blood specimen is obtained, the presence of antibodies may indicate past *or* current infection. Thus a second specimen should be obtained 1 to 2 weeks later to check for a rising antibody titer indicative of current infection. The approach outlined by Mann et al. (1981) is most useful.

5. The way to avoid this stressful situation is by vaccinating all children between 15 months and onset of puberty and by encouraging women of childbearing age to have baseline antibody titer determinations performed.

Mumps

AGENTS

Mumps virus vaccine, live attenuated
  Also in combination:
  Mumps–rubella virus vaccine, live, attenuated
  Measles–mumps–rubella virus vaccine, live, attenuated

AGE TO ADMINISTER

Begin at 15 months of age.

TECHNIQUE OF ADMINISTRATION

Same as for measles.

COMMENTS

• The vaccine was licensed in 1967 and is prepared in cell cultures of chick embryo.
• Because mumps vaccine is available in combined form with measles and rubella vaccines, it should be considered for use at 15 months of age. Otherwise it should be used in susceptible children approaching puberty, in adolescents, and in adults, particularly males who have no history of mumps. See Chapter 27, Infectious Diseases.
• There are no known serious side effects of this vaccine. Occasionally a mild, brief fever and parotitis develop.
• See Contraindications to Routine Immunization, this chapter.

Smallpox

AGENT

Active, live vaccinia virus (nonattenuated).

AGE TO ADMINISTER

Not recommended as routine procedure for individuals residing in the United States. See Comments.

TECHNIQUE OF ADMINISTRATION

The vaccine is supplied as glycerinated vaccine or lyophilized vaccine. For the primary vaccination, a small drop of vaccine is placed on the outer aspect of the upper arm. A series of pressures (8–10) is made with a sterile needle held parallel to the skin, thereby depositing vaccine under the superficial skin. Excess vaccine is wiped away with dry sterile gauze. No dressing is necessary.

COMMENTS

• Successful vaccination depends on the use of a potent vaccine and correct technique. A successful "take" will produce a slowly growing area of erythema after 4 to 5 days which reaches maximal size in 8 to 14 days, acquires a vesicular appearance which then scabs, and usually leaves a recognizable scar. If no vesicle appears do not assume the individual is immune. Repeat the vaccination using another lot (batch) of vaccine.

• Re-vaccination. A similar technique is used but 25 to 30 pressures are recommended. Reaction should consist of vesicular or pustular lesion or definite palpable induration surrounding a central lesion. In endemic areas re-vaccination is recommended every 3 years.

• Routine vaccination is no longer recommended by the U.S. Public Health Service, the American Academy of Pediatrics, and the World Health Organization. Rationale includes the following:

1. There have been no documented cases of smallpox in the United States since 1949.

2. The World Health Organization certified the world free from smallpox in December 1979. The last reported case of endemic smallpox occurred in Somalia in 1977 and the last reported case of laboratory-acquired smallpox in the United Kingdom in 1978.

3. The risks of vaccination outweigh the risks of contracting the disease.

- The Centers for Disease Control (1980) recommend vaccination only for those few laboratory personnel working in WHO smallpox laboratories.
- International Certificate of Vaccination is still required for entry into some countries of Africa and Asia. Current information is obtainable from local health departments.
- Precautions:
  1. Persons with eczema should neither be vaccinated nor exposed to vaccinated persons.
  2. If a client with eczema requires vaccination it is accompanied with a prophylactic dose of vaccinia immune globulin. Consult with a physician before vaccinating.
  3. Do not vigorously cleanse the vaccination site. Danger of skin abrasions and subsequent larger area for virus inoculation result. Do not use alcohol to cleanse the skin. Use acetone.
  4. Do not vaccinate anyone with acute skin lesions (e.g., poison ivy, burns, impetigo).
  5. See Contraindications to Routine Immunization, this chapter.
- Vaccination of young infants:
  1. In a situation of high risk, infants over 2 months of age could be vaccinated after medical consultation. Complication rates appear to be twice as high for children under one year of age.
  2. Young children traveling with parents to countries requiring smallpox vaccination for entry can be spared vaccination by providing a letter from medical authorities advising against vaccination.

DELIVERY OF IMMUNIZATION SERVICES

Informed Consent and Liability

Currently there is much discussion and concern surrounding the issue of informing clients and parents of the possible side effects of immunizations. Informed consent is directed toward providing information, permitting full individual decision-making by the client or parent, and protecting providers from liability. Several issues are of concern:

1. *How much information to provide:* Is it necessary to define in detail every possible complication regardless of how rare?
2. *Format of the information:* Should the information be verbal or written? Should parents sign a consent form? Government-funded programs require written information and written consent.
3. *Effect on the community:* Will the information be misinterpreted and result in refusals, thus jeopardizing the public health?
4. *Liability:* Who should be liable for the unavoidable intrinsic risk associated with vaccine administration?

Parents should definitely be informed of the risks and benefits of immunizations, and it is possible to do so without causing undue alarm or jeopardizing preventive health programs. An example of such basic information is provided in Table 2-4. The Centers for Disease Control (see this chapter, Resource Information) also provides printed information for parents.

The American Academy of Pediatrics has recently proposed a National Vaccine-Injury Compensation Program that would recognize public responsibility for the serious injuries that occasionally and unavoidably follow vaccination (AAP, 1981). At least one state, California, has established a state compensation plan.

Current Immunization Status

As recently as 1977, immunization levels of children 1–4 years of age were dangerously low: DTP 69.5 percent, polio 60.1 percent, measles 63.1 percent, and rubella 59.4 percent (CDC, 1978). As a result, the National Childhood Immunization Initiative was conducted during 1977 and 1979 with impressive results. See Table 2-5. Efforts continue and a new goal has been stated: the elimination of indigenous measles from the United States by the mid-1980s.

Efforts to Improve Immunization Levels

1. Legislation. All states have enacted legislation requiring specific immunizations before school entry. Those states having the

most comprehensive laws and most vigorous enforcement policies have shown the lowest incidence of measles (CDC, 1982). Excluding from school students who have not provided documented evidence of immunity to the disease is the most effective means of enforcement. Documented evidence includes: a physician-documented history of measles, laboratory evidence of measles immunity, or a documented history of vaccination with live measles virus vaccine on or after the first birthday.

2. Accurate reporting of cases to local health departments. This is an important yet frequently overlooked responsibility.

3. Accurate record keeping. Permanent records at health facilities as well as provision of records to parents help identify children at risk.

4. Education of parents and communities.

5. Provision of funds to health department to purchase vaccines.

6. Continued surveillance by health providers of the immunization status of every child they see.

Table 2-4

Benefits and Reactions from Immunization of Children[a,b]

Diseases	Vaccines

Diphtheria
    Occurs primarily in children
    Attacks the throat and nasal
        passages
    Interferes with breathing
    Produces toxin that damages
        heart, kidneys and nerves
    10% of cases are fatal
	Diphtheria–tetanus toxoids (DT,
	    Td)
	    Almost all persons will be pro-
	        tected after completing a
	        primary series and a booster
	    Common reactions include a
	        sore lump at injection site
	        and occasionally fever, 12 to
	        24 hours after vaccination
	    Most severe reactions are very
	        rare

Tetanus (lockjaw)
    Caused by bacteria getting into
        wounds
    Causes painful muscle contrac-
        tions, convulsions
    50% of cases are fatal
	Diphtheria and tetanus toxoids,
	    pertussis vaccine (DTP)[c]
	    Given to children under age 7 yr
	    Most children will be protected
	        after completing a primary
	        series and booster

Table 2-4 *(Continued)*

Diseases	*Vaccines*

Pertussis (whooping cough)
  Most severe in infants less than
    1 year old
  Causes severe coughing spells
    often followed by vomiting
  Often causes pneumonia,
    convulsions
  Very contagious
  Causes serious brain disorder
    in about 1 of every 1,000 pa-
    tients and permanent brain
    damage in 1 of every 10,000
    patients
  2,000 cases each year and 10
    deaths per year in United
    States
	Common reactions include a
	  sore lump at injection site,
	  fever 12 to 24 hours after
	  vaccination
	Causes a fever over 102°F in
	  5% of children vaccinated
	1 in 1750 children vaccinated
	  may have convulsions or
	  shocklike episode (limpness
	  and paleness)
	Rarely, inflammation of brain
	  may occur: 1 in 110,000
	  doses. Very rarely may cause
	  more serious permanent
	  brain disorder: 1 in 310,000
	  doses

Polio
  Attacks the nervous system
  Causes paralysis usually of
    arms or legs, but also the
    muscles you breathe with
  10% of cases are fatal
	Oral polio vaccine[d] (OPV, live,
	  Sabin)
	90% of persons receiving a
	  primary series and booster
	  will be protected
	No common reactions
	A paralytic reaction to the vac-
	  cine occurs in the person
	  vaccinated or a close contact
	  (such as a household mem-
	  ber) about 1 in 4 million doses
	Inactivated polio vaccine (IPV,
	  killed, Salk)
	90% of persons receiving a
	  primary series and booster
	  will be protected
	No common reactions
	Boosters recommended every
	  5 years until age 18
	Recommended for children
	  who have a low resistance to
	  infection or live with persons
	  with a low resistance to
	  infection

Table 2-4 *(Continued)*

Diseases	*Vaccines*
	Sometimes recommended for unimmunized adults whose children are to be vaccinated with OPV
Measles Almost always causes high fever and rash, usually lasts 10 days May cause pneumonia or ear infection in 1 of 10 who have the disease Causes deafness, blindness, convulsions, or brain disorder in 1 of every 1,000 children who get the disease Of children who develop a brain disorder from measles, 1 in 10 dies	Measles vaccine[e] 90% of persons receiving one dose of the vaccine will be protected. 10–20% of children immunized may have mild fever and rash within 10 days. 1 person in 1 million vaccinated may develop brain disorder
Mumps Usually causes fever and swelling of salivary glands May cause inflammation of testicles in adolescent and adult males May cause inflammation of pancreas May cause inflammation of the coverings of the brain and spinal cord in 1 child in 10 Can result in permanent deafness	Mumps vaccine[e] 90% of persons receiving 1 dose will be protected Very rarely, fever and swelling of salivary gland may occur after vaccination
Rubella When contracted by pregnant women can cause miscarriage, stillbirth, or multiple birth defects including deafness, heart disease, blindness	Rubella vaccine[e] 90% of persons receiving one dose will be protected About 1% of young children and 5–10% of teenagers may develop temporary arm, leg, or joint pains 1–3 weeks after getting shot

Table 2-4 *(Continued)*

Diseases	Vaccines
Usually a mild disease with low fever, rash, and swollen glands Can cause joint pains, more frequently in teenagers	About 1 of 7 children will get a rash or some swelling of the neck glands 1–2 weeks after getting the shot Children of pregnant women can be vaccinated **MMR vaccine**[e] Measles, mumps, and rubella vaccines are usually given in combination (MMR) as one shot. Children who have had one of the diseases or vaccines can still be given the combination vaccine to complete their immunization

Source: E. K. Marcuse, "Pediatrician's Immunization Consent Practice, Washington State," Copyright 1983, Children's Orthopedic Hospital and Medical Center, Seattle.

[a]*Special notes:* (1) Children sick with something more serious than a cold should not be immunized without first checking with a doctor. (2) With any drug or vaccine, there is a possibility that an allergic or other more serious reaction or even death could occur. The American Academy of Pediatrics recommends that all normal, healthy children in the United States be immunized against these diseases because it is thought that benefits of these vaccines outweigh their risks. (3) Keep the record of your child's immunization where you can find it: You will need it when you enroll your child in day care or school.

[b]Immunization can prevent crippling or fatal diseases. Outlined below are the dangers of these diseases and the benefits and side effects of immunization. Please review this information carefully. If you have questions, please ask them.

[c]These vaccines should not be given to those who have had a serious reaction to DTP shots before, such as high fever (105°F) or convulsion.

[d]Should not be given to children with cancer, leukemia, or kidney transplant or to those who have other diseases or who take drugs that lower the body's resistance to infection, or to children who live with other persons who have these diseases or take such drugs.

[e]Should not be given to children with cancer, lymphoma, leukemia, or who have other diseases, or who take drugs that lower the body's resistance to infection. Should not be given to children who have had an allergic reaction to eating eggs, or to an antibiotic called neomycin, serious enough to require medical treatment. Should not be given to pregnant females. Children who have received gamma globulin or a blood transfusion in the preceeding 3 months should be scheduled for vaccination later.

Table 2-5
Reported Cases of Specific Diseases in the United States: 1977–1980

Disease	1977	1978	1979	1980
Diphtheria	84	76	59	3
Tetanus	87	86	81	95
Pertussis	2,177	2,063	1,623	1,730
Measles	57,345	26,871	13,597	13,506
Mumps	21,436	16,817	14,225	8576
Rubella	20,395	18,269	11,795	3904
Polio	18	15	34	9

Source: Centers for Disease Control. "Annual Summary 1980: Reported Morbidity and Mortality in the United States," *MMWR 29*:3, September 1981.

Resource Information

1. Local health departments.
2. Manufacturers' inserts. These contain complete information on the use of each specific vaccine.
3. Committee on Infectious Diseases, American Academy of Pediatrics. Their report, the "Red Book," is frequently updated, is very complete, and can be purchased by writing to AAP, P.O. Box 1034, Evanston, IL 60204.
4. Immunization Practices Advisory Committee (ACIP), U.S. Public Health Service, Centers for Disease Control, Atlanta, GA 30333. Telephone: 404-633-3311. CDC publications of particular interest include:
   - *Morbidity and Mortality Weekly Report.*
   - *Health Information for International Travel,* published annually as a supplement to *MMWR,* for sale by the Superintendent of Documents, U.S. Government Printing Office, Washington, DC 20402.

References

American Academy of Pediatrics, Committee on Infectious Diseases. "Concomitant Administration of Vaccines: A Policy Statement." *News and Comment 31*:5, May 1980.

American Academy of Pediatrics. *Report of the Committee on Infectious Diseases,* 19th ed. Evanston, IL, 1982.

American Academy of Pediatrics, Task Force on Compensation for Vaccine-Related Injuries. "Compensation for Vaccine-Related Injuries: AAP Policy Statement." *News and Comment 32*:13, May 1981.

Barkin, R. M. and M. E. Pichichero. "Diphtheria–Pertussis–Tetanus Vaccine." *Pediatrics 63*:256–260, February 1979.

Brickman, H. F. et al. "Timing of Tine Tests in Relation to Immunizations." *Pediatrics 55*:392–396, March 1975.

Centers for Disease Control. "Measles Prevention." *MMWR 31*:217–231, May 7, 1982.

Centers for Disease Control. "School Immunization Requirements for Measles—United States, 1982." *MMWR 31*:65–67, February 19, 1982.

Centers for Disease Control. "Annual Summary 1980: Reported Morbidity and Mortality in the United States." *MMWR 29*:3, September 1981.

Centers for Disease Control. "Measles—Texas." *MMWR 30*:209–211, May 15, 1981.

Centers for Disease Control. "Rubella Prevention." *MMWR 30*:37–47, February 6, 1981.

Centers for Disease Control. "Annual Summary 1979: Reported Morbidity and Mortality in the United States." *MMWR 28*:3, September 1980.

Centers for Disease Control. *United States Immunization Survey 1977.* U.S. Public Health Service, DHEW, Atlanta, GA, 79:8221, October 1978.

Cody, C. L. et al. "Nature and Rates of Adverse Reactions Associated with DTP and DT Immunizations in Infants and Children." *Pediatrics 68*:650–660, November 1981.

Halsey, N. A. et al. "Measles Vaccination." *Pediatrics 63*:346, February 1979.

Hayden, G. F. et al. "Current Status of Mumps and Mumps Vaccine in the United States." *Pediatrics 62*:965–969, December 1978.

Krugman, R. D. et al. "Antibody Persistence after Primary Immunization with Trivalent Oral Polio Vaccine." *Pediatrics 60*:80–82, July 1977.

Krugman, S. "Rubella Immunization: Present Status and Future Perspectives." *Pediatrics 65*:1174–1176, June 1980.

Krugman, S. Personal communication, February 1980.

Krugman, S. "Present Status of Measles and Rubella Immunization in the United States: A Medical Progress Report." *J Pediatr 90*:1–12, January 1977.

Krugman, S. and S. Katz. *Infectious Diseases of Children,* 7th ed. St. Louis: Mosby, 1981.

Lawless, M. R. et al. "Rubella Susceptibility in Sixth Graders: Effectiveness of Current Immunization Practice." *Pediatrics 65*:1086–1089, June 1980.

Mann, J. M. et al. "Assessing Risks of Rubella Infection during Pregnancy: A Standardized Approach." *JAMA 245*:1647–1652, April 24, 1981.

Marcuse, E. K. "Pediatrician's Immunization Consent Practice, Washington State." *Pediatrics 63*:419–422, March 1979.

Marks, J. S. et al. "Measles Vaccine Efficacy in Children Previously Vaccinated at 12 Months of Age." *Pediatrics 62*:955–960, December 1978.

Robinson, R. J. "The Whooping-Cough Immunisation Controversy." *Arch Dis Child 56*:577–580, August 1981.

Salk, J. and D. Salk. "Control of Influenza and Poliomyelitis with Killed Virus Vaccines." *Science* 195:834–847, March 1977.

Shelton, J. D. et al. "Measles Vaccine Efficacy: Influence of Age at Vaccination vs. Duration of Time since Vaccination." *Pediatrics* 62:961–964, December 1978.

Vernon, T. M. et al. "An Evaluation of Three Techniques for Improving Immunization Levels in Elementary Schools." *Am J Public Health* 66:457–460, May 1976.

Wara, D. W. and A. J. Ammann, "The Immunologic System and Immunodeficiency Disorders." In E. H. Waechter and F. G. Blake, editors, *Nursing Care of Children,* 9th ed. Philadelphia: J.B. Lippincott, 1976. Pp. 296–307.

3

Nutrition in Infancy and Childhood

The influence of nutrition on growth and development in infancy and childhood is well known and as knowledge accumulates it becomes more evident that nutrition affects most facets of a person's well-being throughout life.

Parents often lack basic information on nutrition or are confused by the plethora of data, opinions, and material (professional and commercial) aimed at them and at their children. At the same time, there are increasing numbers of parents who have extensive and sophisticated knowledge about nutrition. It is therefore essential for the nurse practitioner to be competent in the area of proper nutrition for infants and children.

Nutrition does not occur in a vacuum. Parents bring with them a whole nutritional past including habits and attitudes toward food that have been influenced by culture, education, and socioeconomic factors and that result in a wide range of variability in infant feeding practices. Approaches to infant, toddler, and school-age feeding practices are discussed in Chapters 5, 6, and 7, respectively.

Acceptance and knowledge of the many individual styles, methods, and approaches to infant feeding are important aspects of the role of the pediatric care provider. However, the primary concern in nutrition counseling must be that of meeting the known nutritional requirements of the infant and child. Reinforcement of the parent's own efforts is mandatory, but when nutritional practices are based on unsound knowledge, counseling and education must be geared toward providing parents with the information and support necessary to meet the normal nutritional needs of their children. Nutrition education is one of the best preventive health care measures available.

This chapter presents information on normal nutritional requirements for infants, children, and adolescents, a review of essential nutrients, guidelines for assessing nutritional status, practical information for parent counseling, and brief discussions of some common nutritional problems. Nutritional needs during pregnancy are briefly presented, since the nurse practitioner is often a source of advice and counsel for pregnant women.

NUTRITIONAL REQUIREMENTS

The science of nutrition continues to expand, and new and revised data continue to emerge in relationship to nutrients and amounts considered essential for optimal growth, development, and health. It is important to recognize that the recommendations made are based on available data and change frequently.

Definitions

- Requirement. The requirement of a person for a specific nutrient is defined as the "least amount of that nutrient that will promote an optimal state of health" (Fomon, 1974, p. 109). Since requirements are expressed in minimal terms, and since these values are estimated and cannot with certainty be used under all circumstances and sets of conditions, they are not used as recommended intakes.
- Recommended Dietary Allowances (RDAs). These values are the levels of intake of essential nutrients considered, in the judgment of the Food and Nutrition Board of the National Academy of Science–National Research Council, to be adequate to meet the

known nutritional needs of almost every healthy person (see Table 3-1). The allowances are intended for general use and are based on the needs of "average" people living in temperate environments and expending "average" amounts of energy. It is recognized that individual nutrient requirements differ and that factors such as age, sex, body size, genetic makeup, physiologic state, and environment affect requirements. These *recommended intakes* are generally higher than the *requirements* and represent amounts of nutrients that are safe and present no hazard. The RDAs do not allow for persons depleted of specific nutrients due to illness or deficiency states.

• Estimated Safe and Adequate Daily Dietary Intakes of Additional Selected Vitamins and Minerals. A major change in the revised 1980 RDAs is the inclusion of estimated ranges of safe and adequate intakes for three minerals, three vitamins, and six trace elements that reflect the best available current knowledge (see Table 3-2).

Essential Nutrients

ENERGY (CALORIES)

Requirements The energy needs of children vary at different ages and under various circumstances. Energy requirements (see Table 3-3) depend on energy expenditures caused by the following events:

• Basal metabolism
• Body activity
• Growth
• Specific dynamic action of food (i.e., the increased heat production after ingestion of food)
• Fecal loss

Distribution of Calories In addition to total requirements, the distribution of calories must be considered so foods chosen will contain all the other dietary essentials. Diets are generally calculated to provide calories as follows:

Table 3-1
Recommended Dietary Allowances, Revised 1980[a]
Designed for the Maintenance of Good Nutrition of Practically All Healthy People in the United States

Age and Sex Group (year)	Weight (kg)	Weight (lb)	Height (cm)	Height (in)	Protein (gm)	Fat-Soluble Vitamins: Vitamin A (µg RE)[b]	Vitamin D (µg)[c]	Vitamin E (mg α TE)[d]	Water-Soluble Vitamins: Vitamin C (mg)	Thiamine (mg)	Riboflavin (mg)	Niacin (mg NE)[e]	Vitamin B6 (mg)	Folacin[f] (µg)	Vitamin B12 (µg)	Minerals: Calcium (mg)	Phosphorus (mg)	Magnesium (mg)	Iron (mg)	Zinc (mg)	Iodine (µg)
Infants																					
0.0–0.5	6	13	60	24	kg × 2.2	420	10	3	35	0.3	0.4	6	0.3	30	0.5[g]	360	240	50	10	3	40
0.5–1.0	9	20	71	28	kg × 2.0	400	10	4	35	0.5	0.6	8	0.6	45	1.5	540	360	70	15	5	50
Children																					
1–3	13	29	90	35	23	400	10	5	45	0.7	0.8	9	0.9	100	2.0	800	800	150	15	10	70
4–6	20	44	112	44	30	500	10	6	45	0.9	1.0	11	1.3	200	2.5	800	800	200	10	10	90
7–10	28	62	132	52	34	700	10	7	45	1.2	1.4	16	1.6	300	3.0	800	800	250	10	10	120
Males																					
11–14	45	99	157	62	45	1,000	10	8	50	1.4	1.6	18	1.8	400	3.0	1,200	1,200	350	18	15	150
15–18	66	145	176	69	56	1,000	10	10	60	1.4	1.7	18	2.0	400	3.0	1,200	1,200	400	18	15	150
19–22	70	154	177	70	56	1,000	7.5	10	60	1.5	1.7	19	2.2	400	3.0	800	800	350	10	15	150
23–50	70	154	178	70	56	1,000	5	10	60	1.4	1.6	18	2.2	400	3.0	800	800	350	10	15	150
51+	70	154	178	70	56	1,000	5	10	60	1.2	1.4	16	2.2	400	3.0	800	800	350	10	15	150

Females																				
11–14	46	101	157	62	46	800	10	8	50	1.1	1.3	15	1.8	400	3.0	1,200	1,200	300	18	15	150
15–18	55	120	163	64	46	800	10	8	60	1.1	1.3	14	2.0	400	3.0	1,200	1,200	300	18	15	150
19–22	55	120	163	64	44	800	7.5	8	60	1.1	1.3	14	2.0	400	3.0	800	800	300	18	15	150
23–50	55	120	163	64	44	800	5	8	60	1.0	1.2	13	2.0	400	3.0	800	800	300	18	15	150
51+	55	120	163	64	44	800	5	8	60	1.0	1.2	13	2.0	400	3.0	800	800	300	10	15	150
Pregnancy	+30				+30	+200	+5	+2	+20	+0.4	+0.3	+2	+0.6	+400	+1.0	+400	+400	+150	h	+5	+25
Lactation	+20				+20	+400	+5	+3	+40	+0.5	+0.5	+5	+0.5	+100	+1.0	+400	+400	+150	h	+10	+50

Source: Food and Nutrition Board, National Academy of Sciences–National Research Council, Revised 1980.

[a] The allowances are intended to provide for individual variations among most normal persons as they live in the United States under usual environmental stresses. Diets should be based on a variety of common foods in order to provide other nutrients for which human requirements have been less well defined. See Table 3-3 for weights and heights by individual year of age and for suggested average energy intakes.

[b] Retinol equivalents: 1 retinol equivalent = 1 μg retinol or 6 μg β-carotene.

[c] As cholecalciferol: 10 μg cholecalciferol = 400 IU vitamin D.

[d] α tocopherol equivalents: 1 mg d-α-tocopherol = 1αTE

[e] 1 N.E. (niacin equivalent) = 1 mg niacin or 60 mg dietary tryptophan.

[f] The folacin allowances refer to dietary sources as determined by *Lactobacillus casei* assay after treatment with enzymes (conjugases) to make polyglutamyl forms of the vitamin available to the test organism.

[g] The RDA for vitamin B₁₂ in infants is based on average concentration of the vitamin in human milk. The allowances after weaning are based on energy intake (as recommended by the American Academy of Pediatrics) and consideration of other factors, such as intestinal absorption.

[h] The increased requirement during pregnancy cannot be met by the iron content of habitual American diets or by the existing iron stores of many women; therefore, the use of 30- to 60-mg supplemental iron is recommended. Iron needs during lactation are not substantially different from those of nonpregnant women, but continued supplementation of the mother for 2 to 3 months after parturition is advisable in order to replenish stores depleted by pregnancy.

Table 3-2
Estimated Safe and Adequate Daily Dietary Intakes of Additional Selected Vitamins and Minerals

Age Group (years)	Vitamins			Trace Elements[a]						Electrolytes		
	Vitamin K (µg)	Biotin (µg)	Pantothenic Acid (mg)	Copper (mg)	Manganese (mg)	Fluoride (mg)	Chromium (mg)	Selenium (mg)	Molybdenum (mg)	Sodium (mg)	Potassium (mg)	Chloride (mg)
Infants												
0.0–0.5	12	35	2	0.5–0.7	0.5–0.7	0.1–0.5	0.01–0.04	0.01–0.04	0.03–0.06	115–350	350–925	275–700
0.5–1.0	10–20	50	3	0.7–1.0	0.7–1.0	0.2–1.0	0.02–0.06	0.02–0.06	0.04–0.08	250–750	425–1,275	400–1,200
Children and adolescents												
1–3	15–30	65	3	1.0–1.5	1.0–1.5	0.5–1.5	0.02–0.08	0.02–0.08	0.05–0.1	325–975	550–1,650	500–1,500
4–6	20–40	85	3–4	1.5–2.0	1.5–2.0	1.0–2.5	0.03–0.12	0.03–0.12	0.06–0.15	450–1,350	775–2,325	700–2,100
7–10	30–60	120	4–5	2.0–2.5	2.0–3.0	1.5–2.5	0.05–0.2	0.05–0.2	0.1–0.3	600–1,800	1,000–3,000	925–2,775
11+	50–100	100–200	4–7	2.0–3.0	2.5–5.0	1.5–2.5	0.05–0.2	0.05–0.2	0.15–0.5	900–2,700	1,525–4,575	1,400–4,200
Adults	70–140	100–200	4–7	2.0–3.0	2.5–5.0	1.5–4.0	0.05–0.2	0.05–0.2	0.15–0.5	1,100–3,300	1,875–5,625	1,700–5,100

Source: From Recommended Dietary Allowances, Revised 1980. Food and Nutrition Board, National Academy of Sciences–National Research Council. Because there is less information on which to base allowances, these figures are not given in the main table of the RDAs and are provided here in the form of ranges of recommended intakes.

[a]Since the toxic levels for many trace elements may be only several times usual intakes, the upper levels for the trace elements given in this table should not be habitually exceeded.

Table 3-3

Mean Heights and Weights and Recommended Energy Intake[a]

Age and Sex Group (years)	Weight		Height		Energy		
					Needs		Range
	kg	lb	cm	in.	MJ	kcal	(kcal)
Infants							
0.0–0.5	6	13	60	24	kg × 0.48	kg × 115	95–145
0.5–1.0	9	20	71	28	kg × 0.44	kg × 105	80–135
Children							
1–3	13	29	90	35	5.5	1,300	900–1,800
4–6	20	44	112	44	7.1	1,700	1,300–2,300
7–10	28	62	132	52	10.1	2,400	1,650–3,300
Males							
11–14	45	99	157	62	11.3	2,700	2,000–3,700
15–18	66	145	176	69	11.8	2,800	2,100–3,900
19–22	70	154	177	70	12.2	2,900	2,500–3,300
23–50	70	154	178	70	11.3	2,700	2,300–3,100
51–75	70	154	178	70	10.1	2,400	2,000–2,800
76+	70	154	178	70	8.6	2,050	1,650–2,450
Females							
11–14	46	101	157	62	9.2	2,200	1,500–3,000
15–18	55	120	163	64	8.8	2,100	1,200–3,000
19–22	55	120	163	64	8.8	2,100	1,700–2,500
23–50	55	120	163	64	8.4	2,000	1,600–2,400
51–75	55	120	163	64	7.6	1,800	1,400–2,200
76+	55	120	163	64	6.7	1,600	1,200–2,000
Pregnancy						+300	
Lactation						+500	

Source: From Recommended Dietary Allowances, Revised 1980, Food and Nutrition Board, National Academy of Sciences–National Research Council, Washington, D.C.

[a] The data in this table have been assembled from the observed median heights and weights of children, together with desirable weights for adults for mean heights of men (70 in.) and women (64 in.) between the ages of 18 and 34 years as surveyed in the U.S. population (DHEW/NCHS data).

Energy allowances for the young adults are for men and women doing light work. The allowances for the two older age groups represent mean energy needs over these age spans, allowing for a 2 percent decrease in basal (resting) metabolic rate per decade and a reduction in activity of 200 kcal/day for men and women between 51 and 75 years, 500 kcal for men over 75 years, and 400 kcal for women over age 75. The customary range of daily energy output is shown for adults in the range column and is based on a variation in energy needs of ±400 kcal at any one age emphasizing the wide range of energy intakes appropriate for any group of people.

Energy allowances for children through age 18 are based on median energy intakes of children of these ages followed in longitudinal growth studies. Ranges are the 10th and 90th percentiles of energy intake, to indicate range of energy consumption among children of these ages.

Normal full-term infant

Protein	6–8 percent
Fat	30–55 percent
Carbohydrate	approx. 50 percent

Adult

Protein	10–15 percent
Fat	30–40 percent
Carbohydrate	50–60 percent

Sources of Calories Calories are provided as follows:

Protein	1 gm yields 4 calories
Fat	1 gm yields 9 calories
Carbohydrate	1 gm yields 4 calories

WATER

Requirements Water requirements vary with energy produced or calories metabolized (e.g., greater need in hot weather). Water balance is affected by fluid intake, protein and mineral content of the diet, renal solute load, metabolic rate, respiratory rate, and body temperature. Table 3-4 presents daily fluid requirements for children and adults under normal conditions.

Deficiency Effects of deficiency include thirst, dehydration, high specific gravity of urine, loss of kidney function, and death.

Excess Effects of excess include abdominal discomfort, headache, cramps, water intoxication, convulsions, edema, and circulatory collapse.

PROTEIN

Definitions There are several important definitions related to proteins:

• *Proteins* constitute a group of complex nitrogenous compounds that contain amino acids as their basic structural units and that are essential for growth and repair of all animal tissue.
• *Essential amino acids* are those that cannot be synthesized by the

Table 3-4
Range of Average Water Requirement of Children at Different Ages
Under Ordinary Conditions

Age	Average Body Weight (kg)	Total Water in 24 hours (ml)	Water per kg Body Wt in 24 hours (ml)
3 days	3.0	250–300	80–100
10 days	3.2	400–500	125–150
3 months	5.4	750–850	140–160
6 months	7.3	950–1,100	130–155
9 months	8.6	1,100–1,250	125–145
1 year	9.5	1,150–1,300	120–135
2 years	11.8	1,350–1,500	115–125
4 years	16.2	1,600–1,800	100–110
6 years	20.0	1,800–2,000	90–100
10 years	28.7	2,000–2,500	70–85
14 years	45.0	2,200–2,700	50–60
18 years	54.0	2,200–2,700	40–50

Source: Reprinted with permission from V. C. Vaughan, R. J. McKay, and R. E. Behrman, editors, *Nelson Textbook of Pediatrics*, 11th ed., Philadelphia: W.B. Saunders, 1979. P. 175.

body to meet the demands for normal growth. They must be obtained from outside sources and must be present simultaneously and in sufficient quantity in the body.

• The *quantity* of protein in a given food is estimated by measuring the amount of nitrogen in that food. The RDAs (Table 3-1) represent baseline values for quantity of protein.

• The *quality* of protein is related to its ability to supply all essential amino acids in sufficient amounts to meet requirements for maintenance and growth.

• *Complete protein* is any protein containing sufficient amounts of the essential amino acids. Most animal protein is complete protein.

• *Incomplete protein* is a protein lacking one or more essential amino acids or supplying too little of an essential amino acid. Most plant protein is incomplete protein.

Deficiency Protein deficiency results in lassitude, abdominal enlargement, edema, depletion of plasma proteins, negative nitrogen balance, kwashiorkor, and marasmus.

Excess Excessive protein intake is primarily of concern in those disorders that involve defects in amino acid and protein metabolism (e.g., phenylketonuria).

Distribution of Calories The following percentage of calories per day should consist of protein:

Infants	6–8 percent
Childhood	10–15 percent

Sources of Protein The best sources of protein include the following foods:

1. Complete protein: egg yolk, milk, liver, kidneys, meat, fish, poultry, soybean, wheat germ, brewer's yeast, garbanzo beans, and cottage cheese
2. Incomplete protein: whole grains, nuts, seeds, legumes, and lentils

FAT

Definitions Important definitions related to fats are as follows:

- *Fats* are organic compounds that function in the body chiefly to provide energy, to protect body organs, to maintain body temperature, enable absorption of the fat-soluble vitamins (A, D, E, K), and provide essential fatty acids necessary for health and growth.
- *Essential fatty acids* are those that cannot be synthesized by the body and must be obtained from outside sources. They are necessary for growth and skin integrity. Essential fatty acids also act as precursors of *prostaglandins,* which function on the vascular system to help regulate blood flow and may also be important in mediating inflammatory reactions and in regulating gastric secretions and release of pituitary hormones. The two essential fatty acids are linoleic and arachidonic.
- *Unsaturated fatty acids* contain one or more "unfilled links" be-

tween the carbon atoms where other substances can be added and can react with the fatty acids. They are better absorbed than saturated fatty acids. There are two types:

1. *Monounsaturated fatty acids* are those with one reactive double-bond linkage.
2. *Polyunsaturated fatty acids* are those with two or more double-bond linkages.

- *Saturated fatty acids* do not contain any open double-bond linkages. They are stable and characteristically firm at room temperature and less easily absorbed by the body.
- *Phospholipids* are waxlike substances essential for cell membrane structure and important in absorption and transport of fatty acids. They are produced in the liver. *Lecithin* is the most well-known phospholipid and is important because it appears to be capable of breaking down fat and cholesterol into tiny particles that can readily pass into tissues.
- *Cholesterol* is an organic compound that appears to have several functions in infancy:

  1. Participates in the process of myelinization
  2. Permits synthesis of steroid hormones and bile acids
  3. Develops regulatory mechanisms for cholesterol metabolism in adult life (Fomon, 1974, p. 174)

Deficiency Deficient fat intake results in a lack of satiety, weight loss, and skin problems if essential fatty acids are not provided.

Excess Excessive fat intake causes obesity. Other concerns related to fat intake are atherosclerosis and hyperlipidemia. See Chapter 18, Cardiovascular Risk Factors in Children.

ATHEROSCLEROSIS The issue of whether reduction of fat intake and cholesterol in infancy and childhood will alter or prevent the development of atherosclerosis is complicated and unsolved. Human milk contains approx. 20 mg/dl* of cholesterol, a relatively

---

*dl = deciliter. One deciliter equals 100 ml. See Appendix for table of measurements in current use.

high amount when compared with commercial formulas (1 to 3 mg/dl) and cow milk (15 to 30 mg/dl). In addition, the ratio of polyunsaturated to saturated fats (P/S) is lower in human milk than in commercial formulas.

Assuming that human milk, with its high cholesterol level and low P/S ratio, is the best nutrition for normal human infants, the most reasonable recommendation is to encourage human milk as the primary nutrient for the first 6 months and as the predominant nutrient from 6 to 12 months. Beyond the first year, it seems prudent to exercise moderate restriction of foods high in cholesterol and saturated fat (Glueck, 1979).

TYPE II HYPERLIPOPROTEINEMIA (FAMILIAL HYPERCHOLESTEROLEMIA) This inherited condition is characterized by increased cholesterol levels. Its consequences include tendon xanthomas (see Chapter 14, Xanthoma) and premature (before age 55) ischemic heart disease. Screening for cholesterol and triglyceride levels should be performed on any child if there is a family history of hyperlipidemia, premature vascular disease, sudden death, or xanthomas in a parent or grandparent, or if the child has xanthomas or unexplained abdominal pain, is 20 percent overweight, has blood pressure greater than 140/90, or systolic or diastolic pressure greater than the 95th percentile (Nora, 1980). Those with serum cholesterol levels above 200 mg/dl or triglyceride levels above 100 mg/dl during the first 10 years or between 125 and 150 mg/dl during the second decade are placed on preventive programs. Current recommendations are that total dietary cholesterol not exceed 300 mg/day, that saturated fatty acids provide not more than 10 percent of total calories, and that total dietary fat not exceed 35 percent of calories (Lieberman, 1980).

Distribution of Calories. The percentage of calories per day that should be fat is as follows:

Infants	30–55 percent
Childhood and adolescence	30–45 percent

The percentage of calories per day that should be linoleic acid is 2 to 3 percent. [*Note:* human milk contains 8 to 10 percent of total calories as linoleic acid.]

Sources of Fat Common sources of fat are the following foods:

1. Unsaturated fatty acids:

   • Monounsaturated: olive oil, peanut oil, human milk, and cow milk
   • Polyunsaturated: corn oil, soy oil, safflower oil, sesame oil, and fish oils

2. Saturated fatty acids: most animal fats (e.g., milk, butter, egg yolk, bacon, meat, cheese)
3. Essential fatty acids: natural vegetable oils (e.g., corn, soybean, cottonseed, safflower, sesame, sunflower), eggs, milk, and poultry
4. Phospholipids (lecithin): natural oils, egg yolk, and liver
5. Cholesterol: animal fats

CARBOHYDRATE

Definitions Important definitions related to carbohydrates are as follows:

• *Carbohydrates* constitute a group of chemical compounds including sugars, starches, and cellulose. They function to provide energy, to store energy in the liver in the form of glycogen, and to provide roughage.
• Carbohydrates are classified as follows:

   1. *Monosaccharide.* A simple sugar (e.g., glucose, fructose) that is most readily used by the body
   2. *Disaccharide.* A sugar that contains two monosaccharides (e.g., lactose, sucrose, maltose)
   3. *Polysaccharide.* A complex sugar that contains many monosaccharides (e.g., starch, cellulose)

Deficiency Lack of sufficient carbohydrate can result in ketosis and weight loss.

Excess Carbohydrates taken in excess contribute to obesity. Sucrose is thought to be the chief cause of dental caries. Deficiencies in specific digestive enzymes will cause corresponding malabsorption of the specific carbohydrate (e.g., galactosemia, lactose intolerance).

LACTOSE INTOLERANCE Lactose intolerance is thought to occur in several situations: in the breast-fed infant, after severe diarrhea, and in congenital form. For a full discussion refer to Chapter 20, Malabsorption: Disaccharide Deficiency.

In the breast-fed infant the high lactose content of human breast milk (37 percent of calories) may explain the characteristic frequent, loose, runny "breast milk stools" of the infant, as the lactose intake may be greater than the ability of the lactase enzyme to digest it completely. By 4 to 6 weeks of age, lactose can be normally digested.

Distribution of Calories Minimum requirements for carbohydrate are not really known. However, infants receiving primarily human milk or milk-based formulas usually receive 35 to 55 percent of their daily calories from carbohydrate, chiefly in the form of lactose.

Sources of Carbohydrate Sources of carbohydrate are as follows:

1. Monosaccharides: honey, molasses, dates, figs, fruits, and vegetables
2. Disaccharides: Lactose—milk, ice cream, and yogurt
   Sucrose—sugarbeets, sugarcane, ripe fruits, jellies, cakes, candy, and commercially prepared baby foods
   Maltose—corn syrup
3. Polysaccharides: corn syrup hydrolysates (dextri-maltose), grains and grain products, legumes, and tuber and root vegetables

VITAMINS

Definitions Important definitions related to vitamins are as follows:

- *Vitamins.*These organic substances occur naturally in plant and animal tissue, and are necessary in small amounts for the control of metabolic processes, for normal growth, and for maintenance of health. They are classified as either fat soluble or water soluble.
- *Fat-soluble vitamins* (A, D, E, K). These vitamins are more stable to

heat and less likely to be lost in cooking and processing. They are not excreted in the urine, so excesses are stored in the body and may result in toxicity.

- *Water-soluble vitamins* (C, B_1—thiamine, B_2—riboflavin, niacin, B_6—pyridoxine, B_{12}, folacin). Excesses of these vitamins are excreted in the urine so toxicity is decreased. Deficiencies develop more rapidly.

Functions, Deficiency, Excess, and Sources The functions, symptoms of deficiency and excess, and sources of the vitamins are presented in Table 3-5.

Advisable Intakes Official recommendations for vitamin intake are found in Tables 3-1 and 3-2. Many parents are reading popular literature regarding nutrition and frequently need guidance to accurately and/or safely interpret the recommendations published in such sources. A popular source of nutrition information continues to be *Let's Have Healthy Children* by Adele Davis. Earlier editions of this book contained questionable recommendations regarding vitamin intake. A new edition, revised since the author's death, contains appropriate recommendations for fat-soluble vitamins. See the References at the end of this chapter. Regardless of the information source, care providers have a responsibility to inform parents of the consequences of excessive intakes of the fat-soluble vitamins (Table 3-5).

Other current dietary trends include the use of large doses of vitamins as nutritional supplements. There is no scientific basis for vitamin intake in excess of RDAs by healthy people and, in fact, reports of harmful consequences are increasing (Committee on Nutrition, 1979).

Megavitamin therapy has also been advocated for prevention of disease, relief of minor symptoms, and, recently as a treatment for mental retardation. Although some specific clinical entities (e.g., steatorrhea, malabsorption, rare inborn errors of metabolism) are treated in part by increasing vitamin dosage, current claims of the success of megavitamin therapy in the treatment of mental retardation, learning disabilities, and childhood psychoses are not justified on the basis of available documented results (Committee on Nutrition, 1979).

Table 3-5

Vitamins: Functions, Symptoms of Deficiency and Excess, and Sources

Vitamin	Function	Deficiency or Excess	Sources
Vitamin A (retinol)	Essential for growth, development and maintenance of normal vision, maintenance of epithelial tissue, tooth development	*Deficiency:* impaired vision including night blindness, dry and scaly skin, problems in respiratory, digestive, and GU membranes, failure to thrive, impaired tooth development *Excess:* anorexia, irritability, increased ICP, headache, nausea and vomiting, hepatomegaly, desquamation of the skin, changes in long bones *Toxic dose:* 18,500 IU of vitamin A given daily for over 1 month. Aqueous suspensions of vitamin A are more easily absorbed, thus toxicity develops with lower doses and in shorter time.	Carotene, a precursor of vitamin A, is found in tomato, carrots, squash, cantaloupe, apricots, yams, all green vegetables (especially chard, kale, and spinach). Vitamin A: human milk, commercially prepared formula, dairy products especially egg yolk, liver, fish liver oils, yellow vegetables, green leafy vegetables, fortified margarine

Vitamin D			
Needed to promote growth, necessary for the absorption of calcium and phosphorus, bone and tooth mineralization *Note*: Anticonvulsant drugs interfere with metabolism.	The American Academy of Pediatrics recommends *against* the use of vitamin A preparations containing more than 6000 IU per dose. *Note*: Excessive intake of carotene may result in carotenemia, which is not harmful. *Deficiency*: rickets, poor growth, poor tooth development, muscular weakness *Excess*: vomiting and diarrhea, symptoms of hypercalcemia, failure to thrive, calcification of soft tissues, renal disorders, cardiac myopathy *Toxic dose*: more than 1,800–3,000 IU/day. Doses over 1,000 IU/day should be avoided.	Fish liver oils, fatty fish (sardines, salmon), fortified milk, sunlight *Note*: Ultraviolet light acting on skin oils produces vitamin D, but it is advised not to depend on this source, especially in infancy. 30–60 minutes of exposure per day is needed to provide sufficient vitamin D.	

Table 3-5 (Continued)

Vitamin	Function	Deficiency or Excess	Sources
Vitamin E (tocopherol)	Required for intact muscles, normal reproduction, resistance to hemolysis. Considered essential for human infant. Needed to prevent unsaturated fatty acids from being destroyed in the body. *Note:* As intake of polyunsaturated fatty acids increases, vitamin E intake must increase.	*Deficiency:* red cell hemolysis in premature infants, weakness and degeneration of skeletal muscle *Excess:* can interfere with vitamin K metabolism, result in prolonged prothrombin time, and predispose to bleeding	Wheat germ, oils of grains, human milk, nuts and seeds, salad oils, margarine, stone-ground whole grain cereals and breads, green leafy vegetables *Note:* Vitamin E cannot be absorbed without fat. Therefore infants on skim milk will not absorb sufficient vitamin E.
Vitamin K	Necessary for normal clotting of blood via formation of prothrombin	*Deficiency:* coagulation problems, hemorrhage *Excess:* unknown	Milk, cabbage, spinach, lettuce, yogurt, pork, liver
Vitamin C (ascorbic acid)	Needed for normal development of collagen (connective tissue) and normal body metabolism, protection from infection (mechanism poorly understood)	*Deficiency:* delayed healing, petechial hemorrhages, irritability, fatigue, swelling of joints and gums, scurvy *Excess:* no harmful effects known; excreted in urine	Citrus fruits, guava, bell pepper, rose hips, cantaloupe, kale, broccoli, strawberries, green vegetables, human milk, tomatoes, potatoes *Note:* Vitamin C is destroyed by food process-

			ing, storage, and heating. Thus vitamin C content of whole cow milk is reduced to negligible amounts by pasteurization, storage, and heating. This applies also to commercially prepared strained baby fruits and vegetables.
Vitamin B₁ (thiamine)	Required for carbohydrate metabolism, promotes appetite	*Deficiency:* fatigue, depression, insomnia, neuritis, headache, beriberi, cardiac problems *Excess:* no harmful effects known, unneeded amounts excreted	Pork, liver, wheat germ, rice polish, brewer's yeast, whole grain cereals, legumes, nuts, milk
Vitamin B₂ (riboflavin)	Required for normal energy metabolism, part of several metabolic enzymes, normal tissue function	*Deficiency:* cheilosis (cracks and splits in tissue of mouth and lips), photophobia, blood-shot eyes and other visual symptoms, skin problems *Excess:* no harmful effects known; excreted in the urine	Liver, yeast, dairy products, cooked leafy vegetables, legumes, whole grains

Table 3-5 *(Continued)*

Vitamin	Function	Deficiency or Excess	Sources
Niacin (nicotinic acid)	Required for cellular metabolism	*Deficiency:* pellagra, psychologic changes (depression, tension, insomnia), skin problems, diarrhea *Excess:* pruritis	Can be synthesized in the body from the amino acid tryptophan; found in brewer's yeast, liver, wheat germ, kidney, cereal grains, nuts, legumes, poultry, green vegetables
Vitamin B$_6$ (pyridoxine)	Serves as coenzyme in metabolism of protein, fat, and carbohydrate	*Deficiency:* seizures, irritability, and headache, mouth, lip, and tongue soreness, seborrheic dermatitis, and anemia *Excess:* no harmful effects known, excreted in the urine	Brewer's yeast, blackstrap molasses, wheat germ, liver, kidney, soybeans, bananas, corn *Note:* B$_6$ is sensitive to heating, processing, and storage.
Vitamin B$_{12}$ (cobalamin)	Required in protein metabolism, folacin metabolism, essential for normal cell function, especially bone marrow cells	*Deficiency:* pernicious anemia, megaloblastic anemia, GI problems, neurologic deterioration *Excess:* no harmful effects known, excreted in the urine	*Only* in animal foods: liver, organ meats, milk, eggs, cheese, meat, fish, human milk

Folacin (folic acid)	Serves as coenzyme in protein metabolism, essential for formation of nucleoproteins which in turn are required for normal erythrocyte maturation, helps in normal growth and reproduction	*Deficiency:* megaloblastic anemia, GI disturbances, and diarrhea *Excess:* no harmful effects known, excreted in the urine	Liver, yeast, leafy green vegetables, human milk, cow milk, dried legumes, nuts, oranges *Note:* Goat milk does *not* have sufficient folacin for the human infant
Other B-complex vitamins: pantothenic acid and biotin	Serve as coenzymes in metabolism of protein, fat, and carbohydrate	*Deficiency:* fatigue, headache, sleep disturbances, personality changes, muscle cramps. *Note:* deficiency very rare because they are so widely distributed in most foods *Excess:* no harmful effect known; excreted in the urine	Exists in all cells of living tissue; especially rich sources are yeast, liver, eggs, wheat germ, nuts, and peas
Choline	Serves in metabolism and catabolism, is an essential component of phospholipids (especially lecithin), vital in lipid metabolism, a constituent of acetylcholine which plays a role in normal nerve function	*Deficiency:* has not been definitively established *Excess:* no harmful effects known, excreted in the urine	Foods that contain phospholipids (i.e., egg yolk, whole grains, legumes, meats, wheat germ)

MINERALS AND TRACE ELEMENTS

Definitions Minerals and trace elements are naturally occurring, inorganic substances, several of which are nutritionally important.

Functions, Deficiency, Excess, and Sources Table 3-6 presents information on functions, symptoms of deficiency and excess, and sources of the most important minerals and trace elements.

Advisable Intakes The actual minimum requirements for most of the minerals and trace elements are not known and, with the exception of iron and fluoride, are not of practical concern since they are found in adequate amounts in normal diets. See Table 3-1 for the RDAs for calcium, phosphorus, iodine, iron, magnesium, and zinc and Table 3-2 for estimated intakes of sodium, potassium, chloride, and the trace elements. Fluoride is also discussed in Chapter 16, the Mouth and Teeth.

INFANT NUTRITION

This section presents data on the nutritional aspects of breast milk, commonly used infant formulas, iron nutrition during infancy, solid foods, and recommended vitamin and mineral supplementation during infancy. See Chapter 5 for additional information on breast feeding and infant feeding. An excellent infant feeding resource for health professionals is "Feeding Guide: A Nutritional Guide for the Maturing Infant," available from Health Learning Systems, Inc., 200 Broadacres Drive, Bloomfield, NJ 07003.

Breast Milk

COMPOSITION

Colostrum This is the initial milk secreted during the first 5 to 10 days after birth. Colostrum differs from mature breast milk in several ways:

1. Lower in energy value (67 Kcal/100 ml)
2. Higher in protein, fat-soluble vitamins, and minerals

Table 3-6

Minerals: Functions, Symptoms of Deficiency and Excess, and Sources

Mineral	Function	Deficiency or Excess	Sources
Calcium	99% of calcium in the body is used in structure of bones and teeth, necessary for blood coagulation, aids in transmission of nerve impulses, aids lactation, muscle contractility, and myocardial function *Note:* Vitamin D necessary for calcium absorption	*Deficiency:* bone demineralization, tooth demineralization, irritability, tetany, rickets, growth retardation, hypocalcemia *Excess:* unknown	Milk, buttermilk, sardines, cheese, canned salmon, mustard and turnip greens, soybeans, blackstrap molasses, cream of wheat, figs, dates, egg yolk, clams, oysters *Note:* One quart of milk will provide approx. 1,000 mg of calcium
Chloride	Formation of hydrochloric acid, maintenance of acid–base balance and electrolyte balance, maintenance of normal irritability of nervous tissue and contractility of muscle tissue	*Deficiency:* alkalosis, dehydration *Excess:* unknown	Table salt, meat, eggs, dairy products
Copper	Essential constituent of many enzymes required for oxidative metabolism, especially iron metabolism	*Deficiency:* hypochromic anemia, neutropenia, bone disease, anorexia, diarrhea, failure to thrive *Excess:* unknown	Meat, eggs, nuts, human milk, drinking water supplied through copper pipes

103

Table 3-6 (Continued)

Mineral	Function	Deficiency or Excess	Sources
Fluoride	Necessary for maximal resistance to dental caries	*Deficiency:* dental caries *Excess:* mottling of tooth enamel, fluorosis, more than 4 mg/day will cause teeth to mottle (See Chapter 16, The Mouth and Teeth)	Most reliable source is fluoridated water—at a level of 0.5–1.0 ppm, fluoride drops or tablets. Seafood is highest food source. Some fish have 6–12 mg/kg, but most is not bioavailable, thus diet alone cannot supply sufficient fluoride
Iodine	Constituent of thyroid hormone, thyroxine; control of basal metabolic rate	*Deficiency:* goiter, cretinism *Excess:* depression of thyroid	Iodized salt, fish, seaweed
Iron	Essential component of hemoglobin for the transport of oxygen to all tissues	*Deficiency:* anemia, low iron stores *Excess:* hemosiderosis, cardiovascular collapse See Chapter 19, Iron Deficiency Anemia.	Liver, kidneys, beef heart, brewer's yeast, wheat germ, lean meats, greens, dried fruits, egg yolk, enriched cereals, and grains See Tables 3-11 and 3-12 for additional dietary sources of iron
Magnesium	Needed for structure of bones and teeth, utilization of fats and carbohydrates, enzyme systems, neuromuscular irritability; regulation of body temperature	*Deficiency:* irritability, muscle weakness, tetany, behavioral disturbances *Excess:* none from dietary intake	Nuts, soybeans, cooked whole grains, leafy green vegetables, milk, cocoa, shellfish *Note:* Magnesium intake is related to calcium intake. The more calcium in the diet, the more magnesium needed.

Mineral	Functions	Clinical Significance	Sources
Phosphorus	80% of body phosphorus is used for structure of bones and teeth, necessary for normal blood pH, constituent of nucleic acids and nucleoproteins, component of phospholipids which promote fat metabolism and cell permeability. *Note:* Vitamin D necessary for phosphorus absorption	*Deficiency:* stunting of growth, poor quality of bones and teeth, muscle weakness. *Excess:* possibility of tetany in newborns on formula with low Ca:P ratio	Liver, yeast, lecithin, wheat germ, dairy products, egg yolk, nuts, cereal grains, meat, fish, dates, raisins
Potassium	Necessary for muscle contraction, nerve impulse conduction, fluid balance, heart rhythm	*Deficiency:* muscle weakness, anorexia, nausea, abdominal distention, nervous irritability, tachycardia, drowsiness. *Excess:* heart block	Meats, poultry, fish, fruits, vegetables, whole grain cereals
Sodium	Maintenance of acid–base balance, electrolyte balance, maintenance of normal irritability of nervous tissue, contractility of muscle tissue	*Deficiency:* dehydration, anorexia, nausea, diarrhea, muscle cramps. *Excess:* edema	Table salt, soy sauce, baking powder, cheese, milk, eggs, shellfish, meat, seasonings, and preservatives
Zinc	Essential constituent of insulin and several enzymes, important for skin keratinization and muscle growth	*Deficiency:* anorexia, retarded growth, delayed sexual maturation, impaired wound healing, intestinal malabsorption. *Excess:* relatively nontoxic	Widely distributed in liver, seafood, nuts, grains

3. Higher in sodium, potassium, and chloride

Colostrum is high in antibodies, especially IgA, which provides protection from enteric infections, particularly enteropathic *Escherichia coli*. It also facilitates the elimination of meconium from the gastrointestinal tract. Between 7 to 10 days postpartum to 2 weeks postpartum, colostrum undergoes the transition to mature milk.

Mature Milk Table 3-7 summarizes and compares the composition of mature human milk and whole cow milk. Among the significant differences are the following:

• *Protein and minerals.* Cow milk is higher in these constituents because the growth rate of the calf is twice as rapid as the growth rate of the human infant. Thus, cow milk has a higher renal solute load, which may tax the infant's kidney function.

• *Casein.* The casein content of cow milk is twice as high as in breast milk. This results in formation of a large and difficult-to-digest mass of curds in the infant stomach unless cow milk is acidified and heated.

• *Fat.* The fat of human milk is more easily absorbed than the butterfat of cow milk. Butterfat contains more saturated fatty acids.

• *Cholesterol.* Human milk is high in cholesterol. See this chapter, Cholesterol.

• *Carbohydrate.* The lactose content of cow milk is lower than that of breast milk. Extra sugar is usually added to cow milk formulas.

• *Vitamins.* Both human milk and cow milk contain *adequate* amounts of vitamin A and the B complex vitamins and *inadequate* amounts of vitamin D (see below, Supplementation). Human milk will contain adequate vitamin C if the maternal diet is adequate in vitamin C-containing foods. Cow milk is inadequate in vitamin C.

• *Iron.* Both human milk and cow milk contain small amounts of iron. The iron in breast milk is well absorbed and may be sufficient during the first 4 to 6 months. See this chapter, Iron Nutrition in Infancy. The iron in cow milk is not well absorbed and is inadequate without supplementation.

- *Fluoride.* Both human milk (0.025 mg/liter)and cow milk (0.03 to 0.10 mg/liter) are inadequate in fluoride content.

- *Antibodies.* Mature human milk protects against enteritis and respiratory infections during the first year of life due to the presence of immunoglobulins, lactoferrin, and bifidus factor (Lawrence, 1980). A study of infants up to 3 months of age who were exclusively breast-fed revealed no bacterial infections, reduced respiratory infections, and essentially no gastrointestinal infections (Fallot et al., 1980).

- *Other protective benefits.* It was recently demonstrated in a well-designed study that breast feeding was associated with a significant protective effect against subsequent obesity (Kramer, 1981). With respect to protection against allergies, breast-fed infants have less opportunity to develop allergies to cow milk, but Kramer (1981) has shown that breast feeding and delayed introduction of solid foods do not protect against atopic eczema.

DISTRIBUTION OF CALORIES

The approximate percentages of calories in mature human milk are as follows:

Protein	6–8 percent
Fat	50–56 percent
Carbohydrate	38–42 percent

SUPPLEMENTATION

Guidelines for vitamin and mineral supplementation (with the exception of fluoride) in normal infants and children are presented in Table 3-8. The rising national awareness of good nutrition as essential to health, the availability of vitamin and mineral supplements without prescription, commercial advertising, and a belief by many that supplementation will remediate any dietary deficiency have led to widespread and often irrational use of such supplements. Supplementation in breast-fed infants will be discussed here, although it should be noted that little to no supplementation is indicated for normal infants fed commercially prepared formulas and normal infants and children over 6 months of age.

Table 3-7
Composition of Mature Human Milk and Cow Milk

Composition	Human Milk	Cow Milk
Water (ml/100 ml)	87.1	87.2
Energy (kcal/100 ml)	75	66
Total solids (gm/100 ml)	12.9	12.8
Protein (gm/100 ml)	1.1	3.5
Fat (gm/100 ml)	4.5	3.7
Lactose (gm/100 ml)	6.8	4.9
Ash (gm/100 ml)	0.2	0.7
Proteins (% of total protein)		
Casein	40	82
Whey proteins	60	18
Nonprotein nitrogen (mg/100 ml)	32	32
(% of total nitrogen)	15	6
Amino acids (mg/100 ml)		
Essential		
Histidine	22	95
Isoleucine	68	228
Leucine	100	350
Lysine	73	277
Methionine	25	88
Phenylalanine	48	172
Threonine	50	164
Tryptophan	18	49
Valine	70	245
Nonessential		
Arginine	45	129
Alanine	35	75
Aspartic acid	116	166
Cystine	22	32
Glutamic acid	230	680
Glycine	0	11
Proline	80	250
Serine	69	160
Tyrosine	61	179
Fatty acids (% of total fatty acids)		
Essential		
Linoleic	10.6	2.1
Major minerals per liter		
Calcium (mg)	340	1170
Phosphorus (mg)	140	920
Sodium (mEq)	7	22
Potassium (mEq)	13	35
Chloride (mEq)	11	29
Magnesium (mg)	40	120
Sulfur (mg)	140	300

Table 3-7 *(Continued)*

Composition	Human Milk	Cow Milk
Trace minerals per liter		
Chromium (μg)	–	8–13
Manganese (μg)	7–15	20–40
Copper (μg)	400	300
Zinc (mg)	3–5	3–5
Iodine (μg)	30	47[a]
Selenium (μg)	13–50	5–50
Iron (mg)	0.5	0.5
Vitamins per liter		
Vitamin A (IU)	1898	1025[b]
Thiamin (μg)	160	440
Riboflavin (μg)	360	1750
Niacin (μg)	1470	940
Pyridoxine (μg)	100	640
Pantothenate (mg)	1.84	3.46
Folacin (μg)	52	55
B_{12} (μg)	0.3	4
Vitamin C (mg)	43	11[c]
Vitamin D (IU)	22	14[d]
Vitamin E (mg)	1.8	0.4
Vitamin K (μg)	15	60

Source: Reprinted with permission from S. J. Fomon, *Infant Nutrition*, 2nd ed., pp. 362–363, © 1974 by the W. B. Saunders Company, Philadelphia.
[a]Range 10 to 200 μg/liter.
[b]Average value for winter milk; value for summer milk, 1690 IU/liter.
[c]As marketed; value for fresh cow milk 21 mg/liter.
[d]Average value for winter milk; value for summer milk, 33 IU

• *Vitamin D.* Although breast milk has been shown to have a vitamin D content inadequate to meet recommended daily requirements of the infant, the report by Lakdawala and Widdowson (1977) suggested that additional vitamin D in an easily absorbable water-soluble form was available in breast milk. Subsequently, the need for vitamin D supplementation on a routine basis was questioned. More recent reports (Greer et al., 1982) have found either no vitamin D sulfate or negligible vitamin D activity in the water-soluble fraction of human milk.

Although it is true that by far most unsupplemented full-term breast-fed infants do not develop nutritional rickets, the disorder does occur. Little (1982) reports six cases between 1970 and 1979, and Edidin et al. (1980) report 10 cases in infants whose mothers were strict vegetarians and did not take vitamin supple-

Table 3-8

Guidelines for Use of Supplements in Healthy Infants and Children[a]

Child	Multivitamin–Multimineral	Vitamins			Minerals
		D	E	Folate	Iron
Term infants					
Breast-fed	0	±	0	0	±[b]
Formula-fed	0	0	0	0	0
Preterm infants					
Breast-fed[c]	+[c]	+	±[d]	±[c]	+
Formula-fed[c]	+[c]	+	±[d]	±[c]	+[b]
Older infants (after 6 mo)					
Normal	0	0	0	0	±[b]
High-risk[e]	+	0	0	0	±
Children					
Normal	0	0	0	0	0
High-risk	+	0	0	0	0
Pregnant teenager					
Normal	±	0	0	±	+
High-risk[f]	+	0	0	+	+

Source: Reprinted with permission from Committee on Nutrition, "Vitamin and Mineral Supplement Needs in Normal Children in the U.S.," *Pediatrics 66*:1017, December 1980. Copyright American Academy of Pediatrics, 1980.

[a]Symbols: +, a supplement is usually indicated; ±, it is possibly or sometimes indicated; 0, it is not usually indicated. Vitamin K for newborn infants and fluoride in areas where there is sufficient fluoride in the water supply are not shown.

[b]Iron-fortified formula and/or infant cereal is a more convenient and reliable source of iron than a supplement.

[c]Multivitamin supplement (plus added folate) is needed primarily when calorie intake is below approximately 300 kcal/day or when the infant weighs 2.5 kg; vitamin D should be supplied at least until 6 months of age in breast-fed infants. Iron should be started by 2 months of age.

[d]Vitamin E should be in a form that is well absorbed by small, premature infants. If this form of vitamin E is approved for use in formulas, it need not be given separately to formula-fed infants. Infants fed breast milk are less susceptible to vitamin E deficiency.

[e]Multivitamin–multimineral preparation (including iron) is preferred to use of iron alone.

[f]Multivitamin–multimineral preparation (including iron and folate) is preferred to use of iron alone or iron and folate alone.

ments. Additional factors such as geographic location, time of year, skin pigmentation, maternal vitamin D intake, and duration of exposure to sunlight also influence vitamin D status in infants. The Committee on Nutrition of the American Academy of Pediatrics (December 1980, September 1981) recommends that vitamin D supplementation of 400 IU/day be considered for infants whose mothers' vitamin D nutrition is inadequate and whose exposure to ultraviolet light is inadequate (see Table 3-5, vitamin D). Other authorities disagree and advise that, since there is no hazard from vitamin D supplementation in recommended amounts and that even a slight possibility of rickets should be avoided, vitamin D supplementation be provided to breast-fed infants from birth (Fomon et al., 1979).

- *Iron.* See this chapter, Iron Nutrition in Infancy.

- *Fluoride.* It is recommended that fully breast-fed infants receive 0.25 mg fluoride per day. See Chapter 16, Fluoride.

- *Vitamin B_{12}.* Maternal diet influences the concentration of certain water-soluble vitamins in breast milk. There are reports of vitamin B_{12} deficiency in breast-fed infants of strict vegetarian mothers. The Committee on Nutrition (June 1980) recommends that breast-fed infants of malnourished vegetarian mothers receive multivitamin supplements. See this chapter, Vegetarian Diets.

HYPERBILIRUBINEMIA

Breast milk jaundice may in some cases be severe, but generally is not a contraindication to breast feeding. See Chapter 19, Breast-feeding Jaundice.

Formulas and Milks

Milks from various species and in many different forms have been employed successfully in infant feeding. Commercially prepared formulas are currently the most popular because of convenience, standardization of ingredients, and fortification with vitamins and minerals.

INFANT FORMULAS

Several types of milk-based and milk-free formulas are used. Since whole cow milk is not a satisfactory food for infants, commercially prepared formulas are attempts to modify milk so they more closely resemble human milk. Table 3-9 analyzes commonly used infant formulas with regard to composition, distribution of calories, and supplementation.

FORMS OF COW MILK AND GOAT MILK

Although it is recommended that infants remain on breast milk or iron-fortified infant formula for most of the first year of life, many parents make the switch to some form of fresh cow milk before 6 months of age. It is important to know the composition of available cow milk so adequate nutritional counseling can be provided. Table 3-10 presents the composition of several forms of cow milk and goat milk. Analysis of these milks reveals several inadequacies related to their use in young infants. These inadequacies are as follows:

• *Whole milk.* See this chapter, Mature Milk.
• *Evaporated milk.* Protein content is high if diluted 1 : 1 with water. See Table 3-9 for the recipe for evaporated milk formula suitable for infants. Iron and vitamin C content are inadequate.
• *Skim milk.* This is not suitable for use in infants under 1 year of age because of:
  1. Insufficient calories due to low fat content (Fomon, 1979, observes that infants fed skim milk consume large volumes of calorically dilute food. Such infants continue to gain weight but less rapidly than do infants fed formula or whole cow milk. Also, skinfold thickness decreases rapidly, suggesting that body energy stores are being depleted.)
  2. Excessive protein
  3. Insufficient essential fatty acids, vitamin C, and iron
• *Two percent or low-fat milk.* This is more suitable than skim milk but still could result in inadequate fat and caloric intake if other foods are not fed. Iron and vitamin C are inadequate.

- *Goat milk.* Even though not widely used in the United States, goat milk is a major source of infant nutrition in many parts of the world. The one major deficiency in goat milk is folacin (folic acid), and infants receiving this milk should be given a daily folacin supplement of 50 μg to prevent megaloblastic anemia. Goat milk is also deficient in iron, vitamin C, and vitamin D.

OTHER FORMS OF MILK

- *Certified milk.* Milk that may be raw or pasteurized but that has been certified as to cleanliness
- *Condensed milk.* Milk that has more sugar and less protein than evaporated milk (It should not be used interchangeably with evaporated milk, nor should it be used in infant feeding)
- *Cultured milk* (e.g., buttermilk, acidophilus milk, yogurt). Milk prepared with added lactic acid and that aids in replacing normal bowel flora
- *Dry milk.* Milk that is a sterile product that can be kept for long periods of time (It is usually made from skim milk, since fat particles present storage problems.)
- *Homogenized milk.* Milk that has gone through a process by which fat globules are broken down in size and are more evenly distributed throughout the milk
- *Pasteurized milk.* Milk that has been sterilized
- *Raw milk.* Milk that has not been heat treated

MILK SUBSTITUTES

- *Filled milks.* These are combinations of skim milk solids and non-milk fat. They may have all the ingredients of regular milk but, if coconut oil is used as the fat, will be deficient in linoleic acid.
- *Imitation milks.* These nondairy creamers consist of water, protein, corn syrup, sucrose, and vegetable oil. They are nutritionally inferior, especially in protein, calcium, and phosphorus, and usually lack vitamin supplementation. Although inexpensive, they should not be used as the chief source of milk. Examples are Mocha Mix and Cereal Blend.

Table 3-9

Analysis of Commonly Used Infant Formulas

Type of Formula	Composition of Formula	Supplementation[a]	Comments
FORMULAS BASED ON COW MILK:			
1. Cow milk with added carbohydrate Evaporated milk	In these formulas cow protein and cow fat (butterfat) are combined with added lactose or corn sugar. This results in a formula that supplies calories as: Protein 14–16% Fat 36–38% Carbohydrate 46–50% (20 calories per ounce)	Unless added will be deficient in vitamins C and iron. Some preparations fortified with vitamin D.	Evaporated milk is the most widely known formula of this type and used to be used extensively in this country. It is still nutritionally sound and an economical approach to infant feeding. Recipe for one day's supply of evaporated milk formula: 13 oz evaporated milk 19 oz water 1½ oz corn syrup Recipe for one individual feeding of evaporated milk formula: 3 oz evaporated milk (100 ml)

2. Nonfat cow milk, vegetable oils, and carbohydrate as lactose Enfamil (Mead-Johnson) Similac (Ross)	Corn oil, coconut oil, and soy oil are generally used and are well absorbed These formulas provide calories as: Protein 9% Fat 50% Carbohydrate 41% (20 calories per ounce)	Available with adequate vitamin supplementation Available with or without iron supplementation	4.5 oz water (130 ml) 2 tsp corn syrup (10 ml) *Note:* After 6 months there is no need to add corn syrup, since infants are usually on solid foods. Formulas containing butterfat may result in higher fat excretion and occasionally in steatorrhea in young infants. Butterfat also causes a sour odor to vomitus. Available as powder, liquid concentrate, or ready-to-feed Suitable for feeding of full-term and premature infants with no special nutritional requirements

Table 3-9 (Continued)

Type of Formula	Composition of Formula	Supplementation[a]	Comments
3. Nonfat cow milk, whey proteins, vegetable oil, and carbohydrate Similac PM 60/40 (Ross) Similac with Whey (Ross) SMA (Wyeth)	These formulas have a protein ratio of whey to casein resembling human milk (60:40). The proteins have also been demineralized so minerals in desired amounts can be deliberately added. This results in mineral concentrations similar to human milk. Calories are supplied as: Protein 9% Fat 48% Carbohydrate 43% (20 calories per ounce)	Available with vitamin supplementation. Check for amount of iron supplementation	Special characteristics of these formulas: 1. Low renal solute load in relation to caloric concentration. 2. Low sodium content This makes them desirable for use in infants with renal disease, congenital heart disease, or congestive heart failure, as well as for normal infants.
4. Milk-based formula for older infants Similac Advance (Ross)	This formula is composed of nonfat cow milk and soy-protein isolate, corn oil, and lactose as carbohydrate with calories supplied as: Protein 26% Fat 27% Carbohydrate 47% (16 calories per ounce)	Fully supplemented with vitamins and iron	Key features of this formula: 1. Low caloric concentration 2. Low percentage of calories as fat 3. Low in saturated fat, cholesterol 4. High percentage of calories as protein

It is designed to be used when infants switch from infant formula to other forms of cow milk. The age at which an infant switches from infant formula is important here since the infant under 6 months of age would be receiving more calories from protein and fewer calories from fat than those amounts advised. Other foods in the diet must be considered in terms of fat content since most commercially prepared baby foods are high in protein and carbohydrate but low in fat.

5. Special milk-based formulas Probana (Mead-Johnson)	Probana is high in protein, high in carbohydrate, and low in fat. Carbohy-	Supplemented with vitamins but does *not* contain iron	Suitable for use in feeding infants and children with celiac disease, cystic

Table 3-9 (Continued)

Type of Formula	Composition of Formula	Supplementation[a]	Comments
	drate is from simple sugars and banana powder. It supplies calories as: Protein 27% Fat 14% Carbohydrate 51%		fibrosis, diarrhea, or other conditions involving steatorrhea or poor fat absorption. Renal solute load is high. Watch for dehydration.
Lonolac (Mead-Johnson)	The special feature of this formula is its very low sodium content. It contains 1 mEq sodium per liter.	Not supplemented. Need to add vitamins C and D and iron	Designed for use in infants with congestive heart failure. The low sodium content makes it unsuitable for long-term use.
MILK-FREE FORMULAS: 1. Soy-based formulas Isomil (Ross) Prosobee (Mead-Johnson) Nursoy (Wyeth) Soyalac (Loma Linda) I-Soyalac (Loma Linda)	These formulas provide protein in the form of soy-isolate or soy flour, fat as soy and coconut oils, and carbohydrate as sucrose or corn sugar. Soy-isolate formulas provide calories as: Protein 12–15% Fat 45–48% Carbohydrate 39–40% (20 calories per ounce)	Most of these formulas have been supplemented with calcium, iodine, vitamins, and all have iron. Labels on individual products should be checked for adequacy of supplementation.	Suitable for use in feeding milk-sensitive infants, or infants who need a lactose-free diet. Prosobee contains no lactose or sucrose. The carbohydrate is in the form of corn syrup solids. Isomil also comes in a sucrose-free form.

Carbohydrate Free (Ross, RCF)	This is a soy-based formula with no carbohydrate. Carbohydrate and water must be added in prescribed amounts.	Supplemented with adequate vitamins and minerals. No iron supplementation	For use in feeding persons unable to tolerate the type or amount of carbohydrate in milk or conventional formulas. Used under physician direction.
2. Nonsoy, milk-free formulas.			
Meat-Base Formula (Gerber)	The protein comes from beef heart, the fat is both animal and vegetable, and the carbohydrate content is low.	Supplemented with calcium, vitamins, and iron	A nutritionally adequate formula for infants and children intolerant to cow and goat milk.
Nutramigen (Mead-Johnson)	The protein is in hydrolyzed form specially processed to remove allergenic substances. The fat is highly refined corn oil and the carbohydrate is from sucrose and tapioca starch. Calories provided as: Protein 13% Fat 35% Carbohydrate 52%	Fully supplemented with vitamins and iron	Suitable for use in infants and children allergic or intolerant to ordinary food proteins. Provides lactose-free feedings in galactosemia.

Table 3-9 (Continued)

Type of Formula	Composition of Formula	Supplementation[a]	Comments
Lofenalac (Mead-Johnson)	The protein has been treated to remove most of the phenylalanine. Calories provided as: Protein 13% Fat 35% Carbohydrate 52%	Vitamins, minerals, and iron added	For use as basic food in low-phenylalanine management of infants and children with phenyl-ketonuria, provides essential nutrients without the high phenylalanine content present in natural food proteins
Portagen (Mead-Johnson)	This formula is essentially lactose free and also uses medium chain tri-glycerides, which are more easily digested and	Fully supplemented with vitamins and iron	For use in the management of children with impaired fat absorption, pancreatic and liver disease

absorbed than conventional food fat.

Calories provided as:

Protein	14%
Fat	41%
Carbohydrate	45%

Fully supplemented with vitamins and iron

Useful in the management of infants and children with severe gastrointestinal abnormalities in which absorption of several nutrients is impaired.

Pregestimil (Mead-Johnson)

Contains protein hydrolysate, medium chain triglycerides, and carbohydrate as corn syrup solids, tapioca starch.

Calories provided as:

Protein	11%
Fat	35%
Carbohydrate	54%

---

[a] Fluoride supplementation. Currently marketed milks and formulas have no fluoride. Need for fluoride supplementation must be evaluated on the basis of the amount of water subsequently added to the milk or formula, the amount of water consumed on its own, and the level of fluoride in the community water supply. See Chapter 16, Fluoride.

Table 3-10

Composition of Several Forms of Cow Milk and of Fresh Fluid Goat Milk

	Cow Milk				Goat Milk (Fresh Fluid)
	Whole Milk	Evaporated Diluted 1:1 With Water	Fresh Fluid Skim Milk	"Two Per Cent"	
Energy (kcal/100 ml)	66	68.5	36	59	67
Major constituents (gm/100 ml)					
Protein	3.5	3.5	3.6	4.2	3.2
Fat	3.7	3.8	0.1	2.0	4.0
Carbohydrate	4.9	4.8	5.1	6.0	4.6
Caloric distribution (% of calories)					
Protein	22	19	40	28	19
Fat	48	50	3	31	53
Carbohydrate	30	31	57	41	28

Minerals/liter					
Calcium (mg)	1170	1260	1210	1430	1290
Phosphorus (mg)	920	1025	950	1120	1060
Sodium (mEq)	22	26	23	27	15
Potassium (mEq)	35	39	37	45	46
Iron (mg)	0.5	0.5	trace	1	1
Vitamins/liter					
Vitamin A (IU)	1025	1850	90	800	2074
Thiamin (μg)	440	280	400	400	400
Riboflavin (μg)	1750	1900	1700	2100	1840
Niacin (mg)	940	1.0	0.9	1.0	1.9
Pyridoxine (μg)	640	370	450	—	70
Pantothenate (mg)	3.46	3.5	3.6	—	3.4
Folacin (μg)	55	55	55	55	6
Vitamin C (mg)	11	5.5	19	10	15
Vitamin D (IU)	400	400	—	400	24
Vitamin E (IU)	0.4	1.3	—	—	—

Source: Adapted with permission from S. J. Fomon, *Infant Nutrition*, 2nd ed., p. 372. © 1974 by the W. B. Saunders Company, Philadelphia.

Iron Nutrition in Infancy

IRON STORES AT BIRTH

The normal birth weight infant of a well-nourished mother is born with adequate stores of iron to meet body needs for hemoglobin production up to 4 to 6 months of age. After this time body stores must be resupplied to ensure proper blood formation and to prevent iron deficiency anemia (see Chapter 19, Iron Deficiency Anemia).

In small and preterm infants who have not had time in utero to build adequate iron stores and who grow rapidly in the early months, neonatal iron stores will be depleted after about 2 months of age.

IRON REQUIREMENTS

The normal healthy infant at birth has approximately 135 mg of iron stored in body tissues. At 1 year of age the infant should have 270 mg of iron, since the red blood cell mass doubles during the first year. Thus, another 135 mg of iron must be absorbed from exogenous sources during the first year. This breaks down to 0.3 mg of iron absorbed per day. Additional but smaller amounts are required for production of other iron compounds and to account for dermal losses (Rudolph, 1982).

ADVISABLE INTAKES

The RDAs (see Table 3-1) for iron intake in infancy are as follows:

Age	Amount
0 to 6 months	10 mg/day
6 mo to 3 yr	15 mg/day

These are amounts that, considering the various rates of absorption from different sources of iron, are sufficient to meet known requirements.

ABSORPTION OF IRON

Absorption of iron varies with age, state of health, form of iron ingested, source of iron, amount of iron, and the interaction of iron with other dietary components and with intestinal secretions (e.g., iron absorption is enhanced in the presence of ascorbic acid and amino acids).

Form of Iron   Absorption occurs in the small intestine in the *ferrous* form. Other forms must be broken down to the ferrous form. The absorption of different forms of iron is as follows:

Good Absorption	*Poor Absorption*
Heme iron (animal)	Vegetable iron (inorganic)
Ferrous iron including:	Ferric iron including:
Ferrous sulfate	Ferric cholinate
Ferrous succinate	Ferric orthophosphate
Ferrous lactate	Sodium iron pyrophosphate
Ferrous fumarate	Reduced iron of large
Ferrous gluconate	particle size
Reduced iron of small	
particle size	
(electrolytic iron	
powder)	

Rate of Absorption   It is generally assumed that from 1 to 20 percent (an average of 10 percent) of ingested iron is absorbed. Vegetable iron (e.g., rice, spinach, beans, corn, wheat, soy beans) is in the lower range of 1 to 10 percent; animal products are in the upper range of 10 to 20 percent. Human breast milk has a small amount of iron (approx. 0.5 to 1.0 mg/liter) but it is well absorbed at approximately 50 percent. Cow milk has a similar amount of iron but is absorbed at a rate of 10 percent. Iron-fortified formulas and cereals have iron absorption rates of about 4 percent.

IRON SUPPLEMENTATION IN INFANCY

To provide sound nutrition and to prevent iron deficiency anemia it is recommended that all infants receive iron supplementation from one or more sources during the first year of life (see Table 3-8). The level of supplementation suggested by the American Academy of Pediatrics (Committee on Nutrition, 1976, p. 765), is as follows:

Term infants	1 mg/kg/day
Preterm infants	2 mg/kg/day up to 15 mg/day

Sources of iron should be introduced not later than 4 months in full-term infants (see below for breast-fed infants) and not later than 2 months in preterm and low-birth-weight infants.

Breast-fed Infants   Since breast milk contains up to 1.0 mg of iron per liter which is absorbed at a rate of 50 percent, most breast-fed infants will absorb sufficient iron per day to meet requirements. Therefore, the infant who is exclusively breast-fed does not need other exogenous sources of iron until 6 months of age. When breast-feeding is discontinued before 6 months of age, an iron-fortified formula and iron-fortified cereal should be given. It is important to note that strong differences of opinion exist. Fomon et al. (1979) recommend daily supplementation with 7 mg ferrous iron beginning in the first month.

SOURCES OF IRON

Iron content of some infant foods and major sources of iron are listed in Tables 3-11 and 3-12. In early infancy when the variety of foods ingested is limited the chief sources of dietary iron supplementation are iron-fortified formulas and dry infant cereals.

Iron-Fortified Formulas   These are adequately fortified with absorbable iron (approx.12 mg/liter) and should be used as long as possible during the first year of life. For the bottle-fed infant, there is no nutritional need for iron-fortified formula before 4 to 6 months of age, but for practical purposes it is reasonable to begin at birth in order to avoid a formula switch later on. When infants are switched to fresh cow milk during the first year there is a high incidence of enteric blood loss which can contribute to iron deficiency. See Chapter 19, Iron Deficiency Anemia.

Infant Cereals   Dry infant cereals are fortified with reduced iron of small particle size which is absorbed at approximately 4 percent. The amount of iron added to the cereal equals 0.45 mg/gm of cereal. If an infant is to absorb at least 0.3 mg/day during the first year (see above, Iron Requirements), at least 17 gm of cereal (7.5 mg of iron) must be ingested daily. It has been calculated that 6 tablespoons of cereal equals 14 gm. Thus, approximately 7 to 8 tablespoons equals 17 gm. It then follows that 4 tablespoons of cereal served twice a day

Table 3-11
Iron Content of Selected Foods Fed to Infants in the United States

Food	Elemental Iron	
	(mg/100 gm of food)	*(mg/100 kcal)*
Milk or formula		
Human milk	0.05	0.07
Cow milk	0.05	0.07
Iron-fortified formula	0.9–1.3	1.2–1.8
Formula unfortified with iron	<0.05	<0.05
Infant cereals		
Iron-fortified (dry) mixed with milk[a]	7–14	7–14
Wet-packed cereal-fruit	1–6	1.3–7.5
Strained and junior foods		
Meats		
Liver and a few others	4–6	4–6
Most meats	1–2	1–2
Egg yolks	2–3	1.0–1.5
"Dinners"		
High meat	<1	<1
Vegetable-meat	<0.5	<0.5
Vegetables[b]	<0.5	<0.5
Fruits[b]	<0.5	<0.5

Source: Reprinted with permission from S. J. Fomon, *Infant Nutrition*, 2nd ed, p. 314, © 1974 by the W. B. Saunders Company, Philadelphia.

[a] Assuming that one part by weight of dry cereal is mixed with six parts of milk
[b] A few varieties of vegetables and fruits provide 1 to 2 mg of iron/100 gm (1 to 3 mg/100 kcal).

will provide sufficient iron to meet most infant's needs. This form of cereal is also recommended for use during the second year of life. See this chapter, Solid Foods, Serving Size.

Medicinal Iron   See Chapter 19, Iron Deficiency Anemia. To reduce the risk of accidental ingestion, no more than a 1-month supply should be kept in the home.

Solid Foods

Infants receiving breast milk or formula with appropriate vitamin and mineral supplements do not need additional foods before 6 months of age. Some authorities use weight (6 to 7 kg) as the criterion (Committee on Nutrition, 1979). No nutritional or psy-

Table 3-12
Typical Foods as Sources of Iron

Food	Size of Serving	Iron, in Milligrams	
		per Avg. Serving	per 100 Grams of Food
Liver			
Lamb, broiled	2 slices (75 gm)	13.4	17.9
Beef, fried	2 slices (75 gm)	6.6	8.8
Chicken, cooked	¼ cup (50 gm)	4.3	8.8
Meats (lean or med. fat)			
Beef, round, cooked	1 lg. hamburger (85 gm)	3.0	3.5
rib roast, cooked	3 slices (100 gm)	2.6	2.6
Pork, chop, cooked	1 med. lg. chop (80 gm)	2.5	3.1
Lamb, shoulder chop	1 chop, cooked (90 gm)	1.6	1.8
Baked beans, canned with			
pork and molasses	½ cup (130 gm)	3.0	2.3
pork and tomato	½ cup (130 gm)	2.3	1.8
Fruits, dried (uncooked)			
Apricots	4 halves, (30 gm)	1.7	5.5
Prunes	4–5 medium, (30 gm)	1.2	3.9
Figs	2 small (30 gm)	0.9	3.0
Raisins	2 tbsp (20 gm)	0.6	3.5
Legumes			
Soy beans, dry	½ cup scant, cooked (30 gm dry)	2.5	8.4
Peanut butter	2 tbsp scant (30 gm)	0.6	2.0
Lima beans, fresh	½ cup, cooked (80 gm)	2.0	2.5

Food	Serving		
Molasses, med.	1 tbsp (20 gm)	1.2	6.0
Eggs, whole	1 med. (50 gm)	1.2	2.3
Leafy vegetables			
Spinach	½ cup, cooked (90 gm)	2.0	2.2
Beet greens	½ cup, cooked (100 gm)	1.9	1.9
Chard	½ cup, cooked (100 gm)	1.8	1.8
Kale (leaves only)	½ cup, cooked (55 gm)	0.9	1.6
Turnip greens	½ cup, cooked (75 gm)	0.8	1.1
Vegetables			
Potatoes, sweet	1 med., baked (110 gm)	1.0	0.9
white	1 med., baked (100 gm)	0.7	0.7
Broccoli	⅔ cup (100 gm)	0.8	0.8
Brussels sprouts	5–6 med. (70 gm)	0.8	1.1
Cauliflower	¾ cup, cooked (100 gm)	0.7	0.7
Carrots	⅔ cup, diced, cooked (100 gm)	0.6	0.6
String beans	¾ cup, cooked (100 gm)	0.6	0.6
Beets	2, 2-in. diam. (100 gm)	0.5	0.5
Bread			
White, enriched	1 slice	0.6	2.5
Whole-wheat	1 slice	0.5	2.3
White, unenriched	1 slice	0.2	0.7
Cereals, whole grain (oats, corn, wheat, rice)	See label on package—range from 0.2 to 0.7 mg unenriched, up to 10 mg enriched, per serving.		
Fresh fruits and fruit vegetables	100 gm serving, mostly	0.3–0.6	
Milk, whole, fluid, cow's	½ pint, or 8 oz glass (244 gm)	0.10	0.04
Human	½ pint, or 8 oz (244 gm)	0.24	0.1

Source: Reprinted with permission from L. J., Bogert, et al., *Nutrition and Physical Fitness*, (Philadelphia: Saunders, © 1973), p. 269.

chologic advantages accrue to infants started on solids during this period. In addition, the cost per unit of calories is considerably more for commercially prepared baby foods than for most milks and formulas. The possibility also exists that early introduction of solids contributes to habits of overfeeding and later overeating. Constipation can occur if solid food intake is high. Another factor involves the possibility of food allergy since foreign proteins in foods can become antigens due to the lack of sufficient IgA production in the infant under 6 to 7 months. Nonetheless, surveys of current infant feeding practices in the United States reveal that most infants are receiving commercially prepared strained foods by 4 weeks of age.

From a developmental perspective, infants by 5 to 6 months of age are interested in chewing, picking up food, and putting everything available into their mouths. These infants are more able to sit with support, have good head and neck control, and are able to communicate interest or satiety. Many parents and professionals feel it is appropriate to introduce solids during this period congruent with developmental level. See Chapter 5, First Solid Foods.

NUTRITIONAL CONSIDERATIONS

The trend toward early introduction of solid foods will not be easily or quickly reversed. Nurse practitioners provide education and support for parents based on current knowledge but must also accept parents who, for a wide variety of reasons (family tradition, peer pressure, competition with neighbors, and others) insist on early feeding of solids. Parents must not be made to feel guilty about their feeding practices. Information that may help parents make informed decisions follows.

Distribution of Calories When solid foods are introduced, it is possible that marked variation in caloric distribution will occur. See Table 3-13. Generally speaking, solid baby foods are rich sources of carbohydrate, moderate sources of protein, and poor sources of fat. When infants are fed solids and also switched to whole cow milk, 2 percent milk, or skim milk, protein calories will be very high (an expensive and inefficient method of providing calories) and, in the case of skim milk, fat calories will be very low (see Table 3-10). Diets that provide excess amounts of protein, sodium, and other

Table 3-13
Caloric Density and Distribution of Calories in Strained Foods Relative
to Human Milk and Infant Formula

Food	kcal/ 100 gm	Percentage of Calories From Protein	Fat	Carbo- hydrate
Egg yolks	196	20	78	2
Meats	105	53	46	1
Desserts and puddings	81	5	10	85
Fruits	63	2	4	94
High-meat dinners	88	29	42	29
Human milk	*75*	*6*	*56*	*38*
Infant formula	*67*	*9*	*48*	*43*
Fruit juices	53	2	2	96
Creamed vegetables	61	17	15	68
Soups and dinners	58	16	28	56
Plain vegetables	36	17	5	78

Source: Adapted from T. A. Anderson, "Are Infants Getting the Right Foods?" in *Year ONE: Nutrition, Growth, Health*, Columbus, OH: Ross Laboratories, 1975, p. 19, and Gerber Products Company, 1979 analyses.

solutes can be a hazard for the infant because they create a large solute load that the infant cannot efficiently excrete unless body fluid reserves are drawn upon. If the infant then becomes febrile, tachypneic, or develops diarrhea, the increased water lost via the skin, lungs, and intestines may not be adequately met from body fluid reserves and the potential exists for hypernatremia or dehydration.

Commercially Prepared Infant Foods

COMPOSITION   The composition and nutritional quality of commercially prepared infant foods vary widely. Without knowledge of the facts or understanding of how to read labels, parents can unknowingly purchase nutritionally inferior products. Some examples are as follows:

1. *Iron content of infant cereals.* Dry cereal preparations (rice, barley, oatmeal, high-protein) contain from 72 to 80 mg of iron per 100 gm of cereal. By contrast, the wet-pack cereals with fruit, often

purchased because parents think they will be more appealing to the infant, contain only 0.2 to 5.3 mg of iron per 100 gm (Fomon, 1974, pp. 410–411).

2. *Combination dinners.* In the combination meat and vegetable dinners the label is the key to nutritional ingredients. Gerber's *Beef with Vegetables* contains 6.1 gm of protein per 100 gm, while Gerber's *Vegetables with Beef* contains 1.6 gm of protein per 100 gm.

3. Single preparations. Single products are usually more nutritional than combinations. For example, plain meats contain from 12 to 15 gm of protein per 100 gm.

Thus, it behooves the nurse practitioner to obtain listings of baby foods and their ingredients to share the facts with parents. Complete listings are available from the major manufacturers (Gerber, Heinz, Beech-Nut).

RECENT CHANGES   In recent years pressures brought by consumers and professionals have resulted in many changes in the manufacture of strained and junior foods. Some of the more significant changes are as follows:

1. *Reduction of excessive sodium content of many infant foods.* The addition of sodium chloride, sodium nitrite, and monosodium glutamate (MSG) has been discontinued.

2. *Reduction of sucrose.* The amount of sucrose added to fruits, desserts, vegetables, and dinners has been reduced but sucrose-containing fruits and desserts are still sold and purchased widely. Beech-Nut has eliminated all added sugar from its products.

3. *Use of more bioavailable forms of iron in infant cereals.* Electrolytic iron powder (reduced iron of small particle size) is now used in most cereals.

4. *Adoption of nutritional labeling.* Products are now required to list the nutrient content on the label or to provide an address from which such information can be obtained.

STORAGE AND REFRIGERATION OF COMMERCIAL BABY FOODS   Guidelines are as follows:

1. *Formulas.* Once a can of liquid ready-to-feed or concentrate has been opened it should be refrigerated, and the unused portion should be discarded after 48 hours.

2. *Baby foods.* After the first portion has been served, the lid should be replaced on the jar, and the jar should be refrigerated. If jars are being saved for another meal, the food should be taken out of the jar for heating. Once a jar has been opened the entire contents should be served in 2 to 3 days, or else it should be discarded.

Home Preparation of Baby Foods Many parents are interested in preparing their own baby foods at home for both economic and nutritional benefits. This practice should be encouraged. Some foods are avoided during the first year because of difficulty with digestion (i.e., cucumbers, onions, cabbage, broccoli). Home-prepared spinach and beets may contain sufficient nitrite to cause methemoglobinemia in young infants (Committee on Nutrition, 1979, p. 151). These vegetables plus turnip, mustard, and collard greens should be introduced later in the first year.

REFERENCES FOR PARENTS The following inexpensive paperback books for parents are recommended:

1. Castle, S. *The Complete Guide to Preparing Baby Foods at Home.* Garden City, NY: Doubleday, 1973.
2. Kenda, M. E. and P. S. Williams. *The Natural Baby Food Cookbook.* New York: Avon, 959 Eighth Ave., 1972.
3. Lansky, V. *Feed Me, I'm Yours.* New York: Bantam Books, 1974.

DIRECTIONS FOR BLENDER PREPARATION A good blender can be purchased for approximately $35.00, and a baby-food grinder is available for under $10.00.

1. Scrub all equipment with hot water and soap and rinse well.
2. Prepare food for cooking, removing skin, pits, or seeds. Bring to a full boil and cook until tender.
3. Add 1 cupful food at a time to blender with ¼ cup liquid (cooking liquid). More water may be needed for meat to permit blades to operate. Care should be taken, however, to use as little water as possible.

Several methods may be used to prepare feedings for a number of days:

• Freeze pureed food (from blender) in ice-cube trays putting 2 tablespoons in one cube, or using 24 tablespoons for a 12-cube tray. When food is frozen the cubes may be stored in a plastic bag in the freezer.

- Place 2 tablespoons of the food in a paper cupcake liner and freeze on a cookie tray. When hard, store as above.
- Wrap 2 tablespoons of the food in a piece of aluminum foil and store in freezer.
- To reheat: Place food in a glass custard cup and heat until very hot in a covered pan of boiling water. Cool before feeding.

BLENDER RECIPES A sample of recipes is included so nurse practitioners can assist parents who have questions.

Meats

½ cup cubed cooked meat

2 tablespoons milk, formula, or liquid from boiled meat

Put ingredients into blender and mix at high speed until perfectly smooth. To test for smoothness, put a small amount on the palm of your hand. Rub with finger. If any large particles can be felt, process again.

Chicken

½ cup cooked chicken, cut in pieces

½ tablespoon cream or milk

Put ingredients into blender and mix to a smooth pulp. Yield: 1 to 2 servings.

Vegetables

½ cup freshly cooked vegetable

2 tablespoons milk or formula

1 teaspoon margarine (optional)

Put ingredients into blender. Run at high speed until perfectly smooth. Test for smoothness. Yield: 1 to 2 servings.

Tomato

1 fresh tomato, peeled

Wash tomato thoroughly. Cut into quarters. Put into blender and blend to a smooth pulp.

Fruits

¾ cup cooked or canned fruit; peaches can be fresh

2 teaspoons liquid from fruit

Put ingredients into blender. Blend at high speed until perfectly smooth.

Serving Size At birth the stomach capacity of the infant is 30 to 90 ml (1 to 3 oz), at 1 month 90 to 150 ml (3 to 5 oz), and by 1 year of age will hold 240 ml (8 oz) of fluid and 1 cup of solids. Small amounts (e.g., a teaspoon) of each new food should be offered and gradually increased as tolerated. After initial introduction, the following quantities are suggested as guidelines for serving sizes during the first year:

- Cereal. Up to 8 tablespoons daily in two servings. The usual dilution of cereal with milk or formula is one part cereal to six parts milk.
- Juices. Begin with 1 to 2 ounces and increase up 4 ounces.
- Strained and junior foods. Serve one third to one half of the jar. Jar sizes of commercial foods are:

Strained foods: 3¾ to 4½ ounces

Meat and egg yolks: 3½ ounces

Junior foods: 7½ to 7¾ ounces

Junior meats: 3½ ounces

Junior high-meat dinners: 4½ to 4¾ ounces

Juices: 4½ ounces

Nutritional Needs of the Low-Birth-Weight Infant

DEFINITION

The low-birth-weight infant is defined as one with a birth weight of less than 2,500 gm.

NUTRITIONAL CONSIDERATIONS

The low-birth-weight infant requires a special approach to nutrition in view of the early cessation of transplacental supply of nutrients, immature metabolic systems, and the potential for an unusually rapid growth rate ("catch-up" growth). Specific features of the low-birth-weight infant related to nutrition include the following:

- Need for increased calories and protein for growth
- Need for increased vitamins and minerals for growth
- Efficient absorption of protein and carbohydrate but decreased absorption of fat (due to liver immaturity) (Vegetable oils and human milk fat are relatively well absorbed.)
- Loss of fat-soluble vitamins and calcium as a result of fecal fat loss
- Early depletion of iron stores predisposing to iron deficiency sometime after 2 or 3 months of age
- Low body stores of vitamin E and poor absorption of vitamin E predisposing to vitamin E deficiency during the first 3 months of life
- Inadequate stores of folic acid during the first 3 to 4 months of life (Dallman, 1974, pp. 750–751)

NUTRITIONAL MANAGEMENT

Early feeding of the low-birth-weight infant should be managed collaboratively with the physician. Nutritional management of the preterm and low-birth-weight infant includes the following guidelines:

- Additional calories. Approximately 110–150 cal/kg/day supplied in formulas calculated to provide 24 to 27 cal per ounce
- Distribution of calories as:

Protein	11 percent
Fat	40–50 percent
Carbohydrate	39 percent

- Vitamin K intramuscularly at birth.
- Daily oral multivitamin supplement that provides the equivalent of the RDAs for term infants, including vitamin E.
- Additional calcium, sodium, phosphorus, and copper.
- Iron supplementation by 2 months of age at 2 mg/kg/day. See this chapter, Iron Nutrition in Infancy.

- Vitamin E supplementation during the first 3 months of life. Alpha-tocopherol acetate (Aquasol E) in a dose of 5 IU/day is recommended unless contained in the multivitamin supplement. This is a water-soluble form of vitamin E and is better absorbed. The requirement for vitamin E increases as the levels of iron and polyunsaturated fats in the diet increase.
- Folic acid supplementation during the first three months of life at a dose of 50 μg/day (Dallman, 1974). Folic acid is not added to liquid multivitamin supplements due to its instability.

NUTRITION IN CHILDHOOD AND ADOLESCENCE

The Toddler and Preschool Period

During this period several factors affect nutritional status. Physical growth rate decreases, motor development matures, and cognitive and personality development increase. Although provision of adequate nutrition remains the parents' responsibility, the child affects the process by developing self-feeding skills, food preferences, and individual patterns of food intake. See Chapter 6, Feeding of Toddlers and Preschoolers. Guidelines for nutrition during this period include the following:

- A balanced diet that meets the RDAs (Table 3-1) should be offered.
- Food may need to be offered five to seven times a day
- Stomach capacity is approximately 500 ml at 2 years of age and gradually increases to adult capacity of 750 to 900 ml (Gundy, 1981).
- Milk intake need not exceed 16 ounces per day.
- The exact amounts of specific foods to be given cannot be rigidly prescribed and depend on the individual child's appetite. Suggestions are given in Table 3-14.
- A useful rule of thumb regarding minimal serving sizes for preschoolers is one bite (or teaspoonful) for each year of age of each food served.

Table 3-14
Recommended Food Intake for Good Nutrition[a]

Food Group	Servings/Day	Average Size of Servings					
		1 year	2-3 years	4-5 years	6-9 years	10-12 years	13-15 years
Milk and cheese (1.5 oz cheese = 1 C milk) (C = 1 cup – 8 oz or 240 gm)	4	½ C	½-¾ C	¾ C	¾-1 C	1 C	1 C
Meat group (protein foods)	3 or more						
Egg			1	1	1	1	1 or more
Lean meat, fish, poultry (liver once a week)		2 Tbsp	2 Tbsp	4 Tbsp	2-3 oz (4-6 Tbsp)	3-4 oz	4 oz. or more
Peanut butter			1 Tbsp	2 Tbsp	2-3 Tbsp	3 Tbsp	3 Tbsp
Fruits and vegetables	At least 4, including: 1 or more (twice as much tomato as citrus)						
Vitamin C source (citrus fruits, berries, tomato, cabbage, cantaloupe)		⅓ C citrus	½ C	½ C	1 medium orange	1 medium orange	1 medium orange
Vitamin A source (green or yellow fruits and vegetables)	1 or more	2 Tbsp	3 Tbsp	4 Tbsp (¼ C)	¼ C	⅓ C	½ C

Other vegetables (potato and legumes, etc.) or	2	2 Tbsp	3 Tbsp	4 Tbsp (¼ C)	⅓ C	½ C	¾ C
Other fruits (apple, banana, etc.)		¼ C	⅓ C	½ C	1 medium	1 medium	1 medium
Cereals (whole-grain or enriched)	At least 4						
Bread		½ slice	1 slice	1½ slices	1-2 slices	2 slices	2 slices
Ready-to-eat cereals		½ oz	¾ oz	1 oz	1 oz	1 oz	1 oz
Cooked cereal (including macaroni, spaghetti, rice, etc.)		¼ C	⅓ C	½ C	½ C	¾ C	1 C or more
Fats and carbohydrates	To meet caloric needs						
Butter, margarine, mayonnaise, oils: 1 Tbsp = 100 calories (kcal)		1 Tbsp	1 Tbsp	1 Tbsp	2 Tbsp	2 Tbsp	2-4 Tbsp
Desserts and sweets: 100-calorie portions as follows: ⅓ C pudding or ice cream 2-3" cookies, 1 oz cake, 1⅓ oz pie, 2 tbsp jelly, jam, honey, sugar		1 portion	1½ portions	1½ portions	3 portions	3 portions	3-6 portions

Source: Reprinted with permission from V. C. Vaughan and R. J. McKay, editors, *Nelson Textbook of Pediatrics*, 10th ed., P. 159. © 1975 by the W. B. Saunders Company, Philadelphia.

[a]Based on Food Groups and the Average Size of Servings at Different Age Levels

- Finger foods should be emphasized. Protein-rich finger foods include peanut butter and crackers, cheese squares, hard-boiled eggs.
- Nuts, bony fish, and popcorn should be avoided in the toddler because of the risk of aspiration or impaction.
- There is little basis for vitamin and mineral supplementation except for iron and fluoride (if water supply is inadequate). Vitamin B_{12} may be indicated in strict vegetarian diets.
- During these two periods when appetite slackens and independence needs of the young child further affect eating patterns, the temporary use of vitamin supplements may reassure the concerned parent of nutritional adequacy.
- Preschool children are at risk for iron deficiency anemia and dental caries. Adequate iron-containing foods must be provided and excessive intake of sweet foods should be avoided.

School Age

The healthy school-age child usually presents few nutritional problems and adapts to family eating patterns. See also Chapter 7, Health Care of the School-Age Child. Table 3-14 gives suggestions for recommended foods and serving sizes for the school-age child. Snacks continue to be a primary source of nutrients, and an increasing amount of nutrition is obtained outside of the home. Assessment of nutritional status is important as undernutrition during this age period can contribute to poor school performance. See this chapter, Individual Nutritional Assessment. Children from deprived families, or at high risk for malnutrition (e.g., anorexia, poor eating habits) may need to receive multivitamin and mineral supplements.

Adolescence

Nutritional needs are greatly influenced by this period of physical and emotional adjustment. It is a time when caloric needs increase due to the adolescent growth spurt; when protein, mineral, and vitamin needs reach adult values; and when female adolescents need increased iron coincident with menarche (see Chapter 19, Iron Deficiency Anemia). It is also a period when rebellion against previously acquired family eating habits is common, when activities outside the home increase and snacking becomes a major source of nutrients, and when strivings for self-identity and concerns over body image lead to extreme diets. The RDAs for adolescents are presented in Table 3-1. See also Chapter 8, Health Care of the Adolescent.

NUTRITIONAL STATUS

Adolescents from ages 10 to 16 years have been found to have the most unsatisfactory nutritional status of any age group (Torre, 1977). Although protein deficiency is not extensive, deficiencies in iron, vitamin A, calcium, vitamin C, riboflavin, and thiamin are common. Food sources of these nutrients are found in Tables 3-5 and 3-6. A guide to nutritional assessment of the adolescent is presented in Table 3-15.

SNACKS

Since adolescents obtain significant amounts of essential nutrients through snacks, suggested snacks include fresh fruits, fruit juices, dried fruits, cheese, milk beverages, peanut butter and crackers, raw vegetables, nuts, and leftover meats. A caloric comparison of popular snacks is found in Table 3-16.

SPECIAL PROBLEMS

Pregnant Adolescent The RDAs for pregnant adolescents are found in Table 3-1. Iron, calcium, folic acid, B vitamins, and vitamins A and C are the nutrients most often lacking in these young women.

Oral Contraceptives Women taking oral contraceptives need increased amounts of vitamin B_6 (pyridoxine), vitamin C, and folic acid. See this chapter, Maternal Nutrition.

Athletes A minimum of 2,300 to 5,000 calories per day may be required for those involved in very strenuous exercise. The optimum distribution of calories is thought to be as follows:

Protein   10–15 percent
Fat   25–35 percent
Carbohydrate   50–65 percent

Table 3-15
Adolescent Nutritional Assessment Guide

History
  Family history
    Obesity, diabetes mellitus, hypertension, or heart disease in close
    family members? Preventive diet may be indicated.
  Dietary history
    Discuss appetite, total daily food intake, special diet, frequency of
    meals, snacking habits, food preferences, food allergies, vitamin
    supplements.
  Medications
    On oral contraceptive? May need increased vitamin C, pyridoxine,
    and folic acid.
  Habits
    Smoke? May need vitamin C supplementation or increased intake
    of ascorbic acid-rich foods.
  Exercise
    Daily exercise patterns, if any.
    Participation in sports? Which sports? How often? May need in-
    creased calories, vitamin C and B complex, and water and salt to
    replace losses in sweat.
  Past health problems
    History of significant weight gain or loss? History of obesity,
    anemia, thyroid imbalance, or diabetes?
  Special considerations
    Pregnant? Consider needs for increased calories, protein, calcium,
    iron, B vitamins, and vitamins C and A.
    IUD in place? May need increased iron to replace losses in men-
    trual flow.
  Review of systems
    If the following symptoms are elicited, consider corresponding min-
    eral and vitamin deficiencies:
      Dryness and cracking of skin or lips, itching of genital area:
        riboflavin
      Nervousness, irritability, insomnia, muscle cramps: calcium
      Indigestion, constipation, nervousness, irritability, fatigue, mental
        depression: thiamine
      Night blindness, roughness of skin, dryness of hair: vitamin A
      Bleeding of gums, slow wound healing, easy bruising: vitamin C
      Fatigue, irritability, anorexia, headache, increased menstrual flow:
        iron

Table 3-15 (Continued)

Physical assessment
 Observe for evidence of poor nutritional status via:
 Height and weight
  Fall far below mean or growth chart for age? Consider protein and
   calorie deprivation.
  Fall far above mean? Consider overweight, obesity.
 Clinical signs
  Lethargy, general depression, dry skin or hair, lesions on lips, skin,
   or genitalia, dental caries, swollen or bleeding gums, tachycardia,
   and enlarged thyroid may indicate nutritional inadequacies.
 Laboratory data
  Consider iron deficiency anemia if hemoglobin or hematocrit levels
   are low.

Source: Reprinted with permission from J. Slattery, G. Pearson, and C. Torre, *Maternal and Child Nutrition: Assessment and Counseling,* East Norwalk, CT: Appleton-Century-Crofts, 1979. P. 203.

Table 3-16
Comparison of Calories in Fast Food and Whole Food Snacks

Fast-Food Snacks	Cal	Whole-Food Snacks	Cal
1 doughnut	230	1 orange	65
1 sweet roll	275	1 apple	85
4 cookies	200	1 banana	100
1 carton flavored yogurt	260	½ cantaloupe	60
1 ice cream cone	300	1 carrot	20
1 chocolate shake	360	1 handful raisins	40
1 slice pizza	185	4 stalks of celery	20
1 Big Mac	541	1 glass low-fat milk	135
1 cheeseburger	300	1 glass tomato juice	45
1 hot dog	270	1 glass orange juice	120
1 bag french fries	210	1 cup popcorn	25
20 potato chips	230	1 frozen juice bar	85

Source: Teen Clinic, Ambulatory Care Center, University of California Medical Center, San Francisco, CA.

CULTURAL CONSIDERATIONS

Food preferences and eating patterns are influenced by many factors. Among the most significant factors are ethnic, racial, and cultural influences. It is impossible to identify an absolute diet pattern for any cultural group, since no two people eat exactly alike. The information presented in Table 3-17 is intended to serve as a guide toward better understanding of predominant food choices of selected major cultural and ethnic groups.

VEGETARIAN DIETS

Types of Vegetarian Diets

Definitions of vegetarian diets are as follows:

1. Lacto-ovo-vegetarian diet is an all-vegetable diet supplemented with milk, cheese, and eggs.
2. Lacto-vegetarian diet is an all-vegetable diet supplemented with only milk and cheese.
3. Pure vegetarian or vegan diet excludes all foods of animal origin.

Nutritional Adequacy

Vegetarian diets can be nutritionally adequate and provide for normal growth and development in children provided they are based on sound nutritional knowledge.

• The protein sources must be varied to supply the essential amino acids and energy requirements. Most plant protein is incomplete protein. Exceptions are: soybeans, garbanzo beans, wheat germ, and brewer's yeast, which are complete proteins. Table 3-18 presents amino acid composition of selected foods. Properly fortified soy milk is strongly recommended for infants and children (ADA, 1980).

Table 3-17
Acceptable Foods of Some Cultural and Ethnic Groups

Food Group	Mexican-Spanish	Chinese	Japanese	Black	American Indian
MILK	Milk (fresh, dry, evaporated), cheese (Cheddar, Monterey Jack, Parmesan, cottage, Mexican), Flan (very sweet custard), ice cream	Milk, especially flavored (usually in small quantities until taste is developed)	Larger quantities of milk are being consumed by the younger generations	Fresh homogenized milk, buttermilk, evaporated, nonfat dry (limited use in food preparation), ice cream, puddings (bread, rice, chocolate, coconut), cheese (Cheddar, cottage, Longhorn, American)	Fresh milk, evaporated (used in cooking), ice cream, cream pies
MEAT Poultry Eggs Legumes Game Fish and Seafoods	Beef, pork, lamb, chicken, tripe, hot sausage, beef intestines, fish, bologna, frankfurters, eggs, nuts, dry beans (especially pinto), chick peas	Pork, fish and shellfish, duck, chicken, organ meats, eggs, soybeans, nuts, red beans, black beans, split peas, bean curd (Tofu), pork sausage (frequently eaten three times a day; also is lower in fat content than regular sausage)	Pork, beef, fish, shellfish, chicken, soya beans, soya cake, red beans, lima beans, Tofu, eggs, nuts	Pork (fresh and cured—all cuts), organs, chitterlings (pork intestines), beef, lamb, tripe, chicken, turkey, duck, goose, fresh fish, tuna and salmon canned, eggs, nuts, cow peas, blackeyed peas, chick peas, beans: navy, red, and pinto, peanut butter, game: rabbit and venison	Pork, beef, lamb, chicken, duck, turkey, goose, fish (fresh and canned), shellfish, eggs, legumes: red, white or black beans, blackeyed peas, sunflower seeds, California walnuts, acorns, pine nuts, peanut butter, rabbit.

Continued on next page

Table 3-17 (Continued)

Food Group	Mexican-Spanish	Chinese	Japanese	Black	American Indian
FRUITS AND VEGETABLES					
Good sources of Vit. A	Spinach, wild greens, tomatoes, carrots, green peppers, yellow corn, pumpkin, peaches	Bok choy (Chinese mustard cabbage), many other leafy greens, green peppers, tomatoes	Sweet potatoes, spinach, carrots, tomatoes, yellow squash	Leafy greens (fresh ones preferred: wild greens, spinach, mustard, chard, beet tops, collards), tomatoes, sweet potato, carrots, pumpkin (if available), yellow squash, green peppers, okra	Tomatoes, pumpkin, carrots, yellow squash, leafy greens (dandelion, mustard), watercress
Good sources of Vit. C	Chili pepper (fresh), green peppers, tomatoes, Guava fruit, oranges, lemons, limes, papaya	Bok choy, green pepper, tomatoes (fresh), fruits (usually not eaten frequently) melons, oranges, papaya, watercress	Tomatoes (fresh), oranges, cabbage (raw)	Oranges (and juice), melons, green peppers, tomatoes, lemons, strawberries, collard, chard, mustard, and turnip greens, cabbage (raw)	Turnips (raw), cabbage (raw), oranges, grapefruit, melons, lemons, strawberries, mustard greens, watercress

Fair sources of Vit. C	Cactus leaves, potatoes, cabbage, cactus fruit, Zapote (a fruit), radishes	Leafy greens, Chinese cabbage, celery	Potatoes (in limited amounts), cabbage (cooked)	Potatoes (sweet and white), cabbage (cooked), turnips (cooked), radishes	Cabbage (cooked), potatoes (sweet and white), turnips (cooked)
Others	Summer squash, green peas, green beans, hominy, beets, celery, onions. When income permits: bananas, apples, fruit juices other than grapefruit or orange, fruit cocktail	Peas in pod, okra, summer squash, green beans, white turnips, mushrooms, eggplant, cucumbers, bamboo shoots, soybean sprouts	String beans, radishes, onions, eggplant, cucumber, pickled vegetables (as dessert), mushrooms, celery	Grapes, bananas, peaches, fruit cocktail, pineapples, apples, string beans, mixed vegetables, beets, turnips, canned green peas, onions, corn	Grapes, bananas, peaches, pears, fruit cocktail, apples, pineapple, green peas, green beans, beets, turnips, onions (green and bulb), cucumbers, eggplant, lettuce, corn
BREADS AND CEREALS	Rice, oats, cornmeal, corn flakes, thin spaghetti, noodles, macaroni, sweet breads, tortilla, biscuits	Rice, millet, oats, wheat, rice cakes, noodles, macaroni, refined bread, rice noodles, rice flour	Rice, rice cakes, crackers, refined bread, noodles	Refined breads, hot yeast breads, cornbread, biscuits, pancakes, cream of wheat, oats, grits, rice, cornmeal, flour, corn flakes and other dry cereals, macaroni	Refined bread, whole wheat bread, biscuits, cornbread, pancakes, cream of wheat, oatmeal, rice, dry cereal

Table 3-18
Amino Acid Composition of Some Foods[a]

Essential Amino Acids	Cheese Eggs Milk Meat	Corn	Cereal	Legumes	Whole Grains (with germ)	Nuts Seed Oils Soybeans	Sesame and Sunflower Seeds	Peanut Protein	Green Leafy Veg. Leaf Prot.	Gelatin[b]	Yeast
Cystine[c]							x				
Methionine	x	x	x	–	x	–	x	–	–	–	x
Isoleucine	x										
Leucine	x										
Lysine	x	–	–	x	x	x	–	–		–	
Phenylalanine										–	x
Threonine	x	–	x	x	–	x		–			
Tryptophan		–	–	–			x			–	
Valine	x										

Source: Reprinted by permission from the *Journal of Nutrition Education*, 2:135–139, Spring 1971, Society for Nutrition Education.

Symbols: x = High amount of amino acid present in that food.

– = Low amount of amino acid present in that food.

Blank spaces indicate a generally good balance of amino acids present with respect to other amino acids in the food.

[a] Be sure to complement a low amino acid with a food high in that amino acid at the same meal.

[b] Gelatin is not a good source of all essential amino acids.

[c] Not essential but added because hard to get in a vegetarian diet. Methionine and cystine can be compared as one.

Table 3-19

Some Vegetarian Sources of Calcium, Iron, and Zinc

Food	Calcium[a] (mg)	iron[a] (mg)	zinc[a] (mg)
Animal protein foods			
hamburger, lean, 3 oz	10	3.0	3.8
liver, beef, 2 oz	6	5.0	2.9'
milk, fluid whole, 1 c	288	0.1	0.9
milk, non-fat dry, ¼ c	219	0.1	0.8
cheese, cheddar, 1 oz	213	0.3	0.5
cheese, cottage, ½ c packed	115	0.3	—
Beans, seeds, nuts			
navy beans, ½ c cooked	48	2.5	0.9
mature soybeans, ½ c cooked	37	1.3	—
sesame seeds, whole, ½ c	1160	10.5	—
sesame seeds, hulled, ½ c	110	2.4	—
sunflower seed kernels, ¼ c	36	2.1	—
almonds, ½ c	166	3.3	—
soybean milk, 1 c	60	1.5	—
Vegetables			
spinach, ½ c cooked	*	2.0	0.8
beet greens, ½ c cooked	*	1.4	—
dandelion greens, ½ c cooked	126	1.6	—
kale, ½ c cooked	74	0.6	—
mustard greens, ½ c cooked	97	1.3	—
turnip greens, ½ c cooked	126	0.8	—
collards, ½ c cooked	144	0.6	—
broccoli, ½ c cooked	68	0.6	—
green peas, ½ c cooked	19	1.5	—
sweet potatoes, 1 sm. (110 gm.)	44	1.0	—
Dried fruits			
dried apricots, ¼ c uncooked	25	2.0	—
dried figs, 1 large, uncooked	26	0.6	—
prunes, 4 uncooked	14	1.1	—
raisins, ½ oz. (1½ tbs)	9	0.5	—
Cereals, breads			
rice, brown, ⅔ c cooked	7	0.3	1.1
oatmeal, 1 c cooked	22	1.4	1.2
oatmeal, dry, ¼ c (18 gm.)	10	0.8	0.7
wheat bran flakes, 40%, 1 oz	21	1.3	1.0
wheat germ, ¼ c	18	2.4	3.6
white bread, enriched, 1 sl	21	0.6	0.2
whole wheat bread, 1 sl	25	0.8	0.5

Source: Copyright December 1975, the American Journal of Nursing Company. Reproduced from the *American Journal of Nursing* 75(12):2168–2173.

[a]RDA for adult male or female for calcium—800 mg.
 RDA for adult male for iron—10 mg; for adult female—18 mg.
 RDA for adult male or female for zinc—15 mg.

*Calcium in spinach and beet greens is present as insoluble calcium oxalate and cannot be absorbed.

—indicates values not reported.

Values for calcium and iron calculated from U.S. Dept. of Agriculture Handbook No. 8, *Composition of Foods,* and U.S. Dept. of Agriculture Home and Garden Bulletin No. 72, *Nutritive Value of Foods.*

Values for soybean milk obtained from U. D. Register and L. M. Sonnenberg, "The Vegetarian Diet." *J Am Dietet Assoc 62*:253–261, Mar 1973.

Values for zinc calculated from E. W. Murphy, B. W. Willis, and B. K. Watt. Provisional Tables on the Zinc Content of Foods. *J Amer Dietet Assoc 66*:345–355, May 1975.

Table 3-20
Sample Menus: Lacto-Ovo-Vegetarian and Typical American

Lacto-Ovo-Vegetarian	Cal.	Pro. (gm)	Fat (gm)	Carb. (gm)
½ c orange juice	60	1	tr	15
1 c oatmeal, cooked	130	5	2	23
1 tsp honey	22	tr	0	6
1 c skim milk	90	9	tr	12
1 sl whole wheat toast	60	3	1	12
1 tbs peanut butter	95	4	8	3
Hot cereal beverage	0	0	0	0
Total	457	22	11	71
1 c meatless split pea soup sandwich	145	9	3	21
2 sl whole wheat bread	120	6	2	24
1 oz cheddar cheese	115	7	9	1
½ tbs mayonnaise	33	tr	3	1
2 lettuce leaves	10	1	tr	2
raw green pepper, ½ pod	7	tr	tr	2
raw apple	70	tr	tr	18
2 fig bars	100	2	2	22
1 c whole milk	160	9	9	12
Total	760	34	28	103

Typical American	Cal.	Pro. (gm)	Fat (gm)	Carb. (gm)
½ c orange juice	60	1	tr	15
1 egg, scrambled	110	7	8	1
2 sl bacon	90	5	8	1
1 sl toast	60	3	1	12
1 pat butter	35	tr	4	tr
1 tbs jelly	50	tr	tr	13
1 c coffee				
(1 tbs cream)	30	1	3	1
(1 tsp sugar)	13	0	0	4
Total	448	17	24	47
1 c chicken noodle soup sandwich	220	8	6	33
2 sl white bread	120	6	2	24
2 sl bologna	80	3	7	tr
½ tbs mayonnaise	33	tr	3	1
2 lettuce leaves	10	1	tr	2
10 potato chips	115	1	8	10
1 choc. chip cookie	50	1	2	7
12 oz soft drink	145	0	0	37
Total	773	20	28	114

	Calories	Protein	Fat	Carbohydrate
Spanish soybeans over rice and bulgur	451	18	17	61
spinach and mushroom salad				
1 c raw spinach	13	1	tr	2
1 tbs oil in dressing	125	0	14	0
1 c skim milk yogurt	125	8	4	13
1 raw peach	35	1	tr	10
1 c apple juice	120	tr	tr	30
⅓ c mushrooms	9	1	tr	1
Total	878	29	35	117
Grand total	2095	85	74	291
% of total calories		16%	32%	55%

	Calories	Protein	Fat	Carbohydrate
3 oz ground beef	245	21	17	0
½ c mashed potatoes	93	2	4	12
½ c green peas	58	5	1	10
iceberg lettuce wedge	15	1	tr	3
1 tbs blue cheese dressing	75	1	8	1
1 slice apple pie	350	3	15	51
1 c coffee	30	1	3	1
(1 tbs cream)				
(1 tsp sugar)	13	0	0	4
Total	879	34	48	82
Grand total	2100	71	100	243
% of total calories		13%	43%	45%

Source: Copyright December 1975, the American Journal of Nursing Company. Reproduced from the *American Journal of Nursing*, 75(12):2168–2173.

- Amino acids in one food can supplement those in another food. For example, wheat is low in lysine but beans are high in lysine, and rice is low in methionine but dried beans are high in methionine. Thus, two or more foods containing incomplete protein may be eaten at the same meal and supply complete protein.
- Folacin and vitamin C sources must be included via a variety of fruits and leafy green vegetables.
- A diet that excludes all animal foods will be deficient in vitamin B_{12}. Symptoms of B_{12} deficiency are soreness of the mouth and tongue, numbness and tingling of the hands and feet, back pain, pernicious anemia. To prevent B_{12} deficiency the vegetarian diet should include some animal protein such as eggs, cheese, or milk. If the vegetarian will not eat these foods, a B_{12} supplement is advised.
- A pure vegan diet will be deficient in vitamin D unless there is adequate daily exposure to sunlight (see Table 3-5, vitamin D).
- A form of iodized salt should be used to provide needed iodine.
- Vitamins and minerals will be supplied adequately if good quality protein (including milk products and eggs), vegetables, and fruit (including dark green leafy, deep yellow, and citrus) are supplied regularly. Vegetarian sources of calcium, iron, and zinc are listed in Table 3-19.

In summary, any vegetarian diet that includes some animal foods (poultry, fish, milk, eggs, or cheese) can be nutritionally sound with careful planning. An infant or child who is growing well and who is in good hematologic status provides an adequate evaluation of dietary status. The strict vegetarian diets must be supplemented with vitamin B_{12} and vitamin D preparations and cannot be considered satisfactory for young children. Severe nutritional deficiencies including kwashiorkor, marasmus, rickets, and death have recently been reported (Zmora et al., 1979; Dwyer et al., 1979).

Sample Vegetarian Diet

A sample vegetarian diet compared with a typical American diet is presented in Table 3-20.

OVERNUTRITION IN INFANCY AND CHILDHOOD (OBESITY)

Assessment

Even though there are more well-fed children in the United States today than ever before, the problem of excessive weight gain and obesity must not be ignored when considering infant nutrition. Not only does obesity have serious physical, psychologic, and social consequences for the affected child, but it is also well known that obesity predisposes to serious disease states in adulthood (e.g., diabetes, hypertension, cardiovascular disease). Evidence currently indicates that 80 to 85 percent of overweight children will continue to be obese as adults (Meyer and Neumann, 1977). Since treatment programs for obesity have proved generally ineffective, the prevention of obesity seems to be the most logical approach.

DEFINITION

Children with weights 10 to 20 percent above the mean for their height and age are defined as *markedly overweight*. Those with weights greater than 20 percent above the mean are defined as *obese* (Rudolph, 1982, p. 255). Some authorities define infantile obesity as weight above the 85th percentile (Brasel, 1979).

ESTIMATION OF OBESITY

Even though obesity can be recognized by inspection—that is, a child who looks fat is probably overweight—documentation using body weight, weight-to-height ratio, and skinfold thickness measured at the mid-triceps or tip of the scapula are useful in determining degree of body fat. See this chapter, Evaluation of Nutritional Status.

INCIDENCE

No definitive statistics are available, but it has been estimated that approximately 10 to 30 percent of American children are affected by obesity. A child with two obese parents has an 80 percent chance of becoming obese as an adult, while a child with one obese parent has a risk of 40 percent.

INFLUENCING FACTORS

All the following factors are thought to play a part in the complex etiology of obesity:

- Activity patterns, energy balance, metabolic rate
- Genetic influences
- Number and size of adipocytes (Adipocytes are those cells of adipose tissue capable of storing fat. They increase in number until puberty when adult values are reached. Obese children have increased cell *size*, and those who are already obese by 1 year of age have marked increases in *number* of cells as well.)
- Nutritional habits (e.g., overfeeding)
- Psychologic factors (e.g., parents who use food as a means of controlling behavior)
- Quantity of food ingested. (This is regulated by caloric requirements for maintenance and growth, attitudes of caretakers, and types of food offered.)

OVERFEEDING IN INFANCY

Calorie Requirements   Many studies have documented the frequency and extent of overfeeding of infants in our society. Two of these studies demonstrated the following:

- Sixty-seven percent of infants under 1 month of age making their first visit to a child health clinic were receiving solid foods. By 2 months of age, 96 percent were receiving solids (Paige, 1975).
- Twenty percent of 130 full-term infants seen at a well-child clinic had been introduced to one or a combination of solid foods by 1 week of age (Paige, 1975).
- All these infants were being fed nutrients in excess of the RDAs.

Attitudes of Caretakers   Attitudes with a significant effect on overfeeding include the following:

- The failure of public and professional encouragement and support of breast feeding is significant. The breast-feeding mother relies on the infant's signals to determine length of feeding and satiety. The mother who is bottle feeding tends to rely on the amount of formula in the bottle and persists until the bottle is empty. This frequently leads to overfeeding.

- The myth persists that a chubby baby is a healthy baby.
- Early introduction of solids is viewed as a sign of developmental progress or else as a way of relieving family and/or peer pressure.

Types of Food Offered   See this chapter, Solid Foods.

OBESITY IN OLDER CHILDREN

Obesity frequently begins during mid-childhood and quite often is associated with a precipitating situational event (e.g., illness, family disruption, move to a new environment). Socioeconomic factors, cultural patterns, lack of activity compounded by extensive TV viewing, and high-calorie snacking also contribute to obesity in this age group. These children tend to have a poor self-image and feelings of inferiority and rejection. As they experience teasing and ridicule from peers, they may become withdrawn, isolated, and even more inactive (Neumann, 1977).

History and Physical Examination   Assessment of the obese child or adolescent (see also Table 3-15) includes the following factors:

- Birth weight
- Early feeding history
- Early growth patterns including record of heights and weights
- Age of onset of obesity
- Precipitating events or circumstances
- Family history of obesity
- History of chronic or serious health problems
- Developmental history
- School history (information from teachers is important)
- Family relationships
- Family attitudes about food and eating
- Nutrition history with 24-hour diet recall (see Table 3-24)
- 24-hour recall of physical activity
- Degree of dependency, maturity, motivation, and self-image of the child (may need formal psychologic assessment)

- Blood pressure
- Height, weight, arm circumference, triceps skinfold
- Stage of pubertal development (Neumann, 1977; Meyer and Neumann, 1977)

Management

PREVENTION IN INFANCY

Attempts at nutritional counseling and education should begin in the prenatal clinic. If a family history of obesity exists, the infant will be at increased risk of developing obesity, and counseling efforts must be intensified. Points to include in counseling are the following:

- Encourage breast feeding
- If bottle feeding, help parents to learn to interpret infants' cues relative to hunger and satiety
- When giving water avoid adding sweeteners
- Delay introduction of solids until 5 to 6 months of age
- Encourage home preparation of solid foods without added sugar
- Avoid the use of commercially prepared mixed dinners, wet-pack cereals, and desserts
- Encourage a range of activity patterns
- Assure parents that 1 pint of milk a day is adequate for an infant over 1 year of age
- Reinforce positive parent–child interactions other than feeding that provide mutual satisfaction
- Explain the normal decrease in appetite and nutritional requirements after 1 year of age
- Use the height–weight grid as a teaching tool. Show parents that their infant is gaining appropriately. Careful monitoring of height and weight and the use of skin calipers will assist in early identification of infants who are gaining too rapidly.

TREATMENT IN INFANCY

If an infant is becoming overweight or has become obese, the goal is not weight loss but a reduction in the rate of weight gain. A regular diet is provided to meet known requirements with a gradual reduction of the total amount of food consumed. Skim milk is not used and low fat milk should be used only in older obese infants. When cultural influences are contributing to overnutrition, sensitivity is critical. A staff member of the same ethnic or cultural background may be useful in these situations.

TREATMENT IN OLDER CHILDREN

The management of obesity in older children requires the combined efforts of the child, family, health provider team, school, and community. Successful programs have been described (Neumann, 1977; Meyer and Neumann, 1977) and include the following components:

- Nutrition and diet education
- Physical activity program (may involve school and community)
- Frequent visits for weight check and follow-up evaluation with continuity provider
- Group counseling and rap sessions for education and expression of feelings
- Family counseling
- Behavior modification techniques
- Psychologic support
- Referral to regular weight-reduction programs (e.g., Weight Watchers)

FOOD ALLERGY

Assessment

Reactions to milk and other foods may result from a wide variety of mechanisms and may be seen as a wide range of signs and symptoms. A full discussion of these factors is beyond the scope of this chapter (see Chapter 26, Allergies). It is possible that the occurrence of food allergies in infants is related to the slow development of IgA barriers, and that after 1 year of age IgA barriers are fully developed, and thus the incidence of food allergies decreases markedly (Rudolph, 1982, p. 476).

COMMON ALLERGENIC FOODS

Certain foods are thought to be commonly allergenic at early ages, and thus parents are advised to avoid them during the early months of life. The most common offenders are the following:

- Cow milk
- Wheat and corn
- Egg whites
- Chocolate
- Citrus products
- Nuts and legumes
- Fish, shellfish
- Beef and chicken

MANIFESTATIONS

Most children show onset of symptoms within 1 month after institution of the antigenic food. Symptoms include diarrhea, rhinitis, abdominal pain, vomiting, allergic skin reactions, and behavioral symptoms (lethargy, irritability, restlessness, moodiness).

HISTORY AND PHYSICAL EXAMINATION

History and physical examination of a child suspected of food allergy include the following data:

- Family history of allergy
- Age of onset of symptoms
- Continuous or intermittent symptoms
- Diet
- Parents' and child's suspicions regarding offending foods
- Infections
- General appearance
- Nutritional status
- Eczema
- Character of feces

Management

INFANTS SENSITIVE TO COW MILK

Elimination of cow milk and milk products from the diet is recommended (see Chapter 26, Milk-Free Diet). Cow milk substitutes, mainly soy formulas, with vitamin and mineral supplementation, have been shown to be very effective and result in normal growth curves. Most children with milk allergy in infancy are able to tolerate cow milk by 3 years of age. Parents should be encouraged to breast-feed for the first 6 months and to limit the introduction of new foods until after 6 months of age when the IgA barrier is close to fully developed.

CHILDREN WITH OTHER FOOD ALLERGIES

A child suspected of having a food allergy is usually placed on an elimination diet of suspected foods until symptoms completely clear. Later foods are reintroduced slowly (one every 6 to 7 days) in a systematic challenge. Once a food has been identified as the causative antigen, strict avoidance is the only effective treatment. See Chapter 26, Allergies, for a full discussion.

EVALUATION OF NUTRITIONAL STATUS

In identifying potential or real health problems and in planning for optimal health care services, evaluation of the nutritional status of individuals and groups must be undertaken by those involved in child care.

Individual Nutritional Assessment

Data to be collected in performing nutritional assessments include family history, birth history, growth history, past and current medical history, nutrition history, physical examination including anthropometric measures (i.e., serial height, weight, head circumference, triceps skinfold, mid-upper arm circumference), and laboratory procedures. Height, weight, and head circumference are

Table 3-21
Approximate Limits for Mid-Upper Arm Circumference
and Triceps Fatfold

Age	Mid-Upper Arm Circumference (3rd to 5th Percentile)[a]		Triceps Fatfold (90th to 97th Percentile)[b]	
	In.	cm	Boys	Girls
0 months	3½	9	10	
3 months	4	10	11	
6 months	4½	11½	12	
9 months	5	12	13	
12 months	5	13	14	
2 years	5	13	13	
3 years	5	13	13	
4 years	5¼	13½	13	
5 years	5¼	13½	13	
6 years	5½	14	12	15
7 years	5½	14	13	16
8 years	5¾	14½	14	17
9 years	6	15	14	18
10 years	6½	16	16	20
11 years	6½	16½	17	21
12–16 years	7–8	17–20	18–20	22–25

Source: Reprinted with permission from A. J. Zerfas, et al., "Office Assessment of Nutritional Status," *Pediatr Clin North Am* 24:253–272, February 1977. Philadelphia: W. B. Saunders.

[a] Under this value suggests undernutrition.
[b] Over this value suggests obesity (values in millimeters).

plotted accurately on appropriate growth charts (see Appendix, Figures 1 to 8). Approximate limits for arm circumference and triceps skinfold are given in Table 3-21. Table 3-22 provides a framework for nutritional assessment of infants and children. Additional information includes knowledge of family economic status, cultural background, educational level, and family food patterns.

NUTRITION HISTORY

A convenient form of recording a nutrition history in infants and toddlers is presented in Table 3-23.

TWENTY-FOUR-HOUR RECALL

Frequently it is difficult for busy parents to remember exactly what a child eats during a 24-hour period. A convenient form for collecting this information is presented in Table 3-24.

GENERAL CHARACTERISTICS OF GOOD AND POOR NUTRITION

Table 3-25 outlines physical manifestations of both good and poor nutrition.

Community Screening Programs

When nutritional screening programs are conducted in communities, data in addition to individual and family information must be collected:

• Demographic data
• Socioeconomic and educational levels
• Racial and ethnic groups
• Source of food and water supplies
• Local food customs

MATERNAL NUTRITION

Nutrition During Pregnancy

Normal physiologic processes are greatly altered during pregnancy and additional demands are imposed on the maternal organism. The objectives of nutrition during pregnancy are as follows:

1. Provide for normal maternal maintenance requirements
2. Provide for growth and development of the fetus
3. Reduce the incidence of complications of pregnancy.

RECOMMENDED DAILY DIETARY ALLOWANCES

The RDAs during pregnancy for women of different age groups are listed in Table 3-1. The pregnant woman needs more calories,

Table 3-22

Levels of Nutritional Assessment for Infants and Children

Level of Approach[a]	History		Clinical Evaluation	Laboratory Evaluation
	Dietary	Medical and Socioeconomic		
	Birth to 24 Months			
Minimal	1. Source of iron 2. Vitamin supplement 3. Milk intake (type and amount)	1. Birth weight 2. Length of gestation 3. Serious or chronic illness 4. Use of medicines	1. Body weight and length 2. Gross defects	1. Hematocrit 2. Hemoglobin

Mid-level	1. Semiquantitative
	   a. Iron-cereal, meat, egg yolks, supplement
	   b. Energy nutrients
	   c. Micronutrients: calcium, niacin, riboflavin, vitamin C
	   d. Protein
	 2. Food intolerances
	 3. Baby foods: processed commercially, home cooked
		1. Family history: diabetes, tuberculosis
		 2. Maternal: height, prenatal care
		 3. Infant: immunizations, tuberculin test
			1. Head circumference
			 2. Skin color, pallor, turgor
			 3. Subcutaneous tissue paucity, excess
				1. RBC morphology
				 2. Serum iron
				 3. Total iron binding capacity
				 4. Sickle cell testing

In-depth level	1. Quantitative 24-hour recall 2. Dietary history	1. Prenatal details 2. Complications of delivery 3. Regular health supervision	1. Cranial bossing 2. Epiphyseal enlargement 3. Costochondral beading 4. Ecchymoses	Same as above, plus vitamin and appropriate enzyme assays, also protein and amino acids, hydroxyproline, etc., should be available
		For Ages 2 to 5 Years		
	Determine amount of intake	Probe about pica, medications	Add height at all levels, add arm circumference at all levels, add triceps skinfolds at in-depth level	Add serum lead at mid-level, add serum micronutrients (vitamin A, C, folate, etc.) at in-depth level
		For Ages 6 to 12 Years		
	Probe about snack foods, determine whether salt intake is excessive	Ask about medications taken, drug abuse	Add blood pressure at mid-level, add description of changes in tongue, skin, eyes for in-depth level	All the above plus BUN

Source: Reprinted with permission from George Christakis, editor, "Nutritional Assessment in Health Programs," Supplement, *Am J Public Health 63*:46, 1973.

[a] It is understood that what is included at a minimal level would also be included or represented at successively more sophisticated levels of approach. However, it may be entirely appropriate to use a minimal level of approach to clinical evaluations and a maximal approach to laboratory evaluations.

Table 3-23
Nutrition History: Birth to 24 Months

NAME: _____

CLINIC: _____

DATE: _____ AGE: _____

Birth weight: _____ Present weight: _____ Percentile: _____

Birth height: _____ Present height: _____ Percentile: _____

Hemoglobin: _____ Hematocrit: _____

(most recent visit)   (most recent visit)

Breast fed: _____ Bottle fed: _____

Any concerns about this method of feeding? _____

BREAST FED

a) For how long is the baby on the breast? _____

b) How much time between feedings? _____

c) Do you supplement breast milk with a bottle? _____

BOTTLE FED

Kind of formula: _____ How is it prepared: _____

Amount of formula taking:

      a) ounces per feeding: _____

      b) number of feedings per day: _____

      c) total milk intake in 24 hours: _____

Do you add anything to the bottle? _____

(let mother respond without suggestions as to kinds of mixtures that might be used)

If yes, what is it?

Cereal: _____ Amount: _____ times per day: _____

Sugar: _____ Amount: _____ times per day: _____

Honey: _____ Amount: _____ times per day: _____

Other: _____ Amount: _____ times per day: _____

If water is offered, do you add anything else? _____

Kind: _____ Amount: _____ times per day: _____

Vitamin supplements:

Kind: _____ Amount: _____ times per day: _____

Solids being given: _____

What do you offer first: milk (bottle or breast) _____ or solids?_____

Commercially prepared baby food: _____ home cooked: _____

Kind: _____ Amount: _____ time of day: _____

Overall feeding schedule: _____

Explore about snack foods: _____

Determine whether salt intake is excessive: _____

Developmental feeding skills: _____

164

Table 3-23 *(Continued)*

INITIAL EVALUATION SUMMARY AND RECOMMENDATIONS
Adequacy of diet in terms of nutrients: _____

_____
_____

Anticipatory guidance (counseling needed for future developmental-
nutritional needs) _____

_____
_____

Follow-up: _____

_____
_____
_____

Date: _____

Source: Reprinted with permission from Yolanda Gutierrez, M.S., Assistant Clinical Professor, Department of Family Health Care Nursing, University of California, San Francisco.

Table 3-24
24-Hour Recall

Name: _____
Date and time of interview: _____
Length of interview: _____
Date of recall: _____
Day of the week of recall: _____
                1-M 2-T 3-W 4-Th 5-F 6-Sat 7-Sun

I would like you to tell me everything you (your child) ate and drank from the time you (he) got up in the morning until you (he) went to bed at night and what you (he) ate during the night. Be sure to mention everything you (he) ate or drank at home, at work (school), and away from home. Include snacks and drinks of all kinds and everything else you (he) put in your (his) mouth and swallowed. I also need to know where you (he) ate the food, and now let us begin.

What time did you (he) get up yesterday? _____
Was it the usual time? _____
What was the first time you (he) ate or had anything to drink yesterday morning? (List on the form that follows.)

165

Table 3-24 *(Continued)*

Where did you (he) eat? (List on form that follows.)
Now tell me what you (he) had to eat and how much?
[Occasionally the interviewer will need to ask:
   When did you (he) eat again? Or, is there anything else?
   Did you (he) have anything to eat or drink during the night?]
Was intake unusual in any way? Yes _____ No _____
(If answer is yes) Why? _____
               In what way? _____
What time did you (he) go to bed last night?
Do(es) you (he) take vitamin or mineral supplements:
   Yes _____ No _____
(If answer is yes) How many per day? _____
             Per week? _____
What kind? (Insert brand name if known)
Multivitamins _____ Iron _____
Ascorbic Acid _____ Other _____
Vitamins A and D _____

Suggested Form for Recording Food Intake

Time	Where Eaten*	Food	Type and/or Preparation	Amount

*Code:
  H—Home
  R—Restaurant, drug store, or lunch counter
  CL—Carried lunch from home
  CC—Child care center
  OH—Other home (friend, relative, babysitter, etc.)
  S—School, office, plant, or work
  FD—Food dispenser
  SS—Social center, e.g. Senior Citizen, etc.

Source: *Screening Children for Nutritional Status: Suggestions for Child Health Programs.* Maternal and Child Health Services, DHEW Publ. No. (HSM) 2158, Washington D.C., U.S. Government Printing Office, 1971. P. 13.

Table 3-25

Characteristics of Good Nutrition and Poor Nutrition

Good Nutrition	Poor Nutrition
Well-developed body	Body may be undersized, or show poor development or physical defects
About average weight for height	Usually thin (underweight 10 percent or more), but may be normal or overweight (fat and flabby)
Muscles well developed and firm	Muscles small and flabby
Skin turgid and of healthy color	Skin loose and pale, waxy, or sallow
Good layer subcutaneous fat	Subcutaneous fat usually lacking (or in excess)
Mucous membranes of eyelids and mouth reddish pink	Mucous membranes pale
Hair smooth and glossy	Hair often rough and without luster
Eyes clear	Dark hollows or circles under eyes or puffiness; eyes reddened
Good natured and full of life	Irritable, overactive, fatigues easily or Phlegmatic, listless, fails to concentrate
Appetite good	Appetite poor
General health excellent	Susceptible to infections Lacks endurance and vigor

Source: Reprinted with permission from L. J. Bogert, et al., *Nutrition and Physical Fitness*, (Philadelphia: Saunders, © 1973), p. 419.

protein, vitamins, and minerals than the nonpregnant woman. For most women on well-balanced diets these increases can usually be met by means of increased caloric intake using the Daily Food Guide as presented in Table 3-26. Supplements are unnecessary except for iron and folic acid. If a careful nutrition history reveals dietary inadequacies, appropriate measures must be taken. Other adjustments must be made on an individual basis considering age, body size, physical status, climate, and cultural factors.

Table 3-26
Daily Food Guide

	Number of Servings		
Food Group	Non-pregnant Woman	Pregnant Woman	Lactating Woman
Protein foods			
animal[a]	2	2	2
vegetable[b]	2	2	2
Milk and milk products	2	4	5
Breads and cereals	4	4	4
Vitamin C rich fruits and vegetables	1	1	1
Dark green vegetables	1	1	1
Other fruits and vegetables	1	1	1

Source: Maternal and Child Health Branch, California Department of Health, June 1977.
[a] 1 serving is 2 oz (60g).
[b] Should include at least 1 serving of legumes.

SUPPLEMENTATION

Iron   Iron is necessary during pregnancy to maintain normal hemoglobin levels and reserves in the mother, to furnish iron requirements to the fetus, and to provide the fetus with sufficient iron stores to be used after birth. To meet these requirements, 6 to 7 mg of elemental iron (usable iron) must be absorbed daily. Diets consumed by American women rarely contain sufficient absorbable iron to meet these needs. Usually pregnant women ingest 13 to 14 mg of dietary iron per day, most of which is not absorbed. See Absorption of Iron, this chapter.

Recommendation. The Committee on Maternal Nutrition of the National Academy of Sciences (1970) recommends iron supplementation during the second and third trimesters. Ferrous iron, 30 to 60 mg daily, is the recommended dose.

Folic Acid   There is evidence that pregnancy is associated with an increased, although small, risk of megaloblastic anemia due to folate deficiency. Other evidence suggests that folate deficiency may predispose toward spontaneous abortion and hemorrhage (Committee on Maternal Nutrition, 1970).

Recommendation. A daily supplement of 200 to 400 µg of folic acid is recommended throughout the course of pregnancy. This should easily prevent folic acid deficiency in practically all women.

WEIGHT GAIN

Limitation of maternal weight gain during pregnancy by limitation of calories has been recognized as potentially hazardous to the fetus. Limiting the weight gain of normal pregnant women to 10 to 14 pounds is not justified. The average acceptable weight gain for a favorable outcome is approximately 11 to 12 kg or 24 to 27 pounds, but a more practical range is 20 to 35 pounds.

SODIUM RESTRICTION

Sodium restriction and/or prescription of diuretics were formerly employed to prevent preeclampsia. This practice is now recognized as potentially hazardous. To meet the increased need for sodium during pregnancy and to avoid sodium deficit, no sodium restrictions are advised. The use of diuretics is also discouraged.

Nutrition During Lactation

RECOMMENDED DIETARY ALLOWANCES

A mother's diet may be quite varied without affecting the composition or volume of breast milk as long as good nutrition is maintained according to the RDAs listed in Table 3-1 and the Daily Food Guide in Table 3-26. If the diet is deficient, there may be decreased quantity of milk, but the quality will remain constant as long as the mother's body stores can supply the missing nutrients.

LACTATION NUTRITION GUIDELINES

A number of important factors should be included in nutrition counseling during lactation:

• Follow the Daily Food Guide (Table 3-26)

- Do not restrict calories
- Drink 2 to 3 quarts of fluid daily
- Take 30 to 60 mg of ferrous iron daily
- Avoid oral contraceptives for 6 weeks postpartum

References

American Dietetic Association. "Position Paper on the Vegetarian Approach to Eating." *J Am Diet Assoc* 77:61–69, July 1980.

Anderson, T. A. "Commercial Infant Foods: Content and Composition." *Pediatr Clin North Am* 24:37–47, February 1977.

Bogert, L. J. et al. *Nutrition and Physical Fitness,* 10th ed. Philadelphia: W. B. Saunders, 1979.

Brasel, J. A. "The Effects of Feeding Practices on Normal Growth, Failure to Thrive and Obesity." In L. J. Filer, editor, *Infant Nutrition: A Foundation for Lasting Health?* Bloomfield, NJ: Health Learning Systems, 1979.

Christakis, G. "Nutritional Assessment in Health Programs," *AJPH Supplement 63,* November 1973.

Committee on Maternal Nutrition, Food and Nutrition Board, National Research Council. *Maternal Nutrition and the Course of Pregnancy.* Washington, D.C.: National Academy of Sciences, 1970.

Committee on Nutrition, American Academy of Pediatrics. "Nutrition and Lactation." *Pediatrics* 68:435–443, September 1981.

Committee on Nutrition, American Academy of Pediatrics. "Vitamins and Mineral Supplement Needs in Normal Children in the United States." *Pediatrics* 66:1015–1021, December 1980.

Committee on Nutrition, American Academy of Pediatrics. "On the Feeding of Supplemental Foods to Infants." *Pediatrics* 65:1178–1181, June 1980.

Committee on Nutrition, American Academy of Pediatrics. *Pediatric Nutrition Handbook.* Evanston, IL: American Academy of Pediatrics, 1979.

Committee on Nutrition, American Academy of Pediatrics. "Fluoride Supplementation: Revised Dosage Schedule." *Pediatrics* 63:150–152, January 1979.

Committee on Nutrition, American Academy of Pediatrics. "Nutritional Needs of Low-Birth-Weight Infants." *Pediatrics* 60:519–527, October 1977.

Committee on Nutrition, American Academy of Pediatrics. "Iron Supplementation for Infants." *Pediatrics* 58:765–768, November 1976.

Dallman, P. R. "Bioavailability of Iron: The Form is More Important than the Quantity." *Pediatric Basics,* No. 17. Fremont, MI: Gerber Products, January 1977.

Dallman, P. R. "Iron, Vitamin E, and Folate in the Preterm Infant." *J Pediatr* 85:742–752, December 1974.

Davis, A. *Let's Have Healthy Children*, revised by M. Mandell. New York: New American Library, 1981.

Dwyer, J. T. et al. "Risk of Nutritional Rickets Among Vegetarian Children." *Am J Dis Child 133*:134–140, February 1979.

Edidin, D. V. et al. "Resurgence of Nutritional Rickets Associated with Breast-Feeding and Special Dietary Practices." *Pediatrics 65*:232–235, February 1980.

Erhard, D. "Nutrition Education for the 'Now' Generation." *Journal of Nutrition Education 2*:135–139, Spring 1971.

Fallot, M. E. et al. "Breast-feeding Reduces Incidence of Hospital Admissions for Infection in Infants." *Pediatrics 65*:1121–1124, June 1980.

Fomon, S. J. *Infant Nutrition*, 2nd ed. Philadelphia: W. B. Saunders, 1974.

Fomon, S. J. et al. "Cow Milk Feeding in Infancy: Gastrointestinal Blood Loss and Iron Nutritional Status." *J Pediatr 98*:540–545, April 1981.

Fomon, S. J. et al. "Recommendations for Feeding Normal Infants." *Pediatrics 63*:52–59, January 1979.

Food and Nutrition Board, National Research Council. *Recommended Dietary Allowances, Revised 1980*, 9th ed. Washington, D.C.: National Academy of Sciences, 1980.

Glueck, C. J. "A Pediatric Approach in High Risk Infants to the Primary Prevention of Atherosclerosis." In L. J. Filer, editor, *Infant Nutrition: A Foundation for Lasting Health?* Bloomfield, NJ: Health Learning Systems, 1979.

Green, M. L. and J. Harry. *Nutrition in Contemporary Nursing Practice*, New York: Wiley, 1981.

Greer, F. R. et al. "Water-Soluble Vitamin D in Human Milk: A Myth." *Pediatrics 69*:238, February 1982.

Gundy, J. *Assessment of the Child in Primary Health Care*. New York: McGraw-Hill, 1981.

Kramer, M. S. "Does Breast-feeding and Delayed Introduction of Solid Foods Protect Against Subsequent Obesity?" *J Pediatr 98*:883–887, June 1981.

Kramer, M. S. and B. Moroz. "Do Breast-feeding and Delayed Introduction of Solid Foods Protect Against Subsequent Atopic Eczema?" *J Pediatr 98*:546–550, April 1981.

Lakdawala, D. R. and E. M. Widdowson. "Vitamin D in Human Milk." *Lancet 1*:167–168, January 22, 1977.

Lappe, F. M. *Diet for a Small Planet*, rev. ed. New York: Friends of the Earth/Ballantine Books, 1975.

Lawrence, R. A. *Breast-Feeding: A Guide for the Medical Profession*. St. Louis: C.V. Mosby, 1980.

Lieberman, E. "Blood Pressure and Primary Hypertension in Childhood and Adolescence." *Curr Probl Pediatr 10*:1–29, February 1980.

Little, J. A. "Water-Soluble Vitamin D in Human Milk: A Myth." *Pediatrics 70*:499, September 1982.

Maternal and Child Health Unit. *Nutrition During Pregnancy and Lactation*. California Department of Health, Sacramento, CA, 1975.

McMillan, J. A. et al. "Iron Sufficiency in Breast-Fed Infants and the Availability of Iron from Human Milk." *Pediatrics 58*:686–691, November 1976.

Mertz, W. "The New RDAs: Estimated Adequate and Safe Intake of Trace Elements and Calculation of Available Iron." *J Am Dietet Assoc 76*:128–133, February 1980.

Meyer, E. E. and C. G. Neumann. "Management of the Obese Adolescent." *Pediatr Clin North Am 24*:123–132, February 1977.

Neumann, C. G. "Obesity in Pediatric Practice: Obesity in the Pre-school and School-age Child." *Pediatr Clin North Am 24*:117–122, February 1977.

Nora, J. J. "Identifying the Child at Risk for Coronary Disease as an Adult: A Strategy for Prevention." *J Pediatr 97*:706–714, November 1980.

Oski, F. A. and H. A. Pearson, editors. *Iron Nutrition Revisited—Infancy, Childhood, Adolescence.* Report of the Eighty-Second Ross Conference on Pediatric Research. Columbus, Ohio: Ross Laboratories, 1981.

Paige, D. M. "Avoiding Overnutrition in Infancy." In *Year ONE: Nutrition, Growth, Health.* Columbus, Ohio: Ross Laboratories, 1975.

Pearson, G. A. "Nutrition in the Middle Years of Childhood." *Am J Maternal Child Nursing 2*:378–384, November/December 1977.

Pipes, P. L. *Nutrition in Infancy and Childhood,* 2nd ed. St. Louis: CV Mosby, 1981.

Rowe, N. R. "Childhood Obesity: Growth Charts vs. Calipers." *Pediatric Nursing 6*:24–27, March/April 1980.

Rudolph, A. M., editor. *Pediatrics,* 17th ed. East Norwalk, CT: Appleton-Century-Crofts, 1982.

Screening Children for Nutritional Status: Suggestions for Child Health Programs. Maternal and Child Health Service, Health Services and Mental Health Administration, DHEW, Rockville, MD, USPHS Publication No. 2158, 1971.

Slattery, J. S. "Nutrition for the Normal Healthy Infant." *Am J Maternal Child Nursing 2*:105–112, March/April 1977.

Slattery, J. et al., editors. *Maternal and Child Nutrition: Assessment and Counseling,* East Norwalk, CT: Appleton-Century-Crofts, 1979.

Taitz, L. S. "Obesity in Pediatric Practice: Infantile Obesity." *Pediatr Clin North Am 24*:107–115, February 1977.

Torre, C. T. "Nutritional Needs of Adolescents." *Am J Maternal Child Nursing 2*:118–127, March/April 1977.

Vaughan, V. C. et al., editors. *Nelson Textbook of Pediatrics,* 11th ed. Philadelphia: WB Saunders, 1979.

Williams, E. R. "Making Vegetarian Diets Nutritious." *Am J Nurs 75*:2168–2173, December 1975.

Zerfas, A. J. et al. "Office Assessment of Nutritional Status." *Pediatr Clin North Am 24*:253–272, February 1977.

Zmora, E. et al. "Multiple Nutritional Deficiencies in Infants from a Strict Vegetarian Community." *Am J Dis Child 133*:141–144, February 1979.

4

Assessment of Parent–Child Interaction

Successful parenting has been defined by Leal (1983, p. 12) as

> that state of being in which a single adult (or a pair of adults) has
> undertaken, by conscious choice or biological demand, the care and
> keeping of a child in such a manner that the child, by objective
> standards, is functioning optimally in accordance with his or her
> stage and phase of psychogenetic, psychosocial, emotional, adaptive,
> and temperamental development and in keeping with the capacities
> of his or her biological integrity and cognitive potential.

It is crucial to realize that achievement of such successful parenting involves multiple and complex variables interacting over time. And, while the nature of the parent–child relationship is central to evaluation of parenting, overemphasis on the impact of early mother–child interaction can lead to unnecessary parental anxiety and guilt.

Practitioners working with parents and children in primary care settings must be knowledgeable about and have perspective on the role of attachment, must recognize that each mother or parent–infant relationship is unique and a function of the individual characteristics of parent, infant, and their environment, and must be able to assess interaction accurately and objectively to predict successful, at-risk, or disturbed situations. With such understanding we enhance our value as supportive figures to parents and contribute more effectively to optimum development.

This chapter reviews the theory of attachment, presents data to be used in assessing parent–child interaction, and discusses implications for management. Parenting in special circumstances is discussed in Chapter 9. Information on failure to thrive and child abuse is found in Chapters 31 and 32.

THEORETICAL CONSIDERATIONS

The relationship between a mother and her newborn infant used to be examined and analyzed mainly in terms of the mother. New mothers were evaluated on their qualities of mothering and motherliness, which are described as follows:

- *Mothering* refers to the many active and practical attitudes necessary to take care of the offspring and to guide its maturation and primary learning.

- *Motherliness* is the characteristic quality of a woman's personality which supplies the emotional energy for maintaining the tasks of mothering. It is the capacity of the mother to receive from her child; her ability to be continuously gratified by this exchange and to use this gratification unconsciously in her emotional maturation (Benedek, 1956).

More current research and study have broadened our knowledge and have identified a wide range of variables which influence the mother–child relationship. Of major importance is recognition that the characteristics of the infant contribute significantly and reciprocally to the development of the mother–infant bond, and that the timing of initial interaction is important. There appears to be a sensitive period in the first minutes and hours of life during which close contact of mother and father with their neonate can significantly enhance the bonding experience (Klaus, 1982). If early separation is necessitated by medical or other emergencies, attachment can be facilitated by thoughtful nursing interventions and parents must be reassured that irreparable harm has not been done. See this chapter, under Management Implications, and Chapter 9, Parenting in Special Circumstances.

Terms

ATTACHMENT AND BONDING

Attachment is the term used to describe the unique emotional relationship between mother and infant. It has been defined by Ainsworth (1970, p. 50) as "an affectional tie that one person or animal forms between himself and another specific one—a tie that binds them together in space and endures over time." The term, bonding, is generally used synonymously. Perhaps the most enduring and strongest affectional relationship in humans is the mother–infant bond.

ATTACHMENT BEHAVIORS

For attachment to occur both mother and infant must demonstrate behaviors which elicit reciprocal and complementary behaviors from each other. These are termed attachment behaviors.

Maternal Attachment Behavior This is defined as "the degree to which a mother is attentive to and maintains physical contact with her infant" (Leifer, 1972, p. 105). It has also been described as the extent to which a mother feels that her infant occupies an essential position in her life (Robson and Moss, 1970).

Infant Attachment Behavior This is behavior which promotes proximity to or contact with the mother figure. Bowlby postulates that an infant's attachment to the mother is a product of the activity of a number of behavioral systems that have proximity to the mother as a predictable outcome. Sucking, clinging, following, crying, and smiling are initial behaviors of the infant that contribute to attachment. It is now known that in the first minutes and hours of life, the neonate is amazingly capable of seeing, hearing, and moving in rhythm to the mother's voice. These behaviors evoke responses from the mother and initiate channels of reciprocal communication essential to the process of attachment (Klaus and Kennell, 1982). Between the ages of about 9 to 18 months these simpler behavioral systems "become incorporated into far more sophisticated goal-corrected systems . . . so organized and activated that a child tends to be maintained in proximity to his mother" (Bowlby, 1969, p. 180).

Classes of Infant Behaviors Mediating Attachment

Attachment serves many important functions, a cardinal advantage being protection of the infant. This protection provides the infant with a sense of security that allows for exploration of the environment. Such exploration is viewed as highly related to later cognitive development. Attachment also is the foundation for the infant's development of self-esteem, and influences the quality of future relationships. Those behaviors which assist the infant in achieving these goals are as follows:

1. *Orientational behaviors.* To keep informed of the mother's whereabouts, the infant orients to her, tracking her movements visually and aurally.
2. *Signaling behaviors.* These behaviors stimulate the mother to come into closer proximity or contact with the infant (e.g., crying, smiling, babbling, calling, and raising arms to her) (Bell, 1972).
3. *Active behaviors.* These are behaviors through which an infant achieves proximity or maintains contact once it has been attained (e.g., clinging, approaching, following, climbing).

Development of Attachment

MATERNAL ATTACHMENT

Klaus and Kennell (1982, p. 9) have identified steps important to the formation of a mother's attachment to her infant:

- Before pregnancy
    Planning the pregnancy
- During the pregnancy
    Confirming the pregnancy
    Accepting the pregnancy
    Fetal movement
    Beginning to accept the fetus as an individual
- Labor
- Birth

• After birth
  Seeing the baby
  Touching the baby
  Giving care to the baby
  Accepting infant as a separate individual

INFANT ATTACHMENT

Attachment develops in phases described as follows:

Phase 1: Orientation and signals without discrimination of figure
Behaviors: During the first few weeks the infant responds to anyone in the vicinity by orienting, tracking with the eyes, grasping, smiling, reaching, and by ceasing to cry on hearing a voice or seeing a face.

Phase 2: Orientation and signals directed toward one or more discriminated figures
Behaviors: The infant behaves as in Phase 1 but in a more marked fashion to the mother than to others. The infant displays differential behavior to the mother's voice; stops crying differentially according to who provides comfort; cries differentially when the mother leaves; smiles and vocalizes differentially; and maintains a differential visual-motor orientation toward the mother.

Phase 3: Maintenance of proximity to a discriminated figure by means of locomotion as well as by signals
Behaviors: When able to crawl and move about, the infant shows differential behaviors such as approaching, following, climbing upon, exploring, and clinging to the mother and uses the mother as a secure base from which to explore and as a safe haven to which to return.

Phase 4: Formation of a reciprocal relationship
Behaviors: By about 4 years of age, when the child's cognitive and judgment abilities improve, the child can predict the mother's movements, infer what her goals are (e.g., to remain close or to leave), and can initiate behavior to attempt to change her goals to fit his or her own (Bowlby, 1969; Ainsworth, 1969).

FACTORS AFFECTING PARENT–INFANT INTERACTION AND DEVELOPMENT OF ATTACHMENT

The mother–infant or father–infant dyad is a reciprocal relationship, with each member contributing to interaction or to lack of interaction. In addition to the characteristics of both parent and infant, environmental factors also influence the interaction and the development of attachment. The following factors are known to affect relationships between mothers and infants and, depending on the context, will exert either positive or negative influence. Very few studies have been done on the impact of pregnancy and birth on fathers, but data do suggest that the period before birth is somewhat similar for fathers and mothers (Yogman, 1980), and that early father–infant interaction is surprisingly similar (McDonald, 1978; Parke, 1979). In addition, the father is forced to reevaluate his roles:

- Provider for the family
- An adult male with responsibility for a dependent
- A model of masculinity for the new child
- A major support for the mother in her adjustment to the maternal role (Brazelton, 1973b).

Parental Factors

PAST EXPERIENCES

These include the following experiences:

1. Own experience being parented, relationship with own parent
2. Genetic and cultural background
3. Incorporation of cultural values and expectations
4. Skill in interpersonal interaction
5. Relationships and experiences with family members, including mate
6. Parity

7. Experiences with previous pregnancies and infants
8. Self-concept, self-image, and level of psychosexual maturity

EXPERIENCES WITH CURRENT PREGNANCY

These experiences include the following:

1. Planned or unplanned pregnancy
2. Acceptance of pregnancy
3. Perception of fetus as a separate individual
4. Fantasies about newborn
5. Age of the mother
6. Health of the mother, physical and emotional reserves
7. Fears and worries about fetus, labor, and delivery
8. Actual labor and delivery, length of labor, amount of pain

NEONATAL PERIOD

Factors during this period include the following:

1. Mother's perception of labor and delivery
2. Physical comfort, level of fatigue
3. Hormonal levels
4. Comparison of fantasized infant and real infant
5. Ability to identify and to accept infant as an individual
6. Ability to perceive infant's cues
7. Feeling of competence to care for infant

Infant Factors

Factors in the infant that influence attachment include the following:

1. Size
2. Sex
3. Gestational age
4. General health
5. Presence or absence of visible blemishes

6. Activity level
7. Perceptual and sensory capacity:

   - Ability to receive stimuli
   - Ability to attend to stimuli
   - Ability to discriminate stimuli
   - Ability to respond to stimuli

8. Temperament: emotional reactivity or behavioral style (see Chapter 5, Differences in Temperament and Personality)
9. Infant state*:

   - Sleep patterns
   - Alert levels
   - Crying behaviors

10. Regularity of infant state: sleep–wakefulness–hunger cycles
11. Arousal and calming characteristics (ease of consolability)
12. Ability to initiate interaction and elicit parenting
13. Reactions to parent's ministrations

External Factors

Other factors influencing attachment include the following

1. Economic status
2. Housing
3. Father's response to mother and infant
4. Support from father, family, peers, and culture
5. Family goals
6. Siblings
7. Societal and cultural values

---

*Infant state: levels of tension or perceptual arousal reflecting both need and availability for contact with the external environment (Clark and Affonso, 1976, p. 553). For a complete discussion of infant state see Barnard, K. E., et al. *Early Parent–Infant Relationships, Module 3, A Staff Development Program in Perinatal Nursing Care,* edited by M. L. Duxbury, White Plains, NY: The National Foundation/March of Dimes, 1978.

8. Other responsibilities (job, home, children)
9. Course of labor, delivery, and immediate postpartum period
10. Behavior and attitudes of hospital staff
11. Hospital policies
12. Time of initial contact with infant
13. Multiple births

The Acquaintance Process

There is a process that occurs at the beginning of all interpersonal relationships and that forms the basis of subsequent interpersonal behavior (Kennedy, 1973). It consists of three steps:

1. Acquisition of information about the other individual
2. Assessment of the other's attitude in relation to oneself
3. Continuous collection of data to validate or to negate initial impressions (Newcomb, 1961)

Parents and infants experience this process, which begins while the baby is in utero and continues after delivery. It is important that the parent acquire valid and sufficient information about the infant and that the assessment of the data be accurate and positive. Otherwise, problematic relationships might develop. In addition, all the factors listed above can influence this process.

Many new, inexperienced, uncertain, or ambivalent parents will need assistance in this initial identification or claiming process to assess accurately their infants' characteristics, cues, and response patterns. The more a parent recognizes and responds to the cues that the infant presents about its needs, the more likely is a sense of attachment and competence to be developed in both.

BEHAVIORAL OBSERVATIONS

Accurate assessment is based on objective data, not intuition. This section presents information about parental and infant behaviors that can be observed to assess and to predict the development of attachment, and parent–child interactive behaviors in early childhood that can be assessed to analyze actual or potential behavior problems.

Parental Behaviors

PRENATAL PERIOD

Observations during this period include the following:

1. Expressions of attitude about changing body image (e.g., pride, discomfort, embarrassment, shame)
2. Verbalizations about fetus

   • Is fetus discussed as a separate individual?
   • Does parent wonder what the baby will be like?
   • Is parent thinking about a name for the baby?
   • Is the fetus referred to by sex?

3. Response to quickening
4. Preparations for baby

   • Purchase of baby supplies
   • Home arrangements for baby
   • Decision on feeding method
   • Interest in learning about infant care

5. Degree of anxiety and fear about labor and delivery
6. Desire for knowledge about labor and delivery
7. Degree of emotional liability

INTRAPARTAL PERIOD

Observations during this period include the following:

1. Spontaneous verbalizations and response at moment of delivery
2. Attempts to see and to touch baby
3. Questions asked about condition, appearance, and behavior of baby
4. Reactions to sex of baby

POSTPARTAL PERIOD

These behaviors have been identified specifically with maternal behavior in the immediate postpartal period, although limited data (Parke, 1979) suggest similar behaviors in fathers. Claiming and identification behaviors to be observed include:

1. Touch. Touch has several aspects as follows:

   Proximal contact:
   - Does the mother touch the infant?
   - How much does she touch the infant?
   - Does she begin by touching the infant's extremities with her fingertips and soon proceed to massaging and encompassing the infant's trunk with her full hand (Kennel and Klaus, 1971)?

   Ventral contact:
   - Does she hold and enfold the infant close to her body?

   Affectionate contact (not associated with feeding):
   - Does she kiss the infant?
   - Does she fondle, cuddle, rock, pat, or caress the infant?

2. Distal contact
   - Does she talk to the infant?
   - What does she say to the infant?
   - Does she express love?
   - Are any special designations used (e.g., "he," "it," "angel," "bad girl," "sour puss")?
   - Does she look, sing, laugh, or smile at the infant?

3. Eye contact
   - Does she attempt eye-to-eye contact with the baby?
   - How often?
   - Does she use the "en face" position?*

---

*"En face" position: the mother's face in such a position that her eyes and those of the infant meet fully in the same vertical plane of rotation (Klaus, 1970, p. 1023).

Note: Visual contact and use of the "en face" position are considered *cardinal* attachment behaviors.

4. Individualization of infant

   • Does she identify the infant's individual characteristics and personality?

   • Does she identify particular features of the infant with herself or with other family members? If so, in a positive or negative way?

5. Caretaking

   • How does she respond to the infant's behavior (e.g., cry, yawn, sleep, cough)?

   • How is the infant held for feeding? What is the feeding procedure?

   • Is the mother aware of the infant's reactions while dressing and undressing?

   • Is the mother able to comfort and to protect the infant?

   • Does mother reluctantly relinquish the infant to the nurse?

PERIOD OF HEALTH SUPERVISION

Observations during early infancy include the following:

• How does the mother hold the baby (e.g., close to her, protecting baby's head, awkwardly)?

• Does she hold the baby or place it on the examining table?

• How often does she glance at the baby?

• What does she do when the baby cries? How quickly does she respond?

• Does she comfort the baby without being told? How does she comfort the baby?

• What does she do during the physical exam (e.g., stay by the baby without being told, back away, ignore procedure)?

• What does she do during the immunization procedure? What is her facial expression? Does she comfort the baby after the procedure?

• How does the mother react when given a compliment about the baby? Where does she look? Facial expression? What does she say (e.g., positive comment, negative comment, change the subject, no response)?

Infant Behaviors

Babies show a series of behavior patterns that are essential for establishing parent–infant interaction. The extent to which the infant takes the initiative in seeking interaction is surprising.

INITIAL BEHAVIORS

Initial behaviors to be observed include the following:

1. Rooting
2. Sucking
3. Grasping
4. Clinging
5. Regular changes between sleep, wakefulness and activity, and crying
6. Smiling and babbling
7. Normal activity level
8. Responds to ministrations by calming
9. Visual alertness (fixes object and briefly tracks)
10. Responds to sensory stimuli with pleasure or displeasure
11. Quiets when presented with parent's face, voice, touch
12. Responds to feeding (sucks eagerly, cuddles, smiles, and sleeps after feeding)

LATER INFANT BEHAVIORS

See this chapter, Development of Attachment.

Descriptions of High and Low Attachment

Conditions of high and low attachment have been described (Lamper, 1974). Examples are provided to demonstrate the range of behaviors that must be assessed before making such evaluations.

HIGH ATTACHMENT

At 28 to 32 days after birth the mother:

1. Is preoccupied and vigilant about the baby
2. Provides appropriate visual, auditory, and tactile stimuli during caretaking activities
3. Is successful at eliciting responses from the baby
4. Fondles the baby and looks at the baby "en face"

At 8 months of age:

1. Mother often takes the baby out with her
2. Mother avoids even brief separations
3. Mother comments on positive features of the baby
4. Mother not observed to physically reject or mistreat the child
5. Baby actively tries to approach the mother after separation
6. Baby seeks contact and initiates interaction
7. Baby is more interested in the mother than in a stranger

LOW ATTACHMENT

At 28 to 32 days after birth the mother:

1. Has limited proximity, contact, and communication with the baby
2. Does not respond to the baby's cry but is likely to let the baby "cry it out"
3. Enjoys leaving the baby with someone else
4. Is detached during the physical exam
5. Is less attentive during feeding

At 8 months of age:

1. Mother rarely takes the baby out with her
2. Mother openly finds fault with the baby
3. Mother comments on negative features of the baby
4. Mother uses physical punishment inappropriately
5. Mother rejects the baby's efforts to establish contact with her
6. Mother interrupts the baby's ongoing activities

7. Infant has little tendency to approach or to contact the mother after separation but may ignore or turn away from her
8. Infant responds to strangers as to the mother
9. Infant may prefer objects to people

Behaviors in Early Childhood

Nurse practitioners assist parents and young children to develop healthy interaction patterns and/or to modify potentially difficult patterns of behavior. The Parenting Program at the Child Development Center, University of Washington includes observational assessment of parent–child interactions as the basis for intervention (Webster-Stratton and Kogan, 1980). See Table 4-1.

DISORDERS IN MATERNAL ATTACHMENT

There are many variables related to the strength and security of attachment and many individual differences in the rate of development of attachment, the ways a child manifests attachment, and the figures to whom attachments are made. Nonetheless, knowledge and experience point to certain observations, signs, symptoms, and environmental factors that predispose to or indicate disturbances in mother-infant relationships. Information (adapted from Green, 1975, and Barbero, 1975) is presented here on predisposing factors to and early manifestations of mothering disabilities.

Predisposing Factors

PAST EVENTS

Events in the mother's past that predispose to mothering disabilities include the following:

1. Poor relationship between the mother and her own mother
2. Emotional deprivation, rejection, lack of affection in the mother's childhood

Table 4-1
Parent–Child Observational Assessment[a]

Attention
1. Watches
2. Does own thing
3. Works together
   Note whether the mother and child play together or whether each works on his own activity independently and ignores the other's activity. Also note whether parent or child attend to and watch each other.

Communication
4. Quiet
5. Comments
6. Shared conversation
7. Clarity and lack of ambiguity
   Do parents and child share in conversation together or is there silence or one-sided talking?
   How clear and effective are the parents in communicating or limit setting?

Acceptance
8. Smiles, enthusiasm
9. Praise
10. Physical warmth
    How much praise, warmth, affection, and positive acceptance occurs from parent to child and child to parent?

Nonacceptance
Emotional:
11. Negative voice, pout
12. Mixed messages[b]
13. Physical hostility
Intellectual:
14. Frustration
15. Actions ignored
16. Negative content
    How much negative commenting, correcting, punishing, judging, and criticism occur? Does either child or parent seem not accepting of himself?

Control
17. Physical intrusion
18. Control and directiveness
19. Competition
    How much ordering or competition for control is there? Who usually takes the lead or initiates suggestions for play?

Submissiveness
20. Approval seeking
21. Active compliance
    Does one member of the pair constantly ask for approval from the other? Does either one accept and go along with rules set by the other?

Source: Copyright © 1980, American Journal of Nursing Company. Reproduced, with permission, from *American Journal of Nursing*, February, Vol. 80, No. 2, Pp. 240–244.

[a] All items are checked for parent and child.

[b] Teasing, smiling at same time as being negative.

3. Long-term emotional disturbance or medical illness in the mother's childhood
4. Loss of parent figures early in the mother's life
5. Death or illness in prior children (unresolved grief)
6. Repeated pregnancies and children at short intervals
7. Previous abortions
8. Marital discord or separation

PREGNANCY

Predisposing factors during pregnancy include:

1. Strongly unwanted pregnancy
2. Attempts to obtain or to induce an abortion
3. Protracted emotional or physical illness
4. Deaths or major illness of key family members
5. Highly unrealistic views of motherhood (e.g., "sheer bliss")
6. Out-of-wedlock pregnancy
7. Geographic move late in pregnancy
8. Lack of social supports

PERINATAL EVENTS

Predisposing factors during the perinatal period include:

1. Complications of parturition. Maternal affectional ties may be easily disturbed in the immediate newborn period by such minor problems as poor feeding, slight hyperbilirubinemia, or mild respiratory distress.
2. Acute illness of the mother or infant
3. Congenital defects
4. Prematurity
5. Multiple births
6. Difficult labor and delivery, unplanned obstetric interventions, use of medications
7. Prolonged separation of the infant from the mother; institutional disruptions
8. Maternal depression in the first year

9. Father psychologically or physically absent
10. Level of infant activity
11. Social isolation
12. Financial stresses
13. Failure of the infant to meet parental expectations
14. Mental illness, alcoholism, drug abuse

Manifestations of Maladaptation of Mothers to Their Infants*

Many mothers may exhibit one or more of these behaviors at different times and for different reasons and are not "maladapted" mothers. However, if constellations of these behaviors exist and persist over time, they may be indicative of maladaptive mothering. Such behaviors are exhibited by mothers who:

1. See their infants as ugly or unattractive
2. Perceive the odor of their infants as revolting
3. Disgusted by drooling of infants
4. Disgusted by sucking sounds of infants
5. Upset by vomiting, but seem fascinated by it
6. Revolted by any of infant's body fluids that touch them or that they touch
7. Annoyed at having to clean up infant's stools
8. Preoccupied by odor, consistency, and number of stools
9. Let infant's head dangle without support or concern
10. Hold infants away from their own bodies
11. Pick up infant without warning by a touch or by speech
12. Juggle and play with infant roughly after feeding even though the infant often vomits at this behavior
13. Think infant's natural motor activity is unnatural

---

*List adapted with permission from M. G. Morris, "Maternal Claiming-Identification Processes: Their Meaning for Mother–Infant Mental Health." Paper presented at a Continuing Education Program for Nurses' Workshop, College of Nursing and University Extension Division, Rutgers, The State University of New Jersey, 1968.

14. Worry about infant's relaxation after feeding
15. Avoid eye contact with infants or stare fixedly into their eyes
16. Do not coo or talk to their infants
17. Think that their infants do not love them
18. Consider that their infants expose them as unlovable, unloving parents
19. Think of their infants as judging them and their efforts as an adult would
20. Perceive their infant's natural dependent needs as dangerous
21. Fears of infant's death appear at mild diarrhea or minor cold
22. Convinced that their infant has some defect, in spite of repeated physical examinations that prove no abnormality
23. Constantly demand reassurance that no defect or disease exists and cannot believe relieving facts when they are given
24. Demand that feared defect be found and relieved
25. Cannot find in their infants any physical or psychologic attribute which they value in themselves (probably the most diagnostic of these signs and readily elicited)
26. Cannot discriminate between infant signs signaling hunger or fatigue, need for soothing or stimulating speech, comforting body contact, or for eye contact
27. Develop inappropriate responses to infant needs:

    • Over- or underfeed
    • Over- or underhold
    • Tickle or bounce the baby when he is fatigued
    • Talk too much, too little, and at the wrong time
    • Force eye contact or refuse it
    • Leave infant in room alone
    • Leave infant in noisy room and ignore infant

28. Develop paradoxical attitudes and behaviors. Example: Bitterly insist that infant cannot be pleased, no matter what is done, but continue to demand more and better methods for pleasing infant.
29. Express serious concern about "bad" behavior of infant and "spoiling" the baby

30. Fail to select a name for the baby or select "impossible" names
31. Unable to give a good history, cannot report what has been going on with baby

Manifestations of Mothering Disabilities in Infants

Infants who are involved in disturbed parent–child interactions exhibit behaviors (adapted from Green, 1975) which include:

1. Feeding problems (anorexia, refusal of solids)
2. Recurrent vomiting or rumination
3. Developmental delay (delayed smiling or motor progress)
4. Failure to gain weight
5. Recurrent diarrhea
6. Irritability or excessive crying
7. Listlessness or lethargy
8. Sleep disturbances
9. Unusual visual alertness ("radar gaze")
10. Decreased cuddliness
11. Baby not physically well cared for
12. Undiscriminating attachment
13. Minimal vocalization

Failures in Attachment

The most extreme manifestations of attachment disorders are represented by the conditions of severe failure to thrive and child abuse. See Chapter 31, Failure to Thrive, and Chapter 32, Child Abuse. Characteristics of "potential" abuse situations are known (Helfer, 1975) and should be assessed to prevent such severe distortions of parenting behavior.

PARENTAL CHARACTERISTICS
Parental characteristics include the following:

1. Neglect or abuse during parent's early childhood resulting in a missing "mothering imprint"

2. Extreme personal and social isolation as exemplified by the absence of friends and supportive relationships
3. Poor marital relationship
4. Low self-esteem
5. Parent–child role reversal. Parents see the child as the source of their emotional support and gratification.

CHILD FACTORS

Failures in attachment as manifested by child factors include the following:

1. Seen as different or difficult by parents
2. Does not respond in the manner expected by parents
3. Was born prematurely or by cesarean section (These children have abuse rates much higher than those of general population.)

PRECIPITATING EVENT OR CRISIS

Abuse situations in a family at risk can occur in the presence of any stress or combination of stresses, major or minor, such as unemployment, financial crisis, and lack of a support system.

ASSESSMENT TOOLS

Care providers must be alert to the behaviors described in the preceding sections and must be able to systematically observe interactions to collect the most reliable data possible. Observation of behavior for purposes of evaluating interaction is a complex and difficult task and should be performed only by professionals with training and skill in this area. When at-risk or maladaptive interaction is observed or suspected, the most effective approach to intervention is via consultation and joint planning with those qualified members of the health team.

Several tools and instruments have been developed to assist in more objective and systematic assessment. A sample of available tools is presented here.

Table 4-2

Tool 1. Categories of Adaptive and Maladaptive Mothering Behaviors

Adaptive	*Maladaptive*

1. Feeding Behaviors
   Offers appropriate amounts and/or types of food to infant.
   Holds infant in comfortable position during feeding.
   Burps baby during and/or after feeding.
   Prepares food appropriately.
   Offers food at comfortable pace for infant.
	1. Feeding Behaviors
	   Provides inadequate types or amounts of food for infant.
	   Does not hold infant, or holds in uncomfortable position during feeding.
	   Does not burp infant.
	   Prepare food inappropriately.
	   Offers food at pace too rapid or slow for infant's comfort.

2. Infant Stimulation
   Provides appropriate verbal stimulation for infant during visit.
   Provides tactile stimulation for infant at times other than during feeding or moving infant away from danger.
   Provides age-appropriate toys.
   Interacts with infant in a way that provides for infant's satisfaction.
	2. Infant Stimulation
	   Provides no or only aggressive verbal stimulation for infant during visit.
	   Does not provide tactile stimulation or only that of aggressive handling of infant.
	   No evidence of age-appropriate toys.
	   Frustrates infant during interactions.

3. Infant Rest
   Provides quiet or relaxed environment for infant's rest, including scheduled rest periods.
   Ensures that infant's needs for food, warmth, and/or dryness are met before sleep.
	3. Infant Rest
	   Does not provide quiet environment or consistent schedule for rest periods.
	   Does not attend to infant's needs for food, warmth, and/or dryness before sleep.

4. Perception
   Demonstrates realistic perception of infant's condition in accordance with medical and/or nursing diagnosis.
   Has realistic expectations of infant.
   Recognizes infant's unfolding skills or behavior.
   Shows realistic perception of own mothering behavior.

5. Initiative
   Shows initiative in attempts to manage infant's problems, including actively seeking information about infants.

6. Recreation
   Provides positive outlets for own recreation or relaxation.

7. Interaction with Other Children
   Demonstrates positive interaction with other children in home.

8. Mothering Role
   Expresses satisfaction with mothering.

4. Perception
   Shows unrealistic perception of infant's condition.
   Demonstrates unrealistic expectations of infant.
   Has no awareness of infant's development.
   Shows unrealistic perception of own mothering.

5. Initiative
   Shows no initiative in attempts to meet infant's needs or to manage problems. Does not follow through with plans.

6. Recreation
   Does not provide positive outlets for own recreation or relaxation.

7. Interaction with Other Children
   Demonstrates hostile-aggressive interaction with other children in home.

8. Mothering Role
   Expresses dissatisfaction with mothering.

Source: Copyright March/April 1976, the American Journal of Nursing Company. Reproduced with permission from *MCN, The American Journal of Maternal Child Nursing* Vol. 1, No. 2.

The Harrison Tools

Characteristics of adaptive and maladaptive behaviors of mothers (Table 4-2) and infants (Table 4-3) have been developed by Harrison (1976). Guidelines for use of these tools are as follows:

1. Purpose: The tools were designed to measure changes in mother and infant behaviors during the course of intervention.
2. When to use: The tools should be used for initial baseline assessment and then at intervals to measure change.
3. How to use: Harrison stresses the value of direct observation in the home setting since the mothering behaviors observed at home are more likely characteristic of the mother's general behavior.

The Neonatal Perception Inventory (NPI)

Broussard and Hartner (1971) have developed two simple questionnaires for mothers that determine the mother's concept of what an "average" baby's behavior is like and then her assessment of what her own baby is like. Guidelines for use of the NPI are as follows:

1. Purpose: This screening instrument can be used in identifying infants at risk for subsequent emotional disorders.
2. When to use: The Neonatal Perception Inventory I (Table 4-4) is administered on the first or second postpartum day. The Neonatal Perception Inventory II (see Table 4-5) is administered when the infant is 1 month of age.
3. Instructions for administering the Neonatal Perception Inventory:

   The Neonatal Perception Inventory is easily and quickly administered by telling the mother:
   "We are interested in learning more about the experiences of mothers and their babies during the first few weeks after delivery. The more we can learn about mothers and their babies, the better we will be able to help other mothers with their babies. We would appreciate it if you would help us to help other mothers by answering a few questions."

Table 4-3

Tool 2. Categories of Adaptive and Maladaptive Infant Behaviors

Adaptive	Maladaptive
1. Sleeping Behavior Receives adequate sleep for normal growth—at least 16 hours per day—without restless sleep patterns or prolonged crying at nap or bedtime after other needs have been met.	1. Sleeping Behavior Receives inadequate sleep for normal growth—less than 16 hours per day. Shows restless sleep patterns and/or prolonged crying at nap or bedtime.
2. Feeding Behavior Actively seeks food offered. Effectively sucks and swallows food. Demonstrates pleasurable relief after eating.	2. Feeding Behavior Resists food offered. Does not suck effectively. Remains fussy after adequate amount of feeding—no pleasurable relief.
3. Response to Environment Demonstrates active response to environment by exploring or reaching-out behavior.	3. Response to Environment Seems apathetic to environment.
4. Vocalizing Demonstrates vocalizations when alert, if developmentally ready.	4. Vocalizing Makes infrequent or no vocalizations during visit although developmentally ready.
5. Smiling Demonstrates smiling behavior if older than two months.	5. Smiling Does not demonstrate smiling behavior during visit.
6. Cuddling Cuddles when held.	6. Cuddling Resists being held or stiffens when held.

Source: Copyright March/April 1976, the American Journal of Nursing Company. Reproduced with permission from MCN, *The American Journal of Maternal Child Nursing* Vol. 1, No. 2.

Table 4-4
Neonatal Perception Inventory I

AVERAGE BABY

Although this is your first baby, you probably have some ideas of what most little babies are like. Please check the blank you think best describes the AVERAGE baby.

How much crying do you think the average baby does?

a great deal	a good bit	moderate amount	very little	none

How much trouble do you think the average baby has in feeding?

a great deal	a good bit	moderate amount	very little	none

How much spitting up or vomiting do you think the average baby does?

a great deal	a good bit	moderate amount	very little	none

How much difficulty do you think the average baby has in sleeping?

a great deal	a good bit	moderate amount	very little	none

How much difficulty does the average baby have with bowel movements?

a great deal	a good bit	moderate amount	very little	none

How much trouble do you think the average baby has in settling down to a predictable pattern of eating and sleeping?

a great deal	a good bit	moderate amount	very little	none

Table 4-4 *(Continued)*

YOUR BABY

While it is not possible to know for certain what your baby will be like, you probably have some ideas of what your baby will be like. Please check the blank that you *think* best describes what *your* baby will be like.

How much crying do you think your baby will do?

| a great deal | a good bit | moderate amount | very little | none |

How much trouble do you think your baby will have feeding?

| a great deal | a good bit | moderate amount | very little | none |

How much spitting up or vomiting do you think your baby will do?

| a great deal | a good bit | moderate amount | very little | none |

How much difficulty do you think your baby will have sleeping?

| a great deal | a good bit | moderate amount | very little | none |

How much difficulty do you expect your baby to have with bowel movements?

| a great deal | a good bit | moderate amount | very little | none |

How much trouble do you think the average baby has in settling down to a predictable pattern of eating and sleeping?

| a great deal | a good bit | moderate amount | very little | none |

Source: Reprinted with permission from E. R. Broussard and M. S. S. Hartner, "Further Considerations Regarding Maternal Perception of the First Born." In J. Hellmuth, editor, *Exceptional Infant: Studies in Abnormalities,* Vol. 2, New York: Brunner/Mazel, 1971. Pp. 442–447.

Table 4-5
Neonatal Perception Inventory II

AVERAGE BABY

Although this is your first baby, you probably have some ideas of what most little babies are like. Please check the blank you think best describes the AVERAGE baby.

How much crying do you think the average baby does?

_____ _____ _____ _____ _____
a great deal   a good bit   moderate amount   very little   none

How much trouble do you think the average baby has in feeding?

_____ _____ _____ _____ _____
a great deal   a good bit   moderate amount   very little   none

How much spitting up or vomiting do you think the average baby does?

_____ _____ _____ _____ _____
a great deal   a good bit   moderate amount   very little   none

How much difficulty do you think the average baby has in sleeping?

_____ _____ _____ _____ _____
a great deal   a good bit   moderate amount   very little   none

How much difficulty does the average baby have with bowel movements?

_____ _____ _____ _____ _____
a great deal   a good bit   moderate amount   very little   none

How much trouble do you think the average baby has in settling down to a predictable pattern of eating and sleeping?

_____ _____ _____ _____ _____
a great deal   a good bit   moderate amount   very little   none

---

Table 4-5 *(Continued)*

YOUR BABY

You have had a chance to live with your baby for a month now. Please check the blank you think best describes your baby.

How much crying has your baby done?

a great deal	a good bit	moderate amount	very little	none

How much trouble has your baby had feeding?

a great deal	a good bit	moderate amount	very little	none

How much spitting up or vomiting has your baby done?

a great deal	a good bit	moderate amount	very little	none

How much difficulty has your baby had in sleeping?

a great deal	a good bit	moderate amount	very little	none

How much difficulty has your baby had with bowel movements?

a great deal	a good bit	moderate amount	very little	none

How much trouble has your baby had in settling down to a predictable pattern of eating and sleeping?

a great deal	a good bit	moderate amount	very little	none

Source: Reprinted with permission from E. R. Broussard and M. S. S. Hartner, "Further Considerations Regarding Maternal Perception of the First Born." In J. Hellmuth, editor, *Exceptional Infant: Studies in Abnormalities Vol. 2*, (New York: Brunner/Mazel, Inc., 1971), pp. 442–447.

The procedures are identical for administering the Average Baby form of the NPI on the first or second postpartum day and the NPI at one month of age. The mother is handed the Average Baby form while the individual administering the Inventory says: "Although this is your first baby, you probably have some ideas of what most little babies are like. Will you please check the blank you *think* best describes what *most* little babies are like."

The tester waits until the mother has completed the Average Baby form and takes it from the mother and then hands the mother the Your Baby form.*

The procedure for administering the Your Baby forms of the NPI is the same at Time I and Time II. However, the instructions given to the mother vary slightly to take into account the time factor. At Time I the tester tells the mother: "While it is not possible to know for certain what your baby will be like, you probably have some ideas of what your bably will be like. Please check the blank that you *think* best describes what *your* baby will be like."

At Time II, she says:

"You have had a chance to live with your baby for a month now. Please check the blank you think best describes your baby."

Method of Scoring

The Average Baby Perception form elicits the mother's concept of the average baby's behavior. The Your Baby Perception form elicits her rating of her own baby. Each of these instruments consists of six single item scales. Values of 1–5 are assigned to each of these scales for each of the inventories. The blank signified *none* is valued as *1* and *a great deal* has a value of *5*. The lower values on the scale represent the more desirable behavior.

The six scales are totaled with no attempt at weighting the scales for each of the inventories separately. Thus a total score is obtained for the Average Baby and a total score is obtained for the Your Baby.

The total score of the Your Baby Perception form is then subtracted from the Average Baby Perception form. The discrepancy constitutes the Neonatal Perception Inventory score.**

The inventories have shown both construct and criterion validity.

---

*The tester remains with the mother during the entire administration procedure.

**Example: Given a total Average Baby score of 17 and a total Your Baby score of 19, the Neonatal Perception Inventory score is −2. One-month-old infants rated by their mothers as better than average (+ score) are considered at Low-Risk. Those infants not rated better than average (− or 0 score) are at High-Risk for subsequent

The Degree of Bother Inventory

The Degree of Bother Inventory (Broussard, 1971) is another easy-to-administer questionnaire useful in assessing infant behavior that is of concern to mothers. Guidelines for use of this tool are as follows:

1. Purpose: The tool (see Table 4-6) is used to assess problems of infant behavior. It is important to note that "since the threshold of parental annoyance varies widely according to a parent's emotional orientation to a child, the ultimate decision as to what constitutes a problem for a specific mother varies among mothers" (Broussard, 1971, p. 435).

2. When to use: The tool is administered when the infant is 1 month of age.

3. How to use: After the mother fills out the inventory the score is calculated by assigning values of 1 to 4 to each of the six items on the inventory and totaling the values. A score of 24 indicates that the mother is easily annoyed by her infant. A score of 6 indicates that the mother is not bothered or annoyed at all by her infant.

The Brazelton Neonatal Behavioral Assessment Scale

It is possible to evaluate some of the integrative processes and determine subtle behavioral responses of the neonate (Brazelton, 1973). General guidelines for the use of the Brazelton Scale are as follows:

1. Purpose: The Brazelton Scale tests and documents the infant's use of state behavior (state of consciousness), the infant's response to various kinds of stimulation, and how the infant affects the environment. It can be used to alert professionals and parents to the potential individual strengths of the neonate.

    "The behavior exam tests for neurological adequacy with 20

---

development of emotional difficulty. (Reprinted with permission from E. R. Broussard and M. S. S. Hartner, "Further Considerations Regarding Maternal Perception of the First Born." In J. Hellmuth, editor, *Exceptional Infant: Studies in Abnormalities, Vol. 2*, New York: Brunner/Mazel, 1971. Pp. 442–447.

Table 4-6
Degree of Bother Inventory

Listed below are some of the things that have sometimes bothered other mothers in caring for their babies. We would like to know if you were bothered about any of these. Please place a check in the blank that best describes how much you were bothered by your baby's behavior in regard to these.

Crying	a great deal	somewhat	very little	none
Spitting up or *Vomiting*	a great deal	somewhat	very little	none
Sleeping	a great deal	somewhat	very little	none
Feeding	a great deal	somewhat	very little	none
Elimination	a great deal	somewhat	very little	none
Lack of a predict- *able schedule*	a great deal	somewhat	very little	none
Other: (Specify)	a great deal	somewhat	very little	none
. . . .	a great deal	somewhat	very little	none
. . . .	a great deal	somewhat	very little	none
. . . .	a great deal	somewhat	very little	none

Source: Reprinted with permission from E. R. Broussard and M. S. S. Hartner, "Further Considerations Regarding Maternal Perception of the First Born." In J. Hellmuth, editor, *Exceptional Infant: Studies in Abnormalities, Vol. 2,* New York: Brunner/Mazel, 1971. Pp. 442–447.

reflex measures and for 26 behavioral responses to environmental stimuli, including the kind of interpersonal stimuli which mothers use in their handling of the infant as they attempt to help him adapt to the new world" (Brazelton, 1973, p. 370).

In the exam, a graded series of procedures (including talking, hand on abdomen, restraint, holding, and rocking) are designed to soothe and alert the infant. The infant's responsiveness to inanimate stimuli (e.g., rattle, bell, red ball, white light, temperature change) is assessed. Estimates of vigor, attentional excitement, motor activity and tone, and automatic responsiveness are assessed as the infant changes state. Over a period of several days the examination outlines:

A. The initial period of alertness immediately after delivery

B. The period of depression and disorganization which follows and lasts for 24 to 48 hours in infants with uncomplicated deliveries and no medication effects

C. The curve of recovery to optimal function. This third period may be the best single predictor of individual potential function and basic central nervous system intactness and organization.

2. When to use:

A. Repeated examinations on any 2 or 3 days during the first 10 days after delivery

B. During pediatric examinations throughout the neonatal period

3. How to use: Special training is required for use of the full scale. Several teaching films are available to assist with training:

A. The Brazelton Neonatal Assessment Scale: An Introduction

B. The Brazelton Neonatal Assessment Scale: Variations in Normal Behavior

C. Self-Scoring Examination

Films may be obtained from E.D.C. Distribution Center, 39 Chapel Street, Newton, MA 02160

It has been suggested (Widmayer and Field, 1981) that using the Brazelton scale and the Mother's Assessment of the Behavior of

Her Infant (MABI)* scale to teach mothers about the skills of their newborn may facilitate more responsive early interactions which, in turn, may contribute to early cognitive development.

Infant Temperament Questionnaire

Based on the work of Thomas et al (1969), Carey (1972, 1981) has developed a simplified questionnaire for measuring infant temperament. Guidelines for the use of this tool are presented in Chapter 5, Health Care of the Infant.

1. Purpose: Information obtained provides a specific temperament profile of the infant which gives parents a more organized picture of their infant's behavior. This data can be used to clarify parental perceptions, provide information on normal individual differences, identify "difficult" and "slow-to-warm" children, and assist parents in adjusting to their particular infant's style.
2. When to use: The Infant Temperament Questionnaire has been standardized for use between 4 and 8 months. Questionnaires have also been developed for use with children age 1 to 3 years, age 3 to 7 years, and age 8 to 12 years.
3. How to use and where to obtain: See Chapter 5.

MANAGEMENT IMPLICATIONS

The primary objective for application of information in this chapter is the prevention of parenting disabilities and attachment problems. Assessments revealing potential risk situations call for early and active intervention (see Chapters 31 and 32). However, all parents deserve the benefits of knowledgeable and sensitive support as they begin to adapt to their new infants, and reinforcement that parenting abilities can be developed and improved.

---

*The MABI is an adaptation of the Brazelton scale and is discussed in T. Field, et al., "Mother's Assessments of the Behavior of Their Infants," *Infant Behav Dev* *1*:156, 1978.

Prenatal Period

• Assessment and supportive measures should begin during the prenatal period.
• Expectant parent classes, rooming-in, and other programs can strengthen preparation for parenthood.

Immediate Neonatal Period

• Careful observations in the very first minutes of mother–newborn interaction can provide helpful data.
• Allowing mothers to hold and nurse their infants on the delivery table can facilitate bonding.
• Mothers need time to form attachments. In the early transition period mothers need time for recovery, and expecting too much too soon can result in anxiety and guilt.
• Fathers need opportunities for early and extensive contact with the infant and mother in the hospital. Privacy for the family is important.
• When premature or sick infants are separated from parents, every effort must be made to provide contact. Parents need to be reassured that the interruption in contact does *not* preclude healthy attachment.
• Active nursing support is essential as new mothers learn to feed and care for their new infants. Mothers should not be left alone. Institutional disruptions should be minimized.
• The nurse should assist the mother in observing and assessing her infant's characteristics, behaviors, and response patterns to provide accurate data to the mother. To do this, nurses need to be able to assess infant state and plan caretaking activities accordingly.
• Mothers need to be aware that the infant contributes to interaction. Often mothers think the source of difficulties is exclusively in their handling of the infant. Parental expectations must be elicited and clarified or corrected.
• Early discharge should be avoided if there are problems in the mother–infant acquaintance period.

Postnatal Period

- A home visit or, at least, a telephone call during the first week at home provides critical feedback and support to new parents.
- Public health nursing referrals may be indicated.
- Infant crying presents the greatest challenge and parents need help to learn how to console their infants and to cope with crying.
- The first well-baby visit should be scheduled by 2 weeks of age, or 2 weeks after discharge from the hospital.
- The focus of the well-baby visits must be on the parents as well as the infant. Consider group or "cluster" visits.
- Mothers must be allowed to verbalize their feelings, positive and negative, related to the infant.
- Mothers' physical and psychic energy should be assessed at early visits. Bishop (1976) suggests that low energy results in low parenting and recommends that data be obtained on the mother's blood pressure, hematocrit, pain, bleeding, infection, general appearance, body language, depression, and availability of adequate support.
- Nurse practitioners must be alert to signs of disturbance in parent and/or infant.
- Parent support groups provide encouragement and reinforcement in the postnatal period.

Resource Information

Film: *The Amazing Newborn.* Health Sciences Communication Center, Cleveland: Case Western Reserve University, 1975. Distributed by Ross Laboratories. An excellent film for parents and professionals showing infant capabilities from birth and summarizing current research in infant behavior.

References

Ainsworth, M. D. S. "Object Relations, Dependency, and Attachment: A Theoretical Review of the Infant–Mother Relationship." *Child Dev* 40:969–1026, December 1969.

Ainsworth, M. D. S. and S. M. Bell. "Attachment, Exploration, and Separation: Illustrated by the Behavior of One-Year Olds in a Strange Situation." *Child Dev* 41:49–65, March 1970.

Barbero, G. "Failure to Thrive." In M. H. Klaus, T. Leger, and M. A. Trause, editors, *Maternal Attachment and Mothering Disorders: A Round Table*. New Brunswick, N.J.: Johnson and Johnson Baby Products Co., 1975. Pp. 9–12.

Bell, S. M. and M. D. S. Ainsworth. "Infant Crying and Maternal Responsiveness." *Child Dev 43*:1171–1190, December 1972.

Benedek, T. "Psychobiological Aspects of Mothering." *Am J Orthopsychiatry 26*:272–278, April 1956.

Binzley, V. "State: Overlooked Factor in Newborn Nursing." *Am J Nurs 77*:102–103, January 1977.

Bishop, B. "A Guide to Assessing Parenting Capabilities." *Am J Nurs 76*:1784–1787, November 1976.

Bowlby, J. *Attachment and Loss*. Vol. 1. *Attachment*. New York: Basic Books, 1969.

Brazelton, T. B. "Assessment of the Infant at Risk." *Clin Obstet Gynecol 16*:361–375, March 1973a.

Brazelton, T. B. "Effect of Maternal Expectations on Early Infant Behavior." *Early Child Develop Care 2*:259–273, 1973b.

Brazelton, T. B. *Neonatal Behavioral Assessment Scale*. Clinics in Developmental Medicine Series, Vol. 50. Philadelphia: J. B. Lippincott, 1973c.

Brazelton, T. B. *On Becoming a Family: The Growth of Attachment*. New York: Delacorte Press/Seymour Lawrence, 1981.

Broussard, E. R. and M. S. S. Hartner. "Further Considerations Regarding Maternal Perception of the First Born." In J. Hellmuth, editor, *Exceptional Infant: Studies in Abnormalities*, Vol. 2. New York: Brunner/Mazel, 1971. Pp. 432–449.

Carey, W. B. "Clinical Applications of Infant Temperament Measurements." *J Pediatr 81*:823-828, October 1972.

Carey, W. B. "Intervention Strategies Using Temperament Data." In C. C. Brown, editor, *Infants at Risk: Assessment and Intervention. An Update for Health-Care Professionals and Parents*. Piscataway, NJ: Johnson and Johnson Baby Products Co., 1981. Pp. 96–106.

Clark, A. L. "Recognizing Discord between Mother and Child and Changing It to Harmony." *Am J Maternal Child Nurs 1*:100–106, March/April 1976.

Durand, B. "Failure to Thrive in a Child with Down's Syndrome: A Clinical Nursing Study." *Nurs Res 24*:272–286, July/August 1975.

Green, M. "A Developmental Approach to Symptoms Based on Age Groups." *Pediatr Clin North Am 22*:571–582, August 1975.

Harrison, L. L. "Nursing Intervention with the Failure-to-Thrive Family." *Am J Maternal Child Nurs 1*:111–116, March/April 1976.

Helfer, R. E. "Relationship between Lack of Bonding and Child Abuse and Neglect." In M. H. Klaus et al., editors, *Maternal Attachment and Mothering Disorders: A Round Table*. New Brunswick, NJ: Johnson and Johnson Baby Products Co., 1975. Pp. 21–26.

Horowitz, J. A. et al. *Parenting Reassessed: A Nursing Perspective*. Englewood Cliffs, NJ: Prentice-Hall, 1982.

Hymovich, D. P. and R. W. Chamberlin. *Child and Family Development: Implications for Primary Health Care*. New York: McGraw-Hill, 1980.

Kennedy, J. C. "The High-Risk Maternal–Infant Acquaintance Process." *Nurs Clin North Am 8*:549–556, September 1973.

Kennell, J. H. and M. H. Klaus. "Care of the Mother of the High-Risk Infant." *Clin Obstet Gynecol 14*:926–954, September 1971.

Klaus, M. H. and A. Fanaroff. *Care of the High Risk Infant,* 2nd ed. Philadelphia: W. B. Saunders, 1979.

Klaus, M. H. and J. H. Kennell. *Parent-Infant Bonding,* 2nd ed. St. Louis: C. V. Mosby, 1982.

Lamper, C. "Facilitating Attachment through Well-Baby Care." In J. E. Hall and B. R. Weaver, editors, *Nursing of Families in Crisis.* Philadelphia: J. B. Lippincott, 1974. Pp. 72–83.

Leal, C. A. "Successful Parenting in the Black Community." In V. J. Sasserath, editor, *Minimizing High-Risk Parenting.* Skillman, NJ: Johnson and Johnson Baby Products Co., 1983. Pp. 11–16.

Leifer, A. J. et al. "Effects of Mother-Infant Separation on Maternal Attachment Behavior." *Child Dev 43*:1203–1218, December 1972.

McDonald, M. A. "Paternal Behavior at First Contact with the Newborn in a Birth Environment without Intrusions." *Birth Fam J 5*:123–132, Fall 1978.

Newcomb, T. *The Acquaintance Process.* New York: Holt, Rinehart, 1961.

Parke, R. D. "Perspectives on Father–Infant Interaction." In J. D. Osofsky, editor, *The Handbook of Infant Development.* New York: Wiley, 1979.

Porter, C. P. "Maladaptive Mothering Patterns: Nursing Intervention." In *ANA Clinical Sessions: Detroit 1972.* East Norwalk, CT: Appleton-Century-Crofts, 1973. Pp. 87–102.

Robson, K. S. and H. A. Moss. "Patterns and Determinants of Maternal Attachment." *J Pediatr 77*:976–985, December 1970.

Snyder, C., et al. "New Findings About Mothers' Antenatal Expectations and Their Relationship to Infant Development." *Am J Maternal Child Nurs 4*:354–357, November/December 1979.

Thoman, E. B. "Development of Synchrony in Mother–Infant Interaction in Feeding and Other Situations." *Fed Proc 34*:1587–1592, June 1975.

Thomas, A., et al. *Temperament and Behavior Disorders in Children.* New York: New York University Press, 1969.

Webster-Stratton, C. and K. Kogan. "Helping Parents Parent." *Am J Nurs 80*:240–244, February 1980.

Widmayer, S. M. and T. M. Field. "Effects of Brazelton Demonstrations for Mothers on the Development of Preterm Infants." *Pediatrics 67*:711–714, May 1981.

Yogman, M. W. "Development of the Father–Infant Relationship." In H. Fitzgerald et al., editors, *Theory and Research in Behavioral Pediatrics,* Vol. 1. New York: Plenum, 1980.

5

Health Care
of the Infant:
0–12 Months

The first year is one of rapid growth and development for the infant and one of drastic change and growth in the life of the parents. Although a time of joy for most parents, it is also a period fraught with anxieties and concerns. Parents need reassurance that their baby is "all right" and explanations of normal variations that are transient and nonpathologic. In their own words, parents "worry about" many aspects of early parenting. They need help with understanding the external and internal forces exerted upon them as parents.

This chapter provides the nurse practitioner with information to perform at a high level, giving comprehensive primary health care. It discusses assessment of the newborn and the growth, development, and feeding of the infant. It includes most of the common problems related to the newborn with the hope that teaching parents to appreciate and gratify their infant's early needs and to understand normal developmental behavior may help avoid some of these problems. To assist the nurse practitioner, a comprehensive schedule for well-child care is provided as a guide, accompanied by appropriate developmental milestones.

211

A COMPREHENSIVE SCHEDULE FOR WELL-CHILD CARE

Recognizing the parents as the true providers of child health care, health professionals assist them in parenting by offering guidance, counseling, and teaching. For this reason health visits are not equated with immunization schedules. Families need individual attention, some will function with fewer visits, and some, especially first-time parents, will need longer visits and/or extra visits. The goals in planning for comprehensive child health care are as follows:

- Recognize that routine health supervision enhances the optimal physical, intellectual, emotional, and social growth of the child.
- Provide direct services to clients and families via a caring relationship and a nonfragmented communicative approach.
- Direct families toward responsible parenting through education in childrearing practices, knowledge of normal child development and emotional needs, awareness of preventive measures such as immunization schedules, safety precautions, and illness care.
- Develop self-confident parents through the provision of encouragement, reassurance, and other measures supportive of the parenting role.
- Use anticipatory guidance to assist parent's adjustment to infant's temperament and individual developmental needs.

To promote better preventive pediatric care, it is recommended that parents be encouraged to visit the pediatric primary health care provider prenatally to discuss similarities and differences of child-care philosophies, options for health care, and knowledge of services of a public health nurse. This relationship is especially recommended for first-time parents who need help soon after the infant's birth.

Ideally, the area used as a waiting room for parents and children should display appropriate toys and books for use. This area can also include a bulletin board for mutual use of parents and agency to announce parenting classes, nursery school locations, and other items. A display case could be used as a teaching aid to demonstrate safety items, nutritional values of infant foods, and other educational information. A few toys may be made available in the examining room for use by the children while the parents are discussing child care with the practitioner.

To make a physical examination more comfortable or convenient for a parent and an infant or child, the infant can be examined on the lap of the parent, the parent can undress the child as necessary to the examination, and the practitioner can use the instruments on a doll or the parent before use on the child.

The child's record should include growth and developmental charts that are kept up to date at each visit. See Appendix and Chapter 24, Developmental Assessment. A small record book can be given to the parents containing entries from each visit that include the child's height, weight, immunizations, appropriate telephone numbers, and educational material.

The following schedule outlines the content of the health visit at different ages. The reader is referred to appropriate chapters for complete information regarding specific topics.

First Visit

The first visit is best made at 2 weeks of age and should occur no later than 1 month of age.

HEALTH ASSESSMENT

See Tables 5-1 and 5-2 for a review of the health assessment at this age.

COUNSELING

Physical Care See this chapter, Physical Care of the Newborn. Discuss the following topics:

- Bathing and the use of lotions, powders, and soaps. (See Chapter 14, General Care of the Skin, and Care of Diapers.)
- Care of the cord. (See this chapter, Physical Care of the Newborn.)
- Elimination. Discuss patterns and colors of stools. (See this chapter, Stool Patterns.)

Table 5-1

Health Assessment at First Visit

Health History Physical Examination	Nutrition	Development	Screening and Immunizations
Parental concerns	Assess caloric needs for optimum growth: 100–110 cal/kg/day	2 weeks: sucking and rooting reflexes, Moro reflex, and tonic neck reflex (TNR) present	Urine ferric chloride for PKU
Prenatal history	Discuss need for iron, vitamins, fluoride	Sensitive to light and noise	Discuss with parents
Birth history	Discuss current feeding methods	Head falls backward or forward when sitting	Discuss immunization schedule and its importance
Neonatal history	See this chapter, Feeding in Infancy	Grasp reflex present	
History of familial diseases			
Interval history			
Family and social history			
Length, weight, and head circumference			
Complete physical examination			
Discussion of normal variants and abnormal physical findings with parents			

Table 5-2

Waechter Developmental Guide: Summary of Average Development during the First Month

Age	Physical and Motor Development	Intellectual Development	Socialization and Vocalization	Emotional Development
1 month	Physiologically more stable than in newborn period	Reflexive	Cries, mews, and makes throaty noises	Response limited generally to tension states
	Waves hands as clenched fists	No attempt to interact with environment	Responds in terms of internal need states	Panic reactions, with arching of back and extension and flexion of extremities
	Objects placed in hands are dropped immediately	External stimuli do not have meaning	Interested in the human face	Derives satisfaction from the feeding situation
	Momentary visual fixation on objects and human face			Maximal need for sucking pleasures when held and pleasure from rocking, cuddling, and tactile stimulation
	TNR position frequent and Moro reflex brisk			Quiets when picked up
	Able to turn head when prone, but unable to support head			
	Responds to sounds of bell, rattle, etc.			
	Makes crawling motions when prone			
	Sucking and rooting reflex present			
	Coordinates sucking, swallowing, and breathing			

Reprinted with permission from E. H. Waechter and F. G. Blake, *Nursing Care of Children*, 9th ed., Philadelphia: JB Lippincott, 1976. Pp. 276–279.

Source: Reprinted with permission from E. H. Waechter and F. G. Blake, *Nursing Care of Children*, 9th ed., Philadelphia: JB Lippincott, 1976. Pp. 276–279.

- Safety. (See this chapter, Accident Prevention and Safety.)
- Out-of-doors. (See Chapter 14, Sunburn, Prevention.)
- Equipment. Discuss need to obtain car seat (See this chapter, Accident Prevention and Safety) and discuss vaporizer. (See Chapter 17, Humidification.)
- Illness prevention. Discuss early rashes and their care, (See Chapter 14, Miliaria, Diaper Rashes) colds, and the need for protection from infection in the early months.
- Protocol of visits. Discuss the components of child health care and immunization schedules and when and how to call for medical care.

Emotional and Mental Development Among the topics to be discussed are the following:

- Gratification of basic infant needs, contact such as holding, singing and talking to, fondling, and rocking, and sucking needs such as amount of time and when to use the pacifier, nonnutritive breast, or bottle sucking
- Differences in infant temperament and the part these play in parental understanding of the infant's behavior (See this chapter, Important Early Needs and Differences in Temperament and Personality.)

Stimulation Infants at this age need and enjoy many levels of stimulation:

- Being moved through space (kinesthesia). A cradle, rocking-chair, carriage, or automobile can be used.
- Sucking to ease discomfort and tension. If the infant needs more non-nutritive sucking, fingers or a pacifier may be used. It may be necessary at times to hold the pacifier in the infant's mouth.
- Having physical contact with the mother, father, or caretaker. The infant should be held, fondled, walked, rocked, and talked or sung to.
- Changing position.
- Observing a mobile.

Parent–Child Relationship   Discuss the following aspects:
- Parental expectations in reference to crying, feeding, elimination, sleeping, and spoiling
- The importance of mother–child attachment

Parenting   Discuss parenting on several levels:
- The shift in the family from two to three members and its meaning to the family
- The need for adopting a philosophy of child care that is mutually agreed upon by parents
- The importance of help in the home for cooking, cleaning, and to relieve the mother for the care of the child
- The need to consider time for the mother's own needs and for rest
- Her feelings of inadequacy, anxiety, resentments, and isolation
- Realistic expectations of the parents for themselves and each other as parents and the changes in their relationship
- The importance of the father's understanding of the physical and emotional changes occurring in the mother and the need for his support
- Active participation of the father in the care of the child as part of his role
- The father's needs and availability of support

Nurse Practitioner Goals   The goals of the nurse practitioner include the following:
- Providing health education about infant care and development
- Recognizing this period as one of greatest apprehension and anxiety for the parents about assuming the responsibility of a dependent infant
- Providing an atmosphere supportive of responsible parenting and a free exchange of ideas
- Listening well and answering all questions fully
- Observing the interactions of the parents with their child and assessing parental understanding of the child's temperament and/or behavior

- Identifying potential and high-risk situations such as extreme parental frustration or anger, and faulty parental bonding (See Chapter 4, References for further reading material.)
- Examining one's own feelings about the family
- Discussing family planning
- Assessing the parents' understanding of the health care system and encouraging both parents to accompany the child to the health visit
- Encouraging the parents' attendance at parenting groups or classes and suggesting appropriate reading material (See this chapter, Booklist for Parents.)

Visit at 5 to 9 weeks

HEALTH ASSESSMENT

See Tables 5-3 and 5-4 for a review of the health assessment at this age.

COUNSELING

Physical Care   This includes a review of the first visit and discussion of the following:

- Sleep patterns and sleeping arrangements
- The meaning of illness, colds, and fever: Teach the use of the thermometer, and when to call for medical care.
- Accident prevention appropriate for age

Emotional and Mental Development   Review basic psychologic needs (see this chapter, Important Early Needs) and discuss the following:

- The child's continued gratification of these needs
- Attachment and its meaning to the infant and mother
- The parents' observations of the child's temperament

Stimulation   The 5- to 9-week-old child needs and enjoys many levels of stimulation:

Table 5-3
Health Assessment at 5 to 9 Weeks

Health History Physical Examination	Nutrition	Development	Screening and Immunizations
Parental concerns	Assess caloric needs for optimum growth	5 weeks: rooting, Moro, and TNR	Diphtheria, tetanus, pertussis vaccine (DTP)
Interval history to include past illnesses, eating, sleeping, elimination, behavior	Discuss parental attitudes and expectations re: solids	May "smile"	Trivalent oral polio vaccine (TOPV)
Family and social history	Discuss need for water	Fist to mouth	
Length, weight, and head circumference		Follows light; tracks sound	
Complete physical exam		9 weeks:	
Discussion of findings with parents		Smiles	
		Vocalizes	
		Hands to midline	
		Listens	
		Follows light past midline	
		Holds head up 90° in prone position	

Table 5-4

Waechter Developmental Guide: Summary of Average Development during the Second Month

Age	Physical and Motor Development	Intellectual Development	Socialization and Vocalization	Emotional Development
2 months	Moro reflex still brisk Posture still toward TNR position Has visual response to patterns Eye coordination to light and objects Follows objects vertically and horizontally Responds to objects placed on face Listens actively to sounds Able to lift head momentarily from prone position Turns from side to back Able to swallow pureed foods	Recognition of familiar face Indicates inspection of the environment Beginning to show anticipation before feeding	Beginnings of vocalization: coos Beginning of social smile Actively follows movement of familiar person or object with eyes Crying becomes differentiated Vocalizes to mother's voice Visually searches to locate sounds of mother's voice	Maximal need for sucking pleasures Indicates more active satisfaction when fed, held, rocked

Source: Reprinted with permission from E. H. Waechter and F. G. Blake, *Nursing Care of Children*, 9th ed., Philadelphia: JB Lippincott, 1976. Pp. 276–279.

- A mobile to watch, later a mirror placed in the crib, and pictures of faces
- A change of scenery: The infant seat may be propped and moved about.
- Nonnutritional sucking of fingers or pacifier
- A prone position to allow lifting of the head (This should occur several times a day.)
- Crib devices that are semirigidly supported and strong enough to withstand abuse (Rattles and hand toys are not good at this age.)
- Opportunities to be held, rocked, talked and sung to, and to have parents repeat the noises made by the infant

Parent–Child Relationship Discuss the following aspects:

- Need for taking time to enjoy and observe the movements, reactions, rhythm, and uniqueness of the child

Parenting Repeat from first visit as necessary and discuss parenting on several levels:

- The mother's need for rest, relaxation, and exercise (She may need help with organizing the day. Discuss her feelings about how things are going.)
- The father's role as supportive (How does he see his role? Discuss his need to become familiar with the infant by gentle handling and playing.)
- The parents' need to be away from the infant occasionally for short periods of time (If the mother returns to work there needs to be joint responsibility for planning care of the infant and care of the home.)

Nurse Practitioner Goals Goals of the nurse practitioner include the following:

- Providing support and reassurance to the parents (In this early period the family rhythm is set by the child. The parents may be worn out from too little sleep. They may feel resentment at the constant attention needed by the infant. They need to know that the infant becomes more secure with their care and therefore easier to manage.)
- Encouraging participation in parenting groups or classes.

Visit at 2½ to 4 Months

HEALTH ASSESSMENT

See Tables 5-5 and 5-6 for a review of the health assessment at this age.

COUNSELING

Physical Care. Discuss the following aspects:

- The need for an organized day and consistency of care
- Sleep and napping needs
- Drooling as a sign of salivary gland maturation and the infant's inability to swallow excessive saliva. It is not necessarily a sign of teething
- The use of jumpers, walkers, and high chairs when the head is held erect

Emotional and Mental Development Review basic psychologic needs (See this chapter, Important Early Needs.) Discuss the following:

- Gratification of basic needs
- Use of the pacifier. The infant may not be as dependent on the pacifier at about 4 months. This is a good time to watch for clues to discontinue its use. (See this chapter, Sucking Need, and Pacifier.)

Stimulation The 2½- to 4-month-old infant needs and enjoys many levels of stimulation:

- Being talked to, played with affectionately, and moved about to various parts of the house (Playpens and cribs are not advisable for long periods of time.)
- Looking at mirrors (These should be of good stainless steel placed about 4 to 5 inches away from the child. This is a particularly good device for the diapering table.)
- Handling, pulling, and grabbing at crib devices
- Kicking and thumping at a large stuffed toy tied to the foot of the crib

Table 5-5
Health Assessment at 2½ to 4 Months

Health History Physical Examination	Nutrition	Development	Screening and Immunizations
Parental concerns	Continued need for iron-enriched formula	2½ mo: holds head and chest to 90° in prone position	DTP and TOPV #2
Interval history	Digestive system now mature enough to handle solids	Laughs, babbles	Hearing: alert to sounds
Family and social history	Introduction of cereal, fruits at 4 mo	TNR and Moro reflex diminishing	Vision: inspects own hands, fixates on cube 1–2 feet away
Length, weight, and head circumference	Teething biscuits may be used, avoid wheat products (See Chapter 3, Food Allergies)	4 mo: holds head erect and steady in sitting position	
Complete physical examination		Bears weight on legs	
Discussion of findings with parents		May roll over	

223

Table 5-6

Waechter Developmental Guide: Summary of Average Development during the Third to Fifth Months

Age	Physical and Motor Development	Intellectual Development	Socialization and Vocalization	Emotional Development
3 months	Frequency of TNR position and vigor of Moro response rapidly diminishing Uses arms and legs simultaneously, but not separately Able to raise head from prone position; may get chest off bed Holds head in fairly good control Beginning differentiation of motor responses Hands are beginning to open and objects placed in hands are retained for brief inspection, able to carry objects to mouth Indicates preference for prone or supine position "Stepping" reflex disappears	Shows active interest in environment Can recognize familiar faces and objects such as bottle, but objects do not have permanence Recognition is indicative of recording of memory traces Beginning of play with parts of body Follows objects visually Beginning ability to coordinate stimuli from various sense organs Shows awareness of a strange situation	More ready and responsive smile Facial and generalized body response to faces Preferential response to adult voices Has longer periods of wakefulness without crying Beginnings of prelanguage vocalizations: babbling and cooing Laughs aloud and shows pleasure in vocalization Shows anticipatory preparation to being lifted Turns head to follow familiar person Ceases crying when mother enters the room	Maximal need for sucking pleasure Wishes to avoid unpleasant situations Not yet able to act independently to evoke response in others

	Physical/Motor	Cognitive	Language/Vocalization	Social
	Landau reflex appears Eyes converge as objects approach face Has necessary muscular control to accept cereal and fruit			
4 months	Ability to carry objects to mouth Inspects and plays with hands Grasps objects with both hands Turns head to sound of bell or bottle Reaches for offered objects Eyes focus on small objects Beginning eye–hand coordination Ability to pick up objects Rooting reflex disappears; TNR disappearing Sits with minimal support with stable head and back Turns from back to side Breathing and mouth activity coordinated in relation to vocal cords	Recognizes bottle on sight Becomes bored when left alone for long periods of time Actively interested in environment Indicates beginnings of intentionality and interest in affecting the environment Indicates beginning anticipation of consequences of action	Vocalizes frequently and vocalizations change according to mood Begins to respond to "no, no" Enjoys being propped in sitting position Turns head to familiar noise Chuckles socially Demands attention by fussing, enjoys attention	Interest in mother heightens Baby is affable and lovable Shows signs of increasing trust and security

Continued

Table 5-6 (Continued)

Age	Physical and Motor Development	Intellectual Development	Socialization and Vocalization	Emotional Development
	Holds head up when pulled to sitting position			
5 months	Begins to drool	Able to discriminate strangers from family	Enjoys play with people and objects	Other members of the family become important as the baby's emotional world expands
	Ability to recover near objects	Turns head after fallen object	Smiles at mirror image	
	Reaches persistently	Shows active interest in novelty	More exuberantly playful, but also more touchy and discriminating	Beginning ability to postpone gratification
	Grasps with whole hand	Attempts to regain interesting action in environment		Awaits anticipated routines with happy expectation
	Ability to lift objects	Ability to coordinate visual impressions of an object		Beginning exploration of mother's body
	Beginning use of thumb and finger in "pincer" movement	Beginning differentiation of self from environment		
	Able to sustain visual inspection			
	Able to sit for longer periods of time when well supported			
	Beginning signs of tooth eruption			
	Ability to sleep through night without feeding			
	Moro reflex and TNR finally disappear			

Source: Reprinted with permission from E. H. Waechter and F. G. Blake, *Nursing Care of Children*, 9th ed., Philadelphia: JB Lippincott, 1976. Pp. 276–279.

Parent–Child Relationship It is helpful to figure out the infant's "life-style." Discuss the following aspects:

• The infant's patterns (Has the infant fairly regular patterns? Is the infant easily satisfied or does he or she react strongly?)
• The infant's developing temperament (Awareness of the infant's temperament and how the parents deal with it is a key aspect of how smoothly the child's development will proceed. See this chapter, Booklist for Parents.)

Parenting Repeat from past visits as necessary and discuss:

• Sharing of child care. The father may diaper and bathe the infant to overcome his fear of handling the infant.

Nurse Practitioner Goals The goals of the nurse practitioner include the same as those of the first visit, with one addition:

• Reassuring the parents that they are doing a good job

Visit at 6 to 9 Months

HEALTH ASSESSMENT

See Tables 5-7 and 5-8 for a review of the health assessment at this age.

COUNSELING

Physical Care Discuss the following topics:

• Accident prevention appropriate to age
• Teething and use of teething toys and crackers (See Chapter 16, Table 16-1.)
• Use of jumpers, swings, and walkers with caution (They should not be used for long periods of time and should be safely constructed.)
• Care of upper respiratory infections and mild diarrhea (See Chapter 17, Upper Respiratory Tract, and Chapter 20, Diarrhea.)

Table 5-7

Health Assessment at 6 to 9 Months

Health History Physical Examination	Nutrition	Development	Screening and Immunizations
Parental concerns Interval history Family and social history Length, weight, and head circumference Complete physical examination Discussion of findings with parents	Limit milk to 24 oz/24 hr Discuss iron-containing foods, finger foods Advise waiting to wean until after 1 year Discuss fluoride, avoidance of sugared foods No bottle in bed (See Chapter 16, Nursing Bottle Mouth)	Laughs, babbles Passes object hand to hand and mouths objects Tooth eruption Turns to voice Rolls over, may get to sitting Beginning stranger anxiety Stronger attachment to mother	DTP, and TOPV #3 optional Hearing sounds laterally in both directions Eye cover test for strabismus (Chapter 15)

Emotional and Mental Development   Discuss the following needs:

- The need for answering all cries within a reasonable period of time
- Stranger anxiety and what it means to members of the family (See this chapter, Stranger Anxiety.)
- Attachment to certain objects as normal, such as blankets and toys
- Consistency, continuity, and sameness (This is very helpful in enabling the infant to start to develop some beginning sense of self-identity.)

Stimulation   Children of this age need and enjoy many levels of stimulation:

- Being physically active.
- Hearing sounds, those of others and the infant's own. Talk to the infant about what is occurring at the moment.
- Grabbing, pulling, and dropping objects.
- Moving about. Allow child space to roam, to roll over, and to crawl, preferably on a blanket on the floor.
- Using walkers and jumpers. These are used with caution. They should be safe and not used for long periods of time.
- Playing with safe small objects, stuffed toys, and jack-in-the-box toys.

Parent–Child Relationship   The child's personality changes with assumption of the upright position. Discuss the following aspects:

- Stranger anxiety. This may create problems with the family, since the infant prefers the mother at this time.
- Parents' attitudes toward messiness, food play, and spoiling.

Parenting   Discuss parenting on several levels:

- Time away from the child for short periods of time. This is not a time for prolonged separation.
- Feelings about getting up at night.

Table 5-8
Waechter Developmental Guide: Summary of Average Development during the Sixth to Ninth Months

Age	Physical and Motor Development	Intellectual Development	Socialization and Vocalization	Emotional Development
6 months	Ability to pick up small objects directly and deftly Ability to lift cup by handle Grasps, holds, and manipulates objects Ability to pull self to sitting position Beginning to "hitch" in locomotion Momentary sitting and hand support When lying in prone position, supports weight with hands Weight gain begins to decline Ability to turn completely over	Increasing awareness of self Responds with attentiveness to novel stimuli Beginning ability to recognize mother when she is dressed differently Objects begin to acquire permanence: will search for lost object for brief period	Very interested in sound production Playful response to mirror Laughs aloud when stimulated Great interest in babbling, which is self-reinforcing Beginning recognition of strangers	Beginning sense of self Increased growth of ego

Age				
7 months	Ability to transfer objects from one hand to another Holds object in one hand Gums or mouths solid foods, shows exploratory behavior with food Ability to bang objects together Palmar grasp disappears Bears weight when held in standing position Sits alone for brief periods Rolls over adeptly	Ability to secure objects by pulling on string Repeats activities that are enjoyed Discovers and plays with own feet Drops and picks up objects in exploration Searches for lost objects outside perceptual field Has consciousness of desires Growing differentiation of self from environment Rudimentary sense of depth and space	Vocalizes four different syllables Produces vowel sounds and chained syllables Makes talking sounds in response to the talking of others Crows and squeals	Beginning to show signs of fretfulness when mother leaves or is in presence of strangers Shows beginning fear of strangers Orally aggressive in biting and mouthing
8 months	Ability to ring bell purposively Ability to feed self with finger foods Beginning tooth eruption Sits well alone Ability to release objects at will	Uncovers hidden toy Increased interest in feeding self Differentiation of means from end in intentionality Has lively curiosity about the world	Listens selectively to familiar words Says "da da" or equivalent Babbles to produce consonant sounds Vocalizes to toys Stretches out arms to be picked up	Plays for sheer pleasure of the activity Anxiety when confronted by strangers indicates recognition and need of mother; attachment behavior begins to be obvious and strong

Source: Reprinted with permission from E. H. Waechter and F. G. Blake, *Nursing Care of Children*, 9th ed., Philadelphia: JB Lippincott, 1976. Pp. 276–279.

- Differences of opinion between parents on child-raising philosophy.
- Problems regarding family planning if necessary.

Nurse Practitioner Goals The goals of the nurse practitioner include the following:

- Continuing to provide appropriate health education
- Reassuring parents in reference to their concerns
- Expressing empathy toward their frustrations in handling infant behavior
- Recognizing that some families need more or longer visits

Visit at 9 to 12 Months

HEALTH ASSESSMENT

See Tables 5-9 and 5-10 for a review of the health assessment at this age.

COUNSELING

Physical Care Discuss the following:

- Accident prevention appropriate to age. (See this chapter, Accident Prevention and Safety.)
- Safe area for child to move about without restricting exploration and satisfaction of normal curiosity.
- Caries prevention. Cleaning teeth daily with gauze, and no bottles at bedtime or nap with milk or fruit juices. (See Chapter 16, Nursing Bottle Mouth.)
- Use of Ipecac. (See Chapter 28, Poison Ingestion.)
- Disadvantages of early toilet training. (It is better to wait until the child is ready. See Chapter 6, Toilet Training.)
- Reasons for not weaning from breast or bottle too early. (See this chapter, Weaning from Breast to Bottle.)

Emotional and Mental Development Discuss the following needs:

- Need for feeling loved and cared for.

Table 5-9

Health Assessment at 9 to 12 Months

Health History Physical Examination	Nutrition	Development	Screening and Immunizations
Parental concerns Interval history Family and social history Length, weight, and head circumference Complete physical examination Discussion of findings with parents	Advise 3 meals/day May introduce cup if child ready, advise waiting to wean until after 1 yr Normal drop in appetite Restriction of sugared foods, milk, and juices in bedtime bottles	Jabbers, babbles Thumb–finger grasp Imitates speech sounds Plays pat-a-cake May pull to stand and/or crawl	Hematocrit, hemoglobin, and RBC indices Sickle cell and G-6-PD No immunizations if up to date Hearing: turns head 45° in direction of sound Vision: eye cover test Hirschberg's light reflex test

233

Table 5-10

Waechter Developmental Guide: Summary of Average Development during the Ninth to Twelfth Months

Age	Physical and Motor Development	Intellectual Development	Socialization and Vocalization	Emotional Development
9 months	Rises to sitting position Creeps and/or crawls, maybe backward at first Tries out newly developing motor capacities Ability to hold own bottle Drinks from cup or glass with assistance Beginning to show regular patterns in bladder and bowel elimination Good ability to use thumb and finger in pincer grasp Pulls self to feet with help	Ability to put objects in container Examines objects held in hand, explores objects by sucking, chewing, and biting	Responds to simple verbal requests Plays interactive games, such as peek-a-boo and patty cake	Mother is increasingly important for her own sake, reacts violently to threat of her loss Begins to show fears of going to bed and being left alone Increasing interest in pleasing mother Active search in play for solutions to separation anxiety
10 months	Ability to unwrap objects Pulls to standing position	Beginnings of imitation Looks at and follows pictures in book	Extends toy to another person without releasing Responds to own name	Has powerful urge toward independence in locomotion, feeding, beginning to help in dressing

Age				
	Uses index finger to poke and finger and thumb to hold objects Finger feeds self; controls lips around cup Plantar reflex disappears Neck-righting reflex disappears Sits without support; recovers balance easily Pulls self upright with furniture		Inhibits behavior to "no, no" or own name Beginning to test reactions to parental responses during feeding and at bedtime Imitates facial expressions and sounds	Experiences joy when achieving a goal and mastering fear
11 months	Ability to hold crayon adaptively Ability to push toys Ability to put several objects in container, releases objects at will Stands with assistance, may be beginning attempts to walk with assistance Beginning ability to hold spoon "Cruises" around furniture	Works to get toy that is out of reach Growing interest in novelty Heightened curiosity and drive to explore environment	Repeats performance laughed at by others Imitates definite speech sounds Uses jargon Communicates by pointing to objects wanted	Reacts to restrictions with frustration, but has ability to master new situations with mother's help (weaning)

Source: Reprinted with permission from E. H. Waechter and F. G. Blake, *Nursing Care of Children*, 9th ed., Philadelphia: JB Lippincott, 1976. Pp. 276–279.

- Separation anxiety (See this chapter, Separation Anxiety.)
- Night crying. Difficulty in putting infant down for nap and at bedtime, and the need for bedtime rituals. (See this chapter, Problems Related to Sleep.)
- Need for satisfaction of normal curiosity. This is not a time for repeated "no's."

Stimulation The 9-month-old child needs and enjoys many levels of stimulation:

- Imitation of sounds, which should be answered in kind by the parent
- Space to crawl about, to touch, and to explore
- Large balls, boxes, blocks, stack toys, jack-in-the-box toys
- Hide-and-seek and peek-a-boo games

Parent–Child Relationship Discuss the following aspects:

- The child's continuing preference for the mother
- Need to respond to the child such as picking up dropped toys, playing peek-a-boo

Parenting Discuss parenting on several levels:

- Feelings and ideas toward weaning, toilet training, masturbation, discipline, and the need to set limits
- Availability of parenting groups or classes

Nurse Practitioner Goals The goals of the nurse practitioner include the following:

- Reassuring and educating parents about their concerns
- Treating their concerns with respect and empathy

Visit at 12 Months

HEALTH ASSESSMENT

See Tables 5-11 and 5-12 for a review of the health assessment at this age.

Table 5-11

Health Assessment at 12 Months

Health History Physical Examination	Nutrition	Development	Screening and Immunizations
Parental concerns	Review basic food groups, table foods, and amounts appropriate for age	Indicates wants	Urinalysis
Interval history		Drinks from cup	Hemogram if not obtained sooner
Family and social history		Pincer grasp	
Length, weight, and head circumference	Lessened appetite	May use spoon	Tuberculin test
Complete physical examination	Milk limited to 16–20 oz/ 24 hr	Says ma-ma, da-da	Hearing: rapid localization of sound
Discussion of findings with parents	Avoidance of sugared foods and drinks	Crawls, walks holding on or alone	Vision: eye cover test

Table 5-12

Waechter Developmental Guide: Summary of Average Development during the Twelfth Month

Age	Physical and Motor Development	Intellectual Development	Socialization and Vocalization	Emotional Development
12 months	Turns pages in book, can make marks on paper Babinski sign disappears Beginning standing alone and toddling "Cruises" around furniture Lumbar curve develops Hand dominance becomes evident Ability to use spoon in feeding	Dogged determination to remove barriers to action Further separation of means from ends Experiments to reach goals not attained previously Concepts of space, time, and causality begin to have more objectivity	Jabbers expressively Has words that are specific to parents Few, simple words Experimentation with "pseudo-words" of great interest and pleasure	Ability to show emotions of fear, anger, affection, jealousy, anxiety Baby is in love with the world

Source: Reprinted with permission from E. H. Waechter and F. G. Blake, *Nursing Care of Children*, 9th ed., Philadelphia: JB Lippincott, 1976. Pp. 276–279.

COUNSELING

Physical Care Discuss the following:

- Accident prevention. House should be made toddler-safe.
- Caries prevention. Clean child's teeth daily with gauze.
- Illness care. Teach bed care, diet, throat examination, and symptoms of an ear problem.

Emotional and Mental Development Discuss the following needs:

- Autonomy: the development of the child's strong will, the need for dependence–independence, increased growth of ego and learning to distinguish between self and parent. (Books helpful to parents may be found in this chapter, Booklist for Parents.)
- The expression of curiosity, which aids in the child's intellectual development

Stimulation The child needs and enjoys many levels of stimulation:

- Being read to
- Naming and pointing to features, such as nose, eye
- Roaming and being allowed to touch, to investigate, and to manipulate objects
- Playing in water and sand with appropriate toys
- Playing and holding dolls and stuffed toys
- Sorting, piling, and dumping small objects from a box

Parent–Child Relationship Discuss the following aspects:

- The parents' feelings toward "education" versus development, discipline–punishment, setting of limits, and temper tantrums.
- Development of autonomy. This begins the age of exploration and sometimes creates a conflict or battle of wills between the parent and the child. The mother may be threatened by the independence shown by her baby or may expect too much in terms of "good" behavior from the child.
- Demands of supervising a mobile infant. How does the mother feel about the constant picking up of toys, and the full-time job of protecting this beginning toddler?

Parenting   Discuss parenting on several levels:

- Any conflicts of opinion between the parents concerning child-rearing practices.
- Changes in parental relationships. The child's need for constant supervision drains energy and emotional reserve. There should be an awareness of the need to maintain closeness and emotional contact with each other, not just in the parental role but in giving to each other as adults.

Nurse Practitioner Goals   The goals of the nurse practitioner include the following:

- Helping parents recognize and deal with their frustrations
- Being alert for signs of anger and resentment toward child
- Re-emphasizing developmental processes as normal

ASSESSMENT OF THE NEWBORN

The nurse practitioner is a key figure in assessing infants for physical characteristics, some that are transient and nonpathologic, for identifying infants who are at risk and may need referral and re-evaluation, and for assisting parents in observing and appreciating their infant's characteristics, temperament, and behavior. This section presents information on assessment and early care of the newborn and includes some specific tools for assessing the term and the premature infant. Other tools for assessing mother–infant interaction and behavior can be found in Chapter 4.

Physical Assessment of the Newborn

A large percentage of infant deaths occur during the first 24 hours after birth. The nurse has the important function of assuming responsibility for immediate and careful observation of the newborn. One of the best means of detecting any abnormality is to proceed with a careful, thorough, and systematic physical examination (see Table 5-13).

Table 5-13

Physical Assessment of the Newborn

Body Part/ Factors	Usual Findings	Normal Variations	Abnormalities
Head			
Size	35 ± 2.5 cm circumference		<33 cm: microcephaly (e.g., anencephaly) >38 cm: macrocephaly (e.g., hydrocephalus)
Shape	Molded, if vaginal delivery, round if cesarean section Palpable anterior and posterior fontanels and sutures	Asymmetry due to molding, hematomas, or edema (e.g., caput succedaneum, cephalohematoma) Posterior fontanel may be closed	
	Anterior fontanel flush with neighboring parts (can be expected to be slightly depressed when child is in sitting position)		Tension of the anterior fontanel (to be determined when child is in sitting position) Depressed (e.g., dehydration) Bulging (e.g., intracranial pressure) *Notify physician immediately* Hemorrhage (intracranial) Depressed skull fracture *Notify physician immediately*
	Sutures are normally felt as ridges immediately after birth or as depressions within 1 day	There may be overriding of the sutures *Observe and notify physician*	

Continued

241

Table 5-13 (Continued)

Body Part/ Factors	Usual Findings	Normal Variations	Abnormalities
Face			
Symmetry	Symmetry between left and right side of face		Asymmetry between left and right side of face (e.g., congenital malformation, hemiplegia)
	Symmetrical contractions of face with infant cries or grimaces		Movement of only one side of face when infant cries (e.g., facial nerve palsy)
Color	Red		Pallor, gray color
			Persistent cyanosis (e.g., congenital cardiac malformations)
Eyes			
Symmetry	Correct placement on face in relation to each other		Centered or deviated to right or left
Eyelids	Edema due to instillation of silver nitrate		Marked edema or inflammation
	Blink reflex present		Drooping
			Setting-sun sign
Discharge	None	Moderate discharge from irritation by silver nitrate	Purulent
Cornea	Bright and shiny		Hazy or dull

Pupils	Round shape		Oval or irregular shape Constricted (e.g., cerebral paralysis) Fixed and dilated
Iris	Equal and reacting to light	Reaction to light discernible	
Sclera	Dark or slate blue Bluish-white		Hemorrhage Jaundice
Retina	Red reflex		Opacity of lens
Coordination	Nystagmus usually present when child rotated laterally Does not persist when replaced in crib	Occasional uncoordinated movements	Persistent uncoordinated movements
Ears			
Shape	Well formed	Preauricular papillomas may be present	Malformations (e.g., branchial clefts)
	Cartilage present	Amount of cartilage varies (lessened amount is usually a sign of prematurity)	
	Upper part of ear should be on same plane as angle of eye	May be folded or creased	Malformations (e.g., low placement)
Hearing	Blinking of the eyes, momentary cessation of activity or starting indicate positive reaction to sound		No response to sound
	Moro reflex		No response to Moro reflex (e.g., intracranial hemorrhage)

Continued

Table 5-13 (Continued)

Body Part/ Factors	Usual Findings	Normal Variations	Abnormalities
Nose			
Symmetry Shape	In midline of face Appears flattened		Deviated to right or left Malformation Unusual flattening
Patency	Infant should breathe easily through nose when mouth closed	Some mucus present in nares may interfere with free breathing	Flaring of nares (e.g., obstructed airway, atelectasis) Check for other signs of respiratory distress
Mouth			
Lips	Pink	May have transient circumoral cyanosis	Malformation (e.g., cleft lip)
Tongue	Rooting reflex Pink Inside mouth		Thrush Protrusion
	Normal volume	Short frenulum linguae (insignificant)	Frenulum linguae extending to tip of tongue (may interfere with sucking) Large and thick (e.g., Down's syndrome)
Palate	Pink and well formed	Epstein's pearls Inclusion cysts	Malformation (e.g., cleft palate or unusually high)
Gums	Pink	Rear gums may be whitish May appear quite jagged Teeth may be present Inclusion cysts	

Salivation	Scant	Excessive and frothy (e.g., tracheoesophageal fistula)
Reflexes	Sucking reflex initiated when lips touched Extrusion reflex Gag reflex initiated by tongue blade	Loss of sucking reflex (e.g., physiologic jaundice)
Neck		
Appearance	Short, straight	Masses Distended veins or edema Webbing
Motion	Head moves freely from side to side and from flexion to extension	Restriction of motion Congenital torticollis Opisthotonus
Chest		
Size	Averages 30 to 37.5 cm	<30 cm: prematurity
Shape	Almost circular	Gross abnormalities Bulging Depressed sternum
Expansion	Symmetry of movement with respirations	Asymmetrical movements (e.g., diaphragmatic hernia)
Respirations	Rate: 40/min	May range from 30 to 60/min Labored breathing Grunting on expiration Retractions with respirations
Breath sounds	Vesicular	Rales Rhonchi Wheezes

Continued

245

Table 5-13 *(Continued)*

Body Part/ Factors	Usual Findings	Normal Variations	Abnormalities
Breast tissue	Present in both sexes	Excessive amount of breast tissue	
Nipples	Symmetrical placement of nipples	Milky secretion may be evident	Asymmetrical placement of nipples (e.g., fracture of clavicle) Signs of infection Presence of supernumerary nipples below nipple line or in axillary region
Heart sounds	Rate: 120 to 150/min Rhythm: irregular after physical or emotional stimulus Quality: first sound (closure of mitral valve and tricuspid valve) and second sound (closure of aortic and pulmonary valve) should be sharp and clear		Sounds of poor quality Extra sounds Heard on right side (sign of dextrocardia) Murmurs accompanying heart beats
Abdomen Shape	Contour cylindrical and relatively prominent		Asymmetry Distention Localized bulging (e.g., hernia) Scaphoid abdomen (e.g., diaphragmatic hernia) *Check for other signs of respiratory distress*

Femoral pulses	Present		
Umbilical stump	Bluish-white Dry within several hours after birth	Umbilical hernia may be present and is usually insignificant	Abnormal redness, bleeding, or infection
Genitalia			
Size	In both sexes, tend to appear large in relation to rest of body	Edema present in breech delivery Size of penis and scrotum varies widely	
Color	Red	May have increased pigmentation in dark-skinned races	
Appearance	Female: labia minora are quite prominent and protrude over labia majora	Smegma	
	Male: prepuce usually adherent to the glans	Vaginal discharge mucoid or blood-tinged	Excessive vaginal bleeding
	Testicles usually in scrotum Scrotum small and firm or fairly loose, relaxed, and pendulous		Malformations (e.g., epispadias, hypospadias, phimosis)
		Cryptorchidism	Hydrocele
	Meatal opening should appear as a slit		Meatal opening appears round

Continued

Table 5-13 (Continued)

Body Part/ Factors	Usual Findings	Normal Variations	Abnormalities
Extremities			
Appearance	Generally flexed but can be put in full range of motion passively	May retain in utero position when sleeping	Limitation of movement in any joint (e.g., fractures, paralysis)
	Alignment of parts and presence of all limbs and extremities		Absence or defects of parts or all of extremities
Color	Cyanosis may last for several hours after birth		Difference of color or temperature between the extremities
Hands	Fists clenched		Malformations (e.g., webbing or presence of extra digits, clubbing of fingers, unusual shortness or curvature of little finger; simian crease on palm of hand)
	Flexion of hand at wrist is ~110°; extension is 80°		
	Grasp reflex		
Arms	Shoulders abduct from trunk about 120°		Limitation of motion (e.g., fracture, paralysis)
	Range of motion at the elbow		
Feet	Plantar fat makes feet appear flat		Malformations (e.g., clubfeet, absence of toes, abnormal spacing between first and second toes)
	Grasp reflex		
	Babinski reflex		

	Normal	Variations	Deviations
Legs	Usually held in varus or valgus attitude but can be straightened without forceful manual stretching Flexion and extension of ankle about 130° Mild degree of bowing or medial rotation Symmetry of medial skin folds on anterior and posterior thigh	May turn in but can be passively turned out	Extra folds or asymmetry (e.g., hip dislocation)
Hip	Range of motion should be about 160° to 170° in flexion and extension Thighs flexed at hip should abduct to an angle of 160° between thighs		Limited abduction of one or both hips (e.g., dysplasia, hip dislocation)
Skin			
General appearance	Red in color Varies with race and ethnic origin Cyanosis of lips, fingernails, toenails, hands, and feet Tendency to be dry	Harlequin sign Erythema toxicum neonatorum Capillary hemangiomas Lanugo Vernix caseosa Desquamation (e.g., if postmaturity)	Pallor: jaundice in first 24 hours of life Generalized cyanosis (e.g., cardiac, neurologic, or respiratory malformations) Tinted vernix caseosa

Continued

249

Table 5-13 *(Continued)*

Body Part/ Factors	Usual Findings	Normal Variations	Abnormalities
Turgor	Skin of back of lower leg or thigh or of abdomen returns to its former position after release of grasp between thumb and index finger of examiner		Fold of skin persists for several seconds after release
Back			
General appearance	Shoulders, scapulae, iliac crests on same plane with each other		Malformations (e.g., spina bifida)
	Spine straight and easily flexed	Pilonidal dimple over coccygeal area	Abnormal curvature of spine Pilonidal cyst or sinus
		Hair over shoulders and back, especially in premature infants	Tufts of hair anywhere over the spine, especially over the sacrum (e.g., spina bifida)
Anus			
Patency	Proved by adherence of meconium on rectal thermometer	Anus may be irritated by frequent rectal temperatures	Imperforate anus Fissures, bleeding

Source: Reproduced with permission from Marcil, V. "Physical Assessment of the Newborn." *Can Nurs* 72(3):22–24, March 1976.

BEFORE THE EXAMINATION

Before the actual examination proceed as follows:

- Review the antenatal history (health of the mother during pregnancy, Rh typing, complications of pregnancy and drugs taken).
- Review the birth history (kind and duration of labor, type of delivery, sedation or anesthesia, resuscitation required, Apgar score, birth weight and length, and gestational age).
- Evaluate the infant's body temperature, respiratory rate, pulse rate, cry, and color.
- Observe the state of consciousness and general activity.

SEQUENCE OF EXAMINATION

This may be adapted to the particular infant and situation. If the infant is sleeping, it may be best to examine the chest and abdomen first.

AFTER THE EXAMINATION

Detailed recording is made to provide valuable baseline data.

Assessment Tools

APGAR SCORE

The Apgar score evaluates the newborn infant using a five-factor score (Apgar, 1955). The Apgar score has stood the test of time as an index of acute severe neonatal impairment at birth (Scanlon, 1973). Commonly used in all delivery rooms at birth, the score is easy to use and to understand. This score is valuable in identifying those infants who are at special risk, need prompt diagnosis and treatment, and need careful watching. It is based on five signs that are evaluated at 1 minute and again at 5 minutes after birth. The five signs are given in Table 5-14 in acronym form for ease of use and for committing to memory.

Table 5-14
Apgar Score

Signs		Scoring		
		0	1	2
Appearance	Color	Blue, pale	Body pink Extremities blue	All pink
Pulse	Heart rate	Absent	Slow Below 100	Over 100
Grimace	Reflex irritability, response to stimuli on sole of foot	None	Some grimace	Cry
Activity	Muscle tone	Limp	Some flexion of extremities	Active motion
Respiration		None	Slow, irregular	Good, strong cry

Source: Reprinted by permission from Apgar, V., "Role of Anesthesiologist in Reducing Neonatal Mortality," *N Y State J Med* 55:2365–2368, August 1955. Copyright by the Medical Society of the State of New York.

Five Signs of Apgar Score

1. Appearance. This may also be described as color. All babies are cyanotic or pale at birth but change to pink within 1 to 3 minutes. Even with prompt onset of respiration and good circulation, the hands, feet, and presenting parts may remain cyanotic for more than a day. Persistent cyanosis of other parts indicates a need for prompt diagnosis and treatment.

2. Pulse. This is also described as heart rate. A heart rate under 100 is a danger signal.

3. Grimace. This may also be described as reflex irritability. Absence of reflex irritability is evidence of a depressed nervous system. It can be tested by slapping the feet tangentially. This should cause the infant to cry or make some motion.

4. Activity. This may also be described as muscle tone. Poor muscle tone is a danger signal. A flaccid baby is usually in shock or narcotized.

5. Respiration. Spontaneous respiration should be well established within 1 minute. Absence of breath sounds or inadequate respirations are indications for immediate assistance.

Scoring At 1 and again at 5 minutes after the complete birth of the infant, the signs are evaluated and a score of 0, 1, or 2 assigned to each. A score of 10 at 1 minute reflects the best possible condition. An infant scoring 0–3 will probably need resuscitation. An infant scoring 4–8 may need only a few whiffs of oxygen.

BRAZELTON NEONATAL BEHAVIORAL ASSESSMENT SCALE

This tool has emerged as an excellent means of assessing the subtler behavioral responses of neonates as they adjust to and shape their environment. It can be used as a predictive tool particularly for high-risk infants, for imparting information that will help parents see themselves as the most important resources for the maximal well-being of their infant. The Brazelton Scale is discussed further in Chapter 4.

CAREY INFANT TEMPERAMENT QUESTIONNAIRE

Based on the work of Thomas et al. (1969, 1977), Carey (1972, 1981) has developed a simplified questionnaire for measuring infant temperament. Carey defines infant temperament as the emotional reactivity, or behavioral style displayed during the early months of life. He believes temperament is an important variable in infant development and is deserving of further attention by child care professionals. Identifying the temperament of the infant makes possible a more individualized approach for helping parents determine alternatives in handling, caring for, and interacting with their infant.

Using the Questionnaire Mothers of infants (4 to 8 months old) are asked to select from three possible choices the one that best describes the infant's behavior in each of nine categories. The categories include activity, rhythmicity, adaptability, approach, sensory threshold, intensity, mood, distractibility, and persistence. The questionnaire is viewed as easy to administer and simple and quick to score, the usual time being 8 to 10 minutes. See also this chapter, Differences in Temperament and Personality.

Obtaining the Questionnaire The objectives of the questionnaire, its important implications in well-child care, and the questionnaire with scoring techniques are well described in Erickson (1976). To obtain copies of the questionnaire, see Resource Information.

CLINICAL ASSESSMENT OF GESTATIONAL AGE (DUBOWITZ SCALE)

This is a scoring system for gestational age (Dubowitz, 1970), based on 10 neurologic and 11 "external" criteria, which is most reliably and effectively used during the first 5 days of life. The scoring system is more objective and reproducible than trying to guess gestational age on the presence or absence of individual signs. The criteria used are easily defined, and the scoring system can be readily learned in about 10 minutes with a little practice.

Indications for Use The scale may be used to assess infants in these instances:

1. Premature or small-for-gestational-age (SGA) infants to determine problems that may occur
2. Large-for-gestational-age (LGA) infants to guard against misjudging gestational age
3. SGA term infants as distinct from appropriately-grown-for-gestational-age (AGA) preterm infants

4. Dehydrated infants to discriminate the malnourished child
5. Full-term infants to assess condition or as a teaching tool to parents

External Criteria The 11 external criteria and their scoring scale are presented in Table 5-15.

Neurologic Criteria Ten criteria (in conjunction with Figure 5-1) are used for scoring purposes:

1. Posture. With the infant quiet and in supine position, the posture is observed and scored. (0: Arms and legs extended. 1: Beginning of flexion of hips and knees, arms extended. 2: Stronger flexion of legs, arms extended. 3: Arms slightly flexed, legs flexed and abducted. 4: Full flexion of arms and legs.)

2. Square window. The hand is flexed on the forearm between the thumb and index finger of the examiner. Enough pressure is applied to get as full a flexion as possible, and the angle between the hypothenar eminence and the ventral aspect of the forearm is measured and graded according to diagram. (Care is taken not to rotate the infant's wrist while doing this maneuver.)

3. Ankle dorsiflexion. The foot is dorsiflexed onto the anterior aspect of the leg, with the examiner's thumb on the sole of the foot and the other fingers behind the leg. Enough pressure is applied to get as full flexion as possible, and the angle between the dorsum of the foot and the anterior aspect of the leg is measured.

4. Arm recoil. With the infant in the supine position, the forearms are first flexed for 5 seconds, then fully extended by pulling on the hands, and then released. The sign is fully positive if the arms return briskly to full flexion (score 2). If the arms return to incomplete flexion or the response is sluggish it is graded as score 1. If they remain extended or are only followed by random movements the score is 0.

5. Leg recoil. With the infant supine, the hips and knees are fully flexed for 5 seconds, then extended by traction on the feet, and released. A maximal response is one of full flexion of the hips and knees (score 2). A partial flexion scores 1, and minimal or no movement scores 0.

Table 5-15

Scoring System for External Criteria

External Sign	Score[a]				
	0	1	2	3	4
Edema	Obvious edema of hands and feet; pitting over tibia	No obvious edema of hands and feet; pitting over tibia	No edema		
Skin texture	Very thin, gelatinous	Thin and smooth	Smooth; medium thickness; rash or superficial peeling	Slight thickening; superficial cracking and peeling, especially of hands and feet	Thick and parchmentlike; superficial or deep cracking
Skin color	Dark red	Uniformly pink	Pale pink; variable over body	Pale; only pink over ears, lips, palms, or soles	
Skin opacity (trunk)	Numerous veins and venules seen, especially over abdomen	Veins and tributaries seen	A few large vessels clearly seen over abdomen	A few large vessels seen indistinctly over abdomen	No blood vessels seen
Lanugo (over back)	No lanugo	Abundant; long and thick over whole back	Hair thinning, especially over lower back.	Small amount of lanugo and bald areas.	At least half of back devoid of lanugo
Plantar creases	No skin creases	Faint red marks over anterior half of sole	Definite red marks over > anterior half; indentations over < anterior third	Indentations over > anterior third	Definite deep indentations over > anterior third

Nipple formation	Nipple barely visible, no areola	Nipple well-defined; areola smooth and flat, diameter < 0.75 cm	Areola stippled, edge not raised; diameter < 0.75 cm	Areola stippled, edge raised; diameter > 0.75 cm
Breast size	No breast tissue palpable	Breast tissue on one or both sides < 0.5 cm diameter	Breast tissue on both sides; one or both 0.5 to 1.0 cm	Breast tissue both sides; one or both > 1 cm
Ear form	Pinna flat and shapeless, little or no incurving of edge	Incurving of part of edge of pinna	Partial incurving whole of upper pinna	Well-defined incurving whole of upper pinna
Ear firmness	Pinna soft, easily folded, no recoil	Pinna soft, easily folded, slow recoil	Cartilage to edge of pinna, but soft in places, ready recoil	Pinna firm, cartilage to edge; instant recoil
Genitals Male	Neither testis in scrotum	At least one testis high in scrotum	At least one testis right down	
Female (with hips half abducted)	Labia majora widely separated, labia minora protruding	Labia majora almost cover labia minora	Labia majora completely cover labia minora	

Source: Reprinted with permission from L. M. S. Dubowitz, V. Dubowitz, and C. Goldberg, "Clinical Assessment of Gestational Age in the Newborn Infant," *J Pediatr* 77:1–10, July 1970.

[a] If score differs on two sides, take the mean.

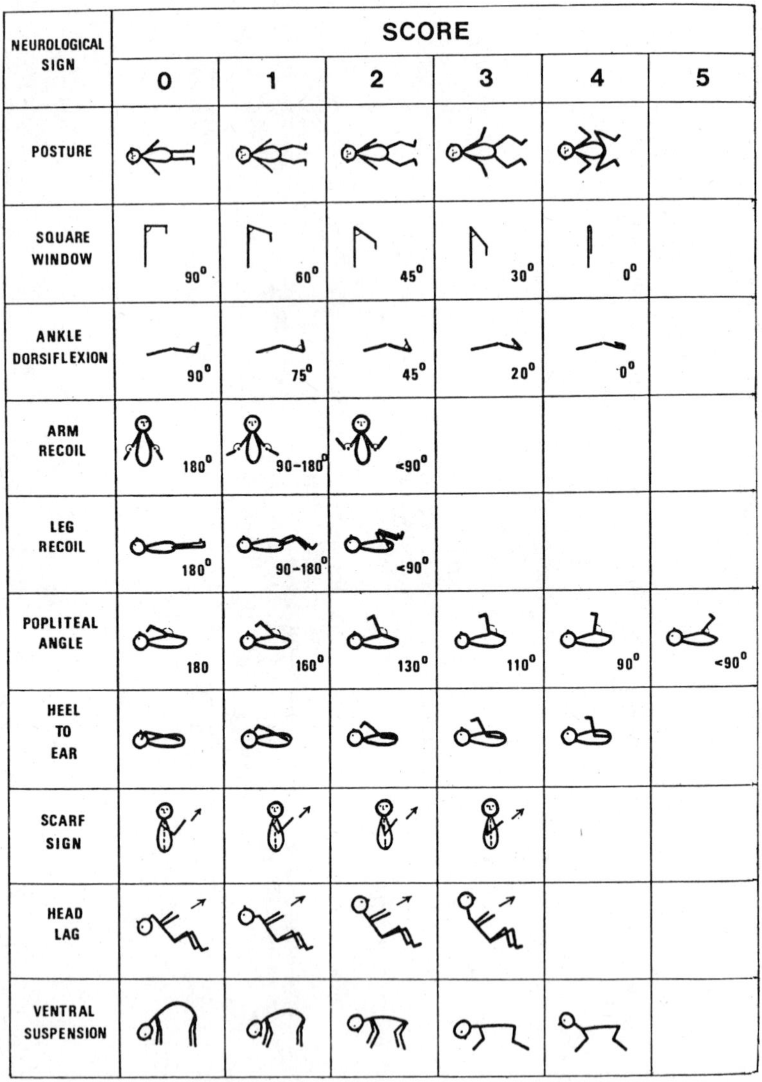

Figure 5-1 Scoring system for neurologic signs. These signs are used together with neurologic criteria. (Reproduced with permission from L. M. S. Dubowitz, V. Dubowitz, and C. Goldberg, "Clinical Assessment of Gestational Age in the Newborn Infant," *J Pediatr* 77:1–10, July 1970.)

6. Popliteal angle. With the infant supine and the pelvis flat on the examining couch, the thigh is held in the knee-chest position by the examiner's left index finger and thumb supporting the knee. The leg is then extended by gentle pressure from the examiner's right index finger behind the ankle, and the popliteal angle is measured.

7. Heel-to-ear maneuver. With the baby supine, draw the baby's foot as near to the head as it will go without forcing it. Observe the distance between the foot and the head as well as the degree of extension at the knee. Grade according to diagram. Note that the knee is left free and may draw down alongside the abdomen.

8. Scarf sign. With the baby supine, take the infant's hand and try to put it around the neck and as far posteriorly as possible around the opposite shoulder. Assist this maneuver by lifting the elbow across the body. See how far the elbow will go across and grade according to illustrations. (0: Elbow reaches opposite axillary line. 1: Elbow between midline and opposite axillary line. 2: Elbow reaches midline. 3: Elbow will not reach midline.)

9. Head lag. With the baby lying supine, grasp the hands (or the arms, if a very small infant) and pull him slowly toward the sitting position. Observe the position of the head in relation to the trunk and grade accordingly. In a small infant the head may initially be supported by one hand. (0: Complete lag. 1: Partial head control. 2: Able to maintain head in line with body. 3: Brings head anterior to body.)

10. Ventral suspension. The infant is suspended in the prone position, with examiner's hand under the infant's chest (one hand in a small infant, two in a large infant). Observe the degree of extension of the back and the amount of flexion of the arms and legs. Also note the relation of the head to the trunk. Grade according to diagrams.

Scoring The steps for establishing gestational age are as follows:

1. The external criteria are scored as shown in Table 5-15.
2. The neurologic criteria are scored as described in the preceding section and in Figure 5-1.

Table 5-16
Total Scores for Neurologic and External Criteria

Neurologic Criteria		External Criteria	
Criterion	Score	Criterion	Score
Posture	0–4	Edema	0–2
Square window	0–4	Skin texture	0–4
Ankle dorsiflexion	0–4	Skin color	0–3
Arm recoil	0–2	Skin opacity	0–4
Leg recoil	0–2	Lanugo	0–4
Popliteal angle	0–5	Plantar creases	0–4
Heel to ear	0–4	Nipple formation	0–3
Scarf sign	0–3	Breast size	0–3
Head lag	0–3	Ear form	0–3
Ventral suspension	0–4	Ear firmness	0–3
		Genitals	0–2
Total	0–35	Total	0–35

3. When the scores are obtained for both categories (see Table 5-16), they are added together and computed using the formula given in Figure 5-2. The resulting gestational age is then recorded on the graph.

If score differs on the two sides, take the mean.

DANGER SIGNS IN THE NEWBORN

These signs can alert the provider of care to identify the high-risk infant. In assessing a newborn any of the signs listed should be considered for reevaluation or referral. See Table 5-17.

Care of the Newborn

FEEDING METHODS

See this chapter, Feeding in Infancy, Breast Feeding, and Problems Related to Feeding. Also see Chapter 3, Nutritional Requirements, Infant Nutrition, Formulas and Milks, Iron Nutrition in Infancy and Solid Foods.

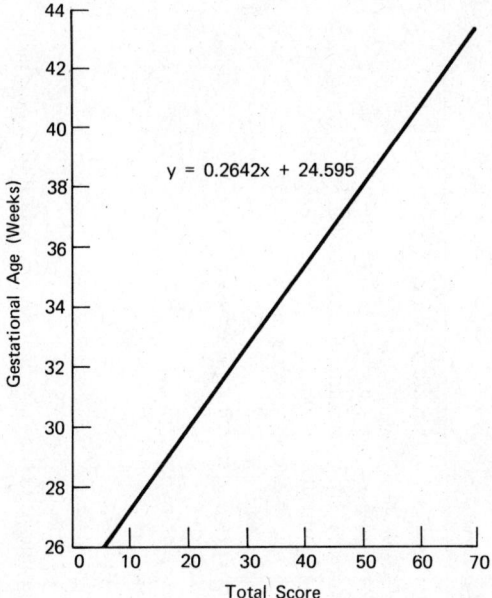

Figure 5-2 Graph for reading gestational age from total score obtained on the gestational age scale. Formula for obtaining gestational age score is shown above, with *x* as the total score and *y* as the gestational age score. (Reproduced with permission from L. M. S. Dubowitz, V. Dubowitz, and C. Goldberg, "Clinical Assessment of Gestational Age in the Newborn Infant," *J Pediatr* 77:1–10, July 1970.)

EARLY PSYCHOLOGIC NEEDS

Among these needs are the need to suck and a feeling of being loved and cared for that includes the following needs:

1. To have a strong attachment to one or more persons
2. To know that someone will answer a cry
3. To have bodily contact and to be held and gently stimulated

For more information, see this chapter, Important Early Needs.

Table 5-17
Danger Signs in the Newborn

Positive family history (e.g. diabetic mother, toxemia)
Complications of gestation and delivery
Abnormal position of the baby
Atypical intrauterine growth
Any congenital malformation (e.g., asymmetry of chest)
Rapid or difficult respirations
Rapid, slow, or irregular pulse
Abnormal cry
Cough
Cyanosis
Low Apgar score
Sweating
Excess salivation
Diarrhea
Vomiting of bile
No meconium stool (for 48 hours)
Delayed or inadequate voiding
Abdominal distension
Cord odor or exudate
Bleeding from circumcision or cord
Single umbilical artery
Full fontanelle (hydrocephalus)
Small head for size
Convulsions, twitching, excessive irritability
Lethargy
Fever or hypothermia
Paralysis
Jaundice
Pallor
Petechiae
Change in behavior or condition ("not looking right")

SAFETY NEEDS

See this chapter, Accident Prevention and Safety.

SLEEPING NEEDS

See this chapter, Table 5-18 and Problems Related to Sleep.

PHYSICAL CARE OF THE INFANT

Bathing the Newborn Unless otherwise indicated, these procedures can be followed:

1. The entire body is bathed daily, especially in deep folds and creases, with warm water and a mild soap. Neutragena soap is recommended.
2. Oils and lotions are not recommended for use on the skin. They tend to interfere with normal skin secretions and may cause rash in the newborn. Dryness of the skin at this age is not an abnormal condition. See Chapter 14, General Care of the Skin.
3. Powder in small amounts may be used in the diaper area only. See Chapter 14, Lotions, Powders. Powder should be applied by hand.
4. Daily shampooing using mild shampoos is recommended to aid in the prevention of cradle cap. See Chapter 14, Cradle Cap.
5. At bath time or whenever necessary the eyes may be wiped using cotton balls and warm water, wiping from the inner canthus to the outer and changing to a clean cotton ball for each eye. Abnormal amounts of tearing or yellow mucous discharge from the eyes should be assessed for the cause.
6. No special attention should be given the nose beyond removing obvious mucous plugs as they appear at the nares. This is done with a clean washcloth or cotton ball. Yellow nasal discharge should be assessed for the cause.
7. Cleaning the ears is done only with a clean washcloth and only on that area that can be easily reached. The ears should not be cleaned with the aid of cotton swabs. Wax (cerumen) lubricates the ear canals, insulates them against temperature extremes, repels insects, keeps water and soap out, and helps prevent itching.

Table 5-18
Normal Sleep Patterns

Age	Number of hr/24 hr	Comments About Sleeping Habits
Newborn	Low: 10 Average: 16½ High: 23 (7–8 short naps)	No child fits into a routinely prescribed sleep pattern.
2–4 months	Low: 8–10/night High: 11–12/night 2–3 naps/day	Release into sleep varies with infants. Some are more tense than others. Although there is no correlation with solid food intake and sleeping through the night, the parent's attitude may make the difference.
6–12 months	11–12/night 2–3 naps/day	There should be an established routine for bedtime. Baby may wake due to illness, teething, or separation anxiety.
12–18 months	8–12/night 1–2 naps/day	There may be waking problems after the mother returns to work, even after several months.
2–3 years	8–12/night 1 nap/day	There is a need for rituals and consistency at bedtime. Active children may not nap after 2½ years.
3–4 years	8–12/night May take 1 nap/day	Some children will wake with dreams. (One fifth of the night is spent dreaming.) Many children will wake and wander at night. Some children will accept a locked half-door on the bedroom. The habit of sleeping with parents should be discouraged.
4 years	8–12/night	This is a good time to shift from crib to bed. Some dreaming and waking may result.
4½–5 years	8–12/night	There may be an increase in bad dreams and night terrors. The child may need considerable attention to get back to sleep. The child may enjoy reading at bedtime before lights out. Dreams may be at a low peak.

Care of the Umbilical Cord   Once or twice daily the cord should be gently lifted and rubbing alcohol applied to its base to facilitate drying. Any discharge, swelling, or bleeding should be assessed for the cause.

Care of the Genitalia   See also Chapter 22, The Genitalia.

FEMALE   The female genitalia are wiped clean using cotton balls or a washcloth, wiped front to back. No excess pressure is necessary; some waxy material may remain. Slight bloody or white mucous discharge is normal. Yellow discharge or frank bleeding should be assessed for the cause.

MALE   Normal bathing of the penis is recommended. It is not necessary to push or to retract the foreskin. See Chapter 22, Phimosis.

Care of the Circumcision   Gentle bathing with warm water and a washcloth is recommended. Immersion in a basin or small tub may be done being careful not to wet the umbilical cord. Vaseline is not used since this causes maceration and delays healing. The plastic bell may remain attached by a threadlike tissue that will release in 4 to 7 days. Excess swelling, redness, yellow discharge, or bleeding should be assessed for the cause. See Chapter 22, Circumcision.

Dressing the Newborn   The infant can be kept warmly snug in a cotton receiving blanket. A loose shirt and diapers should be sufficient clothing. An additional blanket may be used with weather changes. The extremities of the newborn are normally somewhat blue and cold because of immaturity of the small blood vessels in these areas.

Common Conditions of the Newborn

This area consists of a variety of conditions of the skin and other organs found in the newborn assessment, a large number of which are within normal limits or are normal variants. Many of the conditions are transitory and most of them are nonpathogenic. Included here are the most commonly encountered conditions.

BEDNAR'S APHTHAE

Assessment These are ulcers that may be seen on the hard palate posteriorly. Usually bilateral, they are thought to be due to vigorous sucking.

Management None is necessary beyond explanation to the parents.

BRACHIAL PALSY

Assessment This is paralysis of the upper arm with or without paralysis of the forearm and hand. It is caused by an injury to the brachial plexus when traction is exerted on the head during delivery of the shoulder. The child has a characteristic position of adduction and internal rotation of the arm with pronation of the forearm. The biceps reflex and the Moro reflex are absent on the affected side. Differentiation must be made from fractures of the clavicle, fracture and injuries to the humerus, and cerebral injury.

Management If the condition is caused by edema and hemorrhage, a return of function will occur within a few months. If it is due to laceration permanent damage may result. Splinting to prevent deformity and necessary physiotherapy are indicated.

CAFE-AU-LAIT SPOTS

Assessment These are light to dark brown pigmented areas of the skin of various sizes.

Management One or two patches may be within normal limits. Five to seven or more may indicate fibromas or neurofibromatosis and a referral is made to a neurologist.

CAPUT SUCCEDANEUM

Assessment This is clear fluid trapped under the scalp but on top of the pericranium and is not confined to one bone. It is ill defined, pits on pressure, and is not fluctuant. This sometimes occurs with an elongated head and may indicate a long delivery. It is caused by the head pressing on the pelvic outlet in the last period of labor. This fluid disappears in about a week.

Management Beyond explanation to the parents none is necessary.

CEPHALOHEMATOMA

Assessment This is a soft, fluctuant, well-outlined mass of blood trapped beneath the pericranium and confined to one bone. Possibly due to birth trauma, it occurs commonly. It is sometimes not noted until the second postpartum day. A ridge may be felt around the hematoma for as long as 6 months.

Management If the cephalohematoma crosses the midline, further assessment should be made for a possible skull fracture. Infants with large hematomas should receive additional iron in their diet. See Chapter 3, Iron Requirements in Infancy.

CIRCUMORAL CYANOSIS

Assessment This is pallor that occurs around the mouth that may be displayed by an infant when crying or cold during the first few days of life.

Management None is necessary beyond explanation to the parents.

CRANIOTABES

Assessment This is softening of the outer layer of the scalp and may be seen in premature infants. It is felt upon examination as a ping-pong ball sensation as the scalp is pressed with the fingers behind and above the ears. It may indicate a pathologic condition: rickets, syphilis, hypervitaminosis A, or hydrocephaly.

Management Reassessment of the cause and referral are indicated with the presence of craniotabes.

CYANOSIS

Assessment This develops when the hemoglobin is reduced by 5 gm/dl. The newborn usually has high hemoglobin levels, therefore, cyanosis occurs more easily and with less relative oxygen unsaturation than in the older child. Normally, by 4 hours of age cyanosis will show less in hands and feet. Pathologically it may be caused by pulmonary disease, congential heart disease, central nervous system disorders, or hypoglycemia. It is sometimes confused with ecchymosis. Pressure on the cyanotic area will blanch the skin temporarily. The ecchymotic area remains blue with pressure.

Management Continued cyanosis should be reassessed for the cause and referral is indicated.

DESQUAMATION

Assessment This is dryness and peeling of the skin. It occurs normally in the newborn and is felt to denote postmaturity. It is most prominent about the ankles and wrists and over the abdomen. In severe cases, the palms and soles are involved, and sloughing skin may be noted over the entire body.

Management It clears with no special attention generally after a few tub baths.

ECCHYMOSIS

Assessment These marks are evidence of blood under the skin usually due to bruising or birth injuries. See this chapter, Cyanosis.

Management They disappear as the blood is reabsorbed.

EPSTEIN'S PEARLS

Assessment These are small epithelial cysts occurring along both sides of the median of the hard palate or along the alveolar ridge.

Management They are not pathologic and disappear with time.

ERYTHEMA TOXICUM NEONATORUM

Assessment This is a rash consisting of small maculopapular lesions that develops in the first few days of life. It resembles varicella or "flea-bites." Of unknown origin, it is transitory and may disappear within 8 hours.

Management None is neccessary beyond explanations to the parent.

FACIAL NERVE PALSY

Assessment Usually the paralysis is peripheral and results from pressure over the facial nerve in utero during labor or from forceps during delivery. Movement on only one side of the face is noted and the mouth is drawn to that side. Sometimes the eye on the affected side cannot close and the nasolabial fold is absent. Prognosis depends on whether the nerve is intact or whether the nerve fibers are torn. Improvement will occur within a few weeks in the former case.

Management Care of the exposed eye is essential. Frequent irrigations with normal saline solution are recommended. Referral to a neurologist is indicated if severe nerve damage is suspected.

FONTANELS

Assessment Both anterior and posterior fontanels must be assessed.

ANTERIOR This is the unossified membranous space in the skull at the junction of the sagittal, coronal, and frontal sutures or the junction between the frontal and parietal bones. It may be small or absent at birth, then enlarges to an average of 2.5 by 2.5 cm, closing between 9 and 19 months. See Chapter 1, Figure 1-2. Early closure is not a reason for concern so long as the head growth continues normally. Tenseness or bulging of the anterior fontanel may be an indication of a pathologic condition. This is best noted if the infant is in a sitting position.

POSTERIOR This is the junction of the lambdoidal and the sagittal sutures or the parietal and the occipital bones. Often not palpable at birth, it averages 1 by 1 cm and closes approximately by the second month. There are additional fontanels located over the mastoid and the sphenoid areas.

Management If tenseness or bulging of the anterior fontanel occurs, the infant should be further assessed regarding increased intracranial pressure.

FRENULUM (TONGUE-TIE)

Assessment This is the thin mucous membrane that attaches the tongue to the floor of the oral cavity. It is also called frenulum linguae.

Management A referral to the appropriate specialist is recommended only if the frenulum keeps the tongue from reaching the gum line.

HARLEQUIN COLORING

Assessment This is a condition in which half of the newborn's body appears red while the other half appears pale. It may possibly be attributable to poorly developed vasomotor reflexes. It is transitory, usually occurring when the infant cries lustily.

Management This is not significant and needs only an explanation to parents.

HEMANGIOMAS (STRAWBERRY MARKS)

Assessment These are evenly rounded formations of immature blood vessels from 1 to 10 cm or more in transverse measurement. They may be present at birth but more often begin to appear in the first or second month of life. Hemangiomas tend to enlarge diffusely and sometimes rapidly. With large or multiple hemangiomas it must be considered clinically that one or more additional hemangiomas may be present in some internal structure. They should be noted for size and shape.

Management The hemangiomas may reach their maximum size in a few months and slowly start to shrink sometime between 6 and

18 months. For very large ones the process may take 5 years or longer. Referral to the appropriate specialist is recommended if the hemangioma interferes with normal bodily function.

JAUNDICE

Assessment Jaundice is a deposit, in the skin, of unconjugated bilirubin which has built up in the bloodstream. The skin color may range from yellow to orange to sometimes greenish tones.

Management See Chapter 19, Dermal Icterus Index and Jaundice in the Newborn.

LANUGO DISTRIBUTION

Assessment This is the first fine hair to cover the body during fetal life. It is usually found over the shoulders, back, and sacral areas. This hair generally disappears before or shortly after birth and is first lost from the face and anterior trunk, although at term it may still be present over the shoulders. Lanugo is prominent in Mexican-American infants, in whom it may be abundant over the shoulders, arms, and face at term.

Management Parents may need reassurance that it will soon disappear.

LARYNGEAL STRIDOR (CROWING)

Assessment Congenital laryngeal stridor is a noisy, crowing respiratory sound. Common in the neonatal period and during the first year of life, it may be caused by a "flabby" epiglottis. The condition is seldom serious, and the symptoms become less severe, generally disappearing by 1 year.

Management Severe crowing with dyspnea and inspiratory retractions should be further assessed for malformations of the larynx.

MILIA

Assessment These are white pinpoint-size lesions usually found over the bridge of the nose, the chin, or the cheeks. They are caused by retained sebum generally disappearing after the first few weeks of life.

Management No treatment is necessary.

MOLDING (FACIAL ASYMMETRY)

Assessment This is a result of overriding of the sutures at birth due to intrauterine molding or molding during delivery because the bones are soft and pliable. Flattening of part of the head or face may occur in an infant who lies in only one position or who has unusually soft bones. If present at birth, it generally disappears in a few days.

Management If the flattened occiput is due to a static position in the crib, it is recommended that the infant's position in the crib be reversed daily. The infant will turn toward the light, thereby giving equal pressure to the bones on both sides of the head.

MONGOLIAN SPOTS AND OTHER BLUE NEVI

Assessment These are massive aggregations of melanin-rich dark cells that give the affected area a purple-black or blue-black color. There are usually found over the sacrum and coccygeal area of over 50 percent of the newborns of Black, Chicano, and Asiatic-Indian origin. They have no clinical significance. They are distributed though the deep layers of the skin tissues and cannot be disposed of by radiotherapy, freezing, or chemical caustics. They are not malignant. Most disappear with time.

Management Nevi may be distinguished from ecchymosis by their distribution. They may be concealed by cosmetic covering later in life if desired.

MOTTLING

Assessment This is an overall red and white coloration of the skin that generally occurs in fair children who are chilled.

Management No treatment is necessary.

PETECHIAE

Assessment These are tiny, reddish-purple, sharply circumscribed lesions found in the superficial layer of the epidermis. They may be caused by birth injury or can be a sign of severe systemic disease such as sepsis, erythroblastosis fetalis, hemorrhagic disease, thrombocytopenic purpura, or meningococcemia.

Management Petechiae should be assessed immediately for a cause, as mentioned above.

PSEUDOSTRABISMUS

Assessment This is caused by the epicanthal folds (vertical folds of the skin covering the inner canthus of the eye) that make the eye appear "crossed."

Management True strabismus is ruled out with the Hirschberg's light reflex test. The beam of light should normally be reflected in the same position in each eye. See Chapter 15, Pseudostrabismus.

PTOSIS

Assessment This condition is drooping of the upper eyelid usually attributable to a congenital underdevelopment of the lid muscles. It may also be an acquired deformity. If acquired, it may be due to an interference with the cranial nerve as a result of meningitis or encephalitis.

Management Acquired ptosis needs immediate assessment and referral to the appropriate clinic or physician. See Chapter 15, Ptosis.

QUIVERING CHIN

Assessment This is a nonspecific response of the central nervous system after a difficult birth or as a concomitant manifestation of various perinatal problems. In the absence of additional factors, the tremor may be regarded as insignificant.

Management No treatment is necessary.

SCLERAL HEMORRHAGES

Assessment These are slight hemorrhages that are noted on the sclerae, sometimes occurring as a result of a difficult delivery. These hemorrhages are usually of no clinical significance and disappear within a few weeks after delivery.

Management They should be noted on the record and followed until they resolve.

"SETTING-SUN SIGN"

Assessment In this condition the sclerae are exposed above the iris when the eyes are open normally. It can be normal in full-term infants and in many premature infants but may also be found in association with an enlarging head circumference (e.g., hydrocephalus).

Management It should be noted and followed along with careful measurements of head size. The value of the phenomenon in early diagnosis of hydrocephalus is limited because clear clinical signs of intracranial hypertension would have already appeared before the onset of the phenomenon (McMillan et al., 1977, p. 326).

"SNORTING"

Assessment This is a nasal sound made by some infants on respiration. It has no significance and may be attributable simply to thickened nasal mucus.

Management Parents need reassurance, since they may fear that the infant is having difficulty breathing.

SUCKING TUBERCLE

Assessment This may be found in the middle of the upper lip of some infants whether they are bottle- or breast-fed. It is caused by friction and strength of sucking. It appears as small blisters, broken skin, or as a small callus.

Management No treatment is necessary. It will heal spontaneously after weaning.

SUTURES

Assessment The cranium is composed of eight bones joined together by immovable sutures which are spaces between the skull bones. The coronal suture extends from ear to ear across the top of the skull. The sagittal suture divides the parietal bones running at right angles to the coronal suture. The lambdoidal suture separates the parietal bones from the occipital bones. Sutures are frequently palpable at birth and are felt as prominent ridges from the overriding of their edges during the birth process.

Management Sutures generally flatten by 6 months of age. See this chapter, Molding and Fontanels.

SWEATING

Assessment In infants, sweating normally begins after 1 month of age. Under 1 year of age and under normal circumstances sweating may be profuse and is usually due to exercise, crying, eating, or an overly warm atmosphere. See this chapter, Body Temperature Control, and Chapter 18, Signs and Symptoms of Congestive Heart Failure.

Management This is accomplished by changing the atmosphere.

TELANGIECTASIAS (CAPILLARY HEMANGIOMAS, NEVUS FLAMMEUS, PORT-WINE STAIN)

Assessment These are irregular, blotchy, pink capillary lesions of the skin. They may be superficially or deeply involved in the dermis. They are found frequently at the back of the neck, the base of the neck, the base of the nose, the center of the forehead, and on the eyelids. They tend to disappear by 2 years of age after gradually fading.

Management Parents need reassurance and support.

UMBILICAL GRANULOMA

Assessment This is umbilical tissue that persists after the cord has dried and fallen off. It is sometimes white and glistening, or it may be pink to red.

Management   Umbilical granulomas can be removed by an application of silver nitrate followed by a wash of normal saline solution. Large ones with peduncles may be tied off.

UMBILICAL HERNIA

Assessment   This is seen as an opening of the aponeurosis of the obliquus externus abdominis muscle felt under the skin at the umbilical area. The size should be judged by the actual palpated opening. Most hernias decrease by the end of the first year; referral should be made if it has not decreased by the fourth or fifth year.

Management   Explanations to the parents of the cause and aiding them in palpation of the opening are necessary. The size of the hernia is not judged by its appearance when the infant cries. A coin should not be taped to the abdomen, since it may interfere with the closure and cause maceration of the skin.

VAGINAL DISCHARGE

Assessment   A bloody discharge called pseudomenstruation may be attributed to absorption of maternal hormones. This is not usually observed beyond the first month of age. White mucous discharge is a normal discharge. Yellow mucous discharge is an indication of a pathologic condition.

Management   Assessment should be made for the cause if the discharge is yellow.

VERNIX CASEOSA

Assessment   This is a cheesy, white material covering the entire body of the newborn, sometimes occurring only in the skin folds or nail beds. Yellow discoloration of the vernix is an indication of intrauterine distress, postmaturity, or hemolytic disease of the newborn, and occasionally is seen in infants born of breech presentation.

Management   Normal vernix is presently left on the skin for protection. Yellow vernix should be further assessed.

Prematurity

ASSESSMENT

History A complete prenatal and natal history is taken, including length of time the infant spent in the hospital, how the family managed, how the baby was fed, and all treatments and medications received.

Definitions There are several designations for infants based on gestation and weight:

1. *Premature* (preterm) infant is one born before the end of the thirty-seventh week of gestation, regardless of birth weight. The majority of infants who weigh less than 2,500 gm (5 lb 8 oz), and almost all infants below 500 gm are prematurely born.
2. *Term* infant is one born between the beginning of the thirty-eighth week and the completion of the forty-first week.
3. *Postmature* infant is one born at the onset of the forty-second week or any time thereafter.
4. *Low-birth-weight* (LBW) infants are designated as follows:
   • Infants whose rates of intrauterine growth are normal at birth, even though they are small because they are delivered before the end of the thirty-seventh week, are termed *appropriately grown for gestational age* (AGA).
   • Infants whose rates of intrauterine growth are slow, who are delivered at or later than term, and are small are termed *small-for-dates* or *small for gestational age* (SGA).
   • Infants whose rates of growth in utero are retarded, and who, in addition, are delivered prematurely are termed *small-for-dates* and *premature*.
5. *High-birth-weight* infant. An infant who weighs 4,000 gm or more is considered a high-birth-weight. Infants are considered *large for gestational age* (LGA) at any weight when they fall above the ninetieth percentile on the intrauterine growth curves.

Determination of Gestational Age Methods of eliciting this information are listed below:

History of pregnancy. Count the weeks elapsed from the first day of the last menstrual period (LMP). This is valid in 75 to 85 percent of clients. First maternal perception of fetal heartbeat is at approximately 20 weeks; first perception of fetal movement is approximately 16 weeks.

Prenatal tests. Analysis of the amniotic fluid may determine, among other things bilirubin levels, creatinine levels, and the lecithin:sphingomyelin ratio, which is helpful in determining gestational age. Also used is cellular examination for fat-laden cells.

Postnatal examination. Clinical assessment of gestational age (Dubowitz scale) is commonly used. See this chapter, Clinical Assessment of Gestational Age.

Factors Disposing to Prematurity   These factors are as follows:

• Chronic hypertensive disease
• Toxemia
• Placenta previa
• Abruptio placenta
• Cervical incompetence
• Low socioeconomic status, including poor nutrition, chronic infection, fatigue, and generally poor personal and environmental hygiene
• Absence of prenatal care
• Multiple pregnancies
• History of previous premature delivery
• Age (highest incidence is age under 20)
• Order of birth (highest incidence is in first pregnancies)

Mortality and Morbidity   Eighty to 90 percent of prematures are at risk in the first year due to anorexia, birth injuries, hyaline membrane disease, bronchopneumonia, septicemia, and other infections. Because of improved methods of delivering intensive care the survival rate for infants over 2000 gm is 95 percent, for infants weighing 1,500 to 2,000 gm it is 70 percent, and for infants 1,000 to 1,500 gm it is 60 percent. For infants weighing less than 1,000 gm the outlook is not good.

Principal causes of morbidity include hemorrhage, kernicterus, retrolental fibroplasia, anemia, and infection.

MANAGEMENT

The management of prematures is directed at problems that may have been associated with the prematurity, at working with the family to improve relationships if necessary, and at gaining an awareness of the developmental and other factors associated with prematurity.

Temperature Control in Prematurity Premature infants weighing more than 1,000 gm are kept at an optimal incubator temperature that will maintain an axillary temperature of the infant at approximately 36°C (96.8°F). This is usually an air temperature of approximately 31.7°C (89°F). Humidity is maintained between 60 and 70 percent. If an incubator is not available, these conditions of temperature and humidity can be attained by the use of blankets and warm water bottles and by controlling the temperature and humidity of the room (see Chapter 17, Humidification). Prematures can be moved to areas of less heat and humidity only when the gradual change to the new environment is not accompanied by a significant change of temperature, color, or activity. The removal may be only a day or two after birth for some infants or at more than a month of age for the less mature ones. Small-for-gestational-age (SGA) infants with less subcutaneous fat should be kept warmer than larger infants. (See this chapter, Body Temperature Control.)

Follow-up Care For the infant close to 2,500 gm (5 lb 8 oz) who will leave the hospital 5 to 6 days postnatally, the weight should be checked weekly or biweekly for assurance of gain, and the family should be in close contact with the care facility for the first month. This infant's care should not be different from that of a full-term infant. It is preferred that no special attention be given to the prematurity.

Infants of lower birth weight and who have had prolonged illnesses with hospitalization need these extra attentions in follow-up care:

1. More frequent visits are necessary for careful physical and neurologic assessment and follow-up of earlier problems.

2. Length, weight, and head circumference are taken at each visit. Deviations and lags are observed and recorded.
3. Developmental screening tests are done at routine times. Determining the developmental level of the infant is done by subtracting the number of weeks of prematurity from the infant's chronologic age.
4. Added help is offered with nutrition. See Chapter 3, Nutritional Needs of Low-Birth-Weight Infants. Breast feeding is important for its special nutritional and immunologic factors and its effects on maternal-infant relationships. See this chapter, Nursing Premature Infant.
5. The treatment of the skin of the premature does not differ essentially from that of the mature infant. Maceration is the most common factor which may cause disruption of the protective barrier of the stratum corneum. Sometimes there is depigmentation following as simple a procedure as applying or removing adhesive tape. Explanations to the parents should be made to reassure them that the marks will disappear in time.
6. The environment of the premature may need to be considered. Because of their lack of adipose tissue, prematures need to be kept warmer until weight has been restored to normal levels. See above, Temperature Control in Prematurity. These infants may also enjoy a bright, noisy environment for a time following lengthy hospitalization, particularly if most of the time was spent in the intensive care nursery.
7. Incidence of illnesses should be discussed. Because gamma globulin levels are lower, the resistance to upper respiratory infections and diarrhea is low. Although they may go out, infants should be kept away from large groups or from persons with obvious infections. Colic may appear when the infant has reached an age approximately 2 weeks beyond the expected date of delivery.

Referrals   These should be made at appropriate times for the following reasons:

1. A circumcision that may have been deferred at birth may need to be scheduled.

2. Early dental assessment may be required. Stimmler (1973) suggests that structural defects occur in the primary dentition of all children who have suffered from low calcium levels for even a few days. It occurs 12 months after the appearance of the teeth as enamel hyperplasia.
3. Hearing assessment may be necessary. Causes of hearing loss in the premature may occur from incubator noises, high bilirubin levels, or from drugs such as kanamycin, gentamicin sulfate, and furosemide.
4. Ophthalmologic examination is done before the infant leaves the hospital and again at 4 to 6 months by an ophthalmologist to rule out retrolental fibroplasia. Early signs may be observed at this time.

Counseling This includes offering support and reassurance to the family that their child is normal. The parents should be given opportunities to express their feelings and attention should be given the following:

1. Mother–infant relationship. Early separation interferes with the development of normal mothering skills, attitudes, and relationships. Mothers need to be taught that this lack of response is not a reflection of poor mothering so future relationships between mother and infant are not jeopardized. See Chapter 4, Assessment of Parent–Child Interaction.
2. "Prematurity neuroses." Parents need to be cautioned against overprotectiveness of the premature. Brown and Bakeman (1977) suggest that mothers of prematures compensate for the inactivity of their infants and continue to do so even when this is no longer adaptive, and that prematures, therefore, have less opportunity to regulate their own activity patterns. The overprotective feeling may also be fostered by the excessive cautionary advice given the parents by medical personnel.
3. Community resources. The local community should be assessed for sources available to aid the family such as house-keeping help, visiting nurses, developmental disabilities agency, hearing and vision screening, La Leche League, another family with a premature infant as a role model or even a "premature club."

GROWTH AND DEVELOPMENT IN INFANCY

To prepare parents for their role, nurse practitioners must be empathetic to the problems of parenting. Caretakers and parents must understand the vital importance of promoting a philosophy of child care that follows closely the child's physical and psychologic growth. The ultimate aim is to achieve security and independence commensurate with the child's level of development. In this section are listed factors affecting psychologic growth of the infant, including the needs of the parents and the child, the different temperaments of children with implications for child care, and a variety of developmental sequences and behaviors.

Factors Affecting the Psychologic Growth of the Infant

These are instinctive needs upon which the child's subsequent emotional and social adjustments are based. The infant whose psychologic needs are not fulfilled is definitely handicapped in personality growth and in early capacity to trust and to respond to others. The denial of fulfillment of their needs causes some children to develop such common problems as excessive thumbsucking, head banging, and other forms of tensional outlet. In severe cases of unfulfilled needs, marasmus can occur, which exhibits as "wasting away," infantile atrophy, or debility.

IMPORTANT EARLY NEEDS

Early mothering and sucking are the most important needs of the newborn, followed by the needs of feeding, sleeping, and help in the development of specific skills.

Early Mothering Infants need a strong attachment to one person who can be trusted to answer their cries and to give them a feeling of security, of well-being, and of being loved and cared for. This is a continuance of the closeness of the prenatal state with the additional factor of touch or positive contact. The more nearly it imitates the condition before birth the more successful it is. The infant needs periods of close contact with the mother that include being held, rocked, and carried about; being sung and spoken to;

and being fondled and caressed. From being held and allowed to suck freely and frequently, the infant receives reflex stimulation, which primes breathing mechanisms into action and which finally enables the whole respiratory process to become organized under the control of the nervous system.

MOTHERING ATTITUDE A positive attitude of mothering is extremely important. Early mothering needs are best met by a parent without hesitation, without a feeling of duty, without a feeling of sacrifice. The mother (or mother figure) should have a feeling of following her maternal instincts, of being good to herself, and of caring for her "inner child." These feelings bolster the positive attitude, creating a "positive atmosphere or aura" for the infant, the benefits of which will last throughout the child's lifetime. To accomplish this for her child the young mother needs help, support, and understanding from her husband, her family, her friends, and from the primary health care provider. She needs space and time from normal activities to accomplish her goals. That is, she should be free from household duties or other commitments as much as possible in the first month. The parents need to reach a mutually agreed on and compatible philosophy of childrearing to help the mother with her early tasks.

Sucking Need The mouth is the center of the child's universe, the avenue through which hunger and thirst are assuaged. Babies feel with their mouths. The mouth is fundamentally an organ of touch. In the first 6 months sucking is the most satisfying absorbing activity performed by the infant. It assists the infant to breathe, and it increases the amount of blood sent to the brain probably contributing to its development. Tension, which is very evident in early infancy (a fact not well understood), can be relieved by sucking and comfort is restored. Satisfying this need does not develop a dependency, rather, denying this need may contribute to its continuous occurrence in later years, such as thumbsucking beyond the age of 3 or 4 years.

AMOUNT OF SUCKING Infants need a minimum of 2 hours a day, including feeding time, for oral exercise. More time is needed by immature or premature infants. Sucking needs are fulfilled by breast feeding, bottle feeding, and by allowing the infant to suck on a pacifier, which may be held in the infant's mouth if necessary. See this chapter, Use of the Pacifier. Some infants are able to suck their thumbs at birth, but most infants cannot until approximately 3 months of age.

LESSENING OF THE SUCKING NEED Sucking reaches a maximum intensity about the fourth month and, if it has been fully exercised and the child has received good early mothering, the urgency tends to diminish as the child begins to vocalize, to bite, and to grasp. (Parents can look for cues at this time for eliminating the use of the pacifier.)

Overfeeding can develop as a result of misinterpretation of the infant's needs. When infants cry they may be signaling a need to suck separate from a need to eat. For information regarding the needs of feeding, see this chapter, Feeding in Infancy.

Child's Self-esteem The child's self-image is critical to future development. To assure a child's self-esteem, several needs should be met:

1. Thoughtful and adaptive care. Praise, reassurance, companionship, and intellectual stimulation are essential.
2. Consistent and fair treatment.
3. Rights as an individual and acknowledgment as a member of the family.
4. Management from a base of affection and intelligent concern. Limits set by the parents should be reasonable and consistent.
5. A feeling of protection from external dangers as well as from the child's own impulses.

NEEDS OF THE PARENTS

How parents feel about themselves is probably the most important determinant of their child's maturation and development. Certain basics are intrinsic to feeling "good":

1. Understanding themselves better to develop a healthy self-image that will aid them in raising their children
2. Examining their feelings and expectations of parenthood, of each other as parents, and of their child's behavior
3. Being allowed to develop as parents

4. Having their concerns recognized and being given attentive and considerate professional care
5. Understanding the differences in children
6. Appreciating that they haven't necessarily been wrong in their treatment of childrearing
7. Understanding developmental stages of infancy and childhood for better understanding of the underlying causes of problems (see Table 5-19).
8. Establishing mutual agreement on methods of childrearing and on the handling of problems.

INDIVIDUAL CHARACTERISTICS OF THE FAMILY

The environment helps determine the infant's psychologic growth. The characteristics of the family determine the environment. Important among these characteristics are the following:

1. Structure of the family, sex of the child, and whether the child is an only child, a twin, a stepchild, an adopted child, or an illegitimate child
2. Size of the family, presence of relatives in the home, established values and customs, race, and nationality.
3. Whether a child is quick or slow to learn and whether the child is physically healthy or unhealthy
4. Socioeconomic position of the family
5. Marital situation in the home
6. Expectations of the child's behavior by the parents
7. Degree of knowledge of child development by the parents

DIFFERENCES IN TEMPERAMENT AND PERSONALITY

The term temperament designates the behavioral style of the individual irrespective of the content, level of ability, or motivation of the particular activity. The child's temperament influences the behavior and attitudes of peers, siblings, parents, and teachers. In the first few months of life the basic foundation of a child's personality and temperament is being formed. During this time newborns have quick changes of moods; their behavior is fragmented. Each child has a different personality and temperament, and parents

Table 5-19

Tool for Teaching Parents Basic Developmental Concepts and Appropriate Parenting

Age	Stage of Development	Behavior	Methods of Handling Behavior
Birth to 18 months	Basic trust vs. basic mistrust Relationship with mother emphasized Understands own needs Characterized by dependency and a need for consistency	Dependent Cries when mother leaves Demands attention Learns to feel secure Displays needs emotionally Fussy Impatient Won't entertain self Hasn't learned concept of discipline	If you know child is safe, it doesn't hurt him or her to cry Mother needs to teach some separation Meet infant's basic needs Use television for stimulation and/or consolation but not to replace mom Introduce infants to others Spend time with infant, hold, cuddle
18 months to 3 years	Autonomy vs. shame and doubt Learns individualization Begins potty training (muscle development should be adequate) Feels separate and apart from mother Tests limits, forces issue of discipline	Puts everything in mouth Exhibits potty-training problems Says "No!" constantly Has tantrums, expressing anger Not able to verbalize Knows when taking advantage of parent, really wants limits Pulls out furniture drawers and explodes	Try not to make potty training a forced issue Check own reactions to messes Set limits and be consistent For safety put locks on doors Training takes persistent efforts for a period of time Consider permissive vs. strict discipline Isolate child in room as method of handling behavior

Age	Developmental stage	Behaviors	Parenting suggestions
3 years to 6 years	Initiative vs. guilt Learning acceptable behavior Learns concept of discipline Exhibits closeness to parent of opposite sex Organizes activities on own	Blames mistake and misbehavior on others Lies to cover mistakes Has imaginary friends Developing vocabulary, sassy Ask questions about sex	Teach that it is okay to make a mistake Differentiate between fantasy and lying Check parent reaction to language and responses Try to identify imaginary "friend" and need for one Answer questions simply to meet needs Have the punishment fit the crime
6 years to 11 years	Industry vs. inferiority Attends school Reaches plateau period of learning personality Develops interests and explores hobbies Develops ego	Views peer group as important Catches self and changes behavior to "yes" instead of "no" behavior (good) Finds things out for self Asks "why?"	Child needs to have efforts noticed and praised Parent, as teacher, is very important If you don't know, say so Give the child responsibility Show acceptance of child at home Show interest in child's hobbies

Source: Reproduced with permission from McAbee, R. "Rural Parenting Classes: Beginning to Meet the Need," *Amer J Mat Child Nurs*, 2:315–319, Sept/Oct. 1977.

need to be aware of the differences as part of understanding the child's behavior. Thomas et al. (1977) in a study of different personalities found that children show distinct individuality of temperament in the first weeks of life independent of the parent's handling or personality style. The environment heightens, diminishes, or modifies behavior, but the basic temperament is the child's own. The provider of care who fails to acquire a working knowledge of infant temperament is apt to make important errors in judgment about their clients and their handling.

"Easy" Children   Forty percent of the children studied by Thomas et al. (1977) were termed "easy," exhibiting these characteristics:

1. Positiveness of mood
2. Regularity of body functions
3. Low or moderate intensity of reaction, adaptability, and positiveness in a new situation

"Slow-to-Warm-Up" Children   This category included 15 percent of the children studied, who were characterized by the following:

1. Low activity level
2. A tendency to withdraw on first exposure to new stimuli
3. Slow adaptability
4. Somewhat negative mood
5. A low intensity of reaction to situations

"Difficult" Children   This category included 10 percent of the children studied, who were characterized by the following:

1. Irregularity in body functions
2. Intensity in reactions
3. Withdrawal in the face of new stimuli
4. Slow adaptation to change in the environment
5. Negative mood.

Thirty-five percent of the children showed a mixture of traits.

Applications to Child Care   Using these criteria, parents can be taught to provide child care that includes these objectives:

- To respond flexibly to the individual requirements of each child
- To view their children with more objectivity
- To provide firm, steady, and consistent care
- To create a positive, relaxed atmosphere in which the child may grow
- To understand that certain features of their child's development and actions are not the result of something they did or did not do
- To learn to emphasize the positive aspects of their child's temperament

See also this chapter, Carey Infant Temperament Questionnaire.

Specific Developmental Areas of Infancy and Childhood

Listed below are various developmental sequences and behaviors that may be found in this chapter and in other chapters:

- Emotional, intellectual, and mental developments of infancy (See this chapter, A Comprehensive Schedule for Well-Child Care, Waechter's Developmental Guide, Tables 5-2, 5-4, 5-6, 5-8, 5-10, and 5-12.)
- Bladder capacity (See Chapter 21, Bladder Capacity.)
- Eye development (See Chapter 15, Table 15-1, Chronology of Ophthalmic Development.)
- Feeding development (See this chapter, Developmental Sequence of Feeding Behaviors, and Table 5-21, Developmental Stages of Readiness to Progress in Feeding Behaviors.)
- Hearing development (See Chapter 25, Development of Hearing Responses.)
- Language development (See Chapter 25, Development of Language.)
- Infant reflexes (See Chapter 24, Table 24-2, Infant Reflexes.)
- Psychologic development (See this chapter, Factors Affecting the Psychologic Growth of the Infant, and Chapter 6, Development of Aggression, Building Self-Confidence, and The Child's Growing Ego.)
- Sexual development (See Table 5-20, Chronological Develop-

Table 5-20

Chronological Development of the Child's Sexual Needs and
Interests from Birth Through 6 years

Age	Behavior and Attitudes
0–1	Finds touch and oral stimulation a source of gratification When clothes are off, handles genitals
1½–2½	May be unable to function in strange bathrooms Kisses at bedtime Is conscious of own sexual organs and may handle them Shows interest in watching others in bathroom or when they are undressed Distinguishes boys and girls by different postures when urinating, does not verbalize this Shows beginning of interest in physiological differences between sexes Inquires about mother's breasts Notices but does not verbalize that boys and fathers have a distinctive genital and that girls and mothers do not
3–4	Verbally expresses interest in physiologic differences in sexes and in different postures for urinating; girls make one or two experimental attempts to urinate while standing up Exhibits desire to look at or touch certain parts of adults' bodies, especially women's breasts Expresses general interest in babies, what they can do, where they come from, where they are before they are born May not understand that babies grow inside the mother's body May expose genitals or urinate in public Shows interest in other people's bathrooms, demands privacy for self but is extremely interested in bathroom activities of others Questions how baby gets out of mother, may spontaneously think that it is born through the navel
5–6	Shows decreasing interest in sex differences Questions how baby gets in and out of mother's body Demonstrates interest in parents' babyhood, in having a baby brother or sister, in having a baby oneself when one grows up (boys and girls) Asks questions about testicles (boys) Asks factual questions about having a baby, such as "Does it hurt?" May be beginning to show interest in the part the father plays in reproduction.

Source: Adapted from *Infant and Child in the Culture of Today,* Arnold Gesell, Frances L. Ilg, Louise B. Ames. New York: Harper & Row, 1974. Copyright 1974, Gesell Institute of Child Development. Reprinted by permission of Harper & Row.

ment of the Child's Sexual Needs and Interests from Birth through 6 Years.)
- Sleep patterns (See Table 5-18, Normal Sleep Patterns.)
- Stomach capacity (See Chapter 3, Solid Foods, Serving Sizes.)
- Stool patterns (See this chapter, Stool Patterns in Infancy.)
- Tooth development (See Chapter 16, Tooth Development and Table 16-1, Eruption and Shedding of Deciduous Teeth.)

STOOL PATTERNS OF INFANCY

These are generally as follows:

Breast-fed Infant   This infant has many stools per day (sometimes one after each feeding) in the first month or two progressing to one stool a day or even many days (4 or 5 days) in the later months before solid foods are introduced to the diet. The stool resembles pale, yellow curds unless iron is given which makes the stool darker. It is watery and it is explosive in nature; there is no unpleasant odor. A green stool in the neonate who is not taking iron may denote that the infant is not receiving enough milk.

Bottle-fed Infant   This infant has two to four stools per day in the first month progressing to one to three stools or less per day in the later months. The color may be varied shades of green, brown, or yellow depending on the formula and on whether iron or solid food are taken. The color is not important in a well child. The stool is soft and may have an unpleasant odor.

BODY TEMPERATURE CONTROL

This is a function of heat production and of heat loss. Heat production in the newborn is unreliable. The demands of relatively great surface area, the immaturity of sweating and shivering mechanisms (lack of development of the heat-regulating center in the diencephalon), the probable disadvantages of delicate skin, and meager subcutaneous fat are all handicaps to controlling both rate and amount of heat loss.

Shivering and Body Activity   These tend to increase heat production. Vasoconstriction of the surface vessels tends to conserve heat, and perspiration and surface vasodilation tend to reverse the action by disseminating heat.

Maintenance of Normal Body Temperature   A normal infant's temperature should be 36.4° to 37°C (97.5° to 98.6°F). Axillary temperature is 96° to 99°F. The room temperature should be maintained at 74° to 76°F for the newborn. Body heat can be maintained with the swaddling of one soft blanket. Although care should be taken to avoid chilling and a subsequent drop in body temperature, it is now suggested that infants who are protected from chilling at all times may be less able to respond to cold stress later. For normal temperature range see Chapter 11, Fever.

FEEDING IN INFANCY

A positive feeding interaction between a parent and child establishes the basis for a warm, trusting bond. Early parental education and guidance fosters successful feeding experiences and prevents feeding problems. The role of the nurse practitioner is to provide parental guidance in early feeding techniques, to help parents establish adequate nutritional practices for the child's later growth and development and to understand their own attitudes, feelings, and expectations around feeding, and to encourage parental problem solving when feeding questions arise.

Implicit in these roles is the need for regular consultations with parents to assess continuing problems, to offer psychologic support and to instill confidence in the parents' ability to feed their child. For additional information, see Chapter 3, Nutrition During Lactation, Infant Nutrition, Formulas and Milk, Iron Supplementation in Infancy, Table 3-8, Solid Foods, Nutritional Needs of the Low-Birth-Weight Infant, Overfeeding in Infancy, and Food Allergies, and Chapter 16, Methods of Fluoride Supplementation.

Development of Infant Feeding Behavior

Feeding behavior is a function of motor development. For example, the child's ability to suck, chew, and swallow is determined by the acquisition of fine, gross, and oral motor skills. The child's ability to self-feed depends on the motor development of the trunk, arms, and hands. See Table 5-21.

DEVELOPMENTAL SEQUENCE OF FEEDING BEHAVIORS

Feeding behaviors are as follows:

- *Birth to 4 weeks:* The rooting and sucking reflexes are present. The tongue moves in an up-and-down motion.
- *10 weeks:* The child recognizes the bottle or breast as the food source.
- *16 weeks:* Maturation of the sucking pattern with the tongue moving back and forth occurs. The infant shows ability to draw in lower lip as spoon is removed making spoon feeding easier, as well as ability to clasp hands on the bottle
- *24 to 28 weeks:* Beginning of chewing movements and up-and-down jaw movements is shown. This is a critical or sensitive period for learning to eat solids (Illingworth, 1964). Readiness to finger feed is indicated by ability to grasp objects, to put them into the mouth, and to maintain a sitting posture, ability to grasp objects with palm of hand. Ability to obtain the bottle in a sitting posture is shown. Messiness and spilling may conflict with parent's interest. Awareness of the cup is shown.
- *28 to 32 weeks:* Maturation of the tongue is more sophisticated in regard to spoon feeding than drinking from a cup. The infant shows ability to sit alone without support, to reach and grasp objects, and to use fingers to transfer items from one hand to another. Around 32 weeks infant shows ability to bring head forward to receive spoon as it is presented and increased mobility of the tongue allowing increased manipulation of food in mouth before swallowing.
- *36 to 48 weeks:* Further development of the pincer grasp is seen. The infant has ability to manage bottle alone and to rescue it if it gets lost. By 48 weeks, the pattern of eating changes from sucking to beginning rotary chewing movements. There is also a beginning ability to self-feed. Greater tongue mobility allows true drinking action from cup as opposed to sucking action.
- *15 months:* Ability to use spoon is poor due to lack of wrist con-

Table 5-21

Developmental Stages of Readiness to Progress in Feeding Behaviors

Developmental Landmarks	Change Indicated	Examples of Appropriate Foods
Tongue laterally transfers food in the mouth Voluntary and independent movements of the tongue and lips Sitting posture can be sustained Beginning of chewing movements (up and down movements of the jaw)	Introduction of soft, mashed table food	Tuna fish; mashed potatoes; well-cooked mashed vegetables; ground meats in gravy and sauces; soft diced fruit such as bananas, peaches, pears; liverwurst; flavored yogurt
Reaches for and grasps objects with scissor grasp Brings hand to mouth	Finger feeding (large pieces of food)	Oven-dried toast, teething biscuits, cheese sticks, peeled Vienna sausage (food should be soluble in the mouth to prevent choking)
Voluntary release (refined digital grasp) Rotary chewing pattern	Finger feeding of smaller pieces of food Introduction of more textured food from family menu	Bits of cottage cheese, dry cereal, peas, small pieces of meat Well-cooked chopped meats and casseroles, cooked vegetables and canned fruit (not mashed), toast, potatoes, macaroni, spaghetti, peeled ripe fruit

Approximates lips to rim of the cup	Introduction of cup	Food that when scooped will adhere to the spoon, such as applesauce, cooked cereal, mashed potato, cottage cheese
Understands relationship of container and contained	Beginning self-feeding (messiness should be expected)	
Increased rotary movements of the jaw	More skilled at cup and spoon feeding	Chopped fibrous meats such as roast and steak
Ulnar deviation of wrist develops		Gradually introduce raw vegetables and fruit
Walks alone	May seek food and get food independently	Food of high nutrient value should be available
Names food, expresses preferences; prefers unmixed foods		Balanced food intake should be offered and child should be permitted to develop food preferences without concern that they will last forever
Goes on food jags		
Appetite appears to decrease		

Source: Reproduced with permission from P. L. Pipes, *Nutrition in Infancy and Childhood*, (St. Louis: C. V. Mosby, 1977).

trol. Ability to manage cup is still difficult, often tilting cup too rapidly.

- *16 to 17 months:* Ulnar deviation of wrist allows the child to use spoon more effectively and to minimize spilling.
- *18 months:* Ability to lift elbow as spoon is raised and to flex wrist as the spoon reaches the mouth results in only moderate spilling.
- *18 to 24 months:* Ability to tilt cup with finger manipulation is shown. By 24 months, refinement of rotary chewing movements is achieved.

Table 5-21 summarizes the important developmental landmarks and suggests food for appropriate changes in feeding behavior.

BREAST FEEDING

Anatomy and Physiology of the Breast

The breast is composed of approximately 15 to 20 milk-producing glands called milk lobes. Each lobe is divided into lobules that contain alveoli. The alveoli are the basic organs of milk production and excretion. They contain the secretory cells which produce the milk, a cavity that collects the milk, and contractile myoepithelial cells that expel milk from the cavity. The milk is expelled into the ductile system (lacteriferous ducts), which takes it to the lacteriferous sinus or reservoir and through the nipple to the infant.

The nursing infant causes stimulation of afferent nerves in the nipple to stimulate the anterior pituitary to release prolactin hormone which causes the secretory cells of the alveoli to initiate milk production. The posterior pituitary releases oxytocin, a hormone that causes milk to be released from the alveoli into the lacteriferous ducts.

MECHANISM OF DRUG EXCRETION

The excretion of drugs is dependent on the following physiochemical characteristics:

- pH gradient between plasma and milk

- pK_a or degree of ionization of the drug (Generally basic drugs are excreted in higher concentrations in milk, and acidic drugs are excreted in lower concentrations.)
- Lipid–water solubility of the drug
- Distribution of the drug by body transport mechanisms
- Concentration gradient of diffusable drug between plasma and milk (The more easily a drug can be dialyzed, the greater the concentration it will achieve in breast milk.)

Any drug taken orally or administered parenterally and absorbed by the mother will be excreted in her milk. Most drugs achieve insufficient concentration in the milk, but some drugs can achieve high concentrations. Nursing mothers should take medications 15 minutes after nursing or 3 to 4 hours before the next feeding. This allows enough time for most medications to be cleared from the maternal serum and to achieve a relatively low milk concentration. Medications taken 30 to 60 minutes before breast feeding usually achieve peak serum milk concentrations.

The reader is referred to the reference section of this chapter and the following authors: Anderson, Herfindal, Lawrence, and O'Brien, for information concerning specific medications excreted in breast milk and their effect on the nursing infant.

ADVANTAGES OF BREAST FEEDING

Protective Benefits Human colostrum and breast milk contain macrophages that phagocytose microorganisms and kill bacteria. T and B cell lymphocytes are also present in human milk. They react to microorganisms invading the gastrointestinal tract. All classes of immunoglobulins are found in human milk, the highest concentration in the colostrum. Secretory IgA is the most significant and it is thought to protect the gastrointestinal tract against infections. The intestines of breast-fed infants are colonized by *Lactobacillus bifidus*. This is a gram-positive, nonmotile, anaerobic bacillus that helps protect the infant from diarrhea. Human milk contains lysozyme, an antimicrobial enzyme that is bacteriostatic against gram-positive bacteria. Lactoferrin, an iron-binding glycoprotein, is found in colostrum and breast milk. It is bacteriostatic and deprives *Escherichia coli, Staphylococci,* and *Candida albicans* of iron for growth. Breast milk is also thought to contain interferon, an antiviral substance.

Nutritional Benefits Breast milk supplies adequate nutrition for full term infants, in amounts suitable for their needs. However, there is controversy over whether breast milk should be supplemented with vitamin D and fluoride. Rickets have occurred in breast-fed children who have received no vitamin D supplementation and who have had no exposure to sunlight. Rickets in breast-fed children exposed to sunlight is unknown. The American Academy of Pediatrics recommends vitamin D supplementation. In clinical practice it is generally thought that if the infant is exposed routinely to sunlight, there is no need for vitamin D supplementation. However, Fomon et al. (1979) caution against reliance on sunlight during the first 12 months of life and recommend 400 IU of vitamin D daily. Fluoride supplementation is generally recommended. See Chapter 3, Supplementation and Chapter 16, Determining the Need for Fluoride Supplementation.

Maternal Benefits With breast feeding, maternal involution of the uterus is enhanced through stimulation of the hormone oxytocin. There is controversy over whether breast feeding provides protection against breast cancer. An international study showed no protective benefits (MacMahon et al., 1970). The data also do not support claims that breast cancer incidence increases with breast feeding (Fraumeni and Miller, 1971).

Physical Closeness Skin contact and the physical closeness between the mother and infant enhances psychologic bonding during the immediate newborn period. Breast feeding makes for continued stimulation, as the infant observes the mother's face, hears her voice, and feels the warmth of her body.

CONTRAINDICATIONS TO BREAST FEEDING

Galactosemia Infants with galactosemia cannot breast feed because they lack the ability to metabolize lactose. Tyrosinemia and primary lactose intolerance, two rare conditions, are other contraindications to breast feeding.

Hepatitis B Mothers with hepatitis B are those who are hepatitis B antigen positive and asymptomatic carriers should not breast fed because of the possibility of infecting the infant. However, transmission of hepatitis B antigen via breast milk has not been well documented (Smith and Hindman, 1975). See Chapter 27, Infectious Hepatitis.

Pollutants Environmental pollutants such as dichlorodiphenyl-trichloroethane (DDT), polychlorinated biphenyl (PCB), polybrominated biphenyl (PBB), and lead are found in breast milk (Wilson et al., 1973; Miller, 1977; Finburg, 1977; Lam et al., 1973). There are no documented studies on the effects of these pollutants in infants who have been breast fed and they are not a contraindication to breast feeding. However, if the mother has a known exposure to the pollutants, a blood level test is ordered. In the case of PCB exposure, the PCB level should be measured in three weeks time. The advice of state health department officials should be sought in the rare instances in which a high PCB level is found (American Academy of Pediatrics, 1978).

ESTABLISHING A SUCCESSFUL BREAST-FEEDING ROUTINE

Maternal Anxiety The most common deterrent to establishing a successful breast-feeding routine is maternal anxiety. Frequently women feel the cause of their anxiety relates to breast feeding, and in many instances this is not the reason. For example, there may be anxiety over lack of preparation for the maternal role, physical discomfort from delivery and common behaviors of newborns (crying, regurgitation, and passage of flatus). The woman may be anxious because of: fear of rejection by a sleeping newborn, faulty breast-feeding technique, engorgement, and sore nipples.

The reasons for maternal anxiety are assessed. Questions are answered. Encouragement, reassurance, and emotional support are maintained. Support services are initiated including use of family and friends, public health nurse, breast-feeding groups, and health professionals. Continuous support to the mother in the initial period of breast feeding is the most important factor in maintaining breast feeding.

Counseling The pediatric nurse practitioner counsels parents in many different aspects of breast-feeding routines.

GENERAL CONSIDERATIONS Adequate stimulation of the breasts requires feeding every 2 to 4 hours during the day. At night the infant's sleep is not interrupted for feeding. Usually the infant nurses on the first breast for approximately 10 minutes and on the second breast for 10 to 20 minutes. The protein curd of breast milk (lactalbumin) is easier to digest than the protein curd of cow milk (casein), hence the faster emptying time of the stomach and the more frequent breast feedings. A reduction in breast size is a normal physiologic reaction to the establishment of a smoothly functioning breast routine.

MATERNAL POSITION There are several positions that allow for maternal comfort during breast feeding. The woman may lie on her side with one arm under her head and the other arm and hand supporting the breast used for feeding. The infant lies next to the mother. A second position is for the mother to sit up in bed in a semi-Fowler's position or in a chair with a pillow under her arm and resting on her abdomen for support. The infant is held supine in her arms on the pillow.

INFANT POSITION Most infants are fed in the side-lying position with their heads in the antecubital space of the mother's elbow. However, other positions are recommended for problems of sore nipples. The infant in the side lying position is turned 180°, the head is now where the feet normally are (football hold position). The mother can sit up or lie on her side. Another position is to hold the infant sitting up frontally facing the mother's breast. These positions relieve constant pressure on the same area of the mother's nipple.

TECHNIQUE The nurse practitioner discusses stimulation of the rooting reflex: stroking the side of the infant's cheek closest to the mother's nipple. Newborn development in reference to feeding is reviewed: some infants sleep for the first 2 or 3 days and need to be stimulated to nurse; the infant is not expected to nurse for long periods in the first 3 days but to learn through frequent association the feel of the mother's nipple and where the milk is. The mother's hands are washed before nursing. The mother's nipple is made more protuberant for easier grasp by the infant by having her rotate it between the thumb and forfinger. The infant is held in a position most comfortable to the mother. Sleepy newborns are unwrapped from blankets and their feet are gently rubbed to awaken them. When the infant opens his or her mouth, the nipple and part of the areola are inserted. It is normal for newborns to suck for a few moments and then to fall asleep for a few minutes. Sucking is reestablished by having the mother put her finger under the newborn's chin and gently push it upward. A specific area for sucking is established by having the woman place her index and middle finger in a "V" around the margin of the areola. This also establishes an air space for the infant to breathe. To break the suction after nursing, the woman places her small finger in the side of the infant's mouth to release the pressure and removes the breast.

LET DOWN REFLEX Anxiety may deter the release of oxytocin from the posterior pituitary and inhibit milk let-down from the acini (milk-producing glands). The let-down reflex is described by breast-feeding women as a "pins and needles" sensation in the breasts occurring before or at the beginning of feeding. However, many women do not normally experience this sensation. Some authorities recommend oxytocin nasal spray when there is concern that the let-down reflex is not functioning properly. Other ways to help release the let-down are to obtain adequate maternal rest and nutrition and to reduce the causes of anxiety. Ways to relieve anxiety are to establish a nonchaotic home routine, to drink a liquid before and during breast-feeding (warm milk, water, wine, beer, according to La Leche League, 1976), and to use support systems (public health nurse, empathetic family members, La Leche League).

USE OF CREAMS Lanolin creams are used occasionally during pregnancy to help lubricate dry nipples. They are also used after birth for the same reason. The cream is placed on the areola and never directly on the nipple so as to not interfere with milk drainage. Two such creams are Massé and Aloe Vera Gel.

BREAST PUMPS These devices are used to maintain the milk supply through routine stimulation of the breasts when the woman is not able to nurse herself. There is controversy over using hand and electric pumps. Some authorities believe the amount of pressure exerted by the pumps is painful and injurious to the lacteriferous ducts. However, if pain is not present when using the pumps they are recommended by the authors.

HAND EXPRESSION OF MILK A mother may hand express milk when she is away and desires that the infant be given only breast milk, when the infant is ill or premature and cannot nurse, when her breasts are engorged, or when she has sore, cracked nipples.

Gentle pressure (light massage) is exerted with the fingers on all sides of the breast from the proximal portion (top area of the breast) to the distal portion (nipple). This is done five to 10 times on each breast. Oil is used on the fingers to reduce friction. The areolar margin is then grasped with the thumb and index finger and gentle pressure is exerted by the fingers first backward and then downward, 360° around the areolar margin. This causes expulsion of milk from the lactiferous sinus.

The milk is expressed into a sterile container (plastic is more suitable for freezing than glass). It may be stored in the refrigerator for 24 hours or cooled in the refrigerator and then placed in the freezer and stored for as long as 2 weeks.

RELACTATION Some mothers are interested in reestablishing a breast milk supply after a period of not nursing. Mothers who adopt or who have premature or extremely ill infants or women who have decided to breast feed after a period of bottle feeding may consider relactation. The success of reestablishing a milk supply depends on the length of time the mother has not nursed, whether breast tissue has been stimulated by estrogen, as occurs during pregnancy, cooperation of the infant, the mother's motivation and the frequency of nursing. Relactation is usually done under medical supervision to evaluate weight gain and symptoms of dehydration. The practitioner must be both knowledgeable and supportive. Breast preparation by toughening the nipples and manual expression is encouraged. A current regime is to have the infant suckle on the breast while the mother uses a Lact-Aid. See this chapter, Resource Information. This device supplies milk to the infant through a fine plastic tube attached to a sterile bag of formula held by a cord around the mother's neck. When the infant starts to suck on the breast, the tube is inserted into the infant's mouth and formula is obtained from the bag. In one study maternal milk production took from 8 to 58 days (Bose et al., 1981). The most crucial variable to successful relactation appears to be the length of time between the birth of the baby and involution of the breast tissue. The shortest time provides the most successful outcome. Adoptive mothers produce breast milk but may be able to provide only partial nourishment to their infants, because their breasts do not receive the estrogen stimulation that occurs during pregnancy.

Bottle Feeding

FORMULAS

The preparation of formula is reviewed with the parents to identify any mixing errors and to assess the amount of formula received by the infant.

Caloric Needs of Infant Fifty calories per pound of body weight per day is needed by the infant. There are 20 calories per ounce of formula. For example, a 7.5-lb infant needs 375 calories, or 18.7 ounces per day.

RULES OF THUMB Simple methods for explaining to parents include the following:

1. 2½–3½ oz/lb is adequate. For example, 7.5-lb infant receives 4 ounces × 5 per day, or 20 oz ÷ 7.5 = 2.7 oz/lb/day.
2. Age in months plus 3 (up to 6 months) = amount of formula per feeding. For example, 1 month + 3 = 4 oz per feeding

Sterilization of Formula Researchers (Hargrove, 1974; Kendall, 1971) have not found any differences in the incidence of illness or infection in infants fed formulas prepared by the clean technique or by terminal sterilization. The results were found regardless of socioeconomic background or housekeeping methods. Nevertheless, sterilization of formula is often recommended. For a discussion of sterilization methods the reader is referred to any standard pediatric nursing text.

Clean Technique Pipes (1977) recommends this technique:

1. Wash hands carefully before preparing the formula.
2. Thoroughly wash all equipment to be used during the preparation, including cans that contain the milk, bottles, nipples.
3. Cover and refrigerate opened formula cans.

4. Prepare formula immediately before each feeding.
5. Discard any remaining milk not consumed after the formula is heated and the infant is fed.

Care of Equipment   Careful washing of the bottles, nipples, screw rings, and caps with detergent soon after the feeding avoids milk drying in the equipment. Brushes for the bottle and the nipple facilitate cleaning. After the nipples are washed, a toothpick is twisted in each nipple hole to prevent clogging.

Technique of Bottle Feeding   A comfortable chair and position are essential with the baby cradled in the parent's arm. An armchair and a pillow under the elbow are often helpful. Bottle propping is avoided. The bottle is tilted so the milk fills the neck of the bottle to prevent the swallowing of too much air. It usually takes about 20 minutes of continuous sucking for an infant to complete an 8-ounce bottle. To prevent a vacuum that collapses the nipple and makes sucking harder, parents are cautioned not to screw the nipple cap too tightly.

NIPPLE HOLE   A test for the right size of the nipple hole is to invert the bottle and to observe the pattern of milk flow from the nipple. If the milk comes out in a fine spray for 1 to 2 seconds and then switches to drops, the nipple hole is correct. If it continues to spray, the nipple hole is too large. If it starts with slow drops, the nipple hole is too small (Spock, 1976). Parents can enlarge nipple holes as follows (Spock, 1976, p. 151):

1. Stick the dull end of a fine (No. 10) needle into a cork for safety reasons.
2. Hold the cork and heat the needle point in a flame until it is red hot.
3. Stick the needle a short distance into the nipple top.
4. Test the milk flow.

CLOGGED NIPPLE HOLES   A solution to this problem is to purchase nipples with holes that are "crosscut," which means that a small cross has been cut in the tip of the nipple. The edges of the cut remain together until the baby sucks. Parents can make crosscuts on regular nipples as follows:

1. Pinch the nipple tip to form a narrow ridge.
2. Cut across it with a razor blade.
3. Repeat the previous two steps pinching the nipple at right angle to the first pinch.

This problem can occur if parents mix solid foods with formula, for example, cereal mixed with formula. In this case larger nipple holes will not solve the problem. Parents need to be counseled that the desirable way to serve cereal is with a spoon.

Water Supplement Water may be given to an infant between feedings if the child is crying or if the weather is particularly hot. In the past sugar or honey was added to the water. Arnon et al. (1979) note that 10 to 15 percent of all honey has been found to contain botulism spores (see Chapter 27, Infant Botulism). Therefore, honey should not be used in water or substituted for corn syrup in formula preparation for children under 1 year of age.

First Solid Foods

INITIAL INTRODUCTION

Semisolid foods when an infant is 6 months of age are important because they provide sensory stimulation and help desensitize the gag reflex.

See Chapter 3, sections on Solids, Nutritional Considerations, Commercially Prepared Infant Food, Home Preparations of Baby Foods, Blender Recipes, and Serving Sizes.

The first food generally introduced to a baby's diet at approximately 4 to 6 months of age is iron-fortified rice cereal. One teaspoon of cereal is mixed with approximately two teaspoons of warm water or milk to make a smooth, runny paste. The baby is held in an upright position firmly on the mother's lap with both arms gently restrained from batting at the spoon. A small rubber-tipped spoon is used and the baby is fed slowly. The infant may spit it back but can be offered more cereal until successfully swallowing some. The amount of cereal can be increased and thickened gradually until the infant is taking about ½ cup two times a day. Bananas (ripe and brown-speckled) may be introduced next, followed by other cereals, fruits, vegetables, and meats (commercial or home-prepared). They should be added gradually to the diet, not more than one or two new foods in the same week.

LATER FOODS

When the infant is sitting in a high chair and eating well, finger foods should be encouraged. Newspaper can be placed under the high chair. Foods are selected and prepared that can be manipulated in the mouth without the potential of choking or aspirating, for example, well-cooked vegetables, canned fruits, well-cooked ground meats, liverwurst, minced chicken livers, drained tuna, custards, and puddings.

PROBLEMS RELATED TO SOLID FOOD FEEDING

As these problems occur more frequently after the first birthday, more consideration is given to them in Chapter 6. See Prevention of Potential Feeding Problems, and Problems Related to Feeding.

ACCIDENT PREVENTION AND SAFETY

During the first year of life, accidents are the sixth leading cause of death, surpassed only by anoxia, congenital anomalies, complications of pregnancy, immaturity, and pneumonia. Most accidents can be prevented by practicing appropriate safety measures. The counseling of parents on the developmental capabilities and activities of the infant and on the measures needed to provide a safe environment are an important aspect of routine health care visits. This section offers an outline for age-appropriate counseling, Table 5-22, followed by information regarding infant equipment, statistics, and regulations.

Equipment

CRIBS

The U.S. Consumer Product Commission estimates that 150 to 200 infants die every year in the United States from crib accidents.

Table 5-22
Accident Prevention in Infancy[a,b]

Event[c]	Birth–3 months	3–6 months	6–9 months	9 months–1 year
Burns and fires (see Chapter 28, Burns)		Avoid sink or adult tub near hot water faucets for bathing baby.		
		Use small tub with nonskid bottom.	Use rubber nonskid pad in tub.	
		Test bath water until it is comfortable to own elbow before putting infant into tub.		
		Keep one hand on infant at all times.		
		Avoid handling hot liquids, smoking, or cooking while tending or holding infant.		
			Keep all hot foods and drinks away from edges of tables and counters.	
				Turn all pot handles inward on stove.
				Keep all lighters and matches out of infant's reach
				Keep the kitchen door closed or gated.
			Keep vaporizers beyond infant's reach.	
			Never leave infant unattended with fireplace burning.	
			Place guards around all open heaters, registers, floor furnaces, and burning fireplaces.	
			Place safety caps on the unused electrical outlets and eliminate all dangling electrical cords.	
		Install home smoke alarms, one on each level of the house, including the basement.		
		Purchase flame-resistant clothing and furniture. (See this chapter, Flammable Fabrics.)		
		Shelter the infant from burning sun rays. Apply a sunscreen to exposed areas. (See Chapter 14, Sunburn.)		

Continued

Table 5-22 (Continued)

Event[c]	Birth–3 months	3–6 months	6–9 months	9 months–1 year
Choking (see Chapter 28, Asphyxiation)		Avoid bottle propping. Burp the baby well before putting into the crib. Place the infant on the stomach and turn the infant's head to one side or prop on one side by using a blanket. Examine all toys and rattles. They should be too large for the infant to swallow and free from any sharp edges, strings, detachable parts, and toxic paints. (See this chapter, Toys.) Keep the diaper pins out of infant's reach. Make a habit of pinning to own clothing while changing the diapers. Remove button-type eyes and decorations from dolls or stuffed animals. Use only pacifiers that have a large shield at the base. Do not tie pacifier around infant's neck. Do not given the infant hard foods such as raw vegetables, candy, peanuts, popcorn, or bones of any kind. Inspect all toys routinely for loose parts, and discard them appropriately. Keep the floors, counters, and table tops free from all objects that can be swallowed.		
Falls		Always keep one hand on the infant while giving care. Securely fasten the dressing table straps while the infant is on it. Keep the crib sides up and properly fastened whenever the infant is in the crib. Never leave the infant on an elevated surface unattended. If it becomes necessary to turn away from the infant for any reason, put the infant in a crib with the sides up, in a playpen, or on the floor. Put the infant carrier in the playpen or on the floor when the infant is in it. Always strap the infant securely in the carrier (seat).		

308

	Always use the safety strap when the child is in the high chair or stroller.
	Buy and use sturdy high chairs or low feeding tables. (See this chapter, High Chairs.)
	Keep the car windows by the child closed and car doors locked.
	Keep the doors leading to stairs and to the outside locked. Install gates if necessary.
	Keep infant carriers out of grocery carts.
	Make sure that infant is sitting well before allowing to sit in grocery cart.
Injuries and lacerations	Fence outside stairways, decks with wide slats, and areas near water.
	Keep a moving child within eyesight at all times.
	Avoid the use of hanging table cloths. Keep drapery cords away from cribs.
	Check the furniture for sharp corners and pad them if indicated.
	Use plastic rimmed metal "mirrors" in infant crib as developmental toy.
	Keep items such as sharp objects, scissors, and knives out of the infant's reach.
	Keep hallways and staircases well lighted.
	Tack down extension cords and scatter rugs.
Motor vehicle accidents	Always use an infant car seat appropriately installed and adjusted for age and size. (See this chapter, Infant Carriers and Child Car Seats.)
	Keep the car doors locked.
	Keep the car interior free from litter and loose objects.
	Never leave an infant unattended in the car or alone with a toddler.
	Use safety restraints for all passengers and the driver.

Continued

Table 5-22 (Continued)

Event[c]	Birth–3 months	3–6 months	6–9 months	9 months–1 year
Strangulation	Avoid tying anything, including pacifiers, around the infant's neck. Firmly fasten all mobiles above the infant's crib out of reach of the infant. Never tie the infant down. Purchase cribs with slats no more than 2⅜ inches apart. Line the crib with bumper pads securely fastened.			
Poisonings and ingestions (see Chapter 28, Poisonings)	Avoid giving one child the medicine prescribed for another child. Do not refer to medicine as candy. Powder own hand first and then apply to infant. Never shake on infant or on surfaces where baby sleeps. Read all labels before giving the medicine and never give medicine in the dark. Keep all medications in a locked cupboard and replace them to the locked area immediately after use. Discard house plants that are poisonous. Keep syrup of ipecac in the house and understand its use. (See Chapter 28, Syrup of Ipecac.) Lock all insecticides, poisons, plant foods, and harmful cleaning agents in a special cupboard. Keep the area under the sink free of these harmful agents. Keep nail polish and aerosol products away from infant.			

Suffocation	Do not allow infant in bed with sleeping parents.
	Tie all plastic bags in a knot and discard them immediately and safely.
	Be sure gas fixtures do not leak.
	Do not let baby chew or suck on a balloon (inflated or not).
	Remove doors from abandoned refrigerators and lids from unused trunks.
	Remember that accidents are more common during times of stress, fatigue, hunger, and hastiness.
	Keep infants away from strange pets, and teach them to treat own pets gently.
	Keep a list of important telephone numbers on a wall by the telephone.
	Do not leave bathtubs filled or tubs of water around.
	Do not leave an unattended baby in a wading pool.
Additional precautions	

---

[a]For a developmental perspective, see this chapter, The Waechter Developmental Guides. The young infant is helpless and totally dependent and requires absolute protection. The infant moves about by wiggling and squirming and rolling over. The infant's strong natural sucking reflex results in the infant putting everything and anything into the mouth. Dangerous items become more accessible as the older infant crawls, grabs, reaches, and explores. The infant pulls self up and everything else down and is completely unaware of danger.

[b]Specific safety advice is given at the appropriate age. Advice that begins in the left column holds true for the entire first year.

[c]The major events in this age group are burns and fires, choking due to obstruction of the respiratory tract through inhalation of food or an object, falls, motor vehicle accidents, and strangulation.

311

Another 40,000 infants are injured seriously enough to require medical treatment.

Safety Regulations   As of February 1, 1974, a new safety regulation went into effect relating to the design and manufacture of cribs. Important aspects of this regulation are the following:

- Any metal hardware used on the crib must be safe and without rough edges.
- Crib slats must be no more than 2-3/8 inches apart.
- Locks and latches on the dropside must be safe and secure from accidental release or from release by the infant.
- There must be strict warnings on the crib carton, in the assembly instructions, and on the headboard advising you to use only a mattress that fits snugly and properly.

Tips on Purchasing Second-Hand Cribs   These should include points listed below:

- Buy a crib with as narrow a space between slats as possible, preferably no farther apart than 2-3/8 inches. Carry a tape measure with you when you shop.
- Buy a crib with as large a distance as possible between the top of the side rail and the mattress. The sides, when lowered, should be at least 4 inches above the mattress.
- Buy a crib without ornamental balls, bells, and teething rails.
- Check the crib latches and locks. Be certain they cannot be easily tripped.
- Check the mattress fit. It must be snug. If more than two fingers fit between the mattress and the crib, the mattress is too small.
- Check the overall condition of the crib. Be certain all the slats, nuts, bolts, and other fasteners are in place and functioning.
- Check the paint condition of the crib. If in doubt as to the type of paint used, remove the old paint, sand the surface, and repaint with nontoxic paint.

Safety-Proofing the Crib in Use   Several criteria are necessary:

- Fit the crib with bumper guards that go around the entire crib.

- Secure the bumper guards in at least six places using ties or snaps.
- Leave bumper guards in place until the child can pull up to standing and use them as a ladder.
- Set the mattress in the lowest position as soon as the child can pull up to standing.
- Stop use of the crib when the child's height reaches three quarters the height of the side rails.

FLAMMABLE FABRICS

Epidemiology Current statistical data are difficult to locate. However, the U.S. government estimates that annually 750 to 1,250 fatalities and 37,000 to 50,000 injuries occur to children under the age of 10 from fabric fires.

Safety Regulations The U.S. Consumer Product Safety Commission created in 1972 now has broad jurisdiction over product safety, including responsibility and functions of the Flammable Fabrics Act, effective May 1973.

The U.S. Department of Commerce established a separate, more stringent test method standard for fabrics used for sleepwear in the size range 0 to 6x. Under this standard, DOC FF 3-71, effective July 29, 1972, 0 to 6x sleepwear fabric must be essentially flame resistant. This means that the fabric must not support combustion after removal of the flame source. This flame resistance must persist though the useful service life of the garment, or through 50 launderings.

Various states have legislation governing flammable fabrics. It is important that everyone be familiar with their specific state laws. Strong consumer participation is needed in demanding better flammable fabric standards, more specific, clearer, labeling of articles, and very clear laundering instructions to preserve the flame resistance.

Currently there is serious concern regarding the potential cancer-causing properties of some chemicals being used. Studies are being conducted and it is recommended that everyone keep abreast of the findings and purchase accordingly.

Tips on Purchasing Clothing These should include points listed below:

- Avoid loose-fitting garments that swing away from the body. They can easily catch on fire from momentary contact with a burning fireplace, floor heater, other space heater, or open burner. Flame spread increases as the amount of air surrounding the clothing increases.
- Avoid napped surfaces with loose fibers that create air space between them. These ignite rapidly and the flame spread is rapid.
- Keep in mind that flammability is largely determined by fabric structure or weave. Generally, heavier fabrics have higher flame resistance, are slower burning, and are less apt to ignite from momentary contact. Cotton and rayon generally burn the fastest. Synthetics usually burn less fast; however, they may melt and cause body burns. Animal hair, pure silk, wool, and protein fabrics are more flame retardant. Chemically treated cellulose fibers and inherently flame-retardant fibers such as the modacrylic are the least fire hazardous.

HIGH CHAIRS

Epidemiology The U.S. Product Safety Commission estimates that high-chair-related accidents are responsible for 7,000 injuries per year that are serious enough to require treatment in a hospital emergency room.

Safety Regulations Currently no specific safety standards are in effect. The American Society for Testing and Materials is working closely with the manufacturers in the development of voluntary standards.

Tips on Purchasing High Chairs and Their Use *Consumer's Research,* "Handbook of Buying Issue" (1980) includes these tips:

- Be certain that assembly, use, and maintenance instructions come with the chair. Follow them exactly.
- Be certain the chair is comfortable for the child, is equipped with adjustable foot rests, and has a padded seat and a high padded back.

- Be certain the chair is stable and well balanced. The chair should not tip with an active child in it, other children in the house should not be able to tip it over, and any folding high chair must have locks that prevent the chair from collapsing while the child is in it.
- Be certain that the tray is durable and chip and splinter proof, that the distance from the seat back to the tray can be adjusted, that it is adequate in size and shape to provide support to the child's arms and is made of material that is easily cleaned, and that it is equipped with latches that hold it securely in position.
- Be certain the chair has an adjustable harness or safety belt that holds the child securely. The restraint should be easy to apply and should prevent the child from slipping and from standing up on the chair. Both a waist and a crotch restraint are recommended.
- Do not place the chair with the child in it near a stove, electrical appliances, or stairs.
- Never leave the child unattended in the high chair.

INFANT CARRIERS AND CHILD CAR SEATS

Epidemiology   The U.S. Dept. of Health and Human Services and the Insurance Institute for Highway Safety (1981) report that the number one cause of death in persons up to 4 years of age is motor vehicle accidents, especially in the first 6 months except for causes of death at birth.

Safety Regulations   The Federal Motor Vehicle Safety Standard # 213-80 (1971), requiring only static tests for car child restraints has been revised (January 1981) specifying dynamic test criteria. It requires that child restraint systems meet certain strength and performance standards. Look for a label on the restraint that says "dynamically tested."

Tips on Purchasing and Use   For the child's ultimate protection, these instructions should be followed:

- Read and understand all installation and use instructions before purchasing.
- Be certain that proper installation is possible in your automobile.

High back seat restraints often require installation of a top tether that must be securely bolted to a sturdy metal panel to prevent the seat from lurching forward. Some child car seats should not be used in low back auto seats and some should not be used in high-back bucket seats. Know your automobile and choose appropriately.

- Choose another model if installation is too complicated to use the device each time.
- Choose only those devices specifically designed for automobile use. Purchase the one you will use properly each time.
- Place the infant carrier or car seat in the safest part of the automobile. Generally speaking, the center of the seat is safer than the sides and the back seat is safer than the front. Infant carriers, for instance, are designed to face the back of the seat, *never forward*. The type of car must be considered as well as the need for the driver to turn around often to check on the child, thus taking eyes off the road and possibly causing an accident.
- See the pamphlet "Don't Risk Your Child's Life!" published by the Physicians for Automotive Safety, for a discussion of the crash-tested car seats available. Where to buy and how to use these car seats is described in the pamphlet, which is frequently updated. For copies of the pamphlet (25 cents each), write to: Physicians for Automotive Safety, 50 Union Avenue, Irvington, NJ 07111. The car seats, which are made by certain automobile manufacturers, are available at dealers or in department and juvenile specialty stores.
- See the April 1982 issue of *Consumer Reports* for their list of the top models and also the April 1981 issue *Consumer's Research*, "Making Sure the Safety Seat Is Safe."

INFANT CARRIERS These criteria should be observed:

- Choose an infant carrier that is equipped with restraining straps that allow the infant to be cradled in a semireclining position.
- Position the infant carrier facing the rear. Strap to the seat of the car by using the adult seat belts.
- Protect the infant by using an infant carrier until the infant's development is such that the infant can sit up and hold the head erect, about 6 months of age. Some infant carriers can be converted into a child car seat, thus saving an extra purchase.

CHILD CAR SEATS For choosing a proper fit:

• Keep in mind that car seats can be purchased with an impact shield and/or a harness depending on the model. Safety experts prefer the shield, particularly for children under the age of 2 or 3. The impact shield offers protection by distributing the force of the impact over a large area of the body; however, the shield has a tendency to block the child's view and may contribute to the child's restlessness. The conventional car seat utilizes the harness to restrain the child. This harness must fit properly and be adjustable to allow for sloping, underdeveloped shoulders and the wearing of heavy, bulky clothing. This type is suitable for children who are able to sit up unaided and who weigh at least 15 pounds. They can be used until 4 years, or 40 pounds.

• Protect the child with harness alone. This is a 5-point harness secured by a strap around the seat back and is bolted to the floor or to the rear window shelf. It will fit a child who can sit up unaided and weighs 15 to 50 pounds.

• Use adult shoulder straps only if they cross the child's chest and not the face or neck. This is usually possible after the attainment of 55 inches in height.

TOYS

Epidemiology The U.S. Consumer Product Safety Commission estimates that in 1980, 250,000 persons received hospital emergency room treatment for injuries associated with toys. According to a survey sponsored by the National Safety Council, age 5 appears to be the most vulnerable single year for children to receive toy or play injuries. Park and playground equipment such as merry-go-rounds, swings, and jungle gyms account for most injuries to the 2- to 7-year-old child.

Safety Regulations The Child Protection and Toy Safety Act of 1969, effective as of January 1970, authorizes the Food and Drug Aministration to remove and to keep from the market toys and other children's products with electrical, mechanical, and thermal hazards.

The U.S. Consumer Product Safety Commission has the authority under the Federal Hazardous Substance Act as amended to ban hazardous toys from sale. The regulations provide that toys having the following characteristics are banned hazardous substances:

1. Any doll, stuffed animal, or similar toy having parts that could become exposed and cause cuts, punctures, or other similar injuries.
2. Any toy with noise-making parts that could be removed by a child and swallowed or inhaled.
3. Baby bouncers and similar articles that support very young children while sitting, walking, or bouncing, which could cause injury to the child such as pinching, cutting, or bruising.
4. Caps intended for use with toy guns or toy guns that cause noise above a certain level.
5. Lawn darts and other pointed items intended for outdoor use that could cause puncture wounds, unless they have included appropriate cautionary language, adequate directions, and warning for safe use, and are not sold by toy stores or stores dealing primarily in toys and other children's articles.
6. Toys known as clacker balls which could break off or fracture and thereby cause injury.
7. Toy rattles containing rigid wires, sharp points, or loose small objects that could become exposed and cause cuts, punctures, or other injuries.

On September 3, 1973, a safety regulation for electrically operated toys went into effect. This regulation requires and specifies the following:

1. Electrical toys to bear warning labels stating that they are not recommended for children under a certain age (For any toy that contains a heating element, the manufacturer may not indicate that the toy is recommended for children under the age of 8 years.)
2. Reliable electrical construction
3. Maximum temperature for electrical toys

Currently the Commission is developing new regulations that will provide more comprehensive safety standards for all toys and offer special protection for children under the age of 8 years.

To report a product hazard or product-related injury, write to the U.S. Product Safety Commission, Washington DC 20207.

Tips on Toy Purchasing and Use   For playground equipment and toys in general, these criteria should prevail:

• Anchor all playground equipment firmly to the ground.
• Be certain all spaces between moving parts are wide enough not to catch or to pinch fingers or toes.
• Be certain swing sets are strong and have seats with smooth, rolled edges. Swings should be separated a safe distance from each other and be supported by strong chains without open-ended S hooks.
• Check the equipment frequently for wear and tear, and tighten all bolts and lubricate the joints.
• Cover all protruding bolt ends with protective plastic caps.
• Round off any sharp, exposed edges.
• Report any defective public playground equipment to the appropriate department.
• Avoid toys that produce extremely loud noises that can damage hearing, as well as toys that have propelled objects that can injure eyes.
• Check the toy chest for safety. Be certain it has adequate ventilation, has no automatic locking device, has a lightweight lid, and that the hinging action does not present a strong possibility for pinching or squeezing the child's hands or fingers.
• Choose toys appropriate for the child's age and ability. Consider younger siblings who will have access to the toys intended for older children.
• Instruct the child in the proper use of the toy.
• Read the instructions for use before giving the toy to the child.
• Teach the child proper toy care. Insist that the child put the toys away so they do not get broken and so no one else trips or falls on them.
• Remember, there is no substitute for adult supervision.
• Watch out for toys that have sharp edges, small parts, or sharp points.
• Think, teach, and buy toy safety.

COMMON CLINICAL
PROBLEMS OF INFANCY

This section defines and discusses how to deal with common problems and the factors that lead to them. See also this chapter, Child's Self-esteem, Needs of the Parents, Individual Characteristics of the Family, and Differences in Temperament and Personality. See Chapter 6, Determining the Seriousness of Behavior Problems, Avoiding Potential Behavior Problems, Angry Child, Development of Aggression, The Child's Growing Ego, Building Self-Confidence, and Childhood Coping.

Definition of a Common Problem

A common problem may be defined as behavior of the infant or child that disturbs parental expectations, evokes anxieties and insecurities, and causes emotionally charged reactions. In the early parental experience these reactions may produce a "negative atmosphere or aura" that is disturbing to the infant, and that possibly may contribute to tensions that cause the infant to react "negatively," for example, unexplained and prolonged crying.

Many common problems may be classified as follows:

1. Developmental disorders. These are due to the inevitable and characteristic conflicts associated with the successive stages of psychologic development. They are usually transitory and, within certain limits, are to be regarded as part of normal development, such as obstinacy, negativism, or temper tantrums in the toddler years. The intensity and duration of the symptoms vary with the severity of the environmental situation. Treatment usually consists of working with the parents to help them to perceive and to change those attitudes or reactions which are felt to be threatening to the relationship between parent and child.

2. Situational disorders. These stem from abnormal environmental situations with which a child is unable to cope at a given age. Any of the problems that occur as developmental disorders may also be seen in situational disorders. The latter is suspected if

symptoms are severe, persistent, and especially, clearly defined. Treatment consists mainly in alleviation of the disturbed environmental situation. Parents will need to become more understanding to elicit a change in the child's behavior. Older children can be talked to with the aim of increasing their understanding, easing their anxiety, and giving emotional support. Some examples of situational disorders are colic, feeding and sleeping problems, breath holding, and excessive masturbation.

Contributing Factors

Among these factors are:

1. Unrealistic parental expectations of behavior for the child's age. Expectations that are too advanced or below normal for the child's age are obviously a handicap for the child and tend to produce conflicts in the parent–child relationship.
2. Lack of parenting experience and insufficient parental knowledge of the infant's psychologic and physical needs, temperament of the child, and the normal developmental aspects of child behavior.
3. Unrealistic expectations of the parenting role.
4. The emotional impact on the young parent as bonding and attachment occur with realization of the ever-present need for giving full attention to a helpless infant.
5. The age, sex, and temperament of the child as well as what is going on in the family.
6. Parental overconcern with regard to the management of minor problems.

General Management of Common Problems

Factors to consider in the management of common problems are the needs of the child, the needs of the parents, and the individual characteristics of each family that influence the behavior of the family. To be effective, the management of common problems is directed toward several measures:

1. Prevention. This may be accomplished through early and con-

tinued education at parenting groups or classes and by ongoing provision of emotional support by the nurse practitioner.
2. Alleviation of the immediate situation. See the individual problem in this chapter.
3. Identification of the source of the problem. This may be accomplished by careful history taking and interviewing and by additional counseling sessions with the family.
4. Assistance from appropriate specialists as needed. This may be a physician, a psychologist, or a psychiatric social worker.

OBTAINING THE HISTORY

Information about the Family   Information may best be obtained by directing the questions at the factors involved in creating the problem and at the factors that influence the behavior of the family (see above).

Information about the Child   To help in handling behavioral problems, it is necessary to find out more about the child (behavioral problems tend to occur after infancy):

- Where does the child fit in the family?
- What are the child's habits of eating, sleeping, playing, and using spare time?
- How is the child disciplined or punished, and by whom?
- What is the nature of contact with other children?
- How many are in the family, and how is the child treated by the various members?
- What is going on in the family, such as newborn birth, geographic move, divorce, or the death of a family member?
- Are parents in agreement about methods of handling problems?

QUESTIONS COMMON TO MOST PROBLEMS

Questions to ask include the following:

- How is the problem defined in the parent's own words?
- How long has the problem existed?
- What has the parent done so far to deal with it?

- Why does the parent consider it to be a problem?
- What are the parent's expectations of the child?

Parental Concerns of Infancy

BURPING

Assessment   In infancy swallowed air bubbles are trapped in the stomach as infants feed. It occurs more in bottle-fed infants. Although a minor problem, the correct method of burping an infant can help to relieve the stomach of air and to alleviate pain and crying. If crying occurs during a feeding, air should be suspected.

Management   Babies need to be burped frequently, at least before, during, after, or in between feedings if crying occurs. The most satisfactory position for burping is an upright one. The baby sits on the parent's knees. The baby's back is held straight and upright with one hand, while the other hand grasps the baby's distal arm. The baby rests forward against the same wrist which holds the distal arm. The back may be gently rubbed. It should not be slapped or patted. If the baby doesn't burp after a few minutes, try again in 10 to 15 minutes if the infant is still awake.

COLIC

Assessment   Colic is defined as unexplained bouts of crying, sometimes accompanied by abdominal distention, spasms, and/or passing of gas. It generally occurs at the same time of the day, usually at the busiest period of the day. It may be caused by feeding problems, maternal anxiety, or allergy to milk. It is aggravated by tension in the household. The infant is not ill. Something, possibly immaturity of the digestive system, causes hyperactivity of the bowels. It generally lasts for 3 months. Coincidentally the digestive system is more mature and the infant is able to satisfy sucking need with the thumb. Colic is one of the most trying of the common problems along with crying, its chief symptom. See this chapter, Crying, and Gas.

HISTORY   The same history is taken as that for "crying."

Management This is directed at trying to find the source of the problem and at giving support to the parents. There is almost always a reason. Suggestions for helping with suspected colic are as follows:

- Review the basic infant needs. (See this chapter, Important Early Needs.)
- Review feeding methods carefully.
- Keep a record of the time during the day that it occurs. Soothe the child before the crying spell is expected.
- Wrap the infant warmly, including booties.
- Walk or rock the infant or take for a ride in a car.
- Rest the infant with abdomen on a warm and/or hard surface, such as the parent's knees or shoulder.
- Try infant on a soy milk formula if bottle fed.
- Give whiskey 10 to 20 drops in warm water 30 minutes before expected crying spell.
- Change the household routine to produce a quieter environment (if possible) if the colicky spells occur during a very active time.
- Advise a mild sedative only in extreme cases.
- Offer reassurance to the parents that the infant is not ill and that they are giving good care.
- Emphasize that it definitely will go away.

CONSTIPATION IN INFANCY

Assessment The consistency of stools (hard, pebbly, rocklike) defines constipation in infancy. It is not related to the frequency of bowel movements, straining, grunting, or the number of days between movements. See this chapter, Stool Patterns of Infancy, and see Chapter 20, Constipation.

HISTORY Ascertain the consistency, color, and frequency of the stools and if accompanied by any mucus or blood. Review the infant's diet. Ask how the parents feel about regular toileting and what their concept is of constipation.

Management This is directed at educating the parents about normal stool patterns and relieving the cause if the child is constipated. Treatment and guidance include the following:

- The infant may need more liquids in the diet. Offer water between meals. (See this chapter, Water Supplement.)
- The infant may have been introduced to solid foods too soon, or they are being increased too quickly. Discontinue them temporarily until constipation clears up. Begin again with smaller amounts, increasing them very slowly depending on the stool consistency.
- Dark Karo syrup, 1 tsp in 2 to 3 oz of water, may be given.
- Fruit may be given; pureed prunes up to 3 tablespoons may be helpful.
- The parents need reassurance that the child is not ill. Discuss with them their attitude and expectations of toileting habits and discourage the use of stool softeners, laxatives, or enemas.

CRYING

Assessment Periodic crying for unexplained reasons in the neonatal period continues to be one of the most frustrating of the common problems. Crying in the newborn period may assume a definite pattern early. It may be associated with unexplainable tension. It may begin and end at approximately the same time every day (see this chapter, Colic) or it may spread to other hours upsetting the household and provoking feelings of inadequacy and incompetency. The parent may think that the infant is in pain, is hungry, or will hurt him/her self. Crying, aggravated by household tension, may lead to overfeeding, more crying, and more tension resulting in a cycle that leaves parents and infant frustrated and unrelieved. Conflicting advice of relatives and friends adds to the feelings of insecurity of the most secure parent.

HISTORY This should include the following questions:

- At what time and for how long is the crying spell?
- What is the infant fed, how often, and what methods are used? Is the infant bottle- or breast-fed? If bottle, how is it prepared, is the bottle propped or held, how large are the nipple holes, what kind of nipple is used?
- When and how often is the infant burped?
- What is the stool pattern?

- Are the infant's basic needs of contact and sucking met? Does the infant use a pacifier?
- How do the parents handle the cry?
- What are the parents' expectations of crying? Do they agree on methods of handling the cry?
- What is going on in the house? Does the mother have help? Are there siblings?
- Are there allergies in the family?
- Are there any other symptoms?
- How does the parent feel when the infant's cries cannot be stopped?

Management Relieving parental anxiety is the most important aspect of management. Ideally assessment and management of crying of the newborn should not be done by telephone. The parents must be reassured that the infant is not in pain, and physical illness should be ruled out. A careful physical examination should be performed. Keep in mind that the parents are feeling inadequate, and that they need support and understanding. Explanations should include the following:

- Babies cry for a reason. It is their only way to communicate. All cries should be answered. Do not let the baby "cry it out." Answering cries leads to better attachment between mother and child.
- A clear explanation of basic infant needs, both psychologic and physical should be given. See this chapter, Important Early Needs. One or two periods of crying for 5 to 10 minutes a day can be a breathing exercise or a release into sleep. If the child cries longer, needs should be reassessed.
- A positive, relaxed approach to infant care is beneficial. At fussy periods try to produce a quiet household; infants sleep more soundly in a quiet environment.
- A definite pattern of crying can be anticipated and modified by early offering of physical comforts, such as swaddling, soothing talk, holding, rocking, and sucking.
- A review of feeding and burping methods should be given. The infant may need extra fluids.
- Reinforcement should be given to the parents that they are doing

the correct thing and that crying may be a facet of the child's personality.

- If parents are feeling very stressed and frustrated by the infant's crying, respite care and/or around-the-clock availability of the nurse practitioner may be indicated.

GAS (FLATUS)

Assessment This is air in the stomach or intestines that causes abdominal distress and/or distention and discomfort, and may be expelled through the anus. There are several causes:

- Excessive swallowing of air (hyperaerophasia) due to physiologic inability to seal off nasal passages during swallowing. The air may be swallowed while crying, while at breast or bottle, or when sucking the pacifier.
- Overfeeding or underfeeding.
- An allergy to milk.

HISTORY Ascertain the length of feeding time, size of nipple holes, type of bottle used, and methods of feeding. Is the child held or is the bottle propped? Does the baby use a pacifier? How and when is the baby burped? What is the stool pattern?

Management This is directed at locating the cause and, if possible, eliminating it by the following methods:

- Calm the infant and burp with picked up after crying.
- Burp the infant frequently during and after the feedings.
- Enlarge the nipple holes if necessary to cut down on the feeding time.
- Place the baby on the left side to ease the expelling of gas.
- Try the infant on soy milk formula for a trial period of 2 to 3 weeks if allergies are familial or suspected.
- Reassure the parents that the child will outgrow hyperaerophasia.

HICCOUGHS

Assessment Hiccoughs are caused by sudden, sharp, involuntary spasms of the diaphragm, perhaps by small amounts of food being regurgitated into the esophagus. They usually occur after a feeding but may occur anytime. They are more distressing to the parents than to the infant who would cry if distressed.

Management It is not necessary to do anything, but often the hiccoughs will cease if the infant is offered water or a pacifier. The parents can be reassured that the infant is neither suffering nor ill.

PACIFIER

Assessment There are many questions about the use and misuse of pacifiers. Parents misunderstand the infant's need for nonnutritional sucking or use the pacifier beyond the child's need for extra sucking. See this chapter, Important Early Needs, and Sucking Needs.

POSITIVE USE OF THE PACIFIER There are times when the pacifier can and should be used. Parents need to understand the following:

- The pacifier may be used immediately after birth. It helps the infant develop sucking functions of the mouth and aids in establishing breast feeding; it may be held in the mouth if necessary.
- In infancy the pacifier provides a good method for satisfying the sucking need.
- Bottle-fed infants need extra sucking time. They may be held and cuddled at the same time.
- Pacifiers do not become a habit unless the child sucks beyond infancy, becomes ill, or for some reason does not receive enough mothering.
- Some infants will substitute the thumb before or at about 3 month of age.
- Parents can watch for clues to eliminate the use of the pacifier between 3 and 4 months when the infant becomes more active and there is a diminishing need to suck. Stimulation suitable to the age may be substituted.

NEGATIVE USE OF THE PACIFIER Prevention of inappropriate use of the pacifier may be accomplished by stressing the following:

- It should not replace holding and/or stimulation.
- It should not be used constantly without first answering other infant needs.
- The child can suck any type of pacifier, but it is better if the

pacifier nipple is similar to the other nipples being used, for example, the Nuk nipple comes also as a pacifier.

• Parents should try to discontinue the use of the pacifier beyond 4 to 5 months, since a habit may form and may be difficult to overcome. It is preferable that the child suck his/her thumb beyond this time as the thumb may not be used as frequently as when the pacifier is offered by the mother.

SPOILING

Assessment Spoiling may occur if basic needs are not gratified in early infancy. The child continues to need them satisfied beyond a normal time limit thereby developing as a demanding, undisciplined child. Overgratification of needs in later infancy and toddler age caused by anxiety, hesitancy, and ambivalence of the parents in setting limits also results in a demanding, undisciplined child. It is generally held that a child cannot be "spoiled" under 6 months of age, the age when all of the infant needs should have been satisfied. See this chapter, Crying, and Important Early Needs.

HISTORY Ascertain what the parents mean by "spoiling" and how the child is disciplined and by whom. Do the parents agree on methods of disciplining?

Management For concerns regarding "spoiling," counseling should include the following:

• During early infancy, needs must be gratified.
• Gradually a child is able to handle frustrations for longer periods of time, generally at about 6 to 9 months.
• At this time it may be difficult to draw an arbitrary line between indulgence and restriction; it must be gentle and gradual.
• Parents who find it difficult to manage a particularly demanding child should spell each other or secure the help of a babysitter.
• A relaxed, calm approach should be tried.
• It is helpful to attend parenting classes to share concerns of "spoiling" with other parents.

SEPARATION ANXIETY

Assessment This is a gradual process of differentiation of the infant's body from the mother's body. Usually occurring at about 9 to 10 months of age, it signals the beginning of a new attachment to the mother. The infant has not yet learned that when mother goes away she will return.

Management Peek-a-boo games will help the child to cope with the parent's leaving. A child needs at least 30 minutes to 1 hour to become acquainted with a new person. Parents should not "sneak out" to avoid a scene. It is best for the infant and young child to know that their parents leave and return.

STRANGER ANXIETY

Assessment This is anxiety provoked by a strange human face beginning at about 6 to 8 months of age and gradually vanishing over the next year. It is interpreted as indicating that the child has developed a good schema of the mother's face. A stranger is a discrepancy in this schema that the child cannot handle.

Management An infant will exhibit less stranger anxiety if held by the mother in the presence of strangers, and if they all spend time together before the baby is left alone with the stranger (e.g., a new babysitter).

Problems Related to Breast Feeding

INSUFFICIENT BREAST MILK

Assessment The following are considered:
- Why does the mother feel this way?
- How often is the mother nursing?
- How often are supplements given?
- Is the infant taking both breasts?
- What previous experience or education has the mother had concerning breast feeding?
- Is the mother confident in her ability to breast feed?
- Is the mother anxious?
- How adequate is the mother's nutrition, fluid intake, and amount of rest?

- How many wet diapers in 24 hours?
- Is the mother taking any medication that would reduce the milk supply?
- What is infant's present weight compared with birth weight?

Management The following are discussed:

- Nursing more frequently to enhance milk production trying not to feed sooner than every 2 hours
- Eliminating bottle supplements if possible
- Obtaining a balanced diet for mother with lots of fluids.
- Drinking a glass of warm milk before and during feeding and/or a glass of wine to help relax the mother
- Reassuring the mother that six to eight wet diapers in 24 hours is evidence of adequate fluid intake
- Explaining that breast fed infants gain more slowly in the early weeks.

FREQUENT FEEDINGS

Assessment The following are considered:

- How often is the mother feeding?
- Is the feeding causing maternal exhaustion and anxiety?
- Are there problems with lack of privacy and feedings in the home?

Management The following are discussed:

- Normal frequency of breast feeding is usually every 2 to 4 hours. Feeding more frequently than every 2 hours will cause the infant to consume only small amounts of milk and hence to be hungry more frequently.
- Breast-fed babies are routinely fed more often than are bottle-fed babies. Breast milk is easier to digest than cow milk, hence the faster emptying of the stomach.
- Early or frequent supplements with formula enhance maternal anxiety that breast feeding is inadequate. With frequent feedings every 2 to 4 hours during the day, no formula supplements should be given for the first 2 months.

FUSSY, CRYING BREAST-FED INFANT

See this section, Crying.

Assessment The following are considered:

- How frequently is the infant feeding?
- What is the duration of the feeding?
- How often is the baby burped?
- Is the nursing position comfortable for the mother and the infant?
- Has the mother indented a portion of the breast to allow for an unobstructed airway while the infant is feeding?
- Is the nipple and part of the areola in the infant's mouth?
- Are there any symptoms of illness?
- Is the home routine chaotic or peaceful?
- Is the mother getting enough rest, eating a balanced diet, and drinking enough fluids?

Management The following are discussed:

- Usual frequency of feeding: every 2 to 4 hours during the day and letting the infant sleep as long as possible at night
- Frequently burping to eliminate flatus
- Symptomatic relief of crying (Wrap tightly in receiving blanket, use pacifier, rock infant in chair, ride in car or carriage.)
- Eliminating stressful situations in the home
- Obtaining a well-balanced diet with fluids and enough rest for the mother
- Normal infant crying (increases during the first 3 months of life)

INFANT REFUSING ONE BREAST OR SUPPLEMENTS

Assessment The following are considered:

- Is the mother using both breasts at each feeding to allow for equal stimulation? What positions are used?
- After a routine breast feeding pattern has been established how does the infant respond to supplements?

Management The following are discussed:

- Continue to offer the rejected breast at each feeding. Start first with the accepted breast and change after a few minutes to the other breast, or change positions.
- Supplements begin with water or apple juice first. Many infants will accept this rather than cow milk, initially. See this chapter, Bottle Feeding, Water Supplement.

SUBTLE INFLUENCES OF SOCIETY AGAINST BREAST FEEDING

Assessment The following are considered:

- How does the mother respond to busy hospital routine and pressures: Does she ask questions? Are hospital personnel willing to instruct?
- Is the infant's father and other family members encouraging in their attitude toward breast feeding?
- Is mother aligned with other breast-feeding women?

Management The following are discussed:

- Aligning the breast-feeding mother with an empathetic professional, with a woman who has breast-fed, or with a member of La Leche League International or other supportive group.
- Arranging a family conference to discuss parents' feelings about breast feeding and to explain misconceptions
- Obtaining physical rest, adequate nutrition, and psychologic support

WORKING AND BREAST FEEDING

Assessment The following are considered:

- Is the mother motivated to continue breast feeding while working?
- Can she start bottle supplementation at home before returning to work?
- Is she knowledgeable about initial leaking and engorgement of breasts when commencing work?
- Does she know how to handle manual expression of breast milk?

Management The following are discussed:

- Confidence is instilled in the mother by explaining routine. Start bottle supplementation at home during hours she will work. Leaking and fullness will be minimal when she returns to work. Breast-feed infant in AM before work and several times in PM.
- Bra liners should be used for milk leakage. Breast milk can be manually expressed during working hours to relieve fullness.
- Review technique of manual expression of breast milk.

SORE NIPPLES

Assessment The following are considered:

- How many days post partum is the mother?
- Nipples usually become sore between the fifth and fourteenth day, depending on the frequency and duration of nursing.
- Inspection of the nipples ascertains if there is abrasion of the tissue.
- Palpation of the breasts for heat and inspection for erythema helps rule out the presence of mastitis.

Management This is aimed at prevention. These directions should be followed in this order from birth until nipple tissue toughens.

PREVENTION

1. Try not to breast-feed more frequently than every 2 hours.
2. Dry the nipples in room air after each feeding. Dried milk acts as a protective coating to the nipple.
3. Use a gooseneck lamp with a 25-W bulb at a distance of 1 to 2 feet from nipples for a few minutes after above.
4. Apply nipple ointment or cream to nipples. These do not need to be wiped off each time. (See this chapter, Breast Feeding, Use of Creams.) Frequent washing of nipples has a drying effect. Bathe nipples once a day only.

TENDER AND SORE NIPPLES Use the directions listed above as well as the following:

- Manually express a small amount of milk before nursing. This will cause the infant to suck less hard initially in an effort to bring down the milk.

• Use a nipple shield if nipples are very sore or cracked.
• Assume different nursing positions to relieve pressure on various areas of the nipple.
• Do not use soap or alcohol on the nipples and do not wear bras with plastic liners.

ENGORGEMENT

Assessment The following are considered:

• How many days post partum is the mother? (Engorgement is caused by the production of milk usually around the third day and resulting stasis due to insufficient nursing.)
• How comfortable or uncomfortable do the breasts feel upon touch? (Engorged breasts are hard and painful to touch.)

Management The following are discussed:

• Nursing frequently
• Before nursing, application of hot towels to the breasts or a warm shower or tub bath to help stimulate milk flow and dilate ducts
• Before nursing, manual expression of breast milk to soften nipple and areola to allow for easier grasp by the infant.

PREVENTION OF INITIAL ENGORGEMENT If the infant is put to breast within the first hour or two after birth and is allowed to feed at will after the principles set down for prevention of sore nipples, the engorgement is minimal and in some cases nonexistent.

FLAT OR INVERTED NIPPLES

Assessment The nipples are examined.

Management The following are discussed:

• For flat nipples during pregnancy perform nipple rolling exercise: nipple is held between thumb and index finger and is gently pulled out and rolled. Exercise is done two times a day starting in the last trimester.

• After birth use of a nipple shield intermittently to establish suction and to allow the nipple to become more protuberant. Constant use will decrease milk production because of the baby's weak sucking response.
• For inverted nipples as early as possible during pregnancy breast shields are worn inside the bra. These shields have an opening at the areola and nipple site and exert pressure on that area to allow the nipple to become more protuberant. Early shields were called Woolwich breast shields. Currently Netzy Cups, which produce the same physiologic effect, are used in the United States. If they cannot be obtained locally, write to La Leche League International, Franklin Park, IL 60131.

MASTITIS

Assessment The following are considered:

• Are symptoms of infection present: extreme tenderness, erythema, heat in the breast tissue? Cracked and bleeding nipples?
• Is there maternal fever? Lethargy?

Management The following are discussed:

• Prevention by massaging plugged milk ducts (see above, Sore Nipples)
• Applying heat to the breasts with wet compresses or a heating pad
• Forcing fluids and physical rest for the mother
• Nursing continued on the affected breast, to allow release of plugged milk ducts
• Using oral antibiotics to decrease the infection (*Staphylococcus* is the most frequent causative organism.)

NURSING TWINS

Assessment The following are considered:

• Mother's motivation to nurse twins
• Amount of help at home

Management There are two approaches:

- Complete breast feeding. Nurse infants at the same time using one breast for each infant or nurse one infant at different times. If one infant is nursed at different times the mother can experiment with the amount of milk available in the breast. If milk production is adequate she can use both breasts for one infant. If there is inadequate time for milk production she should use only one breast to feed infant.
- Breast-feeding combined with supplements. At feeding time, nurse one infant and bottle-feed the other. At subsequent feedings, breast-feed the infant that was bottle-fed last and bottle-feed the infant that had the breast at the last feeding.

NURSING PREMATURE INFANT

Assessment The following are considered:

- How is the infant currently being fed?
- Is the infant's sucking reflex established?
- Is the mother knowledgeable about manual expression of the breast if the infant is gavage fed?
- Is breast milk nutritionally adequate for long-term supplementation? Breast milk may not be completely adequate in calcium, phosphorus, and protein for long-term feeding in infants weighing less than 1,500 gm (Fleischmann and Finburg, 1979).

Management The following are discussed:

- Manual expression of breast if infant is gavage fed
- Use of breast pump
- Other methods of milk stimulation, possibly having husband help
- Frequent expression of breast milk at least every 4 hours necessary to maintain supply.

HYPERBILIRUBINEMIA

See Chapter 19, Hematopoietic System: Breast-Feeding Jaundice.

WEANING FROM BREAST TO BOTTLE OR CUP

Assessment Weaning from breast to bottle becomes a problem if the parent has ambivalent feelings about weaning or if the infant refuses the bottle.

HISTORY Ascertain the age of the child and a schedule of feedings. Determine who wants the baby weaned (the mother, the father, or both) and why.

Management This is directed at helping the parent to make the decision to wean, and at giving support and advice on methods of weaning.

DECISION TO WEAN When helping a parent to decide when to wean include the following:

• Weaning should be discussed and decided on by both parents.
• It is helpful if the mother makes a contract with herself every 3 months while breast feeding as to whether or not to continue.
• The mother needs a very positive attitude toward weaning.
• The period between 6 to 9 months of age is not the best time to wean because the infant is experiencing separation anxiety and does not react well to major changes.
• The age of 1 year may be a good time to wean since the infant is ready to use a cup and wishes to be more independent. Some children have a continuing need to suck.

ACTIVE WEANING Start weaning by substituting a bottle for the breast one feeding at a time for a few days at a time; for example, drop the 2 PM feeding first for a few days, then the 10 AM feeding followed by the 6 PM feeding, and finally the 6 AM feeding.

RESISTANCE TO WEANING These methods may be tried.

• Give water or juices in the bottle before starting to wean until the infant is used to the bottle.
• Make sure that the nipple being used is similar in type to the pacifier or one which has been used in the past.
• Heat the milk to approximately 98 to 99°F.
• Be firm against succumbing to the infant's demands for the breast.

- Have someone other than the mother give the bottle.
- Keep to a schedule if possible.
- Be firm, positive, and patient.

Problems Related to Bottle or Solid Food Feeding

OVERFEEDING VERSUS UNDERFEEDING IN INFANCY

Assessment Some mothers find it a problem to determine whether a proper amount of milk or solid food is being given to the infant.

HISTORY Obtain a detailed diet history to include the amounts of milk and solid food and by what methods and how frequently the infant is fed. Obtain the infant's birth weight and present weight. Obtain a description of the stools and how frequently the infant urinates. See Chapter 3, Solid Foods.

Management This is directed at educating the parents regarding nutritional needs. They need to be aware of basic foods and how to determine the amounts necessary for optimum growth. (See this chapter, Caloric Needs of Infancy.) They also need to understand the following:

- Some infants will eat more than they require if food is offered whenever they cry. Explain the infant's needs for non-nutritive sucking and contact.
- "Too loose" a demand feeding schedule may be confusing to the parent. Try to adjust the schedule to a reasonable amount of time between feedings.
- Water may be offered between feedings, since the infant may be thirsty. This may postpone the next feeding for a period of time. See this chapter, Water Supplement.
- If the infant is gaining weight, the infant is not underfed.
- True constipation, green stools, or scant urine with a strong odor should be reported to the health facility.

REFUSAL OF SOLIDS

Assessment Parents sometimes feel that once solid foods are introduced the child should eat on schedule; that they must be forced to eat what has been suggested at the health facility. A problem is created for some mothers when the child refuses the offered food.

HISTORY Ascertain the age of the child, diet history including snacks and foods that the child enjoys, and how the parents feel about the refusal of food.

Management See this chapter, First Solid Foods and Chapter 3, Solid Foods. Discuss with the parents the following:

- There is no reason for solids in an infant's diet before 4 to 6 months of age. At this time the child needs to chew and to pick up food and has an added need for iron-containing foods.
- Digestion starts with salivation, which occurs at 3 to 4 months.
- Infants enjoy picking up food and feeding themselves at about 6 months of age.
- Solid food feeding is not necessarily related to sleeping through the night.
- Tongue thrusting is a normal phenomenon, not a refusal of food. It disappears sooner in some babies than in others.
- An infant may resist food if there is a feeling of being forced.
- Solids may be stopped except for the ones enjoyed by the infant.
- Fruits and cereals or other foods may be mixed together or added to the milk in extreme cases.

Discuss with parents their feelings about feeding and messiness. Suggest a calm and relaxed approach.

"SPITTING-UP" (REGURGITATION)

Assessment "Spitting-up" commonly occurs after a feeding. The causes may be air swallowed along with food, possible inability to relax the esophageal sphincter until later, possible overfeeding, or an allergy to cow milk. Persistent regurgitation tends to be outgrown when the child enters the sitting stage of development.

HISTORY Obtain a diet history. Determine how the infant is burped, if the entire feeding is brought up, if it is projectile in nature, if it contains mucus or blood, if the infant is gaining weight, if the baby is always hungry, and how long it has been going on.

Management This is directed at defining the problem and at giving parental support. Parents need to understand the following:

- Correct preparation of the formula, proper nipple hole sizes, or a new nipple may be needed. See this chapter, Bottle Feeding.
- Infants need frequent and regular burping.
- Formula may be changed to one without an iron supplement, to an evaporated milk formula, or to a soy milk formula.
- The child may be kept in an upright position for about 30 minutes after a feeding.
- The formula may be thickened slightly with infant rice cereal.

WEANING FROM BOTTLE TO CUP

Assessment Weaning to the cup successfully is often dependent on the physical and emotional development of the child, the family life style, and stresses within the family. It should be attempted gradually when the child is ready, usually at about the age of 1. Dentists believe that the child continues to need sucking until this age to develop the mouth and jaws properly.

HISTORY Ascertain the age of the child, who wants to wean, what has been tried, how many bottles are given per day, if the child can use a cup, and how the sucking needs are satisfied.

Management This includes support and counseling as follows:

- Children enjoy the accomplishment of using a cup; it is one of their first steps toward independence.
- They may keep one bottle a day until they are ready to give it up. If this bottle is used at bedtime it should contain water only.
- Forcing a child to use a cup may increase the need to suck.
- It is considered to be more detrimental to wean sooner than later.
- Parents should keep a calm, relaxed attitude.

Problems Related to Sleep

SLEEPING IN EARLY INFANCY

Assessment Some infants have problems with release into sleep and may wake frequently during the night to be fed.

Management This is directed at counseling the parents regarding gratification of infant's early needs. See this chapter, Important Early Needs and Table 5-18: Normal Sleep Patterns. Parents need to know that:

- Infants can sleep through the night at about 3 months of age. This is particularly true if baby is bottle-fed. This can be accomplished by a positive parental attitude and an understanding that the baby does not need nourishment during the night at this age.
- Some infants may need to cry for 5 to 10 minutes before falling to sleep.
- Many infants need help releasing into sleep. This can be accomplished by the use of the pacifier, by holding, rocking, or walking the baby to sleep, or by the mere physical presence of the parent.
- A quiet room should be found for the infant to sleep in when the parents can separate the infant from their room.
- A soft cuddly toy or soft blanket may give the baby reassurance and a relief of anxiety.

WAKING DURING LATER INFANCY

Assessment This is ordinarily linked to whatever has been learned from the parent by history and generally has a basis of separation anxiety.

HISTORY Ascertain the baby's age, state of wellness, if fed when wakes, if at day care, how parents handled the problem up to now, and how they feel about it.

Management After discussion of revealed factors the suggestion of a sleep routine can be made particularly if the baby is over 6 months old.

SLEEP ROUTINE When the infant wakes, the parent goes into the room, makes reassuring remarks, such as "I'm here," "It's all right," and "Go to sleep," and pats baby's back but does not pick the infant up. The parent stays with the infant until the baby goes to sleep then returns to own room. It may be necessary to have a cot or a mattress on the floor by the crib for resting until the baby is asleep. Food is not given. Consistency is critical, and parent may need to repeat the routine several times in the beginning (fathers are very successful, especially with breast-fed infants).

Problems Related to Travel

AIR TRAVEL

Assessment Parents who are traveling with children need to be aware of various factors involved, such as: How the child will sleep, eat, play, space allotted, packing and illness problems.

Management These suggestions are made:

- The airlines should be notified ahead of time of the age of the child or children. Bassinets are available for infants under 6 months of age.
- Infant's supplies and food should be carried on plane along with favorite toy or blanket. Older children will be supplied with food by airlines.
- Infants must be held on the lap of an adult during takeoffs and landings.
- Bottle or breast should be offered to infant during takeoffs and landings to relieve air pressure in the ears. Ear problems may be particularly uncomfortable at this time. A decongestant may be given ½ hour before takeoff. Flying is not contraindicated if eardrum has recently been perforated.
- Older children should be told in detail what to expect of air travel, describing the noise, ear sensations when taking off and landing, and limitations of space and foods to expect.

CAR TRAVEL

Assessment This is the way most families travel especially if there are other children. A sick child should not travel.

Management These suggestions are given:

- Plan well ahead for the clothes, water, food, and favorite toys or blanket to be taken along.

- Don't overpack.
- Have formula ready so that warm water from thermos may be added or use ready-to-feed formula and food. Do not save leftovers.
- Make provisions for child to sleep on a long journey.
- Carry a stroller.
- Have first-aid supplies handy.

Booklist for Parents

Infancy and Development

Brazelton, T. B. *Infants and Mothers*. New York: Dell, 1976.

Brazelton, T. B. *Doctor and Child*. New York: Dell, 1976.

Caplan, F., editor. *The First Twelve Months of Life*. New York: Bantam Books, 1973.

Dodson, F. *How to Parent*. New York: New American Library, 1970.

Dodson, F. *How to Father*. New York: New American Library, 1974.

Dodson, F. *How to Grandparent*. New York: New American Library, 1980.

Dreikurs, R. *Children, The Challenge*. New York: Hawthorne Press, 1964.

Fraiberg, S. *The Magic Years*. New York: Charles Scribner's Sons, 1959.

Gesell, A., F. Ilg, and L. Ames: *Infant and Child in the Culture of Today*. Rev. ed. New York: Harper & Row, 1974.

Ilg, F. and L. Ames: *Child Behavior*. New York: Harper & Row, 1955.

Spock, B. *Baby and Child Care*. New York: Hawthorne Books, 1976.

White, B. *The First Three Years of Life*. New York: Avon Books, 1975.

Breast Feeding

Brewster, P. *You Can Breastfeed Your Baby*. New York: Rodale Press, 1979.

Eiger, M. and Olds, S. *The Complete Book of Breastfeeding*. New York: Bantam Books, 1973.

Kippley, S. *Breastfeeding and Natural Spacing*. New York: Penguin Books, 1974.

La Leche League. *The Womanly Art of Breastfeeding*. Franklin Park, IL, La Leche League International, 1963.

McDonald, H. *The Joy of Breastfeeding*, Pasadena, CA, Oaklawn Press, 1979.

Pryor, K. *Nursing Your Baby*. New York: Pocket Books, 1963.

Raphael, D. *The Tender Gift*. New York: Schocken Books, 1973.

Nutrition

Smith, L. *Feed Your Kids Right.* New York: Dell, 1980.

Weiner, M. and Goss, K. *The Art of Feeding Children Well.* New York: Warner Books, 1981.

Winick, M. *Growing Up Healthy.* New York: William Morrow, 1982.

Safety

Green, M. I. *A Sigh of Relief.* New York: Bantam Books, 1980.

Resource Information

Assessment of the Newborn

1. Infant Temperament Questionnaire (4 to 8 months old) can be obtained by writing to or calling:
   William B. Carey, M.D.
   319 West Front Street
   Media, PA 19063   Telephone: (215) 566-6641

2. Toddler Temperament Scale (1- to 3-year-old) can be obtained by writing to or calling:
   William Fullard, Ph.D.
   Dept. of Educational Psychology
   Temple University
   Philadelphia, PA 19122   Telephone: (215) 787-6102

3. Behavioral Style Questionnaire (3 to 7 years old) can be obtained by writing to or calling:
   Sean C. McDevitt, Ph.D.
   Devereux Center
   6436 E. Sweetwater
   Scottsdale, AZ 85254   Telephone: (602) 948-5857

4. Middle Childhood Temperament Questionnaire (8 to 12 years old) is available from:
   Robin L. Hegrik
   307 North Wayne Ave.
   Wayne, PA 19087

5. For information regarding breast-feeding device write to:
   Lact-aid
   Box 6861
   Dept. KA
   Denver, CO 80206

6. Monthly magazine for parents, write to:
   Growing Child
   22 N. Second St.
   P.O. Box 620
   Lafayette, IN 47902

Accident Prevention and Safety

Resource information can be obtained from these sources:

1. Bureau of Product Safety, Food and Drug Administration
   U.S. Department of Health and Human Services
   5401 Westbard Avenue
   Bethesda, MD 20016
2. U.S. Department of Health and Human Services
   Office of Child Development
   Washington, DC 20201
3. National Child Safety Council
   4065 Page Avenue
   P.O. Box 280
   Jackson, MO 49203
4. National Burn Federation
   3737 Fifth Avenue, Suite 206
   San Diego, CA 92103
5. Center for Auto Safety
   1223 Dupont Circ. Building
   Washington, DC 20036
6. National Safety Commission
   425 N. Michigan Avenue
   Chicago, IL 60611

A simple bath thermometer "The Frog Prince" is sold at drug stores or some supermarkets, or may be purchased for $2.25 (plus 50 cents for handling and postage) from Clinitemp, Inc., P.O. Box 40273, Indianapolis, IN 46240

Infant Care When Traveling

Information about traveling with a child can be obtained from Mead Johnson and Co., Public Relations Office, Evansville, IN 47721

References

Agran, P. F. "Motor Vehicle Occupant Injuries." *Pediatrics* 67:838–840, June 1981.
Alexander, M. A. and M. S. Brown. *Pediatric History and Physical Diagnosis for Nurses.* New York: McGraw-Hill, 1979.

American Academy of Pediatrics, Policy Statement. "PCBs in Breast Milk." April 1978.

American Academy of Pediatrics, Committee on Nutrition. "Encouraging Breast Feeding." *Pediatrics* 65:657–658, March 1980.

Anders, T. F. and P. Weinstein. "Sleep and Its Disorders in Infants and Children." *Pediatrics* 50:312–324, March 1972.

Anderson, P. O. "Drugs and Breast Feeding." *Semin Perinatol 3*:271–278, July 1979.

Anderson, P. O. "Drugs and Breast Feeding." *Drug Intell Clin Pharm 11*:208–223, April 1977.

Apgar, V. "Role of Anesthesiologist in Reducing Neonatal Mortality." *NY State J Med 55*:2365–2368, August 1955.

Applebaum, R. M. "The Modern Management of Successful Breast Feeding." *Pediatr Clin North Am 17*:203–255, February 1970.

Arnon, S. S., et al. "Honey and Other Environmental Risk Factors for Infant Botulism." *J Pediatr 94*:331–336, February 1979.

Avery, G. B., editor. *Neonatology.* Philadelphia: J. B. Lippincott, 1977.

Barness, L. E. *Pediatric Physical Diagnosis.* Chicago: Yearbook Medical, 1972.

Battle, C. U. "Sleep and Sleep Disturbances in Young Children: Sensible Management Depends Upon Understanding." *Clin Pediatr 9*:675–682, 1980.

Beckwith, L. "Premature Birth and Caregiver–Infant Interaction." *Pediatr Res 11*:374, April 1977.

Bettelheim, B. *Dialogues with Mothers.* New York: Avon, 1971.

Bose, C. L. et al. "Relactation by Mothers of Sick and Premature Infants." *Pediatrics* 67:565–569, April 1981.

Brazelton, T. B. *Doctor and Child.* New York: Dell, 1976.

Brazelton, T. B. *Toddlers and Parents.* New York: Delacorte, 1969.

Brazelton, T. B. *Infants and Mothers.* New York: Dell, 1967.

Brown, J. V. and R. Bakeman. "Behavioral Dialogues Between Mothers and Infants: The Effects of Prematurity." *Pediatr Res 11*:375, April 1977.

Brown, J. B. "Infant Temperament: A Clue to Childbearing for Parents and Nurses." *Am J Maternal Child Nursing 2*:228–232, July/August, 1977.

Carey, W. B. "Intervention Strategies Using Temperament Data." In C.C. Brown, editor, *Infants at Risk: Assessment and Intervention. An Update for Health Care Professionals and Parents.* Piscataway, NJ: Johnson and Johnson Baby Products, 1981. Pp. 96–106.

Carey, W. B. "Clinical Applications of Infant Temperament Measurements." *J Pediatr 81*:823–828, October 1972.

Chamberlain, R. "Parenting Styles, Child Behavior and the Pediatrician." *Pediatr Ann 6*:50–63, September 1977.

Chess, S. et al. *Your Child Is a Person.* New York: Viking, 1965.

Colombo, L., R. Hopkins, and W. Waring. "Steam Vaporizer Injuries." *Pediatrics* 67:661–663, May 1981.

Consumer Reports. Consumer Union Ratings. "Child Safety Seats." April 1982.

Consumer's Research. "Making Sure the Safety Seat Is Safe." Washington, NJ *64*:22–24, December 1981.

Consumer's Research. Handbook of Buying Issue. "High Chairs." "Cribs." Washington, NJ, 1980, p. 50.

Cordova, A. "The Mongolian Spot." *Clin Pediatr 20*:714–719, November 1981.

Dansky, K. "Assessing Children's Nutrition." *Am J Nurs* 77:1610–1611, October 1977.

Department of Health, Education and Welfare, Publ. No. 79-30034. "Young Children and Accidents in the Home." U.S. Government Printing Office, October 1979.

Dubowitz, L., V. Dubowitz, and C. Goldberg. "Clinical Assessment of Gestational Age in the Newborn Infant." *J Pediatr* 77:1–10, July 1970.

Erickson, M. L. *Assessment and Management of Developmental Changes in Children.* St. Louis: C. V. Mosby, 1976.

Erikson, E. *Childhood and Society.* New York: Norton, 1963.

Finburg, L. "Pollutants in Breast Milk: PCB's: The Ladies Milk Is Not for Burning." *J Pediatr 90*:511–512, March 1977.

Fleischmann, A. and L. Finburg. "Breast Milk for Term and Premature Infants: Optimal Nutrition?" *Semin Perinatol 3*:397–405, October 1979.

Fomon, S., et al. "Recommendations for Feeding Normal Infants." *Pediatrics 63*:52–59, January 1979.

Fraiberg, S. *Every Child's Birthright.* New York: Basic Books, 1977.

Fraiberg, S. *The Magic Years.* New York: Scribner, 1959.

Fraumeni, J. and R. Miller. "Breast Cancer from Breast Feeding." *Lancet 2*:1196, November 27, 1971.

Freidman, A. S. and D. B. Freidman. "Parenting—A Developmental Process." *Pediatr Ann 6*:10–22, September 1977.

Graef, J. W. and T. E. Cone, editors. *Manual of Pediatric Therapeutics.* 2nd ed. Boston: Little, Brown, 1980.

Grimes, D. "Routine Circumcision Reconsidered." *Am J Nurs 80*:108–109, January 1980.

Harris, B. G. "Learning About Parenting." *Nursing Outlook 25*:457–462, July 1977.

Henderson, L. and L. Newton. "Helping Nursing Mothers Maintain Lactation while Separated from their Infants." *Am J Maternal Child Nursing 3*:352–356, November/December 1978.

Herfindal, E. T. *Clinical Pharmacy and Therapeutics.* 2nd ed. Baltimore: Williams & Wilkins, 1979.

Ilg, F. L. and L. B. Ames. *Child Behavior.* New York: McKay, 1972.

Insurance Institute for Highway Safety, "Children in Crashes." November 1981.

Jacobs, A. H. and R. L. Cahn. "Birthmarks." *Pediatr Ann 5*:6–28, December 1976.

Jelliffe, B. D. and E. F. Jelliffe. "Human Milk and Breast Feeding: Recent Highlights." *Trop Pediatr Environmental Child Health 25*:111–113, October 1979.

Jelliffe, B. D. and E. F. Jelliffe. "Current Concepts in Nutrition, Breast is Best: Modern Meanings." *N Engl J Med 297*:912–915, October 27, 1977.

Journal of Insurance, Insurance Information. "Children in Car Crashes." January/ February, 1981.

Korner, A. "Individual Differences at Birth: Implications for Early Experiences and Later Development." *Am J Orthopsychiatry 41*:608–609, August 1971.

Korones, S. B. *High-Risk Newborn Infants.* 2nd ed. St. Louis: C. V. Mosby, 1976.

La Leche League, *The Womanly Art of Breast Feeding.* 2nd ed. Franklin Park, IL: La Leche League International, 1976.

Lam, S., et al. "Lead Content of Milk Fed to Infants." *N Engl J Med 289*:574–575, September 13, 1973.

Lawrence, R. *Breast Feeding—A Guide for the Medical Profession.* St. Louis: C. V. Mosby, 1980.

Lowery, G. H. *Growth and Development of Children.* Chicago: Yearbook Medical, 1978.

MacMahon, B., et al. "Lactation and Cancer of the Breast. A Summary of an International Study." *Bull WHO 42*:185, 1970.

Marcil, V. "Physical Assessment of the Newborn." *Can Nurse 72*:20–24, March 1976.

Matheny, A. P., A. M. Brown, and R. S. Wilson. "Assessment of Children's Behavioral Characteristics: A Tool in Accident Prevention." *Clin Pediatr 11*:437–439, August 1972.

McAbee, R. "Rural Parenting Classes: Beginning to Meet the Need." *Am J Maternal Child Nursing 2*:315–319, September/October 1977.

McMillan, J., P. Nieburg, and F. Oski. *The Whole Pediatrician Catalog.* Philadelphia: W. B. Saunders, 1977.

McMillan, J., J. Stockman, and F. Oski. *The Whole Pediatrician Catalog.* Vol. II. Philadelphia: W. B. Saunders, 1979.

Miller, R. W. "Pollutants in Breast Milk: PCB's and Cola-Colored Babies." *J Pediatr 90*:510–511, March 1977.

National Safety Council. *Accident Facts.* Chicago, 1980.

O'Brien, T. E. "Excretion of Drugs in Human Milk." *J Hosp Pharm 31*:844–854, September 1974.

Parmalee, A. H., W. H. Wenner, and H. Schultz. "Infant Sleep Patterns." *J Pediatr 65*:576–582, October 1964.

Parth, C. M. and L. E. Kaylor. "Temperature Regulation in the Newborn." *Am J Nurs 78*:1691–1693, October 1978.

Physicians for Automotive Safety. *Don't Risk Your Child's Life.* Irvington, NJ, May 1981.

Pipes, P. L. *Nutrition in Infancy and Childhood.* St. Louis: C. V. Mosby, 1977.

Pruett, K. D. and M. F. Leonard. "The Screaming Baby: Treatment of a Psychophysiological Disorder of Infancy." *Am Acad of Psychiatry 78*:289–298, September 1978.

Reisinger, K. S. et al. "Effect of Pediatricians' Counseling on Infant Restraint Use." *Pediatrics 67*:201–206, February 1981.

Ribble, M. *The Rights of Infants.* 2nd ed. New York: Columbia University Press, 1967.

Riordan, J. and B. Countryman. "Part I, Basics of Breastfeeding. Part II, Anatomy and Physiology of Lactation." *J Obstet Gynecol Neonatal Nursing* 9:207–213, July 1980.

Riordan, J. and B. Countryman. "Part III, The Biological Specificity of Breast Milk. Part IV, Preparation for Breastfeeding and Early Optimal Functioning." *J Obstet Gynecol Neonatal Nursing* 9:273–283, September 1980.

Riordan, J. and B. Countryman. "Part V, Self Care for Continued Breast Feeding. Part VI, Breastfeeding Problems and Solutions." *J Obstet Gynecol Neonatal Nursing* 9:357–366, November 1980.

Robinson, L. and A. Brown. "Colic Etc." *Pediatr Nursing* 5:61–64, November/December 1979.

Rudolph, A., editor. *Pediatrics.* 17th ed. East Norwalk, CT: Appleton-Century-Croft, 1982.

Rybicki, L. L. "Preparing Parents to Teach Their Children about Human Sexuality." *Am J Maternal Child Nurs* 1:166–185, May/June 1976.

Scanlon, J. "How Is the Baby? The Apgar Score Revisited." *Clin Pediatr* 12:61–67, February 1973.

Smith, J. L. and S. H. Hindman. "Transmission of Hepatitis by Breast Feeding." *N Engl J Med* 292:1354, June 19, 1975.

Spock, B. *Baby and Child Care.* New York: Hawthorne, 1976.

Stewart, D. and C. Gaiser. "Supporting Lactation When Mothers and Infants are Separated." *Nursing Clin North Am* 13:47–61, March 1978.

Stimmler, L., G. Snodgrass, and E. Jaffe. "Dental Defects Associated with Neonatal Symptomatic Hypocalcaemia." *Arch Dis Child* 48:217–220, March 1973.

Thomas, A. and S. Chess. "Temperament and the Parent–Child Interaction." *Pediatr Ann* 6:26–45, September 1977.

Thomas, A. et al. *Temperament and Behavior Disorders in Children.* New York: New York University Press, 1969.

U.S. Consumer Product Safety Commission. "Bicycles." Washington, DC: U.S. Government Printing Office, 1981.

U.S. Consumer Product Safety Commission. "A Toy and Sports Equipment Safety Guide." Washington, DC: U.S. Government Printing Office, 1980.

U.S. Consumer Product Safety Commission. "Guide to Fabric Flammability." Washington, DC: U.S. Government Printing Office, December 1979.

U.S. Department of Health and Human Services. "Auto Safety and Your Child." Washington, DC: USDHHS, May 1980.

Vorherr, H. "Human Lactation." *Semin Perinatol* 111:191–311, July 1979.

Waechter, E. H. and F. G. Blake. *Nursing Care of Children,* 9th ed. Philadelphia: J. B. Lippincott, 1976.

White, B. *The First Three Years of Life.* Englewood Cliffs, NJ: Prentice-Hall, 1975.

Wilson, D. J. et al. "DDT Concentrations in Human Milk." *Am J Dis Child* 125:814–817, June 1973.

6

Health Care of the Toddler and Preschooler: 1–4 Years

The years of rapid development, separation from parents, and greater independence can cause conflicts within the family because parents do not always understand the readiness of the child for specific behaviors. In the role as a primary care provider, the nurse practitioner guides the parents through this period by helping them develop their philosophy of childrearing. Such a philosophy should be based on an understanding of psychologic development, understanding behavioral activities, and the differences in family coping styles. This is the time that parenting classes and groups are desirable.

This chapter includes well-child care schedules, growth and development charts, feeding practices, and safety measures for the toddler and preschooler, as well as problems and concerns of parents related to this age.

A COMPREHENSIVE SCHEDULE OF WELL-CHILD CARE

For an introduction to health visits and health care philosophy, see Chapter 5, A Comprehensive Schedule for Well-Child Care.

Visit at 15 to 18 Months

HEALTH ASSESSMENT

See Tables 6-1 and 6-2 for the health assessment at this age.

COUNSELING

Physical Care Discuss the following topics:

- Accident prevention appropriate to age (See this chapter, Accident Prevention.)
- Cleaning teeth with gauze or soft brush daily (The child may wish to imitate adult brushing teeth. May pay first visit to dentist.)
- Beginning toilet training if child indicates readiness (See this chapter, Toilet Training.)
- Management of colds and complications, diarrhea, and constipation (See Chapter 17, Upper Respiratory Infections, and Chapter 20, Diarrhea and Constipation.)

Emotional and Mental Development Among the topics to be discussed are the following:

- Age of negativism as a natural aspect of development
- Age of curiosity. Parents should not use repeated "no's."
- Importance of intellectual development at this age
- Beginning interest in peers
- Nursery school

Stimulation This child needs and enjoys many levels of stimulation:

- Push-pull toys, large and small balls, and dolls

Table 6-1
Health Assessment at 15 to 18 Months

Health History Physical Examination	Nutrition	Development	Screening and Immunizations
Parental concerns	Review basic food groups	More than 5–6 words	Measles, mumps, and rubella (MMR) vaccine at 15 months
Interval history	Stress need for iron and avoidance of sugared foods and drinks	Use spoon	DTP #4 and TOPV #3 at 18 months
Family and social history	May feed self	Scribbles on paper	Hearing
Height and weight		Points to one or more parts of body	
Complete physical examination		Climbing, running	
Discussion of findings with parents			

Table 6-2

Waechter Developmental Guide: Summary of Toddler Development

Age	Physical Development	Intellectual and Verbal Development	Emotional and Social Development
18 months	Anterior fontanel closed Trunk long, legs short and bowed Protruding abdomen Walks upstairs with help, creeps downstairs Turns pages of a book Holds cup with digital grasp, lifts cup Beginning to use spoon, but may turn bowl downward Walks without support and with balance Can build a tower of 3 cubes Picks up small beads and places in receptacle Scribbles spontaneously, uses whole hand Closes small box	Imitates words Uses some words to indicate needs, mainly gestures Ability to point to objects named by adult Follows directions, understands requests Imitates adult behavior Ability to retrieve toy out of reach through experimentation Follows a toy through several hiding places Beginning of symbolic thought Egocentrism in thought and behavior "Magical thinking" present Global organization of mental processes Short attention span Imitates nonliving objects, absent objects, and humans Invention of new "means"; symbols increasingly covert Beginning sense of time in anticipation and memory Infers causes from observing effects	Imitates behavior of parents Beginning to test limits Extremely dependent on parents, yet beginning to strive for autonomy Plays "pretending" games, such as peek-a-boo, sleeping Play and imitation fused Explores house area—into "everything" Plays alone, but near others Will have bowel movement when placed on potty at appropriate time Indicates wet pants

Source: Reprinted with permission from E. H. Waechter and F. G. Blake, *Nursing Care of Children*, 9th ed., Philadelphia: J.B. Lippincott, 1976. Pp. 386–387.

- Sand, water, and paper to play with
- Noisy and manipulative toys
- Books and being read to
- Climbing, running, especially out-of-doors
- Encouragement of curiosity

Parent–Child Relationship Discuss the following aspects:

- Period of egocentrism in the child which makes it difficult for the child to appreciate other's point of view
- Permissiveness versus overpermissiveness, handling of discipline, and setting of limits
- The use of substitution and positive reinforcement in place of frequent "no's"
- Sibling relationships, at this age child may show hostility to an older sibling

Parenting Discuss parenting on several levels:

- Attitudes toward coping with negativism, temper tantrums, and obedience.
- Intellectual interests of the child such as books, toys, equipment. This is a key time to encourage the child to explore and for the parents to react enthusiastically to his or her discoveries. Take the time to explain how things work. Intrigue and stretch the child's observations of the world without pushing.

Nurse Practitioner Goals The goals of the nurse practitioner include the following:

- Continuing to provide education re: care and development
- Continuing to offer reassurance
- Assessing parental needs for support measures
- Assessing parents' knowledge of safety precautions
- Identifying high-risk situations

Visit at 2 Years

HEALTH ASSESSMENT

See Tables 6-3 and 6-4 for a review of the health assessment at this age.

COUNSELING

Physical Care   Discuss the following topics:

* Accident prevention appropriate for age
* Care of the teeth (They should be brushed and flossed daily. Primary dental visit may be made.)
* Toilet training, which should be in progress for most children
* Sleeping problems

Emotional and Mental Development   Discuss the following:

* The need for being with peers and the importance of nursery schools
* Nightmares versus night terrors related to fears
* Autonomy-dependency conflict. This child is still interested in the mother (or primary parent-figure) but becomes less "clingy" at age 2½.
* Development of pride in personal accomplishment

Stimulation   This child needs and enjoys many levels of stimulation:

* Practicing skills on small objects, such as fill and dump toys, stacking toys, blocks, and pencils and crayons
* Exploring the world such as playing with the telephone, puppets, and household items
* Carrying on a conversation, being read to, and pretend reading
* Telling stories and singing
* Pretend activity, such as dressing up in adult clothes and playing house
* Playing out-of-doors with sand, water, slides, balls, swings, and climbing equipment
* Watching television

Table 6-3
Health Assessment at 2 Years

Health History Physical Examination	Nutrition	Development	Screening and Immunizations
Parental concerns	Review basic food groups and appropriate amounts for age	May talk well and follow directions	Urinalysis if not done earlier
Interval history		Purposeful markings on paper	Time test
Family and social history	Reduce milk intake to 16 oz/24 hr	Balances 4 blocks	Vision: Allen picture cards: 20/40
Height, weight, and head circumference	Discuss importance of proper snacks (low sugar, high protein)	Performs simple household tasks	Language: DASE
Complete physical examination		Later may throw ball overhand	
Discussion of findings with parents			

Table 6-4

Waechter Developmental Guide: Summary of Toddler Behavior

Age	Physical Development	Intellectual and Verbal Development	Emotional and Social Development
2 years	Holds glass in one hand	Arranges several words together in sentences	"Rituals" and stability of routine important
	Steady gait, runs	"Telegraphic" speech	Extremely vulnerable to changes in physical environment
	Weight is about 28 pounds	Refers to self by pronoun	Extreme use of "no" as assertion of self
	Protruding abdomen less noticeable	Beginning to learn about time sequences	Negativism
	Has about 16 teeth	Searches for new ways to solve problems, "invents means"	Extremely resistant to restrictions on freedom
	Can build a tower of 6 cubes	Global organization of thought processes	"Loves" and "hates" intensely
	Inserts spoon in mouth correctly	Increasing attention span	Beginning cooperation in toilet-ing—anticipates need to eliminate
		Obeys simple commands	Extremely possessive with toys
		Beginnings of symbolic thought	Consumed by own wishes
			Extreme reaction to separation from parents
			Striving for autonomy prominent
			Temper tantrums decreasing
			Dawdling

358

Age	Motor	Language	Social/Emotional
2½	Walks up and downstairs, one step at a time Throws a ball overhand Can jump in place Beginning to ride a kiddie car Pours from pitcher, may spill Teething almost complete Can build a tower of 8 cubes	"Telegraphic" speech continues Speech resembles monologue Increase in vocabulary Beginning knowledge of past, present, and future Egocentrism in thought and behavior Beginning ability to reflect on own behavior	Resistant to bed time; use of transitional object Interested in older children, but has no social skills—parallel play Solitary and parallel play Dawdling continues Temper tantrums continuing, but lessening in quantity and quality Ritualistic behavior at peak Use of "transitional object" to reduce anxiety, e.g., security blanket Fears prominent Extreme reaction to separation from parents; beginning to work on fear of separation Prominent striving for autonomy Continuing negativism Daytime bladder control with accidents when absorbed in play Beginning to acquire nighttime bladder control

Source: Reprinted with permission from E. H. Waechter and F. G. Blake, *Nursing Care of Children*, 9th ed., Philadelphia: J.B. Lippincott, 1976. Pp. 386–387.

Parent–Child Relationship   Discuss:

- The child's moving toward own way of trying to do things. Constant "no's" from the child are not indications of stubbornness but attempts to develop autonomy. Parents need to use alternatives, substitution, and positive reinforcement and should not expose themselves to a battle of wills.

Parenting   Discuss parenting on several levels:

- Coping methods used by parents
- Need for parents to understand that the child must explore and practice constantly

Nurse Practitioner Goals   The goals of the nurse practitioner include:

- Encouraging the use of nursery school for relief for the mother and social development of the child

Visit at 3 Years

HEALTH ASSESSMENT

See Tables 6-5 and 6-6 for a review of the health assessment at this age.

COUNSELING

Physical Care   Discuss the following topics:

- Accident prevention appropriate for age
- Dental care (First visit to the dentist should be scheduled, if not already done, and visits should be every 6 months through time of tooth eruption and period of excessive dental caries at ages 4 to 8.)
- Local park or out-of-doors play for the release of energy (Nursery school should be encouraged.)
- Care of illness, symptoms of common cold and complications, and when to call for medical care
- Lapses in bladder and bowel control

Table 6-5

Health Assessment at 3 Years

Health History Physical Examination	Nutrition	Development	Screening and Immunizations
Parental concerns	Review basic food groups and appropriate amounts for age	Talks well, uses plurals	Tuberculin skin test.
Interval history		Jumps, runs	Urinalysis for girls
Family and social history	Discuss proper snack foods	Pedals tricycle	Hemoglobin or hematocrit
Height and weight, blood pressure		Washes and dries hands	Vision: E chart or Allen picture cards 20/30
Complete physical examination	Eating patterns are influenced by family members	Separates from mother easily	Hearing: Audiometric sweep test
Discussion of findings with parents			Language: DASE

Table 6-6

Waechter Developmental Guide: Summary of Toddler Behavior

Age	Physical Development	Intellectual and Verbal Development	Emotional and Social Development
3	Walks downstairs, alternating feet	Increased attention span	Nighttime bladder control is fairly reliable, but not complete; takes responsibility for toileting, occasional accidents
	Hops on one foot	Uses regular plurals	
	Swings and climbs	Can give first and last name	
	Balances on one foot	Begins to ask "why"	
	Rarely needs assistance in eating	Exploration of the environment outside the home	Reduction of ritualistic behavior
	Rides a tricycle		Beginning interaction with others in play, sharing toys
	Fine motor control increasing, enjoys painting, coloring, etc.	Vocabulary: 1,000 words; speech fluid; sentences of 4 words	Dramatizes, expresses imagination in play
	Eruption of deciduous teeth completed	Centers attention on one aspect of a situation	Interest in conforming to parental expectations
		Transductive reasoning	Greater independence in activities
			Beginning awareness of sex role
			Sense of self as an individual
			Consolidation of autonomy
			Increased ability to separate from parents for short periods

Source: Reprinted with permission from E. H. Waechter and F. G. Blake, *Nursing Care of Children*, 9th ed., Philadelphia: J.B. Lippincott, 1976. Pp. 386–387.

Emotional and Mental Development Discuss the following needs:

- Sexual curiosity (Answers should be appropriate to the questions. Parents should examine their own attitudes.)
- Sibling and peer rivalry
- Beginning of early fears, such as bodily injury, and of imagination, such as imaginary friends
- Interest in language (Child shows ability to notice small details and discrepancies.)
- Ability to anticipate consequences and the ability to deal with abstractions

Stimulation This child needs and enjoys those activities enjoyed by the 2-year-old child as well as other levels of stimulation:

- Getting dressed by self and performing small household tasks
- Growing plants in cans
- Throwing, catching, and playing ball
- Climbing a rope ladder
- Stringing objects, finger-painting, and using play dough
- Creating own art work at drawing board or block building
- Sewing cards and using blunt scissors
- Riding a tricycle
- Going for excursions, such as a bus ride, the zoo, shopping

Parent–Child Relationship Discuss the following aspects:

- Period of high activity level for child, which is wearing to the mother
- Need for youngsters to climb, jump, and run and need for channels to release energy
- Need to permit child to develop at own pace (There is no advantage to pushing nor to overindulgence.)

Parenting Discuss parenting on several levels:

- Role of father in nighttime contact such as playing, reading, bathing, and performing bedtime rituals

- Need of mother for relief from constant care. Nursery school or cooperative child care should be encouraged.

Nurse Practitioner Goals The goals of the nurse practitioner include the previous goals as well as the following:

- Providing education, support, and anticipatory guidance
- Reinforcing parental strengths and resources
- Encouraging joint decision making regarding child health care

Visit at 4 Years

HEALTH ASSESSMENT

See Tables 6-7 and 6-8 for a review of the health assessment at this age.

COUNSELING

Physical Care Discuss the following topics:

- Accident prevention appropriate to age.
- Dental care. Visits to the dentist should be made every 6 months during the period of greatest carious activity, 4 to 8 years of age.
- Recreation, such as going to the local park or out-of-doors activity for release of energy. There is a need for nursery school or excursions.
- Toileting. Forty percent of 4-year-olds continue to bedwet.

Emotional and Mental Development Among the topics to be discussed are the following:

- The process of refinement of abilities rather than the emergence of new abilities at this age
- Need for the child to learn place in the family, as a child with parents, and to accept the boundaries between children and adults
- Need for socialization of the child (The child can no longer function by just listening or voicing own needs and wishes. Parents and society make demands and this presents conflicts. There is a

Table 6-7

Health Assessment at 4 Years

Health History Physical Examination	Nutrition	Development	Screening and Immunizations
Parental concerns	Review basic food groups and appropriate amounts for age	Knows first and last names	Hematocrit and RBC indices
Interval history		Copies circles and crosses	Tuberculin skin test, if not done at 3 years
Family and social history	Continued need for iron-containing foods	Understands prepositions and opposites	Vision 20/20: E chart
Height and weight, blood pressure	Avoidance of sugared snacks and drinks	May dress self	Hearing: Audiometric sweep test
Complete physical examination		Separates from mother easily	Language: DASE
Discussion of findings with parents		Heel to toe walk	

Table 6-8

Developmental Guide: Summary of Toddler Behavior

Age	Physical Development	Intellectual and Verbal Development	Emotional and Social Development
4	Increased coordination and articulation of small muscle movements, as in writing Balances well on toes Coordinates body movements better in independent activities Enjoys stunts	Boasts, exaggerates, threatens Converses with imaginary playmates Knows age, one color, can count to four or more Girls more advanced than boys Verbalizes flight of ideas	Dresses and undresses self and laces shoes Masters own toileting Prefers to play in groups of two to three children Has favorite companion of own sex Puts away own toys Has complicated ideas but does not carry over from day to day

slow process of helping the child to become "socialized" to participate outside of the home.)

Stimulation This child needs and enjoys those activities enjoyed by the 3-year-old as well as other levels of stimulation:

- More peer activity
- Challenge from nursery school and increased excursions, such as bus, train, or plane rides; visits to zoo, airfields, and fire stations
- An increased interest in sports

Parent–Child Relationship Discuss the following aspects:

- Limits set by parents (These are essential to help the child in the struggle to deal with inner feelings. Disappointments, frustrations, and delay are all part of growing up.)
- Methods for handling the child's egotism (It is important to avoid destroying it or creating a battle of wills. Parents should help youngsters to cope by encouraging them to experiment with new tasks. Parents should not "push" development or "cop out" by leaving children alone, signs of overpermissiveness.)

Parenting Discuss:

- Problems within the family that may be disturbing to the child or may be the source of behavioral problems. Family problems may stem from disagreements on methods of discipline, marital problems, older members in the family, sibling rivalry, divorce, moving, or death.

Nurse Practitioner Goals The goals of the nurse practitioner include the following:

- Continuing to listen carefully
- Examining own attitudes about the family
- Helping parents identify needs for support (The practitioner supports what parents are doing whether permissive or strict as long as extremes are being avoided, the approach is consistent, and the child is adapting well to the approach being used.)

GROWTH AND DEVELOPMENT

As the primary health care provider, the nurse practitioner continues to foster positive parental attitudes and development of a healthy child-rearing philosophy. The Waechter Developmental Guides in this chapter outline physical and motor, intellectual, socialization and vocalization, and emotional development. Chapter 5 includes Table 5-16, A Tool for Teaching Basic Developmental Concepts and Appropriate Parenting. In Chapter 5, there is a section dealing with specific developmental areas of infancy and children. For better understanding of toddler and preschool age, this chapter will include areas of psychologic development.

Areas of Psychologic Development

DEVELOPMENT OF AGGRESSION

Infancy Aggression is a normal part of growth. It starts in infancy as a force within children that enables them to grow and develop. Without it children could not learn to cope with their environment. Infants show aggression when they reach out, grab for objects, and put things into their mouths. They spit out what is not pleasant to them and hang on to what they like. As they grow older their aggression is put to the service of their curiosity, they get into everything and learn that way.

Toddler Around 2 years of age, they learn that by giving and withholding at their own will they can control grownups. If the grownups interfere they respond with temper tantrums, stubborn and defiant behavior. As they learn to use language and enjoy it, it becomes a more mature way of tackling the world. Around the age of 4, boys especially need to express the beginning of manliness. They need to test their independence and strength. Although they may seem rebellious, they are expressing a strong need for more physical activity, independence, and admiration. Decisive limitations should be set for them to express their independence and to help keep in check their potentially destructive impulses.

THE CHILD'S GROWING EGO

Children not only get pleasure and enjoyment from controlling and mastering their impulses, but they are also hungry for new experiences and new skills of muscle and mind. Children want to grow up, to be independent, and to be proud of themselves. They need support to develop ego strength. Parents can accomplish this by several means:

• Making demands and setting limits
• Encouraging children's activities to completion
• Helping the children to overcome obstacles
• Remaining consistent in their attitudes

BUILDING SELF-CONFIDENCE

Helping the child achieve a good self-concept involves several measures:

• Using "environmental control" to minimize the need for other methods of discipline, that is, childproofing house, limiting own no's and don'ts
• Giving a child freedom to explore the environment and to assume self-regulation as he or she is able at each stage of development
• Treating the feelings of the child differently from the way one treats the child's actions
• Relying on the powerful force of unconscious imitations
• Giving emotional support to help a child overcome feelings of inadequacy
• Letting the child learn by natural consequences within reasonable limits

CHILDHOOD COPING

Coping refers to one's ability to deal with new situations and stressful experiences; it includes an element of problem solving.

Infancy   Examples of coping strategies in infancy are:

• Changes in position, restlessness, body rocking, toy manipulation, and locomotion

- Turning away from undesirable stimuli
- Generalized gross motor response
- Crying and fussing
- Sucking and hand–mouth activity

Toddlers and Preschoolers Responses to stress in this age group are characterized by these behaviors in this order:

- Separation anxiety and regression
- Denial, repression, and projection
- Aggression, protest behavior, temper tantrums
- Withdrawal, fantasy, and controlling or restructuring the environment
- Trial-and-error experimentation and motor activity

Understanding these phenomena as childhood coping can assist the health provider to look for underlying causes and guide the parents.

FEEDING OF TODDLERS AND PRESCHOOLERS

The mouth, for the first 1½ years, is the principal source of pleasure. As the baby grows many other sources of gratification are found. Appetite for food is influenced by many factors, such as changing rate of growth, illness, amount of physical activity, hunger, emotions, and parental attitudes toward feeding. The nurse practitioner should assess the child's nutritional status, allay any anxieties exhibited by parents, and ideally try to improve the parents' attitude. For nutritional information see Chapter 3, Nutrition in Infancy and Childhood, and especially Nutritional Requirements, The Toddler and the Preschool Period, Table 3-14: Recommended Food Intake for Good Nutrition, Cultural Considerations, Overnutrition in Infancy and Childhood, and Food Allergy.

Assessment of Present Nutritional Status

See Chapter 1, Child Health Assessment, Nutrition, and Chapter 3, Table 3-22: Levels of Nutritional Assessment of Infants and

Children, Evaluation of Nutritional Status, Table 3-23: Nutrition History: Birth to 24 Months, Table 3-24: 24-Hour Recall, Table 3-25: Characteristics of Good and Poor Nutrition.

In addition, the nutritional history should include the following:

• Parental attitudes toward messiness, spilling and quantity of intake
• Parental and other family members' expectations of child's food intake
• Cultural factors
• History of pica

Prevention of Potential Feeding Problem

Parents are often overly concerned about the amount of food their child eats. This can result in feeding problems such as lack of appetite, refusal of new food, or overeating. The nurse practitioner can increase the parents' awareness of their own expectations of the child's food intake, correct misconceptions and explore their understanding of normal growth and development.

CAUSES OF FEEDING PROBLEMS

A feeding problem occurs most often when the child fails to meet parental expectations. Between the ages of one and two, feeding problems are more frequent than at any other period. Parents' impatience at this time may perpetuate a feeding problem and may initiate others. Parents need knowledge of the ages of normal disinterest in food, food preparation and feeding environment.

Lack of Interest in Food   Between approximately 1 and 3 years of age the child becomes disinterested in food and the appetite falls off dramatically. Milk intake usually decreases. The disinterest can last from several months to a few years. Food jags are common and the child's tastes and behaviors become unpredictable. Often a favorite food will be rejected for a period of time, or the child may become more interested in playing at meals. Calcium, phosphorus, iron, and vitamin A intake during the preschool years decreases as iron-fortified infants cereals are omitted, milk intake is decreased, and vegetables are disliked. After 3 to 4 years of age there is a steady increase in all nutrient intake.

Mealtime Rituals They are associated with the preparation and service of food. Often the child may demand that milk be served in the same glass, or that the sandwich be quartered and arranged in a set pattern on the plate.

Evening Meal It is generally the least popular and acceptable meal to children, and it presents the most concern to parents. Preschoolers tend not to eat for the following reasons:

• Tension at mealtime
• Fatigue (parents and children)
• Unrealistic parental expectations
• Inappropriate size of eating utensils
• Pattern of being bribed with sweets if food is not eaten
• Large meal or milk already consumed
• Parental attention received for dawdling or playing with food

PREPARATION OF FOOD

The following is a list of suggestions for parents in the preparation of food:

• Prepare simple menus with a variety of colorful foods.
• Combine dry foods with one or two moist foods, and sharp flavors with mild flavors.
• Combine soft food, crisp food, and chewy foods.
• Offer mild flavors, mildly salted foods, strong-flavored raw vegetables.
• Make foods softer in texture by adding milk to dry, starchy foods.
• Prepare foods that are easy to eat (thickened soups, finger foods).
• Cut pieces of food so they are large enough for the fork yet small enough to be eaten.
• Offer ground meat or frankfurters instead of steak because 2-to-3-year-old children do not grind meat as easily as adults do.
• Serve at room temperature.
• Serve portions smaller than you expect child to eat so the child can gain a sense of accomplishment.

FEEDING ENVIRONMENT

An environment conducive to eating provides positive interactions between parent and child with a minimum of distractions and is physically comfortable for the child. The child should be situated in a sturdy, well-balanced chair with the feet supported. The furniture should fit the child's body contours. The food should be within reach to avoid spilling. The dishes and glasses should be unbreakable, and the glasses should be small enough to allow the child's hands to encircle them.

Utensils A spoon with a round shallow bowl and blunt tip allows the child to push food from a plate. The handle of the spoon should be blunt, short, and easily held in the palm.

A fork with short, blunt tines adapts easily to the child's palm. Sharp tines spear food more easily but may be used as a weapon.

PARENTAL COUNSELING

Meeting the variable and predictable nutritional needs of a growing child is a time-consuming and often unrewarding job. Parents should be counseled to (Lowenberg, 1977):

- Observe the child's hunger pattern and identify the time of day when the child takes the new food most easily
- Be patient, positively reinforcing, and understanding of each attempt with a new feeding process
- Feed individual foods and not mixtures to help the infant learn to appreciate foods for their own textures and tastes
- Prepare individual foods in as many different ways as possible to enlarge the child's experience
- Introduce new tastes and textures slowly
- Serve foods that are well prepared, colorful, tasty, and textured to create a friendly attitude toward the food
- Provide an emotionally and physically comfortable eating environment
- Obtain the entire family's cooperation
- Understand normal behavioral responses, as well as their own expectations and attitudes.

ACCIDENT PREVENTION AND SAFETY OF TODDLERS AND PRESCHOOLERS

According to the National Safety Council, the leading cause of death under 4 years of age is accidents occurring in this order:

1. Motor vehicle
2. Drowning
3. Fires
4. Suffocation
5. Poisonings and ingestion

Counseling of parents toward safety and accident prevention for the ultimate protection of the child is of prime importance in the delivery of primary health care. This section provides an outline for age-appropriate accident prevention and safety (see Table 6-9) and information regarding bicycle and tricycle purchasing and use.

See Chapter 5, Accident Prevention and Safety in Infancy, for sections covering Cribs, Flammable Fabrics, High Chairs, Infant Carriers and Child Car Seats, and Toys. Also see Chapter 5 for a list of accident prevention and safety resources.

Equipment

BICYCLES

Epidemiology The U.S. Consumer Product Safety Commission estimated that nearly 500,000 persons suffered bicycle-related injuries requiring emergency room treatment annually. The major accidents were as a result of:

1. Loss of control of the bicycle due to difficulty in braking; riding a bicycle that was too large; riding double on banana seats, rear fenders, handlebars, or the horizontal top tube; stunting while riding; striking a rut, bump, or obstacle.
2. Mechanical and structural problems including brake failure, wobbling or disengagement of the wheel or steering mechanism, difficulty in shifting gears, chain slippage, pedals falling off, or spoke breakage.

Table 6-9

Accident Prevention with Toddlers and Preschoolers[a,b]

Events[c]	1 to 2 years	2 to 3 years	3 to 5 years
Burns and fires (see Chapter 28)	Teach the child the meaning of hot		
	Avoid the use of flowing clothing near fire or heating devices		
	Recheck all furnaces, radiators, and space heaters for safety of operation and protective guards.		
	Keep vaporizers beyond children's reach.		
			Teach the child what to do if a fire breaks out.
			Conduct routine fire drills.
			Teach child to roll and to smother clothing if it catches fire.
Drowning (see Chapter 28)	Continue to supervise bath time.		
	Supervise swimming even after the child knows how to swim.		
	Teach the child to respect water and seek professional swimming lessons.		
	Never leave the child unattended near any water area including wading pools.		
			Have the child swim where lifeguards are on duty.
			Have the child wear a life jacket if unable to swim and for all water sports.

Continued

Table 6-9 (Continued)

Events[c]	1 to 2 years	2 to 3 years	3 to 5 years
Falls	Lock all windows. Open windows only from the top. Remove from in front of the windows any furniture or other objects that the child could use for a ladder. Permit climbing adventures within the child's capabilities. Provide a smooth surface for landing. Remove from the crib bumper pads and large toys that the child could use for a ladder. Discourage running in the house.		
	Keep the stairs well lighted and free of clutter.		
Motor vehicle accidents (see Chapter 5, Infant Carriers and Child Car Seats)	Use an appropriate child car seat. The child remains too small for adult seat restraints. Install safety lock adapters on the car doors if they are not built in. They may be purchased at automotive supply stores.		
		Keep the child away from unsupervised driveways and streets.	
	Provide a fenced-in play area.		
		Teach the child pedestrian safety. Set a good example. Play to take place in the yard or playground. Never play in the street.	
			Use adult seat belts if the child is over 40 pounds. Use shoulder restraint if the child is over 55 inches tall.

Poisonings and ingestions (see Chapter 28, Poisonings)	Keep syrup of ipecac in the house, at the babysitter's and at the grandparents'. Be certain everyone understands its use. Purchase only medications that are in childproof containers, and keep them in a locked cupboard. Give the house, basement, garage, and garden a good safety check on a routine basis. (An excellent way to do this is to get down on your hands and knees at a child's-eye level and make the rounds, to see what they are likely to get into or be intrigued by.) Be familiar with the play areas the child frequents, and check on the child's activities often and regularly.
Additional precautions	Check the neighborhood for construction sites, trash heaps, large holes, and discarded refrigerators. Keep tricycles, bicycles, and other play equipment in top condition, and instruct the child in their safe use. Never clean a gun or handle a gun in the presence of a child. Preferably, do not keep guns on the premises. Teach the child safety in using simple tools and household equipment.

[a]For a developmental perspective, see this chapter, The Waechter Developmental Guides. The young toddler is at a very active, curious stage of development. The child is packed with energy and is as quick as a flash. Taking things apart becomes part of play. Putting small items in the mouth, ears, and nose is common. The toddler loves water and knows no fear. The child becomes a great imitator as he or she ages, but uncertainty as to what is dangerous and why continues. Big and small animals fascinate the child. At 3–4–5 years of age, the child expands from the house into the neighborhood and is frequently out of sight playing with peers, riding tricycles. Participation in rough games increases.

[b]Specific safety advice is given in the appropriate age group. Advice that begins in the left column holds true for the ages 1 to 5 years.

[c]The major events in this age group are burns and fires, drowning, falls, motor vehicle accidents, and poisonings and ingestions. At age 3 to 5 years, this includes car/pedestrian accidents.

3. Entanglement of hands, feet, or clothing in the bicycle.
4. Foot slippage from the pedals.
5. Collision with a car or another bicycle.

Safety Regulations   The U.S. Consumer Product Safety Commission is developing safety standards governing the performance and construction of bicycle brakes, wheels, steering system, and frame. These include:

- All uncovered sharp edges and jutting points are to be eliminated.
- Brakes will be required on all sidewalk bicycles with seat height of 22 inches or more.
- Reflectors will be required on the front, back, sides, and pedals to make bicycles visible at night.

Tips on Bicycle Purchasing   These include:

1. Avoid buying bicycles with gear controls and other protruding attachments mounted on the top tube.
2. Avoid buying bikes with sharp edges and protruding bolts. Check all hand and foot brakes for fast, easy stops without instability or jamming.
3. Check the bicycle for functioning head and tail lights. Attach them if they are not standard equipment.
4. Check the foot pedals for rubber tread. Avoid buying bicycles with slippery, plastic pedals.
5. Check the seat for appropriate adjustment.
6. Choose a bicycle that matches the child's ability and kind of riding the child will be doing.
7. Choose a bicycle to fit the child's present age and size.

Tips on Bicycle Riding and Maintenance   These include:

1. Assemble the bicycle according to the instructions or have it assembled by a bicycle shop professional.
2. Adjust the seat to the proper height. The rider's feet should touch the ground on both sides.
3. Do not ride double or show off while riding.

4. Do not ride in inclement weather when the brakes may be less reliable.
5. Do not wear loose clothing that may get tangled in the bicycle parts. Use leg clips or bands on the pant legs. Wear a helmet.
6. Keep the bicycle in a sheltered area to avoid rust and moisture damage.
7. Keep tires inflated to a recommended pressure.
8. Observe all traffic laws. Ride in designated bicycle lanes.
9. Set up and adhere to a regular maintenance program. Periodically check wheel alignment and correct all misalignment; clean and oil all moving parts, being careful not to get oil on the rubber parts; replace all broken and nonfunctioning parts; use reflectors that are at least 2 inches in diameter.
10. Use alternative routes rather than riding through busy intersections and heavy or high-speed traffic.
11. Wear rubber-soled shoes for riding. Never ride barefoot or when wearing loose sandals.

TRICYCLES

Epidemiology   The U.S. Consumer Product Safety Commission estimates that approximately 12,000 persons each year sustain tricycle-related injuries serious enough to require hospital emergency room treatment. The major accidents were as a result of:

1. Entanglement in the tricycle's moving parts
2. Inability to stop the tricycle, usually because tricycles are designed without brakes
3. Instability which causes a tricycle to tip over, often at the time of a sharp turn or when speeding up
4. Poor construction or design including breakage while in use, sharp edges, or points
5. Striking obstacles and colliding with other tricycles

Tips on Tricycle Purchasing   These include:

1. Avoid tricycles with sharp edges, particularly on or along the fenders.

2. Look for pedals and handgrips that have rough surfaces or tread to prevent the child's hands and feet from slipping.
3. Match the size of the child to the size of the tricycle. If the child is too large for the tricycle, it will be unstable. If the child is too small, it may be difficult to control the tricycle.
4. Purchase a stable tricycle. Low-slung tricycles with seats close to the ground offer more stability. Widely spaced wheels provide more stability.

Tips on Tricycle Riding and Maintenance   These include:

1. Caution a child against riding double. Carrying a passenger on a tricycle greatly increases its instability.
2. Cover any sharp edges and protrusions with heavy, waterproof tape.
3. Do not leave the tricycle outdoors overnight where moisture can cause rust and weaken the metal parts.
4. Keep the tricycle in good condition. Check it regularly for missing or damaged pedals and handgrips, loose handlebars and seats, broken parts, and other defects. Repair immediately.
5. Teach the child to avoid sharp turns, and to make all turns at low speeds, and not to ride down steps or over curbs or sewer grates.
6. Teach the child about the danger of riding down hill. A tricycle can pick up so much speed that it becomes almost impossible to slow without brakes.
7. Teach the child safe riding habits and check on the child frequently.

COMMON PROBLEMS OF TODDLERS AND PRESCHOOLERS

Most of the parental concerns of this age group are developmental in nature. Many are linked to the child's growing ego and the child's developing aggressiveness and/or the lack of self-esteem.

See Chapter 5, Definition of a Common Problem. For factors that contribute to problems, see Chapter 5, Growth and Development, Child's Self-esteem, Needs of Parents, Individual Characteristics of the Family, Differences in Temperament and Personality, Common Problems, Contributing Factors, General Management and Obtaining the History. See this chapter, Growth and Development, The Child's Growing Ego, Building Self-confidence, Development of Aggression, and Childhood Coping.

The following section includes a table of common childhood behaviors and discusses the assessment and management of common behavioral problems and parental concerns.

Determining the Severity of Behavioral Problems

Whether a behavior is within the realm of acceptable behavior can depend on several criteria (Brink, 1982):

- Age and sex appropriateness.
- Persistence. Longer than 3 months' duration could denote a major problem.
- Life circumstance as precipitating events. Behavior exhibited without relation to developmental transitions or situational crises and without precipitating event may be serious.
- Sociocultural setting. Some behaviors may be within the norm of a sociocultural group but may not be in the norm of a larger society.
- Extent of disturbances. If behavior is one of many disturbances it may be serious.
- Type of symptom. If behavior is threatening to fulfillment of child's basic needs, it may be serious.
- Severity and frequency of symptom. Occasional behavior versus intense and frequent behavior.
- Change in behavior. If behavior occurs in all settings or in one setting to such an extent that there is an inability to function, a problem may be present.

Avoiding Potential Behavioral Problems

SETTING OF LIMITS

Children are not really comfortable with complete freedom to do as they please at all times. Children who are granted complete freedom often feel anxious, overactive, and ill at ease. They feel the need of security, warmth, friendliness and the need for consistency in discipline and limit setting. Limit setting is in order when the child needs protection from harm, when the child is in danger to himself or herself (i.e., overtired, hungry), and when the child's behavior interferes with the comfort and rights of others. See this chapter, Discipline.

TIME WITH PARENT

Children want time alone with a parent that is spent willingly and lovingly. When parents find it necessary to be away from the child over an extended period of time, or if they have been too busy to be with the child, they should spend some time alone with the child in order to build a lasting relationship. A period of undivided attention from a parent will reassure the child of the parent's love and interest. Often this may be all that is necessary for a child to overcome a behavior that the parent may find objectionable.

Common Habits

Many parents feel that well-adjusted children should not have so-called bad habits and feel guilty of poor parenting if bad habits exist in their children. These habits generally bother the parent more than the child. Most of the habits listed in Table 6-10 are classified as developmental or situational disorders; they are also called tensional outlets. Most children have one or more of these habits, depending on their temperament and the environment. Some of the habits develop into problems if the parent participates in a contest of wills with the child. The habits will usually be outgrown if the parents and caretakers accept them with a calm, relaxed attitude as developmental behaviors. Children should not be nagged or have undue attention called to the habit. Parents can better handle the problem if they ask why the child does it rather than how they can stop it.

HABIT FORMATION

Habit formation is often the result of inconsistency on the part of the parents, who may overstimulate the child in one area and inter-

Table 6-10
Common Childhood Behaviors

Age	Behaviors
1 year	Sucks thumb, smears stools, shakes bed, bangs and rocks, and masturbates
2 years	As above. Has temper tantrums, tears books or wallpaper, tears bed apart, removes clothes, runs around, and has many pre-sleep demands
2½ years	Above behavior in lesser degree. Stutters and has disruptive aggressive attacks such as hitting and biting
3 years	Less of the above behaviors
3½ years	Again an increase in some of the above behaviors. Spits, picks nose, bites fingernails, and whines
4 years	Runs away, kicks, spits, bites nails, grimaces, calls names, boasts, brags, uses silly language, has nightmares and fears, needs to urinate in moments of emotional distress, has "belly" pains and may vomit
5 years	A decrease in some behaviors, blinks eye, shakes head, clears throat, and sniffles
5½–6 years	All the above behaviors and increased clumsiness
7 years	Tries to control behaviors and may have headaches
8 years	Picks at fingers, cries with fatigue, and makes faces
9 years	Stamps feet, fiddles, drops and breaks things, picks at self, growls and mutters

fere with gratification in another. The interference usually starts when the child becomes more obviously aggressive, especially during the oedipal phase, from 3 to 5 years. The child then is forced to seek gratification through infantile pathways, such as thumb sucking, bed wetting, nail biting, or nose picking. These behaviors are forms of easy pleasure that indicate that the child has not found satisfaction in his or her day-to-day life. If we stop the behavior, we only succeed in making the pleasure more gratifying. The child will then increase his or her determination to keep the pleasure and resist having it taken away. The habit now becomes fixed in its second purpose, the defeat of the oppressive adult. Management of "bad habits" includes:

- Downgrading the behavior's importance
- Providing more interests and activities in the child's life
- Exploring the causative agent
- Employing behavior modification
- Spending more time alone with the child (See this chapter, Time with Parent.)

Problems Related to Common Habits

MASTURBATION

Assessment   Children masturbate because it feels good; it is a basic part of their normal developmental pattern. Certain parental reactions to this childhood behavior can instill anxiety and guilt, possibly hindering a positive self-image and future sexual enjoyment for the child.

Management   Developmental counseling should include the child's sexual development. See Chapter 5, Table 5-17.

INFANCY   Masturbation is common among infants. Usually their attention later turns to other things in the environment. It does not result in intellectual, emotional, or physical harm, nor does it make the child more susceptible to masturbation later.

TODDLER   Counseling should cover gender identity, the role of toilet training, and striving for independence as related to genital handling. Parents should not spank, scold, or threaten the child. Such a response only heightens confusion and anxiety and may even cause the child to resort to masturbation as a continual, tension-releasing outlet or to repress and eliminate this natural and healthy self-exploration completely. If parents can handle the situation casually and matter-of-factly, the masturbatory activity will not become a developmental problem of future consequence.

PRESCHOOLER Counseling should be handled as for a toddler. Children who are bored or unhappy tend to masturbate more than those whose lives are satisfying. Parents should be encouraged to involve the child in plenty of play activity and have appropriate toys available. See also this chapter, Time with Parent.

NAIL BITING

Assessment A nail-biting child usually expresses anger, resentment, or defiance of order. The habit is a symptom, not a problem in itself.

Management It is futile to scold, humiliate, or apply preventive medications. One cannot force the child to stop. The more fuss is made over bad habits, the worse they get. See this chapter, Habit Formation and Time with Parent.

NOSE PICKING

Assessment The child who continually engages in nose picking in excess of what might be considered usual for maintaining nasal function, and in the absence of disease, has acquired an undesirable habitual behavior. A logical explanation might be the child's curiosity regarding her or his own body and the fascination with putting things in holes.

Management See this chapter, Habit Formation.

STUTTERING

Assessment Primary stuttering is that which occurs in the younger child who is not aware of the problem. Secondary stuttering occurs in an older child after the age of 3 or 4 years when the child becomes aware that the speech is different. It occurs five times more frequently in males than in females. It may start when attention is called to the normal repeating of words as the child begins speech; it may follow a severe trauma; or it may occur as a result of rigid expectations of feeding or toilet training. The words most generally stuttered are long words, words beginning with consonants, first words of a sentence, and adverbs. See this chapter, Habit Formation and Chapter 25, Fluency Assessment.

Management Support is given to the parents. They need to understand the following:

- The child needs plenty of sleep, outdoor activity, good, nourishing food, and a stable home environment.
- The child should not be made to feel that the speech is abnormal and should be given many opportunities to speak, such as a telephone set, a daily game to mimic the parents' speech, or talking and reading aloud in unison.
- The parents should encourage the areas in which the child excels.
- A change of environments is frequently helpful, such as a visit to the grandparents.
- Parents need to watch for the trigger mechanisms and try to avoid them.
- The child should be forewarned of ridicule by classmates.
- If stuttering continues by the age of 5 referral should be made to a speech therapist and/or a psychiatrist.
- The child may need time alone with parent. See this chapter, Time with Parent.

THUMBSUCKING BY TODDLERS AND PRESCHOOLERS

Assessment Sucking in the infant relieves tension and is the foundation for emotional health. All pleasures are difficult to give up and no child does it quickly or easily. All children retreat to earlier stages of development under stress, and occasional stress is inevitable and desirable for growth. As new demands are made with understanding and approval, the child gives up old needs for new ones. By age 4 or 5, the child may still be sucking the thumb when going to sleep or infrequently in moments of fatigue or tension. By 6 or 7 years of age most children have left this need behind. If the thumbsucking occupies the child to the exclusion of other activities, or persists beyond the ages mentioned, then it is an expression of conflict that is not being resolved by the child. See this chapter, Habit Formation.

Management For further discussion of thumbsucking, especially in reference to teeth, see Chapter 16, Mouth and Teeth, and Thumbsucking.

Problems Related to Anger

ANGRY CHILD

Assessment When the temperament and angry expressions of the toddler appear to reflect something other than the typical unevenness of feeling that accompanies her or his developmental phase, and instead appear to be responses to traumatic events, much time must be spent by the health provider reviewing these events with the parent. Some examples of these events are pregnancy, recent birth of a sibling, changes in the family living situation, a marital separation, a new marriage or close relationship, loss of a favorite caretaker, separation from mother and/or significant other person, and attacks from other children.

Management As the factors that may have contributed to the anger are sorted out, the advice to the parent continues to emphasize support and an intensification of warm attachment between parent and child. The recommendation is made that the mother or father establish a daily routine of special time with the child. (See this chapter, Time with Parent.) An angry, distraught, or retaliative parent may require considerable support and encouragement from the practitioner in order to experiment with the special time routine. Clearly, the more complex the dynamic behind the anger in the child, the more detailed guidance the parent needs. (See this chapter, Temper Tantrums.)

BITING, HITTING, AND KICKING

Assessment These occur as a result of aggressive impulses at 2 to 3 years of age. They are usually temporary behaviors often occurring when the child is in a difficult social situation. They may occur when the child is tired or hungry. Too much may be expected of the child regarding social behavior. See above, Angry Child.

Management Besides looking for tense situations and giving support to the parents, they can be advised as follows:

- It is not desirable to bite or to hit the child in retaliation.
- The parent may cup the child's chin as she or he is about to bite and gently push upward, with a verbal reminder against biting as unacceptable behavior.
- The parent can assure the child that it is okay to bite, but not a person. Give the child something hard to bite on or something soft to hit or kick.
- The child may need more time alone with the parent. As little as 10 minutes a day of meaningful time together is helpful.
- The parent may find that temporary isolation for the child in a room is helpful. Many children are looking for limits and enjoy the quiet of a room.
- The child probably should not have too many or many different companions at this age.
- The child may need to verbalize his or her anger.

BREATHHOLDING

Assessment This is usually one of several signals of a disturbed parent–child relationship, possibly characterized by overprotection. It occurs first at about 2 years of age, rarely before 6 months of age; it disappears after 4 years, rarely seen after 6 years. It has a high familial incidence. Two of the causes may be a tense, rigid feeding regimen or prematurely enforced regulation of toilet habits. The child precedes the breathholding with a temper tantrum, holds his breath, and becomes blue in the face. Some children lose consciousness and may have tonic or clonic movements. It should be differentiated from epilepsy. See Chapter 24, Breathholding, and this chapter, Angry Child.

Management This is directed primarily at parent-child guidance and reassurance. Efforts should be made to understand the family situation. Parents should use purposeful neglect to prevent the child from acquiring satisfaction through using breathholding attacks as a means of dominating the family. The child may need more time alone with parent. See this chapter, Time with Parent. The child may need to verbalize anger. See this chapter, Temper Tantrums.

HEAD BANGING, ROCKING, BED SHAKING

Assessment A form of self-stimulation, these behaviors may be classified as situational disorders. They occur in infancy usually as a result of undergratification of the basic infant needs. They occur at bedtime and during the night. The pattern is reinforced if the child goes to sleep during the behavior. Some children may show a tendency to turn inward or withdraw from reality. See this chapter, Angry Child.

HISTORY Ascertain how the infant's cries are handled, if the basic needs have been gratified, how bedtime is handled, if the child is ill or overstimulated, and the family situation.

Management This is directed at ruling out a hyperactive child and the need for further medical attention. Support is given to the family who need to understand the following:

- The basic infant needs should be gratified. See Chapter 5, Important Early Needs.
- The child should not be left to "cry it out" at bedtime. See Chapter 5, Crying.
- If possible, the parent should spend extra time in a relaxed manner with the infant, holding, rocking, or patting the child's back while the child falls asleep. See this chapter, Time with Parent.
- Soft music or a night light in the bedroom may be helpful.

LYING AND STEALING BY THE PRESCHOOLER

Assessment Four-year-olds boast, brag, and exaggerate, and above all, lie. They have a high-energy level. They take things, having no sense of other people's property. They "borrow" from their friends. Acts of vicious lying and stealing are symptoms of deeper underlying rebellion. Ask the parent what is going on in the child's life, how the behaviors are being handled, and how the parent feels about it. See this chapter, Angry Child.

Management Special things may need to be locked away from the 4-year-old. Parental scorn, criticism, and punishment do not teach the child not to lie or steal. This reaction may provide further ammunition and increase the child's desire to do wrong for the sake of power and defeating the parents. Restitution should be made and stolen articles returned. Children's books are often effective in conveying concepts and values in a nonpunitive way.

TEMPER TANTRUMS

Assessment This is classified as a developmental disorder. Temper tantrums usually occur from 18 months to 3 years of age. This is the age of negativism and independence. Temper tantrums may occur when the chid is hungry, tired, or frustrated by a social situation. They may occur because the child's needs are overgratified and the child now needs to have limits set. See this chapter, Setting of Limits.

HISTORY Ascertain the child's age, when the tantrums occur, and how they are being handled. See this chapter, Angry Child.

Management This is directed at finding the underlying cause and prevention. Lead the parent into understanding that behind the anger in the child there is usually anxiety appropriate to the child's developmental phase. The child is learning to separate from the parent and is both frightened and brave at the same time. The child feels unsafe even when becoming an explorer and when becoming frustrated or angry. Firm but warm and supportive containment is needed. The parent is given very specific directions for holding the child.

TEMPER TANTRUM ROUTINE Take the child on your lap with back toward you. Then put one of your legs over the child's legs, and take the child's arms and cross them in front of the child, with your arms over them. Hold firmly, but do not crush. Be alert to the possibility of the child bucking you with her or his head. Take off child's shoes if necessary to avoid a kicking injury. At the same time *talk* to the child, saying, for example, "I can't let you hurt yourself or anybody else, so I am going to hold you until you quiet down." If the parent is too angry or upset, put the child to bed and *stay with the child,* talking as above. In addition to the routine, a parent needs to understand the following:

- A child of this age needs limits. Tantrums demonstrate this need. See this chapter, Discipline, and Setting of Limits.
- A record can be kept of when the tantrums occur, the child's state of hunger, and his frustrations at the time. Intervention may then be made before the actual tantrum begins.
- Isolation by removal of the child to a room is helpful.
- The parents should try to remain calm and unemotional and should examine their own feelings about the tantrum.
- Special time may be spent with the child. See this chapter, Time with Parent.

Problems Related to Feeding

Much of toddlers' refusal of food is determined by their age and the parental attitude. Parents need to understand the following:

- As children grow and become more active they lose interest in food or may refuse to eat as a form of negativism. Parents should resist giving food instead of offering stimulation or taking time to answer other needs of the child.
- Small amounts of food can be offered frequently in place of three meals. There is no reason why the same foods cannot be eaten day after day as long as the nutritional needs are met.
- If possible less milk per day should be offered and non-nutritive snacks should be avoided.
- If milk is refused, powdered milk can be added to solid foods and calcium can be obtained in puddings, yogurt, cheese, ice cream, or via a calcium supplement.
- It should be a pleasure to eat, not a chore; fingers are as good as spoons.

Discuss with the parents their feelings toward food refusal, messiness, and reassure them that the child will grow and stay well. See this chapter, Habit Formation and Time with Parent.

INAPPROPRIATE FEEDING BEHAVIOR (DAWDLING, GORGING, STUFFING)

Assessment This is often an attention-getting device. It may also be an attempt to exert independence. Questions to ask are:

- What initiates the behavior?
- What has the parent done to handle the problem?
- How would the parent describe the feeding milieu at home?
- How much time does the parent spend with the child?

Management Parents need to recognize that it is the child's choice whether to eat or to continue with the behavior. The child is positively reinforced for all attempts at appropriate behavior, and ignored for continuing the inappropriate behavior. See this chapter, Prevention of Potential Feeding Problem. Guidelines for coping with the behavior include:

- Firm limit setting
- Patience
- Rewarding positive behavior

LACK OF APPETITE

Assessment It is a common concern raised by parents of toddlers, and it is also a common indicator of illness. A detailed history of the onset, duration, pattern, and associated symptoms (e.g., nausea, diarrhea, fever) is obtained. In exploring the concern the parent's expectations and meaning of "lack of appetite" are clarified. The nutritional intake (See Chapter 3), feeding environment, pertinent past medical history, development, parent-child relationship, rate of growth, and other physical factors such as fatigue are assessed. Questions to ask include:

- How is the food prepared and served?
- What does the parent do when the child refuses to eat?
- What and when does the child snack (type of food, quantity, time of day, location)?

Management There are no magic solutions to this problem, and patience is often necessary. If the poor appetite is not related to illness, explanations about normal development and patterns of appetite, ideas about food preparation, ways to enhance the feeding environment, and showing the child's growth chart may help. See this chapter, Lack of Interest in Food, Preparation of Food, and Parental Counseling. Parents may need help in exploring their own discomforts with the poor appetite and in anticipating ways to prevent continuing resistance.

If a nutritional deficiency is identified, parents are counseled on foods to prepare. Supplemental vitamins or minerals may also be prescribed. If an obvious cause is not identified and there are associated physical signs and symptoms such as failing to thrive, further medical and laboratory investigation is indicated.

REFUSAL OF A NEW FOOD

Assessment This is a common problem. A description of the behavior that is interpreted as rejection is necessary. For example, inexperienced parents commonly misinterpret tongue thrusting in the infant as food rejection. In the older child refusal may be an attempt at independence and autonomy. Questions to ask are:

- How is the food prepared and served?
- What is the child's behavior when the food is served?
- What is the parent's response when the food is served?
- Does the parent like the new food?

Management Patience and persistence are necessary. Often familiarity with the new food will increase the likelihood of acceptance; however, children will show food preferences just as adults, and it may be that the child dislikes the taste or texture. Pressuring the child to eat the food may set the stage for future resistance. See this chapter, Prevention of a Potential Feeding Problem. The following suggestions are recommended:

1. Introduce the new food calmly and be prepared for its rejection.
2. If rejected, serve the food again several days later prepared differently if possible.
3. Serve the new food with a favorite food.
4. Introduce it when the child is hungry.
5. Compliment the child after trying even a bite.

REFUSAL OF SPECIFIC FOOD GROUPS

Assessment It is not uncommon for a child who likes a specific food group, such as vegetables, to suddenly reject them for several weeks or months. If the child is not pressured, the food group will usually resume favor. Questions to ask are the following:

- How is the food prepared and served?
- What has the child's previous experience been with the food?
- What does the parent do when the child refuses the food?
- What is the child's response?
- Does the parent like the specific food group?

Management This is often a passing stage. It is important not to pressure the child to eat the food group because it may set the stage for future resistance. The parent may need guidance in preparing the food for the child or in selecting another food within the same food group that provides the same nutritive value. For example, vegetables can be served raw in strips and slices or lightly cooked, or if food dislike is for squash, parents can offer carrots. See this chapter, Prevention of a Potential Feeding Problem and Preparation of Food.

SLEEPING PROBLEMS OF THE TODDLER

Assessment Sleeping problems in early childhood are developmental disorders generally due to separation anxiety or to a fear of aggressive impulses. A poor environmental situation has the effect of increasing the child's impulses and fears, thereby causing more severe sleep disturbances. Teething, illness, or television shows of a violent nature can also be causes.

HISTORY Ascertain at what time and how often the problem occurs, if the child has bedtime rituals and consistent care, and what is happening in the family.

Management This is directed at reassuring the child and the parents and at alleviation of the existing environmental situation. See Chapter 5, Waking During Later Infancy. Parents need to understand the following:

- The normal development of separation anxiety. See this chapter, Separation Anxiety. The child should be assured that the parents will be present upon awakening.
- Sleeping in the parents room at this age or parental overpermissiveness may be associated with sleeping disturbances.

- There is a need for a firm, fair, and consistent treatment at bedtime accompanied by regular rituals.
- Boisterous physical activity or stress prior to bedtime should be avoided.
- A night light or soft music may help a child who has difficulty falling asleep. A soft, cuddly toy may give comfort.
- A child who cannot sleep should not be nagged or punished.

NIGHTMARES

Assessment These are frightening dreams from which the child awakens with a feeling of suffocation, fear, and helplessness. They may start about 3 years of age. They occur as a result of increased sexual and aggressive urges and fantasies.

Management Reassure the parent that these dreams are considered to be normal. Usually the child recalls the dream and is easily placated by recognizing the parent or sitter. The child usually needs comforting before returning to bed.

NIGHT TERRORS

Assessment These are dreams that fail to wake the child completely so that the child does not remember the experience the following day. The child acts excited, calls out, may believe that there are animals or strange people in the room, or may not know who he or she is or recognize the parents. After a few minutes the child falls back to sleep. These dreams are rare, occurring mainly between the ages of 2 and 4.

Management The parents need to be reassured. These terrors tend to disappear spontaneously if not to much fuss is made, and if the child is comforted before returning to bed.

Parental Concerns About Toddlers and Preschoolers

Concerns of the parents of this age child are generally developmental in nature. Parents who do not understand the readiness of a child for a specific behavior have ambivalent feelings about handling certain behaviors. They either allow too much freedom or they try to "train" the child before the child is fully developed.

Discipline is necessary for a child's well-being and physical and mental growth but it needs to be differentiated from punishment.

DISCIPLINE

Assessment Discipline is defined as the job of parents to set forth a set of rules for correct and incorrect behavior and for the safety of the child based on the parents' concept of behavior, feelings, and attitudes. It is a setting of limits and controlling of undesirable acts. It is learning to behave in a manner acceptable to others and training that develops self-control and character.

PERMISSIVENESS This is defined as refraining from inhibiting the child's individual development. It produces confidence and an increasing capacity to express feelings and thoughts. It is a form of discipline.

OVERPERMISSIVENESS This is the allowing of undesirable acts or overgratification of needs. Overpermissiveness brings anxiety and increasing demands for privileges that cannot be granted, resulting in "spoiling." In infancy if limits are not set, the child may cry automatically at any slight discomfort or disappointment. In the early school years if children receive censure for everything they do, they learn that they are displeasing and inept. In adolescence if they are not required to be courteous or obedient, they learn to be self-indulgent.

Management The setting of limits should be done in a manner that preserves the self-respect of both parent and child. Some desirable and undesirable methods of discipline are in the following list:

- Do set examples for love, honesty, unselfishness, and good manners.
- Do be aware that discipline is essential to healthy growth and development of self-discipline.
- Do act in a fair, clear, and consistent method; "treat as you would be treated."
- Do agree on methods of discipline.
- Do give simple directions; give warnings; bend a little.
- Do allow the child to express feelings; be permissive.

- Do respect children; praise, approve, and encourage.
- Do not expect behavior beyond the ability or development of the child.
- Do not argue, threaten, promise, sermonize, or give rude teaching of politeness.
- Do not be overpermissive.
- Do not push the child to achieve.
- Do not be too authoritarian or overstrict. According to Carey (1972, p. 37), as the educational level and socioeconomic status of the parents go down, the use of authoritarian methods increases and is the most prevalent method of discipline.

PUNISHMENT

Assessment   This is defined as the method of controlling behavior when limits are exceeded. A child needs to feel guilty if he misbehaves; the guilt reaction will eventually serve to inhibit the impulse to repeat the act. The degree of guilt feelings should be appropriate to the act. Most punishment is meted out as a result of the parent's loss of temper. Parent's own motives should be questioned.

Management   There are methods of punishment that are more acceptable than others. Some of both are listed below:

- Do agree on methods between parents
- Do allow room for a cooling-off period
- Do respect the feelings of the child
- Isolation to a room at the time of the misdemeanor may be helpful
- Do not expect behavior beyond the developmental level of the child
- Do not direct anger at the child, but at the situation
- Do not retaliate by hitting

Corporal punishment leads to child abuse and repetition of the tragic cycle of violence observed so commonly in child-abuse families (see Chapter 32), in which most child battering parents report that they were beaten as children (Weisel, 1980, p. 640).

• Do not belittle, be sarcastic, ridicule, humiliate, or shame the child.
• Do not send the child to bed or force him to go without food.
• Do not deprive the child of parental love.

SEPARATION ANXIETY

Assessment This is a normal behavior of the developmental phase from 9 months, peaking about 14 to 18 months of age. It is characterized by children becoming disturbed by the parent's disappearance. It is based on their attachment to the parent and their conscious awareness of their need for the parent. This behavior takes many forms, crying, touching mother (or parent), visual regard of mother, waking at night and proximity to mother.

NINETEEN MONTHS The child is still concerned with separation and does not part easily from parent or caretaker.

TWO YEARS This is the age when dependence on the mother reaches a peak of satisfaction and the ability to separate becomes more comfortable. The more enjoyable and secure the relationship has been, the easier the separation.

Management The process of appearance–disappearance allows the child to acquire an intellectual control over the environment. See Chapter 5, Separation Anxiety and Problems Related to Sleep. Major changes occurring in the child's life at this time may cause difficulties to arise. The child who wakes at night should be comforted. See Chapter 5, Waking During Infancy. Independence should not be pushed as the child may interpret this as rejection. Reassurance is given to the parent that the child will outgrow this anxiety.

SIBLING RIVALRY (JEALOUSY)

Assessment This is described as hostile and aggressive behavior exhibited more often in a child who is not much older than the sibling. The closer the age, the more hostile and aggressive the behavior. It occurs in children who are not yet old enough to cope with sharing the mother. They compete for the exclusive love of the parent. Jealousy is sometimes expressed by competitiveness, regression of toilet training, or other appropriate behaviors. See this chapter, Table 6-10, and Habit Formation.

Management This is directed at reassuring the parents. They need to understand the following:

• Much is dependent on how the parent reacts to the behavior. They need to understand the child's feeling of displacement.

• The older child needs some time alone with the parent for some part of each day. See this chapter, Time with Parent.

• Each child should be treated as an individual. Older children may enjoy special privileges.

• It is best to space children at least 3 years apart. The 3 year old is better able to cope with the displacement.

• The older child should be prepared for the advent of a new sibling along with the rest of the family and should be given simple explanations.

• It may be helpful if the older child can visit the hospital to see the mother and baby, and be allowed to help with care of the baby.

• It is wiser to accept jealousy as a fact and to learn to deal with it than to deny its existence.

TOILET TRAINING

Assessment Toilet training becomes a concern to parents because they do not understand when to start teaching the child toilet habits, they do not understand the child's development, they wish to be finished with soiled diapers and messiness, and they have social pressures from family and friends. To handle toilet training the parents and practitioner should explore their expectations and must understand the readiness of the child (see Table 6-11). Brazelton (1962), in a study done of 1,170 children over a span of 10 years, published these statistics:

• 12 percent of the children accomplished bowel training first.
• 8 percent of the children accomplished bladder training first.
• 80 percent of the children accomplished both simultaneously.

Table 6-11

Physiologic and Psychologic Readiness of Child for Toilet Training

Physiologic	*Psychologic*
Is able to manipulate sphincter muscles: 1½ to 2 years of age	Sense of self-identity: 1 year of age
Is able to manipulate clothing up and down (needs manual dexterity): 1½ to 2 years	Trust relationship with mother, a need to please: 2 years
Can hold a specific amount of urine in the bladder, up to 5 hours: 2½ years	Sense of independence and wish to do for him/herself: 2 years
Can understand simple questions	Express pride in achievement: 2 years
Can ask to be changed by pulling at pants, grunting: 1½ to 2 years	Emotional capacity to withhold any action or to perform it: 2 years
Can understand simple directions: 1½ to 2 years.	

- Most of the children were trained by 27 to 29 months of age.
- 40 percent of the children were still bedwetting at age 4.
- 30 percent of the children were still bedwetting at age 5.
- A 2 year old voids 12 times in 24 hours, about 2 oz per voiding.
- 3 to 6 year olds void 7 to 8 times in 24 hours, about 3 oz per voiding.

EXPECTATIONS OF PARENTS Since parental expectations affect the attitude of parents, and the attitude of the parents toward toilet training, they should be ascertained when counseling is given at the 9- to 12-month health visit. See Chapter 5, Visit at 9 Months. Find out from the parents the following:

- When had they planned to toilet train?
- Do they expect a female child to differ from a male child?
- Do they understand that toilet training involves both bladder and bowels?
- What are their cultural patterns of toilet training? How were they trained?
- How do they feel about cleanliness, messiness, and modesty?

- What are the pressures from family and friends?
- Are they open to different methods of toilet training?

Management This is directed at counseling regarding unrealistic expectations, the readiness of the child, explaining the types of toilet training, and discussing problems related to toilet training. See Chapter 21, Enuresis.

EARLY TOILET TRAINING The trend is away from teaching the child toileting habits at the early age of 10 to 15 months, and it should be discouraged. Physiologically the child is not ready. Psychologically the mother is, therefore, this is called "mother-training" and should be attempted only if the mother is strongly motivated. She should recognize that the child can be bowel trained only, that accidents are due to her, not to the child, and that the training should not be stressful; the child should not feel forced. Mainly, the attitude about early toilet-training should be discussed.

TOILET TRAINING AT 18 TO 30 MONTHS Toilet training may be started at this age when the time is right, that is, when there are no major changes occurring in the household, when the child shows interest after observing others such as mothers' sitting and fathers' standing, when nursery school friends are trained, or when the child becomes aware of wet and dirty diapers as opposed to clean and dry ones. Physical and psychologic development of the child indicates that this is the correct age for training, and parents can begin in the following ways:

- The child can be introduced to his or her own potty chair. Allow the child to play with it, sit on it in clothes, and later with diapers off. The mother may put the stool from the diaper into the potty as the child observes.
- If there is no resistance, the child may be put on the potty for not longer than 5 to 10 minutes at the time that elimination is expected. If the child is successful or shows interest, the times may be increased to 2 to 3 a day.
- With continued interest and success, training pants may be introduced. Allow the child to sit on the potty on demand or at spaced times during the day.
- At no time should this be a stressful situation. If the child resists, it is best to forget it for a few weeks at a time and to try again.

- Toilet training can be accomplished readily, or it can occur over a long period of time. At all times the parent should have a positive and relaxed attitude.

"NATURAL" TOILET TRAINING There is a trend toward allowing children to train themselves. Parents can bring toileting to the child's attention when it is sensed that the child is ready, but the attitude of "allowing the child to handle the situation all by him/herself" is overcautious. The child needs to know that the parent is willing to help. The child needs limits set at this age and enjoys independence and the feeling of accomplishment.

Problems Related to Toilet Training Some children are not ready at 18 to 30 months, and some parents need support if the training does not progess well. Some of the problems that may occur and their management are listed below:

- A child may play with feces, which is disturbing to the parent. Allow the child to play with soft clay or finger paints for the need to smear.
- Boys may have problems with sitting or standing. It is sometimes easier to start the training by sitting. Other boys may enjoy using a large tin can while standing. (They particularly enjoy the noise this makes.)
- Children may have problems using a large toilet. Efforts should be made for child to have a small potty, one which resembles the large one. A portable toilet seat can be taken on excursions. Use a footstool for the child to climb on and use as a foot support.
- A newly trained child may regress due to stress in the family such as moving, a new sibling, divorce, death, or starting to school. Put the child back in diapers if this is acceptable, and say as little as possible. Give extra attention to the child and start retraining within a few weeks.
- Children continue to need help in the area of cleanliness. Parents should support the child who wishes to be independent and should recognize that cleanliness is not the main concern.
- Odd words may be used for bowel movements and urination, which may cause trouble when the child is not at home. These words should be conveyed to caretakers outside the home.

- Minor problems that may occur during the course of toilet training are messing with food, temporary food dislikes, smearing feces, and constipation or diarrhea.
- A child can learn early to control the environment by controlling bowels. This can lead to attention-getting devices or more serious problems of severe constipation, enuresis, encopresis, diarrhea, or colitis. These conditions need to be handled in collaboration with other professionals. It is imperative to know what is happening in the home and how the toilet training has been handled.

Booklist for Parents*

Ames, L. and Ilg, F. *Your Two-Year Old.* New York: Delacorte Press, 1976.

Ames, L. and Ilg, F. *Your Three-Year-Old.* New York: Delacorte Press, 1976.

Ames, L. and Ilg, F. *Your Four-Year-Old.* New York: Delacorte Press, 1976.

Brazelton, T. B. *Toddlers and Parents.* New York: Dell, 1969.

Bettelheim, B. *Dialogues with Mothers.* New York: Avon, 1971.

Caplan, F. and Caplan, J. *The Second Twelve Months of Life.* New York: Bantam Books, 1977.

Dodson, F. *How to Discipline with Love.* New York: New American Library, 1981.

Dreikurs, R. and Cassel, P. *Discipline Without Tears.* New York: Hawthorne Books, 1970.

Gardner, R. *The Parents' Book about Divorce.* New York: Doubleday, 1977.

Ginott, H. G. *Between Parent and Child.* New York: Macmillan, 1965.

Grollman, E. *Explaining Divorce to Children.* Boston: Beacon Press, 1969.

Grollman, E. *Explaining Death to Children.* Boston: Beacon Press, 1967.

Gruenberg, S. M. *Wonderful Story of How You Were Born.* New York: Doubleday, 1970.

Kelly, G. A. *Your Child and Sex.* New York: Random House, 1964.

Levine, M. and Seligman, L. *What to Tell Your Children About Sex.* New York: Meredith Press, 1968.

McDermott, J. *Raising Cain and Abel Too—Sibling Rivalry.* New York: Wyden Books, 1980.

McNamara, J. *The Adoption Question.* New York: Hawthorne Books, 1974.

Norris, G. and Miller, J. *The Working Mother's Complete Handbook.* New York: Hawthorne Books, 1980.

Rosenbaum, J. and Rosenbaum, S. *Step-Parenting.* New York: Hawthorne Books, 1980.

*See also Chapter 5, Booklist for Parents.

Salk, L. *What Every Child Would Like His Parents to Know.* New York: McKay, 1973.
Weisberger, E. *Your Young Child and You.* New York: Hawthorne Books, 1979.

References

Bettelheim, B. *Dialogues with Mothers.* New York: Avon, 1971.

Brazelton, T. B. *Doctor and Child.* New York: Dell, 1976.

Brazelton, T. B. *Toddlers and Mothers.* New York: Dell, 1974.

Brazelton, T. B. "A Child-Oriented Approach to Toilet-Training." *Pediatrics* 29:121–128, January 1962.

Brink, R., "How Serious is the Child's Behavior Problem?" *Am J Maternal Child Nursing* 7:33–36, January/February 1982.

Chess, S., et al. *Your Child Is a Person.* New York: Viking, 1965.

Dodson, F. *How to Discipline with Love.* New York: New American Library, 1981.

Dreikurs, R. *Children—The Challenge.* New York: Hawthorne, 1964.

Erikson, E. *Childhood and Society.* New York: Norton, 1963.

Freidman, A. S. and D. B. Freidman. "Parenting—A Developmental Process." *Pediatr Ann* 6:10–22, September 1977.

Gallo, A. M. "Early Childhood Masturbation: A Developmental Approach." *Pediatr Nurs* 5:47–50, September/October 1979.

Gessel, A., et al. *The Infant and Child in the Culture of Today.* Rev. ed. New York: Harper & Row, 1974.

Ginott, H. *Between Parent and Child.* New York: MacMillan, 1965.

Ilg, F. L. and L. B. Ames. *Child Behavior.* New York: McKay, 1972.

Klosky, L. "Nose Picking in Children." *Pediatr Nurs* 4:47–48, November/December 1978.

Lowenberg, M. E. "The Development of Food Patterns in Young Children." In P. L. Pipes, editor, *Nutrition in Infancy and Childhood.* St. Louis: C. V. Mosby, 1977. Pp. 85–100.

Murphy, M. A. "Toilet-Training, When and How." *Pediatr Nurs* 1:22–27, November/December, 1975.

National Safety Council. *Accident Facts.* Chicago: U.S. Government, 1980.

Salk, L. *What Every Child Would Like His Parents to Know.* New York: McKay, 1972.

Swanson, J. "A Toddler's Eating Habits." *Pediatr Nurs* 5:52–53, January/February 1979.

U.S. Consumer Product Safety Commission. *A Toy and Sports Equipment Safety Guide.* July 1980.

Verville, E. *Behavior Problems of Children.* Philadelphia: W. B. Saunders, 1967.

Weisel, M. "The Pediatrician and Corporal Punishment." *Pediatrics* 66:639–641, October 1980.

White, B. *The First Three Years of Life.* Englewood Cliffs, NJ: Prentice-Hall, 1975.

7

Health Care of the School-Age Child: 5–10 Years

The school-age period is characterized by an enormous expansion of the child's world, increased independence of thought and behavior, and steady but slow changes in physical growth and maturity. It is the period during which the dependence of the infant and preschool years gives way to the independence of the school years. The child, parents, and caretakers must adjust to increasing separation from the family because of school attendance, outside activities and interests, and peer relationships.

This chapter provides information on health assessment, growth and development, accident prevention and safety, and common problems of the school-age child.

A COMPREHENSIVE SCHEDULE OF WELL-CHILD CARE

Visit at 5–10 Years

HEALTH ASSESSMENT

The purposes of the history are to identify important health problems and to predict or prevent future difficulties. (See Table 7-1.) Information is elicited about the child's physical, emotional, educational, or social problems. How are the child's interactions with family members, teachers, and peers? How is the child's school performance? Does the child have difficulty sleeping? How would the caretaker describe the child's moods?

Gross pathologic conditions are seldom discovered in a child who has been seen regularly in the health care system. However, the nurse practitioner must always be alert for problems.

COUNSELING

Health teaching is directed toward the parents' and child's concerns. The school age period brings into focus problems related to school adjustment, peer relationships, learning difficulties, and emotional difficulties associated with identity, role, and self-image. Parents and caretakers are counseled to be role models and to function as advisors and teachers.

Physical Care   Discuss the following topics:

• Maintenance of self-hygiene with frequent washing of oily skin and hair
• Oral hygiene: brushing after meals and at bedtime; flossing once a day
• Outdoor activity for exercise

Emotional and Mental Development   See Tables 7-2 and 7-3. Discuss the following needs:

• Talking out problems with family members
• Needs of child: positive input from family, setting of appropriate limits and after school chores

Table 7-1

Health Assessment at 5 to 10 Years

Health History Physical Examination	Nutrition	Development	Laboratory Procedures Immunizations/Screenings
Parental and client concerns	Basic food groups: milk, 3 servings; meat (including poultry, fish, eggs, peanut butter, dried beans), 4 servings; fruits, vegetables, 4 servings; breads, cereals, 4 servings	5 to 6 years: balance on one foot for 10 seconds; backward heel to toe walk; draws person with greater than 6 parts; performs self-care activities	DTP and trivalent OPV boosters are given between 4 and 7 years of age
Interval history: illnesses, injuries, major changes in life-style	Food likes and dislikes	6 to 9 years: latency period of physical and psychological growth; questions about sex and conception	Tuberculin testing every 3 years
Review of systems	Types of food used for snacking	9 to 11 years: concrete thinking continues: judges thoughts only in reference to own experience, learns by trial and error	Routine urinalysis and complete blood count if not done within the last 3 years
School history	Sugar intake		
Family and social history	Other considerations: milk fortified with vitamin D; iodized salt; whole grain or enriched breads and cereals; evaluate calcium, fluoride, iron source	Beginning growth spurt: females at approximately 9½ years and males at approximately 10½ years	Screening: visual acuity and audiogram, language (DASE), dental, scoliosis
Weight, height, blood pressure, pulse, and respiration		Females: beginning growth of pubic hair and breast budding; tomboy activities	
A complete physical is done		Males: male-dominated social activity	
Discuss the findings with the parent and client		Average yearly weight gain is about 5½ to 7 lb.	
		Average yearly height increase is about 2 to 3 inches.	

Table 7-2
Personality Development

Child Is	Child Needs
Developing a sense of belonging and a more sophisticated sense of self and family in relation to the outside world.	A home environment that is secure and stable, in which the child can feel safe and relax and regroup energies after a day of learning new skills.
Basing his or her self-concept on things done rather than on things felt.	To take part in new experiences. A child becomes competent by participating in an activity that requires learning new skills, not by waiting until he or she is proficient before being included.
	To be praised for trying something new and making progress, not criticized for not doing it perfectly.
	Freedom to explore new skill areas without feeling more will immediately be expected from the child, who needs a chance to relax and enjoy success.
	To be compared with herself or himself, not measured against others.
	Toys and games that allow for experimentation and risk (i.e., Lincoln Logs, Erector Set, chemistry set).
	An environment stimulating enough to evoke curiosity.
	Experiences that are a result of his or her own actions, not only those based on something someone else has suggested.
Basing a personal assessment and how he or she fits into the world on external factors. Children are unable to evaluate their own performance and depend on the opinions of others.	To be reassured that there are many ways of accomplishing a task and that it is all right to do it in his or her own way.
	Recognition for unique skills.
	Appropriate and congruent affect with verbal messages.
	To be told when he or she does something competently for positive reinforcement.
	Parenting, not punishment. A child needs to be shown that there are alternative ways of doing something, not just criticized for not doing it properly.

Table 7-2 (Continued)

Child Is	Child Needs
	Opportunities for problem-solving, not rigid rules that prevent the child from developing initiative.
Developing a sense of right and wrong. There are three essential components: Authoritarian morality: conformity to avoid censure. Guilt: the result of the strengthening of an internal sense of right and wrong and the development of a concept of the future. Justice: the idea that crime begets punishment.	Solid and consistent limits that are reasonable, are applied fairly, and can be enforced. Good role models to follow to help incorporate societal values (e.g., parents should not talk about cheating on income taxes while telling their child it is wrong to steal). Punishment that fits the "crime." A child needs to learn not only what makes people angry, but to what degree.

Source: Reprinted with permission from Mari Siemon, "Mental Health in School-Aged Children," Am J Maternal Child Nurs 3:211–217, July/August 1978.

- Parents' interest in and participation in school activities
- Importance of peer relationships and group activities
- Outdoor activities as a method to reduce tension and stress

Stimulation and Creativity Table 7-4 lists popular activities and toys of the school-age child. Children of this age need and enjoy many levels of stimulation. Discuss:

- Conversation with parent or caretaker to explore thoughts, feelings, and daily activities
- Going on family trips and doing projects at home: cooking, games, handicrafts
- Instructing in the telling of time, traffic rules, remembering phone number, address

Table 7-3
Cognitive Development

Child Has	Child Needs
Concrete thoughts: he or she is learning to decipher symbols in speech and to recognize multiple meanings of words. Words are taken literally and personally.	Help in separating criticisms of behavior from criticisms of herself or himself (e.g., a parent should say, "I don't like what you did," not "I don't like you"). A clear understanding of words and meanings. Be specific in terms of behavior that is desirable or undesirable (i.e., "be good" may mean something different to an adult than to a child).
Egocentric thoughts: the child has a limited capacity to think for herself or himself and to make decisions. Judgments are based on what the child feels or would like to have happen.	Clear boundaries and limits. To have feelings recognized and accepted while limits are being enforced (i.e., "I know you're angry, but . . . ."). Opportunities to begin assuming responsibilities in order to move from being completely controlled, to being permitted to make limited decisions, to eventual emancipation in decision-making. Good role models to learn how to make decisions and to explore alternative behaviors. This also involves freedom to make mistakes.
Little sense of logic beyond simple cause and effect. Young children have the following view of things: Nonscientific: their ideas are not based on facts. Phenomenalistic: they believe that there is a causal relationship between two events that occur close together in time.	Firm and consistent limits to safeguard against an immature ability to make judgments. Repeated reiteration of rules and requests. Recognition that errors in judgment are attributable to ignorance, not to malice. To have the causes of traumatic events such as a death or divorce explained in order to understand with certainty that he or she was not responsible.

Table 7-3 *(Continued)*

Child Has	Child Needs
The use of magical thinking as an explanatory concept. There are four components: Animism: the belief that there are no accidents or impartial events, but that everything occurs by intent. Omnipotence: thoughts are as powerful as deeds. Compulsiveness: rituals are a way of warding off bad things. Denial: the belief that if you don't think about things, they won't be real.	Rules and structure that establish order in life. To be reassured that thoughts and wishes do not equal deeds. To have personal feelings of anger, fantasies, sibling rivalry, and so forth accepted as normal by adults. To have adults recognize that his or her denials may not be "lies," but may be triggered by an unconscious need for self-defense.

Source: Reprinted with permission from Mari Siemon, "Mental Health in School-Aged Children," *Am J Maternal Child Nurs* 3:211–217, July/August 1978.

School Preparation The nurse practitioner can help parents prepare their child for school. See Chapter 25, Screening Tests for School Readiness. Leve (1980, p. 338) recommends that parents:

- Adopt a positive attitude.
- Allow the child to express anxieties and fears about school.
- Discuss with the child the changes in his or her life.
- Prearrange a school visit for the child to meet the teacher and observe classroom activities.
- Provide concrete symbols of the child's new status.
- Recognize the effect on the child of the older siblings' or friends' attitudes toward school.

Table 7-5 identifies tasks of children, parents, teachers, and nurses in facilitating school adjustment.

Table 7-4
Popular Activities and Toys of the School-Age Child

Activity	6 Years	7 Years	8 Years	9 Years
Group	Adults still control group activity Ring games Chasing games Dramatic play with changing parts or couples (i.e., cops and robbers, mother and father, doctor and patient)	Lessening of adult influence More social play in small groups Dramatic play with some desire for props and stage sets Hide-and-seek; "it" games with increasing control of "it" character	Magic shows Games with rigid rules Board games Guessing games Aimless and wandering exploration with peers Beginning of team games Clubs and rituals	Learn plays with formal roles Team games with complicated rules; beginning of organized sports Intellectual board games
Solitary	Painting, cutting, pasting Dolls Toy farms, gas stations, city scenes TV cartoons Swimming, skating Looking at comic books	Barbie dolls Mechanical toys with action and many parts Coloring books TV cartoons Reading simple stories about real people	Collections such as stamps, cars, insects, match books Simple building Helping with household chores Reading about real-life and faraway characters	Arts and crafts that require special or complex skills and techniques Models Building Reading stories with complicated plots
Stories, Jokes, Humor	Story-telling with complicated plots laced with fantasy Puppets Jokes that juxtapose lines Word rhymes	Stories become more realistic Jokes may still be word plays or simple "moron" and other classic jokes	Stories that play tricks on people Stories that have much action but little resolution Riddles Jokes that pick up weak points or that exaggerate	Stories with some resolution of plot Jokes with some sexual overlay with or without knowledge Beginning interest in poetry

Source: Reprinted with permission from R. R. Wieczorek and J. N. Natapoff, *A Conceptual Approach to the Nursing of Children: Health Care from Birth through Adolescence.* Philadelphia: J.B. Lippincott, 1981. (Adapted in part from B. Sutton-Smith, and S. Sutton-Smith, *How to Play with Your Children,* New York: Hawthorne Books, 1974.)

Table 7-5

Tasks of Children, Parents, Teachers, and Nurses in Facilitating School Adjustment

Statement of Adjustment	Child's Tasks	Parents' and Teacher's Role in Facilitating Task Achievement	Nurse's Role in Assisting Parents, Teachers, Child
Diffusion into larger world (5 or 6–8 yr)	1. Must adapt to differences in teacher's and parents' disciplinary approach and behavioral expectations.	1. Parents and teacher should communicate their respective expectations for the child to identify extreme differences and to work out compromises that permit him or her to meet expectations of each and so that parents and teachers can mutually reinforce their expectations.	1. School nurse can help organize parent–teacher interaction (e.g., preschool roundups; parent–teacher–nurse conferences) or mediate in conflicts. For example, during preschool roundup or school physical examination, determine child's and parents' expectations for school.
	2. Must compete with peers for teacher's attention and approval as teacher replaces parent for large portion of day.	2. Teachers should avoid obvious favoritism in classroom, give individual attention and praise to each child, and avoid comparisons of achievement.	2. School nurse can offer guidance to teachers and intervene in unhealthy child–teacher relationships. For example, during preschool registration or school physical, evaluate parent–child relationship for problems, as these often carry over to teacher–child relationships.

Continued

Table 7-5 (Continued)

Statement of Adjustment	Child's Task	Parents' and Teacher's Role in Facilitating Task Achievement	Nurse's Role in Assisting Parents, Teachers, Child
	3. Must learn to handle blatant, hurtful honesty and downright rudeness of peers without damage to self-concept.	3. Peer activities and behaviors need close adult supervision.	3. Nurse in well-child facilities or schools can provide this guidance to parents and teachers.
	4. Needs to test out new ideas and behaviors in security of home environment.	4. Parents need to recognize developmental function of "trying on" ideas and behaviors incongruent with family's but to set reasonable limits on how much and what type of "trying on" is to be allowed.	4. Nurse in well-child facilities or schools may offer this anticipatory guidance.
Disorganization created by disparities between home and school or peers (8–10 yr)	1. Must learn to concentrate on cognitive achievements as the child settles into school life.	1. Parents and teachers need open communication about cognitive tasks being focused on at any one time and skills the child finds difficult with this task. Investigation of state of health, sensory organ function, and neurologic, physical, and emotional function should follow in order to determine source of problem in achieving task.	1. School nurse observations in classroom will help identify children having difficulty with this task.

2. Must learn to integrate peer values in a manner that does not deny family values and to transfer family values into larger world in socially acceptable ways.

2. Parents and teachers must understand that just as children fall when learning to walk, so will they fall when learning to think. These falls during school age are typically boasting, teasing, fighting, lying, cheating, sassing, and whining.

3. Teachers and parents need to develop the art of overlooking minor falls and feel comfortable seeking help for more serious or persistent falls. Children left alone with their peer group often overcome problems with peer assistance rather than with adult intervention.

2. School nurses should regularly monitor playground and classroom activities to identify dissociated children and then set the task force (parents, teachers, nurses, other pertinent school or health personnel) in motion to uncover source of problem and offer help.

3. Well-child facility and school nurse should evaluate child's behavior patterns and self-concept at each contact to pick up clues that all is not well in the child's emotional and social relationships. Nurse in clinic or school should offer parental/teacher anticipatory guidance regarding handling of behavior problems.

Source: Reprinted with permission from J. J. M. Tackett and M. Hunsberger, *Family-Centered Care of Children and Adolescents.* Philadelphia: W.B. Saunders, 1981. Pp. 1044–1045.

Parent–Child Relationship   Discuss the following aspects:

- Family's ability to grant some autonomy to the child in decision making: choosing own clothes, planning leisure activities
- Importance of chores in helping to establish feelings of responsibility and accomplishment
- Family and child's readiness for separation and school
- Approach to discussion of sexual matters with child

Nurse Practitioner Goals   The goals of the nurse practitioner include the following:

- Being an advocate for the child
- Providing health education about nutrition, development, safety
- Being aware of signs of family dysfunction: noncommunication, school phobia, scapegoating
- Communicating with family and school officials if learning problems are present

GROWTH AND DEVELOPMENT

During the school-age years, there is movement toward the integration of personal, egocentric needs and societal pressures on the child, and an equilibrium develops between the child's emerging independence and adherence to rules leading to increased autonomy. The school-age period is a time of rapid growth and development in intellectual and social maturation. Table 7-6 summarizes the growth and development milestones of the school-age child.

Feeding During the School Years

During the school years, parental supervision of feeding habits decreases and children begin to select some of their own foods and determine their own eating patterns. There are fluctuations in appetite due to growth patterns and activity levels. The school-age child's digestive system demonstrates maturity by having fewer upsets and retaining food for a longer period of time so that the child does not have to be fed as carefully and as promptly. Since growth is slow, the caloric needs, when compared with the stomach size, are not as great as when the child was younger. Parents need to be cautioned that the child will fill up on empty calories and foods that are not conducive to growth, such as excess fats, sugars, and starches. The child should eat foods high in protein, minerals, and vitamins. Caution parents about excessive soft drinks and candy. See Chapter 3, Recommended Daily Dietary Allowances and Recommended Food Intake for Good Nutrition.

Dental Health

The school years are important for dentition. Changes from deciduous to permanent teeth take place during these years. See Chapter 16, Dentition and Dental Referral. Proper nutrition is essential for healthy dentition.

Children should be encouraged to brush their teeth and floss their teeth regularly.

Posture

Posture consists of proportion, symmetry, and alignment. See Chapter 23, Posture. By 6 years of age, most children are walking with a heel–toe motion similar to that of adults. A mild amount of pigeon-toe or knock-knee may be normal. The spine makes a series of subtle bends: forward at the neck, backward at the thorax or ribs, forward at the lumbar area or lower back, and backward at the sacral area or buttocks. Some swayback, potbelly, and knock-knee may be normal (Brower and Nash, 1979, p. 60). There are several signs of posture problems:

• Chronic slumping
• Extreme posture variations
• Feet that excessively point in or out
• Shoes that are pulled out of shape, worn out too quickly, or soles or heels that wear down unevenly
• Unusual head holding angles

Table 7-6

Growth and Development Chart: The School-Age Child

Age (years)	Personal/Social	Fine Motor	Gross Motor	Language	Cognitive
5	Initiates contacts with strangers and relates interesting vignettes Interested in telling and comparing stories about self Peer relations are important ("best friends" abound) Responds to social values by assuming sex roles with rigidity	Ties shoelaces Copies a diamond and a triangle Prints a few letters or numbers May print first name Cuts food	Will not attempt feats beyond ability Throws and catches ball well Jumps rope Walks backward with heel to toe Skips and hops Adept on tricycle and climbing equipment	Vocabulary of 3,000 words 90% of speech is intelligible Asks meanings of words Enjoys telling stories	Thinks feelings and thoughts can happen Intrusions into the body cause fear and anxiety (fear of mutilation and castration)
6–7	Beginning Erikson's stage of "industry vs inferiority" Adheres to predetermined rules Becoming ready to enter the larger society and to venture out into the world of	Painting, cutting, pasting Unable to control small muscle precisely Copies diamond and square Prints words, starting with name	Improved capabilities Larger, stronger muscles Unable to sit for prolonged periods Knows right from left Can walk a chalk mark	Major speech patterns and syntax are established Able to speak the culture's dominant language Considerable increases in new grammatical constructions take place	Egocentric—believes everyone thinks as he or she does Continues preoperational thinking until age 7 Wants to learn all about the body and is interested in functions of such activi-

Age	Social	Motor	Language	Cognitive
	peer groups, school, and clubs Interacts with a small number of neighborhood youngsters in loosely organized groups Able to handle basic impulses, to separate from parents, and to adapt to new situations	Draws a person with 12–16 parts	Can tell stories about monsters and other threats but does nothing about them	ties as growing, running, and sneezing Sees health in concrete terms
7–8	Groups become firmly established, often sex and race segregated Sets own elaborate rules and moral codes Spends many hours with peers Hierarchy emerges with leaders and followers rigidly determined and relatively stable over time	Eye–hand coordination not fully developed Seems a little "clumsy" Cautious when attempting new gross motor activities May be able to swim and ride bicycle Balance improving	Vocabulary continues to increase Story characters begin to respond to threat or trouble but do not really do much for themselves. The trouble just goes away	Thinking becomes operational Cause and effect are understood Will learn to understand that others have thoughts and intentions and that if you hurt someone you may be hurt in return Begins to see the relationship between part and whole

Continued

419

Table 7-6 (Continued)

Age (years)	Personal/Social	Fine Motor	Gross Motor	Language	Cognitive
8–10	Organized sports become popular Adheres rigidly to rules Fantasy and aimlessness decrease Becomes increasingly concerned with techniques and formal activities such as model building	Increasing capabilities with fine motor control Uses both hands independently Draws a person with 18–20 parts	Very energetic Jumps, chases, skips, runs Tends to be more graceful and coordinated Engages in organized sports	Vocabulary continues to increase Story characters begin to react to the danger with specific and successful action	The child's ability to get along with peers coincides with cognitive growth and the ability to understand the other's point of view Can understand weight changes Reversibility—cognitive processes can take place in opposite directions Can go through a chain of events backward to the beginning and understand how it is possible to undo something

Ability to classify objects into a hierarchical arrangement

Can recognize subclasses of a larger group (dog as an animal)

Concepts of birth and death become clearer but are still thought of in concrete terms

Interest grows in the intricacies of bodily functions, in internal organs, and in how things work

Health: able to consider internal factors such as feeling states

Source: Reprinted with permission from R. R. Wieczorek and J. N. Natapoff, *A Conceptual Approach to the Nursing of Children: Health Care from Birth through Adolescence,* Philadelphia: J.B. Lippincott, 1981.

Competitive Athletics and Sports

Guidelines for parents to consider regarding their child's participation in competitive athletics (AAP, 1981) are the following:

1. There should be high-quality supervision:
   - Are there qualified and competent person(s) available to teach and supervise the relative hazards of each sports activity, and to recognize and care for injuries during games and practice?
   - Are there established policies, procedures, and responsibilities for first aid, referral, and follow-up of injured children?
   - Is there attention to physical and emotional stress and fatigue?
2. The child should have a periodic health appraisal every two to three years.
3. The athletic grouping should be done according to the child's weight, size, physical condition, skill, physical maturation, and sex when indicated.
4. The child should have appropriate physical conditioning.
5. There should be adequate and properly fitted equipment.
6. The sports facilities should be suitably maintained.
7. There should be assurance that the athletic program will not interfere with the normal school program.

Children who are injured should be removed from sports play and evaluated. See Table 7-7 for indications for immediate removal from sports play.

Weight Training and Lifting

Weight training is usually employed for physical conditioning for sports. It is a method of resistance conditioning that involves repetitive exercises using various weights, machines, pulleys, and devices. A properly supervised program of exercises can enhance the performance of a postpubertal athlete; however, prepubertal boys benefit minimally. They do not significantly improve strength

Table 7-7

Area of Injury	Indications for Immediate Removal from Play
Eye	Blunt trauma, visual difficulty, pain, laceration, obvious deformity
Head	Loss of consciousness, disturbed sensorium, seeing stars or colors, dizziness, auditory hallucinations, nausea, vomiting, lethargy, severe headache, rising blood pressure, disturbed smell, diminishing pulse, amnesia, hyperirritability, large contusion, open wounds, unequal pupils, leakage of cerebrospinal fluid or blood from ears or nose, numbness of one side of body
Neck or spine	Obvious deformity, restricted motion, weakness of extremity, pain on movement, localized tenderness, numbness of extremity, paresthesias
Shoulders or extremities	Obvious deformity, crepitus, loss of range of motion, loss of sensation, effusion, pain on use, unstable joint, open wounds, significant tenderness, significant swelling
Abdomen	Dizziness or syncope, nausea, persisting pallor, vomiting, history of infectious mononucleosis, abnormal thirst, muscle guarding, localized tenderness, shoulder pain, distention, rapid pulse, clamminess and sweating

Source: Reprinted by permission from J. Greensher, H. C. Mofenson, and N. J. Merlis, "First Aid for School Athletic Emergencies," *NY State J Med* June 1979. P. 1058. Copyright by the Medical Society of the State of New York.

or increase muscle mass in a weight-training program because of insufficient circulating androgens. Girls compete well against boys in endurance exercises, but not as well in strength activities. After menarche, females may develop strength, but weight training does not significantly increase their muscle mass unless anabolic steroids are taken. This practice is not recommended. The reader is referred to the guidelines for safe conduct of weight training detailed by Stone and Kroll (1978).

Weight lifting is a sport designed to demonstrate maximum strength. The potential for injury is high if lifting is not practiced safely and correctly. Parents should be cautioned about the dangers of improperly supervised weight-lifting practice.

Exercise

Dynamic exercises involve rhythmic contractions and relaxations of large muscle masses and are aerobic by nature. By contrast, tension exercises cause prolonged contraction of the muscles as in weight training or wrestling. Dynamic exercises are the preferred form of exercises because they promote aerobic fitness. Normally active children are aerobically physically fit because, by nature, they are so active.

One or more of the following exercises can be chosen by children to train themselves to be aerobically fit:

• Bicycling
• Aerobic dancing
• Cross-country skiing
• Distance running or race walking
• Distance swimming
• Hiking
• Jumping rope

Summer Camp

Guidelines for parents in selecting camps (AAP Newsletter, April 1982) are as follows:

• Ability of the camp to handle emergencies as well as any special health needs of the child.
• Availability and accessibility of qualified health personnel. A nurse should be present if the total number of staff and children exceeds 50. One staff member certified in emergency care should be available for every 200 campers. An infirmary building should be available if there are more than 100 people living at the camp site.
• Availability of first-aid equipment, telephone service, and an emergency communications system.
• Availability of health screening exams for children arriving at camp and leaving the camp.
• Medications are safely locked and dispensed by qualified personnel.

- Programs featured in the camp program.
- Qualifications of the staff.
- Written procedures to ensure safe participation in activities.

Television

Television viewing by children consumes more time than any other activity except for sleeping. Children average 26 hours of television watching each week. The major concern about the tremendous amount of television viewing is the effect of television violence. The causal linkage between television violence and actual aggressive behavior remains elusive. Research, however, has shown that children can learn prosocial, helpful behaviors through television viewing.

Nurse practitioners should encourage and reinforce parents to take an active interest in their children's television viewing habits with the goal of making it a positive influence on the child's development. Parents should *talk* about programs with children as a means of discussing what delighted or upset them about the shows. Discussion will help the child distinguish reality from fantasy. Parents should *choose* the programs with their children, and they should *look* at them together.

The National Coalition on Television Violence is organized to monitor and decrease television violence. Information on this organization can be obtained by writing to NCTV, 1530 P Street NW, P.O. Box 12038, Washington DC 20005.

ACCIDENT PREVENTION AND SAFETY

Developmental Perspectives

The school-age child assumes great responsibility. The child goes to school alone, often using school buses, but also uses public transportation. The child follows peer leaders and will become daring under their pressure. Group activity involvement is important to the child. Increasing participation in sports is seen. Time spent away from home increases and so does the need for assuming greater responsibility for one's well-being.

EVENTS

The major events continue to be burns and fires, drowning, and motor vehicle accidents along with a variety of other events.

COUNSELING

Safety and accident prevention discussion for the school-age child needs to be addressed to both the parent and the child. Safety tips to cover for each event are listed below.

Burns and Fires   See Chapter 28, Burns.

1. Be aware of the tragedy of fire and learn to respect fire.
2. Douse all campfires and barbecues well with water. Supervision by adults of all campfires is essential.
3. Purchase safe camping gear. Look for fire retardant or fire resistant on the label.
4. Eliminate fire hazards in the home.
5. Practice regular fire drills at home and at school.

Drowning   See Chapter 28, Near Drowning

1. Adopt the buddy system for water sports and wear a life jacket while boating and water skiing.
2. Learn to swim under adult supervision, preferably a lifeguard.
3. Be sure water sources are adequately protected.

Motor Vehicle Accidents

1. Be a safe pedestrian. Look both ways before crossing the street. Use a crosswalk. Do not cross on a red light.
2. Do not use the street as a playground.
3. Use auto safety restraints at all times, even for short distances. Avoid horse play in the car.
4. Inspect bus routes, driver qualifications, and adequacy of bus maintenance.

Other Events

1. Be certain the child knows his or her name, address, and phone number.
2. Do not keep firearms in one's possession. If they are about, be certain the guns are not loaded. Keep them locked up.
3. Encourage supervised sports and group activities.
4. Know and abide by the bike-riding laws. Wear bright clothing, preferably with fluorescent patches, while biking. Keep bikes in good repair.
5. Learn the proper use of all household gadgets and equipment.
6. Teach the child not to ride with strangers.
7. Teach the child how to contact the police and the fire department.
8. Teach the child to avoid strange, sick animals, and never to tease an animal or touch one that is sleeping.

SCREENING INFORMATION

For vision screening, see Chapter 15, for hearing screening and language screening, see Chapter 25, and for screening tests for school readiness, see Chapter 25.

PROBLEMS OF THE SCHOOL-AGE CHILD

The physical problems of school-age children are covered elsewhere in this book. They include anemia (see Chapter 19), conjunctivitis (see Chapter 15), dental caries (see Chapter 16), hearing (see Chapter 25), skeletal abnormalities (see Chapter 23), verrucae (see Chapter 14), and vision (see Chapter 15).

Aggressive Conduct Disorder

Assessment This is a behavior disorder characterized by persistent aggressiveness (both physical and verbal), noncompliance, and meanness, destructiveness, or antisocial behavior. The estimated prevalence of this disorder ranges from 1.5 to 7 percent. Twice as many inner-city-area children have this problem as compared with rural-area children. Boys outnumber girls being treated for this problem roughly 6:1. The history usually reveals that the child has been difficult to handle since the first or second year of life. The child is reported to be more demanding than most children, to require more supervision, and to be more volatile. The child is seen as disruptive. The family history usually reveals parents with psychiatric disorders such as antisocial problems, hysteria, anxiety, or schizophrenia.

Management Referral for psychiatric/psychologic help is indicated. The prescribing of stimulant drugs and use of behavior modification are the two commonly used approaches. The value of long-term drug treatment is questionable. Behavior modification may be a more promising form of treatment. Therapy aimed at parents may also be useful since a more positive atmosphere in the home and better attitude toward the difficult child in the long run will help the child.

Attention-Deficit Disorder

See Chapter 25 for a discussion of this problem.

Childhood Depression

Assessment The existence of childhood depression has been debated by mental health professionals. However, clinical observations strongly support the idea that depression in childhood exists. Research still needs to be conducted to truly identify the scope and nature of the problem.

HISTORY Elicit information on school performance, academic functioning; chronic illness; pattern of psychosomatic illness; history of psychopathology; unusual habits such as pulling out of hair; review of systems emphasizing gastrointestinal disturbances, alteration in eating patterns (anorexia, vomiting, overeating), changes in bowel or bladder habits, sleep difficulties, headaches unrelated to organic causes; family structure, dynamics, peer relationships (see Chapter 1, family history), family turmoil (death of family member, loss of pet), social isolation, or peer rejection. Questions include: How significant was this change to your child? What was the sequence of events surrounding this change?

INTERVIEW THE CHILD Explore the child's verbal expressions, fantasies, and moods (Nelms and Brady, 1980). Use direct or open-ended questions. Useful questions include: How do you feel about yourself? Do you think other kids like you? Do you ever want to hurt yourself?

DIAGNOSIS The actual diagnosis of depression is variable and complex. Labelling a child as depressed should be done with great caution. There are no currently established criteria for the diagnosis, although the health history, high risk factors, and behavioral manifestations of depression can indicate the need for psychologic referral. Table 7-8 lists the high-risk factors and Table 7-9 lists behavioral manifestations of depression in school age children. The symptoms may be normal responses to crises as well as indicators of future difficulties. Criteria for further investigation are persistence of a combination of symptoms over several months, and an abrupt change in the child's usual behavior pattern.

Table 7-8
At-Risk Factors

1. Death of a parent
2. Divorce
3. Long-term hospitalization
4. Placement in a foster home
5. Absence or chronic separation of parent and child
6. Parent(s) with psychopathology
7. Learning problems
8. Chronic illness or physical deformity
9. Rigid parents with strict uncompromising standards

Source: Reprinted with permission from A. Child, C. Murphy, and M. Rhyne, "Depression in Children: Reasons and Risks," *Pediatr Nurs* 6(4):9–13 July/August 1980.

Table 7-9
Manifestations of Depression in Children

School-age child
  At home
    Temper tantrums
    Provocative behavior
    Disobedience
    Playing hookey
    Running away from home
    Boredom
    Sad face
    Tearful
    Monotone voice
    Slow movement
    Somatic complaints
    Denial of feeling sad or hopeless
    Lack of any desire for constructive activity
  At school
    Quiet
    Inhibited
    Indecisive expression
    Inevitableness of failure
    Excessive daydreaming
    Seldom asks for help
    Too sensitive
    Cries easily
    Indifference to succeeding
    Sleepiness
    Avoids group activities
    Loss of usual energy
    Conduct problems, especially in boys
    Learning difficulties
    Hyperactivity
    Hypochondriasis
    Difficulty in simple mental activities
    Avoids eye contact when spoken to
    Excessive use of washroom
    Inordinate amount of time to complete assignments
    Passive and submissive relationship toward the teacher
    Restlessness

Source: Reprinted with permission from A Child, C. Murphy, and M. Rhyne, "Depression in Children: Reasons and Risks." *Pediatr Nurs* 6(4):12, July/August 1980.

Management   A full discussion of the management of childhood depression is beyond the scope of this chapter. The reader is referred to child psychiatric texts for in-depth information.

Generally, the management of childhood depression depends on the severity and type of depression, the treatment method chosen, and the nurse practitioner's clinical expertise. The child with acute depression may be managed with counseling, short-term psychotherapy, or careful monitoring of the child's overall mental health. The nurse practitioner skilled in counseling may be able to manage a child with acute depression. A child with chronic depression is referred for psychiatric/psychologic intervention for long-term psychotherapy. The goal of psychotherapy is to help the child develop mastery of his or her current difficulties and to grow optimally.

The family should be involved in the child's treatment and, frequently, family therapy may be initiated. A supportive home environment for the child is important. The family needs ongoing caring, encouragement, and support of the nurse practitioner through this difficult and, often, long and slow recovery process.

Lying

Assessment   A conscious and deliberate misrepresentation of the facts is properly called lying. Children under age 6 to 7 have an active fantasy life, and in the early school years sorting fantasies from real life may be difficult. Normally, most children will tell a lie at some point or another.

Management   The approach to management depends on whether this is a new behavior and on the frequency of occurrence. The motivation for the lying needs to be explored. Appropriate counseling is initiated once the motivation is identified. A problem-solving session with the parents and child may be useful in deterring further events. The nurse practitioner can help the family identify communication patterns within the family that might motivate the child to lie. The nurse practitioner should support parents in their efforts to help their child stop lying. Excessive lying is often a sign of deeper family pathology, and the family should be referred for mental health counseling.

Obsessive–Compulsive Disorder

Assessment Children between 7 and 8 years start to have this problem. Common compulsions are handwashing, bedtime rituals, repeated erasing and rewriting of school assignments. These symptoms frequently occur in children who are anxious or depressed.

Management Referral to child psychiatrist may be indicated.

School Phobia

Assessment School phobia is a persistent and abnormal fear of going to school. Twenty percent of children experience a period in which they prefer not to go to school. This usually occurs in the first 2 or 3 years of attendance. Most of these children master their fears on their own with firm parental support. Less than one-tenth of 1 percent develop such a mortal fear of school that they adamantly refuse to attend or run away if they are taken to school (Stewart, 1980).

Children with school phobias tend to be the oldest or only children from families of higher socioeconomic status. They have higher IQs than children with conduct disorders. This problem occurs more frequently in girls than in boys. The onset may be sudden or gradual. There is evidence that mothers of children with school phobia overprotect and indulge them so that the external world may appear dangerous (Berg et al., 1969; Hersov, 1960).

Stewart (1980, p. 392) offers several diagnostic criteria for school phobia. Criteria nos. 1 and 2 plus three or more of nos. 3–7 should alert the nurse practitioner to a possible school phobia:

1. Attacks of disabling anxiety
2. Specific fears that are disabling
3. Complaints of stomachaches, no appetite, vomiting
4. Complaints of palpitations, dyspnea, chest pain
5. Tiredness or depression
6. Timidity, worrying
7. Difficulty going to sleep

Management The goal of management is to alleviate the child's and parents' anxieties. The child must firmly be made to attend school. Delay in returning to school worsens the prognosis. If upon return to school the child panics, have someone the child trusts go to school and sit in the classroom for several days to desensitize the situation, and then gradually move outside the classroom. This method gradually helps the child to decrease anxiety.

Other interventions include emotional support and parental education. Parents should learn to encourage the child to develop self-help skills, self-reliance, and self-confidence (Fond and Brosnan, 1980). Coordination between the school and health care system is necessary.

Prognosis Mild phobias that start early and those that come on suddenly usually resolve with firm and sympathetic care from parents. Children with more serious and chronic problems have a poor prognosis and should be referred for psychiatric help.

Stealing

Assessment The significance of stealing depends on the child's developmental stage. Once the child has gained control over impulses, the act of taking something that belongs to someone else is properly called stealing. Most children around 7 years of age do go through a period in which they take change from a parent's purse or wallet. This occurs typically during the stage in which they are learning how to make change and are discovering the value of money.

Management Upon discovering that their child has taken money from them, parents should explain and discuss the importance of property rights with the child. The reason for stealing should be explored. Parents should be counseled to handle the situation simply and to clearly express their anger at this behavior. Stories or books can be used to convey the moral or principle involved. Indiscriminate, repeated stealing may require referral to mental health counseling.

Resource Information

USDHHS. *Children and Youth in Action: Physical Activities and Sports.* DHHS Public. No. (OHDS)80-30182, November 1980.

Braga, J. and L. Braga. *Children and Adults: Activities for Growing Together.* Englewood Cliffs, NJ: Prentice-Hall, 1976.

References

AAP Policy Statement. "Competitive Athletics for Children of Elementary School Age. *News and Comment 32* 6:9–10, June 1981.

American Academy of Pediatrics. *School Health: A Guide for Health Professionals, 1981.* Evanston, IL: AAP, 1981.

AAP. "Summer Camp: Make Sure It's Safe and Healthy for Your Children." *Your Child's Health.* Spring 1982.

AAP Policy Statement. "Weight Training and Weight Lifting: Information for the Pediatrician." *News and Comment 33* 7:7–8, July 1982.

Annell, A. L., editor. *Depressive States in Childhood and Adolescence.* New York: Wiley, 1975.

Aradine, C. R. "Books for Children about Death." *Pediatrics 57*:372–378, March 1976.

Berg, I., K. Nichols, and C. Pritchard. "School Phobia: Its Classification and Relationship to Dependency." *J Child Psychol Psychiatry 10*:123–141, October 1969.

Brower, E. W. and C. L. Nash. "Evaluating Growth and Posture in School-Age Children." *Nursing 79* 9:57–63, April 1979.

Child, A. C., C. M. Murphy, and M. C. Rhyne. "Depression in Children: Reasons and Risks." *Pediatr Nurs 6*:9–13, July/August 1980.

Danish, R. "The Case for Television." In D. H. Smith and R. A. Hoekelman, editors, *Controversies in Child Health and Pediatric Practice.* New York: McGraw-Hill, 1981. Pp. 157–166.

Denhoff, E. and S. A. Feldman. *Developmental Disabilities.* New York: Marcel Dekker, 1981.

Fond, K. and J. Brosnan. "School Phobia: The School Anxiety Symptom." *Pediatr Nurs 6*:9–13, September/October 1980.

Gabel, S. and M. Erickson, editors. *Child Development and Developmental Disabilities.* Boston: Little, Brown, 1980.

Hersov, L. A. "Refusal to Go to School." *J. Child Psychol Psychiatry 1*:137–145, June 1960.

Leve, R. *Childhood: The Study of Development.* New York: Random House, 1980.

Lewis, M. *Clinical Aspects of Child Development.* 2nd ed. Philadelphia: Lea & Febiger, 1982.

Mofenson, J., et al. "First Aid for School Athletic Emergencies." *NY State J Med* 79:1058–1062, June 1979.

Nelms, B. C. and M. A. Brady. "Assessment and Intervention: The Depressed School-Age Child." *Pediatr Nurs* 6:15–19, July/August 1980.

Pearson, G. A. "Nutrition in the Middle Years of Childhood." *Am J Maternal Child Nurs* 2:378–384, November/December 1977.

Poznanski, E. O., V. Krahenbuhl, and J. Zrull. "Childhood Depression: A Longitudinal Perspective." *Arch Gen Psychiatry* 23:491–501, June 1970.

Ruttenberg, H. D. "Exercise in Children: Sports Medicine As a Health Service in Pediatrics." In A. J. Moss, editor, *Pediatrics Update*. New York: Elsevier Biomedical, 1983. Pp. 381–397.

Schulterbrandt, G. and A. Raskin, editors. *Depression in Childhood: Diagnosis, Treatment and Conceptual Models*. New York: Raven Press, 1977.

Siemon, M. "Mental Health in School-Aged Children." *Am J Maternal Child Nurs* 3:211–217, July/August 1978.

Stewart, M. "Personality and Psychoneurotic Disorders." In S. Gabel and M. Erickson, editors, *Child Development and Developmental Disabilities*. Boston: Little, Brown, 1980. Pp. 389–409.

Stone, W. J. and W. A. Kroll. *Sports Conditioning and Weight Training*. Boston: Allyn and Bacon, 1978.

Tackett, J. J. M. and M. Hunsberger. *Family-Centered Care of Children and Adolescents*. Philadelphia: W.B. Saunders, 1981.

Welner, L. "Childhood Depression: An Overview." *J Nerv Ment Dis* 166:588–593, August 1978.

8

Health Care of the Adolescent: 11–21 Years

Adolescence is defined as that period in the second decade of a person's life when increased physical growth, beginning development of secondary sexual characteristics, and emotional changes are initiated. Puberty, a term used synonymously with adolescence, refers only to the biologic changes that occur during this period.

Society has recognized the rapid developmental period of adolescence by providing constitutional rights for minors and by lowering the age for some legal responsibilities. Adolescents have also become increasingly verbal in expressing their own feelings about themselves and their futures.

Adolescents are facing problems their parents never dealt with: increasing sexual freedom and its consequences, the uncertainty of future careers in a shrinking job market, and diffuse role models of parents and peers because of rapid social change.

To provide realistic care, the nurse practitioner recognizes society's attitude toward adolescence and understands the developmental tasks that adolescents must deal with to become mature, independent adults.

ADOLESCENT PHYSICAL DEVELOPMENT

Assessment

DEVELOPMENTAL LANDMARKS

Puberty generally starts in girls between 10 and 11 years of age and in boys between 11 and 12 years of age. The normal range is age 8 to 13 for girls and age 9½ to 14 for boys. In most adolescents, the initial pubertal event for the female is breast budding and for the male it is testicular growth. Occasionally for both sexes pubic hair growth may be seen first. Precocious puberty in girls, which is breast development and/or pubic hair growth, occurs before 8 years of age. In boys, precocious puberty, which is growth of the testicles greater than 3 cm in diameter and/or pubic hair development, occurs before age 9. Delayed puberty in girls is lack of development of secondary sexual characteristics after 13 years of age and in boys it is after 14 years of age. The range of menarche is between 10 and 16½ years of age and the mean age in the United States is 12.6 years.

MAJOR EVENTS OF PUBERTY

Secondary sexual characteristics are major pubertal changes. These include development of breasts in girls, enlargement of genitals and appearance of pubic and axillary hair in both sexes, and voice changes in boys. Other major events of puberty include the following:

- Increased acceleration of the skeletal system culminating in the growth spurt or peak height velocity (PHV)
- Increased muscular strength in both sexes, but especially in boys
- Increased development of the circulatory and respiratory systems causing increased strength and endurance, especially for males
- Increased deposit of adipose tissue in the buttocks, thighs, and breasts in girls

TANNER STAGING

The progressive growth of secondary sexual characteristics is internationally measured according to Tanner's developmental stages. The research was done and published in England (Tanner, 1962; Marshall and Tanner, 1969, 1970). Nude photographs were obtained for a group of healthy adolescents starting with puberty. Progressive changes in breast, pubic hair, and genital growth were noted. As a result, Tanner described the categories of changing adolescent development: female breast and pubic hair changes and male penis, scrotal, and pubic hair changes. Each category is divided into five stages from 1 to 5 (see Table 8-1: Developmental Stages of Secondary Sexual Characteristics).

Tanner staging is an important clinical tool for the nurse practitioner because it provides concrete evidence of an adolescent's physical development over a period of time. This helps with ascertaining the stage of the pubertal growth and whether the growth is occurring at a normal rate. Results of Tanner staging are also correlated with other physical developments. For example, in females menarche occurs between Tanner breast stages 4 and 5 and height spurt occurs between breast stages 3 and 4. In males, height spurt occurs between pubic hair stages 3 and 4. This information is helpful to professionals and to adolescents who want to know whether they will grow more or if menarche will occur shortly. Figures 8-1 and 8-2 depict the sequence of events at adolescence in girls and boys. Figure 8-3 shows the sequence of pubertal development in the female. Figure 8-4 shows the sequence of pubertal development in the male.

HORMONAL ACTIVITY

Hypothalamus/Anterior Pituitary The hypothalamus, under the influence of the central nervous system (CNS) and its neurotransmitters, produces neurohormonal substrates called releasing factors or hormones, which are stored in nerve endings (Finkelstein, 1980). At these sites, gonadotropin-releasing hormone (GRH) causes the anterior pituitary to release follicle-stimulating hormone (FSH) and luteinizing hormone (LH).

During childhood, the hypothalamic–pituitary axis and the gonads (ovaries, testicles) are operating at low levels, producing

Table 8-1

Developmental Stages of Secondary Sex Characteristics

Stage	Female Breast Development	Male Genital Development	Male and Female Pubic Hair Development
1	Pre-adolescent: elevation of papilla only	Pre-adolescent: testes, scrotum, and penis are about the same size and proportion as in early childhood	Pre-adolescent: no pubic hair
2	Breast bud stage: elevation of breast and papilla as small mound. Enlargement of areolar diameter	Enlargement of scrotum and testes; skin of the scrotum reddens and changes in texture; little or no enlargement of penis	Sparse growth of long, slightly pigmented downy hair, straight or only slightly curled, appearing chiefly at the base of the penis or along the labia
3	Further enlargement and elevation of breast and areolar with no separation of their contours	Enlargement of penis, which occurs at first mainly in length; further growth of testes and scrotum	Hair darker, coarser, and more curled; spreads sparsely over the junction of the pubes
4	Projection of the areola and papilla to form a secondary mound above the level of the breast.	Increased size of penis with growth in breadth and development of glans; further enlargement of testes and scrotum; increased darkening of scrotal skin	Hair adult in type but area covered is still considerably smaller than in the adult; no spread to the medial surface of the thighs
5	Mature stage: projection of papilla only due to recession of the areola to the general contour of the breast	Genitalia adult in size and shape	Adult in quantity and type

Source: Reprinted with permission from J. M. Tanner, *Growth at Adolescence,* 2nd ed. (Oxford, England: Blackwell Scientific Publications, 1962).

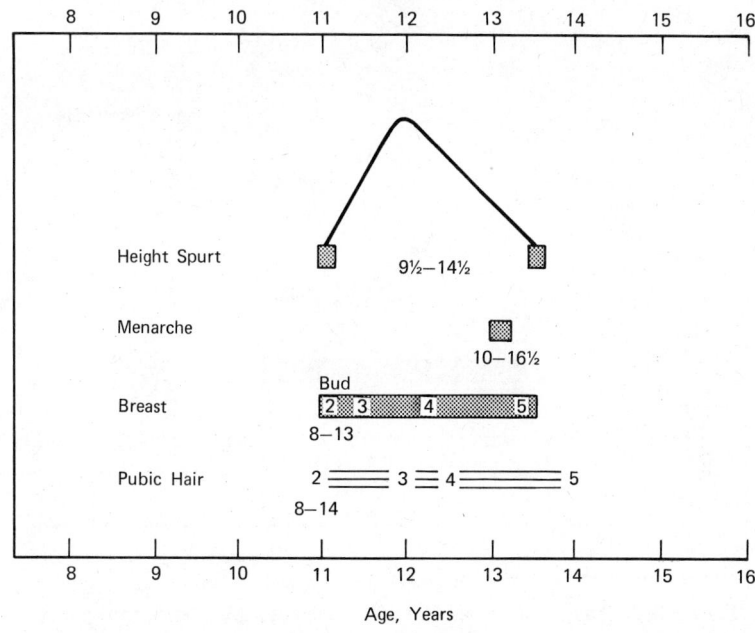

Figure 8-1 Sequence of events at adolescence in girls. An average girl is represented. The range of ages within which each event charted may begin and end is given by the figures placed directly below its start and finish. (Reprinted with permission from J. M. Tanner, *Growth at Adolescence,* 2nd ed., Oxford, England: Blackwell Scientific, 1962.)

FSH, LH, estrogen, progesterone and testosterone. The mechanism is extremely sensitive to negative feedback. When increased levels of estrogen, progesterone, and testosterone are in the blood, the hypothalamic–pituitary axis stops producing FSH and LH, causing levels of estrogen, progesterone, and testosterone to fall. At puberty the system becomes more operational and larger amounts of FSH and LH are in the blood before negative feedback mechanisms are initiated to decrease production of the hormones.

FOLLICLE-STIMULATING HORMONE (FSH) This hormone in the female matures the ovarian follicles to produce estrogen and some progesterone. In males, FSH causes seminiferous tubules of the testicles to produce sperm.

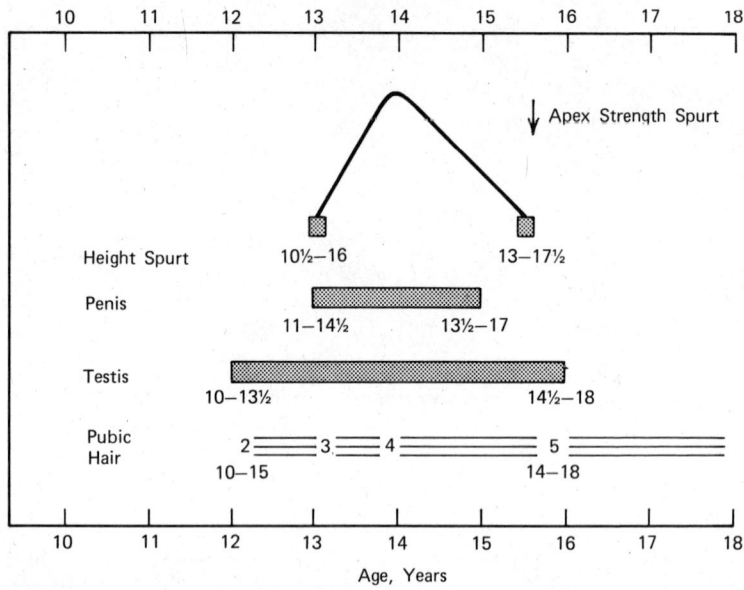

Figure 8-2 Diagram of sequence of events at adolescence in boys. An average boy is represented: the range of ages within which each event charted may begin and end is given by the figures placed directly below its start and finish. (Reprinted with permission from J. M. Tanner, *Growth at Adolescence,* 2nd ed., Oxford, England: Blackwell Scientific, 1962.)

LUTEINIZING HORMONE (LH) This hormone in females forms the corpus luteum of pregnancy in the ovary, which begins the production of progesterone to sustain the pregnancy. LH in the male helps mature the Leydig cells in the testicles to produce testosterone.

Estrogen and Testosterone These hormones—estrogen in the female and testosterone in the male—are responsible for the development of secondary sexual characteristics. They also affect the following:

• Protein. A slight increase in total body protein, resulting in increased height and weight in both sexes
• Skeletal. Increased growth rate of bones, resulting in increased height; also causes early uniting of epiphysis of the long bones,

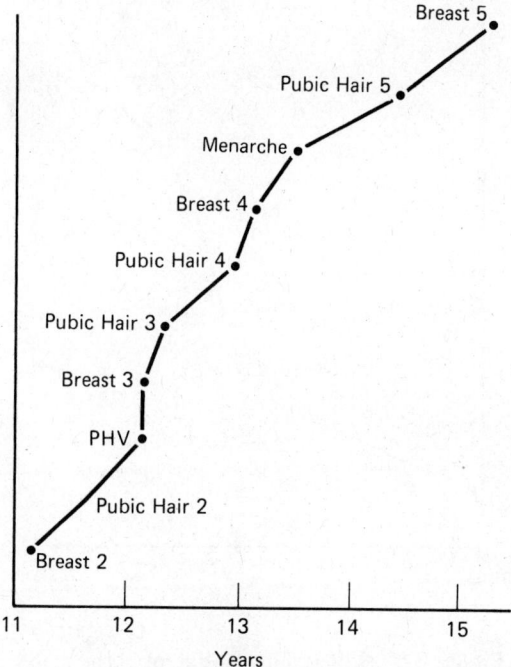

Figure 8-3 Pubertal development in the female. Sequence and mean ages of pubertal events in females adapted from the data of Marshall and Tanner 1969–1970. PHV = peak height velocity. (See Table 8-1 for description of each developmental stage.) (Reprinted with permission from A. Root, "Endocrinology of Puberty," *J Pediatr 83*:1, July 1973.)

thus ending the growth process in both sexes; broadens the pelvic bones in the female

- Muscular. Increase in muscle size, causing increased strength and broadening of the shoulder and thoracic cage in males
- Sexual organs. Increase in the size of the uterus, fallopian tubes, vagina, penis, testicles, and scrotum; increased deposits of adipose tissue on the mons pubis and labia majora; enlargement of the labia minora; and development of endometrium during the

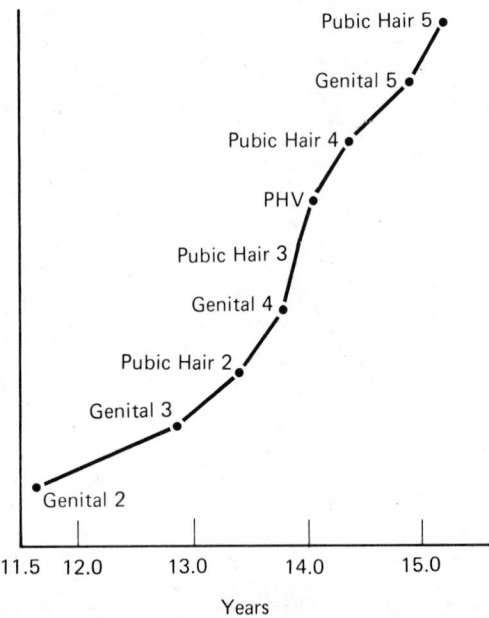

Figure 8-4 Pubertal development in the male. Sequence and mean ages of pubertal events in males, adapted from the data of Marshall and Tanner 1969–1970. (See Table 8-1 for description of each developmental stage.) (Reprinted with permission from A. Root, "Endocrinology of Puberty," *J Pediatr 83*:1, July 1973.)

proliferatory and secretory phase of the menstrual cycle in females
- Breasts. Increase in fat deposits, growth of ductile system, and development of the nipple in females
- Skin. Increased secretion of the sebaceous glands, often resulting in acne in both sexes; increase in adipose tissue in the buttocks, hips, and thighs in females; skin texture becomes more soft, smooth in females; in males, increased thickness of the skin
- Hair. Increased hair distribution in the axillae and pubic region with triangular distribution of pubic hair; in males, hair growth on the face, chest, and extremities
- Libido. Increase in sexual assertiveness and desire in both sexes

- Voice. In males, enlargement of the larynx and vocal cords, resulting in a deeper voice and the characteristic "Adam's apple"

Progesterone   This hormone is secreted by the ovary through the corpus luteum and is active during the secretory phase of the menstrual cycle. During pregnancy progesterone is secreted in large quantities by the placenta. Progesterone is responsible for the following changes:

- Uterus. Prepares uterus for implantation of the fertilized egg; during pregnancy decreases the frequency of uterine contractions
- Fallopian tubes. Promotes secretory changes in the mucosal lining which are necessary for the nutrition of the fertilized dividing ovum
- Breasts. Development of milk lobules and alveoli (milk-producing cells) during pregnancy, resulting in enlargement of breasts

LACTOGENIC HORMONE (PROLACTIN)   This hormone is responsible for the production of breast milk.

GROWTH HORMONE   This hormone is responsible along with estrogen and testosterone for the growth spurt. In females this occurs between 9 and 14 years of age. In males, the growth spurt occurs between 11 and 16 years of age.

Adrenals   The terms androgen refers to male sex hormones. The adrenal gland secretes approximately five different androgens. The masculinizing activity of these hormones is slight, and they do not cause significant masculine characteristics even in women.

TESTOSTERONE   This adrenal secretion helps in the early development of male sexual organs thereby promoting maturity and an increase in size of the penis, scrotum, and testes.

ESTROGEN, PROGESTERONE   The quantity produced by the adrenal gland is too small to exert an effect on the body.

The Menstrual Cycle   Menstruation is a late occurrence in puberty, having been preceded by the continuing development of breast, pubic hair, and genitals. It is defined as the shedding of the uterine lining and is the result of the cyclic production of estrogen and progesterone by the gonadotropic hormones. It occurs in three phases: proliferation of the endometrium, secretory changes of the endometrium, and menstruation.

PROLIFERATION OF THE ENDOMETRIUM After menstruation occurs the cells of the endometrium begin to grow rapidly and to increase in thickness due to estrogen secretion. This occurs in the first half of the menstrual cycle.

SECRETORY CHANGES OF THE ENDOMETRIUM Progesterone and estrogen are secreted by the corpus luteum of the ovaries. These hormones produce a highly secretory endometrium that provides optimal conditions for implantation of the fertilized ovum. This occurs in the second half of the menstrual cycle.

MENSTRUATION The sudden decrease in the production of estrogen and progesterone causes desquamation and bleeding of the endometrial layer. This occurs just before the end of the monthly cycle.

Management

The most common problems relating to physical development in adolescence are delayed puberty, short stature, delayed and irregular menses, and precocious puberty. It is beyond the scope of this book to discuss these conditions comprehensively. The nurse practitioner is referred to medical and endocrine texts for further information. In dealing with problems relating to growth in adolescence, the nurse practitioner works interdependently with medical, endocrine, nutritional, and social service disciplines in comprehensive management of problems of physical development.

ADOLESCENT PSYCHOLOGIC DEVELOPMENT

Assessment and Management

DEVELOPMENTAL TASKS OF ADOLESCENCE

A developmental task arises at a certain period in a person's life and presents a new challenge to the person's current physical and/ or psychologic abilities (Havighurst, 1972). Developmental tasks are attained through physical and social maturation and through personal efforts. There are four major developmental tasks of adolescence:

- Establish an identity.
- Develop a sexual preference.
- Emancipate from family.
- Establish career goals.

During early, middle, and late adolescence certain common developmental problems contribute to completion of the four major developmental tasks of adolescence. The nurse practitioner must be aware of the major developmental tasks and common developmental problems in order to provide comprehensive care to adolescents.

Early Adolescence Early adolescence occurs between the ages of 10 and 13 for girls and between 12 and 14 for boys.

CONCERN WITH CHANGING BODY IMAGE This is the major developmental problem of early adolescence. Increased hormone production initiates the development of secondary sexual characteristics. If the changes occur in a positive manner, the adolescent accepts the body changes as a normal physiologic development toward adulthood and communicates feelings about the process openly with family members and peers.

If the change occurs in a negative manner, the adolescent has fearful and possibly guilty feelings toward the changing body image and may deny that the change is taking place or displace the feelings through psychosomatic complaints. This reaction is usually manifested as noncommunication with family members, avoidance of social activities, and fear of locker-room activity.

Counseling The nurse practitioner discusses with the adolescent feelings about his or her weight, height, and body size, as well as what body proportions he or she would like. The adolescent's Tanner staging is discussed and correlated with developmental parameters, such as growth spurt and menarche.

ABILITY TO THINK ABSTRACTLY Many adolescents progress from concrete thinking to the stage of abstract cognitive development. Thinking in this stage has several characteristics:

- Deductive-hypothetical: able to construct new formulations and thoughts without having prior experience
- Inductive: able to construct theories and make associations between phenomenon
- Reflective: able to analyze thoughts about self and society; able to fantasize
- Futuristic: able to think about the future and realistically plan for it

Counseling The nurse practitioner assesses the adolescent's cognitive level by asking questions about the future: "What do you want to be? How do you go about doing that?" Questions that analyze the adolescent's ability to make associations between phenomena include: "What if a friend is abusing drugs, what would you do? What if a friend became pregnant, how would you help?" If adolescents cannot come up with solutions to problems or cannot project into the future concerning goals, they are probably in the concrete stage of cognitive development. Concrete thinkers need visual methods of health teaching, such as pictures, diagrams, and written materials, in addition to verbal instructions.

MOOD SWINGS/SEXUAL FANTASIES Mood swings occur because of changing hormonal levels and the adolescent's own conflicts with a need for independence from authority figures versus a need to be dependent and nurtured. Other worries contributing to mood swings are fear of establishing an individual identity and of developing a mature sexual orientation.

Sexual fantasies are a defense against acting on sexual/hormonal urges. There may be very little communication with family and peers about the intensity of feelings. Rather, feelings are displayed through sexual jokes and innuendo. The adolescent deals with fantasies by increased physical activity and/or asceticism or sexual relations.

Counseling The nurse practitioner discusses adolescent's degree of conflict with family members, fluctuations between depression and elation, and the availability of time alone at home. The adolescent is reassured about the normalcy of mood swings and sexual fantasies. There is encouragement to initiate dialogue with family members, peers, or professionals around conflicts at home and to discuss own feelings regarding conflicts. The normalcy of erotic urges, wet dreams, and masturbation as well as the importance of daydreaming as a therapeutic escape from emotional tensions are discussed.

Middle Adolescence Middle adolescence occurs between 13 and 16 for girls and between 14 and 17 for boys. Generally this is the period of major psychosocial turmoil because the adolescent is expected to act like an adult when full psychologic maturity is not yet achieved.

INCREASED PEER INTERACTION This is the major developmental problem of middle adolescence. It is through the peer group that the adolescent discusses fears, problems, and feelings. There is conformity to group ideas, dress, and social actions. Peers provide a testing ground for new ideas, outlandish behavior, and experiments. Most importantly, peers provide acceptance, support, and a sense of belonging to a group that thinks, feels, and acts in unison.

There is little intimacy during middle adolescence. Adolescents are still egocentric and narcissistic in personal relationships and have not yet developed the capacity for genuine closeness.

Counseling The nurse practitioner discusses with adolescents the degree of peer interaction and support: type of activity, number of friends, group or single dating, and pressures to conform to group ideas. The importance of peer allegiance and group activities is discussed. Also there is dialogue on ways in which the group conflicts with the adolescent's own goals and how this is resolved by the adolescent.

INCREASED EMANCIPATION FROM FAMILY Along with the strong emergence of the peer group is the adolescent's continuing emancipation from the family. There are conflicts over the degree of independence the adolescent is permitted to assume as well as rebellion against family traditions and values. These conflicts are necessary in order to develop an identity unique to the adolescent; they tend to deviate somewhat from the family's values and culture.

Counseling The nurse practitioner discusses areas of conflict with family and the availability of a family member to act as a friend. Ways to communicate with family to resolve conflicts are discussed: use of "I" statements, letting family members know about personal needs, and use of a contract to clarify agreements between family members and the adolescent concerning their individual behaviors.

BEGINNING IDEALISTIC/ALTRUISTIC THOUGHTS Thinking is directed toward social and idealistic causes and becomes a statement of the adolescent's own identity as distinct from that of the parents. The adolescent's idealism motivates active questioning of society and family values. The adolescent has feelings of cynicism alternating with renewed idealism and occasional anger at authority figures for lack of interest in improving society.

Counseling The nurse practitioner discusses the adolescent's feelings concerning problems and conflicts with family over idealistic pursuits. Ways to help adolescents realize ambitions by working in constructive organizations, volunteering time to political groups, and humanitarian causes are discussed.

Late Adolescence Late adolescence occurs between 17 and 21 for females and 18 and 21 for males. An important task during this period is the achievement of intimacy in relationships. The adolescent also assumes more adult responsibilities, such as driving a car, voting at 18, obtaining a job, and completing planning for career goals.

ABILITY TO LOVE AND BE LOVED The narcissism that was evident in middle adolescent love relationships becomes, in many instances, an intimate union in which the friends mutually communicate and care for one another. There is a desire to date or see one person on a regular basis.

Counseling The nurse practitioner asks adolescents whether they have any desire to have a close relationship with someone, whether they are seeing anyone regularly, or whether they like discussing personal feelings with the same-sex or opposite-sex person over a period of time. For socially isolated adolescents, ways are discussed whereby they can meet people in church, social, or outdoor groups. Courses are discussed in which some adolescents may develop increased social skills. If adolescents are in an intimate relationship, thoughts about future goals and the relationship are discussed.

PLANNING CAREER GOALS Most adolescents have specific plans to achieve career goals. For those who are undecided about a career, attending college or joining the services may be an interim maturing process until a specific career choice is decided on. Some adolescents use the peer group as their escape from planning career goals and hang out on the streets, in cars, or in bars. The lack of plans for a career is a serious psychologic problem in adolescence.

Counseling The nurse practitioner discusses the adolescent's commitment to future goals, for example, what the adolescent sees as his or her life's work and what plans are being made to achieve that goal. Continued ongoing psychotherapeutic support is given to those adolescents who lack future direction or goals.

HEALTH ASSESSMENT

Health History

During each health visit, the adolescent's state of functioning is assessed:

- Relationship with family
- Relationship with peers
- Scholastic achievement

The adolescent should be functioning well in at least two of the above areas. If there are problems in all three areas, continuous professional assessment and management are needed.

Because of high no-show rates with appointments, a call the day before as a reminder may help increase compliance if the appointment is not confidential. Irwin and co-workers (1981) found that adolescent boys under age 15 kept a higher percentage of appointments when they were made by parents. In this way family members can help increase appointment-keeping behavior.

The following history is presented as it relates to the adolescent.

PRESENTING PROBLEM AS DISCUSSED
BY CLIENT AND PARENTS
Past History

1. Illnesses
2. Weight gain or loss
3. Regular smoking or use of alcohol

Birth

1. Gravida, para, gestation
2. Type of delivery
3. Birth weight, Apgar score
4. Resuscitation measures, neonatal course
5. Maternal use of diethylstilbestrol during pregnancy

Developmental Milestones

1. Sat, walked, first words, sentences

Allergies

1. Asthma, hayfever
2. Drugs
3. Food

Communicable Diseases

1. Rubella, mumps, rubeola

Immunizations

1. Dates of last polio, diphtheria, tetanus, rubeola, mumps, rubella immunizations

FAMILY HISTORY

1. Hypertension
2. Heart attacks
3. Diabetes
4. Tuberculosis
5. Cerebrovascular accident

PRESENT HISTORY

Nutrition

1. Basic food groups
   - Milk: three servings

- Meat (includes poultry, fish, eggs, peanut butter, dried beans): four servings
- Fruits and vegetables: four servings
- Breads, cereals, and grains: four servings

2. Types of foods used for snacks and snacking pattern
3. Eating habits: number of regular meals a day, use of crash diets, fasting, food fads, source of protein and iron; knowledge of balanced food choices (See Table 3-1: Recommended Daily Allowances)

Cognitive Development   Assess thinking ability:

Concrete and abstract (See this chapter, Developmental Tasks, Early Adolescence)

School Experience

1. Grade, name of school
2. Success in school: performance in math, reading, spelling, grades in subjects
3. Favorite subject, most difficult subject, best subject
4. Attitude toward school
5. Have client write the name of school, present subjects, and a sentence in reference to why she or he is here
6. School/work goals for the future
7. School social activities

Family Relationships

1. Availability of someone to talk with
2. Areas of conflict and compatibility
3. Compliance with rules and regulations at home
4. Relationships with siblings

Peer Relationships

1. Loner vs many friends; activities with peers
2. Areas of disagreement with peers
3. Pressures from peer group to conform

Outside Interests

1. Work
2. Social activities
3. Hobbies

Sexuality

1. Dating: groups, single partners, one steady partner
2. If dating single partners, ask whether sexually active
3. Knowledge of physiology of conception, reasons for body changes, normalcy of wet dreams, masturbation
4. Knowledge of contraceptive methods, symptoms of venereal disease, prevention, and treatment

Attitudes

1. Smoking
2. Substance usage: alcohol, prescription and nonprescription drugs

Body Worries

1. Height, weight
2. Size of breasts, genitals
3. Skin

Review of Systems

1. General health as described by client
2. Dietary history
3. Skin: acne, history of chloasma
4. HEENT (Head, Eyes, Ears, Nose, Throat): headaches, squint, allergies, problems with vision, thyroid disease
5. Dentition: last dental visit
6. Chest/cardiac: breast cancer, fibrocystic nodules; heart attack, CVA, murmur, rheumatic fever
7. Respiratory: infections, pneumonia, bronchitis
8. Gastrointestinal: abdominal pain, weight loss or gain, changes in bowel patterns, ulcers, hepatitis, adenoma

9. Genitourinary: enuresis, dysuria, urinary tract infection, V.D.
10. Ortho: joint or back pain, sport injuries
11. Neuro: seizures, emotional problems
12. Endocrine: thyroid disease, irregular menses
13. Menstruation (See this chapter, Family Planning)

Physical Assessment

When performing a physical examination, the procedure is explained to the adolescent including examination of the genitals. All clothing is removed, and an examining gown is worn. Adolescents are draped appropriately and their modesty respected. A young adolescent may prefer to have a parent in the room. The examination provides an excellent opportunity to discuss medical problems related to organ systems or body worries, for example, skin problems and worries about breast cancer.

The following physical assessment as it relates to the adolescent is in addition to the general physical (see Chapter 1, Child Health Assessment).

1. Height, weight, heart rate, respiration rate, and blood pressure
2. Skin: acne, scars, icterus
3. Eyes: funduscopic
4. Dentition: caries, occlusion, periodontal disease
5. Neck: thyroid
6. Chest:

   • Females: breast development, Tanner stage (see Table 8-1), masses
   • Males: gynecomastia

7. Back: scoliosis or lordosis
8. Sports assessment (Goldberg et al., 1980):

   • Body fat composition: skin fold calipers
   • Body flexibility: toe touch, toe-in, toe-out, lotus position; shoulder external rotation/forearm supination, elbow extension

- Musculoskeletal: range of motion, muscle strength, ligamentous stability in ankle, knee, shoulder, and elbow joints
9. Genitalia: Tanner stage (see Table 8-1)
10. Pelvis: perineum, vagina, cervix (describe presence of ectopy, erosion), uterus (describe location, size, consistency), adnexa, adenosis with DES exposure

Laboratory

Laboratory studies include CBC, UA, rubella titer (females), VDRL (Venereal Disease Research Laboratory), Papanicolaou smear, cervical *Chlamydia* and *Neisseria gonorrhoea* culture, if sexually active, and sickle cell screening, if black race.

Immunizations

Immunizations include Td (tetanus/diphtheria) and TOPV (trivalent oral polio vaccine) boosters at 14 years of age, if none in the past 10 years.

Screening

1. Visual acuity
2. Audiogram
3. Hemoglobin, if indicated
4. Tuberculin test
5. Periodic Gonococcus (GC), *Chlamydia* culture in females if sexually active

HEALTH MANAGEMENT

Ambulatory Health Maintenance Visits

THE ENVIRONMENT

Adolescent appointments are scheduled on different days from well-baby or young-child visits whenever possible. The environmental milieu provides age-appropriate reading material, and the general overall impression should indicate that adolescents are a part of the client population.

The preceding statements promote the concept of the exclusiveness and individuality of the client and provide subtle influences that the client is valued for his or her own self-worth and individuality.

PROCEDURE FOR VISITS

On the first visit the adolescent and the parent are interviewed first to discuss the chief complaint and the past history. Both the adolescent and the parent are then interviewed separately. Occasionally a social worker may interview the parent while the adolescent is being seen if there are family/social problems. Some adolescents may object to the parent being in the room and should therefore be interviewed alone. The rationale for this approach is that although adolescents are encouraged to assume responsibility for their care, parental information is needed on some visits. The older adolescent is usually seen alone on succeeding visits. Middle and early adolescents are seen with or without parents according to individual situations. The adolescent and the parent are always seen together if the adolescent desires that the parent be present, is extremely anxious, immature, mentally retarded, or has a learning or speech disability. The role of the nurse practitioner is defined to the client. The practitioner is the client's health provider and the client is free to discuss anything he or she wishes. The procedure for future visits is defined, including goals for treatment, approximate number of visits, review of client's progress, and the need for a verbal or written contract.

The nurse practitioner, while being interested in the family concerns, is primarily the client's advocate. This situation encourages a relationship in which the client can assume responsibility in managing his or her own health care.

CONFIDENTIALITY

All matters discussed with the client are confidential except in situations in which the client's actions are threatening to self or society, such as suicide, homicide, or heavy substance abuse. In these situations, parents or guardians are notified. The adolescent is informed of this aspect of health care.

LEGAL ISSUES

The judicial system recognizes the constitutional rights of minors such as due process of law when charged with a criminal act, the right to free speech, and in certain instances the right to self-consent. In the past decade legislation has been passed concerning treatment of venereal disease, substance abuse, contraception, and abortion. All 50 states and the District of Columbia have legislation pertaining to various aspects of obtaining health care without parental permission. The state statutes are extremely variable as to age at which minors can seek health care on their own and what type of health care services can be offered. The nurse practitioner is referred to specific state statutes for further information.

The Mature Minor Rule This law provides legal sanction for certain activities of minors such as driving a car, buying alcohol, enlisting in the armed services, voting, and consenting to marriage, before the majority age of 21. Individual states have various ages at which minors are deemed sufficiently mature. For example: Oregon, 15 years; Arkansas, a female at 16 years; Alabama, 14 years. In reference to health care the mature minor rule states that a minor can effectively consent to medical treatment if the minor understands the nature of the treatment as well as its benefits and possible consequences.

Comprehensive State Statutes Generally these laws define emancipated minors and under what conditions certain medical and surgical procedures may be instituted. They also broadly define other situations where delay or denial of care because of lack of parental permission would increase the risk to the minor's health and life. The first state to enact such a statute was Pennsylvania. It states that any minor 18 and older may consent to any medical or surgical procedures. The age in Alabama is 14, and that statute adds, mental health care.

Emancipated Minors In the case of an emancipated minor seeking health care services the laws of various states generally offer no legal penalties either to the health care agency or to the minor. An emancipated minor is usually defined as having one or some of the following characteristics:

- Away from home with and in some cases without parental consent
- Earning own support
- Married minors
- Minor parents
- Minors in the service
- 15 years or older, depending on individual state statutes
- Working minors at home contributing at least half of their support

Unemancipated Minors It is in this area that health professionals have been reluctant to offer health care services to minors. The laws of the individual states are complex in defining an unemancipated minor and under what conditions an unemancipated minor can be treated. The nurse practitioner is referred to individual state statutes for further information.

Treatment Without Parental Consent A minor's right to consent to medical care depends on the minor's ability to give informed consent, by understanding the nature of the procedure, the risks involved, and the available alternatives. The minor must also demonstrate sufficient intelligence and maturity. If capable of the above, she or he is said to have reached "the age of majority."

Emergencies Courts have held that a physician need not wait to obtain parental consent when an emergency endangers the life or health of a minor. Several states have specific definitions on what constitutes an emergency. However, in many states definitions of emergency care are expanding and are stated in broad general terms.

COUNSELING

The attitude of the nurse practitioner is one of friendliness and concern. Nonverbal cues such as body position, use of hands, facial expression, and movements alert the nurse practitioner to the adolescent's degree of comfort. The practitioner is aware of the client's reluctance to answer personal questions until rapport has been established. The practitioner maintains a degree of professionalism by not taking sides in any conflict or agreeing with the adolescent unconditionally.

Adolescents will not verbalize thoughts completely until they are comfortable with and feel they can trust the nurse practitioner. The adolescent sees the practitioner as a person who views the problems and situations objectively and does not want the practitioner to function as a peer.

Noncommunicative Adolescent   The nurse practitioner discusses the presenting complaint. If the adolescent is unable to add information in this area, the practitioner discusses what the adolescent thinks the parent's reasons are for the visit. A review of systems occasionally elicits some worries of the client. A discussion of the client's interests about school, hobbies, social activities, and sports occasionally initiates responses. The nurse practitioner discusses feelings in response to the adolescent's nonverbal behavior, "I bet you would rather be somewhere else right now."

The nurse practitioner also recognizes the fact that the client does not wish to verbalize and respects this by keeping the visits short. A discussion of the visit routine helps alleviate some anxiety about the unexpected.

Concrete-Thinking Adolescent   These adolescents require that most questions be oriented to the present time. Health education for these clients needs to be written out in addition to any verbal explanations given. The use of other visual aids such as pictures, models, and diagrams is helpful.

Hostile Adolescent   These adolescents require tact and patience. It is important to acknowledge the hostility verbally and to ask why the adolescent is angry. If an explanation is given it can be discussed, possibly resulting in reduction of the adolescent's anger. If the adolescent remains hostile, it is important to accept his or her feelings and to keep the visit short.

Domineering Parents   This situation can occasionally be avoided by seeing the clients and parents separately. If this is impractical parents are counseled separately to ascertain their anxiety in reference to the adolescent. It is important to allow the adolescent to take some direction for the visit. This helps develop capabilities for coping with situations and problems without parental consultation.

Communicating About Sexuality The nurse practitioner initiates discussion about sexuality by asking about body growth and changing body proportions. Hormonal influence on physical changes are explained. It is inappropriate to ask initially about sexual activity without first discussing general aspects of physical/sexual development.

The early adolescent is asked whether he or she is interested in the opposite sex yet. The normalcy of this interest is discussed.

During middle adolescence dating in groups begins. If the adolescent is dating single partners, the nurse practitioner asks whether he or she is sexually active. Methods of birth control for boys and girls are discussed. Societal pressures for sexual activities and the options for adolescents concerning sexual behavior are discussed, including abstinence, sublimation of erotic urges, verbal intimacy, and intercourse.

In late adolescence, in addition to the above questions, prevention of sexually transmitted diseases is discussed (See this chapter, Family Planning).

Many adolescents will be embarrassed about questions concerning sexuality. However, with initiation of the subject by the nurse practitioner, on subsequent visits adolescents may bring up questions themselves.

FAMILY PLANNING

Assessment and Management

Many adolescents are sexually active. They require accurate education concerning birth control methods and a complete health assessment when using contraceptives. One study found that 59 percent of sexually active adolescents used contraception and that the school and parents were the most frequently used resource for obtaining information (Burbach, 1980). Boys and girls are both educated to take responsibility for contraception and are encouraged to come together for health visits. Venereal disease prevention is also discussed as the responsibility of each partner.

Sexual issues and contraception are discussed by the nurse practitioner in a nonjudgmental, confidential manner. Adolescents are encouraged to accept responsibility for their own actions, to review choices in regard to sexual activity, and to acquire knowledge concerning risks and side effects of contraceptive methods.

HEALTH HISTORY/CLIENT CONCERNS

A history is taken and a physical assessment made relating to contraceptive issues. Questions concerning sexuality and contraceptive use are included in the history (See this chapter, Communicating About Sexuality). When seeing young adolescents and older nonsexual adolescents, the questions are omitted, if indicated. Individual concerns are discussed as they are presented by the client.

Past History

1. Illnesses, surgery, hospitalizations, serious injuries, blood transfusions
2. Specific illness: blood clots in the legs or lungs, heart attacks, strokes, angina pectoris, high blood pressure, liver disease, venereal disease, cancer of reproductive organs
3. Maternal use of diethylstilbestrol during pregnancy
4. Infertility problems and evaluations
5. Pregnancies, live births, abortions

Family History

1. Allergy, anemia, cancer: breast, uterine; diabetes, epilepsy, heart attacks, CVA, hypertension, jaundice, severe depression, tuberculosis
2. Oral contraceptive use: acne, gallbladder disease, hyperlipidemia, hyperthyroidism, liver disease, sickle cell anemia, uterine myomata, blood clots in lungs, extremities

Social History

1. Living arrangements: type of housing, persons in household
2. Means of support

3. School/work status
4. Client profile: leisure activities, support systems, goals

Menstruation

1. Date of last menses, length, flow, normality, premenstrual tension, dysmenorrhea
2. Date of previous menses
3. Frequency and regularity of periods
4. Age at menarche, client's feelings about menarche
5. Problems with spotting between periods, menorrhagia, metorrhagia, amenorrhea

Contraceptive Use

1. Methods, duration of use, side effects
2. Reason for termination
3. Client's degree of knowledge about types and effectiveness rates for contraceptives and side effects

Sexuality

1. Number of episodes of vaginitis, venereal disease, pelvic inflammatory disease, urinary tract infection
2. Treatment and follow-up for #1
3. Frequency of sexual activity, number of partners
4. Accurate knowledge of protection against venereal disease and pregnancy

Review of Systems   See this chapter, Health Assessment.

PHYSICAL EXAMINATION

1. Weight, height, heart rate, respiration rate, and blood pressure
2. Thyroid palpation
3. Palpation of breasts
4. Auscultation of the heart
5. Auscultation of the lungs
6. Inspection and palpation of the abdomen

7. Inspection of external genitalia and internal genitalia using a speculum and performing bimanual and vaginal–rectal examinations

During health visits, self-examination of the breast and testicles is taught. This allows the adolescent to become familiar with these body parts. Changes including hard nodules and irregular masses can be quickly reported. For females, the examination is done after the menses. For males it is done monthly.

Pelvic examinations are indicated for the following:

• Sexually active
• Symptoms of venereal disease
• Vaginal discharge
• Menstrual irregularities
• Delayed menstruation
• Adolescent request

LABORATORY

1. Papanicolaou smear, Gonococcus, and *Chlamydia* culture
2. VDRL, CBC, rubella titer, urinalysis
3. Lipid profile, if strong, positive family history of heart attacks before 50 years of age (see Chapter 18, Cardiovascular Risk Factors in Children)

FREQUENTLY USED TERMS

Woman-years (Pearl Index)   In most studies, the efficacy of birth control methods is stated in terms of 100 woman-years. Woman-years are based on 13 cycles per year for one woman or one cycle for 13 women or any combination thereof. Hence 100 woman-years means 1,300 cycles (13 cycles × 1 woman × 100) or (1 cycle × 13 women × 100). For example, the theoretical effectiveness rate of the diaphragm is three pregnancies per 100 woman-years of use, that is, three pregnancies out of 1,300 cycles. The problem with this data collection system is that the longer such a study is run, the lower the failure rate. This is because failures drop out of the study with duration of use (Hatcher et al., 1982, p. 3).

Life Table Failure Rates In these studies, the efficacy of birth control methods is collected for the first year of use and provides an answer to the question, "Of 100 women who start and continue to use contraception, how many will become pregnant in the first year?" (Hatcher et al., 1982, p. 3).

Theoretical Effectiveness Rate This term is used to judge the effectiveness of various birth control methods. It indicates the maximum effectiveness rate of a birth control method without taking into account the element of human error.

Use Effectiveness Rate This term is used to judge the effectiveness of various birth control methods. It indicates the effectiveness rate of a birth control method, taking into account the probability of human error in its use. Use effectiveness rates vary widely, depending on the study cited.

CONTRACEPTIVE DEVICES

In prescribing contraception to adolescents, the nurse practitioner assesses the following:

- Motivation to use contraception
- Frequency of intercourse (may consider mechanical method if not frequent)
- Cognitive development
- Knowledge of contraceptive methods (may consider method that adolescent is most familiar with)
- Knowledge of contraindications and side effects

Combined Oral Contraceptives These contraceptives contain estrogen and progesterone and are more effective in reducing the incidence of pregnancy than is the progestin-only pill. See Table 8-2 for additional information on oral contraceptives and Table 8-3 for contraindications to combined birth control pills. Table 8-4 lists the hormonal content of oral contraceptives.

PROTOCOL FOR INITIAL HEALTH VISIT Height, weight, and blood pressure measurements are obtained. A complete history is obtained and a physical assessment is done. (See Physical Examination in

Table 8-2
Oral Contraceptives

Oral Contraceptives	Mechanism of Action	Effectiveness Rate

Combined pill (see Table 8-3 for contraindications to combined birth control pills containing both an estrogen and a progestin; see Table 8-4 for brand name and dosage of estrogen and progesterone)	Estrogen
	  Inhibits ovulation through suppression of follicle-stimulating hormone (FSH) and luteinizing hormone (LH).
	Postcoitus, high doses of estrogen inhibit implantation and may accelerate ovum transport and cause leuteolysis, the degeneration of the corpus luteum.
	Progesterone
	  Decreases sperm penetration and transport through creation of a thick, cellular cervical mucus.
	Inhibits capacitation, which is the release of spermatic enzymes that allow sperm to penetrate the ovum.
	May decrease ovum transport, implantation, and ovulation.
		Theoretical: Less that one pregnancy per 100 woman-years.
		Use: Approximately 1–4 pregnancies per 100 woman-years.

Family Planning section of this chapter.) A complete pelvic examination is done.

PROTOCOL FOR RETURN VISITS Adolescents are seen more frequently initially. The first return appointment is made in 1 month to discuss pill regimen and side effects and to answer questions. Repeat visits are usually every 3 to 6 months. A repeat physical and pelvic examination is done yearly. Pap smears and a GC culture are obtained according to the protocol of the agency. One study recommends that the initial Pap smear be obtained at the onset of sexual activity or at 18 years of age, to be repeated in 6 months and annually thereafter (American College of Obstetricians and Gynecologists, 1975). Another study recommends that the initial Pap smear be obtained at the onset of sexual activity, or at age 20, followed in 1 year by a second smear. If the two cytologic studies show no abnormal findings, future smears are obtained at 3-year intervals on non-high-risk women, ages 20 to 40 (Gusburg, 1980).

HEALTH TEACHING The following are discussed:

Medication Regimen The pill is started on the fifth day after the menses begins. For the 21-day pack, one pill is taken every day for 21 days, no pills are taken for the next 7 days, and a new package of pills is restarted on the eighth day. For the 28-day pack, one pill is taken every day for 28 days. A new package of pills is started immediately after taking the last pill. In the 28-day pack the last 7 pills of the cycle are placebos or iron tablets. Twenty-eight-day packs are used by women who have difficulty remembering the regimen of the 21-day pill pack. A second backup method of birth control is used on the first cycle of the pill. The pill is taken at the same time every day to keep a continuous level of the drug in the body.

Missed Pills (1) Take the pill as soon as remembered. Take the next day's pill at the regular time. (2) Take two pills as soon as remembered and two pills the next day. Use a second method of birth control until the pack is finished. (3) If three pills are missed, a second method of birth control is started immediately. The old pill pack is thrown away and a new pack is started the following Sunday even if the client has withdrawal bleeding at the time. The second method of birth control can be stopped 2 weeks after being on the new pill pack (Hatcher et al., 1982, p. 58).

Table 8-3
Contraindications to Combined Birth Control Pills
Containing Both an Estrogen and a Progestin

Absolute Contraindications
1. Thromboembolic disorder (or history thereof)
2. Cerebrovascular accident (or history thereof)
3. Coronary artery disease (or history thereof)
4. Known impaired liver function at present time
5. Hepatic adenoma (or history thereof)
6. Malignancy of breast or reproductive system (or history thereof)
7. Known pregnancy

Strong Relative Contraindications
8. Severe headaches, particularly vascular or migraine[a]
9. Hypertension with resting diastolic blood pressure of 90 or greater on three or more separate visits, or an accurate measurement of 110 or more on a single visit[a]
10. Diabetes[a]
11. Prediabetes or a strong family history of diabetes
12. Gallbladder disease, including cholecystectomy[a]
13. Previous cholestasis during pregnancy, congenital hyperbilirubin (Gilberts disease)
14. Mononucleosis, acute phase
15. Sickle cell disease (SS) or sickle C disease (SC)[a]
16. Undiagnosed, abnormal vaginal bleeding[b]
17. Elective surgery planned in next 4 weeks or major surgery requiring immobilization[a]
18. Long-leg casts or major injury to lower leg
19. Age over 40 years[a]
20. Age over 35 years and a history of heavy smoking[a]
21. Impaired liver function within past year

Other Relative Contraindications
May contraindicate initiation of the pill:
22. Termination of term pregnancy within past 10–14 days[a]
23. Weight gain of 10 pounds or more while on the pill[a]
24. Failure to have established regular menstrual cycles[a]
25. Patient with profile suggestive of anovulation and infertility problems: late onset of menses and very irregular, painless menses[a]
26. Cardiac or renal disease (or history thereof)[a]
27. Conditions likely to make patient unreliable at following pill instructions (mental retardation, major psychiatric problems, alcoholism, history of repeatedly taking pills incorrectly)[a]
28. Lactation (oral contraceptives may be initiated as weaning begins and may be an aid in decreasing the flow of milk)[a]

Table 8-3 (*Continued*)

Other Relative Contraindicaions (Continued)
May initiate the pill for women with these problems and observe carefully for worsening or improvement of the problem:

29. Depression[a]
30. Hypertension with resting diastolic blood pressure at a single visit of 90–99[a]
31. Chloasma or hair loss related

to pregnancy (or history thereof)[a]

32. Asthma[a]
33. Epilepsy[a]
34. Uterine fibromyomata[a]
35. Acne
36. Varicose veins[a]
37. History of hepatitis but now normal liver function tests for at least one year

---

Source: Reprinted by permission of Hatcher, et al. *Contraceptive Technology 1982–83*, New York: Irvington Publishers, 1982.

[a]Contraindication to estrogen-containing pills that may *not* be a contraindication to progestin-only pills or may be less of a contraindication to progestin-only pills than to combined pills.

[b]Several reviewers in Hatcher, et al. (above) strongly feel that this should be listed as an absolute contraindication to use of the pill. It remains here since we cannot, in a simple, straightforward manner, define "abnormal." If you, the clinician, believe that the patient's bleeding pattern is "abnormal," and the cause is unknown, do not provide her with birth control pills.

Other Considerations   Absent menses: If pregnancy is not a consideration, continue taking pills for another cycle. Obtain medical consultation if no menses occurs after second cycle. If pregnancy is a possibility obtain a pregnancy test and pelvic examination. Stop pills if positive; if negative, obtain medical consultation. For breakthrough bleeding after the second cycle obtain medical consultation. Self breast examination is taught.

Progestin-Only Pill   This pill contains progesterone only, and the amount is smaller than in the combined pill. It is used for women over 35 years of age and for adolescents who have estrogen and progesterone excess side effects. See Tables 8-3 and 8-5.

PROTOCOL FOR HEALTH VISITS   The same protocol is observed as with the combined pill. A hematocrit is done for excessive breakthrough bleeding, to rule out anemia.

HEALTH TEACHING   The following are discussed:

Medication Regimen   The pill is started on the first day of the menses and is taken continually even when menses occurs. The

Table 8-4

Hormone Content of Oral Contraceptives

Brand Name, No. of Pills per Pack, and Manufacturer	Estrogen (mg/tab)	Progestin (mg/tab)
Combination		
Enovid 10 mg[a] (Searle)[a]	Mestranol .15	Norethynodrel 10
Norinyl 1 + 50 (21, 28) (Syntex)	Mestranol .05	Norethindrone 1.0
Ortho-Novum 1 + 50 (21, 28) (Ortho)	Mestranol .05	Norethindrone 1.0
Ortho-Novum 10 mg (20) (Ortho)	Mestranol .06	Norethindrone 10.0
Enovid 5 mg (20) (Searle)	Mestranol .075	Norethynodrel 5.0
Norinyl 1 + 80 (21, 28) (Syntex)	Mestranol .08	Norethindrone 1.0
Ortho-Novum 1 + 80 (21, 28) (Ortho)	Mestranol .08	Norethindrone 1.0
Enovid E (20, 21) (Searle)	Mestranol .10	Norethynodrel 2.5
Norinyl 2 mg (20) (Syntex)	Mestranol .10	Norethindrone 2.0
Ortho-Novum 2 mg (20) (Ortho)	Mestranol .10	Norethindrone 2.0
Ovulen (20, 21, 28) (Searle)	Mestranol .10	Ethynodiol diacetate 1.0
Loestrin 1 + 20 (28) (Parke Davis)[a]	Ethinyl estradiol .02	Norethindrone acetate 1.0

Zorane 1 + 20 (28) (Lederle)	Ethinyl estradiol .02	Norethindrone acetate 1.0
Loestrin 1.5 + 30 (28) (Parke Davis)[a]	Ethinyl estradiol .03	Norethindrone acetate 1.5
Lo-Ovral (21, 28) (Wyeth)	Ethinyl estradiol .03	Norgestrel 0.3
Zorane 1.5 + 30 (28) (Lederle)	Ethinyl estradiol .03	Norethindrone acetate 1.5
Brevicon (21, 28) (Syntex)	Ethinyl estradiol .035	Norethindrone 0.5
Modicon (21, 28) (Ortho)	Ethinyl estradiol .035	Norethindrone 0.5
Ovcon-35 (28) (Mead Johnson)	Ethinyl estradiol .035	Norethindrone 0.4
Demulen (21, 28) (Searle)	Ethinyl estradiol .05	Ethynodiol diacetate 1.0
Norlestrin 1 mg (21, 28) (Parke Davis)	Ethinyl estradiol .05	Norethindrone acetate 1.0
Norlestrin 2.5 mg (21, 28) (Parke Davis)	Ethinyl estradiol .05	Norethindrone acetate 2.5
Ovcon 50 (28) (Mead Johnson)	Ethinyl estradiol .05	Norethindrone 1.0
Ovral (21, 28) (Wyeth)	Ethinyl estradiol .05	Norgestrel 0.5

Microdose

Ovrette (28) (Wyeth)	None	Norgestrel .075
Micronor (35) (Ortho)	None	Norethindrone .35
Nor - Q.D. (42) (Syntex)	None	Norethindrone .35

[a] Available with iron.

Table 8-5
Progestin-Only Pill

Pill	Mechanism of Action	Effectiveness	Contraindications	Side Effects
Progestin-only pill	Same as progesterone in combined pill (see Table 8-2). Pill is used by woman over 35 and by those with history of hypertension, severe varicose veins, and headaches, and by those with estrogen and progesterone excess side effects. Mini pills contain a smaller amount of progesterone than the combined pills.	Theoretical: 1.25 pregnancies per 100 woman-years. Use: 2–4 pregnancies per 100 woman-years.	Undiagnosed abnormal vaginal bleeding Diabetes, gestational diabetes Mononucleosis Irregular menses Past history of ectopic pregnancy	Irregular menses (increased, decreased, spotting and amenorrhea) Decreased libido Fatigue Appetite increased Progesterone deficiency: delayed onset of menses after last pill, heavy menstrual flow, late breakthrough bleeding Mild headaches Edema Hirsutism

number of pills per pack varies from 28 to 42. The next pack is started immediately.

Missed Pills (1) Take the pill as soon as remembered and use a second method of birth control until the next menses. (2) Take two pills as soon as remembered and two pills the next day. Use a second method of birth control until next menses.

Postcoital Contraception These pills are used to prevent conception after unprotected mid-cycle intercourse. See Table 8-6.

HEALTH TEACHING In prescribing high-dose oral estrogens, the nurse practitioner does so under health care protocols. Several generic estrogen compounds require different dosages. The medication regimen and common side effects are discussed. If menstruation does not occur in 1 month, the protocol is reviewed. If a pregnancy test is positive, recommend therapeutic abortion (TAB). Discuss reasons for TAB: possible teratogenesis of the fetus, possible future genital carcinoma in females.

Intrauterine Devices (IUD) IUDs are prescribed with caution for adolescents. This is because of the side effects of increased incidence of pelvic inflammatory disease (PID) and possible decreased fertility. Some adolescents have multiple sexual partners, and this will increase the possibility of PID. Many adolescents are nulliparous, and most IUDs are unsuitable. See Table 8-7, Contraceptive Devices.

PROTOCOL Height, weight, and blood pressure measurements are obtained. A complete history is obtained and a physical assessment is done. A complete pelvic examination is done. Laboratory screening: see this chapter, Health Assessment.

Insertion This is done by a qualified person. The anterior cervix is held in place with a tenaculum. The uterus is probed with a sound for size and the IUD is then inserted. Some clinicians use a local anesthetic injected paracervically to decrease abdominal discomfort. Responses to the insertion vary according to the person: mild to severe abdominal cramping, occasional vagal nerve response, nausea, vomiting, bradycardia, pallor, clammy skin, dizziness, and fainting. The client sits up slowly after insertion, to decrease vagal nerve response.

Table 8-6
Postcoital Contraception

Estrogen Pill	Mechanism of Action	Effectiveness	Contraindications	Side Effects
High-dose oral estrogens	Presumed to prevent implantation of the blastocyte in the endometrium	Pregnancy rate of 4 out of 546 patients, one study (Hatcher et al., 1982, p. 155).	Breast, genital malignancy Clients' refusal to consider a therapeutic abortion (TAB) if treatment failure occurs	Nausea Vomiting Breast tenderness Headache Menstrual irregularities Possible teratogenic effect on fetus if DES failure occurs

Table 8-7
Contraceptive Devices

Device	Mechanism of Action	Effectiveness	Contraindications	Side Effects
Intrauterine device (IUD)	Presumed to function as a foreign body producing local inflammatory response causing lysis of the blastocyte.	Theoretical: 1–3 pregnancies per 100 woman-years. Use: 4–10 pregnancies per 100 woman-years. The addition of copper to IUDs decreases the pregnancy rate.	Pelvic inflammatory disease, recent or recurrent Pregnancy Multiple sexual partners Abnormal uterine bleeding Purulent cervicitis History of ectopic pregnancy Abnormal Papanicolaou smear Uterine malignancy or premalignancy Decreased response to infection (diabetes, immunosuppressed) Severe anemia Uterine anomalies Allergy to copper	Perforation of uterus Uterine embedment Incidence of spontaneous abortion Increased menstrual flow Urticarial allergic skin reaction (Cu-7) Severe dysmenorrhea Septicemia Ectopic pregnancy Syncope and bradycardia secondary to insertion Spotting, bleeding, hemorrhage, anemia Abdominal cramping

Continued

Table 8-7 *(Continued)*

Device	Mechanism of Action	Effectiveness	Contraindications	Side Effects
Diaphragm (see Table 8-8 for types)	The diaphragm holds the spermicidal agent near the cervical os, and acts as a mechanical barrier to sperm; the agent acts as an antispermicidal medium.	Theoretical: Two pregnancies per 100 woman-years. Use: Varies widely depending on study cited. Generally can expect 2–3 pregnancies per 100 woman-years (Jackson, et al., 1981, p. 141).	Severe anteverted or retroverted uterus Complete uterine prolapse Severe cystocele Severe retrocele Lack of acceptance by client	Possible allergic reactions to rubber or spermicidal agents (rare) Recurrent cystitis or urethritis due to pressure of diaphragm rim against urethra Possible decreased incidence of sexually transmitted disease (STD) due to mechanical barrier
Spermicidal foam, suppositories	Coital movements spread the medium over the cervical os.	Theoretical: Three pregnancies in 100 woman-years. Use: Varies widely depending on study cited; between three and 30 pregnancies in 100 woman-years.	Allergy to foam (rare) Inability to remember to use consistently	Allergic reaction to foam

476

Method	Mechanism	Effectiveness	Disadvantages	
Condom	Over an erect penis the condom is a barrier to the expulsion of sperm into the vagina.	Theoretical: Two pregnancies per 100 woman-years. Use: Ten pregnancies per 100 woman-years.	Allergy to rubber (rare)	Allergy to rubber (rare) It decreases the risk of transmitting or receiving sexually transmitted disease.
Rhythm	Refrain from intercourse during fertile periods (see this chapter, Rhythm).	Theoretical: 15 pregnancies per 100 woman-years. Use: 25–35 pregnancies per 100 woman-years.	Irregular menses Client unacceptance	Psychologic frustration over method
Basal body temperature	Refrain from intercourse during time of ovulation.	Theoretical: 15 pregnancies per 100 woman-years. Use: 15–20 pregnancies per 100 woman-years.	Frequent infections Irregular sleeping habits Tension Use of electric blankets, which may elevate BBT	Psychologic frustration over method
Coitus interruptus	Sperm is deposited away from vagina.	Theoretical: 16 pregnancies per 100 woman-years. Use: 20–25 pregnancies per 100 woman-years.	Lack of self-control Lack of ejaculatory control	Psychologic frustration over method

TYPES The following are commonly used IUDs:

Lippes Loop This device can be left in the uterus indefinitely and does not have to be replaced periodically.

Copper 7 This device is shaped like a number 7 and has fine copper wire wrapped around its stem. The addition of copper wiring enhances its effectiveness. It is contraindicated in clients who are allergic to copper and in those with Wilson's disease, a skin condition thought to be caused by improper copper metabolism. The copper 7 device needs to be replaced every 3 years.

Saf-T-Coil This device has the shortest length and is used in clients with small uteri.

Progestasert This device contains a small amount of progesterone which is released over a period of 12 months. The hormone enhances the effectiveness of the device. The IUD needs to be replaced yearly. The device is well tolerated, but there is an incidence of ectopic pregnancy (Greydanus, 1980).

Copper T or Tatum T This is the most recent IUD on the market. It is not used in women who have an allergy to copper. It may present symptoms in women with undiagnosed Wilson's disease, a rare autosomal recessively inherited disorder characterized by excessive copper storage in liver, kidney, and brain. The incidence is 1 : 200,000.

Diaphragm with Cream or Jelly The diaphragm is a flexible rubber dome encircled by a metal spring. A spermicidal cream or jelly is placed inside the dome and on the rim before insertion. See Table 8-7, Contraceptive Devices.

PROTOCOL FOR INITIAL HEALTH VISIT See this chapter, Health History and Physical Examination. In addition the proximal vagina is measured by the index finger from the posterior fornix to the symphysis pubis. This length is then compared with the appropriate circumference of the various sizes of diaphragms.

HEALTH TEACHING The client is instructed to use one tablespoonful of cream or jelly on the inside and the rim of the diaphragm. It can be inserted 6 hours before use. To insert, the client squats or stands with one leg raised on a chair. The diaphragm is

Table 8-8
Types of Diaphragms

Types	Description	Indications
Flat Spring Ortho-White latex 55-45	Thin, delicate rim; folds flat for inser- tion	Nulliparous females with firm vaginal tone
Coil Spring Koromex, latex Ortho, latex Ramses, gum rubber	Sturdy rim; folds flat for insertion	Multiparous females with average vagi- nal tone
Arch Spring Koroflex, latex Allflex, latex Ramses Bendex, gum rubber	Sturdy rim; folds in arc for insertion	Used in women with lax vaginal tone rectocele and/or cystocele

pinched together at the rim, dome side down, with one hand. The other hand spreads apart the lips of the vagina. The diaphragm is inserted back into the vagina as far as it will go; the front rim is tucked behind the symphysis pubis bone. The index finger then follows the rim of the diaphragm to make sure it is in place and also feels for the cervix through the dome. An applicatorful of spermicidal jelly or cream is inserted into the vagina before each additional act of intercourse. The diaphragm is left in place for 8 hours after intercourse. Douching is not done before then. To remove, the index finger is hooked under the rim of the diaphragm at the symphysis pubis bone and it is pulled out. It is washed with water, dried, and kept in a container when not in use. See Table 8-8 for types of diaphragms.

Spermicidal Foam, Suppositories These preparations contain a foam, jelly, or cream that holds the spermicidal agent against the cervical os and a chemical that immobilizes the sperm. See Table 8-7 for contraceptive devices.

PROTOCOL FOR HEALTH VISITS See this chapter, Health History and Physical Examination.

HEALTH TEACHING The client is instructed to shake the container before use. Two applicators full of the medium are inserted back

Table 8-9
Spermicidal Foams and Suppositories

Type of Agent	Manufacturer
Foams	
Because Contraceptor Vaginal Contraceptive	Shering
Delfen Contraceptive Foam	Ortho
Emko Vaginal and Pre-Fil Vaginal Contraceptive Foam	Shering
Koromex Contraceptive Foam	Holland-Rantos
Suppositories	
Encare Oval	Norwich-Eaton
Intercept Contraceptive Inserts	Ortho
Semicid Contraceptive Suppositories	Whitehall
S'positive Vaginal Contraceptive Suppositories	Jordan-Simner

into the vagina just before intercourse. One applicatorful is inserted before each additional intercourse. If douching is desired, the client waits for 8 hours after intercourse. To increase effectiveness, it is recommended that a condom be used in conjunction with the foam or suppository. Suppositories must dissolve after placement in the vagina for 10 to 30 minutes. See Table 8-9, Commercial Spermicidal Foams and suppositories.

Condoms Condoms are rubber or processed sheaths that fit over an erect penis. They are all the same size, 19 cm in length and 2.5 cm in width. There are two shapes: straight sided or tapered. They come with lubrication (wet jelly or dry powder) or without. See Table 8-7 for contraceptive devices.

PROTOCOL FOR HEALTH VISITS Routine health history and examination if client has not had one in 1 year.

HEALTH TEACHING The condom is placed on the erect penis before insertion into the vagina. One-half inch of empty space is left at the tip of the condom to hold the ejaculate. If lubrication is needed when applying the condom, saliva or K-Y jelly is used, as Vaseline causes the rubber to deteriorate. When withdrawing, the condom is held at the proximal end to prevent leakage of sperm into the vagina.

Rhythm The absence of sexual intercourse or the use of another method is practiced during the fertile period (ovulation). To ascertain the period when ovulation occurs the client needs accurate knowledge of her shortest and longest menstrual cycle. The fertile period is calculated by subtracting 18 days from her shortest cycle and 11 days from her longest cycle. This provides a range in which she is at risk for pregnancy. This method uses the following assumptions: ovulation occurs 12 to 16 days before menstruation, sperm remain viable for 48 hours, ovum will survive for 24 hours. See Table 8-7 for contraceptive devices.

PROTOCOL A routine health history and physical examination is done if client has not had one in 1 year.

HEALTH TEACHING The method to calculate the fertile period is reviewed. Abstinence or a second method of birth control is discussed for use during the fertile period. The effectiveness rate is reviewed. See Table 8-10 for how to calculate the interval of fertility.

Basal Body Temperature (BBT) Method The basal body temperature is the lowest temperature attained by the body during waking hours. Just before ovulation the BBT drops. In 24 to 48 hours after this time there is a noticeable temperature rise. The temperature remains elevated for 3 days. By charting body temperature before getting out of bed in the morning a woman can determine when she ovulates. See Table 8-7. Thermometers that record temperatures lower than 35.1°C (96°F) are used.

HEALTH TEACHING Temperature is taken orally every morning upon awakening and is charted. Charts are reviewed with the couples and interpreted for the first 3 months. Couples refrain from intercourse or use another method at the beginning of a drop in the temperature until after it remains elevated for 3 days.

Coitus Interruptus By withdrawing the penis before ejaculation the male deposits semen away from the vagina. See Table 8-7.

HEALTH TEACHING The semen is released away from the woman's genitals. It is possible that some preliminary ejaculatory fluid can be expelled before ejaculation without the knowledge of either

Table 8-10
How to Calculate the Interval of Fertility

If Your Shortest Cycle Has Been (no. of days):	Your First Fertile (Unsafe) Day Is:	If Your Longest Cycle Has Been (no. of days):	Your Last Fertile (Unsafe) Day Is:
21[a]	3rd day	21	10th day
22	4th	22	11th
23	5th	23	12th
24	6th	24	13th
25	7th	25	14th
26	8th	26	15th
27	9th	27	16th
28	10th	28	17th
29	11th	29	18th
30	12th	30	19th
31	13th	31	20th
32	14th	32	21th
33	15th	33	22nd
34	16th	34	23rd
35	17th	35	24th

Source: Reprinted by permission of Hatcher, et al. *Contraceptive Technology 1982–83,* New York: Irvington Publishers, 1982.

[a]Day 1 = First day of menstrual bleeding.

partner. Sperm can also migrate into the vagina if ejaculation occurred on the external genitalia.

COMMON CLINICAL PROBLEMS

Dysmenorrhea

ASSESSMENT

Definition and Etiology Dysmenorrhea is painful, crampy lower abdominal discomfort before and/or during the initial phase of menstruation. It occurs most frequently 1 to 2 years after menarche, when regular ovulatory cycles are established, and decreases in early adulthood.

The precise causative mechanisms are unknown, but theories

concerning increased intrauterine pressure, hypercontractibility of the uterine muscle, and uterine ischemia have been implicated as causative factors. There is evidence in favor of an increase in prostaglandins during the menstrual cycle. These endogenous substances are composed of fatty acids and are present in many human tissues. They stimulate smooth muscle and myometrial contractibility and are detected in menstrual fluid and plasma of females. Higher levels are associated in some women with dysmenorrhea (Ylikorkala et al., 1978). Prostaglandin production is reduced by either inhibition of prostaglandin synthetase activity or direct antagonistic action on prostaglandin receptors.

Symptoms Premenstrual symptoms include pain in lower back, heavy feeling in pelvic region, weight gain due to fluid retention, fatigue, moodiness, and headaches. They may disappear as soon as menses begin or merge with symptoms of dysmenorrhea which are lower abdominal pain (cramplike), nausea, and headache. Abdominal pain is most severe on the first day of the menses.

MANAGEMENT

Drugs that reduce prostaglandin activity and decrease dysmenorrhea symptoms are indomethacin, naproxen sodium, and mefenamic acid. Because of the potential side effects, including headache, aplastic anemia, and autoimmune hemolytic anemia, these compounds are not routinely recommended for use in adolescents (Klein et al., 1981).

Acetylsalicylic acid (ASA) is also a prostaglandin synthetase inhibitor and has been reported to relieve cramps successfully when started 3 days before menses. The dosage is 600 mg qid. This is usually the first drug of choice with adolescents in treating dysmenorrhea. Oral contraceptives are occasionally used in the management of dysmenorrhea especially in the sexually active adolescent. By suppressing ovulation, oral contraceptives prevent endogenous production of progesterone which may affect prostaglandin liberation from the endometrium (Klein, 1980).

Counseling If medication is prescribed, the regimen is reviewed with the adolescent. Mode of action is explained along with side effects. In addition to medications, other treatment regimens are discussed, including hot baths, adequate sleep, and regular exercise.

Sexually Transmitted Diseases

In an attempt to establish an individual identity, some adolescents may experiment sexually or develop promiscuous behavior. Other adolescents repress their sexual feelings. The women's movement, society's more permissive attitude toward sexuality, and the availability of contraception have all contributed to increased sexuality among adolescents and the resulting increase in sexually transmitted diseases.

ASSESSMENT

Definition Sexually transmitted diseases (STD) are those diseases transmitted between hetero- or homosexual persons through sexual intercourse or intimate contact with the genitals, mouth, or rectum.

Incidence The incidence of STD is increasing among the 16- to 25-year age group (Campbell and Herten, 1981). Because asymptomatic infections, especially *Gonococcus* (GC), are particularly prevalent among adolescents, those clients who are sexually active should be periodically screened for GC. Syphilis accounts for less than 1 percent of STD in adolescents (Oill et al., 1980).

Symptoms Symptoms of STD depend on the causative agent. The adolescent can be asymptomatic, but generally symptoms relate to the genital tract, where there may be lesions, itching, or discharge. There may be associated symptoms of the urinary tract, including frequency, urgency, and pain. Systemic symptoms include abdominal pain, fever, lethargy, and exanthems. See Table 8-11 for further assessment and management of sexually transmitted diseases.

MANAGEMENT

Counseling With the increase of STD, especially in the adolescent population, discussions during visits emphasize prevention of disease. The use of condoms is emphasized with both males and females. Birth control measures besides condoms thought to decrease STD are discussed: birth control pills, vaginal foam, and diaphragm. Multiple sexual partners are discouraged when using the IUD.

Genital cleanliness, involving washing and voiding before and after intercourse, is discussed. The use of cotton, loose-fitting underwear to prevent chafing and irritation and to absorb discharge is explained.

Both sexes are encouraged to discuss openly with their partners ways in which to reduce STD, mutual support for the use of the condom, and feelings concerning anger over transmission of STD. Adolescents are encouraged to seek diagnosis and treatment promptly when symptoms do occur.

Toxic Shock Syndrome

ASSESSMENT

Toxic shock syndrome (TSS) was first reported in 1978 (Todd et al., 1978). The study involved seven children (six girls, one boy) aged 8 to 17 years. Later reports revealed a high incidence in menstruating women who were tampon users. Most commonly the syndrome occurs before 30 years of age.

Etiology There appears to be a relationship between TSS and *Staphylococcus aureus;* the organism has been cultured from the cervix and vagina of women with symptoms of TSS. It is hypothesized that tampons cause microulcerations in the vagina, permitting entry of bacteria (Barrett et al., 1977). Supra-absorbent tampons are believed to cause ulcerations three times over regular tampons (Friedrick and Siegesmund, 1980).

Incidence Between 1975 and 1981, there have been 941 confirmed cases of TSS (Centers for Disease Control, 1981). Ninety-nine percent of cases occurred in females, 98 percent of which occurred during menstruation. The death rate is approximately 8 to 10 percent.

Table 8-11

Sexually Transmitted Diseases

Type and Etiology	Symptoms	Assessment	Management
Chlamydia: caused by bacteria *Chlamydia trachomatis*, involved as a causative agent in nongonococcal urethritis, postgonococcal urethritis, epididymitis, proctitis in males. A causative agent in nongonococcal acute salpingitis, cervicitis in females, often found in mixed infections along with gonorrhea, candida (Klein, 1980)	Generally involves mucosal surfaces. In males: urethral discharge (mucopurulent), dysuria. In females: vaginal discharge and perineal pruritus. With chlamydia cervicitis there are occasionally no distinct symptoms. May be asymptomatic in males.	Papanicolaou smear: if abnormal obtain *Chlamydia* culture. Complement fixation tes⏐	Tetracycline 500 mg qid × 10 days p.o. Erythromycin 500 mg qid × 10 days p.o.
Gonorrhea caused by *Neisseria gonorrhoeae*	Incubation period, 2–8 days. Females: may be asymptomatic. Males and females: symptoms include urinary frequency, urgency, dysuria, mucopurulent	Females: cultures of endocervix and rectum; in those practicing fellatio, culture pharynx. Males: Gram stain of urethral exudate shows gram-negative diplococci; in disseminated	Tetracycline 500 mg po qid × 5 days (Medical Letter, 1982). Penicillin G procaine 4.8 million units IM plus Probenecid 1 gm po × 1 Amoxicillin 3 gm po × 1 plus

	vaginal discharge, abdominal pain, fever with involvement of fallopian tubes, proctitis from implantation of organism during anal intercourse, abscess of Bartholin or Skenes glands in females.	GC, culture blood, joint effusions and skin lesions, if present.	Probenecid 1 gm po × 1 (Medical Letter, 1982) Specinomycin is drug of choice if allergy exists to penicillin, tetracycline.
Herpes simplex caused by Herpes virus, type II (HSV II)	Prodromal symptoms: tingling, burning, and/or painful sensations of genitalia. Active symptoms: vesicles with erythematous base on penis, scrotum, perineum, vagina, or inner thighs; rupture in 2–3 days forming ulcers that crust and heal in 7–10 days; associated symptoms include fever, malaise, anorexia.	Papanicolaou smear Tzanck test: scrape base of ulcer; fix on slide with methyl alcohol then stain with Giemsa; positive if multinucleated giant cells or typical eosinophilic intranuclear inclusions are present. Immunofluorescence test. Viral culture: scrape lesion and culture Serum viral titer: acute and convalescent titers are necessary.	Astringent, drying solutions such as Burows cold compresses or sitz baths; otherwise keep lesions dry and clean to prevent secondary bacterial infection. Topical anesthetics: lidocaine jelly Acyclovir (Zovirax Ointment 5%): antiviral-topical treatment; with initial lesions shows decrease in healing time of lesions; not effective in recurrent infections; used in immunosuppressed persons.

Continued

487

Table 8-11 (Continued)

Type and Etiology	Symptoms	Assessment	Management
			ALSO Refrain from sexual intercourse when active lesions are present. Use condom during prodromal symptoms and for 10 days after lesions heal. Papanicolaou smears are recommended every 6–12 months because of possible link between HSV II and cervical dysplasia and cancer. If active lesions are present and client is at term in pregnancy, cesarean section is performed to prevent transmission of virus to fetus.
Nonspecific urethritis caused by organisms other than gonococcus.	Dysuria Urinary frequency Urethral discharge	Gram stain of urethral discharge to rule out *Neisseria gonorrhoeae*	Tetracycline 500 mg po qid × 7 days. Erythromycin 500 mg po qid × 7 days.

Chlamydia trachomatis most common offending organism, more common in males

Exudates that contain polymorphonuclear leukocytes but no gram-negative diplococci are diagnostic of nonspecific urethritis.

Syphilis caused by *Treponema Pallidum*

Primary: chancre, or painless eroded lesion with raised border on penis, vulva; painless inguinal adenopathy.
Secondary: macular/papular dry, nonpruritic rash on soles, palms; headache, malaise, anorexia, fever, sore throat.
Latent: no symptoms; untreated syphilis that reaches this stage may result 15 or 20 years later in serious and widespread central nervous system and vascular complications (paresis, tabes dorsalis, blindness, and cardiac disease).

Dark-field microscopy of *T. pallidum*.
Positive reagent test for syphilis (VDRL, TPI (*Treponemal Pallidum* immobilization)) becomes positive in 10–90 days after the initial lesion.
FTA-ABS (Fluorescent Treponemal Antibody absorbed) confirms diagnosis and eliminates false-positive VDRL tests.

Early syphilis
Penicillin G Benzatinine
    OR
Penicillin G Procaine 2.4 million units IM × 1.
Tetracycline 500 mg po qid × 15 days.
Erythromycin 500 mg qid po × 15 days.

Symptoms TSS is usually characterized by a rapid onset of symptoms. Death occurs through hypotension, shock, and renal and cardiac failure. Signs and symptoms of TSS as delineated by Price (1981) are as follows:

- Fever greater than 38.8°C (102°F)
- Headache
- Sore throat
- Nausea and vomiting
- Diarrhea
- Abdominal pain
- Hypotension
- Muscle and joint aches (myalgia, arthralgia)
- Erythematous, diffuse rash
- Desquamation of soles and palms

Laboratory Findings Vaginal and cervical cultures for *Staphylococcus aureus* are obtained.

MANAGEMENT

After physical and pelvic examinations are performed and appropriate cultures obtained, the patient is treated with antibiotics that cover *Staphylococcus aureus*. Intravenous therapy with correction of electrolyte imbalances is instituted for those patients with symptoms of shock and severe gastrointestinal disturbances.

Counseling Adolescents have many worries and misconceptions concerning TSS and need education concerning its cause, symptoms, and management. Because of the possible increased occurrence of vaginal ulcerations when tampons are kept in place for long periods of time, adolescents are educated to change them every 2 to 3 hours during the day. At night sanitary pads should be used instead of tampons. The use of high absorbent super tampons is discouraged. Instead, regular tampons are recommended.

Starting in December 1982, federal regulations require that all tampon packages contain a statement saying that tampons are associated with TSS, "a serious and occasionally fatal disease." Symptoms of TSS and ways to decrease the syndrome are discussed in the statement.

Vaginitis

ASSESSMENT

Definition and Etiology Vaginitis is an infection of the vagina caused by a variety of organisms. See Table 8-12 for further assessment and management of vaginitis.

MANAGEMENT

Counseling With symptoms of vaginal discharge, adolescents are urged to seek education, diagnosis, and treatment. Douching is never relied on as an effective treatment measure for vaginitis. Adolescents need to know the difference between physiologic and specific vaginitis (see Table 8-12). Follow-up appointments are made after treatment is completed to re-emphasize preventive measures. These include use of condoms with multiple partners, cotton underpants, decreased use of panty hose, and increased use of skirts. Feminine hygiene sprays or bubble bath are discouraged because of possible irritation and inflammation of the perineum and vagina.

To decrease risk of exposure to vaginitis and STD adolescents are urged to be cautious about new partners, to carry condoms, and to wash before and after coitus. Birth control measures that act as barriers to sperm penetration through the cervix are discussed, such as diaphragm with jelly, foam, and oral contraceptives.

Lice, bacteria, and fungi can be transmitted from the water contained in unclean toilet bowls. Sitting on such toilet bowls exposes the genitals to the backsplash of the contaminated water. Therefore, women should crouch over rather than sit on public toilets.

Table 8-12
Vaginitis

Type and Etiology	Symptoms	Assessment	Management
Monilia (yeast) caused by *Candida albicans*: can be transmitted sexually or can occur because of alterations in vaginal pH because of oral contraceptive or antibiotic use.	Thick, white, curdlike vaginal discharge. Intense itching vagina, labia, perineum.	KOH wet-mount slide, positive for *Candida albicans* pH less than 4.6.	Miconozole (Monistat) cream; one applicator hs × 7 nights. Clotrimazole; one suppository vaginally hs × 7 nights. Mycostatin vaginal suppository; 1 bid × 14 days. Burows solution (aluminum acetate 1:20 dilution), apply to irritated areas qid to decrease irritation; not necessary to treat partner.
Nonspecific vaginitis (Gardnerella) caused by *Hemophilus vaginitis*: can be sexually transmitted but not documented; controversy over whether *Hemophilus* causes vaginitis.	Thin, gray-clear, malodorous discharge.	Saline wet-mount slide, positive for clue cells. Occasional WBCs; pH greater than 4.6.	Ampicillin 500 mg po qid for 7–10 days; only 50% effective; if treatment failure use: Metronidazole (Flagyl) 500 mg bid × 5–7 days Treat partner after initial treatment failure in female.

Physiologic discharge	Thin to thick white-yellow discharge. Occasionally mild odor. Discharge is nonirritating. Develops 6 months before menarche and remains postmenarche depending on fluctuating estrogen levels.	Saline wet-mount slide shows only epithelial cells.	Cotton underwear to absorb discharge. Education as to normalcy of discharge.
Trichomonas caused by *Trichomonas vaginalis*	Thin, yellow-green discharge is mild to moderately irritating. Mild to moderate itching. Transmitted sexually.	Saline wet-mount slide positive for clue cells. Occasional WBCs; pH greater than 4.6.	Metronidazole (Flagyl) 2 grams po in one dose or 250 mg po tid × 7 days (drug of choice) for pregnancy. Clotrimazole two 100-mg vaginal tablets qhs × 7 days.

References

American College of Obstetricians and Gynecologists, Technical Bulletin #29. "The Frequency with which Cervical–Vaginal Cytology Examinations Should Be Performed in Gynecologic Practice." Chicago, 1975.

Barrett, K., et al. "Tampon Induced Vaginal and Cervical Ulceration." *Am J Obstet Gynecol 127*:332, February 1, 1977.

Bettoli, E. "Herpes: Facts and Fallacies." *Am J Nurs 82*:924, June 1982.

Burbach, C. "Contraception and Adolescent Pregnancy." *J Obstet Gynecol Nurs 9*:319, September 1980.

Campbell, C. and J. Herten. "VD to STD: Redefining Venereal Disease." *Am J Nurs 81*:1629, September 1981.

Centers for Disease Control. "Epidemiology Notes and Reports: Follow-up on Toxic Shock Syndrome." *Mortality Morbidity Weekly Rep* January 30, 1981.

Erikson, E. *Identity, Youth and Crisis.* New York: Norton, 1968.

Esman, A. *The Psychology of Adolescence.* New York: International Universities Press, 1975.

Finkelstein, J. "The Endocrinology of Adolescence." *Pediatr Clin North Am, 27*:53, February 1980.

Freud, A. "Adolescence." *Psychoanal Study Child 13*:255, 1958.

Friedrick, E. and K. Siegesmund. "Tampon Associated Vaginal Ulcerations." *Obstet Gynecol 55*:149, February 1980.

Goldberg, B., et al. "Pre-participation Sports Assessment—An Objective Evaluation." *Pediatrics 66*:736, November 1980.

Greydanus, D. "Contraception in Adolescence: An Overview for the Pediatrician." *Pediatr Ann 9*:52, March 1980.

Gusburg, S. President American Cancer Society: Letter to the Medical Profession, Spring 1980.

Guyton, A. *Textbook of Medical Physiology.* 6th ed. Philadelphia: W. B. Saunders, 1981.

Hatcher, R., et al. *Contraceptive Technology 1982–1983.* New York: Irvington, 1982.

Havighurst, R. *Developmental Tasks and Education.* New York: McKay, 1972.

Irwin, C., et al. "Appointment Keeping Behavior in Adolescents." *J Pediatr 99*:799, November 1981.

Jackson, M., et al. *Vaginal Contraception.* Boston: G. K. Hall, 1981.

Katchadourian, H. *The Biology of Adolescence.* San Francisco, W. H. Freeman, 1977.

Kellum, M. and A. Loucks. "Genital Herpes Infections: Diagnosis and Management." *Nurse Pract 7*:14, February 1982.

Klein, J., et al. "The Effect of Aspirin on Dysmenorrhea in Adolescents." *J Pediatr 98*:987, June 1981.

Klein, J. "Update: Adolescent Gynecology." *Pediatr Clin North Am 27*:141, February 1980.

Marshall, W. and J. Tanner. "Variations in the Pattern of Pubertal Changes in Boys." *Arch Dis Child 45*:13, February 1970.

Marshall, W. and J. Tanner. "Variations in Patterns of Pubertal Changes in Girls." *Arch Dis Child 44*:291, June 1969.

Medical Letter. "Treatment of Sexually Transmitted Diseases." *24*:29, March 19, 1982.

Muus, R. *Theories of Adolescence.* 3rd ed. New York: Random House, 1975.

Oill, P., et al. "Symposium on Adolescent Gynecology and Endocrinology: Venereal Diseases in Adolescents and Contraception in Teenagers." *West J Med 132*:39, Jan., 1980.

Price, J. "Update: Toxic Shock Syndrome." *J School Health 51*:143, March 1981.

Root, A. "Endocrinology of Puberty." *J Pediatr 83*:1–19, July 1973.

Tanner, J. *Growth at Adolescence.* Oxford, England: Blackwell Scientific, 1962.

Todd, J., et al. "Toxic Shock Syndrome Associated with Phage Group I Staphylococci." *Lancet 2*:1116, November 25, 1978.

Ylikorkala, O. and M. Dawood. "New Concepts in Dysmenorrhea." *Am J Obstet Gynecol 130*:833, April 1, 1978.

9

Parenting
in Special
Circumstances

Families confront and manage the normal developmental stresses that occur throughout the family life cycle, but occasionally increased burdens tax the coping methods of the family and its individual members. Such situations include the normal circumstances surrounding the birth of the first and subsequent children, having active toddlers at home, independence conflicts with adolescents, the career advancement of either marriage partner, and marital disagreements. At these junctures, families need increased support. These normal developmental stresses are compounded in families whose members are forced to deal with additional stresses, such as chronic illness, single or adolescent parenthood, and the problems of the working mother. For example, the original stress factor may snowball into any of several critical problems:

- Less time for family-related tasks, resulting in decreased communication, recreation, and mutual problem solving
- Family disintegration, as evidenced by disrupted marriages
- Increased resentment of family members because of added stresses and less attention to individual needs

The purpose of this chapter is to provide the nurse practitioner with information to help families cope with parenting in special circumstances. In these stressful situations, increased support by

497

health professionals and by social and community organizations is crucial to family acceptance of and adaptation to the situation. In addition to the roles of professional consultant on family life, health educator, and provider of primary care, the nurse practitioner is called upon to function as a parent to the parents. This supportive professional relationship allows parents and children to develop additional strength to deal with the conflicts and stresses that special circumstances entail.

ASSESSMENT

The goal of the nurse practitioner in working with families is to promote positive parenting through reducing problems, minimizing stresses, and providing quality health care so that the child can develop as normally as possible. It is also important for parents to verbalize feelings and thoughts about the situation in which they are parenting. Such expression provides a catharsis for their feelings as well as providing information for the nurse practitioner on parental reactions and coping mechanisms. The following areas are also explored:

- Parents' specific coping mechanisms in dealing with the circumstance (denial, shock, anger, depression, mourning, withdrawal)
- Knowledge of the prognosis, in the case of chronic illness
- Ways in which the circumstance has or will affect life-style
- Added stresses the parents envision
- Parental/family adjustment
- Past medical/social management regimens
- Ways in which the family feels the nurse practitioner can help

MANAGEMENT

In managing families who are parenting in special circumstances, the nurse practitioner provides care that incorporates the following features:

1. Quality health care appropriate to the physical and emotional needs of the child and family
2. Management plans to correct delays or temporary disruptions related to the impact of the stress on the child's and family's developmental tasks
3. Psychological support and community services offered routinely

CHRONIC ILLNESS

Assessment

Generally, chronic diseases are those illnesses characterized by impairment of body function with stages of exacerbation and remission but with no possibility of complete cure (see Chapter 12, Approach to Chronic Illness).

REACTIONS OF THE FAMILY

The initial fear and anxiety of family members progresses to depression as the impact of the chronic illness is realized (see Chapter 12). Self-blame and resentment as to the parents' alleged contributions to the illness may occur. Parents or caretakers may lose self-confidence in their parenting abilities for awhile. Some parents react to the situation by overprotecting and indulging the child. Parents who experienced their child as normal before the illness occurred may experience a continuous sorrow, that can last for many years, for the loss of their healthy child (Steinhauer et al., 1974). In many families, the feelings and sorrow of one member affect all members, placing added stress on the whole family, and not just the parents (Lawson, 1977). In a few cases family members may even reject the chronically ill child. Siblings may react at times with jealousy because of attention given to the chronically ill sibling. There will be increased financial obligations on the family because of treatments and other added costs of care. Eventually, the biggest psychological task for parents is to accept the child's chronic illness.

Because of the added stress the illness places on family members, past unresolved conflicts may resurface, communication and support to members may be lessened, and severe marital disintegration may develop. After a period of time, some families adapt positively to the illness and its stresses and become a stronger unit. In most cases social activities are decreased because of time limitations and decreased financial resources.

REACTIONS OF THE CHILD

Children react to the impact of chronic illness according to their age and cognitive development (see Chapter 12, Approach to Chronic Illness).

REACTIONS OF HEALTH PROFESSIONALS

Many health professionals feel hopeless and guilty about not being able to cure or at least decrease the symptoms of the illness. This reaction may lead to withdrawal from the family, hence decreased support. Another trap to avoid is overemphasizing the illness and overindulging the family members, which may be counterproductive to carrying out effective diagnostic and treatment regimens. Health professionals may react with anger and hostility toward families if they do not go along with treatment regimens (Martin and Mauer, 1982).

ROLE OF THE NURSE PRACTITIONER

The nurse practitioner who suspects the presence of a chronic illness takes a complete history, including past history, with specific emphasis on the following factors:

- Family history of congenital anomalies
- Intrauterine infections, such as rubella, herpes, toxoplasmosis, and cytomegalic inclusion virus
- Severe perinatal infections
- Damage to central nervous system through infection and/or trauma
- Postnatal and childhood infections
- Prenatal information, such as gestation, infections, use of alcohol, smoking, severe anemia
- Birth circumstances, such as method of delivery, Apgar scores, resuscitation methods

A physical assessment is done, including a complete developmental examination (see Chapter 1, Child Health Assessment, and Chapter 24, The Neuromuscular System). Medical and specialist consultants are obtained as needed to make a diagnosis. The nurse practitioner who follows a child who has a chronic disease assesses several factors:

- The child's course of primary and specialist care
- Who the main provider of continuity of care is
- Alterations in developmental functioning due to disease
- Support measures in the family
- Financial problems for the family

Management

Parenting of children with chronic illness recognizes that illness in one child has major implications on emotional and physical relationships and possibly on the continued existence of the family as well (Steinhauer, 1974). Therefore, the more family members are able to resolve emotional anxieties and resentments and are able to support and communicate with one another realistically, the better their chances of providing continuous, adequate care to the child.

For care to be effective, family members need clear definitions and discussions of the child's major problems and goals for short- and long-term treatment. These discussions should be scheduled at regular intervals in order to review past developments and to discuss any new treatment regimens.

To ensure comprehensive, continuous, and coordinated care, it is important that a health professional be in charge, who coordinates the various personnel involved in the care of the chronically ill child and who helps parents deal with the problems (Pless, 1973). This person, in addition to providing illness management, functions as the ombudsman, communicator, and therapist for family feelings and stresses. The primary provider is also the coordinator and expert consultant on the child's needs with community and supportive agencies. Therefore, the role of the primary care provider encompasses three functions:

- Manager and coordinator of care
- Ombudsman for family
- Coordinator of community agencies

TREATMENT OF THE CHRONIC ILLNESS

The goals for treatment should include the following (Yancey, 1972):

- Treatment of the illness through correction of the cause if possible, as well as control of symptoms and treatment of complications
- Prevention of the illness, treatment regimen, and rehabilitative programs from interfering in the child's normal development
- Prevention of the illness and treatment regimen from disrupting family functioning.

HOSPITALIZATION

Children with chronic illness are hospitalized frequently. This causes separation from the family, peers, and school. Most children become resentful of hospital routine, of being dependent on other people, and of the continuous treatments they are subjected to (Mattsson and Gross, 1972). Several needs must be met for chronically ill children and their parents:

- Truthful comprehensive explanations of diagnostic procedures
- Encouragement to ask questions
- Follow-up on understanding of illness
- Adequate preparation for procedures
- Encouragement of the child to maintain self-care

It is important for nurses to discuss with the family general routines of care after discharge from the hospital. Schedules for treatment regimens, who performs them, and any restrictions and modifications of the child's behavior concerning transgressions are also discussed.

DEVELOPMENTAL NEEDS

Parents of a child with chronic illness must recognize that their child needs to progress with accomplishment of normal developmental goals whenever possible. In order to develop internal coping mechanisms, preschoolers and school-age children need to have normal restrictions placed on their demands to avoid overindulgence of wants. Self-care should be both encouraged and rewarded. Only the most necessary physical restrictions should be placed on the child, with involvement generally encouraged with peers, school, and social activities.

With school-age children and adolescents, involvement in peer groups who have the same illness is helpful. This affords acceptance, group support, and discussion of concerns and questions. Groups can be joined in which the child has an interest, such as boy scouts or girl scouts. New hobbies can be substituted for activities that cannot be accomplished due to physical limitations (Wolfish and McLean, 1974). School activities within the regular institution are encouraged. When this is not possible, regular tutorial services are instituted to maintain cognitive development. By encouraging developmental tasks in their children, parents focus on normal activities in daily living. A number of routines can enhance parenting in chronic illness (Krulik, 1980):

- Prepare the child for changes in appearance, daily routine, environment, and feeling states.
- Encourage participation of the child in decisions about treatment regimen.
- Accept the child as a partner in performing treatments.
- Share management of the illness regimen by the whole family.

COUNSELING

Perhaps the most important aspect of counseling in chronic illness is to listen to and validate the parents' feelings concerning the disease process. In the initial stages, there may be shock and denial. In these situations, acceptance of the feelings without trying to explain their reactions and to move them along to other stages is most helpful. With gradual recognition and initial acceptance of the child's condition, realistic problem solving can be attempted. For example, the nurse practitioner discusses how the family copes with the needs of the child or with problems associated with transportation to school and medical appointments or with sibling resentment.

Open communication concerning feelings and mutual problem solving with all family members may be suggested if this is in line with family response and coping mechanisms. Referral to a social worker or family therapist for ongoing support and communication may help with severe family disruption. Otherwise listening to complaints of both parents and children and helping them to solve their problems within their capacity is therapeutic. In counseling, it is important to reassure family members that their negative feelings are an important response to the stresses of the illness. Continuous and sincere reassurance that they are doing a good job in handling the illness is important. This approach recognizes their contributions and increases support that they are doing the best they can under the circumstances.

COMMUNITY REFERRAL

An essential part of helping parents cope with chronic illness in children is to recognize the significant role played by community organizations in dealing with the chronic illness. Many organizations provide physical equipment, such as beds, commodes, and oxygen tanks. Other organizations provide stimulation and play programs in which infants and young children are taught developmental skills, such as motor control and language development. Equally important, these programs provide for emotional support and health education through parent groups and member activities. Many parents have organized their own support groups around the specific chronic illness of the child. For example, parent groups dealing with asthma, cystic fibrosis, and cancer are helpful (Walsh, 1981). In weekly meetings specific topics are discussed and supports initiated. National organizations have well-defined programs that deal with illnesses, for example, the American Cancer Society's "I Can Cope Program" (Craft et al., 1982).

SINGLE PARENTHOOD

Assessment

The number of single-parent families has increased substantially over the past 10 years. There are approximately nine million single-parent families in the United States, more than 80% of which are managed by women (U.S. Census Bureau, 1978). In 1978 the median income of families headed by women was $8,540, or just less than half the $17,640 median income of all families.

Women become single parents as a result of such situations as death or divorce of a spouse, separation, by adopting, and by natural means, consciously or unconsciously, all of which create special needs. For example, a woman who is widowed or divorced and who has never worked outside the home may have limited knowledge of financially managing a household. She may have minimal job skills and educational preparation. In contrast, a mature woman who consciously makes a choice to become a single parent through having her own child or through adoption may be prepared to manage the added financial burdens and may be organized in management because she has been working for a number of years. This woman may also be able to solve problems more effectively because of her past experiences.

For many women, the pregnancy was unplanned and a therapeutic abortion was not an option. Some of these women have fantasies and unrealistic expectations concerning motherhood. Consequently, they may not be prepared for adjustments in lifestyle, daily routines, employment status, and finances.

PROBLEMS ASSOCIATED WITH SINGLE PARENTHOOD

Society views raising children alone in a negative manner and does not recognize the needs of the single parent. Single households are referred to as broken homes, and children who are unsupervised because of maternal employment are described as "latch-key children" (Duffy, 1982). Few community resources are available to help manage a household. Few communities offer quality child care and, traditionally, women are paid less than men for similar jobs. Society also reinforces the notion that two parents are better than one. Single parents are often labeled as disorganized or as being outside the mainstream of society. Unmarried single mothers are viewed more negatively by society than are divorced or separated parents. The social stigma for single parents is least with widows.

Many single parents find themselves socially isolated and alone. They participate less in community affairs as compared with two-parent families (Smith, 1980). Many are without employment skills and stay at home caring for their families. Consequently, they are socially removed from a peer and support system. Frequently they feel overwhelmed with household chores, managing children, financial concerns, and increased fatigue. Along with these feelings there is a sense of powerlessness. This is increased if the woman does not seek family, peer, or community support. Because of greater psychological stress, she may experience increased illness, including psychosomatic problems. Some parents have verbalized their problems in dealing with loneliness and in feeling guilty in thinking two parents are better than one (Horowitz and Perdue, 1977). In some situations, the father is involved in helping care for the child. In most instances, this help is welcomed and is found supportive. In other situations, because of past couple disharmony or conflicts, there may be intense disagreements about raising the children, about financial problems, and about the amount of support spouses give to one another.

CHARACTERISTICS

Because single parents come from many different life situations, no one set of characteristics can describe their personality and coping mechanisms. Obviously, women who have job skills and careers are more equipped to handle the stresses of employment and managing a household. Other women have little preparation for single parenting. They come from low socioeconomic backgrounds with little experience in adequately managing their own lives. Consequently, these women may be nonassertive, have no job skills, and be socially isolated. Many have decreased self-esteem and ill-defined goals for the future. Some single parents who need emotional support may not be able to express it. They may concentrate instead on the child and worry or have complaints to a disproportionate degree about the child's behavior, state of health, or minor childhood illnesses. They make frequent visits to the health care facility.

HISTORY

In addition to the routine history, the following history is obtained (see Chapter 1, Child Health Assessment):

- Pregnancy planned or unplanned
- Support during pregnancy, delivery, and neonatal period
- Current support systems
- Parental concerns regarding the child's state of health and behavior and their own coping mechanisms

- Goals for self and for child for the next five years
- Parental knowledge of community resources
- Assessment of maternal child interaction (see Chapter 4, Assessment of Parent–Child Interaction)

Because stresses of being a single parent are increased, the potential for child abuse is assessed in all mothers who are extremely isolated or depressed or who exhibit negative interaction with their children.

Management

An important goal for care is to help single parents develop positive self-esteem and an independent self-identity (Duffy, 1982). Independence in identity means seeing oneself as a person apart from one's mate, children, and home. Although all these aspects may contribute to an identity, the recognition of an independent identity includes important self-aspects such as work, professional skills, activities, projects, interests, and future goals. In addition, helping the parent increase skills in caring for the child is an important goal for care.

GENERAL PRINCIPLES

The nurse practitioner provides single-parent families with care that is empathetic and continuous. In health visits, the parent should feel that the environment is supportive, with the focus on increasing self-esteem and parenting skills.

The strengths and weaknesses the woman sees in herself are discussed. Ways and activities to enhance the strengths and decrease the weaknesses are explored. For example, to encourage the ability to be social, a support group is advocated; for lack of job skills, a training program or courses may be discussed.

Adequate communication techniques such as making assertive statements and use of "I" language may need to be role-modeled by the nurse and practiced with the parent. For many parents whose needs are too numerous for one person to handle, a multidisciplinary approach is helpful. In addition to being seen by a nurse practitioner, referral to a social worker, family therapist, or psychologist is mandatory to provide additional support and mutual problem solving.

SUPPORT SYSTEMS

While psychological support is necessary to all persons, it is particularly important to single parents who are socially isolated, lacking in self-esteem, and depressed. Family members are an obvious support if they are available. However, with increased interaction, there may be family conflicts over routines of caring for the children, use of discipline, and the parent's routine and life-style.

Personal friends constitute an invaluable means of support through occasional child care, discussion of problems, and social activities. For some friends who are without children having friends with children increases the variety and richness of their lives. Other friends may have children, and this situation allows for common discussion of interests and problems.

Group supports are extremely helpful in decreasing social isolation, providing emotional support, enhancing self-esteem, and increasing knowledge of child rearing. Some areas have groups specifically relating to the needs of single parents. If available, single parents should be encouraged to join. These groups also encourage continued contact with members between sessions through phone calls and planned group activities, even after the formal meetings have finished. Some group sessions are devoted to practicing skills, such as applying for and interviewing for a job, learning effective communication techniques, and achieving goals that increase self-esteem.

Community resources are supportive. These include community colleges, job training programs, social service departments, child care agencies, and the public school system.

CONTINUITY

In seeing single parents, an important role of the nurse practitioner is to provide coordination of all the services needed by the family. It is also important to develop an atmosphere in which the parent can verbalize concerns, feel nonthreatened, and obtain psychological support. This type of atmosphere is more likely to come about when the care is continuous and frequent. Single parents need not feel that their life-style is second best to that of two-parent families. With motivation, encouragement, and development of their own skills, single parents provide viable, supportive living environments for the growth of healthy children.

THE ADOLESCENT PARENT

In 1978 approximately 1.1 million adolescents became pregnant in the United States. Of these, 543,407 teenagers delivered viable infants, 419,000 had abortions, and 150,000 had miscarriages or other fetal deaths (DHHS, 1980). Sixteen percent of all infants in the United States have teenage mothers. Births to married adolescents account for 56% of all adolescent births (Dryfoos, 1982).

Some adolescents relinquish their infant for adoption or have a family member care for the child. For adolescents who choose to become parents, there are occasionally serious consequences to their future:

- Noncompletion of high school
- Nondevelopment of job skills
- Lack of completion of adolescent developmental tasks
- Welfare status
- Increasing family disharmony over child rearing, and degree of independence of mother.

This section will focus primarily on adolescent mothers. (For additional information see Chapter 8, Health Care of the Adolescent.)

Assessment

EFFECTS ON ADOLESCENT DEVELOPMENT

The younger a teenager is when she has a child, the more serious the consequences concerning normal progression of adolescent development. The adolescent parent is deprived of the moratorium of adolescence (Mercer, 1980). This is the period in an adolescent's life when decisions about the future are delayed so the adolescent can concentrate on achieving developmental tasks.

The time involved in infant care impinges on social time with peers. Early and middle adolescents are extremely narcissistic and do not have the psychologic maturity to cope with the demands of a child. In assessing attachment behavior between teenage mothers and their infants, one study suggested a critical age (18 years) at which mothers develop optimal maternal readiness for quality interaction with their infants (Teberg, 1983). This age coincides with late adolescent development, which focuses on the ability to have an intimate, caring relationship with another person. A study comparing young adolescents (aged 13–16 years) with a group of controls (aged 30 years) was designed to assess problems with parenting that might result in less than optimal mothering (Bingol, 1972). The adolescents showed more brief responses to infants, less eye contact, little verbal encouragement, and less smiling behavior than did the controls. Most of the teenagers were able to meet the infants' needs but were unable to decrease the babies' stress and anxiety. Adolescents may become resentful because of inability to concentrate on their development tasks due to time spent caring for the infant.

Some teenagers do not have the ability to think abstractly until middle or late adolescence. Consequently, the ability to understand relationships between optimal parenting and the child's development or between the need to continue with their own development is faulty.

Being an adolescent mother is believed to restrict the ability of the teenager to pursue nonmaternal activities (Presser, 1980). Continuing with school, developing mature social relationships, and finding substantial employment are all self-growth activities that are difficult to achieve because of motherhood. Many women drop out of school when they become pregnant and become full-time homemakers. This situation can continue for a lifetime. Other adolescents who have a strong desire to continue with school may do so, but have more difficulty in achieving goals of employment than do women who become mothers in their twenties.

Adolescent fathers' involvement with parenting, although increasing, is still marginal. Mothers of adolescent mothers in one study viewed adolescent fathers as not generally supportive (Poole, 1982).

PARENTING ABILITIES

Adolescent mothers are able to cope with parenting and have an increased likelihood of having a positive relationship with their child under certain conducive circumstances:

- Consistent emotional support at home
- Family encouragement to continue own developmental tasks

concerning completion of school, maintenance of some social activities, and development of future goals
• Consistent help with child care

Young mothers under 15 years of age appear to be at greater risk for defective parenting and socioeconomic problems. Their children appear to be at greater risk for medical problems, decreased emotional and intellectual stimulation, and neglect (Bingol et al., 1972).

One study compared the development of infants whose mothers were given either at-home infant care education or job skill training in an infant day care center with the development of a group of controls. The mothers in both intervention groups talked with their infants more, the infants had higher Bayley motor development scores and weighed more than the controls (Field et al., 1982). Some adolescent mothers have unrealistic expectations about an infant's development and have punitive child-rearing attitudes (DeLissovoy, 1973).

Adolescent mothers, when compared with older mothers, are more likely to seek medical advice from their own mothers than from health professionals (Zuckerman et al., 1979). It is therefore important to recognize the impact of family routines, myths, and traditions in providing care and health education. It is believed that the adolescent mother can progress into a positive maternal role if support for abilities as a parent is given by the maternal grandmother (Mercer, 1980).

REACTIONS OF THE ADOLESCENT'S FAMILY

Families react to adolescent parenthood in many ways. Some grandparents may feel that the mother needs to assume total responsibility for the care of the child. Consequently, there is little support for the mother. Other families may encourage educational activities but are negative about social activities with peers. Some families may take over a large part of the care of the child and not allow the adolescent parent much control.

PRENATAL AND WELL-BABY VISITS

If possible, it is important to begin to establish rapport with the adolescent parent during pregnancy. This is most commonly done in a prenatal visit. Discussion focuses on equipment and clothes obtained for the infant, desired type of feeding, support at home, plans for school, past experiences in caring for infants, and use of community resources such as a public health nurse. Many adolescents have fixed their attention on the actual delivery and birth of the infant and are not ready to receive information on infant care.

During well-baby visits, it is important to remember that the adolescent parent has two major tasks:

• To continue her own adolescent development
• To provide to the best of her ability for the care of a child

The first task of continuing with her own development is assessed by asking the following questions:

• What are your plans for school?
• What social activities do you engage in with peers?
• What type of conflicts exist at home with the family?
• Are there concerns about body image?
• Are you using birth control?
• What are your future goals?

The second task of providing care to the infant is assessed through the following history:

• Complications in prenatal, birth, and neonatal periods
• Family/social history
• Nutrition history
• Development
• Immunizations
• Observations of signs of faulty maternal child bonding
• Involvement with community support programs

Management

In providing care to adolescent parents, it is important to recognize that they are adolescents first who need to progress with their developmental tasks and are parents second (Bierman and Street, 1982). Therefore, management regimens are always integrated with the nurse practitioner's knowledge of adolescent cognitive development, coping mechanisms, school/social activities, relationship with family members, and future goals. Adolescents who are responsibly coping with their own development have greater abilities to cope with caring for a child. Other adolescents may discontinue schooling or decrease social activities in order to concentrate on parenting activities.

In whatever coping style the adolescent adopts, the importance of family support should be recognized. Therefore, adolescents who return to school may do so in part because of family encouragement and because the family provides child care and supportive services. If relationships between family members and adolescents are strained, it is imperative to conduct problem-solving sessions with adolescents on ways to increase effective communication, complete assigned tasks at home, and ventilate feelings positively. Occasionally it is useful to encourage family members to come for pediatric visits in order to discuss common problems at home.

PRIORITIES FOR CARE

Comprehensive care to adolescent parents and their children needs to be multidisciplinary. Besides the primary care providers, social workers, if available, provide supportive psychological counseling and problem solving for parents. Community agencies including public health nurses, day-care centers, schools for continuing the adolescent's education, and family planning centers are integrated into the comprehensive care regimen. Role modeling appropriate to parental interaction with the child is an important priority of the nurse practitioner at each visit.

DEVELOPMENTAL TASKS

The adolescent's own developmental tasks are emphasized during pediatric visits. She is encouraged to maintain schooling, plan future goals, enjoy regular peer contact, and work on maintaining viable relationships with family members.

SUPPORT SYSTEMS

Establishing a viable support system for the adolescent is important. It should consist of help from immediate family members, including the child's father, and acceptable outside child care. Obtaining ongoing health care from knowledgeable and supportive professional agencies and home visits from public health nurses is helpful.

HEALTH EDUCATION

Health education concerning infant care is an ongoing part of routine care. Some adolescents may profit from one-to-one consultation during visits. Others may gain more information from group discussion with their peers on well-child care. At some health care facilities, classes are conducted as part of the pediatric visits to provide increased health education to parents. These classes may be held before individual visits or informally while parents are waiting. Topics include nutrition, development, play, immunizations, and family planning (see Chapter 10, Health Education in Primary Care). Implicit in providing health education is the need to recognize the influence and opinions of other family members. If advice given is dissimilar to family opinions, it will probably not be followed. It is therefore important to discuss feelings about baby care and management routines at home before offering health education to the adolescent.

HEALTH CARE OF THE ADOLESCENT

Many adolescents have little accurate knowledge about maintaining their own health. Some are obese, have skin problems, are deficient in immunizations, have faulty diets, smoke, and do not get enough exercise. Although the focus of pediatric visits is on the child, it is appropriate to initiate an appointment for the mother for a general health visit so that adolescent problems can be assessed realistically. Family planning should be discussed (see Chapter 8, Health Care of the Adolescent).

CONTINUITY OF CARE

It is important that adolescent parents see the same health provider if available. This allows, over a period of time, for a more thorough assessment of the family's health status and for the management of problems. More importantly, it enables the adolescent to develop a trusting relationship with the health care provider.

THE WORKING MOTHER

Assessment

In many American families both parents work. More than half the women in the United States with children under age 18 work outside the home. Most of these women are between 24 and 34 years of age, the traditional child-bearing years (Zambrana et al., 1979). During the past decade there has been a heavy influx of women, both single and married, into the labor market. Women employed in 1970 numbered 30.3 million, while in 1980 there were 44.5 million.

There are several reasons why women work. The financial burden of raising a family is lessened when a woman works outside the home. The extra money may also provide an increase in the standard of living of the family. The extra money may also be used to buy convenience appliances and a new car or to take a vacation. Women also work outside the home in order to pursue and stimulate their own interests. Working provides a network of personal interactions in contrast to the social isolation of home that many women find psychologically depressing (Eisenberg, 1975). Other women work because they find housework and the daily routine of the home unfulfilling. Some women obtain work in which they have a special interest. Other women with college degrees pursue work in their respective professions. Most women employed outside the home have underpaid, unskilled, or semiskilled service-related jobs. When women work on a full-time basis they earn only 60% of mens' wages (U.S. Dept. of Labor, 1973).

ADVICE OF CONTEMPORARY CHILD-CARE BOOKS ABOUT WORKING MOTHERS

The following themes can be identified in child-care literature concerning working mothers:

1. Children need a mother in the home for at least the first 3 years of their life (Brazelton, 1969; Fraiberg, 1977; Dodson, 1977). This provides the bonding, love, reassurance, and support for the child's psychological development. This crucial period, if

positive, may help the child to become a loving, caring adult. Popular child-care books imply that only a mother's love can do this.

2. It is suggested that women who have young children should always consider the welfare of the children and sacrifice their own working goals if conflicting with the child's needs (Radl, 1973).
3. Part-time work is always advocated over full-time work.
4. Child-care substitutes do not take the place of a mother's care.

Many women feel guilty about pursuing their own goals when confronted with popular opinions against working from professionals on child care. This guilt may negatively influence their relationships with their husbands and children. Work that should be viewed as personally fulfilling, productive, and ego enhancing becomes for some women negative, worrisome, and guilt producing.

EFFECT OF MATERNAL EMPLOYMENT ON CHILDREN AND MARRIAGE

While the effect of maternal employment on children is difficult to assess objectively, some general statements can be made in view of past research. Mothers who are satisfied with their role, whether working or not, have the best-adjusted children (Etaugh, 1974). With preschool children, the provision of regular and stimulating caretaking arrangements appears to be important for the normal, personal and intellectual development of these children whose mothers do work (Etaugh, 1974). There do not appear to be any consistent data, either positive or negative, on the development of elementary school age children whose mothers work. Middle-class adolescents appear to have the fewest adjustment problems if their mothers work, although lower socioeconomic boys and girls may have slightly more "home-related" problems (Etaugh, 1974). One study that compared marriages of employed mothers with those of full-time housewives found no differences in spouses' happiness or adjustment (Howell, 1973). One study, however, states that working mothers report more conflicts about conversational topics with their husbands and have more thoughts about separation or divorce (Nye and Hoffman, 1965). Another study compared the incidence of depression in working single and married mothers and found that there were both positive and negative aspects. Single mothers were found to be more committed to work and to derive greater emotional benefits from it and did not experience decreased self-esteem. Married mothers were found to experience more conflict with working and household chores and only slightly less depression than that of single mothers (Keith and Schafer, 1982). While the results of many studies on child adjustment are contradictory, the following general factors were evident when investigating effects on children (Zambrana et al., 1979):

- Quality child care and maternal role satisfaction are important.
- Quality of time spent with children is emphasized.
- Parental attitude toward maternal employment and general family stability is crucial.

Many mothers who work run up against role conflict within the family because of the unequal sharing of household tasks between husband and wife. Some women feel guilty if they don't "do everything," or believe their family is short-changed if other people provide care to their families. Other women who desire extra help with household tasks may find it difficult to obtain because of noncooperation on the part of family members or because of lack of finances to employ help outside the family. In some families, husbands and children help with household tasks willingly, and household chores are equitably divided. However, women still have to compromise their careers concerning increased job responsibilities and advancement. This is because they are still the primary persons who coordinate and are responsible for the care of the children (Pozanski et al., 1974). In many families a working mother's career roles are usually sacrificed for the good of the family.

HISTORY

In providing primary care to the children of working mothers, the nurse practitioner assesses the support systems of the mother:

- What arrangements are available for child care? Are these satisfactory?
- Who helps with household tasks?
- What specific responsibilities is the mother relieved of because she works?

- Who is her most supportive person?
- What effect, if any, does she see on the children?
- If given a choice would she rather work or not work?
- Does she feel guilty about working?

Management

Generally there are four options for the working mother (Howell, 1973):

1. The woman continues to assume full responsibility for household tasks while working. This situation leaves little time for quality interaction and play with children or effective communication with other family members.
2. Someone can be hired as mother surrogate to the children and in addition may perform household chores. If the family can afford it, this person may live with the family. In many upwardly mobile professional families who can afford live-in help, this situation works well. The mother surrogate also then becomes the nurturer not only to the children, but occasionally to the parents as well. In addition to providing child care, this person may cook meals, do light house chores, and provide nighttime babysitting.
3. Husbands and wives agree to share tasks in the home.
4. Some families may employ a number of persons to help with house chores, such as cleaning, gardening, and sending laundry out.

The nurse practitioner discusses the above options with parents. If women would like more help from family members but are unable or afraid to ask, the mother and nurse practitioner may practice effective communication techniques, such as using "I" statements, discussing chore assignments at home, and having each family member state wants.

Discussion of results of studies on effects of maternal employment on children may relieve some of the guilt about working that the mother feels. It is also important to review those factors that have a positive influence on children:

- Satisfaction with maternal role, whether working or not
- Importance of consistent, quality day care
- Importance of marital and family harmony

Perhaps in the future, fathers' life-styles may be modified to enable more shared parenting without fear of feeling unmasculine. Until that time comes when both men and women can make realistic choices about career and family goals regardless of sex, one parent, usually the mother, will continue to carry the burden of dual careers: full-time family care and working outside the home.

References

Abram, H. "The Psychology of Chronic Illness." *J Chronic Dis 25*:659–663, December 1972.

Bierman, B. and R. Street. "Adolescent Girls as Mothers—Problems in Parenting." In I. Stuart and C. Wells, editors, *Pregnancy in Adolescence.* New York: Van Nostrand Reinhold, 1982.

Bingol, N., D. Reininger, H. Rich, S. Iosub, and E. Wasserman. "What Happens to the Babies Born to Adolescent Mothers?" *Pediatr Res 6*:328, April 1972.

Brazelton, T. *Infants and Mothers.* New York: Delta Books, 1969.

Craft, M., Davidson, J., Davis, K., and B. Day. "Nursing Care in Childhood Cancer." *Am J Nurs 82*:440–442, March 1982.

DeLissovoy, V. "Child Care by Adolescent Parents." *Child Today 2*:22–25, July/August 1973.

Department of Health and Human Services Publ. No. 18-1120, Vol. 29, No. 1. April 1980. P. 11.

Dodson, F. "How to Discipline with Love." New York: Rawson Association, 1977.

Dryfoos, J. "The Epidemiology of Adolescent Pregnancy: Incidence, Outcomes and Interventions." In I. Stuart and C. Wells, editors, *Pregnancy in Adolescence.* New York: Van Nostrand Reinhold, 1982.

Duffy, M. "When a Woman Heads the Household." *Nurs Outlook 30*:468–473, September/October 1982.

Eisenberg, L. "Caring for Children and Working: Dilemmas of Contemporary Womanhood." *Pediatrics 56*:24–28, July 1975.

Etaugh, C. "Effects of Maternal Employment on Children: A Review of Recent Research." *Merrill Palmer Quarterly 20*:71–98, April 1974.

Field, T., S. Widmayer, M. A. Greenberg, and S. Stoller. "Effects of Parent Training on Teenage Mothers and Their Infants." *Pediatrics 69*:703–707, June 1982.

Fraiberg, S. *Every Child's Birthright: In Defense of Mothering.* New York: Basic Books, 1977.

Horowitz, J. and B. Perdue. "Single Parent Families." *Nurs Clin North Am 12*:503–511, September 1977.

Howell, M. "Effects of Maternal Employment on the Child." *Pediatrics 52*:327–343, September 1973.

Howell, M. "Employed Mothers and their Families." *Pediatrics 42*:252–261, August 1973.

Keith, P. and R. Schafer. "A Comparison of Depression Among Employed Single-Parent and Married Women." *J Psychol 110*:239–247, March 1982.

Krulik, T. "Successful Normalizing Tactics of Parents of Chronically Ill Children." *J Adv Nurs 5*:573–578, November 1980.

Lawson, B. "Chronic Illness in the School-Aged Child: Effects on the Total Family." *Am J Maternal Child Nurs 2*:49–56, January/February 1977.

Martin, G. and A. Mauer. "Interaction of Health Care Professionals with Critically Ill Children and Their Parents." *Clin Pediatr 21*:540–544, September 1982.

Mattsson, A. and A. Gross. "Long Term Physical Illness in Childhood." *Pediatrics 50*:801–811, November 1972.

Mercer, R. "Teenage Motherhood: The First Year." *Journal of Obstetric, Gynecologic and Neonatal Nursing 9*:16–27, January/February 1980.

Nye, F. and L. Hoffman. "The Sociocultural Setting." In Nye and Hoffman, editors, *The Employed Mother in America.* Chicago: Rand McNally, 1965.

Pless, B. "The Challenge of Chronic Illness." *Am J Dis Child 126*:741–742, December 1973.

Poole, C. "Mothers of Adolescent Mothers." *J Adolesc Health Care 3*:41–43, August 1982.

Pozanski, E., A. Maxey, and G. Marsden. "Parental Adaptations to Maternal Employment." *Am Acad Child Psychiatry 13*:319–334, Spring 1974.

Presser, H. "Social Consequences of Teenage Childbearing," in *Adolescent Pregnancy and Childbearing: Findings from Research.* U.S. Dept. HHS Publ. No. 81-2077. Washington, DC: U.S. Government Printing Office, 1980.

Radl, S. *Mother's Day Is Over.* New York, Charterhouse Books, 1973.

Smith, M. "The Social Consequences of Single Parenthood: A Longitudinal Perspective." *Fam Relations 29*:75–80, January 1980.

Steinhauer, P., D. Mushin, and Q. Rae-Grant. "Psychological Aspects of Chronic Ilness." *Pediatr Clin North Am 21*:825–840, November 1974.

Teberg, A., H. Valeta, and W. Wingert. "Attachment Interaction Behavior Between Young Teenage Mothers and their Infants." *J Adolesc Health Care 4*:61–66, March 1983.

U.S. Census Bureau. *Statistical Abstracts of the US.* Washington, DC: U.S. Government Printing Office, 1978.

U.S. Dept. of Labor: Women's Bureau. *Twenty Facts on Women Workers.* Washington, D.C.: U.S. Government Printing Office, 1973.

Walsh, S. "Parents of Asthmatic Kids: A Successful Parent Support Group." *Pediatr Nurs 7*:28–30, May/June 1981.

Wolfish, M. and J. McLean. "Chronic Illness in Adolescents." *Pediatr Clin North Am* *1*:1043–1049, November 1974.

Yancy, W. "Approaches to Emotional Management of the Child with a Chronic Illness." *Clin Pediatr 11*:64–67, February 1972.

Zambrana, R., M. Hurst, and R. Hite. "The Working Mother in Contemporary Perspective: A Review of the Literature." *Pediatrics 64*:862–870, December 1979.

Zuckerman, B., C. Winsmore, and J. Alpert. "A Study of Attitudes and Support Systems of Inner City Adolescent Mothers." *J Pediatr 95*:122–125, July 1979.

10

Health Education in Primary Care

Health education is a major component of nursing practice. Florence Nightingale not only developed nursing schools but devoted a large part of her career to educating physicians and health officials in improving sanitary conditions in hospitals and in maintaining adequate nutrition of patients. Nurses have always educated patients concerning personal hygiene and the benefits of exercise, nutrition, and fresh air to improve well-being. It is from these roots that nurses have expanded health education practices to include broader concepts of health and illness.

Today, health educators provide information, knowledge, and instruction to consumers in maintaining optimal health, preventing disease, managing illness, and developing skills in providing direct, daily health/nursing care to family members.

Health education can also involve aspects of health counseling. Health counseling includes health education but also entails psychologic assessment and support concerning deterrents to the attainment of improved physical and psychosocial health. Health counseling involves mutual exchange of ideas and advice on how to achieve optimal physical/psychologic and social well-being. Although elements of both health education and health counseling are used interchangeably in clinical practice, this chapter will focus on health education rather than on counseling.

In addition to individual health education, nurses teach clients in group classes, including adults, adolescents, and school-age children. Nurses work with groups in hospitals, clinics, private practice, schools, and community agencies. They are also active in maintaining and improving occupational health standards. The major focus is to educate people about unsafe working conditions.

The public has shown an increased interest in becoming more responsible in seeking education about health issues. As uniquely qualified experts in health education, nurses should lead the movement to educate consumers about health care. In pediatric primary care, the nurse practitioner routinely incorporates health education as part of each visit. The main components of health education include:

- Maintaining or promoting the client's optimal health status
- Preventing disease
- Explaining etiology and management of illness conditions
- Discussing the client's future physical and psychosocial development
- Counseling concerning accident prevention
- Informing families of community agencies and their appropriate utilization

This chapter discusses principles of teaching and learning, individual and group health teaching during pediatric visits, and the development of health education classes.

PRINCIPLES OF TEACHING AND LEARNING

Teaching includes those activities and conditions that promote learning. Learning occurs when there is a change in a person's behavior as a result of an experience. Learning is best achieved when a person recognizes a need to know something. Such internally developed learning is more likely to be sustained than is learning that is externally motivated by outside pressures or commitments.

Motivation

Motivation to learn is increased and maintained by providing certain conditions:

- Concise, well-organized, and clear material to the learner
- Frequent, positive feedback (for example, comments about a child's increased vocabulary may motivate parents to continue with activities of verbal stimulation)
- Successful achievement of learning tasks (for example, in discussing weight reduction, the nurse may initially concentrate on one task at a time, such as eating smaller food portions)
- Verbal dialogue, progress checks, tests, and reviewing charts (such as weight-reduction charts)
- Active involvement in a task (for example, in discussing diaper folding or temperature taking, it is best to have parents take part in these activities)
- Client-initiated goals for learning (for example, parents usually ask questions during pediatric visits because they want to know how to care for their child)
- Incentives to learn (for example, the incentive to be a better parent motivates people to learn)

There are several ways to assess a person's motivation to learn:

- Have there been past attempts at learning with successful outcomes?
- Does the person ask questions?
- Does the person have a sense of control over his or her future, as demonstrated by an ability to set and achieve goals, a positive feeling about life, and an ability to care for himself or herself adequately?
- Does the person have multiple stresses in his or her life that would inhibit concentration on learning?
- Is the person coping with survival issues, such as chronic poverty, unemployment, and rehabilitation from substance abuse, which inhibit learning?
- Are there severe worries, depression concerning self, or a life situation that would decrease learning?

Use of Contracts

The use of contracts in providing care motivates clients to accomplish goals. A contract is a nonlegal agreement between a client and a health professional. It states mutually agreed-upon measurable goals that the client will accomplish over a period of time in order to increase the level of wellness. For example, the client agrees to keep a number of pediatric appointments or agrees to carry out a prescribed exercise regimen. In cases in which health care problems are serious and chronic, the use of a contract to state desired objectives may be part of the pediatric visit.

Use of Objectives

Objectives are an important tool in the teaching/learning process, as they clearly define expectations and goals for the learner. An objective is an intent described by a written statement concerning a proposed change in a learner. Objectives describe what learners are to be like when they have completed the learning experience (Mager, 1972). Objectives are clearly written, realistic to the subject matter being taught, and measurable by a standard such as a test or learner demonstration of knowledge. For example, after completing a class on infant care, the learner will read a thermometer correctly two out of three times. The objective describes the learning activity (class on infant care), the behavior to be accomplished (reading the thermometer), and the number of trials needed to accomplish the behavior (two out of three times). Objectives are even more effective when the learner writes them down. This helps increase the responsibility for his or her own education and makes the desired behavior personalized and specific to the learner.

Occasionally it is necessary to distinguish between short- and long-term health education objectives. This distinction helps the client and the nurse practitioner set priorities concerning work to be done both during and between visits. An example of a short-term learning objective for nutrition is for the parent to name age-appropriate iron-containing foods. Short-term objectives involve immediate information that may have a direct effect on the learner's behavior at the moment.

Long-term objectives involve health education toward achieving goals over several visits. An example of a long-term health education objective for birth control might involve naming various methods and side effects of birth control devices over several visits. Behavioral changes of the client are observed over a long period of time.

Specific written objectives for learning are rarely used during routine pediatric visits. Rather, a continuous health education/nursing process takes place during these visits involving identification of parent/child educational needs and discussion of developmental issues in child rearing. Formal written objectives are most often used in health education classes.

Methods of Teaching

The teaching method selected depends on three factors:

- Population. Are the learners homogeneous or heterogeneous? Do they have the same learning needs? Are they motivated to learn?
- Size. How many people are to be taught? Lecture teaching is appropriate for large groups.
- Content. What does the group want to learn? Lecture, discussion, or demonstration are appropriate if learning needs are the same.

The most common methods of teaching are described in the following sections.

INDIVIDUAL INSTRUCTION

Instruction on an individual basis occurs most often during pediatric visits when parents and clients ask specific questions about health issues. The nurse practitioner also presents short, concise health education material concerning health and developmental issues.

GROUP VISITS

Group visits are discussed under "Incorporating Group Health Education Into Primary Care."

FORMAL CLASSES

Nurses are active as health educators with groups of parents, adults, school-age children, adolescents, and other health consumers.

Lecture/Discussion This format allows time for participants to ask questions and to have material clarified. Participants can also learn from one another. The teacher needs clear objectives about what is to be accomplished during the classes.

Demonstration/Practice These sessions give participants an opportunity to see specific actions and then to practice behaviors to achieve these actions. In pediatrics, classes on bathing an infant, on using a baby food processor, or on practicing diaper folding are appropriate for demonstration.

Role Playing This format is used when a problem situation or feeling needs to be better understood by the learners. They reverse roles such that a parent may play an adolescent and a nurse may play a parent. The objective is for the participants to understand the feelings of the other person and thereby reduce the problem situation. This method is used most often with students or in communication classes.

Micro Teaching This method involves teaching small parts of a programmed instruction to a few students for a short period of time. The advantages are that students learn limited material in a concise manner and the teacher concentrates on techniques of teaching without a complex formalized teaching environment (de Tornyay and Thompson, 1982).

Visual Aids Learning is enhanced by the use of a variety of visual aids. These increase the effectiveness of verbal presentations by providing the student with a second teaching stimulus. Writing an outline of the material to be presented on a blackboard or passing out a written outline increases learning by enhancing the verbal presentation. The following visual aids are most commonly used:

- Overhead projectors help clarify and emphasize points made in verbal presentations. They are most effective when a single point is used on each sheet.
- Slides present new material and provide visual variety to presentations.
- Printed material and handouts help emphasize points.

Assessing the Level of Knowledge

Inherent in principles of teaching and learning are the evaluation of the learner's knowledge before instruction begins. This is accomplished by the following methods:

- Pretest. This written test assesses the learner's knowledge before instruction begins.
- Active questioning. Verbal questioning assesses the learner's past educational or practical experience or attendance at similar classes.

Evaluation

Learning is evaluated by the following methods:

- Post-test. This written test assesses the learner's knowledge after instruction is completed. It contains the same questions given in the pretest in order to compare the learner's knowledge before and after instruction.
- Demonstration of teaching activity. The learner demonstrates the correct method for taking a rectal temperature or for inserting and removing a diaphragm.
- Expected parent/client outcomes. These statements are written as a section of formalized standardized procedures or protocols used by nurse practitioners when seeing clients with specific health/illness problems. They provide statements designed to evaluate the client's learning. For example, in a well child protocol, an outcome would be for the parent to state two age-appropriate home safety precautions.

INCORPORATING INDIVIDUAL HEALTH EDUCATION INTO PRIMARY CARE

Individual health education occurs during primary health care visits. It is most often the result of questions asked by the parent or client concerning health and illness. During this process, the parents' learning is increased because they are internally motivated to ask questions.

Frequently, the nurse practitioner also initiates health education topics appropriate to the developmental age of the child, such as toddler behavior at the 12-month visit. Learning will take place only if the parent is receptive to this information.

The advantages of individual health education are as follows:

• The instruction is one to one and more personalized than group teaching.
• Discussion and clarification are immediately available.
• Visual aids such as written instructions, charts, and handouts can be used to enhance verbal discussion.

The disadvantages of individual health teaching during primary health care visits include the following:

• Lack of interest or other stresses may prevent the client or family from being motivated to learn during a particular visit.
• Since the nurse practitioner is initiating health education, rather than the client, the teaching may not be among the client's priorities.
• There may not be enough time for health education because of other visit priorities.

Health Visits

The goal of health visits is to provide motivation and opportunity for families and clients to assume responsibility for the maintenance and promotion of their child's and their own state of health. This is done initially by providing answers to client's questions. Most parents come to visits with questions concerning their child. Adolescents come with questions or worries about their health or because they need forms filled out for school or health insurance. In addition to answering parents' questions, the nurse practitioner has a unique opportunity to stimulate learning by performing health education at these visits (see Table 10-1, Suggested Health Education Topics for Parents at Primary Health Care Visits).

Besides addressing client's questions, health education also addresses developmental issues concerning the child. For example, the nurse practitioner incorporates various aspects of accident prevention appropriate to the client's age, such as toddler-house safety, child-street safety, and adolescent-driving/firearm safety. The client may or may not be interested in this information, since it is being initiated by the nurse practitioner, and it may not be a priority of the client. Nevertheless this information is an important part of education during health care visits.

SETTING PRIORITIES

Health education is most effective when it addresses what clients think they need to know. Clients will be unable to incorporate other health education into specific visits if their concerns are not addressed first. Therefore, routine pediatric visits usually start out with certain open-ended questions by the nurse practitioner:

- What brings you in today?
- How have things been going for you?
- What had you hoped I could do for you today?
- What questions do you have today?

After the client's questions are answered, the nurse practitioner may proceed with other health education priorities appropriate to the visit.

Some families may be acutely stressed because of serious illness, family dysfunction, socioeconomic problems, or having to cope with the realities of single parenting (see "Understanding the Population"). A parent who is struggling to maintain adequate nutrition for the family may not be paying attention to what is being taught concerning toddler development. In this situation, the nurse practitioner may need to bypass some health education priorities so that families can concentrate on and cope with the realities of their life situation.

By helping families solve personal problems, nurse practitioners

Table 10-1
Suggested Health Education Topics for Parents at
Primary Health Care Visits[a]

Age	Topic
1 month	Normal variants in sleeping/bowel movements
	Amount of crying
	Stimulation, both visual and verbal
	Variations in oral intake
	Safety: Falls, and car seats
	Parental cohesiveness
6 months	Visual, verbal, and tactile stimulation
	Use of hard rubber objects for teething and learning hand–mouth motor integration
	Use of infant walker to increase locomotion around the house
	Safety: Falls, objects in mouth
	Nutrition
	Normalcy of exploration of body parts
12 months	Verbal stimulation through naming body parts, objects, and pictures in books
	Toddler development: Decreased appetite, fear of strangers, clinging to mother, and temper tantrums
	Safety: Falls, burns, electrical outlets, and ingestion of pills and poisons
	Nutrition
	Brushing teeth
	Assessment of parental thoughts on toilet training
	Setting limits
2 years	Verbal, visual, and tactile stimulation
	Self-care activities: Feeding, undressing, and nutrition
	Safety: Falls, burns, and poisons
	Night terrors
	Normalcy of masturbation
	Toilet training
	Discipline
3 years	Increased use of pencil-and-paper tasks
	Naming pictures
	Simple puzzles
	Self-care: Dressing self and mastering toilet training
	Helping with simple household chores
	Safety: Falls, drowning, burns, streets, and ingestion of pills and poisons
	Normalcy of being egocentric

Table 10-1 *(Continued)*

Age	Topic
4 years	Stimulation: Reading stories, doing puzzles, and making drawings
	Importance of play activities to increase mastery over tasks and to cope with fearful situations
	Normalcy of being egocentric
	Sibling rivalry
	Safety: Streets, ingestion of pills and poisons
	Instructions to parents on principles of sex education
5 years	Stimulation: Reading stories, playing games to act out sexual roles, fantasies, and fears
	Playing house, playing with dolls, trucks, models of schools, parks, and farms
	Cooking
	Self-care activities: Oral hygiene, helping with tasks around the house
	Safety: Burns, falls, streets, and ingestion of pills and poisons
6–8 years	Stimulation: School projects, increasing gross motor skills through sports, bike riding, and skating
	Importance of peers and sharing activities and of increased ability to compromise with peers
	Nutrition
	Safety: Swimming, bike riding, skating, streets, falls, burns
7–10 years	Importance of participation in school activities and taking trips with family
	Field trips
	Controlled use of television
	Maintaining daily hygiene
	Activities of increased ego strength: Liberal use of praise and encouragement to complete tasks
	Nutrition
	Safety: See 6–8 years
10–12 years	Importance of peers in life to validate feelings and provide friendship
	Review of beginning physical body changes
	Ways to problem solve disagreements with parents and peers
	Safety: See 6–8 years
12–18 years	See Chapter 8, "Health Care of the Adolescent"

[a]For additional information, see Chapter 6, "Health Care of Toddlers and Preschoolers," Tables 6-2, 6-4, 6-6, and 6-8.

increase the family's ablity to concentrate on other activities, such as health education.

UNDERSTANDING THE POPULATION

Teaching is most effective if it is specific to the client population. This makes education more personalized to a particular cultural group and more relevant to their needs. Many large urban populations contain various ethnic groups. In a pediatric outpatient department in San Francisco, one may see families from such cultural backgrounds as white, black, Chicano, Mexican, Latino, Chinese, Middle Eastern, Japanese, Filipino, and Vietnamese. In rural areas, the nurse practitioner may be dealing with similar racial mixes or with families from a more homogeneous background. It is important for the nurse practitioner to understand some of the major cultural norms of each ethnic group he or she comes into contact with. This approach leads to respect for their traditions and to awareness of one's own biases when working with various cultures.

Understanding the economic milieu of families helps focus patient education on their needs. If parents are socioeconomically disadvantaged, health education may need to be modified. Dealing with social service and housing agencies, chronic unemployment and undereducation may take up all the family's emotional and physical resources. The nurse practitioner assesses the most relevant health education needs of such families. Families may need to know about safety measures in less than adequate housing situations. They may need to know that temper tantrums in a toddler are not the result of a dysfunctional family situation. Health education in obtaining adequate nutrition on a low budget is appropriate to families with financial problems and deals specifically with their needs for financial planning.

The nurse practitioner helps families in acute and chronic turmoil deal with and solve some of their problems. This goal may be accomplished through emotional support and problem solving, consultation, and evaluation by social service staff, referral to community agencies, and ongoing management of their health care needs. Health education needs to be modified for a family experiencing an acute crisis, such as recent death of a relative or close friend, divorce, separation, severe marital stress, or loss of a job. Families in these states may be too stressed, and only the most important health education material should be discussed.

Other families may be extremely motivated concerning health education and may want to know everything about parenting and child care. These families take an active role in deciding what they want to know and investigate. The nurse practitioner is a resource to these parents by providing information and direction and by discussing their questions.

EVALUATION

During pediatric visits, evaluations are done by asking oral questions of the parent or client. For example, if the parent has been given health instruction concerning increased iron-containing foods in the diet, then asking the parent to give a 24-hour dietary history helps evaluate learning (see the section, Principles of Teaching and Learning, Evaluation).

Follow-up evaluation is also done by the nurse practitioner. It takes time for information to be assimilated by the client, especially complex education concerning a health or medical issue. Therefore, follow-up phone calls or a return visit in several days might be necessary to evaluate the client's understanding and to answer questions. Follow-up evaluation is indicated with the following:

• Complex medical situations and treatment regimens
• Review of drug therapy
• Review of explanations of illness
• Genetic counseling
• Assessment of client's understanding of previously given information

TEACHING CHILDREN

At each pediatric visit, establishing a trusting relationship with the child provides several positive ends:

• Makes the visit more pleasant for parent, child, and nurse practitioner
• Alleviates any fear the child may have about the visit
• Helps the child see the nurse practitioner as a non-threatening person
• Encourages the less fearful child to be more willing to answer questions

• Allows the nurse practitioner to begin teaching the child about his or her own health care

Trustful relationships begin with greeting the child initially. At the beginning of the visit, age-appropriate play activities such as drawing for a 4-year-old and handling bright objects for a 12-month-old commence between the nurse practitioner and the child. The child is asked questions about school, a new sibling, or names of friends. Toys in the office within easy reach make children feel more comfortable. Toys that teach children about health care and what health professionals do are educational. These include medical kits and books about office visits, nurses, and doctors. Dolls to which children can give injections or apply band-aids or bandages help them express anger and fear on inanimate objects at threatening procedures. Puppets help create a play environment in which children can act out their fear and express their feelings. Children are also taught by asking them questions like, "Do you know when you are wheezing?" This helps them take responsibility for recognizing symptoms of illness and for informing parents when they are ill (Pantell et al., 1982).

Goals of education during pediatric visits for children include the following:

• To help them develop coping mechanisms and mastery over threatening situations
• To help them express their fears verbally or through play so they may be more open to health education
• To encourage the older child to assume some responsibility for his or her own care

Frequently during pediatric visits, parents are asked most of the questions about school-age children. This leaves the child without motivation to learn about his or her health care or to learn mechanisms to cope with illness. Unconsciously it provides the child with decreased ego strength because of lack of dialogue and validation by the nurse practitioner during the visit. In contrast, when the child is made an integral part of the visit at whatever age, whether through play or through verbal interaction, there is increased parent–child satisfaction and a greater willingness to be open to learning situations (see Table 10-2, Play Activities and Health Education Topics for Children at Primary Health Care Visits). During adoles-

Table 10-2
Play Activities and Health Education Topics for
Children at Primary Health Care Visits

Age	Play Activities	Health Education
1 month	Smiling at and talking to infant Touching extremities and body Following rattle	Parent directed
6 months	Talking to infant and handing the child bright, soft toys Having the child reach for objects Playing with feet Transferring objects from hand to hand	Parent directed
12 months	Talking to child Putting toys within easy reach Allowing physical exploration of the room Remaining at a safe distance initially to reduce stranger anxiety Having child observe "movement" toys: windup or pull toys	Parent directed
2 years	Talking to child Providing toys: Stacking blocks, playing with boxes for in–out maneuvers, holding keys Using pen or pencil for scribbling Looking at picture books	Parent directed
3 years	Talking to child Asking questons about age, type of play activities, and TV programs Naming pictures Throwing and catching ball Jumping Naming colors	Parent directed

Table 10-2 *(Continued)*

Age	Play Activities	Health Education
4 years	Questions concerning school, play activities, names of siblings, friends, and TV programs Pencil-and-paper tasks: Drawing a person and writing letters and one's name Jumping, hopping, and catching ball	Child directed Importance of brushing teeth, of not running into street, of telling parent when not feeling well and being able to describe symptoms Dressing/undressing self
5 years	As above	Child directed Brushing teeth Safety: Not playing with matches or drinking or eating medications Not crossing streets alone Fun household tasks Learning to put away articles and helping parent with tasks Helping with cooking, with direction from parent
6–8 years	Activities in school and with friends Having favorite books and TV programs Doing puzzles and reading books	Child directed Self-care activities: Bathing, brushing teeth, and dressing Telling parent symptoms of illness Learning to tell time Helping with light household chores to gain mastery over tasks Street safety: Bicycling and roller skating Nutrition Routine exercise

Table 10-2 *(Continued)*

Age	Play Activities	Health Education
7–10 years	Types of play activities with peers Books read TV programs, recreational activities child likes Subjects and activities child likes/dislikes about school Health history directed partially toward child	Child directed Daily hygiene activities: Teeth and body Self-directed household activities Safety: Climbing, falls, bicycles, and skates Talking about feelings of sadness and happiness to parent
10–12 years	Peer activities Afterschool activities School: Subjects and grades Future goals	Child directed Self-care activities and taking responsibility for own care Making meals and doing household chores Beginning of changing body image
12–18 years	See Chapter 8, "Health Care of the Adolescent"	

cence, the client is asked whether he or she wants the parent present at visits. This recognizes the adolescent's ability to become self-sufficient in taking responsibility for personal health care (see Chapter 8, Health Care of the Adolescent).

INCORPORATING GROUP HEALTH EDUCATION INTO PRIMARY CARE

The use of pediatric well-baby visits to attend to a group of parent–infant pairs is not uncommon in pediatric practice. This type of delivery of primary health care is called group or cluster visits. Three to four parent–infant pairs are seen together and 1½ to 2 hours is allotted for the visit. Such visits are most often planned around infants in the same age range so that parents can discuss similar questions and experiences. Most often these visits are conducted during the child's first year of life because parents have many questions and profit from the experiences of other parents in similar situations. Group visits, however, are also conducted during the second year of life when parents can profit from discussion concerning toddler behavior.

The format for visits begins with generalized discussion concerning the infant's health for approximately 45–60 minutes. Parents' questions are answered, and specific recommendations concerning nutrition, development, and anticipatory guidance are discussed. Each child is then examined to assess further the state of health and determine the presence of illness. Differences in development and temperament are discussed with parents while observing each child. Immunizations are then given. Depending on the cohesiveness of the group, future visits may be conducted in group meetings or may be planned as single visits.

The advantages of group visits are that health education is shared between parents and the nurse practitioner, thereby decreasing the authority role of the nurse. Parents bring to the group unique experiences concerning their child, and this stimulates discussion and increases their motivation to learn. The group situation also allows parents to teach and learn from one another. These increased educational contributions to the group foster their sense of self-worth and mastery as parents.

One study that compared group visits with individual visits found group visits efficient, requiring no more time of the health professional per visit than was true of individual visits (Osborn and Woolley, 1981). The same study showed that group-evaluated parents called less for advice between visits and kept a higher percentage of well-child visits than did the controls (Osborn and Woolley, 1981).

The disadvantages of group visits are that there is less individualized attention and more generalized, collective attention to members in the group. Occasionally a group visit may be dominated by an anxious or extremely verbal parent whose needs may overshadow those of other parents requiring just as much attention. Because of lack of time, all parents' questions might not be answered. Lastly, scheduling may be complicated and time consuming because of various parents' routines.

HEALTH EDUCATION CLASSES

Because of their background and expertise in wellness care and health issues, nurses are logically suited to conduct health education classes. Nurses are knowledgeable about community activities and organizations in addition to being familiar with similar or previous health education classes conducted by these organizations. Nurses are versatile and active in teaching a variety of consumer groups:

- Professional peer groups (topics include establishing health education classes, developmental issues in children and adolescents, and assessment and management of illness in children)
- High school education classes (topics include drug abuse, parenting, common illnesses in children, sexuality, and changing body image)
- Parenting classes (topics include infant–parent classes, toddler–parent groups, and prenatal classes)
- Parent support groups to alleviate social isolation and to increase parents' coping abilities

Principles of Health Education Classes

An open, warm, friendly attitude displayed by the teacher is important in conducting group education classes. This allows for open discussion, answering questions, and the generation of the feeling among participants that they are valued for themselves, their presence at the classes, and the contributions they make. Gutelius and Kirsch (1975) state that factors that tend to enhance learning in parent education classes are personalized frequent contact between health educator and parents and an attitude of friendliness.

During classes an important principle of health education is to repeat important points during discussion, since individualized personal contact is lessened in group classes. Awareness of the population to be taught is important in order that the nurse provide education specifically directed to their needs. If possible, it is important to try to help participants identify their own needs, their questions, and learning objectives through discussion, to help further clarify their own thoughts and feelings.

In classes with adolescent parents, in addition to maintaining an open, friendly attitude, some education may need to be simplified concerning discussion topics. This approach addresses the learning needs of concrete thinking adolescents.

With adolescent parents, it is important to instill a view that they can have control over their own future. This is done by verbally expressing concrete ideas such as continuing with education, setting short-term and long-term goals, taking care of themselves physically and emotionally, and planning for possible emergency situations. With some adolescent parents or with concrete thinking adults, it is important to ask what a particular situation has been like for them rather than to ask how they feel about a situation. This approach helps increase their ability to express thoughts about circumstances and situations on a concrete level without having to deal with abstract or feeling thoughts.

Fostering a sense of self-worth in all participants during health education classes is important. This is done by listening attentively to their questions, commenting briefly on their remarks, and maintaining a nonjudgmental attitude. Considering parents as authorities in caring for their children and the nurse practitioner as the catalyst to help improve their abilities fosters a positive relationship between the participants and the educator.

Developing Health Education Classes

ASSESSING THE NEED

Before any health education class is begun, the nurse practitioner investigates the need for classes by providing answers to several questions:

- Has a questionnaire or poll been conducted to assess client interest in classes?
- Did the potential participants request classes?
- Are the same classes already offered in the community?
- Are there gaps in knowledge of the persons involved that would be rectified by group classes?

- Is the group homogeneous and concentrating on the same learning tasks?
- What time of day or evening would classes be held to encourage participation?
- Would travel arrangements/babysitting be available to encourage attendance at classes?
- Are patient education committees or support personnel available to offer input on past education programs, ways to advertise, areas to include in content, and evaluation procedures?

ASSESSING THE LEVEL OF KNOWLEDGE

Inherent in principles of teaching and learning is the evaluation of the learner's knowledge before instruction begins. In group education classes this is accomplished in the following ways:

- Pre-test. This written test assesses the learner's knowledge before instruction begins. Questions pertain to material that will be presented in class.
- Active questioning. Verbal questioning assesses the learner's past practical experience, attendance at similar classes, or parent/education groups.

DEVELOPING CONTENT

Content develops from the health education needs of the client. Many nurse practitioners are knowledgeable about specific areas of health education such as infant care or adolescent development. Old lectures, conference notes, articles, and books are reviewed to formulate content, and a literature survey is conducted to add new content to old material.

Depending on the client population, the type of presentation is decided on. For adolescent parents, discussion with multiple visual aids is important. In prenatal classes, discussion allowing ample time for questions and demonstrations of various aspects of infant care is appropriate. For adult parenting classes, discussion with some lecture works best.

Visual aids enhance verbal presentations and stimulate learning. Posters and charts that emphasize verbal points are appropriate. Other helpful aids are slides, films, and role playing. In a class for junior high school students on parenting, role playing may be used to develop an understanding in the adolescent's mind of what it feels like to be a parent. For example, one adolescent plays the role of the parent to another adolescent classmate who role-plays being disruptive and uncooperative at home.

For classes that will continue over several sessions, the participation of allied health professionals changes the focus of and adds a different stimulus to the presentation. To that end, nutritionists, pharmacists, play therapists, and physicians may give guest presentations.

DEVELOPING LEARNING OBJECTIVES

The purpose of objectives is twofold: to clarify the goals of the program for the participants, and to create measurable activities that can be evaluated at the end of the program to assess the participants' learning progress. A copy of course objectives are given to participants before the course starts (see section, Use of Objectives).

EVALUATION OF CLIENT'S LEARNING

In health education classes, evaluation is conducted at the end of the course by giving a post-test. This test contains the same questions that were given in the pretest. It is evaluated to see whether there has been improvement in the participants' responses. Other ways to evaluate learning are through direct observation of behavior, especially if demonstrations are used, and through direct questioning of the participants.

EVALUATION OF THE PROGRAM

The most logical way to evaluate a group class is to distribute written evaluation forms at the end of the program. These forms ask participants questions about the content of class material, their degree of understanding of the material presented, evaluation of the instructor and his or her teaching methods, and the ability of the instructor to develop group cohesiveness. Evaluation of a program can also be based on the learning objectives that were written for the classes. The objectives are reviewed to determine whether participants have accomplished them. For example, an objective may state that after observing a class on infant bathing, the student will return a demonstration that includes three principles: proper holding, washing body creases, and assessing water temperature. If participants have fulfilled the above objective and other objectives in the class, the program receives a favorable evaluation.

REVISION OF THE PROGRAM

The program is revised on the basis of the participants' comments and evaluation forms, the ease with which participants were able to accomplish stated objectives, and appropriateness of objectives to participants' interest.

SPECIFIC TEACHING SITUATIONS

When teaching parents about child care, it is important to incorporate developmental models into the teaching activities. The following are some examples:

- Educating about toilet training. The nurse practitioner relates the child's ability to be toilet trained to the physiologic maturity of the gastrointestinal, urinary, and neurologic systems.
- Educating about accident prevention for a toddler. The cognitive development, which includes short attention periods, short memory, and narcissistic temperament, is incorporated into the discussion.
- Educating about methods of discipline in a 4-year-old. The preoperational level of cognitive development requires that simple explanations, immediate discipline measures, and the child's inability to understand another person's point of view be discussed.

In conducting sexuality or health education classes for adolescents in high school, the following are important teaching techniques:

- Have adolescents write questions on paper anonymously to be read and answered by the educator during class. These questions most often address specific and personal concerns of adolescents who may be too uncomfortable to ask them verbally in class.
- Enhance verbal discussion with visual presentations such as fre-

quent use of the blackboard, charts, slides, films, and passing out books during class for review.

• Some junior high school students may be in the stage of concrete cognitive development, necessitating simplified presentations.

In conducting health education classes for elementary school children, presentations are kept simple, with each paragraph illustrating a single idea oriented to the present. In order to make abstract ideas more concrete, drawings are used. For example, in discussing body parts, a simple figure of a person with various body parts is drawn.

References

Billie D. (ed.). *Practical Approaches to Patient Teaching.* Boston: Little, Brown, 1981.

Casey, P., M. Sharp and F. Loda. "Child Health Supervision for Children Under Two Years of Age: A Review of its Content and Effectiveness." *J Pediatr* 95:1–9, July, 1979.

de Tornyay, R. and M. Thompson. *Strategies for Teaching Nursing,* 2nd ed. New York: Wiley, 1982.

Gutelius, M. and A. Kirsch. "Factors Promoting Success in Infant Education." *Am J Publ Health* 65:384–387, April, 1975.

Kemp, J. *Instructional Design.* Belmont: Fearon, 1972.

Mager, R. *Preparing Instructional Objectives.* Belmont: Fearon, 1972.

Osborn, L. and F. Woolley. "Use of Groups in Well Child Care." *Pediatrics* 67:701–706, May, 1981.

Pantell, R. et al. "Physician Communication with Children and Parents." *Pediatrics* 70:396–402, September, 1982.

Redman, B. *Issues and Concepts in Patient Education.* East Norwalk, CT, Appleton-Century-Croft, 1981a.

Redman, B. *Patterns for Distribution of Patient Education.* East Norwalk, CT, Appleton-Century-Croft, 1981b.

Redman, B. *The Process of Patient Teaching in Nursing.* 3rd ed. St. Louis: C.V. Mosby, 1976.

ASSESSMENT AND MANAGEMENT OF COMMON CLINICAL PROBLEMS

In the course of providing comprehensive primary care services to infants and children, the nurse practitioner frequently identifies or is presented with signs and symptoms of illness or abnormality. Many common conditions of childhood can be safely and appropriately managed by the nurse practitioner who practices in collaboration with a physician. Other conditions require referral for medical management and collaboration for subsequent care.

The decision as to which problems are managed by the nurse practitioner depends on a number of factors, and admittedly the scope of practice will vary from setting to setting. Those factors to be considered include the nature of the problem, the experience of the nurse practitioner, the availability of physician consultation, the relationship between the nurse practitioner and physician (e.g., amount of time working together, degree of trust established), the setting (e.g., isolated rural practice, university teaching clinic), the use of standing orders, protocols, or standardized procedures, and the legal statutes of the state.

When referral for medical evaluation and management is indicated, the role of the nurse practitioner does not cease. As the primary care provider for the child and family, the nurse practitioner remains the primary resource person for the family and fulfills that role by coordinating services and by providing the teaching, counseling, and support measures that are the hallmark of nursing services.

Part Two is designed to provide information necessary to identify abnormalities and assess specific conditions of infancy and childhood, to present guidelines for referral, to specify the management role of the nurse practitioner with regard to common clinical problems, and to present pertinent information for parent–child teaching and support during and after diagnosis and treatment.

Detailed information on treatment is presented only for those very common illnesses and problems. In-depth information on treatment of less common or more complicated problems should be obtained from recognized pediatric textbooks. Medications are mentioned as they relate to particular conditions, but dosages are not specified, since so many variables affect determination of dose and since this function is almost universally viewed as a collaborative one with the physician (see Chapter 13).

11

Approach to Minor Acute Illness

EFFECTS OF THE DISEASE ON THE INDIVIDUAL CHILD

Many illnesses during childhood are acute in origin. Respiratory infections are extremely common, and other acute illnesses include gastroenteritis, otitis media, exanthems, conjunctivitis, viral syndromes, and fevers. Because of the youthful resilience of the child's body, recovery from acute illness is usually very rapid.

Physical

In the infant and young child problems attributable to immature organ development are common. The infant frequently regurgitates liquids because of a loose stomach–cardiac sphincter. Frequent middle-ear infections in childhood are caused by a short and straight eustachian tube that provides easy access to infectious agents from the oropharynx. Infants and children require increased fluids during illness in proportion to their weight because of heavy losses of fluids with diarrhea and vomiting and because of increased demands of the basic metabolic processes during illness. It

549

is common for infants and children to lose weight or to gain weight slowly during and immediately after an illness. This effect is most noticeable during the rapid growth pattern of infancy. Generally children can withstand the rigors of high temperatures better than adults, and they recover more rapidly from acute illness.

Psychologic

When illness develops in children their personal sense of security is decreased. This comes about from the illness itself, the child's thoughts about overcoming the effects of the illness, and the possible absence of adequate emotional support from family members. Illness produces a temporary anxiety state, and children may no longer feel that obstacles in the environment can be mastered.

Some children consciously or unconsciously rely on somatic complaints to keep from involving themselves in psychologically traumatizing situations.

Infants exhibit psychologic problems in the face of illness as well. Outbursts of crying and irritability are frequent, and the need for physical and emotional comfort is increased.

EFFECTS OF ILLNESS ON THE FAMILY UNIT

When children become ill the family undergoes increased anxiety and stress. These effects are more intense if the child is chronically ill (see Chapter 12, Approach to Chronic Illness). In acute illness, the family unit may continue their daily routine if the illness is of short duration and not serious.

Family stress associated with illness in children results from the following:

- Increased medical costs
- Time away from work to care for the child
- Inability to complete professional or household tasks
- Concentration on management of the treatment regimen
- Dealing with an irritable, fearful child
- Worry over the child's illness

• Miscommunication and power struggles between family members as a result of the child's illness

ASSESSMENT OF THE PRESENTING SYMPTOM

Symptoms

Presenting symptoms are variable, depending on the infectious agent, the response of the child to the agent, and the child's health status. For some children symptoms may involve only a slight decrease in motor activity or appetite, while other children may actively complain of discomfort or may exhibit symptoms of acute illness.

The most common symptoms of acute illness in children are fever, lethargy, irritability, anorexia, nausea, vomiting, diarrhea, exanthem, rhinorrhea, cough, and discharge from the eyes. In one study, the most positive correlation in overall assessment of febrile children was degree of playfulness (McCarthy et al., 1980).

For infants, the nurse practitioner relies on the parents' information and description of behavior and objective symptoms such as fever to ascertain the presence of illness. While an older child can localize pain to an accurate degree, an infant with pain will be irritable or will try to strike randomly at the area of discomfort.

Infants and young children with fevers do not have chills in contrast to older children and adults. Occasionally a febrile convulsion is the parents' first indication that the child has a fever.

As children mature and are exposed to a larger environment through nursery schools, peer play, and other adults outside the family, the incidence of respiratory infections dramatically increases.

History

Important information to obtain in establishing the data base includes

• Age of the child
• Presence, duration, and severity of symptoms
• Sudden or gradual onset

- Past history of similar symptoms
- Events surrounding the first appearance of symptoms
- Character of symptoms if painful: sharp, dull, radiating, burning
- Location of symptoms
- History of exposure to illness, allergens, travel
- Symptoms increasing or decreasing in severity
- Appearance of child in relation to the symptoms
- Activity level of child
- Presence or absence of appetite
- Recent communications or evaluations with health personnel regarding the symptoms
- Treatment measures at home or in the health care facility
- Pertinent negatives
- Parents' knowledge of infections in the community
- Immunization status

The younger the child the more investigation is exerted in finding a cause of illness. If vague symptomatology such as slight irritability or anorexia is present during the first 3 months of life, sepsis is always considered. Infants and young children cannot respond to sudden loss of fluids and dehydration is a serious complication of illnesses such as prolonged high fevers or gastroenteritis.

Telephone

It is estimated that in pediatric practice the use of the telephone is two times greater than that of other specialties for several reasons:

- Parents with infants need guidance and reassurance initially with the parenting role
- Counseling about home treatment of minor illnesses
- Explanations of immediate treatment in emergency situations
- Information in reference to specific questions
- Reassurance that the child is not seriously ill
- Interpretation of normal developmental variables to parents

In assessing illness situations presented by phone the goals are as follows:

- Ascertain why the parent is calling
- Decide if the child's illness can be managed at home or needs referral to the health agency for further evaluation
- Decide if medical consultation is needed to further assess the illness
- Assess the anxiety level of the parents and their ability to manage the illness if home treatment is indicated.

OTHER CONSIDERATIONS

In assessing illness conditions via telephone consider the following:

- Is the caretaker known to the nurse? This helps the nurse assess how reliable the caretaker is in interpreting the child's symptoms and managing the illness at home.
- How far from the health agency do the caretakers live? In situations where parental anxiety is high, a visit to the health professional is encouraged.
- What is the age of the child? Newborns and infants are seen in the health care agency for illness because of the danger of serious infections such as sepsis.
- Have the symptoms been present over a long period of time? In particularly complicated histories it is important to ask why the caretaker is calling at this particular time and what help the caretaker feels the health agency can offer.
- What are the support measures at home?
- Does the caretaker have the name and phone number of the health care professional and agency for follow-up phone calls?
- How appropriate is the phone call? If the symptom is relatively mild in relation to the concern, other anxieties or problems in the home are investigated.

DISADVANTAGES

The nurse practitioner is not able to evaluate the child's physical condition objectively, to note the child's response to the environment, and to assess physically the severity of parental statements, such as "trouble breathing" and "bad rash" over the telephone.

With parental anxiety the problem can be assessed to some degree over the telephone, but seeing the parent and child in the office affords more opportunity to observe and to discuss the parents' anxiety and its causes and to evaluate the parents' interaction with the child.

An office visit also affords the opportunity to emphasize treatment regimens and instructions to parents both verbally and in writing.

Indications for Referral to the Health Care Agency

- Age. All children under 6 months of age with the following symptoms are referred: fever, lethargy, extreme irritability, anorexia, vomiting, diarrhea, dehydration, chronic feeding problems.
- In situations where a clear history cannot be elicited from the caretakers
- Any condition that indicates that an acute infectious process is present
- Fever of greater than 4 days' duration
- Fluid intake less than 480 cc in 24 hours
- Copious vomiting and diarrhea
- Extreme lethargy and malaise
- Purulent discharge from eyes
- Abdominal or groin distention
- Hives or other exanthems difficult to diagnose over the phone
- Fever of unknown origin
- Extreme parental anxiety
- Parents' asking that child be seen
- Parents' complaining of lack of support with child care
- Emergencies: falls where there is a loss of consciousness, change in behavior, vomiting, asymmetrical movements of extremities; ingestions; burns; auto accidents

When a child is referred to the health care agency, the nurse practitioner, if unable to see the child, establishes and coordinates services between the family and the physician, consults with medical personnel in reference to information obtained over the phone, and continues to assess the child's progress at home and the parents' compliance with treatment regimens after discharge from the health care agency.

Physical Examination

The vital signs are recorded. A weight is obtained if the child's oral intake has decreased or if vomiting and diarrhea are present. The amount of examination done depends on the presenting symptom, how well the child is known to the examiner, and when the last physical was done. See Chapter 1, Child Health Assessment.

Children who are ill need increased emotional and physical support, and it is necessary to proceed slowly with the examination. In some instances, children tolerate examination more comfortably on the parent's lap than on the examining table.

Indications for Laboratory Studies

Depending on the presenting symptoms and the initial physical evaluation, the following procedures are performed:

- Urinalysis to rule out infection
- Hematocrit to rule out anemia
- White blood cell count and differential to aid in assessing presence of infection
- Blood culture to rule out systemic infection
- Lumbar puncture to rule out the presence of meningitis, increased intracranial pressure
- Chest X-ray to rule out infection, foreign body
- Blood electrolytes to help evaluate degree of dehydration, metabolic status

MANAGEMENT

Principles of Management in Acute Illness

The child and not the illness is the main focus of the nurse practitioner when managing sick children. Therefore, physical and emotional needs of the child are considered. The adjustment of both the child and the family to the illness is done by encouraging them to verbalize feelings and by enhancing their coping mechanisms. Other goals in dealing with illness in the family are (Carey and Sibinga, 1972):

- Determine the needs and expectations of the child and the family.
- Help both deal with the illness.
- Promote self-confidence in the family in dealing with the illness.

A primary consideration for the nurse practitioner is that family members be knowledgeable of the treatment regimen and symptoms of increased illness, side effects of medications and mechanisms for obtaining information when questions arise. In acute illness, arrangements are made for short-term disruption of family routine such as time off work or obtaining child care arrangements.

Role of the Family

Illness places added stress on the family. Stress is decreased if various members contribute to management of the child's illness. Effective communication is necessary to decrease misconceptions of the treatment regimen and prognosis. Parents need to communicate their thoughts and ideas concerning medical treatment and to discuss their different opinions without anger. Routines of care are initiated with assignment of responsibilities to various family members. Single-parent families may need help from personal or community support systems to care effectively for their ill child and to allow time for self-nurturing.

Role of the Nurse Practitioner

Illness in itself causes disruption and confusion in family life. The evaluative process of how the family copes with the child's illness starts at the beginning of the visit.

After the diagnosis is established the nurse practitioner instructs parents as to the treatment regimen. Instructions are verbally given and then re-emphasized in writing. Parental questions are answered. Reactions to medications and symptoms of toxicity are discussed. If necessary, temperature taking is reviewed. Parents are instructed as to increased symptoms of illness and where to contact health personnel if necessary.

Role in Collaboration with Medical Personnel

With medical consultation, the nurse practitioner continues to remain the primary health care person for the client and family. In the event of hospitalization, the nurse practitioner functions within the health care team, contributing past and present history, and plans with the team for current management and for follow-up care. The role of the nurse and physician is one of interdependence and shared responsibility for client care mutually agreeing on goals for future management.

The nurse practitioner maintains close collaboration with social service, nutritionists, pharmacists, and dentists. In this role the nurse practitioner accepts responsibility for assessment, management, and teaching regimens that are initiated.

COMMON CLINICAL PROBLEM

Fever

ASSESSMENT

The symptom of fever in infants and children is extremely common. Fever is defined as an elevation in normal body temperature. The amount of fever does not correspond to the severity of the illness, neither does the absence of fever indicate the absence of infection. Fever is a useful defense mechanism that alerts the individual that physiologic changes in the body are occurring in response to a pathologic process. The evaluation and treatment of the underlying cause of the fever is the primary goal.

In infectious processes, it is believed that fever develops because of the release of an endogenous pyrogen from polymorphonuclear leukocytes. The endogenous pyrogen circulates in the blood and acts on the anterior hypothalamus to raise the thermoregulatory setpoint, which controls the fever (Kluger, 1980).

Normal Values Normal body temperature is between 36.2°C and 37.8°C rectally (97°F and 99°F) and 36°C and 37.6°C (96.8°F and 98.8°F) orally. Normal ranges in body temperature can vary as much as 1.5°, depending on the amount of activity, emotional stress, type of clothing worn, and temperature of the environment. With exercise, temperatures can normally rise as high as 39.4°C (103°F) by mouth. At rest, however, temperature is usually below 38°C (100°F) by mouth. Oral readings above this are generally accepted as fever. Hyperpyrexia is temperature greater than 41°C (105.8°F) and is rare in pediatric practice. Children usually become uncomfortable with fevers of 39.5° to 40°C (103° to 104°F).

Body temperature in older children and adults varies in response to diurnal fluctuations, the lowest peak occurring between 2 and 6 AM and the highest peak between 4 and 7 PM. During infancy and early childhood, temperature fluctuations are more common and diurnal variation in body temperature is absent during the first 2 years of life. If the amount and consistency of a child's temperature is in question, the parents are instructed to take the temperature rectally over a period of 2 days several times a day, with the child resting and wearing light clothes.

Etiology   Most fevers are the result of an acute infectious process, with 90 percent being of viral origin (Graef and Cone, 1980). More than half of all fevers involve the upper and lower respiratory tract. Most of the remaining fevers involve the genitourinary and gastrointestinal systems (Graef and Cone, 1980). The most common foci of infection in the respiratory tract are the middle ears, oropharynx, tonsils, larynx, and lungs.

Some illnesses produce characteristically high fevers: roseola, rubeola, pneumonia, pyelonephritis, bacteremia, and pneumococcal infection (Pascoe and Grossman, 1978, p. 360). Persistent low-grade fevers may indicate chronic infections: bacterial gastroenteritis, collagen diseases, blood dyscrasias, and tumors (Ziai, 1975). Tachypnea with fever may be indicative of pneumonia.

In newborns who are septic or who have serious infections fever is usually absent or the infant is hypothermic. Symptoms of poor feeding, lethargy, and irritability are more accurate indications of an infectious process than fever measurements at this age.

Complications   Many parents whose children have fevers worry about seizures and brain damage. Consequently, most parents treat fevers aggressively. The major complications of fever are heat stroke and seizures (McCarthy et al., 1980). Heat stroke develops with temperatures greater than 42°C (107.6°F). Symptoms are delerium, coma, and absence of perspiration (anhydrosis), and there may be sequelae of neurodeficits and ataxia. Febrile seizures occur in 3 to 5 percent of children with moderate and high fevers. There is no convincing evidence of neurologic injury occurring at the time of febrile seizures (Consensus Statement, 1980). See Chapter 24, Febrile Seizures.

History   In obtaining information about fever important questions include the following:

- Age of the child
- Appearance of the child
- Variations in fever during the day
- Activity level and appetite
- Degree of irritability
- Complaints of pain, chills, and other symptoms of illness: rhinorrhea, cough, tachypnea, ear pain, painful voiding
- History of recent immunizations

Questions in reference to exposure include the following:

- Contact with other children who are sick or well
- Contact with sick adults
- Contact with foreign visitors

Questions in reference to treatment measures at home include the following:

- Medications given: prescription, over-the-counter
- Specific home remedies: herbal preparations, vaporizer, sponging

Physical Examination   In assessing fever as a presenting symptom, a complete physical examination is done. A well-lighted area is important, preferably natural light, to ascertain the presence of beginning exanthems. Cerumen is removed from auditory canals for complete visualization of tympanic membranes. The child should be quiet for adequate auscultation of the chest.

Laboratory   If the cause of the fever is found on physical examination, laboratory studies are usually not necessary except to rule out incidental findings such as anemia. If no cause for the fever is found, the following laboratory studies are performed if indicated:

- Routine urinalysis and screening culture to rule out urinary tract infection
- White blood cell and differential counts

    1. Neutrophils (polymorphonuclear leukocytes) are increased in bacterial and early phases of viral infections.
    2. Lymphocytes are increased in viral infections.
    3. Monocytes are increased in the recovery phase of acute infections.

- Nasopharyngeal and throat cultures
- TB test
- X-ray film of the chest
- Lumbar puncture
- Blood culture

MANAGEMENT

Children under 6 months of age presenting with fever are always seen in the health care agency because of the possibility of sepsis. All other children with fever of longer than 3 days' duration are seen for physical assessment and possible laboratory studies. Children with fever of greater than 10 days' duration with unknown etiology may be admitted to the hospital for further evaluation.

There is little correlation between the amount of heat felt on the child's forehead and the reading on the thermometer. Parents are therefore encouraged to use the thermometer when assessing the presence of fever.

The general principle for management is to diagnose and treat the underlying cause. There is controversy as to whether the fever itself should be treated. In discussions against treatment, the following arguments are used:

- Loss of an important diagnostic finding may not justify providing physical comfort for the client.
- Fever may be protective for the host.
- Fever is a symptom causing morbidity and encourages rest and possible medical consultation to determine causes rather than medication to reduce it.

- Some data suggest that fever in viral infections may reduce viral replication and therefore should not be treated (Graef and Cone 1980).
- There are few harmful effects of fever.

Arguments for treatment are as follows:

- Antipyretics make the client more comfortable
- Fever reduction may reduce the incidence of febrile convulsions; however, there is no atual evidence that this is true.

General Measures For management of fever, general measures include removal of excess clothing, bed rest, and clear fluids by mouth. Fevers are treated in a rational manner, and urgency is warranted only for fevers above 41°C (106°F) (Schmitt, 1980). Treatment is recommended for all fevers over 39°C (102.2°F). Sponging with tepid water remains controversial. If this procedure causes chills and shivering, the hypothalamus will respond with increasing the body temperature. However, most authorities recommend sponging for one-half hour every 2 hours with tepid water for fever above 40°C (104°F). Alcohol and ice water are not used for sponging because of the increased incidence of chills and therefore a possible increase in temperature. Ice water enemas are not used because of the possibility of hyponatremia. Sponging or medication is never instituted if the cause of the fever is environmental or mechanical, such as vigorous exercise and increased environmental temperature. In these situations, removal of clothing and rest are more effective.

Indications for Consultations Medical consultation is necessary in the following conditions:

- Infants under 3 months of age with any symptoms of illness
- Infants under 6 months of age with fever only
- All children with fever and vague symptomatology: irritability, poor feeding, lethargy
- Fevers longer than 24 hours without symptoms
- Fevers longer than 72 hours with symptoms
- Child appears ill and toxic

Medications Drugs commonly used in the treatment of fever are: acetylsalicylic acid (aspirin), and para-aminophenol. They are thought to act on the hypothalamus resulting in dilation of the peripheral blood vessels and increased dissipation of body heat.

ASPIRIN Because of its effectiveness in reducing fever aspirin is frequently prescribed in adults. It also has analgesic and anti-inflammatory properties. It is not commonly used in children because of the possibility of side effects and accidental ingestion. Aspirin is metabolized more slowly in children under 2 years of age which makes them more susceptible to its side effects. For this reason aspirin is used with caution, if at all, in low doses in this age group. Side effects include dizziness, drowsiness, hypersensitivity resulting in asthma, angioneurotic edema, and anaphylaxis. Gastrointestinal disorders are common including heartburn, gastrointestinal bleeding, and ulceration. Large doses of aspirin (3 to 8 gm/day) can cause tinnitus (ringing in the ears), vertigo and reduction in plasma prothrombin levels. There is a correlation between aspirin ingestion for varicella infections, respiratory febrile illnesses and an increased incidence of Reye's syndrome. Therefore, Tylenol rather than aspirin is recommended for treating fever in these conditions (Waldman et al., 1982). See Chapter 24, The Neuromuscular System.

PARA-AMINOPHENOLS Para-aminophenols include acetanilid, phenacetin, and acetaminophen. The three are similar in their antipyretic and analgesic properties but acetanilid is no longer used because of the serious side effects of methemoglobin formation. Phenacetin and acetaminophen are similar to the salicylates in their antipyretic effects. When given in combination with salicylates they increase the effectiveness of lowering the body temperature. The anti-inflammatory properties are less than the salicylates, and they are not used in this regard.

ADVANTAGES OF ACETAMINOPHEN Acetaminophen has several advantages over aspirin:

• Stable in liquid preparations
• Used when allergy to salicylates is evident
• Does not cause gastric bleeding
• Less toxic in infants

A massive overdose of acetaminophen can cause hepatotoxicity. In the reduction of fever, studies have shown that acetaminophen is more rapid in onset than aspirin but has a slightly shorter duration of action.

COMMERCIAL PREPARATIONS There are a variety of brand-name children's aspirin tablets. All are chewable and flavored. They contain 1¼ grain (81 mg) acetylsalicylic acid. Bayer children's aspirin and St. Joseph aspirin for children are familiar to many parents.

Commercial preparations of acetaminophen include the following:

- Tylenol: elixir 160 mg acetaminophen in 5 cc, drops 80 mg acetaminophen in 0.8 cc, chewables 80 mg in each tablet (the drops and elixir contain 7 percent alcohol)
- Tempra: elixir 120 mg acetaminophen in 5 cc, drops 60 mg acetaminophen in 0.6 cc, chewables 120 mg in each tablet (the drops and elixir contain 10 percent alcohol)
- Liquipren drops: 120 mg acetaminophen in 2.5 cc (one full dropper), the dropper is also calculated at 1.25 cc (the preparation does not contain alcohol)

SAFETY PRECAUTIONS As with all medications, parents should keep them out of the reach of children and should purchase only those drugs which have safety caps. Medicine should never be called candy. Prolonged use of any drug should not be continued without proper medical supervision.

CALCULATIONS Aspirin is calculated according to age or weight. For age: 1 grain is given per year of age up to 10 years, repeated not more than once every 4 hours. For weight: 10 to 15 mg/kg/dose every 4 hours is prescribed.

Counseling Parents are instructed that fever is a symptom of illness and that the nurse practitioner should be consulted if the child has other increasing symptoms of illness, such as irritability, lethargy, anorexia, and symptoms related to specific organ systems. For general home management of fever, parents are instructed to do the following:

- Increase oral fluid intake to prevent dehydration.
- Dress the child lightly to maximize heat loss through the skin.
- Increase room air circulation.

- Sponge with tepid water rubbing the skin briskly to increase blood flow to the surface where it is cooled.

If an etiology is found for the fever, parents are instructed about specific management.

References

Carey, W. and M. Sibinga. "Avoiding Pediatric Pathogenesis in the Management of Acute Minor Illness." *Pediatrics* 49:553–562, April 1972.

"Consensus Statement: Febrile Seizures." *Pediatrics* 66:1009, December 1980.

DuBois, E. F. *Fever and Regulation of Body Temperature.* Springfield, IL: Charles C. Thomas, 1948.

Graef, J. W. and T. E. Cone, Jr. *Manual of Pediatric Therapeutics, 2nd ed.,* Boston: Little, Brown, 1980.

Kluger, M. "Fever." *Pediatrics* 66:720–724, November 1980.

Marlow, D. R. *Textbook of Pediatric Nursing.* 5th ed. Philadelphia: WB Saunders, 1977.

McCarthy, P., et al. "History and Observation Variables in Assessing Febrile Children." *Pediatrics* 65:1090–1095, June 1980.

Murphy, D. and C. Dineen. "Nursing by Telephone." *Am J Nurs* 75:1137–1139, July 1975.

Pascoe, D. J. and M. Grossman (eds.). *Quick Reference to Pediatric Emergencies,* 2nd ed., Philadelphia: JB Lippincott, 1978.

Porter, D. P. "Without Standing Orders." *Am J Nurs* 73:1559–1561, September 1973.

Schmitt, B. "Fever Phobia." *Am J Dis Child* 134:176–181, February 1980.

Smith, J. W. *Manual of Medical Therapeutics.* Boston: Little, Brown, 1980.

Spivak, J. L. and H. V. Barnes. *Manual of Clinical Problems in Internal Medicine,* 2nd ed. Boston: Little, Brown, 1978.

Waldman, R. et al. "Aspirin as a Risk Factor in Reye's Syndrome." *JAMA* 247:3089–3094, June 11, 1982.

Ziai, M. *Pediatrics.* Boston: Little, Brown, 1975.

12

Approach to Chronic Illness

The care of children with chronic illness is emerging as a primary focus in pediatric primary care because of such factors as increased survival of many children with chronic conditions and change in patterns of childhood morbidity associated with infectious disease, nutritional disorders, and other conditions. These children and their families present major challenges for health care providers and planners who work in a health care system that offers increasingly sophisticated ambulatory management of conditions that were formerly treated in the hospital setting.

Children with chronic illnesses and their families need special attention directed toward their abilities to accept and adjust to the chronic condition. The nurse practitioner is especially suited to support family coping processes in caring for the chronically ill child because of a strong background in counseling, knowledge of growth and development, identification with the psychosocial needs of the family, and pragmatic attention to adjustments of daily living. It is important for the nurse practitioner to emphasize the normal aspects of growth and development and normal health promotion activities. Contact with the health care system is frequent, and many health professionals are involved with the treatment plan. The specific role of the nurse practitioner varies according to knowledge and expertise and the particular health care setting.

This chapter presents an approach to the assessment and management of chronically ill children and their families within the context of primary care. The specific example of asthma is discussed in this chapter under "Common Clinical Problem." The reader is referred to other chapters for discussions of other specific chronic conditions. See Chapter 9, Chronic Illness; Chapter 18, Congenital Heart Disease; Chapter 19, Sickle Cell Disease, Thalassemia, and G-6-PD; Chapter 23, Kyphosis, Lordosis, Scoliosis, and Congenital Dislocation of the Hip; Chapter 24, Cerebral Palsy, Developmental Delay, and Epilepsy; Chapter 25, Attention Deficit Disorder and Hyperactivity; Chapter 26, Allergies; Chapter 27, Tuberculosis; and Chapter 31, Failure to Thrive.

ASSESSMENT

Definition and Prevalence

It is difficult to identify the absolute prevalence of chronic illnesses in children in the United States because of the varying definitions. There is the added problem of statistical computations on incidence that are done for specific diseases or by specific locale rather than on a national basis (Travis, 1976; Kleinberg, 1982).

The Commission on Chronic Illness (1957) defined chronic illness in terms of certain characteristics common to all impairments or abnormalities. A condition possessing one or more of the following characteristics was considered chronic:

• Irreversible pathologic alteration
• Lengthy periods of supervision, observation, or care required
• Permanency
• Residual disability
• Special rehabilitation training

Mattsson (1972, p. 801) defined a disorder as long term or chronic when it has "a protracted course which can be progressive and fatal, or [is] associated with a relatively normal life span despite impaired physical and mental functioning. Such a disease frequently shows periods of acute exacerbations requiring intensive medical attention." Travis (1976) does not consider a handicap or abnormality as synonymous with chronic illness. Green and Haggerty (1977, p. 16) define chronic disorders simply as conditions that persist for more than 3 months.

In spite of these varying definitions, there is consensus that approximately 7–10% of all children have some form of chronic illness (Mattsson, 1972; Pless et al., 1976). This estimate, however, does not include handicapping conditions such as mental retardation and cerebral palsy. If these conditions were included, the percentage of children with chronic conditions would be increased to 20% (Green and Haggerty, 1977).

The National Health Survey (1973) found that one in eight children in the 6–11-year age group, and one youth in five in the 12–17-year age group have one or more significant cardiovascular, neurologic, musculoskeletal, or other physical abnormality. The more frequent category of chronic physical conditions seen is allergic disease, of which asthma is the most serious. Allergies occur in 2–3% of children and account for 35–45% of all chronic disease in children (Green and Haggerty, 1977). The reader is referred to Chapter 26 for specific information on allergies.

Impact of the Chronic Illness on the Child and Family

Chronic illness in a child has a pervasive impact on the family. Established patterns of living without illness come to an end, and new patterns of living everyday with illness evolve for the child, parents, and siblings. The impact of the chronic illness on the child and family can be described in terms of the character of the illness, the family size, structure, relationships, and coping abilities, the age and developmental stage of the child when the diagnosis is made, the child's reaction to stress of illness, and the hospitalizations (Travis, 1976). See Chapter 9 for related information.

CHARACTER OF ILLNESS

Travis (1976) identifies six dimensions that determine the impact of the particular illness on the child and family:

1. *Degree and manner of family burden.* Does the illness mean sleep interruption for long, continuing periods? Are there physical burdens, such as lifting and dressing? Are complicated special

diets required? Is extra housecleaning necessary on a regular basis to maintain an extra-clean environment?

2. *Degree of financial burden.* Is funding available for treatments, equipment, medications, and hospitalizations? What are the sources of income for the family?

3. *Need for housing adaptation.* Are structural changes in the house necessary, such as wheelchair access or accessible bathtubs?

4. *Pain, social isolation, and unpredictability of crises.* Does the illness cause physical pain? Is mobility limited? Does the illness cause physical deformity? Is there depletion of energy? Does the illness prevent full participation in social activities such as eating? Does the illness precipitate unpredictable crises such as asthma or sickle cell anemia?

5. *Differences in school experience.* Is the child enrolled in a special school or special class? Is the child able to attend school regularly?

6. *Factors affecting the manner of death.* Is the illness fatal? How old is the child? Is death sudden or prolonged? Is the child at home or at the hospital? Is the child aware of surroundings, or is the child in a drugged or half-awake state? Does death occur peacefully or uncomfortably?

FAMILY SIZE, STRUCTURE, RELATIONSHIPS, AND COPING ABILITIES

An assessment of the family system is essential (see Chapter 1). The degree to which a family is functioning well before the discovery of the chronic illness will affect the family's ability to cope with the diagnosis.

Smith (1983, p. 38) identifies three indicators for healthy adaptation of the family:

- Adequate support systems in the community
- Good mental health among its members
- Innate capacity to adapt to stress and change

Commonly observed difficulties in families with chronically ill children include the following (Kaplan, 1980, p. 38):

- Abandonment of the child in the hospital due to premature disengagement of the family

- "Flights of activity," such as moving to new communities or divorces or remarriages, which increase the stress load on the family and waste precious energy and resources
- Inaccurate communication about the disease and its prognosis between parent–child and siblings
- Unresolved grief problems among survivors

Travis (1976) identifies two dimensions for assessment:

- *Family size and structure.* Are there two parents? If yes, are they able to share the burden, setting aside periods of respite and time for other activities? What is the family's stage of development? Is this the only child, or are there siblings to help with the child's care and social development?
- *Relationships with the family.* What other events are occurring within the family (divorce, remarriage, pregnancy, job changes, school activities)? If it is a two-parent family, is the father involved in the care and available to the family?

Hymovich (1979) considers three other assessment dimensions:

- *Coping abilities of the family.* How is the family reacting to the diagnosis? Does the family request assurance and support? Does the family provide appropriate limits and discipline for the child? How are the siblings responding to the illness? Does the family seek pertinent information about the illness?
- *Family perception of the illness.* What are the values of the family? What is the culture of the family? How will the illness affect current life-styles? What are the family's religious beliefs?
- *Internal and external resources.* What support systems does the family have? What community resources does the family make use of? Are babysitting arrangements available? Is an extended family available to assist in the care of the child?

The nurse practitioner must be alert to signs that suggest inability to cope. Smith (1983, p. 38) describes four parental patterns indicative of difficulty coping:

- Overconcerned, oversolicitous parent who takes excessive responsibility for the child and the illness. This type of parent fosters excessive regression in the child, hinders the child's development beyond the constraints of the disorder, and prevents the child from assuming control over his or her own care.

- Overly fearful and anxious parent who may inappropriately convey unrealistic fear and anxiety to the child. During hospitalizations, the parent never leaves the bedside or, when fearful, does not come near the hospital to visit.
- Excessively angry parent who is frequently suspicious of medical and nursing competence and constantly challenges decisions and procedures. Health professionals are put on the defensive, creating an uncomfortable environment that may compromise the quality of care.
- Guilty parent who may also exhibit behaviors described above. The parent feels responsible for the illness either because of a family history of the same problem or because of unrealistic thoughts about errors of omission or commission in the previous care of the child.

AGE AND DEVELOPMENTAL STAGE OF THE CHILD AT DIAGNOSIS

The child's age and developmental stage are significant factors in his or her ability to understand the illness. In a study of the relationship between cognitive development and children's understanding of the cause of the illness among chronically ill hospitalized children of normal intelligence between 5 and 12 years of age, Brewster (1982) concluded that understanding of illness is related to cognitive maturation.

The chronically ill child is especially at risk and is vulnerable. Normal developmental continuity is interrupted, and it becomes a special challenge to foster the child's optimum growth and development. A child stricken with a chronic illness nonetheless continues to mature and change. The response of the child to the chronic illness depends on his or her age and the developmental tasks to be mastered.

Infant The diagnosis is frequently made during the first days or weeks of life. Prolonged hospitalization is inevitable after birth. The infant's development of trust is jeopardized as hospital routines discourage participation of parents in the care and the parents themselves go through attachment problems. Parents may not visit the infant as often, may abdicate the parental role to the staff, and may even look for excuses to postpone discharge (Kleinberg, 1982). See Chapter 5 for normal developmental milestones.

Toddler This is a period normally characterized by the struggle to develop autonomy while maintaining strong parental attachment, high energy levels and curiosity, and control over body. A chronic illness during this age affects the toddler's mastery of bodily controls and the drive for independence. It also affects the child's energy levels. For example, an asthma attack consumes the child's energy and pain may limit interest in physical activities. Families may become overprotective and inhibit expression of autonomy and feelings. The child's prolonged separations resulting from hospitalizations may arouse anxiety over abandonment. See Chapter 6 for normal developmental milestones.

Preschooler Chronic illness interferes with the preschooler's awareness of own body, ability to gain mastery of the environment, and development of language and play skills. The chronically ill preschooler's mastery over these normal developmental tasks is thwarted because of the parents' need to retain control and responsibility for physical care. See Chapter 6 for normal developmental milestones.

School-age Child During this period, the child is dealing with issues of industriousness, mastery, and peer relationships. A chronically ill school-age child may suffer from peer criticisms directed towards physical appearance and low energy levels. The ability to participate physically in sports activities may be limited. The chronic illness may hinder the child's desire to accomplish and obtain new skills and to maintain peer relationships because of restrictions and dependency. The child may have difficulty developing a strong self-concept and body image. See Chapter 7 for normal development.

Adolescent This is the period when the self-image coalesces, and the chronically ill adolescent is vulnerable to negative perceptions of bodily limitations and negative peer reactions (Travis, 1976). Factors that influence the adolescent's response to chronic illness include the age at which the condition was initially diagnosed, the severity or degree of visibility of the condition, and the extent of life-style change required to cope successfully with the disorder. See Chapter 8 for normal development.

THE CHILD'S REACTION TO THE STRESS OF ILLNESS

Travis (1976) considers two dimensions in assessing the child's reaction: the nature and degree of stress, and the child's struggle to cope with the illness.

Nature and Degree of Stress   The perceived degree of stress and the child's capacity to adapt determine coping ability. How long has the child been experiencing the stress? Did it occur suddenly? What is the child's stage of development? What is the child's previous experience with stress? How much pain is experienced? Are there associated fears?

Coping Mechanisms   Signs of the child struggling to cope with the illness can be seen in the use of coping mechanisms. Is the child able to express himself or herself? Is the child using denial as manifested by such behavior as disregarding restrictions or expecting miracles? Has the child regressed in behavior? Does the child withdraw from surroundings? Is the child depressed beyond the stage of active, physical illness, pain, or grieving period?

HOSPITALIZATION

The response to hospitalization depends on several factors (Nelms and Mullins, 1982):

1. The child's age and stage of development
2. The family's ability to cope with the hospitalization
3. The reason for the hospitalization
4. Preparation for the experience
5. The hospital environment

   Short hospital stays prevent some of the negative effects of hospitalization; however, the technological advances of care guarantee a hospital stay fraught with intrusive procedures, helplessness, recurring venipunctures, and so on. Preparation of the child and family can reduce stress. Hospital tours and books are useful aids in preparation for a hospital stay.

Education and the Chronically Ill Child

PL 94-142 is a landmark legislation enacted by Congress in 1975. It assures all handicapped children the right to education. The handicapping conditions include learning disabilities (see Chapter 25), mental retardation, and chronic physical conditions such as asthma, epilespy, lead poisoning, or diabetes, which adversely affect a child's educational performance. PL 94-142 requires each state's educational agency to develop guidelines and bylaws for program implementation in the following areas (Kleinberg, 1982):

1. Identification system for children in need of special education services
2. Multidisciplinary assessment tools
3. Placement of these children in the most appropriate educational program in the least restrictive environment
4. Development of an individualized educational plan (IEP)
5. Inclusion of services related to IEP, such as transportation, speech, or physical therapy
6. Involvement of parents in program planning and implementation

MANAGEMENT

The child's response to the chronic illness will depend on his or her age, the severity of the illness, and the family's coping style and communication patterns. Explanations of illness must consider the child's views of the illness and the reasons for treatment. The child is then guided through concepts that are new to the child in a manner appropriate to level of comprehension (Brewster, 1982, p. 361).

Pless and Satterwhite (1975) discovered that children with chronic disorders as well as their families experience adjustment problems and have limited understanding of the chronic illness. As a result, some children are unnecessarily curtailed in their sports activities, experience school difficulties, and have low self-esteem. These problems are not trivial and could have significant impact on the development of the child. The problems are clearly associated with an inadequate understanding of the chronic condition and a lack of guidance in day-to-day management. These researchers suggest that the problems may be related to the health care provided to these children and their families. The problems suggest a deficiency in the amount or kind of support, counseling, and help provided by health professionals. Pless and Satterwhite advocate changes in the health delivery system designed to prevent these problems. The reader is referred to Powell (1975) for a report of a research project in which organizational changes in ambulatory health organizations for care to children with chronic illness were observed. Issues such as staffing are addressed.

Principles of Management

Management of chronic illness involves the entire family, and for this reason it should be family focused. The nurse practitioner must promote independent problem solving by the family, be available to support the family, and foster self-care of the illness.

GENERAL CONSIDERATIONS

The nurse practitioner should act according to certain guidelines:

- Be empathetic with parental reactions to the diagnosis and required care, as acknowledgment of these feelings will facilitate gaining trust and obtaining cooperation of the child and family
- Be patient and understanding of the parents' initial and often continuing reactions of anger, fear, guilt, and sadness
- Communicate with school personnel as necessary
- Inquire about the reactions and responses of siblings
- Promote the child's optimum growth and development

THE HEALTH CARE VISIT

At each visit, the nurse practitioner should be attentive to the normal health care supervision needs of the child. (See the appropriate age-related chapter in this book for a complete discussion of health care supervision.) In addition, the nurse practitioner should demonstrate a caring attitude in a number of ways:

- Allow the child and parents to express their feelings and discuss the situation
- Assess the family's adjustment to the illness
- Be aware of the family's communication patterns
- Inquire about the physical care
- Offer counseling and support about child care
- Respond simply and concisely to inquiries about the illness
- Talk privately with the child when able to express himself or herself verbally

Tips for the Clinic Visit and Medical Procedures   The U.S. Department of Health and Human Services (1982) makes the following suggestions to parents for reducing the stress of the health visit and treatments:

- Accompany the child for medical procedures and treatments.
- Be careful not to discuss with other parents or patients in the waiting room aspects of the child's illness that have not been previously discussed with the child.
- Bring the child's favorite toy, book, crafts, or quiet game.
- Explain the purpose of the visit to the child and the need for any procedures. Do not lie to the child, particularly if the procedure will be painful.
- Maintain a brief personal record of clinic visits, medications, and/ or treatments.
- Maintain home records of the child's health. Include unexplained symptoms, fever, or suspected side effects. Note the incident, date, time, and duration.

CONTINUITY OF CARE

Regularly scheduled visits are important. These enable the family to develop a trusting relationship with the nurse practitioner and allow time for comprehensive assessment, treatment evaluation, and revision of the treatment plan. The visits can be brief, but they should allow time for the expression of feelings of loss, frustration, and sadness. The nurse practitioner should discuss her or his availability to the family and should give the parents telephone number(s) at which she or he can be reached.

COLLABORATION WITH HEALTH PROFESSIONALS

The management plan includes referral to specialists depending on the child's problems and the nurse practitioner's expertise in the particular chronic illness. As the family adjusts to the circumstances surrounding the chronic illness, delicate and sensitive care by health professionals is essential. The nurse practitioner may serve as the primary coordinator of the management plan in conjunction with the pediatrician and other specialists.

PROMOTION OF SELF-CARE SKILLS

Orem (1980, p. 35) defines self-care as "the practice of activities that individuals initiate and perform in their own behalf in maintaining life, health, and well being." The role of the nurse practitioner is to facilitate the development of self-care skills by the child and by the family. Self-care skills increase the confidence of the child and family, decrease health care costs, and minimize the anxiety associated with the chronic illness. There are seven areas of self-care (Orem, 1980; Underwood, 1983):

1. Intake of air, food, and fluids
2. Elimination
3. Rest and activity
4. Balance between solitude and social interaction
5. Body temperature and personal hygiene
6. Prevention of hazards to life, functioning, and well-being
7. Promotion of normalcy

The nurse practitioner works with the child and family to assist them in developing problem-solving and decision-making skills to help the child meet personal needs.

COMMUNITY RESOURCES

No single person can be the sole resource for a family with a chronically ill child. A network of persons and organizational resources is essential. The nurse practitioner should collaborate with other health professionals to identify community resources for the family.

Resources vary according to the community, perceived needs,

and the political and economic climate. The nurse practitioner should become familiar with the current community resources for financial aid and social services, such as the Easter Seal Society, Crippled Children's Services, and the American Cancer Society. There are also resources directed to parents, such as support groups, and resources for children, such as summer camps for diabetics and asthmatics.

COMMON CLINICAL PROBLEM

Asthma

ASSESSMENT

In this chapter, asthma is discussed as a chronic illness. The reader is also referred to Chapter 26, Bronchial Asthma.

Asthma is a major health problem and the most common chronic disease of childhood. It is responsible for one-fourth of all school absences attributable to chronic conditions (Ellis, 1977). It is a complex disease with a multifactorial etiology.

Definition Asthma is a diffuse obstructive disease of the airway characterized by bronchial hyperresponsiveness that reverses either spontaneously or as a result of treatment. Obstruction is caused by mucosal edema of the airway, increased mucus secretion, and smooth muscle bronchospasm in response to extrinsic allergens, such as pollens, dust, and air pollution, and to physical or intrinsic factors, such as exercise or viral respiratory infections. Impaired ventilation and pulmonary gas exchange results.

The psychologic etiology of asthma has certainly been a popular theory over the years, but it is now recognized that while psychologic factors can contribute to the disease, they do not have a primary etiologic role (Ellis, 1977; Kleinberg, 1982).

Age of Onset Approximately 75% of asthmatic children begin to exhibit symptoms of the disease before 4 or 5 years of age. It is difficult to predict at an early age the course and severity of the disease for any given child. Most children will have only occasional attacks of minimal severity that are easy to manage (Ellis, 1977). Seventy to 90% of asthmatic children will be symptom free by adolescence.

History In addition to general history information (see Chapter 1), obtain information about the child's problems with asthma, what bothers the child, the specific treatment for asthma attacks, overview of the child's particular needs and current problems, medications taken regularly, and school attendance and progress.

Clinical Findings The asthmatic child appears small in stature with barrel chest, round shoulders, poor color, and is a mouth breather. A prominent cough may be heard, and clubbing of the fingertips may be present. The chest should be observed for dyspnea, distention, hyperventilation, intercostal and supraclavicular retractions, and a prolonged expiratory phase. Percuss the chest for hyperresonance. On auscultation, listen for prolonged expiratory wheezing with sibilant, musical rales. Inspiratory wheezing may also be present. Wheezing may be diminished or absent if there is severe reduction of air exchange or profound obstruction.

STATUS ASTHMATICUS It is a stage in an asthmatic attack when the child is unresponsive to medications that are usually effective in relieving symptoms, such as epinephrine, isoproterenol, and aminophylline. The child typically has been ill for several days and may have gone back and forth for treatment that has proved inadequate. It is crucial to recognize status asthmaticus because it can lead to death.

X-ray Film of the Chest Mucous plugs may cause complete obstruction and radiographically may be confused with pneumonia.

Laboratory Tests Useful information can be derived from laboratory tests. Table 12-1 identifies the tests used in making initial diagnosis.

Differential Diagnosis Consider the following factors in making the differential diagnosis (Ellis, 1977; Pearlman and Bierman, 1980):

• Bronchiolitis

- Chronic bronchitis
- Congenital malformations
- Croup syndrome
- Foreign body
- Hypersensitivity pneumonitis
- Infectious agents
- Mitral valve prolapse
- Underlying disorder (i.e., cystic fibrosis, immunodeficiency disease)

MANAGEMENT

Refer to the principles of management in the earlier section of this chapter. Asthma requires continuous attention. Management is difficult and requires a comprehensive approach involving the child and the family. The consequences to the child and family are enormous and affect the family's psychologic balance, financial resources, and the child's growth and development.

In 1975, the cost of caring for the approximately 8 million asthma patients in the United States was estimated to be $805,721,000. (National Institute of Allergic and Infectious Diseases, 1979). One survey demonstrated that the cost of asthmatic illness to a family ranged from $1,644 per year to $70,000 per year (Vance and Taylor, 1971). The costs of health care for those suffering from asthma can be controlled through parental and child collaboration and by health teaching that enhances skills for self-management.

The medical regimen is frequently complex and may require several different medications and treatments over an extensive period of time. Recent studies have shown that by improving the understanding and the need for the medical management of asthma, the costs of hospital and emergency room visits are decreased, self-management skills are increased, and asthma care is initiated earlier (Maiman et al., 1979; Fireman et al., 1981).

Therapeutic Goals   These are as follows (Mascia, 1982, p. 73):

- Decrease the length and severity of the asthmatic attacks.
- Enable independence in self-care and improved self-image.
- Help the child and family adjust to the disease.

Table 12-1
Laboratory Tests in Asthma

Test	Possible Abnormalities in Asthma	Comments
Complete blood count	Leukocytosis, occasionally	Induced by infection, epinephrine administration, stress
	Eosinophilia, frequently	Varies with medication, time of day, and adrenal function, not necessarily related to allergy (often higher in intrinsic than in extrinsic asthma)
Sputum examination	Eosinophils	In both intrinsic and extrinsic asthma
White or "clear" and small, yellow plugs	Charcot-Leyden crystals	Derived from eosinophils
	Creola bodies	Clusters of epithelial cells
	Curschmann's spirals	Threads of glycoprotein
Nasal smear	Eosinophils	Suggests concomitant nasal allergy in children
	Lymphocytes, PMNs, macrophages	Replace eosinophils in URIs.
	PMNs with ingested bacteria	Bacterial rhinitis or sinusitis
Serum tests	IgG, IgA, IgM	Often normal, may be abnormal—various patterns seen
	IgE	Sometimes elevated in allergic asthma, often normal
	Aspergillus-precipitating antibody	Suggestive, not diagnostic, of bronchopulmonary aspergillosis
Sweat test	Normal in asthma, performed to rule out cystic fibrosis	Cystic fibrosis and asthma can coexist

Test	Findings	Comments
X-ray film of the chest	Hyperinflation, infiltrates, pneumomediastinum, and pneumothorax, rule out tuberculosis	Indicated once in all children with asthma, indicated on hospitalization for asthma
Lung function tests[a]	$\downarrow$ FEV_1, $\downarrow$ FVC, $\downarrow$ $FEF_{25-75\%}$, $\downarrow$ PEFR, FEV_1/FVC $< 75\%$	Useful for following course of disease and response to treatment
Response to bronchodilators	$> 15\%$ improvement FEV_1, PEFR	Safest diagnostic test for asthma
Exercise tests	Decreased lung function after 6 minutes of exercise: PEFR and $FEV_1 > 15\%$ $\downarrow$, $FEF_{25-75\%} > 25\%$ $\downarrow$	Useful in diagnosing asthma in children, often abnormal when resting lung function is normal
Methacholine inhalation test (Mecholyl test)	20% fall in lung function with dose tolerated by normal subjects	Should be performed only by specialists
Antigen inhalation test	20% fall in lung function immediately after challenge, may cause delayed response 6–8 hours later	Potentially dangerous, performed by specialist only
Allergy skin test	Identifies allergic factors that might be causative factors	Test only likely factors, selected on basis of history
RAST[b]	Same significance as skin tests. [Detects specific IgE antibody.]	More expensive than skin tests

Source: D. Pearlman and C. Bierman, "Asthma (Bronchial Asthma, Reactive Airways Disorder.)" In C. Bierman and D. Pearlman, *Allergic Diseases of Infancy, Childhood and Adolescence*, Philadelphia: W.B. Saunders, 1980. P. 592.

[a] FEV_1, forced expiratory volume in 1 second; FVC, forced vital capacity; FEF, forced mid-expiratory flow; PEFR, peak expiratory flow rate.

[b] RAST, Radio-Allergosorbent-Test.

• Prepare for increased physical demands by strengthening the chest muscles and teaching proper breathing.

Therapeutic Treatment This is aimed primarily at relaxing the bronchi to prevent attacks and removing triggering agents from the environment or minimizing their effects.

Avoidance of Known Irritants It is only a partial therapy because of the complicated nature of asthma and the difficulty in identifying the triggering allergens (see Chapter 26, Environmental Control). Other suggestions for environmental control include the following (Mascia, 1982, p. 77):

• Assure adequate humidification and filtering equipment in environments with forced hot air heating systems.
• Avoid paints, sprays, perfumes, and smoke.
• Control growth of mold in basement crawl spaces, washrooms, and paint soils. Fungicide may be useful.
• Discourage pets, especially from the bedroom.
• Encase pillows and mattresses in zippered plastic covers.
• Use air conditioners during the pollen seasons to avoid outdoor allergens from entering the home through open bedroom windows.

ALLERGY TESTING AND HYPOSENSITIZATION See Chapter 26, Diagnostic Skin Testing and Hyposensitization. Children who manifest clearcut responses to certain foods or substances may obtain benefit from testing and hyposensitization. Hyposensitization injections can temporarily decrease a child's sensitivity to allergens and decrease attacks for a season or year. For continued results, the series must be repeated yearly. If no improvement is seen after 1 or 2 years, the injections should be discontinued.

BREATHING EXERCISES AND POSTURAL RELAXATION Children with asthma tend to develop poor breathing habits and lose mobility in their lower chest. The upper chest becomes overworked, so they need to increase the movement of the lower chest. Breathing exercises are designed to increase abdominal breathing and make for a better exchange of air. Table 12-2 outlines the steps in proper breathing. Also listed are blowing exercises for use by younger children to enhance their abilities to breathe in and out freely.

Table 12-2
Breathing Exercises for Asthmatics

Aim: To help patient get a better exchange of air
Position: On back with hips and knees flexed to relax abdominals
(practice while sitting, standing, and walking):
1. Place one hand on mid-chest, other on abdomen.
2. Keep mouth closed, and breathe in deeply through nose. Let abdomen rise with chest remaining stationary.
3. Breathe out slowly through pursed lips, making soft blowing "ssss" sound. Press abdomen inward and upward, and chest should still remain at rest. (Expiration through pursed lips prevents collapse of bronchial tubes.)
Blowing exercises
1. Blow out candle at varying distances.
2. Blow Ping-Pong balls.
3. Blow bubbles through a straw.
4. Blow musical instrument.
5. Blow party horns and toys.

Source: Reprinted with permission from S. B. Kleinberg, *Educating the Chronically Ill Child.* Rockville, MD, Aspen Systems, 1982. P. 90.

PHARMACOLOGIC THERAPY This is the principal modality of asthma management. Medications are determined in collaboration with the physician. Medication use and amount depend on the age of the child, the severity of asthma, ability to tolerate the drug, allergen exposure, and level of activity. The dosage levels must be adjusted regularly for growth and changes in disease severity.

Acute Attack Follow these steps:

1. Use aerosolized bronchodilator (e.g., isoproterenol) by hand or pressurized nebulizer. It is effective for the relief of acute symptoms before seeking health care at an institution. It is useful especially at night and has also been found helpful in the treatment of exercise-induced asthma. Caution the child and family against excessive use of these agents, because they can increase bronchial obstruction. The need for aerosol treatments more often than every 3–4 hours because of poor or brief bronchodilator response is an indication that the attack is worsening. In that event the child requires prompt medical attention.

2. For the child whose chest feels too tight to inhale the aerosol effectively, give epinephrine 0.05–0.2 ml of 1:1,000 solution subcutaneously every 20 minutes as necessary up to three doses.
3. Administer oxygen, since hypoxemia is usually present. The child is hospitalized if there is a poor response to the ambulatory treatment with adrenergic agents.

Ongoing Therapy   Medications are prescribed both to control asthma and to prevent attacks. Around-the-clock therapy using some form of theophylline is given in a dose of 3–5 mg/kg body weight every 6 hours. If the child is unresponsive to the usual dosage regimen, the plasma or saline theophylline concentrations (10–20 μg/ml of plasma is considered optimum concentration) are monitored to determine whether theophylline dosage is insufficient.

Oral adrenergic agents (e.g., metaproterenol, terbutaline, salbutamol, or ephedrine) are prescribed along with theophylline every 6 hours if sufficient bronchodilator control is not reached. Combination drugs, such as theophylline, ephedrine, and phenobarbital, are not as effective as the use of single entities.

If the child is unresponsive to the regular administration of the medications listed above, a trial of cromolyn sodium may be indicated. Cromolyn sodium has no effect on acute asthma symptoms. It is a prophylactic agent that apparently prevents or decreases the release of histamine and other chemical mediators. It must be taken by inhalation from a device called a Spinhaler.

If the child has chronic, severe airway obstruction that interferes with normal daily activities, such as school attendance, sleeping, or play, corticosteroids may be effective.

Health Teaching for the Child and Family   Health education should occur in a series of small steps and over a period of time. One educational session is insufficient. Reinforcement and motivation to learn are essential (see Chapter 10 for teaching principles). Teaching should include (Fireman et al., 1981) the following aspects:

1. Description of lung anatomy
2. Review of basic pulmonary physiology and pathophysiology
3. Explanation of factors that can provoke asthma, such as allergens, infections, exercise, and irritant inhalants

4. Description of the actions of the medications used

5. Explanation of environmental control, highlighting irritating stimulants and psychosocial factors that give rise to asthma attacks

Self-care Skills Promotion and reinforcement of self-care skills require parental support. Parents should give positive reinforcement to their child for self-care behaviors and negative reinforcement for unnecessarily dependent behaviors. Parents should be encouraged to create opportunities in which the child can practice self-care skills (Parcel and Nader, 1977). The nurse practitioner should help the child and family obtain the following self-care skills:

1. Observation: Be able to recognize situations that might lead to an asthma attack

2. Discrimination: Be able to recognize changes indicative of an impending or actual asthma attack

3. Decision making: Be able to decide to initiate action on his/her own or obtain help to prevent or stop an asthma attack

4. Communication: Be able to inform parents, health personnel, or others what is occurring before and during an asthma attack

5. Self-reliance: Possess a positive attitude about mastering self-care skills

Follow-up Regular monthly visits are indicated after the diagnosis of asthma to reinforce health teaching, to answer questions, and to develop self-care skills. The nurse practitioner should ascertain the child and family's adjustment to the diagnosis and compliance with the medical regimen. Serum theophylline levels are checked at 6–12-month intervals or whenever necessary to permit necessary readjustment of the dosage levels.

References

American Academy of Pediatrics. "Management of Asthma." *Pediatrics* 68:874–879, December 1981.

Asthma and the Other Allergic Diseases. National Institute of Allergy and Infectious Diseases Task Force Report, NIH Pub. No. 79-387. USPHS, National Institutes of Health, 1979. Pp. 7–31.

Brewster, A. "Chronically Ill Hospitalized Children's Concepts of Their Illness." *Pediatrics 69*:355–362, March 1982.

Commission on Chronic Illness. *Chronic Illness in the U.S. Vol. 1, Prevention of Chronic Illness.* Cambridge, MA: Harvard University Press, 1957.

Ellis, E. "Asthma." In M. Green and R. Haggerty, eds. *Ambulatory Pediatrics II.* Philadelphia: W.B. Saunders, 1977. Pp. 325–338.

Examination and Health History Findings among Children and Youths 6–17 Years of Age, 1973. Vital and Health Statistics Series 11, No. 129-08. DHEW Publ. No. 74-1611. P. 26.

Fireman, P. et al. "Teaching Self-Management Skills to Asthmatic Children and Their Parents in an Ambulatory Care Setting." *Pediatrics 68*:341–348, September 1981.

Gode, R. O. and M. S. Smith. "Effects of Chronic Disorders on Adolescent Development: Self, Family, Friends, and School." In M. S. Smith, editor, *Chronic Disorders in Adolescence.* Boston: John Wright–PSG, 1983. Pp. 31–44.

Green, M., and R. J. Haggerty, eds. *Ambulatory Pediatrics II.* Philadelphia: W.B. Saunders, 1977.

Hughes, J. "The Emotional Impact of Chronic Disease: The Pediatrician's Responsibility." *Am J Dis Child 130*:1200–1203, November 1976.

Hughes, J. *Synopsis of Pediatrics.* 5th ed. St. Louis: CV Mosby, 1980.

Hymovich, D. "Assessment of the Chronically Ill Child and Family." In D. Hymovich and M. Bernard, editors, *Family Health Care.* New York: McGraw-Hill, 1979.

Kaplan, D. M. "Early Intervention for Families with Chronically Ill Children." In A. E. Christ and K. Flomenhaft, editors, *Psychosocial Family Interventions in Chronic Pediatric Illness.* New York: Plenum, 1980. Pp. 37–48.

Kleinberg, S. *Educating the Chronically Ill Child.* Rockville, MD: Aspen Systems, 1982.

Maiman, L. A. et al. "Education for Self-Treatment by Adult Asthmatics." *JAMA 241*:1919–1922, May 4, 1979.

Mascia, A. V. "Rehabilitation of the Child with Chronic Asthma." In J. Downey and N. Low, editors, *The Child with Disabling Illness.* 2nd ed. New York: Raven Press, 1982. Pp. 67–89.

Mattsson, A. "Long-Term Physical Illness in Childhood: A Challenge to Psychosocial Adaptation." *Pediatrics 50*:801–811, November 1972.

Nelms, B. C. and R. G. Mullins. *Growth and Development: A Primary Health Care Approach.* Englewood Cliffs, NJ: Prentice-Hall, 1982.

Orem, D. *Nursing: Concepts of Practice.* 2nd ed. New York: McGraw-Hill, 1980.

Parcel, G. S. and P. R. Nader. "Evaluation of a Pilot School Health Education Program for Asthmatic Children." *J. School Health 47*:453–456, October 1977.

Pearlman, D. S. and C. W. Bierman. "Asthma (Bronchial Asthma, Reactive Airways Disorder)." In C. W. Bierman and D. S. Pearlman, editors, *Allergic Diseases of Infancy, Childhood and Adolescence.* Philadelphia: W.B. Saunders, 1980. Pp. 581–604.

Pless, I. B. and B. B. Satterwhite, "Chronic Illness." In R. J. Haggerty, K. J. Roghmann, and I. B. Pless, editors, *Child Health and the Community.* New York: Wiley, 1975. Pp. 78–94.

Pless, I., B. Satterwhite, and D. Van Vechten. "Chronic Illness in Childhood: A Regional Survey of Care." *Pediatrics* 58:37–46, July 1976.

Powell, F. D. *Theory of Coping Systems: Change in Supportive Health Organizations.* Cambridge, MA: Schenkman, 1975.

Rudolph, A., ed. *Pediatrics.* 17th ed. East Norwalk, CT, Appleton-Century-Crofts, 1982.

Sedlacek, K. "Helping the Asthmatic Child in School." *Am J Maternal Child Nursing* 3:207–210, July/August 1978.

Smith, M. S., ed. *Chronic Disorders in Adolescence.* Boston: John Wright–PSG, 1983.

Travis, G. *Chronic Illness in Children: Its Impact on Child and Family.* Stanford, CA: Stanford University Press, 1976.

Underwood, P. *Self-Care Manual.* San Francisco: University of California, Department of Mental Health Community Nursing, 1983.

U.S. Department of Health and Human Services. *Young People with Cancer: A Handbook for Parents.* NIH Publ. No. 82-2378, April 1982.

Vance, V. J., and W. F. Taylor. "The Financial Cost of Chronic Asthma." *Ann Allergy* 29:455–459, September 1971.

Wieczorek, R. R. and J. N. Natapoff. *A Conceptual Approach to the Nursing of Children. Health Care from Birth through Adolescence.* Philadelpha: J.B. Lippincott, 1981.

13

Approach
to Medications
in Childhood

The use of medications in infants and children raises several issues of concern to health professionals and to parents. Obviously, there is no question about the validity of specific drug therapy in the treatment of many childhood illnesses, and the development of effective therapeutic agents has greatly reduced morbidity and mortality in childhood. Yet, it is clear that medications are frequently prescribed inappropriately and without adequate consideration of benefit, risk, and cost factors. One study reports that "approximately 95 percent of physicians will issue one or more prescriptions to a patient whom they diagnose as having a 'common cold' and almost 60 percent of these prescriptions will be for an antibiotic" (Asnes and Grebin, 1974, pp. 84–85). Other studies conducted in the pediatric outpatient department of a large medical center revealed that "46 percent of all patients seen in 1972 during the day received at least one prescription. Interestingly, this figure rose to 70 percent during the evening" (Asnes and Grebin, 1974, p. 81).

In addition, the notion that there is a "pill for every ill" has become widespread in the United States. This attitude is reinforced by massive advertising through communications media and by the availability of hundreds of over-the-counter medications in pharmacies, supermarkets, department stores, and health food stores.

589

It frequently results in parents pressuring the care provider for medications and in parental dissatisfaction if medication is not prescribed. Nurse practitioners are in a position to influence the medication practices, habits, and attitudes of families they see. The guiding philosophy behind the use of medications is based on considerations of benefit and risk.

With adequate teaching and support it is possible to enable parents and children to manage minor symptoms without the use of medications. It is a more time-consuming effort than writing a prescription or suggesting an over-the-counter remedy but a more useful effort in terms of assisting families to develop their own self-care skills and reducing the expensive and potentially dangerous use of inappropriate and ineffective drugs.

Given such a philosophical stance, this chapter will present information on general guidelines for medication use in infants and children and suggestions for assuring that children receive the medications they need when they need them.

ASSESSMENT

Guidelines for Drug Use in Infants and Children

The effective use of medications depends on considerations of a number of factors including the parents, the child, the health professional (physician and/or nurse practitioner), and the drug selected.

PARENTAL FACTORS

- *Attitudes.* Some parents think that unless medications are prescribed the child has not received sufficient care. On the other hand there are parents who are suspicious and fearful of medications and do not want to medicate their children.
- *Reliability.* The parents must be reliable to handle certain responsibilities (Asnes and Grebin, 1974):

1. Have the prescription filled
2. Administer the medication

3. Prepare the correct dosage and administer it at the correct time intervals

4. Continue administration of the medication for the full prescribed dose

- *Demographic factors.* Age, sex, socioeconomic status, educational level, religion, occupation, marital status, and ethnic background per se are not predictive of compliance with prescribed medical regimen but may interact to provide obstacles to implementing recommendations. For example, a study of the reading level of mothers bringing their children to a large urban pediatric emergency room revealed that at least 45 percent could not read beyond the sixth grade level (Wingert et al., 1969). Since most health education materials are written at above eighth grade levels (eighth to thirteenth grade), it is obvious that such information is incomprehensible to almost half the population studied.

CHILD FACTORS

- *Acute or chronic illness.* Diseases causing malabsorption or hepatic or renal dysfunction may affect drug absorption, metabolism, and excretion.
- *Age.* As a general rule in children under 2 years of age, medications should be used only when absolutely necessary. Infants are more susceptible to toxicity (e.g., an overdose of salicylates leads to metabolic acidosis in infants, rarely in adults) and have limited ability to detoxify drugs (e.g., renal and hepatic functions are not fully developed). Signs of toxicity are difficult to identify early, since reactions are less predictable and the child cannot communicate specific distress. The margin for error in dosage is very narrow so slight miscalculations assume greater import.
- *Allergy.* Hypersensitivity reactions to drugs occur in children as well as in adults. History should include information on past drug allergies or adverse drug reactions.
- *Genetic characteristics.* Some children have genetic characteristics that may influence various stages of drug absorption, metabolism, and excretion. G-6-PD deficiency (hemolytic anemia with primaquine-type drugs) and mongolism (increased response to atropine) are examples.

- *Growth and development.* The child's level of growth and development influences the form of drug prescribed and the method of administration.

HEALTH PROFESSIONAL FACTORS

- *Communication.* The ability to communicate in writing and verbally is essential to avoid errors in medication administration.
- *Knowledge.* "Rational drug therapy involves prescribing the right drug, for the right patient, at the right time, in the right amount, with due consideration for cost" (Asnes and Grebin, 1974, p. 85). Such practice requires extensive knowledge and demands that practitioners keep their information current. See this chapter, Resource Information.
- *Relationship with client.* See this chapter, Compliance.

DRUG FACTORS

- *Cost.* The cost of drugs is increasing and public attention has focused on the high percentage of mark-up included in the price of retail medications. Generic prescribing, rather than designating a proprietary brand, permits the selection of less expensive forms of the same medication. Both types conform to United States Pharmacopeia (USP) and National Formulary (NF) standards for identity, purity, and strength of products. However, there is some concern that this practice does not guarantee that the form selected will have similar biologic and clinical equivalency.
- *Drug incompatibilities.* The simultaneous use of multiple medications can cause adverse drug reactions. Persons prescribing medications must possess knowledge of the mechanisms of drug interaction and must know all the medications a client is taking.
- *Toxicity.* All drugs have toxic effects. Thus, the selection of a drug involves choosing the *least* toxic drug that will produce the desired therapeutic effect.

Basic Formulary

It is recommended that prescribers become familiar with a select number of therapeutic agents and use them consistently. In providing primary care to normal children the types of medications necessary to treat *most* conditions are as follows:

- Analgesic-antipyretic, e.g., acetaminophen
- Antibiotic, systemic, e.g., ampicillin, amoxicillin
- Antibiotic, topical, e.g., Neosporin
- Antifungal, e.g., nystatin
- Antihistamine, e.g., chlorpheniramine maleate (Chlor-Trimeton), diphenhydramine (Benadryl)
- Decongestant, e.g., pseudoephedrine hydrochloride (Sudafed), phenylephrine hydrochloride (Neo-Synephrine)
- Emetic, e.g., syrup of ipecac
- Iron, e.g., Fer-In-Sol
- Steroid, topical, e.g., hydrocortisone
- Vitamin preparation

Over-the-Counter Medications

Millions of people spend billions of dollars yearly for self-prescribed over-the-counter (OTC) drugs. Analgesics, cough and cold preparations, topical preparations, vitamins, and laxatives are the most common varieties purchased. The practice of self-treatment of minor illnesses is not to be discouraged if it is based on adequate knowledge. Unfortunately, the use of OTC drugs may be inappropriate, ineffective, and even dangerous, especially in children. Some of the potential problems are listed.

- The tendency exists to abuse such drugs (i.e., take more than the recommended dosage). Consequently, manufacturers cut down on the published recommended dose to the extent that frequently the dose is not pharmacologically effective.
- For infants and young children doses are not recommended, and many parents guess at an approximate dose.
- Most OTC cold preparations contain multiple ingredients, as many as seven different ingredients (e.g., antihistamine, decongestant, analgesic, vitamin, caffeine, alcohol, flavoring), which makes accurate dosage difficult and evaluation of allergic or toxic side effects confusing.

- The numbers of medications available in homes compounds the dangers of accidental poisoning in young children. See Chapters 5 and 6, Accident Prevention and Safety, and Chapter 28, Emergencies.

Compliance

When the indications for drug therapy exist and medication is prescribed, the therapeutic effect will be achieved only if the child receives the medication as prescribed. Many factors mitigate against compliance with medication regimens, and in a study of 300 children being treated for acute otitis media in an urban medical center clinic it was found that only 7.3 percent (22 children) received the prescribed dose of antibiotic for the full 10-day course (Maₜ'ar et al., 1975). Compliance with a 10-day course of antibiotic has been reported as 66 percent in private practice settings (Charney et al., 1967).

GENERAL COMPLIANCE

Factors known to influence general compliance with therapeutic regimens include the following (Mattar and Yaffe, 1974):

- Parents' perception of the severity of the illness
- Degree of incapacity caused by the illness: direct correlation
- Number of medical restrictions imposed: direct correlation
- Complexity and duration of therapy: inverse correlation
- Number of drugs prescribed: inverse correlation
- Interaction with the caretaker. If the parents are dissatisfied they are less likely to follow recommendations.

COMPLIANCE WITH MEDICATIONS

Factors influencing incomplete administration of medications to children include the following:

- Difficulties having prescriptions filled (e.g., pharmacy closed, problems with Medicaid reimbursement, transportation problems)

- Difficulties in getting children to take the medication
- Dispensing errors (e.g., less than prescribed amount dispensed, incomplete or erroneous labeling)
- Financial problems
- Inaccurate measuring devices (e.g., household teaspoons hold volumes from 2.5 to 9 ml)
- Inadequate understanding by parents, often compounded by language barriers
- Other family stresses (e.g., emotional factors, single working parent)
- Deliberate noncompliance (e.g., therapy conflicts with cultural or individual beliefs)

MANAGEMENT

Role of the Nurse Practitioner

Administration of medications prescribed by physicians has long been a traditional nursing role, and content in pharmacology is part of basic nursing knowledge. The development of the nurse practitioner role, which involves collaboration with physicians, has resulted in an expansion of the nurses' responsibility in relation to medications. Many nurse practitioners are prescribing medications for some minor illnesses by use of jointly developed protocols and standing orders, and in some states where prescribing laws have been changed, they are able to independently prescribe certain medications. Responsibility and accountability for this function demands increased knowledge of the many factors involved in safe and effective drug use.

Current acceptable practice models available to nurse practitioners include the following:

- *Individual consultation.* In settings where the nurse practitioner and physician work in close proximity, the nurse practitioner consults with the physician when medication is indicated, and the physician either writes and signs the prescription or signs it after the nurse practitioner has written it.

- *Protocols and standing orders.* In some settings, approved standard procedures are used to manage specific clinical entities and the nurse practitioner can implement the procedure independently once the diagnosis has been confirmed.
- *Telephone consultation.* When distance separates the nurse practitioner and physician, consultation by telephone and physician communication with the local pharmacy is accepted practice. The use by nurse practitioners of pre-signed blank prescription forms is, simply, bad practice.

Additional role functions of the nurse practitioner include parent and child teaching for optimum compliance and advising clients about the appropriate use of OTC drugs and their potential adverse effects.

The Prescription

Medication errors can be reduced by precisely communicating the instructions on the prescription and label. Prescription writing (Asnes and Grebin, 1974) should include the following essential information:

1. Date and time written.
2. Name of drug. The official generic or trade name must be spelled correctly.
3. Form of drug. Specify capsules, tablets, suspension.
4. Dosage expressed in metric system (e.g., 125 mg/5 ml).
5. Amount of drug to be dispensed. If 125 mg is to be taken 4 times a day for 10 days, and the drug comes as 125 mg/5 ml, then at least 200 ml must be prescribed and dispensed.
6. Route of administration.
7. Directions. Specify amount and time of administration. Use exact hours according to a schedule worked out with the family rather than "three times a day." Specify duration of administration (e.g., "for 10 days" or "until bottle empty"). Do not write, "Take as directed."
8. Indication for drug. If the drug is to be taken "as necessary," specify the indication for its use and the maximum amount to be taken in 24 hours.

9. Special precautions or requirements in administration of the drug (e.g., "store in refrigerator").
10. Refills. Specify the number of refills or "no refills."
11. Label. The name of the drug should be placed on the label.
12. Signature.

Improving Compliance

INTERPERSONAL RELATIONSHIPS

The relationship between the family and the care provider is of prime importance in the outcome of a therapeutic plan. Parent cooperation is likely to be enhanced when the provider:

1. Is known to the family, is a continuity figure
2. Is approachable and conveys warmth
3. Communicates interest and concern
4. Elicits the chief concerns and expectations of the parent and child
5. Acknowledges the parent's anxiety and feelings
6. Provides time for open discussion, questions, and explanations

DEVELOPING THE CARE PLAN

Joint development of the care plan is more likely to promote compliance than a unilateral prescription of orders. The care provider who believes that parents are responsible participants in the care of their child will attend to the following:

1. Obtain information about past illnesses of the child and family and the family's reactions to them
2. Determine how the parents have managed minor illnesses at home
3. Determine what medications are routinely kept in the home and how they are used
4. Reinforce those practices that are appropriate
5. Assess the parents' understanding of the current illness
6. Provide clear information on the illness and rationale for treatment

7. Elicit the parents' ideas on what approaches to treatment will be most effective for the particular child.

PARENT TEACHING RELATED TO MEDICATIONS

When medications are prescribed the care provider can improve the probability of safe and effective compliance in several ways:

1. Limiting the number of medications prescribed
2. Providing verbal and written instructions at the parents' level of comprehension
3. Telling parents the name of the medication. Parents have the right to know what drugs are being given, and such information is essential in managing questions by telephone and in assessing emergency situations (e.g., accidental ingestions).
4. Informing parents of the possible consequences if the drug is not administered
5. Informing parents of the side effects, what to do if they appear, when to call, and when to stop the drug
6. Providing a standard measuring device (e.g., a calibrated dropper, standard teaspoon)
7. Planning dosage schedule in accordance with the family's daily routine
8. Providing a chart, calendar, or checklist for keeping track of doses given
9. Discussing methods of administering the drug and what to do if the child refuses. An excellent guide to giving oral medications to young children is found in the article by Ormond and Caulfield, 1976. See this chapter, References.
10. Discussing storage and preparation (e.g., shaking, diluting) of drug
11. Instructing parents on disposal or storage of the drug on completion of treatment
12. Reviewing safety measures regarding drugs in the home (see Chapters 5 and 6, Accident Prevention and Safety, and Chapter 28, Emergencies)
13. Asking parents to repeat instructions to clarify misunderstandings

14. Encouraging parents to call with any questions or problems
15. Providing a starter dose (sample) if the visit is at night or pharmacies are closed

Resource Information

Drug information is readily available from a variety of sources and the nurse practitioner should select and become familiar with at least one or two reliable references. Manufacturer's inserts also contain information specific to the particular preparation. In some settings the availability of a clinical pharmacist in the pediatric unit has proven very beneficial for staff and families (Levin, 1972).

In addition to medical, nursing, and pharmacology journals and textbooks, some sources of pharmacotherapeutic information are:

1. American Hospital Formulary Service, American Society of Hospital Pharmacists, 4630 Montgomery Avenue, Washington DC 20014.
2. *Drugs of Choice*, W. Modell, editor, C. V. Mosby, St. Louis, MO.
3. *Handbook of Nonprescription Drugs*, American Pharmaceutical Association, 2215 Constitution Avenue NW, Washington DC 20037.
4. *Physician's Desk Reference (PDR)*, and *Physician's Desk Reference for Non-Prescription Drugs*, Medical Economics Company, Oradell, NJ 07649.
5. *FDA Drug Bulletin*, Department of Health and Human Services, Public Health Service, Food and Drug Administration, Rockville, MD 20857.
6. *United States Pharmacopeia Dispensing Information*, U.S. Pharmacopeial Convention Inc., Drug Information Division, 12601 Twinbrook Parkway, Rockville, MD 20852.

References

Aaron, H. and M. M. Lipman, Editors of Consumer Reports. *The Medicine Show.* Mount Vernon, NY: Consumers Union, 1976.

Ames, J. T., et al. "Parents' Conception of Their Use of Over-the-Counter Medicines." *Clin Pediatr 21*:298–301, May 1982.

Asnes, R. S. and B. Grebin. "Pharmacotherapeutics: A Rational Approach." *Pediatr Clin North Am 21*:81–94, February 1974.

Brown, M. S. and M. Collar. "Over-the-Counter Drugs for Upper Respiratory Symptoms." *Nurse Practitioner 2*:18–42, January/February 1977.

Charney, E., et al. "How Well do Patients Take Oral Penicillin? A Collaborative Study in Private Practice." *Pediatrics 40*:188–195, August 1967.

Kennedy, D. L. and M. B. Forbes. "Drug Therapy for Ambulatory Pediatric Patients in 1979." *Pediatrics 70*:26–29, July 1982.

Korsch, B. M., E. H. Gozzi, and V. Francis. "Gaps in Doctor-Patient Communication, 1. Doctor–Patient Interaction and Patient Satisfaction." *Pediatrics* 42:855–871, November 1968.

Levin, R. H. "Clinical Pharmacy Practice in a Pediatric Clinic." *Drug Intelligence and Clinical Pharmacy* 6:171–176, May 1972.

Marston, M. V. "Compliance with Medical Regimens: A Review of the Literature." *Nurs Res* 19:312–323, July/August 1970.

Mattar, M. E., et al. "Inadequacies in the Pharmacologic Management of Ambulatory Children." *J Pediatr* 87:137–141, July 1975.

Mattar, M. E. and S. J. Yaffe. "Compliance of Pediatric Patients with Therapeutic Regimens." *Postgrad Med* 56:181–188, November 1974.

Ormond, E. A. R. and C. Caulfield. "A Practical Guide to Giving Oral Medications to Young Children." *Am J Maternal Child Nursing* 1:320–325, September/October 1976.

Pagliaro, L. A. and R. H. Levin. *Problems in Pediatric Drug Therapy.* Hamilton, IL: Drug Intelligence Publications, 1979.

Wingert, W. W., J. P. Grubbs, and D. B. Friedman. "Why Johnny's Parents Don't Read." *Clin Pediatr* 8:655–660, November 1969.

14

The Skin

Diseases of the skin and allergic skin conditions are closely related. Most of the minor or transient skin disorders treated in the health care facility may be seen and managed by the nurse practitioner. Skin disorders need to be distinguished from more severe problems, many of which are of allergic origin, and may need to be referred for further diagnosis and treatment. This chapter will deal with the assessment and management of common skin problems and with health education of parents in reference to general skin care.

ASSESSMENT

Because of the relationship of skin and allergic conditions, components of the history and physical examination necessarily include aspects of both areas. See Chapter 26, Allergies.

History

PRESENT CONCERNS

If the rash is the primary complaint obtain a family history, drug history (specifically aspirin), and allergic history. If the rash is a secondary complaint, it is important to describe it accurately, since the skin is the mirror of many internal diseases. See Chapter 11, Assessment of Presenting Symptom.

PAST HISTORY

Obtain information about rashes, allergies (see Chapter 26, History), communicable diseases, immunizations, frequency of upper respiratory infections, nutrition in infancy and related feeding problems, "spitting up," colic, and constipation.

FAMILY HISTORY

Obtain information about skin problems and about allergies.

NUTRITION HISTORY

Obtain information about diet, food allergies, and new foods recently added to diet. If the child is being nursed, ask about presence of food allergies in the mother or recent excessive intake of a particular food in her diet.

ALLERGY HISTORY

See Chapter 26, History.

Physical Examination

SKIN

In examining the skin,

- Observe color (normal pigmentation is due to melanin, a dark pigment in the skin), erythema, jaundice, carotenemia, pallor, or flushing.
- Palpate for temperature and state of hydration.
- Observe scars, birth marks, bruises, scratches, bites, swelling, or lumps.
- Observe and palpate texture of the skin to determine if it is smooth, rough, branny, or scaly.
- Observe and describe any rash fully including color, size of le-

sions, location, and distribution. See this chapter, Commonly Used Terms.

Skin Characteristics of Yellow-Skinned or Dark-Pigmented Children
Characteristics of the skin of these children may be observed as follows:

1. Infants of dark-skinned parents are lightly pigmented at birth but grow progressively darker with age until pigmentation peaks at about 6 to 8 weeks of age.
2. Some dark-skinned children may have normal blue coloring of the lips or gums.
3. Blacks may have brown frecklelike pigmentations of the buccal mucosa.
4. Pallor or paleness can be detected in the nail beds, conjunctivae, oral mucosa, or tongue, which are normally reddish pink.
5. Jaundice, which can be various shades of yellow or green, is best seen by looking at the sclerae or mucous membranes in daylight.
6. Carotenemia, which does not color the sclera, may be noted periorally, on the palmar surfaces of the hands, and on the plantar surfaces of the feet. See Chapter 3, Table 3-1, Vitamin A.
7. Rashes that are difficult to visualize may be palpated to aid in assessment.
8. Hypopigmentation or depigmentation in the diaper area may be observed following diaper rash.

Methods and Tools   For observation of the skin daylight is best. It may be necessary at times to take the child to a window to better visualize a rash. Additional tools for assessing skin lesions are as follows:

1. White or yellow overhead light or gooseneck lamp, with at least a 60-watt bulb, is the next choice.
2. A magnifying glass can be useful to distinguish tiny eruptions or to identify the parasites of scabies or the lice of pediculosis.
3. A glass slide or magnifying glass can be used for blanching the skin. This is helpful in identification of petechiae, ecchymoses,

or underlying jaundice that would otherwise be masked by flushed skin that is suffused with blood.

4. An ultraviolet lamp (Wood's lamp) when used in a darkened room detects some fungi and causes them to appear fluorescent. A greenish color of the lesion is positive for tinea (ringworm).

5. KOH (potassium hydroxide) preparation is used to aid in the diagnosis of fungal infections. Scrapings from the edge of an active lesion are put on a slide; 20 percent KOH is added; the slide is heated gently and then examined under the microscope for the branching filaments (hyphae) of fungus.

EYES

Observe for swelling of the lids, crusty lids or lashes, discharges, conjunctivitis, and dark circles below the eyes.

NOSE

Observe presence and type of mucous discharge, excoriation of nares, color and state of turbinates, and patency. Nasal mucosa that is red and swollen may suggest acute rhinitis, while pale, gray, or bluish mucosa may indicate an allergic etiology for rhinitis. Nasal polyps may also lead one to suspect an allergic etiology.

MOUTH

Observe the buccal mucosa for lesions and state of hydration; the uvula for color and size; the tonsils for condition and color. See Chapter 16, Physical Examination.

LYMPH NODES

Palpate for enlargement or tenderness of cervical, axillary, and inguinal nodes. These can range from pea size to lima bean size. Nodes should be described in terms of location, size, consistency, mobility, erythema, presence of heat, and degree of tenderness.

LUNGS

Auscultate for rhonchi, rales, or wheezes.

NAILS

The chief function of nails is protection. Findings that may indicate problems are listed below.

1. *Nail biting, cuticle biting, and playing with the nails or cuticles.* These are common habits which produce considerable damage to the nails.
2. *Brittle nails.* This may be due to lack of water vapor similar to chapping. Little is known about the cause.
3. *Splitting into layers.* This may be due to overimmersion in water.
4. *White spots.* These may have a number of causes, trauma being the most common. The presence or absence of these spots is of no value as an assessment of health.
5. *Staining.* This is usually caused by external substances.
6. *Separation of nail.* This may indicate the start of a fungal infection, trauma, atopic dermatitis, or psoriasis.
7. *Ingrown toenail.* Trauma is the major factor.
8. *Toenail deformity.* This may be the result of ill-fitting shoes or a congenital deformity.

Commonly Used Terms

bulla(ae): a vesicle larger than 1 cm, a "blister."

circinate: having a sharply circumscribed and somewhat circular margin.

confluent: a running together, becoming merged in one.

dermatitis: a term applied to all types of skin inflammation regardless of etiology, characterized by a combination of cutaneous reactions, such as erythema, oozing, drying, and scaling.

dermatosis: any disorder of the skin.

emollient: soothing and softening, a soothing medicine.

erosion: the superficial destruction of a surface area of tissue by inflammation, ulceration, or trauma.

erythema: any redness of the skin.

excoriation: mechanical removal of the epidermis leaving the dermis exposed; a scratch or scrape.

fissure: a narrow opening, chasm, or crack of some length and considerable depth.

induration: an increase in the fibrous elements of; hardening

keratosis: a fine papular eruption limited to sebaceous orifices giving the skin a rough, grainy texture; often associated with vitamin A deficiency.

lichenification: the process by which the skin becomes hardened and leathery usually as a result of chronic irritation.

maceration: a condition of softened, moist, excoriated areas of the skin usually in the intertriginous areas.

macule: a flat, colored skin lesion less than 1 cm.

melanin: dark pigment from choroid, hair, and other dark tissues.

nodule: a moveable, firm mass under the skin.

nummular: resembling a pile of coins.

papule: a raised, circumscribed lesion, less than 1 cm, which may be a variety of red colors.

petechiae: small reddish purple spots in the superficial layers of the skin which do not blanch; formed by effusion of blood.

pityroid: a branny, rough texture of the skin associated with pityriasis.

pustule: an elevated, sharply circumscribed lesion, less than 1 cm, filled with purulent material.

seborrhea: a discharge of sebaceous matter on the skin; an inflammatory process.

ulcer: a break in the skin or mucous membrane that is characterized by loss of surface tissue on an inflammatory base and by disintegration and necrosis of epithelial tissue; associated with slow healing.

vesicle: a small, sharply defined blister, less than 1 cm, filled with clear fluid.

vitiligo: a depigmentation of the skin of unknown origin; lesions are usually small and nummular.

wheal: an elevated white to pinkish ridge, commonly circular; associated with allergies it is usually pruritic (e.g., mosquito bite).

xanthoma: small yellow plaques or tumors of various sizes occurring as a result of local accumulation of fatty material.

MANAGEMENT

Care of the Diapers

The following method can be used for the proper cleaning of diapers:

1. Soak the dirty diapers in a solution of Borateen or Borax, ½ cup to 1 gallon of water, or use Diaper Sweet, Diaper Pure.
2. Prerinse in the washing machine.
3. Wash in the full cycle, separate from family wash, using mild soap such as Ivory Flakes, Lux Flakes, or Ivory soap. These soaps are not irritating to the skin. Detergents or softening agents containing strong acids or alkalis can be irritants and should not be used.
4. Rinse diapers two to three times. Vinegar or bleach, ¼ cup, may be added to the last rinse for acidification of the diapers.
5. Dry diapers in the sun whenever possible. If diapers are dried by machine, avoid fabric softener products because their perfumes and other ingredients are frequently allergenic.

COST FACTORS OF DIAPER CARE

Approximate costs of the different methods are as follows:

- Home laundry: 25 percent less than the cost of 100 disposable diapers
- Diaper service and disposable diapers are about equal in cost

COMMERCIAL DIAPER SERVICE

Positive factors for the employment of a diaper service include the following:

1. High sterilization standards of services
2. More professional approach to sanitation and conditioning to meet infant skin needs
3. Superior to home management in many cases
4. Ecologically preferred over disposable diapers
5. Cost factor equal to that of disposable diapers

DISPOSABLE DIAPERS

In comparison with cloth diapers there are several positive factors to the use of disposable diapers:

1. Better fit
2. More absorbency
3. Ease of transportation
4. No need for pins, plastic or rubber pants, or liners
5. Less complicated to manage for the uninitiated

   Negative factors of disposable diapers include:

1. Unsound ecologically
2. Higher cost
3. Potential allergies

Tips on Disposable Diaper Use

1. Elasticized diapers (Luvs, Huggies) may cause some slight irritation due to pressure on the infant's thighs. Nighttime, when infants tend to wet less, offers an opportunity to use nonelasticized diapers to relieve the pressure.
2. If the infant develops a contact diaper rash after the use of elasticized disposable diapers, switch to a nonelasticized disposable diaper that will permit more circulation of air.

General Care of the Skin

BATHING

Bathing is beneficial to the skin for these reasons:

1. It returns moisture to the skin as it cleans. However, overbathing dries the skin because it removes oil from the keratin barrier.
2. It relaxes muscles, relieves soreness, and eases tension.
3. It may help prevent and control minor skin problems such as diaper rashes, seborrheic dermatitis, minor bacterial infections, intertrigo, and miliaria. The present lax attitude about daily, or at least necessary, bathing for infants and children is contributing to these problems.

General Considerations   Some factors to consider in bathing children are as follows:

- Infants can be bathed and shampooed daily, using warm water and a mild soap, unless they have unusually sensitive skin or are suffering from atopic dermatitis.
- Alkaline soaps can be irritating to the normal acidic skin (pH 4.5 to 5.5) and should be thoroughly rinsed off, being careful to protect the child's eyes at all times.
- Tub soaking causes maceration of the skin and is not advised for more than 10 to 15 minutes.
- Lotions, creams, and powders are not necessary following a bath unless they are prescribed. In fact, powders in the diaper area and axillae can be very irritating.
- Bubble bath products are drying and irritative to the skin.
- Older children may bathe as frequently as needed at the parents' discretion following the principles stated above.

DRY SKIN

The significant protective barrier of the skin is limited almost entirely to its outermost layer, the dry stratum corneum. In infancy the stratum corneum is very thin, containing about 15 percent water. Dry skin indicates a lack of both water and oil. Fissures and cracks develop which disrupt the protective function of this layer, and scaliness and itchiness may occur.

Cause of Dry Skin   Dryness and roughness may be due to:

- Too frequent bathing, improper rinsing, or the use of rough, grainy, alkaline soaps
- Cold weather or overexposure to the sun
- Overexposure to air conditioning
- Contact with woolly clothes or dressing too warmly

Prevention   Preventive measures include:

- Avoiding preceding items to a practical degree
- Soaking in warm water 3 to 5 minutes using superfatted soaps (Basis, Oilatum) or baby oil (¼ cup) and applying a moisturizing lotion

- Using a humidifier or vaporizer, especially at night
- Increasing fluid intake and eating a proper, nutritious diet rich in vitamins A, C, D, and E.
- Getting regular outdoor exercise to stimulate the flow of blood to carry oxygen to the skin.

SOAPS

Most soaps are alkaline (pH 9 to 10) sodium or potassium salts of fatty acids. They emulsify fats with water and help to remove foreign particles from the skin. Their surfactant and alkaline properties may lead to primary irritation of the skin. The skin must be well rinsed to remove them.

Selection of Soaps   Soaps are chosen carefully for skin type:

1. Normal skin:
   - Mild soaps such as Ivory, Conti, and Castile
   - Neutral soaps (pH of 7.5 or less) such as Dove, Neutragena, or Sayman's
2. Dry skin:
   - Less alkaline soaps such as Alpha-Keri and Lubriderm
   - Superfatted soaps (also less alkaline) such as Basis and Oilatum
3. Sensitive skin:
   - Cetaphil lotion (see Chapter 26, Pharmacologic Therapy, Lotions)
   - Lindora: a liquid soap substitute, bubble bath, and shampoo
   - Neutragena. In addition to the soap, Neutragena Hand Cream can be used

SHAMPOOS

Shampoos are liquid soaps or detergents used for cleansing and/or therapeutic measures and should be well rinsed from the hair. Eyes of children should be well protected during their use.

Shampoos Suitable for Children   Among these are Earthborn, Head and Shoulders, Wella, and Protein 21. Baby products such as

Johnson's Baby Shampoo or Mennen's Baby Shampoo are also used extensively.

Dandruff Shampoos Among these are Sebulex, Ionil, Head and Shoulders, and Fostex Cream. Selenium- and cadmium-containing shampoos are not indicated for use with children. See this chapter, Dandruff.

POWDERS

Powders are soothing and absorb moisture. They increase evaporation, and provide antipruritic and cooling sensations. They are used chiefly for prophylaxis in intertriginous areas. Some authorities think powders are not helpful and their use should not be encouraged.

Common Powders There are several powders:

- *Talc.* This is the most lubricant but does not absorb water.
- *Cornstarch.* This is less lubricant and absorbs water but tends to cake and to irritate the skin, providing an excellent medium for growth of bacteria and fungi, especially *Candida albicans*. It is not recommended for use at any time on the skin.
- *Zeasorb.* This is a medicated powder. It is useful for its water-absorbing capacity and also because it is mildly antibacterial and antifungal. Other commonly used medicated powders are Caldesene and Desitin.

Application of Powder Powder should first be put on the parent's hand and then applied to the child as a fine film which will not cake or form lumps when wet. Powders used improperly may be inhaled causing respiratory problems or may cake in the body creases causing excoriation of the skin. Powders should not be applied to the child while in sleeping area because excess powder will similarly cause respiratory problems.

LOTIONS

Lotions are suspensions of powder in water that usually require shaking before application. They provide a protective, drying, and cooling effect and may act as a vehicle for other agents. The addition of alcohol increases the cooling effect. Available lotions include Cetaphil, Dermabase, Keri, Alpha-Keri, and Lubriderm.

Commonly Used Creams and Ointments Some useful vanishing creams are Lubriderm cream, Unibase, Keri cream, and Nivea cream. Commonly used ointments are Caldesene, Desitin, Vaseline, and zinc oxide.

Use of Petroleum Jelly Although a popular home remedy for years, petroleum jelly (Vaseline) is *not* advised for use in the diaper area to prevent or to treat diaper rash. It is occlusive, prevents air from reaching the skin, and can cause skin maceration, which predisposes to yeast infections.

Use of Boric Acid Because of the possibility of systemic poisoning boric acid should never be used in ointments or powders.

COMMON CLINICAL PROBLEMS

Early Skin Problems

CRADLE CAP

Assessment It is a form of seborrheic dermatitis in the newborn usually occurring because the parent is reluctant to scrub over the anterior fontanel. See this chapter, Seborrheic Dermatitis.

Management Treatment includes daily shampoo, removal of the "cap," and medication for secondary infection.

MILD CASES The head is shampooed daily with warm water and mild soap using firm pressure on the scalp. It is rinsed well and patted dry. The cap can be loosened by massaging warm mineral oil or baby oil into the scalp and allowing 15 to 20 minutes to elapse before shampooing. This treatment may need to be repeated for several days. Combing the scalp with a fine comb after applying the oil may be helpful.

SEVERE CASES The treatment is as follows:

1. Antiseborrheic shampoo is used daily, then two to three times a week. Sebulex or Ionil shampoos may be used.
2. Topical steroids can be helpful. See this chapter, Seborrheic Dermatitis.
3. Antibiotic therapy may be indicated for secondary infection.

Counseling The parents should be reassured that vigorous rubbing of the infant's scalp will not injure the fragile-appearing skull.

DIAPER DERMATITIS (DIAPER RASH)

General Definition This is a term used for all rashes of infancy that occur in the diaper area. These include rashes caused by the following:

1. Contact with sensitizing agents
2. Effects of ammonia and/or water (sweat)
3. Fungal infection

To facilitate their recognition and treatment, the assessment and management of these three types will be presented separately immediately following this section. Since preventive measures are key factors in the management of all types of diaper rashes they will be presented here.

General Preventive Measures The overall objective is to keep the diaper area dry, clean, and aerated. Measures to accomplish this include the following:

- Thick diapers and absorbent pads are used as blotters and to drain away wetness. Frequent changing of diapers is recommended. Plastic or rubber pants are not recommended because they keep the area wet and warm.
- Buttocks, thighs, and abdomen are cleansed with water after each diaper change. Emphasis must be placed on the need for this cleansing following each diaper change. Mild soap and water can be used following a bowel movement.
- A thin film of powder may be used to promote dryness. Caldesene powder, an antifungal and antibacterial powder, is rec-

ommended. Cornstarch is not recommended for the prevention or treatment of diaper rashes. See this chapter, Powders.

• The diapers can be removed for short periods during the day, while the infant lies on a pad, to expose the area to air.
• The diapers should be well washed. See this chapter, Care of Diapers.

CONTACT DIAPER RASH

Assessment   It is characterized by erythematous patches of maceration found in the intertriginous areas of the groin, buttocks, inguinal region, and sometimes on the abdomen. This rash is also called "irritative" or "infant" diaper rash. It may occur as the result of contact with disposable diapers, soaps, fabric softeners used for washing diapers, plastic or rubber pants, acids of feces and bacteria of urine from infrequent cleansing of the skin, or diarrhea.

Management   The treatment of contact diaper rash includes preventive measures as listed above, the application of healing ointments, and/or sitz baths.

OINTMENTS   The recommended ointments include Desitin, A & D, or zinc oxide. (Zinc oxide can be drying.) These ointments are to be washed off and reapplied at each diaper change.

SITZ BATHS   These baths may be helpful if the rash is extensive and severe. The child is lowered gently into warm water for a few minutes several times a day. After the area is patted dry, the ointments may be applied. If the rash worsens, the baths should be discontinued.

CONTRAINDICATED TREATMENTS   These are several contraindicated treatments:

• Cornstarch application. See this chapter, Powders.
• Vaseline ointment applications. See this chapter, Creams.
• Other topical ointments. These are potential sensitizers. Sometimes exacerbation of an eruption can be traced to ointments used in treatment. If topical ointment is used for a severe rash the "use" test should be employed. See Chapter 26, Pharmacologic Therapy, Corticosteroids.

AMMONIACAL DIAPER RASH

Assessment This is characterized by an erythematous papulo-vesicular rash sometimes with ulcerating reactions. It is found on the buttocks, thighs, and the abdomen of infants usually over the age of 7 months. It is caused by the irritative effects of ammonia produced by urea-splitting bacteria in the diaper or on the skin. The odor of ammonia is prominent. In the male ulceration of the external urethral meatus can occur. A history of care of the diapers is obtained.

Management The treatment of ammoniacal rash includes preventive measures and healing ointments. See this chapter, Diaper Dermatitis. It also includes the use of dry heat and the acidification of the urine and the diapers as follows:

1. Dry heat is applied by placing a lamp with a 25-watt bulb about 12 inches from the rash area for 10 to 15 minutes, four times a day. Care must be taken to prevent burning the skin.
2. Acidification of the urine is accomplished by adding 1 to 2 ounces of cranberry juice daily to the diet. More water can be added to the diet to further dilute the urine.
3. Acidification of the diapers is accomplished by adding ¼ cup of vinegar or bleach to the final rinse water. See this chapter, Care of the Diapers.
4. Neomycin or bacitracin ointments may be used on infected rashes. Neomycin, however, is a leading allergy producer.

FUNGAL DIAPER RASH

Assessment This is characterized by a smooth, shiny, "fire-engine" red, papular and nummular rash that has well-circum-scribed borders and occasional satellite lesions appearing in the inguinal creases. The causes of fungal rash include the following:

- Monilial (*Candida albicans*) infection in the mother's vagina
- Associated oral thrush in the infant
- Prolonged antibiotic therapy which destroys the normal flora
- Use of cornstarch in treatment of contact or ammoniacal diaper rashes. See this chapter, Powders.

Management   The treatment of fungal diaper rash includes preventive measures, keeping the area as dry as possible, and the use of specific medications. For preventive measures see this chapter, Diaper Dermatitis.

MEDICATIONS FOR FUNGAL DIAPER RASH   These are as follows:

1. Caldesene powder. This is a choice in mild cases.
2. Nystatin (Mycostatin) cream or lotion. It is used two to three times a day for 7 to 10 days for severe cases. This treatment may have to be repeated. If the rash persists after treatment, consider atopic dermatitis, cutaneous thrush, or congenital syphilis. Since yeast in the intestines is the source of infection, one may wish to give nystatin orally for a severe case.

INTERTRIGO

Assessment   Intertrigo is characterized by redness and maceration, which occur where the cutaneous surfaces are in opposition, such as the groin, the buttocks, the axillae, and the neck. The raw surface may ooze serous fluid or be complicated by a bacterial infection. It is seen commonly in fat babies. Intertrigo may be caused by the combination of sweating and chafing and may be aggravated by the presence of urine and stools. *Candida albicans* may be a secondary invader.

Management   The treatment is mainly preventive as follows:

1. The child is bathed daily. A protective, drying, antifungal powder such as Caldesene may be used. If the rash worsens, the powder should be discontinued.
2. The affected areas are exposed to the air frequently to permit complete evaporation of moisture.
3. The clothes are kept light and porous.
4. The following should be avoided:
   - Plastic or rubber pants, since these hold in moisture and heat
   - Ointments, except as prescribed, since they cause further maceration
   - Cornstarch, since this may contribute to fungal infection. See this chapter, Powders.

MILIARIA (PRICKLY HEAT)

Assessment Miliaria is inflamed sweat glands. It is characterized by small, erythematous, papular lesions with tiny vesicles or pustules at the center, usually found on the face, the neck, the shoulders, and the chest. It appears suddenly and can subside as quickly with proper treatment. It is extremely common and often causes undue concern to the parents. It is caused by inflamed and obstructed sweat glands often precipitated by excessive body warmth due to hot weather, too much clothing, or overheated homes.

Management The treatment is mainly preventive as follows:

1. Tepid baths without soap are given as frequently as necessary to cool the child.
2. The skin is dried by patting. Powder is to be used sparingly. Cornstarch is not recommended. See this chapter, Powders.
3. The use of ointments or lotions can aggravate this condition.
4. The child should not be kept overdressed or kept in overheated rooms.
5. The parents are taught about the sensitivity of the infant's skin due to the immaturity of the temperature control system. Infants do not sweat until 1 month old. See Chapter 5, Body Temperature Control.

SEBORRHEIC DERMATITIS

Assessment Seborrheic dermatitis is a common skin rash with a predilection for areas well supplied with sebaceous glands. The lesions are usually multiple, discrete, circumscribed oval or nummular patches covered with fine, yellowish, slightly oily scales on an erythematous base. Intertriginous areas of involvement may become macerated, leading to oozing and crusting, and it may resemble atopic dermatitis (see Chapter 26, Table 26-6). It can be found on the scalp, the eyebrows, behind and in the ears, on the chest, neck, and in the axilla.

Seborrheic dermatitis is due to excessive discharge from the sebaceous glands, but the cause is not really understood. It may be secondarily infected with *Candida albicans*. It appears in infancy between 2 and 12 weeks of age and usually clears spontaneously by

8 to 12 months of age. Examples of seborrheic dermatitis are cradle cap, dandruff, blepharitis, and otitis externa.

Management Treatment includes skin care and medications as follows:

1. Areas are bathed daily or as often as necessary.
2. Greasy ointments should be avoided since they may cause further maceration.
3. Hydrocortisone-containing ointments are used if the rash persists.
4. Antibiotics may be necessary if the rash becomes infected.

Common Communicable Skin Disorders

IMPETIGO

Assessment This is a condition involving the superficial layers of the skin seen as follows:

- It first appears as discolored spots of various sizes and shapes. Then small vesicles or bullae form and break, spreading germ-laden fluid to the surrounding area.
- The weeping lesions rapidly form yellow, honey-colored, seropurulent crusts and scabs. The tissue around them is red.
- The lesions may be on any part of the body but most often are seen on hands, face, or perineum, as a complication of diaper rash, or as a complication of dermatitis
- The regional lymph nodes may be palpably enlarged.

ETIOLOGY It typically begins in a dirty scratch or some other superficial lesion. The pathogenic invaders are staphylococci and streptococci. It may be spread by direct contact with infected persons or insects.

INCUBATION PERIOD This is from 2 to 10 days.

LABORATORY Culture is performed on fluid from an intact vesicle or pustule or the base of a lesion after the crust is removed.

DIFFERENTIAL DIAGNOSIS This includes ringworm, herpes simplex, or other vesicular or ulcerating lesions.

COMPLICATIONS Acute glomerulonephritis may follow infection if the strain of Streptococcus is nephritogenic.

Management If treatment includes antibiotic therapy, it is managed collaboratively with a physician. Treatment includes several measures:

1. *Preventive measures.* The child's washcloth, towels, drinking glass, and bed linen are isolated. Hands are washed before and after treatment, and nails are kept short and clean.
2. *Topical treatment.* Crusts are soaked with warm water compresses 5 to 10 minutes before removing them. Bacitracin or neomycin ointment is rubbed into lesions including the surrounding areas.
3. *Antibiotic therapy.* If the child has many lesions, this treatment may be indicated. Antibiotic therapy is determined by results of culture. If the culture indicates pure streptococci or a mixture of staphylococci and streptococci, treatment is with penicillin. If pure staphylococci are found, cloxacillin may be used. Erythromycin is the alternative drug in patients allergic to penicillin.
4. *Follow-up.* The child should be seen in 3 days if no improvement is evident.

PITYRIASIS ALBA

Assessment This is characterized by one or more sharply circumscribed, slightly erythematous, scaly, branny, hypopigmented patches of unknown origin on the cheeks, chin, and forehead. The cause is unknown. It most commonly occurs in pigmented skin of children between 3 and 12 years of age. Hypopigmented areas may slowly repigment but in rare instances may be permanent.

Management It is treated with application of any bland moisturizer and time. It takes 3 to 4 months to fade and always clears at puberty.

PITYRIASIS ROSEA

Assessment This is a common, mild, inflammatory disorder characterized by round or oval, discrete and confluent, pale pink, slightly scaly macules or rings. It is branny to the touch. It may be itchy and somewhat resembles ringworm. Patches of rash are distributed on the trunk and on the thighs. A "herald spot," a larger, more prominent patch is present and may appear as early as 10 days before the generalized rash.

Pityriasis rosea is thought to be viral in origin, but the cause is not clear. It is usually found in older children and in young adults. The onset of the eruption is sometimes coincident with mild malaise and symptoms of a viral respiratory tract infection. Mildly infectious, moderate outbreaks are not uncommon. Recovery is spontaneous and uncomplicated, occurring within 8 to 10 weeks. It leaves no marks or scars.

Management   Treatment involves care of the skin as follows:

1. Calamine lotion or witch hazel applications can be used for pruritus.
2. Tepid baths of colloidal starch (1 cup Linit starch to 1 tub of water) or oatmeal (Aveeno) can be taken. Hot baths are irritative to the condition, causing more pruritus.
3. Sun exposure to the point of mild erythema shortens the course of the disorder. Care must be taken to avoid sunburn.

SCABIES

Assessment   The basic lesions are papules or small nodules, plus secondary inflammation due to skin bacteria, urticaria, or scratch dermatitis. Scabies typically occurs on the genitals and buttocks, between the fingers, and in the folds of wrists, elbows, armpits, and beltline.

ETIOLOGY   Scabies is caused by a parasite, female itch mite, *Cicaris scabiei* or *Sarcoptes scabiei*. It burrows into the stratum corneum of the skin and lays eggs in the tunnel.

CLINICAL PICTURE   The characteristic burrows appear as fine, wavy lines from a few millimeters to a centimeter in length. Barely visible to the naked eye, they are grey to pink in color, and can be identified with a good magnifying glass or by scraping the skin and examining the scrapings under a microscope. Pruritus, the main symptom, is most severe at night. Scabies is highly contagious and is spread through clothing and bedding, as well as by human contact.

Management All family members should be examined and treated as needed. Treatment includes the following:

1. The scabicide of choice is 10 percent crotamiton (Eurax). Apply cream or lotion to all skin from the neck down; 12 hours later, without rebathing, repeat the application. It should be noted that, although gamma benzene hexachloride (Kwell) is an excellent scabicide, it is concentrated in the central nervous system and may cause seizures (Solomon et al., 1977), therefore alternative scabicides are recommended for infants and young children under the age of three.
2. Clothing should be washed or dry-cleaned as appropriate.
3. After scabicide treatment, the lesions recede slowly. Although the treatment with a scabicide has been successful, itching may persist due to the body's continuing reaction to the dead bodies of the parasite. An antihistamine may be prescribed in severe cases.

TINEA CAPITIS (RINGWORM OF THE SCALP)

Assessment Tinea capitis is a fungal infection which presents as one or more bald patches, 1 to 5 cm in diameter, with mild erythema, grey scaling, and crusting accompanied by broken stumps of hair. It can cause permanent scarring baldness.

ETIOLOGY Tinea capitis is commonly caused by *Microsporum canis,* which is transmitted by cats and dogs, or *Trichophyton tonsurans,* which is transmitted by humans.

LABORATORY Procedures are used as follows:

1. Ultraviolet lamp (Wood's lamp) is used to fluoresce *Microsporum* infections. *T. tonsurans* does not fluoresce.
2. Microscopic examination of a hair shaft with KOH will show round spores. See this chapter, Methods and Tools.
3. Microscopic culture will confirm the diagnosis.

Management The treatment of choice is ultramicrofine griseofulvin (Fulvicin). Local remedies add little to the results obtained from griseofulvin alone.

FOLLOW-UP   The child should be seen after 2 weeks of treatment and the patches should be recultured.

PREVENTION   Preventive measures are as follows:

1. Avoid exchange of headgear
2. Treat infected animals and re-examine them
3. Wash scalp after barbershop haircuts

TINEA CORPORIS (RINGWORM OF THE BODY)

Assessment   Tinea corporis is a fungal infection which presents with a small macule and enlarges by peripheral extension with central healing to form slightly scaly, circular lesions, 0.4 to 5 cm in size. One or more lesions may be found on the face, upper extremities, or the trunk. Dry types tend to become scaly. The moist type becomes vesicular or pustular. Pruritus, when it occurs, is mild.

ETIOLOGY   The most common cause is *Microsporum canis,* which is transmitted by cats or dogs.

LABORATORY   Microscopic examination with KOH will show hyphae. See this chapter, Methods and Tools.

Management   Treatment consists of the following:

1. Tolnaftate 1 percent solution (Tinactin) for weeping lesions
2. Tolnaftate 1 percent cream (Tinactin) rubbed into chronic lesions. The cream may be used also on weeping lesions as the solution stings.

PREVENTION   Preventive measures include the following:

1. Avoiding contact with infected animals
2. Avoiding exchange of clothing without adequate laundering
3. Avoiding community showers or bathing places

TINEA PEDIS (ATHLETE'S FOOT)

Assessment   This fungal infection is seen as a vesicular or even bullous eruption with maceration of the skin between the toes. It is rare in young children. Foot dermatitis in children may be contact dermatitis caused by allergy to some component of the shoe or atopic dermatitis.

ETIOLOGY Tinea pedis is caused by species of *Trichophyton.*

LABORATORY Microscopic examination with KOH will show hyphae. See this chapter, Methods and Tools.

Management Treatment includes:

1. General measures
   - Thoroughly drying between the toes after bathing
   - Use of white, cotton socks, which are changed daily or more frequently as necessary
   - Wearing of well-ventilated shoes or sandals with exposure of feet to the air when possible.
   - Wearing of rubber or wooden sandals in community shower or bathing places

2. Antifungal agents
   - Tolnaftate 1 percent solution (Tinactin) is gently massaged into lesions twice a day after washing and drying
   - Desenex or Tinactin powder is sprinkled on mild lesions twice a day or is used as a prophylactic measure

Other Common Skin Disorders

ACNE VULGARIS

Assessment Acne is the formation of comedones (blackheads and whiteheads) and pustules caused by the increased keratinization and plugging of the pilosebaceous follicles with sebum. Acne is found on the face, the chest, and the back, usually in adolescence and young adulthood.

ETIOLOGY Influences in the etiology of acne are the increased levels of free fatty acids that contribute to comedone and pustular formation, the increased levels of androgens in males and to a lesser extent in females, and the presence of *Propionibacterium acnes,* the bacterial causative agent.

INCIDENCE Acne occurs most often during adolescence because of increased sebum production and androgen levels. In 80 percent of cases the incidence and severity decline after 22 years of age (Hurwitz, 1979).

LESIONS The characteristic lesions of acne are:

* *Open comedone (blackhead):* This is composed of an epithelium-lined sac filled with sebum and keratin, which escapes to the surface.
* *Closed comedone (whitehead):* This contains sebum and keratin in an epitheal lined sac; because of the microscopic opening the contents cannot come to the surface and the follicle ruptures and expels sebum into the surrounding dermis.
* *Pustule (inflammatory acne):* It is formed by the inflammatory process in the dermis as a result of the rupture of the closed comedone.
* *Scarring.* This is caused by severe acne formation through burrowing of remnants of the sebaceous follicle into the dermis.

Management The management of acne emphasizes control rather than cure. Clients benefit from an interested, enthusiastic health professional and responsibility for carrying out their management program.

TOPICAL MEDICATIONS This treatment regimen may be just as effective as oral antibiotics for clients with mild to moderate acne (*Medical Letter,* 1980):

1. Tretenoin (Vitamin A acid, retinoic acid, Retin-A) is a comedolytic agent that is the most effective topical drug for noninflammatory and inflammatory acne. It is well tolerated by clients with sensitive skin. In the first few weeks of therapy, comedones become pustules followed by clearing of the skin. Apply 0.05 to 0.15 percent cream or 0.01 percent gel initially two or three times a day after washing. If this regimen is tolerated, it may be applied once daily. Side effects are erythema and increased reaction to sunburn. Sunscreens are recommended.
2. Benzyl peroxide is an oxidizing agent effective in inflammatory acne and causes desquamation of the skin. It turns over the stratum corneum of the follicular duct thus preventing the op-

portunity for accumulation of sebum that helps to form comedones. It is antibacterial against *Propionibacterium acnes.* Apply 5 to 10 percent lotions or gels to the face two to three times a day. For severe cases, use in combination with tretenoin.

3. Sulfur and/or salicylic acid-containing preparations are keratolytic agents that desquamate the skin, cause peeling and erythma but are less effective than tretenoin or benzyl peroxide.

4. Topical tetracycline is effective in mild acne, inhibiting the growth of *P. acnes* and decreasing the formation of comedones, papules and pustules. A side effect is yellow discoloration of the skin.

ANTIBIOTICS Broad-spectrum antibiotics are the most effective treatment for inflammatory acne. They inhibit the growth of *P. acnes* and reduce levels of free fatty acids. Side effects are nausea, diarrhea, cramps, and anemia, neutropenia and eosinophilia as rare complications, and a possible increase in bacterial and fungal infections. These antibiotics are listed below:

1. *Tetracycline.* Taken 1 hour before or after meals and at bedtime. The dosage is 250 mg. and therapy continues for three to six weeks.

2. *Erythromycin.* Taken with meals three or four times a day. The dosage is 250 mg. for two to six weeks. It is used when tetracycline is ineffective or contraindicated.

3. *Lincomycin and clindamycin.* These drugs have been used in the treatment of acne with moderate success.

ESTROGENS Oral female contraceptives reduce acne through suppression of sebum production. A therapeutic effect is not evident for three or more months.

DIET There is no convincing evidence that single or multiple dietary items contribute to acne (Frank, 1979).

COMEDONE REMOVAL This procedure is done professionally and under aseptic conditions. When comedones are removed the risk of future inflammatory reactions such as pustules is reduced.

COUNSELING Adolescents benefit from empathetic concern and professional advice concerning acne. Emphasis is placed on the maintenance of self esteem and a reminder that physical attributes are only one facet of a person. Maintaining regular habits of hygiene are discussed: daily and frequent bathing of oily skin areas with soap; adequate rest and good nutrition; and the reduction of stressful events. Adolescents are seen often: collaboratively with a physician for review of the medication regimen; and for education and support.

DANDRUFF

Assessment A form of seborrheic dermatitis, dandruff is a fine, flaky, slightly oily desquamation of the scalp which may spread to the forehead and eyebrows. True dandruff is seldom found in children before adolescence. Generally only a dry scalp with slight scaling is observed in young children.

Management Two or three shampoos a week using a commercial antiseborrheic shampoo are recommended. Shampoos containing tar are recommended for severe cases:

1. Shampoos containing sulfur and/or salicylic acid (Ionil, Meted, Sebaveen, Sebulex, Vanseb)
2. Shampoos containing antiseptic agents only (Head and Shoulders, Metasep, Zincon)
3. Shampoos containing tar (Ionil-T, Vanseb-T, Sebutone). Shampoo is left on the hair and scalp for 5 to 10 minutes before rinsing well.
4. Topical corticosteroids may be needed in severe cases.

FOLLICULITIS

Assessment Folliculitis is inflammation and abscess of hair follicules. The lesions consist of pinhead-size or slightly larger pustules surrounded by a narrow area of erythema. Many pustules are usually present in the same area. It is found usually on the scalp or the extremities. It may be mildly pruritic. It is frequently caused by *Staphylococcus aureus* and is most often secondary to intertrigo or chronic irritation of the skin.

Management Treatment consists of the following:

1. Warm compresses of saline, tap water, or Burow's solution several times a day

2. Topical application of Neosporin ointment
3. Systemic antibiotics for cases with fever and complicating cellulitis
4. Referral for recurrent folliculitis

FURUNCULOSIS (BOILS)

Assessment Furuncles are deep-seated infections of the sebaceous glands or hair follicles which gradually approach the surface and appear red, elevated, and painful. After several days the skin in the center becomes thin and a pustule may form. A "core" of necrotic material along with liquid purulent discharge is evident when the furuncle ruptures or is incised. Furuncles are most often seen on the neck, face, axillae, and buttocks. The fusion of several furuncles produces a carbuncle. Fever and general malaise may be present.

ETIOLOGY The cause of furunculosis is frequently *Staphylococcus aureus*. The disease is strongly familial. Bouts in children may continue to recur over several years; the reason is unknown.

COMPLICATIONS Complications of furunculosis are spread of the disease and recurrence.

Management Treatment consists of:

1. Soaking lesions for 1 hour, not less than four times daily, using warm tap water or saline compresses
2. Continuous compresses until boil comes to a point if spontaneous drainage or resolution does not occur
3. Incision and drainage when boils come to a point, followed by continuous moist compresses for several days
4. Systemic antibiotics for severe furunculosis

Treatment is continued for 7 to 10 days. Referral is made for recurrent furunculosis.

PEDICULOSIS CAPITIS (HEAD LICE)

Assessment This is louse infestation presenting with severe itching of the scalp, excoriation, secondary infection, and enlargement of occipital and cervical nodes. It is caused by head lice, which may appear as "nits" on the hair shaft. They appear as small, round, gray lumps, difficult to see in blonde hair. The area behind the ears and the back of the scalp should be examined closely.

Management The treatment of choice is Kwell shampoo (gamma benzene hexachloride 1 percent). Since gamma benzene hexachloride is concentrated in the central nervous system and central nervous system toxicity from systemic adsorption in infants has been reported, the following modification of gamma benzene hydrochloride is recommended for head lice. A shampoo preparation is left on the scalp 5 minutes and rinsed out thoroughly. The hair is then combed with a fine-toothed comb to remove nits (Silver et al., 1980, p. 198). Treatments are repeated in 24 hours and hair is rechecked for nits. Nits are removed by soaking hair in diluted vinegar (vinegar and water 1 : 1) and combing with fine tooth comb daily. Hats, combs, and hair brushes are thoroughly cleaned. Family members must be examined and treated. A pediculicide alternative is A-200 Pyrinate.

PEDICULOSIS CORPORIS (BODY LICE)

Assessment This louse infestation, which presents with intense itching, multiple scratch marks, and excoriation of the skin, is very rare. Close examination reveals hemorrhage points (small, red puncta) where lice have extracted blood. It may be complicated by urticaria or superficial bacterial infection. Lesions are most common on the upper back, sides of the trunk, and the upper, outer arms. The insects live in the folds of clothing.

Management Treatment is as follows:

1. Gamma benzene hexachloride 1 percent (Kwell) cream or lotion is applied to the entire body for 4 hours following a hot, soapy bath or shower. See treatment above. Skin is dried before application. Freshly laundered or dry-cleaned clothing is worn. The medication remains on for 12 to 24 hours and the treatment is repeated.
2. Clothing is thoroughly washed or dry-cleaned.
3. Bed linen and toilets are scrupulously cleaned.
4. Family members are treated as necessary.

5. Scratch dermatitis can be relieved with oral or intramuscular corticosteroids.
6. Topical antibiotic ointment, Bacitracin, can be used for secondary infections.
7. Treatment may be repeated in 4 days if necessary.

PEDICULOSIS PUBIS ("CRABS")

Assessment   This is louse infestation which presents with intense itching of pubic and rectal areas, resulting in excoriation and secondary dermatitis. Small bluish marks may appear on skin of the trunk, the eyebrows, lashes, and axillary area. Origin of the infection is usually venereal. "Crabs" are extremely rare in children.

Management   The treatment of "crabs" is essentially the same as that for body lice. See this chapter, Pediculosis Corporis.

POISON IVY, POISON OAK, POISON SUMAC

Assessment   A contact dermatitis, the lesions can be multiple vesicles, papules, and bullae on an erythematous base, accompanied by intense itching and burning. Lesions appear in linear streaks. Severe, systemic attacks present with swelling and burning pain.

ETIOLOGY   Poison oak, ivy, and sumac dermatitis are caused by an allergen, the oleoresin which is present in the leaves, stems, and roots of the vines. It can result from contact with smoke or burning leaves, contaminated clothes, tools, or the fur of a cat or dog.

CLINICAL PICTURE   Lesions usually appear on exposed areas of skin, face, and extremities but may be found elsewhere. They appear from several hours to a few days after contact and last from 2 to 4 weeks. The severity of the dermatitis depends on the amount of sap that gets on the skin and on the degree of sensitivity of the person. It is not spread from one part of the skin to another by scratching, or from one person to another by skin-to-skin contact, or by contamination by the blister fluid.

Management   Treatment consists of relieving the pruritus and removing oils from the skin as quickly as possible by bathing with mild soap and lots of water. Strong "yellow" soaps are not beneficial and may be irritating to the skin. Some methods used to relieve itching are as follows:

1. Applications of cool, wet compresses (1 tablet or package of Domeboro to 1 pint of water).
2. Application of menthol- or phenol-containing lotion such as Calamine lotion. Use of preparations containing the "caine" anesthetic are not recommended due to possible sensitivity reaction. Caladryl, which contains Benadryl, an antihistamine, is not recommended.
3. Cool baths using starch colloidal preparation (1 cup of Linit starch to tub of water) or oatmeal baths such as Aveeno. See Chapter 26, Pharmacologic Therapy, Baths.
4. Cleansing and opening of large blisters.

REFERRAL For severe attacks immediate referral to a physician, preferably a dermatologist, is recommended. Oral or parenteral hydrocortisone or prednisone in sufficient amounts to afford relief of symptoms may be indicated.

PREVENTION Preventive measures include the following:

1. Avoidance of offending plants
2. Learning to identify offending plants
3. Destruction of plants by chemical means when possible
4. Wearing rubber gloves when handling exposed clothing or tools
5. Decontamination of clothes, tools

Desensitization "shots" or antipoison pills have not proven to be effective and are not recommended.

SUNBURN

Assessment The stages of sunburn are described as follows:

1. Mild or first-degree type sunburn consists of erythema, tenderness, and mild pain of sun-exposed areas.
2. More severe sunburn progresses with more redness, pain, swelling, and blisters.
3. Very severe sunburn includes extensive areas of sunburn, inability to tolerate contact with clothing or sheets, and constitutional symptoms of nausea, tachycardia, chills, and fever.

This history is usually adequate to explain the clinical picture. Factors which predispose to sun sensitivity, such as drug administration or systemic illnesses, need to be ruled out.

COMPLICATIONS Sunburn may include several complications:

1. Fluid and electrolyte loss
2. Systemic toxicity
3. Infection of ruptured bullae
4. Heat exhaustion

Management A very severely sunburned child should be referred immediately to a physician or to a hospital clinic for supervision of possible complications.

TREATMENT Mild to severe sunburn is treated as follows:

1. Cold water or saline solution compresses are applied for 20 minutes, three to four times daily or more frequently as needed.
2. Low-strength corticosteroid cream or ointment (Synalar, Kenalog, or Aristocort) are used to reduce inflammation and pain.
3. Skin emollients, such as Alpha-Keri, Domol, Lubriderm, or Nivea, may be used for dry skin.
4. Blisters may be opened after careful cleansing of the skin.
5. Local anesthetic sprays that are effective are Americaine, Burn Tame, Tega Caine, although these carry the risks of sensitization.
6. Aspirin or acetaminophen in dosage appropriate to age may be given every 4 hours for pain.

PREVENTION Skin is exposed to ultraviolet rays whether sunny or overcast. Limited and gradual exposure allows the skin to build up protection naturally by moving melanin (which absorbs ultraviolet light and makes one look tan) up to the surface. Black skin, with greater supply of melanin, is best equipped to withstand ultraviolet radiation, followed by brunettes, redheads, blondes, and nontanners who suffer from radiation soonest.

Infancy The following measures are used to prevent overexposure to the sun in infancy:

1. Attention is given to the color of hair and skin of the child.

2. Infants may sun out-of-doors or indoors near an opened window. Active rays will not penetrate through window glass.
3. Infants should be kept out of the sun when ultraviolet rays are strongest, generally 11 AM to 3 PM.
4. Infants should be positioned with their eyes away from the sun.
5. Exposure to the sun may begin at 2 weeks of age for a few minutes daily and increased until 10 to 15 minutes daily is reached. The child is observed for overexposure or overheating.
6. Hats or sunbonnets should be used if an infant must be exposed for a long period of time. Sunscreens may be used to help protect the skin from ultraviolet rays.

Young Children   Young children should be protected from over-exposure to the sun while playing out-of-doors. The color of the child's skin should be considered, hats and clothing should be used for protection, and sun screens may be used.

Sun Screens   These are recommended to protect the skin from overexposure to the ultraviolet rays. The effective agent which prevents burning is para-aminobenzoic acid (PABA). Lotions and creams used for sun-screening purposes should contain PABA. Some of these products are listed below:

1. Pre-sun and Pabanol protect against short-wavelength ultra-violet rays. Light tanning is possible.
2. Uval and Solbar protect against short-wavelength ultraviolet rays and partially against longer waves. Moisturizing lotions may be applied 10 to 15 minutes following the application of sun-screens since many lotions contain alcohol and tend to be drying to the skin.
3. Zinc oxide ointment is a sun block, effectively preventing the ultraviolet rays from reaching the skin.

VERRUCAE (WARTS)

Assessment   Verrucae are sharply circumscribed and raised clusters of tiny papillomas, greyish in color, and sometimes crusty. They are seen on any part of the body; however, they are more commonly found on hands, and fingers, or sometimes on the ball of the foot (plantar warts). Clinical diagnosis is aided under the following conditions:

1. Normal "fingerprint" lines of skin are disturbed or obliterated by the lesion.
2. Small black dots are seen throughout the lesion; these are the thrombosed blood supply of the wart lesion.

Verrucae are caused by a virus and are benign. They occur in 10 percent of children and young adults and have a tendency to recur. Often there is a spontaneous remission, although this may take years.

Management If the verrucae are small, they do not need treatment. Referral is made in the following instances:

1. If danger signs of itching, bleeding, or changes in size or color are apparent.
2. If treatment by acid, cryotherapy, or excision is indicated.

Autoinoculation is many times more common than is infection of another person. No special isolation or protection procedures are necessary.

References

Alexander, M. M. and M. S. Brown. *Pediatric History Taking and Physical Diagnosis for Nurses.* New York: McGraw-Hill, 1979.

Arndt, K. A. *Manual of Dermatologic Therapeutics,* 2nd ed. Boston: Little, Brown, 1978.

Barness, L. A. *Pediatric Physical Diagnosis,* 4th ed. Chicago: Yearbook Medical Publishers, 1972.

Dixon, P. N. "Role of *Candida albicans* Infection in Napkin Rashes." *Br Med J* 2:23–27, April 1969.

Feingold, B. F. *Introduction to Clinical Allergy.* Springfield, IL: Charles C. Thomas, 1973.

Frank, S. *Acne Update for the Practitioner.* New York: York Medical Books, 1979.

Gellis, S. S. and B. M. Kagan. *Current Pediatric Therapy.* Philadelphia: Saunders, 1980.

Graef, J. W. and T. E. Cone. *Manual of Pediatric Therapeutics,* 2nd ed. Boston: Little, Brown, 1980.

Hurwitz, S. "Acne Vulgaris." *Am J Dis Child 133*:536, May 1979.

Jacobs, A. "Eruptions in the Diaper Area." *Pediatr Clin North Am 25*:209–224, May 1978.

Jacobs, P. "Fungal Infections in Childhood." *Pediatr Clin North Am* 25:357–370, May 1978.

Kempe, C. H., H. K. Silver, and D. O'Brien. *Current Pediatric Diagnosis and Treatment*, 6th ed. Los Altos, CA: Lange Medical Publications, 1980.

Livesey, R. P. "The Contribution of Diaper Service Accreditation to Infant Health Care." *Clin Pediatr* 11:541–543, September 1972.

Medical Letter, "Drugs for Acne." *22*:31, April 4, 1980.

Moschella, S. L., et al. *Dermatology*. Vol. 1. Philadelphia: W.B. Saunders, 1975.

Orkin, M. and H. Maibach, "Scabies in Children." *Pediatr Clin North Am* 25:371–385, May 1978.

Physician's Desk Reference for Nonprescription Drugs, 1st ed. Oradell, NJ: Lytton Industries Inc., 1980.

Rasmussen, J. E. "A New Look at Old Acne." *Pediatr Clin North Am* 25:285–302, May 1978.

Rudolph, A., editor. *Pediatrics*, 17th ed. East Norwalk, CT: Appleton-Century-Crofts, 1982.

Solomon, L. M., L. Fahrner, and D. West. "Gamma Benzenehydrochloride Toxicity." *Arch Dermatol* 113:353–357, March 1977.

Vaughan, V. C., et al., editors. *Nelson Textbook of Pediatrics*. 11th ed. Philadelphia: W.B. Saunders, 1979.

15

The Eye

The evaluation of vision and the detection of eye disorders are integral components of every health supervision visit. The absence of vision has a devastating effect on a person's life, and the impairment of vision causes continuous readjustments in life routines. The role of the nurse practitioner in the assessment and management of eye problems is severalfold:

- To evaluate visual acuity for refractive errors
- To detect the presence of amblyopia
- To evaluate with medical consultation the presence of organic eye disease
- To refer to the ophthalmologist those conditions that require further evaluation and management

ASSESSMENT

Ophthalmic Development

Approximately 75 to 80 percent of infants at birth are hyperopic (farsighted) (Kempe et al, 1982, p. 202). Normal vision of 20/20 is achieved at 4 to 5 years of age.

Newborns exhibit random eye movements because of immature retinal development and inability to fixate centrally (Ziai, 1975, p. 709). These movements disappear by 3 months of age. Binocular vision begins to develop between 4 and 6 months of age and becomes firmly established during the second 6 months of life (Kempe et al., 1982, p. 202).

A pupillary reaction to a light stimulus is evidence of a functioning retina and optic nerve, but does not rule out cortical blindness.

Tearing in infants is usually due to lacrimal duct obstruction until 3 to 4 months of age.

See Table 15-1 for chronology of ophthalmic development.

History

In the newborn, common eye problems include those related to birth injuries, anatomic asymmetries, lacrimal duct obstruction, and conjunctivitis. In assessing these conditions, questions include description of symptoms, length of time present, frequency, discharge, tearing of eyes, increased blinking, fever, other symptoms of illness; past history of eye disorders, treatment measures, and recent eye medications. In assessing visual disturbances, questions include the following:

1. *In infancy:* specific concerns of the parents, presence of nystagmus, inability to fixate and to follow a bright object momentarily, and presence of a history of cross eyes
2. *In toddlers:* presence of cross eyes, inability to ambulate without bumping into objects, frequent blinking, rubbing, squinting, and holding objects near to eyes
3. *In school-age children:* headaches, eye pain, double vision, and blurred words with reading, blinking, rubbing eyes, or squinting, when reading or for distant vision, and cross eyes

In assessing organic eye disease questions include presence of nystagmus, inability to fixate on objects, cross eyes, white pupil, and bulging eye orbit.

Physical Examination

Each eye is always assessed separately to rule out defective vision in one eye that might not be apparent when both eyes are examined

Table 15-1
Chronology of Ophthalmic Development

Age	Level of Development
Birth	Awareness of light and dark; the infant closes his eyelids in bright light
Neonatal	Rudimentary fixation on near objects (3–30 inches)
2 weeks	Transitory fixation, usually monocular at a distance of roughly 3 feet
4 weeks	Follows large conspicuously moving objects
6 weeks	Moving objects evoke binocular fixation briefly
8 weeks	Follows moving objects with jerky eye movements; convergence is beginning to appear
12 weeks	Visual following now a combination of head and eye movements; convergence is improving; enjoys light objects and bright colors
16 weeks	Inspects own hands; fixates immediately on a 1-inch cube brought within 1–2 feet of eye; vision 20/300–20/200 (6/100–6/70)
20 weeks	Accommodative convergence reflexes all organizing; visually pursues lost rattle; shows interest in stimuli more than 3 feet away
24 weeks	Retrieves a dropped 1-inch cube; can maintain voluntary fixation of stationary object even in the presence of competing moving stimulus; hand-eye coordination is appearing
26 weeks	Will fixate on a string
28 weeks	Binocular fixation clearly established
36 weeks	Depth perception is dawning
40 weeks	Marked interest in tiny objects; tilts head backward to gaze up; vision 20/200 (6/70)
52 weeks	Fusion beginning to appear; discriminates simple geometric forms, squares and circles; vision 20/180 (6/60)
12–18 months	Looks at pictures with interest
18 months	Convergence well established; localization in distance crude–runs into objects which he sees
2 years	Accommodation well developed; vision 20/40 (6/12)
3 years	Convergence smooth; fusion improving; vision 20/30 (6/9)
4 years	Vision 20/20 (6/6)

Source: Reproduced with permission from C. H. Kempe, H. K. Silver, and D. O'Brien, editors, *Current Pediatric Diagnosis and Treatment*, 4th ed., (Los Altos, Calif.: Lange), 1976.

together. A condition called suppression amblyopia develops when a child uses one eye consistently because of conditions such as strabismus or refractive errors. The unused or idle eye develops decreased vision because the brain blots out the interfering double image it is receiving in the poor eye. See this chapter, Strabismus.

EXTERNAL EXAMINATION

Lids Inspect for ptosis, asymmetry, ability to close, presence of sties (hordeolum/s), tearing, ectropian (rolling out of lids), entropian (rolling in of lids), and epicanthal folds (vertical folds of skin covering the inner canthus).

Eyelashes Inspect for presence of discharge, inflammation, and lice.

Eyeball Examine for size, color, prominence, inflammation, and discharge. A sunken eye orbit is an indication of a severely dehydrated or malnourished child.

Conjunctiva Examine palpebral portion (lines upper and lower eye lids) for inflammation, erythema, edema, and discharge. Bulbar portion (lies over the sclera): examine for erythema and secretions. Cover-uncover and Hirschberg's tests for strabismus. See this chapter, Strabismus.

Ocular Muscles Examine movement by having the child's eyes follow a bright object in four quadrants of vision: upper, lower, inner, outer.

Cornea Examine for clouding, enlargement, ulceration, irritation, and injury.

Sclera Examine for white color. At birth, the sclera is relatively thin and the underlying uvea imparts the blue tone.

Iris Examine for color and shape. Heterochromia (irises of different colors, bilaterally), can be normal or can be associated with specific syndromes or low-grade infections.

Pupil Examine for size. Anisocoria (difference in pupil size) can be normal, or it can be associated with CNS disease, and if found on examination, should always be referred. Examine for color and constriction to light. A white pupillary reflex can indicate retinoblastoma, cataract, detachment of the retina, and abscess in the vitreous humor. Examine for involuntary movements such as nystagmus. See this chapter, Common Clinical Problems.

Lens Examine for cataracts. They can be detected by shining a light into the eye from an angle or by using an ophthalmoscope. If a cataract is present, the reflex will be white instead of red.

FUNDUSCOPIC EXAMINATION

The fundus, the posterior, inner portion of the retina is examined with an ophthalmoscope. The examination is extremely difficult to perform on infants and can only be adequately done with pupillary dilation. Funduscopic examination of the newborn is not routinely done unless there is a specific indication such as congenital nystagmus, impaired vision, or ocular disease.

Funduscopic examination is performed on all children old enough to cooperate by holding their eyes on a distant object. The optic discs are normally round or slightly oval, the margins are normally sharp, and the color is usually creamy pink. Darker pigmentation exists in black races. In papilledema, a symptom of increased intracranial pressure, the discs are swollen and red in color. The physiologic depression is in the center of the optic disc and the optic nerve emanates from this area. The macula is a small circular area in the disc which contains the fovea centralis, the area of the most accurate acuity. The blood vessels in the fundus are the arteries and veins. The veins are slightly wider than the arteries and show a pulsation.

For examination the room is dark. The nurse practitioner looks into the child's right eye with his or her own right eye. The reverse is true for the left eye. The dial on the ophthalmoscope is at $+8$ at the beginning of the examination. The red reflex is obtained and opacities on the lens are noted. The dial is turned to the smaller plus numbers while the nurse practitioner comes closer to the child's eye.

Screening for Visual Acuity

The nurse practitioner assesses the eyes for presence of organic eye disease, amblyopia, and refractive errors. It is difficult to perform vision screening for refractive errors on children before the age of 3 years because of their inability to cooperate with instructions. In all visual screening it is imperative that each eye be tested separately to rule out amblyopia.

VISUAL ACUITY

Screening for visual acuity is done through the use of the Snellen illiterate "E" chart or the alphabet chart.

PROCEDURE FOR SNELLEN EYE CHART SCREENING

Snellen eye chart screening usually cannot be done until the child is 3 to 4 years of age because of the child's inability to understand instructions and their general impatience. If visual screening cannot be done adequately at 4 years of age, the parent is instructed to practice the procedure at home, teaching the child to point the fingers in the direction of the "E" on the chart. The visual acuity is then assessed in two months.

The child wears glasses if they have been prescribed. If the child wears glasses but does not have them at the time of the visit, screening is done at a later date. If glasses are prescribed and are worn infrequently, screening is done, and a note is written on the chart explaining why the glasses are not worn. The child keeps both eyes open and does not press the cover card against the covered eye. Each eye is tested individually.

Ideally one symbol or one line is exposed at a time. The child is instructed to read from left to right. If the child misses a symbol on a line, the line is repeated having the child read from right to left. If the examiner is using the Snellen "E" chart, the child is asked to show with the fingers which way the legs of the "E" are pointing. The child is asked to read all the lines including the 20 foot line. The last line on which the child can read three out of four symbols or four out of six symbols is recorded. During the screening the child is observed for blinking, squinting, rubbing, and complaints of eyes hurting.

In testing young children between 3 and 5 years of age, describe the screening procedure as a game. Have a practice session first to explain the procedure. In order to assure maximum cooperation of the child, two people are needed, one to stand at the chart and point to the letters or pictures and one to stand by the child to verbally encourage responses.

Visual acuity is recorded as a fraction. The top number is the distance the child stands from the chart. The bottom number is the last line read correctly.

INDICATIONS FOR REFERRAL

If the first screening is unsatisfactory or the visual acuity is 40 or worse, the child is screened at a later date. If the second screening shows continued poor visual acuity, the child is referred to an ophthalmologist. Generally, all children who cannot see half the letters or worse on the 20/40 line are referred to an ophthalmologist. Children who screen 20/30 and complain of eyestrain, headaches, and eye pain are also referred. Children wearing glasses should be seen for yearly eye examinations.

MANAGEMENT

General Eye Care

There are no specific routines for eye care except wiping away any mucoid discharge with a moist cotton ball when it is apparent in the inner canthus. This commonly occurs during the newborn period. Occasionally, during this period, an eyelash is seen on the cornea. It is removed by the natural bathing mechanism of the lacrimal duct. It is unwise to instill any drops or ointments in the eyes unless prescribed by a physician.

Counseling

The nurse practitioner discusses with parents symptoms of possible eye disorders.

OBSERVATIONS FOR DEVIATIONS

The frequency and duration of differences in the range of gaze such as inward or outward turning of the eyes are noted by the parents. Symptoms of conjunctivitis are discussed, including discharge, erythema, and tearing. Tearing without crying is a symptom of lacrimal duct obstruction. Parents also observe for anatomic differences between the eyes. Consult the primary care provider if deviations occur.

SYMPTOMS OF POOR VISUAL ACUITY

In older children complaints of headache and painful eyes indicate a strain on ciliary muscles used in accommodation. Blurred vision for near and far objects, rubbing, squinting, and frequent blinking are also symptoms of inadequate vision.

Medications

For adequate visualization of the inner eye during diagnostic procedures, pupillary dilation is required.

MYDRIATICS

These medications dilate the pupil without paralyzing the ciliary muscle of accommodation. They are used in refraction and in general ophthalmoscopic examinations, especially in infants. They are contraindicated in clients with glaucoma and hypertension because of the side effects of increased intraocular pressure. Pupillary dilation causes photophobia and blurring of near objects. The maximal duration of effect is up to 1 hour and the recovery time depending on the strength of the solution is 3 to 6 hours.

Common mydriatics are phenylephrine (Neo-Synephrine), 1 to 2 percent, ephedrine (0.1 percent), and hydroxamphetamine, 1 percent.

CYCLOPLEGICS

These medications dilate the pupil (mydriasis) and produce paralysis of accommodation (cycloplegia). They are used in refraction and in the treatment of acute inflammations of the iris and ciliary body. Toxic reactions occur and can be fatal especially in children with mongolism and brain damage.

Common cycloplegics are atropine sulfate, 0.25 to 2 percent, scopolamine hydrobromide, 0.2 percent, and cyclogyl, 1 percent.

TOPICAL ANTIBIOTICS

Topical antibiotics are used in response to a specific causative organism whose sensitivity has been established. When possible, antibiotics are used that are seldom employed systemically to decrease the risk of hypersensitivity reactions. Broad-spectrum antibiotics and the sulfa drugs seldom produce sensitivity.

Some common agents are bacitracin (Baciquent), erythromycin (Ilotycin), and sulfacetamide sodium.

TOPICAL CORTICOSTEROIDS

Topical corticosteroids are effective in treating allergic blepharitis, conjunctivitis, contact dermatitis of the eyelids, interstitial keratitis, and iritis. However, there are complications from short- and long-term corticosteroid usage: decreased healing of corneal abrasions, aggravation of herpes simplex keratitis, glaucoma, and possible cataract formation. Prolonged use of topical steroids necessitates management by an ophthalmologist.

Weak steroid preparations include medrysone, 1 percent, hydrocortisone, 0.5 to 1.5 percent, and prednisolone, 0.125 percent. Strong preparations include dexamethasone, 0.1 percent, prednisolone, 1 percent, and triamcinolone, 0.1 percent.

SOLUTIONS AND OINTMENTS

The advantages of ointments are that they remain in the eye with tearing, are comfortable with initial instillation, have less absorption into lacrimal passages, and are used less frequently since contact time is much longer. The disadvantage is that they interfere with vision by producing a film over the eye.

The advantages of solution are that they do not interfere with vision, and they cause fewer allergic reactions. A disadvantage is that they must be instilled at frequent intervals because they are washed away easily with tearing.

INSTILLATION OF MEDICATIONS

To instill medications in the eye during infancy, two people are needed. One person leans over the infant securing the legs, trunk, and arms with the body and holds the head straight with the hands. The second person retracts the lids with the fingers of one hand and drops the medication into the palpebral conjunctiva with the other hand.

COMMON CLINICAL PROBLEMS

Amblyopia

See this chapter, Strabismus.

Blepharitis

ASSESSMENT

Blepharitis is a chronic inflammation of the margins of the eyelids. The common types are: seborrheic (nonulcerative) and staphylococcal (ulcerative). Symptoms of seborrheic blepharitis are oily, easily removed scales at the lid margins. This condition is often associated with dandruff of the scalp. In staphylococcal blepharitis, the scales are dry and hard to remove with occasional ulcers and pustules. In both conditions there is edema, erythema, crusting, and irritation of the lid margins.

MANAGEMENT

For seborrheic blepharitis, dandruff is controlled and if inflammation is present a sulfonamide medication is prescribed. For staphylococcal blepharitis, antibiotic, sulfonamide medication, or a steroid combination topical ointment is prescribed.

Counseling   The parents observe for increased symptoms of infection. Instillation of eye medication is reviewed.

Chalazion

ASSESSMENT

Chalazion is a chronic granulomatous inflammation of the tarsal gland which is a modified sebaceous gland located between the skin and the conjunctiva of the upper lid. The cause is not known. Symptoms are slight tenderness, erythema, and a swelling on the conjunctival surface of the lid.

MANAGEMENT

Occasionally the lesion may reabsorb spontaneously after application of warm compresses. Local excision is sometimes necessary.

Counseling The parents are instructed to apply warm compresses to the lid four times a day. Symptoms of infection are reviewed.

Color Blindness

ASSESSMENT

Etiology Color blindness is an X-linked recessive trait. Females are carriers because they have one normal and one defective gene for color vision. Since the male Y chromosome carries no gene for color discrimination, the single gene the female contributes, if it is defective, will cause color blindness. Therefore, half of the female's sons on the average will be color blind. (See Chapter 29, Genetics.)

Incidence Approximately 7.5 percent of white males, 4 percent of black males, and only 0.5 percent of all females are color blind.

Classifications There are three inherited types of color blindness:

- Protan: affects red, blue, green color sensitivity
- Deutan: affects green, purple color sensitivity
- Tritan: affects yellow, blue color sensitivity. It is extremely rare.

Screening This is done by having the child name several colors. If speech development is normal and the child cannot accurately name colors, screening is done with pseudoisochromatic tests which have children trace lines or numbers on colorful backgrounds.

MANAGEMENT

There is no treatment for color blindness. However, it is important to make parents, teachers, relatives, and peers aware that the child's perception of color is not the same as others' with accurate color discrimination. Affected individuals have problems with matching clothing colors, particularly light shades.

Counseling The nurse practitioner discusses with the family the results of the color vision screening. Individuals who are protan types may not see the red brake lights of cars. They confuse red, brown, and black colors. Deutan types may not be able to distinguish green traffic lights from street lamps. They confuse green, brown, and purple colors.

Conjunctivitis

ASSESSMENT

Conjunctivitis is an inflammation and infection of the conjunctiva producing erythema, mucoid, or mucopurulent discharge, tearing, itching, and irritation. The discharge occasionally results in caking and sticking together of the lids. Conjunctivitis is classified according to the causative agent or the age at which it occurs.

MANAGEMENT

A search for the causative agent is undertaken through smears and conjunctival scrapings for culture. The child is placed on broad-spectrum antibiotics or sulfonamides while awaiting the results of the culture. If the causative agent is not readily identified, the medications are continued until the discharge is gone to decrease the incidence of secondary infection. Topical medications such as drops are given as frequently as every 2 hours. The usual frequency for ointments is every 4 hours. In young children eye ointment is easier to apply, and there is less chance of overdosage. Older children tolerate drops during the day, since it does not interfere with vision.

Role of the Nurse Practitioner   It is of primary importance to assess the degree of infection and to obtain cultures. Health education is provided to the parents as to the etiology, methods of contagion, and the treatment regimen. The correct procedure for instilling topical ophthalmic medications is reviewed. See this chapter, Instillation of Medications.

NEISSERIA GONORRHOEAE CONJUNCTIVITIS

Assessment   This condition is a rarity in the United States because prophylactic AgNO$_3$ drops or antibiotics are placed in the eyes of all newborns. However, if it occurs, it requires prompt diagnosis and treatment, since untreated it can cause corneal ulceration, panophthalmitis (inflammation of all eye structures), and occasionally septicemia. Symptoms are copious, purulent discharge, edema of the lids, and intense erythema. Diagnosis is by smear which shows gram-negative intracellular diplococci and a positive culture for *Neisseria gonorrhoeae*.

Management   Topical antibiotics are given every 1 to 2 hours. Systemic antibiotics are given four times a day for 5 days. The conjunctival sac is irrigated with saline solution and cycloplegics are used in cases where there is corneal involvement.

CHEMICAL CONJUNCTIVITIS

Assessment   This condition is caused by AgNO$_3$ drops, and it is the most common type of ophthalmia neonatorum. Symptoms are erythema, chemosis (edema of the conjunctiva), and a mucoid discharge. It is a sterile inflammation which occurs during the first 24 to 48 hours after birth and clears spontaneously in 3 to 4 days.

Management   There is none except to wipe away discharge from the eye with moist cotton.

ADENOVIRUS CONJUNCTIVITIS

Assessment   This condition is occasionally associated with pharyngitis and preauricular adenopathy. Symptoms are erythema and chemosis of the conjunctiva, mucoid discharge, and enlargement of lymphoid follicles on the lower palpebral conjunctiva. In the newborn, viral conjunctivitis occurs 5 to 10 days after birth.

Management Topical antibiotics or sulfonamides are used to prevent secondary infection but have no other therapeutic value.

CHLAMYDIA CONJUNCTIVITIS

Assessment This condition is caused by the bacterium *Chlamydia trachomatis*. Symptoms are diffuse erythema and edema of the lids with thin, watery discharge. Scarring of the conjunctiva later develops with corneal vascularization and opacification. Conjunctival scrapings are stained with Giemsa solution and show typical cytoplasmic inclusion bodies in epithelial cells. In older children, the conjunctivitis is characterized by early enlargement of the lymphoid follicles of the lower palpebral conjunctiva. The acute phase may last for several weeks and if not treated may progress to a chronic keratoconjunctivitis.

Management Topical sulfonamide or erythromycin is used until one day after inflammation and discharge subsides. The infant is also treated with oral erythromycin to prevent pneumonitis, a possible sequela after chlamydia conjunctivitis. Parents are also treated with oral tetracycline or erythromycin for 7 days to decrease complications of chlamydia cervicitis or salpingitis in females and epididymitis in males (Rowe et al., 1979).

HERPES SIMPLEX CONJUNCTIVITIS

Assessment This viral conjunctivitis can affect the eye with or without accompanying generalized herpes infection. Symptoms are discharge, keratitis (inflammation of the cornea), and chorioretinitis (inflammation of the choroid and retina). Diagnosis of herpes keratitis is confirmed by observing "Chinese characters" on the corneal surface after staining with fluorescein. An ophthalmologist is consulted if there is involvement of the eye structures other than the conjunctiva.

Management Idoxuridine (IDU) is applied topically when there is corneal involvement. Adenosine arabinoside (Ara-A), an antiviral topical medication, is used in cases of IDU-resistant herpes ocular infections.

BACTERIAL CONJUNCTIVITIS

Assessment The most common causative agents are *Staphylococcus aureus*, hemolytic *Streptococcus, Neisseria gonorrhoeae, Koch-Weeks bacillus, Pneumococcus,* and *Hemophilus influenzae.* Symptoms are copious, purulent discharge, which accumulates on lashes causing them to stick together, and erythema of the bulbar and palpebral conjunctiva. Other names used to denote bacterial conjunctivitis are pinkeye and acute catarrhal conjunctivitis. In the newborn, bacterial conjunctivitis occurs 2 to 5 days after birth.

Management Culture and sensitivity studies are obtained and the appropriate antibiotics are prescribed.

ALLERGIC CONJUNCTIVITIS

See Chapter 26, Allergies.

Dacryocystitis

ASSESSMENT

Dacryocystitis is secondary to dacryostenosis and occurs because of the accumulation of mucus and tears in the lacrimal sac with resulting bacterial infection. Symptoms are excessive tearing without crying, and purulent discharge.

MANAGEMENT

Lacrimal sac massage is instituted and topical antibiotics are applied after cultures are taken. Severe infection of the lacrimal sac is treated with systemic antibiotics. After treatment, probing of the lacrimal duct is occasionally necessary to open it.

Counseling The technique of massage and the application of topical antibiotics is demonstrated to the parents. See the following section, Dacryostenosis.

Dacryostenosis

ASSESSMENT

Dacryostenosis or lacrimal duct obstruction occurs in the newborn period and during infancy. Symptoms are chronic tearing (epiphora) and a mucoid discharge from the lacrimal puncta near the inner canthus.

MANAGEMENT

To remove accumulated tears and mucus from the duct, massage with firm pressure is instituted along the side of the nose toward the eye, four times a day. If tearing or mucoid discharge persists after 6 months of age, the infant is referred to an ophthalmologist for probing to open the lacrimal duct.

Counseling   Parents are shown the technique of massage and are instructed to observe for symptoms of infection. Massage is done three to four times a day.

Emergencies

A pediatrician assesses and manages eye emergencies such as corneal abrasions and nonpenetrating foreign objects. All other emergencies are referred to an ophthalmologist. The role of the nurse practitioner in eye emergencies is to offer accurate information to parents when they call in reference to first aid measures such as washing eye with water, if appropriate, or covering eye, and to make referrals to the appropriate individuals.

CORNEAL ABRASIONS

Assessment   With any irritation or denudement of the corneal surface an abrasion occurs. Fluorescein strips are used to detect the extent of the abrasion, and they stain epithelial defects light green.

Management   Cycloplegic drops are used to maintain pupillary dilation and to rest the eye. Antibiotic ointment is applied, and the eye is patched for 24 to 48 hours or until the epithelium is healed.

CONJUNCTIVAL FOREIGN BODY

Assessment The most common site is the furrow immediately behind the margin of the upper lid.

Management The usual method of removal is to evert the upper lid and with a moist cotton tip applicator lift out the foreign body.

INJURIES

Fracture of the Eye Orbit Symptoms are bone tenderness and displacement of the globe. Examination of extraocular movements will facilitate the diagnosis, especially if the eye is unable to gaze upward. Eye X-rays and ophthalmologist referral are indicated.

Chemical Burns of the Cornea and Conjunctiva The eye is irrigated with saline or boric acid solution. Occasionally a topical anesthetic is instilled into the eyes to relieve blepharospasm before the irrigation is started. After irrigation the eye is inspected for obvious injury. Antibiotic ointment is instilled and the eye is re-examined in 24 hours.

Thermal Burns of the Cornea This condition is usually caused by a cigarette. The burn becomes a white eschar on the corneal surface. Treatment consists of topical anesthetic application, removal of the eschar with a cotton tip applicator, and the application of antibiotic ointment to the eye.

Hordeolum (Sty)

ASSESSMENT

External hordeolum is an abscess of the sebaceous gland of the eyelash follicle at the lid margin. It is caused by *Staphylococcus aureus*. Symptoms are erythema, edema, and tenderness. Occasionally the abscess ruptures spontaneously.

Internal hordeolum is an abscess of the meibomian glands, which are sebaceous glands located in the upper eyelids.

MANAGEMENT

Warm compresses three to four times a day are prescribed for both types of hordeolum. Occasionally antibiotic or sulfonamide ophthalmic medication is used during the acute stage. If spontaneous rupture does not occur, the sty is incised when it is large and edematous.

Counseling Application of warm compresses is discussed with parents as the most important part of the treatment. Application of eye medication is demonstrated (see this chapter, Instillation of Medication). Washing hands after contamination to prevent recurrence is emphasized.

NYSTAGMUS

ASSESSMENT

Nystagmus is an involuntary movement of the iris and pupil. Intermittent periods of nystagmus in an infant up to 3 months of age are normal. Continuous nystagmus before 3 months of age and nystagmus in older infants and in children is abnormal and is referred for further evaluation.

Types of Movements The following are the most common movements:

- Horizontal, vertical, rotatory, or mixed
- Jerky (rhythmical), slow drifting movement in one direction followed by a quick corrective movement in the opposite direction
- Pendular, to and fro movements equal in each direction with jerking movements when the eyes are moved to the side

Etiologies Most often the etiologies are associated with defective vision.

- Congenital nystagmus exhibits movements, which may be in all directions of gaze. The condition is present at birth, but is not commonly detected before 2 to 3 months of age, and may indicate organic eye disease.

• Neurologic nystagmus exhibits jerky, horizontal, or rotatory movements. They are secondary to lesions in the vestibular apparatus, the cerebellum, or the brainstem.

• Ocular nystagmus exhibits pendular movements, which prevent the development of normal fixations. Causes include albinism, congenital anomalies of the optic nerve, total color blindness, and congenital opacities of the cornea or lens.

Opticokinetic Nystagmus These movements indicate functioning neural receptors in the retina and intact neural pathways and are a normal finding in infants. They are produced by having the infant fixate on a rotating object. The movements are slow in the direction of the moving stimulus and quick in the reverse direction. This procedure is important in assessing the presence of vision in infants.

MANAGEMENT

For intermittent nystagmus occurring past 3 months of age and for continuous nystagmus before 3 months of age, the child is referred for ophthalmologic consultation.

Ptosis

ASSESSMENT

Ptosis is a drooping of the upper eyelid. It may affect one or both eyes. Congenitally the cause is a defective levator palpebral superior muscle. It is often inherited as an autosomal, dominant trait. Acquired causes include birth trauma, encephalitis, pineal tumors, and Horner's syndrome. Occasionally the ptosis can be so severe as to interfere with vision and cause amblyopia.

MANAGEMENT

If the ptosis interferes with vision, surgical correction is advised as soon as possible. If there is no visual compromise, surgical correction is done between 3 and 4 years of age.

Counseling Parents are counseled about the causes and usual treatment regimens. They observe for symptoms of amblyopia: squinting, frequent blinking, and rubbing the eyes.

Refractive Errors

ASSESSMENT

The leading causes of visual impairment in childhood are refractive errors. There are three types:

- Astigmatism, in which light rays diffuse on the retina due to inconsistent curvatures of the cornea; it is associated with hyperopia or myopia
- Hyperopia (farsightedness), in which light rays fall behind the retina due to a short anterior–posterior diameter of the eyeball or due to a lens which is too thin and flat and light rays are not bent adequately
- Myopia (nearsightedness), in which the light rays fall in front of the retina due to a long anterior–posterior diameter of the eyeball or due to a lens which is too thick and the light rays are not bent adequately

At birth most infants are hyperopic, which increases until 7 to 8 years of age when the farsightedness gradually decreases. Between 9 and 11 years of age, emmetropia (parallel light rays brought to a pinpoint focus on the retina) is established. Myopia does not develop until 8 to 10 years of age and increases until 20 to 30 years of age. At 1 year of age, a child's visual acuity is 20/100, at 2 years of age 20/60, and at 4 years of age 20/20. See Table 15-1. Pupillary dilation is required for accurate assessment of refractive errors.

Astigmatism This condition produces headaches, vertigo, frowning when reading, chronically irritated lids, and various degrees of visual defects, according to the amount of hyperopia or myopia present. Significant degrees of astigmatism can be detected through screening for visual acuity with the Snellen chart.

Hyperopia This condition is more common than myopia and is the natural accommodation of the eyes until approximately 9 years of age. Occasionally one eye may be more hyperopic than the other eye, causing amblyopia. Esotropia is frequently associated with hyperopia in childhood. Efforts to accommodate the visual strain may cause headaches, tired eyes, and blurring vision. Generally, hyperopia is more difficult to diagnose in children because they can accommodate this defect more effectively. Hyperopia is associated with complaints of eyestrain and headaches after long periods of reading or writing. It cannot be diagnosed by visual screening with the Snellen charts. It is suspected with the following history: eyestrain and pain, headaches, and lines running together when reading. Referral to an ophthalmologist for refraction is indicated.

Myopia This condition is seen initially between the ages of 8 and 11 years and can be evident by complaints of not seeing the chalkboard at school, holding books close to the face, and not catching a bounced ball at play. It can be diagnosed through visual acuity screening with the Snellen chart.

Other Symptoms of Refractive Errors These symptoms include frequent rubbing of the eyes, complaints of double vision, burning and tearing eyes, frowning, words running together while reading, tired eyes (asthenopia), and squinting to create a pinhole effect to help bring the eye into more accurate accommodation.

Screening for Refractive Errors See this chapter, Procedure for Snellen Eye Chart Screening.

MANAGEMENT

All children whose visual acuity chart screening shows inability to see half the letters on the 20/40 line after a second screening are referred to the ophthalmologist. Children are also referred whose history indicates hyperopia.

Glasses The correct treatment for refractive errors is glasses. Their use, however, does not prevent a progression of the visual defect. Visual changes continue to develop because of the ophthalmic changes due to the rapid growth during childhood and adolescence. Therefore, when glasses are worn, yearly ophthalmic examinations are necessary to evaluate the status of the refractive error. After 20 years of age, the same glasses can be worn until middle age. Contact lenses can be routinely worn by children when they are old enough to place in their own eyes.

Counseling The cause of the visual impairment is discussed with the parents, what objections if any they or the child have in reference to wearing glasses, and the reasons for yearly follow-up eye examinations. The symptoms of poor vision because of refractive errors are reviewed, and the need for repeat visual acuity screening is stressed if the symptoms persist.

Strabismus

ASSESSMENT

Definition Strabismus is the crossing or squinting of the eyes. It can occur when there is any disorder or disruption of binocular vision. A condition called suppression amblyopia develops when a child uses one eye constantly, as in strabismus. The unused eye develops decreased vision because the brain blocks out the interfering double image it is receiving in the poor eye.

Pathophysiology Double vision or diplopia occurs in strabismus because the image viewed does not fall on corresponding parts of the retina in each eye. To avoid diplopia, the child learns to suppress vision in the deviating eye, resulting in decreased vision. This eye then becomes amblyopic (impaired vision because of disuse). The earlier strabismus is diagnosed, the greater the prevention of suppression amblyopia and the acquisition of normal vision.

Pseudostrabismus This condition occurs when there are epicanthal folds or a wide bridge across the nose. In these instances, a slight portion of the medial aspect of the eye is covered and the illusion of cross-eye results. Pseudostrabismus is differentiated from true strabismus by the cover-uncover and Hirschberg tests. There is no treatment.

Etiology The most common cause is imbalance of the muscle alignment of the eyes. Other causes include brain tumor, infection, retinoblastoma, cataracts, uveitis, ocular injury, and optic nerve atrophy.

Incidence Strabismus occurs in 5 percent of all children. It can be congenital, and 50 percent of all cases are familiar.

Classifications The following are common types of strabismus:

- *Nonparalytic (comitant).* This is the most common type of strabismus. The deviation is the same in all fields of gaze.
- *Paralytic (noncomitant).* This type is due to paralysis of the ocular muscles. The eyes are straight except when moved in the direction of the paralyzed muscles.
- *Accommodative.* There are two types:

  1. *Convergent.* This internal deviation occurs when there is hyperopia and the eyes overaccommodate to remove the error. In doing so, the eyes exert an abnormal degree of overconvergence on the muscles and strabismus develops.
  2. *Divergent.* This external deviation is associated with slight or no refractive error and is often present at birth. The deviation occurs when the child looks at distant objects or daydreams.

- *Monocular.* This type is due to paralysis of the ocular muscles. One eye deviates permanently while the other eye fixates normally.
- *Alternating.* In this type either eye is used for fixation while the other eye deviates. Vision develops equally in both eyes since each eye is used for normal vision part of the time.

Terms The following are used to describe abnormal positions of the eye:

1. Tropias are active frank misalignments of the eyes when the subject is staring straight ahead. Examples are esotropia, exotropia.
2. Phorias are latent, intermittent misalignments of the eyes which become active (tropias) only when binocular vision is impeded. Examples are esophoria, exophoria.

History In the newborn period parents may complain that the infant looks cross-eyed. In an older child, in addition to cross-eye, parents may describe frequent blinking, rubbing, squinting, over-reaching objects, and tripping. All observations of the parents are investigated. Occasionally parents relate that the preceding symptoms occur only when the child is tired. This situation is due to a latent deviation (phoria) becoming an active deviation (tropia).

Cover-Uncover and Hirschberg's Tests Strabismus is evident when there is a positive cover-uncover test. This examination is done by bringing a bright object in front of the child's eyes at a distance of approximately 30 cm. When the child fixes on the object, the nurse practitioner covers one of the eyes with a cover card or finger. Quickly uncover the covered eye and observe for movement. If the uncovered eye moves to fixate while the other eye is covered, there is a strong suspicion that the moving eye has a strabismus. Repeat the test with the second eye. If the child pushes the examiner's hand away while it is covering the good or seeing eye, this can also be a strong suspicion for amblyopia. This examination is most accurate if done after 5 months of age. The Hirschberg test involves shining a penlight into the child's eyes or above the nose. The light reflection should come from corresponding parts of the cornea if strabismus is absent.

MANAGEMENT

All cases of true strabismus are referred to an ophthalmologist. The goal of treatment is to develop adequate vision in each eye. Conservative management consists of patching the good eye so that the deviant eye develops normal vision through continued use. The length of time the eye is patched depends on the age of the child when the diagnosis was made. If before the first year of life, patching may only be used for a few weeks. The success of patching depends on the ability of the child to cooperate with a patch over the eye.

Glasses Corrective lenses help to focus the object on the retina and relieve accommodative effort. The successful wearing of glasses also depends on the cooperation of the child.

Surgery Usually surgery is indicated in those children whose strabismus is not corrected by glasses. There is a trend toward earlier surgery because of a better prognosis for binocular vision (Taylor, 1980). Occasionally, multiple surgical procedures are necessary to adjust the ocular muscles.

Counseling Evaluation of pseudo- or true strabismus is made. If pseudostrabismus is present, counseling is directed toward the explanation and the necessity of no treatment. Parents' questions are answered.

After medical consultation and ophthalmologist referral for true strabismus, parents are counseled in reference to their understanding of the etiology and the rationale for management. If the child requires operative treatment, the nurse practitioner remains in contact with the family to reinforce the physician's explanations, to define procedures, to interpret medical and nursing management, and to assist in planning home management.

References

Fraunfelder, F. *Current Ocular Therapy.* New York: W. B. Saunders, 1980.

Freman, S. *Handbook of Pediatric Ophthalmology.* New York: Grune & Stratton, 1978.

Gilman, A., et al., editors. *Goodman and Gilman's The Pharmacologic Basis of Therapeutics,* 6th ed., New York: MacMillan Co., 1980.

Kempe, C. H., H. K. Silver, and D. O'Brien, editors. *Current Pediatric Diagnosis and Treatment.* 7th ed. Los Altos, CA: Lange Medical Publications, 1982.

Pascoe, D. J. and M. Grossman, editors. *Quick Reference to Pediatric Emergencies.* 2nd ed. Philadelphia: J. B. Lippincott, 1978.

Rowe, D. S., et al. "Purulent Ocular Discharge in Neonates: Significance of Chlamydia Trachomatis." *Pediatrics 63*:628–632, April 1979.

Sagaties, M. J. "Screening for Strabismus and Amblyopia." *Nurse Practitioner 10*:19–22, April 1982.

Taylor, D. "Squint. Practical Aspects of Diagnosis and Management." *Practitioner 224*:587–590, June 1980.

Ziai, M. *Pediatrics.* 2nd ed. Boston: Little, Brown, 1975.

16

The Mouth
and Teeth

Dental problems continue to rank as the most common health problem of children today. Caries is remarkably prevalent and about half of school-age children have some form of malocclusion or gingival disease. Most oral diseases are preventable through adequate dental care and the establishment of preventive practices in the home. Nurse practitioners can play an active role in the early identification of problems and facilitation of appropriate referrals. This chapter includes assessment and management of common problems of the mouth and teeth in addition to basic dental information.

ASSESSMENT

History

PRESENT CONCERNS

Obtain information pertaining to the individual presenting problem following suggestions contained in Chapter 11, Assessment of Presenting Symptom.

PAST HISTORY

Obtain information on methods of infant feeding (breast or bottle, length of time), pattern of tooth eruption, history of mouth breathing, thumb sucking (length of time), brushing habits, dental visits, dental problems, mouth diseases, and upper respiratory infections.

BIRTH HISTORY

Obtain information on congenital deformities of the nose and mouth, cleft lip or palate, supernumerary teeth, and maternal medication.

FAMILY HISTORY

Obtain information on congenital deformities, malocclusion, mouth breathing, and periodontal diseases.

NUTRITION HISTORY

Obtain information on carbohydrate and fluoride intake and bottle habits (use at bedtime, what the bottle contains), snacking habits.

Physical Examination

POSITIONING THE CHILD

To obtain an adequate examination of the mouth and throat:

1. Place a cooperative child in a sitting position on the examining table or on the parent's lap.
2. Place an infant or uncooperative child flat on the table. Have a parent hold the child's arms above and beside the head as the examiner immobilizes the child's body with her or his own body and arms.

FACIES

Observe for symmetry, jaw size, swellings, and discolorations.

MOUTH

Observe for ability to open, extent of opening, and odors. To examine the mouth:

1. Use a tongue depressor to inspect under the tongue and between the tongue and the cheeks.
2. Have a young child say "aa" as in "apple" to obtain a clear view of the tonsils, uvula, and epiglottis. Children prefer that a tongue depressor not be used for this purpose.

LIPS

Observe for symmetry (purse lips), size, color, fissures, bleeding, edema, and hydration.

Common Findings

1. *Cracked, bleeding lips (cheilitis).* This is a sign of illness or chapping due to wind and frequent licking of the lips.
2. *Dry, scaly patches.* Observed at lip corners, they may be caused by nutritional deficiencies.
3. *Maceration and fissures.* Observed at lip corners, they may indicate onset of a fungal infection.

GUMS (GINGIVAE)

Observe for color, texture, bleeding, and lesions.

Normal Variants

1. *Extension of the septum (alveolar frenulum).* Observed on the upper gum, it may cause a separation between the central incisors. It corrects itself with growth.
2. *Melanotic (dark pigmentation) line.* It is observed along the gums of black children.

Abnormal Findings

1. *Bleeding gums.* This may be a sign of poor dental hygiene.
2. *Overgrowth of gums (hyperplasia).* See this chapter, Gum Hyperplasia.
3. *Purple, bleeding gums.* This is a sign of scurvy.
4. *Blue-black margin.* This is a sign of lead poisoning.

BUCCAL MUCOSA

Observe for color, lesions, and hydration.

TONGUE

Observe for movement, papillae changes, dryness, coating, color, and frenulum. See Chapter 5, Frenulum.

Normal Variants

- *Fissured tongue.* Fissure may run parallel to or at right angles to the central grooves. Ten percent of the population manifests at least two fissures. Fissuring may follow scarlet fever, syphilis, or typhoid fever.
- *Geographic tongue.* The dorsum of the tongue shows characteristic smooth, shiny, erythematous areas which are slightly depressed below the surrounding normal papillae. Noticed in 1 to 6 percent of the population, they disappear and reappear in different areas and at different times of a person's life.

Abnormal Findings

- *Coated tongue.* This is caused by the accumulation of food debris and bacteria among hypertrophied filiform papillae. The tongue has a smooth appearance until the age of 5 because the filiform papillae are normally short. In a child under 5 the cause should be sought for any coating of the tongue.
- *Dry coated tongue.* This is a result of failure of secretion by the salivary and lingual glands and is one of the best clinical signs of dehydration. The color may vary from white to brown.
- *Furry tongue.* This is seen early in states of mild dehydration and low-grade fever.
- *White strawberry tongue.* This is a transitional stage from the white-coated tongue to the raw red tongue. The appearance is of an unripe strawberry. The engorged and enlarged fungiform papillae appear prominently above the level of the white, desquamating filiform papillae. It is seen early in scarlet fever and other acute states. See Chapter 27, Scarlet Fever.

HARD PALATE

Observe for color, lesions, and high arching.

SOFT PALATE

Observe size and movement of uvula, or if bifid.

TONSILS

Inspect for color, edema, size, symmetry, coating, crypts, and exudate.

Tonsil Size Tonsillar lymphoid tissue is not prominent in the 1 to 2 year old. Tonsils appear largest in the 3 to 4 year old, and tissue is again small in the 10 year old. A method for recording tonsillar size is as follows:

1 + edges seen
2 + larger
3 + touching uvula
4 + meeting at midline (kissing tonsils)

POSTERIOR PHARYNX AND EPIGLOTTIS

Inspect for color, swelling, and exudate.

TEETH

Observe number, extra or missing, staining, caries, bite (occlusion), or overbite (malocclusion). See this chapter, Malocclusion and Caries.

Notched Teeth "Hutchinson teeth" (notched upper central incisors) and "mulberry molars" in which the cusps are crowded together may be found as a result of congenital syphilis.

Staining Stains observed on teeth are as follows:

• *Black stain.* This may occur as a result of iron ingestion. It is a temporary staining which disappears when the diet contains less iron. Iron or acid medications should be taken through a straw. See Chapter 19, Iron Deficiency Anemia.
• *Green stain.* A greenish color of the enamel may result from intense neonatal jaundice. The deciduous teeth may be completely green except for the portion developed postnatally. Green stains may occur on the labial surfaces of the anterior teeth near the gingivae in children who lack satisfactory care. This can be removed by a dentist.
• *Yellow-gray, bright yellow, and gray-brown stains.* These discolorations may occur as a result of tetracycline therapy during the

period of tooth formation. Tetracyclines have caused tooth defects when administered to the mother in the last trimester of pregnancy while the teeth are forming in utero, through milk from a nursing mother, or directly to the child up to age 8. Tetracyclines at levels exceeding 75 mg/kg nearly always cause enamel hyperplasia. Although no treatment is necessary, severe hyperplasia may require dental restoration of teeth.

Dentition

TOOTH DEVELOPMENT

The process of normal tooth development begins in utero and continues into early adulthood. Basic facts of tooth development are as follows:

- Each tooth undergoes four successive periods of development during its life cycle: growth, calcification, eruption, and attrition. Normal eruption and shedding of primary teeth, and eruption of permanent teeth are presented in Table 16-1.
- Calcification of the central and lateral incisors of the deciduous (primary) teeth begins about the fifth fetal month. These are the first deciduous teeth to erupt at about the infant's fifth or sixth month of age.
- Calcification of the first molars of the permanent (secondary) teeth begins at birth. These are the first permanent teeth to erupt at the child's sixth or seventh year of age.
- Normal variants include premature eruption, delayed eruption, and congenital absence of some teeth.
- The formation of healthy tooth structure is fostered by a diet adequate in protein, calcium, phosphate, and vitamins (especially C and D), and requires strenuous chewing of foods such as hard breads, raw fruit, and vegetables. It is important to establish good eating habits early: rewards other than sugary snacks given for good behavior/accomplishments, decreased frequency of between-meal snacks, and low-sugar or no-sugar alternatives when snacks are given, e.g., diabetic canned fruits, sugarless gum, candy, soda pop.
- Nutritional disorders and prolonged illness in infancy may interfere with calcification of deciduous and permanent teeth.

Table 16-1

Normal Tooth Eruption and Shedding

Eruption and Shedding of Primary Teeth			Eruption of Permanent Teeth	
Upper	*Eruption*	*Shedding*	*Upper*	
Central incisor	8–12 months	6–7 years	Central incisor	7–8 years
Lateral incisor	9–13 months	7–8 years	Lateral incisor	8–9 years
Cuspid	16–22 months	10–12 years	Cuspid	11–12 years
First molar	13–19 months	9–11 years	First bicuspid	10–11 years
Second molar	25–33 months	10–12 years	Second bicuspid	10–12 years
			First molar	6–7 years
			Second molar	12–13 years
			Third molar	17–21 years
Lower			*Lower*	
Second molar	23–31 months	10–12 years	Third molar	17–21 years
First molar	14–18 months	9–11 years	Second molar	11–13 years
Cuspid	17–23 months	9–12 years	First molar	6–7 years
Lateral incisor	10–16 months	7–8 years	Second bicuspid	11–12 years
Central incisor	6–10 months	6–7 years	First bicuspid	10–12 years
			Cuspid	9–10 years
			Lateral incisor	7–8 years
			Central incisor	6–7 years

Source: Copyright by the American Dental Association. Reprinted by permission.

IMPORTANCE OF THE PRIMARY TEETH

The primary teeth play an important role for the following reasons:

- Each primary tooth is needed to occupy a space for a permanent tooth. The most common disturbance in the eruption of teeth is caused by premature loss or extraction of neglected primary or permanent teeth. Early loss of a primary tooth impairs mastication and may result in improper eruption or impaction of the permanent tooth. When teeth are lost prematurely, construction of a space maintainer by the dentist is necessary.
- Speech development depends on primary teeth. Proper pronunciation of at least 18 of the 26 letters requires the proper alignment of the teeth.
- Primary teeth round out the shape of the face by supporting facial muscles and ligaments, contributing to the growth and development of the jaws.
- Cosmetic appearance: emotional impact of negative feedback.

MANAGEMENT

Plaque

Plaque is a colorless, transparent, sticky, organic layer which firmly coats the surface of the teeth. It supports the growth of destructive bacteria that cause decay and periodontal disease. It accumulates along the gums and at the site of cracks and rough spots.

CAUSES OF PLAQUE

High carbohydrate intake, sweet sticky foods taken between meals, and poor dental hygiene contribute to plaque formation. Plaque adheres to enamel in 24 hours. The amount of sweet foods ingested is not as important to the health of the teeth as is the time of contact between sweet substances and the teeth. Thus, long-lasting suckers, mints, and sticky caramels are more damaging because they are in contact with the teeth for extended periods.

PLAQUE REMOVAL

Plaque is removed only by brushing and flossing the teeth and should be removed at least once in 24 hours.

Toothbrushing Toothbrushing will remove plaque from the outer, inner, and biting surfaces of the teeth. Methods of toothbrushing are as follows:

- The parent may first start cleansing the child's teeth by rubbing them gently with gauze wrapped around a finger.
- Children should begin brushing between 18 months to 3 years of age or when they are able to stand at the sink on a stool. An egg timer may be used to help the child to spend enough time at brushing. The child may need help until 4 or 5 years of age.
- The older child may use a "disclosing tablet," a vegetable dye that colors the plaque red and indicates areas where plaque has not been removed.
- Teeth are brushed thoroughly after each meal and after eating sweets. If unable to brush the mouth should be rinsed with water.
- With the bristle tips at a 45° angle against the gum line, the brush cleans the teeth and gums at the same time. Short strokes are used in a gentle back-and-forth scrubbing motion. Chewing surfaces are also brushed with the same scrubbing strokes.

SELECTION OF TOOTHBRUSH This includes the following:

1. *Type of brush.* A brush with a straight handle, a flat brushing surface, and soft, round-ended bristles is recommended. The head of the brush should be small enough to provide easy access to every tooth. Both hand brushes and powered brushes can be effective for plaque removal; powered cordless brushes may be especially appealing and useful to children.
2. *Size of brush.* Children need brushes smaller than those designed for adults; however, the handle should be large enough to hold easily.
3. *Replacement of brush.* Toothbrushes should be replaced when they soften and the bristles are slightly frayed, probably as often as every 2 to 3 months or sooner.

Flossing This is the most effective method for removing plaque from between the teeth. Methods used to aid in flossing are as follows:

- The floss is gently guided against the side of the tooth into the space between the teeth until resistance is felt. It is then curved into a C shape around the side of the tooth and scraped up and down against the surface of each tooth.
- Children may find it easier to hold the floss when the ends have been tied together to form a circle about 10 inches in diameter.
- Care is taken to floss gently but firmly as improper flossing can be injurious to the gums.

Water Irrigation "Water pik" is recommended for removing food particles which are stuck between the teeth and cannot be removed with brushing or flossing. Water irrigation is especially effective for wearers of braces or permanent bridges. "Water pik" does not remove plaque.

Fluoride

The ingestion of fluoride during the period of tooth development has been shown to reduce significantly the incidence of dental caries, in some cases by as much as 80 percent. To achieve the greatest benefits from fluoride, sources of fluoride must be introduced in infancy and provided systematically until at least 16 years of age.

METHODS OF FLUORIDE SUPPLEMENTATION

Water Fluoridation The fluoridation of community water supplies is the most efficacious method of assuring consistent intake of fluoride. Approximately 1 ppm of fluoride in drinking water has been specified as the recommended concentration for the partial control of dental decay; however, optimal concentrations will vary (0.7 to 1.2 ppm) depending on the annual mean maximum daily temperature of the area (American Dental Association, 1979, p. 318).

Medicinal Fluoride See this chapter, Recommended Intake of Fluoride.

Topical Fluoride Applications This fluoride, which is applied by the dentist, becomes part of the tooth enamel, making it more resistant to decay-causing acids. In fluoridated water areas it provides an additional 17 percent protection to the teeth. Parents should know of its importance.

Fluoride Toothpastes The American Dental Association recommends the use of these toothpastes, and reports show that they reduce the incidence of new carious lesions.

DETERMINING THE NEED FOR FLUORIDE SUPPLEMENTATION

The need for and the amount of supplementation depends on the age of the child, the level of fluoride concentration in the local water supply, and the amount of water in the child's diet.

Guidelines for Supplementation Supplementation is necessary and should begin at birth (see below, Breast-Fed Infants) when:

1. Community water contains less than 0.3 ppm. The use of prescribed supplements should be limited to children whose drinking water contains a concentration of fluoride ion no higher than 70 percent of the optimal level necessary for community water fluoridation in the geographic area. See Table 16-2.
2. The diet does not contain sufficient fluoridated water, as with infants fed cow's milk or commercially prepared formulas, and the many children who do not drink sufficient water.

Breast-Fed Infants There is controversy over the issue of when to begin fluoride supplementation in breast-fed infants. Very little fluoride is transmitted in breast milk, yet the reduction in dental caries that has occurred in children in naturally fluoridated communities has occurred without fluoride supplementation during breast feeding. Hess (1977) and Waitrowski et al. (1975) recommend that fluoride supplementation in the breast-fed infant be delayed until 6 months of age. Fomon et al. (1979) and the American Academy of Pediatrics Committee on Nutrition are currently recommending fluoride soon after birth for full breast-fed babies. See Table 16-2.

Table 16-2
Supplemental Fluoride Dosage
Schedule (mg/day)^a

Age	Concentration of Fluoride in Drinking Water (ppm)		
	<0.3	0.3–0.7	>0.7
2 wk to 2 yr	0.25	0	0
2–3 yr	0.50	0.25	0
3–16 yr	1.00	0.50	0

Source: American Academy of Pediatrics, Committee on Nutrition, Fluoride Supplementation: Revised Dosage Schedule, *Pediatrics* 63:150–152, January 1979. Copyright American Academy of Pediatrics, 1979.
^{a}2.2 mg sodium fluoride contains 1 mg fluoride ion.

RECOMMENDED INTAKE

The Committee on Nutrition of the American Academy of Pediatrics (1979) and the Council on Dental Therapeutics (1979) recommend optimal dosage of fluoride supplementation. See Table 16-2.

Medicinal Fluoride Fluoride preparations are available either singly or in combination with vitamins. The fixed proportion of ingredients in the combination makes it more difficult to adjust approximately the amount of fluoride prescribed in areas where the drinking water contains substantial but inadequate levels of fluoride. These examples of available preparations will contain fluoride only:

1. Luride Drops (Hoyt Laboratories): 8 drops = 2.2 mg sodium fluoride
   Luride Lozi-Tabs:
   0.25 mg = 0.55 mg sodium fluoride
   0.5 mg = 1.1 mg sodium fluoride
   1.0 mg = 2.2 mg sodium fluoride
   Luride SF Lozi-Tabs: Each tablet contains 2.2 mg sodium fluoride; contains no artificial color or flavors.
2. Flura-Drops (Kirkman Laboratories): 4 drops (or 0.18 ml) = 2.2 mg sodium fluoride

Flura-Loz: Each lozenge contains 2.21 mg sodium fluoride plus coloring and flavoring agents.

Flura-Tablets: Each tablet contains 2.21 mg sodium fluoride.

DOSAGE FOR CHILDREN UNDER 2 YEARS OF AGE It is necessary that water containing 1 ppm fluoride be prepared with tablets or drops and this water be used for the child's drinking water and for the preparation of food or formula. One 2.2-mg tablet of sodium fluoride completely dissolved in 1 quart of water will provide infants with fluoridated water containing approximately 1 ppm (American Dental Association, 1979, p. 321).

DOSAGE FOR CHILDREN 2 TO 3 YEARS OF AGE This is one half the amount recommended for the 3 year old and older.

DOSAGE FOR CHILDREN 3 YEARS OF AGE AND OLDER Sodium fluoride tablet 2.2 mg, 1 tablet daily to be chewed and swished before swallowing. *Caution.* Sodium fluoride should be stored out of reach of children nor should more than 264 mg be dispensed at one time.

Excessive Fluoride Mottling of the teeth occurs when the fluoride content of the water is higher than 2.5 ppm or when a child receives an overdose of medicinal fluoride (over 4 mg/day) (see this chapter, Fluorosis). To avoid the possibility of mottling, the prescribed dietary supplement should be adjusted downward in proportion to the concentration of fluoride in the drinking water. See Table 16-2.

Dental Referral

INITIAL VISIT

It is recommended that the child be seen first at least by age 3. Most children should be seen at an earlier age if possible since 36 percent of children have caries by age 3. Parental attitude creates the mood of the first visit. One should speak of the dentist as a friend who helps to keep the teeth healthy. "Overpreparing," urging, bribing, or forcing the child are not recommended.

LATER VISITS

The child should visit the dentist on a regular basis, at least every 3 or 4 months, during the ages of 4 to 8 because the greatest incidence of caries occurs between these years and because of the speed with which caries develop.

SPECIAL REFERRALS

Referrals are made to the dentist for a child of any age if the following occur:

1. The child falls and injures a tooth or the jaw. The tooth is kept moist and taken to the dentist. See this chapter, Injury to Teeth.
2. The child complains of pain in teeth or gums.
3. The teeth become discolored.
4. Caries is present upon examination.
5. Malocclusion is severe, or the child's tongue thrusts, and the child has not previously had dental care.

COMMON CLINICAL PROBLEMS

Mouth

DROOLING (SALIVATION)

Assessment In infancy cells of the salivary glands do not mature until 3 to 6 months of age at which time the flow of saliva is increased. The infant has not learned to swallow efficiently, therefore drooling occurs. Excessive salivation is more evident with teething, as a reflex to anticipated pain, from nausea, or from irritation of lesions in the mouth. It may also follow administration of mercurial compounds and occurs in certain nervous disorders such as encephalitis and chorea.

Management The parents are given an explanation of salivation.

GINGIVITIS

Assessment There are several forms of gingivitis to consider. Among these are early, moderate, and severe gingivitis, which are caused by the bacteria that forms dental plaque.

1. *Early gingivitis.* This consists of eruption and marginal gingivitis. Eruption gingivitis is temporary gingivitis seen during decidu-

ous tooth emergence. See this chapter, Teething in Infancy. Eruption of the permanent teeth is often accompanied by a mild gingivitis possibly because the surrounding gingivae receive little protection from the tooth during eruption. The gingivae become inflamed by the continued irritative and abrasive action of food. Marginal gingivitis in children is usually associated with poor oral hygiene and, at times, with the presence of abnormal occlusion.

2. *Moderate gingivitis.* Inflammation is present. The gingiva is red, glazy, and bleeds with manipulation.
3. *Severe gingivitis.* The gingiva is red and enlarged, covering more of the tooth than is normal. It may bleed spontaneously and ulcerations may be present.

Management Treatment is aimed at relief of soreness and improvement of oral hygiene. Mouth rinses are given using warm normal saline solution and improved toothbrushing and flossing techniques are recommended for removal of plaque. Water pik may be used for irrigative purposes. In severe gingivitis, fibrous enlargement of the gingiva must be surgically removed.

JUVENILE PERIODONTITIS

Periodontal disease, inflammatory disease affecting the gum tissue and supporting bony structures of the teeth, frequently occurs in children. Poor or inadequate nutrition is almost always a primary or secondary factor. The basic cause is inflammation produced by subgingival bacterial colonization. The long-term ultimate consequence of this process is resorption of supporting bone and/or root abscesses.

Assessment The gingiva may appear normal and the only symptom is increased tooth mobility. The permanent first molars and lower incisors are primarily affected. There is extensive bone loss evident on radiologic examination.

Management Periodontitis may be prevented by strict attention to proper dental care. Recognition of the disease is an indication for referral to a dentist.

THRUSH

Assessment Oral candidiasis (thrush) is caused by the fungus *Candida albicans*. Infections are transmitted from the vaginal canal of mother, from poorly sterilized bottles or nipples, mother's breast, or attendant's hands, or result from long-term suppression of the natural oral flora through infections and use of antibiotics. Oral candidiasis in a child over 1 year of age, if recurrent, raises the possibility of immunodeficiency.

SIGNS OF THRUSH Thrush presents with white, milky, or cheesy patches on the tongue and/or on the buccal mucosa. If scraped, a red, bleeding lesion results. Microscopic examination of cheesy material mixed with 10 percent potassium hydroxide will show hyphae of the organism and will confirm the diagnosis. If diaper rash appears in association with thrush, fungal diaper infection is suspected.

Management Antifungal agents are used as follows:

1. Installation in the mouth of nystatin (Mycostatin) in suspension in dosage prescribed by the physician.
2. Local applications of 1 percent methylrosaniline chloride (gentian violet) solution, q.i.d. with a soft cotton swab. A fresh swab is used with each application. This treatment is less effective than nystatin and can discolor the skin and clothing. Relapse is not uncommon and calls for further course of medication.

TRAUMA TO THE TONGUE

Assessment Some causes of trauma to the tongue are accidental biting of the tongue, injuries by sharp objects such as toys, and burns by hot foods. Symptoms may include swelling and redness, blisters, or ulcers which disappear in a few days.

Management Ice may be used for swelling. A mild antiseptic mouthwash, such as 1 percent tincture of iodine in physiologic saline solution, may be used. Food is kept cool and in liquid form until the trauma is healed.

Dental Problems

BRUXISM (NIGHT GRINDING)

Assessment Bruxism is involuntary grinding, clenching, or gnashing of the teeth during sleep. It is caused by malocclusion in an effort to find a more comfortable position for the teeth or is triggered by anxiety or emotional disturbance. It can result in especially rapid attrition (the normal wearing of the teeth) and can lead to periodontal disease, facial pain, and, sometimes, loss of teeth.

Management Treatment consists of the following:

1. *Equilibration.* This is done by the dentist who grinds down high chewing surfaces and/or builds up low ones to restore proper alignment. Orthodontia may be required.
2. *Exercise.* An exercise that helps the problem with psychologic roots is to clench the teeth tightly for 5 seconds, relax for 5 seconds, and repeat six times each day for 2 weeks.
3. *Counseling.* The cause of the emotional disturbance should be sought.

CARIES (TOOTH DECAY)

Assessment Dental caries are progressive lesions of the calcified dental tissues characterized by loss of tooth structures.

CAUSATIVE FACTORS Three definitive factors necessary to produce tooth decay are *bacteria, carbohydrate,* and *plaque.* The bacteria are classified into three groups:

1. Acidogenic organisms that produce the acids upon the tooth surface which decalcify the hard tissues. *Lactobacillus acidophilus* and certain streptococci are the most frequent.
2. Proteolytic organisms that digest the organic matrix after its decalcification and produce the characteristic discoloration and odor of caries.
3. *Leptotrichiae* organisms that form plaque on the smooth surfaces of the teeth where the acidogenic organisms are harbored.

Carbohydrates are the major food factor. These are sticky, refined carbohydrates that are eaten between meals and remain on the tooth surface for long periods of time. Acidogenic bacteria quickly produce acid from these sugars. Mealtime sugars are buffered by saliva and other foods that tend to neutralize the acid. Feigal et al. (1981) suggest that liquid and chewable drug preparations used over a long period of time for chronic conditions are a risk for the development of caries.

INCIDENCE The incidence of caries in children ranges from 5 percent at age one to 75 percent at age 5. (Silver et al., 1980, p. 231). The periods of greatest carious activity are 4 to 8 years of age in deciduous dentition and 12 to 18 years of age in the permanent dentition.

SIGNS OF TOOTH DECAY Caries are seen as discolored areas or actual cavitations in the pits and fissures of the chewing surface of the posterior teeth or between the teeth and, in a badly neglected mouth, at the neck of the tooth at the junction of the gingivae. Many caries are not visible upon inspection of the teeth. Dental equipment and X-rays provide more reliable detection.

Management Management is directed toward prevention of caries:

1. Plaque removal by brushing and flossing after each meal, rinsing mouth with water when impossible to brush or floss
2. Fluoridation of community water or oral fluoride supplementation by drops or tablets
3. Topical application of fluoride by the dentist
4. Use of toothpastes containing fluoride
5. Early introduction to dental care with frequent supervisory visits
6. Proper, nutritional diet containing limited carbohydrates

FOODS TO RECOMMEND FOR SNACKS These include food groups as follows:

• Milk group. Milk, cheese, cheese dips, cheese curls
• Meat group. Luncheon meats, salami, smoked sausages, clam dip, nuts of all kinds
• Fruit and vegetable group. Raw fruits and vegetables, unsweetened fruit juices and vegetable juices.

- Bread and cereal group. Crackers, toast, pretzels, corn chips, popcorn, teething biscuits.

FOODS TO AVOID These include the following:

- High carbohydrate content foods such as infant formula with added sugar and sweet, sticky snacks taken in between meals ("trigger" foods). These snacks are candy, cake, cookies, pie, pastry, ice cream, sundaes or cones, candied popcorn, candy apples, candy-coated gum, peanut butter and jelly sandwiches, honey graham crackers, dried fruits and raisins.
- Products such as hard candies, lollipops, breath mints, and cough drops that are held in contact with teeth over a period of time.
- Lemons, if they are sucked or eaten, bring teeth into contact with acid.

CONGENITAL ABSENCE OF TEETH (ANODONTIA)

Assessment Congenital absence of teeth occurs frequently as a genetic anomaly. The permanent absence of the third molars, the upper lateral incisors, and/or the lower and upper bicuspids is attributed to evolutionary causes. Absence of other teeth may be indicative of some hereditary systemic disease such as arachnodactyly, cleidocranial dyostosis, or congenital ectodermal dysplasia.

Management Consultation and/or referral are indicated.

DELAYED ERUPTION

Assessment The first tooth normally erupts between the fifth and twelfth month. A first tooth that does not appear by the twelfth month suggests disturbances of nutrition or endocrine origin. Rickets, Down's syndrome, and congenital syphilis should be ruled out.

Management Referral to or consultation with the physician is indicated.

FLUOROSIS

Assessment "Mottling" of the teeth results from excess exposure to fluoride. This occurs when the fluoride content of the community water is over 2.5 ppm or when the diet contains more than optimal levels of fluoride (see this chapter, Fluoride). Fluorosis occurs only in children during the tooth development ages from birth to 14 years. Teeth affected in childhood remain affected throughout life. The types of fluorosis are as follows:

1. *Mild fluorosis.* "Mottling" of the teeth is a cosmetic defect in which opaque paper-white areas appear on the surface of normally translucent teeth.
2. *Moderate fluorosis.* This occurs when brown stains begin to appear.
3. *Severe fluorosis.* This occurs when brown stains appear, the teeth become pitted, and, eventually, the enamel erodes.

Management   There is no actual treatment. Prevention includes a careful assessment of the child's diet, looking for the following:

1. A diet containing large amounts of fluoridated water, such as drinking water, foods reprocessed in water, or diets rich in fish, tea, and mineral water
2. An overdosage of supplemental fluorides (see Table 16-2)

GUM HYPERPLASIA

Assessment   This is defined as overgrowth of gums due to prolonged periods of Dilantin therapy, mouth breathing, or vitamin deficiency. The gums may bleed as the child stops brushing, thereby aggravating the problem.

Management   Treatment includes meticulous attention to dental hygiene with the use of soft toothbrushes and digital pressure to the gums several times a day.

INJURY TO TEETH

Assessment   Teeth may be broken, cracked, pushed out of alignment, or knocked out of the mouth (evulsion).

Management   In case of an evulsed tooth, these four steps should be followed:

1. Find the tooth.

2. Wash the tooth under running water; hold by crown; do not scrub.
3. Insert tooth into socket gently or place it under the child's or parent's tongue. Saliva is the best transport to maintain periodontal ligament viability.
4. Go directly to the dentist. The child may hold the tooth in place with a finger. The driver should be cautioned to drive carefully.

For other injuries the child should be referred to the dentist.

PREVENTION A child engaging in sports should wear a helmet, wear tooth protectors, be referred to an orthodontist if the front teeth protrude.

LIP BITING

Assessment Habitual sucking or nibbling on the lower lip tends to force the lower incisors backward. This habit may occur as a tensional outlet.

Management Lip pomade can be applied frequently, to serve as a reminder not to bite lips and to promote healing of chapped mucosa. The abnormal position of the teeth tends to rectify itself spontaneously with growth. It is best not to pay undue attention to this habit. See Chapter 6, Common Habits.

MALOCCLUSION

Assessment Malocclusion refers to irregularities of tooth alignment and the improper fitting together of the teeth on chewing. Abnormal jaw relationships, and abnormal and deforming muscle function, both inherited and acquired, may result in malocclusion. Deciduous teeth or first permanent teeth may be widely spaced or may overlap. This is usually temporary as the teeth tend to realign spontaneously with growth. Malocclusion is not common in deciduous teeth.

NORMAL OCCLUSION This is present when the top posterior teeth (molars) meet and rest snugly on the opposing bottom posterior teeth and when the upper anterior teeth (incisors) barely overlap and touch the bottom anterior teeth. The examiner should observe the jaw structures of the parents as a clue.

CAUSES OF MALOCCLUSION These include the following:

1. Incompatibility of tooth size and jaw size may be due to genetic factors that may result in spacing, crowding, or irregularity of teeth
2. Prolonged retention of primary teeth that may result in delayed eruption of permanent teeth
3. Neglected primary or permanent teeth that may be lost prematurely
4. Lip biting, mouth breathing, tongue thrusting, teeth grinding, thumb sucking, or improper sleeping habits over a long period of time may exert pressures that interfere with good growth patterns

Management Referral is made when malocclusion is present, which interferes with the proper chewing of foods, or when there is obvious jaw deformity in the family.

PREVENTION Preventive measures include the following:

1. Parental encouragement to meet early sucking needs in the first year and discouragement of weaning to the cup before 1 year to promote better development of mouth and jaw
2. Removal of the thumb or fingers from child's mouth while sleeping
3. Positioning of the child in sleep so his/her cheek does not rest on small, hard, firm objects such as fists or toys

MOUTH BREATHING

Assessment Mouth breathing may occur as a result of habit or nasal obstruction. The tongue normally lies against the roof of the mouth. When the tongue is suspended between the dental arches or on the floor of the mouth, development of the teeth and jaws are affected. These effects include the following:

1. Elongation of the face with dropping of the mandible
2. Narrow and pinched nostrils from disuse
3. Dull and drawn expression

Young children normally sleep with their lips open; this is not considered to be mouth breathing. To determine whether a child is mouth breathing, a wisp of cotton is held to the child's nose and mouth.

Management Referral is made to an otolaryngologist if nasal obstruction is present. Surgical removal of the obstruction (adenoidectomy) and muscular exercises to strengthen the lips and to maintain closure may be necessary. Orthodontia is frequently necessary.

NURSING BOTTLE MOUTH

Assessment This condition is a form of rampant caries associated with frequent, prolonged use of a nursing bottle containing carbohydrate liquids which are in contact with the teeth. These liquids may be milk, apple juice, or other fruit juices. Nursing bottle mouth may occur in children as early as 18 months of age. The history may reveal that the child has a well-regulated diet and the teeth are brushed, but the child is put to bed with a nursing bottle. The bottle often remains in the mouth most of the night, and/or through naptime. Because of reduced salivary flow while sleeping, oral clearance is reduced. The lactose content of both human and bovine milk can be cariogenic if the milk is allowed to remain in contact with the teeth.

SIGNS OF NURSING BOTTLE MOUTH

1. Severe to mild decay of all primary upper anterior teeth
2. Decay of upper and lower first molars and lower primary canine teeth in extensive cases

Management Prevention includes the following:

1. Early health education of parents and early dental assessment
2. Elimination of milk or juice in nursing bottle at nap or bedtime. If child needs additional sucking, water in the bottle is preferable; child should be held while given bottle feeding
3. Guidance may be necessary if bedtime sucking continues beyond infancy

PREMATURE ERUPTION

Assessment Natal teeth or neonatal teeth are usually lower incisors. They may be of two different types. Predeciduous teeth are supernumerary teeth, structurally defective, nearly always loose; only the crowns are calcified and the roots are absent or poorly formed. True deciduous teeth occur more frequently and are normal. An x-ray will reveal which type of tooth is present.

Management Removal of predeciduous teeth is usually recommended, especially if looseness entails danger of aspiration, or if they are painful or interfere with nursing. True deciduous teeth should not be extracted.

TEETHING IN INFANCY

Assessment Primary or deciduous tooth eruption begins at about 6 months of age with the lower central incisors, closely followed by the lower lateral incisors and the upper central incisors. Teething continues with teeth erupting approximately every 2 months until 2 years of age. See Table 16-1.

SIGNS OF TEETHING They are not always clear. Some children teethe without pain and with few physical signs. Other children are uncomfortable, irritable, cry, and rub at the gums. Upon inspection, red and swollen gums are evident. Teething can cause daytime restlessness, increase in finger sucking, gum rubbing, drooling, and possibly loss of appetite. When fever, excessive irritability, and other manifestations of illness are attributed to teething, a serious illness may be overlooked.

PHYSIOLOGIC AND DEVELOPMENTAL FACTORS Occurring coincidentally in the infant are factors some parents find difficult to disassociate from teething. These factors are as follows:

1. Excessive salivation: occurs normally at 3 to 4 months of age
2. Lowering of the level of maternal antibody protection: fevers do not occur as a result of teething and should be separately assessed
3. Fussiness, sleep disturbances, and separation anxiety
4. Reaching for and mouthing objects

Management Chewing on clean, hard objects to relieve tension felt in the gums is recommended. Some favorite objects are:

• Hard, rubber teething rings
• Hard, rubber teething beads

- Ridged rubber or plastic teething toys
- Hard rolls or crusts of bread
- Teething pretzels

Rubbing gums with teething lotions which contain benzocaine has been recommended. Rubbing gums with whiskey is a time honored and most frequently recommended treatment. Some teething appliances made of plastic with liquid filling are not recommended since infants may chew through the plastic and may ingest the liquid. Further search should be made for fever or other manifestations of illness.

THUMB SUCKING

Assessment   Thumb sucking is suspected if upper incisors markedly protrude over lower teeth. The thumb or other fingers may exhibit calluses. Holding the thumb in the mouth the greater part of the day and/or night can permanently distort the jaws and teeth. The child's age and severity of the habit determine whether or not sucking is harmful to the facial contours and structures. In 75 percent of all cases the dental deformity will be remolded and corrected spontaneously if the thumb sucking ceases before the age of 6.

Sporadic sucking is essentially innocuous, and regular sucking until age 2 or 3 is considered to be normal. Excessive sucking beyond the age of 6 may be caused by an emotional disturbance. See Chapter 6, Habit Formation.

Management   Practical suggestions are as follows:

1. The thumb or fingers may be removed from the mouth after the child is asleep.
2. Parents and well-meaning relatives and friends are cautioned against pulling the thumb from the mouth or against ceaselessly reminding the child to remove it.
3. Unpleasant tasting medications used to coat the thumb or appliances which prevent sucking are ineffective and may cause further emotional damage.

COUNSELING   Factors to consider for counseling about excessive sucking are as follows:

- The child may need more activity or playtime with other children, or may need more time alone with parents.

- The child may be jealous of a sibling.
- The child may be left for lengthy periods with a caretaker.
- The child may be bored, tired, thirsty, hungry.
- The child may be feeling the effects of a family problem.
- The child may need more time with a parent. See Chapter 6, Time with Parent.

TONGUE THRUST

Assessment   Tongue thrust occurs as a result of the habit of bracing the tongue against the upper and lower incisors at each swallow. In time this causes the teeth to protrude. It may be a manifestation of tension. It may interfere with the acquisition of clear speech.

SIGNS OF TONGUE THRUSTING   Suspect tongue thrusting if both upper and lower incisors protrude enough to leave an oval space when the jaw is closed. If this condition is arrested early, the abnormal position of the teeth may rectify itself spontaneously with growth.

Management   Referral to the dentist is made if signs of tongue thrusting are evident. Orthodontia may be necessary.

COUNSELING   The source of tension may need to be discussed with the parents if the habit continues. It is advised not to call the child's attention to the habit. See Chapter 6, Common Habits.

Resource Information

Resource information can be obtained from these organizations:
1. American Dental Association, 211 E. Chicago Avenue, Chicago, IL 60611.
2. American Society of Dentistry for Children, 211 E. Chicago Avenue, Chicago, IL 60611.
3. College of Physicians and Surgeons, 344 14th Street, San Francisco CA 94118.
4. Semantodontics, Box 15668, 3712 E. Indian School Rd., Phoenix, AZ, 85060

References

Alexander, M. M. and M. S. Brown. *Pediatric History Taking and Physical Diagnosis for Nurses.* New York: McGraw-Hill, 1979.

THE MOUTH AND TEETH • 687

American Academy of Pediatrics. Committee on Nutrition. "Fluoride Supplementation: Revised Dosage Schedule." *Pediatrics* 63:150–152, January 1979.

American Dental Association. Council on Dental Therapeutics. "Prescribing Fluoride Supplement." *Accepted Dental Therapeutics.* 38th ed. Chicago, 1979.

Berkowitz, R., S. Ludwig, and R. Johnson. "Dental Trauma in Children and Adolescents." *Clin Pediatr* 19:166–171, March 1980.

Curson, M. E. J. "Dental Implications of Thumbsucking." *Pediatrics* 54:196–200, August 1974.

De Weese, D. D. and W. H. Saunders. *Textbook of Otolaryngology.* St. Louis: C. V. Mosby, 1973.

Feigal, R. M., M. Jensen, and C. Mensing. "Dental Caries Potential of Liquid Medications." *Pediatrics* 68:416–419, September 1981.

Fomon, S. J., et al. "Recommendations for Feeding Normal Infants." *Pediatrics* 63:52–58, January 1979.

Graber, T. W. *Orthodontics, Principles and Practice.* Philadelphia: W. B. Saunders, 1966.

Hess, J. "Fluoride Therapy in Children." Unpublished material, Dept. of Pediatrics, Grand Rounds, University of California, San Francisco, June 16, 1977.

Honig, P. "Teething—Are Today's Pediatricians Using Yesterday's Notions?" *Pediatrics* 87:415–417, September 1975.

Kempe, C. H., H. K. Silver, and D. O'Brien. *Current Pediatric Diagnosis and Treatment.* Los Altos, CA: Lange Medical Publications, 1980.

Lowery, G. H. *Growth and Development of Children.* Chicago: Yearbook Medical Publishers, 1978.

Morris, A. L. and H. M. Bohannon. *The Dental Specialties in General Practice.* Philadelphia: W. B. Saunders, 1969.

Sweiger, J. L., J. W. Lang, and J. W. Schweiger. "Oral Assessment: How to Do It." *Am J Nurs* 80:654–657, April 1980.

van der Horst, R. L. "On Teething in Infancy." *Clin Pediatr* 12:607–610, October 1973.

Vaughan, V. C., et al., editors. *Nelson Textbook of Pediatrics.* 11th ed. Philadelphia: W. B. Saunders, 1979.

Waitrowski, E., et al. "Dietary Fluoride Intake of Infants." *Pediatrics* 55:517–522, April 1975.

Your Child's Teeth. Chicago: American Dental Association, 1971.

17

The Respiratory System

The most common cause of illness in infancy and childhood is infection of the respiratory tract. Infections of the upper respiratory tract alone account for more than one half of the acute illnesses treated in pediatric ambulatory health facilities. This chapter provides information to assist the nurse practitioner in the assessment and management of common acute problems of the respiratory tract in collaboration with a physician. Complete discussion of respiratory tract problems is beyond the scope of this chapter and is available in major pediatric textbooks. Related information is found in the corresponding chapters on allergy, the gastrointestinal system, infectious diseases, and the mouth and teeth.

ASSESSMENT

A careful history and physical examination determine whether the child can be managed on an ambulatory basis or whether further investigation is warranted prior to deciding on the plan of management.

History

PRESENT CONCERN

Obtain a precise chronologic history of each presenting symptom. (See Chapter 11, Assessment of the Presenting Symptom.)

Cough Obtain information about onset, duration (acute, chronic), type (dry, productive, hacking, moist, barking), progress (better or worse), pattern (day or night), pain (location), postnasal drip, sputum (color, consistency, amount, bloody, odor, frequency), associated symptoms (sore throat, respiratory distress, nasal discharge, fever), medications (type, frequency, duration), past history of cough, and exposure (illness in family).

Respiratory Difficulty See this chapter, Respiratory Distress. Obtain information about onset (abrupt, gradual), duration, pattern of respiration (rapid, slow), type of difficulty (inspiratory, expiratory), associated sounds (wheezing, grunting, stridor, barking cough), nasal flaring, cyanosis, associated symptoms (fever, abdominal pain, rhinorrhea, anorexia, headache, malaise), and past history of respiratory difficulty (diagnosis, treatment), and cardiac condition (see Chapter 18).

Rhinorrhea Obtain information about onset, duration, description of discharge (color, consistency), progress (better, worse), pattern (completely clears and then returns), associated symptoms (sore throat, respiratory distress, fever, cough), medications (type, frequency, duration), previous history of nasal congestion and discharge.

Sore Throat Obtain information about onset, duration, progress (better, worse), treatment (lozenges, salt-water gargles), exposure (illness in other family members), and dysphagia.

Associated Symptoms Obtain information on associated symptoms, such as fever, vomiting, and diarrhea.

PAST HISTORY

Obtain information on immunization status and on previous problems of the respiratory tract (diagnosis, treatment, frequency, hospitalization).

FAMILY HISTORY

Obtain information about familial respiratory tract disorders and illness (allergies, asthma).

HOME ENVIRONMENT

Obtain information on available resources (family, friends, financial), the family's ability to follow a management plan, to make observations of the child's respiratory status, and to return for follow-up care.

Physical Examination

A thorough general physical examination is performed. See Chapter 1, Child Health Assessment. The focus of the examination is to determine the severity of the illness and the location of the abnormality. Table 17-1 summarizes the signs which are helpful in localizing the respiratory tract abnormality. The key diagnostic technique is observation. Table 17-2 summarizes the observed physical signs which help to differentiate between an upper and lower airway obstruction.

MEASUREMENTS AND VITAL SIGNS

Obtain weight, temperature, heart rate (see Chapter 18), and respiratory rate.

Respiratory Rate Normal resting respiratory rates are listed in Table 17-3. Obtain the respiratory rate when the child is quiet and relaxed. Take full 1-minute counts since the rate may normally be uneven. In assessing the rate consider factors such as activity level, anxiety, and fever. Note rhythm, depth, positions of discomfort, and breath odors. The active or febrile infant often has a respiratory rate that is more rapid than the resting rate.

Table 17-1
Signs Helpful in Localizing Respiratory Tract Abnormality

Site of Abnormality	Signs Evident from Simple Observation of Patient	Signs Evident on Further Exam
Nose	Noisy respirations (nasal congestion) Rhinorrhea Occasional cough (secondary to postnasal drip or associated pharyngitis) No signs of respiratory distress except in young infants who may have obligatory nasal breathing	Nasal mucosa edematous and either red (suggesting infection) or pale (suggesting allergic rhinitis) Nasal discharge (usually thin, clear). Chest clear to auscultation except for transmitted sounds
Paranasal sinuses (ethmoid and maxillary sinuses clinically most significant in children < 6 yrs of age)	Mucopurulent nasal discharge Choking cough (↑ at night, occasionally productive of mucopurulent material) Older children may report postnasal drip and/or pain—frontal, temporal, retro-orbital, or in upper incisors.	Nasal mucosa usually red, edematous Mucopurulent nasal discharge May see mucopurulent discharge in midline of pharynx (postnasal drip)
Pharynx, tonsils	Dysphagia (in severe tonsillopharyngitis) Older children may complain of sore throat; however, sore throat may also result from pain referred from the middle ear, parotid gland	Pharynx red Tonsils enlarged, red, with or without whitish or yellow exudates Petechiae on soft palate (suggesting streptococcal infection) Discrete ulcers on anterior tonsillar pillars or pharynx (suggesting enteroviral infection, herpangina) Anterior cervical lymph node enlargement (with or without

Structure	Symptoms	Signs
Larynx (edema, spasm)	Hoarseness Barking ("croupy") cough Inspiratory stridor Dysphagia, drooling (in epiglottitis) May have signs of respiratory distress (See Croup Syndromes)	Decreased breath sounds Supraclavicular and suprasternal retractions relatively more pronounced (compared to intercostal and subcostal retractions)
Trachea and bronchi (edema, mucus)	Deep ("hacking") cough No signs of respiratory distress unless other areas of respiratory tract are also involved	Rhonchi
Bronchioles (edema, mucus, spasm)	Wheezing (expiratory whistling sound); may be absent in severe airway obstruction Hyperexpansion of chest, with increased anterior-posterior diameter and shallow respirations May have signs of respiratory distress	Hyperresonance to percussion Decreased breath sounds Prolonged expiratory phase Musical rales: sonorous sibilant
Alveoli (exudate, edema, collapse)	May have signs of respiratory distress	Over involved lung, *may* have: dullness to percussion decreased breath sounds coarse and fine rales
Pleura	"Splinting" of chest May have signs of respiratory distress	Over involved pleura, *may* have: dullness to percussion decreased breath sounds friction rub

Source: Reprinted with permission from D. S. Rowe, unpublished material, 1973.

Table 17-2

Differentiation Between Upper and Lower Airway Obstruction by Simple Observation

Physical Sign	Upper Airway Obstruction	Lower Airway Obstruction
Voice	Hoarse[a]	Normal
Cough	Barking (croupy)[a]	Deep (hacking)
Sounds made during breathing	Stridor (high-pitched, crowing sound), more pronounced during inspiration than expiration	Wheezing (whistling sound), more pronounced during expiration than inspiration
Inspiratory/expiratory ratio	Prolonged inspiratory phase	Prolonged expiratory phase
Chest retractions	Supraclavicular, suprasternal, and sternal retractions relatively pronounced (compared with intercostal and subcostal retractions)	Intercostal and subcostal retractions relatively pronounced
Chest configuration	Normal	Increased anterior-posterior diameter
Respiratory rate	Relatively less rapid (rarely over 60/min)	Often very rapid (frequently over 60/min)

Source: Reprinted with permission from E. Waechter and F. Blake, *Nursing Care of Children*, 9th ed. Philadelphia: J.B. Lippincott, 1976. P. 457.

[a]Hoarseness and a characteristic barking cough are present only when the vocal cords are involved. Children with epiglottitis are usually not hoarse.

Table 17-3
Normal Resting Respiratory Rate Per Minute[a]

Age (years)	Boys (Mean ± 2 SD)	Girls (Mean ± 2 SD)
0–1	31 ± 16	30 ± 12
1–2	26 ± 8	27 ± 8
2–3	25 ± 8	25 ± 6
3–4	24 ± 6	24 ± 6
4–5	23 ± 4	22 ± 4
5–6	22 ± 4	21 ± 4
6–7	21 ± 6	21 ± 6
7–8	20 ± 6	20 ± 4
8–9	20 ± 4	20 ± 4
9–10	19 ± 4	19 ± 4
10–11	19 ± 4	19 ± 4
11–12	19 ± 6	19 ± 6
12–13	19 ± 6	19 ± 4
13–14	19 ± 4	18 ± 4
14–15	18 ± 4	18 ± 6
15–16	17 ± 6	18 ± 6
16–17	17 ± 4	17 ± 6
17–18	16 ± 6	17 ± 6

Source: From A. Iliff and V. A. Lee, Pulse rates, respiratory rates, and body temperatures of children between 2 months and 18 years. *Child Development, 23*:238, 1952. By permission of The Society for Research in Child Development, Inc.

[a]Data of Iliff and Lee from both fed-sleeping and fasting-awake children.

GENERAL APPEARANCE

Assess the overall appearance of the child (prostrate, inactive, apathetic, apprehensive, agitated).

EAR

Inspect the pinna for position, symmetry, anatomic deformities of helix, antihelix, tragus, lobe, and the external canal for size, shape, cerumen, discharge (white, cheesy material, thin or thick purulent material), foreign body, lesions. Examine the internal canal by tugging the auricle posterosuperiorly with one hand and moving the tragus forward with the other. Observe the tympanic membrane with a brightly illuminated pneumatic otoscope using the largest speculum that will fit comfortably in the ear. Note color (reddish to grayish-yellow), thickness, vascularity, contour, bony landmarks (presence, prominence, absence), mobility in the posterosuperior quadrant of the tympanic membrane, and fluid level. See Chapter 25 for hearing tests.

Tympanometry The performance of tympanometry is an important advancement in the diagnosis of middle ear disease. Tympanometry is the objective measurement of the mobility of the tympanic membrane as a function of air pressure change in the external auditory canal. The mobility of the tympanic membrane is a function of the air pressure on either side of the tympanic membrane. A tympanogram graphically records the mobility of the tympanic membrane at specified values of air pressure between plus and minus 200 mm H_2O.

To obtain the tympanogram, an electroacoustic impedance meter is attached to the child's head by an audiometry-type earphone set. A tone of fixed qualities is sent through a small probe that has been inserted, airtight, into the external auditory canal. While the external canal pressure is artificially varied, the mobility of the tympanic membrane is electronically measured. The resulting graphic representations distinguish a normal ear from an abnormal one.

Tympanometry is also used to evaluate middle ear pressure, to identify tympanic membrane perforations, to follow the progress of otitis media, and to confirm the patency of ventilation tubes placed in the tympanic membrane.

NOSE

Inspect for nasal flaring, discharge, color of the mucous membrane, patency, polyps and foreign body.

PHARYNX AND TONSILS

Inspect pharynx for redness, swelling, postnasal drip, abscess, petechiae on the soft palate, discrete ulcers on the anterior tonsillar pillars or pharynx. Examine tonsils for redness, exudate, size. Listen for hoarseness. Watch for drooling, a symptom of epiglottitis. Do not examine the pharynx if epiglottitis is suspected.

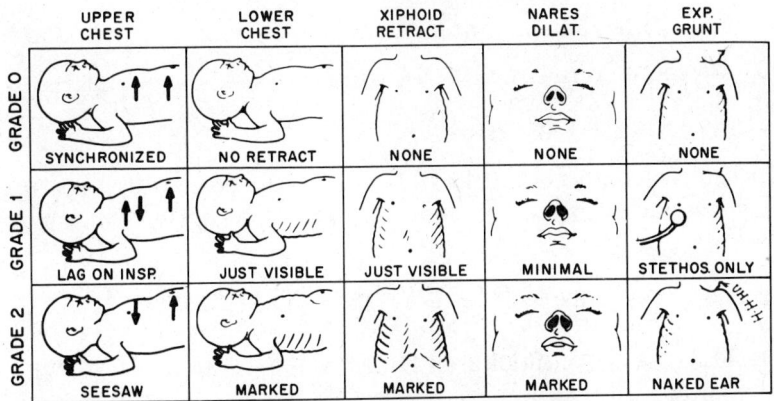

	UPPER CHEST	LOWER CHEST	XIPHOID RETRACT	NARES DILAT.	EXP. GRUNT
GRADE 0	SYNCHRONIZED	NO RETRACT	NONE	NONE	NONE
GRADE 1	LAG ON INSP.	JUST VISIBLE	JUST VISIBLE	MINIMAL	STETHOS. ONLY
GRADE 2	SEESAW	MARKED	MARKED	MARKED	NAKED EAR

OBSERVATION OF RETRACTIONS

Figure 17-1 Retraction scoring. An index of respiratory distress is determined by grading each of five arbitrary criteria. Grade 0 indicates no difficulty, grade 1 moderate difficulty, and grade 2 maximum respiratory difficulty. The "retraction score" is the sum of these values; a total score of 0 indicates no dyspnea, whereas a total score of 10 denotes maximal respiratory distress. (From W. Silverman, *Dunham's Premature Infants*, 3rd ed., 1961. Courtesy of Paul B. Hoeber, Inc.)

CHEST

Inspect for pattern of breathing (rate, depth, rhythm, ease), retractions (intercostal, subcostal, supraclavicular, and suprasternal), decreased breath sounds, abnormal auscultatory chest sounds (rales, rhonchi, wheezing), tachypnea, prolonged inspiratory or expiratory phase. See Figure 17-1 for diagram of retraction scoring.

Laboratory Procedures

CULTURES

See Chapter 27, Infectious Diseases. Nasopharyngeal, sputum, and throat cultures are frequently obtained and often of little help except for identifying beta-hemolytic streptococcus in pharyngitis. For example, a nasal culture will probably show a high bacterial count. This is often mistaken for bacterial disease rather than mere colonization. Interpretation of culture results should consider the origin of the culture (flora of the respiratory tract mucosa normally contain pathogenic organisms) and the possibility of contamination.

X-RAY FILM OF THE CHEST

It is usually indicated if the physical examination of the chest reveals any abnormalities or signs of pulmonary dysfunction.

Basic Principles of Infections of the Respiratory Tract

1. Etiologic classification is of limited value due to the large number of different organisms that cause similar clinical symptoms and the few distinctive clinical syndromes.
2. A single organism is capable of producing clinical symptoms of varying severity and extent. The factors that affect the clinical symptoms are age, sex, previous exposure to the infectious agent, allergy, and nutritional status. For example, illnesses in family members may be simultaneously manifested as the common cold in the parents, bronchiolitis in the infant, and pharyngitis and a subclinical infection in siblings (Vaughan et al., 1979).
3. Most acute respiratory tract infections are caused by viruses and *Mycoplasma*. The only bacterial agents capable of producing primary nasal or pharyngeal disease are various streptococci and the diphtheria organism (Vaughan et al., 1979, p. 1172). Lower respiratory illness is also caused mainly by viral agents; however, pneumonia may be caused by the pneumococcus, *Hemophilus influenzae* and, rarely, other bacterial pathogens. Table 17-4 outlines the ecology of infections, the seasonal pattern, the epidemiology, and the risk of re-infection.

MANAGEMENT

General Measures

Minimize exposure to others. Rest in bed.

FLUIDS

A generous amount of fluids, water in particular, is important. Prevention of dehydration will help prevent thickened mucus. Recommended clear liquids include water, juice, weak tea, cola, Jell-o, broth, and ginger ale. See Table 3-4 in Chapter 3 for the amount of fluid required daily. Caution parents about forcing fluids or awakening child.

HUMIDIFICATION

Generally, inspired, humidified air soothes the respiratory mucosa, decreases the viscosity of upper respiratory secretions, and relieves cough and hoarseness of laryngitis. Methods for humidifying air include steam (boiling water, hot shower) and vaporizer (cool-mist, steam). There is no therapeutic difference between cool-mist and steam vaporizers. A carefully improvised canopy arranged over the crib can prevent dissipation of the vapor throughout the room and direct it toward the child (Hughes, 1980, p. 327). The vaporizer should be placed longer than the child's arm or leg length away from the crib to prevent the child from touching it. It should be within 3 to 4 feet of the child's head with the nozzle directed toward the head of the crib. The height of the vaporizer should be at the height of the crib mattress.

Cool-Mist Vaporizer It is preferred for safety reasons, and the mist can be directed toward the child. It is noisier and humidifies the air more slowly than steam vaporizers. Following each use, it is drained and cleaned carefully according to instructions to avoid bacterial overgrowth. As a precaution against excessive moisture, nearby surfaces are protected with towels or absorbent pads.

Steam Vaporizer It emits steam and produces moisture quickly. Additives (designated by manufacturer) are necessary to control the vapor output. The models are designed to meet safety requirements to prevent tipping over on a 30-degree incline regardless of water level and to prevent water from being scaldingly hot if it should spill. For safety reasons it is still advisable to avoid handling the steam vaporizer unless it is unplugged. It should be placed on the floor to prevent hot steam from reaching the child's face and to

Table 17-4

Ecology of Infection with Various Respiratory Tract Pathogens

Group	Serotype	Usual Time of Primary Infection	Person-to-person Spread	Pattern of Infection	Risk of Indicated Illness during Primary Infection	Reinfection
Myxovirus: Influenza	A,B	Infancy and childhood; any age for minor antigenic variants	Highly effective	Epidemic—every 2–4 years, usually winter	Influenza—75%	Common with new variants—less common with same variant
Parainfluenza	1,2,3,4	Infancy—type 3; Childhood—types 1,2,4	Highly effective—type 3; less effective—types 1,2,4	Endemic or sporadic—occasionally epidemic (types 1,3)	Febrile respiratory illness—50–75% (types 1,2,3)	Common—can be associated with URI
Resp. syncytial	—	Infancy	Highly effective	Epidemic, every year—fall, winter or spring	Febrile lower respiratory tract illness—45%	Common—often associated with URI

Adenovirus	1,2,3,5,7	Infancy—types 1,2 Childhood—types 3,5,7	Effective—types 1,2,5 or moderately effective—types 3,7	Endemic (occasionally epidemic types 3,7)	Febrile respiratory disease—55–90%	Uncommon
Picornavirus: Coxsackie B		Infancy and childhood	Moderately effective	Epidemic—summer	Not known	Not known
Rhinovirus	60 or more	All ages	Unknown	Endemic sporadic flurries of different types	URI 50%[a]	Occurs
M. pneumoniae	—	2nd and 3rd decades	Ineffective	Endemic or occasionally epidemic	Pneumonia 3—10%[a]	Uncommon

Source: From V. C. Vaughan, R. J. McKay, and R. E. Behrman, *Nelson Textbook of Pediatrics*, 11th ed., p. 1173, © 1979 by the W. B. Saunders Company, Philadelphia. Table modified from R. M. Chanock and R. H. Parrott: *Pediatrics*, 36:21, 1965.

[a]Data for adult infection.

avoid accidental tripping. Frequent cleaning is advisable to prevent malfunctioning due to mineral deposits. See Chapter 5, Accident Prevention and Safety.

COUNSELING Ideally, vaporizers are purchased before a crisis so a suitable model can be purchased at an economic price. Suggestions for using a vaporizer are as follows:

1. Direct the vapor toward the child
2. Clean unit after each use

MEDICATION

See Chapter 13, Approach to Medications in Childhood.

Cough Suppressants They are used to depress the cough reflex. They can be useful with a dry, nonproductive, hyperactive, and annoying cough; however, there are very few indications for the use of suppressants. Codeine and dextromethorphan hydrobromide are the common ingredients of suppressant medications.

CODEINE It is considered the most useful narcotic antitussive agent. It has a drying effect on the respiratory mucosa. Side effects include nausea, drowsiness, and constipation. It is contraindicated in children with chronic pulmonary disease.

DEXTROMETHORPHAN HYDROBROMIDE It is considered to be as effective as codeine but does not depress respiration or predispose to addiction. Side effects are mild and infrequent. The most common complaints are drowsiness and gastrointestinal upset.

Decongestants They are of questionable value, and their use remains controversial (Lampert et al., 1975; West et al., 1975). They are either applied topically or administered orally to decrease the edema of the nasal mucosa and to relieve symptoms.

NOSE DROPS Phenylephrine hydrochloride (e.g., 0.25 percent Neo-Synephrine Hydrochloride) is the common ingredient used in topical products. Nose drops must be used with great caution. They may be instilled 4 or 5 times each day not to exceed 5 days. Overuse may cause rebound edema of the nasal mucosa. They should be avoided during the first 3 months of life.

ORAL PRODUCTS Pseudoephedrine hydrochloride (e.g., Sudafed) is commonly used in cold products. It should not be used for more than 10 days. Side effects are uncommon, but nervousness, restlessness, or sleeplessness may occur. This medication is not recommended in the presence of high blood pressure, heart disease, diabetes, or thyroid disease without physician consultation. The usual dosage for over-the-counter decongestants is as follows:

- 2 to 5 years: 15 mg, three to four times per day
- 6 to 12 years: 30 mg, three to four times per day
- >12 years: 60 mg, three to four times per day

Expectorants They are of questionable effectiveness. Glyceryl guaiacolate is the most common ingredient of expectorant medication. It is seldom associated with gastric upset and nausea.

Antimicrobial Therapy A common error is to institute antimicrobial therapy indiscriminately. Such practice increases the costs of health care, encourages the growth of resistant bacteria, and carries the risk of adverse reactions to the medication (Hughes, 1980, p. 327). Use of antimicrobial therapy should be instituted judiciously. See the specific common respiratory problem for the antimicrobial agents used.

OTHER SYMPTOMATIC MEASURES

1. A bulb syringe is useful for removal of nasal discharge in infants below 3 to 4 months. Drops of physiologic saline prepared by a pharmacist are put into each nostril to liquefy the dried mucus. Wait 1 to 2 minutes. The bulb is squeezed prior to insertion into the nostril. Let it expand while inside the nostril. The mucus is then squirted onto tissue paper, and the process is repeated as necessary. If a pharmacy is not easily available, physiologic saline may be prepared at home, but parents should be cautioned about making the solution too strong. Written instructions should be carefully reviewed with the caretakers. To prepare the saline solution, add ¼ measured teaspoon of salt to one measured cup of boiled water (10 minutes). The solution is covered and cooled. Refrigeration can be used to speed cooling. The saline solution is then poured into a clean jar and capped (Bridgewater and Voignier, 1979).

2. Hard, sour candies or popsicles relieve cough or sore throat.
3. Warm, saline gargles several times a day relieve sore throat.
4. Fever reduction. See Chapter 11, Approach to Illness in Childhood.

Counseling

The first illness is often a problem of the respiratory system. This is an opportune time to counsel parents about the care of their sick child. Their ideas and practices in the care of their own respiratory illnesses are explored, and good practices are reinforced. Therapeutic measures are practically reviewed. The use of over-the-counter preparations is discussed. See Chapter 13, Approach to Medications in Childhood.

COMMON CLINICAL PROBLEMS

Upper Respiratory Tract

The upper respiratory tract consists of the structures above the larynx: nasal cavity, paranasal sinuses, pharynx, and middle ear.

EPISTAXIS (NOSEBLEEDING)

Assessment   The anterior medial nasal septum is the most common site for bleeding. Epistaxis is most often secondary to trauma, an upper respiratory infection (URI), dry air, or nose picking. Other causes include the following:

- Allergic rhinitis
- Benign or malignant tumor of the nose and paranasal sinuses
- Blood dyscrasias (i.e., leukemia, hemophilia, ITP)
- Clotting/bleeding problems
- Dilated vessels in the nasal septum
- Foreign body in the nose
- Nasal polyps
- Severe hypertension

- Trauma
- Winter indoor heating

Epistaxis rarely occurs in infancy, but it is common in childhood and decreases after puberty.

Management Most nosebleeds stop spontaneously. The following steps are followed to control bleeding:

1. The child is positioned in a sitting posture if possible, and instructed to breathe through the mouth while pressure is applied to the nose.
2. Direct, firm pressure is applied for 2 to 10 minutes from the lateral side of the nose against the septum in the area of Kesselbach's plexus.
3. If bleeding persists, other measures are necessary to constrict the nasal vessels such as local application of epinephrine (1:1,000) with or without topical thrombin. Once bleeding is controlled, a silver nitrate stick may be used to prevent further difficulties if a bleeding site is identified. If bleeding still persists, a nose packing by an otolaryngologist may be necessary (Vaughan et al., 1979; Graef and Cone, 1980, p. 531).
4. Petroleum jelly is applied to the nasal mucosa to alleviate crusting of blood and further excoriation.

Consultation with a physician is indicated if a bleeding site is not identified. If a significant amount of blood was swallowed, the parents are warned that the child might pass a dark, tarry stool or might vomit bloody material.

FOREIGN BODY

Ear

ASSESSMENT Symptoms may include discharge from the external canal, decreased hearing in the affected ear, and symptoms of inflammation. There may be a history of the child putting objects in the ears. Failure to remove the foreign body may lead to otitis externa. Examination requires good visualization.

MANAGEMENT Consultation is obtained. If it is a nonvegetable object, irrigation with water helps to remove the object. If it is a vegetable object, irrigation with water is contraindicated because it may cause the object to swell. A referral to an ENT specialist may be indicated.

Nose

ASSESSMENT Symptom is unilateral rhinorrhea that is purulent, foul smelling, and unresponsive to antimicrobial therapy. Examination requires good visualization. A foreign body that is not removed can induce an acute inflammatory process.

MANAGEMENT Referral to a physician is indicated if the foreign body cannot be removed easily or if high fever is present. The child may need to be sedated before the removal of the object.

Trachea or Bronchial Tree

ASSESSMENT Sudden onset of severe coughing without previous history of fever or nasal discharge suggests inhalation of a foreign body. X-rays may be indicated, although a normal X-ray does not rule out the possibility of a foreign body because many substances are not radiopaque. The cough may become quiescent but may recur later accompanied by fever and possibly dyspnea. Pneumonia may ensue. The problem does not resolve until the foreign body is removed.

MANAGEMENT ENT and/or surgical consultation is indicated.

IMPACTED CERUMEN

Assessment The question of how vigorously to pursue visualization of the tympanic membrane is a most common problem. Indication for removal of impacted cerumen include a history of upper respiratory symptoms, fever, or decreased hearing.

Management To remove cerumen hold the child securely. There are two basic techniques to remove cerumen: dry and wet.

DRY TECHNIQUE Use a No. 00 blunt ear curet. Do not use a sharp curet. Gain the cooperation of the child by showing the curet and stroking it lightly over the back of the hand, cheek, and pinna. It is essential that the child be restrained well. Clean the canal under direct vision through otoscope. If the wax is clinging to the walls of the canal, pass the curet beyond it and gently retract the curet with light pressure on the skin of the ear canal. If there is a large mass of wax, pass the curet superior to the mass and position it just behind the mass. For very hard wax, the use of hydrogen peroxide or mineral oil for 15 minutes will soften the wax for easier removal. Pull the wax mass out of the canal. Parents should be prepared for the possibility of bleeding. The dry technique is successful 95 percent of the time (Graef and Cone, 1980, p. 525).

WET TECHNIQUE If the wax is pushed firmly against the tympanic membrane, irrigate with water at body temperature with a metal or plastic ear syringe or a Water Pik. Body temperature is important to avoid vertigo. The wet technique is messier and may frighten children. Do not use this technique if a perforation of the tympanic membrane is suspected because wax may be inadvertently blown into the middle ear.

MEDICATION Triethanolamine polypeptide oleate-condensate (Cerumenex) is sometimes prescribed to soften ear wax. Allow the drops to remain in the ear no longer than 15 to 30 minutes because of its potential caustic and allergenic effects. Debrox, hydrogen peroxide, or mineral oil are used to soften hard, dry cerumen. Instill four to five drops two to three times each day for 4 to 5 days.

COUNSELING Education about ear hygiene is part of routine ambulatory care. Cotton Q-tips are useful for cleaning the external ear, but they should *not* be inserted into the ear canal. If it is necessary to remove cerumen during the clinic visit, the process is explained to the parent and to the child. Prophylactic medication is sometimes prescribed for installation several days prior to the next clinic visit.

INFLUENZA

See Chapter 27.

NASOPHARYNGITIS (THE COMMON COLD)

Assessment Fifty percent of upper respiratory infections are "the common cold." In acute nasopharyngitis there is usually a history of recent exposure to a respiratory illness, and the symptoms completely resolve. It is difficult to differentiate allergic rhinitis from recurrent upper respiratory infection. Predisposing factors include individual susceptibility, respiratory allergy, poor nutrition, and environment (Wasserman and Gromisch, 1981, p. 231). Refer to Chapter 26, Allergic Rhinitis, for more discussion.

INCIDENCE The number of respiratory infections in children under 6 years ranges from 0 to 15 per year with an average of 7 per year (Dingle, 1964). After the age of 6 the number of colds decreases to 4 to 5 yearly.

ETIOLOGY Viruses are the primary cause of nasopharyngitis. Refer to Table 17-4. Of the relatively few bacteria implicated in nasopharyngitis, group A beta-hemolytic streptococcus is the only one that occurs frequently enough to require serious consideration in the general population (Waechter and Blake, 1976).

CLINICAL FINDINGS Nasal congestion, rhinorrhea, and sneezing are the common symptoms. Other symptoms may include fever, sore throat, headaches, muscle aches, intermittent coughing, mouth breathing and decreased appetite. The physical findings include inflammation and edema of the nasal mucosal membranes, redness of the pharynx, tonsils, and palpebral conjunctivae, redness and congestion of the tympanic membrane, enlargement of cervical lymph glands.

COURSE OF ILLNESS The incubation period is usually 2 to 4 days. Sneezing, nasal obstruction and discharge, and sore throat follow. Nasal congestion and cough usually persist for about 1 to 2 weeks. Other symptoms rarely last beyond 2 to 3 days. Persistence of symptoms beyond 2 weeks suggests the possibility of complications.

COMPLICATIONS The most common complications are secondary bacterial infections of the middle ear and paranasal sinuses. Suppurative cervical adenitis may also occur. A secondary bacterial infection is suspected if fever persists or returns after 3 days.

Management Management is supportive and symptomatic. See this chapter, General Measures. Antibiotics are not used except in cases of proven streptococcal infections. Cold preparations and remedies are largely ineffective, and their value remains unproven. Humidification may prevent drying of the nasal mucosa. Nasal mucus can be removed with the bulb syringe in the young infant or with a soft tissue.

COUNSELING Openly share with parents the current knowledge on nasopharyngitis. Education should include information about the course of illness, signs, and symptoms indicative of bacterial complications and the need for re-evaluation, and the use of medications (see Chapter 13, Approach to Medications in Childhood).

OTITIS EXTERNA (SWIMMER'S EAR)

Assessment It is a painful infection of the external auditory canal. It frequently follows ear trauma caused by fingernails, cotton tip applicators, or a foreign body. There is usually a history of water in the external auditory canal. The most common causative agent is *Pseudomonas aeruginosa* and fungi such as *Candida* and *Aspergillus*. The most common clinical findings are pain upon movement of the tragus, pain with chewing, edema, and a whitish cheesy discharge. Removal of all exudate and discharge is necessary for examination of the external canal and the tympanic membrane. Visualization may be difficult due to edema and stenosis. Otitis externa may follow perforation of tympanic membrane.

Management

MEDICATION Eardrops containing cortisone and antibiotics specific for *P. aeruginosa* and staphylococcus are given as follows: three drops three times per day for 7 to 14 days. Analgesics are given to relieve pain.

COUNSELING Education is provided about the causes of external otitis, administration of eardrops, and signs and symptoms which indicate the need for further evaluation. Gentle cleansing of the ear canal is done as needed (usually one to two times each week). Cotton is placed in the canal while drainage is present to prevent dermatitis of the pinna. Swimming is not allowed. If treatment is unsuccessful in 2 weeks or symptoms increase, suspect sensitivity to the medication and substitute another one (Graef and Cone, 1980).

PHARYNGOTONSILLITIS

Assessment It is uncommon in children less than 2 years of age. Thirty to fifty percent of the cases of acute pharyngitis in school age children seen at the health care facility are streptococcal in origin. The incidence of streptococcal pharyngitis increases during the winter and spring months. Note any history of recent exposure to Streptococcus as well as history of penicillin allergy.

ETIOLOGY Viruses are the most common causes of acute pharyngotonsillitis. The only common bacterial cause of acute pharyngitis is group A beta-hemolytic streptococcus.

CLINICAL PRESENTATION Distinguishing a viral infection from a bacterial infection requiring antimicrobial therapy is difficult. Table 17-5 summarizes the major differences. In scarlet fever, a characteristic scarlatiniform rash sometimes develops within the first 12 hours after the onset of symptoms, and may occur up to 2 days later. (See Chapter 27, Table 27-1). The peritonsillar lymph nodes are tender and enlarged. The symptoms usually subside within 24 to 48 hours and rarely continue after 4 to 5 days even without antibiotic therapy.

Table 17-5
Differentiation of Viral and Streptococcal Pharyngotonsillitis

	Viral Pharyngotonsillitis	Strep Pharyngotonsillitis
Age	Any age	Usually over 3 years
Onset	Gradual	Sudden
General appearance	Mild to moderate toxicity and malaise	Moderate to severe toxicity and malaise
Fever	Slight to moderate (38.3°C to 39.4°C)	Moderate to high (38.9°C to 40.6°C)
Symptoms	Cough, conjunctivitis, hoarseness, rhinitis, sore throat	Sore throat, abdominal pain, headache, vomiting
Physical findings	Minimal to moderate tonsillar erythema, none or small exudate (except in infectious mono), minimal to moderate enlargement and tenderness of anterior cervical nodes	Moderate to extensive tonsillar erythema, small to extensive exudate (rule out diphtheria if extensive), petechial mottling of soft palate, moderate to extensive enlargement and tenderness of anterior cervical nodes

Source: Compiled from Eichenwald, 1976a; Green, M. & R. Haggerty, *Amb Peds II*. Phil: Saunders, 1977 and Waechter, 1976.

THROAT CULTURE   A throat culture is the most reliable method of identifying a streptococcal infection. Criteria for when to obtain a throat culture in children below 3 years of age are poorly defined since the incidence is less and complications are uncommon. One guideline is to obtain a throat culture from infants who have a prolonged illness with thin nasal discharge or who have exudative tonsillitis (Waechter and Blake, 1976, p. 450). Honikman and Massel's (1971) guidelines for obtaining throat cultures in school age children are useful in communities in which streptococcal infection and its complications are common. A throat culture is obtained from any child with the following:

1. A pure or predominant sore throat and fever of any degree (over 37.3°C orally)
2. Associated oral temperature of 38.3°C or higher

If there is any question about the etiology, a throat culture is taken.

COMPLICATIONS
Suppurative:

• Cervical adenitis
• Otitis media
• Peritonsillar abscess (uncommon but serious)
• Sinusitis

Nonsuppurative:

• Acute poststreptococcal glomerulonephritis
• Acute rheumatic fever

Management   Medication is best delayed until throat culture results are available, even when streptococcal pharyngitis is strongly suspected. Antimicrobial therapy is still effective in preventing acute rheumatic fever even if treatment is delayed up to 9 days after the onset of symptoms.

ANTIMICROBIAL THERAPY   Penicillin is the drug of choice for 10 days for acute streptococcal pharyngotonsillitis. The choice of route of administration depends on the ability and willingness of the child to take the oral medication and on the parents' ability to comply with the 10-day treatment. See Chapter 13, Compliance. Erythromycin is given to children with a documented penicillin allergy.

Sulfonamides are effective prophylactically but are ineffective in the treatment of streptococcal infections.

SUPPORTIVE THERAPY See this chapter, General Measures. For sore throats warm, normal saline gargle several times each day soothes irritated mucosa. Hard, sour candy is useful with a dry, raspy throat since it acts as a demulcent by increasing the flow of saliva. Hot or cold compresses to tender cervical nodes may comfort the child.

EXPOSED CONTACTS Throat cultures are indicated for symptomatic family members; but if recurrent streptococcal pharyngitis occurs within the family, all family members should be cultured.

COUNSELING Education should include information about the course of illness, the necessity for a full 10-day course of treatment if Streptococcus is the etiologic agent, side effects of the antibiotic, and signs and symptoms indicative of bacterial complications.

SEROUS OTITIS MEDIA

Assessment It is a noninfectious condition with an accumulation of fluid in the middle ear. It is the most common chronic problem of childhood. Suspect its presence in any child who does not "pay attention," or who adjusts the volume of the television to uncomfortable levels.

ETIOLOGY It is caused by allergy, nasopharyngeal inflammation, or barotrauma (such as rapid descent in a nonpressurized aircraft cabin). It is often a sequela of suppurative otitis media. There are several predisposing factors (Rudolph, 1982, p. 892):

• Allergy
• Craniofacial abnormalities, i.e., cleft palate
• Inflammation of the upper respiratory tract
• Nasopharyngeal masses
• Systemic diseases, such as hypothyroidism, renal failure, and heart failure
• The horizontal position and flaccid cartilaginous support of the eustachian tube in children

CLINICAL FINDINGS A marked conductive hearing loss that continues for weeks or months is the principal symptom. The fluid produces a sensation of fullness in the ear, decreasing hearing, and a "popping" sound with swallowing. The tympanic membrane is retracted, translucent, and dull. Fluid may or may not be evident behind the drum. Decreased mobility of the drum is evident with pneumatic otoscopy or electronic tympanometry.

COMPLICATIONS

• Delayed language and speech development
• Behavior and coordination changes
• Recurrent acute suppurative otitis media
• Erosion of the ossicles and formation of cholesteatoma

Management Attention is directed toward the identification of the cause of serous otitis media. Oral decongestants are frequently prescribed, but their efficacy is unproven. See Decongestants, this chapter. Children with a history of allergies can be treated with a traditional program of environmental control and antihistamines. Follow-up visits are important to assess the resolution of the problem. If the serous otitis media is not resolved, referral to ENT is indicated. Insertion of small plastic tubes in the tympanic membrane for chronic conditions does temporarily aerate the middle ear and improve hearing; however, the problem may recur upon removal of the tubes.

SINUSITIS (ACUTE)

Assessment Acute bacterial sinusitis is seen as a complication of acute viral nasopharyngitis. The signs occur shortly after the acute phase of the illness, just when the child should be improving.

ETIOLOGY It may be viral or bacterial in origin. In young children *H. influenzae*, pneumococcus, group A streptococcus, and staphylococcus are the primary organisms.

CLINICAL FINDINGS Mucopurulent nasal discharge, often unilateral, is the most common finding. Fever, headache, and localized sinus pain are rarely seen in early childhood. A postnasal discharge tends to precipitate coughing attacks. Pain of the upper teeth and cheeks may indicate maxillary sinusitis, and increased pain on bending the head forward may indicate frontal sinusitis.

LABORATORY STUDIES X-ray studies confirm the diagnosis in children after 5 years of age. Before this age the X-ray films are difficult to interpret. CBC, culture and smear of nasal discharge may be helpful.

COMPLICATIONS

• Acute orbital cellulitis
• Meningitis, subdural abscess, epidural abscess
• Cavernous sinus thrombosis

Management There is no specific therapy for acute viral sinusitis.

MEDICATION

1. A short course of topical decongestant may be helpful in shrinking swollen nasal mucosa and facilitating sinus drainage. See this chapter, Decongestants.
2. Ampicillin for 10 to 14 days is the drug of choice for bacterial sinusitis.

COUNSELING Parents are educated about the course of the illness, signs and symptoms of secondary bacterial infection (mucopurulent discharge, persistent cough, malaise), and the necessity for the 10- to 14-day course of therapy if antibiotics are prescribed.

SUPPURATIVE OTITIS MEDIA

Assessment It is the most common acute infectious illness with the exception of the cold. It is a common complication of an upper respiratory infection. One factor which is popularly considered to be a cause of the high incidence of middle-ear infection is the anatomic difference in the eustachian tube. In the infant the eustachian tube is shorter and more horizontal compared to the adult. Suppurative otitis media is most prevalent in the first 6 years of life with a peak incidence between 6 and 36 months.

ETIOLOGY Recent research (Henderson et al., 1982) demonstrates that respiratory infections caused by respiratory syncytial virus, influenza viruses, and adenoviruses are antecedents to acute suppurative otitis media. The causative organisms vary with age. During the first 6 weeks of life, the most common causes are gram-negative enteric bacilli, in addition to *Streptococcus pneumoniae* and

Hemophilus influenzae, the most common causes in older infants and children.

CLINICAL FINDINGS Nasal congestion, irritability and cough are often the only presenting symptoms. Fever is absent in 30 to 50 percent of bacterially proven otitis media. Other associated symptoms include vomiting, diarrhea, severe deep ear pain, and difficulty in hearing.

DIAGNOSIS The diagnosis is based on the proper assessment of the tympanic membrane using a pneumatic otoscope. There is an outward bulging of the tympanic membrane which obscures the normal body landmarks and light reflex, and decreased mobility in the posterosuperior quadrant. The redness of the tympanic membrane alone is insufficient evidence to establish the diagnosis. Tympanometry can be used to establish the diagnosis. See this chapter, Tympanometry.

COMPLICATIONS

- Chronic serous otitis media
- Facial nerve paralysis
- Hearing loss
- Mastoiditis (rare)
- Meningitis (rare)
- Perforation of the tympanic membrane
- Serous labyrinthitis

Management

MEDICATION Selection of an antibiotic is based on the age of the child.

Antimicrobial Therapy

Neonatal Period Therapy is aimed at *S. pneumoniae, H. influenzae,* group B streptococci, and gram-negative enteric bacilli. For infants during the first week of life or who have risk factors associated with pregnancy and delivery such as low birth weight, therapy is a combination of penicillin and an aminoglycoside to provide efficacy for the targeted organisms. For infants in good health and who are not toxic, therapy is either ampicillin or amoxicillin. (Klein, 1981, pp. 228–229)

6 Weeks to 6 Years Therapy is aimed at *S. pneumoniae* and *H. influenzae.* Ampicillin (50 to 100 mg/kg/24 hr in four divided doses) or amoxicillin (20 to 40 mg/kg/24 hr in three divided doses) for 10 days are the preferred drugs. For those children allergic to penicillins, an alternative is a combination of oral erythromycin (50 mg/kg/24 hr) and either triple sulfonamides (100 mg/kg/24 hr) or sulfisoxazole (150 mg/kg/24 hr) in four divided doses for 10 days. The combination of trimethoprim (8 mg/kg/24 hr) and sulfamethoxazole (40 mg/kg/24 hr) in two divided doses for 10 days can also be used for children who are penicillin sensitive or in cases in which the causative agent is ampicillin resistant.

Older Children (>6 Years) Penicillin or erythromycin alone may be given. To cover the possibility of *H. influenzae,* the antimicrobial therapy recommended for children 6 weeks to 6 years of age may be given.

Ampicillin Rash The onset of the rash can occur any time from 24 hours to 16 days after the initiation of treatment. The rash almost always occurs first on the trunk of the body. In over one-half the cases the face and extremities are involved. The palms, soles, and mucosal surfaces are usually not affected. The rash is likely to be maculopapular, mildly pruritic with the absence of systemic symptoms. Ampicillin therapy in this situation can be continued. These children should not be labeled as allergic to penicillin. If the rash is florid or urticarial, immediately discontinue therapy. The incidence of a rash increases in children with infectious mononucleosis, cytomegalovirus infection, or acute lymphocytic leukemia who receive ampicillin (Kerns et al., 1973, p. 187).

Decongestants They are frequently prescribed as adjuncts to the antibiotic therapy; however, their efficacy has not been proven. See this chapter, Decongestants.

MYRINGOTOMY It is rarely performed. The major indication for myringotomy is severe ear pain unrelieved by analgesic medication.

FOLLOW-UP Improvement should occur within 2 to 3 days. A telephone call is useful in confirming resolution of the illness. If improvement is not seen, further investigation is indicated. A follow-up visit is scheduled 2 to 3 weeks after the initiation of therapy to re-evaluate the middle ear and check hearing response.

RECURRENT SUPPURATIVE OTITIS MEDIA Approximately 50 percent of infants and children have at least one other middle-ear infection within 4 months following the diagnosis of the first one, caused by a different organism. This suggests that the second episode is a new infection, not an exacerbation of the previous episode. Referral to an otologist is indicated for frequent recurrent episodes of suppurative otitis media.

Prophylactic antimicrobial therapy is sometimes used for children with recurrent otitis media. However, the long-term effects of such a practice have not been studied.

COUNSELING Education should include information about the causes and complications of otitis media, the side effects of the antibiotic, the importance of giving the antibiotic for the entire course of therapy, and the need to return for a follow-up evaluation.

Lower Respiratory Tract

Conditions affecting the larynx, trachea, bronchi, and bronchioles warrant careful evaluation because of the potential interference with ventilation.

RESPIRATORY DISTRESS

Assessment   It indicates lower respiratory tract abnormality and may require emergency measures.

ETIOLOGY

1. Respiratory tract infection (i.e., bronchiolitis, acute epiglottitis, spasmodic laryngitis, acute laryngotracheobronchitis, pneumonia)
2. Noninfectious respiratory tract abnormality (i.e., asthma, atelectasis, aspiration, pneumothorax)
3. Cardiac disorders (i.e., congestive heart failure). See Chapter 18

4. Generalized metabolic disorders (i.e., acidosis, salicylate poisoning, shock.)
5. Neurologic disorders (i.e., encephalitis, intracranial hemorrhage, meningitis)
6. Sepsis

CLINICAL EVALUATION Signs of respiratory distress are: cyanosis, expiratory grunting, inspiratory chest retractions (subcostal, intercostal, suprasternal, supraclavicular), nasal flaring, and tachypnea (the most sensitive indicator). A consistently elevated respiratory rate is more important than the specific rate. Guidelines for determining tachypnea are as follows:

Age	Respiratory Rate
Newborn	>50
1 year	>36
5 years	>25
Adolescent	>22

See Figure 17-1, Retraction Scoring.

Management Immediate referral to a physician is indicated. Treatment is directed toward the basic disease as well as the administration of oxygen. Local paramedics or the fire department may be the quickest source.

SUPPORTIVE MEASURES See this chapter, General Measures. Oral hydration and humidification are essential. Oxygen therapy is almost always indicated. Specific additional therapy depends on the etiology of the respiratory distress.

COUNSELING Parents are often frightened when their child is in respiratory distress. Education should include observational guidelines for assessing the condition of the child, including how to count respiratory rates, positions for easier breathing, and possibly pulmonary resuscitation measures.

BRONCHIOLITIS

Assessment It is a viral infection of the small bronchi and bronchioles characterized by lower airway obstruction. Obstruction is caused by edema, accumulation of mucus, and bronchospasm.

INCIDENCE It occurs during the first 2 years of life with a peak incidence at 6 weeks of age. The highest incidence occurs during the winter and early spring months.

ETIOLOGY The causative agent in over 50 percent of the cases is respiratory syncytial virus (RSV). Other viruses include parainfluenza type 3, adenovirus, and rhinovirus type 2.

CLINICAL PICTURE The infant suddenly develops respiratory difficulty after 1 to 2 days of coryza and cough. Respiratory difficulty is characterized by prolongation of expiratory phase and wheezing. The acute phase is usually 24 to 48 hours after the onset of wheezing. The peak severity of RSV bronchiolitis is generally in 48 to 72 hours (Rudolph, 1982, p. 596). Usually within a few days the wheezing subsides, but a deep, hacking cough may persist for 2 to 3 weeks. Fever is rarely higher than 38.3°C and may even be absent. The degree of respiratory distress is variable. Physical findings may include tachypnea, cyanosis, flaring of the alae nasi, shallow intercostal and subcostal retractions, and inspiratory rales. See Figure 17-1 for retraction scoring.

LABORATORY Chest films are obtained. Blood gas determinations may be necessary to rule out other causes of severe respiratory distress.

DIFFERENTIAL DIAGNOSIS

• Asthma (one injection of epinephrine to test reversible bronchospasm may be helpful)
• Primary pneumonia
• Foreign body aspiration
• Anaphylactic reactions to drugs, food proteins, or other allergic substances
• Poisoning

COMPLICATIONS

• Pneumonia (more than 30 percent of hospitalized infants with bronchiolitis have X-ray films of the chest revealing pulmonary infiltrates)
• Atelectasis
• Cardiac failure
• Dehydration

- Pneumomediastinum (rare)
- Pneumothorax (rare)
- Respiratory acidosis
- Subcutaneous emphysema (rare)

Management   If the child is severely ill, hospitalization is indicated for treatment with humidified oxygen and observation of respiratory status. Indications for hospitalization include infants less than 2 months, the presence of cyanosis, and respiratory rate greater than 60. Mild infections can be managed supportively at home.

HYDRATION   See this chapter, General Measures. Oral fluids are important to prevent dehydration and thickening of mucus in the lower respiratory tract; they are contraindicated in severe respiratory distress because vomiting may be induced and aspiration pneumonia may ensue.

HUMIDIFICATION   See this chapter, General Measures. Cold steam is traditionally used, although there is good evidence that the water particles do not reach the bronchioles.

MEDICATION   Bronchodilators and corticosteroids have not been proven effective in the management of bronchiolitis. Antimicrobials are not indicated unless a superimposed bacterial pneumonia is present.

COUNSELING   Caring for a child in respiratory distress is a frightening experience for parents. They need clear instructions for managing the child at home. Explanations should be given about the course of the illness and the signs and symptoms which indicate progressive respiratory distress. Often asking parents "What are you most afraid of?" will provide directions for further counseling.

CROUP SYNDROMES

Assessment   The term "croup" refers to syndromes or diseases that present with inspiratory stridor. These conditions are further characterized by a "brassy" or "barking" cough, hoarseness, and respiratory distress. The three forms of the croup syndromes are:

acute epiglottitis, spasmodic laryngitis, and acute laryngotracheo-bronchitis (LTB). Diphtheria must be considered in the differential diagnosis of every child with acute infectious croup. A history of complete immunizations rules out the diagnosis. Table 17-6 summarizes the clinical presentation, clinical findings, and treatment for each of these croup syndromes.

ACUTE EPIGLOTTITIS   Physician referral is essential. *This is a medical emergency.* It is a rapidly progressing supraglottic obstruction due most commonly to *H. influenzae,* type b. The child characteristically sits with her or his chin extended and breathes slowly through the mouth. Swallowing is painful and drooling is common. X-ray films of the soft tissue of the neck may help to confirm the diagnosis. It is essential, however, that a physician capable of performing an emergency cricothyroidectomy (see Chapter 28, Tracheostomy) attend the child to the X-ray department in the event of complete airway obstruction. Examination of the posterior pharynx is deferred until the personnel and equipment are available to perform an emergency endotracheal intubation or tracheostomy in the event of complete obstruction. A tracheostomy should not be performed on a child with epiglottitis until the trachea has been intubated.

SPASMODIC LARYNGITIS   This infection causes acute inspiratory obstruction of the vocal cords. The child typically awakens during the night with a barking cough, hoarseness, and marked inspiratory stridor. The attack lasts several hours, subsides, and may recur during the next several nights. The examination of the posterior pharynx reveals minimal inflammation.

ACUTE LARYNGOTRACHEOBRONCHITIS (LTB)   This is the most common croup syndrome in young children 6 months to 3 years of age. It usually occurs during winter months. The child usually has nasal congestion and occasional cough for 1 to 2 days prior to the development of inspiratory stridor. Inspiratory stridor results from edema of the subglottic area. The cautious examination of the posterior pharynx reveals a mildly reddened and mildly edematous epiglottis. The attack reaches maximal severity within 24 hours. Stridor and chest retraction diminish within 3 to 4 days, but the paroxysmal, barking cough may persist for 2 to 3 weeks.

Table 17-6
Croup Syndromes

	Epiglottitis (Acute)	Spasmodic Laryngitis	Acute LTB
Primary age	>3 years	1 to 3 years	6 months to 3 years
Etiology	Usually H. influenzae, occasionally Pneumococcus or viruses	Uncertain, possibly viral	Virus (RSV, parainfluenzae, influenzae)
Onset	Rapid (4 to 12 hr)	Sudden, usually at night	Gradual (may become progressively severe over 24 hr)
Presenting complaints	High fever (39.0 to 41.0°C), acute inspiratory stridor, drooling, dysphagia, general malaise	No fever, severe inspiratory stridor, "barking" cough, hoarseness	"Barking" cough, hoarseness, grad. increasing inspiratory stridor, low or absent fever
Physical examination	Pharynx inflamed, diminished breath sounds, pallor, inspiratory rhonchi, severe respiratory distress; toxic appearance	Diminished breath sounds, labored respirations, respiratory distress, accelerated pulse	Diminished breath sounds, inspiratory rales, respiratory distress, expiratory phase of respiration labored and prolonged
Laryngeal findings	Inflammation of supraglottic structures, grossly edematous, red epiglottis (raspberry)	Spasm of vocal cords (glottic), inflammation minimal	Edema of subglottic area, mildly reddened and mildly edematous epiglottis
Clinical course	Rapidly progressive (within 6 to 12 hr), total airway obstruction	Self-limited, usually within hours, but may be recurrent the following night	Moderate airway obstruction may persist, rapid respiratory failure may develop
Bacterial complications	Common when causative agent is H. influenzae and Pneumococcus	None	Rare
Treatment	Antibiotics and airway maintenance, hospitalization is mandatory, cool-mist, oxygen, tracheotomy or ET tube may be necessary.	Cool or warm humidification, oxygen, relief of laryngospasm may be obtained from racemic epinephrine from IPPB machine.	Cool-mist, oxygen, bed rest, hydration, stridor relieved by racemic epinephrine via IPPB machine, tracheotomy is rarely necessary.

Source: Information gathered from Eichenwald, 1976a; Tooley and Lipow, 1977; Vaughan et al., 1979; and Rudolph, 1982.

Management

ACUTE EPIGLOTTITIS See Table 17-6. The child is hospitalized. Intravenous ampicillin (150 mg/kg/day) and chloramphenicol (50 to 100 mg/kg/day) are administered. Improvement occurs within 24 hours after initiating treatment. Within 2 to 5 days the tracheostomy or ET tube can be removed.

SPASMODIC LARYNGITIS See Table 17-6. Warm steam from a hot shower can bring immediate relief. If this is unsuccessful, the child is taken to the emergency room. Racemic epinephrine administered by intermittent positive pressure brings relief.

ACUTE LARYNGOTRACHEOBRONCHITIS See Table 17-6. Therapy includes cool-mist, hydration, and bed rest. See this chapter, General Measures. Hospitalization may be necessary. Systemic steroid treatment has been frequently used, but its value has not been proven in controlled trials. Nebulized racemic epinephrine by IPPB causes short-term relief of stridor but may need to be repeated at 4-hour intervals. Emergency tracheostomy or endotracheal intubation may be necessary before the development of severe hypoxia or complete airway obstruction.

COUNSELING Stridor, coughing, and laryngeal spasms are frightening to the child and to the parents. The child needs the emotional closeness of a protective person. Holding infants and children securely in the arms helps to relax them and to make them feel safe. Education should include information about the course of illness of the specific croup syndrome, observational guidelines for respiratory distress, and supportive measures.

PNEUMONIA

Assessment It is one of the common serious childhood infections. The presentation of pneumonia is highly variable depending on factors such as the age of the child and the etiologic organism. Any child with suspected pneumonia should be evaluated by a physician. Refer to any standard pediatric textbook for more specific information.

ETIOLOGY The causative agents are viruses (cause of the majority of pediatric pneumonias), *Streptococcus pneumoniae*, *Mycoplasma pneumoniae* (common cause in children 5 to 15 years of age), staphylococcus (most common in infants under 2 years), *Diplococcus pneumoniae* (most frequent cause for all ages of the bacterial pathogens). The common viruses are respiratory syncytial, adenovirus, influenza, and parainfluenza. *Mycobacterium tuberculosis* should be considered as the etiologic agent for any age.

CLINICAL PICTURE   The manifestations of pneumonia in infants and children are highly variable. Some children appear very sick while others do not seem ill at all. The most common presenting symptoms are fever and cough. Other symptoms include dyspnea, tachypnea, chills, chest or abdominal pain. Young infants may have just vomiting or diarrhea initially. The physical findings may or may not reveal signs of respiratory distress, rales, or decreased breath sounds over the inflamed area. In spite of the variability of signs and symptoms, pneumonias caused by *D. pneumococcus, Mycoplasma pneumoniae,* and staphylococcus have characteristic clinical pictures.

Mycoplasma pneumonia   It is more common in older children (5- to 19-year age group). The early clinical features include insidious onset, malaise, headache, fever, sore throat, nonproductive cough, and normal chest findings during the early course of the illness. The illness is often protracted with symptoms lasting 3 to 4 weeks on the average with a range of 1 to 16 weeks. Hospitalization is rarely necessary. The chest X-ray findings include interstitial pneumonitis and areas of consolidation.

Pneumococcal pneumonia   It occurs at all ages. It typically presents after 1 or 2 days of mild nasal discharge and cough with an abrupt high fever, chills, chest pain, tachycardia, and respiratory distress. Inflammatory edema and the exudation of serum and red cells into the alveoli result in early consolidation. The X-ray film of the chest is usually positive for infiltrates. The chest examination may be unremarkable. There is dullness to percussion over the affected lung, and breath sounds are diminished. The white blood cell count is usually elevated.

Staphylococcal pneumonia   It is a life-threatening illness that is most common in infants under 2 years. The typical history is of an infant who abruptly develops respiratory distress following a variable period of a mild respiratory illness. Within a few hours the infant's condition rapidly deteriorates. The signs include rapidly evolving respiratory distress (see Fig. 17-1, Retraction Scoring), cyanosis, pallor, and abdominal distention. Fever is either low grade or absent. Auscultation of the chest is often not helpful. The X-ray film of the chest may show no abnormalities or show only faint focal mottling.

LABORATORY PROCEDURES

- Blood cultures (for etiologic diagnosis)
- X-ray film of the chest
- Tuberculin skin test (rule out *Mycobacterium tuberculosis*)

UNDERLYING ABNORMALITIES The possibility of a foreign body aspiration should be explored with the parents. If pneumonia is recurrent or persistent, consideration is given to the following:

- Asthma
- Bronchiectasis
- Congenital anomalies
- Immune deficiency states

COMPLICATIONS

- Fluid in the pleural space (pleural effusion, empyema)
- Pneumothorax

Management Consultation and referral to the physician is indicated. The child's age and condition, severity of the symptoms, causative agent, and availability of adequate home care determine the management plan. There should be conscientious follow-up to determine presence of fever or tachypnea. A follow-up visit is scheduled upon completion of antibiotic therapy for checkup and repeat X-ray.

INDICATIONS FOR HOSPITALIZATION

- Empyema or pleural effusion
- Infants under 6 months of age
- Possible staphylococcal pneumonia
- Severe respiratory distress
- Toxic appearance
- Inadequate home care

MEDICATION Antimicrobial therapy depends on the age of the child and on the causative agent. Expectorants and antitussives are of questionable value. See this chapter, Medication.

SUPPORTIVE CARE See this chapter, General Measures. Adequate hydration is necessary to prevent thickening of secretions. A vaporizer may provide some relief but its value is questionable. The child should rest in bed.

Prevention The polyvalent polysaccharide vaccine against disease caused by *Streptococcus pneumoniae* was licensed in 1977 and has been shown in selected populations to reduce by approximately 80 percent the incidence of pneumonia with bacteremia caused by the *S. pneumoniae* types contained in the vaccine. Current recommendations regarding its use in children are for persons 2 years of age and older who are at risk of severe or overwhelming pneumococcal infection. This includes children with sickle cell disease, postsplenectomy children, and children with nephrotic syndrome, severe congenital cardiac conditions, and other chronic illnesses. Routine use in the general population is not recommended at this time because of insufficient data (Granoff, 1980; Centers for Disease Control, 1981).

Counseling Education should include information about the course of the illness, side effects of the medication, observational guidelines for respiratory distress, and specific supportive measures.

References

American Pharmaceutical Association. *Handbook of Prescription Drugs.* 5th ed. Washington DC, 1977.

Bass, J. W., et al. "Streptococcal Pharyngitis in Children." *JAMA 235*:1112–1116, March 15, 1976.

Bierman, C. W. and D. S. Pearlman, editors. *Allergic Diseases of Infancy, Childhood and Adolescence.* Philadelphia: W.B. Saunders, 1980.

Bishop, B. "How to Make a Home Croup Tent." *Pediatr Nurs 4*:37–38, March/April 1978.

Bluestone, C. D. "Otitis Media in Children: To Treat or Not to Treat?" *N. Engl J Med 306*:1399–1403, June 10, 1982.

Bridgewater, S. C. and R. Voignier. "For Stuffy Nose." *Pediatr Nurs* 5:57: September/October 1979.

Centers for Disease Control. "Pneumococcal Polysaccharide Vaccine." *Morbidity Mortality Weekly Rep* 30:410–419, August 28, 1981.

Cowan, M. J., et al. "Pneumococcal Polysaccharide Immunization in Infants and Children." *Pediatrics* 62:721–726, November 1978.

Dingle, J. F., G. F. Badger, and W. S. Jordan. *Illness in the Home: A Study of 25,000 Illnesses in a Group of Cleveland Families*. Cleveland: Case Western Reserve University Press, 1964.

Editors of Consumer Reports. *The Consumers Union Guide to Buying for Babies*. New York: Consumers Union, 1975.

Editors for Consumer Reports. *The Medicine Show*. Rev. ed. New York: Consumers Union, 1976.

Eichenwald, H. P. "Respiratory Infections in Children." *Hosp Pract* 11:81–90, April 1976a.

Eichenwald, H. P. "Pneumonia Syndromes in Children." *Hosp Pract* 11:89–96, May 1976b.

Graef, J. W. and T. E. Cone, Jr. *Manual of Pediatric Therapeutics*. 2nd ed. Boston: Little, Brown, 1980.

Granoff, D. M. "Pneumococcal Vaccine in Children." *Clin Pediatr* 19:96–98, February 1980.

Green, M. *Green & Richmond Pediatric Diagnosis*. 3rd ed. Philadelphia: W. B. Saunders, 1980.

Henderson, F. W., et al. "A Longitudinal Study of Respiratory Viruses and Bacteria in the Etiology of Acute Otitis Media with Effusion." *N Engl J Med* 306:1377–1383, June 10, 1982.

Hoekelman, R. A., editor-in-chief. *Principles of Pediatrics: Health Care of the Young*. New York: McGraw-Hill, 1978.

Honikman, L. H. and B. F. Massell. "Guidelines for the Selective Use of Throat Cultures in the Diagnosis of Streptococcal Respiratory Infections." *Pediatrics* 48:573–582, October 1971.

Hughes, J. G. *Synopsis of Pediatrics*. 5th ed. St. Louis: C.V. Mosby, 1980.

Illiff, A. and V. A. Lee. "Pulse, Respiratory Rate, and Body Temperature of Children between Two Months and Eighteen Years." *Child Dev* 23:237–245, December 1952.

Kerns, D. L., et al. "Ampicillin Rash in Children: Relationship to Penicillin Allergy and Infectious Mononucleosis." *Am J Dis Child* 125:187–190, February 1973.

Klein, J. O. "Optimal Treatment: Viewpoint 1." In D. Smith and R. Hoekelman, editors, *Controversies in Child Health and Pediatric Practice*. NY: McGraw-Hill, 1981, pp 221–230.

Lampert, R. P., D. S. Robinson, and L. F. Soyka. "A Critical Look at Decongestants." *Pediatrics* 55:550–552, April 1975.

Levy, J. S. and G. Lovejoy. "Management of Pharyngitis by Pediatric Nurse Practitioners." *Clin Pediatr* 15:415–418, May 1976.

Lipow, H. W. "Respiratory Tract Infections." In M. Green and R. J. Haggerty, editors, *Ambulatory Pediatrics. II.* Philadelphia: W. B. Saunders, 1977. Pp. 36–72.

McCracken, G. H. Jr. "Managing Neonatal Infections." *Hosp Pract 11*:49–57, February 1976.

McMillan, J. A., P. I. Nieburg, and F. A. Oski. *The Whole Pediatrician Catalog.* Philadelphia: W. B. Saunders, 1979.

Rowe, D. S. "Acute Suppurative Otitis Media." *Pediatrics 56*:285–294, August 1975.

Rowe, D. S. "Signs Helpful in Localizing Respiratory Tract Abnormality," unpublished material. San Francisco: University of California, June 1973.

Rudolph, A., editor. *Pediatrics.* 17th ed. East Norwalk, CT: Appleton-Century-Crofts, 1982.

Russo, R. and V. J. Gururaj. *Practical Points in Pediatrics.* 3rd ed. Fresh Meadows, NY: Medical Examination Publishing Co., 1981.

Sataloff, R. T. and C. M. Colton. "Otitis Media: A Common Childhood Infection." *Am J Nurs 81*:1480–1483, August 1981.

Silver, H. K., et al. *Handbook of Pediatrics.* 13th ed. Los Altos, CA: Lange Medical Publications, 1980.

Silverman, W., editor. *Dunham's Premature Infants.* 3rd ed. New York: Hoeber, 1961.

Stevens, D., et al. "*Mycoplasma pneumoniae* Infections in Children." *Arch Dis Child 53*:38–42, January 1978.

Stool, S. E. and C. S. McConnell Jr. "Foreign Bodies in Pediatric Otolaryngology." *Clin Pediatr 12*:113–116, February 1973.

Tooley, W. H. and H. W. Lipow. "Specific Diseases Causing Obstruction." In A. Rudolph, editor, *Pediatrics.* 16th ed. New York: Appleton-Century-Crofts, 1977. Pp. 1554–1571.

Vaughan, V. C., et al., editors. *Nelson Textbook of Pediatrics.* 11th ed. Philadelphia: W. B. Saunders, 1979.

Waechter, E. and F. Blake. *Nursing Care of Children.* 9th ed. Philadelphia: J. B. Lippincott, 1976.

Wasserman, E. and D. Gromisch. *Survey of Clinical Pediatrics.* 7th ed. New York: McGraw-Hill, 1981.

Welliver, R. C. and D. T. Wong, "*Mycoplasma pneumoniae* Infections of Children and Adolescents." In A. J. Moss, editor, *Pediatrics Update.* New York: Elsevier Biomedical, 1983.

West, S., et al. "A Review of Antihistamines and the Common Cold." *Pediatrics 56*:100–107, July 1975.

18

The Heart

Approximately 8 to 10 of every thousand live-born children have a congenital cardiac disorder. Some cardiac defects are detectable at birth or during early infancy. In fact, about 90 percent are diagnosed under one year of age but some do not become manifest until later in childhood when symptoms of cardiac decompensation occur.

The role of the nurse practitioner in relation to the cardiovascular system is to identify those children with signs or symptoms of congenital and acquired heart disease and to refer them immediately for medical evaluation. This chapter presents information that will assist the nurse practitioner in screening children for cardiac disease and in providing counsel and support to affected families. A complete discussion of specific congenital cardiac defects is beyond the scope of this book and may be found by consulting the major textbooks listed under References.

ASSESSMENT

Normal Values

Pulse rate, respiratory rate, and blood pressure vary considerably from infancy through childhood. Measurements need to be obtained with the child at rest since exercise or crying will affect values. The average pulse rates and blood pressure levels for chil-

Table 18-1
Average Pulse Rates at Rest

Age	Lower Limits of Normal		Average		Upper Limits of Normal	
Newborn	70		120		170	
1–11 months	80		120		160	
2 years	80		110		130	
4 years	80		100		120	
6 years	75		100		115	
8 years	70		90		110	
10 years	70		90		110	
	Girls	*Boys*	*Girls*	*Boys*	*Girls*	*Boys*
12 years	70	65	90	85	110	105
14 years	65	60	85	80	105	100
16 years	60	55	80	75	100	95
18 years	55	•50	75	70	95	90

Source: From V. C. Vaughan and R. J. McKay, editors. *Nelson Textbook of Pediatrics,* 10th ed., Philadelphia: W. B. Saunders, 1975. P. 1003.

dren are shown in Tables 18-1 and 18-2 respectively. Average respiratory rates are found in Chapter 17, The Respiratory System, Table 17-3. Concern about blood pressure control and the early origins of cardiovascular disease have led to attempts to monitor blood pressure closely from childhood onward. Figure 18-1 (A and B) are charts of percentiles of blood pressures for children ages 2 to 18 years. The charts are recommended for use in plotting blood pressures during growth and maturation as a mechanism for determining patterns over time (Blumenthal et al., 1977). They may be obtained from National High Blood Pressure Education Program, Landow Building, 13th floor, 7910 Woodmont Avenue, Bethesda, MD 20014.

History

PAST HISTORY

Obtain information on maternal infection during pregnancy (e.g., rubella), fetal distress, Down's syndrome, Turner's syndrome, or

Table 18-2
Normal Arterial Blood Pressures at Different Ages

Age	Systolic		Diastolic	
	50th Percentile (mm Hg)	95th Percentile (mm Hg)	50th Percentile (mm Hg)	95th Percentile (mm Hg)
Birth–6 months	80	110	45	60
3 years	95	112	64	80
5 years	97	115	65	84
10 years	110	130	70	92
15 years	116	138	70	95
Adults	120	140	80	90–95

Source: Reprinted with permission from A. M. Rudolph, editor, *Pediatrics*, 16th ed., New York: Appleton-Century-Crofts, 1977. P. 1485. Adapted from Londe: *Clin Pediatr* 5:71, 1966; Moss and Adams: *Problems of Blood Pressure in Childhood*. Springer, IL: Charles C Thomas, 1962; Zinner et al: *N Engl J Med 284*:401, 1971.

other genetic syndromes, signs or symptoms of congenital heart disease, heart murmurs, group A beta-hemolytic streptococcal infections, rheumatic fever, kidney disease, hypertension, smoking, and exercise patterns.

FAMILY HISTORY

Obtain information on incidence of heart attack (include age of occurrence), high cholesterol levels, type II hyperlipoproteinemia (familial hypercholesterolemia), high blood pressure, xanthomas, stroke, obesity, congenital heart disease in sibling or other family member, and rheumatic fever.

Physical Examination

GENERAL APPEARANCE

Observe activity levels and degree of fatigability. Measure height, weight, and head circumference.

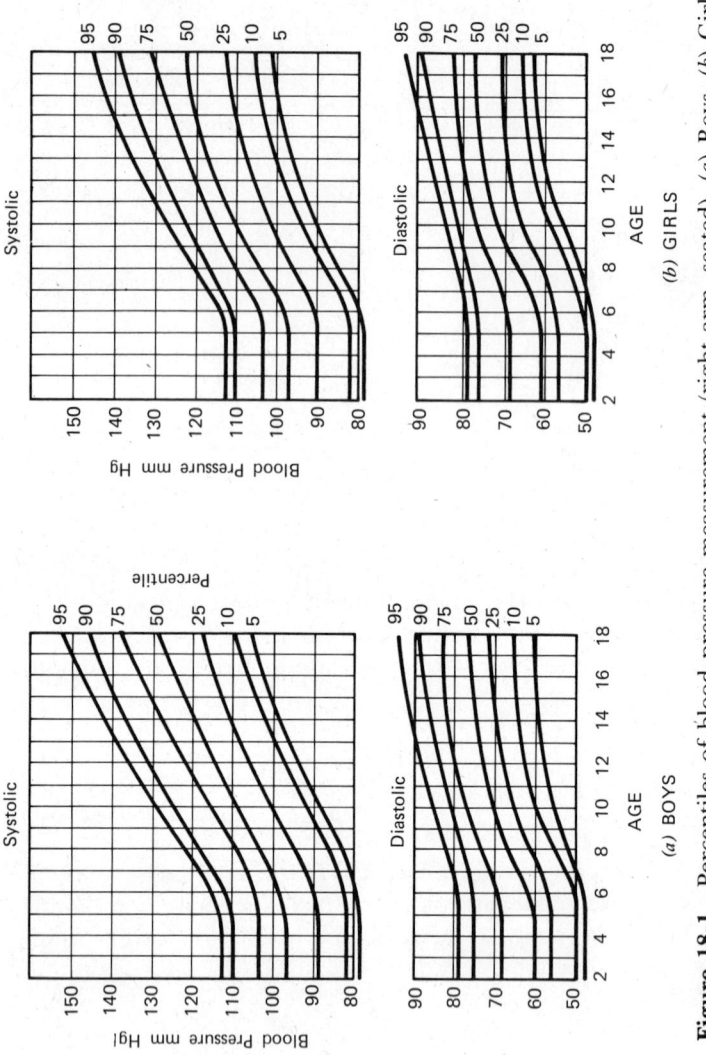

Figure 18-1 Percentiles of blood pressure measurement (right arm, seated). (*a*) Boys. (*b*) Girls. (Reprinted with permission from S. Blumenthal et al., "Report of the Task Force on Blood Pressure Control in Children," *Pediatrics*, Supplement, Vol. 59, Part 2, May 1977, p. 803.)

VITAL SIGNS

Obtain pulse rate, respiratory rate, and blood pressure. If the respiratory rate in a quiet, resting child is above 50, suspicion index should rise.

• Blood pressure. The cuff must cover two thirds of the upper arm and should comfortably encircle the girth of the arm without leaving a gap. The blood pressure should be measured on the right arm with the child seated and relaxed so that, when plotted on the grids shown in Figure 18-1, the data will be comparable. In neonates and small infants, blood pressure may be obtained using palpation, the flush method, or the more accurate Doppler ultrasound technique.

EYES

Observe for periorbital edema. Examine fundus for arteriolar changes.

SKIN

Observe for pallor, cyanosis, and excessive perspiration. Cyanosis may be particularly notable in mucous membranes, nail beds, and extremities.

CHEST

Observe for retractions, chest deformity. Listen for rales. See also Chapter 17, Physical Examination.

HEART

Inspect and palpate for evidence of cardiac enlargement (precordial bulging, distended or pulsating neck veins), location and character of apex beat, and presence of heaves or thrills. Percussion is not generally useful in infants and small children. Auscultate heart sounds for rate and rhythm. Note character and intensity of each heart sound (S_1 and S_2). Listen for extra sounds and note timing, intensity, and pitch. Listen for murmurs and describe timing (systolic or diastolic), location, radiation (use the "inching" technique to follow sound to axillae, back, and neck), quality, and intensity. Note whether the murmur changes with position change from supine to sitting. Grade the murmur according to the following scale (Bates, 1979, p. 154).

- *Grade 1.* Very faint and heard only after the examiner has "tuned in"; may not be heard in all positions
- *Grade 2.* Quiet but heard immediately upon placing the stethoscope on the chest
- *Grade 3.* Moderately loud; not associated with a thrill
- *Grade 4.* Loud and may be associated with a thrill
- *Grade 5.* Very loud; associated with a thrill
- *Grade 6.* Heard with the stethoscope off the chest; associated with a thrill

ABDOMEN

Palpate for hepatomegaly and splenomegaly.

EXTREMITIES

Observe for clubbing of fingers and toes; edema. Palpate pulses (radial, femoral, carotid, popliteal, and pedal) for regularity and intensity. Absent femoral pulses suggest coarctation of the aorta. Palpate for xanthomas.

Signs and Symptoms of Congenital Heart Disease

INFANCY

The findings in infancy include anorexia, cyanosis, delayed development, enlarged heart or liver, exertional dyspnea during feeding, failure to gain weight, heart murmurs, persistent tachycardia (over 150 to 200 beats per minute at rest), bradycardia, rapid respiratory rate (over 50 to 60 respirations per minute at rest), recurrent respiratory infections, and respiratory distress.

CHILDHOOD

In older children additional findings include clubbing of the fingers and toes, decreased exercise tolerance, dyspnea, poor physical development, and squatting (a position in which the child crouches with legs drawn up closely to the body).

Signs and Symptoms of Congestive Heart Failure

Any child suspected of congestive failure should be treated as an emergency. Symptoms include dyspnea, fatigue, weakness, irritability, weak cry, cough, poor feeding, and sweating (prominent on exertion). Signs include pallor, duskiness, cyanosis, enlarged heart, hepatomegaly, neck vein distention, tachycardia (pulse over 140 in sleeping infants, over 100 in sleeping older children), tachypnea (50 to 100 or faster), and retractions. Late findings include facial and periorbital edema, pulmonary edema, and pulmonary rales.

Signs and Symptoms of Rheumatic Fever (Acquired Heart Disease)

Rheumatic fever is an inflammatory disease that can cause cardiac damage. It occurs most commonly between 5 and 15 years of age. It is usually a sequel to a preceding group A beta-hemolytic streptococcal infection.

JONES CRITERIA

The presence of two major or one major and two minor manifestations with evidence of a preceding streptococcal infection indicates a high probability of rheumatic fever (Kempe et al., 1982, p. 355). However, children with fewer manifestations may also have rheumatic fever.

Major Manifestations

1. *Carditis.* Significant new murmur, tachycardia, evidence of congestive heart failure, and enlarging heart
2. *Polyarthritis.* Two or more joints affected by heat, redness, swelling, severe pain, and tenderness
3. *Chorea.* Emotional lability and involuntary movements appearing most often in prepubertal girls usually several months after streptococcal infection
4. *Erythema marginatum.* Macular erythematous rash with a serpiginous pattern primarily on the trunk and extremities
5. *Subcutaneous nodules.* Joints, scalp, and spine are affected

Minor Manifestations

1. Clinical findings:
   - Previous rheumatic fever or rheumatic heart disease
   - Fever
   - Polyarthralgia

2. Laboratory findings:
   - Increased erythrocyte sedimentation rate (ESR) or C-reactive protein (CRP)
   - Increased white blood count (WBC) and anemia
   - Prolonged PR interval on electrocardiogram (ECG)
   - Increased antistreptolysin titer (ASLO), positive throat culture, recent scarlet fever

Cardiovascular Risk Factors in Children

CORONARY HEART DISEASE

During the past decade, major attention has been focused on the control and prevention of ischemic (coronary) heart disease. Data point to a combination of genetic and environmental factors that interact to increase the potential of coronary heart disease. Although conclusive evidence of a causative relationship between dietary factors (fat and cholesterol) and atherosclerotic disease does not exist, some authorities believe it important to identify children at risk so that risks can be reduced through preventive programs (Nora, 1980). Others express concern at labeling children as being at risk until long-term studies determine whether there is a direct relationship between lowered cholesterol and reduced morbidity and mortality from coronary heart disease (Holtzman, 1980).

SCREENING

See this chapter, History and Physical Examination, and Chapter 3, Type II Hyperlipoproteinemia for indications for obtaining cholesterol and triglyceride levels. Routine laboratory screening is not recommended for all children.

PREVENTION

Although the genetic component (family history) is fixed, the environmental components are subject to intervention, and avoiding such risks may reduce risk to the minimum level. Health education that emphasizes exercise, weight control, prudent diet (including breastfeeding, late introduction of appropriate solids, control of salt intake, and reduced animal fat intake), stress control, and avoidance of smoking is the best preventive approach.

HYPERTENSION

The role of hypertension in cardiovascular disease has also been stressed in recent years along with the possibility that, if a trend toward fixed hypertension is detectable during early life, intervention to prevent or delay its development may be effective. As with coronary heart disease, fixed hypertension results from an interplay of genetic and environmental factors with estimates that genetic factors are responsible for 60 percent of the variance of blood pressure (Lieberman, 1980).

SCREENING

The Task Force on Blood Pressure Control in Children (Blumenthal et al., 1977) recommends that blood pressure measurements be obtained annually on all children 3 years of age and older and plotted on the appropriate grids (Fig. 18-1).

- *High-normal pressure* is the term applied to an asymptomatic child whose initial blood pressure measurement is greater than the 95th percentile but below the arbitrary cutoff point currently used to define hypertension (140/90 in children 0 to 13 years and 150/100 in children 13 years and older). This child should receive at least two follow-up blood pressure measurements within 3 to 5 months to determine whether this is a single, isolated elevated value. If the subsequent readings fall below the 95th percentile, the child is followed routinely.

- *Sustained elevated blood pressure* is the term applied to an asymptomatic child who has had blood pressure levels above the 95th percentile on at least three consecutive occasions using the same criteria for measurement, that is, same arm, same cuff, same position (Lieberman, 1980). This child should have a history and physical examination oriented toward hypertension-related factors. Recommended laboratory evaluation includes urinalysis, BUN or creatinine, ECG, X-ray film of the chest, and fasting serum lipids.

PREVENTION

Regular health maintenance and health education are warranted. Counseling should emphasize weight control, salt and sodium reduction, alteration in fat content if lipid levels are elevated, active exercise on a regular basis, avoidance of smoking, and avoidance of pressor agents, for example, cold and asthma remedies, birth control pills, steroids.

MANAGEMENT

An infant or child who manifests signs or symptoms of heart disease is referred for medical evaluation. The diagnosis of congenital or acquired heart disease requires specialized medical management and supervision. Once the referral is made, the role of the nurse practitioner remains active. The objectives of care are listed below:

1. To provide ongoing preventive and health maintenance services in collaboration with the physician
2. To provide support for the family during diagnosis and treatment (Gottesfeld, 1979).
3. To assist the family to understand the diagnosis and treatment plan
4. To provide opportunity for family members to express their feelings and concerns
5. To provide the teaching necessary for parents to care for the child at home including the following:
   - Reduction of the work load of the heart
   - Reduction of respiratory distress
   - Recognition of symptoms of congestive heart failure
   - Prevention of respiratory infections
   - Maintenance of nutrition

6. To initiate public health nursing referral where indicated
7. To initiate referral for genetic counseling when indicated

COMMON CLINICAL PROBLEMS

The Innocent Murmur

ASSESSMENT

By far the most common clinical situation encountered in pediatric primary care settings is the identification of innocent heart murmurs in infants and young children. An innocent heart murmur is a cardiac murmur occurring in the absence of significant heart disease or structural abnormality of the heart. At least 30 percent of children may have innocent murmurs detected at a single, random examination (Vaughan et al., 1979, p. 1251).

General Characteristics of Innocent Murmurs   The characteristics of innocent murmurs which help to distinguish them from significant murmurs include the following (Caceres and Perry, 1967, pp 99–100):

- Usually systolic in timing except for the venous hum
- Duration usually short
- Loudest usually at the lower left sternal border or at the second or third left intercostal space
- Variation in loudness and presence from visit to visit
- Usually soft (no more than grade 2/6) and localized
- Rarely transmitted
- Changes in loudness with position change
- Heard best in the recumbent position, during expiration and after exercise, except the venous hum
- Heart sounds normal
- Normal pulses, respiratory rate, and blood pressure.

Additional Features   With increased body temperature there is increased heart rate, increased cardiac output, and increased velocity of flow. Consequently, the intensity of innocent murmurs may increase during acute infections associated with fever or after vigorous exercise. Soft murmurs also may develop during acute illness or severe anemia and disappear during convalescence.

Types of Innocent Murmurs Common innocent murmurs are described. Intensity of these murmurs is seldom over grade 2/6.

1. Still's murmur is a soft, low-pitched, mid-systolic, musical murmur heard best at the apex and lower left sternal border with the child lying down.
2. Basal ejection systolic murmur is a high-pitched blowing systolic murmur heard best at the pulmonic area (upper left and upper right sternal borders) with the child lying down. It will get softer when the child sits up.
3. Carotid bruit is a very common, soft, blowing, high-pitched, early systolic murmur heard above the clavicles along the carotid arteries with the child lying down.
4. Physiologic peripheral pulmonic stenosis is a short systolic murmur heard best in the axillae and back. It disappears by 3 to 4 months of age as the pulmonary arteries enlarge.
5. Venous hum is a humming, continuous, systolic/diastolic murmur heard best just below the clavicles with the child sitting up, and in the neck. It can be abolished by having the child lie down. Intensity may reach grade 3–4/6.

MANAGEMENT

When a murmur is detected, its presence and nature should be confirmed by the physician. Since innocent murmurs do not indicate heart disease and require no treatment, the clinical issue that arises is *whether* and/or *what* to tell the parents. Many parents have difficulty in understanding the meaning of an innocent murmur and the information that their new baby or young child has a heart murmur, however innocent, generates fear and anxiety. One study (Bergman and Stamm, 1967) revealed that in a group of children with innocent murmurs, 40 percent had been restricted in normal activities by their parents. The parents had misinterpreted the diagnosis and believed their children had "something wrong" with the heart or heart disease. The philosophy basic to this book is that parents should be fully informed about their children's health status and be participants in decisions about care. Yet, the decision to inform parents of the presence of an innocent murmur needs to be made on an individual basis.

Informing Parents   In deciding when and how to inform parents about an innocent murmur the following factors should be considered:

1. Knowledge of the family

   - Is there a family history of heart disease? If so, who has or had it and what was the outcome?
   - How much anxiety can be expected?
   - Is this the first visit of the child and family? It can be argued that the first well-baby visit is not the time to discuss an innocent murmur due to the many normal anxieties faced by new parents during this period of adjustment.
   - If the family is known, how have illness situations been handled in the past?
   - Are the parents calm, overreactive, faced with other stresses?
   - What is the level of understanding of the parents?
   - Are there language or other communication barriers? The dangers of misinterpretation of information are present even without language barriers.

2. Source of health care and follow-up

   - Does the family plan to receive further health care at the specific agency or office?
   - Will the child be followed by one primary person or team?
   - What other health care facilities are used by the family? If the parents use another agency (e.g., the local emergency room) when the child is ill, it is likely that they will be questioned about the murmur. If they have not been informed previously, this may result in increased anxiety over the child's condition, anger at not having been told before, and suspicion that previous caretakers "missed" the murmur.

Parent Counseling   When the decision is made to inform the parents it must be stressed that the innocent murmur is a normal phenomenon that may be exaggerated at times; that the child does *not* have heart disease; and that no restrictions are necessary. The murmur can be described as the sound that blood makes while moving through the heart. A helpful analogy is to compare the sound with that made by water flowing through a garden hose; usually it is not heard unless a person's ear is very close to the hose or unless there is a kink in the hose obstructing the flow of water. Ample opportunity for questions and discussion must be provided at the time and at subsequent visits to ensure correct interpretation of this common clinical finding.

Patent Ductus Arteriosus (PDA)

ASSESSMENT

Patent ductus arteriosus is a common congenital cardiac anomaly which occurs as an isolated defect or is frequently associated with maternal rubella during early pregnancy and with small preterm infants. Because the ductus fails to close soon after birth, aortic blood is shunted (left-to-right) into the pulmonary artery and is recirculated through the pulmonary circulation. Consequently the left ventricle must work harder to meet the needs of the peripheral tissues.

Clinical Signs and Symptoms   Findings vary with the size of the defect.

1. *Small defects.* A small opening will usually not affect physical growth and development. The only finding may be a murmur that is similar to a venous hum.
2. *Larger defects.* With larger defects and shunts, symptoms may be progressive exertional dyspnea, left ventricular failure, or congestive heart failure. Physical signs include a wide pulse pressure, prominent radial pulses, and limited growth and activity. The classic murmur is a machinery, humming, harsh sound beginning in systole, reaching maximum intensity at the end of systole, and waning in diastole, heard best under the left clavicle and in the pulmonic area.

MANAGEMENT

Spontaneous closure of the ductus after infancy is extremely rare and even asymptomatic PDAs are not benign. Life expectancy is reduced and subacute bacterial endocarditis is a frequent complication. Therefore, surgical closure of the defect is usually indicated. The objectives of primary care nursing management are those presented earlier in this chapter.

Resource Information

Information on educational materials and services available for children with cardiac conditions can be obtained from:

1. American Heart Association, 205 E. 42nd Street, New York, NY 10017.
2. Crippled Children's Services, State Health Departments.
3. Lieberman, E. *A Handbook for Pediatric Hypertension.* Available from the American Heart Association, Greater Los Angeles Affiliate, 2405 West Eighth Street, Los Angeles, CA 90057.

References

Bates, B. *A Guide to Physical Examination.* 2nd ed. Philadelphia: J. B. Lippincott, 1979.

Bergman, A. B. and S. J. Stamm. "The Morbidity of Cardiac Nondisease in Schoolchildren." *N Engl J Med 276*:1008–1013, May 4, 1967.

Blumenthal, S. et al. "Report of the Task Force on Blood Pressure Control in Children." *Pediatrics* Suppl *59* (5), Part 2, May 1977.

Caceres, C. H. and L. W. Perry. *The Innocent Murmur.* Boston: Little, Brown, 1967.

Gottesfeld, I. B. "The Family of the Child with Congenital Heart Disease." *Am J Maternal Child Nursing 4*:101–104, March/April 1979.

Haddock, N. "Blood Pressure Monitoring in Neonates." *Am J Maternal Child Nursing 5*:131–135, March/April 1980.

Holtzman, N. A. "Hyperlipidemia Screening and Semmelweis Re-visited." *Pediatrics 66*:838–839, December 1980.

Kempe, C. H., et al. *Current Pediatric Diagnosis and Treatment.* 7th ed. Los Altos, CA: Lang Medical Publications, 1982.

Lieberman, E. "Blood Pressure and Primary Hypertension in Childhood and Adolescence." *Curr Probl Pediatr 10*:1–35, February 1980.

Nora, J. J. "Identifying the Child at Risk for Coronary Disease as an Adult: A Strategy for Prevention." *J Pediatr* 97:706–714, November 1980.

Rudolph, A. M., editor. *Pediatrics.* 17th ed. East Norwalk, CT: Appleton-Century-Crofts, 1982.

Smith, K. M. "Recognizing Cardiac Failure in Neonates." *Am J Maternal Child Nursing* 4:98–100, March/April 1979.

Vaughan, V. C., et al., editors. *Nelson Textbook of Pediatrics.* 11th ed. Philadelphia: W. B. Saunders, 1979.

19

The
Hematopoietic
System

The hematopoietic system is complex and disorders can involve many organs and organ systems. The disorders most commonly encountered in primary pediatric settings are neonatal jaundice and the anemias of childhood including hemolytic disease of the newborn, nutritional anemias, and the hemoglobinopathies. This chapter presents information basic to understanding jaundice and anemia, normal blood values related to these conditions, and data necessary for assessment and management. With such information the nurse practitioner can provide appropriate health education to individuals, families, and groups regarding prevention of anemia and explanation of common blood disorders.

ASSESSMENT

Normal Blood Values

Red blood cell values for hemoglobin, hematocrit, and mean corpuscular volume at different ages are presented in Table 19-1. Different agencies and laboratories may have established slightly different standards depending on the population sampled and the

Table 19-1
Estimated Normal Mean Values and Lower Limits of Normal
(Mean Minus 2 SD) for Hemoglobin, Hematocrit,
and Mean Corpuscular Volume[a]

Age (yr)	Hemoglobin (gm/dl) Mean	Hemoglobin (gm/dl) Lower Limit	Hematocrit (%) Mean	Hematocrit (%) Lower Limit	Mean Corpuscular Volume (fl) Mean	Mean Corpuscular Volume (fl) Lower Limit
0.5–1.9	12.5	11.0	37	33	77	70
2–4	12.5	11.0	38	34	79	73
5–7	13.0	11.5	39	35	81	75
8–11	13.5	12.0	40	36	83	76
12–14						
female	13.5	12.0	41	36	85	78
male	14.0	12.5	43	37	84	77
15–17						
female	14.0	12.0	41	36	87	79
male	15.0	13.0	46	38	86	78
18–49						
female	14.0	12.0	42	37	90	80
male	16.0	14.0	47	40	90	80

Source: Reprinted with permission from A. M. Rudolph, editor, *Pediatrics,* 17th ed., East Norwalk, CT: Appleton-Century-Crofts, 1983. P. 1036.
[a]*Note:* All values are based on data obtained from venous blood by electronic counter primarily in Caucasian individuals. Selection of the populations in general was likely to exclude individuals with iron deficiency. The mean ±2 SD can be expected to encompass 95 percent of the observations in a normal population.
[Compiled from Dallman, S. *J Pediatr 94*:26, 1979; Saarinen, S. *J Pediatr 92*:412, 1978, and Williams et al: *Hematology,* 2nd ed., New York: McGraw-Hill, 1977.]

methods of sampling and analysis used. These standards are those used at the University of California Medical Center, San Francisco, California.

History

PRESENT CONCERNS

Presenting symptoms are evaluated according to the guidelines outlined in Chapter 11, Assessment of Presenting Symptoms.

PAST HISTORY

Factors to be elicited in the past history include prematurity, any blood loss, jaundice, bruising, or petechiae at birth or later; anemia, pallor, irritability, malaise, weight loss, chemical ingestions, drugs, recurrent infections, chronic disease, and parasitic infections. A nutrition history is obtained. See Chapter 3, Nutrition History.

FAMILY HISTORY

Important factors in the family history include race; geographic country of origin; any previous infants with jaundice, anemia, or exchange transfusions; familial diseases (e.g., sickle cell anemia); maternal blood type, Rh factor, and maternal nutritional status during pregnancy.

Physical Examination

GENERAL APPEARANCE

Observe physical development and nutritional status. Obtain height, weight, and vital signs.

SKIN

Observe for pallor, jaundice, bruises, petechiae, and hematomas.

EYES, MOUTH, NOSE, THROAT

Observe sclera, conjunctiva, and mucous membranes for color and evidence of bleeding.

HEART

Palpate and auscultate for murmurs, tachycardia, and signs of congestive failure.

ABDOMEN

Palpate for hepatomegaly and splenomegaly.

Metabolism of Bilirubin

When red blood cells break down, hemoglobin is released and further broken down into iron, protein, and bilirubin. Iron and protein are stored and re-used by the body. The bilirubin resulting from this breakdown of hemoglobin is unconjugated, indirect bilirubin. Unconjugated bilirubin is fat soluble, not water soluble, so it cannot be excreted by the kidneys. Being fat soluble it can permeate the membranes and enter tissues (i.e., subcutaneous and brain tissue) where it can become neurotoxic at certain concentrations. This is especially dangerous in premature infants who lack subcutaneous fatty tissue.

The normal mechanism for converting unconjugated to conjugated bilirubin begins with the binding of unconjugated bilirubin to serum albumin. It is then transported to the liver, and there is acted upon by enzymes (e.g., glucuronyl transferase) and converted to direct, conjugated bilirubin. Direct bilirubin, which is water soluble, is soluble in body fluids and is easily excreted through bile ducts to the gut. It does not enter the cells so is not toxic. The laboratory tests used to detect levels of bilirubinemia react *directly* only with the water soluble or conjugated form of bilirubin. The test for unconjugated, fat-soluble bilirubin is *indirect* because an alcohol solvent must be added before the test can be performed. See below, Common Laboratory Procedures for Jaundice.

Jaundice

Jaundice results from the accumulation in the skin of bilirubin pigment. Jaundice can be detected clinically when bilirubin levels exceed 4 to 5 mg/dl. It is best assessed in daylight. In infants with dark pigmented skin, it can be detected in the sclera and posterior palate and by blanching the palms and soles. The causes of jaundice are:

1. Any factor that increases the load of bilirubin to be metabolized by the liver (e.g., erythroblastosis fetalis, hemolytic anemias, infection)
2. Any factor that may damage or may reduce the activity of the enzyme, bilirubin glucuronyl transferase (e.g., anoxia, infection)

3. Any factor that may compete for or block the enzyme (e.g., drugs such as nitrofurantoin or other substances requiring glucuronic acid conjugation for excretion)
4. Any factor leading to absence or decreased amounts of the enzyme (e.g., genetic defect, prematurity) (Vaughan et al., 1979, p. 443)

Common Laboratory Procedures for Jaundice

Data useful in the assessment of jaundice include the following:

1. *Total serum bilirubin.* This is the sum of unconjugated and conjugated bilirubin. Normal values of total bilirubin are as follows:

Age	Term Infant	Premature
Birth	<2 mg/dl	<2 mg/dl
0–1 day	<6 mg/dl	<8 mg/dl
1–2 days	<8 mg/dl	<12 mg/dl
3–5 days	<12 mg/dl	<16 mg/dl
Thereafter	<1 mg/dl	<2 mg/dl

After the newborn period total bilirubin is normally less than 1 mg/dl.
2. *Direct bilirubin.* This measures the amount of conjugated bilirubin. After 1 month of age values are 0 to 0.3 mg/dl.
3. *Indirect bilirubin.* This measures the amount of unconjugated bilirubin. Normally, 90 percent of total bilirubin is in unconjugated form. After 1 month of age values are 0.1 to 0.7 mg/dl.
4. *Direct Coombs test.* This detects the presence of antibody attached to red blood cells. A positive result in the newborn indicates that the newborn's red blood cells are coated with maternal antibodies and is diagnostic of isoimmunization (e.g., Rh incompatibility, ABO incompatibility).
5. *Indirect Coombs test.* This is used to detect anitbodies in the mother's serum by mixing her serum with cells of known antigenic type. A positive result indicates maternal antibody in the infant's blood but does not confirm incompatibility with the infant's red blood cells. It is not used often in infants.

DERMAL ICTERUS INDEX

The prevention of bilirubin encephalopathy requires careful recognition of hyperbilirubinemia in the newborn.

Definition In newborn infants, progressive hyperbilirubinemia is accompanied by a caudad advancement of dermal icterus which begins at the face and proceeds to the trunk, the extremities, and finally the palms and soles. In 1969, Kramer noted that there is a positive relationship between the concentration of serum bilirubin and the caudad progression of dermal icterus which suggests that simple inspection of the skin of the newborn infant provides useful information about the actual bilirubin level. See Table 19-2 and Figure 19-1. Additional findings by Kramer include the following:

1. Dermal icterus is not discernible at serum bilirubin levels of less than 4 mg/dl. At higher bilirubin concentrations a predictable direct relationship between bilirubin levels and the cephalopedal progress of dermal icterus has been noted.
2. The cephalopedal progression of dermal icterus was noted to continue only as long as the concentration of serum bilirubin increased.
3. The point of most distal skin icterus remains unchanged as serum bilirubin levels remain at a fixed level.
4. The dermal staining always fades gradually in all affected skin

Table 19-2
Indirect Serum Bilirubin Concentration and Its Relationship to the
Progression of Dermal Icterus

Dermal Zone	Full-Term Infants Bilirubin (mg/100 ml) Range	Infants of low birth weight Bilirubin (mg/100 ml) Range
1	4.3–7.8	4.1–7.5
2	5.4–12.2	5.6–12.1
3	8.1–16.5	7.1–14.8
4	11.1–18.3	9.3–18.4
5	15	10.5

Source: Reprinted with permission from L. I. Kramer, "Advancement of Dermal Icterus in the Jaundiced Newborn," *Am J Dis Child 118*:454–458, September 1969. Copyright 1969, American Medical Association.

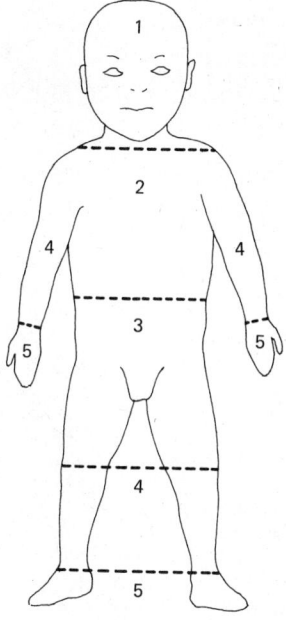

Figure 19-1 Dermal zones of progressive cephalopedal icterus. 1, Head and neck; 2, trunk to umbilicus; 3, groin, including upper thighs; 4, knees to ankles and elbows to wrist; 5, hands and feet, including palms and soles. (Reprinted with permission from L. I. Kramer, "Advancement of Dermal Icterus in the Jaundiced Newborn." *Am J Dis Child 118*:454–458, September 1969. Copyright 1969, American Medical Association.)

areas at the same time as the serum bilirubin concentration begins to fall from its peak level.

5. Some infants of low birth weight show a more rapid progression of skin icterus than do full-term infants, and the variation in the pattern of skin staining in some low-birth-weight infants reduces the usefulness of determining serum bilirubin levels by dermal inspection.

Comments   This dermal zone method of inspection is not meant to replace laboratory determinations. This method depends on the inspection of the undressed infant under blue-white fluorescent lighting. The mechanism for the cephalopedal progression of dermal icterus in newborn infants with rising levels of serum bilirubin is not fully understood.

Anemia

Anemia is defined as "a lower than normal value for hemoglobin, hematocrit, or number of red blood cells per cubic millimeter. The lower limit of the normal range is set two standard deviations below the mean at any given age" (Rudolph, 1982, p. 1040). See Table 19-1. Since anemia is a manifestation of an underlying process it is important that the cause be determined.

Etiologic classification of anemias (from Rudolph, 1982, p. 1040):
   I. Impaired Production of Red Cells and Hemoglobin
      A. Nutritional anemias
         1. iron deficiency
         2. megaloblastic anemia
      B. Anemia of infection and chronic disease
      C. Aplastic and hypoplastic anemia
  II. Accelerated Destruction of Red Cells
      A. Extracorpuscular defects
         1. erythroblastosis fetalis
         2. autoimmune and drug-induced hemolytic anemia
         3. abnormalities of the vasculature or plasma
         4. splenic enlargement
      B. Intracorpuscular defects
         1. abnormalities of hemoglobin structure and synthesis
         2. abnormalities of the red cell membrane
         3. abnormalities of red cell metabolism
 III. Blood Loss

Common Laboratory Procedures for Anemia

Information in this section comes primarily from the data of Dallman and Koerper. (See this chapter, References.) Laboratory data useful in assessment of anemia include the following:

1. *Hematocrit.* This is a measurement of the percentage of red blood cells in the total blood volume. The hematocrit is generally equal to the hemoglobin times 3.

2. *Hemoglobin.* This is a measurement of the concentration by weight of hemoglobin in each deciliter of whole blood. With the use of electronic counters, the hemoglobin is a more accurate measurement than the hematocrit.

3. *Red blood cell count (RBC).* This is the measurement of the number of red blood cells found in each cubic millimeter of blood.

4. *RBC indices.* Indices provide an estimate of the size (volume),

amount of hemoglobin, and hemoglobin concentration of the average red blood cell:

- Mean corpuscular volume (MCV) is the volume of the average RBC expressed in femtoliters (fl). It is the most useful index in the diagnosis of anemia.
- Mean corpuscular hemoglobin (MCH) is the absolute amount of hemoglobin by weight in the average RBC expressed in picograms (pg).
- Mean corpuscular hemoglobin concentration (MCHC) is the concentration of hemoglobin in the average RBC expressed in grams per deciliter.

5. *Peripheral blood smear.* A stained smear of blood gives information about the morphology (size, shape) and hemoglobin content (color) of the red blood cell, the level of platelets, indices, and types of leukocytes present. Terms used to describe red blood cells are:

- *Anisocytosis:* cells of unequal size
- *Poikilocytosis:* cells of abnormal shapes
- *Microcytic:* cells that are smaller than usual
- *Hypochromic:* cells that are paler than normal

6. *Reticulocyte count.* Reticulocytes are young, newly formed RBCs that normally comprise about 1 percent of total RBCs. An increase may indicate that the bone marrow is compensating for some problem by producing more RBCs.

7. *Free erythrocyte protoporphyrin (FEP).* The FEP rises in conditions that interfere with the final step in the synthesis of heme, the combination of iron and protoporphyrin. When the RBC does not have enough iron to make heme, the FEP becomes elevated and rises markedly as the concentration of hemoglobin falls. It rises before anemia becomes severe enough to be detected by traditional means (e.g., hemoglobin and blood smear). Values above 3 μg/gm of Hb are abnormal and occur in iron deficiency, chronic inflammatory disease, and lead intoxication.

8. *Serum iron (SI).* This measurement indicates iron concentration in serum or plasma. It is not the most helpful test because

values fluctuate during the day, being higher in the morning. Mean values for children are 30 to 70 μg/dl. For adults they are 65 to 110 μg/dl (Koerper, 1977).

9. *Total iron-binding capacity (TIBC)*. This indicates how many binding sites are available for iron. Normal values for children and adults are 200 to 400 μg/dl.

10. *Transferrin saturation*. This is the ratio of serum iron to total iron-binding capacity (SI/TIBC × 100). It is expressed as percent saturation and is more helpful than either measure taken separately. In iron deficiency, the SI decreases, and the TIBC increases, resulting in a lower percent saturation. In adults, 16 percent is the lower limit of normal; in children between 6 months and adolescence, the corresponding values are 7 percent or 10 percent. A value below 7 percent strongly suggests iron deficiency.

11. *Serum ferritin concentration (SF)*. This indicates the level of iron stores in the liver, spleen, and bone marrow. Ferritin is a large molecule that carries iron to storage sites. When iron is deficient none will go for storage since it is being used to synthesize hemoglobin. At all ages, values below 10 or 12 μg/liter indicate depletion of iron reserves.

12. *Stool examination for occult blood*. Guaiac testing is only sensitive enough to pick up more than 5 ml of occult blood. The benzidine test is very sensitive. A 1+ reaction (4+ is maximum) is considered normal and not indicative of occult blood.

COMMON CLINICAL PROBLEMS

Jaundice in the Newborn (Hyperbilirubinemia)

The nurse practitioner provides well-baby and/or follow-up care for infants who have had some form of hyperbilirubinemia and often is the first to identify breast-feeding jaundice in normal newborns. See this chapter, Dermal Icterus Index. The information presented here will assist the nurse practitioner in monitoring the progress of such infants and in explaining the infant's condition to parents. Before beginning such explanations it is essential to ask the parents to describe their understanding of what happened while the infant was in the nursery and what they were told about the infant's condition.

PHYSIOLOGIC JAUNDICE

Assessment Jaundice is the result of the breakdown of fetal red cells plus the immaturity of liver enzymes to conjugate and to excrete bilirubin (see this chapter, Metabolism of Bilirubin, and Jaundice). Jaundice appears in the full-term infant on the second to fourth day, may reach levels of 6 to 10 mg/dl, and resolves by the seventh day. In the premature infant jaundice appears on the third or fourth day, may reach levels of 10 to 12 mg/dl by the fifth to seventh day, and resolves by the ninth day or longer. The infant is otherwise healthy. Levels of bilirubin exceeding 10 mg/dl in the term infant and 14 mg/dl in the premature infant suggest that other factors are superimposed on the normally occurring physiologic jaundice (Rudolph, 1982, p. 1007). See below, Hyperbilirubinemia of the Newborn.

Management The infant needs adequate hydration. Phototherapy is usually not required in physiologic jaundice.

HYPERBILIRUBINEMIA OF THE NEWBORN

Assessment This is a more severe form of physiologic jaundice and suggests additional contributing factors such as blood group incompatibility, cephalohematoma, or infection. The primary problem usually is deficiency or inactivity of bilirubin glucuronyl transferase causing abnormal elevation of unconjugated bilirubin. Jaundice appears during the first week and may persist. Bilirubin levels may exceed 15 mg/dl and present the dangers of kernicterus. The incidence of bilirubin levels higher than 15 mg/dl is greater in low-birth-weight infants.

LABORATORY Laboratory assessment of newborns with hyperbilirubinemia includes (Rudolph, 1982, p. 1007):

1. Maternal blood group and Rh type
2. Infant blood group and Rh type, and direct Coombs test
3. Total and direct-reacting serum bilirubin

4. Hemoglobin or hematocrit
5. Reticulocyte count and white blood count
6. Red cell morphology
7. Urinalysis

Management Phototherapy and/or exchange transfusion may be indicated.

PHOTOTHERAPY Blue light waves assist the breakdown of unconjugated bilirubin in the skin into nontoxic, excretable by-products. The infant is undressed and placed under a bank of fluorescent lights. The eyes are carefully patched to protect them from the intense light. Position is changed systematically so all body surfaces are exposed. Loose stools, lethargy, skin rashes, and temperature changes are side effects of phototherapy. The therapy is usually discontinued in 1 to 3 days when unconjugated bilirubin has been reduced to levels considered safe in terms of the infant's age and condition.

Parents need ample explanations of what is happening to their infant, and opportunities to care for and feed the infant during hospitalization.

EXCHANGE TRANSFUSION Infants who have had exchange transfusions for blood group incompatibilities need to be observed closely for 6 to 8 weeks to monitor the degree of anemia. Serial hematocrit or hemoglobin determinations are performed until a sustained rise is demonstrated. Supplemental iron and/or blood transfusion may be necessary.

BREAST-FEEDING JAUNDICE

Assessment One of every 200 breast-fed infants develops severe and prolonged hyperbilirubinemia which is thought to be caused by the secretion of a substance in the mother's milk which inhibits the activity of bilirubin glucuronyl transferase. Increased bilirubin levels develop after the third day, and levels may peak by the seventh to tenth day or as late as 2 to 3 weeks of age. Levels may reach 15 to 20 mg/dl. The infant is otherwise well and kernicterus has not been reported with breast-feeding jaundice.

Management If bilirubin exceeds 15 mg/dl during the first 3 weeks it is recommended that a bilirubin level be obtained 2 hours after a breast feeding, breast feeding be discontinued for up to 12 hours to permit the enzyme to become active, and then a repeat bilirubin obtained. If the bilirubin has dropped 2 mg/dl, the infant can resume breast feeding (Lawrence, 1980, p. 210). Resumption of nursing may produce only a small increase and then a slow decline in bilirubin. If the child is well and the bilirubin is less than 15 mg/dl and falling, there is no need to interrupt breast-feeding. If the bilirubin rises while off the breast, other causes must be investigated.

COUNSELING The breast-feeding mother will worry that her milk is not good for the infant or is harming the infant and may be anxious about resuming breast-feeding. Clear explanations, and ample encouragement and support are required. The mother will need instruction on manual expression of milk during the period of formula feeding. See Chapter 5, Breastfeeding.

HEMOLYTIC DISEASE OF THE NEWBORN (ERYTHROBLASTOSIS FETALIS)

Assessment This condition results from exaggerated erythrocyte destruction.

Rn INCOMPATIBILITY The hemolytic process occurs as the result of (Lin-Fu, 1975, p. 6):

1. Immunization of an Rh-negative woman caused either by the inherited Rh factor in the red blood cells of her fetus or by transfusion of Rh-positive blood resulting in the production of anti-Rh antibodies by her immune system
2. Transplacental transfer of the woman's anti-Rh antibodies to the fetus causing hemolysis of the red blood cells and other pathologic processes both in utero and in the neonatal period

The hemolysis causes an increased load of unconjugated bilirubin to be metabolized by the liver, and hyperbilirubinemia may develop rapidly. Jaundice at birth or appearing during the first 24 hours should be considered to be due to erythroblastosis fetalis until proven otherwise. Firstborn babies are usually not affected since the degree of maternal sensitization is slight unless the mother has previously been transfused with Rh-positive blood or has had an abortion. Subsequent infants are at greater risk, often are severely affected, and may require multiple exchange transfusions.

ABO INCOMPATIBILITY Usually the mother is type O and the infant is type A or B. These incompatibilities result in milder disease and often require no treatment other than phototherapy. Occasionally exchange transfusion may be required. Jaundice may be the only clinical manifestation and appears during the first 24 hours.

Management The goals of management are as follows:

1. To prevent death of the affected infant from the complications of severe anemia and to avoid the toxic effects of hyperbilirubinemia, namely, kernicterus. Exchange transfusions and phototherapy are the major therapeutic modes.

2. To prevent immunization of Rh-negative women by the injection of Rh immunoglobin (RhoGAM), an IgG containing high titers of anti-Rh antibodies. This is possible only in nonsensitized women. The recommendation of both the U.S. Public Health Service and the American College of Obstetricians and Gynecologists is that any Rh-negative woman whose serum does not contain anti-Rh antibodies be given an intramuscular injection of Rh-immunoglobulin within 72 hours after delivery or abortion. The dangers of immunization following abortion often have been overlooked, but studies indicate that transplacental hemorrhages do occur during both spontaneous and induced abortions (Lin-Fu, 1975, p. 13). The injection of RhoGAM is intended to destroy any circulating fetal Rh factor before the woman's own immune system can respond to the factor. If the fetus's Rh factor is successfully destroyed within the mother, her immune system will remain quiescent during the next pregnancy should the fetus be Rh-positive. In order to avoid erythroblastosis fetalis, RhoGAM must be given after each subsequent pregnancy in which the fetus is Rh-positive.

KERNICTERUS

Assessment Kernicterus refers to the neurologic damage that occurs when unconjugated bilirubin is deposited in certain brain tissues. Symptoms usually develop during the first week of life and include lethargy, poor feeding, weak Moro reflex, high-pitched cry, and opisthotonos. Advanced and terminal symptoms are apnea, convulsions, and respiratory arrest. Mortality is high, and survivors show various signs of central nervous system damage. The risk of kernicterus exists with serum bilirubin levels above 18 to 20 mg/dl. Low-birth-weight and premature infants may be susceptible at lower levels.

Management Prevention of kernicterus is the best management. Exchange transfusions and phototherapy are indicated to keep unconjugated bilirubin levels below neurotoxic levels.

Anemia

PHYSIOLOGIC ANEMIA OF INFANCY

Assessment At birth the normal newborn has high hematocrit and hemoglobin levels which gradually decline to a low point (Hb 11 gm/dl) between 2 and 3 months of age. See Table 19-1. At about 3 to 4 months of age the bone marrow begins active erythropoiesis, and levels begin to increase. The same phenomenon operates in premature infants, but the drop in hemoglobin levels is more severe and may go to 9 gm/dl.

Management No medical intervention is indicated unless the anemia is severe. The premature infant may require a blood transfusion if hemoglobin falls to 6 to 7 mg/dl and/or if the infant shows signs of early heart failure. On general principle it is important that all premature infants receive dietary sources of iron, folic acid, and Vitamin E so normal hematopoiesis can occur. See Chapter 3, Nutritional Needs of the Low-Birth-Weight Infant, and Iron Nutrition in Infancy.

IRON DEFICIENCY ANEMIA

Assessment This condition results when the body lacks sufficient iron for hemoglobin synthesis.

ETIOLOGY Lack of sufficient iron can be the result of any of several factors:

1. Insufficient iron stores at birth due to prematurity, twinning, blood loss from perinatal hemorrhage, or a severely iron-deficient mother

2. Insufficient iron in the diet to meet demands for expanding body mass and blood volume, for example, during catch-up from prematurity, infancy, adolescence, pregnancy

3. Blood loss after birth due to hemorrhage or to chronic cow milk-induced enteric blood loss. The latter is considered to be the possible etiology in 25 to 50 percent of the cases and is caused by the combination of ingestion of large quantities of whole non-heat-treated cow milk plus intestinal sensitivity to a protein component in the milk.

4. Parasitic infestation

INCIDENCE It is most prevalent between 6 months and 3 years of life and during the adolescent growth spurt but is increasingly being found in school age children. Although it is found in children from all socioeconomic groups, the highest incidence of anemia is found in lower socioeconomic populations.

PHYSIOLOGY Iron deficiency develops in predictable stages over a period of time. Depletion of iron stores is followed by a fall in serum iron and a concurrent increase in iron binding capacity which results in a decreased transferrin saturation. This ultimately results in the decreased production of hemoglobin that is clinically recognized as anemia (Rudolph, 1982, p. 1046). As hemoglobin production decreases the newly formed cells become smaller (low MCV) and less well filled with hemoglobin (low MCH). The anemia that develops is a delayed manifestation of iron deficiency and becomes clinically evident only after months of suboptimal hemoglobin production, since red cells that were produced under conditions of iron adequacy live out their normal 120-day life span.

CLINICAL SIGNS AND SYMPTOMS Infants with slowly developing anemia usually do not show any clinical symptoms and appear well. They are frequently identified by routine screening tests during health supervision visits. Children with moderate to severe anemia (Hb below 6 to 7 gm/dl) may exhibit pallor, fatigue, listlessness, constipation, or anorexia. They are sometimes described by their parents as "obnoxious." They may be poor feeders and refuse to take solids. They may be fat and have poor muscle tone, or may be underweight. Pica may be present. Children with severe untreated anemia (Hb 2 to 3 mg/dl) may be very irritable and develop tachycardia, cardiac murmurs, cardiorespiratory distress, and cardiac failure. Preliminary reports suggest that iron deficiency can affect attention span, alertness, and learning in young children (Smith et al., 1974; Oski and Honig, 1978).

NUTRITION HISTORY Essential to the diagnosis is a thorough diet and nutrition history. Use of a 24-hour diet recall is helpful (see Chapter 3, Nutrition History). The history will probably reveal a diet high in milk intake (more than 1 quart per day) and low in iron-containing solid foods.

Laboratory Laboratory investigation includes the detection of mild iron deficiency, documentation of anemia, and differentiation between iron deficiency and beta-thalassemia minor.

Detection of Mild Iron Deficiency Mild iron deficiency is not reliably detected by traditional laboratory procedures (e.g., hemoglobin, peripheral blood smear). The tests that are most helpful in identifying mild deficiency are the MCV (using an electronic counter), FEP, and serum ferritin (see this chapter, Common Laboratory Procedures for Anemia, and Fig. 19-2).

Detection of Iron Deficiency Anemia The laboratory definition of iron deficiency anemia depends on the age of the child. Hemoglobin, hematocrit, and MCV values below the lower limits of normal (-2 SD) for age are generally used. See Table 19-1. The recommended approach includes:

1. *Complete blood count.* It will reveal low values for hemoglobin, hematocrit, RBC, MCV, and MCH. The MCHC goes down only when the hemoglobin is 8 gm/dl or lower.

2. *Peripheral blood smear.* It will show hypochromic, microcytic cells with marked variation in size and shape, but only when the anemia has become moderate to severe.

3. *Reticulocyte count.* This may be normal in mild anemia and low in moderate to severe anemia.

4. *Stool guaiac or benzidine tests.* At 2 months of age up to 80 percent of infants being fed fresh cow milk will have stools positive for occult blood. By 6 months of age, 60 percent will have positive findings, and by 1 year of age, 20 percent will have positive findings (Koerper, 1982).

DIFFERENTIATION BETWEEN IRON DEFICIENCY AND BETA THALASSEMIA MINOR The determination of MCV values by electronic particle counter is

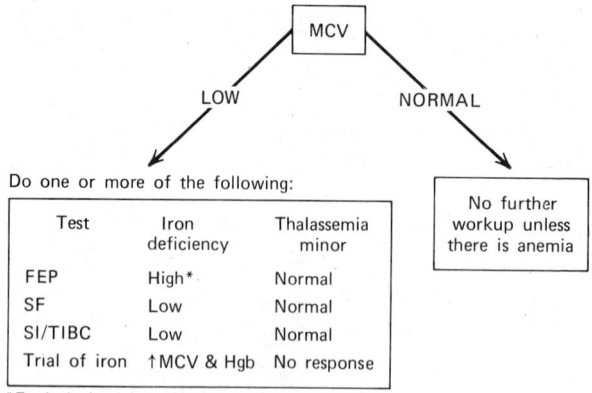

*Exclude lead intoxication

Figure 19-2 Screening for childhood anemia based on the MCV. (Reprinted with permission from P. R. Dallman, "New Approaches to Screening for Iron Deficiency," *J Pediatr 90*:678–681, April 1977.)

becoming more widespread in screening programs for childhood anemias. When the MCV is low, the differential diagnosis is chiefly between iron deficiency and beta thalassemia minor (see this chapter, Beta Thalassemia). Figure 19-2 illustrates the diagnostic process that will differentiate between the two. Another differentiating factor is the red blood cell count. If the MCV is low and the RBC is low, iron deficiency can be assumed. If the RBC is over 5.5 million/cu mm, thalassemia minor needs to be investigated (Koerper, 1982).

Management The management of iron deficiency includes prevention of the condition, screening for early identification of iron deficiency states, and treatment of actual cases.

PREVENTION Prevention of iron deficiency is the best management and involves provision of adequate exogenous sources of iron. See Chapter 3, Iron Nutrition in Infancy.

SCREENING The process outlined in Figure 19-2 represents an approach to identifying iron deficiency with a high degree of accuracy. A hemoglobin is also obtained, and the likelihood of iron deficiency is greater if both the Hb and MCV are low. In settings where the electronic counter is not available, screening is done by obtaining hemoglobin and hematocrit levels. Screening is performed between 9 and 12 months of age, during adolescence, and if warranted by history (Koerper, 1982).

TREATMENT When clinical and laboratory assessment reveals iron deficiency anemia the plan of management includes specific medication therapy and parent counseling as follows:

Medication The procedures for therapy and follow-up are described.

1. Iron in the ferrous form is the drug of choice. Recommended doses of oral iron are presented in Table 19-3. Available liquid oral iron preparations are listed in Table 19-4. Medication is given for 3 months or for 2 months after Hb reaches normal levels so that iron stores can be replenished. The more severe the anemia, the longer the treatment.

2. In mild anemia (Hb > 9 mg/dl), the child should be seen and the hemoglobin checked at 1-month intervals until the anemia has been corrected. In moderate to severe anemia, the child should be seen in 1 week for hemoglobin and reticulocyte count. The reticulocyte count will show a response within 3 to 7 days if the anemia is truly based on iron deficiency, and if the medication is being given and absorbed. Hemoglobin should rise 0.5 to 1 gm/dl per month. If no therapeutic response is present after 1 to 2 months of reliably administered iron, therapy should be stopped, and other causes of anemia should be investigated.

Table 19-3
Recommended Doses of Oral Iron in Infants

Hb (gm/dl)	Dose (Elemental iron/kg/day)	Comments
>9	2–3 mg	Can be given in a single dose
8–9	3–4 mg	Can be given in a single dose
<8	5–6 mg	Given in divided doses to decrease side effects
<4–5		Admission to hospital for transfusion, danger of cardiac problems, congestive failure

Source: M. Koerper, Personal communication, March 1982.

Table 19-4
Common Oral Iron Liquids

Proprietary Name	Active Ingredient	Elemental Iron (mg/cc)
Mol-Iron Liquid	Ferrous sulfate	10
Feosol Elixir	Ferrous sulfate	8
Fer-In-Sol Syrup	Ferrous sulfate	6
Fer-In-Sol Drops	Ferrous sulfate	25
Fergon Elixir	Ferrous gluconate	7

Source: Adapted from *Physician's Desk Reference for Nonprescription Drugs*, 1st ed., Oradell, NJ: Medical Economics Co., 1980.

3. Once blood levels have returned to normal, medication should be continued an additional 6 to 8 weeks to replenish iron stores. The child should be seen again at the end of treatment and hematocrit, hemoglobin, and indices checked.

Parent Counseling Parents need instructions on medication therapy and diet modification.

Medication Instructions may be written and given to parents. Points to include are:

1. The exact dose and how to measure it should be written out.
2. Medication should be given between meals for better absorption. Giving it shortly after meals is helpful in reducing gastric irritation.
3. Large amounts of milk should be avoided since milk can interfere with absorption.
4. If the taste is unpalatable, the medication can be given with juice. Older children may prefer chewable tablets.
5. The teeth may be temporarily stained, but this can be reduced by placing the medicine with a dropper on the back of the tongue, by using a straw, and by rinsing the mouth or brushing the teeth after taking the medicine.
6. The stools may turn black.
7. The full course of medication must be taken, even though the child is well.

8. The medicine must be kept out of reach since accidental ingestions can result in serious side effects including hemorrhage and death. See Chapter 13, Parent Teaching Related to Medications.

Diet Education of parents regarding feeding practices is essential and should be on-going.

1. Breast feeding or the use of iron-fortified infant formula should be encouraged during the first year. Fresh cow milk should be avoided.
2. Daily milk intake should be restricted to one third of the total calories. This would limit milk intake of young children to little more than 1 pint per day.
3. Iron supplementation. See Chapter 3, Iron Nutrition in Infancy.
4. A list of iron-containing solid foods should be provided and their use encouraged. See Chapter 3, Iron Nutrition in Infancy.
5. Parents must be supported in their efforts to change or to modify feeding patterns.

SICKLE CELL ANEMIA AND TRAIT

Assessment Each person inherits one gene from each parent that governs the synthesis of hemoglobin. The protein (globin) portion of the normal adult hemoglobin A molecule contains two pairs of polypeptide chains (two alpha chains and two beta chains). The sickle cell hemoglobin molecule (Hb S) is abnormal and results from single amino acid substitution on the beta chain caused by inheriting a defective co-dominant gene.

SICKLE CELL TRAIT If only one co-dominant gene is inherited, Hb S will be formed in small proportion to Hb A (35 percent S to 60 percent A). This person is said to be heterozygous and has sickle cell trait, a benign condition which does *not* cause anemia and disease. Trait is present in 8 to 10 percent of American blacks, and a decreased incidence is found in some Mediterranean, Latin, and Oriental populations. Hemoglobin and hematocrit values are normal. Sickling does not occur except in rare instances when hypoxia may occur from shock or flying at very high altitudes in unpressurized aircraft.

SICKLE CELL ANEMIA The term sickle cell disease includes several disorders in which sickling of erythrocytes produces a chronic hemolytic anemia and obstruction of the microcirculation. These are, in order of decreasing frequency, sickle cell anemia (SS disease), sickle-hemoglobin C disease (S-C disease), and sickle-beta thalassemia (S-B thalassemia) (Vichinsky and Lubin, 1980). Only sickle cell anemia will be discussed here. If two co-dominant genes are inherited, Hb S will account for up to 70 to 90 percent of the hemoglobin. This person is homozygous and will have sickle cell anemia which is a severe, chronic, hemolytic anemia.

Incidence At birth, one in 600 American blacks has sickle cell anemia. In adult blacks the incidence is one in 1875 due to the mortality of the disease. It is also found in geographic areas throughout the world in which malaria is endemic.

Clinical Picture The presence of Hb S with decreased oxygen concentration deforms the normal red blood cell into an abnormal crescent-shaped cell. These cells lead to increased blood viscosity, retarded capillary flow, damage to the fragile cells, and increased red cell destruction (the sickle erythrocyte may have a life span as short as 20 days). The degree of anemia remains fairly constant unless red blood cell production decreases (aplastic crisis) or blood viscosity increases (vaso-occlusive crisis). Symptoms usually do not appear until the latter part of the first year of life since the presence of large amounts of fetal hemoglobin (Hb F) in the early months tends to obscure the presence of Hb S. The child is asymptomatic for periods of time until a crisis occurs. Crises are precipitated by infection, dehydration, trauma, hypoxia, exposure, and strenuous exertion. Vaso-occlusive crises are the most common and symptoms include anorexia, pallor, weakness, jaundice; severe pain and swelling in the hands, feet, abdomen, joints, and extremities; fever; and anemia. Chronic anemia and repeated vaso-occlusive episodes lead to varied and severe problems as children grow older. These include complications in the central nervous system (cerebrovascular accidents), cardiovascular system (cardiac enlargement), genitourinary tract (hyposthenuria, which is constant secretion of urine of low specific gravity, enuresis, UTIs), impaired pulmonary function, impaired liver function, ocular abnormalities, skeletal problems, and skin ulcers. These children are extremely susceptible to infection, and many die in early adulthood.

Table 19-5
Transmission of Sickle Cell Disease

Genotype of Parents	Probability of Abnormal Hemoglobin in Offspring		
	Normal	Trait	Disease
1 parent with trait	50%	50%	0
Both parents with trait	25%	50%	25%
1 parent with trait, 1 parent with disease	0	50%	50%
Both parents with disease	0	0	100%

Source: Reprinted with permission from L. S. Brunner and D. S. Suddarth, *The Lippincott Manual of Nursing Practice*, Philadelphia: J. B. Lippincott, 1974. P. 1164.

Laboratory   Initial laboratory diagnosis includes peripheral blood smear (reveals 10 to 15 percent irreversibly sickled cells), complete blood count (hemoglobin ranges from 6 to 9 gm/dl), red cell indices (MCV is elevated), reticulocyte and platelet counts (elevated), and hemoglobin electrophoresis (Vichinsky and Lubin, 1980).

GENETIC IMPLICATIONS   The mode of transmission of sickle cell trait and anemia is autosomal co-dominant (see Table 19-5). It is *co-dominant* because there *are* effects of the trait as well as of the disease. Definite probabilities exist with each pregnancy that the offspring will inherit the disease, the trait, or neither. See Chapter 29, Genetics.

Management   Management includes treatment of the child with sickle cell anemia and screening for detection of sickle cell trait.

SICKLE CELL ANEMIA   Management of crises and prevention of further crises are the important components of care. See Vichinsky and Lubin, 1980.

Vaso-occlusive Crisis   The child requires pain medication and increased fluid intake.

General Management   In addition to regular health maintenance care, prevention of vaso-occlusive and anemic crises is the goal. Measures include:

1. Avoiding dehydration.
2. Treating fevers as emergencies. If an unexplained fever over 38.5°C (101°F) occurs, blood cultures should be obtained and antibiotics should be begun immediately. Parents may keep penicillin at home and treat the first sign of fever or infection. This is because of the high incidence of sudden onset of pneumococcal septicemia which can be overwhelming and cause death in a matter of hours. Immunization with pneumococcal vaccine is effective in minimizing *Streptococcus pneumoniae* infections; however, the vaccine does not protect against all serotypes (see Chapter 17, Pneumonia) and is not effective in children under 2 years of age.
3. Transfusion therapy. Transfusions have been effective in treating severe complications as they decrease the number of sickle cells.
4. Avoiding low-oxygen environments. Flights on regular pressurized aircraft are permitted, but unpressurized aircraft are not advised. Prolonged underwater swimming or breath holding can also precipitate problems.
5. Parent education and counseling. Clear information communicated in understandable ways is essential, as is compassionate support.

SCREENING Screening for sickle cell is a complicated issue and many differences of opinion exist. The most reasonable approaches to prevention of transmission and prevention of morbidity are presented.

Sickle Cell Anemia It is now possible to diagnose sickle cell anemia prenatally using amniocentesis and fetal blood sampling, but these techniques are not widely available and fetal blood sampling carries a 5 to 10 percent risk of fetal loss (Kan and Dozy, 1978). Neonatal screening for detection of infants with sickle cell anemia is suggested to counsel parents regarding optimal infant care and early detection of crises. This may reduce the high risk of morbidity and mortality in children between 6 months and 3 years of age. There is a special procedure available that can differentiate trait from disease at birth (Bailey et al., 1974; Smith et al., 1973).

Sickle Cell Trait The purpose of screening for trait is to identify those parents or prospective parents who are carriers and may produce offspring with sickle cell disease and to provide the information and counseling necessary for these persons to make informed decisions about childbearing.

When to Screen The question about when to perform screening is currently at issue. Many agencies perform screening for sickle cell on all Afro-American children during the latter part of the first year of life. Since screening before 1 year of age may be inaccurate if levels of fetal hemoglobin persist, some authorities recommend that screening be performed after 1 year of age (Koerper, 1982).

Implications of Early Screening Identification of infants and young children with sickle cell trait means that parents must be educated about the consequences of childbearing. Parents then have the responsibility of informing their children when they reach childbearing age. Unless continuity of health supervision is maintained, the risks of parental misinterpretation of such information, of placing unnecessary restrictions on themselves and on their children, and the anxiety and worry produced are real dangers.

Screening in Adolescence Some authorities suggest that screening programs be directed toward adolescents who have been exposed to an educational program which accurately describes the consequences of sickle cell trait and disease and the reproductive alternatives available to persons with the genetic trait (birth control, abortion, artificial insemination, or assumption of a 25 percent risk with each pregnancy of producing a child with sickle cell disease). This approach runs the risk of being too late in populations where sexual activity results in early adolescent pregnancies. Additional recommendations for screening are at the time of entry into the armed forces, during routine antepartum care, as a part of premarital examinations, and when persons are admitted to the hospital (Smith et al., 1973). Screening must be voluntary and performed only with informed consent.

Positive Results Every person with a positive screening test should have a hemoglobin electrophoresis test to provide definitive information on the types of hemoglobin present.

Counseling Points to include in counseling persons with sickle cell trait are:

1. Individuals with the trait must be counseled that they do *not* have the disease, that they do *not* have to alter their normal life activities, and that their life span is normal.

2. There is reason to mention risks associated with unusual hypoxia. It has been reported that unaccustomed, vigorous exercise at high altitudes (above 4,000 feet) resulted in the deaths of four black males (Smith et al., 1973). Increased risk of vaso-occlusive episodes also exists when flying in unpressurized aircraft or when snorkeling or diving if hypoxia occurs.

3. Persons with trait may be blood donors but should acknowledge the presence of trait so the blood will not be used for newborn exchange transfusions.

4. Before undergoing anesthesia, persons with trait should inform health personnel.

5. Screening information is kept confidential.

RESOURCES   Information on sickle cell disease and trait is available from the following resources:

1. Chief, Health Staff, Job Corps, Manpower Administration, U.S. Department Labor, Washington, DC.

2. Foundation for Research and Education in Sickle Cell Disease, 423–431 West 120th Street, New York NY 10027.

3. The National Foundation–March of Dimes, P. O. Box 2000, White Plains NY 10602.

BETA THALASSEMIA

Assessment   Beta thalassemia is a hereditary defect in the rate of production of the beta globin portion of the hemoglobin molecule. It is inherited as an autosomal co-dominant trait in a manner similar to sickle cell disease (see Table 19-5). The defect results in decreased production of normal beta chains of hemoglobin. The defect is found in persons of Mediterranean and Oriental origin with a 1 percent incidence in American blacks.

BETA THALASSEMIA MAJOR (COOLEY'S ANEMIA)   This is the homozygous condition in which there is severely deficient production of the beta chain of hemoglobin and overproduction of the delta chain. Red blood cells have a shortened life span and reduced hemoglobin levels.

Clinical Signs and Symptoms   These result from severe, progressive hemolytic anemia and chronic hypoxia and develop during the second 6 months of life. They include pallor, irritability, poor growth, greenish brown complexion, and enlarged liver and spleen. Hypertrophy of the blood-forming tissues results in widening of the flat bones of the face and skull, which gives a characteristic facies and causes bone pain. Puberty rarely occurs. Prognosis is poor due to side effects of frequent transfusions. Cardiac failure develops in late childhood and adolescence.

Laboratory   These children have low hemoglobin levels (about 6 gm/dl), low MCVs and low red blood cell counts.

BETA THALASSEMIA MINOR (THALASSEMIA TRAIT)   This is the heterozygous condition in which there is a mild deficiency in the production of the beta chain of hemoglobin. Mild hypochromic anemia occurs which may be confused with iron deficiency. See this chapter, Iron Deficiency Anemia. Most children are asymptomatic.

Laboratory   Smaller red blood cells are produced resulting in a low MCV. To compensate for the small cells the body produces more red cells and the RBC is high (over 5.5 million/cu mm). Hemoglobin and hematocrit levels are normal or slightly below normal.

Management   Management depends on whether the condition is homozygous or heterozygous.

BETA THALASSEMIA MAJOR   The management of beta thalassemia major includes:

1. Transfusions of packed red blood cells are given often enough to keep the hemoglobin above 10 to 11 gm/dl. This level should permit a reasonable level of activity, school attendance, alleviation of the severe symptoms of anemia, and fairly normal growth and development in early childhood.
2. Iron-chelating agents to relieve the effects of iron overload (hemosiderosis) are being evaluated and are only being used under research protocol.
3. Splenectomy is often necessary because of massive splenomegaly, but this procedure predisposes the young child to severe septicemia.
4. Counseling. The child must receive on-going support from parents and care providers. Any chronically ill child worries about self-image, repeated medical procedures, being different from

peers, and ultimate survival. Parents also need support to cope with the changes in family life occasioned by the care of a chronically ill child, to help the child lead as normal a life as possible, and to deal with their fears about the child's anticipated death.

BETA THALASSEMIA MINOR The management of beta thalassemia minor involves identifying carriers, providing genetic counseling, and avoiding inappropriate iron therapy.

Screening   Screening for thalassemia trait is indicated in high-risk populations to facilitate genetic counseling (see Chapter 29, Genetics). The process for distinguishing beta thalassemia minor from iron deficiency is presented in Figure 19-2. If the MCV is low and the RBC is over 5.5 million/cu mm, a hemoglobin electrophoresis is done to determine the presence of increased levels of Hb A_2 and/or Hb F, which occur in the beta thalassemias.

ALPHA THALASSEMIA TRAIT

Assessment   This condition is common in Southeast Asia, and from 2 to 7 percent of American blacks are heterozygotes for alpha thalassemia. The condition is due to deletion of one or more of the four alpha globin genes normally present and results in decreased synthesis of alpha chains. Thus, there are four possibilities of clinical expression as indicated in Table 19-6.

CLINICAL IMPLICATIONS   Alpha thalassemia trait is most often confused with beta thalassemia and/or iron deficiency anemia. Hemoglobin electrophoresis which is normal in alpha thalassemia will distinguish between alpha and beta thalassemia. Neither alpha nor beta thalassemia will respond to iron therapy.

Management   It is suggested that black newborns be screened for alpha thalassemia. If the MCV at birth is less than 94 fl/dl, a hemoglobin electrophoresis should be performed. Approximately 67 percent of these infants will be heterozygotes for the trait (McMillan et al., 1977, p. 132). If a child is found to possess alpha thalassemia trait, the parents should be screened to determine the chances of producing a child with all four alpha globin genes missing.

Table 19-6
Alpha Thalassemia

Condition	No. of Genes Deleted	Hb	MCV	RBC	Clinical Findings
Silent carrier	1	nl	nl	nl	None
Alpha thalassemia trait	2	nl–sl ↓	↓	↑	Microcytosis, occasional mild anemia
Hb H disease	3	mod ↓ (8–10 gm/dl)	↓	nl	Chronic hemolytic anemia
Homozygous alpha thalassemia	4				Anemic and hydropic in utero and are stillborn or die at birth

Source: M. Koerper, Personal communication, April 1977.

GLUCOSE 6-PHOSPHATE DEHYDROGENASE DEFICIENCY (G-6-PD)

Assessment This genetically inherited condition is a deficiency of the enzyme G6PD in red blood cells which results in hemolysis of red cells after exposure to certain substances having oxidant properties. Although it is a sex-linked trait, female carriers may also be symptomatic (see Chapter 29, X-Linked Inheritance). About 10 percent of American black males and 2 percent of American black females have the defect. It occurs also in Mediterranean, Middle Eastern, and Oriental populations. Symptoms of hemolytic anemia usually occur only during severe infection or following exposure to the offending substances listed in Table 19-7. They resolve following discontinuation of exposure. Occasionally the anemia may be severe enough to require transfusion.

Management Prevention of hemolysis by avoiding offending substances is the best treatment. This requires identification of persons with the enzyme deficiency and education of such persons regard-

Table 19-7

Drugs Provoking Hemolysis in G6PD Deficient Red Cells

Acetanilid
Acetophenetidin (phenacetin)
Acetylsalicylic acid (aspirin)
N_2 acetylsulfanilamide
Antipyrine
Colamine
Fava bean
Furazolidone
Isoniazid
Naphthalene (moth balls)
Naphthoate
Nitrofurantoin (Furadantin)
Pamaquine
Para-aminosalicylic acid
Phenacetin
Phenylhydrazine
Primaquine
Probenecid
Pyramidone
Quinine
Quinidine
Salicylazosulfapyridine
Sulfamethoxypyridazine (Kynex)
Sulfacetamide
Sulfisoxazole (Gantrisin)
Sulfoxone
Synthetic vitamin K compounds
Thiazolsulfone

Source: Adapted with permission from J. W. Graef and T. E. Cone, *Manual of Pediatric Therapeutics,* Boston: Little, Brown, 1974. P. 325.

ing drugs to be avoided. A list of substances should be given to every affected family. A screening blood test is available and should be performed on all black children and those of Mediterranean, Middle Eastern, and Oriental extraction.

References

Bailey, E. N., et al. "Screening in Pediatric Practice." *Pediatr Clin North Am 21*:123–165, February 1974.

Brunner, L. S. and D. S. Suddarth. *The Lippincott Manual of Nursing Practice.* Philadelphia: J. B. Lippincott, 1974.

Dallman, P. R. "New Approaches to Screening for Iron Deficiency." *J Pediatr* 90:678–681, April 1977.

Graef, J. W. and T. E. Cone. *Manual of Pediatric Therapeutics.* Boston: Little, Brown, 1974.

Kan, Y. W. and A. M. Dozy. "Antenatal Diagnosis of Sickle Cell Anaemia by DNA Analysis of Amniotic Fluid Cells." *Lancet* 2:910–911, October 28, 1978.

Kim, H. C. "Laboratory Identification of Inherited Hemoglobinopathies in Children." *Clin Pediatr* 20:161–171, March 1981.

Koerper, M. A. Personal communication, March 1982.

Koerper, M. A. Personal communication, April 1977.

Koerper, M. A. and P. R. Dallman. "Serum Iron Concentration and Transferrin Saturation in the Diagnosis of Iron Deficiency in Children: Normal Developmental Changes." *J Pediatr* 91:870–874, December 1977.

Koerper, M. A., et al. "Developmental Changes in Red Blood Cell Volume: Implications in Screening Infants and Children for Iron Deficiency and Thalassemia Trait." *J Pediatr* 89:580–583, October 1976.

Kramer, L. I. "Advancement of Dermal Icterus in the Jaundiced Newborn." *Am J Dis Child* 118:454–458, September 1969.

Lawrence, R. A. *Breast-Feeding: A Guide for the Medical Profession.* St. Louis: C.V. Mosby, 1980.

Lin-Fu, J. S. *Prevention of Hemolytic Disease of the Fetus and Newborn Due to Rh Isoimmunization.* Rockville, MD: DHEW Publication No. (HSA) 75-5125, 1975.

McMillan, J. A., et al. *The Whole Pediatrician Catalog.* Philadelphia: W.B. Saunders, 1977.

Oski, F. A. and A. Honig. "The Effects of Therapy on the Developmental Scores of Iron-Deficient Infants." *J Pediatr* 92:21–25, January 1978.

Physician's Desk Reference for Nonprescription Drugs. 1st ed. Oradell, NJ: Medical Economics Co., 1980.

Reeves, J. D., et al. "Screening for Iron Deficiency Anemia in One-Year-Old Infants: Hemoglobin Alone or Hemoglobin and Mean Corpuscular Volume as Predictors of Response to Iron Treatment." *J Pediatr* 98:894–898, June 1981.

Rudolph, A. M., editor. *Pediatrics.* 17th ed. East Norwalk, CT: Appleton-Century-Crofts, 1982.

Smith, N. J. and E. Rios. "Iron Metabolism and Iron Deficiency in Infancy and Childhood." *Adv Pediatr* 21:239–280, 1974.

Smith, W. B., et al. "Identifying and Counseling Patients with Sickle Trait." *Calif Med* 119:1–7, July 1973.

Vaughan, V. C., et al., editors. *Nelson Textbook of Pediatrics.* 11th ed. Philadelphia: W. B. Saunders, 1979.

Vichinsky, E. P. and B. H. Lubin. "Sickle Cell Anemia and Related Hemoglobinopathies." *Pediatr Clin North Am* 27:429–447, May 1980.

20

The Gastrointestinal System

Parents are frequently concerned during infancy and childhood about commonly occurring maladjustments of the gastrointestinal (GI) system such as regurgitation, constipation, diarrhea, and abdominal pain. While these conditions occasionally cause only minor problems, they can also herald the beginning of more serious pathologic conditions. The nurse practitioner is continuously alert to the presence of symptoms that indicate more serious progression of disease processes, obtains medical consultation when indicated, and discusses with parents the management plan.

ASSESSMENT

Normal Values

BOWEL MOVEMENTS

There is a wide variation in stool patterns from individual to individual. Frequency and consistency are determined to a large extent by the type and amount of oral intake and by the variability in the GI pattern of absorption and motility. There is no correct number of bowel movements a person should have over a period of days. Color of stools also varies according to oral intake and physiology of the GI tract. Normally stools are brown. Black stools may indicate the presence of blood, iron, lead, charcoal, or bismuth preparations. Red stools may indicate frank bleeding of the large intestine or anal fissures or may be due to certain foods such as undigested beets. Clay-colored stools may indicate biliary obstruction or infectious hepatitis. For normal patterns of stools in infancy, see Chapter 5, Stool Patterns of Infancy.

History

PAST

Obtain information on past illnesses, colic, infant feeding problems, constipation, melena, surgical procedures, failure to thrive, chronic diarrhea, indigestion, vomiting, family allergies, and foreign travel.

PRESENT

Obtain information regarding the age of the child, initial symptoms (location, progression, severity, and duration), the quality of pain (intermittent or continuous, radiating, dull, or sharp), symptoms associated with eating, drinking and if relieved by such, number and consistency of bowel movements, family's feelings in reference to normalcy of elimination, presence of blood, mucus, or pus in the stools, medications taken, previous treatments, current oral intake, and presence of vomiting and description (color, projectile or nonprojectile).

BIRTH

Discuss complications of pregnancy, labor, and delivery, gestational age, birth weight, early elimination patterns, description of bowel movements, and feeding problems in the hospital, including poor sucking, copious regurgitation, vomiting.

FAMILY

Discuss familial diseases (cystic fibrosis, celiac disease), family members with similar symptoms of the presenting complaint.

Physical Examination

The nurse practitioner performs a complete physical examination. See Chapter 1, Child Health Assessment.

Laboratory

STOOL ANALYSIS

Examination of the stool is helpful in evaluating disease entities such as bacterial and parasitic infections, malabsorption, and ulcerative colitis. Frank examination of the stool includes inspection for the following:

- Mucus, blood, or pus: this could suggest a bacterial infection.
- White flecks and beanlike curds: this could indicate a protein allergy.
- Oil in stool: this could indicate steatorrhea indicative of cystic fibrosis and celiac disease.

Other examinations of the stool include the following:

- pH and reducing substances (sugar): pH below 6.0 and sugar in the stool could indicate disaccharide intolerance.
- Stool smear for leukocytes: their presence could indicate bacterial infection or ulcerative colitis.
- Stool for ova and parasites: a positive result indicates infection.
- Stool for bacterial culture
- Seventy-two hour stool collection for quantitative fat determination: a fat content of more than 10 percent of fat ingested in the previous 24 hours could indicate the presence of malabsorption.

OTHER LABORATORY EXAMINATIONS

- Complete blood count to rule out infection, anemia
- Sweat test to rule out cystic fibrosis
- Disaccharide tolerance test to rule out disaccharide intolerance
- D-Xylose tolerance test to rule out small bowel malabsorption
- Barium enema to rule out Hirschsprung's disease, malrotation, and colitis
- Jejunal biopsy to rule out mucosal disease of the intestine

MANAGEMENT

Diet

Diet therapy is an important aspect of any management plan in the GI system. Depending on the specific disease entity, the dietary management may include nothing by mouth, clear liquids, or a modified or routine diet.

Counseling

Disease of the GI tract, while extremely common, can occasionally become life threatening. Examples include intractable diarrhea, undetected malabsorption syndromes, appendicitis, Hirschsprung's disease, and intestinal obstruction. The nurse practitioner educates parents about the symptoms of severe illness: dehydration, extreme lethargy, severe abdominal pain, copious blood in the stools, severe vomiting, and abdominal distension. Parents are counseled to seek medical consultation if these conditions occur.

Hospitalization

In situations when hospitalization occurs, the nurse practitioner continues to offer psychologic support, explanations of the medical regimen, and plans with the parents and hospital staff for discharge and follow-up care.

Ambulatory Care

If ambulatory management is indicated, the nurse practitioner follows closely with the parents the progression of symptoms, is alert to increased symptoms of illness, and reinforces explanations of management.

Medications

LAXATIVES

Laxatives are rarely used for simple constipation. Instead families are counseled in establishing proper bowel habits, increasing high residue foods in the diet, and increasing the oral fluid intake. Laxatives are never used in infants. In school age children they are used when constipation is a symptom of conditions like encopresis and anal fissures.

Stimulant   These laxatives increase the peristaltic activity of the intestine by irritation of the mucosa. Examples are cascara, senna compounds glycerine suppositories and castor oil.

Emollient   These laxatives permit the mixture of fat and water in the intestines which helps soften the stool. An example is dioctyl sodium sulfosuccinate (Colace).

Lubricant   These laxatives soften the stools by preventing colonic reabsorption of water. Examples of lubricants are mineral oil and olive oil. With prolonged use mineral oil is absorbed through the GI tract and can penetrate the mesenteric lymph nodes, liver, and spleen causing chronic inflammation (American Pharmaceutical Association, 1979, p. 43). If given with meals, mineral oil may decrease the absorption of vitamins A and D. There is also the danger of aspiration into the lungs in young children.

ANTIEMETICS

Medications to control vomiting are rarely used in infants and children because they can mask symptoms diagnostic of potentially serious diseases such as intestinal obstruction. Judicious use of antiemetics is at the discretion of the physician. Examples are dimen-hydrinate (Dramamine), and bismuth compounds which coat the intestines and decrease nausea.

ANTIDIARRHEALS

Occasionally medications are used in the management of diarrhea in older children, but never in infants and toddlers. Medications do not lessen the amount of fluid loss and mask the severity of the diarrhea by making the stools appear more firm. Some medications decrease abdominal cramps and bowel motility. The following are some commonly used drugs:

- Opiates (paregoric and tincture of opium) increase smooth muscle tone and decrease bowel motility. Chronic use increases the possibility of addiction.
- Absorbents (Kaopectate) absorb excess water in the stools.
- Antispasmodics (Lomotil) decrease bowel motility.
- Lactobacillus preparations (yogurt) are thought to help restore normal flora in the colon after acute infections.

COMMON CLINICAL PROBLEMS

Anal Fissures

ASSESSMENT

Definition Anal fissures are small tears in the anal mucosa and occur as a result of the passage of hard stools. Occasionally, children will try to hold back stools because of painful defecation with resulting increased constipation. Occasionally, small streaks of bright red blood are seen in the bowel movement.

Physical Examination With a good light and a magnifying lens, fissures can usually be seen with the child in knee-chest position and with the buttocks spread apart. A digital examination is done to rule out anal sphincter stenosis.

Differential Diagnosis   Anal fissures account for over 50 percent of all causes of blood in the stool. Other causes include intussusception, diverticulum, volvulus, diarrhea, and ulcerative colitis. Rarely is malignancy a cause of rectal bleeding in childhood. Gross red blood in stools is usually associated with lower intestinal bleeding, while tarry stools are usually associated with gastric or small intestinal bleeding.

MANAGEMENT

Diet   The diet is increased in roughage-containing foods such as fibrous vegetables, fruits, and bran flakes.

Medication   The consistency of the stool is altered to permit passage through the rectum without difficulty. Stool softeners, such as mineral oil, between meals so as not to interfere with vitamin A and D absorption, and dioctyl sodium sulfosuccinate (Colace), are prescribed.

Sitz Baths   These warm tub baths reduce anal discomfort and are prescribed three times a day.

Counseling   Parents are counseled to continue the medication regimen until stools are soft. Dietary management is reviewed. In cases where the anal sphincter is tight manual dilation by the child or parent while the child is taking a sitz bath is recommended.

Appendicitis

ASSESSMENT

Definition   Appendicitis is an inflammation of the small appendage of the cecum. It is rare before the age of 2 years.

Symptoms   Frequently, the symptoms are varied, vague, and atypical. However, the child usually complains of persistent, localized lower-right-quadrant pain. There may or may not be vomiting, slight fever, anorexia, diarrhea, or constipation. Physical examination reveals abdominal tenderness over the appendiceal area. Rebound tenderness, a sign of peritoneal irritation, may be present.

Differential Diagnosis Other causes of abdominal pain include viral and bacterial gastroenteritis, urinary and pelvic infections, food poisoning, and respiratory disease.

Laboratory Blood leukocytes seldom reveal values greater than 15,000/cu mm. X-ray film of the chest and urinalysis are obtained to rule out respiratory and urinary tract infection which can cause abdominal pain.

Physical Examination A complete physical is done, including a rectal examination.

MANAGEMENT

Appendectomy is performed and the prognosis is excellent. If the appendix ruptures, either localized or generalized peritonitis results, and the treatment is intensive antibiotic therapy.

Constipation

ASSESSMENT

Definition Constipation is frequently interpreted by parents as straining, grunting, or any difficulty with stool passage especially during infancy. While these symptoms are frequent, true constipation is defined as hard, rocklike bowel movements regardless of difficulty of passage. See Chapter 5, Constipation in Infancy.

Etiology The most common cause during infancy is dietary mismanagement. Other causes in childhood include faulty toilet habits (retaining stool), pain on defecation, cultural beliefs, frequent use of laxatives and enemas, and psychogenic problems related to elimination. Medical causes include Hirschsprung's disease, hypothyroidism, renal-tubular acidosis, anal fissures, and strictures, and excessive vomiting.

Physical Examination Occasionally on examination a distended abdomen and a rectum full of feces is present.

MANAGEMENT

Diet   During infancy and childhood the amount of water and high residue foods such as fruits, fibrous vegetables, and bran flakes is increased.

Medication   For chronic constipation the lower bowel is cleansed with enemas and stool softeners are prescribed. See this chapter, Medications.

Encopresis

ASSESSMENT

Definition   Encopresis is fecal incontinence occurring on a regular basis. The bowel movements are usually constipated and some children have fecal impactions. Children with primary encopresis have never been toilet trained, while children with secondary encopresis had at one time established complete control of bowel patterns.

Etiology   Chronic constipation or psychogenic problems such as an attention-gaining behavior or regression are frequent causes of encopresis. Rarer causes include spinal cord lesions, anorectal stenosis, hypothyroidism, and cerebral palsy.

Epidemiology   Generally the condition appears in children over 5 years of age, and males are more commonly affected. Children state that they are unaware that they are having a bowel movement. Girls with encopresis may have a history of urinary tract infections due to contamination from soiling.

Physical Examination   A complete physical is done, including rectal examination for anal strictures.

MANAGEMENT

Bowel Routine   The establishment of a regular bowel routine is mandatory. Fecal impactions are removed through enemas, and a high residue diet is prescribed. A daily toilet routine is established in which the child sits on the toilet and tries to defecate at regular intervals.

Medication   Stool softeners are given daily to ensure easy passage of stool and to help retrain bowel habits.

Family Therapy   If the condition continues the family is referred for therapeutic counseling and investigation of psychogenic causes.

Role of the Nurse Practitioner   In management the nurse practitioner provides education in reference to adequate nutrition, monitors compliance to the medication regimen, and allows the family to discuss feelings of frustration and anger.

Diarrhea

ASSESSMENT

Definition   Diarrhea is defined as watery, copious bowel movements which are usually green in color and have a foul odor. Occasionally the diarrhea contains blood, pus, or mucus, and this can indicate bacterial infection. Diarrhea is prevalent during infancy and childhood and is of particular concern during the first 12 months of life because of the infant's inability to tolerate fluid losses which result in dehydration and electrolyte imbalance.

Etiology   There are multiple causes of diarrhea:

- Nonbacterial, nonspecific, or viral
- Dietary mismanagement
- As a symptom of other illnesses: otitis media, urinary tract infection, meningitis (in infants)
- Complication of antibiotic therapy: ampicillin, neomycin, tetracycline
- Bacterial: *Campylobacter, Salmonella, Shigella,* enteropathic *Escherichia coli* gastroenteritis
- Malabsorption: mono- and disaccharide deficiencies; cystic fibrosis, celiac disease
- Milk allergy
- Food poisoning
- Chronic ulcerative colitis

- Parasite infections
- Intestinal obstruction
- Intussusception
- Hemolytic uremic syndrome

History In assessing diarrhea the following are included:

- Caretakers' definition of diarrhea
- Onset of symptoms
- Number and size of bowel movements in 24 hours
- Consistency and color including presence or absence of blood, pus, mucus, or water ring
- History of exposure in family, community
- Current oral intake
- Presence or absence of other symptoms: fever, irritability, cold, cough, lethargy, anorexia, vomiting, abdominal pain, or frequency in voiding
- Symptoms of dehydration
- Treatment regimens at home
- Parental degree of concern

Physical Examination A complete physical examination is done to rule out the presence of contributing disease conditions. The degree of hydration is evaluated. Special attention is given to the following areas:

- *Skin:* dry, hot, degree of turgor
- *Head:* anterior and posterior fontanel: bulging, full, flat, or sunken
- *Mouth:* mucous membranes, moist or dry
- *Eyes:* orbits sunken, presence or absence of tearing
- *Neck:* supple or rigid
- *Ears:* presence of middle ear infection
- *Abdomen:* presence or absence of organomegaly, tenderness, bowel sounds
- *Neurologic:* tone, normal, hypo- or hyperactive, symmetry of movement, general state of awareness

Complications   The following can be severe complications of diarrhea.

DEHYDRATION   This condition is defined as the percentage of body weight lost as water. For example, a child who is 10 percent dehydrated has lost 100 cc of water for every kilogram of body weight. Most children with diarrhea are less than 5 percent dehydrated. Clinical signs of dehydration are as follows:

Body weight lost as water	Symptoms
5 percent	Dry mucous membranes, lack of tear formation
7–10 percent	Decreased skin turgor, sunken eyes, sunken fontanel, increased pulse rate
10–15 percent	Low blood pressure

METABOLIC ACIDOSIS   This condition occurs because of excessive fluid and electrolyte losses. The bicarbonate concentration and the pH of the blood decreases causing hyperventilation, tachypnea, tachycardia, and extreme irritability. Blood electrolyte studies show a low bicarbonate level and a relatively normal chloride level.

Indications for Referral   It is difficult to assess the problem of diarrhea over the phone if parents or the caretakers are unfamiliar to the nurse practitioner. Newborns with diarrhea and children with increased symptoms of illness are seen in the primary health care facility.

MANAGEMENT

Goals   The goals of management are to provide decreased irritation to the GI tract, to prevent dehydration, and to correct electrolyte imbalances.

Diet   Diet modification is a major management component of diarrhea.

LIQUIDS   Clear liquids are prescribed for 24 hours and include water with nonlactose sugar, apple juice, flat, diluted ginger ale, and flavored gelatin. Commercial preparations such as Lytren or

Pedialyte contain carbohydrates and electrolytes in correct amounts and are also prescribed.

AMOUNTS Amounts of clear liquids given are approximately 150 cc per kilogram of body weight up to 1 year of age. For fluid requirements over 1 year of age see Chapter 3, Table 3-4, Range of Average Water Requirement. If vomiting is present, small amounts of fluids are given frequently, 15 to 30 cc every 30 to 60 minutes. With diarrhea large amounts of fluids are given infrequently.

FOOD PROGRESSION If diarrhea continues after 24 hours without clinical evidence of dehydration, solids such as rice cereal, applesauce, and bananas are added to the diet to promote bulk in the stools. If the diarrhea is decreasing, the diet is slowly advanced on the second or third day to include half-strength formula. If the diarrhea has been prolonged some authorities recommend a soy formula for several months because of secondary lactose intolerance.

Medication See this chapter, Medications.

Stool Culture Cultures are obtained on all children whose symptoms last longer than 5 days, whose history is positive for exposure to bacterial gastroenteritis, and whose stools contain blood, mucus, or pus.

Secondary Lactose Intolerance Because of gastrointestinal inflammation, lactase, the enzyme which changes lactose into the simple sugars fructose and galactose, cannot function properly. This leads to transient intolerance of lactose with secondary diarrhea. Since human and cow milk contain lactose as the carbohydrate, a nonlactose soy formula is substituted until the diarrhea is abated. See this chapter, Malabsorption: Disaccharide Deficiencies.

Counseling Monitoring the temperature is discussed with the parents. The amount and frequency of oral fluids are reviewed. Parents are counseled to observe for increased symptoms of illness: reduced fluid intake, increased water in bowel movements, fever, lethargy, symptoms of dehydration and electrolyte imbalance, irritability, and anorexia.

Indications for Hospitalization   Medical consultation is necessary and possible hospitalization is indicated if the client is an infant and exhibits symptoms of dehydration, electrolyte imbalance, or sepsis.

Gastroenteritis

See Table 20-1.

Inguinal Hernia

ASSESSMENT

Definition   Inguinal hernias occur when peritoneal fluid or abdominal contents penetrate the inguinal canal. A direct inguinal hernia bulges through the inguinal canal at the external ring of the canal. An indirect inguinal hernia enters into the inguinal canal at the internal ring of the canal. The process vaginalis is the lower portion of the peritoneal sac which envelops the testes. It remains open in many infants and peritoneal fluid or abdominal contents may be forced into it, becoming an indirect inguinal hernia.

Occurrence   Inguinal hernias occur most often during the first 10 months of life. There is a 9:1 ratio between males and females. Incarceration is more common in females. The hernia sac may contain an ovary in females.

Symptoms   There is painless, reducible inguinal swelling which increases in size with crying or coughing. With incarceration there is tenderness and pain and the swelling cannot be reduced. Abdominal distention and obstruction can occur with incarcerated inguinal hernias.

Physical Examination   A complete physical is done. An experienced examiner may elicit the silk-glove feel of the rubbing together of two walls of the empty hernia sac in the inguinal canal.

MANAGEMENT

Surgical   Surgical repair of the inguinal hernia is done. The opposite side of the inguinal canal is also explored since in 25 percent of cases contralateral hernias exist.

Counseling An explanation of the cause of inguinal hernia and reasons for surgical repair are given to the caretakers. The nurse practitioner follows the child during hospitalization, explains procedures, answers questions and plans follow-up care with the physician.

Intussusception

ASSESSMENT

Definition Intussusception is the telescoping of a segment of the intestine into another segment. Most commonly the terminal ileum prolapses into the cecum.

Occurrence The most frequent occurrence is between 4 and 9 months of age. It is unusual to occur after 2 years of age. Males are affected three times more frequently than females.

Symptoms There is sudden, acute crying with legs flexed onto the abdomen in an otherwise healthy infant. The intense crying is suggestive of severe abdominal pain and occurs at regular intervals usually every 15 to 20 minutes. Vomiting follows. Initially there may be a normal stool but after symptoms progress they are mucoid and bloody and are described as "currant-jelly." Later symptoms are anorexia, lethargy, and shock.

Physical Examination A complete physical is done. On abdominal examination a mass in the upper right quadrant might be palpated. On rectal examination there may be blood on the examining finger.

MANAGEMENT

Conservative Barium enema may be used to reduce the telescoping if there are no clinical symptoms of strangulated bowel, perforation or severe shock.

Surgical Removal of the telescoped bowel is performed.

Counseling The nurse practitioner ascertains the family's understanding of the condition, offers explanations and provides psy-

Table 20-1
Gastroenteritis

Type	Transmission	Symptoms and Diagnosis	Treatment and Counseling
Campylobacter Causative agent: *Campylobacter jejuni*; gram-negative rod	Fecal/oral route through contaminated water and food, also by direct contact with fecal material from infected animals or humans	Mild: last 24 hours, diarrhea, occasionally bloody Severe: diarrhea, stools may be grossly bloody; abdominal pain, fever, nausea, vomiting, lethargy Obtain stool culture	Mild: disease is self-limited; no treatment Severe: antibiotics; erythromycin is drug of choice; other drugs include tetracycline, aminoglycosides, clindamycin Observe for increased symptoms of illness: high fever, dehydration, severe lethargy, peritoneal signs
Enteropathic *Escherichia coli* Causative agent: *Escherichia coli*; gram-negative bacteria	Fecal/oral route through contaminated water and food; high prevalence in areas with poor sanitary conditions	Mild: diarrhea only Severe: copious stools may contain mucus but blood or pus are usually absent; vomiting, fever, abdominal pain Obtain stool culture	Mild: clear liquids Severe: IV fluids for fluid and electrolyte imbalances Observe for increased symptoms of illness: high fever, dehydration, severe lethargy, peritoneal signs

Salmonella Causative agent: *Salmonella;* gram-negative bacteria	Fecal/oral route through contaminated water and food and through infected animals such as pet turtles	Diarrhea, occasionally contains blood or pus Obtain stool culture	The disease is self-limited and lasts 5 to 7 days; clear liquids, IV fluids for fluid and electrolyte imbalances; antibiotics are given if there is secondary infection or in children with chronic bowel or sickle cell disease; bacillus is shed in the stools of asymptomatic children for several weeks to months and some may become chronic carriers; therefore need to obtain periodic stool cultures; when carriers return to school need to wash hands after toilet use
Shigella Causative agent: *S. dysenteriae, S. boydii, S. sonnei, S. flexneri*	Fecal/oral route through contaminated water and food	Mild: diarrhea, mild fever Severe: diarrhea; watery, green with blood or mucus; vomiting, abdominal pain, headache, delerium Obtain stool culture	Clear liquids or IV fluids for fluid and electrolyte imbalances; antibiotics given Observe for increased symptoms of illness: high fever, dehydration, severe lethargy; handwashing after toilet use
Viral	Fecal/oral route through contaminated food, infected persons; also by infected air droplets	Diarrhea: watery; abdominal pain, fever	Clear liquids, by mouth Observe for increased symptoms of illness: high fever, dehydration, severe lethargy

chological support and education during hospitalization and follow-up care.

Malabsorption: Disaccharidase Deficiencies

ASSESSMENT

Definition The disaccharides lactose and sucrose are broken down by specific enzymes called disaccharidases, which are located in the brush border of the epithelial cells of the small intestine. The enzymes change lactose, sucrose, and maltose to glucose, galactose, and fructose for absorption from the GI tract. In disaccharidase deficiency, the disaccharidases are impaired, and the disaccharides cannot be absorbed. It is speculated that the unabsorbed disaccharide causes an increased osmotic load in the colon, leading to increased intestinal fluid secretion and diarrhea.

Classification and Etiologies Disaccharide deficiencies are classified into primary and secondary etiologies.

PRIMARY The primary deficiencies are congenital and are characterized by the absence of the enzyme in the small intestine. Primary sucrase deficiency is the result of an autosomal recessive disorder. The genetic inheritance of primary lactase deficiency is not yet known.

SECONDARY The secondary deficiencies occur in any disease involving damage to the mucosa of the small bowel which results in impaired action of the enzymes. Examples are gastroenteritis, ulcerative colitis, irritable colon, cystic fibrosis, celiac disease, malnutrition, and impaired GI tract functioning after gastric surgery. Drugs such as neomycin, kanamycin, and colchicine also affect the mucosa of the small bowel. While all the disaccharidases are affected, lactase is the most severely damaged and is the slowest to recover.

Incidence Primary sucrase and lactase deficiency is extremely rare. Secondary lactase deficiency occurs in approximately 10 percent of American whites and in 70 percent of American blacks. Secondary sucrase deficiency symptoms are usually masked by those of lactase.

Symptoms   In infants, watery diarrhea is the most striking symptom. It is usually frothy and copious. Other symptoms are vomiting, abdominal distension, and dehydration. In more severe cases, failure to thrive, electrolyte imbalance, metabolic acidosis, lethargy, and irritability are evident. In older children symptoms include intermittent diarrhea and abdominal pain. Steatorrhea, excessive fat in the stool, occurs in some children, and it is usually an indication that the intestinal mucosa has suffered extensive damage.

Laboratory   The following tests are done:

REDUCING SUBSTANCES   The stool is examined for the presence of undigested sugar (reducing substance). In testing the stool for the presence of lactose 10 drops of water and 5 drops of watery stool are mixed. One Clinitest tablet is added, and the test is read the same as when testing urine for sugar.

In testing the stool for the presence of sucrose, 10 drops of 1 normal hydrochloric acid and 5 drops of stool are mixed. The mixture is allowed to react for a few minutes before the Clinitest tablet is added. The test is read the same as when testing urine for sugar.

pH   The stool is also tested for pH since in disaccharide intolerance the pH is less than 6.0. These tests if positive, however, are not considered diagnostic of disaccharide malabsorption.

DISACCHARIDE TOLERANCE TEST   A more specific test of disaccharidase function is the oral disaccharide tolerance test. Two grams of lactose or sucrose per kilogram of body weight are given orally. A rise in blood glucose of 20 to 25 mg/100 ml or greater indicates normal hydrolysis of disaccharides. A blood glucose rise of less than 20 mg/dl indicates that the disaccharide has not been hydrolyzed and remains unabsorbed from the GI tract. A complication of this test can be severe diarrhea.

Physical Examination   A complete physical is done.

MANAGEMENT

Diet   For lactase deficiency a lactose-free diet is prescribed. Since lactose is the sugar in human and cow milk the child is placed on a soy formula. Foods are also excluded which contain lactose such as

Table 20-2
Composition of Various Carbohydrates in Liquid Preparations

Lactose	Sucrose	Glucose	Corn Syrup (contains glucose, maltose, dextrin)
Breast milk	Nutramigen	Pregestimil	Lofenalac
Cow milk	Meat Base	Soyalac	Nursov
Goat milk	Neomullsoy	Prosobee	Prosobee
Human milk	Nursov	Bakers	Neomullsoy
Similac	Prosobee	Isomil	Soyalac
Similac PM	Soyalac	Meat Base	Isomil
Enfamil	Isomil		Portagen
SMA	Portagen		Bakers
Lonalac			Meat Base
Bakers			

whey, dry milk solids, cheese, ice cream, and yogurt. Parents are instructed to read labels on all products including baby food preparations to make sure that they do not contain lactose.

In sucrase deficiency the diet is more complicated since sucrose is present in many foods including various fruits, vegetables, cooked and dry cereals, and canned foods. Oral antibiotic preparations and aspirin contain sucrose.

Counseling The nurse practitioner counsels parents about dietary management. After gastrointestinal infections the nurse is aware that several months are needed for the small intestine to regenerate sufficiently for the disaccharidase to return to normal function. Therefore dietary management is continued for 3 to 4 months. Table 20-2 shows the composition of various carbohydrates in liquid preparations.

Pyloric Stenosis

ASSESSMENT

Etiology The circular muscle of the pylorus valve of the stomach is thickened and elongated, causing disruption in passage of stomach contents into the small intestine. Spasm of the valve occurs causing projectile vomiting.

Incidence This condition occurs in approximately 1 in 500 births. Males are four times more affected, and firstborns are more susceptible than later children.

Symptoms The most common symptoms are listed below:

- Projectile vomiting after feeding. Vomiting most commonly begins after the third to fourth week of life, and it might not occur after every feeding
- Slow weight gain or weight loss
- Avidly hungry infant
- Dehydration
- Constipation

Physical Examination Occasionally the hypertrophied pyloric valve can be palpated in the upper right quadrant of the abdomen and is felt as an olive-sized tumor. The abdomen is observed for distension in the upper right quadrant. Gastric peristaltic waves due to gastric contractions are occasionally observed after feeding. They are seen as rhythmical waves moving across the abdomen.

Diagnostic Studies An X-ray film of the abdomen shows a large gas-filled stomach. Fluoroscopy with barium shows an elongated and narrowed pylorus valve with a delayed opening. However, many authorities rely on the history of sudden occurrence of projectile vomiting, the presence of visible peristaltic waves, and a palpable pyloric mass as symptoms diagnostic of the condition.

MANAGEMENT

Surgery Dehydration and electrolyte imbalance is corrected before surgery. The operation consists of an incision into the hypertrophied pyloric valve (pyloromyotomy). Depending on the extent of the surgery, the infant may be fed intravenously for several hours or for 1 to 2 days. When oral feedings are begun they are instituted slowly and in small amounts.

Counseling The nurse practitioner is alert to the symptoms of pyloric stenosis. Since this condition occurs frequently with firstborn children, emotional support to anxious parents is provided. The nurse encourages the parents to hold and to care for the infant and offers explanations about management procedures during hospitalization. Support and routine health education continue after hospital discharge.

Regurgitation

ASSESSMENT

Definition Regurgitation is a common occurrence in the first year of life. It is the nonforceful, nonprojectile, effortless expulsion from the stomach of a small quantity of liquid or food after feeding. Refer to Chapter 5, "Spitting Up" (Regurgitation) for more information.

Etiology Regurgitation is caused by air swallowed with food, overfeeding, allergy to cow milk, or a relaxed stomach cardiac sphincter muscle. Because of the lax muscle, milk is expulsed with bubbling. Occasionally significant regurgitation continues past 6 months of age, and close observation of weight gain is necessary.

Diagnostic Studies If the condition continues past 12 months of age, an upper gastrointestinal series is helpful in determining the severity of the regurgitation and to rule out gastroesophageal reflux. Hemoglobin determination is sometimes necessary because of occasional iron deficiency anemia from coexistent esophagitis secondary to hydrochloric acid bathing the lower esophagus.

Physical Examination A complete physical is done.

MANAGEMENT

Counseling Parents are counseled to thicken oral liquids with cereal and to bubble the child frequently during feeding. The child remains upright after feeding for 30 minutes.

Stomachache

ASSESSMENT

Etiology   During childhood, organic causes of stomachache are found in less than 10 percent of all cases. They include the following:

- Appendicitis
- Cholelithiasis
- Constipation
- Malrotation of the bowel
- Meckel's diverticulum
- Parasitic infection
- Peptic ulcer
- Regional enteritis
- Ulcerative colitis
- Urinary tract infection or anomaly

Causes of recurrent stomachache include the following:

- Idiopathic
- Psychogenic

  1. Attention mechanism
  2. Phobias
  3. Stress
  4. Unconscious diversion to keep family from solving other problems

Incidence   Complaints of stomachache occur in 1 of 10 children. The most common ages are 5 to 10 years.

Symptoms   The most common symptom is pain usually around the umbilicus or in the lower abdomen. Pain in this area is less likely to have an organic cause than pain that is lateral. The pain is not usually related to stressful situations, does not awaken the child from sleep, and is rarely related to meals. Frequency varies from several times a day to weekly or monthly. Occasionally there is pain in other areas of the body. This usually indicates a psychogenic rather than an organic cause.

Physical Examination A complete physical is done. Occasionally this procedure has reassuring qualities for the parents in knowing that a thorough examination was completed even though no organic cause is found.

Laboratory Diagnostic studies are considered after evaluating the results of the physical examination, the chronicity of the symptoms, and the psychosocial milieu.

MANAGEMENT

Organic If organic lesions are found, appropriate management is initiated. If no evidence of organic or familial dysfunction is found, the child is periodically seen for re-evaluations, since an organic pathologic condition may be more easily diagnosed at a later date.

Psychogenic If physical and laboratory values are normal, the presence of family dysfunction is further investigated. Common factors to consider are recent death or separation of family members, amount and frequency of illness in the family, marital disharmony, too strict or too inconsistent discipline, lack of attention toward the child, alcoholism or drug abuse, and financial problems. If serious family dysfunction is evident, the family is referred to a behavioral pediatrician for further counseling.

Vomiting

ASSESSMENT

Definition Vomiting is the forceful retching of gastric contents. It may be projectile or nonprojectile. Projectile vomiting may indicate serious organicity, such as pyloric stenosis or increased intracranial pressure. Vomiting is occasionally confused with regurgitation. See this chapter, Regurgitation. The presence of green vomitus may indicate intestinal obstruction.

Etiology In association with the GI tract, the following etiologies are considered:

• Appendicitis
• Chalasia

- Intestinal obstruction
- Overfeeding
- Pyloric stenosis

In association with infection, the following etiologies are considered:

- Gastroenteritis
- Meningitis
- Parasitic
- Respiratory
- Septicemia
- Urinary tract

Other causes of vomiting include the following:

- Congenital adrenal hyperplasia
- Diabetic acidosis
- Drugs: digitalis, aspirin, some antibiotics, sulfonamides
- Increased intracranial pressure
- Migraine headache

History Include the following information:

- Age of the child
- Frequency, amount, and time of occurrence
- Length of time symptom is evident
- Nature of vomitus: color, presence of blood, mucus, pus
- Projectile or nonprojectile
- Forceful or effortless
- Other associated symptoms: diarrhea, respiratory infection, dehydration, fever, constipation
- Feeding techniques: frequency of burping, sitting up after feeding
- Home treatment: use of medications, types of food given

Physical Examination A complete physical examination is done.

MANAGEMENT

Diet After a serious organic pathologic cause is ruled out, management begins with dietary modifications. Infants and children are given clear liquids for 6 hours initially. See this chapter, Diarrhea, Dietary Management. Liquids are given in small amounts 15 to 30 cc, frequently every 30 to 60 minutes. If the child retains fluids over a period of time larger amounts of clear liquids are added. After 12 to 24 hours bland foods may be added such as cooked cereal, applesauce, crackers, and bananas. If vomiting continues after 6 hours the child is seen in the health care agency.

Medication Rarely are antiemetics or sedatives used to control vomiting in infants and children. These medications cause drowsiness and therefore decrease the fluid intake. They also can mask possible serious progression of the vomiting. See this chapter, Medications.

Counseling The nurse practitioner monitors the frequency of vomiting along with the parent, educates the parent in reference to increased symptoms of illness, and assesses parents' understanding of dietary management. Parents are counseled to bring infants below 6 months of age who exhibit true vomiting to the acute care facility to investigate etiologies and to assess hydration.

References

American Pharmaceutical Association. *Handbook of Nonprescription Drugs.* 6th ed. Washington, DC: American Pharmaceutical Association, 1979.

Apley, J. *The Child With Abdominal Pains.* London: Blackwell Scientific Publications, 1975.

Blaser, M. and L. B. Reller. "Campylobacter Enteritis." *N Engl J Med* 22:1444–1452, December 10, 1981.

Ewerbeck, H. *Differential Diagnosis in Pediatrics.* New York: Springer-Verlag, 1980.

Graef, J. W. and T. E. Cone, Jr. *Manual of Pediatric Therapeutics.* 2nd ed. Boston: Little, Brown, 1980.

Grant, M. and W. M. Kubo. "Assessing a Patient's Hydration Status." *Am J Nurs* 75:1306–1311, August 1975.

Green, M. and R. J. Haggerty. *Ambulatory Pediatrics. II.* Philadelphia: W.B. Saunders, 1977.

Illingworth, R. *Common Symptoms of Disease in Children.* 3rd ed. Oxford: Blackwell Scientific Publications, 1971.

Kempe, C. H., H. K. Silver, and D. O'Brien. *Current Pediatric Diagnosis and Treatment.* 7th ed. Los Altos, CA: Lange Medical Publications, 1982.

Levine, M. "The Schoolchild with Encopresis." *Pediatr Rev* 2:285–290, March, 1981.

Rudolph, A. M. editor, *Pediatrics.* 17th ed. East Norwalk, CT: Appleton-Century-Crofts, 1982.

Smith, D. W. and R. E. Marshall. *Introduction to Clinical Pediatrics.* Philadelphia: W.B. Saunders, 1977.

Walker, W. "Benign Chronic Diarrhea in Infancy." *Pediatr Rev* 3:153–158, November, 1981.

Wallack, J. *Interpretation of Diagnostic Tests.* 3rd ed. Boston: Little, Brown, 1978.

21

The Urinary System

The two major functions of the kidneys are to excrete most of the end products of body metabolism and to control the concentrations of most of the components of body fluids. Urinary disorders (including congenital malformations, structural anomalies, and infections of the urinary tract) are significant in relation to their potential for interrupting these functions and contributing to renal disease. For this reason, any deviations from normal urinary function should be evaluated in collaboration with the physician. This chapter presents information on assessment of the urinary tract with special emphasis on two common problems in primary care pediatrics: enuresis, and urinary tract infection. The role of the nurse practitioner is to participate in management, coordinate treatment, and provide follow-up and health teaching to the child and family.

ASSESSMENT

Normal Values

BLADDER CONTROL

Ninety-nine percent of infants urinate within the first 48 hours of life. Voiding is completely involuntary until sometime during the

805

second year of life when bladder sensation develops. Complete neuromuscular control of urination is achieved in most children by 4 to 5 years of age.

BLADDER CAPACITY

Approximate bladder capacity in infants and children is as follows (Schauffler, 1958):

At birth	60 cc
3 months	115 cc
1 year	285 cc
12 years	840 cc

ROUTINE URINALYSIS

The specimen should be the first morning specimen (because it is concentrated) and should be examined within a few hours of collection.

General Appearance The urine should be clear. If it is cloudy, it may be abnormal sediment or may be an "old" specimen.

Color Normal urine is pale yellow or amber. Pink or reddish color may indicate red blood cells, ingestion of beets, blackberries, certain vegetable dyes and drugs. Orange-red or reddish-brown color may indicate bilirubin, blood. Red or red-brown is the most common abnormal color.

Odor Acetone odor indicates ketonuria. Ammonia or fecal odor indicates bacterial infection.

Specific Gravity Normal values are 1.010 to 1.030. Abnormally low values indicate lack of ability to concentrate urine. Abnormally high values indicate dehydration.

pH Urine is usually acidic (pH 5–6) in the fasting state. Normal range is 4.6 to 8.

Glucose, Protein, Ketones, Blood Screening tests for these substances should be negative. However, approximately 5 percent of children will have a trace or 1+ protein which can be caused by exercise, fever, dehydration, infection, cold temperatures. It is usually transient. A second specimen (first morning specimen) should be examined and if proteinuria is persistent or above 2 +, the child needs further evaluation.

Sediment   The specimen is centrifuged and examined microscopically for sediment.

- *Red blood cells.* More than 2 to 3 cells per high power field is abnormal. A repeat specimen is obtained.
- *White blood cells.* More than 5 cells per high power field is abnormal and indicates a suppurative process. A repeat specimen is obtained with special care in cleansing the perineal area. *Pyuria* is defined as 5 to 8 white blood cells per cubic millimeter in an uncentrifuged sample of a clean catch, midstream urine specimen, *or* 5 to 10 white blood cells per high power field on a centrifuged specimen.
- *Epithelial cells.* These are seen commonly but probably are urethral or vaginal cells.
- *Casts.* These are clumps of cells formed in the nephron, and their presence indicates some pathologic state in the kidney. Physician consultation is indicated. Red cell casts suggest glomerular injury and renal bleeding; white cell casts suggest pyelonephritis; hyaline casts suggest proteinuria of glomerular origin; granular casts suggest a degenerative process.
- *Crystals.* These are normally not present. Most are of no significance although some acid urine crystals may be suggestive of kidney stones.
- *Bacteria.* Bacteriuria is evaluated by direct microscopic examination of the urinary sediment. Any bacteria present in an unspun specimen is indication for obtaining a urine culture and consideration of urinary tract infection.

History

FAMILY HISTORY

Obtain information on incidence of renal disease, diabetes, deafness, hypertension, structural abnormalities of the urinary tract, and syndromes having associated urinary tract abnormalities.

PAST HISTORY

Obtain information on congenital anomalies; infections, especially past urinary tract infections and streptococcal infections; abdominal pain or mass; vomiting; diarrhea; fever of undetermined origin; failure to thrive; trauma to abdomen, lower back, or genitalia; changes or abnormalities in micturition including frequency, dribbling, dysuria, urgency, enuresis, daytime incontinence, increased or decreased urine volume; change in color or odor of urine; edema; toilet training. In the older child, obtain information about sexual activity.

Physical Examination

GENERAL

Obtain vital signs, blood pressure. Evaluate growth patterns.

SKIN

Observe for pallor, sallow complexion, dehydration, and edema.

EARS

Inspect for low-set or deformed ears.

CARDIOVASCULAR

Check for tachypnea, hypertension, and circulatory congestion.

ABDOMEN

Palpate for enlargement of kidneys, costovertebral angle (CVA) tenderness, flank or suprapubic tenderness, abdominal masses, and ascites. Palpate lower abdomen over the bladder and observe for dribbling.

GENITALIA

Observe for abnormalities of the external genitalia, including signs of trauma or abuse: in the female, irritation, discharge, and/or large vaginal opening; in the male, irritation and/or discharge. Observe process of voiding, looking for dribbling, difficulty in starting or stopping midstream.

NEUROLOGIC

Examine for innervation abnormalities in the lower extremities. See Chapter 24, The Neuromuscular System.

MANAGEMENT

Every child with symptoms or findings suggestive of urinary tract anomaly or kidney disease must be referred for thorough evaluation. Parents and child need interpretation of diagnostic procedures and treatment plans. They also need education aimed at preventing urinary infections. See this chapter, Urinary Tract Infection.

COMMON CLINICAL PROBLEMS

Enuresis

ASSESSMENT

Enuresis is involuntary urination in a child whose age and development are such that control would be expected. *Primary* enuresis occurs in children who have never achieved bladder control. *Secondary* enuresis occurs in children who previously have achieved bladder control for at least 3 months to 6 months and then lose it. *Enuresis* usually refers to involuntary wetting during sleep; *diurnal enuresis* refers to wetting during the day and when it occurs in children over 5 years of age, a significant pathologic state (e.g., urinary tract infection) must be suspected. Since the complete neuromuscular control of urination is attained by most children by 4 to 5 years of age, the diagnosis of enuresis should be made for involuntary urination beyond the age of 5 years in girls and 6 years in boys.

Incidence Twenty-five percent of children will have some relapse bedwetting that usually occurs at times of illness or stress and is self-limiting. Beyond this, surveys indicate that up to 15 percent of 6 to 7 year olds and 3 percent of 13 to 14 year olds may still wet the bed more than once a month (Starfield, 1972). Males are affected more than females in all age groups.

Etiology Etiology is complex and not completely understood, but several factors are thought to contribute.

1. *Developmental delay.* An inherited tendency toward delayed development of adequate neuromuscular control is thought to be a major factor in primary enuresis. Strong familial tendencies exist; these children have small functional bladder capacity sometimes called "irritable bladder," and most are cured spontaneously as maturation occurs. Twenty-five percent of children having one enuretic parent will themselves be enuretic and 50 percent if both parents were enuretics.

2. *Organic factors.* Most cases of enuresis involve no organic basis, but organic etiology must be ruled out. Disorders that may cause enuresis include obstructive lesions of the genitourinary tract, urinary tract infections, lumbosacral disorders which affect bladder innervation, conditions in which the ability to concentrate urine is impaired (e.g., diabetes mellitus, diabetes insipidus, sickle cell anemia, and allergic disorders).

3. *Deep sleep.* One hypothesis suggests that some enuretic children have a high threshold for nocturnal arousal and it is known that enuresis occurs during the predream non-rapid eye movement (non-REM) state of sleep (Starfield, 1978).

4. *Psychologic–emotional factors.* Situational crises (e.g., divorce, death of a parent, birth of a sibling, move to a new surrounding) may cause temporary regression in bladder control. Too early, too vigorous or other inappropriate approaches to toilet training may result in enuresis. Enuresis may also be symptomatic of more serious behavioral disorders, significant family stress, or psychopathology. Parental attitudes commonly associated with an enuretic child are punitiveness, neglect, oversubmissiveness, and perfectionism. See Chapter 6, Habit Formation, and Toilet Training.

History   A detailed account of the enuresis includes information regarding:

1. Number of nights per week or month that bedwetting occurs
2. Fluid intake
3. Sleep patterns
4. Voiding patterns
5. Any related events or stress; recent urinary tract infection
6. Occurrence at home and/or away from home
7. Management techniques used by family
8. Child's response to enuresis: ask the *child*
9. Family attitudes and response to enuresis
10. Emotional climate in the home
11. Details of toilet training
12. Presence or absence of family history of enuresis.

Past medical history, review of systems, and physical examination should include areas mentioned previously in this chapter. In addition, inquire about a history of sickle cell disease, since children with sickle cell anemia usually have a urine concentrating defect and excrete large amounts of dilute urine, which may cause bedwetting.

Laboratory   Routine urinalysis and measurement of specific gravity after an overnight fast are performed. Functional bladder capacity should be measured as a baseline. Functional bladder capacity is determined by having the child refrain from voiding as long as possible and then measuring the amount voided. Adequate nighttime bladder control cannot be attained if bladder capacity is significantly less than 10 ounces. Urine culture is obtained if suspicion of infection exists. If an underlying organic disorder is suspected, appropriate blood and urine studies should be carried out with referral to the appropriate specialists.

MANAGEMENT

Most children will be best managed by the primary care provider who has rapport with the family since a positive relationship may be the most important therapeutic tool. The approach must be geared to the individual situation considering the child's age, severity of symptoms, and severity of family disruption. Since the cause of the enuresis is often obscure or difficult to assign with certainty, the most frequent approach to therapy is to attempt to alleviate the symptom. The method chosen must be planned with the child's and family's active participation and consent. If the child is not interested in nor motivated to achieve control, all attempts will fail. Regardless of the method chosen, it must be presented and undertaken with optimism for success. The family may need to be seen frequently for follow-up and reinforcement.

Counseling and Support A survey (Shelov et al., 1981) of 1435 parents revealed that most parents have unrealistic expectations in relation to urinary control. The average age at which parents expected children to be dry was 2.75 years, and 90 percent of parents expected nighttime dryness at or before 4 years of age. The survey also showed that parents think emotional causes are important and are less likely to accept small bladder size as the etiology. Therefore, an initial goal of counseling is to elicit parental knowledge, expectations, and attitudes and provide appropriate health teaching about normal development of urinary control. See Chapter 6, Table 6-11.

When dealing with actual enuresis, expression of the feelings of both child and parents should be encouraged and acknowledged. Parents need to be reassured that the child cannot help the enuresis, that the child is not "bad," and that it isn't their fault. If punitive or shaming techniques have been used in the past, parents should not be made to feel more guilty but need explanations that this approach just does not work. The objectives of counseling should include the following:

1. Parental understanding of the multifactorial nature of enuresis and its common occurrence
2. Parental acceptance of the child and the symptoms to provide maximum emotional support
3. Conveyance to the child and family of a sense of optimism
4. Acceptance by the child of the symptom accompanied by identification of the child's strengths in other areas of functioning

5. Development of an appreciation in the child that control of the enuresis can be achieved

Psychotherapy is indicated when there is evidence of significantly disturbed parent-child relationships.

Simple Measures   Activities such as restricting fluids after supper, voiding before bedtime, and rousing to void before the parents' bedtime and at other intervals during the night are frequently suggested, but there is no evidence that they hasten the onset of a spontaneous cure. They may even result in additional conflict between parent and child.

Conditioning   Devices such as the Enuretone apparatus are being used more frequently. A bed mattress device sensitive to moisture is connected to an alarm bell which goes off and wakes the child upon initiation of wetting. Over time this can condition the child to awaken before voiding. Relapses occur frequently, but dryness is attained more quickly and even permanently with a second course. The child may develop a rash on the buttocks or perineum. Use of this technique may be impractical in homes where the sleep of other family members becomes a problem. Studies have shown that this procedure is not psychologically harmful to children (Cohen, 1975).

Bladder Stretching Exercises   School age children with decreased functional bladder capacity have responded well to a regimen of bladder training. The ideal candidate for this approach is the child with a history of frequent daytime voiding of small amounts (less than 4 ounces) or urine. Starfield (1972) has developed a procedure which involves the child in a 6-month program. Once a day the child holds urine for as long as possible. The child drinks a lot of fluid during this period. When the child must void, the urine is measured and the amount recorded in a daily log. Dry nights are also recorded. The recording serves as reinforcement for the child. Wall charts can be kept and the child encouraged to break previous records and gold stars given for successes. In Starfield's study one third of children were cured, and all children had increased functional bladder capacity after 6 months.

Medications If the previous methods are not successful, medication may be considered. Imipramine (Tofranil) has been successful in the control of enuresis in a significant number of cases. The mode of action is unclear but is thought to be either an anticholinergic effect on bladder muscle or an antidepressant effect on the central nervous system. Side effects are nervousness, sleep disorders, and mild GI disturbances. More alarming are the toxic effects, sometimes fatal, which have been associated with accidental ingestion of an overdose by a younger sibling of the enuretic child. Many physicians are wary of prescribing this drug also because of the increasing abuse of mood-altering drugs.

Urinary Tract Infection (UTI)

ASSESSMENT

Bacterial infections occur both in the presence of structural abnormalities in the urinary tract and in normal urinary tracts.

Incidence During infancy about 1 percent of children will develop bacteriuria, and about two thirds of these are boys. After infancy the incidence is much more common in girls. It has been conservatively estimated that from 5 to 10 percent of girls and less than 1 percent of boys will have at least one UTI before 18 years of age (Kunin, 1977). Recurrent infections, abnormalities of the urinary tract, and infections of the upper urinary tract (pyelonephritis) carry guarded prognoses as far as renal damage is concerned.

Etiology Bacteria enter the urinary tract either through the blood stream (more common in young infants who cannot localize infections well) or through the urethra. Infection may develop in the urethra (urethritis), bladder (cystitis), or kidney (pyelonephritis).

PREDISPOSING FACTORS Predisposing factors to invasion of bacteria through the urethra are as follows:

1. Shortness of female urethra
2. Obstructive uropathy
3. Foreign bodies

4. Fecal contamination, poor perineal hygiene
5. Stasis of urine, incomplete emptying of the bladder
6. Chemical irritants, bubble bath, detergent
7. Pinworms
8. Indwelling catheters, catheterization
9. Sexual intercourse
10. Pregnancy

COMMON ORGANISMS The most common organisms that infect the urinary tract:

1. *Escherichia coli* accounts for 80 to 85 percent of acute uncomplicated infections and 50 to 70 percent of recurrences.
2. Gram-positive organisms (e.g., *Staphylococcus aureus*) account for 5 to 10 percent of uncomplicated infections.
3. *Klebsiella, Enterobacter, Pseudomonas,* and *Proteus* occur less commonly and are associated with more complicated infections (i.e., with presence of structural abnormalities).

Clinical Signs and Symptoms Presenting signs and symptoms vary considerably and onset may be gradual or abrupt. A large number of children are asymptomatic, and infection is detected on routine urine screening. Infants may have nonspecific symptoms and may appear lethargic, irritable, and septic with vomiting, diarrhea, fever, and failure to thrive. Young children may have GI symptoms of anorexia, vomiting, diarrhea, abdominal pain, as well as fever, irritability, loss of previously attained bladder control, urgency, frequency, hematuria, burning on urination, dribbling, foul-smelling urine. Fever, chills and flank pain may occur when the infection is in the kidney.

Laboratory The diagnosis is confirmed primarily by the presence of significant bacteria on urine culture. The presence of more than 100,000 (10^5) colonies of a single bacteria per ml of urine in a correctly collected and plated specimen indicates infection. One such culture in a child with symptoms is the minimal criterion for confirmation of infection. If the colony count is between 10,000 and 100,000 per ml, a repeat specimen is obtained. In an asymptomatic child at least three consecutive cultures with greater than

100,000 colonies of the same bacteria per ml should be obtained to confirm the diagnosis. If a suprapubic tap (direct aspiration of the bladder) has been performed, the presence of *any* bacteria indicates infection. Positive urine cultures are also tested for sensitivity of the organisms to drugs.

Specimen Collection The importance of correct technique in obtaining urine for culture cannot be overemphasized. In infants it is difficult to obtain adequate samples due to the obvious possibilities for contamination. Suprapubic aspiration may be considered. In children who are toilet trained, a midstream urine after cleansing of the external genitalia is usually sufficient. If the specimen cannot be cultured within 30 minutes, it is refrigerated and plated within 24 hours. If the specimen is brought from home it should be kept on ice en route.

MANAGEMENT

After diagnosis of a urinary tract infection, nurse practitioners are involved in coordinating treatment and follow-up with the child and family. The goals of management are:

1. Eradication of the infection
2. Prevention and/or treatment of recurrences
3. Identification and correction of structural anomalies

Medication Choice of medication, dosage, and length of course will be decided by the physician based on the offending organism, age and weight of the child, whether the infection is the first or a recurrent one, and sensitivity of the organism to the drug. Usually the drug is prescribed for 2 weeks in a first infection. Longer courses may be necessary in recurrent or complicated infections. The school nurse should be informed when children are on longterm drug therapy.

Medications commonly used are listed below:

1. Sulfisoxazole (Gantrisin)

   • *Organisms.* Effective against *E. coli, Klebsiella, Proteus,* and *Staphylococcus*
   • *Contraindications.* Not to be used in infants less than 2 months

of age, in pregnancy or lactation, or in persons with G-6-PD deficiency (see Chapter 19, G-6-PD)

- *Side effects.* Blood dyscrasias, allergic reactions, GI symptoms, and occasionally CNS reactions
- *Practical points.* It is low in cost. It must be stored in the refrigerator. Increased fluid intake is necessary during the course of medication to prevent crystalluria and stone formation.

2. Ampicillin

- *Organisms.* Effective against *Escherichia coli, Proteus,* and *Klebsiella*
- *Contraindications.* Not to be used in persons with previous hypersensitivity to penicillin or during pregnancy
- *Side effects.* GI symptoms, particularly diarrhea, and hypersensitivity with skin rash
- *Practical points.* It is low in cost. Reconstituted suspensions are stable for 7 days at room temperature and for 14 days with refrigeration.

3. Nitrofurantoin (Furadantin)

- *Organisms.* Effective against *Escherichia coli, Staphylococcus aureus, Klebsiella, Proteus, Pseudomonas,* and enterococci
- *Contraindications.* Not to be used in infants under 1 month of age, during pregnancy or lactation, or in persons with G-6-PD deficiency.
- *Side effects.* GI distress, hypersensitivity reactions (pulmonary), skin rashes, hemolytic anemia; 10 to 15 percent of children develop nausea and vomiting
- *Practical points.* It is moderate in cost. The suspension can be given with water, milk, juices, or food to decrease GI irritation.

4. Cephalexin (Keflex)

- *Organisms.* Effective against *Escherichia coli, Proteus,* and *Klebsiella*
- *Contraindications.* Not to be used in pregnancy or in persons with hypersensitivity

- *Side effects.* Diarrhea and other GI symptoms, hypersensitivity reactions
- *Practical points.* It is more expensive than other medications. It can be given without regard to meals.

5. Trimethoprim and sulfamethoxazole (Bactrim, Septra)

- *Organisms.* Effective against *E. coli, Klebsiella, Enterobacter, Proteus*
- *Contraindications.* Not to be used in infants under 2 months of age, during pregnancy and lactation, in persons with hypersensitivity to either drug, in G-6-PD, in severe allergy or asthma, in folate deficiency, and in renal or hepatic impairment.
- *Side effects.* Blood dyscrasias, allergic reactions, GI reactions, occasionally central nervous system reactions
- *Practical points.* Increased fluid intake is necessary to prevent crystalluria and stone formation. It is recommended that initial episodes of uncomplicated urinary tract infection be treated with a single effective antibacterial agent rather than the combination.

Supportive Care   During the symptomatic period children need increased fluids and increased rest.

Follow-up Care   Once drug therapy has been initiated the child is seen in 48 to 72 hours to determine if the symptoms have subsided and to reculture the urine. Urine should be sterile at this time. If not, a new medication may need to be selected. The child should then be seen shortly after completing the course of medication (within 1 to 2 weeks) and another urine culture obtained. If this culture is negative, the infection is considered cured. Since the recurrence rate of UTIs is high, long-term follow-up is indicated. A suggested protocol is as follows:

After resolution of infection, follow-up visits are scheduled at:

2 weeks	Culture, urinalysis
6 months	Culture, urinalysis
12 months	Culture, urinalysis, and physical examination
24 months	Culture, urinalysis, and physical examination

Indications for Further Diagnostic Studies Significant urinary tract abnormalities have been discovered via radiologic examinations in approximately 15 percent of children at the time of their first diagnosed UTI. Yet, there is considerable debate over the indications for such studies and other urologic procedures. Consultation should be obtained routinely from the pediatrician and/or urologist on the need for further studies. Existing guidelines suggest that when there is no evidence of urinary tract dysfunction except infection:

1. All males have an intravenous pyelogram (IVP) and voiding cystourethrogram (VCUG) after resolution of the first infection.
2. Females less than 1 year of age have an IVP and VCUG after resolution of the first infection.
3. Females from 1 year to menarche have an IVP and VCUG after resolution of the first infection if symptoms suggest kidney involvement; if cystitis only, may or may not have IVP.
4. Postmenarchal females have an IVP after the second documented infection. If the symptoms indicate cystitis only, IVP may not be performed.
5. Postmenarchal females with clinical signs of pyelonephritis or a history suggesting previous undocumented UTIs have an IVP after resolution of the first documented UTI.

PREPARATION FOR DIAGNOSTIC PROCEDURES Should any child be required to undergo IVP or VCUG, the nurse practitioner must tackle the significant task of preparing both the child and the family for these intrusive procedures. In addition to teaching and support geared to the child's developmental level some additional suggestions are:

1. The child must be assured, especially if loss of bladder control is one of the symptoms, that the tests are not punishment.
2. The nurse practitioner needs to investigate and to be familiar with the way children are handled in the radiology unit. Efforts to assure humane treatment of children may need to be a larger project for the nurse practitioner.
3. Where possible the parent and child should be accompanied

through the procedures. Often student nurses are available and can learn as well as act as advocate for the family.

4. The child and parent must be given the opportunity to express their feelings, perceptions, and fears before and after the procedures.

Prevention

SCREENING The objective of screening is to identify those children with asymptomatic bacteriuria. The timing and frequency of routine urinalyses are being reevaluated, but the American Academy of Pediatrics (1982) recommends one urinalysis during each of the following time periods: infancy (1 to 12 months), early childhood (15 months to 4 years), late childhood (5 to 12 years), and adolescence (14 to 20 years). Several direct culture techniques which are simple, inexpensive, and can be performed at home are on the market (Kunin, 1977, p. 168). In addition a nitrite dip-strip test is available for use at home (Kunin, 1976).

PARENT TEACHING Perineal hygiene in girls should be taught from infancy. The technique of wiping from front to back should be stressed. Abundant fluid intake and regular voiding practices are important as is complete emptying of the bladder with each voiding. Harsh detergents and bubble baths may irritate perineal and urethral tissue and lead to inflammation and infection. In children who have had one UTI, parents need to know that subsequent symptoms should be promptly investigated and regular follow-up carefully obtained. Because the severity of symptoms in childhood is poorly correlated with the ultimate course, follow-up into adulthood is advised. Parents may ask about giving the child cranberry juice since it has some ability to suppress bacteria in the urine. It takes 2 gallons of cranberry juice per day to suppress bacteria in an adult which makes it an unrealistic and unnecessary therapy (Bergman, 1969).

References

American Academy of Pediatrics, Committee on Practice and Ambulatory Medicine. "Guidelines for Health Supervision." *News and Comment 33*:6, May 1982.

Bergman, A. B., editor. *Urinary Tract Infections in Childhood: Report of the First Ross Roundtable on Critical Approaches to Common Pediatric Problems.* Columbus, OH: Ross Laboratories, 1969.

Cohen, M. W. "Enuresis." *Pediatr Clin North Am* 22:545–560, August 1975.

Ginsburg, C. M. and G. H. McCracken. "Urinary Tract Infections in Young Infants." *Pediatrics* 69:409–412, April 1982.

Krugman, S. and S. L. Katz. *Infectious Diseases of Children.* 7th ed. St. Louis: C. V. Mosby, 1981.

Kunin, C. M. *Detection, Prevention and Management of Urinary Tract Infections.* 3rd ed. Philadelphia: Lea and Febiger, 1979.

Kunin, C. M. "Urinary Tract Infections." In M. Green and R. J. Haggerty, editors, *Ambulatory Pediatrics II.* Philadelphia: W. B. Saunders, 1977. Pp. 165–171.

Kunin, C. M., et al. "Detection of Urinary Tract Infections in 3- to 5-Year Old Girls by Mothers Using a Nitrite Indicator Strip." *Pediatrics* 57:829–835, June 1976.

McCoy, J. A. "Preliminary Diagnosis of Urinary Tract Infection in Symptomatic Children." *Nurse Practitioner* 7:28–48, January 1982.

Ruble, J. A. "Childhood Nocturnal Enuresis." *Am J Maternal Child Nurs* 6:26–31, January/February 1981.

Schauffler, G. C. *Pediatric Gynecology* 4th ed. Chicago: Yearbook Publishers, 1958.

Shelov, S. P., et al. "Enuresis: A Contrast of Attitudes of Parents and Physicians." *Pediatrics* 67:707–710, May 1981.

Starfield, B. "Enuresis: Focus on a Challenging Problem in Primary Care." *Pediatrics* 62:1036–1037, December 1978.

Starfield, B. "Enuresis: Its Pathogenesis and Management." *Clin Pediatr* 11:343–350, June 1972.

Thomas, C. K. "Childhood Urinary Tract Infection." *Pediatric Nursing* 8:114–119, March/April 1982.

22

The Genitalia

Genital problems are not uncommon in childhood and, regardless of severity, must be assessed and managed with gentleness and sensitivity because of the degree of concern likely to be felt both by parents and children. Examination of the genital organs in the neonatal period must be done with care and with attention to the parent's spoken or unspoken concerns. Many new parents will have questions and/or fears about the appearance of their infant's genitals and may be hesitant to touch or to manipulate the genital area for proper hygiene. The first examination with the parents present is an excellent opportunity for demonstrating techniques of care and for eliciting concerns. Obviously, such an approach is used for any child regardless of age. See Chapter 8, Health Care of the Adolescent, for information on sexually transmitted diseases and vaginitis.

ASSESSMENT

History

MALE

Factors to ascertain in the male are any history of pain in the penis, testicles, or rectum, disturbances in micturition, hematuria, urethral discharge or bleeding, swelling, inflammation, and trauma.

FEMALE

Factors to ascertain in the female are any history of itching, burning, irritation, discharge, or pain in the perineal area, and menstrual history. For both males and females, information on sexual activity and sexual abuse needs to be elicited. See Chapter 8, Health Care of the Adolescent, and Chapter 32, Child Abuse.

Physical Examination

EXTERNAL GENITAL ORGANS, MALE

Inspect for size, configuration, symmetry, cleanliness. Note presence or absence of circumcision. If uncircumcised, gently check retractibility of the foreskin to observe position of the urethral meatus. Note size of the meatus and any discharge from it. Palpate genital area for masses. Note presence of phimosis, hypospadias, hydrocele, hernia, and cryptorchidism (see this chapter, Common Clinical Problems).

Testes   Palpate testes from above downward for location and size. The testes may have to be "milked down" from the inguinal canal. The environment and the examiner's hands should be warm as an active cremaster reflex may simulate cryptorchidism. To abolish this reflex, have the child sit crosslegged on the examining table. Parents may have more success in palpating the testes at home with the child in a warm bath.

Scrotum   Note the size of the scrotum and any swelling or fullness. Any swelling of the scrotum other than the testicle should be checked by transillumination. The room is darkened and a beam of light from a flashlight is directed from behind the scrotum through the mass. Transmission of light will appear as a red glow. Swellings caused by serous fluid will transilluminate; those caused by blood or tissue will not.

Older Males   Note pubertal changes. Check pubic hair for pediculosis.

EXTERNAL GENITAL ORGANS, FEMALE

Inspect for size, configuration, symmetry, and cleanliness. Separate the labia fully to inspect clitoris, urethral meatus, vaginal orifice, and hymen. Note mucous or skin tags. Note presence of vaginal discharge, vulvar or labial adhesions, imperforate hymen, clitoral hypertrophy, presence of hair and distribution, pubertal changes. Palpate area for any masses. Check pubic hair for pediculosis.

MANAGEMENT

Health concerns and problems related to the genitalia require sensitive and supportive approaches by the nurse practitioner. There are two major areas of management: education and counseling regarding normal development, including masturbation, sex education (see Chapter 5, Table 5-20, Chronologic Development of Sexual Needs and Interests from Birth Through 6 Years; and Chapter 6, Masturbation), and personal hygienic care of the genitals, as well as teaching, support, and coordination of care when genital abnormalities are present.

Parents need careful explanations of medical and surgical procedures and treatments. Their fears must be elicited and appropriate counseling provided, bearing in mind that most parents will have concerns about the possible impact of the specific condition on their child's sexual or reproductive intactness.

The child must receive age-appropriate explanations and support. Age-related fears (e.g., punishment, castration) must be recognized and reassurance provided. Since procedures involving the genitalia are generally perceived as intrusive and traumatic by young children and by parents too, it is important that the role of the nurse practitioner include protection of the child from the sometimes impersonal and insensitive approaches of others.

COMMON CLINICAL PROBLEMS

Adhesions, Labial and Vulvar

ASSESSMENT

Adhesions are usually associated with the hypoestrogenic state of childhood or with vulvovaginitis, and appear as a membrane of epithelium that may cover the urethral meatus. They are found in young girls and will disappear at puberty with the onset of endogenous estrogen. It is important to assess adequacy of urinary stream.

MANAGEMENT

No treatment is indicated unless urinary function is impaired. If treatment is required, local application of an estrogen cream (Dinestrol, Premarin) daily for 7 to 14 days is usually effective. Parents must be counseled not to prolong treatment since the use of estrogen cream for 2 to 3 months will cause a systemic effect and breast tenderness.

Circumcision

ASSESSMENT

Circumcision is the surgical removal of the prepuce (foreskin) from the penis. Although the most common surgical procedure in male infants in the United States, the medical indications for circumcision have not been established. Parents elect the procedure because of religious or cultural beliefs, social pressure, custom, cosmetic purposes, or because it has "always been done." Some parents believe that circumcision is required by law and is mandatory hospital policy (Grimes, 1980).

Arguments in Favor of Circumcision Rationale put forth by those who favor circumcision states that circumcision:

1. Promotes cleanliness of the glans penis and will result in decreased incidence of cervical carcinoma in sexual partners
2. Prevents penile cancer
3. Prevents balanitis (infection of the foreskin), adhesions, phimosis, and occlusion of the urethral meatus
4. Makes boys feel more normal since most American boys are circumcised.

Arguments Against Circumcision Those who do not favor routine circumcision state that:

1. The level of hygiene in both male and female does seem to be a factor in the etiology of cancer of the cervix, but "noncircumcision is not, of itself, of primary etiologic significance" (AAP, 1975, p. 611).

2. Cancer of the penis can be prevented by circumcision but also by good penile hygiene.
3. There is no convincing evidence that circumcision reduces the incidence of cancer of the prostate.
4. Circumcision leaves the glans and urethral meatus exposed to the effects of ammonia in wet diapers. This may result in a caustic burn or, in some cases, meatal stenosis.
5. The only medical indications for circumcision are extreme phimosis that could lead to obstructive uremia or intractable paraphimosis.
6. Two to ten percent of males with true phimosis may need circumcision before starting school.
7. Significant complications occur in 1 of 500 newborns circumcised (Gee and Ansell, 1976, p. 826).
8. Cultural norms are changing and more accepting of normal penile anatomy.

Contraindications Contraindications to circumcision are:

1. Exstrophy of the bladder
2. Epispadias or hypospadias. The foreskin may be needed if plastic surgery is necessary.
3. Ambiguous genitalia
4. Neonatal illness
5. Premature birth
6. Familial bleeding disorders

Complications Complications of circumcision include the following:

1. Hemorrhage
2. Meatal ulceration leading to meatal stenosis
3. Local infection that can lead to septicemia, significant hemorrhage, mutilation, or death (Cleary and Kohl, 1979)
4. Cautery burns
5. Urethral fistula, as a result of too deeply placed sutures
6. Surgical trauma to penis, amputation of the glans, excessive removal of penile skin.

MANAGEMENT

Care of the Circumcision When performed in the immediate neonatal period (after 24 hours of age), the incision is covered with sterile dressing and petrolatum, or Vaseline gauze, to prevent infection and to prevent irritation from the penis sticking to the diapers. Parents should observe for: adequacy of urinary stream, hematuria, bleeding, signs of infection. The incision usually heals quickly within 3 to 4 days.

Counseling It is the responsibility of the nurse practitioner to provide parents, before delivery, with factual options regarding circumcision. The known long-term medical effects of circumcision and noncircumcision should be presented. Ultimately it is the parents who make the final decision. Education for penile hygiene is necessary if noncircumcision is elected (see this chapter, Phimosis). Some parents may have concerns or emotional fears about manipulating the child's penis during cleansing. Assistance with verbalizing such discomfort and demonstration of cleansing techniques will reassure these parents.

Cryptorchidism

ASSESSMENT

Cryptorchidism is the absence of one or both testes from the scrotal sac. It is important to differentiate undescended from retractile testes. Retractile testes can be manipulated into the bottom of the scrotum. Undescended testes may represent delayed descent, prevention of descent by mechanical lesions (e.g., adhesions, narrow inguinal canal, fibrous bands, or diversion of descent into the perineum or femoral area). They are usually unilateral. Twenty percent are bilateral and are frequently associated with hernias. Endocrine causes are rare. Secondary sex characteristics develop normally as androgen production usually is normal.

Incidence Approximately 4 percent of term male newborns and 30 percent of premature males have undescended testes at birth, but during the first weeks and months of life about 80 percent of all undescended testes will be in the scrotum. Spontaneous descent after infancy is uncommon and even if it does occur, damage to the testes may have occurred. Late descent is neither to be expected nor desired.

MANAGEMENT

Any child with undescended testes is referred to a physician for evaluation and treatment. Differences of opinion exist as to the best age for medical and surgical treatment.

Medical Treatment In the case of *bilateral* undescended testes, medical treatment consists of a short term series of injections of human chorionic gonadotropin to precipitate descent of the testes when the child is about 5 years of age. One third of the children so treated will respond. If the testes do not descend, surgery is performed. Medical treatment is not recommended in unilateral cryptorchidism.

Surgical Treatment Orchidopexy is the surgical procedure for bringing the testis down into the scrotum. Since some cellular changes and degeneration are found to occur in the undescended testis during early childhood, it is recommended by many authorities that surgery be performed before 5 years of age. It cannot be said with certainty that correction of the condition will absolutely prevent infertility or sterility as some testes may have been defective to begin with. Indications for orchidopexy (Hoekelman et al., 1978, p. 1305) include the following:

1. Possibility of infertility in bilateral undescended testes
2. Association of inguinal hernia
3. Increased incidence of neoplasia in an undescended or ectopic testis
4. Greater risk of trauma
5. Emotional problems associated with appearance of the scrotum.

Counseling Whatever the course of management selected, the nurse practitioner is a key figure in interpreting the plan to both child and parents and in preparing them for eventual surgery. See this chapter, Hypospadias. The child and parents should be helped to verbalize their concerns about possible defective sexual ability.

Hydrocele

ASSESSMENT

A hydrocele results from the accumulation of peritoneal fluid in the scrotal sac. Normally, in utero, as the male testis descends toward the scrotum, it is preceded by a sac of peritoneal tissue called the processus vaginalis. Once the testis reaches the scrotum the processus vaginalis atrophies and is usually obliterated at the time of birth.

Noncommunicating Hydrocele Frequently at birth some residual peritoneal fluid remains after closure of the processus vaginalis. This is called a *noncommunicating hydrocele*. The scrotal sac appears full, fluctuant, tense, and clear on transillumination. The fluid gradually absorbs during the first year of life and no treatment is necessary. Since the processus vaginalis is closed off, there is no danger of hernia.

Communicating Hydrocele A *communicating hydrocele* exists when the processus vaginalis remains open. Fluid may not be noticed in the scrotum until some time after birth. The patent passageway to the abdomen is often associated with an inguinal hernia and surgical repair is more frequently required.

MANAGEMENT

Parents need simple, clear explanations of the enlarged scrotum. Parents are frequently frightened by the size of the scrotum, fearing that it means their sons will have abnormally large genitals in adulthood. Assurance that the fluid will resorb during the first year brings great relief. With a communicating hydrocele, parents must be instructed to observe for signs of potential inguinal hernia. See Chapter 20, Inguinal Hernia.

Hypospadias

ASSESSMENT

In hypospadias the urethral opening is on the ventral (lower) surface of the penis. In mild cases the opening is on the glans or corona. In severe cases the urethra opens on the shaft of the penis, at its base, or on the perineum. It is frequently associated with chordee, a ventral bowing of the penis. Incidence is about 1 in 500 male infants. Most cases are mild.

Clinical Signs   The child is unable to urinate with the penis in the normal elevated position and usually must sit to void.

MANAGEMENT

Surgery is indicated to correct the chordee and to reposition the urethral opening. Since the foreskin is used in this repair, infants with this condition must not be circumcised. It is essential that the repair be performed prior to school entry so the boy will be able to void standing up like his peers.

Preparation for Surgery   Preparation of the young child for genital surgery must consider the age of the child, stage of development, level of understanding, fears and fantasies, correction of misconceptions, assurance that he is not to blame for his condition nor being punished for anything—especially masturbation, opportunities for expression of feelings verbally or through play, and assistance to parents so they can fully prepare and support their child.

Paraphimosis

ASSESSMENT

Paraphimosis occurs when the prepuce has been retracted, usually by the parent, child, or vigorous examiner, and cannot readily be replaced over the glans. Blood supply to the glans is constricted; edema, bluish discoloration, pain, and dysuria result. Gangrene can occur.

MANAGEMENT

Application of cold compresses to reduce swelling is indicated. Physician consultation is obtained. If manual attempts to replace the foreskin are unsuccessful, surgical release may be required.

Phimosis

ASSESSMENT

Phimosis occurs when the preputial opening of the foreskin is narrowed so that the foreskin cannot be retracted over the glans of the penis. Straining at urination may result. In most normal uncircumcised males there is some degree of adherence of the foreskin during the first year, which will disconnect by 1 year of age. In fact, at birth only 4 percent of boys have a fully retractable foreskin, at 6 months of age 15 percent, and at 1 year of age 50 percent. It is not until 3 to 4 years of age that most boys have a completely retractable foreskin. Approximately 1 percent of 16- to 17-year-old uncircumcised boys continue to have phimosis.

MANAGEMENT

If this adherence does not interfere with urination, no manipulations are necessary. Parents should be instructed in hygienic care of the penis, which includes gentle retraction, cleansing, and return of the foreskin to its regular position. By the time the child is 4 to 5 years of age, he can be expected to perform this part of his bath for himself (Osborn et al., 1981). If the phimosis is severe, the preputial opening may be widened by incision, or circumcision may be performed.

Vulvovaginitis, Nonspecific

ASSESSMENT

Vulvovaginitis is the most common gynecologic problem of childhood and refers to infections of the vulva, vagina, and occasionally the urethra (Altchek, 1972). Vulvitis is characterized by excoriation of the labia majora, labia minora, clitoris, and introitus. Vaginitis is characterized by discharge or bleeding not attributed to trauma, menses, or neonatal estrogen withdrawal (Paradise et al., 1982). Such infections are most frequent after the second year of life (median age 5.8 years) and are the result of bacterial or monilial infection, poor hygiene, pinworms, local varicella lesions, local trauma from insertion of foreign bodies, masturbation, and sexual abuse. See Chapter 32, Child Abuse, and Chapter 8, Sexually

Transmitted Diseases. Symptoms may include urinary frequency, enuresis, inflammation with discharge, pruritus, and swollen mucous membranes. The young child may be irritable, restless, scratching the genital area, or rubbing against furniture. Vaginal swabs should be obtained for bacterial/fungal cultures and for ova and parasites.

MANAGEMENT

Local cleansing measures (gentle bathing with warm water and bland soap twice a day) are effective in treating many nonspecific, mild infections. Cleansing after each bowel movement and frequent changing of loose, white cotton panties are indicated. For severe infections wet dressings or irrigations using water, saline, Aveeno Colloidal in water, or other topical agents are used (see Chapter 26, Topical Therapy). If the condition has not cleared after 2 weeks of perineal care, further investigation is warranted. Systemic antibiotic therapy is indicated if bacterial or fungal infection is present.

References

Altchek, A. "Pediatric Vulvovaginitis." *Pediatr Clin North Am 19*:559–581, August 1972.

American Academy of Pediatrics, Committee on Fetus and Newborn. "Report of the Ad Hoc Task Force on Circumcision." *Pediatrics 56*:610–611, October 1975.

Bates, B. *A Guide to Physical Examination.* 2nd ed. Philadelphia: J.B. Lippincott, 1979.

Cleary, T. G. and S. Kohl. "Overwhelming Infection with Group B Beta-hemolytic Streptococcus Associated with Circumcision." *Pediatrics 64*:301–302, September 1979.

Gee, W. F. and J. S. Ansell. "Neonatal Circumcision: A Ten-Year Overview." *Pediatrics 58*:824–827, December 1976.

Grimes, D. A. "Routine Circumcision Reconsidered." *Am J Nurs 80*:108–109, January 1980.

Hoekelman, R. A., et al., editors. *Principles of Pediatrics: Health Care of the Young.* New York: McGraw-Hill, 1978.

Osborn, L. M., et al. "Hygienic Care in Uncircumcised Infants." *Pediatrics 67*:365–367, March 1981.

Paradise, F. E., et al. "Vulvovaginitis in Premenarcheal Girls: Clinical Features and Diagnostic Evaluation." *Pediatrics 70*:193–198, August 1982.

Redman, J. F. and N. K. Bissada. "How to Make a Good Examination of the Genitalia of Young Girls." *Clin Pediatr* 15:907–908, October 1976.

Rudolph, A. M., editor. *Pediatrics.* 17th ed. East Norwalk, CT: Appleton-Century-Crofts, 1982.

Terris, M. F., et al. "Relation of Circumcision to Cancer of the Cervix." *Am J Obstet Gynecol* 117:1056–1066, December 1973.

Vaughan, V. C., et al., editors. *Nelson Textbook of Pediatrics.* 11th ed. Philadelphia: W. B. Saunders, 1979.

23

The Skeletal System

Minor orthopedic abnormalities and developmental variants are common problems for management in pediatric ambulatory care. Although definitive diagnosis and treatment of orthopedic problems fall within the realm of the orthopedist, early detection of these conditions is the responsibility of the nurse practitioner. This chapter describes the most common orthopedic problems, with emphasis on methods of assessment.

ASSESSMENT

History

PRESENT CONCERN

See Chapter 11, Assessment of Presenting Symptom.

PAST HISTORY

Obtain information about injuries or deformities, webbing of the neck, fractures, nerve injuries, shoulder or arm paralysis, hip or foot deformities or problems, and nutrition pertinent to vitamin D and calcium intake.

BIRTH HISTORY

Obtain information about congenital abnormalities, birth injuries, abnormal presentation (breech), prematurity, or anoxia in the neonatal period.

FAMILY HISTORY

Obtain information about congenital abnormalities of the hip, foot or back problems, limps, painful joints, or "twisted spine."

Physical Examination

The general screening examination in infancy and childhood includes components of the skeletal examination. This can be found in Chapter 1, Child Health Assessment. Specific screening examinations for hip, leg, and spinal disorders can be found in this chapter under the specific problem. Included here are examination techniques for assessing range of motion of limbs, flexibility of foot and ankle joints, posture, and gait.

EXAMINATION FOR RANGE OF MOTION

Full range of motion (extension, flexion, and rotation) of limbs and joints, both active and passive, is performed. Range of motion is described by degrees of a circle with neutral position at 0° (see Figure 23-1). Note deviations, rigidity, stiffness, or pain.

Normal Limits   Normal limits of range of motion are as follows:

Shoulder abduction	0°–90°
Shoulder backward extension	0°–60°
Shoulder forward flexion	0°–180°
Shoulder rotation	0°–90°
Hip flexion and extension (knee flexed over chest)	0°–120°
Hip extension (leg extended and back)	0°–30°
Ankle dorsiflexion, newborn	0°–30°
Ankle dorsiflexion, adolescent	0°–10°
Ankle plantar flexion	0°–30°–45°
Foot inversion	0°–35°
Foot eversion	0°–15°

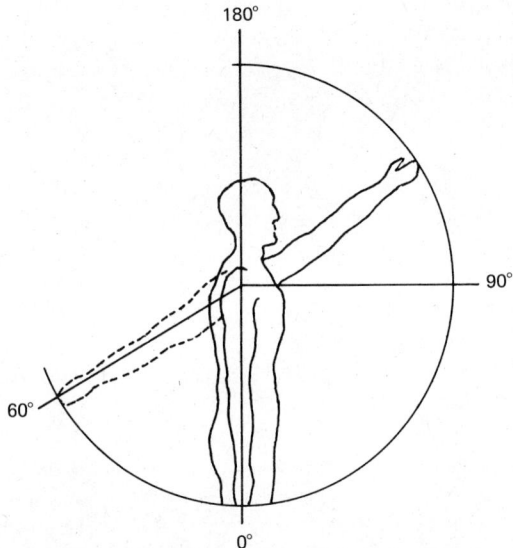

Figure 23-1 Range of motion of limbs described by degrees of a circle. (Reproduced with
permission from "Joint Motion: Method of
Measuring and Recording," Chicago: American
Academy of Orthopaedic Surgeons, 1965. P. 33.)

EXAMINATION FOR FLEXIBILITY OF FOOT AND ANKLE

Flexibility of the foot and ankle is examined both actively and
passively (Fig. 23-2) and by eliciting the tonic foot reflexes. Tonic
foot reflexes are elicited by using an ordinary applicator and lightly
stroking areas of foot indicated in Figure 23-3. Observe foot or
ankle joints for rigidity, stiffness, or pain. Rigidity is indicated by
eversion or inversion when the foot does not move beyond the
neutral position (Figure 23-3) and does not respond to toe-
grasping or by dorsiflexing.

EXAMINATION FOR POSTURE

To examine for posture (see Fig. 23-4):

1. Have the child undress to panties
2. Observe from the front, back, and sides

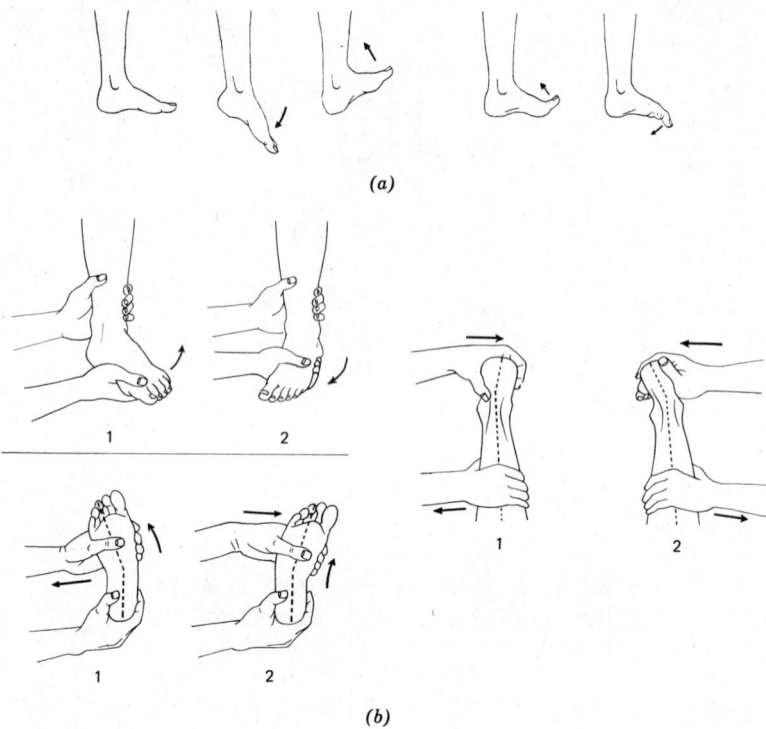

Figure 23-2 Examination for flexibility of the foot. (*a*) Active flexion of foot and toes. (*b*) Passive flexion of foot: (1) eversion, (2) inversion. (Reproduced with permission from R. J. Ducroquet et al., La marche et les boîteries, Paris: Masson, 1965. English translation: J. B. Lippincott, 1969.)

3. Note the following:
   • From the front, whether the pelvis and hips are level, shape of the legs, amount of space between the knees and ankles, and whether the feet turn in, out, or pronate
   • From the back, curvature, masses of the spinal column, level of the hips and shoulders, whether the hips and shoulders are level, and whether the legs are straight over the heels
   • From the side, whether the head is held straight over the shoulders with the chin in, chest up and over the hips, abdomen taut, buttocks tucked in, and feet straight forward

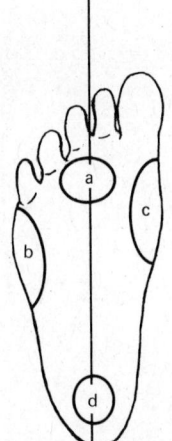

Figure 23-3 Tonic foot reflexes. Areas of foot stroked to elicit tonic foot reflexes: (*a*) plantar or toe grasping, (*b*) eversion, (*c*) inversion, (*d*) dorsiflexion. Midline bisects the second and third toes indicating the neutral position of the foot. (Adapted from G. P. Furlong and G. W. Lawn, "Evaluation of Foot Deformities in the Newborn," *GP* *31*:89–97, November 1965.)

EXAMINATION FOR GAIT

To examine a child for gait:

1. Observe the child walking backward and forward
2. Note deviations of gait, knock-knees, bowlegs, or pronation of feet. For a description of abnormal gaits see this chapter, Limps.

Normal Gait of a Child Beginning to Walk   Characteristics of early gait are as follows:

1. Normal base width heel to heel is 15 to 20 cm
2. Feet turn out and the femurs are in eversion. As the child ages and step becomes steadier the femurs turn in to their normal base width.
3. Steps off with knee bent, leg held high, and arms held up for balance. Sometimes a child pushes off with one foot, slightly

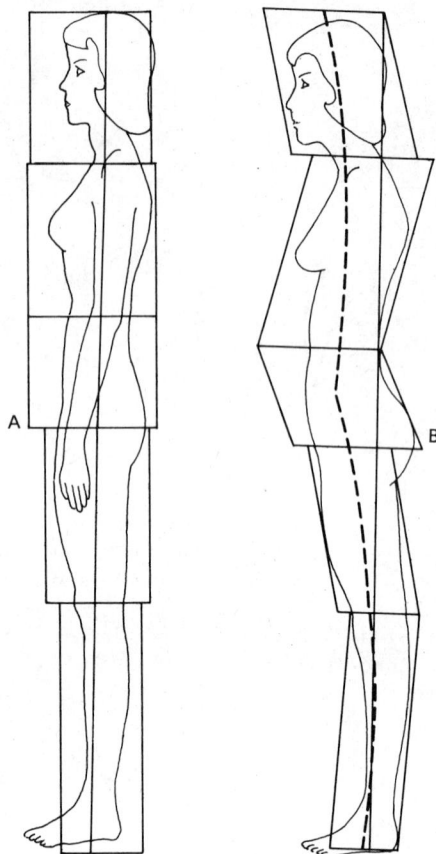

Figure 23-4 Good and poor standing posture. (*a*) In good standing posture, the weight-bearing line (line of gravity) passes just anterior to the ear, through the shoulder joint, just posterior to the hip joint, and slightly behind the patella; it strikes the floor just anterior to the external malleolus. (*b*) Poor standing posture illustrating malalignment of the body segments and a distorted weight-bearing line. Note forward position of the head, round shoulders, increased lordosis, and protruding abdomen. (Reprinted with permission of C. B. Larson and M. Gould. *Orthopedic Nursing*, 8th ed., St. Louis: C. V. Mosby, 1974. By M. Joan Popp, University Microfilms, 300 N. Zeeb Road, P.O. Box 1346, Ann Arbor, Michigan 48106. Copyright registration No. A912364S.)

dragging the other, and this is considered to be a normal deviation.

Normal Gait of an Older Child Characteristics of mature gait are as follows:

1. Normal base width is 5 to 10 cm heel to heel
2. Pelvis rotates 40° forward in the swing phase of gait
3. Knee remains flexed during all components of gait
4. Pelvis and trunk shift laterally approximately 1 inch

Potential Orthopedic Risks

DISLOCATIONS AND FRACTURES

Parents and health personnel need reminding that some common habits can lead to these problems:

1. Radial head dislocations. These can be caused by pulling, jerking, or swinging infants and toddlers by their arms, or by taking them down from one's shoulders after a "piggy back" ride.
2. Fractures and injuries. Playground equipment can be hazardous to children. Parents must locate a safe place where children can play. Centrifugal swings, teeter-totters, swings with wooden seats, black-top playground surfaces, trampolines, and skateboards are particularly hazardous.

DEVELOPMENTAL PROBLEMS

Positioning and "poor" posture contribute to these potential risks:

1. *Femoral anteversion.* In infancy this may be caused by the child's sleeping on haunches with buttocks in the air and feet turned in. In an older child it is caused by sitting in "TV squat," or "tailor fashion" on haunches with legs tucked under and feet turned in. Infants should sleep in different positions, on back and both sides. Older children should be taught to sit "yoga" style. See this chapter, Femoral Anteversion.
2. *Muscular "hip pockets."* These are common upper thigh bulges often seen in adolescent girls and adult women. These are caused by standing or walking with the knees rigid and hy-

perextended (locked) as a result of poor posture. Good posture can be maintained with emphasis on taut abdominal and gluteal muscles and flexed knees.

3. *Pronated feet, lordosis, and knock knees.* These defects may develop in young children and adolescents due to obesity. Obesity can also cause fatigue, backache, or limps.

Commonly Used Terms

abduction: drawing away from the midline.

adduction: drawing together, or toward the midline.

anteversion: displacement so the whole axis is directed farther forward than normal.

dorsiflexion: movement of toes/feet or finger/hand toward the dorsal surface (up).

dysplasia: abnormality of development.

epiphysis: a part or process of a bone that ossifies separately and later becomes ankylosed to the main part of the bone.

eversion: a turning out or inside out.

external rotation: turning anterior surface or limb out or laterally.

internal rotation: turning anterior surface or limb in or medially.

inversion: a turning up, supination.

luxation: complete displacement of a part, dislocation.

malleolus: either of the two rounded prominences on either side of the ankle joint, lateral (external or outer) and medial (internal or inner).

plantar flexion: movement of the toes/foot or fingers/hand toward the plantar surface (down).

pronation: palmar surface of hand turned downward or toward posterior surface of the body; plantar surface of foot turned outward.

supination: palmar surface of hand turned upward or toward anterior surface of the body; plantar surface of foot turned inward.

torsion: the act or state of twisting.

valgus: deviation away from the midline.

varus: turned inward to an abnormal degree.

MANAGEMENT

Counseling

Early identification of skeletal abnormalities is important to prevent future problems, for example, dislocation of the hip. When abnormalities are detected at birth, parents will need information and counseling beginning in the early postpartum period. This is a very sensitive time, especially for parents of a first child, and the nurse practitioner needs to be aware of factors that may be involved:

1. Parents, particularly mothers, normally experience feelings of inadequacy as they adjust to their infants. If abnormalities, even minor, are discovered, strong feelings of guilt and frustration may develop as the parents react to the suggestion that their child is not perfect. These feelings must be appreciated and dealt with in a delicate manner.

2. The nurse practitioner may be taken unaware by the discovery of an abnormal finding and feel overanxious. It may be expedient to take a few minutes to collect one's thoughts by continuing with the examination, then returning to the area in question before giving an explanation.

3. The findings may not be definitive until there is further evaluation. While this may make the parents more anxious, their anxiety can be greatly eased if the nurse practitioner intervenes to smooth the way to the appropriate consultant. For example, if an additional appointment has to be made with an orthopedist, the nurse can make the call to the clinic or physician to facilitate the process.

Besides providing support and understanding the nurse practitioner may choose to be available at all times for parental questions or problems.

Exercise

Daily exercise is essential to good growth and development by providing muscular activity to stimulate the flow of blood to carry oxygen throughout the body. Exercise for fun and competition can be superior to forced exercise.

INFANCY

The infant exercises by kicking, stretching, crying, and squirming. This activity should occur several times a day on a firm surface, without the restriction of clothes and with the child in the supine position. Limits must be set for safety when the child begins to crawl and to walk, but the baby needs more space than is provided by a "play-pen" which is mainly a convenience for the parent.

TODDLERS AND PRESCHOOLERS

These children need safe areas indoors and outdoors in which to run, to climb, and to explore. Neighborhood parks can provide this space if the child is confined to apartment living. A method designed to exercise and straighten the spine consists of a removable bar placed in a doorway from which a child can hang freely by the hands.

SCHOOLS

Most schools provide opportunities for organized exercise and for group and competitive sports. Ice-skating classes and dancing classes are excellent choices for obtaining exercise. Afterschool exercise is important if the child has been sitting for most of the day.

PARENTS

Parents can encourage active forms of play, participation in school sports, and act as examples to their children. Activities and sports children can continue for the rest of their lives such as swimming, bicycling, hiking, dancing, tennis, skiing, soccer, and kickball are good forms of exercise for the entire family.

Posture

GOOD POSTURE

Good posture exists when body alignment is such that the musculoskeletal system of the body can function with efficiency and with a minimum of effort. See Figure 23-4. It is nonfatiguing, painless, and can be maintained for periods of time. It creates a more pleasing appearance and also provides for correct functioning of the weightbearing joints. It lessens the possibility of strain to joints and ligaments by preventing uneven distribution of body weight.

FACTORS INFLUENCING POSTURE

Of factors that influence posture there are three that supersede all others in their prevalence and frequency:

1. *Familial-hereditary.* These include postures, variations in ligamentous laxity, and muscle tone.
2. *Structural abnormalities.* These may be congenital or acquired, skeletal, muscular, or neurologic, and static or progressive.
3. *The posture of habit and postural training by parental control or educators.* These lay the groundwork of ultimate adult posture.

POOR POSTURE

Some factors that influence poor posture are as follows:

1. *Obesity.* This may produce sway-back (lordosis), knock-knees, or pronated feet.
2. *Chronic illness or chronic fatigue.* These may lead to slumping or sagging.
3. *Unusual tallness.* This may make some adolescents insecure and cause slouching or ducking of the head.
4. *Insecurity or lack of self-esteem.* These may be due to criticism at home, difficulties in school, or an unsatisfactory social life.
5. *Diseases.* Among these are rickets, poliomyelitis, tuberculosis of the bone, or developmental problems such as scoliosis or slipped epiphysis.

MAINTAINING GOOD POSTURE

Parents should be encouraged to help the child to maintain good posture from birth. Some areas for education include the following:

1. *Bedding.* Use of firm mattresses beginning with the crib, the bassinet, or the carriage is recommended. No pillow is necessary for babies.

2. *Lying position.* Lying in the prone position is not recommended. When the child sleeps in the prone position the feet are often adducted, the buttocks are elevated, the hips and knees are in complete flexion, and the child is at risk for tibial torsion. Later these children tend to sit on the adducted feet and may prolong the presence of metatarsus adductus or femoral anteversion (Ponseti and Becker, 1966, p. 709).

3. *Sitting position.* Back and feet should be supported while the child is sitting at the table, in a high chair, on a toilet seat, or in a car seat. Poor sitting positions help to develop lordosis, protruding abdomens, and rounded backs. Infants should not be propped or left sitting in canvas swings for long periods of time.

4. *Infant and baby equipment.* Infant carriers, slings, infant seats, swings, and strollers are not considered to be potentially risky for posture if they are used as directed and for short periods of time.

5. *Child's self-esteem.* Parents need to understand its importance for the child's well-being.

6. *Proper diet and exercise.* Proper nutrition is important for the normal growth and development of bones and muscles. See this chapter, Exercise.

7. *Parental example.* This should include posture, diet, and exercise.

8. *TV watching.* Activity level of children and adolescents has dropped severely in recent years and is attributed to long hours of television watching.

9. *Regular health visits and physical examinations.* These should be conducted on a regular basis.

Shoes

FIRST SHOES

Neither high top nor low quarter shoes are necessary until the foot needs warmth or protection. Booties, slippers, fabric shoes, or moccasins can be used to keep the feet warm. They do not give support, but permit full motion of the foot if they are not so small or tight as to turn under the toes. Care should be taken that the soles are not too slippery for a child attempting to walk.

LATER SHOES

After the child walks and needs protection for the feet, shoes should have a thin leather sole sufficient to protect the foot, and uppers and soles flexible enough to permit normal motion and use of muscles. For toddlers high-top shoes help keep the shoe on the foot and are used if the child tends to pronate or walks on toes beyond an initial period.

Low Quarter Shoes   These shoes should be narrow enough in the heel to fit snugly, and long and broad enough so the ball of the foot is accommodated at the widest part of the shoe. They should be flexible enough to bend at this point and give good support. The big toe should be a thumb's width from the end of the shoe in the weightbearing position. The width is determined in the weight-bearing position by the pinch test. The leather over the widest part should be supple enough and wide enough to allow a small amount to be pinched.

Sneakers and Sandals   These shoes are adequate if they do not interfere with the movement of the foot or if the child does not have foot problems. There is no evidence that they cause "fallen arches."

High-Heeled Shoes   These shoes may cause in-toeing if worn for long periods of time by throwing the body forward and resulting in poor posture, calluses, and strained metatarsal arches.

Corrective Shoes   Significant differences of opinion among pediatric orthopedists, orthopedists, pediatricians, and podiatrists concerning the best treatment for flexible flat feet, metatarsus adductus, intoeing, and leg-length differences are known to exist. Shoe modifications are rarely appropriate, and properly fitted regular shoes that allow a position resembling barefootedness are appropriate for most children (Staheli and Giffin, 1980).

EVALUATION OF SHOES

When the child is being examined the shoes should be carefully observed for worn areas on the soles and heels. These areas should be evenly centered. If corrective shoes are used, the length of time since they were prescribed should be ascertained and their need reassessed if 2 or more years have elapsed. Ill-fitting shoes can cause corns (due to pressure on the little toe), calluses, and overriding toes. Painful feet and limps in children are most commonly caused by ill-fitting shoes.

Cast Care

Parents need help with caring for a child in a cast. Some suggestions for improved care include not only care of the cast but also care of the child's skin and the child's well-being.

CARE OF THE CAST

Casts must be kept clean, dry, and free from odors and sharp edges. Suggestions for care are as follows:

1. Loose cotton can be placed under the cast edges. This can be removed and replaced as necessary to keep the cast dry or clean.
2. Plastic material may be used on the cast edges to maintain dryness.
3. Hair-dryer may be used for drying small areas.
4. Edges of the cast may be overlapped with small strips of adhesive tape to keep edges clean and free from sharp areas. They are replaced as necessary.
5. Dirty areas can be washed with Zephiran Chloride 1:1000 to clean and to eliminate some of the odor-causing bacteria.

CARE OF THE SKIN

Daily bathing keeps the child clean and comfortable. Special care of the skin includes the following steps:

1. More frequent cleaning of the anal area of an infant or young child who wears diapers
2. Massaging areas of redness with rubbing alcohol. Alcohol is not used if the skin is broken
3. Avoiding oils and lotions since they cause maceration
4. Avoiding powders since they cake and crumble causing irritation
5. Positioning the crib at a tilt to prevent the infant or child from lying in accumulated urine
6. Keeping the skin exposed to the air

CARE OF THE CHILD IN A CAST

Special measures are as follows:

1. The child who wears a cast should be kept cool, preferably indoors. Insects and heat are a problem outdoors.
2. The physician or medical clinic should be called if the child develops pressure sores, a fever, or a foul odor from the cast.
3. The child's position should be changed frequently if immobilized. The body should be kept in good alignment.
4. Small babies need to be played with, held, and cuddled.
5. The child should be given an opportunity to talk about the experience of being immobilized.

COMMON CLINICAL PROBLEMS

Most of the common problems, except for the very minor ones, are treated by the orthopedist. Quick detection and rapid referral are in the province of the nurse practitioner. Assessment of specific symptoms and signs is included with many of these common problems.

Birth Injuries

BRACHIAL PALSY

Assessment Brachial palsy occurs when traction for vertex delivery is exerted on the head during delivery of the shoulder; for breech delivery when the head is extracted by strong lateral flexion of the trunk and neck. Injury to the brachial plexus may cause paralysis of the upper arm with or without paralysis of the forearm and hand. Most commonly the injury is limited to the fifth or sixth cervical nerves. The infant loses the power to abduct the arm from the shoulder, to rotate the arm externally, and to supinate the forearm. The usual position is adduction and internal rotation of the arm with pronation of the forearm. Recovery can be expected by 18 months in mild cases. Poorer prognosis exists when the entire plexus is involved or when the lower plexus in involved.

SIGNS OF BRACHIAL PALSY   Extension of the forearm in retained, the biceps reflex is absent, and the Moro reflex is absent on the affected side. On examination the arm which lies limply close to the body and does not come around when stimulated for Moro reflex is a key sign.

DIFFERENTIAL DIAGNOSIS   Cerebral injury, dislocation, epiphyseal separation of the humerus, fracture of the arm or clavicle, and septic arthritis of the shoulder must be ruled out.

Management The arm and joints are put through full range of motion several times daily. Referral may be made to a physiotherapist or the parent is taught to mimic the actions of the other arm as a model.

COUNSELING   The nurse practitioner supports the parents by providing explanations sufficient to their understanding of the problem, by assisting them to reach the orthopedist as needed, by making sure that the exercises are performed, and by requesting the aid of the public health nurse when necessary. Parents need to understand that this child is to be played with, held, and cuddled. Parents also need to be reassured that it is not their fault or the result of "poor performance" during labor and delivery.

FRACTURE OF THE CLAVICLE

Assessment Fracture of the clavicle occurs during a difficult delivery of the shoulders. The clavicle is fractured more frequently than any other bone.

CLINICAL SIGNS Signs of a fractured clavicle are the following:

1. Infant fails to move the affected side
2. Crepitus may be elicited
3. The Moro reflex is absent
4. Spasm of the sternocleidomastoid muscle is present
5. Callus forms within a week and may be the first observed clinical sign presenting as a mass on the affected side
6. Diagnosis is confirmed by X-ray film

Management Treatment, if any, may be immobilization of the arm and shoulder of the affected side. Parental support is given with explanation of the cause, callus formation, treatment, and prognosis. Parents need to understand that this child is to be played with, held, and cuddled. See this chapter, Brachial Palsy.

FRACTURES OF OTHER LONG BONES

Assessment These bones include the humerus, femur, forearm, or leg.

CLINICAL SIGNS Signs of fractures are as follows:

1. Spontaneous movements of the affected limb ("pseudoparalysis") are usually absent
2. The Moro reflex is absent in the involved extremity
3. Callus may be felt as a mass
4. Associated nerve damage may be present
5. Diagnosis is confirmed by X-ray

Management Treatment may vary:

1. *Humerus.* Strapping arm to side or chest, or application of a spica cast
2. *Femur.* Application of Bryant's traction or Buck's extension
3. *Forearm or leg.* Application of splints

COUNSELING Parents need support with explanations of cause, callus formation, treatment, and prognosis. They need to understand that this child is to be played with, held, and cuddled. See this chapter, Brachial Palsy.

FOLLOW-UP At subsequent health visits the nurse practitioner can inspect the child for cleanliness, abrasions of the skin due to appliances, and inspect the splints or straps for tightness or sharp edges. Reassurance and added support are given the parents at each visit.

TORTICOLLIS

Assessment Congenital muscular torticollis is unilateral contracture of the sternocleidomastoid muscle. It is an asymmetrical deformity of the head and neck, in which the head is tilted toward the side with the shortened muscle and the chin rotated toward the opposite side. Torticollis means "twisted neck." "Wryneck," a lay term, is used to describe torticollis arising from any cause. The condition is more common in girls than in boys. The majority resolve spontaneously within the first year of life.

ETIOLOGY The immediate cause of the deformity is fibrosis within the sternocleidomastoid muscle in which there is subsequent contracture and shortening. The question is now being raised whether breech presentation is a predisposing factor.

CLINICAL SIGNS Signs of torticollis are as follows:

1. Firm swelling (mass) 1 to 2 cm in diameter is present in the midportion of the sternocleidomastoid muscle.
2. The child tilts head toward the affected side and rotates it toward the opposite shoulder.
3. Possible facial deformity is present with the affected side smaller.

Management Correction can be obtained by persistent stretching in the opposite direction. Parents are advised to position the baby in the crib with the head turned away from light (window). The infant will attempt to turn toward the light thereby stretching and exercising the neck muscles.

COUNSELING See this chapter, Brachial Palsy.

Congenital Orthopedic Deformities

CONGENITAL HIP DISLOCATION (CHD)

Assessment Congenital hip dislocation or subluxation is complete or partial displacement of the femoral head out of the acetabulum. The basic abnormality is hip dislocation. Secondary to the dislocation, representing a recovery stage, is hip dysplasia or acetabulum dysplasia.

ETIOLOGY CHD is not related to trauma or to other musculoskeletal disease. The potential for dislocation exists at birth. It is a multifactorially determined trait that becomes manifest under the influence of certain environmental factors. Among the genes involved are those which tend to produce ligamentous laxity. Levels of female hormones may be elevated in affected infants.

INCIDENCE The incidence varies greatly with genetic background. Reports of instability of one or both hips range from 1:60 to 1:1,000 live births. There is a strong familial tendency with greater risk in a sibling. There is a higher incidence in firstborns, breech deliveries, and in girls.

SIGNS OF CHD IN INFANCY Primary signs include dislocation of the femoral head by the examiner (Barlow's maneuver) and reduction of the femur by the examiner (Ortolani's maneuver). See this section, Screening for CHD. These maneuvers are performed to demonstrate the instability of the joint and are best performed in the nursery or in the first week when the infant is more "floppy." After this period contracture of the muscle begins to take place.

Secondary signs are better noted after the first week, and are:

1. Limitation of full abduction of the hip. See this section, Screening for CHD.
2. Apparent shortening of the femur. See this section, Screening for CHD.
3. Asymmetry of thigh, labial, and inguinal creases. These signs are insignificant if occurring alone. Occasional inguinal or labial creases and 33 percent of thigh creases are normal.
4. Prominent trochanter on the affected side.
5. Hollow over the acetabulum. This may be felt with the thumb in the groin of the affected side.

6. Diagnosis by X-ray film in the neonatal period may or may not be reliable as the femur may slip in or out with maneuvering.

SIGNS OF CHD IN THE OLDER CHILD These signs include the following:

1. Limitation of abduction with obvious adductor contracture.
2. Apparent short leg.
3. Delayed walking.
4. Limp with waddling gait. Gait is flat-footed with the knee on the normal side slightly bent.
5. Positive Trendelenburg sign. See this section, Screening for CHD.
6. Diagnosis is confirmed by X-ray film.

SIGNS OF BILATERAL CHD IN THE OLDER CHILD These include the following:

1. Marked lordosis.
2. Prominent abdomen.
3. Very prominent buttocks, "cute little wiggle or bottom."
4. Bilateral prominent trochanters.
5. Very wide perineum and stance.
6. Limited abduction bilaterally.
7. Diagnosis is confirmed by X-ray film.

SCREENING FOR CHD There are several signs that need careful screening. Such screening is accomplished by the various maneuvers described below.

Dislocation of the Femoral Head (Barlow's Maneuver) With one hand grasping the symphysis in front and the sacrum in back, lateral pressure is applied to the medial thigh with the thumb of the other hand while longitudinal pressure is applied with the palm to the knee on the side being examined. The hip, which has been flexed 90° is then abducted. A positive sign is a sensation of abnormal movement, indicating dislocation of the femoral head from the acetabulum. The hands are reversed for examining the other hip.

Reduction of the Femur (Ortolani's Maneuver) After provocation of a dislocation by Barlow's maneuver, the hip should be abducted to about 80° while the proximal femur is lifted anteriorly with the fingers placed along the lateral thigh. A positive sign is a sensation of a jerk or snap with reduction into the socket. A click is not necessarily heard and a click heard without a sensation of abnormal motion is probably not significant.

Limitation of Full Abduction of the Hip With the child flat on the back, the hips are abducted one at a time, then together. A phase of limited abduction is normal for 20 percent of children (Sharrard, 1979, p. 336). Many black children have tight adductor tendons, but the incidence of CHD in black children is low (Williams, 1975) to virtually nonexistent (Specht, 1974). Assessment is as follows:

1. Normal limits of hip abduction are as follows:

   Some children with comfort   70°–80°
   Most children   60°
   Some children   <60°

2. "Gray" area of limits of hip abduction is 40°–60°. Assessment should include whether or not it is bilateral, the state of relaxation of the child, and whether or not it is consistently present on repeated examinations.
3. Suspicious (abnormal) limits are in the range of 20°–40°.
4. Positive sign for CHD is limitation of abduction in the range of 0°–20°. See Figure 23-5.

Apparent Shortening of the Femur This is assessed using the following maneuvers:

1. Allis' sign. With the child lying on the back with pelvis flat and both knees flexed and feet planted firmly, the knees are observed. If a knee projects further anteriorly, the femur is longer; if a knee is higher than the other, the tibia is longer.
2. With the child lying on the back both legs are extended out straight with pressure on the knees. The heels are matched together and observed for equal or unequal length.
3. Trendelenburg sign. With the child standing on one leg, the pelvis is observed. When the child stands on the abnormal leg, the pelvis drops on the normal side (the gluteal fold lowers). Observe dimples overlying the posterior superior iliac spine for rise or fall. See Figure 23-6.

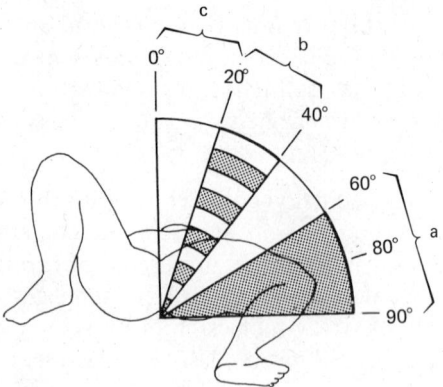

Figure 23-5 Degrees of abduction of the hip: (*a*) normal limits, (*b*) abnormal (suspicious) limits, (*c*) positive sign for CHD. (Reprinted and adapted with permission from M. O. Tachdjian, *Pediatric Orthopedics*, Vol. 1, Philadelphia: W. B. Saunders, 1972. P. 136.)

PROGNOSIS OF CHD This is dependent on the age of the child when diagnosed and treated as follows:

1. If treated in first 6 months, there is a good chance of complete recovery.
2. If treated at 6 months to 1 year, there is variation in the prognosis. The child may or may not have a normal hip.
3. If treated after walking age, the child will continue to have problems.

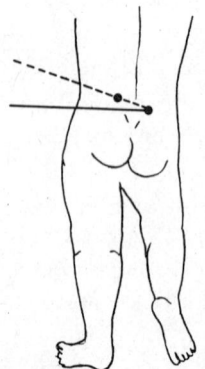

Figure 23-6 Positive Trendelenburg sign. (Reprinted and adapted with permission from J. D. Lowell, et al., "Congenital Hip Dysplasia," *Clin Pediatr* 3:279–287, May 1964. P. 282.)

Management In infancy early identification and referral are the most important aspects of management.

REFERRAL Immediate referral is made upon finding positive signs. Intervention may be necessary to assure that child is seen by the orthopedist within 24 hours. Positive findings that require referral are as follows:

1. Positive primary signs (dislocation and reduction of femur, Barlow's and Ortolani's maneuvers).
2. Several secondary signs. These include limitation of abduction, apparent shortening of the femur, unequal gluteal and labial folds, and higher trochanter.
3. Apparent shortening of the femur. This is referrable with or without other findings.
4. Limited abduction of the hip, 20° or less.

TREATMENT Initial treatment consists of reducing the hip(s), proving it is reduced by X-ray, and maintaining reduction through some means of abduction as follows:

1. Double or triple diapering may be advised if borderline subluxation is suspected. To keep down the cost factor, the parent is taught to put one diaper on with plastic material or pants between it and the extra diapers. The diapers are folded into rectangles and doubled over in front.
2. A Frejka splint is used for the infant under 3 months. This is a square pillow filled with kapok and held in place by a "romperlike" garment. It maintains the thighs in flexion, abduction, and external rotation but allows for some movement. The splint must be removed and reapplied after each diaper change. Plastic pants may be worn to protect the splint. A second cover is needed for laundering purposes. The splint may be worn 3 to 10 months until a normally developed hip joint is shown on X-ray film.
3. Abduction braces may be used if the hip is not stable after treatment with a splint.
4. Traction is usually necessary to stretch the leg muscles and tendons and place the femoral head in a better position for reduction before application of a cast. This is usually necessary in the treatment of a child over 3 months of age.

5. A spica cast is used following traction. The legs are put in flexion and abduction. Because of rapidity of growth at this age several cast changes are invariably required.
6. Surgery may be necessary in those hips that do not reduce through gentle manipulation and traction or in those that do not stay reduced.

ROLE OF THE NURSE PRACTITIONER   Early detection and fast referral are of the utmost importance. From discovery of the first positive sign, support and reassurance are given to the parents. This should be accomplished by explaining the cause, treatment, and prognosis of CHD, and by keeping in close contact with the family through the period of further diagnostic measures and treatment. If possible the nurse practitioner should be present when the child visits the orthopedist or is hospitalized. The parents are given an opportunity to express their feelings. Close relationship with the orthopedist is maintained regarding treatment and progress.

FOLLOW-UP   At subsequent health visits the nurse practitioner can do the following:

1. Remove the splint or harness to inspect the skin for cleanliness, excoriation, abrasion, or pressure sores.
2. Inspect the cast for cleanliness, wetness, tightness, or sharp edges. See this chapter, Care of the Cast.
3. Explain the need for the child to be played with, held, and cuddled. Suggest different methods for sitting in the cast to eat and to play.
4. Request earlier follow-up appointment with the orthopedist at own discretion.
5. Request visits to family from the public health nurse as necessary.

METATARSUS ADDUCTUS (VARUS)

Assessment   In metatarsus adductus the forefoot is turned in or adducted, the longitudinal arch may be exceptionally high, and the space between the first and second toes may be wider than normal. The origin is usually congenital. This toeing-in (pigeon-toe) occurs as a result of *rigidity* and *tightness* of the muscles and ligaments of the forefoot. It is commonly associated with tibial torsion. It is most

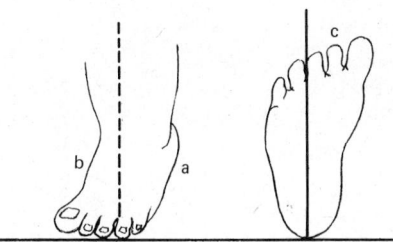

Figure 23-7 Signs of metatarsus adductus: (*a*) convex lateral border of foot, (*b*) concave medial border of foot with possible wrinkling, (*c*) space may exist between the large toe and second toe, (*d*) midline bisects third and fourth toes.

common in a mild form, and many straighten spontaneously with growth.

CLINICAL SIGNS Signs of metatarsus adductus are described in Figure 23-7. In addition the forefoot does not move past neutral position. See Figure 23-3.

SCREENING FOR METATARSUS ADDUCTUS The examination consists of testing the foot for flexibility and eliciting tonic foot reflexes, especially eversion reflex. See this chapter, Examination for Flexibility of Foot and Ankle.

Management When the condition is flexible, it should be observed for spontaneous resolution which often occurs in the first few weeks or months of life. Reversing shoes is not recommended since it merely pushes the toes over and may start a new foot problem. In the interim before the child reaches the orthopedist, the parent can be instructed to elicit the eversion reflex as a passive stretching exercise at each diaper change.

REFERRAL AND TREATMENT OF RIGID METATARSUS ADDUCTUS Referral is made as soon as possible when rigidity and tightness prevent the foot from moving past the neutral position. Full correction should be achieved either spontaneously or by casting before 12 months of age. Following cast immobilization reverse-last shoes may be ordered (Staheli and Giffin, 1980).

COUNSELING Much of the outcome of treatment depends on the parents' understanding. The nurse practitioner can keep close contact with the orthopedist to better understand and explain the treatment. Explanation should be given that the child needs to be played with, held and cuddled.

FOLLOW-UP On subsequent health visits:

• Inspect the skin for cleanliness or the presence of pressure sores.
• Review care of the skin, care of the cast and correct method of diapering.
• Reiterate the child's need for normal activities and being held.

PES PLANUS (FLAT FEET)

Assessment In pes planus the longitudinal arch of the foot appears flat on the floor when the child is weight bearing. Nearly all infants and the majority of young children exhibit pseudo flat feet. Flat feet are described as follows:

1. *Pseudo flat feet.* The plantar fat pad is normal until ages 2 to 3 years. The feet are flexible and exhibit hypermobility of the joint and an anatomic low arch. Pseudo flat feet are strongly familial.
2. *Rigid flat feet.* Extremely uncommon, this foot presents with tightness of the heel cord or *tarsal coalition* (a cartilaginous fibrous or bony connection between various bones). It is congenital but not visualized at birth.

SCREENING FOR PES PLANUS The procedure is as follows:

1. Observe the feet in weighted and unweighted positions.
2. Stand the child on his toes. In flexible flat foot the arch disappears with weight bearing. It reappears when the child stands on his toes. See Figure 23-8.
3. Elicit dorsal and plantar flexion to rule out tight heel cord.
4. Elicit eversion and inversion flexion to rule out tarsal coalition. For range of motions of ankles see this chapter, Examination for Flexibility of Foot and Ankle.

Management Referral is indicated for rigid flat feet. Shoe wedges, special heels, and shoe inserts are not recommended for hyper-

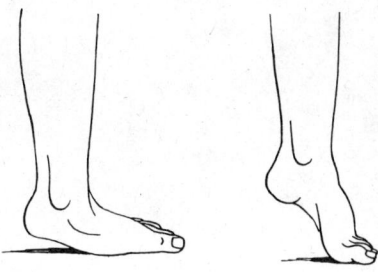

Figure 23-8 Pseudo flat feet. The flat arch disappears with child on toes. (Reproduced with permission from R. J. Ducroquet et al., *La Marche et les Boîteries*, Paris: Masson, 1965; English translation: J. B. Lippincott, 1968.)

mobile flat feet. Exercises are not necessary as this is not a muscular problem.

TOE-WALKING

Assessment Some children walk normally on their toes. The most common cause of toe-walking is spastic cerebral palsy. Less common causes of toe-walking are congenital shortening of the Achilles tendon, dystonia musculorum deformans, early muscular dystrophy and infantile autism.

Management Muscular, reflex, and neurologic tests are performed to rule out abnormalities.

Developmental Variants

Children can be afflicted with a variety of different congenital and developmental abnormalities of the legs, feet, and toes. Unborn babies lie cramped in utero. As a result, for the first week or two, a leg or foot may present in a distorted asymmetric position. A minimal degree of inversion or eversion is not significant. Joint laxity or hypermobility and torsional (twisting) forces on the limb are responsible for a number of variants seen in young children.

FEMORAL ANTEVERSION

Assessment This is a relatively common cause of intoeing in the child between 3 and 7 years of age. It is often caused by TV squat position assumed by children, see Figure 23-9. Occasionally the condition is familial and a second tortional deformity may be present. Increased femoral anteversion may be compensated by external tibial torsion during mid and late childhood. In others it is

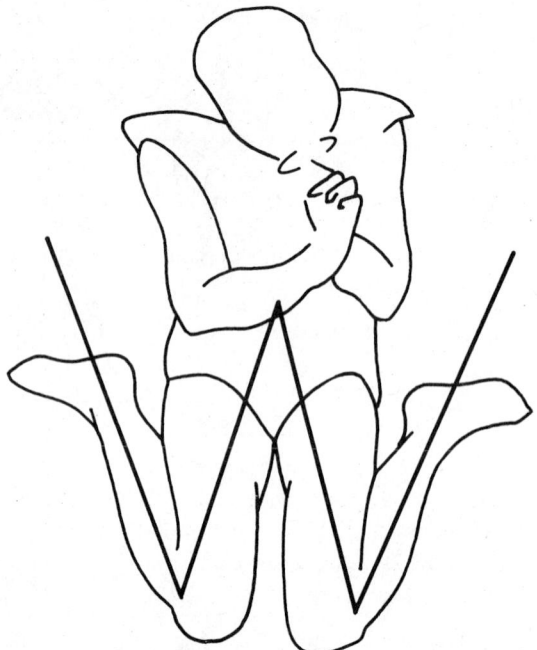

Figure 23-9 Reverse tailor, "TV squat," or "W" sitting position. (Reprinted with permission of the publisher of *Pediatric Nursing*, Vol. 5, No. 4, July/August 1979.)

aggravated by internal tibial torsion resulting in significant intoeing. Most commonly femoral anteversion is bilateral and symmetrical and is more often seen in girls. Normally, in early infancy external rotation and anteversion are at their peak due to intrauterine positioning.

SCREENING FOR INCREASED FEMORAL ANTEVERSION Examine the legs for internal and external hip rotation (see Figs. 23-10a and 23-10b). Increased internal rotation is evidence of increased femoral anteversion. The deformity is considered mild in values between 70° and 80°, moderate between 80° and 85°, severe if greater than 85°. Normally in infancy external rotation is close to 90°, decreasing with advancing age.

Management Referral is made if the deformity is severe or greater than 85° after the child has been observed at least 1 year to determine whether the deformity is improving.

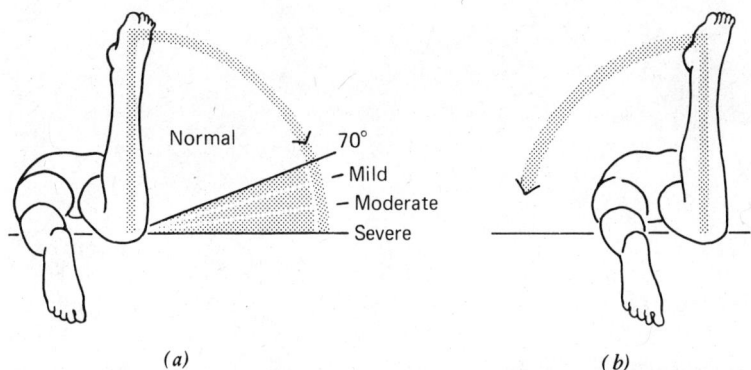

(a)   *(b)*

Figure 23-10 *(a)* Internal hip rotation, *(b)* external hip rotation. Internal rotation is normally less than 70°. The sum of internal and external rotation is roughly 100°; therefore, when internal rotation is increased, external rotation is correspondingly less. (Reprinted with permission from L. Staheli, "Tortional Deformity," *Pediatr Clin North Am 23*:799–812, November 1977. P. 805.)

TREATMENT This consists of a major surgical procedure that is justified only if the deformity is severe.

GENU VALGUM (KNOCK-KNEES)

Assessment Knock-knees are described as a more than 10° to 15° deviant axis of the thighs and calves. "Physiologic" knock-knees are considered to be familial, developmental, and are associated with pronated feet, ligamentous relaxation, and overweight. Severe genu valgum (12 inches or more between the malleoli with femoral condyles touching) may be attributed to rickets or epiphyseal injury. Knock-knees are considered normal from ages 2 to 6 while physiologic genu varum is correcting itself and overcompensation is occurring.

SCREENING FOR GENU VALGUM The procedure is as follows:

1. Elicit range of motion of legs and flexibility of ankles. See this chapter, Physical Examination.
2. With the child standing observe axis of thighs and calves. Normally they are parallel with a 10° to 15° deviance. See Figure 23-11.
3. From the front and back observe the space between the knees. Normally this is approximately 1½ inches.

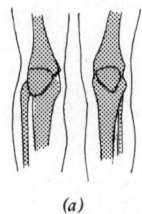 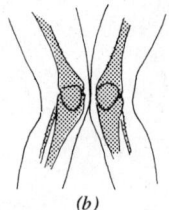 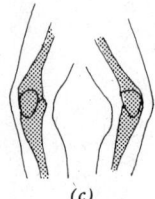

(a)   (b)   (c)

Figure 23-11 Axis of thigh and calf: (*a*) normal axis, (*b*) deviant axis exhibiting knock-knees (genu valgum), (*c*) deviant axis exhibiting bow-legs (genu varum). (Reproduced with permission from R. J. Ducroquet et al., *La Marche et les Boîteries,* Paris: Masson, 1965; English translation: J. B. Lippincott, 1968.)

4. From the front and back observe the space between the ankles. Normally the space between the medial malleoli at the heels is approximately 2 inches.

Management Referral is made if the knees are touching and the ankles are widespread with a corresponding axis deviation of thigh and calf of more than 10° to 15°. Knock-knees in children under the age of seven may be safely ignored unless it is excessive (angle mentioned above), asymmetric, or accompanied by shortened stature. Otherwise normal footwear is appropriate.

GENU VARUM (BOWLEGS)

Assessment Genu varum is due to a deviant axis of the thighs and calves. See Figure 23-11. Bowlegs are defined as follows:

1. *"Physiologic" bowlegs.* This condition often occurs with internal tibial torsion and normal genu valgum. It is congenital, familial, or postural in origin. It is common and considered normal until the ages of 2 or 3 with spontaneous correction occurring with growth.
2. *"Pathologic" bowlegs.* This condition is rare and may be due to rickets, epiphyseal injury, achondroplasia, Morquio's disease, or Blount's disease.

SCREENING FOR BOWLEGS The same procedure is followed as for knock-knees. See this chapter, Screening for Genu Valgum.

Management Referral is made if the knees are widely spaced and the axis deviation of thigh and calf is more than 10° to 15°. See this chapter, Internal Tibial Torsion. Bow legs that are unilateral or asymmetric beyond the age of 2 years, particularly in black infants, may represent pathological conditions that require further investigations (McDade 1977, p. 831). The risks of not treating are degenerative arthritis and bunions in later life.

TREATMENT This varies with the consulting physician. Children with a strong familial pattern are generally treated with a Denis-Brown splint.

FOLLOW-UP See this chapter, Internal Tibial Torsion.

INTERNAL TIBIAL TORSION

Assessment Internal tibial torsion is usually accompanied by metatarsus adductus and may occur as a result of the following:

1. Twisting or torsion of the tibia due to lying in "position of comfort" in utero with relaxed tendons. It may continue as a distorted asymmetric position for a few weeks after delivery.
2. External forces applied to the tibia such as sleeping or sitting in position with haunches up, feet turned in. If these forces are removed, there is a natural tendency for the condition to improve. If the child continues these postural habits, then the deformity may persist.

SCREENING FOR INTERNAL TIBIAL TORSION The procedure is as follows:

1. Examine the legs for range of motion and flexibility of the ankle. Elicit the tonic foot reflexes. See this chapter, Physical Examination.
2. Hold the knee firmly with the foot in the neutral position. Observe the medial and lateral malleoli. See Figure 23-12. The normal angle between them is approximately 15° to 20°.

Management Referral is made if the angle between the malleoli is much less than 15° to 20°, and if there are positive findings for metatarsus adductus. See this chapter, Metatarsus Adductus.

TREATMENT This varies with the consulting physician and may include treatment with a night splint. The nurse practitioner may recommend:

1. Changing sleeping position of the infant from supine to prone or onto side.

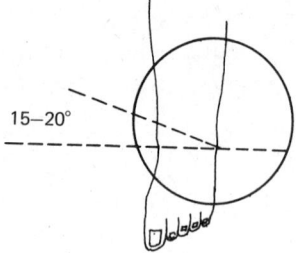

Figure 23-12 Normal angle between medial and lateral malleolus.

2. Changing position of the young child who sits on feet (reverse "tailor" or "TV squat," see Fig. 23-9) to a "yoga" position.
3. Cutting holes in the heels of infant's shoes and tying them together at night. This will change the tortional force. During the day regular shoes are worn.

   FOLLOW-UP   If a Denis-Brown splint is used in treatment, it may be removed to inspect for cleanliness, abrasions, or evidence of tight straps or shoes. If evidence is present, consult with the orthopedist for changing the angle of the splint.

OVERRIDING TOES

Assessment   In infancy this is usually a hereditary problem. In the older child it may occur as the result of ill-fitted shoes. See this chapter, Shoes.

Management   It may be corrected by splinting the overriding toe to an adjoining toe.

PRONATION

Assessment   Pronation is a common postural disturbancé evidenced by flattened or depressed position of the longitudinal arch. It presents as "walking on the inside of the foot" and is usually familial. Pronation may be seen in the normal child under age 3, and with overweight children.

   SCREENING FOR PRONATION   This is determined by eliciting range of motion of feet and ankles and observing for tight heel cords. From the back observe child walking. Normally ankles are directly over heels. Shoes may be observed for wear on the inner aspects.

Management   Referral is made if the child is over age 3, is overweight, or if pronation is associated with other foot problems such as genu valgum.

TREATMENT   This may include high-top shoes, with a hard sole and an inner heel wedge with a longitudinal arch. If associated with tight heel cord, exercise may be necessary.

TOEING-IN

Assessment   Toeing-in may be caused by any of several factors:

1. *Metatarsus adductus.* If not found at an earlier age, it presents when child first starts to walk. This common problem is discussed fully in this chapter, Metatarsus Adductus.
2. *Internal tibial torsion.* See this chapter, Internal Tibial Torsion.
3. *Increased femoral anteversion.* A combination of mild metatarsus adductus and internal tibial torsion together with increased femoral anteversion may produce a severe toeing-in. See this chapter, Femoral Anteversion.

SCREENING FOR TOEING-IN   See this chapter, Metatarsus Adductus, Internal Tibial Torsion, and Femoral Anteversion.

Management   See this chapter, Metatarsus Adductus, Internal Tibial Torsion and Femoral Anteversion. In addition attention is given to sitting and sleeping positions. The child needs to be taught the "yoga" position for sitting on the floor. An infant should sleep on back or sides.

Spinal Problems of Children

KYPHOSIS

Assessment   Kyphosis is an exaggerated convex curve in the thoracic region of the spine. It represents a developmental lesion and may cause backache and pain. The most common form is "postural." Children assume bizarre sitting and standing attitudes which aggravate existent kyphosis. It is especially common in the adolescent female. It may be secondary to congenital deformity such as scoliosis, tumor, trauma, infection, decompressive laminectomy, the chondrodystrophies, or cretinism and achondroplasia.

Management   Referral of postural kyphosis and lordosis is made to a physiotherapist who is experienced with the emotional problems of growing up. Postural sports are recommended, weight lifting, dancing or swimming. Success depends on motivation and on the parent–child relationship. See this chapter Scoliosis, Psychological Aspects of Scoliosis. If it is obvious that the deformity is increasing (even slightly), referral is made to the orthopedist. Deformities that are minimal and mobile can be treated with Milwaukee braces. Congenital kyphosis needs early surgical intervention. Parents need help with understanding the cause and treatment.

LORDOSIS

Assessment   Lordosis is an exaggerated concave curve in the lumbar region of the spine almost always occurring in combination with postural kyphosis. Severe lordosis may cause a limp or pain. The lumbar lordosis is largely attributable to the failure of hip flexors to stretch and elongate. Normally children with protuberant abdomens have a slight degree of lumbar lordosis, and it is observed normally more in black children.

Management   Referral is made if the lordosis causes a limp and/or pain. See above, Kyphosis.

SCOLIOSIS

Assessment   Scoliosis is described as an S-shaped lateral curvature of the spine with rotation of the vertebral bodies. There are two basic classifications:

1. *Structural scoliosis.* This means a curve that is less flexible and not usually completely or nearly completely corrected by postural changes (such as with bending X-ray films). There are three types of structural scoliosis:

   • *Congenital scoliosis.* These curves include hemivertebral, vertebral failure of formation, failure of segmentation, and extra ribs. These curves often have a poorer prognosis.

   • *Paralytic scoliosis.* Mainly associated with polio, it is now seen with other neuromuscular disorders. These children usually have secondary lung dysfunction problems. This type tends to become worse after bone maturity.

- *Idiopathic scoliosis.* This is the most common variety. It has a high familial history. Once thought to be a disease of adolescence, it is now also found at the 4 to 9-year-old level.

2. *Functional or nonstructural scoliosis.* There is no specific structural change. It may be due to shortening of one leg as a result of an old fracture, to asymmetrical growth of the legs, to flexion fractures about the hip, knee, ankle, or foot, to poor posture, or to avoidance of pain.

INCIDENCE Scoliosis occurs in 5 to 10 percent of the general population; of this 15 percent occurs in the 10-year-old to adult group. It is more frequent in girls than in boys with a large percentage of occurrence in siblings.

SCREENING FOR SCOLIOSIS Early detection and early treatment are necessary to prevent secondary lung pathology and future back ailments. Pain is not a presenting symptom. The procedure for examination is as follows:

1. Dressed in underwear have the child bend in a 50 percent forward flexing position, with shoulders drooping forward, and arms and head dangling. Observe the child from above the head. Inspect for any lateral curvature of the spine and for any prominence or projection of the rib cage which appears only on one side. This examination should start at the earliest age possible as projection of the rib cage is detectable before the spine curvature is visible. See Figure 23-13.
2. With the child standing erect and with weight equal on both feet observe for the following:

   - Difference in levels of shoulders, scapulas, and hips
   - Prominence of either scapula or hip
   - Differences in the size of the spaces between the arms and the trunk
   - A curve in the vertebral spinous process alignment. If given permission, the examiner may mark each process with a pen to aid in detection.

Common factors may delay detection: (1) failure of healthy-looking youngsters of preadolescent age to have yearly physical examinations, (2) the process of curvature is slow and may not be

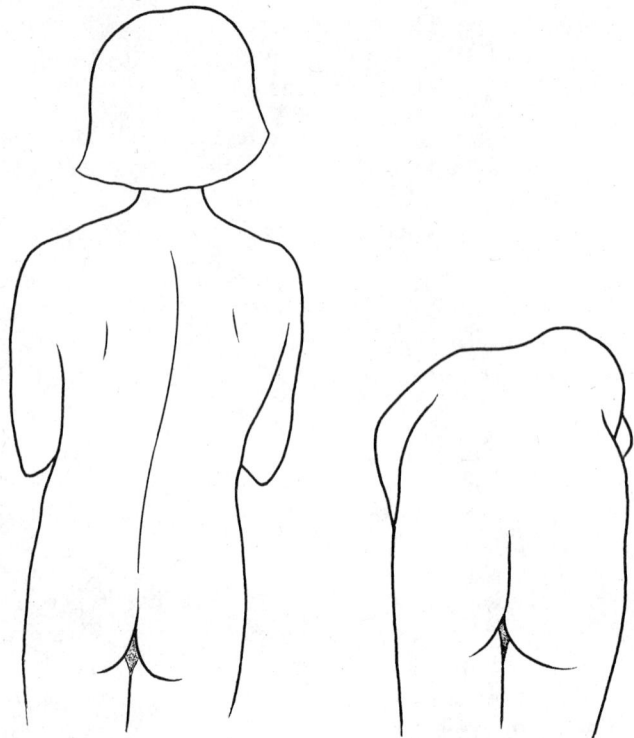

Figure 23-13 Examination for scoliosis. Structural scoliosis is best demonstrated observing the child bending over. (Reprinted with permission from *Report of the Third Ross Roundtable on Critical Approaches to Common Pediatric Problems,* in collaboration with the Ambulatory Pediatric Association, 1972.)

noticed by child or family, and (3) children have fears of being different from their peers and do not report a change. A common observation by parents is the need to alter hems in dresses or to alter sleeve length.

Management Referral is made immediately on detection of a curve or an increased muscle mass in the posterior thoracic region.

TREATMENT The aim of treatment is to prevent increasing deformity. Treatment includes the following:

1. The Milwaukee brace, in general, is prescribed for structural curves that show some mobility or correction with bending in a child who hasn't reached maturity and whose curve is severe.
2. Traction and casting before surgery may be helpful.
3. Surgery may be indicated if the curve continues to progress.

ROLE OF THE NURSE PRACTITIONER This includes the following:

1. Explaining the problem and the need for immediate referral and treatment. The speed of the child's growth and development causes the problem to worsen rapidly.
2. Attending the child's first referral visit for one's own understanding of the process of treatment and for support to the child and family.
3. Preparing the child and parents for hospitalization by arranging a visit to the hospital so procedures of treatment can be explained and the child can be shown some of the equipment to be used.
4. Visiting the child in the hospital and maintaining a close relationship with ward personnel and physician.
5. Contacting the public health nurse as necessary for home care.
6. Being available at all times to the family for support and information.
7. Being aware of the psychologic aspects of scoliosis treatment and providing guidance to the family in this area.
8. Offering an opportunity to teenagers to discuss their feelings.

FOLLOW-UP At follow-up visits the following are included:

1. The braces and harness are observed for sharp edges or tightness; the skin is examined for pressure sores.
2. For more comfort in braces the child is advised to wear a T-shirt or undershirt under the brace to keep leather from chafing the skin. Bras may be worn under the T-shirt. Underpants may be worn over the brace since elastic and wrinkles cause pressure sores.

PSYCHOLOGIC ASPECTS OF SCOLIOSIS Because of the disabling effects of scoliosis and the need for long-term treatment these youngsters and their families face multiple problems of adjustment.

Problems for the Children

1. Lowering of self-esteem as they see themselves as "different"
2. Handling feelings of hostility and anger over the need for treatment, curiosity of strangers, and invasion of privacy
3. Trying to understand fully the problem and treatment
4. Worrying about acceptance by peers and friends, and concern about attractiveness to the opposite sex
5. Wondering about their physical, occupational, and sexual future
6. Worrying about clothes, and participation in sports and schoolwork

Problems for the Parents

1. Guilt for not detecting the problem sooner
2. Concern about inflicting unnecessary pain and treatment on the child
3. Necessity to face the child's hostility and anger
4. Concern about siblings and their need for attention and consideration
5. Concern about expenses
6. Need to express their own feelings

Some Helpful Suggestions   Independence for the child should be fostered by the parents and by health care personnel. Hospital, clinic, and medical office personnel should show friendly support and interest in child's progress. Improvement of self-image may occur if the child is given an opportunity to master a new hobby or sport or to go to camp for the summer.

LIMPS

Assessment   The cause of a limp may be an organic problem or a simple problem such as a shoe which is ill-fitting, abnormally worn, or has a wrinkled lining. Socks, also, should be investigated for wrinkles or holes. A limp is usually associated with accompanying pain which may be referred to the knee or leg.

CAUSES OF LIMPS IN CHILDREN

1. 1 to 2 years: Congenital dislocation of hip, cerebral palsy
2. 2 to 5 years: Monarticular synovitis, muscular dystrophy

3. 5 to 12 years: Legg-Perthe's disease
4. 12 to 15 years: Slipped femoral epiphysis
5. All age groups: Osteomyelitis, trauma, neurologic disorders (polio and peroneal muscular atrophy), spinal deformity, rheumatoid arthritis, tumors, and functional disorders.

SCREENING FOR LIMPS

1. Examination of posture and gait. See this chapter, Physical Examination.
2. Observation of general coordination both walking and running
3. Observation of method of arising from the supine to the erect position
4. Thorough neurologic assessment. See Chapter 24, Physical Examination.
5. Inspection of the spine, pelvis, and joints of the lower extremities
6. Measurement of leg length and inspection of shoes for wear
7. Test for Trendelenburg sign for hip flexion deformity. See this chapter, Screening for CHD.

COMMON ABNORMAL GAITS

1. *Spastic gait.* This gait is associated with hemiplegia or diplegia of cerebral palsy. The spastic hemiplegic tends to walk on the toe of the affected leg and the spastic diplegic tends to scissor. See Chapter 24, Cerebral Palsy.
2. *Trendelenburg or "waddle" gait.* This is a short leg limp associated with a pelvic tilt in standing and bending of the normal knee in walking.
3. *Drop-foot gait.* This gait is high-stepping with the toes clearing the floor (seldom seen today with the disappearance of poliomyelitis).
4. *Antalgic gait.* This gait may represent an attempt to avoid a painful lesion in the lower extremity, so the child tends to get off that leg as quickly as possible in what is virtually a hop.
5. *Bizarre gaits.* These may occur in a normal child who is unconsciously mimicking an abnormal gait in a member of the family or friend.

Management   Except for a minor limp due to a shoe problem the diagnosis and treatment of a limp is managed collaboratively with a physician.

Resource Information

A helpful publication is:
Cast Care Booklet, Children's Rehabilitation Center, University of Virginia Hospital, Route 250 West, Charlottesville, VA 22903.

References

Alexander, M. M. and M. S. Brown. *Pediatric History Taking and Physical Diagnosis for Nurses.* New York: McGraw-Hill, 1979.

Asher, M. "Orthopedic Screening," *Pediatr Clin North Am 24*:713–721, November 1977.

Bunch, W. H. "Common Deformities of the Lower Limb." *Pediatr Nurs 5*:18–22, July/August 1979.

Chung, S. "Diseases of the Developing Hip Joint." *Pediatr Clin North Am 24*:857–870, November 1977.

Ducroquet, R. J., et al. *Walking and Limping.* Philadelphia: J. B. Lippincott, 1968.

Dunn, B. H. "Common Orthopedic Problems of Children." *Pediatr Nurs 1*:7–10, November/December 1975.

Furlong, G. P. and G. W. Lawn. "Evaluation of Foot Deformities in the Newborn." *GP 31*:89–97, November 1965.

Hensinger, R. "Limp." *Pediatr Clin North Am 24*:799–812, November 1977.

Hill, R. M. and L. S. Romm. "Screening for Scoliosis in Adolescents." *Am J Maternal Child Nursing 2*:156–159, May/June 1977.

Hoppenfield, S. *Physical Examination of the Spine and Extremities.* East Norwalk, CT: Appleton-Century-Crofts, 1976.

"Joint Motion: Method of Measuring and Recording." Chicago: American Academy of Orthopaedic Surgeons, 1965.

Klein, H. "Back Deformities." *Pediatr Clin North Am 24*:871–880, November 1977.

Lane, P. "A Mother's Confession—Home Care of a Toddler in a Spica Cast: What It's Really Like." *Am J Nurs 71*:2141–2143, November 1971.

Larson, C. B. and M. Gould. *Orthopedic Nursing.* 8th ed. St. Louis: C. V. Mosby, 1974.

Lowell, J. D. "Congenital Hip Dysplasia." *Clin Pediatr 3*:279–287, May 1964.

McDade, W. "Bowlegs and Knock Knees." *Pediatr Clin North Am 24*:825–839, November 1977.

Mignogna-Love, S. "Scoliosis." *Nursing '77 7*:50–55, May 1977.

Ponseti, J. V. and J. R. Becker. "Congenital Metatarsus Adductus: The Results of Treatment." *J Bone Joint Surg* 48A:702–711, June 1966.

Salter, R. B. *Textbook of Disorders of the Musculoskeletal System.* Baltimore: Williams & Wilkins, 1970.

Sharrard, W. J. *Paediatric Orthopaedics and Fractures.* Vol. 1, 2nd ed. Oxford: Blackwell Scientific Publications, 1979.

Sherk, H., P. Pasquariello, and W. Walters. "Congenital Dislocation of the Hip." *Clin Pediatr* 20:513–520, August 1981.

Specht, E. "Congenital Dislocation of the Hip." *American Family Physician* 9:88–96, February 1974.

Staheli, L. "Tortional Deformity." *Pediatr Clin North Am* 23:799–812, November 1977.

Staheli, L. and L. Giffin. "Corrective Shoes for Children: A Survey of Current Practices." *Pediatrics* 65:13–17, January 1980.

Tachdjian, M. O. *Pediatric Orthopedics.* Vols. 1 and 2. Philadelphia: W. B. Saunders, 1972.

Vaughan, V. C., R. J. McKay, and R. E. Behrman. *Nelson Textbook of Pediatrics.* 11th ed. Philadelphia: W. B. Saunders, 1979.

Weiss, J., et al. "Purchasing Infant Shoes: Attitude of Parents, Pediatricians and Store Managers." *Pediatrics* 67:718–720, May 1981.

Williams, R. A. *Textbook of Black-Related Diseases.* New York: McGraw-Hill, 1975.

24

The Neuromuscular System

Neuromuscular problems are not uncommon in childhood and encompass a broad range of symptoms and defects. The consequences of central nervous system pathology are also variable. They may be minimal (the child who experiences one simple febrile seizure) or they may involve major and life-long sequelae (the child with cerebral palsy or mental retardation). Early identification of such problems is critical for optimum management.

The nurse practitioner is involved in identifying children with neuromuscular problems and, in the role of primary care provider, is in a position to offer long-term support, education, and guidance to affected families. Because of a strong background in growth and development, the nurse practitioner can work with the child, family, school personnel, and other involved professionals to maintain a focus on those aspects of the child that are normal in order to promote optimum development.

This chapter presents information on the systematic assessment of the neuromuscular system and the management of some common neuromuscular problems. Refer to Chapter 23, The Skeletal System, and Chapter 25, Language and Learning Disabilities for related information.

ASSESSMENT

History

PRESENT CONCERNS

Presenting symptoms include delayed development, feeding problems, head enlargement, muscle weakness, vomiting, abdominal pain, seizures, visual or auditory changes, vertigo, headache, changes in personality or behavior, changes in activity, changes in achievement, pain or paresthesias (numbness, tingling), ataxia, changes in gait, abnormal sphincter function, and abnormal involuntary movements.

Obtain information in accurate chronologic detail beginning at the earliest onset of symptoms and including descriptions of symptoms and associated events as follows:

1. Has the symptom been present since birth?
2. If not, when did it first appear?
3. Did the symptom develop suddenly or slowly?
4. How has the symptom progressed?
5. Are there periods when the child is entirely well?
6. Has development arrested?
7. Has previous attainment of function been lost?
8. In older children, has there been a deterioration in school performance, irritability, or emotional lability?
9. What has been done so far?

BIRTH HISTORY

Obtain information on complications of pregnancy (illness, infections, drugs, irradiation, injuries, bleeding), previous abortions, labor and delivery (duration, presentation, anesthesia, forceps), gestational age, birth weight, Apgar scores, resuscitation, trauma, jaundice, infections, convulsions, muscle tone (stiffness, limpness), and congenital anomalies.

PAST HISTORY

Obtain information on previous illnesses, injuries (especially head trauma), fevers, headache, convulsions, vision and hearing development, motor development, behavior or personality changes, and school performance.

GROWTH AND DEVELOPMENT HISTORY

Obtain information on serial weight, height, and head circumference; developmental milestones, personality development, and behavior. See Chapters 5, 6, and 7, Growth and Development.

FAMILY HISTORY

Obtain information on family members with similar symptoms, neurologic diseases, abnormal gaits, causes of death, "spells," motor or sensory disturbances, mental retardation, inherited disorders, patterns of growth and development, congenital anomalies, and institutionalizations.

Physical Examination

The complete neurologic examination in infancy and childhood includes components of the entire general physical examination as well as the specific elements of the neurologic examination. All the observations made during an encounter with a child contribute to determining the integrity of the nervous system.

SCREENING NEUROLOGIC EXAMINATION

The complete neurologic examination is complex, time consuming, and unnecessary in most instances. The data collected by history and general physical examination indicate whether or not a complete neurologic evaluation is warranted. A reasonable screening neurologic examination is presented in Chapter 1, Child Health Assessment.

COMPONENTS OF THE NEUROLOGIC EXAMINATION

Behavior and Mental Status Assessment begins with a general description of the child's abilities and responsiveness as follows:

1. State of consciousness. Assess alertness by response to commands, name, speech, and pinprick. Note irritability, drowsiness, or lethargy.
2. Orientation. Ask the child to identify self by name, place, and

approximate time of day. Check short-term memory; for example, "What did you have for lunch today?"

3. Affect. Note appropriateness of mood, ability to relate to others, depression, remoteness, flat affect, euphoria, or lability.
4. Intellectual abilities. Depending on age and developmental level assess:

- Expressive speech. Assess the child's spontaneous verbalizations for fluency, vocabulary, and grammar; ability to name objects and colors and to repeat phrases verbatim.
- Receptive speech. Have the child carry out verbal commands.
- Memory. Ask the child to repeat digits or phrases. Ask what was eaten for dinner the preceding night.
- Ability to read. Ask the child to read from graded reading paragraphs. See Chapter 25, Educational Testing.
- Ability to write, to draw, and to copy shapes. Geometric shapes can be copied as follows:

> Circle or cross at 3–4 years
> Square   at 4–5 years
> Triangle   at 5–6 years
> Diamond   at 6–7 years

- Ability to add and subtract.
- In the child under 6 years of age many of these areas can be assessed using the Denver Developmental Screening Test. See Figure 24-1.

Cranial Nerve Function The twelve pairs of cranial nerves innervate muscles of the eyes, face, and swallowing, and carry somatic sensory fibers from the face and from the special sensory organs. They are described as follows:

1. Cranial nerve I (Olfactory nerve)

- *Function:* Determines the sense of smell.
- *Assessment:* Be sure both nasal passages are patent. Have the child close eyes. Occlude each nostril in turn and test the open nostril by presenting a variety of familiar odors (e.g., peppermint, peanut butter, coffee, onions, or oranges). Colds and allergies with nasal congestion can interfere.

2. Cranial nerve II (Optic nerve)

   • *Function:* Transmits visual signals; necessary for vision.
   • *Assessment:* Test for visual acuity and visual fields and perform funduscopic examination. See Chapter 15, The Eye.

3. Cranial nerves III, IV, and VI (Oculomotor, Trochlear, and Abducens nerves)

   • *Function:* Innervate all eye muscles; control constriction and dilation of the pupils and elevation of the eyelids.
   • *Assessment:* Test for extraocular movements (EOMs) by having the child follow a finger with the eyes while it is moved to all quadrants of vision. Eye movements should be conjugate with both eyes fixed on the finger. Note any nystagmus. Check pupillary reaction to light by shining a light at one pupil. Observe constriction of the pupil receiving the light and consensual constriction of the other pupil. Note unequal pupil size. Note ptosis.

4. Cranial nerve V (Trigeminal nerve)

   • *Function:* Conveys sensation, including touch and pain, to the face; innervates the muscles of mastication; contains the sensory component of the corneal reflex.
   • *Assessment:* Test sensory function by applying light touch (cotton wisp), pressure, temperature (test tubes filled with hot and cold water), and pain (pinprick) to the forehead, cheeks, and jaws. Test motor function by having the child bite hard on a tongue blade as an attempt is made to withdraw it. Test the corneal reflex by touching the cornea with a wisp of cotton. Both eyes should close.

5. Cranial nerve VII (Facial nerve)

   • *Function:* Innervates most of the facial muscles, lacrimal gland, and stapedius muscle of the ear and provides the sense of taste to the anterior two thirds of the tongue and sensation to the external auditory canal.
   • *Assessment:* Ask the child to smile, to look at the ceiling, to raise the eyebrows, to show teeth, to squint, to wrinkle the forehead, and to puff out the cheeks. Note strength and symmetry. Note faulty tearing or ringing in the ears. Test taste by using sugar and salt.

1. Try to get child to smile by smiling, talking or waving to him. Do not touch him.
2. When child is playing with toy, pull it away from him. Pass if he resists.
3. Child does not have to be able to tie shoes or button in the back.
4. Move yarn slowly in an arc from one side to the other, about 6" above child's face.
   Pass if eyes follow 90° to midline. (Past midline; 180°)
5. Pass if child grasps rattle when it is touched to the backs or tips of fingers.
6. Pass if child continues to look where yarn disappeared or tries to see where it went. Yarn
   should be dropped quickly from sight from tester's hand without arm movement.
7. Pass if child picks up raisin with any part of thumb and a finger.
8. Pass if child picks up raisin with the ends of thumb and index finger using an over hand
   approach.

9. Pass any en-   10. Which line is longer?   11. Pass any   12. Have child copy
   closed form.   (Not bigger.) Turn   crossing   first. If failed,
   Fail continuous   paper upside down and   lines.   demonstrate
   round motions.   repeat. (3/3 or 5/6)

When giving items 9, 11 and 12, do not name the forms. Do not demonstrate 9 and 11.

13. When scoring, each pair (2 arms, 2 legs, etc.) counts as one part.
14. Point to picture and have child name it. (No credit is given for sounds only.)

15. Tell child to: Give block to Mommie; put block on table; put block on floor. Pass 2 of 3.
    (Do not help child by pointing, moving head or eyes.)
16. Ask child: What do you do when you are cold? ..hungry? ..tired? Pass 2 of 3.
17. Tell child to: Put block on table; under table; in front of chair, behind chair.
    Pass 3 of 4. (Do not help child by pointing, moving head or eyes.)
18. Ask child: If fire is hot, ice is ?; Mother is a woman, Dad is a ?; a horse is big, a
    mouse is ?. Pass 2 of 3.
19. Ask child: What is a ball? ..lake? ..desk? ..house? ..banana? ..curtain? ..ceiling?
    ..hedge? ..pavement? Pass if defined in terms of use, shape, what it is made of or general
    category (such as banana is fruit, not just yellow). Pass 6 of 9.
20. Ask child: What is a spoon made of? ..a shoe made of? ..a door made of? (No other objects
    may be substituted.) Pass 3 of 3.
21. When placed on stomach, child lifts chest off table with support of forearms and/or hands.
22. When child is on back, grasp his hands and pull him to sitting. Pass if head does not hang back.
23. Child may use wall or rail only, not person. May not crawl.
24. Child must throw ball overhand 3 feet to within arm's reach of tester.
25. Child must perform standing broad jump over width of test sheet. (8-1/2 inches)
26. Tell child to walk forward, ⟳⟲⟳⟲➝ heel within 1 inch of toe.
    Tester may demonstrate. Child must walk 4 consecutive steps, 2 out of 3 trials.
27. Bounce ball to child who should stand 3 feet away from tester. Child must catch ball with
    hands, not arms, 2 out of 3 trials.
28. Tell child to walk backward, ⟵⟳⟲⟳⟲ toe within 1 inch of heel.
    Tester may demonstrate. Child must walk 4 consecutive steps, 2 out of 3 trials.

DATE AND BEHAVIORAL OBSERVATIONS (how child feels at time of test, relation to tester, attention
span, verbal behavior, self-confidence, etc,):

Figure 24-1 Directions for Administering the Denver Developmental
Screening Test. (Reprinted with permission from W. K. Frankenburg
and J. B. Dodds, University of Colorado Medical Center, © 1969.)

6. Cranial nerve VIII (Auditory–vestibular nerve)

- *Function:* Controls hearing and balance.
- *Assessment:* Test for hearing acuity, bone conduction, and air
  conduction. See Chapter 25, Language and Learning Disabilities. Testing for vestibular function is not routinely done.
  It involves instilling cold water into the external ear canal to
  elicit vertigo or nystagmus.

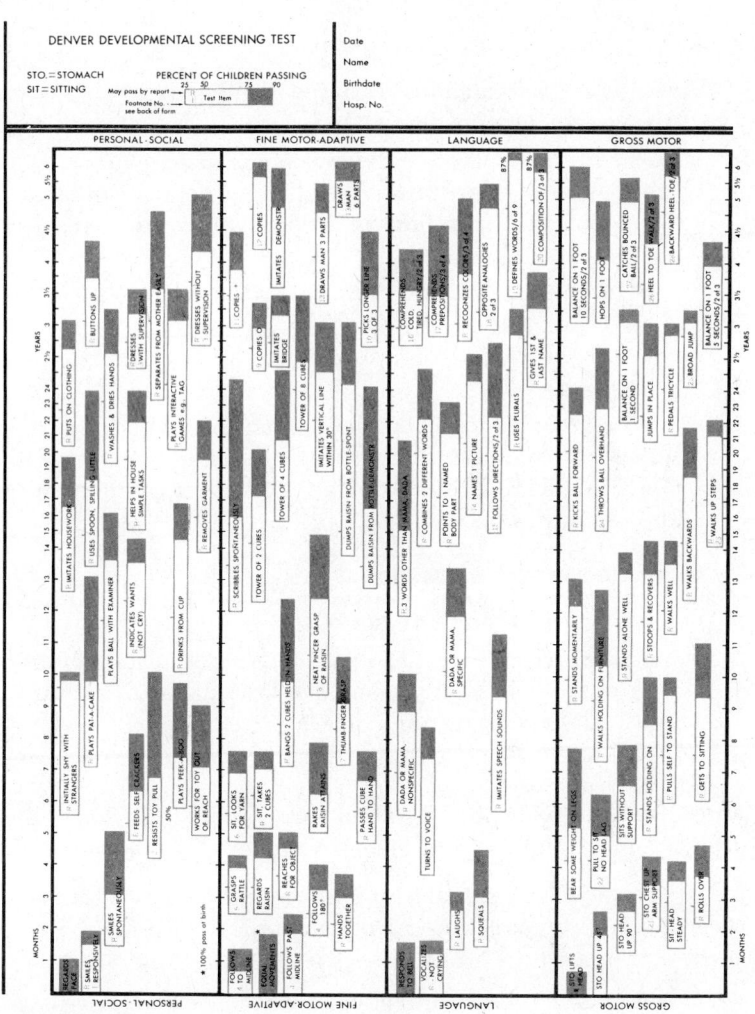

Figure 24-1 (*Continued*)

7. Cranial nerves IX and X (Glossopharyngeal and Vagus nerves)

   • *Function:* Innervate muscles in the mouth and throat and control swallowing and phonation.
   • *Assessment:* Have the child elevate the palate voluntarily (say "ah"), swallow, and speak. Elicit the gag reflex. Note hoarseness, pooling of secretions in oropharynx, or excessive drooling. Note position of uvula.

8. Cranial nerve XI (Spinal accessory nerve)

   • *Function:* Provides motor supply to sternocleidomastoid and trapezius muscles
   • *Assessment:* Have the child elevate the shoulders against pressure of the examiner's hands. Have the child turn the head to one side and resist the examiner's attempts to turn it in the opposite direction.

9. Cranial nerve XII (Hypoglossal nerve)

   • *Function:* Innervates muscles of the tongue
   • *Assessment:* Have the child stick out the tongue and observe it for symmetry. Note any tremors or fasciculations (involuntary contractions or twitchings). Have the child press the tongue against each cheek as the examiner pushes in on the cheek.

Motor Function   The motor system is assessed for size (bulk), tone, strength, and abnormal movements as follows:

1. *Size.* Inspect and palpate for distribution of muscle mass and symmetry in muscle mass. Note any reduction in muscle mass, hypertrophy, or atrophy of muscles.

2. *Tone.* Observe posture and adequacy of movement during normal activities. Do both active and passive range of motion and note *tone* (the resistance offered to the examiner's movements). Note involuntary resistance, spasticity, flaccidity, rigidity, or limitations of range of motion.

   • *Spasticity:* increased resistance to passive movement which gives way suddenly (clasp-knife response)
   • *Rigidity:* an increase in resistance throughout passive movements of a joint

3. *Strength.* Have the child stand up from a lying position and walk on tiptoes and heels. This tests strength in the lower extremities, back, and hips. Observe for Gower's sign (i.e., the child "climbs up on his/herself" when getting up from the floor). This suggests Duchenne muscular dystrophy. To test shoulder muscles, lift the child with hands in the child's axillae. Test upper extremity muscle groups by having the child move fingers, hands, arms, and shoulders against resistance. Have the child reach up to comb hair.

4. *Abnormal movements.* Observe for *tremors* (rapid, regular, repetitive involuntary movements, usually of the distal extremities). Some tremors occur with the child at rest; some occur only when voluntary motion is attempted (intention tremor). Most commonly, tremors may occur in infants, in bursts and without obvious cause. Observe for *chorea* (quick, irregular, jerking and writhing movements; often in trunk, major joints, and face; with irregular gait and associated with decreased muscle tone), *tic* (a stereotyped sudden movement always involving the same muscle group), *athetosis* (a slow writhing movement, more marked in the distal extremities; consisting of alternating supination-pronation and flexion-extension of limbs; and associated with increased muscle tone), *dystonia* (involuntary, sustained spasms; slow twisting movements of the neck, limbs, and trunk; a tendency toward hyperextension of the joints especially when trying to walk; abnormal posture). These involuntary movements are accentuated during emotional stress and disappear during sleep. Other abnormal movements are constant overshooting of movements and clonic or tonic convulsive movements.

Cerebellar Function The cerebellum controls balance and coordination. Assessment includes tests of fine motor coordination, gait, and posture control as follows:

1. *Fine motor coordination.* Young children can be observed while playing, stacking blocks, picking up raisins, dressing, undressing, buttoning, manipulating toys, and drawing. After 4 to 6 years of age tests of rapid alternating movements are used, including rapid supination and pronation of hands, touching finger to nose to examiner's finger (note tremor, past-pointing),

touching finger to nose with eyes closed, touching each finger to thumb of same hand, and touching index finger to adjacent thumb crease. Have the child run the heel of one foot down the shin of the opposite leg. These movements should be done smoothly.

2. *Gait.* Observe gait and standing position. Normal gait is narrow based with smooth movements. Balance is easy and arms swing at sides. Have the child walk a line in toe-to-heel fashion. If there is difficulty with this, have the child stand with feet together, eyes closed, and arms folded across chest. Note ability to maintain upright posture with minimal swaying. This is the Romberg test, and the child should be able to maintain balance without the aid of vision. Have the child walk normally and turn around rapidly. Note ataxia. To rule out tight Achilles tendons, note whether child walks on toes.

3. *Posture control.* By the age of 4 to 5 years the child should be able to stand on one foot for 5 seconds, by 6 years stand on one foot for 5 seconds with arms folded across chest, and by 7 years stand on one foot with eyes closed.

Sensory Function   Sensory assessment is limited in the infant and young child but in older children (4 to 5 years and above) includes the *primary sensory modalities:* superficial tactile sensation (touch), pain, temperature, vibration, pressure, and response to motion and position; and *secondary (cortical) sensation:* two-point discrimination, point localization, stereognosis, and graphesthesia. The child's eyes are closed during assessment which is conducted as follows:

1. Primary sensations:
   - *Superficial tactile sensation.* Stroke various parts of the body with a piece of cotton and compare responses. Check symmetrical areas.
   - *Pain.* Observe reaction to light pin prick.
   - *Temperature.* Touch various parts of the body with a cold tuning fork and observe responses.
   - *Vibration.* Touch vibrating tuning fork to various body parts and have the child note when vibration ceases.
   - *Pressure.* Apply pressure to calves, arms, and Achilles' tendon and observe the child's response.

- *Motion and position.* Grasp the child's toe or finger and move upward and backward. Have the child identify the direction of movement.

2. Secondary cortical sensation:

    - *Two-point discrimination.* Check the child's ability to tell whether two parts of the body are being touched simultaneously.
    - *Point localization.* Have the child identify what spot on the body is being touched.
    - *Stereognosis.* Place a familiar object (key, paper clip, coin, comb) in the child's hand and have the child identify by feel.
    - *Graphesthesia.* Have the child identify numbers or letters written on the palm of the hand with the examiner's finger.

Reflex Function Superficial, deep tendon, and pathologic reflexes are evaluated for presence, symmetry, and strength. Primitive reflexes are discussed in Infant Neurologic Examination which follows. Reflex changes or abnormalities can indicate spinal cord lesions and disorders of peripheral nerves or muscles. Assessment is as follows:

1. *Superficial and deep tendon reflexes.* Table 24-1 lists superficial and deep tendon reflexes, where to apply the stimulus, and expected reactions. Superficial reflexes are elicited by stroking the skin. Deep tendon reflexes are elicited by stretching the tendon by a quick tap with a reflex hammer. Reflexes are graded on a scale of 0 to 4 plus, with 1, 2, and 3 being normal. Absence of reflexes or exaggerated reflex response indicates dysfunction (Waechter and Blake, 1976, pp. 632–633).
2. *Pathologic reflexes.* The Babinski reflex and ankle clonus reflex are described in Table 24-2.

INFANT NEUROLOGIC EXAMINATION

At birth and during the infancy period the neurologic examination is modified since the central nervous system is immature and functions largely at subcortical levels (brainstem and spinal cord). Neurologic development is characterized mainly in terms of motor development and performance. The most significant elements of

Table 24-1

Deep and Superficial Reflexes

Reflexes		Stimulus	Normal Results	Involved Segment
Deep	Superficial			
Biceps muscle	—	Tap biceps tendon.	Forearm flexes at elbow.	C5-C6
Forearm pronator muscles	—	Tap palmar side of forearm medial to styloid process of radius.	Forearm pronates.	C6
Triceps muscle	—	Tap triceps tendon.	Forearm extends at elbow.	C6-C7
Brachioradial muscle	—	While holding forearm in semipronated position, tap styloid process.	Forearm flexes at elbow.	C7-C8
Finger (flexion)	—	Tap palm at tip of fingers.	Fingers flex.	C7-T1
Abdominal muscles	—	Tap inferior thorax, abdominal wall, and symphysis pubis.	Abdominal wall contracts; leg adducts when symphysis pubis is tapped.	T8-T12
—	Abdominal muscles	Stroke upper, middle, and lower skin on abdomen.	Abdominal muscles contract with retraction of umbilicus toward stimulated side.	T8-T12
—	Cremasteric muscle	Stroke medial upper leg in adductor region.	Testicles move up.	L1-L2
Adductor muscle	—	Tap medial condyle of tibia.	Leg adducts.	L2-L4
Quadriceps muscle (knee jerk)	—	Tap tendon of quadriceps femoris muscle.	Lower leg extends.	L2-L4
Triceps sural muscle (ankle jerk)	—	Tap Achilles tendon.	Plantar flexion of foot occurs.	L5-S2
—	Plantar area	Stroke lateral side on sole of foot.	Plantar flexion of toes occurs.	S1-S2

Source: Reprinted with permission, from B. L. Conway, *Pediatric Neurological Nursing,* St. Louis: C. V. Mosby, 1977. P. 139.

the infant neurologic examination are described. See also Chapter 5, Assessment of the Newborn.

Head Circumference This is checked routinely during the first 3 years of life for abnormal head size. See Chapter 1, Child Health Assessment.

Transillumination of the Skull In a darkened room a flashlight beam is applied to the skull at various points. Local or generalized areas of transillumination beyond the periphery of the flashlight indicate the need for referral.

Anterior Fontanel It is usually soft and slightly depressed with the infant in a sitting position. A tense and bulging fontanel indicates increased intracranial pressure. The anterior fontanel is usually closed by 18 months to 2 years of age. See Chapter 1, Child Health Assessment.

General Appearance Positioning, activity, quality of cry, alertness, and response to environmental stimuli are noted and described. Spontaneous activity should be symmetrical. Orientation may be assessed by recognition of the mother's face and later of familiar objects and people.

Head, Eyes, Ears Auscultate for bruits. Palpate fontanels and sutures. Observe for dimples, clefts, and asymmetry. Note close-spacing or wide-spacing of eyes, epicanthal folds. Note a small or recessive chin, low set ears. Head control is poor in the neonate although when lying on the abdomen the newborn can turn the head and lift the face. Head control is stable by 4 months.

Neck and Back Palpate for masses, asymmetry, or injury (fractured clavicle, brachial plexus injury). See Chapter 23, The Skeletal System. Note dimpling at the base of spinal cord.

Extremities The normal newborn has increased flexor tone and holds hands in a clenched fist position with extremities drawn up on the trunk. Note palmar creases. Move each body joint through range of motion noting symmetry, tone, and dislocations.

Table 24-2
Infant Reflexes

Reflex	How to Elicit	Response of Infant	Clinical Implications
Acoustic blink	Produce a sharp loud noise (a clap of the hands) about 30 cm from the head.	By second or third day of life infant will blink both eyes. Disappearance of reflex is variable.	Absence may indicate decreased hearing.
Ankle clonus	Flex the leg at the hip and knee, sharply dorsiflex the foot, and maintain pressure.	Rhythmic flexions and extensions of the foot at the ankle.	Abnormal if more than 10 beats during the first 3 months; or more than 3 beats after 3 months. Sustained clonus indicates upper motor neuron disease.
Babinski	Stroke lateral aspect of the plantar surface of foot from heel to toes. Use a blunt object.	Hyperextension or fanning of toes occurs. As myelinization is completed, the normal response becomes flexion (downward curling) of all toes; the positive (pathologic) sign is hyperextension (dorsiflexion) of the great toe with or without fanning of the remaining toes.	After 2 years of age a positive sign is the most significant clinical sign of the presence of an upper motor neuron (pyramidal tract) lesion.
Blinking	Shine a light suddenly at the infant's open eyes	Eyelids close in response to light. Disappears after first year.	Absence may indicate poor light perception or blindness.

Reflex	Procedure	Normal Response	Abnormal Findings
Landau	Suspend infant carefully in prone position by supporting infant's abdomen with examiner's hand.	By 3 months of age the expected response consists of extension of head, trunk, and hips. Head is slightly above horizontal plane. Disappears by 2 years of age.	If newborn collapses into a limp concave position, it is abnormal.
Moro	1. With infant in supine position, gently support head and lift it a few cm off the surface. As soon as neck relaxes, suddenly release the head and let it drop back to the surface, *or* 2. Produce sudden loud noise, or jar the table or crib suddenly.	Normal response is present at birth and is one in which the arms extend outward, the hands open, and then are brought together in midline. The legs flex slightly. Usually disappears by 3 to 4 months. Infant may cry.	Asymmetry indicates possible paralysis. Absence suggests severe neurologic problem. Persistence beyond 4 months may indicate neurologic disease. If it lasts longer than 6 months, it is definitely abnormal.
Neck righting	With infant in supine position turn head to one side.	Infant's trunk rotates in direction in which head is turned. Appears at 4 to 6 months. Disappears at 24 months.	Absent or decreased reflex may indicate spasticity.
Palmar grasp	With infant's head positioned in midline, place examiner's index fingers from ulnar side into infant's palm and press against palm.	Normal response is flexion of all fingers around examiner's fingers. Present at birth and disappears by 4 months when infant is ready to reach.	Note symmetry and strength. Persistence of grasp beyond 4 months suggests cerebral dysfunction.

Table 24-2 *(Continued)*

Reflex	*How to Elicit*	*Response of Infant*	*Clinical Implications*
Parachute	Infant is held in a prone position and is quickly lowered toward the surface of the examining table or floor.	Normal response is extension of arms, hands, and fingers, as if to break a fall. Appears by 9 months and persists.	Asymmetry or absence of response is abnormal.
Perez	Infant is held in a suspended prone position in one of the examiner's hands. The thumb of the other hand is moved firmly from sacrum along entire spine.	Normal response is extension of head and spine, flexion of knees on the chest, a cry, and emptying of the bladder. Present at birth and disappears by 3 months.	Absence indicates severe neurologic disease.
Placing	Infant is held erect and the dorsum of one foot touches the undersurface of the examining table top.	Infant flexes hip and knee and places stimulated foot on top of the table. Present at birth and disappears by 6 weeks or variable.	Absent in paralysis or in infants born by breech delivery.
Plantar grasp	Examiner's finger is placed firmly across base of infant's toes.	Toes curl downward. Present at birth and disappears by 10 to 12 months.	Absent in defects of lower spinal column. Infant cannot walk until this reflex disappears.
Rooting	Infant is held in supine position with head in midline and hands against chest. Examiner strokes perioral skin at corner of mouth or cheek.	Infant opens mouth and turns head toward stimulated side. Present at birth and disappears by 3 to 4 months (awake); by 7 months (asleep).	Absence indicates severe CNS disease or depressed infant.

Rotation test	Infant is held upright facing examiner and rotated in one direction and then the other.	Infant's head turns in the direction in which the body is being turned. If head is restrained the eyes will turn in the direction in which the infant is turned.	If head and eyes do not move, it indicates a vestibular problem.
Spontaneous crawling (Bauer's response)	Infant is lying prone and examiner presses soles of feet.	Infant makes crawling movements. Present at birth.	Crawling is absent in weak or depressed infants.
Stepping	Infant is held upright and soles of feet are put in touch with solid surface.	Infant "walks" along surface. Present at birth and disappears at 6 weeks.	Absence indicates depressed infant, breech delivery, or paralysis.
Sucking	With infant in supine position place nipple or finger 3 to 4 cm into mouth.	Vigorous sucking of finger or nipple. Present at birth and disappears by 3 to 4 months (awake) and 7 months (asleep). Tongue action should push finger up and back. Note rate of suck, amount of suction, and patterns or groupings of sucks.	Absence in term infants indicates CNS depression. Weak reflex may lead to feeding problems.
Tonic neck	With infant in supine position passively rotate head to one side.	Arm and leg on side to which head is turned extend, and opposite arm and leg flex (fencer's position). Present sometimes at birth but usually by 2 to 3 months. Disappears by 6 months.	Obligatory response is always abnormal. Persistence beyond 6 months is abnormal and indicates central motor lesions, e.g., cerebral palsy.

Table 24-2 (Continued)

Reflex	How to Elicit	Response of Infant	Clinical Implications
Trunk incurvation (Galant's)	Infant is held prone in examiner's hand. With the other hand the examiner moves a finger down the paravertebral portion of the spine, first on one side, then on the other.	Infant's trunk should curve to the side being stimulated. Present at birth and disappears by 2 months.	Presence of spinal cord lesions will interrupt this reflex.
Vertical suspension positioning	Infant is held upright, head is maintained in midline.	Legs are flexed at the hips and knees. Present at birth and disappears after 4 months.	Scissoring or fixed extension indicate spasticity.

Source: Adapted from M. L. Powell, *Assessment and Management of Developmental Changes and Problems in Children*, 2nd ed., St. Louis: C. V. Mosby, 1981, and from B. L. Conway, *Pediatric Neurological Nursing*, Philadelphia: J. B. Lippincott, 1977.

Neuromotor Function This develops in cephalocaudal progression. A simple schema for assessment, keeping individual variation in mind, is as follows:

Age (± 2 weeks)	Activity	Progression
1 month	Eyes focus and follow	Eyes
2 months	Social smile	Face
3 months	Early head control	Neck
4 months	Reaches	Arms, hands
5 months	Trunk control	Trunk
6 months	Sits when placed	Trunk, legs
7 months	Uses thumb to grasp	Fingers
10 months	Stands with support	Legs
12 months	Walks with support	Legs, feet

More complete information on growth and development of infants and young children is found in Chapters 5 and 6, Growth and Development.

Sensory Function The newborn perceives tactile stimuli both soothing and painful. Visual acuity is poor, but the newborn follows large moving objects and will blink in response to a bright light. Pupils are equal and react to bright lights. The normal newborn startles to a sudden, loud noise, and other auditory stimuli evoke changes in spontaneous motor activity.

Reflex Function A large number of primitive reflex patterns are found in the normal newborn or appear shortly after birth. Absence of these reflexes may indicate general depression of central or peripheral motor functions. Asymmetrical reflexes may indicate focal lesions. Abnormal persistence of these reflexes beyond the point when voluntary motor functions should be present indicates general developmental lag or central motor lesions. Table 24-2 describes certain of these reflexes and how to assess them.

Developmental Assessment

NORMAL GROWTH AND DEVELOPMENT

The term, development, incorporates two concepts: (1) observable increases in size and structure of an organism over time, and (2) progressive changes in an individual's adaptation to the environment (Waechter and Blake, 1976, p. 50). Children universally follow the same pattern of development and over the years developmental standards have been established based on studies of the age levels at which normal children achieve various motor, language, adaptive, and social behaviors. Excellent and comprehensive summaries of growth and development during the infancy and preschool periods, the Waechter Developmental Guides, are presented in Chapters 5 and 6. The information contained in these tables should be an integral part of the repertoire of all pediatric care providers.

DEVELOPMENTAL SCREENING

A critical part of the neurologic examination is assessment of developmental functioning. Several screening tests are available which can be used to determine which children need more comprehensive developmental evaluation. Interpretation of the results of screening tests requires recognition of the range of normality, individual variations, and the variables present in the test situation (O'Pray, 1980).

Denver Developmental Screening Test This test (see Fig. 24-1) has gained wide acceptance as an economical, simple, and accurate tool for developmental screening of children from birth to 6 years. It gives a quick visual picture of the child's strengths and weaknesses in four areas of behavior: gross motor, fine motor, language, and personal–social. Recently, an abbreviated and revised form of the DDST has become available. The test consists of 12 items pertinent to the child's age and can be administered in 5 to 7 minutes. The recording form has been revised to permit a graphic portrayal of the rate of a child's development, similar to the charts used in plotting height and weight (Frankenburg et al., 1981). All test materials, including the instruction manual, can be obtained from LADOCA Project and Publishing Foundation Inc., East 51st Street and Lincoln Street, Denver, CO 80216.

The Developmental Profile This tool can be used from birth through 12 years of age to determine objectively a child's level of functioning. It consists of 217 items that, to large extent, can be obtained by report from anyone familiar with the child. The items are grouped into five scales: physical, self-help, social, academic, and communication. The results provide an individual profile that can be used to stimulate development in weak areas. The tool is available from Psychological Development Publications, 7150 Lakeside Drive, Indianapolis, IN 46278.

The Neonatal Behavioral Assessment Scale   Developed by T. Berry Brazelton, M.D., this tool is discussed in Chapter 4, Assessment of Parent-Child Interaction.

Normal Laboratory Values

CEREBROSPINAL FLUID

Lumbar puncture and examination of cerebrospinal fluid (CSF) is probably the most important laboratory procedure in the evaluation of neurologic disorders. Normal values include the following:

- Appearance: Colorless, odorless
- Specific gravity: 1.007 to 1.009
- Pressure: 50 to 180 mm of water (with child relaxed and in lateral recumbent position)
- Cell count: WBC 0 to 5/cu mm
- Protein: 15 to 45 mg/dl
- Sugar: Varies with level of serum glucose, CSF value about 50 to 75 percent of the serum glucose level
- Culture: negative

Meningeal Signs

Inflammation of the meninges is a serious condition in infants and young children and must be identified as early as possible. Two specific maneuvers are used to detect meningeal inflammation:

1. *Kernig's sign.* With the child in the supine position, flex one leg at the hip and knee so that the thigh is flexed on the hip and the leg is flexed on the knee, then straighten (extend) the knee. Note resistance or pain when knee is extended. If either is present, it suggests meningeal inflammation.

2. *Brudzinski's sign.* With the child in the supine position, rapidly flex the neck. Note pain or resistance in the neck and flexion of the hips and knees. This sign indicates meningeal irritation.

Other meningeal signs include stiffness of the neck (nuchal rigidity), inability to touch chin to chest, and inability to sit up normally (stiffness of the back). These signs are frequently difficult to elicit in young infants. Evaluation must include symptoms of severe irritability (not being comforted in parent's arms), fever, lethargy, and "looking sick." See Chapter 27, Meningitis.

Neurologic "Soft" Signs

See Chapter 25, Language and Learning Disabilities.

MANAGEMENT

When a child is suspected of or found to have a problem involving neuromuscular functioning, impact on the child and family will be significant. Fear, guilt, and anxiety are common especially if the condition may be life-long or if impaired physical or intellectual functioning is involved. The nurse practitioner can be of invaluable assistance to these families by maintaining the primary care role, working to coordinate evaluation and treatment services, serving as advocate for the family, collaborating with the many disciplines that may be involved, and making referrals to appropriate resources. A most important aspect of management is the need to maintain a focus on the normal features of the child in order to promote optimal growth and development and healthy adaptation.

COMMON CLINICAL PROBLEMS

Breath-Holding

ASSESSMENT

Breath-holding attacks are periods of apnea followed by brief unconsciousness, usually occurring in response to emotional insult or unexpected painful stimuli. They are distinguished from syncope as follows:

- *Cyanotic breath-holding attack.* A situation that precipitates fear, anger, or frustration leads to violent crying. The crying is interrupted by a sudden gasp, apnea, cyanosis, rigidity, and frequently brief unconsciousness with loss of body tone. Opisthotonos and convulsive movements may occur if unconsciousness is prolonged. Prompt restoration to full awareness follows. Complete episodes last less than 1 minute. Episodes lasting longer than 1 minute may indicate epilepsy.
- *Syncope (fainting).* This is usually precipitated by stress or excitement and begins with lightheadedness and pallor. Temporary loss of vasomotor tone and bradycardia caused by transient cerebral ischemia results in brief loss of consciousness. Recovery is spontaneous and physical examination is normal in most cases. Impending attacks can be aborted by lowering the head.

The parent–child relationship should be evaluated to determine the presence or absence of disturbances which may be contributing to the incidence of attacks.

Incidence Up to 5 percent of children experience breath-holding attacks. Age range is from 6 months to 4 to 5 years with peak incidence from 1 to 3 years of age. A history of breath-holding in a near relative is present in approximately 25 percent of the cases.

Differential Diagnosis Features that distinguish breath-holding spells from idiopathic epilepsy are described in Table 24-3.

MANAGEMENT

Medication Treatment with anticonvulsants is not indicated unless there is evidence of epilepsy.

Counseling Breath-holding attacks are terrifying to most parents and frequently lead to oversolicitation and overprotectiveness by parents. This can lead to manipulative behavior by the child. It is important to reassure parents that the attack will spontaneously cease and the child will resume breathing. They do not have to slap the child on the back, do mouth-to-mouth resuscitation, or call an ambulance. The child should not be punished for having an attack.

Table 24-3

Differentiation between Epilepsy and Breath-holding Attacks

	Grand Mal (Idiopathic Epilepsy)	Anoxic Convulsion (Breath-holding Spell)
Age of onset	Rarely in infancy	Often begins in infancy
Family history	None or positive for epilepsy	Often positive for breath-holding spell or fainting
Precipitating factors	Usually absent (or specific sensory stimuli or nonspecific stresses)	Usually present (specific emotional or painful stimuli)
Occurrence during sleep	Common	Never
Posture	Variable	Usually erect
Sequence and patterns	Single cry (may be absent) with loss of consciousness→tonic→clonic phases, cyanosis may occur later in attack; flushed at first, pale after attack	Long crying or single gasp, cyanosis or pallor→loss of consciousness→limpness→clonic jerks→opisthotonos→clonic jerks
Perspiration	Warm sweat	Cold sweat
Heart rate	Markedly increased	Decreased, asystole, or slightly increased
Duration	Usually >1 minute	Usually 1 minute or less
Incontinence and tongue biting	Common	Uncommon (but may occur)
Postictal state	Confusion and sleep common	No confusion. Fatigue common
Interictal EEG	Usually bilateral discharges	Usually normal
Ictal EEG	Generalized, high-voltage polyspike discharges, gradually subsiding into slow waves and depression for several minutes	Isoelectric pattern preceded and followed by diffuse high-voltage delta waves, promptly reverting to normal pattern upon recovery of consciousness

Source: Adapted with permission from C. T. Lombroso and P. Lerman, "Breathholding Spells (Cyanotic and Pallid Infantile Syncope)," *Pediatrics* 39(4):579 April 1967, Copyright 1967, American Academy of Pediatrics.

The most effective approach includes an attitude of calmness during the attack and a subsequent ignoring of the attack. Parents initially need tremendous reassurance and support to develop this approach.

Referral Unprovoked apneic attacks and children whose breath-holding results in frequent loss of consciousness or convulsions need to be referred for further evaluation. Persistence of breath-holding beyond 5 to 6 years with family disruption indicates the need for psychiatric referral.

Cerebral Palsy

ASSESSMENT

Cerebral palsy is the comprehensive term used to designate a group of nonprogressive neuromotor disorders which are the result of antecedent insults to the central nervous system. In addition to motor deficits, cerebral palsy may include mental retardation (50 to 75 percent), seizures (60 percent), speech disorders, visual disorders (more than two thirds), and auditory disorders. It is important to remember that, although they are often severely handicapped, their intellectual abilities may not be similarly affected.

Etiology In many cases the exact etiology is never determined, but causative and risk factors include the following:

1. *Prenatal factors.* Maternal anoxia, maternal bleeding, Rh or ABO incompatibility, irradiation during pregnancy, maternal infection (rubella, toxoplasmosis, cytomegalic inclusion disease), injuries, and genetic factors
2. *Perinatal factors.* Prematurity, asphyxia, cerebral trauma, hemorrhage, low birth weight, and kernicterus
3. *Postnatal factors.* Trauma, hemorrhage, anoxia, meningitis, encephalitis, and poisonings

Incidence Approximately 25,000 children each year are affected, or 1 to 2 of every 1000 births.

Clinical Manifestations The clinical findings are related to the area of the brain that has been damaged and are described according to the nature of the observed motor deficit as follows:

1. *Spastic cerebral palsy.* This is the most common type (70 to 75 percent of affected children); it is due to involvement of upper motor neurons and is characterized by increased muscle tone, exaggeration of deep tendon reflexes, clonus, abnormal persistence of neonatal reflexes, and a tendency toward contractures.

   - Spastic quadriplegia. All four extremities are affected. Mental retardation, convulsions, speech defects, and swallowing disorders are commonly associated.
   - Spastic hemiplegia. Both extremities on one side are involved with the upper extremity more severely affected.
   - Spastic diplegia. Scissoring of the legs, tightening of the Achilles' tendon, flexion contractures of the knees, and toe gait are characteristics. All four extremities are involved but the lower extremities are more severely affected. It is frequently associated with low birth weight.
   - Atonic diplegia. It is characterized by hypotonia, normal or increased deep tendon reflexes, marked delay in developmental milestones, and mental retardation. Muscle tone changes with age and by late childhood may be normal or hypertonic.
   - Spastic paraplegia. Both legs are involved and the upper extremities are normal.
   - Monoplegia (one extremity involved) and triplegia (three extremities involved) are rare.

2. *Dyskinetic (athetoid) cerebral palsy.* This type is the result of basal ganglia or extrapyramidal tract lesions and occurs in 15 to 20 percent of affected children. It causes impairment of volitional activity by uncontrolled, uncoordinated, and purposeless movements that disappear during sleep. Athetoid movements are the most common. Speech and swallowing are impaired, and walking exaggerates the involuntary movements. The combination of motor handicap and disturbed speech may lead to the faulty impression of mental retardation. Intellectual ability must be carefully evaluated before assuming mental defect.

3. *Ataxic cerebral palsy.* Two to five percent of affected children have this type which is the result of a cerebellar lesion and is characterized by ataxic signs from early childhood. Hypotonia and decreased tendon reflexes are present in infancy. Later the

child develops a wide-based gait, has difficulty turning rapidly, and performs coordinated rapid movements (e.g., finger-to-nose test) poorly. Prognosis for improvement is better than for other types.

4. *Mixed cerebral palsy.* More than one form of cerebral palsy may be present in the same child. The combination of spasticity and athetosis is most common.

Presenting Symptoms In infancy the common presenting symptoms are feeding problems, sucking and swallowing difficulties, prolonged drooling, early handedness, irritability, motor delay, decreased spontaneous movements, hypertonicity, asymmetry, and persistent toe-walking. The presence of any of these symptoms plus the presence of any of the risk factors listed earlier indicate the need for a careful and thorough neurologic evaluation.

MANAGEMENT

The management of cerebral palsy depends on the child's age, the type of cerebral palsy, the extent of involvement, the presence or absence of related abnormalities (e.g., seizures), and the degree of mental functioning. Problem areas can be categorized generally in the areas of: feeding, safety, physical care, promotion of optimum development, and adjustment of the child and family to lifelong disability. An extensive guide to management is Finnie's book, *Handling the Young Cerebral Palsied Child at Home.* See Resource Information. See also Chapter 12, Approach to Chronic Illness. It should be noted that often a child affected by cerebral palsy may be quite normal appearing in early childhood. The brain damage that occurred is not manifest because that area of the brain has not been called into use. Later, as new areas of the brain are called upon for new activities, the damage presents itself. Parents must be prepared to deal with this apparently "progressive" aspect of the condition.

Feeding Difficulties in sucking and swallowing are often present in the infant and may be combined with hyperextension of the neck and spasticity in the extremities. This makes the feeding situation frustrating and challenging. The nurse practitioner must acknowledge the difficulties the parents are having and plan a joint effort with them to improve the feeding experience. Suggestions for improving the feeding situation include the following:

- Maintain the infant in a flexed position, sitting cross-legged in the mother's lap to minimize the pathologic extensor reflexes.
- Provide a feeding environment that is quiet, calm, and non-stimulating.
- Develop patience and a slow pace.
- Place food on the back of the tongue for easier swallowing.
- Cut food into small pieces.
- Serve foods that stick to the spoon (e.g., mashed potatoes, apple sauce).
- Slowly guide the spoon to the child's mouth.
- Obtain necessary special equipment (e.g., special handles, non-skid plate and glass holders).
- Use a straw for liquids.
- Try to disregard the mess.

Safety   Routine safety measures are discussed in Chapters 5, 6, and 7, Accident Prevention and Safety. The child with ataxic cerebral palsy or associated seizures may need special head gear to protect against head injury due to falls. Seizure precautions are discussed in this chapter under Epilepsy.

Physical Care   Frequent change of position lessens irritability and increases comfort. Prevention of contractures is accomplished by appropriate exercises, passive range of motion, encouragement of active motion via play, and the use of splints, braces, and back supports. Medications to reduce spasticity and abnormal movements and to relax skeletal muscle are occasionally used but are frequently unsuccessful.

Promotion of Optimum Development   Provision of routine health maintenance care is important and assists the family to focus on the child's assets. Suggestions for age-appropriate activities and interactions contribute to promotion of developmental potential.

Adjustment of the Family to Life-long Disability   The nurse practitioner provides primary care to many children with severe and chronic handicapping conditions and can help parents, over time, to understand their feelings and to adjust to the situation. Questions that help elicit parental feelings are as follows*:

What is your understanding of the cause?

Do you think you are/were at fault?

Was this child a planned baby?

When did you first find out that there was something wrong?

What did the doctor say at first? Did you understand what the doctor said at the beginning?

How long after the birth of the baby did you see your child (if there is a birth defect)?

What do you think about your child's problem?

How does your husband/wife feel about it?

What did your mother say?

Did anyone suggest institutionalizing your child?

Did you ever think it would have been better if the baby had died?

Did you feel uneasy about showing your baby to relatives and friends?

Were your friends helpful? Do they stay away?

Was the baby difficult to care for in early infancy?

Do you and your husband/wife feel the same way about your child's condition?

What do you disagree about?

Do you feel comfortable now about taking your child out in public?

Do you and your husband/wife share in the care of the child?

Do you ever get an opportunity to be away from home to do something you would like for yourself?

Does anyone ever babysit for your child?

How often do you and your husband/wife go out together?

Do you feel that this child takes up most of your time?

---

* Reprinted with permission from C. U. Battle, "Chronic Physical Disease: Behavioral Aspects," *Pediatr Clin North Am* 22:525–531, August 1975. © 1975 by the W. B. Saunders Company, Philadelphia.

Do you think that your normal children resent the time you spend with your child?

What worries you about the future of your child? What are your plans for the future of your child?

Coordination of Care   The total management of the child with cerebral palsy or any chronic handicapping condition involves several disciplines and separate specialists. Integration and coordination of care by the nurse practitioner who is the continuity figure for the family are important role functions. Additional information on assisting families with chronically ill children is found later in this chapter under Epilepsy, and in Chapter 12, Approach to Chronic Illness.

Dermal Sinus

ASSESSMENT

Interference with the development of the spinal cord during the first three weeks of gestation results in defects of closure of the neural tube. Spina bifida and meningomyelocele are examples of severe defects. Dermal sinus tracts are small closure defects. They are epithelial-lined sinus tracts that may be located at any point along the spine but are most common in the lumbosacral area or the occipital region of the head. They are significant if they penetrate into the subarachnoid space, as this can be a route of entry for bacteria and recurrent meningitis. Most dermal sinuses, including the low sacral pilonidal cysts, end blindly and do not communicate with the nervous system. They are, however, susceptible to periodic local infection.

Clinical Signs   Skin markings along the spinal column include dimpling, tufts of hair, or small hemangiomas.

MANAGEMENT

Sinus tracts above the sacral level should be surgically explored and excised. Noncommunicating pilonidal cysts require careful hygiene to prevent infection.

Developmental Delay

ASSESSMENT

Developmental delay is a term frequently used to describe a wide spectrum of clinical findings that may (or may not) indicate abnormalities in the functional status of infants and young children. It is a symptom of subnormal function of the central nervous system whether due to damage, altered physiology, environmental deprivation, or abnormally slow maturation. When developmental delay is suspected thorough developmental history and neuro/developmental assessment are indicated. See this chapter, Physical Examination, and Developmental Assessment. It is of critical importance, however, to recognize that individual variations exist within established norms, and that development is influenced by both heredity and environment. Consequently, it is often difficult to assess with certainty the significance of developmental variations.

Types of Developmental Delay   Some guidelines for considering various forms of developmental delay are as follows:

1. Multiple, global, or major delay in all areas usually signifies an underlying central nervous system disorder, such as mental retardation or cerebral palsy. It may also indicate severe systemic illness causing weakness, malnutrition, emotional disturbance, deprivation or other difficult environmental factors, or benign congenital hypotonia (see this chapter, Hypotonia). And finally, it may indicate prematurity and failure of the examiner to correct for gestational age. The weeks a child is born prematurely are subtracted from the chronologic age to determine age norms.

2. Specific delays in any one of the areas of development indicate specific disorders or may, in fact, be normal variations in which case the child eventually catches up.

3. Delayed gross motor function occurs in cerebral dysfunction; muscle, spinal cord, or peripheral nerve disorders; or other physical disorders (e.g., a dislocated hip).

4. Delayed fine motor function may indicate sensory loss, blindness, or peripheral nerve disorders.

5. Delayed speech occurs with brain disorders, hearing loss, bilingualism, and lack of stimulation.
6. Poor social and adaptive behavior implies diffuse brain disturbance or psychosocial disturbance.

Warning Signals Even though specific developmental variations may be within the normal range for an individual child, certain indicators should alert the care provider to pursue an in-depth developmental evaluation. Some indicators in the first 2 years of life are as follows:

At 6 weeks	Asymmetry in movements, tone, or neonatal reflexes (see Table 24-2)
	Excessive head lag
At 3 months	Does not react to noise
	Does not lift head when lying on abdomen
At 6 months	Does not laugh or smile
	Does not localize sound
	Does not fix and follow objects
	Does not reach out and transfer
At 10 months	Does not sit without support
	Does not bear weight when held
At 12 months	Does not respond to interactive play
	Does not imitate speech sounds
	Does not pull to standing position
At 18 months	Does not vocalize spontaneously
	Does not try to feed self with spoon
	Drools persistently
At 2 years	Does not have recognizable words
	Avoids eye contact
	Does not engage in imitative play
	Engages in excessive rocking or headbanging

MANAGEMENT

Obvious Delays Obvious delays in development are readily identified and, with careful history and physical examination, can often be specifically diagnosed and appropriately managed. Children who are mentally retarded present complex management challenges to family, health professionals, and community. Major areas of management are similar to those discussed elsewhere (see this chapter, Cerebral Palsy, Epilepsy, Chapter 12). Detailed discussions of comprehensive management can be found in Barnard and Erickson (1976) and Powell (1981) (see this chapter, References).

INFANT STIMULATION AND PRESCHOOL EXPERIENCE Up to 80 percent of developmental retardation occurs in children from environmentally deprived backgrounds. Since most intellectual development occurs before school age, the importance of infant stimulation programs and preschool learning and socialization experiences is great. All children with developmental delays should be referred to such programs.

Subtle Delays The subtle delays are more difficult to assess and to manage. Many times nurse practitioners are faced with children who present marginal or subtle findings of developmental delay, who, based on the nurse's experience and intuition, just do not seem "quite right," or about whom an experienced parent is concerned. When thorough examination fails to reveal any significant findings, the concern does not go away. These are uneasy situations to manage. There are no definite rules to follow, but experienced nurse practitioners should pay attention to their hunches and provide close follow-up until subsequent development either confirms or negates the concern. A suggested protocol for following such children is as follows:

1. Consult with the physician and consider referral to the neurologist when abnormal developmental screening (DDST) persists for more than two visits scheduled at least 1 month apart.
2. Evaluate the parent–child relationship. See Chapter 4, Assessment of Parent–Child Interaction.
3. Make a home visit to evaluate the child in the normal environment.
4. Consider referral to community resources providing play and stimulation experiences.

Epilepsy

ASSESSMENT

Epilepsy refers to a symptom complex characterized by recurrent, paroxysmal attacks of unconsciousness or impaired consciousness, usually with a succession of tonic or clonic muscular spasms or other abnormal behavior, produced by abnormal and excessive neuronal discharge occurring in the brain. If the cause is known the disorder is termed *organic* epilepsy; if the cause is unknown (the majority of cases), it is termed *idiopathic* epilepsy. Approximately 7 percent of children will have had one or more seizures by the age of 5 years (Green, 1977), and somewhat above 4 percent of all children between infancy and adolescence (Brill and Mitchell, 1981).

Classification of Seizures An extensive discussion of the various forms of seizures is beyond the scope of this book, but since the nurse practitioner may be providing primary care services to children being treated for epilepsy, and since long-term medications are prescribed according to the type of seizure, the classification of seizures based on cerebral localization of neuronal discharge is presented (Waechter and Blake, 1976, p. 651):

International Classification of Epileptic Seizures
  I. Partial seizures that begin locally (focal)
     A. Simple: motor, sensory, or autonomic
     B. Complex: temporal lobe
     C. Partial seizures that rapidly become generalized
 II. Generalized seizures without local onset
     A. Absences, petit mal
     B. Myoclonic jerks
     C. Infantile spasms
     D. Clonic
     E. Tonic
     F. Tonic-clonic
     G. Atonic drop attacks (brief), atonic absence (longer)
     H. Akinetic (loss of movement), no loss of tone
III. Unilateral (or mainly unilateral), usually in children
 IV. Undefined

Causes of Seizures The etiologic factors associated with epilepsy are multiple and are presented in Table 24-4.

History The history is obtained bearing in mind the etiologic factors listed in Table 24-4. Additionally, the history of the paroxysmal episode is especially important for accurate diagnosis. Information to be obtained includes:

Table 24-4
Etiologic Factors Associated with Epilepsy

Prenatal Factors
Genetic
  Genetic epilepsy
  Inborn errors of metabolism
    Carbohydrate: glycogen
      storage disease,
      hypoglycemia
    Protein: phenylketonuria,
      maple syrup urine disease
    Fat: cerebral lipidoses,
      leukodystrophies
  Heredofamilial diseases:
    myoclonus epilepsy
Congenital structural anomalies
  Porencephaly
  Vascular malformations
  Neurocutaneous syndrome
  Developmental defects of brain
Fetal infections
  Viral encephalopathy: rubella,
    cytomegalic inclusion disease
  Protozoan
    meningoencephalitis:
    toxoplasmosis
Maternal diseases
  Toxemia of pregnancy
  Chronic renal disease
  Diabetes mellitus
  Radiation during pregnancy
  Drug usage and drug
    intoxication
  Trauma

Perinatal Factors
  Trauma
  Hypoxia
  Jaundice
  Infection
  Prematurity
  Drug withdrawal

Postnatal Factors
  Primary infection of central
    nervous system
  Infectious diseases of childhood
    with encephalopathy (eg,
    measles, mumps)
  Head trauma
  Circulatory diseases
    Vascular anomalies
    Occlusive diseases: arterial,
      venous
    Hemorrhage
    Hypertensive encephalopathy
  Toxic encephalopathy
    Thallium
    Lead
    Convulsogenic drugs: INH,
      steroids
  Allergic encephalopathy
    Immunization reactions
    Drug reactions
  Physical and metabolic
    encephalopathies
    Fever and febrile convulsions
    Anoxia and hypoxia
    Prolonged convulsions with
      cyanosis
    Electrolyte disturbance
    Acute porphyria
    Hypoglycemia
    Hypocalcemia
    Hypomagnesemia
    Hyponatremia and
      hypernatremia and others
    Pyridoxine deficiency or
      dependency
  Degenerative diseases of the
    brain
  Tumors

Source: Reprinted with permission from A. M. Rudolph, editor, *Pediatrics,* 16th ed., New York: Appleton-Century-Crofts, 1977. P. 1842.

1. Events preceding the attack. What was the child doing prior to the attack? Was the child anxious, excited, or crying? Was there an aura, warning sensation, or change in mood? Did the child become dizzy, drowsy, or uncoordinated? What was happening in the environment? What was the time of day?
2. Events during the attack. How long did the attack last? What was the position of the head, trunk, and extremities? Where did the movements begin and what kind of movements were involved? What were the eye movements like? Were there pupillary changes? Was there cyanosis, perspiration, or drooling? Did the jaw clamp shut? Was there any respiratory problem, loss of consciousness, or incontinence?
3. Events after the attack (postictal state). Was there drowsiness, sleep, or rapid recovery? Was there any impairment in speech or motor function? Could the child recall any events during the seizure?
4. Related information. If not the first attack, how often do attacks occur? Is the child receiving medication? If so, what type and dose?
5. Consider other causes of paroxysmal behavior (e.g., breath-holding attacks, syncope, migraine headaches, or sleep disturbances).

Physical Examination A thorough general physical examination and complete neurologic examination are performed.

Laboratory Techniques The data obtained from the history and physical examination will determine which laboratory procedures are indicated. Electroencephalogram (EEG) is routinely performed. CT scanning has largely replaced X-ray films of the skull and isotope brain scans. Additional procedures include lumbar puncture, blood and urine chemistries, and angiography.

MANAGEMENT

The Acute Convulsive Episode Major objectives of care are protection of the child from injuries and observation of the event. Protective measures during a seizure are as follows:

1. Maintain an airway.

2. Protect the head from trauma by placing a soft object beneath the head.
3. Loosen restrictive clothing around the neck.
4. Position the child on the side to prevent aspiration of secretions.
5. Do not restrain body movements.
6. Protect the mouth, tongue, and teeth if possible. Padded tongue depressors are used to prevent injury to the tongue and other oral tissues but are useful only during the initial moments of a seizure before the teeth clamp down. If the teeth have already shut, do not force the jaw open as it can cause further damage to mouth and teeth.
7. Provide oxygen and suction as necessary in a prolonged seizure.
8. Comfort and reassure the child and parents as the child rouses from the episode.

Long-term Management This is directed at prevention of seizures and promotion of normal psychosocial development in the child and family. It is a collaborative effort involving the family, nurse practitioner, physician, school personnel, and other appropriate professionals.

MEDICATION The goal of drug therapy is complete seizure control with no significant drug-related side effects (Brill and Mitchell, 1981). With the correct choice of medication and sufficient dosage, this can be attained in most children. The duration of drug therapy depends on the nature and severity of the underlying disease but generally is long term (i.e., several years). Since long-term drug therapy poses risks to children with epilepsy (see below), the issue of when or whether to stop therapy and risk recurrent seizures is a difficult one and must be considered on an individual basis (Emerson et al., 1981). Management of drug therapy is the role of the physician, but the nurse practitioner needs to be aware of the drugs used to identify drug-related problems and to teach the child and family effectively. Only the most commonly used medications are discussed here.

1. Phenobarbital
   - *Use:* Most commonly used anticonvulsant in children because of its broad spectrum (focal, generalized, and psychomotor seizures), low toxicity, and low cost

- *Side effects:* Up to 40 percent of children have side effects or toxic reactions including behavioral changes (i.e., hyperactivity, extreme irritability), disturbed sleep patterns, and interference with cognitive functions such as memory, attention span, and general comprehension (Freeman, 1980). Drowsiness, skin rash, fever, and ataxia may also occur.

2. Phenytoin (Dilantin)
   - *Use:* Effective in treatment of generalized tonic-clonic (grand mal), focal, and psychomotor seizures
   - *Side effects:* Gum hyperplasia occurs in about 50 percent of children. Good dental hygiene and firm massage of the gums help to alleviate the symptom. Nausea and vomiting can be minimized by giving the drug after meals. Hirsutism, acne, and coarse facial features occur to some degree in most children on long term therapy. Parents have complained of behavioral and learning difficulties which become noticeable in retrospect (i.e., after the drug has been discontinued). Ataxia, incoordination, diplopia, and tremor are other side effects. Hypersensitivity reactions (rash, fever, and glandular involvement) may occur.

3. Ethosuximide (Zarontin)
   - *Use:* Drug of choice in the treatment of petit mal epilepsy
   - *Side effects:* Anorexia, abdominal pain, hiccoughs, drowsiness, skin rash, and irritability. Aplastic anemia is rare side effect.
   - *Comment:* The drug comes only in 250-mg capsules. In young children the drug may be dissolved in 1 to 2 ounces of fluid, but this mandates that the child drink all the fluid and demands careful calculation of the small pediatric dose. Another suggestion for improved accuracy is to freeze and then to cut the capsule into desired amounts (Conway, 1977, p. 243).

Teaching Related to Medication   When teaching the child and family about the medication therapy:

1. Stress the importance of taking the medication as prescribed and the necessity for long-term therapy, even after seizures are controlled.

2. Include the fact that it may take several months of regulation before control is achieved.
3. Elicit feelings and attitudes about drug therapy.
4. Stress safety precautions relative to storage of drugs at home.
5. Discuss side effects and when to call for assistance.
6. If the child is school age, plan for administration of the drug at school and involve the teacher and school nurse.
7. See Chapter 13, Approach to Medications in Childhood

COUNSELING   General guidelines and considerations in the supportive counseling of families include those listed below:

1. Presentation and interpretation of the diagnosis. Both parents should be present.
2. Explanation of treatment and follow-up plans. Repeated opportunities must be provided for parents and child to ask questions.
3. Consideration of the impact of the diagnosis. The care provider should try to comprehend the illness as a human experience from the family's point of view.
4. Consideration of the prior life-style of the family and the effect of adaptations to long-term illness.
5. Exploration of attitudes about epilepsy. Reactions of guilt, denial, shame, hostility, and fear can be expected. Most fears will be unspoken so parents and child need assistance to verbalize them. Fears about brain damage and mental retardation are among the most common.
6. Provision of support during an initial period of dependency as the family begins to face the problem and adapt.
7. Planning of normal activities consistent with safety.
8. Review of medications, what to do during an acute seizure, and seizure precautions.
9. Anticipation of crisis periods requiring extra support for the family (e.g., school entry, adolescence).
10. Planning with parents and child for informing school personnel.
11. Provision of information on specific resources (e.g., epilepsy organizations). See this chapter, Resource Information. Assistance in overcoming social, educational, legal, and economic obstacles will be necessary.

Table 24-5

Characteristics of Benign and Nonbenign Seizures

	Simple, Benign	*Nonbenign*
Character	General, major motor, symmetrical, clonic; duration less than 5 minutes; single occurrence	Similar to simple seizure but duration more than 5 minutes; repeated seizures during one febrile illness; may be asymmetrical or focal
Family history	History of simple febrile seizure in one third of cases	History of nonfebrile seizures
Age	3 months to 5 years, peak age 18 months	Wider age range. Onset may be before 6 months or after 5 years
Past history	Birth, developmental, injury, illness history usually not significant	May be positive or negative
Physical examination	Negative; EEG normal; skull films normal	Physical exam, EEG, and skull films may be positive.
Precipitating illness	Extracranial; abrupt rise in temperature with fever over 39.5°C (103.2°F)	May have intracranial infection. May have lower seizure threshold.

More detailed information on counseling is available in major references (Vaughan et al, 1979; Conway, 1977).

Febrile Seizures

ASSESSMENT

Up to 5 percent of children will develop a febrile seizure during childhood. It is important to distinguish whether the seizure is a simple benign febrile seizure or a nonbenign seizure. The characteristics of each type are listed in Table 24-5. The pathophysiology is poorly understood, but an age-dependent sensitivity of the nervous system permits triggering of the seizure by fever. Positive family history in many cases indicates a genetic factor (Brill and Mitchell, 1981).

Laboratory Techniques Lumbar puncture is performed if CNS infection is suspected. EEG, CBC, serum electrolytes, calcium, glucose, X-ray films of the skull, and CT scanning are thought to be of limited usefulness in the uncomplicated febrile seizure (Consensus Statement, 1980).

Risk and Prognosis Most children will subsequently be normal. There are, however, two significant risks associated with febrile seizures: a 30 to 40 percent risk of recurrent febrile seizures if prophylactic medicaton is not provided and a slightly increased risk (2 to 3 percent) of later epilepsy.

MANAGEMENT

The goals of management are to prevent recurrence of seizures, to lower fevers during acute illness (see Chapter 11, Approach to Minor Acute Illness) and to treat the underlying infection.

Prevention of Recurrent Seizures The risk of recurrence can be reduced by continuous daily phenobarbital at dosage sufficient to maintain a blood level of 15 μg/ml for at least 2 years or one year after the last seizure, whichever is the longer period of time. However, the NIH Consensus Panel (Consensus Statement, 1980, p. 1011) recommends that this therapy be considered under the following conditions:

1. In the presence of existing abnormal neurologic development (e.g., cerebral palsy, mental retardation)
2. When a febrile seizure is longer than 15 minutes, or focal, or followed by transient or persistent neurologic abnormalities
3. When there is history of nonfebrile seizures of genetic origin in a parent or sibling.

There is no evidence that prophylaxis reduces the risk of subsequent nonfebrile seizures.

Immunizations In children with a history of febrile seizures, DTP immunizations may be omitted, postponed, or given in fractional doses. Physician consultation is required.

Counseling For most children, the approach to management should include complete education and counseling of the family as to the benign nature of febrile seizures, the management of fever, and first aid for seizures if necessary (see this chapter, Epilepsy).

Handedness

ASSESSMENT

Handedness is never established before 1 year of age and usually by 18 months to 2 years. If a young infant demonstrates handedness before this age, concern and attention must be directed toward the opposite hand to determine paralysis, palsy, or other neuromuscular problem preventing use of the extremity.

The more frequent problem related to handedness is the desire and/or concern of parents that the child learn to use a preferred extremity, usually the right hand. The reasons for this social-cultural preference for the right hand remain mysterious.

MANAGEMENT

Parents need to be reassured that natural dominance is most appropriate, will be fairly consistent by 6 years of age and fully stable by 10 years. Mixed dominance or the use of one hand for one task and the other hand for another task are of no significance.

Headache

ASSESSMENT

Headache in children requires careful assessment of both organic and psychosocial factors, since the cause may be benign or very serious. A useful classification of the types of headache (adapted from Vaughan et al, 1979, p. 1761) is as follows:

1. Vascular headache
   - Migraine
   - Headache secondary to fever
   - Hypertensive headache
2. Headache related to epilepsy

3. Headache related to changes in intracranial pressure
   - Brain tumor headache
   - Low CSF pressure headache
4. Headache due to inflammatory disease of the central nervous system (e.g., meningitis)
5. Tension headache
6. Headache related to psychiatric disease
7. Headache due to eye strain
8. Headache due to sinusitis, ear infection, allergies, impacted teeth, or severe dental caries
9. Headache due to drugs, e.g., glue sniffers, "uppers"
10. Post-traumatic headache

History Data obtained by history should reflect the causes of headache outlined above. Specific factors include mode of onset (sudden, gradual), character of the pain (throbbing, dull), intensity of the pain (severe, mild), location, timing (when it begins, how long it lasts), frequency, factors that aggravate the headache (sudden movement, certain foods), symptoms that accompany the headache, coexisting disease processes, medications used, and family history. Morning headache in children and localization of pain (e.g., occipital pain) are suspicious of brain tumor. Most children do not accurately detail their symptoms of headache, thus functional headache should be considered in a child who offers great detail about the headache. Organic headache is usually intermittent; functional headache is more apt to be continuous and generalized. Low CSF pressure headaches are usually due to persistent leak of CSF after a spinal tap and appear as the child sits or stands up. The pain is relieved when the child lies down.

Physical Examination General physical examination and neurologic examination are performed. Facial expression (e.g., depression) should be noted. Blood pressure, careful funduscopic, visual-field, and visual-acuity examinations are important. The young child who cannot describe symptoms may demonstrate behaviors such as irritability, troubled facial expression, ear pulling, head-banging, or rolling.

Laboratory Techniques Routine studies are not indicated unless a specific disease is suspected. Similarly, X-ray films of the skull, CT scanning, EEG, angiography, and pneumoencephalography are reserved for suspicious and worrisome indicators.

Migraine Headache Approximately 4 percent of children have recurrent paroxysmal migraine headaches. Initial symptoms usually appear between 6 to 14 years of age. A positive family history is present in 70 to 90 percent of children.

- Common migraine is the more frequent type. There is indistinct or less pronounced aura, the pain is steady, severe, throbbing, usually unilateral, and may last several hours.
- Classic migraine includes a prodrome or aura, frequently visual (e.g., "sparkling lines"), but also sensory, motor, or behavioral. The aura is followed by throbbing, unilateral pain that can become generalized and by nausea or vomiting. The pain may last for several hours. The child may withdraw into a quiet, darkened room and go to sleep.

MANAGEMENT

The management of headache varies with the cause. For detailed information see S. Diamond et al, *Postgraduate Medicine*, September 1974; and J. A. Thompson, *Current Problems in Pediatrics*, August 1980.

Counseling Most cases of recurrent headaches occur in school age and adolescent children, are tension related, and include a psychosocial component. Thus the counseling role of the primary care provider is the most important aspect of management. Such counseling requires a family approach with investigation and understanding of the past and current family situation, identification of current stresses, and empathetic discussion of the relationship between feelings and symptoms. Some parents may have difficulty accepting psychologic causes for their child's headache. Support and reassurance are imperative, and comparisons with adult "tension headaches" will often assist parents to understand the role of stress in children as well.

Migraine Headache Migraine headaches are managed with a combination of medication and support.

MEDICATION Aspirin or acetaminophen should be tried first. Phenobarbital in maintenance doses is used in some young children if they consistently are missing out on normal activities. A combination of ergotamine and caffeine (Cafergot) is widely used in older children and adolescents and is administered early in the attack.

COUNSELING Most children do reasonably well on medication. The benign nature of the condition should be stressed. The environment may need modification if there are precipitating events or if the secondary gain that accrues to the child in terms of sympathy and attention results in more frequent headaches.

Hypothyroidism, Congenital

ASSESSMENT

Congenital hypothyroidism results from deficient production of thyroid hormones. Since thyroid hormones are critical for normal physical and mental development, the consequences of thyroid deficiency are severe physical and mental retardation. Although the severity of symptoms and their reversibility depend on the degree and length of thyroid deprivation, thyroid replacement therapy, if begun in the early newborn period, can have positive effects on growth and development. Thus early identification is extremely important.

Early Signs Warning signs in the immediate newborn period include the following:

1. Gestation over 42 weeks and/or birth weight greater than 4.0 kg
2. Large posterior fontanel
3. Respiratory distress
4. Hypothermia, 35°C or less
5. Peripheral cyanosis
6. Hypoactivity, lethargy, poor feeding
7. Lag in stooling beyond 20 hours of age
8. Abdominal distention and/or vomiting

9. Jaundice beyond 3 days of age
10. Edema

The presence of three or more of these signs is highly suspicious of congenital hypothyroidism and a T$_4$ (thyroxine) blood test should be performed. Thyroid screening is performed routinely at birth in many settings.

Signs During the First 3 Months of Life   If the diagnosis is not made in the nursery, the following signs may develop during the first 3 months:

1. A feeling of coldness to the touch
2. Mottling of the skin*
3. Decreased activity
4. Feeding problems
5. Enlarged tongue
6. Hoarse cry
7. Constipation*
8. Dry skin
9. Umbilical hernia*
10. Unusually large anterior fontanel for age*
11. Poor growth

MANAGEMENT

Dessicated thyroid medication is given as replacement therapy on a continuous basis.

Hypotonia (The Floppy Infant)

ASSESSMENT

Hypotonia, or decreased muscle tone, is a frequent presenting symptom in a variety of neuromuscular disorders. The clinical picture of limpness in the neonatal and early infancy period and subsequent delay in achieving motor milestones is produced by

---

*Present in at least 50 percent of patients.

problems at the cerebral, spinal, peripheral, or muscular levels. The most common causes are probably nonspecific mental retardation, perinatal hypoxia, and chromosomal disorders (e.g., Down's syndrome, hypothyroidism). There is a form called *benign congenital hypotonia* in which the infant is hypotonic at birth but appears normally alert, has depressed deep tendon reflexes, and has delayed sitting and walking, but has normal muscle fibers, no muscle atrophy, and eventually develops normally. Also, infants of mothers who have received depressant medications may appear hypotonic. Infants with congenital laxity of the ligaments (double-jointed) may appear hypotonic at birth. Recently, attention has been directed toward botulism as a cause of infant hypotonia and weakness (Arnon et al, 1977). *Clostridium botulinum* toxin was recovered from the feces of six infants under 4 months of age whose clinical findings included constipation followed by neurologic signs of weakened sucking, swallowing, and crying; diminished gag reflex, and generalized weakness. See Chapter 27, Infant Botulism.

Evaluation of Muscle Tone   The hypotonic infant shows the following characteristics:

1. May exhibit poor sucking
2. When supine, lies in a frog-leg position with hips abducted and knees flexed. This position is normal following breech delivery.
3. When eliciting the Landau reflex, droops or collapses over the examiner's hand and looks like an inverted "U"
4. May have absent or depressed deep tendon reflexes
5. Exhibits increased range of joint movement
6. Has muscles that feel flabby to palpation

Laboratory Techniques   These include muscle biopsy, EEG, electromyography, serum enzymes, nerve conduction velocity studies, spinal tap, and T_4 (thyroxine) test.

MANAGEMENT

The underlying cause determines total management. If the cause is benign, the parents may be completely reassured. Most nonbenign causes of hypotonia involve long-term neuromuscular problems, and management includes those principles already discussed elsewhere in this chapter. See this chapter, Developmental Delay.

Lead Poisoning (Plumbism)

ASSESSMENT

In 1981, 535,000 children were tested for lead poisoning, 22,000 of whom were found to have elevated levels (Centers for Disease Control, 1982). Lead poisoning occurs when abnormal amounts of lead are absorbed in the body. The amount of lead ingested, the degree of exposure, and repeated ingestion over time are factors affecting the manifestation of clinical symptoms.

Abnormal Levels   Blood lead levels and erythrocyte protoporphyrin (EP) levels are the most commonly used techniques for measuring lead absorption. Normal blood lead levels are below 30 μg/dl (Hoekelman et al., 1978; Rudolph, 1982) and result from normal exposure to lead in food, water, and air. Abnormal levels and guidelines for treatment are presented in Table 24-6.

Symptoms   Lead toxicity manifests itself in several body systems: hematologic, renal, neurologic, skeletal, and gastrointestinal. In young children the symptoms usually develop insidiously and progressively. Hyperirritability, anorexia, decreased activity, ataxia, vomiting, weight loss, anemia, constipation, personality changes, and developmental delay or reversal make up the constellation of early signs. Late manifestations are acute encephalopathy (cerebral edema, convulsions, coma) which is most common in children 1 to 3 years of age and occurs with lead levels over 70 to 100 μg/dl; and chronic encephalopathy in older children including seizure disorders, hyperkinetic behavior disorders, and developmental regression.

Sources of Lead   Ingestion and/or inhalation of lead occurs most commonly from flaking lead-based paint and from plaster or putty in dilapidated housing. Other sources include the following:

1. Artists' oil paints
2. Face powders
3. Fruit tree spray insecticides

Table 24-6
Lead Levels and Implications

Blood Lead (μg/dl)	EP (μg/dl of Whole Blood)	Implications
<30	<50	Normal. No effect.
30–49	50–109	Uncertain risk. Increased lead absorption and indicative of lead toxicity. Check for evidence of iron deficiency (Chapter 19). Minimal effect on heme synthesis. Remove child from hazards and monitor every 3 months.
50–69	110–249	Significant risk. Moderate inhibition of heme synthesis. Early symptoms and X-ray findings in some. Consider inpatient management and chelation therapy.
≥70	≥250	Substantial and urgent risk. Regardless of other factors (with or without symptoms) hospitalize and treat with chelation therapy. Danger of encephalopathy.

Source: Adapted from Hoekelman, R. A., et al. *Principles of Pediatrics: Health Care of the Young,* New York: McGraw-Hill, 1978. P. 1834. Also Rudolph, A. M., editor, *Pediatrics,* 17th ed., East Norwalk, CT: Appleton-Century-Crofts, 1982. P. 741.

4. Fumes and dust from leaded gasoline and from burning casings of storage batteries
5. Lead nipple shields
6. Lead-soldered cooking utensils
7. Lead shots, fishing weights, leaded jewelry
8. Leaded paint used in newspapers, magazines, books
9. Pottery glazed with lead
10. Water stored in lead-lined containers

These sources alone rarely cause symptomatic lead poisoning but do contribute to increased lead absorption.

MANAGEMENT

Increased Lead Absorption and Lead Poisoning   Children with elevated EP and blood lead levels are referred for further medical evaluation. Treatment is described by Hoekelman et al., 1978, and Rudolph, 1982.

Screening Screening for increased lead absorption can prevent death and disability from lead poisoning by:

1. Identifying children who have absorbed undue amounts of lead from their environment
2. Reducing their exposure to lead by removing hazards from the environment or removing susceptible children from the hazardous environment
3. Medically treating those children who have ill effects or are in danger of developing ill effects of absorbed lead

WHOM TO SCREEN Children to be screened include all children between the ages of 1 and 6 who live in poorly maintained buildings built before 1950, who visit relatives, friends, or babysitters, or who obtain day care in such buildings. Other children who should be screened are those who:

1. Are known to be exposed to other sources of lead
2. Exhibit pica
3. Exhibit unexplained, aberrant behavior, central nervous system symptoms, gastrointestinal symptoms, or anemia
4. Are members of a household in which another member has developed lead poisoning
5. Are residents of inner cities

WHEN TO SCREEN Children at risk should be screened yearly after their first birthday. In very high-risk environments children from 1 to 3 years of age ideally should be screened every 6 months and yearly thereafter. Children with lead levels near or slightly above normal, who continue to be exposed to lead hazards, need to be retested and examined frequently until lead hazards are removed or until they mature sufficiently to avoid such hazards.

POSITIVE RESULTS Both blood lead and erythrocyte protoporphyrin (EP) tests are used in screening. EP is considered preferable because it is a simple, reliable, and inexpensive test. With elevated EP levels (>60 μg/dl), however, iron deficiency must be ruled out. See Chapter 19. Children with positive screening tests should be evaluated by a physician skilled in the diagnosis and treatment of lead poisoning.

Environmental Control Local governmental agencies, community and professional groups must act together to identify hazards and to work for housing rehabilitation and environmental control. When a child at risk cannot be separated from the sources of lead (usually the home), the family can take measures to reduce the hazards:

1. Frequent cleaning of floors, window sills, and bannisters
2. Damp mopping and dusting
3. Covering hazardous surfaces (repainted cribs, window sills) with wall board or heavy contact paper.

Reye's Syndrome

ASSESSMENT

Definition Reye's syndrome is a noncontagious disease characterized by fatty degeneration of the liver and acute encephalopathy. Although not common, it is estimated that approximately 3,500 cases occur annually in the United States, about 1,200 of which progress to coma. Of those who persist with coma, about 250 will die and 120 will be significantly brain-damaged (Partin, 1981).

Epidemiology The disease attacks primarily healthy children under the age of 19 years, with peak incidence between 3 and 11 years. There is a definite association between Reye's syndrome and certain viral infections. Outbreaks occur regularly during seasonal epidemics of influenza A, influenza B, and varicella (chickenpox). See Chapter 27, Infectious Disease. Recent reports (AAP, 1982) indicate that there is "strong epidemiologic evidence for an association" between Reye's syndrome and the prior taking of salicylate medication, but further study is required before definite statements can be made.

Clinical Picture The child, who has had a viral illness, appears to be recovering for a few days when there is sudden onset of persistent vomiting. Fatigue, listlessness, and personality/behavior changes occur shortly thereafter. Confusion, agitation, combative-ness, delirium, and coma rapidly ensue unless treatment is begun immediately.

MANAGEMENT

Early Detection   The key to management is early detection. Nurse practitioners and other primary care providers must be aware of the warning signs and refer to a physician immediately. Care providers must:

1. Be on the lookout for the disease during the winter months when influenza-like respiratory disease is prevalent.
2. Suspect Reye's syndrome in every chickenpox patient who vomits.
3. Ask for a history of prodromal illness in every child whose parent complains of the child's persistent vomiting or in whom the parent's anxiety about vomiting seems unusual. Parents may recognize soft neurologic signs before anyone else (Partin, 1981).
4. Refer any child with suspicious findings to the physician for physical examination and liver function studies.
5. Be aware of the possible association between Reye's syndrome and aspirin. The advisory group formed by the Centers for Disease Control (AAP, 1982) recommends that until the nature of this association is clarified, salicylates should be avoided, when possible, for children with varicella infections and during influenza outbreaks. It also cautioned that all antipyretic medications for these illnesses be avoided except when the need to reduce high temperature outweighs other considerations. In such cases, acetaminophen should be used.

Treatment   Treatment of Reye's syndrome involves hospitalization and intensive care. When diagnosis and treatment occur early, most children recover completely.

Counseling   The National Reye's Syndrome Foundation (see this chapter, Resource Information) is actively involved in educating parents to be alert to the possibility of the disease, to avoid giving aspirin, and to seek prompt medical attention if any of the above indicators is present.

Resource Information

Booklist for Parents

Brown, D. L. *Developmental Handicaps in Babies and Young Children: A Guide for Parents*. Springfield, IL: Charles C Thomas, 1972.

Finnie, N. R. *Handling the Young Cerebral Palsied Child at Home*. 2nd ed. New York: Dutton, 1975.

Lagos, J. C. *Seizures, Epilepsy and Your Child*. New York: Harper & Row, 1974.

Stewart, M. A. and S. W. Olds. *Raising a Hyperactive Child*. New York: Harper & Row, 1973.

Strauss, S. *Is It Well With the Child? A Parents' Guide to Raising a Mentally Handicapped Child*. Garden City, NY: Doubleday, 1975.

Organizations

Literature and information on available resources can be obtained from a variety of national organizations:

1. American Epilepsy Foundation, 77 Reservoir Road, Quincy, MA 02169.

2. Epilepsy Foundation of America, 1828 L Street N.W., Washington DC 20036.

3. Muscular Dystrophy Associations, Inc., 1790 Broadway, New York, NY 10019.

4. National Association for Retarded Children, 420 Lexington Avenue, New York, NY 10017.

5. National Epilepsy League, 203 N. Wabash Avenue, Chicago, IL.

6. National Multiple Sclerosis, Inc., 257 Park Avenue South, New York, NY 10010.

7. National Reye's Syndrome Foundation, 8293 Homestead Road, Bezonia, Michigan 49616.

8. National Society for Crippled Children and Adults, Inc. (Easter Seals), 2023 W. Ogden, Chicago, IL 60612.

9. United Cerebral Palsy Association, 66 E. 34th Street, New York, NY 10016.

10. United Epilepsy Association, 113 W. 57th Street, New York, NY 10019.

References

Alexander, M. M. and M. S. Brown. "Physical Examination: Part 17, Performing the Neurologic Examination." *Nursing 76* 6:38–43, June 1976.

American Academy of Pediatrics, "Reye's Syndrome and Aspirin." Memo to AAP Membership, February 1982.

Arnon, S. S., et al. "Infant Botulism: Epidemiological, Clinical and Laboratory Aspects." *JAMA* 237:1946–1951, May 2, 1977.

Barnard, K. E. and H. B. Douglas. *Child Health Assessment Part 1: A Literature Review*. DHEW Publ. No. (HRA) 75-30. Bethesda, MD: U.S. Dept. HEW, Public Health

Service, HRA, Bureau of Health Resources Development, Division of Nursing, December 1974.

Barnard, K. E. and M. L. Erickson. *Teaching the Child with Developmental Problems: A Family Care Approach.* 2nd ed. St. Louis: C. V. Mosby, 1976.

Bates, B. *A Guide to Physical Examination.* 2nd ed. Philadelphia: J. B. Lippincott, 1979.

Battle, C. U. "Chronic Physical Disease: Behavioral Aspects." *Pediatr Clin North Am* 22:525–531, August 1975.

Brill, C. B. and M. H. Mitchell. "Seizures and Other Paroxysmal Disorders." *Advances in Pediatrics 28*:441–489, 1981.

Centers for Disease Control. "Surveillance of Childhood Lead Poisoning—United States." *MMWR 31*:118–119, March 12, 1982.

Cherry, F. F., editor. *Childhood Lead Poisoning Prevention and Control.* New Orleans: Dept. of Health and Human Resources, Office of Health Services and Environmental Quality, 1981.

Chisholm, J. J. "Management of Increased Lead Absorption and Lead Poisoning in Children." *N Engl J Med 289*:1016–1018, November 8, 1973.

Consensus Statement. "Febrile Seizures: Long-Term Management of Children with Fever-Associated Seizures." *Pediatrics 66*:1009–1012, December 1980.

Conway, B. L. *Pediatric Neurological Nursing.* St. Louis: C. V. Mosby, 1977.

Diamond, S., et al. "Symposium Issue: Current Concepts of Headache." *Postgrad Med 56*(3), September 1974.

Emerson, R., et al. "Stopping Medications in Children with Epilepsy." *N Engl J Med 304*:1125–1129, May 7, 1981.

Frankenburg, W. K., et al. "The Newly Abbreviated and Revised Denver Developmental Screening Test." *J Pediatr 99*:995–999, December 1981.

Frankenburg, W. K. and A. F. North. *A Guide to Screening for the EPSDT Program under Medicaid.* Washington DC: Social and Rehabilitation Service, Dept. HEW, 1974.

Frankenburg, W. K., et al. "The Revised Denver Developmental Screening Test: Its Accuracy as a Screening Instrument." *J Pediatr 79*:988–995, December 1971.

Freeman, J. M. "Febrile Seizures: A Consensus of Their Significance, Evaluation, and Treatment." *Pediatrics 66*:1009, December 1980.

Green, J. B. "Seizures." In M. Green and R. J. Haggerty, editors, *Ambulatory Pediatrics II.* Philadelphia: W. B. Saunders, 1977. Pp. 306–320.

Haynes, U. *A Developmental Approach to Casefinding.* DHEW Publ. No. (HSA) 79-5210. Washington DC: U.S. Dept HEW, Public Health Service, Office for Maternal and Child Health, 1978.

Hoekelman, R. A., et al. *Principles of Pediatrics: Health Care of the Young.* New York: McGraw-Hill, 1978.

Lombroso, C. T. and P. Lerman. "Breathholding Spells (Cyanotic and Pallid Infantile Syncope)." *Pediatrics 39*:563–581, April 1967.

O'Pray, M. "Developmental Screening Tools: Using Them Effectively." *Am J Maternal Child Nursing 5*:126–130, March/April 1980.

Partin, J. C. "Reye's Syndrome: Early Detection Can Now Save Up to 97% of Patients." *Pediatr Consult* 2:3–12, 1981.

Peterson, H. de C. "Diagnosis of Hypotonia in Children: Types, Differential, Diagnosis and Management." *Pediatr Ann* 5:30–38, May 1976.

Powell, M. L. *Assessment and Management of Developmental Changes and Problems in Children.* 2nd ed. St. Louis: C. V. Mosby, 1981.

Rudolph, A. M., editor. *Pediatrics.* 17th ed. East Norwalk, CT: Appleton-Century-Crofts, 1982.

Smith, D. W., et al. "Congenital Hypothyroidism—Signs and Symptoms in the Newborn Period." *J Pediatr* 87:958–962, December 1975.

Starko, K. M. "Reye's Syndrome and Salicylate Use." *Pediatrics* 66:859–864, December 1980.

Thompson, J. A. "Diagnosis and Treatment of Headache in the Pediatric Patient." *Curr Probl Pediatr* 10:5–50, August 1980.

Vaughan, V. C., et al. editors. *Nelson Textbook of Pediatrics,* 11th ed. Philadelphia: W. B. Saunders, 1979.

Volk, D. M. "Reye's Syndrome: An Update for the Practicing Physician." *Clin Pediatr* 20:505–511, August 1981.

Waechter, E. H. and F. G. Blake. *Nursing Care of Children.* 9th ed. Philadelphia: J. B. Lippincott, 1976.

25

Language and Learning Disabilities

Approximately 10 to 20 percent of all school-age children experience learning difficulties in school. The causes are complex, multifactorial, and often intangible. Significant changes have occurred in the study of language, learning, and reading over the past 20 years, which have emphasized the role that language plays in learning and in other aspects of child development.

The 1969 Children with Specific Learning Disabilities Act defines learning disabilities:

> Children with special learning disabilities exhibit a disorder in one or more of the basic psychological processes involved in understanding or in using spoken or written language. These may be manifested in disorders of listening, thinking, reading, writing, spelling, or arithmetic. They include conditions which have been referred to as perceptual handicaps, brain injury, minimal brain dysfunction, dyslexia, developmental aphasia, etc. They do not include learning problems which are due primarily to visual, hearing, or motor handicaps, to mental retardation, emotional disturbance, or to environmental disadvantage.

This chapter highlights information for the nurse practitioner on the early identification, referral, and management of children with language and learning disabilities. For a comprehensive review of language and learning disabilities the reader is referred to the reference list at the end of this chapter.

ASSESSMENT

Children with language and learning difficulties are a heterogenous group presenting with a variety of complex symptoms. The comprehensive evaluation of a child with a language and learning disability involves specialists in language, education, psychology, and family dynamics. The nurse practitioner in collaboration with the pediatrician often functions as the primary coordinator of the evaluation and provides follow-up with the school and the family.

Initially the nurse practitioner gathers observational reports from the school, performs a thorough history and physical examination, and uses selected neurodevelopmental screening tools. If further evaluation is indicated, the nurse practitioner refers the child for a more thorough and sophisticated assessment.

History

A complete history is performed with careful attention to the areas listed below (see Chapter 1, Child Health Assessment).

PARENTAL CONCERN

Allow the parents to describe their concerns in their own words. Elicit a description and onset of the child's behavior that presents problems for them. Look for a pattern of difficulty and stress. Be alert to concerns of difficulty sleeping or feeding, poor health, delayed speech acquisition, poor coordination or concentration, short attention span, restlessness, and behavioral problems.

SCHOOL

Inquire about the child's successes and difficulties in school, most difficult subject, easiest subject, dislike for or reluctance to attend school, poor grades, complaints about performance or academic skills from the teacher, problems in peer relationship, and poor self-concept.

FAMILY HISTORY

Obtain history of familial reading, spelling, speech or behavior disorders, childrearing practices within the family, parental ideas about discipline, conflicts in the management of the child, life-style, and psychologic disorders.

PREGNANCY AND BIRTH HISTORY

Obtain information about complications during pregnancy (bleeding, preeclampsia, infectious or viral diseases), prenatal ingestion of medication, labor or delivery (hypoxia, prematurity), nature of the labor, condition of the baby at delivery, and birth weight.

INFANCY

Obtain information on temperament characteristics, attachment behaviors, colic, feeding problems, abnormal crying, excessive sleeping, and increased irritability.

DEVELOPMENTAL HISTORY

Obtain information about specific growth landmarks (sit, walk, tie shoes, ride a tricycle, ride a bicycle), language development (onset, quality and quantity of babbling and consonant sounds, use of isolated words, phrases, sentences, ability to use meaningful words in speech, ability to let parents know what is wanted, ability to follow directions, different native tongue or dialect), toilet training, temper tantrums, approach to new tasks, and motor coordination (small and large muscle). Look for signs of maturational delay.

PAST MEDICAL HISTORY

Inquire about history of frequent colds, chronic ear infections, hoarseness, serious illness or hospitalizations, seizures, medications used, lead poisoning, chronic illness, physical handicaps, enuresis, encopresis, and accidents.

Physical Examination

A complete physical examination is performed (refer to Chapter 1, Child Health Assessment). Screening for visual acuity (see Chapter 15) and hearing are performed. Significant physical findings for language difficulties are: structural deviations, asymmetry, malformed ear, cleft palate, submucous cleft (a large notch in the upper hard palate), a bifid uvula, tongue-tie, microglossia, tongue thrust, malocclusion, or tongue paralysis. Significant physical findings for learning difficulties are discussed below.

Supplementary Neurologic Evaluation

Refer to Chapter 24, The Neuromuscular System, for the neurologic examination. A supplementary neurologic evaluation is done to measure higher cortical function and elicit "soft" neurologic signs. The diagnostic value of "soft" signs is controversial. The term "soft" neurologic signs has been used to describe perceptual or cognitive behaviors that are present beyond the usual chronologic age in development, such as the persistence of left-right confusion beyond 9 years of age. It has also been used in the description of nonspecific entities such as clumsiness (Conway, 1977). "Soft" neurologic signs reflect developmental and maturational differences in the central nervous system and may indicate abnormalities in the maturational development of the central nervous system of the child. While they do not necessarily indicate a pathologic condition or injury, the presence of these signs may indicate maturational delay. More than half the children with hyperactivity have some "soft" neurologic signs such as clumsiness, short attention span, impulsivity, distractability, hyperactivity, and social immaturity (Ross and Ross, 1982, p. 79). The evaluations of fine-motor coordination, special sensory skills, and laterality and orientation in space are taken from the amplified neurologic examination used at the Child Study Unit, University of California, San Francisco.*

EVALUATION OF FINE-MOTOR COORDINATION

Observe the child during the following activities:

1. Undressing, unbuttoning
2. Tying shoes

---

*Adapted from H. F. Gofman and B. W. Allmond: Learning and Language Disorders in Children. Part II: The School-Aged Child, in L. Gluck, editor, *Current Problems in Pediatrics*, September 1971. Copyright © 1971 by Year Book Medical Publishers, Chicago. Used by permission.

3. Rapid alternating touch of fingertips by thumb
4. Rattle of an imaginary doorknob
5. Unscrewing of an imaginary light bulb
6. Pencil grasp and use; penmanship
7. Rapid tongue movements
8. Hand grip
9. Inversion of both feet (Look for similar movements of the hands. See below.)
10. Repeating several times rapidly: "kitty, kitty, kitty"; "pa, ta, ka" (Accurate reproduction of these sounds generally indicates adequate articulatory coordination.)

Note

- The child's general facility and coordination with these small muscle tasks.
- On items 3, 4, 5, 8, and 9, any marked movement of other parts of the body that mirror or duplicate movements of the test side. Such movements are called associated motor movements, mirror movements, adventitious overflow movements, or synkinesia. When marked they are felt to represent, particularly after 8 to 10 years, a lack of normal cortical inhibition.
- Excessive pressure on the pencil point or a pencil held too lightly. Fingers placed directly over the point, or fingers placed too far (greater than 1 inch) from the point may all indicate difficulty with the coordination of fine musculature within the hands.
- Presence of dysdiadochokinesia, noting speed, accuracy, and sequencing of maneuvers.

EVALUATION OF SPECIAL SENSORY SKILLS

Dual Simultaneous Sensory Tests (Face–Hand Testing) With the child's eyes open demonstrate items 1 and 2 below. Ask the child where she/he has been touched. Then with the child's eyes closed, simultaneously perform items 3, 4, 5, 6.

1. Touch both cheeks.
2. Touch both hands.
3. Touch right cheek and contralateral hand.
4. Touch right cheek and homolateral hand.

5. Touch left cheek and contralateral hand.
6. Touch left cheek and homolateral hand.

   Note

- Rostral dominance: failure to perceive hand stimulus when the face is simultaneously touched. Approximately 80 percent of normal children are able to perform this test without rostral dominance by age 8 years.

Finger Localization Test (Finger Agnosia Test)   Touch two fingers or two spots on one finger simultaneously with the child's eyes closed, after demonstrating first with eyes open. Ask the child: "How many fingers am I touching—one or two?"

   Note

- The number of correct responses in four trials for each hand: six correct answers out of eight is accepted as a "pass." One half of all children pass this test by age 6 years, 90 percent by age 7½ years. This test reflects a child's orientation in space, concept of body image, praxic ability, sensation to touch, and position sense.

EVALUATION OF CHILD'S LATERALITY AND ORIENTATION IN SPACE

Imitation of Gestures   Have the child imitate the following gestures performed by the examiner, emphasizing first that the child must use the same hand as the examiner:

1. Extend index finger.
2. Extend little and index finger.
3. Extend index and middle finger.
4. Touch two thumbs and two index fingers together simultaneously.
5. Form two interlocking rings, thumb and index finger of one hand with thumb and index finger of other hand.
6. Point index finger of one hand down toward the cupped fingers of the opposite hand held below.

   Note

- Difficulty with fine finger movements, manipulation, and/or reproduction of correct gesture.

- After approximately age 8 years, there should not be marked right-left confusion with regard to examiner's right and left. This test reflects a child's ability with finger discrimination, postural praxis, awareness of self-image, and right–left, front–back, up–down orientation.

Following Directions   Ask the child to do the following:

1. Show me your left hand.
2. Show me your right ear.
3. Show me your right eye.
4. Show me your left elbow.
5. Touch your left knee with your left hand.
6. Touch your right ear with your left hand.
7. Touch your left elbow with your right hand.
8. Touch your right cheek with your right hand.
9. Point to my left ear.
10. Point to my right eye.
11. Point to my right hand.
12. Point to my left knee.

Note

- Items 1 through 8 are mastered by approximately age 6 years; items 9 through 12 are mastered by approximately age 8 years.
- Aside from correct versus incorrect responses, any difficulty with following the sequence of directions.

EVALUATION OF PERCEPTUAL–MOTOR FUNCTION

Visual-Motor   Ask the child to copy a circle, square, triangle, and diamond. Observe the child's ability to draw the shapes in a smooth motion, turn corners, especially at right angles, change directions, and accurately reproduce the figure. Also observe eye–hand coordination, spatial and directional organization, and visual–motor coordination. See Chapter 24, Behavior and Mental Status for the average skill response by age.

Auditory-Motor   Ask the child to reproduce in writing the verbal phrases and sentences heard; for example: "My name is
_____." "Write the numbers from 1 to 10." "Write the letters

of the alphabet." "A cat saw a bird." Observe the child's ability to complete the task, to produce and to organize the symbols, and to space the letters. Note any letter or word reversals. A child of 6 years is able to print the first and last names, write the numbers from 1 to 10, and the letters of the alphabet. By 7 years of age the figures are in a horizontal line and become more evenly spaced. By 8 years of age reversals are infrequent.

Gross Motor   Ask the child to lie down in a supine position, stand, walk about 30 steps forward and backward, walk about 25 steps on alternating heels, stand on one foot and hop, skip, and gallop. Observe posture, head tilting, position of hands, legs, toes, straightness of spinal column, exaggerated or asymmetric arm swinging, clumsiness, or problems in balance. By 6 years the child is able to walk on alternating heels. By 8 years the child is able to stand on one foot, hop, skip, and gallop.

ELECTROENCEPHALOGRAM (EEG)

An EEG is sometimes indicated to provide for a more complete evaluation of the nervous system, to confirm the "organic" nature of the learning disorder, to rule out a hidden seizure disorder, to provide a baseline for future evaluation, and to better ensure the safety of a trial of medication which may precipitate a seizure (Whitsell, 1969).

Screening Tests for School Readiness

Screening tests are designed to evaluate the child's educational preparedness and are constructed to assess specific school-related skills, particularly the ability to read and do arithmetic. The target group for which these tests are designed is children 5 to 6 years of age. Administration of a screening test for school readiness can identify a child at risk for school problems, and thereby permit early intervention.

PRESCHOOL INVENTORY

It is designed to measure abilities in areas generally considered necessary for success in the first year of school. It tests performance and is particularly useful with disadvantaged children aged 3 to 6 years. The inventory consists of 64 items that can be divided into four subtests: (1) personal–social responsiveness, (2) associative vocabulary, (3) concept activation–numerical, and (4) concept activation–sensory.

It requires fifteen minutes for administration and scoring. The test is available from Educational Testing Service, 1947 Center Street, Berkeley, CA 94604.

SPRIGLE SCHOOL READINESS SCREENING TEST (SSRST)

The screening test is designed specifically for use by physicians and nurses to measure readiness for school entrance by children 4 years, 6 months of age to 6 years, 9 months of age. The test takes 15 to 20 minutes to administer. Nine areas are examined: verbal comprehension, size relationships, visual discrimination, reasoning, understanding of numbers, analogies, information, vocabulary, and spatial relations. For test materials write to Herbert A. Sprigle, Ph.D., and James Lonier, M.D., Learning to Learn School, Inc., 1936 San Marco Blvd., Jacksonville, FL 32207.

Communication Assessment

This involves assessment of one or all of the dimensions of communication: hearing, language, articulation, fluency, and voice.

HEARING ASSESSMENT

The ability to hear is critical for the development of speech, language, and learning. Early diagnosis of a hearing impairment is essential since even minimal loss may significantly affect the development of language. The response to frequencies of sound in the human ear ranges from 20 to 20,000 Hertz (cycles per second) with the speech range from 500 to 2,000 Hertz (Northern and Downs, 1978).

Hearing Loss

TUNING FORK TESTS Tuning forks can be used to distinguish between conductive and sensorineural hearing loss in a cooperative older child. However, tuning fork tests are difficult to interpret:

- The Weber test is done by striking the tuning fork and placing the handle on the center of the forehead. The child is asked to indicate in which ear the sound can be heard. Normally, the sound should not lateralize to one ear more than to the other.
- The Rinne test is done by striking the tuning fork and placing the handle first on the mastoid process and then near the external ear without interfering with the sound waves. The child is asked to indicate when the sound disappears in each position. Normally, the child should hear the sound longer near the ear canal than on the mastoid bone (+ Rinne), since air conduction is longer than bone conduction. If the sound is heard longer on the mastoid bone, the Rinne test is negative.

CONDUCTIVE HEARING LOSS   Conductive hearing defects are most often secondary to problems in the external or middle ear that impair the normal conduction of sound to the inner ear. The primary effect of the conduction loss is a reduction in the sound without distortion of clarity. The Weber test lateralizes to the poor hearing ear and the Rinne test is negative. An audiogram confirms the hearing loss. These are the most common hearing impairments in children. The impairment is often mild and responds to medical or surgical intervention.

SENSORINEURAL HEARING LOSS   In children, it is generally inherited and can be produced by diseases of the inner ear or of the eighth cranial nerve. The principal result is that the sounds are distorted, making discrimination difficult. Only certain frequencies may be involved, and the child may respond to most sounds at ordinary levels of loudness. The high frequencies tend to be more affected than the low tones unless there is severe involvement, which then causes both high and low tones to be impaired. The Weber test lateralizes to the good ear and the Rinne test is positive. The impairment is rarely responsive to treatment and is generally a greater handicap to communication than are conductive defects.

HIGH-RISK INDICATORS FOR HEARING LOSS

1. Parental concern about hearing problems such as paying little attention to parental requests
2. Family history of childhood hearing impairment

3. History of bleeding or infectious episodes in the early months of pregnancy such as rubella, syphilis or cytomegalovirus.
4. Anatomic malformations involving the head or neck (e.g., pinna abnormalities, cleft palate), birth weight 1,500 gm, hyperbilirubinemia at level exceeding indications for exchange transfusions, or severe asphyxia (e.g., Apgar scores 0 to 3).
5. History of fluid accumulation in the middle ear, treatment with ototoxic drugs such as kanamycin, streptomycin, or neomycin in infancy, or chronic nasal obstruction
6. Environmental history of continuous loud noise
7. History of bacterial meningitis, especially *H. influenzae*

Development of Hearing Responses   Weiss and Lillywhite (1981, p. 106) identify two distinct stages of hearing maturation by age:

Age	*Response Stage*
3–6 months	Reflexive responses to loud, sudden noises such as eye blinks, body jerks, toe and finger spreading, crying, sighing, breathing rate changes, and sometimes smiling
7–12 months	Listening responses to locate the sound source by turning the head, searching with the eyes, quieting behavior

For more specific hearing developmental responses, the reader is referred to Table 25-1, Landmarks of Hearing Development.

Hearing Screening   Hearing testing has progressed to such a level of sophistication that even infants can now be reliably evaluated.

ELECTROPHYSIOLOGIC AUDIOMETRY (EVOKED RESPONSE)   This is used with children who are unable to cooperate. Hearing acuity is determined with a fairly high reliability. The response to an electrical stimulation is recorded on computer graphs.

IMPEDANCE AUDIOMETRY   This measures the pressure in the middle ear, performance of the tympanic membrane or presence of perforation, patency of the eustachian tube, and the integrity of the ossicular chain. Tympanometry is one of the tests that make up impedance audiometry (see Chapter 17). It does not measure hear-

Table 25-1
Landmarks of Hearing Development

3 months	Is *startled* by loud sounds and soothed by mother's voice. Lateral turning to the side of the sound: turning in the general direction, but not looking directly at the sound source.
6 months	Turns eyes and head *to search* for location of sound, but does not necessarily find the sound source on the first attempt. Responds to mother's voice, own name, imitates own noises, and enjoys soundmaking toys.
8 months	Turns eyes and head in a *sweeping motion* to the sound source. Whereas at 6 months child turned in the general direction of the sound source and then attempted to locate it, child now attempts to look in the direction of the sound source and locate it all in one sweeping motion of the eyes and head.
10 months	Turns eyes and head in a *direct diagonal motion* to locate the sound source. Looks directly, promptly, and predictably to the sound source. Also responds to own name, telephone ringing, and someone's voice.
12 months	Begins to show *voluntary control over responses to sound;* may or may not respond, or may delay response. This behavior of selectively responding should not be interpreted as a hearing loss as long as it is intermittent and of recent origin. This might be considered the beginning of listening refinement.
18 months	Has begun to develop *gross discriminations* by learning to distinguish between highly dissimilar noises such as a doorbell and a train, or a barking dog and an automobile horn, and mother's or father's voice.
24 months	Although normative information is not available at this age level, you can expect the child to *refine gross discriminative skills.*
36 months	Starts to *distinguish dissimilar speech sounds,* such as the difference between /ee/ and /er/, although there may be some difficulty with the concepts of "same" and "different."
48 months	Begins to make *fine discriminations* among similar speech sounds, such as between /f/ and /th/ or between /f/ and /s/. The child has matured enough to be tested directly with an audiometer. At this age formal hearing testing can usually be carried out. Not only has hearing developed to its optimum level, but listening has become considerably refined as well.

Source: Reprinted with permission from C. E. Weiss and H. S. Lillywhite, *Communicative Disorders,* 2nd ed., St. Louis: C. V. Mosby, 1981. P. 65.

ing, but it can determine approximate hearing thresholds. Although it can be performed on a child of any age, it is unreliable in the newborn period because of the pliability of the external ear canal (Rudolph, 1982).

Suggested guidelines for hearing screening:

1. In a well child without any of the high-risk indicators, administer at least once during the first year, and then yearly.
2. In an infant or child with some high-risk indicators, refer for a hearing evaluation and follow regularly.
3. In a child who has an ear infection or who has been treated with a known ototoxic drug, administer as part of the follow-up plan.

A child with a high-frequency loss may be mistakenly regarded as hearing normally. Such a child may respond to lower frequency sounds including soft environmental noise, soft speech in the lower frequencies, and may partially compensate for the high frequency loss by reading lips or using context clues. Hearing losses can also vary in accordance with an associated upper respiratory infection or exacerbation of allergic symptoms. Be wary that normal audiograms recorded when the child is free of symptoms do not guarantee normal hearing at other times. For best results:

1. Test infants between feedings.
2. Test older infants and toddlers with sound stimuli that are interesting and familiar such as jingle bells, spoons, or tissue paper.
3. Use more than one stimulus in a particular range if the child does not respond to the first noisemaker. The lack of response may be due to disinterest with the particular sound.
4. Check the squeeze toy for air flow to prevent a positive response from the air flow rather than the sounds.

NEWBORN TO 3 MONTHS Reflexive auditory responses do not eliminate the presence of mild, moderate, and even moderately severe bilateral hearing loss. Central auditory impairments that may later retard language growth and speech development may also be present with reflexive auditory responses (Lillywhite, 1970). Infants who are at high risk for auditory disorders should be referred to an audiologist for a more precise evaluation. As mentioned previously, electrophysiologic devices such as brain stem audiometry are now available. Such devices are expensive and are usually found in regional medical centers, but they are essential to use in infants with high-risk indicators. Some communities have found that a high-risk registry affords early identification and treatment of hearing-impaired infants (Bergstrom et al., 1977).

3 MONTHS TO 12 MONTHS Observations are made of the child's ability to localize the source of the sound. A response indicates only that a child is not deaf. It does not indicate how well the child hears.

Technique The hearing response is tested in a quiet room with the child seated on the parent's lap, supported under the arms, and held so the infant has freedom for head movement. Two examiners are required. The first examiner visually distracts the child with a silent bright-colored toy, while the other examiner delivers the sounds with the noisemaker as softly as possible on one side about 36 inches out of the child's field of vision. The first examiner observes for a response. If the child does not react, increase the loudness of the noisemaker. The test is repeated on the other side. The first responses are the most consistent.

Test Stimuli Environmental sound stimuli are the most satisfactory. Examples are the crinkle of cellophane or tissue paper, the soft scrape of a spoon in a cup, squeeze toys, and small bells.

1 TO 3 YEARS The child's activity level and alertness are increased so special care must be taken to keep the noisemakers out of the field of vision.

Technique Two examiners may be needed. With the child in the parent's lap the child is either visually distracted or allowed to play with the toys. The second stimulus is delivered to the right and left ears. Noisemakers of known frequency and intensity are used. Test materials can be measured at most speech and hearing departments and electronic laboratories.

Test Stimuli In addition to noisemakers listed previously, speech signals may be used as test items. Examples are softly voicing syllables such as "puh," "baa," "bu," "ga," or sounds such as "s" and "sh."

Indications for Referral A child should be referred for further evaluation if the following occur:

1. Failure to respond

2. Inconsistent responses

3. Any doubt on the part of the examiner

Referral of a deaf child before the age of 9 months or 1 year is critical to provide every opportunity for the child to develop normal speech (Fry, 1966).

3 YEARS AND OLDER Formal electronic testing is available for children of this age group. The most common screening procedure is pure-tone audiometry. An audiogram indicates the results of this procedure. It provides a visual profile of the child's audiometry acuity or hearing level, and it can also provide information about the type of hearing loss. The minimum intensity of a tone at which the child responds correctly 50 percent of the time is defined as the *threshold of hearing*, specified in decibels (dB). The average hearing level of "normal" young adults is 0 dB. Normal hearing ranges from 0 dB to 15 dB between 250 and 8,000 Hz (frequency or pitch). Table 25-2 categorizes hearing losses and the resulting speech problem. Numerous sources are available which describe the screening audiometry technique. Several resources (Lillywhite, 1970; Caulfield, 1976) are listed at the end of ths chapter.

LANGUAGE ASSESSMENT

The most effective assessment approach is to obtain a representative sample of the child's oral language interacting with people.

Table 25-2
Categorization of Hearing Losses

Category	Threshold (dB)	Classification	Speech Problem
1	15–30	Mild hearing impairment	Difficulty with faint speech
2	31–50	Moderate hearing impairment	Difficulty with normal intensity speech
3	51–80	Severe hearing impairment	Difficulty with loud speech
4	81–100	Profound hearing impairment	Difficulty with amplified speech

Source: Reprinted with permission from C. E. Weiss and H. S. Lillywhite, *Communicative Disorders*, 2nd ed., St. Louis: C. V. Mosby, 1981. P. 103. Modified from J. Northern and M. Downs, *Hearing in Children*, 2nd ed., Baltimore: Williams & Wilkins, 1978.

Methods for obtaining language samples include having the child play with toys, having the child describe or label pictures, having the child define words or carry out simple commands, or taping the child's conversations. Table 25-3 outlines the development of language comprehension and Table 25-4 outlines the development of language usage.

Indicators for referral of receptive language problems include the following (Weiss and Lillywhite, 1981, p. 143):

Age	*Indicator*
15 months	No response to name, "no-no," "bye-bye," and "bottle."
21 months	Incorrect response to "Give me that," "Sit down," "Stand up."
24 months	Unable to understand and point, on command, to mouth, nose, hair, and ears.
30 months	Unable to understand and demonstrate, on command, in, on, under, front, and back.
48 months	Incorrectly answers the questions: "What do we sleep on?" "What do we sit on?" "What do we cook on?" "What is your name?" "What do you do when you are hungry?" "What do you do when you are thirsty?" Inability to distinguish boy from girl, big from little, one object from two or more objects.
60 months (5 years)	Unable to tell the use of book, stove, house, and key. Cannot distinguish soft from hard and smooth from rough and cannot tell why we have a chair, house, dress, and window.
72 months (6 years)	Unable to explain the reason for having eyes, ears, and legs. Does not have number concepts up to 5.
84 to 96 months (7 to 8 years)	Does not know differences such as the difference between a bird and a dog, the youngest and the oldest, cannot recognize likenesses such as how an apple and an orange are alike.

Table 25-3
Development of Language Comprehension

Chronological Age[a]	Comprehension
6 months	Responds by raising arms when mother says come here and reaches toward the child. Responds appropriately to friendly or angry voices. Moves or looks toward family member when named, such as "Where's daddy?"
12 months	Up to 10 words. No, bye-bye, pat-a-cake, hot, own name. One simple direction such as "Sit down," or "Give it to me." These commands are usually accompanied by gesture.
18 months	Up to 50 words. Recognizes between 6 and 12 objects by name such as dog, cat, show, bottle, and ball. Identifies three body parts such as eyes, nose, and mouth. Understands "now" and simple commands unaccompanied by gesture, such as "Give me the doll," "Open your mouth," and "Stick out your tongue."
24 months	Up to 1,200 words. In, on, under. Identifies dog, ball, engine, bed, doll, scissors, hair, mouth, feet, ear, nose, hand, eye, cat, button, cup, spoon, chair, box, car, key, and fork. Distinguishes between one and many. Formulates negative judgment (a knife is not a fork); understands soon, simple stories. Follows simple directions; responds by pointing to show-me questions. Is beginning to make distinctions between "you" and "me."
30 months	Up to 2,400 words. Identifies action in pictures and objects by use. Carries out one- and two-part commands, such as "Pick up your shoe and give it to mommy." Knows what we drink out of, what goes on our feet, what we can buy candy with, what we can cut with, ride in, and what we use to iron clothes with, cook on, sleep on, sit on, and sweep the floor with. Understands plurals, questions, difference between boy and girl, the concept I, up, down, run, walk, jump, throw, fast, more, and my.
36 months	Up to 3,600 words. Understands both, two, not today, what we do when we are thirsty, hungry, sleepy, why we have stoves, wait, later, big, new, different,

Table 25-3 *(Continued)*

Chronological Age[a]	Comprehension
	strong, today, another, and taking turns at play. Carries out two- and some three-item commands such as "Give me the ball," "Pick up the doll," and "Sit down." Identifies several colors. Is aware of past and future.
42 months	Up to 4,200 words. Knows such words as what, where, how, see, little, funny, we, all, surprise, secret. Knows first name, number concepts to 2, and how to answer questions appropriately, such as "Do you have a doggy?" "Which is the boy?" "Which is the girl?" "Where is the dress?" and "What toys do you have?"
48 months	Up to 5,600 words. Carries out three-item commands consistently. Knows why we have houses, books, stove, umbrella, key. Knows nearly all colors, words such as somebody, anybody, even, almost, now, something, like, but, bigger, too, at least one nursery rhyme, full name, one or two songs, number concepts to 4, and understands most preschool children's stories. Can complete opposite analogies such as brother is a boy, sister is a _____; in daytime it is light, at night it is _____; father is a man, mother is a _____; the sun shines during the day, the moon at _____.
54 months	Up to 6,500 words. Knows what a house, book, window, chair, and dress are made of and what we do with our eyes and ears. Understands differences in texture and composition such as hard, soft, rough, and smooth. Begins to name or point to penny, nickel, and dime. Inconsistently understands if, because, when, why.
60 months	Up to 9,600 words. Knows numbers to 5. Knows and names colors. Defines words in terms of use, such as a horse is to ride. Also defines wind, ball, hat, and stove. Consistently understands words such as if, because, and when. Knows what the following are for: house, fork, and legs. Begins to understand right and left.

Table 25-3 *(Continued)*

Chronological Age[a]	Comprehension
66 months	Up to 13,500 words. Knows number concepts to 7. Knows right and left. Understands most simple, compound, and complex sentences if not too long. Knows functions of body parts (eyes, ears, etc.). Understands dependent clauses, such as "When I open the door, put the cat out."
72 months	Up to 15,000 words. Knows number concepts to 10 (this includes meaning and relationships of numbers). Understands the meaning of morning, afternoon, night, summer, and winter. Can relate differences between objects, animals, and clothing. Is beginning to answer a few similarities correctly, for example, "In what way are _____ and _____ alike or the same? apple and peach? piano and violin? airplane and bus?" Understands differences such as how are a dog and a bird different.

Source: Reprinted with permission from C. E. Weiss and H. L. Lillywhite, *Communicative Disorders*, 2nd ed., St. Louis: C. V. Mosby, 1981. P. 55.

[a]Chronological age assumes normal or average intellectual functioning. If the child is mentally retarded or has superior intelligence, then perhaps the concept of mental age would be more appropriate.

Table 25-4
Development of Language Usage

Chronological Age[a]	Expression
6 months	Repeats self-produced sounds. Imitates sounds. Vocalizes to persons. Uses 12 different phonemes.
12 months	Up to 3 words besides mama and dada. May say such words as bye-bye, hi, baby, kitty, and puppy. Uses up to 18 different phonemes.
18 months	Up to 20 words and 21 different phonemes: jargon and echolalia are present. Uses names of familiar objects, 1-word sentences such as go or eat, gestures, words such as no, mine, eat, good, bad, hot, cold, nice, here, where, more; and expressions such as oh oh, what's that, and all gone; the use of words may be quite inconsistent.

Table 25-4 *(Continued)*

Chronological Age[a]	Expression
25 months	Up to 270 words and 25 different phonemes. Jargon and echolalia are almost gone. Averages 75 words per hour during free play. Talks in words, phrases, and 2- to 3-word sentences. Averages 2 words per response. First pronouns appear, such as I, me, mine, it, who, and that. Adjectives and adverbs are just beginning to appear. Names objects and common pictures. Enjoys Mother Goose. Refers to self by name such as Bobby go bye-bye. Uses phrases such as I (or me) want, go bye-bye, want cookie, up daddy, nice doll, ball all gone, and where kitty.
30 months	Up to 425 words and 27 different phonemes. Jargon and echolalia no longer present. Averages 140 words per hour. Names words such as chair, can, box, key, and door. Repeats two digits from memory. Average sentence length is about 2½ words. Uses more adjectives and adverbs. Demands repetition from others such as do it again. Almost always announces intentions before acting. Begins to ask questions of adults.
36 months	Up to 900 words in simple sentences averaging 3 to 4 words per sentence. Averages 170 words per hour. Uses words such as when, time, today, not today, new, different, another, big, strong, surprise, and secret. Can repeat three digits, name one color, say name, give simple account of experiences, and tell stories that can be understood. Begins to use plurals. Uses some prepositions and uses more pronouns, adjectives, and adverbs. Describes at least one element of a picture. Is aware of past and future. Uses commands such as you make it, I want, you do it, and like that. Also uses expressions such as I can't, I won't tell you, I don't want to, and I'm busy. Verbalizes toilet needs and expresses desire to take turns. Communication includes criticism, commands, requests, threats, questions, and answers.

Table 25-4 *(Continued)*

Chronological Age[a]	Expression
42 months	Up to 1,200 words in mostly complete sentences averaging between 4 and 5 words per sentence. Has been heard to use all 50 phonemes. Seven percent of sentences are compound or complex. Averages 203 words per hour. Rate of speech is faster. Relates experiences and tells about activities in sequential order. Uses words such as what, where, how, see, little, funny, they, we, she, he, some, any, several, and too. Can say a nursery rhyme. Asks permission, such as "Can I?" or "Will I?"
48 months	Up to 1,500 words in sentences averaging 5 to 5½ words. Averages 400 words per hour. Counts to 3, repeats four digits, names three objects, and repeats 9-word sentences from memory. Names the primary colors, some coins, and relates fanciful tales. Enjoys rhyming nonsense words and using exaggerations. Demands reasons for why and how. Questioning is at a peak, up to 500 a day. Passes judgment on own activities. Can recite a poem from memory or sing a song. Uses such words as even, almost, now, something, like, and but. Typical expressions might include "I'm so tired," "You almost hit me," and "Now I will make something else."
54 months	Up to 1,800 words in sentences averaging 5½ to 6 words. Now averages only 230 words per hour and is satisfied with less verbalization. Does little commanding or demanding. Likes surprising. About one in 10 sentences is compound or complex, and only 8 percent of the sentences are incomplete. Can define 10 common words and count to 20. Common expressions are "I don't know," "I said," tiny, funny, surprised, and because. Asks questions for information and learns to control and manipulate persons and situations with language.

Source: Reprinted with permission from C. E. Weiss and H. L. Lillywhite, *Communicative Disorders*, 2nd ed., St. Louis: C. V. Mosby, 1981. P. 57.

Indicators for referral of expressive language problems include the following (Weiss and Lillywhite, 1981, pp. 143–144):

Age	Indicator
18 months	Unable to say at least six words with appropriate meaning.
24 months	Unable to combine words into phrases, such as "Go bye-bye," "Want cookie."
30 months	Unable to use short sentences, such as "Mommy see dolly," "Daddy go bye-bye."
36 months	Does not ask simple questions.
48 months (4 years)	Uses telegraphic, reversed, or confused sentences, such as "Me car go," "Baby loud crying," "Candy me want." Does not use auxiliary verbs, such as "is," "have," and "can," with main verbs.
60 months (5 years)	Does not use the personal pronoun "I" such as "Me (instead of I) want a cookie," or uses name instead of pronoun, such as "Bobby (instead of I) want a drink."
	Consistently uses past tenses, plurals, and pronouns incorrectly, such as "Them throwed a balls." Possesses a limited and shallow expressive vocabulary of fewer than 200 to 300 simple words.

Additional indicators include failure to improve in sentence length, complexity, and accuracy within any 6-month period after 2 years of age, and difficulty in self-expression, according to age level or concern about language used.

ARTICULATION ASSESSMENT

Articulation refers to the clarity, intelligibility, accuracy of a unit of speech sound (phoneme) when used alone or combined in words, the use and perception of speech sounds, phonological rules, linguistic features, contrastive features, and nonsegmental characteristics of verbal communication (Weiss and Lillywhite, 1981, p. 75). Nonsegmental characteristics include aspects such as facial and bodily expressions, posture, eye contact, vocal inflection, pitch, loudness, quality, resonance, rhythm, and rate.

Evaluation of articulation requires that the nurse practitioner be able to discriminate speech sounds. Misarticulations are described in terms of omissions, substitutions, or distortions. Assessment is also made with respect to the position of the consonant sound in syllables or words. Misarticulated consonant sounds may be referred to as occurring in the beginning, middle, or end positions in words. Table 25-5 identifies key words containing consonant phonemes in the different positions. By 24 months of age, all the vowels are present, while the consonants continue to develop in an orderly sequence until the child is 8 years and older. Table 25-6 lists the sequence of consonant development in speech.

The most common communication disorders are articulatory problems. Weiss and Lillywhite (1981, p. 114) offer these preventive measures for the child:

• Demonstrate awareness of when different sounds are learned and emphasize the sound at the appropriate age. See Table 25-6.

• Demonstrate the importance of clearly spoken words and provide the child with many opportunities to experiment using his or her vocal cords.

• Provide a good speech model: adults should speak clearly and slowly with careful phrasing and intonation. During the infancy period, adults should babble using precise sounds and allowing time for imitation. A daily period of time should be set aside specifically for making sounds, listening, and talking. Toys, objects, pictures, and books are useful for naming and discussing exercises.

• Use a variety of facial expressions and other forms of nonverbal communication.

SCREENING TESTS FOR SPEECH AND LANGUAGE DEVELOPMENT

Caution should be exercised when using screening tests, and the results should be judiciously interpreted and generalized. Selected screening tests are presented here.

Denver Articulation Screening Examination (DASE): 2½ to 6 years
This is a screening tool for use by personnel other than therapists. It is basically a word-imitation test of 22 items complete with pictures. In this test the examiner says the word and asks the child to repeat it. Test materials are available from: LADOCA Project and Publishing, Inc., 51st Avenue and Lincoln Street, Denver, CO 80216.

Table 25-5
Key Words Containing Consonant Phonemes
in the Different Positions

Phoneme	Initial	Medial	Final
/p/	pig	puppy	cup
/b/	bottle	baby	bib
/m/	mittens	lemon	arm
/n/	nose	banana	spoon
/ng/	—	singing	ring
/w/	window	sandwich	—
/h/	hoarse	grasshopper	—
/t/	tongue	butter	boat
/d/	dog	ladder	dad
/k/	cat	chicken	milk
/g/	gun	wagon	pig
/f/	fork	telephone	knife
/v/	vacuum	shovel	stove
/y/	yellow	onion	—
/th/	thumb	bathtub	teeth
/th/	that	mother	bathe
/l/	lamp	balloon	ball
/r/	rabbit	carrot	ear
/s/	sun	pencil	house
/z/	zipper	scissors	nose
/ch/	chair	pitcher	watch
/j/	jar	pajamas	orange
/sh/	shoe	washing	fish
/zh/	—	treasure	garage

Consonant blends: Airplane, clock, blocks, tree, ice cream, drum, squirrel, brush, flag, sleeping, stove, string, bridge, pray, frog, glass, grass, spoon, spring, skate, scratch, snow, small, swing.

Source: Reprinted with permission from C. E. Weiss and H. L. Lillywhite, *Communicative Disorders*, 2nd ed., St. Louis: C. V. Mosby, 1981. P. 76.

Table 25-6
The Development of Consonants in Children's Speech[a]

Consonant	Age 2	Age 3	Age 4	Age 5	Age 6	Age 7
/p/	I	F				
/b/	I	F				
/d/	I		F			
/h/	I					
/w/	I					
/m/	I&F					
/n/	I	F				
/t/		I&F				
/k/		I		F		
/g/		I		F		
/f/		I	F			
/l/			I		F	
/y/			I			
/j/			I		F	
/ng/			F			
/v/				I	F	
/th/(voiceless)				I	F	
/s/				I		F

Source: From H. F. Gofman and B. W. Allmond, Learning and Language Disorders in Children. Part I: The Preschool Child, in L. Gluck, editor, *Current Problems in Pediatrics*, August 1971. Copyright © 1971 by Year Book Medical Publishers, Inc., Chicago. Used by permission.

[a]This table indicates the age by which approximately 90 percent of children produce each consonant in words with reasonable consistency. *I* indicates that the consonant is produced in the initial position in syllables; *F* indicates that the consonant is produced in the final position in syllables.

Denver Developmental Screening Test (DDST): 1 month to 6 years
This is a test for overall development and includes limited screening sections for receptive and expressive language development. Refer to Chapter 24, The Neuromuscular System, for more information on the DDST. Test materials available from LADOCA Project.

Developmental Profile: Birth to 12½ years   This is a reliable overall screening of child development, utilizing a structured interview method. The communication scale is designed to assess the expressive and receptive language skills of the child. Test materials are available from: Psychological Development Publications, 7150 Lakeside Drive, Indianapolis, IN 46278.

Peabody Picture Vocabulary Test This is a test of the child's single word receptive vocabulary. The child is required to point to one of four drawings in response to the examiner's stimulus word. Test materials available from: American Guidance Service, Inc., Publisher's Building, Circle Pines, MN 55014.

Photo Articulation Test This is a test of the child's ability to articulate consonants. The examiner points to a picture and the child is asked to name it. The examiner listens for the child's articulation of the consonant which is presented in three different positions. Test materials available from: King Co. Publishers, 2414 W. Lawrence Avenue, Chicago, IL 60625.

Predictive Screening Test of Articulation (PSTA) This is designed to differentiate those children with articulation problems who will benefit from therapy. It is useful for first-graders only and takes 7 to 8 minutes to administer. The test consists of 47 items that sample articulation of certain sounds, tongue movement independent of the jaw, discrimination of frequently confused phonemes in word pairs, and imitation of hand-clapping rhythm. Available from Continuing Education Office, Western Michigan University, Walwood Union, Kalamazoo, MI 49001.

Sequenced Inventory of Language Development (SILD): Birth through 3 years This diagnostic tool allows the examiner to assess systematically the child's language skills and to estimate the child's level of receptive and expressive language functioning (Barnard, 1974). Test information is in the publication: D. L. Hedrick and E. M. Prather, *Sequenced Inventory of Language Development* (Seattle: University of Washington Press, 1970).

Templin-Darley Test of Articulation This is designed to evaluate articulation in children 3 to 8 years of age. The test consists of a screening test, a diagnostic test, and a test of oral pressure for speech sound production. Tests are available from the Bureau of Educational Research and Service, Division of Extension, University of Iowa, Iowa City, IA 52242.

Verbal Language Development Scale: 1 month to 15 years This test assesses the development of the child's speech and language using the informant interview method. It is an extension of the communication section of the Vineland Social Maturity Scale by Edgar A. Doll. Test materials available from: American Guidance Service, Inc., Publishers Building, Circle Pines, MN 55014.

FLUENCY ASSESSMENT

The assessment of fluency is difficult because the development of fluency patterns is so highly individualized. Also, fluency patterns change rapidly during the child's early years, and the degree of fluency is so variable from child to child. Most children are initially dysfluent. There are basically two types of fluency disorders: stuttering and cluttering. Stuttering is a rhythm disorder and cluttering is a rate disorder. The disorder of greater concern is stuttering because it is so apparent to the listener.

Stuttering Stuttering is a complex, multidimensional communication problem involving the rate and rhythm of speech, which is improperly timed and patterned. It occurs more frequently in females. If untreated, the problem progresses and becomes worse. Up to 80 percent of children outgrow stuttering spontaneously during the first 11 years of life. Fewer than 1 percent of all persons stutter. A child beyond 7 years of age should not have any rate or fluency problems. By this age, individual fluency is well established and will remain so unless something unusual occurs to disrupt it. The nurse practitioner should be alert to sudden fluency change at any age. Referral to a speech-language specialist is indicated as soon as the problem is identified for evaluation and intervention.

VOICE ASSESSMENT

Voice is assessed according to loudness (too soft or too loud), quality (nasality, hoarseness, breathiness, harshness), flexibility (intonation, emphasis), and pitch (if not consistent with age and sex). The broad age-range characteristics of voice development used as a guide to assess voice are as follows (Weiss and Lillywhite, 1981, pp. 98–99)*:

---

*Reprinted with permission from C. E. Weiss and H. S. Lillywhite, *Communicative Disorders*, 2nd ed. St. Louis: C. V. Mosby, 1981. Pp. 98–99.

Age	Milestone
Birth to 12 months	A distinctive cry develops for each need such as hunger, pain, anger. Vocal patterns develop to fit various needs, mood changes, and behavior states.
12 to 36 months	Voice becomes more facile and varied. Speaking patterns develop. Toward 36 months, children normally increase the volume and raise the vocal pitch during exciting play or stressful situations.
36 to 60 months	Voice does not change much with the exception that the child may speak in an extremely loud and high-pitched voice. This is usually a result of increased excitement, activity, and enthusiasm.
5 to 11 years	Voice usage stabilizes and levels off. Shouting may continue, but shrill, high-pitched screaming should taper off.
11 to 16 years	Voice changes affected by unstable periods and the pitch fluctuates between the preadolescent and the mature voice.

INDICATIONS FOR REFERRAL

Parental concern is the primary indication for referral. In addition, Lillywhite recommends referral to a speech pathologist or audiologist for detailed evaluation for the following conditions*:

1. If the child is not producing any intelligible speech by age 2
2. If speech is largely unintelligible after age 3
3. If there are many omissions of initial consonants after age 3
4. If there are no sentences by age 3
5. If sounds are more than a year late in appearing, according to expected developmental sequence
6. If there is an excessive amount of indiscriminate, irrelevant verbalizing after 18 months

*From V. C. Vaughan and R. J. McKay, *Nelson Textbook of Pediatrics*, 10th ed. © 1975 by W. B. Saunders Company, Philadelphia.

7. If there is consistent and frequent omission of initial consonants at any age
8. If there are many substitutions of easy sounds for difficult ones after age 5
9. If the amount of vocalizing decreases rather than steadily increases at any period up to age 7
10. If the child uses mostly vowel sounds in his speech at any age after 1 year
11. If word endings are consistently dropped after age 5
12. If sentence structure is consistently faulty after age 5
13. If the child is embarrassed and disturbed by his speech at any age
14. If the child is noticeably nonfluent (stuttering) after age 5
15. If the child is distorting, omitting, or substituting any sounds after age 7
16. If the voice is a monotone, extremely loud, largely inaudible, or of poor quality
17. If the pitch is not appropriate to the child's age and sex
18. If there is noticeable hypernasality or lack of nasal resonance
19. If there are unusual confusions, reversals, or telescoping in connected speech
20. If there are abnormal rhythms, rate, and inflection after age 5

The referral information should include impression of the child's mental status, developmental progress, emotional maturity, past illnesses, physical problems, and family and environmental factors (Lillywhite, 1970).

Resources Help can be found at speech and hearing clinics affiliated with a university or college, community centers, medical centers, child guidance centers, child development programs, special education departments of public schools, or certified speech and hearing specialists in private practice. A Certificate of Clinical Competence from the American Speech and Hearing Association held by a speech and hearing specialist attests to adequate training and experience. The annual directory of the American Speech and Hearing Association lists the certified status of the members. Copies of the directory can be obtained from American Speech and Hearing Association, 9030 Old Georgetown Road, Washington DC 20014.

ILLINOIS TEST OF PSYCHOLINGUISTIC ABILITIES (ITPA): 2 YEARS 4 MONTHS TO 10 YEARS 3 MONTHS This is a common test used by speech and language specialists. It is a diagnostic test of specific cognitive abilities used to identify areas of difficulty in communication and to provide the basis for developing a remedial program. It tests the receptive, expressive, and organizing processes in the acquisition and use of language. Results are categorized according to the learning problem the child demonstrates, such as academic (reading, writing, arithmetic), nonsymbolic (perceptual–expressive), or symbolic (linguistic difficulty in the reception or idea expression) (Conway, 1977).

Academic Evaluation

BEHAVIOR

A description of the child's behavioral response to a new situation and to a comfortable situation provides insights into the child's ability to master the academic tasks of learning to read, to write, and to spell. Observations are made of the child's attention span and concentration while engrossed in a task, and in free play. Gofman and Allmond (1970, p. 40) state that

> Before a child is required to begin the task of learning to read, write and spell he should at least:
> Be intelligible to his teacher and classmates when he talks.
> Be able to follow oral directions made up of at least 3 different commands.
> Be able to listen to a story and tell about the events in logical sequence.
> Be able to copy simple geometric shapes such as a circle, square, cross.
> Be able to sit still and attend for at least 15 minutes.
> Be able to accept limits and tolerate some frustrations and delayed gratification.

CENTRAL NERVOUS SYSTEM

Optimum learning and language development requires intact visual–motor, auditory–vocal, tactile–kinesthetic processes, and a knowledge of two-dimensional spatial relationships. For example, intact visual–motor processes enable a child to transfer the word "pad" from the chalkboard onto paper by using the following skills (Gofman, 1971):

1. Ability to see the word on the chalkboard
2. Ability to visually discriminate the word form from the figure background
3. Ability to develop a visual memory for forms, letters, the correct sequence of letters and eventually of entire words so a "p" always looks like a "p" to the child
4. Ability to develop a feel for the spatial orientation of forms and letters so the child knows the configuration of "p" as well as the sequence of "p-a-d" in the traditional left-right order.

EDUCATIONAL TESTING

Teachers are central figures in the entire evaluation-remediation process. The goal of the teacher's evaluation is to provide an educationally usable assessment of the child's areas of strengths and weaknesses. Standard tests used are:

• Durrell Analysis of Reading Difficulty. Materials available from Harcourt Brace Jovanovich, Test Department, 757 Third Avenue, New York, NY 10017
• Grays Oral Reading Test. Materials available from Bobbs-Merrill Co. Inc., Indianapolis, IN 46206
• Monroe Reading Achievement Test. Materials available from Houghton Mifflin Co., 777 California Avenue, Palo Alto, CA 94304

Graded reading paragraphs and spelling lists adapted from the California State Series Spelling List are included below. Observations are made of the child's ability to recognize words, comprehend words and paragraphs, decipher the sound or spelling of unknown words, discriminate sounds and letters, and write the letters of the alphabet. Following are eight graded reading paragraphs:*

MY   DOG   SEE   BOY

---

*From H. F. Gofman and B. W. Allmond: Learning and Language Disorders in Children. Part II: The School-Age Child, in L. Gluck, (ed.): *Current Problems in Pediatrics*, September 1971. Copyright © 1971 by Year Book Medical Publishers, Inc., Chicago. Used by permission. Adapted from California State Series Spelling List.

1. A little girl had a pet cat. The cat liked to sit in the sun. It played with a red ball. One day the cat ran away. The little girl saw it and said, "I see you."†

2. My friend lives in a new house. She goes to a new school. I am going to sleep at her house tomorrow. She has a big doll to play with. We will have fun.

3. My daddy bought a new car. We will drive it to the country to visit my cousins next week. They asked us to come on Saturday. I hope they like our new red car. We think it is beautiful.

4. Six boys went on a vacation together. They went fishing in a blue boat. One boy caught a big fish. The others did not catch a thing. They decided to go home.

5. A man built a house in the woods. It was almost winter before it was finally finished. He couldn't make up his mind about the furnace. Should he use gas or electricity? Which would you choose?

6. Ann and Bert decided to plant a garden. Their father declared it an excellent project. He advised them to start with a strip of ground by the fence. They worked hard and by the end of summer they had fresh beans, onions, peas, and cabbage for the table.

7. The Indians and the first white settlers knew how to conserve our natural resources. They took from nature only what was necessary for their food, clothing, and shelter. Recently we have come to realize that these resources are becoming scarce. Conservation is a national responsibility.

8. Have you chosen your vocation yet? Long ago man had little choice. His job was to provide food, clothing, and shelter for his family. Today there are many special skills required to keep our present economy going. A person is happier and more prosperous if he has chosen his vocation carefully. There are many people ready to help you if you ask their advice.

The graded spelling list is as follows:*

†The number of the paragraph and of the spelling list indicates the grade appropriate for mastery of these reading paragraphs and spelling words.

*From H. F. Gofman and B. W. Allmond: Learning and Language Disorders in Children. Part II: The School-Age Child, in L. Gluck (ed.): *Current Problems in Pediatrics*, September 1971. Copyright © 1971 by Year Book Medical Publishers, Inc., Chicago. Used by Permission. Selected from California State Series Spelling List.

1	2	3	4
all	mother	teacher	many
bird	little	come	does
let	run	get	head
home	house	Saturday	bring
she	bring	daddy	where
tell	dress	until	water
pin	cows	brother	horse
was	letter	told	wanted
out	ran	ask	please
girl	school	every	think

5	6	7	8
young	lace	chew	sold
building	cart	pity	curious
hair	driving	flames	lovely
interesting	habit	cough	shoot
report	ruler	spite	studying
class	knee	view	believe
read	lemon	suddenly	between
receive	bandage	tale	whom
Monday	tramp	crime	probably
knew	motor	organization	eight

Psychologic Evaluation

An evaluation with a sensitive, astute psychologist provides insights into the child's learning style and coping behavior.

TESTS

A standard intelligence test is administered to evaluate the child's language skills, manipulative abilities, eye–hand coordination, memory, and visual and auditory attention. Examples of tests commonly used in standard evaluations include the following:

- Bayley Scales of Infant Development (2 to 30 months of age)
- Cattel Infant Intelligence Scale (up to 2½ years of age)
- Stanford-Binet Intelligence Scale (2 to 16 years of age)
- Wechsler Intelligence Scale for Children—Revised (WISC-R) (6 to 16 years of age)

Additional tests are performed by the psychologist to verify the suspected areas of difficulty. For example, paper and pencil skills are evaluated by tests such as the following:

- Bender Visual Motor Gestalt Test. Tests the child's ability to combine more than one geometric figure in a contiguous order.
- Boehm Test of Basic Concepts (BTBC). Tests the child's mastery of concepts considered necessary for achievement in the early school years.
- Developmental Test of Visual Motor Integration (BEERY). Given to children who are unable to do the Bender test.
- Frostig Developmental Test of Visual Perception. Tests the visual perceptual functions in children from 4 to 8 years.

Evaluation of Family Interaction

A sensitive interview with the entire family should explore the dynamics of their interactions and the effects of the child's difficulties on the family. This provides a context with which to understand the child and family. Psychiatric consultation may be indicated in cases where questions exist about the emotional stability of the child and family interactions.

RESOURCES

Resources for family therapists or psychiatric referrals include family therapy centers affiliated with a university or college, community centers, medical centers, or family therapists in private practice.

Commonly Used Terms

agnosia: the inability to interpret sensory input.

aphasia: impairment of the ability to use or understand oral language; usually associated with an injury or abnormality of the speech centers.

astereognosis: a form of agnosia in which there is an inability to recognize objects or their forms by touch.

auditory discrimination: the ability to detect similarities and differences in sound stimuli.

auditory reception: auditory decoding of words spoken by another person.

auditory sequencing: the ability to recall details in correct order, such as correctly repeating digits.

disphasia: an organic communicative disorder that refers to the inability to comprehend and/or to express language orally.

dispraxia: an organic communicative disorder that refers to an inability to program the speech musculature for voluntary speech purposes.

dysarthria: the inability to articulate speech sounds intelligibly, usually due to central nervous system impairment in speech/motor musculature.

dysdiadochokinesis: the inability to perform repetitive fine motor movements such as finger tapping.

dysgraphia: the inability to perform handwriting skills in an organized and legible manner.

dyskinesia: impairment of the power of voluntary movements which manifests itself in fragmented, poorly coordinated and sequenced movements.

dyslalia: functional impairment of speech due to defective speech organs.

dyslexia: the inability to read or to understand printed symbols, visually or orally; used when neurological dysfunction is suspected.

echolalia: an involuntary, parrotlike dysfunction manifested in repetition of words or phrases spoken by another, without understanding the meaning of the language.

figure-ground discrimination: the ability to select a specific configuration from the total input of incoming stimuli by sorting out the important features, figures, and characteristics.

intelligence quotient (IQ): the score obtained using the MA/CA formula: $100 \times$ (Mental Age/Chronological Age).

laterality: internal awareness of the two sides of the body and their distinctness; frequently refers to the establishment of one dominant side, such as lefthandedness.

minimal brain dysfunction: descriptive term for a child of average intelligence who has learning disabilities resulting from a possible minimal insult to the central nervous system; differentiated from major brain dysfunctions such as epilepsy or cerebral palsy.

perseveration: the continued repetition of words or motions that is no longer appropriate.

reading disability: the inability to read at a level that corresponds to the child's measured intellectual capacity and estimated reading level by about a year or more.

receptive language: ability to understand spoken, written, or sign language through listening, reading, and observing.

word-attack skills: a child's approach to unfamiliar words by a phonetic approach or contextual clues to arrive at the correct pronunciation.

MANAGEMENT

The nurse practitioner is often the primary coordinator of the evaluation and management. The primary goals in developing the management plan are to increase the child's self esteem and to continue the successful education of the child. The nurse practitioner frequently visits with school officials to present the findings of the evaluation. The educational psychologist and the teacher in special education are responsible for developing a specific program of management and treatment for the learning problem.

The nurse practitioner may be the best person to explain the problem to the parents and to assist them in providing an atmosphere which is conducive and supportive of the child's best development. The child is followed regularly for health maintenance and to monitor the child's progress.

Communication with the Family

The family with a learning disabled child requires a tremendous amount of continuing support and guidance. The parents need help with anxieties, misunderstandings, and fears about the child's school difficulties. They also need encouragement to verbally express their anger, frustration, and disappointment. Results of the evaluation may initially be difficult to grasp. Clarification of the parent's interpretation of the findings is essential. They may need further guidance in accepting and planning for the child.

Communication with School Personnel

Communication with school personnel is vital and must be done directly and tactfully. Sharing findings about the child's level of functioning and special needs in educationally usable terms enables the school personnel to make the appropriate decision about special programs.

Medication

For the learning disabled child with symptoms of hyperactivity, treatment with a stimulant drug such as dextroamphetamine sulfate or methylphenidate may be useful. Medication, however, has not been found helpful in children who do not exhibit hyperactive behavior. For more information, refer to Attention Deficit Disorder with Hyperactivity, this chapter.

COMMON CLINICAL PROBLEM

Attention Deficit Disorder (ADD) with Hyperactivity

The 1980 Diagnostic and Statistical Manual of Mental Disorders (DSM III) has replaced Hyperkinetic Reaction of Childhood with Attention Deficit Disorder with and without Hyperkinesis. This change reflects the results of intensive research in which the emphasis has shifted from hyperactivity to impaired attention as the central diagnostic concept. ADD refers to a spectrum of behaviors which interferes with attention span. Hyperactivity is often, but not necessarily present. The common symptoms are short attention span, distractibility, unpredictability, emotional lability, and impulsivity. Hyperactivity is one of the most common symptoms of behavior problems and learning disabilities in childhood, and for this reason is the focus of this section.

ASSESSMENT

Hyperactivity is best described by a pattern of behavior in which the child demonstrates increased motor activity, short attention span, poor concentration, and impulsivity. The child is emotionally labile, easily distracted by visual and/or auditory environmental stimuli regardless of the environment, prone to mood swings, and temper outbursts. Symptoms of hyperactivity are sometimes accompanied by learning difficulties and "soft" neurologic signs. See this chapter, Supplementary Neurologic Evaluation. Risk factors include prematurity or low birth weight, perinatal anoxia, head injury with unconsciousness, prolonged febrile seizure, and meningitis. High blood lead levels (David et al., 1972, 1976) and maternal alcohol intake (Voorhes et al., 1979) have been implicated in the etiology of hyperactivity. It is seen more frequently in males than females.

Diagnosis The documentation of the symptoms requires careful history taking of development and observation of the child in a variety of situations. Information from both teachers and parents is essential. Table 25-7 lists the diagnostic criteria for ADD with hyperactivity. Signs of developmentally inappropriate inattention, impulsivity, and hyperactivity should be reported by adults in the child's environment, particularly teachers and parents. The symptoms are variable. They may be absent in new or one-to-one situations, but may worsen when self-application to a task is required, as in the school situation. The number of symptoms specified in Table 25-7 is for children between the ages of 8 and 10 years. In younger children, more symptoms are usually present and in more severe forms, whereas in older children the severity and number both tend to diminish. For a review of instrumental and observational measures and rating scales of activity level, refer to Ross and Ross (1982).

MANAGEMENT

Medication The use of stimulant drugs in the treatment of hyperactivity is controversial. Most experts agree, however, that a

Table 25-7

Diagnostic Criteria for Attention Deficit Disorder with Hyperactivity

Inattention	Impulsivity	Hyperactivity	Other Criteria
At least three of the following:	At least three of the following:	At least three of the following:	The following: Onset before the age of 7 years.
1. Often fails to finish things he or she starts.	1. Often acts before thinking.	1. Runs about or climbs on things excessively.	Duration of at least 6 months.
2. Often doesn't seem to listen.	2. Shifts excessively from one activity to another.	2. Has difficulty sitting still or fidgets excessively.	Not attributable to schizophrenia, affective disorder, or severe or profound mental retardation.
3. Easily distracted.	3. Has difficulty organizing work (not attributable to cognitive impairment).	3. Has difficulty staying seated.	
4. Has difficulty concentrating on schoolwork or other tasks requiring sustained attention.	4. Needs a lot of supervision.	4. Moves about excessively during sleep.	
5. Has difficulty sticking to a play activity.	5. Frequently calls out in class.	5. Is always "on the go" or acts as if "driven by a motor."	
	6. Has difficulty awaiting turn in games or group situations.		

Source: Reprinted with permission from the American Psychiatric Association, *Diagnostic and Statistical Manual of Mental Disorders*, 3rd ed., Washington, D.C. APA, 1980.

school-age child with persistent hyperactivity and a short attention span is likely to benefit from treatment with stimulants (Council of Child Health of the American Academy of Pediatrics, 1975). The benefits for preschool children are not as clear. Dextroamphetamine sulfate (Dexedrine) and methylphenidate (Ritalin) are the two most commonly used medications in the control of hyperkinesis. Both drugs can reduce inattention and hyperactivity, and therefore increase the ability to attend in the home and the school setting. Close monitoring and evaluation of effectiveness of the drugs are essential.

METHYLPHENIDATE (RITALIN)   It is most commonly used. The recommended daily dose is 0.2 to 0.3 mg/kg/24 hr for increasing attention span and 1.0 mg/kg/24 hr for decreasing antisocial behavior. The daily dose should not exceed 60 mg. If a definitive response does not occur after 1 month, the drug is discontinued. Side effects occur in approximately 10 to 15 percent of hyperactive children. They include insomnia, anorexia, increased blood pressure; initial period of irritability, tearfulness, and increased sensitivity to outbursts of aggressiveness, periods of extreme fearfulness, and an increased incidence of seizures. The medication should be given at least 30 minutes before meals. Studies by Safer and colleagues (1972, 1973) have indicated that long-term treatment on high doses of methylphenidate causes a slowing of weight and height gain in children but others have questioned the methodological rigor of the studies (Roche et al., 1979). Compensatory rebound has been observed when the medication was discontinued for several months (Safer et al, 1975).

DEXTROAMPHETAMINE SULFATE (DEXEDRINE)   It is available in a long-acting preparation that enables a child to take the drug once a day. Side effects include a high incidence of insomnia and anorexia. The recommended dose is 0.25 to 1.0 mg/kg/24 hr. Actions include decrease of extraneous body movements, improving fine-motor activity, and increasing attention span.

Diet and Hyperactivity   The relationship between diet and hyperactivity is controversial. The research evidence that an additive-free, salicylate-low diet leads to decreased hyperactivity is not definitive. Scientifically controlled studies (Harley et al., 1978a,b; Mattes and Gittelman, 1981; Connors, 1980) do not support the hypothesis, initially propounded by allergist Feingold (1975), that foods containing artificial colors, artificial flavors, and salicylates were responsible for childhood hyperactivity. However, an occasional child, typically a young child, who is sensitive to these ingredients, may show dramatic improvement. Feingold's hypothetical link spoke to a toxic as opposed to allergic effect, that is, toxins cause direct damage to the body and an allergy causes an alteration of the body's response to a substance producing an immunologic defense mechanism.

Health food purveyors exploit the inaccurate concept that foods that are artificially produced have added chemicals, whereas foods that are naturally occurring are chemical free. Denhoff and Feldman (1981, p. 164) emphasize that this inaccuracy forms the basis for the popularity of health food and of the additive-free diet. Foods, however, are composed of chemicals and there are no differences in the chemicals whether natural or synthetic. Parents need to understand that all foods, such as potatos, are natural chemicals and that additives are synthetic chemicals. The Federal Drug Administration (FDA) insists that food additives serve a useful function and cannot substantially reduce the nutritional value of the food. In addition, they cannot be used to deceive or mask inferior ingredients or faulty preparation.

Long-Term Management There are no simple solutions to this problem. A total management plan should include an eclectic approach: medication if it works, parental counseling regarding behavior modification techniques, communication and intervention with school personnel, and support for the child.

PARENTAL COUNSELING The major task for the parents is to pursue a socialization plan individualized to the needs, problems, and abilities of their child. Schmitt (1977) offers useful guidelines for living with a hyperactive child:

1. Accept your child's limitations.
2. Provide outlets for the release of excess energy.
3. Keep the home existence organized.
4. Avoid fatigue in these children.
5. Avoid formal gatherings.
6. Maintain firm discipline.
7. Enforce discipline with nonphysical punishment.

8. Stretch his or her attention span.
9. Buffer the child against any overreaction by neighbors.
10. Periodically get away from it all.

An excellent source of information for parents on the hyperactive child is *Raising a Hyperactive Child,* by Stewart and Olds (1973).

Resource Information

Information for parents is available from these organizations:
1. Association for Children with Learning Disabilities, 5225 Grace Street, Pittsburgh, PA 15236.
   Write for: Becker, W. *Parents are Teachers.* Urbana, Illinois: Research Press, 1971. ($3.75)

2. *Closer Look.* (National Information Center for the Handicapped. A project of the U.S. Department of Health, Education and Welfare, Office of Education, Bureau of Education for the Handicapped). Box 1492. Washington DC 20013.

3. *The Orton Society, Inc.* (organization dedicated to informing public and professionals about speech and language disabilities), 8415 Bellena Lane, Towson, MD 21204.

4. Quebec Association for Children with Learning Disabilities, P.O. Box 22, Montreal 29, P.Q.
   Write for: Golick, M. *A Parent's Guide to Learning Problems.* ($0.50)

5. Science Research Associates, Inc., 259 East Erie Street, Chicago, IL 60611.
   Write for: Van Riper, C. *Helping Children Talk Better.* Chicago: Science Research Associates, 1951.

References

Adamson, W. C. and K. K. Adamson, editors. *A Handbook for Specific Learning Disabilities.* New York: Gardner Press, Inc., 1979.

American Academy of Pediatrics. "Position Statement 1982, Joint Committee on Infant Hearing." *Pediatrics* 70:496–497, September 1982.

Aram, D. M. and J. E. Nation. *Child Language Disorders.* St. Louis: C. V. Mosby, 1982.

Barnard, K. and H. Douglas, editors. *Child Health Assessment Part 1: A Literature Review.* Bethesda, MD: U.S. Department of Health, Education and Welfare, 1974.

Bergstrom, L., W. G. Hemenway, and M. P. Downs. "A High Risk Registry to Find Congenital Deafness." *Otolaryngol Clin North Am* 4:369, June 1977.

Bosco, J. J., and S. S. Robin. "Hyperkinesis: Prevalence and Treatment." In C. K. Whalen and B. Henker, editors, *Hyperactive Children: The Social Ecology of Identification and Treatment.* New York: Academic Press, 1980. Pp. 173–187.

Brown, M. S. "Testing of a Young Child for Articulation Skills—Detecting Early Danger Signs." *Clin Pediatr 15*:639–644, July 1976.

Butler, K. G. and G. P. Wallach, editors. *Language Disorders and Learning Disabilities.* Rockville, MD: Aspen Systems Corporation, 1982.

Carrow-Woolfolk, E. and J. I. Lynch. *An Integrative Approach to Language Disorders in Children.* New York: Grune & Stratton, 1982.

Caulfield, C. "Hearing Screening in Children: A Self-Study Guide for Nurse Practitioners." *Nurse Practitioner 1*:22–27, March/April 1976.

Conners, C. K. *Food Additives and Hyperactive Children.* New York: Plenum, 1980.

Conway, B. L. *Pediatric Neurologic Nursing.* St. Louis: C. V. Mosby, 1977.

Council on Child Health of the American Academy of Pediatrics. "Medication for Hyperactive Children." *Pediatrics 55*:560–562, April 1975.

David, O. J., J. Clark, and K. Voeller. "Lead and Hyperactivity." *Lancet 2*:900–903, 1972.

David, O. J., et al. "Lead and Hyperactivity. Behavioral Response to Chelation: A Pilot Study." *Am J Psychiatry 133*:1155–1158, 1976.

Denhoff, E. and S. A. Feldman. *Developmental Disabilities: Management through Diet and Medication.* New York: Marcel Dekker, 1981.

Douglas, V. I. "Stop, Look and Listen: The Problem of Sustained Attention and Impulse Control in Hyperactive and Normal Children." *Can J Behav Sci 4*:259–282, 1972.

Downs, M. and H. Silver. "The A.B.C.D.'s to H.E.A.R." *Clin Pediatr 11*:563–565, October 1972.

Feingold, B. "Hyperkinesis and Learning Disabilities Linked to Artificial Food Flavors and Colors." *Am J Nurs 75*:797–803, May 1975.

Feingold, B. *Why Your Child Is Hyperactive.* New York: Random House, 1975.

Fry, D. B. "The Development of the Phonological System in the Normal and the Deaf Child." In F. Smith and G. A. Miller, editors, *The Genesis of Language.* Cambridge, MA: MIT Press, 1966. Pp. 187–206.

Gabel, S. and M. T. Erickson, editors. *Child Development and Developmental Disabilities.* Boston: Little, Brown, 1980.

Gofman, H. F. and B. W. Allmond. "Learning and Language Disorders in Children, Part I: The Preschool Child." In L. Gluck, editor, *Current Problems in Pediatrics 1*:3–45, August 1971.

Gofman, H. F., and B. W. Allmond. "Learning and Language Disorders in Children, Part II: The School-Age Child." In L. Gluck, editor, *Current Problems in Pediatrics 1*:3–60, September 1971.

Goldstein, A. "School Readiness and Achievement." In W. K. Frankenburg and B. W. Camp, editors, *Pediatric Screening Tests.* Springfield, IL: Charles C. Thomas, 1975. Pp. 477–538.

Greaser, F. B. "Minimal Brain Dysfunction: Learning Disabilities." In J. J. M. Tackett and M. Hunsberger, editors, *Family-Centered Care of Children and Adolescents.* Philadelphia: W. B. Saunders, 1981. Pp. 1144–1149.

Harley, J. P., et al. "Hyperkinesis and Food Additives: Testing the Feingold Hypothesis." *Pediatrics 61*:818–828, June 1978a.

Harley, J. P., C. E. Mathews, and P. Eichman. "Synthetic Food Colors and Hyperactivity in Children: A Double-Blind Challenge Experiment." *Pediatrics 62*:975–983, December 1978*b*.

Hedrick, D. L. and E. M. Prather. *Sequenced Inventory of Language Development*. Seattle: University of Washington Press, 1970.

Huessy, H. R. and A. Cohen. "Hyperkinetic Behaviors and Learning Disabilities Followed over Seven Years." *Pediatrics 57*:4–10, January 1976.

Lenneberg, E. H. *Biological Foundations of Language*. New York: Wiley, 1967.

Lillywhite, H. S., N. B. Young, and R. W. Olmstead. *Pediatrician's Handbook of Communication Disorders*. Philadelphia: Lea & Febiger, 1970.

Mattes, J. A. and R. A. Gittelman. "Effects of Artificial Food Colorings in Children with Hyperactive Symptoms." *Arch Gen Psychiatry 38*:714–718, June 1981.

McElroy, C. *Speech and Language Development of the Preschool Child: A Survey*. Springfield, IL: Charles C. Thomas, 1972.

McNamara, J. J. "Hyperactivity in the Apartment Bound Child." *Clin Pediatr 11*:371–372, July 1972.

Mosse, H. L. *The Complete Handbook of Children's Reading Disorders: A Critical Evaluation of Their Clinical, Educational, and Social Dimensions*. Vols. 1 and 2. New York: Human Sciences Press, 1982.

Northern, J. L. and M. P. Downs. *Hearing in Children*. 2nd ed. Baltimore: Williams & Wilkins, 1978.

Parrill-Burnstein, M. *Problem Solving and Learning Disabilities*. New York: Grune & Stratton, 1981.

Roche, A. F., et al. "The Effects of Stimulant Medication on the Growth of Hyperkinetic Children." *Pediatrics 63*:847–850, June 1979.

Rogers, M. "Early Identification and Intervention of Children with Learning Problems." *Pediatric Nursing 2*:21–26, January/February 1976.

Ross, D. M. and S. A. Ross. *Hyperactivity: Current Issues, Research, and Theory*. 2nd ed. New York: Wiley, 1982.

Rudolph, A., editor. *Pediatrics*. 17th ed. East Norwalk, CT: Appleton-Century-Crofts, 1982.

Safer, D. J., R. P. Allen, and E. Barr. "Depression of Growth in Hyperactive Children on Stimulant Drugs." *N Engl J Med 287*:217–220, July 1972.

Safer, D. J. and R. P. Allen. "Factors Influencing the Suppressant Effects of Two Stimulant Drugs on the Growth of Hyperactive Children." *Pediatrics 51*:660–667, April 1973.

Safer, D. J., R. P. Allen, and E. Barr. "Growth Rebound after Termination of Stimulant Drugs." *J Pediatr 86*:113–116, January 1975.

B. Schmitt. "Guidelines for Living with a Hyperactive Child" (letter). *Pediatrics 60*:387, September 1977.

Silver, L. B. "Acceptable and Controversial Approaches to Treating the Child with Learning Disabilities." *Pediatrics 55*:406–415, March 1975.

Smith, D. and R. A. Hoekelman. *Controversies in Child Health and Pediatric Practice*. New York: McGraw-Hill, 1981.

Stewart, M. A., and S. W. Olds. *Raising a Hyperactive Child.* Hagerstown, MD: Harper & Row, 1973.

Taichert, L. *Childhood Learning, Behavior, and the Family.* New York: Behavioral Publications, 1973.

Templin, M. "Development of Speech." *J Pediatr 62*:11–14, January 1963.

Thomas, A., et al. "Cross-Cultural Study of Behavior in Children with Special Vulnerabilities to Stress." In D. Ricks, A. Thomas, and M. Roff, editors, *Life History Research in Psychopathology.* Vol. 3. Minneapolis: University of Minnesota Press, 1974. Pp. 53–67.

Vaughan, V. C. et al, editors. *Nelson Textbook of Pediatrics.* 11th ed. Philadelphia: W. B. Saunders, 1979.

Voorhes, C. V., R. L. Brunner, and R. E. Butcher. "Psychotropic Drugs as Behavioral Teratogens." *Science 205*:1220–1225, September 21, 1979.

Weiner, J. "Techniques for Enhancing Social Skills." In D. Kronick, editor, *Social Development of Learning Disabled Persons.* San Francisco: Jossey-Bass, 1981. Pp. 162–194.

Weiss, C. E. and H. S. Lillywhite. *Communicative Disorders: Prevention and Early Intervention.* 2nd ed. St. Louis. C. V. Mosby, 1981.

Whitsell, L. "Learning Disorders As a School Health Problem." *Calif Med 111*:433–445, December 1969.

26

Allergies

Allergy is one of the most common and complex entities encountered in the health care of children. Depending on the source, the incidence of allergy in the pediatric population has been estimated at 10 to 20 percent. Management of the allergic child is shared with the primary care physician with appropriate referrals to an allergist. The nurse practitioner can obtain the history, perform the physical examination, initiate diagnostic procedures, follow through with treatments, and counsel the child and parents.

ASSESSMENT

Definition of Allergy

Allergy means increased sensitivity to a substance that in ordinary amounts would cause no problem in most people (e.g., egg sensitivity, pollen sensitivity). See Chapter 2, The Immune System and Chapter 27, Table 27-8. The allergic disorders of children include a large, dissimilar group of conditions which have in common immunologic hypersensitivity of the child to molecular substances foreign to the child. These foreign molecules serve as *antigens* which, when they produce symptoms in the susceptible individual, are designated as *allergens*. When a particular allergen is absorbed by the body, it eventually comes in contact with lymphocytes which produce allergy antibodies, probably IgE, which react specifically

979

with it. These allergy antibodies become attached to mast cells and basophils, cells rich in histamine and other mediators of the allergic reaction. On reexposure the allergen comes in contact with the antibody on the cell surface resulting in the release of the mediators. This produces an irritation in the susceptible tissues (e.g., the nose, the bronchial tubes, the skin).

Basic Principles

The development of allergic symptoms depends on inheritance, the nature of the allergen, and the degree, duration, and nature of the exposure. Some basic principles are as follows:

- Sensitivity usually occurs only after repeated exposure to the substance.
- Allergic persons may be sensitive to more than one allergen.
- The tendency to be sensitized or allergic to some foreign substance is usually inherited.
- A person who has inherited the tendency may develop sensitivities to different allergens at different age periods. The previous sensitivities may remain or may be lost.
- Allergic persons who tolerate some exposure to their allergens without developing symptoms are considered to be in allergic equilibrium or allergic balance, that is, the amount of allergens taken in is balanced by the person's "tolerance" or "resistance." Nonallergic factors may place an additional burden on such persons and thus disturb allergic equilibrium. Respiratory infections, such as common colds, may increase the total load to a point beyond a person's tolerance and thus upset what was previously a balanced allergic state. Fatigue, emotional tensions, excitement, exertion, cold foggy weather, and many other factors may also increase the burden, upset the balance, and allow an allergic attack to develop.

HOW ALLERGENS ENTER THE BODY

In order of frequency, allergens enter the body through several routes:

1. Ingestion, as foods, drinks, and drugs. Common drug offenders are aspirin, barbiturates, and antibiotics.
2. Inhalation, as dust, pollens, and fumes (air pollution and cigarette smoke). See this chapter, Environmental Control.
3. External contact, as clothes, cosmetics, and industrial products. See this chapter, Environmental Control.
4. Injection, as drugs and sera. Common allergic injectables are vaccines, animal serums, animal saliva, and venoms.

FACTORS THAT INCREASE ALLERGIC REACTIONS

Seasons The seasons and allergens that cause increased reactions are as follows:

- Winter: animals, house dust, and molds; food allergies are worse in winter.
- Spring: pollen of trees and grasses.
- Summer: air pollution, grass pollens, insect bites, sun, and poison oak or poison ivy.
- Fall: pollen of ragweed, and molds.

Weather High fronts can cause an increase in asthma, sinusitis, and rhinitis. Prophylactic decongestants should be increased at this time.

Emotions Emotional disturbances usually play a part but do not cause allergic attacks.

Time of Day When the condition is worse in the morning, suspicion should develop that the allergen is in the bedroom.

ALLERGY IN INFANCY

Predisposing Factors Factors that predispose to the development of hypersensitivity in the infant include the following:

1. Heredity or the atopic hypersensitivity (see this chapter, Definition of Allergy). The most common allergic conditions in infancy are atopic dermatitis, gastrointestinal disturbances, and nasal sniffles.

2. State of the digestive tract. The digestive tract has not fully matured and is more permeable, permitting the assimilation of undigested food proteins.
3. Nature of the diet. Foods are the most common and most important allergens in infancy. Milk is the most common, followed by eggs, orange juice, wheat, corn, and beef.
4. Environment. Less common than food as a factor, an infant may be allergic to both food and environmental allergens.
5. Infection. Infection is a provocative agent not a primary allergen. Gastrointestinal infection serves to increase the permeability of the gut to undigested proteins which may induce sensitivity. See Chapter 2, Immunity.

Familial Incidence The probabilities of inheriting allergic problems are as follows:

1. If neither parent has allergies, the children have less than a 10 percent chance of having an allergic problem.
2. If one parent has a history of allergies, 50 percent of the offspring may eventually manifest allergies.
3. If both parents are allergic, the incidence rises to 75 percent.

ALLERGY IN CHILDHOOD

Predisposing Factors Factors that predispose to allergic problems in childhood are similar to those in infancy, including a history of infantile allergic problems. Environmental factors are the leading cause of allergic conditions in childhood.

Signs and Symptoms Signs and symptoms suggestive of allergic diseases are listed below:

1. Tension-fatigue syndrome. This includes extreme fatigue, lassitude, listlessness, and irritability; facial pallor without anemia; and circles of discoloration under the eyes, "allergic shiners." In most cases the allergens are pollens, environmentals, and foods.
2. Recurrent otitis media and recurrent serous otitis media. See this chapter, Allergic Serous Otitis Media, and Chapter 17, Serous Otitis Media.

3. Upper respiratory symptoms:
   - Feature of the tension-fatigue syndrome
   - "Allergic salute." Itching of the nose and rubbing of the nose upward, which may lead to a crease across the nose just above the tip
   - Excoriated nares and sometimes epistaxis caused by excessive nose picking
   - Rhinorrhea with a seromucoid discharge
   - Postnatal mucous discharge which may cause elongation of the uvula leading to a tickling cough followed by a productive cough
   - Nasal congestion leading to mouth breathing with pursing of the lips, facial deformity, and malocclusion

4. Recurrent laryngitis. Occurs with sudden onset usually at night; may be present with crowing respirations and, at times, suprasternal retractions.

5. Lower respiratory tract. Allergic bronchitis is the commonly observed form of allergic pulmonary disease. Bronchial asthma and status asthmaticus are less frequent.

6. Skin disturbance. Urticaria occurs infrequently in children during the prepubescent period but increases in girls at menarche. Whealing of insect bites is often mistaken for urticaria.

7. Atopic dermatitis. See this chapter, Common Clinical Problems.

History

PRESENT HISTORY

Obtain information pertaining to the area of involvement following suggestions contained in Chapter 11, Assessment of the Presenting Symptom. In addition, obtain information on colic, spitting-up, vomiting, diarrhea, constipation, weight loss or gain, and skin problems. Obtain information on frequency of upper or lower respiratory infections, alterations in taste, smell, or hearing; listlessness, fatigue; night or seasonal coughs; infections of the ears; recurrent nosebleeds; allergies of the skin, eyes, or gastrointestinal system;

unusual reactions to drugs, insect bites, or inhalants; behavior or learning problems; and the time of day and season of the year that symptoms are worse. Additional information regarding the environment can be found in this chapter, Environmental Control.

PAST HISTORY

Obtain information on gastrointestinal disturbances or skin problems in infancy. Obtain information on communicable diseases and immunizations.

NUTRITION HISTORY

Obtain a detailed diet history. See Chapter 3, Nutrition History. Be aware of cultural differences. Emphasis is placed on identifying foods which contain additives and preservatives. For more information, see this chapter, Diet Control.

FAMILY HISTORY

Obtain information about any family members with rashes, migraine headaches, hay fever, asthma, gastrointestinal disturbances, eye problems (such as itching, crusting of lids), food allergies, and food habits of the mother (excessive eating of a particular food during pregnancy can sensitize an unborn infant by transplacental transfer).

Physical Examination

Multiple involvement of organs is the common pattern for allergies.

SKIN

Observe for pallor, dryness, scaliness, lichenification, rashes, irritations, inflammations, and scratches.

EYES

Inspect for discharges; scleral redness; conjunctival swelling, redness, or tiny, grainy, palpebral conjunctival papules (cobblestoning); periorbital swelling; crusting of lashes; tears, discoloration below the eyes (allergic shiners), styes, long, silky lashes, and rubbing or excessive blinking of the eyes.

EARS

Inspect tympanic membranes for retraction, scarring, and evidence of serous otitis media. Observe for crusting or discharge behind the ears or in the auditory canals. Test for hearing loss.

NOSE

Inspect nasal mucosa and turbinates for color, swelling, redness, dryness, bogginess, pallor, and nasal polyps. Observe for nose twitching, allergic salute, and transverse nasal crease. Inspect for discharges noting color, consistency, and crusting.

MOUTH

Inspect for mouth breathing, malocclusion, and jaw deformity. Observe for geographic tongue, gingival hyperplasia, and swollen lips or tongue.

NECK

Palpate for lymph nodes.

THROAT

Inspect for postnasal drip noting color and consistency, elongated pale uvula, lymphoid hyperplasia of the postpharyngeal wall, color, and enlarged tonsils or tonsillar tags.

LUNGS

Auscultate for rhonchi, rales, and expiratory wheezing.

ABDOMEN

Auscultate for increased bowel sounds (some gastrointestinal allergies present first with symptoms of an upper respiratory infection).

MANAGEMENT

Immunotherapy

Immunotherapy consists of diagnostic skin testing and hyposensitization. It is usually managed by an allergist. Referral is made when children have severe and persistent allergic reactions (e.g., severe asthma). The decision for referral is generally made collaboratively with a physician. Mild cases are often treated successfully using environmental control and, at times, dietary measures.

DIAGNOSTIC SKIN TESTING

Techniques commonly used for skin testing are the scratch test, patch test, and intradermal test. Skin testing can be helpful in some cases (e.g., severe atopic dermatitis, asthma) and can provide additional data to consider in the overall assessment of the child.

Positive Tests These are only clues to the allergens and must be interpreted cautiously, since they are not always reliable.

Negative Tests These do not always prove a substance harmless. The final answer depends on a therapeutic trial by removal of the suspected allergen through diet and environmental control.

Skin Testing for Food Allergies This is believed to be unreliable possibly because digestive breakdown products of whole food are the true sensitizers, whereas extracts of naturally occurring foods are used in skin testing. Skin testing of a food when there is a clinical history of marked sensitivity to that food is dangerous and should not be done. An example is egg white, which is a very antigenic material that even in minute quantities can induce violent reactions.

HYPOSENSITIZATION

This consists of a series of injections of extracts of specific antigens to which the child is sensitive and that cannot otherwise be controlled. Its value is limited mainly to atopic disorders and to severe bee sting allergy. The injections begin with a very dilute solution and are increased at 50 percent strength once or twice a week until a top dose is reached and then maintained. Injections may be given at regular intervals throughout the year or before the season associated with greatest symptoms.

Diet Control

Evaluation of data from the physical examination and a carefully taken diet history may provide sufficient evidence to warrant removing a suspected allergen (e.g., milk) from a child's diet. This simple form of diet control, in addition to symptomatic treatment, may be all that is necessary in most mild allergic problems. However, in the treatment of more severe cases, it may be necessary to follow a more stringent regimen.

HISTORY

A detailed diet history remains one of the chief tools in searching for a food offender. The diet history should include the following:

1. Foods eaten daily (consider cultural differences) and food excesses
2. Any unusual foods eaten recently and family food disagreements
3. Previous food intolerances, intense food dislikes, frequency of questionable foods
4. Foods that contain additives or preservatives (See next section, Elimination Diets.)

INDICATIONS FOR USE OF AN ELIMINATION DIET

The indications for proceeding with an elimination diet are as follows:

1. A history of food allergies
2. Failure to control symptoms with immunotherapy and environmental control
3. A recurrence of symptoms not attributed to a reaction to hyposensitization or an infraction of environmental control
4. A history of nasal polyps

5. A history of recurrent otitis media
6. A history of aspirin intolerance (Many food additives and preservatives contain salicylates.)

PROCEDURE FOR AN ELIMINATION DIET

Infancy   Extensive elimination diets should be used as a diagnostic tool only for a short period of time. Suggested extensive elimination diets for infants are as follows:

1. Under 3 months of age: milk substitute only
2. Three to 6 months of age: milk substitute and rice cereal
3. Six months to 1 year of age: milk substitute with vitamin supplementation, rice cereal, applesauce and pears, carrots, squash and lamb.

In 7 to 10 days if there has been no change symptomatically the diet is abandoned. If the allergic syndrome disappears or markedly improves, foods can be added to the diet one at a time by food family groups at intervals of 4 to 5 days. If any food exacerbates the allergy, that food should be eliminated from the diet for 6 months before another trial.

Older Child and Adolescents   The procedure is as follows:

1. A diary of each food, beverage, or medication which is ingested at meals or between meals without alteration in customary patterns is to be recorded for 7 to 10 days.
2. Constituents of all home-prepared foods must be listed as well as ingredients of all packaged foods. Concealed foods may be included in prepared products (see Table 26-1).
3. Symptoms are also recorded for 7 to 10 days. By correlating symptoms with the information in the diary, the nurse practitioner frequently can determine the elimination diet suitable for the particular case, for example milk-free, salicylate-free, or others. See next section, Elimination Diets.
4. The elimination diet is initiated.
5. Two weeks following the start of an elimination diet, the client is interviewed and the diet is reviewed. Improvement can be

Table 26-1
Eggs as an Example of Concealed Foods

Eggs occur in the following:
  Eggnogs, and other egg drinks
  Custard, puddings of various types
  Ice cream and sherbet
  Mayonnaise, hollandaise, and tartar sauce
  Egg noodles
  Cakes and cookies made with eggs
  Pastries and bakery goods
  Pancakes, waffles, muffins, sweet rolls
Eggs may be found in:
  Soups: for clarifying
  Baking powder: some brands
  Coffee: eggs and eggshells can be used for cleaning
  Root beer: for foaming
  Candies: for glazing jelly beans and some chocolate candies
  Meats: egg is used as a binding agent in many prepared meats
  Salad dressings: many contain eggs
Egg protein can be found in:
  Albumin
  Ovoglobulin
  Livetin
  Ovomucin
  Ovomucoid
  Powdered or dried eggs
  Yolk
  Vitellin or ovovitellin
Labels should be carefully checked.

---

expected within 2 to 3 weeks if the correct food has been eliminated.

6. Two weeks later another interview and review are conducted.

7. If symptoms have not subsided, the program is abandoned and another diet regimen is implemented.

8. If the diet is successful in eliminating symptoms it should be continued for at least 2 months before attempting additions of new foods to the diet.

9. New foods can then be added individually every 5 to 7 days.

10. If symptoms return, the food should be discontinued.

11. If the second attempt at introducing the food is not successful, the food should be permanently excluded from the diet.

12. This procedure is repeated with other foods, each one taken individually, until a well-balanced and varied diet is provided for the client.

13. The diet diary should be continued for a few months, if possible, in the event of a recurrence of symptoms.

14. All labels, especially of prepared foods, must be read carefully.

15. Home-prepared foods are preferable because the ingredients can be controlled.

16. Absolute adherence to the diet is imperative. If undesirable weight loss occurs, more of the prescribed carbohydrates, sugar, fats, and oils must be taken. This may require eating four to five meals a day.

17. Caution should be taken not to place a child on a nutritionally deficient diet for long periods of time when no specific results have been obtained.

ELIMINATION DIETS

Examples of some elimination diets follow.

Elemental Diet   This is recommended for children who have been tried on other diets without success and for children who have a serious or life threatening disease in which it is urgent that the role of food hypersensitivity be determined as soon as possible. Vivonex (Eaton Laboratories), a mixture of synthetic amino acids, simple sugars, safflower oil, vitamins, and minerals is used. This is given for 2 weeks unless symptoms completely disappear before that time. If the symptoms persist unchanged during this time, hypersensitivity to ingested foods can generally be ruled out. Once symptoms have completely cleared, additional foods may be added, one every second day (Gellis and Kagan, 1973, p. 662).

Hypoallergenic Diet   If the history does not suggest a specific food as an allergen this diet may be recommended to start the elimination diet. After the first 2 weeks of using this diet different foods are slowly started and reassessed. See Table 26-2.

Table 26-2
Hypoallergenic Diet for Infants and Young Children (Foods Permitted)

Food Category	Specific Foods
Milk	Nonmilk formulas: Nutramigen, Pregestimil (Mead Johnson); see this chapter, Milk Allergy. Prosobee (Mead Johnson) Isomil (Ross) Soyalac (Loma Linda)
Cereals	Rice, oat, corn, barley, rye, poi
Breads	Rye, Rye-Krisp, Baltic rye
Vegetables	Beets, carrots, broccoli, asparagus, peas, green beans, white and sweet potatoes, yams; soups made from these vegetables
Fruits	Apples, pears, plums, bananas, apricots, grapes, juices of these fruits
Meats	Lamb, pork, veal, capon, tom turkey and rooster (young fryers and roasters) (no hens or hen turkeys)
Desserts	Fruits listed and their gelatin products
Spreads	Oleomargarine (most have additives and milk); jellies of the listed fruits
Vitamins, synthetic	Tri-Vi-Sol, Poly-Vi-Sol, Decca-Vi-Sol (Mead Johnson)

Source: Reprinted and adapted with permission from H. I. Lecks, "Allergic Gastrointestinal Disease," in S. S. Gellis and B. M. Kagan, *Current Pediatric Therapy* 7. © 1973 W. B. Saunders Company, Philadelphia.

Milk-Free Diet See Table 26-3. This diet is recommended for children with sensitivities to milk or penicillin (milk can be contaminated with penicillin via treatment of cow's udders; natural cheeses which contain mold may cross-react with penicillin) or as a trial in a child with a history of recurrent serous otitis.

Salicylate-Free Diet This diet is recommended for clients who are allergic to aspirin and foods containing natural salicylates (see Table 26-4), or who have a history of nasal polyps. Feingold (1975, p. 797) has reported that hyperactive children and possibly those with learning disabilities are helped with this diet. This has not been proved conclusively.

Table 26-3
Milk-Free Diet

Foods Allowed	Foods Not Allowed
Milk substitutes: soy milk formulas, Mocha Mix, Coffee Rich	Milk: fresh, dry, evaporated Yogurt
Unprocessed mature cheese such as cheddar and parmesan	Cream cheese, cottage cheese, cheese snacks, processed cheese
Eggs	
Oils, lard, chicken and bacon fat, pure vegetable margarines (diet margarine, Willow Run, Nucoa)	Butter, cream, most margarines, foods dipped in butter or margarine for frying
Meats and fish	Meat with milk sauces, gravies, processed or packaged meats, sausages, frankfurters
All vegetables, cooked without milk or butter	Instant mashed potatoes
All fruits and fruit juices	
Breads and cereals containing wheat, rye, corn, rice, oatmeal, semolina, tapioca	Bread containing milk; check commercial and baby cereals and teething biscuits
Breads (Hillbilly by Colonial, Longhorn and Dark Hollywood by Wonder, water bagels)	
Fruit jellies, gelatin, pastry made with water (milk substitutes are not generally suitable for use in cooking)	All pastries, puddings, cakes, custards, biscuits, commercial packaged products, ice cream and sherbet, "milk" chocolate, muffins, sweet rolls, pancakes, cookies
Jam, honey, syrup, sugar, water ices, peanut butter, nuts	
Meat and vegetable soups	All soups containing milk
Tea, coffee, carbonated beverages, cocoa powder	Check chocolate and caramel flavorings
Herbs and seasonings	Check commercial dressings and mayonnaise
	Check labels for milk in some form: caseinate, casein, sodium caseinate, curds, lactoalbumin, lactoglobulin, lactose and whey

Table 26-4
Salicylate-Free Diet

Foods Allowed	Foods Not Allowed
Grapefruit, lemon, pears, bananas, dates, limes, figs, papayas, melons, and pineapple	Almonds, apples, apricots, blackberries, cherries, currants, gooseberries, grapes or raisins, nectarines, oranges, peaches, plums or prunes, raspberries, strawberries, cucumbers and pickles, tomatoes
All vegetables except cucumbers and tomatoes	
All meats, except those artificially flavored, such as frankfurters, bologna	
All fish except fish sticks	Ice cream, oleomargarine, gin and all distilled beverages except vodka, cake mixes, bakery goods (except plain bread), jello, candies, gum, frankfurters, cloves, mint flavors, jam or jelly, lunch meats (salami, bologna, etc.), licorice
Eggs	
Milk and milk products—may have Brockmeyer's vanilla or carob ice cream	
Pure maple syrup, all vegetable oils, distilled white vinegar, salt, pepper, and sugar	
	Breakfast cereals with artificial color or flavoring
	Wine and wine vinegars, all tea, diet drinks and supplements, cider and cider vinegars, Kool-aid and similar beverages, soda pop (all soft drinks)
Butter or Willow Run margarine	
Plain bread, rice, potato	
Bisquick mix	Flavorings (omit artificially flavored and colored foods, drinks, and drugs)
Coffee, 7-Up, water, milk	Drugs—all medicines containing aspirin, such as Bufferin, Anacin, Excedrin, Alka-Seltzer, Empirin, Darvon Compound
Drugs—Tylenol for fever or pain	Perfumes
	Toothpaste and tooth powder (a mixture of salt and soda can be used), oil of wintergreen, lozenges, mouthwash.

Source: Reprinted with permission from B. F. Feingold, *Introduction to Clinical Allergy,* 1973. Courtesy of Charles C. Thomas, Springfield, IL.

Environmental Control

INDICATIONS

Those children in whom environmental control should be instituted include those with the following:

1. Positive skin test findings for environmental allergens
2. Pollenosis (Most pollen-sensitive children also react to environmental factors.)
3. A strong history of atopic allergy in the parents
4. A clinical history of significant allergy symptoms (nasal, bronchial, atopic dermatitis)

GENERAL CONSIDERATIONS

General considerations related to environmental control are as follows:

- The child with an hereditary atopic constitution may react to every potential allergen in the environment.
- Food sensitivity is rarely observed without inhalant allergy, either to environmentals, pollens, or both.
- Environmental control includes elimination (avoidance) of inhalants such as pollens, dust, animal dander, and fumes (air pollution, cigarette smoke, and wood-burning fires); and all environmental factors found within the home, the school, and places visited. See Table 26-5.
- Control of the home should not be restricted to the child's room; all rooms including the basement and garage must be considered.
- The emotional upheaval caused by the removal of a pet must be tempered by the fact that the child's allergic symptoms can serve as an even greater potential for causing emotional disturbances.
- Failure to exercise environmental control is one of the most frequently encountered reasons for the failure of immunotherapy in the treatment of allergic diseases.

HOW TO "DESENSITIZE" A ROOM

Ordinary house dust is a mixture of many things. See Table 26-5. Practically everything that can wear out can produce dust. A dustfree environment for even part of a 24-hour period will be substantially beneficial for the dust-sensitive child. This is usually the bedroom where the most concentrated amount of time is spent. Suggestions that follow for a bedroom can be applied to other rooms.

1. All clothes are kept in closets, never lying about the room. Closet and all other doors are kept closed. The closet should be cleaned well before clothes are placed inside. Some authorities prefer the closets emptied and sealed with clothes stored elsewhere.
2. No ornately carved furniture, books, or bookshelves should be in the room.
3. Unholstered chairs are replaced with rubberized canvas or plastic chairs.
4. Wood or linoleum floors (no rugs) are permitted. The walls should be scrubbed initially and the floor waxed.
5. No fabric toys or stuffed animals are permitted. Toys may be of wood, plastic, or metal. They may be stuffed with polyesters or old nylons as these are washable.
6. No pennants, pictures, or other dust-catchers are permitted on the walls.
7. The beds are made with allergen-proof encasings for pillows, mattress, and box springs. See Resource Information. The mattress and pillow covers are vacuumed frequently. Fuzzy blankets, quilts, and comforters are avoided. Washable cotton or synthetic blankets are best. The blankets are washed every 4 to 6 weeks. Blanket covers should be of sheeting or washable fabrics. No mattress pad is used on the bed. Dreft or White King D detergents may be used in the washing machine.
8. No kapok, feather, or foam rubber pillows are used. Dacron or other synthetics are substituted. Foam rubber grows mold, especially in a damp area.
9. Air-conditioning window units or central air conditioning may be installed. Windows are kept closed, especially in summer. No electric fans are used.
10. Roll-up, washable, cotton or synthetic window shades are installed. No venetian blinds should be used.

Table 26-5
Commonly Encountered Environmental Factors

Items	Where Found
Grass pollens	
Weed pollens	
Tree pollens	
Cotton linters	Not the same fibers used in cotton cloth. Linters are used in cotton wadding or batting to make pads, cushions, comforters, mattresses, upholstery and some varnishes.
Feathers and down	Pillows, down cushions, couches, and other upholstered articles, birds, sleeping bags
Coconut fiber	Tropical furniture, doormats, gymnasium mats, mattresses, box springs
Cat hair	Cats, toy animals, "imitation" furs, some fur caps, ear muffs, slippers, gloves
Cattle hair	Rugs, rug pads, blankets, carpet padding
Dog hair	Dogs—all dogs produce dander.[a]
Goat hair	Mohair, angora, cashmere, alpaca
Hog hair	Rug and carpet pads, hair brushes, furniture stuffing, mattresses, auto cushions
Horse hair	Horses, carpet padding, some blankets, some antique furniture
Rabbit hair	Fur coats, trimmings sold under trade name Coney or Lapin, toy animals, fabrics, some felts
Hemp	Rope, carpet pads, used as sisal in mattresses and box springs, rugs
Kapok	Kapok is a plant fiber used in cushions, mattresses, sleeping bags, pillows, upholstery
Wool	Raw wool and coarse woolens of all kinds should be avoided. Avoid wool blankets and knitting with wool yarn.
Flaxseed	Some cereals, laxatives, wave sets, paints, varnishes, linseed oil, furniture stuffings
Jute	Carpet pads, carpet backing, burlap, gunny sacks, crocus cloth, "Polynesian" articles such as grass skirts, handbags, place mats, cushions
House dust	A mixture of all the above agents. In addition, it in itself has factors that cause allergy. Control of the above factors in part controls the potency of house dust.

[a]The belief that hairless dogs are not allergenic is a myth. It is the dander and not the hair that is allergenic. There is no difference among species of dogs.

Table 26-5 (*Continued*)

Items	Where Found
Orris root	All ladies' and men's cosmetics, talcum, dusting powder, perfume, deodorants, gin factories, bakeries, toothpaste and powders
Pyrethrum	Insect sprays (almost all—check label)
Vegetable gums	Mucilage, bakery products
Acacia gum	
Karaya gum	In denture adhesive—check labels; also in cream cheeses
Tragacanth gum	Confections, gum drops, pastries and pies
Molds (fungi and mildew)	Dark, damp, cool places as shower stalls, bathrooms, cabinet under sinks, refrigerators, basement, windows, eaves of houses; also in the air and in cheeses. Check around for musty (mildew) odors. Clean thoroughly and spray repeatedly with Lysol

Source: Reprinted with permission from B. F. Feingold, *Introduction to Clinical Allergy*, 1973. Courtesy of Charles C. Thomas, Springfield, IL.

11. Easily washed cotton or fiberglass curtains are used and washed daily. No draperies are used.

12. In houses with forced hot air, a centrally installed electrostatic air filter may be used or a filter of damp cheesecloth is put over the air inlet and changed weekly.

13. Newly developed products, such as Allergex, which inhibit dust formation on furniture, rugs, drapes, and blankets may be used. These products immobilize old dust, retard the formation of new dust, and are applied with simple spray equipment.

14. The room should be damp mopped and dusted, including all parts of the bed, daily with a thorough and complete cleaning once a week.

15. Clothes and shoes are brushed before storing in this room. They may carry pollens and dusts. Other clothes are aired before storing.

16. All dogs, cats, birds, and other pets are removed from the house.

17. No insect sprays or powders are used. Odoriferous substances, such as camphor, tar, and room deodorants, should be avoided.

Parents faced with the rigorous task of desensitizing a room need help and support from health personnel. They need to be encouraged and reassured that their difficult task will afford relief of symptoms for an ill child.

HUMIDITY IN THE HOME

Proper humidification of inhaled air is extremely important to the function of the lungs; and humidified air combats the allergic effect of house dust. A relative humidity of 50 percent has a lethal effect on nearly all infective bacteria and viruses. Efficient functioning of the cilia is dependent on optimal humidity (45 to 50 percent). Ideally the entire house should be humidified, but it is needed most in the bedroom. It is not necessary to have the child's room dripping with moisture to produce the desired conditions. In regions where humidity is not too low, no provision for added moisture is necessary. In dry climates, additional moisture can be added to the room by placing a container of water with a large exposed surface in the room. When a vaporizer is used, the concentration of moisture should be checked. Excessive moisture, particularly over prolonged uninterrupted periods, predisposes to the growth of molds which can complicate the clinical picture. See also Chapter 17, Humidification.

Pharmacologic Therapy

DRUG THERAPY

Drug therapy is no substitute for prevention. In most allergic conditions drug therapy is a relatively secondary aspect of the treatment. Treatment of allergic illnesses by drugs is managed in close collaboration with a physician. However, the nurse practitioner must know the implications of these drugs as applied to allergic diseases.

Antihistamines Antihistamines are used for acute rhinorrhea, allergic rhinitis, hay fever, and pruritus. They may be used as a preventive for the rhinorrhea preceding asthma attacks but are not used once wheezing is established. Effective use of antihistamines depends on achieving a balance between the desired histamine antagonism and the undesirable side effects of which sedation and drying are the most notable. Susceptibility to the side effects varies among clients, and generally, many different preparations are tried before the most effective one is found. Some clients have a prolonged and significant therapeutic effect from low dosages but experience associated sedative symptoms; others tolerate and need much higher quantities. The side effects may subside with continued use, while effectiveness persists. On the other hand some clients will benefit from alternating use of different groups of antihistamines from week to week. A therapeutic effect occurs within 30 minutes with a duration of 3 to 6 hours, but a prolonged effect (8 to 12 hours) can be obtained from sustained release preparations.

PRESCRIPTION PREPARATIONS Some frequently used antihistamines are the following:

1. Benadryl (diphenhydramine hydrochloride). Benadryl is not for use in premature or newborn infants.
2. Dimetane (brompheniramine)
3. Actidil (triprolidine)

OVER-THE-COUNTER (OTC) PREPARATIONS Commonly used OTC antihistamine preparations containing chlorpheniramine in various amounts and some combinations are Alleroid, Contac, Coricidin, Dristan, Novahistine, and Chlor-Trimeton.

Antitussives These drugs are contraindicated for the treatment of bronchial allergies because they suppress the cough and may aggravate the condition. Coughing is the major mechanism for removing bronchial secretions and mucous plugs.

Barbiturates These drugs are contraindicated in the treatment of bronchial allergies because they depress the respiratory center and may aggravate the condition.

Bronchodilators See Sympathomimetics.

Corticosteroids The most common use of steroids is to bring an end to status asthmaticus in infants or in severe asthma in children. The dangers lie in reliance on steroids as a substitute for a thoughtful and searching program of conventional management of childhood allergies and the side effects of steroids.

INJECTABLE STEROIDS These are not recommended for children because of the risk of retardation of bone development and growth.

OPHTHALMIC STEROIDS These are not used topically to treat minor disorders of the eye(s) of children because they are potentially toxic agents.

OTIC STEROIDS These are not recommended because of their potential sensitizing effect.

TOPICAL STEROIDS Topical steroids are of undisputed value as anti-inflammatory and antipruritic agents. Topical steroids are useful in the treatment of small, localized patches of dermatitis. However, those containing parabens as a preservative may cause contact dermatitis. Application of topical antibiotics, especially neomycin, with or without steroids is not recommended. The risk of sensitization is very great. The steroids offer no protection against the development of such sensitivities.

The "Use" Test The "use" test should be employed when using topical ointments which may contain known sensitizers. Before applying a cream or ointment to a large area, apply the medication to an area the size of a dime and watch for several hours for signs of primary irritation (Gellis and Kagan, 1973, p. 715).

Preparations Some topical steroid preparations which are recommended are triamcinolone acetonide (Aristocort, Kenalog), flurandrenolide (Cordran), and fluorometholone (Oxylone). Some which do not contain parabens are dexamethasone (Decadron), and fluocinolone (Synalar).

Decongestants See Sympathomimetics.

Expectorants Expectorants are given to aid in the liquefaction and mobilization of the bronchial secretions. Expectorants are commonly combined with bronchodilators. The most important expectorant is water.

WATER Adequate hydration increases the watery secretions in the bronchioles which thins mucous secretions. This thinning allows for easier removal of mucus and decreased formation of mucous plugs. Effective delivery of water to the lungs depends on adequate oral intake. Additional benefit may be gained from vaporizers and cool-mist humidifiers. (See Chapter 17, Humidification.)

PREPARATIONS Drugs included in this group are potassium iodide, guaifenesin (Robitussin), and iodinated glycerin (Organidin).

Opiates See Barbiturates

Sedatives See Barbiturates. They have no place in routine treatment of children. If there is a specific indication for sedation a nonbarbiturate sedative may be safer to use (e.g., chloral hydrate).

Sympathomimetics These drugs include bronchodilators and decongestants. They produce dilation of the air passages and tend to correct the edema of the mucous membranes. They are used in the treatment of allergic rhinitis and bronchial allergies. Children with asthma who take these medications must concurrently increase their fluid intake.

PREPARATIONS The two sympathomimetics used most often in the treatment of asthma are epinephrine and ephedrine. Both drugs have side effects of tachycardia, sometimes mild muscular incoordination, and stimulation of the central nervous system. These side effects are sometimes perceived by the child as feelings of anxiety which engender further anxiety. A word of explanation to the child that these sensations are normal, and that they mean the medicine is taking effect is indicated. Epinephrine is the most physiologic sympathomimetic. The therapeutic effects are felt in about 15 to 20 minutes after an injection. Ephedrine is the most commonly used sympathomimetic sometimes in combination with aminophylline or theophylline, a sedative, and an expectorant. Benefits from ephedrine may be delayed 45 minutes or more.

Ephedrine Compounds   Some frequently used ephedrine compounds are listed below:

1. Theophylline, ephedrine sulfate, and hydroxyzine hydrochloride (Marax)
2. Theophylline, ephedrine sulfate, and phenobarbital (Tedral)
3. Theophylline, anhydrous (Slo-phyllin)

Combined with Antihistamines   Preparations which contain these drugs in combination with antihistamines are:

1. Triprolidine hydrochloride and pseudoephedrine hydrochloride (Actifed Syrup)
2. Brompheniramine maleate, phenylephrine hydrochloride, and phenylpropanolamine hydrochloride (Dimetapp Elixir)
3. Phenylpropanolamine hydrochloride, pheniramine maleate, and pyrilamine maleate (Triaminic Syrup)

Eye Preparations   Decongestant eye preparations are phenylephrine hydrochloride (Neo-Synephrine) and Visine and Vasocon-A.

Nasal Sprays and Nose Drops   Sympathomimetic amines are used topically as nasal sprays and nose drops. Used in this form vasoconstriction and relief of swelling is much more dramatic and rapid than in the systemic use of these amines. However, there is often a rebound vasodilation occurring an hour or so after the use of the topical agents, and long-term use should be avoided because of the hazard of resulting atrophy of mucosal tissues. There is little justification for their use in children. A commonly used preparation is phenylephrine (Neo-Synephrine).

Nebulizers   These are aerosol inhalators containing isoproterenol, a bronchodilator. They are used in some cases of bronchial allergies. Nebulizers have been associated with worsening of symptoms; use or misuse has also been associated with sudden death, either from toxicity or from sudden severe bronchospasm. They may be used by an older, more stable child. They are more effective when used very early in the development of an asthmatic paroxysm rather than later in the attack. It is important that the parents and the care provider know exactly how they are to be used, and that use is reasonably monitored. There is no justification for their use in young children. See Chapter 12, Pharmacologic Therapy.

Tranquilizers These agents should be used in the allergic child only for those who present serious neurotic traits or other behavior disturbances with anxiety or hyperactivity as outstanding features.

TOPICAL THERAPY

Baths For treatment of a widespread dermatitis, baths are anti-pruritic and mildly anti-inflammatory. The tub is half filled with lukewarm water and the child is bathed for 15 to 30 minutes.

COMMON PREPARATIONS There are several common bath preparations:

1. Water alone.
2. Linit starch, half a box to one tub. This is used for generalized dermatoses.
3. Aveeno colloidal oatmeal. This is used in the treatment of widespread poison ivy or oak dermatitis, diaper rash, atopic dermatitis, and contact dermatitis. One cup is added to a tub of warm water once or twice daily. For infants, 1 or 2 tablespoonfuls are added to the bathinette. The oilated type is not used for treatment of acute oozing dermatitis.
4. Soyaloid colloidal bath. This is a colloidal soya protein complex with 2 percent polyvinlypyrrolidone. It is very valuable for the treatment of diaper dermatitis, poison ivy or poison oak, and sunburn. One packet is dissolved in a tub of warm water, or 2 to 3 tablespoonfuls to each gallon of warm water for an infant's bath.

LUBRICATING BATHS These baths are useful for treatment of dry or pruritic skin as in atopic dermatitis. They can also be used after showering or sponge bathing, and also for general cleansing of the skin. Some lubricating baths are Alpha-Keri, Domol, Lubath, and Nutraspa.

Lotions Lotions are suspensions of a powder in liquid. As the liquid evaporates, a coating of powder remains on the skin surface. Evaporation cools the surface and the powder soothes, protects, and dries the skin. Lotions are useful in the treatment of acute dermatitis but must be avoided on oozing surfaces and in hairy or intertriginous areas. They are most often applied with fingers, gauze, or with a small paint brush, in which case they should be dispensed in a widemouthed bottle. They are applied evenly and removed by soaking, not by peeling, the dried material from the skin. If used for more than 3 or 4 days, shake lotions may cause chapping. The "caine-type" anesthetic lotions should be avoided because of potential sensitivity.

PREPARATIONS Some commonly used lotions are those listed below:

1. Aveeno Lotion. In acute and subacute dermatoses, Aveeno Lotion forms a flexible adherent coating which does not crack or flake off.
2. Calamine Lotion USP. Calamine lotion is inexpensive and has a wide and well-deserved reputation. Its disadvantages are that it tends to dry and to cake, especially in the presence of oozing.
3. Cetaphil Lotion. Cetaphil Lotion is a lipid-free lotion used commonly for atopic dermatitis. It is used as a waterless cleaner, for the relief of itching, and as a vehicle for various active ingredients, especially hydrocortisone.
4. Cordran Lotion. Cordran Lotion (flurandrenolide) is easy to apply and useful in acute and subacute dermatoses. It is rather expensive.
5. Kenalog Lotion. Kenalog Lotion (triamcinolone acetonide) is very effective for seborrheic dermatitis on the face and in the intertriginous areas.

Occlusive Dressings Occlusive dressings are very effective in the treatment of chronic dermatitis, such as atopic dermatitis. Treatment usually is overnight for a period of 8 to 12 hours. No more than 10 percent of the body should be treated at any one time, since significant systemic absorption may occur, especially with the fluorinated corticosteroids. Complications include an objectionable odor, folliculitis, sweat retention, secondary irritation, and infection. Late sequelae may include atrophy and striae.

METHODS Some methods for applying occlusive dressings are as follows:

1. Topical steroids are covered with a thin plastic film followed by a covering of stockinette, cotton glove, stocking, T-shirt, pair of shorts, or Ace bandage.

2. Cordran tape is useful for the treatment of small and medium-size lesions of chronic dermatoses. Before application the area must be cleansed gently to remove scales, crusts, dried exudate, and any traces of medications. Dry the skin thoroughly and apply the tape smoothly against the skin, usually leaving it in place for about 12 hours.

Open Wet Dressings (Compresses and Soaks) Open wet dressings, the mildest form of topical therapy, cool the skin by evaporation, relieve itching, and clean the surface by loosening and removing crusts and debris. Used on acute blistered dermatitis, open wet dressings often may be the only treatment possible. The treatment ordinarily has a duration of 30 minutes to 1 hour, three to four times daily. Ordinary tap water is used and it is not necessary to sterilize the water or the dressings. The solution is kept at room temperature and mixed immediately before each treatment. It is not kept overnight, since it may become unstable and more concentrated on standing.

METHOD The method for applying wet dressings is as follows:

1. Kerlix gauze, plain gauze without absorbent cotton, thin white handkerchiefs, any soft cotton cloth, or strips of bed linen are used with a solution. See following section for solutions.

2. The dressings are moistened in the solution and applied, wet but not runny, flat and smooth against the skin of the affected area. They are left uncovered. One layer is usually sufficient. The fingers are wrapped separately; the arms and legs are wrapped so that the elbows and knees can bend. No more than one third of the body is covered at a time, and chilling is avoided. The child must be comfortable during treatment and positioned so some form of play activity is possible.

3. When evaporation begins to dry the cloth, after 5 to 10 minutes, the entire dressing is removed, resoaked, and reapplied to the inflamed area. The solution is never poured directly over the dressings.

4. After treatment, the skin is dried by patting with a towel or washcloth. At this time a lotion or other medication may be applied.
5. Wet dressings are usually discontinued after 36 to 48 hours. If they are continued longer than this, drying of the skin can result.

SOLUTIONS Solutions commonly used for open wet dressings include the following:

1. Water alone.
2. Burow's solution. A 1:20 solution (i.e., 1 tbsp to 1 quart) is prepared by mixing one packet of powder or one tablet in 1 quart of tap water. The more concentrated solutions indicated on the package directions may be irritating. Burow's solution is mildly astringent and antiseptic and leaves a fresh, dry feeling.
3. Dalibour solution. The contents of one powder packet are dissolved in 1 quart of water, making a 1:16 solution.
4. Silver nitrate. A 0.1 percent to 0.25 percent solution for infected or ulcerated skin is used. Stains are removed by painting the skin with tincture of iodine, washing off, and rubbing with hypertonic saline.
5. Soyboro powder packets. One packet of powder in a quart of tap water provides a soothing and cleansing wet dressing combining Burow's solution with a soya protein complex. This preparation is highly acceptable to clients.

Prophylaxis of Allergy in Infancy

Onset of symptoms in a child of allergic parents may be significantly delayed by advising the following measures:

1. Breast feeding
2. Artificial feeding with non-milk formula
3. Exclusion of milk, citrus, eggs, beef, and wheat for the first 9 to 12 months
4. Introduction of new foods to the diet every 7 days, keeping a careful history of reactions
5. Exclusion of pets from the environment

6. Avoidance of feathers, jute, and Kapok in home furnishings
7. Filtration of heating outlet in child's room

While this subject is debatable, these measures can be practiced without risk and give the parent and primary health provider alternative approaches to the problem.

Psychologic Aspects of Allergy

Each client presenting with a complaint must be evaluated from an organic standpoint and on a psychologic basis. Psychiatric factors related to allergic diseases have been frequently misinterpreted and have led to much misinformation. When symptoms of allergy and of nervous tension are present, there are four major theoretical possibilities:

1. The allergy may cause the behavioral symptoms. For example, children with hay fever may misbehave and be resistant to normal discipline. The dyspnea of severe bronchial asthma is a frightening experience. Often relief from symptoms will greatly improve the behavior.
2. A psychic illness associated with a state of nervous irritability may accentuate the allergic symptoms. Psychic factors as well as weather changes, infection, and endocrine disturbances act as aggravating, secondary, or precipitating factors in the production of allergic symptoms. Commonly there will be a flare-up of allergic diseases after periods of stress. Immunologic and pharmacologic management alone will fail unless the psychologic aspects are considered.
3. The two conditions may have nothing other than a coincidental relationship. For example, it is not necessary to be emotionally unstable to have hay fever.
4. Both conditions may be attributable to some third factor or combination of factors. A genetic predisposition to both allergies and tensional stress merits consideration.

Studies have shown the following results (Patterson, 1972):

1. There is not an allergic personality pattern.
2. Chronically ill children with any major illness present with similar neurotic problems.

3. Maternal rejection is no different in allergic illness than with other medical problems.
4. Methodologic problems, lack of standardization of techniques of allergic and psychiatric treatment, and insufficient follow-up have hampered the meaningful interpretation of research results in this field.

Counseling

The nature of allergic illness is both crisis-ridden and chronic, frequently producing anguish and stress within the family. Parental concerns which are most frequent are: contagiousness, disfigurement, malignancy, and inheritance. Reassurance plays an important role in the successful outcome of the therapeutic program. The nurse practitioner can be of great assistance to the child and to the family in the following ways:

• Be sure that the child and parents know exactly what is expected of them and give them explicit written directions.
• Explain the many aspects of the illness such as genetic basis, day-to-day management, psychologic factors, and prognosis.
• Explain that the amount of relief from symptoms is often in direct proportion to the thoroughness with which the allergens are removed from the environment or diet.
• Teach them safe and appropriate use of medications and when to seek medical assistance.
• Be aware that ideal situations may be recommended but that many families are unable to follow through with directions because of lack of understanding, lack of motivation, or pressures within the family.
• Recognize the difficulties faced and the impact on the family. Help them find a level of symptom that is tolerable for the child and that can be tolerated by the entire family.
• Maintain good communications. Be available to work with them when they encounter behavioral and discipline problems with the allergic child.
• Help them to recognize when hospitalization of the child is necessary.

- Keep informed of the hospitalized child's progress and relate the progress to the parents.
- Assist parents to seek help from local agencies for counseling, household help, or financial aid.
- Visit the home to evaluate the physical and emotional climate or request help from the public health nurse agency.
- Act as liaison to the school for interpreting symptoms and treatment as necessary.

COMMON CLINICAL PROBLEMS

Allergic Skin Disorders

ALLERGIC DERMATITIS

Assessment   Allergic dermatitis is dermatitis caused by increased IgE antibodies as a result of hypersensitivity to specific allergens such as pollens, environmentals, and foods. The types of allergic dermatitis are atopic dermatitis and contact dermatitis.

The term "eczema" is used in a variety of ways in relation to skin disorders. Some use it to mean allergic dermatitis; some to mean atopic dermatitis; and others to mean any dermatitis or dermatosis. Eczema is a descriptive term and should be applied when describing the typical rash of atopic dermatitis. See this chapter, Atopic Dermatitis.

CLINICAL FINDINGS   The symptoms of allergic dermatitis are as follows:

1. Acute form: erythema, edema, oozing, and crusting vesiculation.
2. Chronic form: dryness, scaliness, *hyperkeratosis* (thickening of the keratinized layer of the skin, the stratum corneum), and *lichenification* (thickening of the skin with exaggeration of its normal markings so that striae form a crisscross pattern; it is a response to chronic rubbing and scratching).
3. Both forms: pruritus. This is the most important single nonspecific factor that leads to histopathologic changes in the skin. Some people have a low threshold of tolerance, scratch easily,

and traumatize the skin. To others, the intensity of itching depends on the intensity of the allergic reaction, or even the emotional state of the person.

SECONDARY INFECTION   Secondary infection of dermatitic skin may be subtle and easily overlooked. Children with atopic dermatitis are particularly likely to develop secondary pyogenic infection. Often the dermatitis is improved following childhood communicable diseases. It will recur after convalescence from the secondary disease; the reason is unknown. Infants with allergic dermatitis are very susceptible to infection with herpes virus (see Chapter 27, Viral Infections) and vaccinia virus. Strict avoidance of individuals with either herpes or recent vaccination is necessary. *Neither children with dermatitis nor their siblings should be vaccinated for smallpox.*

LABORATORY FINDINGS   Those common to the diagnosis of allergic dermatitis are:

1. Atopic reactivity (increased IgE antibodies). These are generally found on skin testing.
2. Eosinophilia. More than 10 percent is common in association with allergic dermatitis. (Eosinophilia is the accumulation of unusual numbers of eosinophil cells in the blood or in nasal or ear secretions.)
3. Streptococci or staphylococci. These are commonly revealed on cultures of the skin.

Management   Most of the management of children with allergic dermatitis can be assumed by the nurse practitioner. Consultation is recommended for severe or complicated cases and when corticosteroids are indicated. Referral to a specialist is recommended for management by immunotherapy. See this chapter, Immunotherapy. Treatment may also include diet and environmental control, prevention of pruritus, and topical and systemic therapies.

DIET AND ENVIRONMENTAL CONTROL   See this chapter, Diet Control, and Environmental Control.

PREVENTION OF PRURITUS   Measures that help prevent scratching and further itching are as follows:

1. Fingernails are cut short, elbows are splinted as needed, and the bed is covered with a thick plastic sheet to prevent rubbing.

2. Cotton clothing and socks are worn; wool is an irritant.

3. Exposure of the child to heat, cold, wind, moisture, sunlight, physical effort, or emotional disturbances is avoided as possible.

TOPICAL TREATMENT (See this chapter, Pharmacologic Therapy.) Topical treatment is managed as follows:

1. Cool compresses or soaks are helpful for small areas of involvement.

2. Tepid baths are used for generalized involvement. Given two to four times daily for 10 to 20 minutes, the times are reduced as the condition improves. Cetaphil Lotion may be used following the baths.

3. Topical steroids may be used for small areas of involvement. The "use" test is employed.

4. General use of soap and water is avoided. Dehydration of the skin tends to improve allergic dermatitis; overhydration to make it worse. The use of a waterless cleanser such as Cetaphil Lotion is recommended.

5. Lotions, oils, or greasy ointments should not be used on the affected areas. These can cause increased itchiness and redness.

SYSTEMIC TREATMENT (See this chapter, Pharmacologic Therapy.) Systemic treatment is managed as follows:

1. Pruritus and/or burning pain are reduced with aspirin, usually in combination with antihistamines. "Caine" anesthetics may produce further sensitization.

2. Secondary infection is handled with antibiotics.

3. Sedation can be achieved with antihistamines.

4. Severe and extensive cases are treated with corticosteroids.

COUNSELING Parents should be reminded that these children need care and affection. They should be played with, held, and cuddled. For further counseling measures see this chapter, Counseling, and Psychologic Aspects of Allergy.

ATOPIC DERMATITIS, INFANTILE

Assessment (See above, Allergic Dermatitis.) Infantile atopic dermatitis is a form of allergic dermatitis. Its onset is commonly associated with the introduction of new foods to the diet, especially milk and eggs, but it may be due to environmentals such as wool, dust, and others. It is uncommon in breast-fed babies. See this chapter, Milk Allergy.

INCIDENCE Infantile atopic dermatitis rarely appears before 6 weeks of age, more often after 2 to 3 months of age. There is a strong familial history. Approximately 70 percent of patients with atopic dermatitis have a family history of atopic dermatitis, asthma, or hay fever.

CLINICAL FINDINGS The rash of atopic dermatitis develops in the following pattern:

1. The initial lesion is a small erythematous, papular patch over one or both cheeks.
2. There is intensification of the redness, coalescence of lesions, and development of minute vesicles which give the skin a ground-glass appearance.
3. Oozing and weeping of the lesions become pronounced and the drying exudate forms honey-colored crusts.
4. Excoriation which appears as denuded, raw, and bleeding patches results from itching, scratching, and rubbing.
5. Nodes near the affected areas may become enlarged. This may be due to an immune response; the nodes are neither tender nor suppurative.
6. Secondary infection of bacterial or viral origin may occur. It is usually low grade. Impetigo is the most common and upper respiratory infections are also common.

PROGRESSION OF THE DISEASE The rash begins on the face and forehead but soon extends to the neck, the postauricular areas, and particularly to the bends of the arms (anticubital fossae) and the legs (popliteal fossae). With a more severe reaction, the torso or entire body may show involvement. The circumoral and periorbital regions, and diaper area may be free of rash. The disease may continue without remission for the first 2 years of life, or it may wax and wane with brief periods of clearing of the skin. As the second year approaches, the disease may clear spontaneously. If it continues, the lesions may lose their acute character and become a mixture of acute and chronic forms.

DIFFERENTIAL DIAGNOSIS Skin disorders that resemble infantile atopic dermatitis (see Table 26-6) and that must be ruled out include the following:

1. Contact dermatitis
2. Seborrheic dermatitis

Management The treatment of infantile atopic dermatitis is essentially the same as that outlined for allergic dermatitis. See this chapter, Allergic Dermatitis, for indications for consultation and referral, prevention of pruritus, topical and systemic treatments, and counseling.

ATOPIC DERMATITIS, CHILDHOOD

Assessment (See also this chapter, Allergic Dermatitis.) Atopic dermatitis which occurs beyond the age of 2 or 3 has a more chronic character. It may continue from infancy; however, infantile atopic dermatitis usually clears spontaneously by 2 years of age. It may be caused by environmental allergens and, sometimes, food. A history of familial allergens or infantile atopic dermatitis is common.

CLINICAL FINDINGS The skin, which assumes chronic characteristics of the disease, appears as follows:

1. Lesions appear with scaling papules with crusted summits, hypertrophy, and lichenification.
2. The skin may become leathery, fissured, and striated.
3. A greyish discoloration of the involved area is frequently observed.
4. Scratch marks capped with crusted blood are present.
5. Itching may become intolerable. Itching is caused by obstruction of the sweat glands and occurs in any situation which causes increased sweating.

PROGNOSIS Atopic dermatitis is subject to remission and may reappear at pubescence, adolescence, and/or young adulthood.

Management The treatment of atopic dermatitis is essentially the same as that for allergic dermatitis. See this chapter, Allergic Der-

Table 26-6

Distinguishing Characteristics of Atopic Dermatitis, Seborrheic Dermatitis, and Contact Dermatitis

	Atopic Dermatitis	Seborrheic Dermatitis	Contact Dermatitis
Age of onset	After 2 months	Any age	Any age
Family history of eczema or asthma	Positive	Negative	May be either
Cause	Allergenic	Nonallergenic	May be either
Clinical features	Erythema, edema, oozing, crusting, vesiculation, or lichenification	Erythema, yellowish, scaly lesions; may ooze and crust	Slight to intense erythema; vesicles, or bullae
Distribution	Cheeks, forehead, limbfolds; may extend to extremities and torso	Scalp, forehead, behind and in ears; chest, neck, and axilla	Exposed areas, regional areas, diaper area; may be unilateral
Pruritus	Marked	Mild	Slight to burning pain
Prognosis	May lead to severe dermatitis or asthma	Clears with treatment	Clears with treatment

matitis, for indications for consultation or referral, prevention of pruritus, topical or systemic treatment, and counseling.

CONTACT DERMATITIS

Assessment (See also this chapter, Allergic Dermatitis.) Contact dermatitis can be classified as one of two types:

1. *Nonallergic or irritant.* This form is induced by any substance that is irritating to the skin. The mechanism is either mechanical or chemical. Any part of the body may be affected, and the intensity of the skin reaction depends on the strength of the irritant and the duration of the exposure. The skin response is immediate with no history of previous exposure.
2. *Allergic.* This is a manifestation of the delayed type of hypersensitivity. The latent period, the period of no reactivity, may extend to weeks or longer.

ETIOLOGY Contact dermatitis can be induced by anyone holding the child, through bedding or floor material, or from such items as plastic toys or foods. See below, Suggested Contactants. A careful history of exposure to offending agents is taken.

CLINICAL FINDINGS Common positive signs of contact dermatitis in infancy are involvement of only one cheek, or involvement of knees, anterior surfaces or legs, anterior abdomen, and chest (from crawling on floor). Other signs are as follows:

1. Lesions may range from slight erythema to intense redness, through various degrees of inflammation, and from vesiculation to bullae.
2. Pruritus, at times burning and painful, may be evident.
3. Hypertrophy, hyperplasia, and lichenification may be present.
4. Regional distribution can be a clue.

SUGGESTED CONTACTANTS Some regional areas with suggested contactants (adapted from Feingold, 1973, p. 132) are the following:

1. Forehead: hat bands.
2. Eyes: eyedrops.
3. Eyelids: fingernail polish, hair dyes, rinses, shampoos, cosmetics of all kinds.

4. Ears: perfumes, shafts of eyeglass frames (postauricular eruption).
5. Nose: eyeglass frames.
6. Face and neck: smoke of burning poison oak or ivy; aerosol sprays, paint sprays, dusts, and pollens.
7. Neck: scarves, coat, permanent press garments.
8. Apex of the axilla: antiperspirants, deodorants, clothing, fabric dyes, and permanent press materials.
9. Arms: lateral surfaces from leaning on plastic, lacquered or varnished table or desk tops, or chromium trim on tables. Forearm from ladies purses. Whole arm from clothes lining; inner aspect of arm from upholstered material.
10. Body: girdles, bras, garter belts, cosmetics, suntan lotions, or pollens (the exposed parts of the body).
11. Anogenital region: suppositories, contraceptives, douches, rectal and vaginal discharges, perfumes, soaps, bubble bath, and detergents.
12. Legs (lateral surfaces): floor covering.
13. Feet: the glue and dye in shoes; foot powders and deodorants.

Management Rapid clearing of the skin usually follows elimination of the offending contactant. Patch testing is limited to children for whom the elimination of the suspected items has not been successful. Further treatment of contact dermatitis is essentially the same as that outlined for allergic dermatitis. See this chapter, Allergic Dermatitis, for indications for consultation or referral, prevention of pruritus, topical or systemic treatment, and counseling.

BITES OF ARACHNIDS AND INSECTS

Insects attack by direct bites, penetrating stings, injected venom, or tunnel-like burrows. The skin reaction to the bite itself is due to hypersensitivity and is species specific. There may be an immediate or delayed response. The first step in diagnosis is to determine if the eruption is an expression of a systemic disease such as varicella, response to allergens, or is an insect bite. Clues come from careful history, geography, season, and knowledge of the environment. Distribution of the lesions is a clue; mosquito, gnat, fly, flea, and hornet bites appear on exposed parts of the body; body parasites establish themselves in covered areas; different insects can have identical-appearing lesions. If systemic reactions or anaphylaxis occur, treatment must be carried out as soon as possible, preferably in collaboration with a physician. For further information regarding specific insects see Table 26-7.

URTICARIA

Assessment Urticaria is a mechanism of hive formation: tissue fluid leaks into tissues and causes raised, edematous areas. They seem to be expressions of sensitivity to an irritant or allergen of some sort, although this cannot always be identified. There is a familial factor. Skin tests are generally of little value. These children do not usually have eosinophilia and sometimes give no other signs of being allergic. Chronic urticaria is not associated with atopy and may not have an allergic etiology.

CLINICAL FINDINGS The wheals are of variable sizes. They are usually multiple and may be painful or stinging. They may change in size and shape within hours or may lie in deep tissue layers of the skin and cause large areas of swelling in such parts as the face (angioedema), an extremity, the back, the throat, or the scrotum.

CAUSATIVE AGENTS

1. Alcohol
2. Allergies
3. Cancers, lymphomas, and leukemias (rare)
4. Cosmetics, soaps, and lotions
5. Foods (strawberries, spicy foods, peanuts, butter, and dairy products)
6. Insect bites (mosquito bite)
7. Low-grade infection (strep throat, cystitis)
8. Medications (long-lasting penicillin, sulfas, antibiotics, aspirin)
9. Sunlight, extremes of heat or cold, emotions, and exercise

TYPES OF URTICARIA

1. Angioedema. This presents as subcutaneous edema. It is seen on the eyes, the cheeks, the ear lobes, and the genitalia and may lead to anaphylaxis.

Table 26-7

Insect Bites: Assessment and Management

Insects	Assessment	Findings	Management
Black widow spider (Arachnida)	Neurotoxic. Most deaths attributed to anaphylaxis with a mortality of 4 percent. Likes dark places, wood piles, and latrines. May bite on genitalia or buttocks. Has a red hourglass configuration on abdomen.	*Local:* pin-prick sensation followed by dull pain. Puncture points red and edematous. Pruritus and urticaria may occur. *Early systemic:* abdominal rigidity in 15–30 min. *Later systemic:* weakness, tremor, sweating, and salivation. Skin sensitive. Excruciating pain in limb. Bradycardia and feeble pulse leading to anaphylaxis.	*Local: do not apply tourniquet or attempt to remove venom by incision and suction.* Use an antiseptic and apply ice. Hydrocortisone ointment may be applied for pruritus and urticaria. *Supportive:* hospitalization imperative. Prolonged warm baths and injections of 10 ml of 10 percent calcium gluconate for over 6 months of age, repeated at 4-hour intervals for pain. *Anaphylaxis:* see Chapter 28, Anaphylaxis. *Antivenom: test for equine serum hypersensitivity.* Give the entire contents of a restored vial of Antevenin, 2.5 ml IM. If the child is under 12 years of age or is in shock, give the antivenom intravenously in 10–50-ml saline solution over a 15-min period.

Continued

Brown recluse spider (Arachnida)

Necrotoxic, and in severe cases, hemolytic. Fairly common, it is also called house spider. It has a violin-shaped configuration on its back.

Local: mild stinging at instant of bite. Erythematous vesicle develops with ischemic center. Mild to severe pain develops in 2–8 hr. Star-shaped area develops in 3–4 days, changing to deep purple eschar, firm to the touch.

Systemic: generalized reactions may occur, such as fever or scarlatiniform rash. Hemolysis can occur and be fatal.

Preventive:

1. Area may be sprayed with Malathion.
2. Anaphylactic kit that contains epinephrine should be readily available.
3. Medic-Alert bracelet or necklace engraved with appropriate information should be worn. See this chapter, Resource Information.

Local: mild local symptoms do not require treatment at the site.

Supportive: if reported within 24 hr, administration of parenteral antihistamine and steroid may limit the effect of necrotoxin to the surface of the bitten area, may prevent fatal systemic reactions, and may minimize depth of the disfiguring scar. Tetanus prophylaxis should be considered in nonhealing lesions.

Table 26-7 (Continued)

Insects	Assessment	Findings	Management
Scorpion (Arachnida)	Venom consists of neurotoxin, cardiac toxin, and agglutinins. If scorpion is seen, it should be caught for identification. Found mainly in the Southwest.	*Local:* wound is caused by the sting. Sharp pain followed by local "pins-and-needles" sensation. *Systemic:* itching of the nose, mouth, and throat develops with speech impairment if no immediate first-aid is given. Numbness and weakness generally occur in affected limb. Lymphangitis and lymphadenitis may be observed proximal to the wound. Severe reactions are involuntary twitching progressing to muscular spasms with pain, nausea, and vomiting, and convulsions. Symptoms may last 48 hr. Prognosis is optimistic after 3 hr.	*Preventive:* the area may be sprayed with Malathion. *Local:* use antiseptic and apply ice. Use a tourniquet with momentary releases. This will slow down the absorption of the toxin. The wound should not be incised nor suction applied. *Supportive:* the body is kept warm. Opiates are not given. Injections of barbiturates or calcium gluconate solution may be given to control convulsions. Anti-inflammatory and antipruritic ointment may be used. *Antivenom:* Antivenin is particularly indicated for children. See this chapter, Black Widow Spider. (A specific antivenom for

| | | Southwest scorpions is prepared by Laboratories Myn, Av. Cocoacan 1707, Mexico 12, D. F.) |

Chigger (mite) (Arachnida)	Called harvest bug or red bug. Abound in tall grass, decaying matter, and underbrush. Adhere to clothing, or near hair follicles or sweat glands. Pierce skin, suck off tissue juices, and fall off. Identified with a hand lens as tiny red dots.	*Local:* intense itching, formation of a macule, papule, vesicle, or wheal 1–2 cm in diameter. Secondary infection may occur as a result of scratching.	*Local:* antibacterial and antipruritic medications are used. Starch baths and topical anesthetics are used for severe pruritis. *Supportive:* a mild barbiturate may be given to relieve tension and induce sleep.
Tick (Arachnida)	Wood tick, Eastern tick, and Lone star tick cause toxic manifestations. Live on dogs or in woods. Climb up clothing and attach to the neck. Usually the child is unaware.	*Local:* at times the bite can be painful. Lesion at the site of attachment becomes red and indurated. Petechial hemorrhages may be noted. Tick may be attached. *Systemic:* flaccidity and a slowly ascending motor and sensory paralysis are experienced that can culminate in a fatal outcome. Removing the tick reverses the symptoms.	*Local:* tick is removed (do not crush) with a forceps after application of alcohol or oil (Vaseline). Incomplete removal can lead to the formation of a nodule requiring surgical incision. *Preventive:* after a trip to the woods, clothing, child, and dogs should be closely inspected for the insect.

Continued

Table 26-7 (Continued)

Insects	Assessment	Findings	Management
		Complications: a rare complication of tick bite is Rocky Mountain spotted fever. A rickettsial infection, it is transmitted by the bites of certain species of ticks if they themselves are infected. It occurs in late spring and early summer. The incubation period is 2–14 days. Any child who becomes ill with fever and chills after a known tick bite should be observed for a macular skin rash which will occur 2–4 days after the prodromal symptoms.	
Human and dog fleas (Siphonaptera)	Lesions are found on the arms or legs or in areas where clothing fits tightly. Diagnosis confirmed by seasonal incidence, distri-	*Local:* lesions appear grouped in an irregular pattern producing itching and papular urticarial eruptions, some with a	*Local:* antipruritics and cool, wet compresses are used. Secondary infections require topical antibiotic ointment.

	bution of lesions, presence of household pets, and abatement of eruptions when child is removed from suspected source.	central punctum. Lesions are 3–10 mm in diameter and are often excoriated from scratching.	*Preventive:* hyposensitization may be instituted for repeated attacks of papular urticaria. Pets are dusted with flea powder and given flea collars. Residual insect sprays are used for severe household infestations.
Hornet, honeybee, wasp, and yellow jacket (Hymenoptera)	If stinger is noted, the insect is a honeybee (bumblebee); absence of a stinger indicates yellow jacket (which is more likely to produce anaphylaxis), wasp, or hornet. Hymenoptera cause about 40 fatalities annually in the United States. Reactions occur more frequently in August.	*Local:* sharp pain, edema (very pronounced on loose tissue), redness with later induration, and itchy swelling for days. Detached "stinger" can be identified as a black dot at the center. *Systemic:* present within 15 min to 1 hr. Child itches all over and face feels hot. Urticaria present on face and chest followed by dyspnea, weakness, feelings of anxiety, nausea, abdominal cramps, loss of consciousness, and anaphylactic shock.	*Local:* stinger is picked off except for honeybee, which should be flicked off. For relief of pain and itching the following steps are recommended: 1. Apply alcohol, ice, or a 10 percent solution of ammonia. 2. Moisten the area and rub an aspirin into it. When the first analgesia has worn off, moisten the area again and the relief will persist (Fikar, 1981). 3. Rub the area with meat tenderizer (contains papain, an enzyme that destroys insect venoms) (von Witt, 1980).

Continued

1023

Table 26-7 (Continued)

Insects	Assessment	Findings	Management
			Supportive: when the lesion is on an extremity, a tourniquet is applied proximally to slow absorption. In severe cases, soluble antihistamine is injected to prevent further absorption. Child is removed to a healthy facility. *Anaphylaxis:* epinephrine is administered immediately. See Chapter 28, Anaphylaxis. *Preventive:* 1. Wear white or light-colored clothes and shoes out-of-doors. Avoid scented soaps and cosmetics. Avoid insect breeding

grounds, such as flower beds and orchards with ripe fruits. Spray garbage areas with rapid-acting insecticide.

2. Hyposensitization by an allergist is recommended. Specific antivenom therapy is used, thus identification of the insect is desirable.

3. Anaphylactic kit should be available and the child should carry an aerosol insecticide spray. See this chapter, Resource Information.

4. Medic-Alert tag with appropriate information is worn. See Resource Information.

2. Papular urticaria. This is seen on the extensor muscles of the arms and legs or on the trunk. It comes seasonally and is due to insect bites.
3. Erythema multiforme. It is an allergic reaction. It forms papules and is bullous.

Management   Systemic and long-term treatment is managed collaboratively with a physician. Treatment consists of the following:

1. Local.

   • Calamine lotion is applied. Topical antihistamines, such as Caladryl, are never applied because they are potent sensitizers.
   • Lukewarm or cool water is helpful. Extremes of hot and cold are avoided.
   • Starch baths may be given.
   • Antihistamines and aspirin are given for itching.
   • If infection is the basic cause, the urticaria will disappear as the infection is treated.

2. Systemic. Treatment is for anaphylaxis. See Chapter 28, Anaphylaxis.

Food Allergies

Food allergy occurs more frequently in infants and children than in adults. It is believed that the frequency of food allergy in children is due to incompletely digested food protein that passes into the circulatory system. Food allergies should be suspected in cases of urticaria, angioedema, suspected gastrointestinal allergy, unexplained and sporadic respiratory allergies, and atopic dermatitis.

TYPES OF REACTIONS

The two types of reactions to food allergies are described as follows:

1. The rapid appearance of symptoms which appear within a few minutes after the offending food is eaten; a reaction may occur before the food is swallowed. Fish and seafoods, berries (espe-

cially strawberries), nuts, and sometimes egg white are the most common offenders.

2. A delayed reaction in which hours or, rarely, a day or more elapse between ingestion of the allergen and the appearance of the symptoms.

COMMON FOOD ALLERGENS

Foods that are commonly responsible for allergic reactions are wheat, corn, milk, eggs, beef, white potato, orange, pork, chocolate, and legumes. Almost all foods may be responsible for allergic reactions. Although reactions to chocolate are observed, this is not a strong antigen and does not deserve the reputation it has as a very common cause of food allergy.

FACTORS IN DIAGNOSIS OF FOOD ALLERGY

Factors that should be considered in diagnosing food allergy are listed below:

1. Quantitative factor. Small amounts of food can be tolerated without difficulty whereas larger amounts will precipitate symptoms.
2. Degree of cooking. Rare-cooked or raw foods are more allergenic.
3. Cumulative factor. The child may react if allergenic foods are eaten on successive days.
4. Cyclic factor. After a reaction there may be a refraction period during which ingestion of the allergen will not provoke symptoms.
5. Multiplicity factor. A reaction may occur if several foods to which child is allergic are eaten at the same time, but not if eaten separately.

GASTROINTESTINAL ALLERGIES IN INFANCY

Assessment Many infant feeding problems can be attributed to allergy. Milk is the primary offender; other common allergens are egg, wheat, and citrus. This disturbance occurs mainly in artificially fed infants, and rarely in breast-fed infants. However, if large amounts of one food such as orange juice or eggs are ingested by the mother, the allergen can be transmitted via the breast milk to the child. A careful diet history and behavioral history are taken. Food allergies should be suspected in infants with signs and symptoms that do not clear in a reasonable length of time. See also Chapter 3, Food Allergy.

CLINICAL FINDINGS Infants may show these signs:

1. Irritability and fussiness
2. Crying and pain which is spasmodic and similar to colic
3. Spitting up
4. Loose stools
5. Constipation

PROGNOSIS In some infants this problem will abate after the first or second year. In others the area of involvement may change to problems of the skin, respiratory tract, or ear. If symptoms appear in later life, consideration is given to the possibility that the identical allergens are the cause.

Management There are several goals of management:

1. Removal of the offending food (see this chapter, Diet Control). This usually brings quick relief.
2. Substitution of commercial cow milk formula with non-milk formula. Among those in order of recommendation are the following:

   • Protein hydrolysate with added corn oil, sugar, starch, vitamins and minerals such as Nutramigen or Pregestimil (Mead Johnson). These formulas are recommended for the more severe cases.
   • Soybean formulas. Soybean is a member of the legume family and itself can be allergenic. Some recommended soy formulas are Isomil (Ross), Prosobee (Mead Johnson), and Soyalac (Loma Linda). All soy formulas contain corn oil (a known sensitizer) except I-soyalac (Loma Linda) and Nursoy (Wyeth).

3. Control of the mother's diet if allergy is suspected in the breast-fed baby. Mothers need to follow a diet free of egg, wheat, milk, nuts, and chocolate.

4. Consideration of environmental factors if the infant fails to respond to dietary changes.

MILK ALLERGY

Assessment See also Chapter 20, Malabsorption: Disaccharide Deficiencies. Milk tolerance occurs in 0.3 to 7 percent of all children. In infancy milk intolerance is attributed to the increased permeability of the gut which permits passage of undigested proteins into the serum. The cow milk protein, casein, found in commercially prepared infant formula and fresh cow milk, is the sensitizing agent. Contamination of milk with extraneous substances such as fodder containing grasses and pollens can be a factor in cow milk. Breast milk is not allergenic; however, foods eaten by the mother, especially egg, may be excreted in the milk to produce symptoms in allergic children. See above, Gastrointestinal Allergies in Infancy.

CLINICAL FINDINGS Milk intolerance symptoms may include the following:

1. Frequent loose stools, colic, and gas
2. Frequent upper respiratory infections, especially serous otitis media
3. Skin manifestations such as allergic dermatitis
4. Allergic rhinitis or bronchial asthma in older children

PROGNOSIS Milk allergy may subside at about 2 to 3 years of age. Children with early milk allergy may develop other manifestations of allergy in later life, and the former intolerance should be a consideration in the diagnosis.

Management Milk intolerance in infancy is managed by the elimination of all milk products from the diet.

INFANCY These measures should be taken:

1. Cow milk or cow milk formula is substituted with breast milk or nonmilk formula. See above, Gastrointestinal Allergies in Infancy, for formula discussion.
2. Reintroduction of milk may be attempted in 6 months if the

1030 • ASSESSMENT AND MANAGEMENT OF COMMON CLINICAL PROBLEMS

allergy has been mild, in 12 months in case of moderate allergy, and in 1 to 2 years in case of severe allergy.

3. When the infant starts to eat solid foods, a diet is followed that excludes wheat, eggs, fish, milk, and beef for at least 9 to 12 months. At that time, these foods may be started very slowly, introducing one food at a time in small, increasing amounts. See this chapter, Diet Control. Care is taken to avoid other dairy products. See this chapter, Table 26-3. All labels should be read carefully.

CHILDHOOD A milk-free diet is followed, being careful to read labels of all foods not prepared at home. It is recommended that foods be home prepared. See Table 26-3.

Ocular Allergies

ACUTE ALLERGIC CONJUNCTIVITIS

Assessment Allergic conjunctivitis is one of the most common forms of eye allergy. The airborne allergens induce immediate reactivity. A swab of eye scrapings may show marked eosinophils.

TYPES OF ALLERGIC CONJUNCTIVITIS These include three types:

1. Atopic. The usual causes are pollens, dust, animal hair, and occasionally foods.
2. Drug. The most common offenders are atropine and neomycin.
3. Vernal. It occurs in spring and summer in older children and adolescents and frequently coexists with other atopic diseases.

CLINICAL FINDINGS These include acute and chronic symptoms. Acute symptoms, which are almost always bilateral and rarely occur as an isolated event, include the following:

1. Marked injection and redness of the conjunctivae
2. Edema of the mucosa and profuse tearing, at first watery but may later become mucopurulent
3. Intense itching, burning, rubbing, and occasional pain of varying degrees
4. Edema and pallor of the nasal mucosa

Chronic symptoms are as follows:

1. Itching and burning
2. Photophobia and dryness
3. "Cobblestoning" of upper eyelids

Management   Generally, a search is made for the causative agents through smears and conjunctival scrapings. The child may be placed on broad-spectrum antibiotics or sulfonamides if bacterial conjunctivitis is suspected, while awaiting the results of the cultures.

MEDICATIONS   Drugs used in treatment are as follows:

1. Topical vasoconstrictors and topical corticosteroids may be used as eye drops or eye ointments. The medication may be given as often as every 2 hours for severe reactions. The usual frequency is every 4 hours. In young children eye ointment is easier to apply with less chance of overdosage. Older children tolerate drops during the day.
2. Topical antihistamines afford some relief in mild cases. Failure to respond to antihistamines suggests an infection.

COUNSELING   Parents are taught the correct procedure for instilling topical eye medications. Explanations are provided about the causative agent, expected results of medication (see Chapter 15, The Eye), handwashing techniques to decrease the possibility of contagion, and symptoms of increased severity of the disorder, such as fever, increased discharge, keratitis, and erythema.

Respiratory Allergies

It is frequently difficult to distinguish between upper respiratory symptoms due to allergies and upper respiratory symptoms due to an infectious process. The distinction is important to make since treatment will differ as well as plans for long-term health maintenance care (e.g., the child with symptoms on an allergic basis is a safe candidate for routine immunizations; the child with an upper respiratory infection is not). Table 26-8 outlines features useful in differentiating the two conditions.

Table 26-8
Differentiation Between Allergies and Upper Respiratory Infections

Features	Allergies	Upper Respiratory Infections (Common Cold)
Onset	Sudden	Gradual
Attacks	Multiple, recurrent, or constant	Occasional, free of symptoms between colds
Symptoms	Sneezing, nasal itchiness, stuffy nose, irritative cough, seasonal or perennial	Nasal symptoms progress to chest and cough; duration less than 2 weeks
Fever	No	Maybe
Nasal discharge	Thin, watery, profuse	Thin to thick, maybe mucopurulent
Nasal mucosa	Pale, greyish pink, boggy, moist, swollen	Red and swollen
Exposure to infection	No	Yes
Exposure to environment	Yes	No
Associated allergies or family history	Yes	Not necessarily
Eosinophilia more than 10 percent	Usually	No

ALLERGIC RHINITIS

Assessment   In infancy allergic rhinitis may be due to hypersensitivity to food caused by IgE, or occasionally to inhalant factors. After 1 or 2 years it can be traced to environmental factors as dust, feathers, animal danders, house plants, or molds. When the symptoms persist throughout the year, the condition is known as allergic rhinitis; when the symptoms occur seasonally from pollens, the condition is known as "hay fever." The symptoms are sometimes worse in the winter when the child spends more time indoors.

CLINICAL FINDINGS   These include acute symptoms as well as other more chronic signs.

Acute symptoms:

1. Stopped-up, itchy nose
2. Paroxysms of sneezing
3. Irritating, watery, nasal discharge
4. Conjunctivitis
5. Possible sore throat, hoarseness, and thirst
6. Irritable and short-tempered disposition
7. Possible headache

Chronic signs:

1. The "allergic salute" and "allergic shiner"
2. Thicker nasal discharge. Some children may develop nasal polyps in later childhood.
3. Swollen and pale nasal mucous membranes which may partially or completely block the passages
4. Red and excoriated nares
5. Thickened nasal sinuses
6. Inflammatory sinusitis with a purulent discharge due to complication with bacterial infection
7. Conjunctivae showing evidences of chronic irritation such as itchiness and dryness

SKIN TESTING Testing for food allergens is unreliable. Testing for pollens and environmentals is reliable and may be instituted if the history so indicates.

Management Initially the treatment is aimed at making the child comfortable. Later the offending allergens may be sought by skin testing and hyposensitization may be instituted. Diet and environmental control may be instituted.

MEDICATIONS Decongestants are given to relieve swelling and to promote drainage. Antihistamines are given to relieve itching. Antibiotics are given to treat chronic infections. Sometimes this will interrupt the vicious cycle of allergic reaction and infection. Applications of corticosteroids may be used to treat nasal polyps.

SURGICAL INTERVENTION Chronic infections or polyposis may be indications for surgical intervention as follows:

1. Chronic ear infection may need myringotomy.
2. Chronically infected tonsils and adenoids may be removed, but this is done only when all other methods fail to control the obstructions or infections.
3. Nasal or sinus polyps may be removed.

HAY FEVER

Assessment The name hay fever is a legacy from earlier times. "Fever" was a term of illness, and "hay" pointed to the relationship to grasses and harvesting. It is an allergic (IgE) reaction to one or more inhalants, typically very small windborne pollens. The condition is known as "hay fever" when pollens are in the air. When the symptoms persist throughout the year, the condition is called allergic rhinitis.

INCIDENCE Hay fever usually starts in late childhood or early adolescence. Skin lesions of atopic dermatitis usually fade away at about the time hay fever begins. Offending pollens, early in the spring, are mainly from birches, oak, alders, and hazels. Grass pollens are less time related. One may have symptoms from timothy, redtop, orchard, sweet vernal, blue grass, Russian thistle, sugarbeet, and ragweeds. Ragweed is the primary offender in the eastern and midwestern United States and occurs in the autumn. Pollens tend to be thrown off on sunny days and are carried miles by the wind. Many children have their worst symptoms after sundown.

CLINICAL FINDINGS The symptoms are usually of an acute nature:

1. Stopped-up, itchy nose
2. Paroxysms of sneezing
3. Irritating, watery, nasal discharge
4. Congested and tearing conjunctivae
5. Hoarseness and thirst, possible sore throat
6. Irritable disposition
7. Possible headache
8. Possible cough
9. Bronchitis or asthma

SKIN TESTING This is usually reliable for pollen.

Management This is directed initially at easing the discomforts of the ailment. Environmental control may be instituted. Later skin testing may be done followed by hyposensitization.

MEDICATIONS Decongestants are given to relieve swelling and to promote drainage. Antihistamines are given to relieve itching. Systemic antibiotics or sulfonamides are used to treat secondary infections.

PREVENTION Preventive measures are also part of the treatment:

- The child should be kept indoors in the evenings, on windy days where possible, and when the pollen count is especially high.
- Windows that face the winds should be kept closed.
- The child's room should be air-conditioned using a fine-meshed, "anti-allergy" air filter.
- Automobile rides, especially to the country, should be avoided.
- Open land near the home should be cleared of suspected weeds, grasses, and plants.
- Written notes should be kept of the dates of onset and subsidence of hay fever symptoms in the child. The pattern after 1 or more years will be a valuable clue to the caretaker.

ALLERGIC BRONCHITIS

Assessment In allergic bronchitis the tracheobronchial mucous membrane is chronically sensitized and irritated by continued exposure to molds, pollens, danders, and dusts. The irritated membranes are more readily invaded by bacteria, and the lower respiratory infection is difficult to cure. Sometimes an upper respiratory infection will trigger the bronchial symptoms. If it becomes chronic, permanent bronchial damage may result leading to bronchiectasis.

CLINICAL FINDINGS Symptoms and signs are as follows:

1. Cough, the most prominent sign, that tends to be worse at night
2. Malaise and loss of appetite

3. Wheezing or rhonchi
4. Sibilant or musical rales

DIFFERENTIAL DIAGNOSIS Because the cough is the most distinctive feature of allergic bronchitis it may be confused with other diseases. These diseases should be ruled out:

1. Acute bronchitis. Cough with sudden onset and fever, wheezing, and sibilant rales is not necessarily associated with allergies. This illness may develop following flu or similar virulent respiratory tract infection and may last a week or more or may exhibit other features (including X-ray changes) indicative of bronchopneumonia.
2. Chronic bronchitis. This manifests with a persistent dry cough without malaise or fever, with the chest negative on physical or X-ray examination.
3. Chronically infected tonsils, adenoids, or nasal sinuses. Postnasal drip is a symptom.
4. Pertussis cough. This is a paroxysmal cough not always terminated with a distinctive "whoop."
5. Cystic fibrosis cough. This is paroxysmal with wheezing from viscid mucus in the tracheobronchial tree.

Management Treatment is managed collaboratively with a physician and is directed at several factors:

1. Correcting the obstruction. This should not be achieved by suppressing the respiratory center and the cough reflex or by drying the mucosa. For these reasons sedatives, antitussives, and antihistamines are contraindicated. The medications of choice are bronchodilators and decongestants (sympathomimetics), epinephrine and ephedrine, and expectorants which will liquefy the secretions. See this chapter, Pharmacologic Therapy.
2. Humidifying the home. See this chapter, Humidity in the Home and Chapter 17, Humidification.
3. Keeping child moderately active if afebrile. Moving about and breathing more energetically help to free the mucus from the bronchial tract.
4. Cautioning against smoking to older children and adolescents with a tendency to allergic bronchitis.

5. Eventually identifying and removing allergens through environmental and diet control.

BRONCHIAL ASTHMA

Assessment Bronchial asthma is the extreme form of bronchial allergy. The interaction of the antibody IgE with a specific allergen induces the release of histamine and SRS-A (slow-reacting substance, which is a strong contractor of bronchial smooth muscle equal to that of histamine but with a more prolonged action). These induce tissue changes resulting in edema, stimulation of glands to increase mucus secretion, and bronchospasm.

INCIDENCE The condition begins at any age although less often in infancy. Bronchospasm in infancy is usually secondary to infection rather than to an allergic reaction. It is variable in frequency and duration. Children may have only one or two attacks a year associated with an upper respiratory infection during hay fever season. Others may have it often, usually irregularly.

ETIOLOGY Contact with or exposure to known or suspected allergens that enter the body through the respiratory system can cause asthma. Allergens may be pollen, dust, smoke or fumes, mold, animal danders, or a drug or food taken internally. Asthma may be brought on by upper respiratory viral infections (respiratory syncytial virus). Asthma attacks brought on by weather changes (cold, wind), excitement, or psychologic factors are sometimes referred to as "intrinsic" or "nonallergic."

CLINICAL FINDINGS The signs and symptoms are as follows:

1. The attack may be preceded by rhinitis, sneezing, or coughing, or may begin abruptly (this suggests an inhalant as the allergen). It may occur at night.
2. The attack may occur as intense, sudden, paroxysmal episodes of dry, irritating cough, wheezing, and dyspnea. The bronchospasm causes airway obstruction and interference with respiration, particularly expiration which is prolonged.
3. Wheezing may be audible. Those who have continuous wheezing which is refractory to medication are in "status asthmaticus," a medical emergency.
4. Epigastric pain may be present, or the child may have anorexia,

nausea, and vomiting. Often gastrointestinal symptoms can be indicative of food allergy.
5. The child is anxious and may be more comfortable in a sitting position.
6. Low fever, headache, malaise, and irritability are nonspecific symptoms that are often found.
7. The child who has had asthma a long time may exhibit emphysematous or barreled-shaped chest with widened anteroposterior diameter.

LABORATORY FINDINGS Common findings are as follows:

1. Eosinophilia can often be demonstrated in the peripheral blood, nasal secretions, and sputum.
2. Polymorphonuclear leukocytosis may be present with infection.
3. Pulmonary function studies will disclose diminished maximal breathing capacity and timed vital capacity.
4. There may be an increase in serum Pco_2 and bicarbonate level and a decreased pH in severe asthma indicating respiratory acidosis.

DIFFERENTIAL DIAGNOSIS These diseases may occur in children who have asthma as well:

1. Spasmodic croup. This disturbance is in the larynx rather than in the bronchi and bronchioles. See Chapter 17, Croup Syndrome.
2. Cystic fibrosis. See this chapter, Allergic Bronchitis.
3. Foreign body in lungs. The chest signs resemble asthma but are typically one-sided, have a sudden onset, and the aspirated object will show in the X-ray film of the chest, if it is opaque.
4. A semihysterical behavior pattern with hyperventilation (breathing shallowly and rapidly with excessive anxiety).
5. Mediastinal lesions. These may compress the trachea or bronchi.

Management Asthma is managed collaboratively with a physician.

ACUTE ATTACK During the acute attack attention is paid to environment, diet, medication, and counseling. In order to judge the efficacy of the treatment, spirometry is often performed upon presentation, then repeated and compared.

Environment and Diet

1. The child is placed on bed rest, if possible, in an allergen-free room with optimal humidity of 35 to 50 percent. See this chapter, Humidity in the Home.
2. Cold foods or drinks are avoided since changes in temperature aggravate allergic reactions.

Medications   See this chapter, Pharmacologic Therapy.

1. Bronchodilators (sympathomimetics) are given as soon as possible to relax the smooth muscle of the bronchioles and relieve the spasm. They may be given orally, by injection, by nebulizer, or in some cases sublingually. Initially with wheezing the child may receive one to two doses of aqueous epinephrine at 20- to 30-minute intervals.
2. Expectorants should be administered separately. Water as an expectorant is superior. Without adequate fluid intake the various expectorants are ineffective.

Medications Contraindicated

1. Antihistamines. Valueless and contraindicated, the atropinelike action of the antihistamines has a drying effect on secretions which leads to further airway obstruction. Prophylactic administration of antihistamines is used in children in whom an asthmatic episode is commonly preceded by acute rhinorrhea. In these children prompt use may prevent the asthmatic paroxysm.
2. Barbiturates and sedatives. In general these should be avoided because of their depressant effect on the respiratory center.
3. Cough mixtures. They are not recommended. In such mixtures one constituent counteracts the effect of another.
4. Aerosol inhalation preparations. They have no application to symptoms unless the condition is complicated by chronic pulmonary changes. In asthma care must be taken in the use of these preparations to avoid the induction of bronchospasm. Instructions must be read carefully before advising the use of these medications.

Counseling   A severe paroxysm of asthma may be anxiety provoking to both child and parents. Some parents and some caretakers may overdramatize the occasion. The caretaker must discern whether parents reflect a warm and insightful manner or whether a program of education as to the child's real needs is indicated. When a child is hospitalized, the continued presence of a member of the family may allay anxiety. If conflicts and anxieties in the family perpetuate the child's asthmatic paroxysms, psychiatric consultation should be sought.

LONG-TERM MANAGEMENT

1. Environmental and diet control (See this chapter, Diet Control, Environmental Control.)
2. Immunotherapy as necessary
3. Psychotherapy as needed
4. Medication (e.g., bronchodilators)

Psychologic Aspects of Asthma

Effect on the Child and Family   Williams (1975) has investigated the impact of asthma on the child and family.

> Behavioral disturbances in the child, the mother-child and family relationships, and family social structure were studied in a representative sample of the whole range of asthmatic children and compared with a control group of normal children.
>
> Behavioral disturbances occurred more frequently and at a statistically significant level only in the small group of children with severe and continuing asthma. These children were those with severe chronic airway obstruction as assessed physiologically and also had the most severe allergic manifestations.
>
> The predominant mother-child relationship was an overconcern to protect the child's health in those children with continuing asthma at 14 years of age.
>
> The families of the very severely affected group of children exhibited evidence of more stress than other families.
>
> Socioeconomic conditions were not significantly different in any group of asthmatic children compared with the control group. (Williams and McNicol, 1975, p. 51)

Working with the Child and Family   The parents as well as the child require repeated and comprehensible information about etiologic, clinical, and therapeutic aspects of asthma. Parents need instruction to develop in their child with asthma an increasing responsibility for self-care and to promote the goal of raising the child as normally as possible. Appropriate activities with other children and regular schooling are essential. The primary caretaker should inquire about how the various family members react and relate to the asthmatic child and pay attention to the healthy siblings' common feelings of resentment, anxiety, and overconcern regarding their ill brother or sister. Finally, one must call attention to parental attitudes of overprotection, lenient discipline, rejection, or neglect which may endanger the child's personality development as well as the asthmatic condition.

The long-range management of childhood asthma requires a close working relationship between the primary provider, the allergist, and the psychiatrist (or other mental health worker) regarding those children where psychosocial factors significantly contribute to the course of asthma.

Sports and Asthma There is no justification for keeping the child with asthma from participating in school or in competitive athletics (Cropp, 1975). Regular participation in sports is extremely important for the physical and emotional development of children. Since exercise-induced asthma can be prevented effectively in most asthmatics by the administration of isoproterenol aerosol or selected oral bronchodilators shortly before exercise, these attacks do not have to be feared. Sports which elicit no or relatively mild exercise-induced asthma should be encouraged. Year round swimming, skiing, and touch football are well tolerated by asthmatic children. Physical education teachers and coaches should be advised to include asthmatic children in all sports activities and should permit the children to premedicate themselves prior to exercise. The choice and use of medications should be under the direction of a physician.

Referral for Psychosocial Evaluation Referral for psychosocial evaluation of a family with an asthmatic child is indicated in the following situations:

1. Children in whom emotional factors seem to be of precipitating and aggravating importance
2. Children whose asthma perpetuates individual and family psychopathology and maladaptation
3. Behavioral problems in a child seemingly unrelated to asthma (Mattsson, 1975)

RESOURCE INFORMATION FOR ASTHMA See Resource Information for pamphlets and for the name of a special camp for asthmatics.

ALLERGIC SEROUS OTITIS MEDIA ("ALLERGIC EAR")

Assessment See Chapter 17, Serous Otitis Media. Allergic serous otitis media is most commonly secondary to obstruction of the auditory tube caused by edema and lymphoid hyperplasia of the upper respiratory tract on an allergic basis. Less commonly it occurs in response to a primary allergic reaction of the mucosal lining of the middle ear.

SIGNS AND SYMPTOMS Included are children who have a strong family history of allergy and those who have any of the classic allergic symptoms and signs (rhinitis, "allergic shiners," "allergic salute") and exhibit the following findings most likely have "allergic ear." Symptoms of hearing loss, fullness or crackling in the ears, tinnitus, vertigo, or earaches are noted. Hearing loss is the most common and may be responsible for delayed speech development or short attention span.

The tympanic membranes are often tan, yellow, or varying shades from amber to dark blue. The surface may be dull, shiny, or waxy. The drums are often retracted, but sometimes are flat or bulging. Bubbles or fluid levels may at times be seen through the drums.

Management See Chapter 17, Serous Otitis Media. In addition to symptomatic medication there are three methods:

1. Environmental control
2. Diet control
3. Immunotherapy (This is used only if the problem is seasonal or if it is perennial and nonresponsive to home and diet changes.)

Resource Information

Allergies

General allergy information can be obtained from the following sources:

Allergy Foundation of America
801 Second Avenue
New York, NY 10017

Allergy Rehabilitation Foundation, Inc.
805 Atlas Building
Charleston, WV 25301

American Lung Association
1740 Broadway
New York, NY 10019 (Contact local association)

National Institute of Allergy and Infectious Disease
National Institutes of Health
Bethesda, MD 20014

Recommended books for general allergy are:

Giannini, A. V. et al. *The Best Guide to Allergy.* East Norwalk, CT: Appleton-Century-Crofts, 1981

Somekh, E. *A Parent's Guide to Children's Allergies.* Springfield, IL: Charles C Thomas, 1972

Asthma

Pamphlets can be obtained by writing to:

Mead Johnson Laboratories
Evanston, Illinois, 47721

Cooper Laboratories, Inc.
Wayne, New Jersey, 07470

Information on an asthma camp can be obtained by writing or calling:

Camp Broncho Junction
810 Atlas Building
Charleston, West Virginia, 25301

Diet Assistance

Further diet assistance can be obtained from:

Chicago Dietetic Supply, Inc.
405 E. Shawmut Avenue
LaGrange, Illinois, 60525

Department of Dietetics,
University of Michigan
Ann Arbor, MI 48109

Dietary Department of Mass. General Hospital
32 Fruit Street
Boston, MA 02114

West Laboratories and Diet Bakeries, Inc.
176 Sherman Avenue
Jersey City, NJ 07307

U.S. Department of Agriculture,
Consumer and Food Economics Research Division,
Agricultural Research Services
Beltsville, MD 20705

Recommended books for diet assistance are:

Allergy Recipes (Wheat, Milk and Egg Free), Publication B0305, The American Dietetic Association, 430 North Michigan Avenue, Chicago, IL 60611 (No charge)

Isomil Cookbook for Infants (Milk free), Ross Laboratories, Department 441, 625 Cleveland Avenue, Columbus, OH 43216 (No charge)

Soyalac (Milk-free), Loma Linda Foods, Medical Products Division, Riverside, CA 92505 (No charge)

The Milk-Free Cookbook for Infants, Syntex Laboratories Inc. Nutritional Products Division, Palo Alto, CA 94304 (No charge)

Wheat, Milk and Egg Free, Quaker Oats Company, Consumer Service, Merchandise Mart Plaza, Chicago, IL 60654 (No charge)

125 Great Recipes for Allergic Diets, Good Housekeeping, Bulletin Service, Box 2317, FDR Station, New York, NY 10150 (75 cents charge)

Diets Unlimited for Limited Diets, Allergy Information Association, Room 7, 25 Poynter Drive, Western, Ontario M9R1K8, Canada ($5.00 charge)

Conrad, M. L. *Allergy Cooking*. New York: Pyramid, 1968

Emerling, C. G. and E. D. Jonekers. *The Allergy Cookbook*. Garden City, NY: Doubleday, 1969

Little, B. *Recipes for Allergies*. New York: Grosset and Dunlap, 1971

Identification Items

Various identification items as necklaces and bracelets may be obtained from:

American Medical Association
535 N. Dearborn Street
Chicago, IL 60610

Medic Alert Foundation
P. O. Box 1009
Turlock, CA 95380

National Identification Company
3955 Oneida Street
Denver, CO 80207

Insect Sting Kits

Kits for those highly allergic to insect bites that contain emergency supplies including a syringe or a syringe loaded with epinephrine 1:1,000 are available by prescription from:

Center Laboratories
35 Channel Drive
Port Washington, NY 11050
Hollister-Stier Laboratories
P.O. Box 19957
Atlanta, GA 30325
"Personal" Insect Sting Kit®
International Medications Systems
South El Monte, CA 91733

Nonallergic Products

Products such as allergen-proof pillow casings can be obtained from:

Allergen-Proof Encasings
1450 E. 363rd Street
Eastlake, OH 44094

References

Aas, K. *The Allergic Child.* Springfield, IL: Charles C. Thomas, 1971.

American Academy of Pediatrics, Committee on Nutrition. "On Feeding of Supplemental Foods to Infants." *Pediatrics* 65:1178–1181, June 1980.

Bierman, C. W. and D. S. Pearlman, editors. *Allergic Diseases of Infancy, Childhood and Adolescence.* Philadelphia: W. B. Saunders, 1980.

Bridgewater, S. and R. Voignier. "Allergies in Children: Teaching." *Am J Nurs* 78:620–621, April 1978.

Bridgewater, S. and R. Voignier. "Allergies in Children: Recognition." *Am J Nurs* 78:614–616, April 1978.

Cropp, G. D. A. "Exercise-Induced Asthma." *Pediatr Clin North Am* 22:63–76, February 1975.

Feingold, B. F. *Introduction to Clinical Allergy.* Springfield, IL: Charles C. Thomas, 1973.

Feingold, B. F. "Hyperkinesis and Learning Disabilities Linked to Artificial Food Flavors and Colors." *Am J Nurs* 75:797–803, May 1975.

Fikar, C. "Insect Sting Treatment." *Pediatrics* 68:744, November 1981.

Frazier, C. A. *Insect Allergy: Allergic and Toxic Reactions to Insects and Other Arthropods.* St. Louis: Warren H. Green, 1969.

Gellis, S. S. and B. M. Kagan. *Current Pediatric Therapy.* Philadelphia: W. B. Saunders, 1973.

———. *Current Pediatric Therapy,* 10th ed., Philadelphia: W. B. Saunders, 1982.

Glaser, J. and D. E. Johnstone. "Prophylaxis of Allergic Disease in the Newborn." *JAMA* 153:620–622, October 1953.

Halpern, S. R. et al. "Development of Childhood Allergies in Infants Fed Cow's

Milk." *J Allergy Clin Immunol 51*:139–151, March 1973.

Johnstone, D. E. and A. M. Dutton. "Dietary Prophylaxis of Allergic Disease in Children." *N Engl J Med 274*:715–719, March 1966.

Kempe, C. H., H. K. Silver, and D. O'Brien. *Current Pediatric Diagnosis and Treatment,* 6th ed. Los Altos, CA: Lange Medical Publications, 1980.

McGovern, J. P., T. J. Hayward, and A. A. Fernandez. "Allergy and Secretory Otitis Media." *JAMA 200*:124–128, April 1967.

Mattsson, A. "Psychologic Aspects of Childhood Asthma," *Pediatr Clin North Am 22*:77–88, February 1975.

Miller, J. B. *Food Allergy, Provocative Testing and Injection Therapy.* Springfield, IL: Charles C. Thomas, 1972.

Moss, E. "Atopic Dermatitis." *Pediatr Clin North Am 25*:225–237, May 1978.

Parker, C. "Food Allergies." *Am J Nurs 80*:262–265, February 1980.

Patterson, R. *Allergic Diseases: Diagnosis and Management.* Philadelphia: J. B. Lippincott, 1972.

Rapaport, H. G. and S. M. Linde. *The Complete Allergy Guide.* New York: Simon and Schuster, 1970.

Rapp, D. J. and I. F. Fahey, "Allergy and Chronic Secretory Otitis Media." *Pediatr Clin North Am 22*:259–264, February 1975.

Rudolph, A. M., editor. *Pediatrics,* 17th ed. East Norwalk, CT: Appleton-Century-Crofts, 1982.

Shirkey, H. C., editor. *Pediatric Therapy,* 5th ed. St. Louis: C. V. Mosby, 1975.

Tuft, L. and H. L. Mueller. *Allergy in Children.* Philadelphia: W. B. Saunders, 1970.

Vaughan, V. C. and R. E. Behrman, editors. *Nelson Textbook of Pediatrics,* 12th ed. Philadelphia: W. B. Saunders, 1983.

von Witt, R. "Topical Aspirin for Wasp Stings." *Lancet 2*:1379, December 1980.

Waechter, E. H. and F. G. Blake. *Nursing Care of Children,* 9th ed. Philadelphia: J. B. Lippincott, 1976.

Williams, H. E. and K. N. McNicol. "The Spectrum of Asthma in Children." *Pediatr Clin North Am 22*:43–52, February 1975.

27

Infectious Disease

Infection is the largest single cause of illness in infants and children. A complete understanding of infectious disease requires basic knowledge of immunologic principles, infectious agents, the infectious process, epidemiology, manifestations of infection, treatment, control of infection, and preventive measures. Such complete information is beyond the scope of this chapter and is available in major pediatric texts. The purpose of this chapter is to provide information that will assist the nurse practitioner to assess and to identify common infectious diseases, to obtain appropriate medical consultation and intervention, and to provide adequate counseling for home management. Discussions of respiratory, urinary tract, gastrointestinal, and skin infections are found in the corresponding chapters. Immunizations are discussed in Chapter 2.

ASSESSMENT

History

PAST HISTORY

Obtain information on past infections, communicable diseases, immunodeficiency states, and immunization status.

PRESENT CONCERN

See Chapter 11, Assessment of Presenting Symptom. What is the age of the child? Does the child look sick? Obtain a chronologic history of the signs and symptoms, exposures (other family members, schoolmates, neighbors, babysitters), what treatment has been tried, and what the parent thinks it is (older parents and grandparents remember polio and pertussis). If a rash is present, where did it begin, where did it spread, what does it look like, and does it itch? Inquire as to recent travel to other countries or geographic areas.

Physical Examination

- A thorough general physical examination is performed. See Chapter 1, Child Health Assessment.
- Age and general appearance of the child are clues to potential seriousness or toxicity. Fever and/or infection in any site in an infant under 4 months of age is serious. Sepsis, meningitis, and bacterial diarrheas must be considered.
- Painful swallowing, drooling, and slow mouth breathing are suspicious of acute epiglottitis. Pharyngeal examination is deferred and medical consultation obtained immediately. See Chapter 17, Croup Syndromes.
- Petechial rash associated with meningeal signs is suggestive of meningococcemia. Medical consultation is obtained immediately.

MANAGEMENT

General Measures

Specific treatment measures exist for bacterial infections and are discussed in subsequent sections. Infectious diseases, whether of bacterial or viral origin, are usually associated with a variety of constitutional symptoms: fever, upper respiratory symptoms (cough, rhinorrhea, sore throat), anorexia, headache, malaise, irritability, pain, generalized aching, and rash. The provision of symptomatic relief is accomplished by the following general measures.

FEVER

See Chapter 11, Fever.

1. Antipyretic medication
2. Tepid sponge baths
3. Liberal fluid intake
4. Rest and limited activity

UPPER RESPIRATORY SYMPTOMS

See Chapter 17, The Respiratory System.

1. Liberal fluid intake
2. Cool-mist vaporizers
3. Decongestants
4. Warm gargles, saline mouth and throat irrigations, cool liquids, and soft foods for sore throat
5. Petrolatum jelly to protect skin around the nares
6. Cough preparations generally ineffective and contraindicated in infants and young children

GENERALIZED ACHING AND MALAISE

1. Rest and limited physical activity
2. Warm baths
3. Body massage
4. Cold compresses for headache
5. Analgesic medication

ANOREXIA

1. Small, frequent feedings of favorite foods and liquids
2. A relaxed attitude about oral intake; forcing foods and fluids usually counterproductive

RASH

See Chapter 26, Topical Therapy, Pharmacologic Therapy.

1. Proper hygiene and bathing to reduce incidence of secondary infection
2. Cool baths, local applications of calamine lotion, and mild anesthetic ointments or systemic antihistamines to relieve pruritus
3. Fingernail care, including frequent cutting and cleaning, to reduce effects of scratching; gloves or mittens helpful at night for younger children
4. Saline or viscous xylocaine mouthwashes if mucous membranes are involved

Isolation

The prevention of the spread of communicable infectious diseases is attempted through various isolation techniques. Whether or not the child is isolated in the hospital or at home depends on the specific disease, the severity of symptoms, the home environment, including the presence of susceptible persons, and the ability of the parents to carry out the necessary procedures.

STRICT ISOLATION

A private room is necessary, and the door must be kept closed. Gowns, masks, and gloves must be worn by all persons entering the room. Hands must be washed on entering and leaving the room. Articles must be discarded or wrapped before being taken out for disinfection.

RESPIRATORY ISOLATION

A private room is necessary, and the door must be kept closed. Gowns and gloves are not necessary. Masks must be worn by all susceptible persons entering the room. Hands must be washed on entering and leaving the room. Articles contaminated with secretions must be disinfected.

ENTERIC PRECAUTIONS

A private room is necessary for children only. Gowns and gloves must be worn by all persons having direct contact with the client. Masks are not necessary. Hands must be washed on entering and leaving the room. Special precautions are necessary for articles contaminated with urine and feces. Articles must be disinfected or discarded.

SECRETION PRECAUTIONS, LESIONS

Private room, gowns, masks, gloves are not necessary. Hands must be washed before and after contact with client. Articles: double bagging technique is used for soiled dressings and equipment.

SECRETION PRECAUTIONS, ORAL

Private room, gowns, masks, gloves are not necessary. Hands must be washed before and after client contact. Articles: disposable handkerchiefs are discarded in bags, which should be sealed before being placed in the trash.

COMMON INFECTIOUS DISEASES

Bacterial Infections

INFANT BOTULISM

Assessment Infant botulism is a newly recognized disease, first reported in 1976, caused by *Clostridium botulinum*. It occurs in infants under 8 months of age and is characterized by constipation and neuromuscular symptoms of varying severity, which may progress to respiratory failure. The infant apparently ingests the *C. botulinum* organism, which germinates in the gastrointestinal tract and releases neurotoxin. This differs from the more usual botulism, or "food poisoning," which results from ingestion of food that has been contaminated by preformed toxin.

EPIDEMIOLOGY Knowledge is incomplete but there appear to be no sex differences or feeding method differences. Botulism spores, widespread in soil and agricultural products, are resistant to heat, radiation, and drying and remain viable for long periods. Exposure is common after handling soil or eating unwashed fruits and vegetables. The organism has been revealed on autopsy in a small number of infants whose deaths were classified as Sudden Infant Death Syndrome (Arnon et al., 1978) and has been associated in California with the use of honey in infant feeding (Arnon et al., 1979). Ten to 15 percent of all honey has been found to contain spores.

CLINICAL PICTURE The most frequent presenting symptom is constipation for 3 or more days. This is followed by tachycardia and muscle weakness manifested by loss of head control, difficulty feeding, weak cry, and depressed gag reflex (see Chapter 24, Hypotonia). In severe cases, peripheral motor weakness is followed by diaphragmatic weakness and potential respiratory failure. Signs and symptoms resolve in reverse order of presentation over a period of 10 days to 8 weeks and recovery is usually complete. The only reported deaths have been due to respiratory arrest.

LABORATORY Precise diagnosis is obtained by isolation and identification of *C. botulinum* in stool specimens.

Management Infants with mild symptoms require minimal care and may be managed as outpatients if careful follow-up examinations are arranged (L'Hommedieu and Polin, 1981). Infants with progressive, sequential loss of neurologic functions are at risk for respiratory failure and must be hospitalized.

PREVENTION Parents should be advised not to feed honey to infants under one year of age. Specifically, pacifiers should not be dipped in honey, and honey should not be substituted for corn syrup in formula preparation.

CELLULITIS

Assessment Cellulitis is an invasive infection of the skin that involves both the dermis and subcutaneous tissues. See Chapter 14, The Skin, for a discussion of impetigo and furunculosis. In children it is caused by *Staphylococcus aureus*, group A beta-hemolytic streptococci, or *Hemophilus influenzae* and is frequently an infection secondary to impetigo or other local skin lesions. Since it is a deeper infection than impetigo, it is less likely to be communicable, but more likely to lead to septicemia. It may occur in orbital, periorbital, and cheek areas of younger children in association with otitis media or sinus infections.

CLINICAL PICTURE The affected area is warm, tender, erythematous, swollen, and indurated. Fever, malaise, and lymphadenopathy are present. Lymphangitis ("streaking") may be seen on the extremities.

LABORATORY Blood cultures and/or needle aspiration of the lesion are done for culture and gram stain. X-ray films of underlying bone may be done to rule out osteomyelitis.

Management Specific treatment is appropriate systemic antibiotic therapy, which frequently requires hospitalization. The cephalosporins have been found useful, especially with ampicillin-resistant *H. influenzae* (Santos et al., 1981). In addition, application of warm compresses and immobilization (if the lesion is on an extremity) are recommended. If the organism is streptococcal, family members should be examined to detect carriers.

DIPHTHERIA

Assessment This is an acute infectious disease caused by *Corynebacterium diphtheriae,* which produces a virulent exotoxin. It is characterized by sore throat and formation of a membrane that may cover the tonsils, pharynx, and larynx. The membrane is the result of necrotic epithelial cells and inflammatory exudate coagulating on the surface of the affected structures.

EPIDEMIOLOGY

Mode of Transmission Transmission is by direct contact via coughing, sneezing, and talking with a person who has the disease or is a healthy carrier.

Incubation Period It is 2 to 4 days with a range from 1 to 6 days.

Period of Communicability It is variable: 2 to 4 weeks in untreated individuals, 1 to 2 days in treated persons.

Population at Risk This depends on the immune status of the population. Infants born of immune mothers are relatively immune for about 6 months. Where children are routinely immunized the incidence is predominantly in adults whose immune levels have diminished with time. Recent outbreaks have occurred among poor populations without adequate access to health care services. Crowding enhances spread.

Seasonal Patterns   It is most common in the autumn and winter months in temperate zones.

CLINICAL PICTURE   Signs and symptoms vary with the site of localization.

Nasal Diphtheria   The major symptom is unilateral or bilateral nasal discharge, serous at first and then serosanguinous and mucopurulent, which excoriates the anterior nares and upper lip. Systemic symptoms are slight. A membrane may be visible on the nasal septum. In cases with unilateral discharge, a foreign body in the nose may be confused with nasal diphtheria and should be ruled out.

Tonsillar and Pharyngeal Diphtheria   Malaise, anorexia, sore throat, and low-grade fever precede the formation of the membrane (white to gray-green in color), which may involve both tonsils, pharynx, soft palate, and uvula. Swelling of the neck may result from marked lymphadenopathy. Pulse rate is rapid. Mild cases last about a week, then the membrane sloughs off and recovery ensues. Severe cases involve severe toxemia and may lead rapidly to prostration, stupor, coma, and death within 6 to 10 days.

Laryngeal Diphtheria   It is often associated with severe pharyngeal diphtheria but occurs alone as well. It is the most dangerous form. It resembles croup or acute laryngitis. Fever, hoarseness, and cough may be followed by airway obstruction, congestion, and edema, with inspiratory stridor, retractions, dyspnea, and cyanosis. The membrane may progress down into the tracheobronchial tree and contribute to airway obstruction. If pharyngeal diphtheria is present, the course involves both obstruction and toxemia.

LABORATORY   The diagnosis is confirmed by culture of the organism from the nose and throat. The swab must be rubbed firmly over the lesions and, if possible, inserted under the membrane.

COMPLICATIONS   Up to 50 percent of cases develop myocardial involvement within 2 weeks after onset, since the toxin has an affinity for heart muscle. Nervous system complications (neuritis) occur less frequently and as late as 6 weeks after onset. Soft palate paralysis is the most common but usually subsides completely.

Management Management includes medication therapy, supportive care, care of exposed persons, and preventive measures.

MEDICATION Medication therapy includes the following:

1. Diphtheria antitoxin. This must be given as soon as possible to neutralize the toxin while it is still circulating. Once toxin becomes fixed to tissues, antitoxin has no effect. Hypersensitivity to horse serum must be determined before therapy is begun. By the second to third day after onset, the fatality rate rises sharply if antitoxin is not given.
2. Antibiotic therapy. This is given as a supplement to antitoxin therapy. Antibiotics act against the organism and decrease the numbers of people who remain carriers after recovery. Penicillin and erythromycin are used.
3. Diphtheria toxoid. Adequate immunity does not develop in many persons recovering from diphtheria. A Shick test should be performed and, if positive, immunization with diphtheria toxoid is indicated. A negative Shick test indicates immunity to diphtheria toxin.

COUNSELING FOR HOME CARE

Supportive Care Severely ill children are hospitalized. Complete bed rest is of particular importance for at least 12 days in all children with diphtheria because of the possibility of myocarditis. Diet should be high carbohydrate as blood sugars are frequently low. Other supportive measures are presented earlier in this chapter under General Measures.

Isolation Strict isolation is required and is continued following completion of antibiotic therapy until two or three successive nose and throat cultures taken at least 24 hours apart are negative.

EXPOSED CONTACTS All intimate contacts and household members should be isolated until nose and throat cultures and Shick tests are performed.

• Contacts with negative cultures and negative Shick tests are immune and uninfected and need not be isolated.

- Contacts with positive cultures and negative Shick tests are considered carriers and should be treated with antibiotics in an attempt to eradicate the carrier state.
- Contacts with positive cultures and positive Shick tests should be treated with diphtheria antitoxin and antibiotics.
- Contacts with negative cultures and positive Shick tests should receive active immunization (Krugman and Katz, 1981, p. 23).
- Previously immunized children should be given diphtheria toxoid boosters.
- Persons who completed the primary series more than 10 years previously should also receive a booster.

PREVENTION Active immunization. See Chapter 2, Immunizations.

MENINGITIS, BACTERIAL

Assessment Bacterial meningitis is an acute infection of the meninges following invasion of the spinal fluid by a variety of bacteria. It is a serious disease with etiology, morbidity, and mortality dependent on the age of the child, the causative agent, the severity of the illness, and the rapidity with which effective treatment is begun. The younger the child, the more serious is the prognosis.

ETIOLOGY Causative organisms vary with age. In the neonate the most common causes are enteric organisms: *Escherichia coli* and group B streptococci. In infants and young children the three most common causes are *Hemophilus influenzae, Neisseria meningitidis,* and *Streptococcus pneumoniae.*

EPIDEMIOLOGY

Mode of Transmission Neonatal meningitis reflects the environment of the fetus and newborn infant (e.g., a maternal infection, exposure in the nursery from equipment or unrecognized infection in other infants or personnel). In infants and children the route of infection is most often via the bloodstream, the result of bacteremia due to invasion of bacteria in another part of the body. Infections in the region of the brain (otitis media, mastoiditis, sinusitis, facial infections) may also spread by direct extension. Meningococcal meningitis begins in the nasopharynx, and transmission occurs by droplet spray from the mouth or nose of healthy carriers or those with a mild URI caused by the meningococcal organism.

Other Factors   Seasonal patterns exist with *H. influenzae* meningitis as the incidence of upper respiratory infections is greatest in the autumn and winter. Any situation leading to high incidence of URIs will increase the incidence of meningitis (e.g., crowding, ill health, malnutrition). Only meningococcal meningitis occurs in epidemic form.

CLINICAL PICTURE   Presentation of this disease varies with age and with the type of organism.

Neonates   Unfortunately, the clinical signs in neonates are vague and nonspecific, and the process is insidious. The infant may look well at birth but within a few days may appear to be "doing poorly." Fever may or may not be present. The infant may manifest poor tone, poor sucking with feeding difficulties, vomiting, poor cry, irritability, and either drowsiness or hyperactivity and jitteriness. The fontanel may be full, tense, or bulging. Other meningeal signs may be absent. See Chapter 24, Meningeal Signs. Jaundice, if present, is associated with sepsis, and if sepsis is suspected, meningitis must also be considered. See this chapter, Sepsis in the Newborn. If the diagnosis is not established the mortality is high (65 to 75 percent). Neurologic sequelae (hydrocephalus, brain damage) occur frequently if the infection is detected late in its course.

Infants   The classical presentation of meningitis is rarely seen in infants from 3 months to 2 years of age, although the incidence is highest in this age group. Any unexplained febrile illness should arouse suspicion of meningitis. A previous respiratory or gastrointestinal infection may be present. The infant may become increasingly irritable. Fever, anorexia, vomiting, drowsiness, and high-pitched cry are common. Convulsions may occur. The fontanel may be bulging, but if the infant is dehydrated or the fontanel has closed, this sign may not be seen. Nuchal rigidity, and Kernig's and Brudzinski's signs may be difficult to elicit in this age group.

Older Children   The classic picture begins usually with fever, chills, vomiting, severe headache, and stiff neck. Irritability, convulsions, stupor, and coma may occur. Meningeal signs are present consistently and as nuchal rigidity progresses opisthotonos may develop. Photophobia, blurred vision, and papilledema may be present.

Meningococcemia Children with meningococcal meningitis have sudden onset of high temperature and frequently demonstrate a petechial rash. See Table 27-1. The presence of a rapidly developing petechial rash associated with a shocklike, toxic state in children between 3 months to 6 years indicates fulminant meningococcemia and represents a *true medical emergency.*

LABORATORY Definitive diagnosis is made by examination of cerebrospinal fluid (CSF) and a lumbar puncture is indicated if a reasonable suspicion of meningitis is present. The characteristic findings are as follows:

• Cloudy appearance
• Increase in white cells (polymorphonuclear leukocytes); cell count is usually well over 1,000/cu mm (Krugman and Katz, 1981, p. 173)
• Decreased glucose; blood glucose is obtained for comparison with CSF glucose
• Increased protein
• Culture and smear positive for a pathogenic causative organism; the organism can also be recovered from blood, nasopharynx, and, in the case of meningococcemia, the petechiae

COMPLICATIONS Mortality rates and complications have been reduced since the advent of antimicrobial therapy, but if early treatment is not initiated, the danger remains. Hydrocephalus, cerebral edema leading to permanent damage to cranial nerves and other structures, subdural effusions, peripheral circulatory collapse, shock, and respiratory failure are most common. Persistent fever may be attributable to brain abscess, drug reaction, or continued sepsis.

Management Whatever work setting the nurse practitioner is in, protocols for prompt referral and priority service should be established with appropriate medical sources. Bacterial meningitis is a medical emergency. At the first suspicion of meningitis the nurse practitioner must refer to the physician. The child is hospitalized immediately.

MEDICATION Antibiotic therapy depends on the causative agent and on the age and weight of the child. Weights should be obtained early. Consult a pediatric text for full discussion of the acute care of the child with meningitis. Of note, however, is the recent recognition of widespread ampicillin-resistant strains of *H. influenzae,* which have modified the treatment approach in children under 5 years of age (Munoz, 1980).

COUNSELING During the acute process and the long-term follow-up period, both child and family require support and teaching. Bacterial meningitis is a frightening diagnosis, and parents will have realistic fears about the outcome.

• Teaching should include discussion of the disease process and symptoms and care of the child at home during the convalescent period: restoring resistance to infection, adequate nutrition, health maintenance care, resumption of school and recreational activities, and follow-up procedures.
• Follow-up should include careful developmental appraisals every few months for a year to identify any residual damage. Vision, hearing, and cognitive evaluations should also be performed.

EXPOSED CONTACTS Close contacts of persons with confirmed meningococcal disease are at increased risk, one third of secondary cases occurring within 4 days. Persons at highest risk are household contacts, nursery or day care contacts, and medical personnel who resuscitated, intubated, or suctioned the child before antibiotics were initiated. Current recommendation for prophylaxis is early institution of rifampin or sulfa (if the organism is known to be sensitive to sulfa). Meningococcal vaccine should be considered as an adjunct to prophylaxis for high-risk contacts of persons with serogroup A or C disease (Centers for Disease Control, March 1981).

There is also significant risk of secondary cases of *H. influenzae* type b disease for similar contacts, and these contacts should be under close surveillance for at least one week. The American Academy of Pediatrics is currently recommending rifampin prophylaxis for all household contacts (excluding pregnant women) in households where there are children less than 4 years of age. Nurs-

Table 27-1

Differential Diagnosis of Common Exanthematous Diseases

Disease	Incubation Period	Prodrome	Exanthem	Other Characteristic Signs
Measles	9–14 days	3–4 days of malaise, fever, conjunctivitis, cough, and coryza	Reddish-brown or purple-red maculopapular rash appearing first on face, hairline, forehead, and neck (confluent) and proceeding to trunk, extremities, and feet (discrete). Duration of rash is 5–7 days. Desquamation may occur but not on hands and feet.	Koplik's spots (bluish-white dots with red areola) appear about 12 hours before the rash on buccal mucosa and sometimes on labial mucosa. They usually fade and disappear by the second day of the rash. They are pathognomonic for measles.
Rubella	14–21 days	Usually none	Pink-red maculopapular, discrete rash appearing first on face and neck and rapidly progressing to trunk and extremities. Lasts 3–5 days with earliest lesions fading first so that on the third day the face and neck may be clear. No desquamation.	Lymphadenopathy with postauricular or occipital nodes is characteristic.

Scarlet fever	2–4 days (range: 1–7 days)	12 hours to 2 days with abrupt onset of fever, sore throat, vomiting, headache, chills, and malaise	Bright red, punctate lesions that blanch on pressure. Rough, sandpaperlike texture. Appears within 12–48 hours of fever, first on the flexor surfaces and rapidly becomes generalized. Most intense on neck, axillary, inguinal, and popliteal folds. The face is smooth, red, and flushed, with circumoral pallor. Duration is approximately 7 days, followed by desquamation, including hands and feet.	Tonsils and pharynx are beefy red and may have exudate. Tongue has a white coating which peels off as the papillae become red and swollen, and assumes the "strawberry tongue" appearance. Petechiae may be present on pharynx and palate. Pastia's sign (hyperemic lines on flexor surfaces at wrists, elbows, and groin) are characteristic.
Roseola (exanthem subitum)	10–14 days	3–4 days of high fever and irritability. Fever may go to 40°C.	Rose-pink, maculopapular; discrete rash may begin on chest and trunk, then spread to face and extremities. Duration from several hours to 2 days. Rash immediately follows the rapid fall of temperature to normal levels.	May be first seen with a febrile convulsion. Cervical and occipital lymph nodes are enlarged.

Table 27-1 *(Continued)*

Disease	Incubation Period	Prodrome	Exanthem	Other Characteristic Signs
Erythema infectiosum (Fifth's disease)	6–14 days	None	Rash erupts in three stages: 1. Bright red, confluent, maculopapular rash on face, especially cheeks, with circumoral pallor 2. Discrete maculopapular rash on upper and lower extremities 3. After the rash has subsided (a week or more), it tends to recur following a variety of skin irritants.	"Slapped cheek" appearance in an otherwise well child, lacelike appearance as the rash fades
Meningococcemia	Variable depending on primary infection.	24-hour period of fever, vomiting, irritability, nuchal rigidity, bulging fontanel	Rash is maculopapular but becomes petechial and purpuric. Distribution is variable.	Petechial rash associated with meningeal signs suggests meningococcemia. See text, Meningococcemia.

Enteroviral infections (ECHO and Coxsackie)	Variable but usually brief	Variable; can be absent or include 3–4 days of fever, irritability	Rash resembles the rubella rash, is maculopapular, discrete, and generalized.	Concurrent family illness, gastroenteritis, and local epidemics are commonly associated. Incidence highest in summer and fall. See Chapter 17, The Respiratory System.
Varicella (Chickenpox)	14–16 days (range: 11–20 days)	Usually none. Adolescents may have 1–2 days of fever, headache, and malaise.	Fever, malaise, and rash appear simultaneously. Rash rapidly evolves from macules to papules to vesicles to crusts. Lesions are centripetal in distribution, profuse on trunk, and occur in successive crops over a 3–5-day period. Lesions in all stages are present simultaneously. Lesions are present on scalp, hairline, and mucous membranes. All lesions eventually crust and dry up.	Rash is pruritic.

Source: Based on information from S. Krugman and S. Katz, *Infectious Diseases of Children*, 7th ed., St. Louis: C. V. Mosby, 1981.

ery school and day-care contacts (children and adults) should be considered as part of the household.

PREVENTION Meningococcal polysaccharide vaccines effective against two serogroups (A and C) of meningococcal disease are licensed for use in the United States. They have been given routinely to military recruits since 1971. Routine vaccination of civilians is not recommended when risk of infection is low. However, serogroup-specific monovalent vaccines should be used to control outbreaks caused by *N. meningitidis* serogroup A or C. The usefulness of the vaccine in children is hampered by poor immune response in children under 2 years of age. There is no vaccine for serogroup B, which currently causes the majority of cases (Brook, 1980). See Chapter 17, Pneumonia, for information on pneumococcal vaccine.

PERTUSSIS (WHOOPING COUGH)

Assessment Pertussis is an acute infection of the respiratory tract caused by *Bordetella pertussis*. It is characterized by a prolonged period of respiratory symptoms progressing to repetitive paroxysms of coughing that often end with a spasmodic inspiratory whoop and, frequently, vomiting. It is a serious disease, especially in infancy.

EPIDEMIOLOGY

Mode of Transmission Direct contact with an infected person through coughing, sneezing, or talking is the most common mode of spread.

Incubation Period It is from 5 to 21 days, but almost uniformly within 10 days.

Period of Communicability This extends from 7 days after exposure to 3 to 4 weeks after onset of paroxysms. Most spread occurs during the catarrhal period.

Population at Risk Little to no immunity is transferred via the placenta. Thus, infants and children under 4 years are most susceptible, and the disease is most serious in infants under 1 year. Severe attacks can occur in elderly people. Pertussis is highly contagious for unimmunized persons. Attack rates in unimmunized family contacts are up to 90 percent on exposure to an index case in the family. Morbidity and mortality are higher in females. Naturally acquired immunity is highly effective.

Seasonal Patterns   There is less seasonal variation than for other respiratory infections as it maintains a high incidence during spring and summer.

CLINICAL PICTURE   The complete course lasts 6 to 8 weeks and includes three stages.

Catarrhal Stage   Symptoms of an upper respiratory infection are present, and pertussis may not be suspected until the cough continues to worsen rather than to improve during the second week.

Paroxysmal Stage   The coughing paroxysms (bursts of short, rapid coughs on one expiration, red or cyanotic face, sudden inspiration with whoop, dislodgement of mucous plug, and vomiting) are exhausting and anxiety producing and may be precipitated by a variety of stimuli (movement, swallowing, speech, pressure on the trachea). The paroxysms occur from four to five times a day in mild cases to 40 or more in severe cases. This stage may last from 4 to 6 weeks.

Convalescent Stage   Whooping and vomiting gradually diminish, and the cough becomes less severe, although it persists for 2 or 3 weeks.

LABORATORY   Although the paroxysmal episode and whoop are seldom mistaken, earlier diagnosis may be possible if there is a history of contact with a known case and isolation of the organism from the nasopharynx. White blood count is very high with predominant lymphocytosis.

COMPLICATIONS   Pneumonia is a common complication and is responsible for significant mortality in children under 3 years of age. Hemorrhages (nose bleeds, conjunctival hemorrhage), hernia, rectal prolapse, and trauma to the tongue may result from increased pressure during paroxysms. Intracranial hemorrhage is rare. Nutritional disturbances, malnutrition, and weight loss secondary to exhaustion and vomiting are not infrequent. Neurologic complications are serious and include encephalopathy, brain damage related to asphyxia from severe paroxysms, and seizures.

Management Small infants or those with severe disease and frequent exhaustive paroxysms require hospitalization where equipment for oxygen therapy, suctioning, and resuscitation is available and where continuous nursing surveillance is possible.

MEDICATION Medication therapy includes the following:

1. Pertussis immune globulin. This is recommended for all children under 2 years and for older children with severe cases. Its efficacy is questioned but some beneficial effect may occur.
2. Pertussis vaccine. This is not of value once symptoms have begun.
3. Antibiotics. These are not effective in shortening the paroxysmal stage or in modifying the severity of the disease but can eliminate the organism and decrease contact spread.

COUNSELING FOR HOME CARE Mild cases can be cared for at home.

Supportive Care The child should rest in bed as tolerated. Stimuli that precipitate paroxysms must be kept to a minimum: activity, excitement, smoke, and sudden changes in temperature. Small, frequent feedings are indicated, and re-feeding after vomiting is recommended as another paroxysm is less likely at that time.

Isolation Respiratory isolation is required for the period of communicability. Since family members have high attack rates, no infant under 2 years of age should be brought into the household.

EXPOSED CONTACTS In small infants pertussis immune globulin may be attempted as soon after exposure as possible, but the preventive effects are questionable. Erythromycin is also recommended for 5 to 7 days. Once the full incubation period has passed, active immunization should be instituted. Pertussis in adults is usually a mild to moderate disease and incidence is low. Thus, pertussis vaccine is not routinely given to persons over 6 years of age.

PREVENTION Active immunization. See Chapter 2, Immunizations.

SCARLET FEVER (SCARLATINA)

Assessment Scarlet fever is an infection caused by an erythrogenic toxin-producing group A hemolytic streptococcus in an individual who does not have antitoxin antibodies. The toxin produces a characteristic rash.

EPIDEMIOLOGY

Mode of Transmission   Spread is through direct contact with airborne droplets from the respiratory tract of a symptomatic or asymptomatic individual.

Incubation Period   It is 2 to 4 days with a range of 1 to 7 days.

Period of Communicability   This is variable but is greatest during the acute respiratory illness until a day or 2 after the start of antibiotic therapy.

Population at Risk   Streptococcal infections are uncommon in children under 2 years of age. Incidence is highest in children 6 to 12 years of age.

Seasonal Patterns   It is more common during winter and early spring in temperate areas.

CLINICAL PICTURE   Table 27-1 describes the clinical features of several exanthematous diseases, including scarlet fever.

LABORATORY   Throat culture is obtained for group A hemolytic streptococci. During convalescence antistreptolysin (ASO) titer will rise.

COMPLICATIONS   Complications occur when the streptococcal organism enters adjacent tissues or the bloodstream and establishes metastatic lesions. Early complications usually result from delayed diagnosis and treatment. Common ones include cervical adenitis, otitis media, and sinusitis. More infrequent complications are pneumonia, mastoiditis, osteomyelitis, and septicemia. Late sequelae are rheumatic fever and acute glomerulonephritis, believed to be caused by a hypersensitivity reaction to the organism or its byproducts. They occur 1 to 3 weeks after the disease and may follow mild as well as severe infections.

Management   The child can usually be cared for at home.

MEDICATION   Penicillin is the drug of choice. Erythromycin or a cephalosporin are used if allergy to penicillin exists. Treatment must continue for a minimum of 10 days to eradicate the organisms. Even though the child appears well in 3 to 4 days, the importance of the full course of medication must be emphasized. If family disorganization or lack of comprehension raise questions about the reliability of medication administration, parenteral therapy is indicated.

COUNSELING FOR HOME CARE

Supportive Care   See this chapter, General Measures. Bed rest used to be mandatory and is still recommended during the febrile period. The difficulties of imposing bed rest on a young child who feels well are obvious, and often the child becomes more restless ·han if allowed some natural activity. Thus, bed rest should not be insisted upon as the child feels better. Parents should be prepared for the period of skin desquamation.

Isolation   Respiratory isolation for 1 day after the start of treatment is recommended. The child may return to school upon clinical recovery but not less than 7 days from onset.

Follow-up   The child should be seen within 2 to 4 weeks and examined for signs of rheumatic fever (careful cardiac examination) and glomerulonephritis (urine specimens).

EXPOSED CONTACTS   Prevention of streptococcal infection in exposed susceptible contacts is desirable, but the guidelines are unclear. It is advisable to obtain throat cultures on intimate household contacts. Contacts with a previous history of rheumatic fever should receive penicillin prophylaxis.

SEPSIS IN THE NEWBORN

Assessment   Neonates up to 1 month of age are particularly susceptible to septicemia because of their immunologic immaturity and their exposure to a new environment. This susceptibility to bacterial invasion, which can rapidly disseminate to multiple organ systems, makes neonatal sepsis a very serious disease entity. Like bacterial meningitis (see this chapter), early identification and prompt treatment are critical.

ETIOLOGY   The predominant causative agents include gram-negative organisms (especially *Escherichia coli*) and gram-positive organisms (especially Group B streptococci).

EPIDEMIOLOGY There is a highly significant preponderance among male newborns (Krugman and Katz, 1981). Infection is usually acquired in two primary ways. Infections in the immediate postpartum period probably result from maternal organisms (e.g., vaginal flora, infected amniotic fluid, premature rupture of the membranes, genitourinary infections) that invade via the infant's gastrointestinal tract, respiratory tract, skin, or umbilicus. Infections that develop later in the nursery stay, especially the intensive care nursery, probably are the result of environmental organisms (e.g., contaminated nursery equipment, water in bottle warmers, oxygen sources, isolettes, humidifiers, and from treatments involving catheters and life-support procedures).

CLINICAL PICTURE Signs and symptoms are subtle and likely to be vague and nonspecific, especially in the premature infant. The first indication may be failure to thrive, an infant who "is not doing well" as evidenced by poor feeding, regurgitation, and lethargy or irritability. Fever and meningeal signs may be absent. When any infant exhibits these signs, the mother's chart should be checked quickly for maternal infection or difficult delivery. Other signs include vomiting and diarrhea, abdominal distention, jaundice, hepatomegaly, respiratory difficulty, fullness of the fontanel, and occasionally skin lesions (e.g., cellulitis, impetigo, subcutaneous abscesses).

LABORATORY Cultures of amniotic fluid, blood, spinal fluid, and skin lesions are obtained. White blood count and differential are useful.

COMPLICATIONS AND PROGNOSIS Meningitis is the most important complication of neonatal sepsis and, since it develops simultaneously with sepsis, should be considered from the outset. Case fatality rates have declined to approximately 35 percent, but with sepsis complicated by meningitis, the fatality rate is from 40 to 75 percent, with 60 to 85 percent of survivors having sequelae including encephalopathy, hydrocephalus, and long-lasting neurologic deficits.

Management Once cultures have been obtained, immediate antibiotic therapy is initiated. Gram-negative and gram-positive organisms are covered until the specific organism is identified.

PREVENTION Environmental sources must be searched for the identical bacteria.

COUNSELING Added support is given the parents of an infant with neonatal sepsis following those guidelines outlined for prematurity. See Chapter 5, Prematurity.

TETANUS (LOCKJAW)

Assessment Tetanus is an acute infection caused by the virulent toxin produced by *Clostridium tetani*. The organism enters through a break in the skin, and the toxin travels and binds to central nervous system tissue causing tonic muscular spasms, stiffness of skeletal muscles (especially the jaw), and convulsions.

EPIDEMIOLOGY

Mode of Transmission The organisms are found in soil, horse, cattle, and sheep manure, and street dust. Spores may also be found in contaminated heroin (Krugman and Katz, 1981). The organisms are spread through direct or indirect contamination of an obvious or unrecognized wound. Puncture wounds, scratches, burns, crushing injuries, and the umbilicus of the newborn are favorable portals of entry.

Incubation Period It is variable; from 1 to 2 days to 5 to 12 days to longer periods.

Period of Communicability None.

Population at Risk All unimmunized persons are susceptible and no lasting immunity results after an attack of the disease. Maternal transfer of passive immunity to the infant is of short duration. In many developing countries, tetanus neonatorum is a serious problem that could be alleviated by proper handling of the umbilical cord, health education, and immunization.

CLINICAL PICTURE The minor local wound usually shows nothing unusual. The onset is insidious and initial symptoms are muscle stiffness in the neck and jaw. There is difficulty in opening the mouth and difficulty in swallowing. Within 24 hours the disease becomes full-blown with generalized muscle rigidity. Various stimuli (lights, sounds, movement) initiate paroxysmal spasms which become frequent and painful as the disease progresses. During spasms trismus (lockjaw), risus sardonicus (sardonic grin caused by distortion of face), and opisthotonos are marked. In fatal cases, death usually results from respiratory failure within 3 to 4 days.

LABORATORY No specific laboratory procedures are generally useful, and the diagnosis is made primarily on clinical grounds.

COMPLICATIONS In persons who survive, pulmonary complications may occur from laryngospasm, respiratory obstruction and asphyxia, or tracheostomy. Seizures may result in tongue lacerations or thoracic vertebral fractures. Malnutrition may also occur. Long-term sequelae are not common.

Management The child with tetanus requires hospitalization, and meticulous nursing and medical care. See major texts for full discussion. Control of muscular spasms, antitoxin and antimicrobial therapy, wound care, respiratory care, and general supportive care are required.

ANTITOXIN THERAPY This is the most specific therapy, and human tetanus immune globulin (TIG) is the recommended agent. If human globulin is not available, tetanus antitoxin is used after determining hypersensitivity to horse serum.

COUNSELING In the United States the incidence of tetanus in children is extremely rare, and the nurse practitioner may never have occasion to support a family affected by this serious disease. If the situation does occur, support appropriate to the care of a critically ill child is required. In children who survive, the convalescent period may be lengthy but is usually uneventful in terms of complications.

PREVENTION See Chapter 2, Immunizations. Active immunization, when achieved and maintained, effectively prevents tetanus.

TUBERCULOSIS

Tuberculosis is a serious infectious disease, still widespread throughout the world, which can cause major and chronic disability among the population. It is a complicated entity, and for a complete discussion the reader is referred to major texts listed at the end of this chapter. The purpose of this section is to present a brief description of the disease in children and to consider management procedures for the most common clinical situations the nurse practitioner encounters in practice; specifically, the infant or child with a positive tuberculin test, the child who has been exposed to active tuberculosis, and procedures for routine screening.

Assessment Tuberculosis is caused by the bacilli *Mycobacterium tuberculosis* and *M. bovis*. The bacillus is unique in several ways. It is capable of survival for long periods of time in the environment and is resistant to drying, although sunlight and ultraviolet light will destroy it. Once bacilli enter the body, they "escape body defenses by taking up sequestered positions deep in the tissues where they remain inactive for years but are able to revive and produce new disease in favorable circumstances" (Waechter and Blake, 1976, p. 469). This ability to remain dormant accounts in large part for the insidious nature of tuberculosis.

EPIDEMIOLOGY

Incidence   In 1977, the new active case rate in the United States was 13.9/100,000. In 1979, 27,669 cases were reported. Current immigration patterns may affect case rates. Tuberculosis is prevalent in Latin America and a recent study (Hageman et al., 1980) reports that 40 percent of recent Indochinese refugees have positive tuberculin tests and 1 to 2 percent have active tuberculosis.

Mode of Transmission   An adult or adolescent with active pulmonary tuberculosis is the usual source of infection in children. Coughing and sneezing spray droplets that are inhaled into the lungs. Transmission depends on the number of bacilli discharged into the atmosphere, and this depends on the number of organisms in the sputum, the amount of sputum, the frequency of the cough, and conscientiousness in hygiene while coughing. Also, the frequency and intimacy of exposure affect transmission. Children rarely transmit the disease.

Predisposing Factors   Only a small percentage of persons infected with tubercle bacilli develop overt disease. Factors affecting host resistance and the degree of illness include the following:

1. Numbers of tubercle bacilli and virulence
2. Possible genetic factors

3. Age (increased morbidity and mortality in adolescent girls)
4. Nutrition
5. General state of health
6. Intercurrent infections (e.g., measles)
7. Physical and mental stress (e.g., chronic fatigue)
8. Environmental and socioeconomic circumstances (e.g., poverty, crowding, poor sanitation)
9. Administration of immunosuppressive and corticosteroid drugs
10. Cellular immunity

Incubation Period for Primary Tuberculosis   It is 3 to 5 weeks with a range of 2 to 8 weeks.

PATHOGENESIS When an infected droplet is deposited in the alveolus of a susceptible person, a nonspecific, asymptomatic area of bronchopneumonia—the primary focus—develops initially. These tubercle bacilli then drain from the primary focus to regional lymph nodes. Subsequently, the bacilli enter the systemic circulation and, potentially, can spread to all body organs. Rarely, this lymphohematogenous spread of large numbers of bacilli throughout the body may lead to miliary tuberculosis and other extrapulmonary manifestations. The most common result of the initial infection is healing with granuloma formation. In most persons, the healed granulomas remain stable, in time may calcify, and overt disease never occurs. In 5 to 15 percent of cases, one of the granulomas breaks down, the bacilli multiply and the person becomes ill with tuberculosis (Glassroth et al., 1980). During the initial infection, as bacilli multiply and die, a change occurs in tissue reaction to the bacilli and hypersensitivity develops. This takes about 4 to 8 weeks, which is when the tuberculin test will convert to positive.

CLASSIFICATION OF TUBERCULOSIS The American Thoracic Society (1975) distinguishes between tuberculosis infection and tuberculosis disease as follows:

0 No tuberculosis exposure, not infected (no history of exposure, negative tuberculin skin test)
1 Tuberculosis exposure, no evidence of infection (history of exposure, negative tuberculin skin test)

2 Tuberculosis infection without disease (positive tuberculin skin test, no symptoms, negative bacteriologic studies, no X-ray findings compatible with tuberculosis)

3 Tuberculosis infection with disease (one or more body organs involved and confirmed by bacteriologic, X-ray, and other studies; positive tuberculin skin test)

TUBERCULIN TESTING

The tuberculin test measures the presence or absence of delayed hypersensitivity to the protein portion of the tubercle bacillus.

Tuberculin Material   Two types are available: old tuberculin (OT) and purified protein derivative (PPD). Both materials are effective, but question about the variable potency of different batches of OT has resulted in the widespread use of PPD.

Methods of Testing

1. Intradermal test (Mantoux). If done properly this is the most accurate and reliable test. Old tuberculin or PPD is injected intradermally into the volar surface of the forearm. The dose is 0.1 ml of the desired concentration (strength). First strength is used if an individual is thought to be highly sensitive, intermediate strength is the standard, and second strength is used to exclude the diagnosis if a negative reaction occurs with intermediate strength.
2. Multiple puncture tests (Heaf test, Tine test, Applitest, Monovacc). The exact amount of tuberculin is difficult to measure. These tests are suitable for mass screening but should not be used for making specific diagnoses. Positive reactions should be confirmed via Mantoux testing.
3. Jet injection test. A jet gun deposits PPD intradermally under high pressure. This is useful for mass screening.

Interpretation of Standard-Dose Tuberculin Tests   Tests are read 48 to 72 hours after administration.

1. Intradermal and jet injection tests. Erythema without induration is not significant. Induration is measured at the maximum transverse diameter. Reactions of less than 5 mm are negative; 5 mm to 9 mm are doubtful and a repeat test is done at a different site. If still doubtful and the child has close contact with a per-

son with active tuberculosis, or has clinical or X-ray evidence of disease, the results should be treated as positive. Ten mm or more is a positive reaction, and the test is not repeated for confirmation.

2. Multiple puncture tests. Induration is measured using the diameter of the largest single reaction. If the reaction consists of discrete papules, the individual diameters should not be added together. Reactions of less than 2 mm are negative; 2 mm to 4 mm are doubtful and Mantoux testing is done. Reactions of 5 mm or more indicate a positive test which may be confirmed by Mantoux testing.

Unreliable Tuberculin Testing   Negative test results in the presence of the disease may occur in the following situations:

1. Children on immunosuppressive drugs
2. During the 4- to 8-week incubation period of primary tuberculosis infection
3. For up to 4 weeks after onset of measles or following measles immunization
4. Errors in administration and/or reading of the test; factors relating to test material

Significance of Positive Tuberculin Test   A positive test indicates that the individual has been infected with the tubercle bacillus and is allergic or hypersensitive to its protein. It does not prove the presence of active infection. After identification of tuberculin sensitivity, the following procedures are required.

1. Locate, if possible, any and all lesions
2. Determine whether infection is active, quiescent, or healed
3. Detect any tuberculosis contacts

Therefore, in the child with a positive tuberculin skin test the procedures instituted by the nurse practitioner include:

1. Referral to the physician
2. X-ray film of the chest to detect evidence of pulmonary infection; if X-ray film is abnormal efforts to recover the tubercle bacilli are made (cultures of sputum, gastric contents, spinal fluid, urine)

3. Careful history of all contacts to determine exposure to active tuberculosis

Management

ACTIVE TUBERCULOSIS Children with positive skin tests and demonstrable active lesions are treated with antimicrobial drugs and general supportive measures. Isoniazid and rifampin are the most effective and least toxic drugs. See major references for full discussion.

PREVENTION OF PROGRESSIVE TUBERCULOSIS In children with positive skin tests and no clinically demonstrable disease, prophylactic treatment with isoniazid (INH) for 1 year is indicated in the following cases:

1. Children under 4 years of age with positive skin tests
2. Any child who has recently converted from a negative to a positive skin reaction
3. Any child with a positive skin test and a known exposure to active tuberculosis
4. Any child with inactive primary tuberculosis who has never been treated

CONTACTS Members of the household and other close associates of a person with active tuberculosis should be skin tested. Those with positive reactions are treated. Those with negative skin tests are re-tested in 6 weeks and at least every 3 months for the duration of the contact. Those removed from the contact should be tested 8 to 10 weeks after removal. Isoniazid may be recommended regardless of tuberculin status. Infants should be removed from contact with the infected person until at least 6 months after all cultures are reported as negative.

SCREENING In order to control tuberculosis, persons ill with the disease must be discovered and rendered noninfectious, persons who are infected but not ill must be prevented from becoming infectious, and persons not yet infected must be prevented from acquiring infection (Glassroth et al., 1980). Tuberculin skin testing is, therefore, essential. The Centers for Disease Control and the American Lung Association claim that routine screening of children is inefficient and ineffective as a public health measure on epidemiologic grounds, since the yield is less than 1 percent. Nonetheless, the American Academy of Pediatrics recommends routine tuberculin testing of children beginning at approximately 12 months of age and yearly or every other year thereafter. This is certainly justified in terms of the individual child and the low cost. A recent study (Kraut et al., 1979) of tuberculin screening in an urban pediatric clinic reported that of 1,233 children screened with Tine tests, eight new converters were discovered. Since children with primary tuberculosis rarely have symptoms, tuberculin testing is the only way to identify them. Adults who have consistent contact with children (e.g., school and day-care personnel, babysitters) should be tested routinely.

VACCINATION Bacillus Calmette-Guerin (BCG) is used in many areas of the world to produce active artificial immunity to tuberculosis. The immunity is variable and not complete but lasts several years and does provide protection, particularly in reducing the risks of serious complications. The efficacy of the vaccines currently available is thought to be about 75 percent. BCG vaccination results in hypersensitivity to tuberculin which may last for several years. Thus the value of skin testing in the diagnosis of tuberculosis is lost. It is felt that in the United States, where incidence of tuberculosis is low, the importance of tuberculin test sensitivity is greater in terms of diagnosing infection than in the provision of artificial immunity. Exceptions might be individuals who are at increased risk because of repeated exposure (e.g., infants of mothers with tuberculosis) and persons in groups with high incidence of tuberculosis (e.g., drug addicts, alcoholics, migrant workers). "It is recommended that those who have been vaccinated with BCG be retested periodically with tuberculin and the reactions recorded so that comparisons can be made that will be helpful in differentiating subsequent changes" (Rudolph, 1982, p. 478). Since there is associated risk of tissue necrosis in this situation, it is not a procedure that the nurse practitioner would institute without physician consultation.

Viral Infections

HEPATITIS

Assessment Viral hepatitis is a clinical condition commonly found in the United States. Up to 60,000 cases are reported each year but the real incidence is likely much higher. It is estimated that 200,000 persons, primarily young adults, are infected with hepatitis each year. The infection is caused by at least four distinct agents: hepatitis A virus, hepatitis B virus, and non-A, non-B viruses. Table 27-2 compares the major features of hepatitis A and hepatitis B. Non-A, non-B types clinically resemble hepatitis B.

CLINICAL PICTURE The prodromal period may resemble a respiratory or gastrointestinal infection. Then, during this pre-icteric phase, symptoms of fever, malaise, anorexia, nausea, vomiting, headache, and abdominal pain are common. Urticaria and arthralgia may be present in type B. If the individual smokes, lack of taste for cigarettes occurs. The liver may be enlarged and tender. These symptoms usually begin 4 to 5 days before the appearance of jaundice (icteric phase). During the icteric phase the urine becomes darker and the stools may become clay colored. Jaundice of sclera and skin may last from a few days to as long as a month. In moderate to severe cases, significant weight loss may occur. The vast majority of individuals have an uneventful recovery and complete regeneration of liver cells is observed after 2 or 3 months. Children usually have milder disease than adults and are less likely to develop jaundice (Krugman and Katz, 1981).

LABORATORY Abnormal liver function and other laboratory tests are presented in Table 27-2.

COMPLICATIONS About 10 percent of persons with type B, non-A, and non-B hepatitis develop chronic disease. In severe cases acute hepatic failure may develop. If drowsiness occurs after the onset of jaundice, it indicates possible pre-hepatic coma and the individual must be hospitalized. Chronic infection may lead to cirrhosis.

DIFFERENTIAL DIAGNOSIS Before the appearance of jaundice, infectious mononucleosis, acute appendicitis, salmonellosis, shigellosis, and influenza may be considered.

Management

COUNSELING FOR HOME CARE Most children can be cared for at home, and the treatment is entirely symptomatic and supportive. Adequate rest and a well-balanced, calorically sufficient diet are the two most appropriate measures to aid in regeneration of damaged

Table 27-2

Hepatitis A and Hepatitis B: Comparison of Major Features

Features	Hepatitis A	Hepatitis B
Synonym	Infectious hepatitis	Serum hepatitis
Incubation period	15–40 days	50–180 days
HBAg (Australia antigen in blood)	Absent	Present in incubation period and acute phase
Age group	Usually children and young adults	All age groups
Mode of transmission	Primarily fecal-to-oral route; some parenteral spread (blood products); contaminated water, food, infected shellfish	Primarily parenteral (transfusion of blood or blood products, drug inoculation); nonparenteral (body fluids of infected persons)
Seasonal	Fall and winter predominantly but also throughout the year	Any season
Onset	Usually acute	Usually insidious
Fever	Common; precedes jaundice	Less common
Jaundice	Rare in children; more common in adults	Rare in children, more common in adults
Severity	Usually mild	Often severe
Abnormal SGOT and SGPT	Transient: 1–3 weeks	More prolonged: 1–8 months
Thymol turbidity	Usually elevated	Usually normal
IgM levels	Usually increased	Usually normal
Virus excretion		
Blood	Present during late incubation period and early acute phase	Present during late incubation period and acute phase; may persist for months and years
Feces	Present during late incubation period and acute phase	Probably present but no direct proof
Value of gamma globulin prophylaxis	Good	Uncertain
Carrier state	No	Yes
Immunity		
Homologous	Present	Present
Heterologous	None	None

Source: Adapted from S. Krugman and S. Katz, *Infectious Diseases of Children,* 7th ed., St. Louis: C.V. Mosby, 1981, p. 101; and D. H. Carver and D. S. Y. Seto, "Hepatitis A and B," *Pediatr Clin North Am 21*:674, August 1974.

liver tissue. Restriction of fat intake is not necessary. Vitamin supplements, particularly B complex, are recommended.

ISOLATION

Hepatitis A   The virus is excreted in the feces as early as 3 weeks before onset and into the early part of the icteric phase. Therefore, enteric precautions are required during the acute illness and at least 1 week after the onset of jaundice. See this chapter, Enteric Precautions. A single room with private bath is recommended for any person with the disease.

Hepatitis B   Infectivity is present in persons with acute hepatitis during the latter part of the incubation period and during the acute phase of the infection. It is also present in persons who are healthy chronic carriers. Household contacts are at greatest risk. Handwashing and avoidance of sharing personal hygiene items (e.g., razors, toothbrushes, towels, washcloths) are essential. Enteric and secretion precautions are required during the acute illness. The virus may be present in the blood for variable and long periods of time and careful screening of blood donors is imperative.

PREVENTION AND PROPHYLAXIS

Hepatitis A   Immune serum globulin (ISG) is effective in prevention and/or modification of hepatitis A when given during the incubation period. See Table 27-3. Family members and other intimate contacts should receive injections of ISG preferably within 1 week of exposure. Even if a clinically inapparent infection results, it is believed that such persons do not contribute to transmission of the disease. Protection with ISG is also recommended for persons who will experience prolonged exposure (e.g., travel to endemic areas).

Hepatitis B   Specific hepatatis B immune globulin (HBIG) is being evaluated and has proved efficacious for the prevention or modification of hepatitis B infection. Persons with definite exposure to hepatitis B should receive HBIG within 48 hours after exposure. ISG has had variable and inconsistent effectiveness in the prevention of hepatitis B but should be used if HBIG is not available. Screening of blood donors and the appropriate care of equipment used to break the skin (syringes, needles, stylets) are the best preventive measures.

Table 27-3

Immune Serum Globulin (ISG) in Prophylaxis of Viral Diseases for Exposed Susceptibles

Disease	Indication	Dosage	Efficacy
Measles	Close contact within 5 days	0.04 ml/kg 0.25 ml/kg	Modification Prevention (recommended for high-risk patients only)[a]
Hepatitis A (infectious hepatitis)	Single or short-term exposure[b] (<2 months)	0.04–0.06 ml/kg Adults: 3–5 ml (total dose)	Modification or prevention depending on exposure, dose, time interval between exposure and administration
	Prolonged or continuous exposure (>2 months)	0.12 ml/kg Adults: 6–10 ml (total dose)	Modification or prevention depending on degree of exposure, dose, time interval between exposure and administration
Varicella	Close contacts at high risk (within 3 days)	0.6–1.2 ml/kg for patients on corticosteroids for various diseases, on immunosuppressive drugs, with leukemia or other disseminated malignancies, or impaired delayed hypersensitivity	Possible modification[c]

Source: Adapted from J. W. Graef and T. E. Cone, *Manual of Pediatric Therapeutics,* Boston: Little, Brown, 1974, p. 190, and S. Krugman and S. Katz, *Infectious Diseases of Children,* 7th ed. St Louis: C. V. Mosby, 1981, p. 116.

[a] When ISG is indicated it should be given as soon as possible following exposure. It is of no proven value in the prophylaxis of rubella and mumps.

[b] Exposure is defined as intimate physical contact with an infected person or that person's secretions.

[c] Varicella-Zoster Immune Globulin (VZIG) is preferable. See Tables 27-4 and 27-5.

Recent screening data indicate that 12 percent of Indochinese refugees entering Canada are positive for hepatitis B surface antigen (HBsAg). Most of these individuals are asymptomatic and are chronic carriers. Testing for HBsAg should be part of the health assessment of each Indochinese refugee after arrival in the United States (Krugman and Katz, 1981, pp. 121–122).

Pregnant women who have hepatitis B or are HBsAg carriers may infect their infants in utero or at the time of birth. HBIG may be effective in preventing neonatal hepatitis B. Additionally, breast feeding by these mothers has been implicated as a possible source of newborn infection. Medical opinion differs on whether infants or carrier mothers should be breast fed. Krugman and Katz (1981, p. 124) recommend that, in the United States where hepatitis B is not endemic and commercial formulas are safe and available, these mothers not breast feed. Lawrence (1980, p. 239) advises against breast feeding in mothers who have active hepatitis at delivery or during the third trimester, but suggests obtaining an infectious disease consultation in the case of mothers who are chronic carriers.

Active Immunization Inactivated hepatitis B vaccine has been found safe and effective in the prevention of the disease and was licensed in the United States in November 1981. Recommendations for its use include health care workers in high-risk environments, clients and staff of institutions for the mentally retarded, hemodialysis patients, homosexually active males, illicit injectable drug users, household and sexual contacts of HBV carriers, high-risk populations (especially Alaskan Eskimos and Asian and sub-Saharan African immigrants and refugees), inmates of long-term correctional facilities, and infants of mothers who are chronic carriers (Centers for Disease Control, 1982).

HERPES SIMPLEX

Assessment Herpes simplex viruses are common infectious agents which cause a variety of clinical diseases. Primary infection occurs in susceptible persons, predominantly in children between 1 and 4 years of age, and usually is inapparent. If clinical disease occurs, it can affect the skin, mucous membranes, eyes, genitals, or brain. In newborns who contract the disease from genital herpes in the mother, herpes simplex is a very serious, disseminated disease with a high mortality (Whitley et al., 1980).

PRIMARY INFECTION Gingivostomatitis is the most common primary herpetic infection in children.

Epidemiology The mode of transmission is thought to be by direct body contact and introduction of the virus through a break in the skin (e.g., kissing a teething baby). The incubation period is from 2 to 12 days. It is more common in overcrowded environments.

Clinical Picture Onset is abrupt with fever, irritability, anorexia, and sore mouth. The gums are red, swollen, and bleed easily. Multiple small vesicles appear on the palate, tongue, buccal mucosa, and gums which rupture and become white ulcerations. Eating and swallowing are painful. Symptoms usually subside within 10 days.

RECURRENT INFECTION After the primary infection antibodies develop, but this disease is unusual in that the virus remains dormant in the host and can be reactivated when the body is under stress. Reinfections are localized and commonly take the form of "cold sores," "fever blisters," or "canker sores." Genital herpes is also a manifestation of recurrent infection. See Chapter 8, Sexually Transmitted Diseases.

COMPLICATIONS Herpes stomatitis, if severe, may result in dehydration. Children with atopic dermatitis who develop eczema herpeticum can have very serious disease.

Management The child with herpes stomatitis is severely uncomfortable for several days (3 to 4) and presents a challenge to parents who want to provide relief. Treatment is supportive with primary attention to care of the mouth. Cool liquids and soft, bland foods are offered. Citrus juices are avoided. Oral hygiene with mouthwashes and rinses is indicated. Viscous xylocaine 2 percent may be used as a topical anesthetic for mucous membranes of the mouth and pharynx. Analgesics may relieve the pain. Infants should be watched carefully for signs of dehydration. Older children will probably not take sufficient food or fluid, but parents can be reassured that they will soon recover. Secretion precautions are indicated.

Care of recurrent lesions is also symptomatic. Petroleum jelly is soothing and protective and is used if lesions appear at corners of the mouth and tend to crack and bleed.

HERPES ZOSTER (SHINGLES)

Assessment Herpes zoster is caused by varicella-zoster virus and is thought to be a reactivation of a latent virus after an attack of chickenpox. It is characterized by pain and crops of vesicles confined to an area of distribution of one of the spinal or cranial sensory nerves.

EPIDEMIOLOGY It is spread by direct contact with infected vesicle fluid. It is not as contagious as chickenpox but is communicable for 5 to 7 days after the vesicles appear. It is uncommon in children under 10 years of age and incidence increases with age.

CLINICAL PICTURE The individual usually has pain along the involved dermatone. Malaise and fever may occur. Then, within a few days the first vesicles develop. The vesicles may be itchy. Successive crops of vesicles continue to appear for 1 to 4 days. The vesicles erupt and crust over and skin clears within 1 to 2 weeks.

LABORATORY Isolation of varicella-zoster virus from vesicular fluid will differentiate the condition from herpes simplex infection.

Management No specific therapy is available. Wet compresses or calamine lotion may soothe the lesions. Aspirin is given for pain. Vesicles covering the tip of the nose require referral to an opthalmologist.

ISOLATION Contact with lesions is to be avoided until all lesions have crusted and dried. Some also recommend respiratory isolation.

EXPOSED CONTACTS The primary concern is to protect susceptible infants and immunodeficient children from developing chickenpox after a significant exposure to varicella-zoster virus. Varicella-zoster immune globulin (VZIG) was licensed in 1981 and, although limited in supply, is available through American Red Cross Blood Services. Table 27-4 lists indications for use of VZIG and Table 27-5 lists the regional distribution centers.

INFLUENZA

Assessment Influenza is an acute disease of the respiratory tract caused primarily by influenza viruses A, B, and C. The viruses vary

Table 27-4
Indications and Guidelines for the Use of Varicella-Zoster Immune
Globulin (VZIG) for the Prophylaxis of Chickenpox (Varicella)

1. One of the following underlying illnesses or conditions:
   a. Leukemia or lymphoma
   b. Congenital or acquired immunodeficiency
   c. Under immunosuppressive treatment
   d. Newborn of mother who had onset of chickenpox <5 days before delivery or within 48 hours after delivery.
2. One of the following types of exposure to chickenpox or zoster patients:
   a. Household contact
   b. Playmate contact (>1 hour play indoors)
   c. Hospital contact (in same 2- to 4-bed room or adjacent beds in a large ward)
   d. Newborn contact (newborn of mother who had onset of chickenpox <5 days before delivery or within 48 hours after delivery)
3. Negative or unknown prior history of chickenpox
4. Age of <15 years, with administration to older patients on an *individual* basis
5. Time elapsed after exposure is such that VZIG can be administered within 96 hours

Source: Centers for Disease Control, "Varicella-Zoster Immune Globulin—United States," *Morbidity and Mortality Weekly Report 30*:22, January 23, 1981.

in their antigenic stability and several distinct strains of types A and B exist. Since viruses have this ability to change their dominant antigenic properties, cyclic epidemics can be expected. This factor mitigates against simple influenza immunization programs.

EPIDEMIOLOGY

Mode of Transmission   The virus is spread by airborne droplet and direct contact.

Incubation Period   The incubation period is from 1 to 2 days.

Period of Communicability   Infected persons are communicable from the first to the fifth day of the disease, including the incubation period.

Population at Risk   Since mutant strains of influenza virus A and B occur at intervals, new groups of susceptible hosts accumulate

Table 27-5

Distribution Centers for Varicella-Zoster Immune Globulin (VZIG), as of February 1981

Service Area	Regional Center	24-Hour Telephone Numbers
Massachusetts	Massachusetts Public Health Biologic Laboratories Jamaica Plain, MA 02130	617-522-3700
Connecticut, Maine, New Hampshire, Rhode Island, Vermont	American Red Cross Blood Services Northeast Region 60 Kendrick St. Needham, MA 02194	617-731-2130
New Jersey, New York	The Greater New York Blood Program 310 E. 67th St. New York, NY 10021	212-570-3067 (day) 212-570-3068 (night)
Delaware, Pennsylvania	American Red Cross Blood Services Penn-Jersey Region 23rd and Chestnut Sts. Philadelphia, PA 19103	215-299-4114
Maryland, Virginia, Washington, DC, West Virginia	American Red Cross Blood Services Washington Region 2025 E St., NW Washington, DC 20006	202-857-2021
Alabama, Georgia, Mississippi, North Carolina, Puerto Rico, South Carolina	American Red Cross Blood Services Atlanta Region 1925 Monroe Dr., NE Atlanta, GA 30324	404-881-9800
Florida	John Elliott Community Blood Center 1675 Northwest 9th Ave. P.O. Box 420100 Miami, FL 33142	305-324-8341

Indiana, Michigan, Ohio	American Red Cross Blood Services Southeastern Michigan Region 100 Mack Ave. P.O. Box 351 Detroit, MI 48232	313-833-4440
Iowa, Minnesota, Nebraska, North Dakota, Northern Illinois (Chicago), South Dakota, Wisconsin	The Blood Center of Southeastern Wisconsin 1701 W. Wisconsin Ave. P.O. Box 10G Milwaukee, WI 53201	414-933-5000
Arkansas, Kansas, Kentucky, Missouri, Southern Illinois, Tennessee	American Red Cross Blood Services Missouri-Illinois Region 4050 Lindell Blvd. St. Louis, MO 63108	314-658-2136
Louisiana, New Mexico, Oklahoma, Texas	Gulf Coast Regional Blood Center 1400 La Concha Houston, TX 77054	713-791-6250
Arizona, Hawaii, Southern California	American Red Cross Blood Services Los Angeles-Orange Counties Region 1130 S. Vermont Ave. Los Angeles, CA 90006	213-384-5261
Colorado, Nevada, Northern California, Utah, Wyoming	American Red Cross Blood Services Central California Region 333 McKendrie St. San Jose, CA 95110	408-292-6242
Alaska, Idaho, Montana, Oregon, Washington	Puget Sound Blood Center Terry at Madison Seattle, WA 98104	206-292-6525

Source: Centers for Disease Control, "Varicella-Zoster Immune Globulin—United States," *Morbidity and Mortality Weekly Report* 30:21–22, January 23, 1981.

during these intervals. When major antigenic changes occur, susceptibility is universal. Between epidemics, smaller outbreaks occur in new young susceptible children and in others who escaped the previous epidemic.

Seasonal Patterns   Epidemics of influenza occur during the winter months every 2 to 3 years.

CLINICAL PICTURE   The onset is rapid with chills, fever, headache, generalized aches and pains, malaise, anorexia, and prostration. Vomiting and diarrhea may be the major symptoms in young children. A hacking cough and rhinitis may develop. The eyes may be painful. The lungs are clear, but severe infections may involve the lower respiratory tract and cause pneumonia. Uncomplicated cases usually clear in 3 to 4 days.

COMPLICATIONS   There have been close temporal relationships between influenza types A and B and Reye's syndrome in school age children. See Chapter 24, Reye's Syndrome.

Management   Treatment is entirely symptomatic. See this chapter, General Measures. Effective isolation is largely impractical in epidemic situations.

PREVENTION   Annual influenza vaccination is recommended for those at greatest risk of serious illness or death. These include chronically ill children and adults, and persons over the age of 65.

MEASLES (RUBEOLA)

Assessment   Measles is a highly contagious disease of childhood which can cause severe morbidity and serious complications.

EPIDEMIOLOGY

Mode of Transmission   It is spread by respiratory droplets and by contact with articles freshly contaminated by secretions from the nose, throat, mouth, and eyes.

Incubation Period   It is 9 to 14 days.

Period of Communicability   Children are contagious for at least 7 days after onset of the first symptom.

Population at Risk Unimmunized persons are at risk. In crowded urban areas infants and preschool children have the highest incidence. In less populated areas school age children have the highest incidence. In the late 1970s, more than 25 percent of cases occurred in those over 15 years of age. Infants under 4 to 5 months of age whose mothers had measles rarely contract the disease because of passive immunity transmitted via the placenta. Infants of mothers who never had measles are susceptible. In underdeveloped countries severe measles epidemics still occur. One attack of measles infection generally produces permanent immunity.

Seasonal Patterns Peak incidence occurs during winter and spring months. In the past epidemics occurred at 2- to 3-year intervals as new groups of susceptibles developed. Since introduction of measles vaccine in 1963, epidemics have declined, but concern presently exists over inadequate levels of immunization in some population groups. See Chapter 2, Immunization Levels.

CLINICAL PICTURE Approximately 9 to 10 days after exposure the prodrome begins with fever, malaise, cough, coryza, and conjunctivitis. These symptoms increase in severity, peak on the fourth day coincident with the appearance of the rash, and persist until the second or third day of the rash. See Table 27-1 for description of the rash and Koplik's spots. During this period the child may be extremely uncomfortable and look miserable. Fever may be high; cough and coryza are severe. The conjunctivae are swollen and inflamed and photophobia may result. Nausea, vomiting, headache, and myalgia are common. In uncomplicated measles the temperature falls by the third day after onset of the rash, other symptoms begin to subside, and within a few days the child feels well. Fever that persists may indicate complications.

LABORATORY Measles HI titer, if performed, will demonstrate a rise in antibodies by the second or third day of the rash. Peak titers are reached 2 to 4 weeks later.

COMPLICATIONS Complications result from extensive viral inflammation and/or secondary bacterial infection. Otitis media is one of the most common complications. Other respiratory complications include mastoiditis, pneumonia (leading cause of fatality), and laryngotracheobronchitis. Acute encephalitis, a serious complication, occurs in about 0.1 percent of cases (or one in 2,000 to 3,000 cases), and mortality or severe sequelae are frequent.

Management

COUNSELING FOR HOME CARE

Supportive Care   Treatment is symptomatic. Bright lights should be avoided if photophobia is present. Warm water is used to cleanse the eyes. See this chapter, General Measures.

Isolation   Respiratory and discharge precautions are recommended from the onset of the catarrhal stage through the third day of rash. Isolation may also serve to prevent exposure of the infected child to secondary bacterial infection.

Return to School   The child may resume school attendance upon clinical recovery and at least 5 days after appearance of rash.

EXPOSED CONTACTS

Active Immunization   Measles vaccine given within 24 hours of exposure can prevent infection.

Passive Immunization   Immune serum globulin given within 5 days after exposure can modify or prevent measles in susceptible persons by inducing passive immunity of approximately 4 weeks duration. See Table 27-3. Modified measles usually results in lasting immunity so the recommendation is to give a modifying dose of ISG to susceptible persons of all ages. Complete protection is indicated for infants and children with chronic illness because of the dangers of severe complications. Subsequently, normal infants should receive active immunization at 15 to 18 months of age or at least 2 to 3 months after ISG injection. High-risk, chronically ill children can best be protected by active immunization of their regular contacts.

PREVENTION   Active immunization can effectively prevent measles. See Chapter 2, Immunizations.

MONONUCLEOSIS, INFECTIOUS

Assessment   Infectious mononucleosis is an acute infectious disease occurring primarily in adolescents and young adults, caused by the Epstein-Barr virus (EBV).

Mode of Transmission   The virus is not very contagious and is spread through oropharyngeal secretions and intimate contact (e.g., kissing).

Incubation Period   Eleven days is average with a range of 4 to 14 days.

Period of Communicability   This is uncertain, since the source and time of contact are usually unknown, but it is probably only during the acute illness.

Population at Risk   Adolescents and young adults, particularly college students, are most susceptible. EBV infections occur in infancy and childhood but are likely to be mild and unrecognized. By young adulthood 50 to 80 percent of persons have developed antibodies to EBV.

CLINICAL PICTURE   The illness is generally benign. Onset is abrupt or insidious with mild symptoms of headache, malaise, and fatigue. *Fever* rises gradually and may persist. Sore throat with *exudative pharyngitis* occurs by the end of the first week, and the tonsils are enlarged, reddened, and covered with a shaggy membrane. The membrane peels off in 5 to 8 days. *Lymphadenopathy* and *splenomegaly* are common. Erythematous maculopapular skin rash, hepatomegaly, jaundice, pneumonitis, and CNS involvement are less frequent manifestations of the disease. Most cases clear by the end of the third week although weakness and fatigue may persist for several weeks.

LABORATORY   Blood smear will show atypical lymphocytes accounting for more than 10 percent of the field. Leukocyte count may be markedly elevated. Heterophile antibodies appear in blood serum by the end of the first week of illness and persist for variable periods of time. Liver function tests are often abnormal. A rapid slide test (MONO spot) has been developed which detects antibody and is a valuable diagnostic aid.

COMPLICATIONS   Severe cases may be associated with severe dysphagia, dyspnea, myocarditis, hepatitis, hemolytic anemia, and CNS involvement. Rarely, rupture of the spleen occurs.

Management

MEDICATION Corticosteroids are used in severe and toxic cases to relieve symptoms. They are not recommended for routine cases.

COUNSELING FOR HOME CARE

Supportive Care Symptomatic treatment is indicated. See this chapter, General Measures. Bed rest with gradual increase in activity is recommended. Social contact may resume after the acute phase. Strenuous physical activity is contraindicated while the spleen remains significantly enlarged.

Isolation None is required.

MUMPS

Assessment Mumps (epidemic parotitis) is caused by a virus that has affinity for glandular and nervous tissue. It is characterized most commonly by enlargement of the salivary glands, but 30 to 40 percent of persons develop inapparent infection.

EPIDEMIOLOGY

Mode of Transmission Intimate contact is required with spread occurring through droplets of saliva.

Incubation Period It is usually 16 to 18 days but may be up to 3½ weeks.

Period of Communicability It is less communicable than measles, pertussis, and chickenpox. The period of infectivity is uncertain but may be from 6 days prior to 9 days after the appearance of parotid swelling. In persons with inapparent infections, virus has been recovered in saliva between the fifteenth and twenty-fourth days after exposure.

Population at Risk The disease is endemic in urban populations at all times and people of all ages are susceptible. The highest incidence is in unimmunized children between 5 and 15 years. One attack usually results in lifelong immunity.

Seasonal Patterns It has year round occurrence but is more prominent in winter and spring months.

CLINICAL PICTURE Mild cases may not have a prodrome. When a prodrome exists, it consists of fever, headache, anorexia, malaise, and muscle pain. Within 24 to 48 hours local pain around the ear and jaw develops. This is followed by swelling of the parotid gland which reaches maximum size in 1 to 3 days. One or both parotid glands may be involved. Twenty-five percent have unilateral parotitis. The ear lobe is distorted upward and outward by the swelling. Pain and tenderness may be severe. Other glands (submaxillary, sublingual) also may swell. The swelling gradually subsides over a period of 3 to 7 days. This is the "classic" case, but there is much individual variation in the clinical signs and symptoms.

Epididymo-orchitis This is a common manifestation (20 to 30 percent) in adolescent and adult males. The orchitis is usually unilateral and develops within the first 2 weeks of the infection. Testicular swelling may occur as the only manifestation of mumps. The inflammation and swelling subside as the fever disappears. Some testicular atrophy occurs in about half the cases. Complete atrophy of both testicles is so rare that the concern about sterility and sexual impotence has no basis.

Meningoencephalitis This occurs in over 10 percent of cases. It may be the only clinical expression of mumps, but it usually follows parotitis by 3 to 10 days. The signs and symptoms of fever, headache, nausea and vomiting, nuchal rigidity, and Kernig's and Brudzinski's signs are similar to aseptic meningitis and usually clear entirely. Rarely a secondary encephalitis develops after the mumps, and paralysis, particularly of cranial nerves, may occur along with drowsiness and coma.

LABORATORY Mumps antibody can be identified most reliably by the complement fixation test.

COMPLICATIONS Complications are rare but include deafness, usually unilateral (once in every 300 to 400 cases), postinfectious encephalitis with serious sequelae, myocarditis, pancreatitis, hepatitis, neuritis, and arthritis.

Management

COUNSELING FOR HOME CARE

Supportive Care Citrus fruits and fluids should be avoided. Pain may be relieved by aspirin, codeine, and warm or cold compresses. See this chapter, General Measures.

Isolation   Respiratory precautions are recommended until swelling subsides, but the value of isolation is questionable.

Return to School   Children may return to school after the first week of the illness.

EXPOSED CONTACTS   Mumps immune globulin and ISG are not efficacious in protecting exposed susceptibles. There is no evidence that vaccination with live attenuated vaccine will protect exposed susceptibles but there is no contraindication to its use in this group, as it will provide long-lasting active immunity.

PREVENTION   Active immunization. See Chapter 2, Immunizations.

POLIOMYELITIS

Assessment   Poliomyelitis is a viral infection (enterovirus) that used to be widespread throughout the world. There are three types of virus: Type 1 is the most virulent; Types 2 and 3 are less virulent. Prior to polio vaccine most of the population were exposed to and developed immunity to the virus through contact with wild natural polio virus strains. It is primarily a mild, nonspecific febrile illness or a completely asymptomatic infection, but occasionally a severe paralytic form occurs that can leave lifelong sequelae or can cause death. With the advent of poliovirus vaccine, it has become a preventable disease.

EPIDEMIOLOGY

Mode of Transmission   Polio virus is a wild virus that circulates in the population and multiplies in the human intestinal tract. Direct contact via the fecal-oropharyngeal route is the principal mode of spread.

Incubation Period   The average is 7 to 10 days with a range of 5 to 35 days from the time of exposure to the onset of CNS symptoms. Minor illness has an incubation period of 3 to 5 days.

Period of Communicability   Virus is present in throat, blood, and feces 3 to 5 days after exposure and is excreted in the stools in large concentration for 6 to 8 weeks after onset of abortive, nonparalytic, and paralytic infections.

Population at Risk   Young unvaccinated children are especially susceptible. See Chapter 2, Oral Poliovirus Vaccine. The disease is all but eliminated in temperate zone countries with effective vaccination programs, but is emerging as a serious problem in some less developed tropical and subtropical areas where immunization programs are unsatisfactory.

Seasonal Patterns   The summer and early autumn months have the greatest incidence.

CLINICAL PICTURE   Exposure of a susceptible person to polio virus results in one of the following responses listed in order of frequency:

1. Asymptomatic infection.
2. Abortive poliomyelitis. A picture of fever, sore throat, headache, nausea and vomiting, and abdominal pain lasting 24 to 72 hours represents the entire course of the disease and never is identified as polio.
3. Nonparalytic poliomyelitis. The above symptoms may be more severe. Pain and stiffness occur in the neck, back, and legs.
4. Paralytic poliomyelitis. Minor illness occurs as described above (abortive illness) and may be followed by 1 to 7 days of feeling well. Then symptoms return accompanied by weakness and paralysis in one or more muscle groups. Respiratory difficulties may occur from a variety of causes. Site of paralysis depends on the area of the CNS affected as follows:

   • Spinal form affects muscles supplied by motor neurons in the spinal cord.
   • Bulbar form affects muscles supplied by the cranial nerves or the medulla, which are concerned with respiration and circulation.
   • Encephalitic form affects higher cortical centers.

Once the fever subsides, the spread of weakness and paralysis stops. Spontaneous improvement will occur but if full muscle power has not returned by 18 months to 2 years, the residual is usually permanent. Consult major references for a full discussion of the manifestations and management of this disease.

Management There is no specific treatment. Abortive and non-paralytic cases are treated symptomatically at home.

COUNSELING FOR HOME CARE

Isolation   Enteric precautions are recommended for several weeks.

Return to School   Return to school is permitted 1 week after onset of symptoms or after defervescence, whichever is longer.

EXPOSED CONTACTS   See Chapter 2, Oral Poliovirus Vaccine. Protection of susceptible individuals during polio outbreaks can be enhanced by avoiding:

1. Visits to families and communities where the disease is prevalent
2. Overexertion and chilling
3. Fruits and vegetables that have not been thoroughly washed
4. Tonsillectomy and other operations in the nasopharynx and mouth
5. Unnecessary injections and routine immunizations with other than poliovirus vaccine

PREVENTION   Active immunization. See Chapter 2, Immunizations. The virus serotype should be identified and the corresponding monovalent vaccine given on a community-wide basis to all persons over 2 months of age.

ROSEOLA (EXANTHEM SUBITUM)

Assessment   Roseola is an acute, benign viral infection of infants and young children. It is the most common exanthem in infants between 6 months and 2 years of age.

EPIDEMIOLOGY

Mode of Transmission   Contact is probably respiratory, but the pattern is unclear.

Incubation Period   It is probably between 10 to 15 days.

Period of Communicability   The degree of contagiousness is unclear. Transmission to siblings and other close contacts is rare.

Population at Risk   Ninety-five percent of cases occur in children between 6 months and 3 years of age.

Seasonal Patterns   It occurs year round with peak incidence in spring and autumn.

CLINICAL PICTURE   The onset is sudden with an abrupt rise in temperature to high levels (40 to 41°C). Initial presentation may be with a febrile convulsion. Anorexia, irritability, and mild pharyngitis may be present. After 3 to 4 days of high fever, the temperature rapidly falls and coincides with the appearance of the rash. See Table 27-1 for description of the rash. Occipital and postauricular lymph nodes are commonly present. A feature of the disease is the lack of physical findings sufficient to explain the fever. The child looks alert and nontoxic in spite of the high fever. Recovery is uneventful and complete.

COMPLICATIONS   Febrile convulsion is the most common complication.

Management

COUNSELING FOR HOME CARE   Treatment is symptomatic. See this chapter, General Measures. Parents need support to survive the anxiety of 3 to 4 days of unresponsive fever. No isolation is necessary. Permanent immunity results from the attack.

RUBELLA (GERMAN MEASLES)

Assessment   Rubella is a common viral infection characterized by mild constitutional symptoms, a 3-day rash, and lymphadenopathy. It is of note, primarily, because of its severe effects in the fetus if contracted by a susceptible pregnant woman during the first trimester.

EPIDEMIOLOGY

Mode of Transmission   The infection spreads directly by airborne droplets or by contact with infected persons.

INCUBATION PERIOD   Incubation period is 14 to 21 days.

PERIOD OF COMMUNICABILITY   Rubella is communicable from 7 days before to about 5 days after the rash. Greatest communicability is 3 days before the rash.

Population at Risk   Unimmunized persons are susceptible. The infection is rare in infancy and, since mass vaccination programs, uncommon in preschool children. Highest incidence occurs in school age children, adolescents, and young adults. In the United States 80 to 85 percent of women of childbearing age are immune. The fetus of a susceptible mother is at greatest risk.

Seasonal Patterns   It is endemic in populated areas. Most cases occur during the spring months in temperate zones.

CLINICAL PICTURE   Often the infection goes unnoticed. If there is a prodrome, it consists of mild catarrhal symptoms (fever, malaise, sore throat, coryza). Typically the first manifestation is postauricular, occipital, and posterior cervical adenopathy. The rash usually appears shortly after lymph nodes become enlarged and tender. See Table 27-1 for description of the rash. Women and adolescents may experience polyarthralgia or polyarthritis, but this is uncommon in children. As the rash fades, complete recovery follows. Nodes may be palpable for several weeks.

LABORATORY   Rubella infection is confirmed by virus isolation or by rising titers of rubella antibody in the serum (rubella HI antibody test). Antibody is usually detectable by the third day of the rash.

COMPLICATIONS   Complications are very rare in postnatally acquired rubella but arthritis, encephalitis, and purpura have occurred.

CONGENITAL RUBELLA SYNDROME   The risks of rubella syndrome after maternal rubella are not clear but are thought to be significant: 30 to 50 percent if contracted during the first 4 weeks of gestation; 25 percent during the first 5 to 8 weeks; 8 percent during the first 9 to 12 weeks. Overall risk in the first trimester is 20 percent (Krugman and Katz, 1981, p. 326). Manifestations of congenital rubella include growth retardation, eye defects, congenital heart disease, deafness, CNS defects, mental retardation, thrombocytopenic purpura, bone defects, and others. Infants who survive remain infective for many months (up to and beyond 18 months) and present hazards to susceptible caretakers.

Management

Supportive Care   The disease is usually so mild that symptomatic treatment is not necessary.

Isolation   None is required except that women in the first trimester of pregnancy should not be exposed.

Return to School   Quarantine is not usually imposed. The child may return to school after the rash disappears.

PREGNANT WOMEN EXPOSED TO RUBELLA   See Chapter 2, Rubella.

PREVENTION   Active immunization. See Chapter 2, Immunizations.

VARICELLA (CHICKENPOX)

Assessment   Varicella is a highly contagious disease caused by a primary infection with varicella-zoster virus (see this chapter, Herpes Zoster). The characteristic feature is the generalized, pruritic, vesicular rash.

EPIDEMIOLOGY

Mode of Transmission   Direct contact with persons infected with varicella and herpes zoster is the predominant mode. Respiratory spread also occurs.

INCUBATION PERIOD   It is 14 to 16 days with a range of 10 to 21 days.

Period of Communicability   Transmission occurs from 1 day before the rash until 5 to 6 days after onset of the rash when all vesicles have crusted.

Population at Risk   Highest incidence is in children between 2 and 8 years, but all ages are susceptible. It is much more severe in adults. It may occur in early infancy despite a history of previous chickenpox in the mother.

Seasonal Patterns   There is a higher incidence during the winter and spring.

CLINICAL PICTURE The rash is generally the first symptom. See Table 27-1 for description of the rash. Fever, headache, malaise, and anorexia parallel the severity of the rash. Once an individual lesion dries, a crust forms and falls off within 5 to 20 days, depending on the extent of the lesion. Usually there is no scarring but lesions that become secondarily infected (usually by vigorous scratching with dirty fingernails) may leave permanent scars.

COMPLICATIONS Complications are not common in children. Secondary bacterial skin infections occasionally lead to impetigo, furunculosis, cellulitis, erysipelas, or conjunctivitis. Children with leukemia, deficiencies in cell-mediated immunity, or on immunosuppressive medications may develop encephalitis, pneumonia, or disseminated varicella. Reye's syndrome (see Chapter 24) has been associated with preceding varicella infection.

Management

COUNSELING FOR HOME CARE

Supportive Care Care of the skin is paramount. Itching may be relieved by tepid water baths, cornstarch, Aveeno or baking soda baths, systemic antipruritic medication such as diphenhydramine (Benadryl) and topical lotions (calamine). See this chapter, General Measures and Chapter 26, Topical Therapy. Rinses, gargles, and viscous xylocaine can be used for oral lesions. Occurrence of secondary skin infection can be reduced by bathing with soap and water, changing bed linens and clothes frequently, keeping fingernails short and clean, and using mittens while the child sleeps.

Isolation The child should be kept at home and isolated from susceptible pregnant women and immunosuppressed persons until the vesicles have dried. Respiratory and secretion precautions are advised.

Return to School Return to school is permitted not sooner than 7 days after onset.

EXPOSED CONTACTS In most instances exposure occurs before the disease is detected. Due to its inevitability and benign nature, protection or isolation of healthy susceptible contacts is not warranted. Infants and high-risk children require strict protection from exposure. If exposure occurs Zoster Immune Globulin given within 3 days of exposure is effective in modifying varicella. See Tables 27-3, 27-4, and 27-5.

PREVENTION A live attenuated varicella vaccine has been developed in Japan and used effectively in normal children, chronically ill children, and leukemic children. Studies to further determine safety, efficacy, and noncommunicability of the vaccine are in progress (Asano and Takahasi, 1977).

Parasitic Infections

Infections caused by parasites (helminths, protozoans) are less common in the United States than in tropical and subtropical parts of the world, but they do occur, especially with the increase in intercontinental travel and the large numbers of immigrants and refugees from Latin America and Indochina. Children are affected more frequently than adults. Prevalence varies with climate, sanitation, and socioeconomic conditions. Information on some of the most common parasitic diseases is briefly presented in Table 27-6. For more extensive discussion, including specific medical treatment, refer to major pediatric texts listed in the References.

ENTEROBIASIS (PINWORMS)

Assessment See Table 27-6.

Management

MEDICATION Since the infection is so easily transmitted, many physicians recommend medication for the entire family. The following medications are commonly used:

1. Pyrantel pamoate (Antiminth). 11 mg/kg orally in a single dose. Maximal dose is 1 gm. It comes in suspension form. Side effects may be nausea, vomiting, and abdominal cramps.
2. Pryvinium pamoate (Povan). 5 mg/kg orally in a single dose and repeated in 2 to 3 weeks. It comes in suspension form. Stool becomes red. Vomiting and abdominal cramps may occur.
3. Mebendazole (Vermox). 100-mg tablet in a single dose. Abdominal pain and diarrhea may occur. It should not be used in

Table 27-6

Common Parasitic Infections

Disease and Name of Parasite	Mode of Transmission	Mechanism of Infection	Clinical Findings	Diagnosis	Comments
Protozoan infections:					
Amebiasis (*Entamoeba histolytica*)	Cysts contained in human feces are ingested via contaminated food or water.	Cysts deposit in colonic mucosa causing ulcers. Ulcers cause erosion of blood vessels and also permit amebae to enter the portal system and invade the liver.	Many are asymptomatic or have mild symptoms. Diarrhea, abdominal pain, and dysentery occur. May develop liver abscess.	Stool reveals cysts or trophozoites (vegetative stage of the amebae).	Children in institutional settings are especially vulnerable. Food handlers must use careful handwashing. In environments with unsanitary conditions, do not eat raw food or drink water without precautions.
Giardiasis (*Giardia lamblia*)	Cysts contained in human feces are ingested via direct contact or contaminated food and water.	Trophozoites inhabit the duodenum, upper jejunum.	May be asymptomatic. May have anorexia, nausea, flatulence, abdominal pain. In severe cases, protracted mucous diarrhea, fever, weight loss, and malabsorption can occur.	Diarrheal stool reveals trophozoites. Formed stool reveals cysts.	See Amebiasis, above. Sanitary disposal of feces is important.
Helminthic infections:					
Ascariasis (Roundworm; *Ascaris lumbricoides*)	Ingestion of ova contained in soil contaminated with human feces via dirt, food, water.	Ova hatch in small intestine. Larvae penetrate bowel wall, enter portal system, migrate to the liver and eventually the	May be asymptomatic. May have abdominal distress, malaise; cough during the lung stage. Pneumonia and	Detection of ova in stool. Eosinophilia is marked during migration.	Common in Gulf Coast states, Ozark area, and southern Appalachia. Stress sanitary disposal of feces.

	Mode of Transmission	Life Cycle	Signs and Symptoms	Diagnosis	Comments
		lungs. From the lungs they ascend to the oropharynx and are swallowed. Thus the adult worm inhabits the jejunum.	intestinal obstruction can occur in severe cases.		
Enterobiasis (Pinworm: *Enterobius vermicularis*)	Ova are swallowed either after the child scratches the anal area and transfers fingers to mouth, or by inhalation of ova while handling contaminated bed linens or clothing.	Mature worms inhabit the large intestine and the female migrates to the anus and lays eggs on the perianal and perineal skin.	Nocturnal perianal pruritus. Usually no systemic symptoms, although irritability, anorexia, and loss of sleep can occur. Girls have vulvitis, vaginitis.	Scotch tape test. Press clear tape on perianal skin, transfer tape to glass slide, and observe ova under a microscope.	Up to 30% of children in the United States have pinworms. See text, this chapter, for management.
Hookworm (*Necator americanus*)	Eggs passed in infected feces develop into larvae in the soil. Larvae penetrate human skin, usually through bare feet.	From the skin they enter the blood stream and then pass through the lungs, ascend to the pharynx, and are swallowed. The adult worms attach to intestinal villi and feed on blood.	Small infestations may be asymptomatic. May have dermatitis of feet, cough, fever, abdominal pain, diarrhea. Chronic and large infestations may lead to anemia, iron deficiency, malnutrition.	Detection of ova in stool. Elevated eosinophilia.	Prevalent in the southern United States. Stress sanitary disposal of feces. Encourage wearing of shoes.
Trichinosis (*Trichinella spiralis*)	Ingestion of infected pork, insufficiently cooked.	Larvae emerge in small intestine, mature, and burrow into intestinal wall. New larvae are produced and migrate throughout the body and invade striated muscle.	During the intestinal phase, gastroenteritis is seen. subsequently periorbital and facial edema, headache, fever, conjunctivitis, photophobia, severe muscle pain and tenderness may develop. Cardiac and CNS symptoms may also develop.	History of eating raw or partially cooked pork. Muscle biopsy. Serologic tests. Marked eosinophilia.	In the United States, meat is *not* inspected for this worm. Cook pork thoroughly.

children under 2 years of age or in pregnant women. This is a broad-spectrum antihelmintic that kills a wide variety of worms, including whipworm, hookworm, and roundworm.

4. Piperazine citrate (Antepar). 65 mg/kg orally for 7 days. It is given in the morning before breakfast. It comes in syrup, wafer, and tablet forms. Vomiting, diarrhea, and visual disturbances have been reported.

COUNSELING FOR HOME CARE

Hygienic Care   Eradication is difficult because of the ease of reinfection and transmission. Some authorities recommend vigorous hygienic measures such as daily boiling of bed linens, underwear, and pajamas, and thorough vacuuming. Such measures are probably of little value, but scrupulous parents may feel better carrying out such a regimen. The most reasonable and effective means of reducing infection is personal hygiene including handwashing and fingernail cleaning and cutting.

Supportive Care   Most parents react with shock and revulsion when told their child has "worms." Mothers often feel it must be a reflection of their mothering abilities and become defensive. The nurse practitioner can allay guilt and support parents by explaining the benign nature of pinworms, the high incidence in young children, and the causative factors. Reassurance is necessary that it occurs in all types of families and has no stigma attached.

Recurrent Infections

PRIMARY IMMUNODEFICIENCY DISEASE

Assessment   Children with primary immunodeficiencies affecting cell-mediated immunity or antibody-mediated immunity usually present between the ages of 2 months and 2 years with increased numbers of infections which are unusually severe. These children also never seem to completely recover from one infection before the next one begins. They appear to be "sick all the time." Table 27-7 shows the common clinical signs and symptoms in such children. It is important to obtain a detailed history of all infections, the intervals between infections, environmental factors (e.g., expo-

Table 27-7
Common Clinical Findings in Children with Primary
Immunodeficiency Disease

Common Symptoms	Less Common Symptoms	Occasional Symptoms
Recurrent respiratory infections	Chronic pneumonitis or bronchiectasis	Pneumocystis carinii pneumonia
Recurrent bilateral otitis media	Irritability and pallor Pyoderma	Nonspecific skin rashes, hair loss, and eczema
Unusually severe bacterial infections (sepsis and meningitis)	Lack of lymph nodes and tonsils Oral apthous ulcers	Severe viral disease
Recurrent diarrhea		Arthritis
Fungal skin infections (thrush)		Enlarged liver and spleen
Developmental retardation and failure to thrive		Enlarged lymph nodes Increased or decreased white blood cell count, decreased platelets, and anemia

Source: Reprinted with permission from: E. H. Waechter and F. G. Blake, *Nursing Care of Children*, 9th ed., Philadelphia: J. B. Lippincott, 1976, p. 301.

sure to sources of infection), and parental expectations and ideas about illness in their children. Some parents may have unrealistic notions and fears about childhood illness and may think their child is chronically sick when, in fact, the child is experiencing the normal number of routine infections.

LABORATORY If suspicion of primary immunodeficiency disease exists, diagnostic tests include the following:

1. Complete blood count with total lymphocyte count. Normal lymphocytes number 1,200 or more. If the lymphocyte count is less than 1,200, cellular immune deficiency is likely.
2. Quantitative immunoglobulins. See Table 27-8.

Management The child with primary immunodeficiency disease needs specialized care by qualified physicians. It is the nurse prac-

Table 27-8
Levels of Immune Globulins in Normal Persons at Various Ages

	Newborn	4–6 mo	7–12 mo	6–8 yr	12–16 yr	Adult	Comments
IgG (mg/100 ml)	1031 ± 200[a]	427 ± 186	661 ± 219	923 ± 256	946 ± 124	1158 ± 305	Adult level at birth reflects placental transfer from mother. Drops to low levels by 3 months, then as maternal antibodies disappear, infant's humoral system begins to function and levels increase rapidly for 2 years, then increase less rapidly. Predominant antibody of serum; protects newborn temporarily from diseases for which mother has sufficient antibodies.
IgM (mg/100 ml)	11 ± 5	43 ± 17	54 ± 23	65 ± 25	59 ± 20	99 ± 25	Increases rapidly after birth and throughout first year. Is the chief immune globulin synthesized by the neonate. Responsible for initial antibody response to antigens, especially bacteria. Does not cross placenta.
IgA (mg/100 ml)	2 ± 3	28 ± 18	37 ± 18	124 ± 45	148 ± 63	200 ± 61	Increases slowly during infancy and childhood. Found in colostrum, breast milk. Will protect the breastfed infant from respiratory and GI infections. Produced along the GI tract.

Source: Adapted with permission from E. R. Stiehm and H. H. Fudenberg, "Serum Levels of Immune Globulins in Health and Disease: A Survey," *Pediatrics* 37:717, May 1966. Copyright American Academy of Pediatrics, 1966.

[a]Mean ± SD.

1106

titioner's responsibility to consider these deficiency diseases in the child with recurrent infections and obtain medical consultation.

Resource Information

The most up-to-date information on infectious diseases is available from: Centers for Disease Control, Atlanta, GA 30333   (404) 633-3311. See Chapter 2, Resource Information.

References

American Academy of Pediatrics. *Report of the Committee on Infectious Diseases.* 19th ed. Evanston, IL, 1982.

American Thoracic Society, Ad Hoc Committee to Revise Diagnostic Standards. *Diagnostic Standards and Classification of Tuberculosis and Other Mycobacterial Diseases.* New York: American Lung Association, 1975.

Arnon, S. S., et al. "Honey and Other Environmental Risk Factors for Infant Botulism." *J Pediatr 94*:331–336, February 1979.

Arnon, S. S., et al. "Intestinal Infection and Toxin Production by *Clostridium botulinum* as One Cause of Sudden Infant Death Syndrome." *Lancet 1*:1273–1276, June 17, 1978.

Asano, Y. and M. Takahasi. "Clinical and Serologic Testing of a Live Varicella Vaccine and Two-Year Follow-up for Immunity of the Vaccinated Children." *Pediatrics 60*:810–814, December 1977.

Brook, I. "Meningococcal Meningitis: Control through Antibiotics and Active Immunization." *Clinical Proceedings CHNMC 36*:123–131, May/June 1980.

Brunner, L. S. and D. S. Suddarth. *The Lippincott Manual of Nursing Practice.* Philadelphia: J. B. Lippincott, 1974.

Carver, D. H. and D. S. Y. Seto. "Hepatitis A and B." *Pediatr Clin North Am 21*:669–681, August 1974.

Centers for Disease Control. "Inactivated Hepatitis B Virus Vaccine." *Morbidity Mortality Weekly Rep 31*:317–328, June 25, 1982.

Centers for Disease Control. "Meningococcal Disease—United States 1981." *Morbidity Mortality Weekly Rep 30*:113–115, March 20, 1981.

Centers for Disease Control. "Varicella-Zoster Immune Globulin—United States." *Morbidity Mortality Weekly Rep 30*:15–23, January 23, 1981.

Glassroth, J. G., et al. "Tuberculosis in the 1980s." *N Engl J Med 302*:1441–1449, June 26, 1980.

Graef, J. W. and T. E. Cone. *Manual of Pediatric Therapeutics.* Boston: Little, Brown, 1974.

Hageman, J. H., et al. "Congenital Tuberculosis: Critical Reappraisal of Clinical Findings and Diagnostic Procedures." *Pediatrics* 66:980–984, December 1980.

Kraut, J. R., et al. "Assessment of Tuberculin Screening in an Urban Pediatric Clinic." *Pediatrics* 64:856–859, December 1979.

Krugman, S. and S. Katz. *Infectious Diseases of Children.* 7th ed. St. Louis: C. V. Mosby, 1981.

Lawrence, R. A. *Breastfeeding: A Guide for the Medical Profession.* St. Louis: C. V. Mosby, 1980.

L'Hommedieu, C. L. and R. A. Polin. "Progression of Clinical Signs in Severe Infant Botulism: Therapeutic Implications." *Clin Pediatr* 20:90–95, February 1981.

Malarkey, L. M. "Ridding School Children of Parasites—A Community Approach." *Am J Maternal Child Nursing* 4:363–366, November/December 1979.

Munoz, A. I. *"Hemophilus influenzae* Infections: A Brief Review." *Clin Pediatr* 19:86–90, February 1980.

Rodman, M. J. and D. W. Smith. *Pharmacology and Drug Therapy in Nursing.* 2nd ed. Philadelphia: J. B. Lippincott, 1979.

Rudolph, A., editor. *Pediatrics.* 17th ed. East Norwalk, CT: Appleton-Century-Crofts, 1982.

Santos, J. I., et al. "Cellulitis: Treatment with Cefoxitin Compared with Multiple Antibiotic Therapy." *Pediatrics* 67:887–890, June 1981.

Smith, D. H., et al. "Bacterial Meningitis: A Symposium." *Pediatrics* 52:586–600, October 1973.

Stiehm, E. R. and H. H. Fundenberg. "Serum Levels of Immune Globulins in Health and Disease: A Survey." *Pediatrics* 37:715–725, May 1966.

Vaughan, V. C., et al., editors. *Nelson Textbook of Pediatrics.* 11th ed. Philadelphia: W. B. Saunders, 1979.

Waechter, E. H. and F. G. Blake. *Nursing Care of Children.* 9th ed. Philadelphia: J. B. Lippincott, 1976.

Whitley, R. J., et al. "The Natural History of Herpes Simplex Virus Infection of Mother and Newborn." *Pediatrics* 66:489–494, October 1980.

28

Emergencies

A medical emergency is any situation which requires immediate medical attention to preserve life or health or to alleviate suffering. Many medical conditions require prompt but not immediate attention and are better considered situations of urgency rather than emergency. Care must be taken not to abuse the term to expedite the treatment of conditions which do not warrant emergency care.

Anticipating all presentations of medical conditions requiring immediate attention is not possible. This chapter includes a brief discussion of problems most likely to present as emergencies. In many situations the threat to life and limb will be obvious: for example, coma, major trauma, hemorrhage, and near-drowning. The nurse practitioner serves as an intermediate care provider until the child arrives at a health care facility or until the emergency is resolved and helps the family cope with the emergency. Management of these conditions by the nurse practitioner will usually involve "first aid," that is, nonsurgical and nonpharmacologic intervention designed to help the child until more sophisticated care is available. Some situations, such as sudden upper airway obstruction and cardiac arrest warrant more vigorous intervention and the use of emergency techniques.

See Chapter 15 for eye emergencies, Chapter 18, Congestive Heart Failure and Chapter 26, Bites of Arachnids and Insects.

ASSESSMENT

The first step in emergency care is accurate assessment. Different aspects of the child's condition are assessed in order of priority as expeditiously as possible. The coexistence of concomitant serious conditions must be considered.

History

Determine if the child is in immediate jeopardy. If so, proceed to appropriate supportive and emergency measures. If not, proceed to elaborate on the history. Be alert to contributory factors and openminded about the possible causes of the immediate problem. Often overlooked is the possibility of poisoning, infection, or nonaccidental injury.

TELEPHONE

The person who calls the health care facility for help is often frantic and upset and needs a calm approach and clear, simple directions. Obtain the following information in writing as soon as possible:

1. Name of the caller and relationship to the child
2. Phone number where the caller can be reached
3. Location of the child

Ask the following questions to assess the seriousness of the child's condition:

1. What is the caretaker concerned about?
2. What is the child's age?
3. Is the child having difficulty breathing?
4. Is the child unconscious?
5. What has already been done for the child? Any medications given? Amount? Results?
6. When did the emergency occur and exactly how did it happen?
7. What symptoms does the child have? For example, rapid pulse, rash, or fever? How long has the child had these symptoms?
8. Are there any physical or other medical problems?

Physical Examination

The nurse practitioner must be alert to the signs that indicate a serious or potentially serious condition. Presentation of the signs listed in Table 28-1 warrants immediate referral to a physician. Rapidly evaluate in order of priority:

1. The cardiorespiratory system: cardiac and respiratory rates, adequacy of ventilation, skin color, blood pressure, degree of agitation, and hemorrhage. With acute airway obstruction, respiratory movement may be exaggerated. With carbon monoxide poisoning, the child may be bright red rather than blue. Agitation may be a sign of carbon dioxide retention.
2. The neurologic system: state of consciousness, orientation, localizing neurologic signs.
3. The rest of the child: state of hydration, urinary output, other injuries.

MANAGEMENT

Emergency First Aid

Institute necessary life-saving measures:

1. Assure adequate airway, respiration, and circulation
2. Control hemorrhage
3. Immobilize injured parts
4. Relieve pain
5. Provide for the child's comfort, with caution to avoid worsening the child's condition

Emergency Techniques

CARDIOPULMONARY RESUSCITATION (CPR)

A precise description of CPR techniques is beyond the scope of this chapter. The reader is referred to "Standards and Guidelines for Cardiopulmonary Resuscitation (CPR) and Emergency Cardiac

Table 28-1
Signs Which Indicate Need for Physician Referral

Signs	Condition
Absent or poor chest movements and breath sounds, weak or absent pulses and heart sounds, marked bradycardia or tachycardia, cyanosis or pallor, loss of consciousness, fixation of pupils	Cardiopulmonary arrest
Poor skin turgor, dry mucous membranes, sunken eyes, sunken fontanelle, tachycardia, tachypnea, hypotension, shock, oliguria	Dehydration
Coma, convulsions, aberrant behavior, pinpoint pupils	Drug abuse
Tachycardia, hypotension; pale, ashen appearance; cold, sweaty skin; pale, cold extremities; weak, thready pulse; oliguria, anxiety, agitation, anxiousness, restlessness	Hypovolemic shock
Rising pulse rate, restlessness, increased retractions, cyanosis	Hypoxia
Bulging fontanelle, prominent veins, nausea, vomiting, headache, papilledema	Increased intracranial pressure
Irritability, bulging fontanelle, severe headache, projectile vomiting, stiff neck, positive Brudzinski, positive Kernig, lethargy, focal neurologic signs, convulsions, petechial or purpuric rash	Meningitis
Rapid onset of fever, headache, lethargy, tachycardia, petechial rash, shock	Meningococcemia
Restlessness, irritability, nasal flaring, intercostal retraction during inspiration, flaring of lower rib margins, absent breath sounds over involved areas, or noisy breath sounds with rales, sitting with head forward, mouth open and drooling	Respiratory distress
Early signs: hyperventilation, depressed level of consciousness, warm flushed skin, decreased urine output, fever, chills, normal blood pressure	Septic shock
Late signs: hypotension, tachycardia, cold clammy skin with peripheral mottling and cyanosis, marked lethargy, oliguria to anuria	

Source: Compiled from D. Pascoe and M. Grossman, editors, *Quick Reference to Pediatric Emergencies,* Philadelphia: J.B. Lippincott, 1973; J.W. Graef and T.E. Cone, Jr., editors, *Manual of Pediatric Therapeutics,* Boston: Little, Brown, 1974.

Care," *JAMA* 244:453–509, August 1, 1980, for further information. Reprints are available from the American Heart Association, Distribution Department, 2005 Hightower Drive, Garland, TX 75041. The American Heart Association offers courses in basic and advanced resuscitation. Annual review is recommended. Basic points will be reviewed here:

Airway Place the child on the back on a firm surface. Remove any obstruction from the mouth and pharynx. Keep the tongue out of the airway by using the head tilt-chin lift. Further forward displacement of the jaw (thrust) may be necessary if the head tilt-chin lift is ineffective in opening the airway. Do not exaggerate extension in young children because occlusion may occur with full extension, since the larynx is pliable (Greensher et al., 1979). For victims with a possible neck injury, use jaw thrust without head tilt technique. Keep the head in a neutral position. Establish breathlessness while maintaining the open airway position by placing one's ear over the victim's mouth and nose and observing the chest rise and fall, listening for air escaping during exhalation, and feeling for the flow of air on one's cheeks. Rescue breathing is initiated if breathing does not occur.

Breathing Once an airtight seal has been established, deliver four gentle breaths in rapid succession without allowing for full lung deflation. These four breaths serve as a check for airway obstruction. Limit ventilation to the amount of air needed to raise the chest. If air enters with the four breaths and the chest rises, the airway is patent. If air does not enter freely, even after readjustments in positioning, an obstruction should be suspected. For management of an obstruction in the airway, see this chapter, Choking.

Circulation Initiate circulatory support when peripheral pulses are not palpable or the pulse is less than 60 per minute. Check the carotid pulse in the older child, or, in the infant, the brachial pulse located on the inside of the upper arm midway between the elbow and the shoulder (*JAMA*, 1980).

INFANTS Support the back of the thorax with both hands and compress the midsternum ½ to 1 inch (1.3 to 2.5 cm) with the thumbs, at the rate of 100 compressions per minute. The ratio of compressions to respiration is 5:1. Count compressions as follows: 1,2,3,4,5, breathe.

CHILDREN   Support the back with a board or place the child on the floor. Compress the lower sternum 1 to 1½ inches (2.5 to 3.8 cm) with the heel of the hand, at the rate of 80 compressions per minute. The rate of compressions to respiration is 5:1. Count compressions as follows: 1 and, 2 and, 3 and, 4 and, 5 and, breathe.

HEIMLICH MANEUVER

The Heimlich maneuver is described here for the reader's information. The preferred method of handling aspiration of a foreign body is discussed in this chapter, under Choking. The Heimlich maneuver is used to dislodge a foreign body impacted in the hypopharynx, larynx, or trachea. The rescuer should first attempt to retrieve the foreign matter from the victim's mouth, taking care not to push it deeper. If unsuccessful, the rescuer then grasps the victim from behind, clenching the palms of the hands together over the upper abdomen in the midline. The hands should never be placed on the xiphoid process of the sternum or on the lower margins of the ribcage. The rescuer then compresses the victim's abdomen with a *quick upward thrust*. The thrust is repeated as necessary. The thrusting movement is *NOT* a punch, bearhug, or squeeze (Block and Block, 1976). Do not use this technique on infants or pregnant women. Use chest thrust (place fist over the sternum) on pregnant women. Infants are placed over the hand and forearm.

ENDOTRACHEAL INTUBATION

Endotracheal intubation is one of the quickest and easiest ways to ensure a patent airway. Its use is restricted to health personnel who are highly trained and skilled in this procedure. It prevents aspiration and guarantees delivery of concentrated amounts of oxygen to the lungs. Indications for this procedure include cardiac arrest, respiratory arrest, ineffectiveness of simpler airway methods, coma, and prolonged artificial ventilation (Lanros, 1983).

TRACHEOSTOMY

A tracheostomy may be necessary in cases of laryngeal spasm or edema, epiglottitis, foreign body in the larynx, or crushing injury to the larynx. It is, however, inferior to endotracheal intubation and should not be performed until it can be done under suitable conditions.

An emergency cricothyroidotomy is a vertical incision between the cricoid and thyroid cartilages into the trachea in the subglottic area (Kempe et al., 1980). It allows for the introduction of a tracheostomy tube or improvised airway.

Emotional Support of the Family

Health personnel should be sensitive to parental feelings of guilt, helplessness, and responsibility for the emergency. Parents need a firm and gentle touch. During the crisis, parents should be informed of the child's progress. Adjustment to the reality of the crisis usually evolves through the following stages:

1. Emotional shock. The nurse practitioner must not assume that the parents' or child's comprehension of what is said is complete or accurate.
2. Denial. The nurse practitioner may find the parent or child acting in a manner inconsistent with the gravity of the situation.
3. Anger. The child or parent may react emotionally or even physically to those attempting to help.
4. Resignation. Often, only at this state of adjustment will the family or child begin to develop rapport with the health team.
5. Integration. The family will often begin to seek the real causes of shock or loss, and the nurse practitioner may find it possible to enlighten the family about prevention of accidents and illness.

Emotional Support of the Child

Support of the child in a situation of acute emotional stress requires an understanding of the particular fears of children with regard to threatened loss of life, limb, or love. Children fear bodily harm and loss of control.

The child's anxiety response is influenced by developmental maturity, previous medical experiences, and parental reaction to the situation.

INFANTS AND TODDLERS

Loss of the parent is feared. The child may cry, cling to the parent, avoid eye contact, and be restless and combative. The following may decrease anxiety:

- Include the parents in treatment procedures when appropriate
- Permit the parents to remain with the child
- Reassure the child that the parents will return as soon as the procedure is completed
- Have available an object the child associates with the parent

PRESCHOOL THROUGH SCHOOL AGE CHILDREN

The major fear is of pain or bodily harm. The child may protest, scream, clench the teeth, reach for parent, and be combative. The following may decrease anxiety:

- Address the child at eye level
- Allow the child to play with equipment and materials prior to use
- Allow the child to sit up rather than lie down for procedures whenever possible
- Allow the expression of pain
- Encourage the child to verbalize fears
- Reward bravery and accept fear

Legal Aspects of Emergency Care

Most states protect the health professional who renders "roadside" emergency care from liability except in cases involving the utmost negligence. These legal protections, however, do not protect the person from being sued. The basic tenet of emergency care is *do no further harm.*

Any unconscious victim is assumed to consent to lifesaving treatment. If a child needs emergency treatment, and no guardian is available to give consent, care should be given nonetheless with careful documentation in the medical record to substantiate the necessity of emergency treatment.

If a guardian refuses to provide consent for lifesaving treatment (e.g., blood transfusion), authorization by a superior court magistrate can and should be obtained. A parent does not have the right to jeopardize the life of the child for religious or philosophical reasons. The aid of law enforcement officers may be necessary to ensure the provision of such care to the child.

In the absence of consent by a guardian who may reasonably be expected to give consent once contacted, one should not render more than care of the emergency problem. When such consent cannot be obtained by a reasonable effort, arrangements should be made for temporary custody of the child, usually through an agent of the local social services welfare department.

COMMON CLINICAL PROBLEMS

Avulsion (Amputation)

ASSESSMENT

Avulsion, or amputation, is a loss of tissue, such as ears, fingers, feet, toes, and large areas of skin that have been totally torn away or left hanging as a flap.

MANAGEMENT

Attempt to stabilize the situation. Keep the child quiet. Control bleeding (see this chapter, Hemorrhage) and prevent further contamination of the wound. Preserve avulsed tissue at home as follows:

1. Roll it up with the skin layer facing the outside in waterproof material such as plastic wrap. Do not place in water.
2. Protect it from drying and heat.

Quickly transport the child and the avulsed part to the health facility. At the health facility the avulsed tissue should be preserved by placing it in a gauze wrap that has been moistened with sterile, normal saline solution. The wrap should then be sealed in a plastic bag and the bag placed in iced, normal saline (Lanros, 1983).

Anaphylaxis

ASSESSMENT

Anaphylaxis is the sudden, life-threatening reaction to an antigen, which may be injected, ingested, or inhaled. It should be suspected if the child has received a systemic injection and reacts in any way. The reaction is mediated through the release of histamine, brady-kinin, and other vasoactive substances. The reaction may encompass pruritus, urticaria, agitation, bronchospasm, edema, and cardiac arrest. See this chapter, Shock.

MANAGEMENT

Emergency Treatment   The following steps are necessary:

1. Application of tourniquet proximal to the site of intramuscular injection secure enough to restrict venous return but not hamper arterial flow.
2. Administration of aqueous epinephrine 1:1,000, subcutaneously in a dose of 0.01 ml/kg, up to 0.5 ml. Repeat in 20 minutes if necessary. Corticosteroids and antihistamines may also be indicated.
3. Immediate transportation of the child to a hospital. Emergency intubation or cricothyroidotomy may be necessary to relieve airway obstruction from laryngospasm. Have equipment ready.

Preventive Measures

1. Identify and avoid known allergens in a hypersensitive person. Obtain a history of reactions to drugs and other foreign substances such as insect stings, and record clearly on the front of the child's chart.
2. When practicable, administer medications orally rather than parenterally to reduce the likelihood of anaphylaxis.
3. Desensitize those who have experienced systemic reactions to allergens such as insect stings. Observe the child receiving a desensitization injection for 15 to 20 minutes following the injection. See Chapter 26, Bites of Arachnids and Insects, for specific preventive measures. Help family obtain a bee sting kit where appropriate, and educate the patient and family members as to its use. See Chapter 26, Resource Information.

4. Recommend the use of a Medic Alert bracelet or wallet card which indicates the allergen. See Chapter 26, Resource Information.
5. Be ready for allergic reactions when using parenteral drugs.

Burns

ASSESSMENT

Burns may be thermal or chemical injuries, external or internal (lye ingestion, hot smoke inhalation, aspiration of hot liquid). Abuse is not an uncommon cause. Table 28-2 summarizes the burn hazards for children.

The history should provide information necessary for the nurse practitioner to reconstruct the incident. The explanation should be plausible, with respect to the child's development, the pattern of the burns, and the possibility of events happening as described.

Burn Surface Area The surface area burned is estimated by the "rule of nines" (Table 28-3) or, preferably, with age-specific tables (see Figure 28-1). Palmar surface of hands at all ages represents 1 percent of the body surface area.

Burn Depth Burns are rated by degree:

First degree: epidermis not irreversibly damaged, no blistering, erythematous, painful.
Second degree: epidermal necrosis, blistering, erythematous, painful.
Third degree: dermis damaged irreversibly, eschar formation, painless.
Fourth degree: tissue damage extending to underlying organs and tissues, eschar, painless.

Burn Classification (Kempe et al., 1980).

Minor burns: first- and second-degree burns of less than 10 percent of the body surface that do not involve the hands, the feet, the perineum, or the face.
Major burns: second- or third-degree burns involving more than 10 percent of the body surface.

Table 28-2
Burn Hazards of Children

Group	Type of Burn	Hazard	Time/Place
Infants and toddlers (6–24 mos)	Scalds	Playing underfoot in kitchen, overturning cups, pulling electric cords of coffee pots, frying pans; bath water too hot; parents (neglect/abuse)	Daytime/home
	Electric burns	Chewing extension cords	
Young child (2–6 yrs)	Flame burns	Playing with matches, climbing on stove, warming with heating source	Early morn/ kitchen, bedroom
	Scalds	Water too hot	
Older child (6–14 yrs)	Flame burns	Playing/working with gasoline, campfires, barbecues, chemistry sets, firecrackers, rockets, matches; reaching over stove, candles, making candles, "innocent bystander" (observing others play with fire or gasoline).	After school, holidays/ outdoors, indoors

Morn, eve/ kitchen; after school/yard |
| | Electric burns | Climbing around high-tension wires (usually fatal) | |
| All children | Flame burns | House fires; gas tank explosion during auto accident | Usually night; anytime |

Source: Adapted from material courtesy of Northern California Burn Council.

Table 28-3
Estimating Burn Surface Area Using the "Rule of Nines"

Age and Body Area	Percent of Total Body Surface Area	
Over 12 years		
Head and neck	9%	
Each upper extremity	9%	
Anterior trunk	18%	
Posterior trunk	18%	
Each lower extremity	18%	
Under 12 years		
Head and neck	9%	*plus* 1% for each year
Each upper extremity	9%	under 12
Anterior trunk	18%	
Posterior trunk	18%	*minus* ½% for each year
Each lower extremity	18%	under 12

Source: Reprinted by permission from E. H. Waechter and F. G. Blake, *Nursing Care of Children*, 9th ed., Philadelphia: J.B. Lippincott, 1976. P. 433.

MANAGEMENT

First Aid Parents should be instructed to dribble ice water, which lessens pain and cleanses the wound. Then, ideally, sterile gauze bandages should be used to cover the burned areas. If sterile bandages are not available, the cleanest cloth available is used to cover the burned areas and cloth strips are used to hold them on. Ice water should be dribbled every few minutes until medical care is obtained.

Minor Burns These can be managed on an ambulatory basis. Plain petrolatum or antibiotic-impregnated gauze and clean dressings are applied. Dressings should be changed every 48 hours.

Hospitalization is indicated for children with burns of the hands and feet to allow proper splinting of the extremity and careful wound care. A baseline hematocrit is indicated if 10% of body surface areas is involved. Urine specific gravity is obtained at 24 to 48 hours to determine hydration.

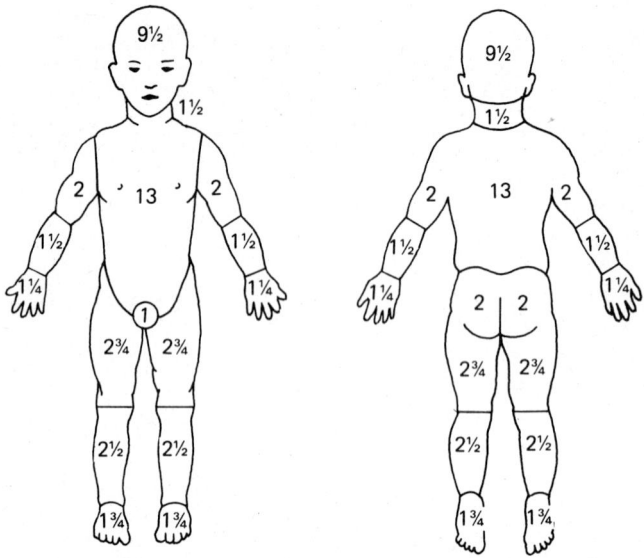

Infant Less Than One Year of Age

Figure 28-1 Lund and Browder modification of Berkow's scale for estimating extent of burns. (Reprinted with permission from H. K. Silver, et al. *Handbook of Pediatrics*, 14th ed., Los Altos, CA: Lange Medical Publications, 1983, p. 718.)

Major Burns These burns require expert medical evaluation. Emergency measures are initiated on the way to the hospital (Kempe et al., 1980).

1. Run cool water immediately over the burn area to cool it.
2. Transport the child wrapped in a clean sheet to a hospital.
3. Administer analgesics if necessary.

Preventive Counseling See Table 5-22, Table 6-9, and Chapter 7, Burns and Fires.

Cardiac Arrest

ASSESSMENT

Cardiac arrest is the sudden cessation of cardiac function. The principal forms are ventricular fibrillation, asystole, and electromechanical dissociation. Causes include myocardial infarction, electrolyte abnormalities, and electrical shock. Relevant historical information includes the name of any medications the child has been taking as well as a search for an immediate insult.

Physical signs are those of asphyxia and absence of pulse and blood pressure. In electromechanical dissociation, organized electrical activity persists until the heart becomes too ischemic to generate it.

MANAGEMENT

Cardiopulmonary resuscitation must begin immediately. See this chapter, Cardiopulmonary Resuscitation.

Choking

ASSESSMENT

The inhalation of foreign objects is the second greatest cause of home accidental death in children less than 5 years of age (National Safety Council, 1979). Aspiration of a foreign body in the upper airway is life-threatening and requires immediate removal.

MANAGEMENT

Do *not* intervene if the child can speak, breathe, and is coughing. Perform the following steps if the child is unable to breath or make a sound (American Academy of Pediatrics, 1981):

1. Turn the child's head and place the child's face down over your knees or on the floor. Infants should be placed over the rescuer's forearm.
2. Forcefully give four back blows.
3. If this fails to clear the airway, deliver four chest thrusts rapidly.
4. Repeat these procedures as necessary if there is no response.
5. Transport quickly to health facility if these measures fail.

Do not probe the mouth with fingers unless the foreign body is visualized.

Counseling Caretakers should be taught to follow these precautions with children:

- Cut food into small pieces.
- Keep small objects away from toddlers.
- Remind children to chew slowly and thoroughly.
- Teach children not to laugh or talk while chewing and swallowing.
- Teach children not to run, walk, talk, or play when they have food or small objects in their mouths.

Coma

ASSESSMENT

Coma has numerous causes, including uncontrolled diabetes mellitus, hypoglycemia, the postconvulsive state, electrolyte imbalance, infection of the central nervous system, cerebrovascular accident, head trauma, Reye's syndrome, hypoxia from hypoperfusion or asphyxia, and drug and poison ingestion. The Glasgow Coma Scale (see Figure 28-2) is a simple, generally applicable assessment schema designed to rate both depth and duration of impaired consciousness and coma. That someone is indeed comatose rather than sleeping or malingering may be determined by firm rubbing of the sternum with the examiner's knuckles.

MANAGEMENT

Until the child arrives at a hospital, attentions should be focused on the maintenance of vital bodily functions and prevention of aspiration of vomitus. Utmost care must be taken with the comatose trauma victim to prevent inadvertent injury to the spinal cord. Comatose diabetics may have injectable glucagon on their persons. Its use can only help.

Convulsions

See Chapter 24, Epilepsy.

Epiglottitis

See Chapter 17, The Respiratory System.

	Date						
Time	0 – 24 Hours	Time	Time	Time	Time	Time	Time
Best Motor Response	5 Obeys commands 4 Localizes response 3 Flexor response 2 Extensor posturing 1 No response						
Best Verbal Response	5 Oriented 4 Confused conversation 3 Inappropriate speech 2 Incomprehensible sounds 1 No response						
Eye Opening	4 Spontaneous 3 In response to speech 2 In response to pain 1 No response						

Figure 28-2 "Glasgow Coma Scale" for recording assesment of coma and impaired consciousness. (Adapted from G. Teasdale and B. Jennett, "Assessment of Coma and Impaired Consciousness," *The Lancet* *II*:81–83, July 13, 1974. P. 83.

Fractures

ASSESSMENT

Obtain history about the child's position prior to the injury, circumstances surrounding the injury, source of pain or tenderness, hearing or feeling of bone snap.

Clinical Findings The signs of a fracture include the following:

- Deformities such as angulation, crookedness, shortening or rotation of an extremity or an open wound over a bone
- Pain or tenderness to touch at the site of the suspected fracture
- Swelling and discoloration of the overlying skin due to hemorrhage

Fractures of bones may have threatening aspects. Vertebral fractures may injure the spinal cord, especially when the child is being moved. Basilar skull fractures often result in hemorrhage into the middle ears, which is visible through the tympanic membrane. Parietal fractures may lacerate the middle meningeal artery resulting in intracranial hemorrhage. Rib fractures may perforate the lung or the chest wall, resulting in a pneumothorax. Almost any fracture may produce internal hemorrhage, which is difficult to detect, especially in the thigh.

MANAGEMENT

Until definitive treatment is available, immobilize the injured area, and apply cool compresses to reduce swelling. See this chapter for information on head injuries.

Frostbite

ASSESSMENT

Frostbite is the injury resulting from the freezing of tissue. The affected part will be numb, hard, and blue. Earlobes, nose, cheeks, hands, and feet are the areas most likely to suffer frostbite. Early signs of frostbite are shivering, loss of flexibility, dull ache, numbness, and low body temperature. Progressive signs are drowsiness, apathy, loss of consciousness, cold, cyanotic, or mottled skin, and hard and inflexible skin and muscle. Advanced frostbite is painless.

Classification and Findings

First degree (frostnip): erythematous skin, edema of the affected part, absent blister formation, tissue damage insignificant

Second degree: formation of blister and bulla

Third degree: necrosis of the epidermis, dermis, and subcutaneous tissues without loss of the body part

Fourth degree: complete necrosis with gangrene and loss of body part

MANAGEMENT

"Frost nip" (Mild Skin Blanching) Rewarm with a warm hand, blow through cupped hands, or place frost-nipped fingers in the armpit.

Deep Frostbite Rapidly rewarm the frostbitten areas in warm water bath with temperature between 37.8 to 40.6°C (100° to 104.9°F). Loosen clothing. Avoid rubbing the cold-injured part with the hands or with snow to prevent damaging thawing tissue irreparably. Do not place the limb over a fire or a hot radiator. If there is a possibility that thawing could be followed by refreezing, do not thaw the frozen part to avoid further loss of tissue. Elevate affected part. Drink warm beverages.

Head Injury

ASSESSMENT

There are three types of head injuries:

- Concussion is the most common type of serious head injury. It is characterized by a transient loss of consciousness, amnesia for the event, and no structural brain damage.
- Contusion is a severe head injury in which there is structural damage to the brain including hemorrhage and swelling of the brain tissue. The immediate neurologic deficit depends on the area of the brain involved. Seizures may occur acutely or from residual damage after healing is complete.
- Intracranial hemorrhage is an accumulation of blood within the cranium. It may result from a seemingly insignificant head injury and may occur several weeks after the initial insult. Signs of intracranial hemorrhage include lethargy progressing to coma, focal neurologic deficits, pupillary dilation, intractable headache, nausea, emesis, bradycardia, hypertension, and even cardiorespiratory failure. Rapid onset of symptoms within hours to sev-

eral days post injury is indicative of acute epidural hemorrhage. Slow onset of symptoms indicates chronic subdural hemorrhage.

Classification of Head Injuries by Symptoms (Lanros, 1983)

Mild: hits head, cries a few moments, and resumes normal activity. No loss of consciousness, no vomiting or change of color. May complain of a mild headache.

Moderate: brief loss of consciousness and return to normal alert state. Decreased level of consciousness for some time and the child needs rousing. One or two episodes of vomiting shortly after the injury. The child needs to be seen immediately if any of the following occur within the next 48 hours: persistent vomiting, unequal pupil size, excess drowsiness or lethargy, weakness of an arm or leg, continuous crying, change of color from normal to pale.

Severe: immediate hospitalization is indicated for any of the following signs: loss of consciousness and remains so, persistent vomiting, convulsions, irregular respirations, pale color, bleeding from the external ear canal (basal skull fracture), worsening of any of the symptoms of moderate head injury.

History Information to be obtained includes the following:

1. The child's age
2. What happened and exactly how it happened
3. The nature of the impact (Was it a massive force such as a moving vehicle or a fall from a considerable height?)
4. The child's behavior since the injury
5. States of consciousness since the injury
6. Presence of a neurologic condition that may have contributed to the injury

Clinical Evaluation Consistent, repeated observation is the key to establishing the neurologic status of the child and determining the progress of the child's condition. Table 28-4 highlights the observations to be made at regular intervals and lists the abnormal responses.

Radiology Whether or not to obtain skull X-rays is a diagnostic dilemma. Absence of radiographically visible fracture does not

Table 28-4
Clinical Evaluation of a Head Injury

Observation	Abnormal Response
Physical examination of the head	Swelling, depression, crepitus, scalp injury, bleeding
Level of consciousness	I. Alert; II. Arousable; III. Unarousable, normal reflexes; IV. Abnormal reflexes; V. No reflexes
Cardiovascular system	↑ Blood pressure, persistent bradycardia (below 60), Cheyne-Stokes respirations, central neurogenic hyperventilation (rapid, deep, regular), apnea
Pupillary response	Asymmetry of pupils, dilation of pupils
Optic disks	Retinal hemorrhage, papilledema (unusual before 6 hours)
Eye movements	No spontaneous movements in all fields of gaze
Tympanic membranes	Presence of blood
Spinal cord integrity	Babinski sign, altered sensation, increased or decreased deep tendon reflexes

preclude a severe brain injury. Indications for obtaining a skull X-ray include a palpable deformity, a significant open scalp wound, a suspicion of the presence of other injuries in addition to the head injury, especially if abuse is suspected, and uncertainty about the severity of the injury.

MANAGEMENT

Superficial Scalp Injuries Bring the edges together and apply pressure if the skull is not depressed. Raise the head and shoulders if possible. Do not bend the neck since a fracture may be present. Gently cover the wound with a snug, preferably sterile dressing.

Suspected Brain Injury Ensure respiration and circulation. Maintain the child in the position in which found. Promptly obtain medical assistance, and request a spinal splint. Identify other injuries. Observe and record the extent and duration of unconsciousness. Do not give fluids by mouth. Keep the child warm. Hospital admission for observation and treatment is indicated for significant injury, including concussion.

Home Observation   The decision to observe the child at home will be influenced by all the following (Shillito, 1977):

1. Emesis less than three times immediately after injury
2. Short duration to no loss of consciousness
3. Stability of vital signs
4. Stability or improvement of mental status and alertness
5. Negative neurologic examination
6. Responsive pupillary reaction
7. No evidence of penetrating skull injury, spinal fluid otorrhea or rhinorrhea, blood behind the ear drums, or bleeding from the external canals
8. Competency of parents

COUNSELING   If the decision is made to follow the child at home, parents are given specific written instructions on the danger signals for which to observe. Rapid transportation to the hospital must be assured in anticipation of complications. An appointment to return is scheduled. For preventive counseling tips, see Table 5-22 and Table 6-9.

DANGER SIGNS   Parents are instructed to return the child immediately to the health care facility if any of the following occur (Shillito, 1977):

1. Excessive drowsiness (initially test at 15-minute intervals arousing the child by methods oridinarily used to awaken from a deep sleep)
2. Changes in vital signs: slowing of pulse, irregular respirations with short periods of apnea, increasing temperature
3. Persistent vomiting
4. Weakness on one side, limping
5. Worsening headache
6. Double vision
7. Difficulty speaking
8. Pupillary constriction or dilation or inequality

9. Convulsion

10. Appearance or progression of swelling beneath the scalp

Hemorrhage

ASSESSMENT

Hemorrhage is significant if more than 20 percent of the total circulating blood volume (approximately 5 liters for the average adult male) is lost internally or externally (see this chapter, Fractures). The signs and symptoms of massive bleeding are extreme paleness, rapid and weak pulse, thirst, restlessness, possibly tenderness over the affected area, and shock. Signs of internal bleeding are as follows:

• Bright red blood in the urine (acute bleeding, infection, post trauma)

• Copious amount of bright red blood in the stools (lower bowel)

• Pink, foamy tinges of blood in vomitus (lung)

• Severe vaginal bleeding (menstrual bleeding, miscarriage, ruptured tubal pregnancy)

• Smokey appearance to the urine (bladder, kidneys, or urethra)

• Tarry stools (upper regions of the colon and small intestine)

MANAGEMENT

It is important to remember that a person can bleed to death in seconds. Immediate transport to a health facility is indicated. Institute measures to control bleeding. There are five techniques to control bleeding: direct pressure, elevation, pressure points, splinting, and tourniquet (Judd and Ponsell, 1982).

Direct Pressure   Blood takes approximately 5 to 10 minutes to clot, so the applied pressure must be maintained until the body's natural clotting system takes effect. Position your hand directly over the injured site using a suitable cloth (e.g., gauze pads, handkerchief). A bandage can also be used to apply direct pressure, and enables the nurse practitioner to institute other care measures.

Elevation   This technique in conjunction with direct pressure is used for hemorrhaging from an extremity which is not fractured. Do not elevate an extremity if a fracture is suspected.

Pressure Points   If bleeding is uncontrolled by direct pressure and elevation, apply pressure to a pressure point (brachial or femoral) proximal to the injury. The arterial walls are pressed against the bone to diminish the blood flow to the extremity sufficiently to enable direct pressure and the body's clotting system to take effect.

Splinting   Early splinting of a fracture controls bleeding by stabilizing the broken bone ends and decreasing soft tissue damage.

Tourniquet   This method should be used *only* when all other techniques fail. It is rarely needed. If it is necessary, apply the tourniquet as far distally as possible for no longer than 15 minutes at a time.

Heat Stroke (Hyperpyrexia)

ASSSESSMENT

Heat stroke is an immediate life-threatening problem due to an accumulation of body heat and a disturbance of the sweating mechanism. It results in generalized cellular damage to the central nervous system, liver, kidneys, and the clotting mechanism.

Clinical findings include temperature of 40.5 to 41°C (104.9 to 105.8°F), profuse sweating (skin may be hot and dry), convulsions (about 60 percent of the cases), delirium to coma, ataxia, incontinence, hypotension, rapid pulse, shock, oliguria or renal failure, vomiting, diarrhea, headaches, dizziness, and abdominal pain.

MANAGEMENT

Therapy   Remove all clothing and rapidly cool the child by continuous sponging on the bare skin with cool water or immersing the child in cool water (do not add ice) until the temperature is sufficiently lowered (39°C [102.2°F]). Do not bring the temperature below 39°C. Carefully avoid shivering as this produces heat. Obtain medical assistance. Treat shock (see this chapter). Administer oxygen. Massage extremities to maintain peripheral circulation.

Prevention Advise parents about the following precautions:

1. During exercise cool off, rest, and drink fluids. Do not exercise in heavy-weight clothing.
2. During hot spells and when the humidity index exceeds 87 reduce activity. The humidity index is available from the local weather bureau.
3. During hot weather never leave the child alone in a car with inadequate ventilation, and ensure adequate hydration on car trips in hot weather also.
4. During hot weather slowly acclimate the body to the increased heat by gradually increasing periods of work or exercise.
5. During illnesses, particularly gastrointestinal illnesses, avoid heavy activity.

Infections

Infections of several types may present as medical emergencies. More complete discussion will be found in Chapter 27, Infectious Disease. Septic shock may result from infection with enteric bacteria, *Streptococcus pneumoniae, Streptococcus viridans,* usually through the mediation of endotoxins. Children without spleens, including those with sickle cell disease, are at a high risk for *S. pneumoniae* and sepsis. Meningitis may present as intractable headache, coma, or shock. It may present atypically without fever, nuchal rigidity, or even without obvious abnormality of the cerebrospinal fluid.

Near Drowning

ASSESSMENT

Near drowning in fresh or salt water presents many of the same problems in emergency management. Deaths are caused by asphyxia and fluid aspiration or asphyxia and laryngospasm. Electrolyte concentrations are of little importance at the site of the accident and compensation usually occurs rapidly. For more information the reader is referred to standard pediatric texts.

MANAGEMENT

The cornerstone of emergency treatment is immediate, persistent cardiopulmonary resuscitation. Vomitus is often present in the hypopharynx, and the rescuer should search for it. Mouth-to-mouth resuscitation may begin in the water, especially if the rescuer has a flotation device. External chest compression should not be attempted in the water unless the rescuer has had special training. Artificial resuscitation should be initiated as soon as possible. Hypothermia should be rapidly corrected. Emergency cricothyroidotomy may be necessary if laryngospasm persists. Victims who recover well after a near-drowning episode should be seen by a physician due to the potential for complications such as pneumonia. See also this chapter, Choking, Cardiac Arrest, and Cardiopulmonary Resuscitation. For water safety information and preventive counseling tips, see Table 6-9, and Chapter 7, Drowning.

Resource Information Water safety information can be obtained from these sources:

1. Public Enquiries, National Center for Urban Industrial Health, 222 East Central Parkway, Cincinnati, OH 45202.
2. American Red Cross Association: local chapter.

Poisoning: Ingestion, Inhalation, Contact

ASSESSMENT

Poisoning may result from ingestion, inhalation, or contact. It should be considered whenever a child presents with otherwise inexplicable symptoms.

Epidemiology Poisonings are complicated episodes involving a victim, a poison, and a location. The victim is most often a child under 5 years of age with a peak incidence at 2 years of age. The poison (a drug, home remedy, or household product) is often not in its usual place, occasionally not in the original container, or insecurely stored. Fifty percent of poisonings occur in the kitchen, 20 percent in the bathroom, and 10 percent in the bedroom. The ingestion often occurs when the environment is in upheaval due to cleaning, repairing, or moving or because the family is under stress (Pascoe and Grossman, 1977).

The Unknown Poison   Poisoning is considered when the following conditions exist (Mofenson and Greensher, 1974):

- Abrupt onset of illness
- Child is between 1 to 4 years of age
- Previous history of ingestion
- Involvement of several organ systems which are inconsistent with a specific disease entity

When the poison is unknown the health care provider must depend on the child's signs and symptoms (odors, pupil evaluation, and skin evaluation are especially helpful) and laboratory evaluation to provide the clues to the poisonous agents.

To help in the recognition of emergency signs and symptoms, the reader is referred to Table 28-5 and to Table 28-6, which list the combination of signs and symptoms (toxidromes) in children that are commonly encountered and the agents that can reproduce them.

MANAGEMENT

Swift, effective management requires knowledge of pharmacologic principles of toxicology and handy resource information. A poison ingestion requires medical management. Initial ambulatory management information is presented here. For in-depth information, the reader is referred to reference texts listed under Resource Information.

Ipecac   Ipecac should be part of every family's first-aid kit. The nurse practitioner should teach parents when and how to use syrup of ipecac.

If ipecac is necessary to induce vomiting, give the following instructions:

- Give 15 ml of syrup of ipecac.
- Give 6 to 8 oz of water.
- Keep the child active.

Table 28-5

Emergency Symptoms and Signs Which May be Encountered in a Poisoning

ABDOMINAL COLIC
Black widow spider bite
Heavy metals
Narcotic depressant withdrawal

ATAXIA
Alcohol
Barbiturates
Bromides
Carbon monoxide
Diphenylhydantoin
Hallucinogens
Heavy metals
Organic solvents
Tranquilizers

BREATH ODOR
Acetone: acetone, alcohol (methyl, isopropyl), phenol, salicylates
Alcohol: alcohol (ethyl)
Bitter almonds: cyanide
Coal gas: carbon monoxide
Garlic: arsenic, phosphorus, organic phosphate insecticides, thallium
Oil of wintergreen: methyl salicylate

MOUTH
Salivation
Arsenic
Corrosives
Mercury
Mushrooms
Organic phosphate insecticides
Thallium

OLIGURIA-ANURIA
Carbon tetrachloride
Ethylene glycol
Heavy metals
Hemolytic poisons (naphthalene, plants)
Methanol
Mushrooms
Oxalates
Petroleum distillates
Solvents

PARALYSIS
Botulism
Heavy metals

Dryness
Atropine
Amphetamines
Antihistamines
Narcotic depressants

Petroleum: petroleum distillates
Violets: turpentine

COMA AND DROWSINESS

Alcohol—ethyl
Antihistamines
Barbiturates and other hypnotics
Carbon monoxide
Narcotic depressants (opiates)
Salicylates
Tranquilizers

CONVULSIONS AND MUSCLE TWITCHING

Alcohol
Amphetamines
Antihistamines
Boric acid
Camphor
Chlorinated hydrocarbon insecticides (DDT)
Cyanide
Lead
Organic phosphate insecticides
Plants (lily-of-the-valley, azalea, iris, water hemlock)
Salicylates
Strychnine
Withdrawal from barbiturates, benzodiazepine (Valium, Librium), meprobamate

Plants (coniine in poison hemlock)
Triorthocresyl phosphate

PULSE RATE

Slow
Digitalis
Lily-of-the-valley
Narcotic depressants

PUPILS

Pinpoint
Mushrooms (muscarine type)
Narcotic depressants (opiates)
Organic phosphate insecticides
Nystagmus on Lateral Gaze
Barbiturates
Minor tranquilizers (meprobamate, benzodiazepine)

Rapid
Alcohol
Amphetamines
Atropine
Ephedrine

Dilated
Amphetamines
Antihistamines
Atropine
Barbiturates (coma)
Cocaine
Ephedrine
LSD
Methanol
Withdrawal-narcotic depressants

Continued on next page

Table 28-5 *(Continued)*

RESPIRATORY ALTERATIONS		*SKIN COLOR*		
Rapid	*Slow or Depressed*	*Jaundice* (hepatic or hemolytic)	*Cyanosis*	*Red Flush*
Amphetamines	Alcohol	Aniline	Aniline dyes	Alcohol
Barbiturates (early)	Barbiturates (late)	Arsenic	Carbon monoxide	Antihistamines
Carbon monoxide	Narcotic depressants (opiates)	Carbon tetrachloride	Cyanide	Atropine
Methanol	Tranquilizers	Castor bean	Nitrites	Boric acid
Petroleum distillates		Fava bean	Strychnine	Carbon monoxide
Salicylates		Mushroom		Nitrites
Wheezing and Pulmonary Edema	*Paralysis*	Naphthalene		
Mushrooms (muscarine type)	Organic phosphate insecticides	Yellow phosphorus		
Narcotic depressants (opiates)	Botulism	*VIOLENT EMESIS OFTEN WITH HEMATEMESIS*		
Organic phosphate insecticides		Aminophylline		
Petroleum distillates		Bacterial food poisoning		
		Boric acid		
		Corrosives		
		Fluoride		
		Heavy metals		
		Phenol		
		Salicylates		

Source: Adapted with permission from H. Mofenson and J. Greensher, "The Unknown Poison," *Pediatrics 54*:340–341, September 1974. Copyright © 1974, American Academy of Pediatrics.

Table 28-6
Diagnosis by Toxidromes

Poison	Toxidrome
Amphetamines	Excessive activity, argumentativeness, tremors, headache, diarrhea, dry mouth with foul odor, sweating, tachycardia, arrhythmia, dilated pupils
Aspirin	Vomiting, hyperpnea, fever
Atropine-like agents (LSD, STP, scopolamine)	Agitation, hallucinations, dilated pupils, beet-red color, dry skin, fever
Barbiturates and tranquilizers	Slurred speech, nystagmus, slightly constricted pupils, skin vesicles, ataxia, sleepiness, coma
Cyanide (insecticides, silver polish, seeds of apple, peach, apricot, plum, cherry)	Silver polish (bitter almonds) odor; GI, CNS, and respiratory symptoms; coma, convulsions, abnormal ECG, bradycardia, heart block, dilated pupils, protrusion of eyes
Heroin	Coma, depressed respirations, pinpoint pupils
Imipramine (tricyclate antidepressants)	Coma, convulsions, cardiac arrhythmias
Organic phosphates	Pinpoint pupils, salivation, lacrimation, pulmonary congestion, abdominal cramps
Phenothiazine	Uncoordinated spasmodic movements, tremor, ataxia, postural hypotension, rhythmic body movements

• Closely monitor the child so the proper position is maintained when vomiting occurs and the risk of aspiration is minimized.
• Repeat the 15 ml dose of ipecac if vomiting does not occur in 15 to 20 minutes.

Telephone It is usually the first contact in case of possible poisoning involving a child under 5 years of age. The pertinent history must be obtained quickly to identify the ingested substance and to determine its potential toxicity so initial management can be quickly initiated and a decision made about whether or not the child should be seen. The steps are:

1. Obtain the following information and write it down:
   - Caller's name, address, and telephone number
   - Child's age, weight, and condition
   - Name of ingested substance if known (look at the label) or any identifying information (prescribing physician, pharmacy)
   - Amount ingested
   - Time of ingestion

2. Reassure the caller if the ingested substance is nontoxic. Refer to Table 28-7 for representative nontoxic commercial products.

3. If the toxicity is unknown, call the nearest Poison Control Center immediately (see this chapter, Poison Control Information) and consult a toxicology text. See references listed under Resource Information, this section.

4. If poison is inhaled, carry the child to fresh air.

5. If poison is on the skin, remove the clothing and flood the involved parts with water. Wash with soapy water and soft washcloth or sponge and rinse thoroughly.

6. If poison is in the eye, irrigate the eye with plain water immediately from a glass or pitcher held 3 to 4 inches from the eye for 15 to 20 minutes or hold the head back over the sink and direct a gentle stream of water into the eye from the water tap. Transport the child for ophthalmologic examination.

7. If the poison is ingested, administer milk or water immediately if a strong acid or alkaline agent has been ingested.

8. Use a toxicity rating scheme to aid in a decision to induce vomiting, lavaging, or instituting a specific treatment. Refer to Table 28-7 for a listing of the representative commercial products in each toxicity class and to Table 28-8 for a toxicity rating chart. Remove the gastric contents for toxicity ratings greater than two, unless a contraindication exists. Contraindications for the induction of emesis are:
   - A caustic substance (i.e., lye, acid)
   - A comatose or convulsing child

- Mineral seal oil or signal oil (found in furniture or oil polishes)
- Strychnine (may induce convulsions)

9. If treatment requires induction of emesis instruct the caller to induce vomiting, give ipecac. See above, Ipecac, for instructions.

   - If ipecac is unavailable, have the child drink a glass of water and then insert a finger down the throat or gently tickle the back of the throat with a spoon or similar blunt object. Do not use salt water because fatal salt poisoning can occur.

10. Instruct the caller to bring the child, the container with the poisonous agent, and any vomitus to the closest emergency facility.

Health Care Facility Management of ingestion at a health care facility requires prompt efforts to retard absorption. Gastric lavage is more effective than emesis and protects the airway in a comatose, convulsing patient. A specific antidote is given if known (see Table 28-9); otherwise, activated charcoal should be given, except with strong acids and strong alkali. A thin, pasty solution is prepared with 1 to 2 tablespoons of any USP activated charcoal product in 6 to 8 oz of water. *Caution:* activated charcoal binds ipecac, so it is recommended that emesis with ipecac precede administration of activated charcoal (Bayer and Rumack, 1983). Cathartics are used to speed evacuation of that portion of the toxin that has not been removed by emesis or lavage.

Specific Poisonous Agents

COMMON POISONS The clinical findings and management of specific poisons are summarized in Table 28-10. For a discussion of lead poisoning, the reader is referred to Chapter 24, The Neuromuscular System.

Follow-up If transportation to a hospital is not indicated, which is most of the time, it is essential to call the parent at 1 and 4 hours after ingestion to assess the child's progress. If the toxin is unknown and the child is gradually becoming comatose, transportation to the hospital is indicated. A follow-up phone call to begin

Table 28-7
Representative Commercial Products in Each Toxicity Class

Class 1
(Practically Nontoxic)
Abrasives
Candies
Candles
Chalk
Cosmetics (especially baby
  products, lipstick, rouge, eye
  makeup)
Crayons (marked AP or CP)
Fish bowl additives
Foods
Lead pencils
Modeling clay
Mucilage and pastes
Paint (latex)
Pure soaps
Putty
Sweetening agents (saccharin)
Toothpaste

Class 2
(Slightly Toxic)
Adhesives (most)
Ballpoint pen inks
Bleaches (less than 6% Na
  hypochlorite)
Bubble bath soaps (detergents)
Caps (toy pistol)
Cigarettes or cigars (tobacco)
Contraceptive pills
Cosmetics (most) (colognes,
  perfumes)
Dehumidifying packets
Deodorants
Deodorizers (spray and
  refrigerator)
Detergents (most—not electric
  dishwasher)
Fabric softeners
Incense

Inks (most)
Iodophil disinfectant
Lubricants (most)
Lubricating oils
Matches (book)
Mineral oil
Paint—indoor (less than 1% lead)
Phenolphthalein laxatives (Ex-Lax)
Polaroid picture coating fluids
Polishes (porcelain, some furniture)
Porous tip ink markers (felt tip
  markers)
Shampoos
Shaving creams
Soap products
Thermometer mercury
Vitamins with or without fluoride

Class 3
(Moderately Toxic)
Adhesives (rubber, linoleum,
  roofing, plastic cement)
Agricultural chemicals (many)
Antifreeze
Bleach (oxalate type and greater
  than 6% Na hypochlorite)
Brake fluids
Cleaners (window, stain removers)
Cosmetics (depilatories, permanent
  wave neutralizers, nail polish
  removers and enamel)
Disinfectants (bathroom, toilet,
  garbage can)
Indelible inks
Lighter fuels
Mothballs (most)
Motor fuels
Polishes (metal, wood, shoe, stove)
Preservatives (brush, canvas, roof)
Stain removers

Continued on next page

Table 28-7 (Continued)

Class 4 (Very Toxic)	Class 5 (Extremely Toxic)

Agricultural chemicals (many)
Ammonia
Bleach—commercial
Degreasers (metal, etc.)
Depilatories (some)
Dishwasher granules—electric
Disinfectants (acid, alkali, halogen,
   pine oil, and phenolic types)
Drain cleaners (some)
Dry cleaner solvents (some)
Fire extinguisher liquid
Leather dyes
Moth repellents (naphthalene)
Petroleum products (most)
Radiator cleaners
Rust removers
	Drain and sewer cleaners (caustics)
	Insecticides (some)
	Fireplace flame colors (blues and
	   greens)
	Fungicides (some)
	Herbicides (some)
	Rodenticides (some)
	
	Class 6
	(Super Toxic)
	Fungicides ⎫
	Herbicides ⎬ a few
	Insecticides ⎭
	Rodenticides
	Botanicals (nicotine, strychnine)
	Inorganic chemicals (cyanide,
	   phosphorus, arsenic, thallium,
	   fluoride)

Source: Reprinted with permission from H. Mofenson and J. Greensher, "The Unknown Poison," *Pediatrics* 54:338, September 1974. Copyright © 1974, American Academy of Pediatrics.

poison prevention education is important if the child is at home or in the hospital (Rumack and Peterson, 1980).

Prevention of Poisoning It is the responsibility of adults to make certain that children are not exposed to potentially toxic substances. Remind parents to safetyproof the household. The following are useful suggestions:

• Avoid calling medicine "candy."
• Keep chemicals in original containers.
• Keep the phone number of the primary care provider, Poison Center, hospital, police department, and fire department or emergency medical services system near the phone.
• Read labels on products and heed warnings.
• Separate food from cleaning products.
• Store household cleansers, medicines, garage products, and insecticides beyond the reach of children. If possible, lock them.

Table 28-8

Definitions of Toxicity Rating: Toxicity Rating Chart

Signal Word[a]	Toxicity Rating or Class	Probable LETHAL DOSE (human) for 70-kg Man (150 lb)
No label	1 Practically nontoxic	Above 15 gm/kg—more than 1 qt
No label	2 Slightly toxic	5 to 15 gm/kg—between 1 pt and 1 qt
Caution	3 Moderately toxic	0.5 to 5 gm/kg—between 1 oz and 1 pt (or 1 lb)
Warning	4 Very toxic	50 to 500 mg/kg—between 1 tsp and 1 oz
Danger Poison	5 Extremely toxic	5 to 50 mg/kg—between 7 drops and 1 tsp
Danger Poison	6 Super toxic	Under 5 mg/kg—a taste (less than 7 drops)

Source: Reprinted with permission from H. Mofenson and J. Greensher, "The Unknown Poison," *Pediatrics 54:*337, September 1974. Copyright © 1974, American Academy of Pediatrics.

[a]Based on Federal Insecticide, Fungicide and Rodenticide Act of 1947.

Table 28-9
Specific Antidotes

Poison	Antidote
Carbon monoxide	Oxygen
Cocaine	Propranolol
Cyanide	Cyanide poison kit (contains amyl nitrite, sodium nitrite, sodium thiosulfate); available from American Cyanamid Company and Eli Lilly and Company
Iron	Deferoxamine
Lead	EDTA
Methanol, ethylene glycol	Ethanol
Methemoglobin-producing agents (nitrates, nitrites, phenacetin)	Methylene blue
Narcotics	Naloxone hydrochloride (Narcan) 0.01 mg/kg IV
Organophosphates	Atropine sulfate Pralidoxime chloride (Protopam)
Phenothiazines	Diphenhydramine
Tricyclic antidepressants, anticholinergics	Physostigmine

For specific developmental preventive counseling tips, see Table 5-22 and Table 6-9.

Resource Information

Reference Texts

Arena, J. *Poisoning: Toxicology, Symptoms, Treatment.* 4th ed. Springfield, IL: Charles C Thomas, 1979.

Driesbach, R. H. *Handbook of Poisonings.* 11th ed. Los Altos, CA: Lange Medical Publishers, 1983.

Gosselin, R. and H. Smith. *Clinical Toxicology of Commercial Products.* 4th ed. Baltimore: Williams & Wilkins, 1976. (Toxicity ratings are listed.)

Handbook of Common Poisonings in Children. U.S. Department of Health, Education, and Welfare, Public Health Service, 5600 Fishers Lane, Rockville, MD 20857, HEW Publ. No. (FDA) 76-7004, 1976. $1.50.

Table 28-10
Common Poisonings

Poison	Symptoms	Treatment	Comments
Caustics (lye in washing powders, drainpipe cleaners, paint removers, Clinitest tablets)	Burning pain from mouth to stomach, difficulty swallowing, edema of mucous membranes, bloody vomitus, weak, rapid pulse, increased respirations	Emesis is not induced. Preferably milk or water is given. Olive oil may ease the pain. Esophagoscopy is indicated. Corticosteroids may be given to reduce inflammation and decrease scar tissue formation	
Petroleum distillates (kerosene, mineral seal oil, charcoal igniting fluid, turpentine, gasoline, naphtha, fuel oils, lubricating oils)	*Large ingestions:* pulmonary symptoms (cough, respiratory distress, pulmonary edema, cyanosis), central nervous system symptoms (irritability, lethargy progressing to coma, convulsions)	*Small ingestions:* emesis is not induced. *Large ingestions:* emesis is indicated in an alert child. Antibiotics are indicated in the treatment of secondary bacterial infections. Epinephrine is contraindicated due to cardiac sensitivity.	Emesis is indicated in large ingestions because toxic central nervous system or cardiac effects may be produced.

Iron	Vomiting, epigastric pain, diarrhea, weak, rapid pulse, pallor, cyanosis, coma, respiratory depression, and massive hemorrhage	Emesis is induced with ipecac syrup. Gastric lavage is also indicated using a concentrated solution of sodium bicarbonate, 5% disodium phosphate, or milk. Lab studies of blood levels are done. Deferoxamine may also be used.	Lethal dose is about 40 mg/kg of iron. Mortality is 30–50%.
Salicylates (aspirin, methyl salicylate, oil of wintergreen)	Rapid, deep breathing; vomiting; extreme thirst; profuse sweating; fever; confusion; severe circulatory collapse; oliguria or anuria; hemorrhage	Emesis or gastric lavage is performed immediately. Activated charcoal is used. Severe poisonings will require IV fluids with careful monitoring of urine output, metabolic and electrolytes status, and glucose.	Salicylates can be detected in urine using Phenistix or Nitrazine paper. Potential fatal serum levels are 100–150 mg/100 ml. One tsp of methyl salicylate equals 21 five-grain aspirin tablets.

1147

Poison Control Information

1. Food and Drug Administration, Office of Drugs, Poison Control Branch, 5600 Fishers Lane, Rockville, Maryland 20857, 301-443-6260. Directory of United States Poison Control Centers and Services can be obtained from this office.
2. *Poisindex*, Denver, CO 80204. The *Poisindex* outlines the management of certain poisons on paper and microfiche.
3. Certified Regional Poison Control Centers, January 1983. The American Association of Poison Control Centers has certified the following regional centers. For more information about the American Association of Poison Control Centers, contact Anthony S. Manoguerra, Pharm. D., Director, Professional Services, San Diego Regional Poison Center, University of California Medical Center, 225 Dickinson Street, San Diego, CA 92103, 619-294-3666.

Arizona Poison Control System
College of Pharmacy
University of Arizona
Tucson, AZ 85724
Service: 916-626-6016
        800-852-7221 (Arizona)
Administration: 602-626-7899
Theodore Tong, Pharm. D., Director

Regional Poison Center
University of California Davis Medical Center
2315 Stockton Blvd.
Sacramento, CA 95817
Service: 916-453-3692
        800-852-7221 (No. Calif.)
Administration: 916-453-3414
Judith Alsop, Pharm. D., Coordinator

San Diego Regional Poison Center
University of California Medical Center
225 Dickinson St.
San Diego, CA 92103
Service: 619-294-6000
Administration: 619-294-3666
Anthony S. Manoguerra, Pharm. D., Director, Professional Services

San Francisco Bay Area Regional Poison Control Center
San Francisco General Hospital Medical Center
1001 Potrero Avenue
San Francisco, CA 94110

Service: 415-666-2845
  800-792-0720 (No. Calif.)
Administration: 415-821-8324
Gerald Joe, Pharm. D., Acting Program Director
Charles Becker, M.D., Medical Director

Rocky Mountain Poison Center
Denver General Hospital
West 8th and Cherokee
Denver, CO 80204
Service: 303-629-1123
  800-525-5042 (Montana)
  800-332-3073 (Colorado)
Administration: 303-893-7774
Barry H. Rumack, M.D., Director

National Capital Poison Center
Georgetown University Hospital
3800 Reservoir Rd. NW
Washington, D.C. 20007
Service: 202-625-3333
Administration: 202-625-6073
Toby Litovitz, M.D., Director

Georgia Poison Control Center
P.O. Box 26066
80 Butler St. SE
Atlanta, GA 30335
Service: 404-588-4400
  800-282-5846
  404-525-3323 (Deaf-only TTY line)
Albert P. Rauber, M.D., Director

St. John's Hospital Regional Poison Resource Center
800 East Carpenter Street
Springfield, IL 62769
Service: 217-753-3330
  800-252-2022 (Illinois)
Administration: 217-544-6464, ext. 4615 (Medical Director)
David Kerwin, R.N., Supervisor

Indiana Poison Center
1001 West 10th St.
Indianapolis, IN 46202
Service: 317-630-7351
  800-382-9097 (Indiana)
Administration: 317-630-6382
James B. Mowry, Pharm. D., Director

Poison Control Center
University of Iowa Hospitals and Clinics
c/o Pharmacy Department
Newton Road
Iowa City, IA 52242

Service: 319-356-2922
  800-272-6477 (Iowa)
Administration: 319-356-2922
Robert Dick, M.S., Director

Maryland Poison Center
University of Maryland School of Pharmacy
636 W. Lombard Street
Baltimore, MD 21201
Service: 301-528-7701
  800-492-2414 (Maryland)
Administration: 301-528-7604

Massachusetts Poison Control System
300 Longwood Avenue
Boston, MA 02115
Service: 617-232-2120
  800-682-9211 (Massachusetts)
Administration: 617-735-6607
Frederick H. Lovejoy, M.D., Director

Poison Control Center
Children's Hospital of Michigan
3901 Beaubien Blvd.
Detroit, MI 48201
Service: 313-494-5711
  800-462-6642 (Michigan)
  800-572-1655 (Michigan)
Administration: 313-494-5335
Regine A. Aronow, M.D., Director

Western Michigan Poison Center
1840 Wealthy, SE
Grand Rapids, MI 49506
Service: 616-774-7854
  800-632-2727 (Michigan)
Administration: 616-774-7851
Walter D. Meester, M.D., Ph.D., Director

Hennepin Poison Center
701 Park Avenue
Minneapolis, MN 55415
Service: 612-347-3141
Administration: 612-347-3144
Edward P. Krenzelok, Pharm. D., Director

Poison Control Center
The Children's Mercy Hospital
24th and Gillham Rd.
Kansas City, MO 64108
Service: 816-234-3000
Administration: 816-234-3664
George W. Wise, M.D., Director

CGMH St. Louis Regional Poison Center
Cardinal Glennon Memorial Hospital for Children

1465 South Grand Blvd.
St. Louis, MO 63104
Service: 314-772-5200
Administration: 314-772-8300
Robert W. Jaeger, B.S. Pharm., Associate Director

Omaha Regional Poison Control Center
Children's Memorial Hospital
8301 Dodge Street
Omaha, NE 69114
Service: 402-390-5400
     800-642-9999 (Nebraska)
     800-228-9515 (Iowa and surrounding NE)
Administration: 402-390-5429 (Medical Director)
     402-490-5434 (Coordinator)
Matilda McIntire, M.D., Medical Director

New Mexico Poison, Drug Information and Medical Crisis Center
University of New Mexico
Albuquerque, NM 87131
Service: 505-843-2551
     800-432-6866 (New Mexico)
Administration: 505-277-4261
William G. Troutman, Pharm. D., Director

Long Island Regional Poison Control Center
Nassau County Medical Center
2201 Hempstead Turnpike
East Meadow, NY 11554
Service: 516-542-2323
Administration: 516-542-3909
Howard C. Mofenson, M.D., Director

New York City Poison Control Center
Department of Health, Bureau of Laboratories
455 First Avenue
New York, NY 10016
Service: 212-340-4494
     212-764-7667
Administration: 212-340-4497
Dr. Bernard Davidow, Director

Finger Lakes Regional Poison Control Center
P.O. Box 651
University of Rochester Medical Center
Rochester, NY 14642
Service: 716-275-5151
Administration: 716-275-2972
Ruth A. Lawrence, M.D., Medical Director

Texas State Poison Center
The University of Texas Medical Branch
Galveston, TX 77550

Service: 713-765-1420 (Galveston)
713-654-1701 (Houston)
800-392-8548 (Texas)
Administration: 713-765-3332
Michael D. Ellis, M.S., Director

Intermountain Regional Poison Control Center
50 North Medical Drive
Salt Lake City, UT 84132
Service: 801-581-2151
800-662-0062 (Utah)
Administration: 801-581-7504
Joseph C. Veltri, Pharm. D., Director

Seattle Poison Control Center
Children's Orthopedic Hospital and Medical Center
P.O. Box C-5371
Seattle, WA 98105
Service: 206-634-5252
Administration: 206-634-5252
Stephen R. Bobbink, R.Ph., Supervisor

Kentucky Regional Poison Center of Kosair Children's Hospital
NKC, Inc.
P.O. Box 35070
Louisville, KY 40232
Service: 502-562-7278
Administration: 502-562-7278
George C. Rodgers, M.D., Ph.D., Medical Director

4. Local poison control information center: call directory assistance.

Poisoning: Plant

ASSESSMENT

The common house and garden plants that cause poisonings are listed in Table 28-11.

MANAGEMENT

Treatment of plant poisonings is difficult due to the problems in plant identification and inadequate experience with plant toxicity. Plant ingestions should be considered as potentially toxic, and vomiting should be induced even prior to identification of the plant. References that are useful in plant identification and toxicity are listed in Resource Information at the end of this section. A local expert in plant identification is a valuable community resource.

Prevention Instruct parents about these practical rules (*The Sinister Garden*, 1966):

• Eat only properly prepared foods from well-known sources.
• Learn to identify the poisonous plants in your neighborhood and home.
• Never chew on jewelry made from imported seeds or beans.
• Never eat any part of an unknown plant.
• Never use anything prepared from nature as a medicine or "tea."
• Supervise toddlers carefully in gardens, patios, and public parks.

Resource Information

Reference Texts

Kingsbury, J. *Poisonous Plants of the United States and Canada*. Englewood Cliffs, NJ: Prentice-Hall, 1964.

The Sinister Garden: A Guide to the Most Common Poisonous Plants. New York: Wyeth Laboratories, Division of American Home Products Corporation, 1966.

Respiratory Arrest

ASSESSMENT

It is the cessation of effective ventilation. It can be caused by acute airway obstruction, central nervous system depression, or neuromuscular paralysis. Apnea and cyanosis are the cardinal signs of respiratory arrest.

MANAGEMENT

Pulmonary resuscitation is begun immediately. See this chapter, Cardiopulmonary Resuscitation.

Shock

ASSESSMENT

Shock is a generalized circulatory disorder characterized mainly by hypotension. It may be caused by hemorrhage, cardiac failure, dehydration, poisons (including bacterial endotoxin), adrenal insufficiency, anaphylaxis, hypoxia, and neurovascular derangement. Physical findings include rapid, weak pulses, diaphoresis, ashen

Table 28-11

Poisonous Parts of Common House and Garden Plants

Plant	Toxic Part	Symptoms
		Flower Garden Plants
Autumn crocus (meadow crocus)	All parts	Vomiting, nervous excitement
Azalea	All parts	Produces nausea and vomiting, depression, difficult breathing; may be fatal
Bleeding heart (Dutchman's breeches)	Foliage, roots	May cause convulsions and difficult breathing when eaten in large quantities
Christmas rose	Rootstocks, leaves	Inflammation of skin, numbing of oral tissues, gastric distress and nervous effects
Daffodil	Bulb	Nausea, vomiting, diarrhea; may be fatal
Delphinium	Seeds, young plants	Stomach upset, nervous excitement or depression if eaten in large quantities; toxicity decreases with age of plant
Four-o'clock	Roots, seeds	The powdered root is an irritant to the skin, nose and throat
Foxglove	Leaves, seeds	One of the sources of the drug digitalis, used to stimulate the heart. In large amounts, the active principles cause dangerously irregular heartbeat and pulse, usually digestive upset and mental confusion. May be fatal.
Hyacinth	Bulb	Nausea, vomiting, diarrhea; may be fatal

Plant	Part	Effect
Iris (blue flag)	Underground stems	Severe, but not usually serious, digestive upset
Jonquil	Bulb	Nausea, vomiting, diarrhea; convulsions and death if eaten in large quantities
Larkspur	Seeds, young plants	Digestive upset, nervous excitement, depression; may be fatal
Lily-of-the-valley	Leaves, flowers	Irregular heart beat and pulse, usually accompanied by digestive upset and mental confusion
Monkshood	Roots, seeds, leaves	Digestive upset and nervous excitement
Morning glory	Seeds	Produce LSD-like effects and may cause mental disturbances when ingested in large quantities
Narcissus	Bulb	Nausea, vomiting, diarrhea; may be fatal
Oleander	Leaves, branches	Dizziness, nausea, irregular heartbeat; may be fatal
Peony	Roots	Juice can cause paralysis
Star-of-Bethlehem	Bulb	Vomiting and nervous excitement
Violet (pansy)	Seeds	In quantity, the cathartic effects can be serious to a child

House Plants

Plant	Part	Effect
Castor bean	Seeds	Burning of mouth and throat, excessive thirst, convulsions. One or two seeds are near the lethal dose for adults.
Dieffenbachia (dumbcane, caladium)	All parts	Intense burning and irritation of the mouth and tongue. Death can occur if base of tongue swells enough to block the air passage of the throat.
Jequirity bean	Seeds, especially orange spot	Stomach pains, irregular pulse, cold sweat. Usually fatal. Does not grow in the U.S., is used for native type jewelry and necklaces.

Table 28-11 (*Continued*)

Plant	Toxic Part	Symptoms
Mistletoe	Berries	Acute stomach and intestinal irritation with diarrhea and slow pulse; may be fatal
Mother-in-law	Leaves	Produces swelling of tongue
Poinsettia	Leaves	Severe irritation to mouth, throat and stomach; may be fatal
Rosary pea	Seeds	Stomach pains, irregular pulse, cold sweat; may be fatal
Ornamental Plants		
Daphne	Berries, bark, leaves	Upset stomach, abdominal pain, vomiting, bloody diarrhea, weakness, convulsions and kidney damage
Golden chain	Bean-like capsules in which seeds are suspended	Severe poisoning; excitement, staggering, convulsions, nausea and coma; may be fatal
Lantana (red sage, wild sage)	Green berries	Affects lungs, kidneys, heart and nervous system; grows in southern U.S. and in moderate climates; may be fatal
Magnolia	Flower	Headache and depression
Rhododendron (western azalea)	All parts	Nausea, vomiting, depression, difficult breathing, prostration and coma; may be fatal
Wisteria	Seeds, pods	Mild to severe digestive upset
Yellow jessamine	Berries	Digestive disturbance and nervous symptoms; may be fatal
Yew	All parts, especially seeds except fleshy red pulp of fruit	Convulsions with rapid death

Trees and Shrubs

Plant	Toxic Part	Symptoms
Apple	Seeds	Releases cyanide when ingested in large quantities; may be fatal
Black locust	Bark, sprouts, foliage, seeds	Children have suffered nausea, weakness and depression after chewing the bark and seeds
Cherry	Leaves, twigs, seeds	Contains a compound that releases cyanide when eaten; difficult breathing, excitement, paralysis of voice and prostration; may be fatal
Elderberry	All parts, especially roots	Nausea and digestive upset
Oak	Foliage, acorns	Affects kidneys gradually; symptoms appear only after several days or weeks; takes a large amount for poisoning.
Peach	Leaves, twigs, especially seeds	Contains a compound that releases cyanide when eaten; difficult breathing, excitement, paralysis of voice and prostration; may be fatal

Vegetable Garden Plants

Plant	Toxic Part	Symptoms
Potato	All green parts	Cardiac depression; may be fatal
Rhubarb	Leaf blade	Kidney damage. Large amounts of raw or cooked leaves can cause convulsions, coma, followed rapidly by death.
Tomato	Green parts	Cardiac depression; may be fatal

Wild Plants

Plant	Toxic Part	Symptoms
Baneberry	All parts	Stomach and intestinal irritation, spasms
Buttercup	All parts	Irritant juices may severely injure the digestive system

Continued on next page

1157

Table 28-11 (Continued)

Plant	Toxic Part	Symptoms
Jack-in-the-pulpit	All parts	Intense irritation and burning of mouth and tongue
Jimson weed (thornapple)	All parts	Abnormal thirst, distorted sight, delirium, incoherence and coma; may be fatal
Marsh marigold (cowslip)	All parts	Irritation of oral tissues, digestive upset, diarrhea, respiratory depression and convulsions
Moonseed	Berries	Blue, purple color, resembling wild grapes; severe digestive upset and abdominal pain
Mushrooms (fly agaric, death cap, and several *Amanita*)	All parts	Stomach cramps, thirst, difficult breathing. Fatal. AVOID ALL WILD MUSHROOMS UNLESS POSITIVE OF THEIR IDENTITY.
Nightshade	All parts	Intense digestive disturbances and nervous symptoms; may be fatal
Poison hemlock	All parts	Digestive disturbances; may be fatal
Poison ivy, oak, sumac	All parts	Itching, burning, redness
Skunk cabbage	Leaves, rhizomes	Burning and swelling of mouth, tongue and throat; large quantities may cause stomach and intestinal irritation
Water hemlock (cowbane)	All parts	Diarrhea, convulsions; may be fatal

Source: Reproduced with permission of The National Association of Retail Druggists, Washington D.C.

color, oliguria, hypothermia, and altered sensorium. Prolonged shock can lead to irreversible organ damage.

MANAGEMENT

The immediate measures to reverse shock include specific therapy for the cause of the shock and assurance of perfusion of vital organs. See this chapter, Anaphylaxis. The latter is aided by placing the child in a recumbent position, preferably with the head lower than the body. Administration of salt and fluids by mouth is to be done only in the extreme situation and with the utmost caution, since the danger of loss of consciousness with subsequent aspiration of vomitus is high. Supportive measures include judicious administration of oxygen if available and maintenance of body temperature. Transportation to a hospital is necessary.

Snakebites

ASSESSMENT

The mortality rate from a snakebite is 1 percent. Most of the snakebites occur between March and October, and between 3 PM and 9 PM because snakes prefer nocturnal activity. Snakes usually await their prey and can strike very fast (Judd and Ponsell, 1982). Two primary types of poisonous snakes are (1) neurotoxic (coral snake, cobra), and (2) hemotoxic (rattlesnake, water moccasin, and copperhead). Identification of the snake is easier if the head is not disfigured. Signs of venom in the body (envenomization) are:

1. Edema around the bite.
2. Tissue surrounding the bite turns red within a few minutes.

MANAGEMENT

Bites by a neurotoxic snake are immediately managed as follows (Judd and Ponsell, 1982):

1. Maintain the extremity in a dependent position, lower than the heart.
2. Reassure and calm the child.
3. Immobilize the affected area as much as possible.

4. Cleanse the wound carefully with soap and water.
5. Monitor the vital signs.
6. Transport to a health facility.

Bites by a hemotoxic snake are managed as follows (Judd and Ponsell, 1982) if transport is possible within one hour: perform all the steps listed above, and in addition treat for shock and given oxygen if available. Attempt to identify the snake. If transport is unavailable within the hour, perform these additional measures (Judd and Ponsell, 1982):

1. Observe the bite for signs of envenomization.
2. Within the first 5 minutes place a tourniquet (i.e., rubberband) approximately 2 inches above and below the bite. Be careful not to seal off pulses to the extremity.
3. If help is 4 to 5 hours away, minor incisions with a clean blade may be necessary to allow the rescuer to suck the venom in the area. This should be done within 30 minutes after the bite and with a physician's instruction. *Do not perform this step if medical assistance will be available within 4 to 5 hours.*

For related information see Chapter 26, Bites of Arachnids and Insects.

Syncope (Fainting)

ASSESSMENT

Syncope is a transient, usually sudden episode of unconsciousness, loss of body tone, and falling due to cerebral ischemia. See Chapter 24, Breath-Holding.

Etiology Syncope is most commonly due to a sudden and marked fall in the blood pressure. Other causes include the following:

• Anemia
• Breath-holding
• Cardiac causes (rare)
• Epilepsy (syncopal episode usually lasts longer than 30 seconds)
• Heat
• Hyperventilation

- Hypoglycemia
- Hysteria

Clinical Picture Fainting is heralded by dizziness, feeling of weakness, numbness of the hands and feet, extreme pallor, nausea, sweating, coldness of the skin, and occasionally visual disturbances. Clonic movements may follow if the child remains unconscious longer than 20 seconds or if the child is positioned in a semi-erect posture.

MANAGEMENT

No specific management is indicated except to keep the child in a horizontal position or tilt the head downward at a 45° angle until recovery.

Trauma

ASSESSMENT

First aid assessment considers these principles:

1. Extent of the injury: ascertain degree and type of damage and the presence of underlying medical problems such as diabetes, cardiac condition.
2. Onset of life-threatening conditions: examine the child thoroughly and observe for conditions such as airway obstruction, cardiac arrest, and shock.

Trauma is too extensive to discuss fully here. Refer to other appropriate references, including other chapters in this book, for further information. (See also Hemorrhage, Shock, Fractures.) Penetrating chest wounds bear specific mention. These may result in pneumothorax, with subsequent deflation of the lung. If only the chest wall is penetrated, compression of the chest followed by closure of the wound can reduce the degree of air accumulation in the pleural space. If the lung is also penetrated, air should be drained from the pleural space to prevent a tension pneumothorax, which is more serious. Internal injuries pose the additional hazard of lack of recognition and thus delay in treatment. Large amounts of blood may be lost into the chest, abdomen, and thigh almost imperceptibly.

The abdominal viscera are poorly protected from blunt trauma, and their rupture should be considered following significant trauma. Even minor trauma can rupture an inflamed or swollen spleen.

MANAGEMENT

There are three basic principles of management of a traumatic injury (Greensher et al., 1979):

1. Immobilization of the injured area.
2. Application of pressure to stop bleeding and cool compresses to reduce swelling.
3. Elevation of injured area to reduce swelling and bleeding.

For open wounds, control the hemorrhage (see this chapter), prevent infection, and determine the extent of trauma until definitive care can be administered at a health facility. Then cleanse the wound, apply an antiseptic, and cover the wound with a sterile dressing.

References

Abrams, M. "Introduction: Traumatic Injuries in Children." *Pediatr Ann* 5:10–11, October 1976.

American Academy of Pediatrics. Committee on Accident and Poison Prevention. "First Aid for the Choking Child." *Pediatrics* 67:744, May 1981.

American National Red Cross. *Advanced First Aid and Emergency Care.* 1973.

Arena, J. *Poisoning: Toxicology, Symptoms, Treatment.* 4th ed. Springfield, IL: Thomas, 1979.

Arena, J. *The Treatment of Poisoning.* Summit, NJ: Ciba Pharmaceutical Company, 1977.

Bayer, M. S. and B. H. Rumack, editors. *Poisoning and Overdose.* Rockville, MD: Aspen Publications, 1983.

Block, C. R. and C. E. Block. "Help, My Child is Choking." *Pediatr Nurs* 2:48–49, September/October 1976.

Brown, W. "Emergency Management of the Injured Child." *Pediatr Ann* 5:22–34, October 1976.

Canright, P. and M. J. Campbell. "Nursing Care of the Child and His Family in the Emergency Department." *Pediatr Nurs* 3:43–45, July/August 1977.

Cohen, S. A. *Pediatric Emergency Management: Guidelines for Rapid Diagnosis and Therapy.* East Norwalk, CT: Appleton-Century-Crofts, 1982.

Corby, D. G. and W. J. Decker. "Management of Acute Poisoning with Activated Charcoal." *Pediatrics 54*:324–329, September 1974.

Dietz, P. E. and S. P. Baker. "Drowning Epidemiology and Prevention." *Am J Public Health 64*:303–312, April 1974.

Done, A. K. "Salicylate Intoxication: Significance of Measurements of Salicylate in Blood in Cases of Acute Ingestion." *Pediatrics 26*:800–807, November 1960.

Gellis, S., editor. *The Year Book of Pediatrics.* Chicago: Year Book, 1977.

Goldberg, A. H. "Cardiopulmonary Arrest." *N Engl J Med 290*:381–385, February 14, 1974.

Graef, J. W. and T. E. Cone Jr. *Manual of Pediatric Therapeutics.* Boston: Little, Brown, 1974.

Greensher, J., H. C. Mofenson, and N. J. Merlis. "First Aid for School Athletic Emergencies." *NY State J of Medicine 79*:1058–1062, June 1979.

Hardin, J. and J. Arena. *Human Poisoning from Native and Cultivated Plants.* Durham, NC: Duke University Press, 1973.

Heimlich, H. J. "Update on the Heimlich Maneuver." *Emergency Medical Services. 6*: 11–20, January/February 1977.

Judd, R. and D. Ponsell. *The First Responder: The Critical First Minutes.* St. Louis: C.V. Mosby, 1982.

Kempe, C. H., H. K. Silver, and D. O'Brien. *Current Pediatric Diagnosis and Treatment.* 6th ed., Los Altos, CA: Lange Medical Publications, 1980.

Lampe, K. F. and R. Fagerstrom. *Plant Toxicity and Dermatitis.* Baltimore: Williams & Wilkins, 1968.

Lanros, N. E. *Assessment and Intervention in Emergency Nursing.* 2nd ed. Bowie, MD: Robert J. Brady, 1983.

Mayer, B. and N. Schlackman. "Organophosphates—A Pediatric Hazard." *AFP 11*:121–124, May 1975.

Mennear, J. H. "The Poison Emergency." *Am J Nurs 77*:842–844, May 1977.

Metropolitan Life Insurance Company. "Accidental Drownings by Age and Activity." *Stat Bull 58*:2–4, May 1977.

Mofenson, H. and J. Greensher. "The Unknown Poison." *Pediatrics 54*:336–342, September 1974.

National Safety Council. *Accident Facts.* Chicago: National Safety Council, 1979. Pp. 81–82.

Pascoe, D. and M. Grossman, editors. *Quick Reference to Pediatric Emergencies.* 2nd ed. Philadelphia: J.B. Lippincott, 1977.

Peterson, B. "Morbidity of Childhood Near-Drowning." *Pediatrics 59*:364–370, March 1977.

Phelan, W. "Camphor Poisoning: Over-the-Counter Dangers." *Pediatrics 57*:428–430, March 1976.

Rudolph, A., editor. *Pediatrics,* 17th ed. East Norwalk, CT: Appleton-Century-Crofts, 1982.

Rumack, B. and H. Matthew. "Acetaminophen Poisoning and Toxicity." *Pediatrics* 55:871–876, June 1975.

Rumack, B. and R. Peterson. "Poisoning." In C. H. Kempe, et al. *Current Pediatric Diagnosis and Treatment* 6th ed. Los Altos, CA: Lange Medical Publications, 1980. Pp. 879–907.

Shillito, J. Jr. "Head Injuries." In M. Green and R. J. Haggerty, editors. *Ambulatory Pediatrics. II.* Philadelphia: W.B. Saunders, 1977. Pp. 247–252.

Silver, H. K., C. K. Kempe, and H. B. Bruyn. *Handbook of Pediatrics.* 14th ed. Los Altos, CA: Lange Medical Publications, 1983.

"Standards and Guidelines for Cardiopulmonary Resuscitation." *JAMA* 244:453–509, August 1, 1980.

Sumner, S. M. and P. E. Grau. "Emergency! First Aid for Choking." *Nursing 82* 12:40–49, July 1982.

Teasdale, G. and B. Jennett. "Assessment of Coma and Impaired Consciousness." *The Lancet* II:81–83, July 13, 1974.

The Sinister Garden: A Guide to the Most Common Poisonous Plants. New York: Wyeth Laboratories, Division of American Home Products Corporation, 1966.

Vaughan, V. C., et al., editors. *Nelson Textbook of Pediatrics.* 11th ed. Philadelphia: W.B. Saunders, 1979.

Waechter, E. H. and F. G. Blake. *Nursing Care of Children.* 9th ed. Philadelphia: J.B. Lippincott, 1976.

Wheatley, G. M. "Childhood Accidents 1952–1972: An Overview." *Pediatric Annals* 2:10–30, January 1973.

29

Genetics

Up to 5 percent of all births in the United States involve physical or mental defects of varying severity. Birth defects may be inherited, may result from environmental factors, or may reflect a combination of both heredity and environment. Expanding knowledge of human genetics makes it possible now to identify carriers of defective genes, to predict the potential for transmitting defective genes, and to determine the presence or absence of defects in the fetus for a growing list of inherited disorders. Nurse practitioners need to understand basic patterns of genetic inheritance, the objectives of genetic counseling, and the indications for referring families for genetic counseling. Indications for genetic screening are discussed throughout the book under specific conditions (e.g., screening for sickle cell disease is found in Chapter 19, Sickle Cell Anemia and Trait). For a full discussion of genetics, consult this chapter, References.

ASSESSMENT

Basic Patterns of Genetic Inheritance

CHROMOSOMES

The nucleus of every cell in the human body contains 46 chromosomes (23 pairs). Chromosomes are composed of linear structures which carry the genetic material, deoxyribonucleic acid (DNA), or

1165

genes. Before fertilization the gametes (egg and sperm cells) undergo a process of cell division resulting in separation of each pair of chromosomes. The mature gametes, therefore, each contain a set of 23 chromosomes which combine when fertilization occurs to provide the zygote with 46 chromosomes. Forty-four chromosomes are referred to as autosomes and the other two are the sex chromosomes. Chromosomal errors can occur, particularly during formation of reproductive cells, and as a result the zygote may contain chromosomes in abnormal number or structure. Down's syndrome is an example of a deviation in number of autosomal chromosomes. Turner's syndrome and Klinefelter's syndrome result from abnormal number of sex chromosomes. Structural chromosomal abnormalities are less well-defined and have more diverse manifestations (e.g., children who "don't look right").

GENES

Genes are the functional hereditary units that transmit all the inherited characteristics from parents to children. There are thousands of genes on each chromosome, and each individual gene determines a specific hereditary characteristic. The genes, like the chromosomes, exist in pairs, one contributed by the mother and one by the father. The two genes in a pair work together to determine the outcome of a specific hereditary trait. The two members of each gene pair may carry similar or different instructions regarding the trait which they determine. If the members of a pair are the same, the person is *homozygous*. If the members of a gene pair supply different instructions, the person is said to be *heterozygous* for that trait. In this case the specific trait is determined by only one member of the pair, and the gene that is expressed is called *dominant*. The gene that is not expressed is called *recessive*. Most traits require the interaction of many gene pairs, but for some only a single pair is involved. Mendelian principles indicate the outcomes that can be predicted in most single-gene inheritance patterns. See Tables 29-1 through 29-7.

MUTATIONS

DNA is remarkably precise in duplicating or copying itself for transmission of genetic blueprints to the next cell or next generation. However, there are times when a slight error in replication results in a mutant gene and an altered *genotype* (basic genetic constitution) or an altered *phenotype* (observable appearance of the organism). Unless the mutation is harmful enough to be lethal, the mutant DNA material will also be faithfully transmitted through countless generations.

AUTOSOMAL DOMINANT INHERITANCE

Genetic defects caused by dominant inheritance are relatively rare and occur when one parent carries a dominant gene for the disease and expresses the disease him or herself. The other parent almost always is free of the same pathologic trait. In such a family there is a 50 percent chance that each offspring will manifest the defect. See Table 29-1. Some cases of autosomal-dominant defects occur as new mutations. In other words, the parents are unaffected, but a mutation has occurred in the germ cell of one parent which causes the defect in the child. The parents in this case have no significant risk of producing further affected offspring, but the affected child carries a 50 percent chance of transmitting the defect to each of his or her children.

Examples of pathologic conditions inherited as dominant traits are achondroplasia (dwarfism), Huntington's chorea, neurofibromatosis, osteogenesis imperfecta, tuberous sclerosis, polydactyly, and retinoblastoma.

AUTOSOMAL RECESSIVE INHERITANCE

Genetic disorders caused by recessive inheritance occur when each parent carries the harmful recessive gene. Both parents are usually unaffected although genotypically abnormal. Each child of such

Table 29-1
Autosomal Dominant Inheritance

Parents	Children
Dn[a]	Dn (disease state)
nn	Dn (disease state)
	nn (normal)
	nn (normal)

[a] D = dominant faulty gene; n = normal gene.

Table 29-2
Autosomal Recessive Inheritance

Parents	Children
Nr[a]	NN (normal)
Nr	Nr (heterozygous: carrier state)
	Nr (heterozygous: carrier state)
	rr (homozygous: disease state)

[a] N = normal dominant gene; r = recessive faulty gene.

parents has a 25 percent risk of manifesting the disease (and if affected will be homozygous for the disease), a 25 percent chance of not inheriting the gene from either parent, and a 50 percent chance of receiving only a single defective gene and becoming a carrier. See Table 29-2. Other possibilities for combinations of recessive and dominant genes and their probable outcomes are illustrated in Table 29-3. Examples of diseases inherited as autosomal recessive traits are adrenogenital syndrome, albinism, Tay-Sachs disease, cystinuria, cystic fibrosis, galactosemia, and phenylketonuria.

Table 29-3
Possible Combinations of Dominant and
Recessive Inheritance

Parents	Children
1. NN[a]	NN (normal)
Nr	Nr (heterozygous: carrier state)
	NN (normal)
	Nr (heterozygous: carrier state)
2. Nr	Nr (heterozygous: carrier state)
rr	Nr (heterozygous: carrier state)
	rr (homozygous: disease state)
	rr (homozygous: disease state)
3. NN	Nr (heterozygous: carrier state)
rr	Nr (heterozygous: carrier state)
	Nr (heterozygous: carrier state)
	Nr (heterozygous: carrier state)

[a] N = normal dominant gene; r = faulty recessive gene.

Table 29-4
X-Linked Recessive Inheritance:
Female Transmission[a]

Parents	Children
Xx[a]	XY (normal son)
XY	XX (normal daughter)
	Xx (carrier daughter)
	xY (affected son)

[a]x = faulty gene on X chromosome; X = normal chromosome; Y = normal chromosome.

X-LINKED INHERITANCE

Normal females have two X chromosomes. Normal males have one X and one Y chromosome. The X chromosome carries many genes related to inherited traits other than sex. The Y chromosome seems to have no other function except for determining masculinity. Consequently, in the male, the genes on the X chromosome are not matched by corresponding genes on the Y chromosome. Therefore a defective gene on the X chromosome, even if recessive, can manifest itself since there is no normal gene on the Y chromosome to mask its effects. In females, a recessive faulty gene might be masked by a dominant normal gene on the other X chromosome.

The most common X-linked abnormalities occur when the mother carries a faulty gene on one of her X chromosomes. In this case each son has a 50 percent risk of inheriting the gene and manifesting the disease. Each daughter has a 50 percent chance of becoming a carrier capable of transmitting the disease to *her* sons. See Table 29-4.

If a male with a pathologic recessive gene on his X chromosome and a normal female produce offspring, all sons will be normal having received a normal X chromosome from their mother. All the daughters will appear normal but will carry the faulty recessive gene on one of their X chromosomes. See Table 29-5. These daughters then transmit the gene to their offspring as illustrated in Table 29-4. X-linked dominant inheritance patterns are shown in Tables 29-6 and 29-7.

Examples of disorders transmitted by X-linked recessive inher-

Table 29-5
X-Linked Recessive Inheritance:
Male Transmission[a]

Parents	Children
XX[a]	XY (normal son)
xY	XY (normal son)
	Xx (carrier daughter)
	Xx (carrier daughter)

[a]x = faulty gene on X chromosome; X = normal chromosome; Y = normal chromosome.

itance are agammaglobulinemia, color blindness, diabetes insipidus, Duchenne type muscular dystrophy, hemophilia, and G6PD. Vitamin D-resistant rickets is acquired by X-linked dominant inheritance.

MULTIFACTORIAL INHERITANCE

There are genetic disorders which result from the combined interaction of multiple genes and environmental factors. Patterns of transmission are complicated, but it is known that the probabilities of recurrence are quite low. With one affected child, chances of another having the same defect are 5 percent or less. Examples of conditions resulting from multifactorial inheritance are cleft lip and palate, pyloric stenosis, congenital dislocation of the hip, clubfoot, spina bifida, hydrocephalus, diabetes mellitus, asthma, and schizophrenia.

Table 29-6
X-Linked Dominant Inheritance:
Female Transmission[a]

Parents	Children
Xx	XY (normal son)
XY	XX (normal daughter)
	Xx (affected daughter)
	xY (affected son)

[a]x = faulty gene on X chromosome; X = normal chromosome; Y = normal chromosome.

Table 29-7
X-Linked Dominant Inheritance:
Male Transmission[a]

Parents	Children
XX	XY (normal son)
xY	XY (normal son)
	xX (affected daughter)
	xX (affected daughter)

[a]x = faulty gene on Y chromosome; X = normal chromosome; Y = normal chromosome.

Prenatal Diagnosis of Genetic Defects

Prenatal evaluation of hereditary diseases and congenital defects is possible by placental aspiration/fetoscopy, serial ultrasonography, and, most commonly, amniocentesis.

AMNIOCENTESIS

Amniocentesis is the transabdominal withdrawal of amniotic fluid from the uterus during pregnancy. The prenatal diagnosis of many inherited defects is possible by subjecting the amniotic fluid to tissue culture, biochemical analysis, and chromosomal analysis.

Indications for Amniocentesis When the following situations exist, amniocentesis may be indicated:

1. Parental concern over known possibility of occurrence of a serious genetic abnormality
2. Parents who have given birth to a child with a chromosomal disorder or multiple major malformations
3. Parents who are known carriers for chromosomal, genetic, or X-linked diseases
4. Women over 35 years of age
5. Parents who have had a child with a neural tube defect
6. Pregnancies in couples who have had three or more spontaneous abortions
7. Pregnancies at risk for X-linked hereditary disorders

Procedure Between the thirteenth to sixteenth week of pregnancy, under local anesthesia, approximately 10 to 12 cc of amniotic fluid is aspirated from the uterus. Before inserting the needle the physician determines fetal and placental position by palpation, ultrasound, and sometimes X-ray. Analysis of the fluid takes 3 to 4 weeks.

Risks Even in experienced hands there are risks:

1. Direct damage to the fetus
2. Placental puncture and hemorrhage with secondary damage to the fetus
3. Stimulation of premature labor
4. Amnionitis (occurs about once in 1,000 procedures)
5. Maternal sensitization to fetal blood (can be prevented by giving Rh immunoglobulin)

It is suggested that amniocentesis be reserved for those cases in which the estimated value of the findings will outweigh the risks.

MANAGEMENT

Genetic Counseling

GOALS OF GENETIC COUNSELING

Genetic counseling aims to do the following:

1. Provide individuals and families with sufficient and correct medical information about a specific disorder so they can understand the nature of the disorder, and the risk of occurrence
2. Provide guidelines for action so individuals and families can use the information wisely in making decisions about future offspring.
3. Assist parents to deal with the impact of the information and to guide them toward effective coping
4. Reduce the number of affected persons

PROCESS OF GENETIC COUNSELING

1. Data collection includes an accurate medical history, detailed family pedigree, and laboratory data obtained from clinical procedures (e.g., dermatoglyphics, chromosome analysis).

2. Once the nature of the defect is established, predictions on the probability of recurrence of a given abnormality in the same family can often be made using the basic laws governing heredity and knowledge of the frequency of specific birth defects in the general population.

3. The genetic counselor (physician, nurse, geneticist) then provides this information to the individuals and families concerned. The manner in which the information is delivered is crucial and demands effective communication skills with sensitivity to the psychologic impact on the family. Repeated conferences for reinterpretation and support are usually necessary.

INDICATIONS FOR REFERRAL FOR GENETIC COUNSELING

The nurse practitioner has the responsibility to identify and refer individuals and families for genetic counseling. Referrals are indicated in the following situations:

1. A family that has a child with a congenital malformation or a group of congenital anomalies

2. A family that has one or more children who are mentally retarded

3. A family in which a medical problem has affected more than one member

4. A family in which a previously diagnosed condition is known to be genetic in origin

5. A child who "doesn't look right" or has delayed or abnormal development

6. Parents of children who have died at birth for unknown reasons

7. Related couples who want to know the risks of having defective children

8. Persons concerned about exposure to environmental agents that may cause abnormalities

9. Couples seeking advice before marriage
10. Persons with known defects who desire information
11. Individuals or families who have received genetics information but are not comfortable with it
12. Parents who have experienced multiple spontaneous abortions
13. Pregnancy in women over 35 years old
14. Families of ethnic background known to influence certain conditions (e.g., Tay-Sachs disease in Jewish populations, sickle cell disease in blacks, thalassemia in Mediterranean and Oriental groups)

Resource Information

Genetic counseling units have been established in many medical centers and teaching hospitals. Current information about specialized genetics services is available in the "International Directory of Genetic Services," published by The National Foundation/March of Dimes, Box 2000, White Plains, NY 10602. Local March of Dimes chapters can provide information on available local services and written material for families.

References

Golbus, M., et al. "Prenatal Genetic Diagnosis in 3000 Amniocenteses." *N Engl J Med* *300*:157–163, January 25, 1979.

Reisman, L. E. and A. P. Matheny. *Genetics and Counseling in Medical Practice*. St. Louis: C. V. Mosby, 1969.

Riccardi, V. M. *The Genetic Approach to Human Disease*. New York: Oxford University Press, 1977.

Sahin, S. T. "The Multifaceted Role of the Nurse as Genetic Counselor." *Am J Maternal Child Nursing* *1*:211–216, July/August 1976.

Selwyn, A. *Genetic Counseling*. White Plains, NY: The National Foundation/March of Dimes.

Summer, G. K. and C. R. Shoaf. "Developments in Genetic and Metabolic Screening." *Family and Community Health* *4*:13–29, February 1982.

Vaughan, V. C., et al., editors. *Nelson Textbook of Pediatrics*. 11th ed. Philadelphia: Saunders, 1979.

Waechter, E. H. and F. G. Blake. *Nursing Care of Children*. 9th ed. Philadelphia: J. B. Lippincott, 1976.

Winchester, A. M. *Genetics: A Survey of the Principles of Heredity*. 4th ed. Boston: Houghton Mifflin, 1972.

30

Sudden Infant
Death Syndrome

Sudden infant death syndrome (SIDS) remains one of the most perplexing and agonizing problems facing affected families and health care providers. The etiology of the syndrome and the identification of infants at risk are crucial areas in which knowledge is incomplete. In the past and, unfortunately, all too often in the present, the management of families who experience this tragedy has been insensitive, accusatory, and punitive. Information is presented here to assist the nurse practitioner in the supportive management and counseling of families who lose an infant to SIDS.

ASSESSMENT

DEFINITION

SIDS is the sudden death of any infant or young child which is unexpected by history and in which a thorough postmortem examination fails to demonstrate an adequate cause for death.

Etiology

Although more than 70 theories of causation have been proposed to explain SIDS, the specific cause remains unknown, and there is no known way to prevent it. Several prominent theories are reviewed here, since parents of young infants may query the nurse practitioner as to what causes SIDS and what can be done to prevent it.

CURRENT THEORIES

Theories and epidemiologic factors currently mentioned and being studied include the following:

- Allergic reactions or immunopathology
- Chronic hypoxia and hypoxemia
- Depressed CO_2 sensitivity, which may fail to stimulate respiratory drive during periods of apnea or hypoxia
- Elevated levels of tri-iodothyronine (Chacon and Tildon, 1981)
- Increased incidence in infants born to narcotic-addicted mothers (Valdes-Dapena, 1980)
- Increased incidence in infants discharged from neonatal intensive care units, indicating a relationship between intrauterine and perinatal factors and SIDS
- Infant botulism as the cause of SIDS in a small subgroup of infants (Arnon et al., 1978)
- Instantaneous interruption in central control functions for respiratory and/or cardiac action
- Nasal obstruction in infants who are obligate nose breathers (under 5 months of age) and who make no attempt to open their mouths to breathe (Shaw, 1970)
- Neurologic problem in which the laryngeal sensory receptors, when stimulated by fluid or regurgitated gastric contents, reflexively inhibit breathing and cause respiratory arrest
- Oropharyngeal occlusion of airways during sleep as a result of deep muscle relaxation of the tongue and soft palate, and displacement of a hypermobile mandible (Tonkin, 1975)
- Respiratory instability and normal prolonged apneic periods occurring during REM sleep as a result of muscle relaxation (Steinschneider, 1972)
- Subtle physiologic handicaps originating before birth, as in CNS dysfunction (particularly the brainstem), respiratory abnormalities, temperature regulation problems, myocardial conduction abnormalities

- Viral infection affecting laryngeal nerves causing laryngeal spasm and sudden closure of the vocal cords during sleep (Bergman, 1972)

DISPROVEN THEORIES

Theories that have been disproven or that have yielded insufficient proof include the following:

- Accidental suffocation by bedclothes. Even very young infants can clear their airways if obstructed by bedclothes.
- Infant feeding methods. Breast feeding, even when done exclusively, does not protect against SIDS.
- Nutritional deficiency or infection per se, although viral infection may serve as a trigger mechanism in an infant at risk.
- Traumatic and toxic causes.

Infants At Risk

No reliable screening mechanism exists for identifying infants at risk for SIDS. It is an occurrence that "for any specific infant, cannot be predicted with any degree of certainty" (Valdes-Dapena, 1980, p. 602). However, recent studies have shown that infants referred to as "near-miss" infants probably constitute a group that is at increased risk. These infants demonstrate both central and obstructive types of stopped breathing episodes and are thought to exhibit autonomic nervous system dysfunction. The issue of apnea monitors arises in this regard. Controversy exists concerning the value of at-home monitoring, but some feel it an appropriate intervention for this group of infants. There is no justification for advocating the general use of home monitoring systems to prevent SIDS.

Another group of infants at special risk for SIDS is the subsequent siblings of infants who have died from SIDS. There appears to be a three- to fourfold increased risk.

INCIDENCE

It is estimated that SIDS claims approximately 7,500 infants per year in the United States or between two and three infants per

1,000 live births. It occurs most often between 2 to 4 months of age and is uncommon before 1 month and after 7 to 8 months of age. It occurs more frequently in males, in low-birth-weight infants, in twins, in low socioeconomic groups living in overcrowded conditions, and during times of the year when colder temperatures and upper respiratory illnesses abound.

CLINICAL PICTURE

Most of these infants die at home, during the night while sleeping, silently, without struggle, and unobserved. Approximately one half have had symptoms of a cold in the week before death, but the other 50 percent have not. Parents or caretakers discover their presumably healthy infant lying lifeless in the crib, in a state of disarray, often with frothy, blood-stained fluid in the nose, mouth, and on the bedclothes. Thus begins the agonizing human experience of coping with the sudden and unexplained death of an infant.

MANAGEMENT

Management is aimed at preventing the potentially crippling psychologic effects of SIDS on parents and family members.

Immediate Management

THE GRIEF PROCESS

Acute grief reactions are intense and include predictable symptoms and behaviors. They may be more intense when the event is unexpected. Initial reactions include shock, denial, anger, guilt, emotional disintegration, and remorse. During the first few days after the death a sense of emotional numbness may develop with depression, insomnia, inability to carry on with daily routines, fatigue, anorexia, preoccupation with the lost child, and continued re-examination of what could or should have been done to prevent the tragedy. Feelings of disbelief may last for several weeks. As the acute stress abates, parents are able to talk about the experience and will be ready for more detailed information.

EMERGENCY ROOM CARE

1. When a dead infant arrives in the emergency room, presume the parents innocent until proved otherwise. Accusations or implications of child abuse are devastating to these parents.
2. Provide a room and privacy for the family and explanations of what procedures are being carried out. Answer questions simply.
3. Offer emotional support and accept the anger expressed without retaliation. Knowing the "right words" is not as important as simply being there, communicating concern and involvement.
4. When SIDS is presumptively diagnosed, emphasize that it was not anyone's fault and could not have been prevented.
5. Obtain permission for an autopsy.
6. Before leaving the emergency room provide parents with printed material on SIDS. The pamphlets put out by the National Foundation for Sudden Infant Death, Inc., are most helpful. Have a supply on hand. See this chapter, Parent Groups.
7. Inform the family that arrangements for a home visit by a public health nurse (or other supportive professional) will be made within the following week.
8. Parents' religious beliefs will significantly affect their response to SIDS and efforts to contact the appropriate clergy should be made after consultation with the family.

AUTOPSY

Autopsy is necessary to confirm the diagnosis of SIDS and should be performed on all infants. Characteristic autopsy findings include congestion and edema of the lungs, intrathoracic petechial hemorrhages on the surfaces of the lungs, pericardium, and thymus, microscopic inflammatory changes in the respiratory tract, minor pharyngeal erythema, and findings indicative of chronic hypoxia and chronic hypoxemia. Autopsy results should be relayed to families within 24 hours.

LEGAL ASPECTS

In most jurisdictions, any unexplained death mandates an autopsy, but whether or not the procedure is mandatory, the death certificate should read, "sudden infant death syndrome." Procedures for death investigations vary from state to state and often cause untold trauma to grief-stricken families. An excellent model for a humane system exists in the state of Oregon. It is available from the Oregon State Deputy Medical Examiner, 301 N.E. Knott, Portland, OR.

Follow-Up Counseling

Nurses are frequently the most available and appropriate professionals to assist families through the grief process following SIDS. Such support and counseling may be required for long periods. A group of parents surveyed after the loss of an infant to SIDS reported this as the most severe crisis ever experienced. It took an average of 8.2 months for them to regain their previous levels of functioning and family organization (DeFrain and Ernst, 1978).

INTERVALS FOR VISITS

The first visit with the family is best accomplished in the family home within 1 week of the infant's death. During this and subsequent visits the objectives of care are as follows:

1. Provide emotional support during the grieving period
2. Listen empathetically
3. Provide information on SIDS to the family as they are ready for it
4. Anticipate normal grief reactions and reassure parents that their reactions are normal
5. Answer all questions asked by parents and give printed material on SIDS
6. Assist parents in dealing with siblings and relatives
7. Put parents in touch with parent groups and The National Foundation for Sudden Infant Death
8. Support the family during the pregnancy and infancy period of a subsequent child
9. Refer parents for psychiatric referral if abnormal reactions exist and persist

INDICATIONS FOR PSYCHIATRIC REFERRAL

1. Parent who shows no emotion
2. Parent who overintellectualizes, for example, is obsessed by the scientific details
3. Parent who persistently denies the infant's death
4. Continuing inability of parent to resume previous responsibilities and level of functioning

QUESTIONS MOST FREQUENTLY ASKED BY PARENTS

- What is SIDS?
- How can a healthy baby die so suddenly?
- Was it my fault?
- Did the baby suffocate in the bedding?
- Did the baby vomit and choke?
- Did the baby suffer?
- Why was there blood around the baby's nose and mouth?
- Could the baby have cried and I didn't hear?
- Was it something infectious?
- Should I have breast-fed the baby?
- What if we have another child? Could it happen again?

These and other questions are answered simply and directly in materials available from the National Foundation for Sudden Infant Death. See this chapter, Parent Groups.

SIBLINGS

Siblings also are affected by SIDS. Although the child's age and developmental level determine the concept of death and the nature of the mourning process, all siblings will normally experience guilt feelings about the loss of the infant. Toddlers may fear that a similar fate awaits them and may become clinging and demanding. A detailed explanation is inappropriate at this age, but love, attention, and reassurance that they are safe will promote a feeling of security.

Older children need encouragement to express what they are feeling, need explanations and facts geared to their level of understanding, and need reassurance that they were in no way responsible and that they are safe and loved. Regressive behavior, nightmares, bedwetting, difficulty at school, and depression might be anticipated and indicate presence of continued guilt and insecurity. Professional counseling may be required.

PARENT GROUPS

A significant source of comfort can be contact with other parents who have experienced and successfully coped with SIDS. Two major national organizations exist and can be contacted for local chapter resources.

1. National Sudden Infant Death Foundation, 310 S. Michigan Avenue, Chicago, IL 60604.
2. Council of Guilds for Infant Survival, 1800 M Street NW, Washington, DC 20037.

SUBSEQUENT CHILDREN

Parents are frequently concerned about whether or not to have a subsequent child. This decision should be deferred until the grief work involving the lost infant is successfully completed. The new child must *not* be considered a replacement child. The odds of having SIDS recur in the same family are thought to be increased (see this chapter, Infants at Risk) and this information must be provided.

When a subsequent pregnancy occurs and during the subsequent child's first year of life, parents will need continual support and counseling to master their fears and concerns. The pamphlet, "The Subsequent Child," by Carolyn Szybist, R.N., is most helpful in providing guidelines for this support. See this chapter, References.

Anticipatory Counseling

Occasionally new parents with their first, healthy newborn show exaggerated concern about their infant's well-being. Normal findings such as nasal congestion, sneezing, mucus, or noisy breathing during sleep result in the parent asking repeated questions without seeming to be satisfied with the answers. The nurse practitioner who identifies such a situation can simply say, "You seem worried about your baby's breathing. Is there any particular reason?" If the parent is vague about the reason for the concern, then ask, "Are you worried about crib death?" This often brings a rush of feelings and fears to the surface that have been occasioned by experiences with neighbors, relatives, or friends who have lost an infant to SIDS, or by media publicity. Once the unspoken fears are verbalized, teaching and reassurance are heard.

Resource Information

Current information on all aspects of SIDS is available from:

Sudden Infant Death Syndrome Clearinghouse
1555 Wilson Boulevard, Suite 600
Rosslyn, VI 22209
703-522-0870

References

Arnon, S. S., et al. "Intestinal Infection and Toxin Production by *Clostridium botulinum* as One Cause of Sudden Infant Death Syndrome." *Lancet 1*:1273–1276, June 17, 1978.

Bergman, A. B. "Sudden Infant Death." *Nurs Outlook 20*:775–777, December 1972.

Bergman, A. B. "Sudden Infant Death Syndrome: An Approach to Management." *Primary Care 3*:1–8, March 1976.

Chacon, M. A. and J. T. Tildon. "Elevated Values of Tri-iodothyronine in Victims of Sudden Infant Death Syndrome." *J Pediatr 99*:758–760, November 1981.

DeFrain, J. D. and L. Ernst. "The Psychological Effects of Sudden Infant Death Syndrome on Surviving Family Members." *J Family Pract 6*:985–989, May 1978.

Patterson, K. and M. R. Pomeroy. "Nursing Care Begins After Death When the Disease Is: Sudden Infant Death Syndrome." *Nursing 74 4*:85–88, May 1974.

Rudolph, A. M., editor. *Pediatrics.* 17th ed. East Norwalk, CT: Appleton-Century-Crofts, 1982.

Shaw, E. B. "Sudden Unexpected Death in Infancy Syndrome." *Am J Dis Child 119*:416–418, May 1970.

Steinschneider, A. "A Reexamination of 'the Apnea Monitor Business.' " *Pediatrics 58*:1–5, July 1976.

Steinschneider, A. "Prolonged Apnea and the Sudden Infant Death Syndrome: Clinical and Laboratory Observations." *Pediatrics 50*:646–654, October 1972.

Szybist, C. *The Subsequent Child.* Chicago: National Sudden Infant Death Foundation, 1972.

Tonkin, S. "Sudden Infant Death Syndrome: Hypothesis of Causation." *Pediatrics 55*:650–661, May 1975.

Valdes-Dapena, M. A. "Sudden Infant Death Syndrome: A Review of the Medical Literature 1974–1979." *Pediatrics 66*:597–614, October 1980.

31

Failure
to Thrive

The syndrome of failure to thrive (FTT) is not uncommon in pediatric practice, and the assessment and management of this condition is sometimes complex. There are multiple etiologies to investigate, and hospitalization may be necessary to establish the cause. Management occasionally involves long-term care, depending on the specific organic etiology. If the etiology is nonorganic, there is also long-term management with a multidisciplinary approach including medical, nursing, social service, and community agency involvement.

The role of the nurse practitioner in this syndrome is to provide primary care to the child and psychosocial support and education to the child and family. The nurse practitioner also coordinates multidisciplinary and community agency involvement.

ASSESSMENT

Definition

In any child who consistently decelerates in weight on the growth curve or who falls below the third percentile ($-2\frac{1}{2}$ SD), a suspicion of FTT is considered. Occasionally FTT may be severe enough to cause decelerated growth on height and head circumference also.

Organic FTT refers to those pathologic, organic conditions that cause lack of growth. *Nonorganic* FTT includes those conditions where no organic etiology can be demonstrated. Environmental deprivation is the most common cause of nonorganic FTT (Sills, 1978). The incidence of organic FTT compared with nonorganic FTT varies depending on the study cited, but nonorganic causes are always more prevalent (Cupoli, 1980).

The above conditions are monitored over a period of weeks or months, depending on the age and the nutritional and developmental status of the child. Labels of FTT based on very short periods of observation are not substantial.

Establishing a Diagnosis

The following variables are considered in establishing a diagnosis (Rowe, 1977):

- There are frequent shifts in growth patterns of infants and toddlers.
- Length measurements are frequently inaccurate.
- Many large newborns do not remain large during the first 6 months of life.
- Acute and/or chronic illnesses influence growth patterns.
- Some racial groups have smaller bone structures and therefore weigh less.
- Growth charts may not be representative of the clinical population. For example, many growth grids used in the USA reflect measurements of white middle-class children. When comparing measurements of other racial and ethnic groups with these grids, discrepancies occur. The nurse practitioner should be aware of the representative population used in the growth grid in the health care agency.

Normal Growth Patterns

NEWBORNS

Newborns can normally lose up to 10 percent of their birth weight in the first few weeks of life through fluid losses: urination, defecation, respiration, and through normal decreased nutritional intake. If an infant has not regained his or her birth weight by 3 weeks of age, etiologies are investigated. Normally newborns gain at a rate of approximately 175 to 245 gm a week (5 to 7 oz), or 17 to 30 gm a day (½ to 1 oz); 1 oz equals approximately 30 gm.

INFANTS AND TODDLERS

Infants gain ½ to 1 oz (15 to 30 gm) per day during the first six months of life. Generally infants double their birth weight between 4 and 6 months and triple it by 12 months of age. Toddlers quadruple their birth weight by 2 years of age. After 2 years of age, there is little difference in the weight and height of premature and full-term infants.

CHILDHOOD

During the ages of 2 and 9 years the annual increase in weight averages approximately 2.6 kg (5 lb).

The average child grows approximately 25.4 cm (10 inches) in the first year of life, 12.7 cm (5 inches) in the second year, 7.6 to 10.2 cm (3 to 4 inches) in the third year, and 5.1 to 7.6 cm (2 to 3 inches) per year until puberty (Kempe et al., 1982).

A practical method to predict a child's approximate adult height is to double the child's height in inches at 2 years of age for males. For females the height at 2 years is also doubled, and 4 inches are subtracted.

The rate of growth after the first year of life reduces considerably and during childhood the rate is slow but steady. The nurse practitioner is referred to developmental texts for specific growth averages during childhood.

ADOLESCENCE

During adolescence a height spurt commences with females at approximately 9½ years of age, peaking at approximately 12 years of age, and stops at approximately 14 years of age. The height spurt in boys commences at approximately 10½ years of age, peaks at approximately 14 years of age, and stops at approximately 16 years of age (Tanner, 1962). See Chapter 8, Adolescent Physical Development.

Etiology

Chronic renal disease, cardiac and central nervous system deficits, severe anemia, genetic short stature, cystic fibrosis, diabetes, gastrointestinal malabsorption, and inflammatory bowel disease are the most frequent causes of organic FTT. Decreased nutritional intake due to psychosocial factors such as faulty parent-child bonding, chronic poverty, and unemployment is the cause of nonorganic FTT. Cupoli (1980) states that nonorganic FTT is a form of infantile depression that occurs in two forms. Under 2 years of age, it is due to maternal deprivation with an elevated fasting growth hormone and possible decreased caloric intake. Over 2 years of age, it is classified as deprivation dwarfism with low levels of ACTH and growth hormone.

When FTT is due to decreased caloric intake or to malabsorption, the weight decelerates more than the height, and the head circumference continues to accelerate. When FTT is due to genetic short stature, the length decelerates more than or equal to the weight, and the head circumference continues to accelerate. When FTT is due to a central nervous system deficit, chromosome abnormalities, endocrine malfunction, or intrauterine growth retardation, weight, height, and head circumference decelerate.

Other etiologies are numerous but infrequent. See Table 31-1 for a complete list of the possible causes of FTT. In determining the possible etiologies the nurse practitioner does the following:

- Obtains a health history (see this chapter, History)
- Assesses the child's nutritional intake
- Assesses the parent–child relationship
- Collects a family history in reference to adult height and weight
- Performs a physical examination to rule out anomalies
- Assesses the child's development
- Obtains appropriate laboratory studies

History

PARENTAL CONCERNS

Elicit the parents' concerns about the child's condition. This provides the practitioner with clues to the parents' feelings and insight into the problem.

FEEDING

- Review current nutritional intake including frequency of feedings, amounts and types of foods, snacks, how the child is fed: bottle (propped or held), spoon, or self-fed. See Chapter 3, Evaluation of Nutritional Status.
- Investigate eating habits that are suggestive of emotional deprivation such as eating spoiled foods, garbage, and nonfood items (pica).

PRESENT AND PAST HEALTH

Obtain information on the following:

- Frequency and duration of acute illnesses
- Exposure to infectious diseases
- Fevers
- Frequency of hospitalizations
- Severe injuries
- Allergies
- Stool pattern, including frequency, consistency, and color
- Occurrence of vomiting, regurgitation, and rumination
- Sleep problems

PARENT–CHILD DYAD

Assess how parents see the child in reference to the following:

- Difficulty with feedings, burping, vomiting
- General responses of the child to the parents: degree of cuddling, amount of crying, ability to be comforted
- Relation to other siblings, amount of rivalry
- Behavior suggestive of decreased stimulation: rocking, head banging, spinning
- Reaction to methods of discipline

PREGNANCY AND BIRTH

Ascertain the following information:

- Age of parents
- Gravida and para of the mother
- Date trimester prenatal care commenced

Table 31-1
Causes of Failure to Thrive

Maternal child deprivation
Socioeconomic
1. Poverty, unemployment
2. Drug, alcohol problems

Feeding problems
1. Organic abnormalities: cleft palate, mental retardation
2. Inadequate breast-feeding techniques or formula preparation

Low birth weight
1. Prematurity
2. Intrauterine growth retardation

Idiopathic short stature
1. Constitutional (familial) short stature
2. Delayed maturation and adolescence

Cardiovascular
1. Congenital heart defects

Gastrointestinal
1. Chronic diarrhea
2. Malabsorption syndromes
   Disaccharide deficiency
   Glucose–galactose malabsorption
   Celiac disease
   Disorders causing dysphagia, regurgitation, and vomiting: anatomic malformations, chalasia, pyloric stenosis

Renal
1. Chronic renal insufficiency
2. Renal tubular acidosis
3. Infections

Neurologic
1. Tumors including diencephalic syndrome
2. Perinatal central nervous system trauma
3. Developmental disorders
4. Subdural hematoma
5. Idiopathic

Endocrine
1. Thyroid disorders
   Hypothyroid
   Hyperthyroid
2. Hypopituitarism
   Idiopathic
   Organic lesions in hypothalamus or pituitary
3. Adrenal insufficiency

Table 31-1 (*Continued*)

Addison's disease
Adrenogenital syndrome (salt-losing form)
Prolonged steroid therapy
Hyperparathyroidism
Hematologic
1. Iron deficiency anemia
2. Hemaglobinopathies
Chronic or recurrent infection
1. Intrauterine: rubella, cytomegalovirus, toxoplasmosis, syphilis
2. Frequent, minor infections
3. Immunodeficiency syndromes
4. Phagocytic disorders
Genetic
1. Trisomies
Respiratory
1. Asthma
Metabolic
1. Rickets
2. Hypercalcemia
3. Galactosemia
4. Hereditary fructose intolerance
5. Glycogen storage disease
6. Phenylketonuria
Musculoskeletal and connective tissue abnormalities
1. Juvenile rheumatoid arthritis
2. Mucopolysaccharidoses
3. Myopathies
4. Hypophosphatasia
5. Pseudohypoparathyroidism

Source: From D. S. Rowe, Unpublished material.

• Trimester prenatal care was commenced
• Maternal nutrition during pregnancy, weight gain
• Amount of smoking, drug, or alcohol use.
• Hospitalizations, illnesses, including

1. Infections: syphilis, rubella, toxoplasmosis
2. Toxemia
3. Hypertension
4. Anemia

    5. Congenital heart disease

    6. Renal disease

- Amount of emotional support given to the mother during pregnancy
- Gestation in weeks, birth weight and length, type of delivery, type of anesthesia, postpartum and neonatal course

DEVELOPMENT

Discuss milestones appropriate for age: head up prone, smiles responsively, rolls over, sits, walks, first words.

FAMILY

Discuss the following with the parents:

- Familial diseases: allergies, heart disease, anemia, epilepsy, diabetes, congenital malformations
- Heights, weights, and developmental history of all family members
- Deaths of other siblings
- Deprivation of parents when they were children

GROWTH OF CHILD

Plot as many measurements as are available on the growth grid; discuss with parents their observations in reference to the child's height and weight as compared with peers.

SOCIAL/PSYCHOLOGIC

Discuss family unit, type housing, means of financial support, single parenting, relatives and friends available for help, degree of cohesiveness, depression of family members, chronic unemployment, and recent or past loss of family member of close friend. Assess family interaction with the child and the environmental milieu during a home visit.

REVIEW OF SYSTEMS

- Cardiorespiratory: shortness of breath, slow feeding, tiring easily with feeding, diaphoresis

- Gastrointestinal (bowel movements: presence of mucus, blood, fat, foul odor); presence of vomiting, rumination, regurgitation
- Neurologic: delayed developmental milestones
- Renal: chronic kidney infection
- Endocrine: Turner's syndrome, growth hormone deficiency
- Hematologic: severe anemia

Physical Examination

The physical examination and history are the most valuable tools in establishing a diagnosis (Sills, 1978). In addition to a complete examination, the following areas are emphasized:

- Weight, height, and head circumference accurately measured
- As many measurements as are obtainable plotted on the growth grid
- The number of teeth counted and correlated with the chronologic age
- Intellectual development correlated with age
- Sexual development correlated with age
- Thorough assessment of any physical defect
- Complete neurologic examination
- Complete developmental assessment
- Swallowing observed to establish pharyngeal–esophageal competence

Laboratory

Initial laboratory tests include the following:

- Complete blood count and smear to rule out anemia, hematologic disorders, infection
- Urinalysis and culture to rule out impaired kidney function
- Creatinine, BUN to rule out impaired kidney function
- Serum electrolytes and CO_2 to rule out renal tubular acidosis, dehydration
- Stool analysis for:

1. Occult blood to rule out possible cow milk intolerance, inflammatory bowel disease
2. Ova and parasites
3. Reducing substances and pH to rule out mono- and disaccharide deficiency
4. Fat to rule out malabsorption

- Tuberculin test

Other laboratory studies if indicated include the following:

- X-ray films for bone age to help ascertain growth hormone deficiency, dystrophies, malnutrition
- Sweat chloride to rule out cystic fibrosis
- PBI and T_4 to rule out hypothyroidism
- Buccal smear in short-stature children with delayed pubescence to rule out Turner's syndrome
- Fat analysis and stool trypsin of 72-hour stool to rule out malabsorption
- Liver function studies
- Upper GI series to rule out anatomic anomalies
- Lower GI series to rule out ulcerative colitis, Hirschsprung's disease
- X-ray films of the skull to rule out increased intracranial pressure, hematomas, tumor

While laboratory studies provide additional information in determining the etiology, the initial nutritional, developmental, family/psychosocial histories, and physical examination determine most etiologies. Sills (1978) found that in 2,607 laboratory studies on 185 cases of FTT only 10 studies (0.4 percent) helped establish the diagnosis. Therefore, when the clinical examination suggests a nonorganic etiology, laboratory studies are of questionable significance.

Indications for Hospital Admission

Children are hospitalized with FTT for the following reasons:

- Child at risk nutritionally and needs immediate treatment

- Observation of parent–child interaction, infant behavior, feeding routines, clarification of nutritional intake
- Performance of complex diagnostic procedures
- Observation of weight gain, if any, when removed from the home
- Interrupt dysfunctional parent–child relationship, if evident
- Provide respite for caretakers

Cupoli (1980) recommends hospitalization within 1 to 2 months of steady deceleration on the growth curve.

Common Problems with Short-Term Hospitalization

The following list is from Rowe (1977). See References in this chapter.

- Multiple caretakers in the hospital are frequently confusing to the parents.
- It is difficult to consistently observe mother–infant interaction and feeding techniques in a busy hospital.
- Occasionally, hospital staff are unfriendly or punitive toward parents.
- Diagnostic procedures interfere with feeding routines and nurturing.
- It may be difficult for parents to visit the child in the hospital due to lack of transportation, baby-sitting problems at home, and lack of financial resources.
- Parents may feel threatened if the child improves clinically.

MANAGEMENT

Specific management depends on the results of the history, observations of the parent-child relationship, social/psychologic assessments, physical examination, and laboratory studies.

Ambulatory

If no organic cause for FTT is found, the initial steps in management are to provide adequate calories and to measure the child's caloric intake. If the nurse practitioner has any confusion about the oral intake, a 3-day dietary history is written by the parent at home. See Chapter 3, Evaluation of Nutritional Status. The nurse practitioner discusses with parents feeding difficulties such as regurgitation, chalasia, and vomiting and advises frequent burping and sitting up after feeding.

Social/psychologic problems are managed according to the specific problem. Public health nurses provide increased education, home evaluation, and psychologic support. Social service helps correct economic concerns and provides counseling for unemployment and psychologic problems.

Hospital

Hospitalization is indicated only if a diagnosis cannot be determined on an outpatient basis or if the child is at risk nutritionally or socially. Oral intake is more accurately monitored in the hospital than in the home. Depending on the cause of FTT, support services, if needed, can be instituted by social service. After a period of observation on a therapeutic nutritional regimen, the following conclusions are drawn:

- Adequate intake with normal weight gain indicates past history of inadequate feeding with decreased calorie intake due most commonly to dysfunctional parent–child relationship.
- Adequate intake with no weight gain indicates possible malabsorption problem, chronic infection, kidney malfunction, and psychosocial problems.
- Inadequate intake with no weight gain indicates possible anatomic abnormalities: cleft palate, micrognathia, tracheo-esophageal fistula, congenital heart disease, neurologic disorder.

Follow-Up Care

FTT children generally require long-term follow-up. It is helpful for these clients to see the same health professionals for ambulatory management after hospital discharge. Other personnel helpful in providing support services are the public health nurse, community agencies with programs for children with congenital defects, and day-care nurseries for role modeling and respite services for the parents.

ROLE OF THE NURSE PRACTITIONER

Organic Etiology The nurse practitioner's responsibilities are as follows:

- Provides psychologic support and counsel in helping the family cope with the child
- Monitors compliance with the management plan
- Assesses the need for additional health education and support services

Nonorganic Etiology The nurse practitioner's responsibilities are as follows:

- Establishes a therapeutic, nonthreatening, long-term relationship with the family
- Intervenes and reverses the faulty parent–child relationship by:
  1. Nurturing the parents
  2. Acting as a nonthreatening role model in demonstrating how to care for the child
  3. Developing a nonpunitive approach in teaching nutrition, stimulation, and play
  4. Helping the family to understand their stresses and to seek solutions
  5. Referring family to appropriate social agencies when indicated

COMMON CLINICAL PROBLEM

Failure to Thrive (FTT) Due to Parental Deprivation

ASSESSMENT

Definition The term parental deprivation rather than maternal deprivation is used in this chapter. This recognizes the fact that both men and women are sharing the responsibility of child rearing. Men are also more numerous as single parents than in the past. Because of economic realities, in most families both parents work to support the family financially. Therefore, the job responsibilities and sexual roles of each parent as caretaker of the children are less defined and more complexly integrated into behaviors that involve both male and female traits.

The concept of parental deprivation has evolved over a period of years. Originally it was thought to be the cause of failure to thrive in children who were receiving institutionalized care. Gradually, the concept of parental deprivation has been expanded to include any situation in which there is insufficient interaction, be it physical or emotional, between the child and the parent figure.

Patton and Gardner (1962) state that family dysfunction and specific disturbances with parental deprivation results in the syndrome of FTT in which, besides having severe growth retardation, there is delayed skeletal maturation and retarded motor and intellectual development. Other data suggest that these deprived infants are underweight because of not being offered enough calories rather than because of an organic or psychologically induced defect in absorption or metabolism (Whitten et al., 1969).

Psychodynamics An understanding of the underlying factors is essential for adequate management of the problem.

MATERNAL Implicit in the way women respond to the needs of their children is the way in which they themselves were nurtured as children. Normally the mother or maternal figure nurtures and cultivates in the child a responsiveness, closeness, and sense of trust in human beings. Women lacking in adequate emotional support and nurturing during their childhood emerge into adulthood with a severe lack of self-esteem and with a failure to establish and to maintain satisfying relationships with those who are close to them. Hence, their inability to adequately care for and to nurture their own children. Frequently they are also isolated and without satisfying recreational outlets or emotionally supportive peer relationships. The pregnancy most often is unplanned. Frequently they are chronically depressed and are burdened by stresses: financial, marital, and emotional. They have difficulty recognizing the needs of their infant and have problems in performing adaptive mothering behaviors that support maternal infant bonding, such as smiling, cooing at the infant, maintaining eye contact, holding the infant close, and formulating adequate feeding routines. See Chapter 4, Assessment of Parent–Child Interaction. Many mothers are easily frustrated by the infant's response to their mothering, which may not always be positive. For example, some infants may continue to cry when held or may regurgitate frequently.

PATERNAL Fathers or paternal figures are usually unsympathetic and not understanding of the mother's social and psychologic situation. They offer the mother little physical and emotional support. They may also feel overburdened with the responsibilities of parenting. If fathers are single parents, there are the added stresses of possible financial problems, job responsibilities, child-care problems, and social isolation.

FAMILY There are usually family stresses, including single parenting, social isolation, unemployment, financial or marital problems, transient family members, chronic illness, drug or alcohol use, and depression.

History In considering parental deprivation as a cause of FTT, the following information is obtained.

PAST HISTORY Discuss general health during pregnancy, trimester at which care was first obtained, if pregnancy was planned, mother's emotional reaction when she learned she was pregnant, emotional support received by mother during pregnancy, whether therapeutic abortion was considered, illnesses, hospitalizations, injuries during pregnancy length of labor, type of delivery, anesthesia, rooming-in in hospital, when mother first began to care for the baby in the hospital, and paternal support.

NUTRITION Discuss type and amount of foods, difficulties in feeding routines as perceived by parents, child's reaction to food, difficulties with swallowing, sucking, regurgitation, and vomiting, type and consistency of bowel movements.

FAMILY Discuss current support measures available to parent, routine of daily life, current familial stresses: financial, social, unemployment, use of drugs, alcohol, illness in family.

Observation of Parent-Child Interaction Observe if the mother or father holds the child close to the body, if there is eye contact, if the parent smiles or plays with the child; ask the parent if there are any complaints about the child: cries too much, dirty, bad; ascertain if the parent has time away from the infant; changing diapers, bathing the baby; ascertain if the parent is an able historian in reference to the child's daily routine.

Observation of Infant Behavior Observe if the infant cuddles toward the parent and gives responses either verbally or facially when stimulated; observe the child's response toward food; observe whether the child looks to the parent for comfort and security in stressful situations; ascertain the child's general developmental status.

Physical Examination In addition to a complete physical examination, a developmental assessment is done to determine the degree of social interaction and covert developmental delays.

Behavioral Manifestations Authorities cite various behavioral manifestations in FTT children. Growth retardation is strongly associated with disturbances in eating and abnormalities in sleeping and elimination with the most noticeable differences in eating behaviors: less regular meals, small amount of food served at mealtimes, and meals more often skipped (Pollitt, 1976). Children are understimulated and retarded in motor and social skills and show little differentiation between strangers and caretakers (Rhymes, 1966). Evidence shows environmental deprivation, marital instability, and a high proportion of mothers with character disorders (Fischhoff et al., 1971). There is an increased incidence of FTT in abused and premature children (Fanaroff et al., 1972). Infantile posture in FTT children due to sensory deprivation is occasionally observed. In this posture, the elbow joints are flexed 90° or more, the humerus is abducted and rotated outward, the hands are pronated and positioned at the side of the head (Kreiger and Sargent, 1967).

Home Visit The purpose of the home visit is to:

• Assess parental child interaction over a longer period of time than is permissible in an office visit
• Observe feeding techniques
• Assess the home environment in reference to safety, availability of infant care items (sleeping area, toys, utensils for feeding, bathing)
• Discuss with other family members their availability to support parents

- Continue to develop a relationship based on nurturing and the establishment of trust
- Act as a nonthreatening role model, in reference to age-appropriate play activities, stimulation, feeding techniques, nutrition, development of parenting behavior.

MANAGEMENT

Hospitalization See this chapter, Common Problems with Short-Term Hospitalization. FTT children with suspicion of psychosocial causes are admitted to the hospital for the following:

- To perform further diagnostic tests to determine if organic etiology is also present
- To allow for possible weight gain away from the home environment
- To obtain further social and psychologic assessment of the family milieu
- To explore family stresses
- To provide respite for the family
- To assess family's ability to care for the child
- To provide role modeling in caring for and nurturing the infant
- To encourage the parents to become active in the child's care and to support them in their attempts at parenting
- To explore with the family community resources for support after hospitalization
- To offer an ongoing therapeutic regimen for the family

Role of the Nurse Practitioner The long-term follow-up demands active participation of the nurse practitioner in all areas of management.

INPATIENT During hospitalization the nurse practitioner is involved in the hospital conferences with the family and helps plan for the child's discharge by formulating a plan for care, implementing the follow-up, and establishing the family with available community services.

COUNSELING To promote a feeling of acceptance and self-worth in parents of FTT infants, the nurse practitioner listens and exhibits sincere interest in the parent as a person. In order not to intimidate the parents, the nurse does not act as an authority figure on any aspect of child care. The primary focus of the nurse's role is to nurture the parents. It is in this consistent and therapeutic contact that parents are able to form a trusting relationship with the nurse and therefore begin to develop a positive self-image. In discussing feeding and play regimens, the nurse assumes a role of collaboration with the parents where ideas and suggestions are mutually discussed and accepted or discarded. The parents are encouraged to find solutions to their questions and are praised for any attempt at communication however slight. The nurse assesses the parents' understanding of age-appropriate nutritional requirements and play activities. The nurse discusses the child's physical and emotional needs and together with the parents outlines ways to meet these needs.

The nurse initiates discussion around the parents' past experience in nurturing and their own relationship with their parents. The nurse discusses current stresses in the parents' life and helps to formulate possible solutions. Acceptance of the parents' feelings both positive and negative toward the child is necessary.

In all discussions the nurse acts as a trusted friend teaching by role modeling and suggestions about child caring rather than by threatening, didactic instruction. Social service is involved in counseling when needed for further support and for psychologic evaluation.

HOME VISIT In the management of any complex health problem adequate reversal of negative trends cannot be accomplished without reinforcement of positive aspects of the office visit through follow-up home visits. In FTT due to parental deprivation the consistency of a limited number of caretakers is desirable to aid the parent in establishing a relationship. Therefore it is advisable to have the home visiting done by a person who will be involved with the parent on a long-term basis. The goals of home visiting are discussed under Assessment.

ROLE MODELING To help the parents become more nurturing the nurse is a role model in projecting nurturing, caring, and supportive behavior toward the child in a manner that is nonthreatening to the parent. Although the child is the object of the discussions, the main focus of attention continues to be the parents, and they are encouraged and supported in whatever response they make toward the child.

Projecting nurturing behavior encompasses a variety of actions:

- Feeding: holding the infant close, positive eye contact, smiling and cooing
- Stimulation: initiating verbal behavior, repeating the child's sounds, stroking and touching the child, providing age-appropriate visual stimulatory objects
- General care: inadvisability of propping the bottle, importance of maintaining routine feeding times, asking for support when needed

Role of the Family Improved interactions between parent and child cannot be accomplished without the inclusion of other family members into the management milieu. If they are unable to accompany the parents on ambulatory visits, or if they are not available during home visits, it is advisable to do the following:

- Encourage their direct participation in providing support to the parents
- Discuss possible stressful situations in the family that may hinder adequate establishment of parent-child bonding
- Offer resources in reference to further discussion of family or interpersonal stresses

Community Community agencies assist parents in helping to further establish an identity, to cope with the demands of living, and to provide occasional respite from parenting. The goals of referral are to offer the parents the following solutions:

- Other therapeutic relationships where parents can discuss fears and feelings
- A constructive outlet to enhance feelings of self-worth in areas such as job training, part-time and volunteer work, and school

Agencies helpful in accomplishing some of these tasks:

- Talk or crisis lines where parents can call at any hour for support and counsel
- Local child abuse councils
- Parent discussion groups at local health centers or hospital clinics
- Adult education

- Child development classes
- Local community agencies that are advocates for increased funding for day care, support for single parenting
- Day-care nurseries
- Infant stimulation programs

References

Barbero, G. and C. Shaheen. "Environmental Failure to Thrive: A Clinical View." *J Pediatr 71*:639–644, November 1967.

Barnard, M. and L. Wolf. "Psychosocial Failure to Thrive." *Nurs Clin North Am 8*:556–565, September 1973.

Cupoli, J. "Failure to Thrive." *Curr Prob Pediatr 10*:2–43, September 1980.

Fanaroff, A., J. Kennell, and M. Klaus. "Follow-Up of Low Birth Weight Infants: The Predictive Value of Maternal Visiting Patterns." *Pediatrics 49*:289–290, February 1972.

Fischhoff, J., C. Whitten, and M. Pettit. "A Psychiatric Study of Mothers of Infants with Growth Failure Secondary to Maternal Deprivation." *J Pediatr 79*:209–215, August 1971.

Harrison, L. L. "Nursing Intervention with the Failure to Thrive Family." *Am J of Maternal Child Nursing 1*:111–116, January/February 1976.

Johnson, P. "Role of the Pediatric Nurse Practitioner in Early Recognition of Failure-To-Thrive Infants Due to Maternal Deprivation." Unpublished masters thesis, University of California, San Francisco, 1976.

Kempe, C., H. Silver, and D. O'Brien. *Current Pediatric Diagnosis and Treatment.* 7th ed. Los Altos, CA: Lange Medical Publications, 1982.

Kennedy, J. "The High-Risk Maternal-Infant Acquaintance Process." *Nurs Clin North Am 8*:549–556, September 1973.

Krieger, I. and D. A. Sargent. "A Postural Sign in the Sensory Deprivation Syndrome in Infants." *J Pediatr 70*:332–339, March 1967.

Leonard, T. "Failure to Thrive in Infants: A Family Problem." *Am J Dis Child 111*:600–612, June 1966.

Money, J. "Dwarfism, Questions and Answers in Counseling." *Rehabilitation Literature 28*:134–138, May 1967.

Patton, R. and L. Gardner. "Influence of Family Environment on Growth: The Syndrome of Maternal Deprivation." *Pediatrics 30*:957–962, December, 1962.

Pollitt, E. "Behavioral Disturbances Among Failure to Thrive Children." *Am J Dis Child 130*:24–29, January 1976.

Pollitt, E., A. Eichler, and C. K. Chan. "Psychosocial Development and Behavior of Mothers of Failure to Thrive Children." *Am J Orthopsychiatry 45*:525–537, 1975.

Rhymes, J. P. "Working with Mothers and Babies Who Fail to Thrive." *Am J Nurs* *66*:1972–1976, September 1966.

Rowe, D. S. Unpublished material, February 1977.

Sills, R. "Failure to Thrive." *Am J Dis Child 132*:967–969, October 1978.

Smith, D., et al. "Shifting linear growth during infancy: Illustration of genetic factors in growth from fetal life through infancy." *J Pediatr 89*:225, August 1976.

Tanner, J. M. *Growth at Adolescence*. Oxford: Blackwell Scientific Publications, 1962.

Whitten, C., M. Pettit, and J. Fischhoff. "Evidence That Growth Failure from Maternal Deprivation is Secondary to Undereating." *JAMA 209*:1675–1682, September 15, 1969.

32

Child Abuse

Child abuse is the physical or mental injury, sexual abuse, or negligent treatment of a child under 18 years of age. In recent years the concept of abuse has been expanded to include neglect. While it is consistently harder to document and prove neglect in a court of law, these cases usually involve the following:

- Failure to thrive children where no medical/biologic causes can be found
- Parental deprivation syndromes
- Chronic neglect which results in frequent, serious injury to the child
- Children with no committed, consistent daily care

The possibility of child abuse was considered in 1940 when John Caffey, M.D., noted frequent associations of chronic subdural hematomas in infants with multiple fractures of the long bones (Rudolph, 1982). National attention was brought to the issue of child abuse by C. Henry Kempe, M.D., in 1962 when he coined the phrase "battered child syndrome." Since then, the public has become increasingly aware of the phenomenon of child abuse as one of the major causes of death and permanent disability in children.

The assessment and management of this complex problem require an understanding of the psychodynamics of child abuse and the development of a therapeutic, nonthreatening relationship with the family. Occasionally the decision is made that the child's welfare is more secure away from the family. However, the focus is to have the child reunited with the family after rehabilitation has begun.

The nurse practitioner is an integral part of the multidisciplinary team approach to the assessment and long-term management of child abuse. The nurse offers psychosocial support to the parents, acts as a role model for nurturing the child, investigates community support services for the family, and is the continuity person for consistent management and follow-up care.

ASSESSMENT

Incidence

While no exact statistics are currently available, it is estimated that one to three percent of children in the United States are abused or neglected (Sturner, 1980). Four thousand children die each year from abuse. In addition to the fatalities that occur, a large number of abused and neglected children suffer permanent physical, neurologic, and emotional retardation.

Epidemiology

Children below the age of 3 years are the most frequent victims of abuse. It is estimated that one third of abuse occurs in infants under 6 months, one third occurs in children between 6 months and three years, and one third occurs over 3 years of age (Schmitt and Kempe, 1975).

Women are more frequent abusers than men because they are usually the primary caretakers. Men abuse more severely and are involved in sexual abuse. Occasionally other relatives and friends commit abuse. Ninety-five percent of abuse is committed by parents or a boyfriend (Schmitt and Kempe, 1975). Abuse occurs in all races and socioeconomic classes, but statistics report a higher incidence in lower socioeconomic classes. However, these clients use facilities where reporting is routinely done, in contrast to private physicians where only approximately 2 percent of all cases are reported.

Psychodynamics

SOCIAL

A crisis usually precipitates the abusive occurrence. The crisis is in line with a long series of frustrations and inabilities to cope, such as living in poverty, marital disharmony, single parent, heavy drug and alcohol use, isolation, unemployment, too many children, and chronic illness. It is believed that social isolation may be the principal contributor to child abuse (Ellerstein, 1981). Occasionally the crisis may be a relatively minor event, but one that carries enough force to result in the abuse of a child. Sometimes, the injury is premeditated.

PARENTS

Most parents do not want to cause injury to their children (Heindl, 1981). Injury generally occurs when there is a loss of self-control by the parent. Retrospective studies on abusive parents show low self-esteem, increased life stress, free expression of aggressive impulses, early marriages, and abuse during their own childhood. A prospective study of 1,400 low socioeconomic mothers showed that 23 of the women in the sample later became abusers. The abusive mother's behavioral traits were compared with the rest of the women in the study who served as controls. In contrast to retrospective studies on abusive mothers, this study showed only slightly less self-esteem than the controls, no social isolation, and no history of abuse as a child. The study showed that mothers had negative relationships with parents, unrealistic expectations of the child, less money than the controls, and a history of alcohol and drug abuse (Altemeier, 1982). Since the results of these studies are not definitive, more prospective research needs to be done on attributes of abusing parents.

Parents exhibit a lack of trust toward other people and see the child as the person who can provide the love, support, and nurturing they lack in their own lives. They may also exhibit feelings of anger, ambivalence, and rejection toward the child. Generally, parents have little self-esteem and are in need of constant reassurance. This lower self-concept may be compensated for by trying to be a perfect parent and setting unrealistic standards for a child's performance. Some may have high expectations of their child similar to their own treatment in their childhood (Rosen and Stein, 1980).

Abusive parents usually visit several health care agencies for treatment and initially may bring in the child for minor complaints before abuse is commenced. They usually demonstrate little concern about the injury and understand little in reference to the child's development. Generally, they have poor impulse control.

CHILD

The child is singled out as someone who is different. Although it is common for several children in one family to be abused, there is usually one child who is more abused than others. This child is quite possibly chronically ill, was premature at birth, has a physical deformity, is hyperactive, and generally more difficult to manage.

Abused children show a high degree of ability, in reference to their age, in caring for the parent and in responding to the parents' need for nurturing. Occasionally, abused children show overall poor hygiene. They sometimes exhibit unusual fear and will not look at the parents for reassurance in unfamiliar situations. Some children have a vacant stare and show a lack of reaction during invasive medical procedures. They may not cry when disciplined. Some children are smarter than their parents which causes hostility between parent and child.

Approach to Interviewing the Parents

An attitude of empathy is necessary in interviewing parents of children with suspected nonaccidental injuries. Knowledge of social and psychologic dynamics of child abuse helps the interviewer to develop an objective, nonpunitive approach toward the parents.

It is not relevant to obtain an admission from the parents if abuse took place and who committed it. As an ego defense to the guilt, fear, and inadequacy they feel, parents frequently use the mechanisms of denial and projection in child abuse situations. Antagonizing the parents with interrogating questions will create further denial, hostility, and an inability to establish a relationship of trust with the health team.

If the facts surrounding the injury are confusing to the interviewer it is best to assume that for whatever reasons, there is, or has been, a family or social crisis. The expression of a sympathetic attitude and recognition that the parents have been trying to do their best in the worst of circumstances focuses attention on the parents' needs and problems and avoids discussing the child and the injuries. This course of action begins the therapeutic and supportive relationship that must be established if meaningful interventions are to be produced. A therapeutic interview allows the parents to maintain their sense of esteem.

Depending on the parent's response and attitude, the interviewer proceeds to gain insight into the family situation, possible stressful occurrences, degree of isolation felt by the parents, and availability of support measures. If the parent is hostile, distrustful, or resentful to the interviewer, it is best to discuss this with the parent using "I feel that you are very angry" language. The interviewers maintain a calm attitude and let the parents know of their desire to help and to be supportive.

Some parents will deny that there are any problems. In this situation after initial attempts to establish rapport have failed, it is best not to proceed further and to allow the parent time with the denial mechanism.

Hospitalization is approached from the standpoint of observation of the child and the necessity to perform other diagnostic procedures. The best time to discuss the suspicion of child abuse is debatable. This situation depends on the attitude of the parents, the degree of injury, and the possibility that the parents might leave with the child. In many instances the parents are informed after the child is admitted into the hospital. If rapport has been established with the parents in the emergency room, occasionally they are told at that time. In telling the parents a simple statement is best: "Because injuries like this can be nonaccidental, or in cases where child abuse or neglect is suspected, I am required by law to report it to the proper authorities." Further explanations are given to the parents about the usual follow-up procedures when appropriate.

If there is any reason to believe that the parents will leave with the child, a police hold is obtained for a period of 72 hours by calling the local child protective agency or, if at night or on weekends, the local police department. If the parent attempts to leave with the child, he or she should not be stopped, and the police should be called immediately.

History

History suspicious of child abuse includes the following:

- An injury that cannot be explained
- Different histories from parents and/or partner or baby sitter
- Explanation of self-injury in infant under 6 months of age (rolled over on leg and broke it)
- Delay in seeking medical attention
- Past history of suspicious injury
- No one with responsibility for caring for child

The history investigates circumstances surrounding the injury, past history of accidents or similar injuries, other agencies used in the care of the child, accidents with siblings, time of occurrence of injury, and time of arrival at the health agency; there is usually a long delay between the two in child abuse cases. Questions are asked about the number of people in the family, support measures for child care, recent family stresses, or financial burdens.

Physical Examination

A complete physical examination is done, including the following:

- Skin: observe for abrasions, burns, belt marks, bites, bruises (fresh or old, variation of color, healing stages), outlines of blunt instruments, ropes or cords, slap or grab marks
- HEENT: mouth, upper lip, and frenulum: bruises in various healing stages; fundoscopic examination for occult injury to retina
- Chest: bruises around breast
- Abdomen: palpate for tenderness, organomegaly, observe for distention, ascultate bowel sounds

- Extremities: observe for symmetrical movements, full range of motion; palpate bones for tenderness
- Genitalia: tears, lacerations, hematoma, erythema of clitoris, labia, vagina; discharge from vagina; unusually large opening; presence of venereal warts; vagina–anus: peri-anal abrasions, hematomas, lacerations, ecchymoses.
- Neurologic: assess gross motor, fine motor abilities; symmetrical DTRS
- Height/weight: deviations noted

Common Clinical Findings

- Skin: old scars, ecchymosis, soft tissue swelling, human bites, burns: cigarette, dry contact burns from heater, usually second degree, water burns (child held and dropped into scalding water, hands and feet usually spared)
- Fractures: skull, rib, limb, presence of old fractures on X-ray films, epiphyseal separations
- Subdural hematomas
- Intestinal injuries: tears of mysentery of small intestines from punch or blow; ruptured spleen or liver from crushing forces; vomiting, abdominal distention, absent bowel sounds
- Trauma to genitals
- Growth retardation
- Poor hygiene
- Shaken infant syndrome caused by manual shaking of trunk or extremities resulting in intraocular and intracranial hemorrhage or neck injury (Caffey, 1974).

Rare Injuries

- Subgaleal hematomas caused by pulling of braids or hair (Kempe, 1975b)
- Bruise of upper lip, floor of mouth, and frenulum caused by forceful feeding (Schmitt and Kempe, 1975)
- Traumatic pancreatic cysts and rupture of liver caused by abdominal blows (Kempe, 1975b)

- Hypernatremic dehydration in older children in instances where a psychotic parent withholds water to decrease bed wetting (Kempe, 1975)
- Intential poisonings (Dine and McGovern, 1982).

Laboratory

- Full-body X-ray films
- Complete blood count
- Urinalysis
- Electrolytes
- Toxicology screen
- PT, PTT, platelets, if bruising present

Differential Diagnosis

- Accidental trauma
- Rare bone diseases: osteogenesis imperfecta
- Scurvy
- Rickets
- Syphilis of infancy

Risk Screening

See Tables 32-1, 32-2, 32-3, and 32-4, and Chapter 4, Assessment of Parent–Child Interaction.

MANAGEMENT

Prevention

Because deaths, serious injuries, and long-term defects occur from child abuse, because rehabilitation is lengthy and costly to individuals and society, and because the emotional trauma to families, health professionals, and the community is long lasting, prevention of child abuse is the most effective management.

Table 32-1
Observations of Parents-To-Be in Physician's Office or Prenatal Clinic

1. Are the parents overconcerned with the baby's sex?
2. Are they overconcerned with the baby's performance? Do they worry that he will not meet the standard?
3. Is there an attempt to deny that there is a pregnancy (mother not willing to gain weight, no plans whatsoever, refusal to talk about the situation)?
4. Is this child going to be one child too many? Could he be the "last straw"?
5. Is there great depression over this pregnancy?
6. Is the mother alone and frightened, especially by the physical changes caused by the pregnancy? Do careful explanations fail to dissipate these fears?
7. Is support lacking from husband and/or family?
8. Where is the family living? Do they have a listed telephone number? Are there relatives and friends nearby?
9. Did the mother and/or father formerly want an abortion but not go through with it or waited until it was too late?
10. Have the parents considered relinquishment of their child? Why did they change their minds?

Source: Reprinted with permission from C. H. Kempe, "Approaches to Preventing Child Abuse," *Am J of Dis in Child 130*:941–947, 1976; copyright 1976, American Medical Association.

There are three types of prevention: primary, secondary, and tertiary.

PRIMARY PREVENTION

This involves community health education classes, especially in junior and senior high schools, with topics on parenting, family development, birth control, and interpersonal relationships. Other classes to increase the effectiveness of parenting include prenatal and postnatal groups, infant and toddler child development courses, and parent effectiveness training (PET). Community support services such as self-help groups, nursery schools, telephone hot lines, or parental stress counseling services help in primary prevention of child abuse. Encouraging postpartum rooming in, birthing centers, and prolonged visiting to prematures helps increase bonding between parent and child.

Table 32-2
Observations to be Made at Postpartum Check-ups and Pediatric Check-ups

1. Does the mother have fun with the baby?
2. Does the mother establish eye contact (direct en face position) with the baby?
3. How does the mother talk to her baby? Is everything she expresses a demand?
4. Are most of her verbalizations about the child negative?
5. Does she remain disappointed over the child's sex?
6. What is the child's name? Where did it come from? When did they name the child?
7. Are the mother's expectations for the child's development far beyond the child's capabilities?
8. Is the mother very bothered by the baby's crying? How does she feel about the crying?
9. Does the mother see the baby as too demanding during feedings? Is she repulsed by the messiness? Does she ignore the baby's demands to be fed?
10. What is the mother's reaction to the task of changing diapers?
11. When the baby cries, does she or can she comfort him?
12. What was/is the husband's and/or family's reaction to the baby?
13. What kind of support is the mother receiving?
14. Are there sibling rivalry problems?
15. Is the husband jealous of the baby's drain on the mother's time and affection?
16. When the mother brings the child to the physician's office, does she get involved and take control over the baby's needs and what's going to happen (during the examination and while in the waiting room) or does she relinquish control to the physician or nurse (undressing the child, holding him, allowing him to express his fears, etc)?
17. Can attention be focused on the child in the mother's presence? Can the mother see something positive for her in that?
18. Does the mother make nonexistent complaints about the baby? Does she describe to you a child that you don't see there at all? Does she call with strange stories that the child has, for example, stopped breathing, turned color, or is doing something "on purpose" to aggravate the parent?
19. Does the mother make emergency calls for very small things, not major things?

Source: Reprinted with permission from C. H. Kempe, "Approaches to Preventing Child Abuse," *Am J of Dis in Child* 130:941–947, 1976; copyright 1976, Amrican Medical Association.

Table 32-3
Positive Family Circumstances

1. The parents see likeable attributes in the baby and perceive him as an individual.
2. The baby is healthy and not too disruptive to the parents' life-style.
3. Either parent can rescue the child or relieve one another in a crisis.
4. The parents' marriage is stable.
5. The parents have a good friend or relative to turn to, a sound "need-meeting" system.
6. The parents exhibit coping abilities, ie, the capacity to plan, and understand the need for adjustments because of the new baby.
7. The mother is intelligent and her health is good.
8. The parents had helpful role models when they grew up.
9. The parents can have fun together and with their personal interests and hobbies.
10. The parents practice birth control; the baby was planned or wanted.
11. The father has a steady job. The family has its own home, and living conditions are stable.
12. The father is supportive of the mother and involved in the care of the baby.

Source: Reprinted with permission from C. H. Kempe, "Approaches to Preventing Child Abuse," *Am J of Dis in Child 130*:941–947, 1976; copyright 1976, American Medical Association.

Table 32-4
Special Well-Child Care for High-Risk Families

1. Promote maternal attachment to the newborn.
2. Phone the mother during the first two days at home.
3. Provide more frequent office visits.
4. Give more attention to the mother.
5. Emphasize nutrition.
6. Counsel discipline only for accident prevention.
7. Emphasize accident prevention.
8. Use compliments rather than criticism.
9. Accept phone calls at home.
10. Arrange for regular home visits by a public health nurse or a lay health visitor.

Source: Reprinted with permission from C. H. Kempe, "Approaches to Preventing Child Abuse," *Am J of Dis in Child 130*:941–947, 1976; copyright 1976, American Medical Association.

SECONDARY PREVENTION

This involves knowledge of families who are at risk for child abuse. These include isolated or single parents and families with psychiatric, substance abuse, economic, and social problems. For these families, providing frequent social service support and counseling, increasing the number of pediatric visits to include more health education and support, providing public health nursing visits, encouraging support from family and friends, and working with community agencies to help decrease family and social problems is mandatory.

TERTIARY PREVENTION

This involves prevention of re-injury to the child once primary injury has occurred. This may be accomplished by foster care of the child by court mandate or until the family is rehabilitated, through psychologic counseling and child development classes. Lay health visitors, a service developed by C. Henry Kempe, M.D., in Denver, advocates lay community persons to visit daily to act as helpers and supporters and deflectors of stress in the families' lives.

Reporting

It is mandatory that all cases of suspected abuse and neglect in the United States be reported to the proper authorities. Physicians commonly report child abuse, but in various states paraprofessional or lay persons can also report. All persons reporting child abuse are immune from court action for civil liability. Failure to report suspected cases can result in prosecution.

Generally, cases are reported to child protective agencies of the local or state government. The objectives of this agency are to prevent and to investigate child abuse and to provide social services to help rehabilitate abusive parents. It also refers those cases to juvenile court when parents are unable or unwilling to use the help offered by the agency. Occasionally cases are reported to the local police department, but most authorities recommend reporting to the child protective agency. Their approach is less punitive and more psychotherapeutically oriented. The agency is called first, and a written report follows within 36 hours.

Legal Definitions

1. A protective police hold for 72 hours from the police department is obtained when there is concern that the parents may leave with the child before assessment is completed or that parents may re-injure the child if child is left with them or when parents refuse to cooperate with hospitalization.
2. A dependency hearing (petition) is a legal maneuver that permits the child protective agency to request temporary custody of the child. If the petition is granted, the child becomes a ward of the state, and the court can insist that the parents undergo a rehabilitation program before the child is returned to the home. The case is reviewed in 6 months.
3. Placement is when a ward of the court is placed in a foster home due to the parents' inability to care for the child. The goal is eventual re-uniting of the family, after rehabilitation is evident.

Goals of Management

- Protection of the child
- Support and rehabilitative regimens for parents and caretakers
- Returning the child to the home when it is judged safe
- Eliminating social ills from society that contribute to child abuse

Hospitalization

Medical problems resulting from abuse are treated. Social service assessment is initiated and plans are made for follow-up care. Photographs from the police department crime laboratory are obtained to document injuries.

Placing the child in the hospital even for minor suspicious injuries accomplishes several objectives. It gives the health professional time to investigate the family's psychologic milieu, methods of functioning with one another, and current life stresses. It also separates the family and the child which is therapeutic in that it gives the family a rest and it protects the child.

During hospitalization, the parents' attitudes are continuously assessed for their desire and cooperation in participating in the care plan. If they exhibit symptoms of psychosis or extreme neurosis, a psychiatric evaluation is made.

Role of the Health Care Team

Management of child abuse is provided by a multidisciplinary team involving physicians, nurses, social workers, and protective service agencies. Other disciplines are involved as needed including a psychiatrist, lawyer, and community representatives.

Generally, principles of care include the following:

• Maintaining an empathic, nonauthoritarian approach toward families
• Setting simple goals for increasing effective parenting
• Correcting unrealistic parental expectations of the child
• Encouraging family, friends, and community support for parents
• Maintaining social service and legal counsel for evaluating progress in rehabilitation efforts

The role of the team is to develop a therapeutic relationship with the family, to evolve a care plan for the protection of the child, to rehabilitate the abusive caretakers as much as possible, and to provide consistent follow-up care.

The protective services agency and public health nurse or nurse practitioner remain involved with the family after hospital discharge to assess the continued potential for abuse and to provide therapeutic and emotional support.

Nurse practitioners evaluate their own feelings about child abuse victims and recognize their own anger toward the abusers. Understanding the psychopathology of child abuse helps nurses to realize the large amount of stress in the families' lives. In most situations, treatments are successful and abusers are rehabilitated. This outcome increases positive attitudes in health professionals concerning abuse (Heindl, 1981).

Follow-Up Care

The child is returned to the home when the following conditions prevail:

- Social/psychologic problems are being treated and families exhibit traits of rehabilitation.
- The family crisis is resolved and future episodes are handled more therapeutically.
- The parents exhibit a positive, caring attitude toward the child.
- Consistent nurturing is provided for the parents to help improve their self-esteem.
- Parents demonstrate the willingness and knowledge to use available support services in the community.
- A routine follow-up plan is determined.
- In families where psychosocial problems still exist, the child may be returned to the home if there are family support services available, if there is a plan for frequent follow-up visits, and if the courts agree.

Community Services

In some cities, depending on funds available, there are sheltered residencies where parents are rehabilitated through behavior modification techniques, role modeling, and educational experiences (Fontana and Robinson, 1976). Other services include the following:

- Lay community workers offer nurturing, friendship, and support to the family for several months
- Crisis nurseries offer intermittent respite from child care
- Parents Anonymous offers 24-hour counsel and support
- Day-care centers offer child care skills and parent–child nurturing

SEXUAL ABUSE

Assessment

DEFINITION

Sexual abuse, as defined by the Child Sexual-Abuse Victim Assistance Project in Philadelphia, includes the following (Simrel et al., 1979):

1. Incidents with sexual assault and physical force to children 16 years of age and younger
2. Sexual contact such as intercourse, fondling, sodomy, exhibitionism between a child and another person of any age where the child's participation was obtained through threats, bribery, coercion, or similar tactics
3. Sexual contact between a child and an adult even with the free cooperation of the child when such contact is prohibited by law

SUSPICION OF SEXUAL ABUSE

Sexual abuse is strongly suspected when the following occur:

- Evidence of physical abuse
- Perineal lesions, itching, or pain
- Vaginitis, urethritis in children under 12
- Child describes sexual encounter

HISTORY

The nurse practitioner obtains history from the parents and/or other involved adults. Information concerning why they think the child is sexually abused, the actual incident(s), person(s) they think may be involved, child's immediate reaction, physical symptoms exhibited by the child, and recent changes in the child's behavior. See this chapter, Physical Examination.

Contributory history includes sleep problems, exaggerated clinging behavior, complaints of painful urination or defecation, anorexia, increased fearfulness, and anxiety.

The child, if age appropriate, is also interviewed alone. Trust is established by first asking questions of a general nature and proceeding to the specific incidence of sexual abuse.

PHYSICAL EXAMINATION

A complete physical examination is done. A general description of the child's physical appearance, including evidence of torn clothing and emotional state is noted. The external genitalia are inspected and deviations are noted. If genital trauma is suspected, an internal vaginal and rectal examination is necessary to rule out internal trauma and presence of foreign body.

LABORATORY

Because of the possibility of legal prosecution, and in situations where sexual abuse occurred less than 72 hours before, specimens are collected, labeled, and transmitted to laboratories under strict, proper technique to ensure their admissibility as evidence in a court of law.

The following laboratory examinations are done:

- Cultures for *N. gonnorrhea* (from vagina, anus, oropharynx), *Chlamydia, Trichomonas,* and *C. albicans*
- Serologic test for syphilis
- Pregnancy test, if indicated

Management

The nurse practitioner working with sexually abused children needs to be knowledgeable concerning the condition and sensitive to the needs of the child and the parents. The principles of management include the following (Pascoe, 1979):

- Care for medical problems of the child
- Care for the emotional problems of the child and family
- Guard child from any threat of further sexual abuse
- Formulate follow-up care
- Fulfill legal requirements

REPORTING

Reporting suspected sexual abuse is mandatory under law. Generally, all suspected cases are reported to the local or state offices of social welfare/child protective services. If serious risks to the child's welfare exist, hospitalization is mandatory to allow additional time for investigation and for possible temporary removal from the home.

ROLE OF THE HEALTH CARE TEAM

Management of sexual abuse is provided by a multidisciplinary team involving physicians, nurses, social workers, community workers, and personnel from protective service agencies. During the assessment and management, the health professionals are empathic to the parents' and the child's situation. The goal of care is that the child will be restored, as much as possible, to optimal physical and psychologic health, the offending individual(s) will be apprehended and the child will be returned to an environment that is safe. It is the focus of the courts and not the health profession to prove that sexual abuse has occurred. Therefore, intimidating questions and a confrontive atmosphere are to be avoided. Rather, a supportive dialogue is established in which the health professional recognizes the parents' distress and proceeds in a manner that shows evidence of concern and competence. Establishing trust and open communication also encourages the attainment of follow-up appointments. See this chapter, Follow-up Care.

References

Altremeier, W., et al. "Antecedents of Child Abuse." *J Pediatr 100*:823–829, May 1982.

Caffey, J. "The Whiplash Shaken Infant: Manual Shaking by the Extremities with Whiplash-Induced Intracranial and Intraocular Bleedings, Linked with Residual Permanent Brain Damage and Mental Retardation." *Pediatrics 54*:396–403, October 1974.

Caipoli, J. and C. Newberger. "Optimism or Pessimism for the Victim of Child Abuse." *Pediatrics 59*:311–312, February 1977.

Dine, M. and M. McGovern. "Intentional Poisoning of Children—An Overlooked Category of Child Abuse: Report of Seven Cases and Review of the Literature." *Pediatrics 70*:32–35, July 1982.

Ellerstein, N., editor. *Child Abuse and Neglect: A Medical Reference.* New York: Wiley, 1981.

Fontana, V. J. and E. Robinson. "A Multidisciplinary Approach to the Treatment of Child Abuse." *Pediatrics 56*:760–764, May 1976.

Graef, J. W. and T. E. Cone. *Manual of Pediatric Therapeutics.* Boston: LIttle, Brown, 2nd ed. 1980.

Green, F. C. "Child Abuse and Neglect: A Priority Problem for the Private Physician." *Pediatr Clin North Am 22*:329–339, May 1975.

Greenburg, N. "The Epidemiology of Childhood Sexual Abuse." *Pediatr Ann 8*:289–299, May 1979.

Heindl, M. "Dealing with Feelings: Who is the Victim?" *Nurs Clin North Am 16*:117–125, March 1981.

Joyner, E., "Child Abuse: The Role of the Physician and the Hospital." *Pediatrics 51*: 799–803, April 1973.

Kempe, C. H. "Approaches to Preventing Child Abuse." *Am J Dis Child 130*:941–946, September 1976.

Kempe, C. H. "Family Intervention: The Right of all Children." *Pediatrics 56*:693–694, November 1975a.

Kempe, C. H. "Uncommon Manifestations of the Battered Child Syndrome." *Am J Dis Child 129*:1265, November 1975b.

Kempe, C. H., H. Silver, and D. O'Brien. *Current Pediatric Diagnosis and Treatment.* 7th ed. Los Altos, CA: Lange Medical Publications, 1982.

Kempe, C. H. and J. Hopkins. "The Public Health Nurse's Role in the Prevention of Child Abuse and Neglect." *Public Health Currents 15*:1–4, May 1975.

Kempe, C. H. and R. E. Helfer. *The Battered Child.* 3rd ed. Chicago: University of Chicago Press, 1980.

Newberger, E. "Knowledge and Epidemiology of Child Abuse: A Critical Review of Concepts." *Pediatr Ann 5*:140–144, March 1976.

Pascoe, D. "Management of Sexually Abused Children." *Pediatr Ann 8*:309–316, May 1979.

Rosen, B. and M. Stein. "Women Who Abuse Their Children." *Am J Dis Child 132*:947–950, October 1980.

Rudolph, A. M., editor. *Pediatrics.* 17th ed. East Norwalk, CT: Appleton-Century-Crofts, 1982.

Schmitt, B. and C. Kempe. "The Pediatrician's Role in Child Abuse and Neglect." *Curr Probl Pediatr 5*:33–47, March 1975.

Simrel, K., R. Berg, and J. Thomas. "Crisis Management of Sexually Abused Children." *Pediatr Ann 8*:317–325, May 1979.

Sturner, W. "Pediatric Deaths." In W. Curren, A. McGarry, and C. Petty, editors. *Modern Legal Medicine: Psychiatry and Forensic Science.* Philadelphia: F. A. Davis, 1980.

Wolf, P. H. "Mother-Infant Interactions in the First Year." *N Engl J Med 295*:999–1001, October 1976.

Appendix

CONVERSION TABLES

GROWTH CHARTS

Table 1
Weights and Measures: Metric System

Mass

1000	grams	= kilogram	$(kg)^a$
1.0	$gram^a$	=	(g)
0.001	gram	= milligram	$(mg)^a$
10^{-6}	gram	= microgram	$(\mu g)^a$
10^{-9}	gram	= nanogram	(ng)
10^{-12}	gram	= picogram	(pg)

Capacity

1000	cubic centimeters	= liter	$(l)^a$
100	cubic centimeters	= deciliter	(dl)
10	cubic centimeters	= centiliter	(cl)
1.0	cubic centimeter^a	= milliliter	(ml, cc)
0.001	cubic centimeter	= microliter	(μl)
		cubic millimeter	(cmm)

^{a}Commonly employed units.

Table 2
Metric and Apothecaries' Equivalents[a]

1 milligram	=	1/65 grain	(1/60)
1 gram	=	15.43 grains	(15)
1 kilogram	=	2.20 pounds	[avoirdupois]
1 milliliter	=	16.23 minims	(15)
1 grain	=	0.065 gram	(60 mg)
1 ounce	=	31.1 grams	(30)
1 minim	=	0.062 ml	(0.06)
1 fluid ounce	=	29.57 ml	(30)
1 pint	=	473.2 ml	(500)
1 quart	=	946.4 ml	(1000)

[a]Figures in parentheses are approximate values and are *not* used in compounding prescription orders.

Table 3
Household Measures

Measure	Approximate Metric Equivalents
1 drop[a]	1/20 ml
1 teaspoon[b]	5 ml
1 dessertspoon	8 ml
1 tablespoon	15 ml
1 wineglass	60 ml
1 glass	250 ml

[a]The USP does not sanction the prescribing of doses in drops. An official standardized USP dropper is available for those who wish to use it. If it is necessary to prescribe oral medications in "drop dosage," the pharmacist should be instructed to mark the medicine dropper to deliver the desired amount of drug or to supply a calibrated dropper.
[b]The size of the household teaspoon varies considerably, and a given teaspoon will yield different volumes of medicine. The USP specifies that for household purposes an American standard teaspoon may be regarded as containing 5 ml.

Table 4
Celsius (Centigrade) and Fahrenheit Temperatures

Centigrade (Celsius)	Fahrenheit
0	32
36.0	96.8
36.5	97.7
37.0	98.6
37.5	99.5
38.0	100.4
38.5	101.3
39.0	102.2
39.5	103.1
40.0	104.0
40.5	104.9
41.0	105.8
41.5	106.7
42.0	107.6

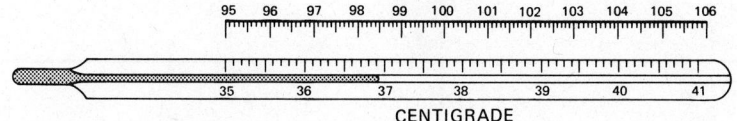

To convert degrees F. to degrees C.
  Subtract 32, then multiply by 5/9
To convert degrees C. to degrees F.
  Multiply by 9/5, then add 32

Table 5
Conversion of Pounds to Kilograms

Pounds→	0	1	2	3	4	5	6	7	8	9
0	0.00	0.45	0.90	1.36	1.81	2.26	2.72	3.17	3.62	4.08
10	4.53	4.98	5.44	5.89	6.35	6.80	7.25	7.71	8.16	8.61
20	9.07	9.52	9.97	10.43	10.88	11.34	11.79	12.24	12.70	13.15
30	13.60	14.06	14.51	14.96	15.42	15.87	16.32	16.78	17.23	17.69
40	18.14	18.59	19.05	19.50	19.95	20.41	20.86	21.31	21.77	22.22
50	22.68	23.13	23.58	24.04	24.49	24.94	25.40	25.85	26.30	26.76
60	27.21	27.66	28.12	28.57	29.03	29.48	29.93	30.39	30.84	31.29
70	31.75	32.20	32.65	33.11	33.56	34.02	34.47	34.92	35.38	35.83
80	36.28	36.74	37.19	37.64	38.10	38.55	39.00	39.46	39.91	40.37

90	40.82	41.27	41.73	42.18	42.63	43.09	43.54	43.99	44.45	44.90
100	45.36	45.81	46.26	46.72	47.17	47.62	48.08	48.53	48.98	49.44
110	49.89	50.34	50.80	51.25	51.71	52.16	52.61	53.07	53.52	53.97
120	54.43	54.88	55.33	55.79	56.24	56.70	57.15	57.60	58.06	58.51
130	58.96	59.42	59.87	60.32	60.78	61.23	61.68	62.14	62.59	63.05
140	63.50	63.95	64.41	64.86	65.31	65.77	66.22	66.67	67.13	67.58
150	68.04	68.49	68.94	69.40	69.85	70.30	70.76	71.21	71.66	72.12
160	72.57	73.02	73.48	73.93	74.39	74.84	75.29	75.75	76.20	76.65
170	77.11	77.56	78.01	78.47	78.92	79.38	79.83	80.28	80.74	81.19
180	81.64	82.10	82.55	83.00	83.46	83.91	84.36	84.82	85.27	85.73
190	86.18	86.68	87.09	87.54	87.99	88.45	88.90	89.35	89.81	90.26
200	90.72	91.17	91.62	92.08	92.53	92.98	93.44	93.89	94.34	94.80

Table 6
Conversion of Pounds and Ounces to Grams

Pounds	Ounces 0	1	2	3	4	5	6	7	8	9	10	11	12	13	14	15
0	—	28	57	85	113	142	170	198	227	255	283	312	340	369	397	425
1	454	482	510	539	567	595	624	652	680	709	737	765	794	822	850	879
2	907	936	964	992	1021	1049	1077	1106	1134	1162	1191	1219	1247	1276	1304	1332
3	1361	1389	1417	1446	1474	1503	1531	1559	1588	1616	1644	1673	1701	1729	1758	1786
4	1814	1843	1871	1899	1928	1956	1984	2013	2041	2070	2098	2126	2155	2183	2211	2240
5	2268	2296	2325	2353	2381	2410	2438	2466	2495	2523	2551	2580	2608	2637	2665	2693
6	2722	2750	2778	2807	2835	2863	2892	2920	2948	2977	3005	3033	3062	3090	3118	3147
7	3175	3203	3232	3260	3289	3317	3345	3374	3402	3430	3459	3487	3515	3544	3572	3600
8	3629	3657	3685	3714	3742	3770	3799	3827	3856	3884	3912	3941	3969	3997	4026	4054
9	4082	4111	4139	4167	4196	4224	4252	4281	4309	4337	4366	4394	4423	4451	4479	4508

	0	1	2	3	4	5	6	7	8	9	10	11	12	13	14	15	
10	4536	4564	4593	4621	4649	4678	4706	4734	4763	4791	4819	4848	4876	4904	4933	4961	10
11	4990	5018	5046	5075	5103	5131	5160	5188	5216	5245	5273	5301	5330	5358	5386	5415	11
12	5443	5471	5500	5528	5557	5585	5613	5642	5670	5698	5727	5755	5783	5812	5840	5868	12
13	5897	5925	5953	5982	6010	6038	6067	6095	6123	6152	6180	6209	6237	6265	6294	6322	13
14	6350	6379	6407	6435	6464	6492	6520	6549	6577	6605	6634	6662	6690	6719	6747	6776	14
15	6804	6832	6860	6889	6917	6945	6973	7002	7030	7059	7087	7115	7144	7172	7201	7228	15
16	7257	7286	7313	7342	7371	7399	7427	7456	7484	7512	7541	7569	7597	7626	7654	7682	16
17	7711	7739	7768	7796	7824	7853	7881	7909	7938	7966	7994	8023	8051	8079	8108	8136	17
18	8165	8192	8221	8249	8278	8306	8335	8363	8391	8420	8448	8476	8504	8533	8561	8590	18
19	8618	8646	8675	8703	8731	8760	8788	8816	8845	8873	8902	8930	8958	8987	9015	9043	19
20	9072	9100	9128	9157	9185	9213	9242	9270	9298	9327	9355	9383	9412	9440	9469	9497	20
21	9525	9554	9582	9610	9639	9667	9695	9724	9752	9780	9809	9837	9865	9894	9922	9950	21
22	9979	10007	10036	10064	10092	10120	10149	10177	10206	10234	10262	10291	10319	10347	10376	10404	22

Table 7
Approximate Metric and Imperial Equivalents

Useful approximate metric and imperial equivalents

  1 cm = 0.39 inches 1 in = 2.54 cm
  1 meter = 1.1 yards 1 ft = 30.48 cm

To convert centimeters to inches

 Divide the length in centimeters by 2.54.

 Example: The average newborn infant measures 50.8 cm:

$$= \frac{50.8}{2.54} = 20 \text{ inches}$$

To convert inches to centimeters

 Multiply the length in inches by 2.54.

 Example: The average newborn infant measures 20 inches:

$$= 20 \times 2.54 = 50.8 \text{ cm}$$

Table 8
Conversion of Inches to Centimeters

Inches	Centimeters	Inches	Centimeters	Inches	Centimeters
10	25.40	15	38.10	20	50.80
10½	26.67	15½	39.37	20½	52.07
11	27.94	16	40.61	21	53.34
11½	29.21	16½	41.91	21½	54.61
12	30.48	17	43.18	22	55.88
12½	31.75	17½	44.45	22½	57.15
13	33.02	18	45.72	23	58.42
13½	34.29	18½	46.99	23½	56.69
14	35.56	19	48.26	24	60.96
14½	36.83	19½	49.58		

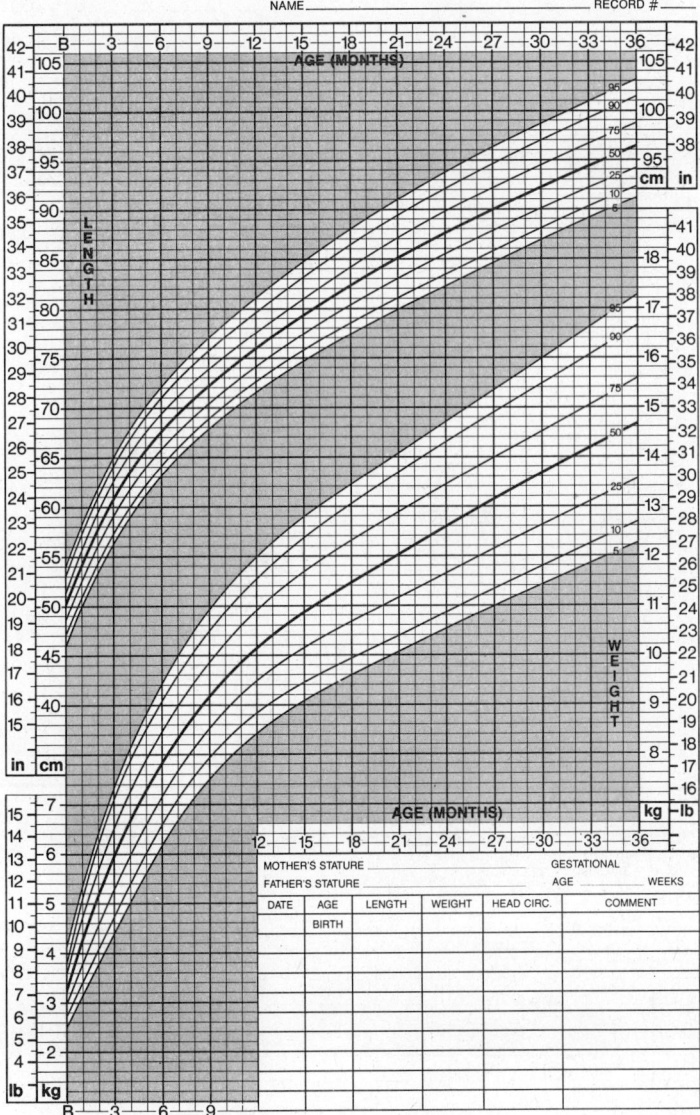

Figure 1 Boys: birth to 36 months physical growth NCHS percentiles.

Source: Adapted from P. V. V. Hamill, T. A. Drizd, C. L. Johnson, R. B. Reed, A. F. Roche, W. M. Moore: "Physical Growth: National Center for Health Statistics Percentiles," *Am J Clin Nutr* 32:607–629, 1979. Data from the Fels Research Institute, Wright State University School of Medicine, Yellow Springs, Ohio. © 1982 Ross Laboratories. Courtesy of Ross Laboratories, Columbus, Ohio.

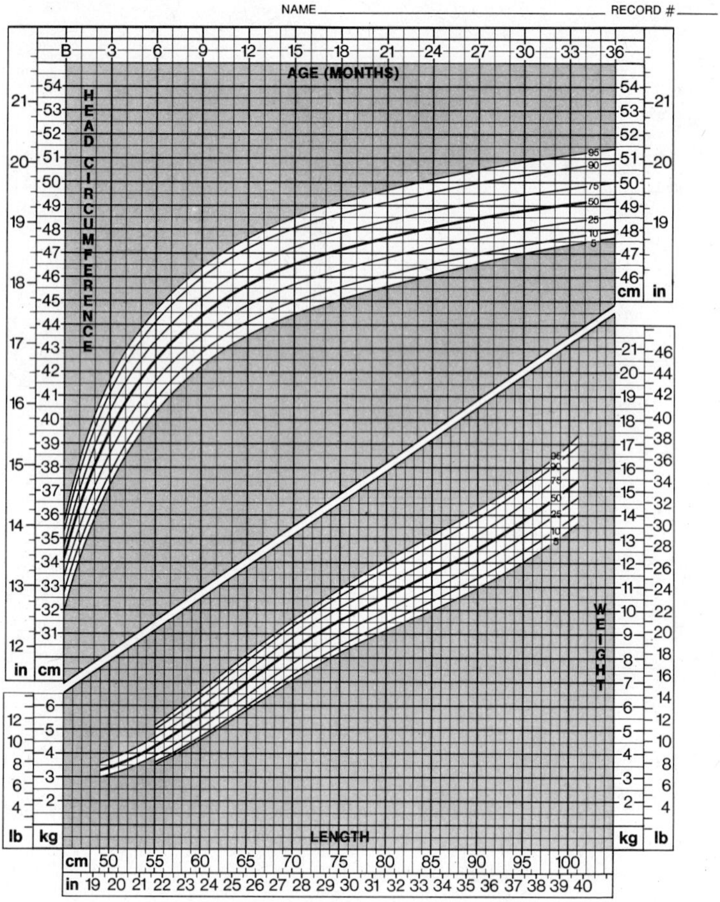

DATE	AGE	LENGTH	WEIGHT	HEAD CIRC.	COMMENT

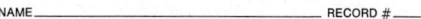

Figure 2 Boys: birth to 36 months physical growth NCHS percentiles.

Source: Adapted from P. V. V. Hamill, T. A. Drizd, C. L. Johnson, R. B. Reed, A. F. Roche, W. M. Moore: "Physical Growth: National Center for Health Statistics Percentiles," *Am J Nutr 32*:607–629, 1979. Data from the Fels Research Institute, Wright State University School of Medicine, Yellow Springs, Ohio, © 1982 Ross Laboratories. Courtesy of Ross Laboratories, Columbus, Ohio.

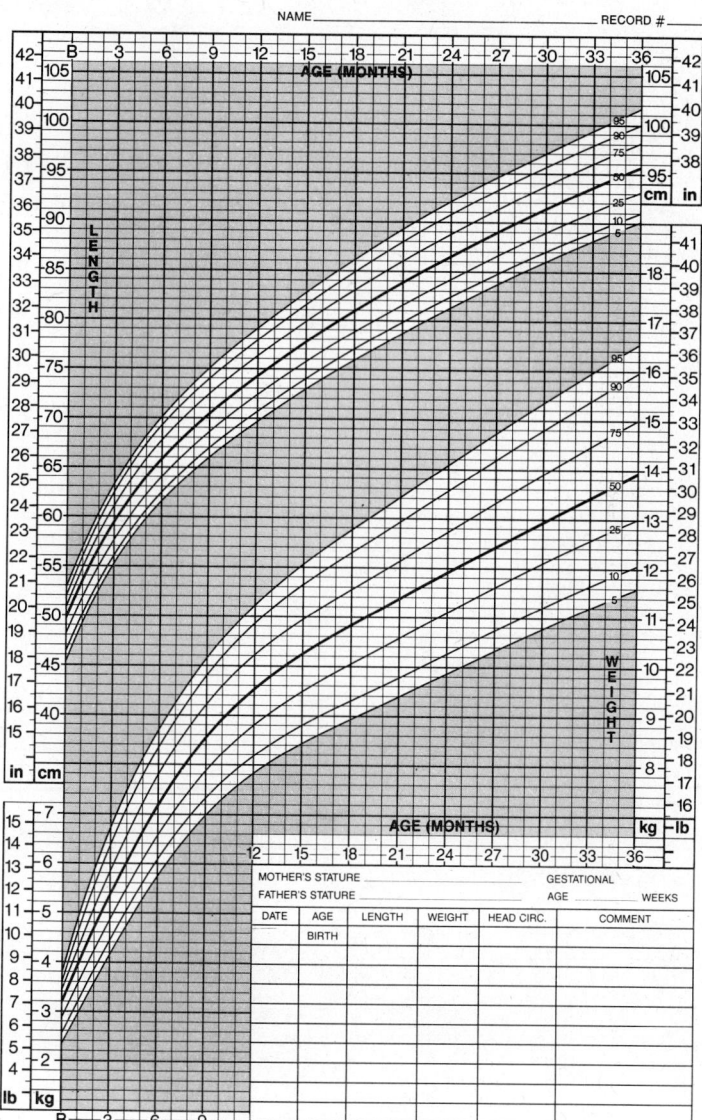

Figure 3 Girls: birth to 36 months physical growth NCHS percentiles.

Source: Adapted from P. V. V. Hamill, T. A. Drizd, C. L. Johnson, R. B. Reed, A. F. Roche, W. M. Moore: "Physical Growth: National Center for Health Statistics Percentiles," *Am J Clin Nutr* 32:607–629, 1979. Data from Fels Research Institute, Wright State University School of Medicine, Yellow Springs, Ohio. © 1982 Ross Laboratories. Courtesy of Ross Laboratories, Columbus, Ohio.

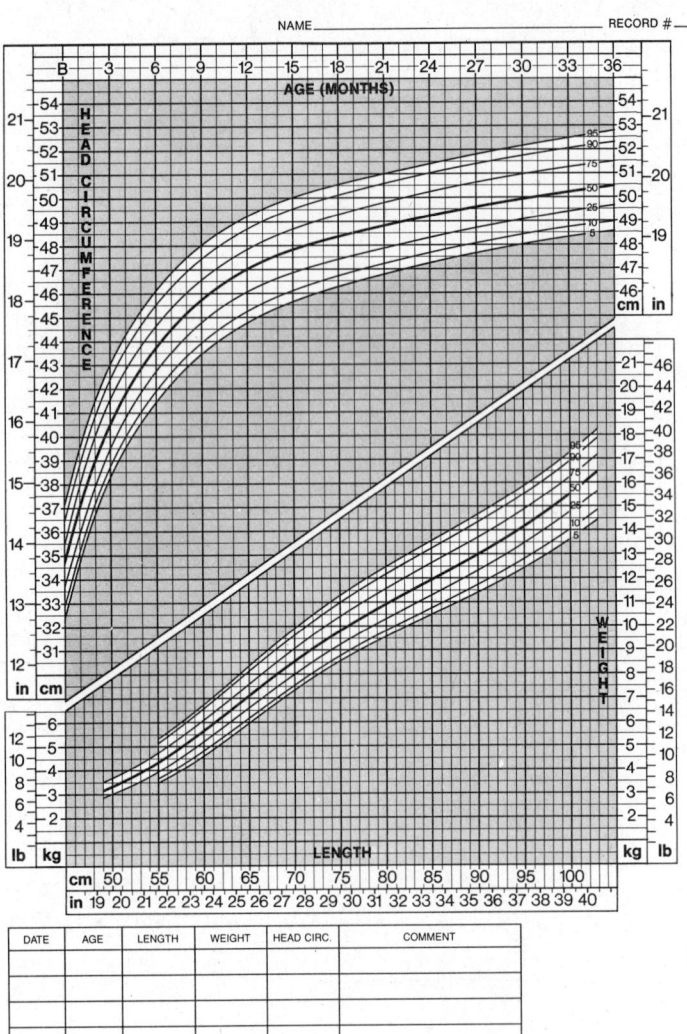

NAME_____ RECORD #_____

Figure 4 Girls: Birth to 36 months physical growth NCHS percentiles.

Source: Adapted from P. V. V. Hamill, T. A. Drizd, C. L. Johnson, R. B. Reed, A. F. Roche, W. M. Moore: "Physical Growth: National Center for Health Statistics Percentiles," *Am J Nutr* 32:607–629, 1979. Data from the Fels Research Institute, Wright State University School of Medicine, Yellow Springs, Ohio, © 1982 Ross Laboratories. Courtesy of Ross Laboratories, Columbus, Ohio.

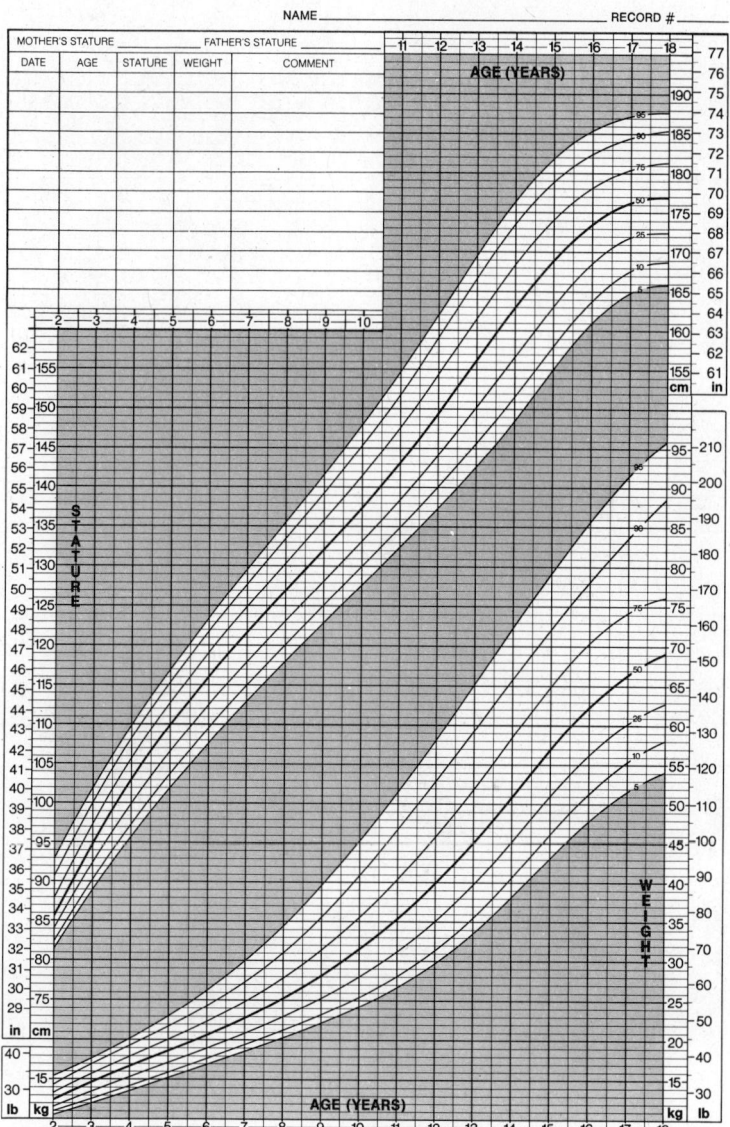

Figure 5 Boys: 2 to 18 years physical growth NCHS percentiles.

Source: Adapted from P. V. V. Hamill, T. A. Drizd, C. L. Johnson, R. B. Reed, A. F. Roche, W. M. Moore: "Physical Growth: National Center for Health Statistics Percentiles," *Am J Nutr 32*:607–629, 1979. Data from the Fels Research Institute, Wright State University School of Medicine, Yellow Springs, Ohio, © 1982 Ross Laboratories. Courtesy of Ross Laboratories, Columbus, Ohio.

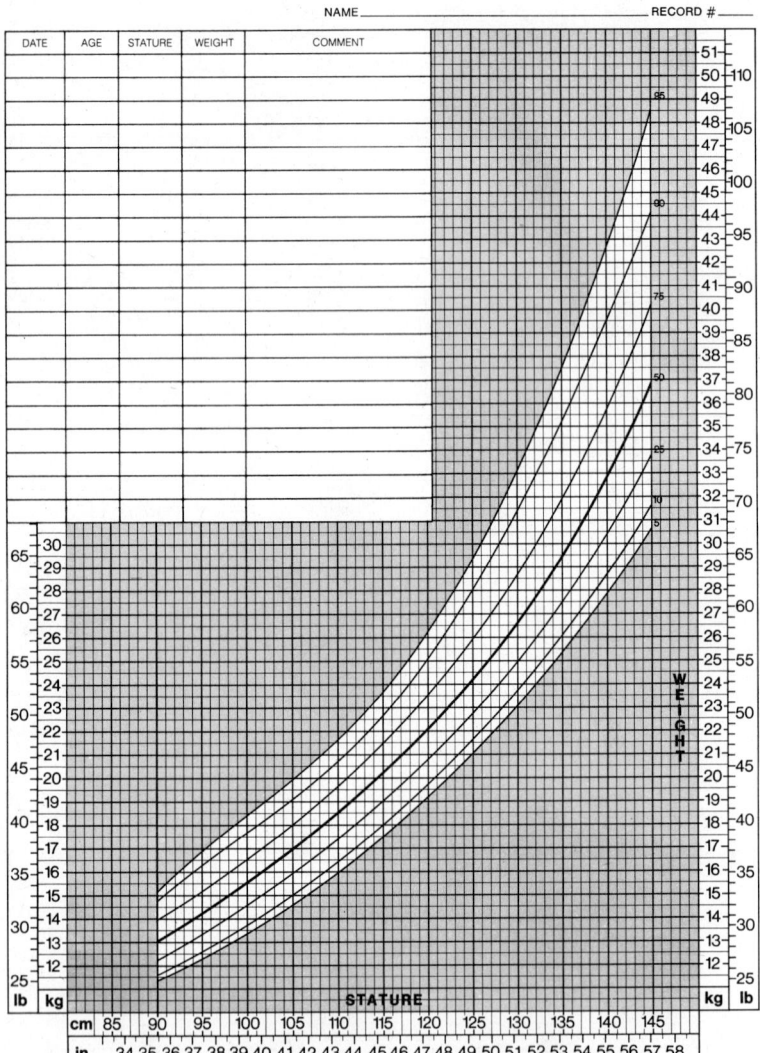

Figure 6 Boys: prepubescent physical growth NCHS percentiles.

Source: Adapted from P. V. V. Hamill, T. A. Drizd, C. L. Johnson, R. B. Reed, A. F. Roche, W. M. Moore: "Physical Growth: National Center for Health Statistics Percentiles," *Am J Nutr 32*:607–629, 1979. Data from the Fels Research Institute, Wright State University School of Medicine, Yellow Springs, Ohio, © 1982 Ross Laboratories. Courtesy of Ross Laboratories, Columbus, Ohio.

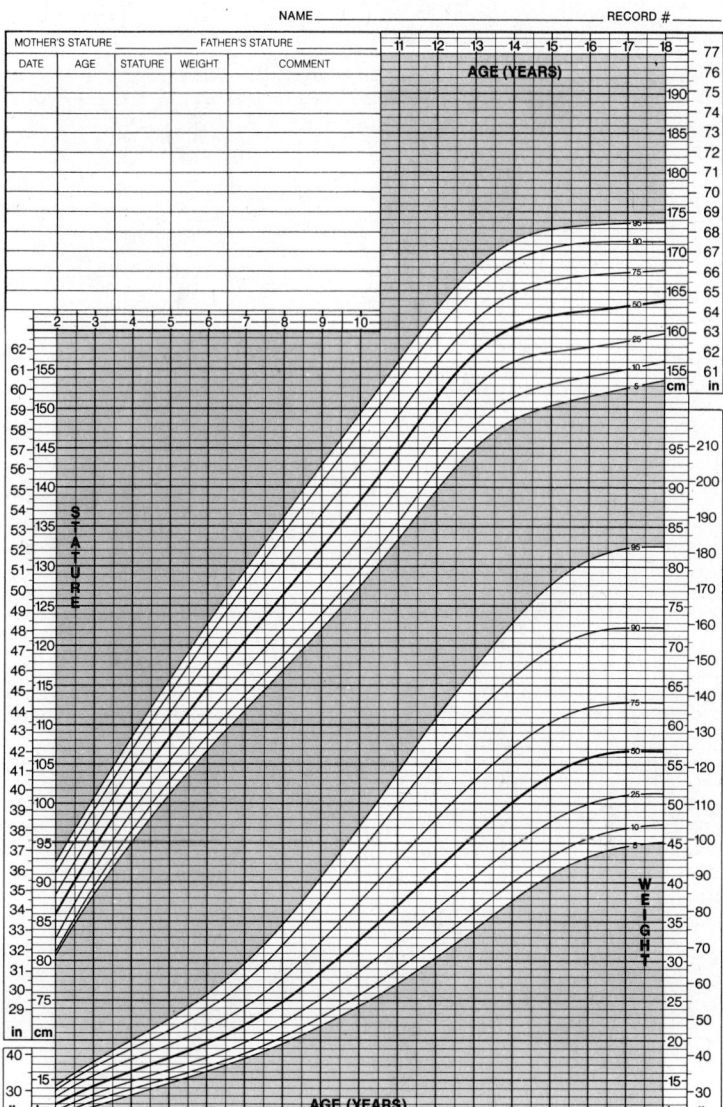

Figure 7 Girls: 2 to 18 years physical growth NCHS percentiles.

Source: Adapted from P. V. V. Hamill, T. A. Drizd, C. L. Johnson, R. B. Reed, A. F. Roche, W. M. Moore: "Physical Growth: National Center for Health Statistics Percentiles," *Am J Nutr 32*:607–629, 1979. Data from the Fels Research Institute, Wright State University School of Medicine, Yellow Springs, Ohio, © 1982 Ross Laboratories. Courtesy of Ross Laboratories, Columbus, Ohio.

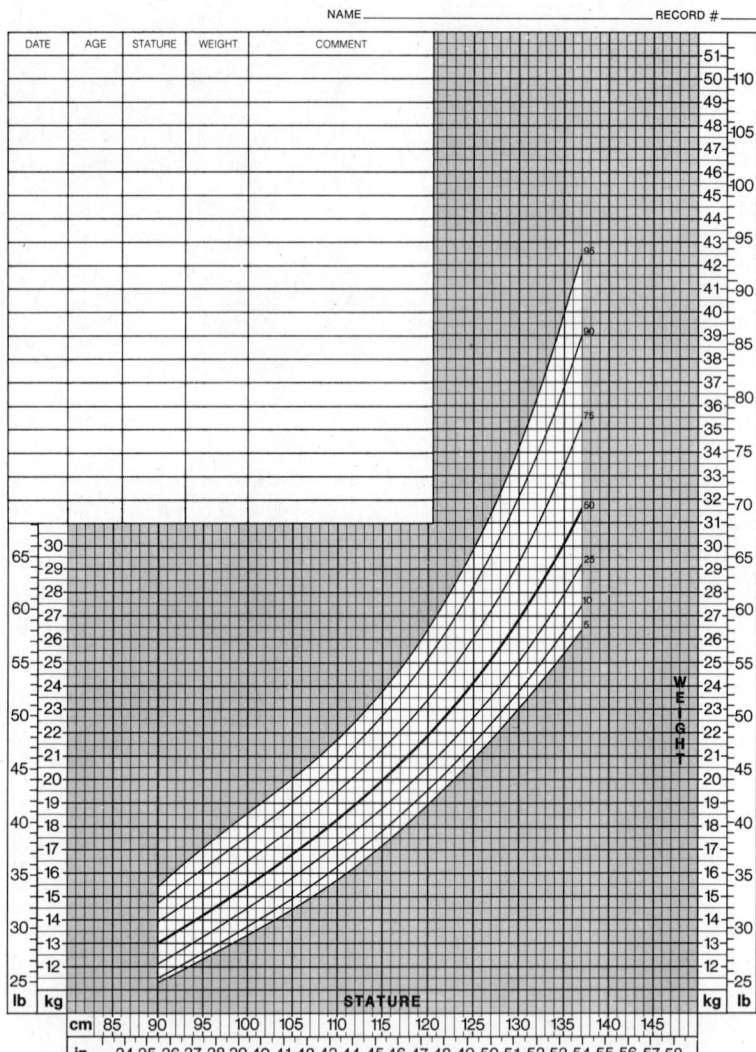

Figure 8 Girls: prepubescent physical growth NCHS percentiles.

Source: Adapted from P. V. V. Hamill, T. A. Drizd, C. L. Johnson, R. B. Reed, A. F. Roche, W. M. Moore: "Physical Growth: National Center for Health Statistics Percentiles," *Am J Nutr 32*:607–629, 1979. Data from the Fels Research Institute, Wright State University School of Medicine, Yellow Springs, Ohio, © 1982 Ross Laboratories. Courtesy of Ross Laboratories, Columbus, Ohio.

Index